A Scholar's Guide to Geographical Writing on the American and Canadian Past

University of Chicago Geography Research Paper no. 235

Series Editors

Michael P. Conzen
Chauncy D. Harris
Neil Harris
Marvin W. Mikesell
Gerald D. Suttles

A Scholar's Guide to Geographical Writing on the American and Canadian Past

Michael P. Conzen
Thomas A. Rumney
Graeme Wynn

The University of Chicago Press
Chicago and London

Michael P. Conzen is professor of geography and chairman of the Committee on Geographical Studies at the University of Chicago.

Thomas A. Rumney is associate professor of geography in the Center for Earth and Environmental Sciences at the State University of New York at Plattsburgh.

Graeme Wynn is professor of geography and associate dean of the faculty of arts at the University of British Columbia.

The University of Chicago Press, Chicago 60637
The University of Chicago Press, Ltd., London
© 1993 by The University of Chicago
All rights reserved. Published 1993
Printed in the United States of America
01 00 99 98 97 96 95 94 93   5 4 3 2 1

ISBN: 0–226–11569–0

Library of Congress Cataloging-in-Publication Data

Conzen, Michael P.
    A scholar's guide to geographical writing on the American and Canadian past / Michael P. Conzen, Thomas A. Rumney, Graeme Wynn.
        Includes indexes.
            p.   cm.
        1. United States—Historical geography—Bibliography.
    2. Canada—Historical geography—Bibliography.   I. Rumney, Thomas A.   II. Wynn, Graeme, 1946–   .   III. Title.
    Z1247.C66   1993
    [E179.5]
    016.91173—dc20   92-23520
                                                                                    CIP

♾ The paper used in this publication meets the minimum requirements of the American National Standard for Information Sciences—Permanence of Paper for Printed Library materials, ANSI Z39.48-1984.

Contents

PART V.   UNITED STATES

PART VI.   INDEXES

ORGANIZATION OF THE TOPICAL SECTIONS
within each regional, state, and provincial section

STANDARD HEADINGS	CATEGORY INCLUDES:
GENERAL	"Historical geography of . . . ," "Geography of . . . ," etc.
ENVIRONMENTAL CHANGE	Human modification; natural hazards
NATIVE PEOPLES & WHITE RELATIONS	Prehistoric cultures, economy and settlements; European contact, trade, war; reservations and modern conditions
EXPLORATION & MAPPING	"Discovery . . . ," cartographic surveys, map trade
POPULAR IMAGES & EVALUATION	Perceptions; preferences; photography
REGIONAL SETTLEMENT	Colonization, pioneering and frontier settling; sequent occupance; rural settlement morphology
POPULATION	Demography; geographical mobility and migration; regional ethnic distributions
RURAL SOCIAL GEOGRAPHY	Ethnicity as community; religion; education; health; social customs
POLITICAL & ADMINISTRATIVE	Territorial boundaries; political ideology and economy; government activities and programs; legal; military
ECONOMIC DEVELOPMENT	General (only); multiple factors in regional development
RESOURCE MANAGEMENT	Natural resource conservation; water use; energy management
LAND AND LAND USE	Survey, tenure, use, value
EXTRACTIVE ACTIVITY	Fishing; fur trade; lumbering, forestry; mining; quarrying
AGRICULTURE	Cultivation; ranching; orchards; truck farming; vineyards
LANDSCAPE	Rural buildings and architecture; fields and fences; highways and other cultural features
COMMUNICATIONS	Trade; transport; postal service; newspapers; electronic media
MANUFACTURING & INDUSTRIALIZATION	All types, viewed regionally or by activity
URBAN NETWORKS & URBANIZATION	Systems of cities; urban hierarchies; hinterland relations
TOWN GROWTH	Focus on individual places; special function towns; areal spread (suburbanization)
URBAN ECONOMIC STRUCTURE	Land use (including parks); infrastructure; services; employment
URBAN SOCIAL STRUCTURE	Ethnicity; residential patterns; organizations; urban politics
TOWNSCAPE	Ground plan; building pattern; land development; housing; architecture
RECREATION & TOURISM	Spas and resorts; sports; touring
PLANNING	Formal planning, generally at the local and municipal levels
PLACE NAMES	Place-name cover; origins and generics; Indian names

Preface

Scholarly guides and bibliographies are generally undertaken as a service to a discipline and to researchers interested in penetrating a specialized field. They can be viewed as a way of drawing together the intellectual accomplishments of a research tradition, and of assessing the declarations and silences of that body of work. Most regard compiling bibliographies as prosaic, but while the rewards of scholarship accrue properly to substantive work, most researchers also recognize the underlying value of such research tools.

It is more than twenty-five years since Douglas R. McManis's much-used and long out-of-print *Historical Geography of the United States: A Bibliography* appeared.[1] That work, arranged regionally and topically, offered sound selections of material by geographers wherever possible, supplemented with books and articles by historians and others on topics where work by geographers was lacking. In the interest of balanced thematic coverage, the resulting proportion of entries by historians was so high, in fact, as to leave little doubt how much interpretive work in American historical *geography* remained to be done. While there is a long tradition of historical writing from a geographical perspective, the absolute number of scholars consistently active in the field has long formed, comparatively speaking, but a minute fraction of those laboring within history, conventionally defined. Nevertheless, interest, and work, in American historical geography have developed steadily.

The maturing of the field in recent times was well captured a decade ago through the publication of Ronald E. Grim's *Historical Geography of the United States: A Guide to Information Sources.*[2] Prepared as an orientation for the general reader, that book made accessible major themes in American historical geography through a stringent selection of key works, suitably annotated, and it highlighted a wide range of primary sources. The growing secondary literature, however, has been appearing in many publication outlets previously unutilized; most notably, geographers have placed their work more and more in regional historical journals and interdisciplinary periodicals during the decade that has followed. By the late eighties it seemed reasonable to propose that the time had come to assess the enlarged scope of the literature, and to do so in ways that met a variety of goals.

Accordingly, the present guide aims to present as nearly comprehensive a view as practical of the evolved character of geographical writing about the North American past. The focus is squarely upon the contributions that geographers have made to understanding the historical experience on this continent. Needless to say, questions of interdisciplinary inclusion at the margins arise. There have been historians and others writing from time to time with such evident geographical awareness and so-

---

[1] Douglas R. McManis, *Historical Geography of the United States: A Bibliography, Excluding Alaska and Hawaii* (Ypsilanti: Eastern Michigan University Press, 1965)

[2] Ronald E. Grim, *Historical Geography of the United States: A Guide to Information Sources* (Detroit: Gale Research Co., 1982).

phistication that their work, appearing both in geographical outlets and elsewhere, deserves inclusion. Yet the new scale of geographers' work on the past leads us to keep such inclusions to a reasonable minimum.

Second, the bibliography seeks to present a cumulative picture of writing in North American historical geography. Hence considerable effort has been made to track down material as far back in time as possible that fulfills the criteria for inclusion. Much early writing did not fall under a self-conscious "historical geography" label, but dealt with applicable themes nonetheless. The inclusion of qualified writing of any vintage served to highlight the evolving pattern of interest in and analytical approaches to various topics. Subsequently, this deepened our curiosity about the course of that evolution, and the two essays that open this guide examine some of the leading trends in historical-geographical writing over the decades.

A third concern has been to focus on substantive research, offering direct understanding of real-world places and historical-geographical processes. There is, of course, a broad continuum between heavily empirical studies, luxuriating in "thick description," at one extreme and studies devoted to the conceptual, methodological, and historiographical issues that surround the practice of scholarship at the other . A suitable dividing line is extremely hard to establish, but we have chosen to concentrate on broadly interpretive studies of substantive problems, and to collect material engaged primarily in methodological review in a compact introductory section.

A fourth interest has been to cater to the needs of researchers interested in finding out what historical-geographical writing has been done on any topic in any part of the United States and Canada. Hence, we have worked to include material at all geographical scales and in all relevant localities. This has produced a bibliography far larger and more complex than the earlier one by McManis, but one incorporating its organizational principles. The present work covers both the United States and Canada, reflecting the value of comparing the historical geography of the two largely English-speaking nations sharing the continent—with sufficient similarities and contrasts to make their comparison enlightening.[3] Mexico, however, was excluded because its cultural traditions tie it more firmly to regions to the south, notwithstanding the recurrent patterns of contact and intermingling with essentially Anglo culture in the United States. Within these territorial parameters, we hope that researchers will be able to find quite detailed coverage of topics at often very local scales, whether as the basis for initiating new research projects, field reconnaissance, or more general enlightenment.

This guide stems initially from conversations between Michael Conzen and Tom Rumney in the spring of 1989 that led to a formal agreement in January 1990 to pursue the project. Extensive library work followed, including joint labors in

---

[3] To refer to the United States and Canada as *largely* English-speaking is, of course, not to ignore the formal status or functional significance of other languages, primarily but not limited to Spanish and French, in the life and regions of the two countries.

Chicago during June, when the conceptual and organizational character of the bibliography was worked out. In July, a request for personal lists of relevant publications was circulated to historical geographers in the United States and Canada. It became apparent that Graeme Wynn, meanwhile, was engaged on a somewhat parallel effort covering Canada. Consultations followed and led to Wynn's joining the binational project, with responsibility for melding and augmenting the Canadian material from the two efforts into a single component. Conzen and Rumney retain responsibility for the United States portion.

The research that went into this study would not have been possible without the cooperation of numerous colleagues, librarians, and other individuals. The exceptional collections of the Joseph Regenstein Library and the Crerar Science Library at the University of Chicago proved indispensable to the project. The holdings of worldwide geographical periodicals at Regenstein Library have few equals in the Western hemisphere, and made the scope of this bibliography feasible. Christopher Winters, bibliographer for geography, anthropology, and maps at the library, provided excellent assistance in running down obscure references and hunting tardy journal accessions. In the reference department, Sandra Roscoe, Beverly A. Sperring, Jennette Rader, and Melissa D. Trevvett rose to challenges large and small with unfailing resourcefulness, and were crucial in solving puzzles on the last shortlists of missing and mangled information. Linda S. Lim and Glenn M. Richard rendered superb service as successive research assistants for the work in Chicago. Chauncy D. Harris, world authority on geographical bibliography and incomparable colleague, gave valuable advice at various stages of the work. Marvin W. Mikesell, judicious student of American cultural-historical geography and incomparable teacher, gave freely of his knowledge on the history of American geographical research. We could not have had two more supportive colleagues at Chicago.

Work in Chicago was supplemented with research forays to neighboring geographical and historical centers. At the University of Wisconsin, Miriam Kerndt, head of the geography library, and Mary Galneder, head of the map collection, were particularly helpful, and Onno Brouwer, head of the cartographic laboratory, extended several helpful professional courtesies. Professor James C. Knox gave advice that served to augment our listings in environmental historical geography. We also wish to acknowledge the assistance of Geoffrey J. Martin (Southern Connecticut State College), William A. Koelsch (Clark University), and Martin S. Kenzer (Florida Atlantic University) in making some suggestions for the "Benchmark Scholars" portion of the work. Jeanne C. Kay (University of Waterloo) offered a number of suggestions on the historical geography of gender. Edward H. Dahl, early cartographic specialist at the National Archives of Canada, reviewed a preliminary draft of the "General Sources" section and made many useful suggestions.

Also essential in completing this volume have been the reference librarians and collections of the State University of New York at Plattsburgh (SUNY), the University of Vermont, and McGill University in Montreal. Tom Rumney is grateful to the staff members of these institutions, and also to SUNY–Plattsburgh for a sabbatical leave that allowed the time away from classes and committees both to travel to Chicago in the summer of 1990 for work at Regenstein Library, as well as to organize and record the vast amounts of raw information that collectively we gathered.

Graeme Wynn wishes to acknowledge with gratitude the research assistance of Yasmeen Qureshi, Maria Cavezza, and Christine Watson, as well as the staff of the university library at the University of British Columbia.

We are indebted to the many professional colleagues who responded to our requests for help, whether through the questionnaire or other specific queries. Those who provided thesis lists include: Alan G. Brunger (Trent University), Rosemary Cann (University of British Columbia), John Clarke (Carleton University), Serge Courville (Laval University), Richard S. Harris (McMaster University), Audrey L. Kobayashi (McGill University), William A. Koelsch (Clark University), David C.-Y. Lai (University of Victoria), Robert D. Lewis (McGill University), D. Aidan McQuillan (University of Toronto), John J. Mannion (Memorial University of Newfoundland), Jean Martin (Laval University), D. Wayne Moodie (University of Manitoba), Brian S. Osborne (Queen's University), John P. Radford (York University), Roger A. Roberge (University of Ottawa), Hansgeorg Schlichtmann and Randy W. Widdis (University of Regina), Peter J. Smith (University of Alberta), W. Robert Wightman (University of Western Ontario), and Susan Wurtele (Queen's University), and the staffs of geography departments at the University of Wisconsin–Madison, University of British Columbia, York University, Simon Fraser University, and the University of Chicago.

To expedite matters, we contacted a number of journal editors during the fall of 1990 for advance information about possible historical material in their closing 1990 issues. We gratefully acknowledge responses from Alvar W. Carlson (*Journal of Cultural Geography*), Howard A. Deller (*Wisconsin Geographer*), Dennis J. Dingemans (*Yearbook of the Association of Pacific Coast Geographers*), Donald Floyd (*California Geographer*), David B. Frost (*NESTVAL Proceedings*), Gerald Green (*Ohio Geographers*), Jesse O. McKee (*Mississippi Geographer*), C. Nicholas Raphael (*Geographical Bulletin*), Jill Thomas (*Bulletin of the Illinois Geographical Society*), and John J. Winberry (*Southeastern Geographer*).

The authors of the two historiographical essays are grateful to several colleagues who commented on early drafts: Carville V. Earle (Louisiana State University); Gary S. Dunbar (Cooperstown, N.Y.); Donald W. Meinig and John A. Agnew (Syracuse University); Cole Harris, David Demerrit, and Marlene Shore (University of British Columbia); David Ward (University of Wisconsin); Marvin W. Mikesell and Kathleen Neils Conzen (University of Chicago); and the anonymous reviewers.

In the editorial phases of this work, two individuals have been of paramount importance: Penelope Kaiserlian, associate director of the University of Chicago Press, has from the outset supported this project with great understanding and patience; and Carol F. Saller, editor for the Geography Research Papers, has brought a skill and resourcefulness to the job of editing, formatting, proofing, and otherwise preparing this volume for printing second to none, made all the more memorable by her good-humored tolerance of the authors' foibles and other complications. Reine Mikesell and Ilse Mueller proofed and corrected the French and German material in the bibliography respectively. In the Committee on Geographical Studies at the University of Chicago, Susan B. Alitto, administrative assistant, Betty McCarthy, secretary to the committee, and Anne Mini, willing assistant in the office, all helped in numerous ways to speed this, at times unwieldy, project toward completion. They all deserve our lasting thanks.

M. P. C.

T. A. R.

G. W.

PART I

INTRODUCTION

The Historical Impulse in Geographical Writing about the United States
1850-1990

Michael P. Conzen

In the United States there is more space where nobody is than where anybody is. This is what makes America what it is. Does it make human nature what it is? If not, it does make the human mind in America what it is.

—Gertrude Stein[1]

What Americans have lacked in a sense of time they have tried to make up by an enlarged sense of space. Their thoughts tend not to run backward into an antiquity they do not know but rather outward into a larger geographical theater of action, the theater not of the past but of the future.

—Richard Hofstadter[2]

A peculiarity of our American geographical tradition has been its lack of interest in historical processes and sequences, even their outright rejection. . . . Knowledge of human processes is attainable only if the current situation is comprehended as a moving point, one moment in an action that has beginning and end. . . . All human time is involved in the field, and any predilection for considering the present as intrinsically most important misses the expressed aim of human geography as a genetic science.

—Carl Sauer[3]

As we live through the last decade of the twentieth century there seems less consensus over the philosophy and content of the human sciences than in any period within living memory. It might be useful, therefore, to examine the changing character of the borderland of two disciplines—geography and history—which have contributed significantly in the past to such consensus, to see how differing perspectives have defined ostensibly common ground, drawn assistance from each other, and offered ideas helpful in building larger understanding. Since classical times, geography and history in the Western tradition have been regarded as dual and complementary means by which to organize and explain the character of the external world and the nature of civilization. Long seen as intellectually distinct but symbiotic, the two fields of knowledge were professionalized during the nineteenth century in Europe and North America, and have continued to expand as disciplines through more specialized study and continual reinterpretation. It is virtually impossible, of course, to write history without at least some sense of spatial context, as it is

---

[1] Gertrude Stein, *The Geographical History of America* (New York: Random House, 1936; Vintage Books Edition, 1973), pp. 53–54.

[2] Richard Hofstadter, *The Progressive Historians: Turner, Beard, Parrington* (Chicago: University of Chicago Press, Phoenix Edition, 1979), p. 6.

[3] Carl O. Sauer, "Foreword to Historical Geography," *Annals of the Association of American Geographers*, vol. 31, 1 (1941), pp. 2, 9, and 13.

hard to write geography without coping with the effects of time. The scholarly juncture between history and geography has almost always drawn interest from both vantage points, and from time to time major ideas in one field have profoundly affected thought in the other. As a result, geography has developed a vigorous and sometimes contentious field of historical geography, and history has on occasion given strong voice to ideas in geographical history.[4]

The exchange between the two fields has been particularly unstable in the United States—the youngest of the societies in which geography was consciously modernized by indigenous initiative. Unfortunately, knowledge of the extent to which historical awareness has variously shaped American geography[5] over the last century and a half has developed only intermittently and in broad outline.[6] Reviews of short-term developments in the field of historical geography are plentiful, especially for the last two decades or so, but they offer little or no picture of the often tortuous path that long-term development of fundamental ideas and scholarly orientations has taken, or of the consequences that the choices reflected in that path have had for contemporary patterns of thought. This essay seeks to advance that understanding by exploring the changing role that historical thinking has played, as an intellectual approach, in the development of geographical knowledge and concepts in American geography, illustrated with examples drawn from geographical writing

---

[4] Alan R. H. Baker, ed., *Progress in Historical Geography* (Newton Abbott, England: David & Charles, 1972); and Fernand Braudel, *The Mediterranean and the Mediterranean World in the Age of Philip II*, trans. Siân Reynolds, 2 vols. (London: Collins, 1972). These adjectival terms exist today in professional asymmetry: geographical history is much less recognized as a mode of inquiry in history than historical geography is within geography. Indeed, Robert S. Lopez, in reviewing *History in Geographic Perspective: The Other France*, by Edward Whiting Fox, wrote in the early 1970s of the "murder of geography" and "its expulsion from history" (*American Historical Review*, vol. 77 [1972], p. 1086). For an early discussion of the distinction between geographical history and historical geography, see Walter S. Tower, "Scientific Geography: The Relation of Its Contents to Its Subdivisions," *Bulletin of the American Geographical Society*, vol. 42, 11 (1910), p. 821. A view of the changing usage of these and related terms is offered in Gary S. Dunbar, "Geosophy, Geohistory, and Historical Geography: A Study in Terminology," *Historical Geography*, vol. 10, 2 (1980), pp. 1–8.

[5] "America" and "Americans" in this essay will refer, for the sake of brevity, to the United States and its residents, while acknowledging that, continentally speaking, Mexicans and Canadians are also, of course, North Americans.

[6] The chief historical assessments appear in chapters contributed to three state-of-the-art collections. The first two are: Andrew H. Clark (chairman of the editorial committee and principal author), "Historical Geography," in Preston E. James and Clarence F. Jones, eds., *American Geography: Inventory and Prospect* (Syracuse, N.Y.: Syracuse University Press for the Association of American Geographers, 1954), pp. 71–105; and, for the period after 1950, his "Historical Geography in North America," in Baker, *Progress*, pp. 129–143 (see n. 4, above). The 1954 statement, in a bid for intellectual lineage, devotes considerably more attention to the Old World antecedents of American historical geography and to its post-1925 character than to its formative years (1850–1925) in the United States. The 1972 overview covers both the United States and Canada for the period 1945–1970. Neither chapter, written by a key protagonist in the events described, fully recognizes the development and coexistence of distinctive and competing research traditions, or schools, of historical geography. The third assessment, a much-needed modern introduction to the subject, provides an all-too-brief review of methodological trends and a splendid, though general, summary of substantive themes (lacking references) through the mid-1980s: see Robert D. Mitchell, "The North American Past: Retrospect and Prospect," in Robert D. Mitchell and Paul A. Groves, eds., *North America: The Historical Geography of a Changing Continent* (Totowa, N.J.: Rowman & Littlefield, 1987), pp. 3–21. Most other overviews of the field (see listings in the "General Sources" section of the *Guide*) cover only brief periods of development or discuss particular research topics.

about the American past. It will be built upon the premise that choosing suitable ways of coping with the time dimension in geography has continuously bedeviled scholarly writing since the middle of the nineteenth century, and that successive attempts to dismiss historical explanation from geographical method have foundered against the time-boundedness of process. Consideration of work in the borderlands of the two fields by professional historians—contributions to geographical history, broadly defined—will for practical purposes be limited to a few key instances of interdisciplinary exchange, while recognizing that that aspect of the subject merits much further examination.

The preferences of fashion in geography have swayed to and fro between periods when historical interpretations commanded the discipline and times when they were openly attacked for their lack of contemporary relevance or explanatory power. Throughout, there has been impressive secular increase in the volume of work in historical geography, growing professional awareness among self-styled historical geographers, and several defining moments when geographers at large have acknowledged the value of a historical perspective in pursuing their work. How these features have modulated the methodological and substantive enthusiasms of the discipline as revealed by the contributions to the historical geography of the United States will add further interpretive crosscurrents to this essay. In light of the numerous recent assessments of the subfield, discussion of current ideological, methodological, and substantive enthusiasms will be considered only in summary form, since the purpose of this review is to trace the origins and importance of longer-run and rather deeper-seated patterns of thought.[7]

American historical geography emerged from no one source and followed no single line of development. It evolved through a series of overlapping creative phases, beginning in the early nineteenth century. Each phase reflected current developments in science, geography, and history at large, and the salience of each phase depended on the power of its core ideas in relation to competing concepts. A long, diffuse period of gestation during the last century gave way to a parade of paradigms of notable authority and resilience during the first two-thirds of this century, followed by twenty-five years of laissez-faire eclecticism which recently has come under increased epistemological and ideological challenge.[8] Throughout, geography and

---

[7] Recent reviews of current thought in American historical geography, often embedded in discussions of general trends in the English-language literature of the field as a whole, can be found in Gary S. Dunbar, "Historical Geography: Its Status and Concerns," *Environmental History Newsletter*, vol. 3, 1 (1976), pp. 15-17; Joseph A. Ernst and H. Roy Merrens, "Praxis and Theory in the Writing of American Historical Geography," *Journal of Historical Geography*, vol. 4, 3 (1978), pp. 277-290; R. Cole Harris, "The Historical Geography of North American Regions," *American Behavioral Scientist*, vol. 22, 1 (1978), pp. 115-130; Michael P. Conzen, "Historical Geography: North American Progress during the 1970s," *Progress in Human Geography*, vol. 4, 4 (1980), pp. 549-559; and "Historical Geography: Changing Spatial Structure and Social Patterns of Western Cities," *Progress in Human Geography*, vol. 7, 1 (1983), pp. 88-107; Donald W. Meinig, "The Historical Geography Imperative," *Annals of the Association of American Geographers*, vol. 79, 1 (1989), pp. 79-87; and Carville Earle et al., "Historical Geography," in Gary L. Gaile and Cort J. Willmott, eds., *Geography in America* (Columbus, Ohio: Merrill Publishing Co., 1989), pp. 156–191.

[8] This schema, which guides the present essay, bears a loose but limited relation to that offered for American geography as a whole in Geoffrey J. Martin, "Paradigm Change: A History of Geography in the

history have followed generally independent paths, but they have intersected often enough to enliven occasionally the margins of both, though with variable long-term implications.

Protean Ancestors and Proto-Historical Geography

Geography mattered a great deal to Americans in the nineteenth century. Claiming half a continent in the name of Manifest Destiny, they had scientific and practical reasons to respect and exploit geographical knowledge at all levels. Curiosity and capitalism had by then transformed exploration into big business worldwide, but in no region on Earth was exploration accompanied by so contingent a colonization, mounted on so grand a scale, but so loosely articulated. The gathering of reliable geographical information was pursued at all levels by many individuals and institutions. Following the Louisiana Purchase, government-sponsored geographical expeditions and surveys were organized with considerable frequency, and their reports, from Pike to Schoolcraft, and Powell to Wheeler, increased place knowledge, documented Indian cultures, laid the groundwork for resource development, and built prestige for the fields of physiography, geology, and other natural sciences.[9] What was not recorded by government survey was collected, updated, and arranged by private parties, whose books and manuals on states and regions found a ready market among the legion of would-be settlers and entrepreneurs seeking to participate in the colonization and economic development of the nation's expanding territory.[10]

This market for geographical knowledge had both practical and disinterested sides: there was need for literature to give guidance in the field, and also to inform citizens everywhere of the broad nature and potential of the national domain over which the society they belonged was asserting control. This civic interest bred an appetite for geographical texts for home and school use, supplied by Jedidiah Morse and his successors, and ensured a place for geography, in addition to history, in the

United States, 1892–1925," *National Geographic Research*, vol. 1, 2 (1985), p. 217. Martin's era of "teleological theodicy," prior to 1859, saw little writing that qualifies as historical geography; thereafter, his break points, around 1892, 1925, and 1957, fall fairly close to turning points in the field of historical geography per se.

[9] Carl O. Sauer, "On the Background of Geography in the United States," in *Festschrift für Gottfried Pfeifer, Heidelberger Geographische Arbeiten*, vol. 15 (1967), pp. 59–71, reprinted in Carl O. Sauer, *Selected Essays, 1963–1975* (Berkeley: Turtle Island Foundation, 1981), pp. 241–259. See also Herman R. Friis, "The Role of Geographers and Geography in the Federal Government: 1774–1905," in Brian W. Blouet, ed., *The Origins of Academic Geography in the United States* (Hamden, Conn.: Archon Books, 1981), pp. 37–56; Edmund W. Gilbert, *The Exploration of Western America, 1800–1850: An Historical Geography* (New York: Cambridge University Press, 1933); William H. Goetzmann, *Exploration and Empire: The Explorer and the Scientist in the Winning of the American West* (New York: Alfred A. Knopf, 1966); and John L. Allen, *Passage through the Garden: Lewis and Clark and the Image of the Northwest* (Urbana: University of Illinois Press, 1975). John Wesley Powell deserves a footnote in the development of American historical geography for his interest in Indian ethnology; his account of "The Philosophy of the North American Indians," *Journal of the American Geographical Society*, vol. 8 (1878), pp. 251–268, hints at a broad historical understanding of Indian culture.

[10] James F. Chamberlain, "Early American Geographies," *Yearbook of the Association of Pacific Coast Geographers*, vol. 5 (1939), pp. 23–29; Marcus Baker, "A Century of Geography in the United States," *Science*, n.s. vol. 7, 173 (1898), pp. 541–551; and Robert C. Bredeson, "Landscape Description in Nineteenth-Century American Travel Literature," *American Quarterly*, vol. 20, 1 (1968), pp. 864–894.

emerging schools and academies of the early nineteenth century. Indeed, in an era when there were no professors of geography at American colleges to conceptualize and pursue advanced research, it is to the leaders of primary and secondary education that we must look for the first indigenous steps in cultivating the common ground between history and geography. A pioneer in linking the nation's young history explicitly to its geographical context was Emma Hart Willard, founder of the Troy Female Seminary (1821), who authored the first histories that incorporated maps as essential tools for interpreting historical events for schoolchildren. Willard recognized that events needed locating in space to become concrete and properly connected in the mind, and her books enjoyed wide and sustained popularity (fig. 1).[11] By 1845, George Stillman Hillard, a Boston man of letters, would contribute the first learned American discussion in print dealing specifically with the interdependence of geography and history, read at a meeting of the American Institute of Instruction.[12] Neither the locational emphasis of Willard nor the concern for the distributional character of the environment of Hillard reached beyond the broadest of generalizations, but the dissemination of their views engendered a climate of opinion receptive to more rigorous concepts introduced in subsequent years.[13]

The explosion of geographical knowledge about the United States in this era not only produced vast stores of new data but also initiated a search for pattern and relationship. To descriptive works about regions were added the first serious attempts to relate nature to the development of human society. The influence of the renowned geographer Carl Ritter in Germany and his concept of unity in diversity, grasped through regional geography—which laid the foundation for modern geography in the Western world—was felt in America, in particular through the writings of his student and disciple Arnold Guyot, who held a chair in physical geography and geology at Princeton from 1854 to 1880 (the earliest chair of geography in the United States).[14] Similarly, Charles Darwin's theory of evolution helped shape the

[11] Emma Hart Willard, *History of the United States: or Republic of America Exhibited in Connexion with Its Chronology and Progressive Geography, by Means of a Series of Maps* (New York: White, Gallaher & White, 1828, abridged edition, 1845). For a discussion of Emma Willard and her frequent collaborator, William C. Woodbridge, and their publications, see Daniel H. Calhoun, "Eyes for the Jacksonian World: William C. Woodbridge and Emma Willard," *Journal of the Early Republic*, vol. 4, 1 (1984), pp. 1–26.

[12] George S. Hillard, *On the Connection between Geography and History* (Boston: William D. Ticknor & Co., 1846), 43 pp. This essay focuses largely upon the Old World, but ends with a spirited review of the significance of coastlines, rivers, mountains, climate, soil, and minerals in shaping the contrasting human geography of the American North, South, and West.

[13] See Murry R. Nelson, "Emma Willard: Pioneer in Social Studies Education," *Theory and Research in Social Education*, vol. 15, 4 (1987), pp. 245–254; and Frank J. Manheim, "George Stillman Hillard—An Early American Apostle of Human Geography," *Bulletin of the Geographical Society of Philadelphia*, vol. 35, 1 (1937), pp. 1–7.

[14] Arnold Guyot, *The Earth and Man: Lectures on Comparative Physical Geography in Its Relation to the History of Mankind* (Boston: Gould & Lincoln, 1849). A seminal collection of Ritter's geographical essays, first published in Germany in 1852, became available to American readers nine years later: *Geographical Studies, by the Late Professor Carl Ritter of Berlin*, transl. Rev. William L. Gage (Cincinnati: Van Antwerp, Bragg & Co., 1861), and only six years later a full biography in English was available: William L. Gage, *The Life of Carl Ritter* (New York: Charles Scribner & Co., 1867). For a discussion of Ritter's influence upon American geographers in the nineteenth century, see Richard Hartshorne and Klaus D. Gurgel, "Zu Carl Ritters Einfluß auf die Entwicklung der Geographie in den Vereinigten Staaten von Amerika," in Manfred

context within which a scientific geography could take root in America. The concept that environmental factors regulate how organisms develop from simple to more complex forms had immediate implications for human geography.[15]

During the second half of the nineteenth century some noted generalists interpreted the interplay of environment and humankind for a broad scholarly and lay audience. Chief among these were George Perkins Marsh and Nathaniel Southgate Shaler, proto-geographers before most sciences were well delineated.[16] Marsh paid special attention in *Man and Nature* (1864) to the destructive effects of human occupation on the environment; Shaler, in a more regionally focused book, *Nature and Man in America* (1891), stressed the loss of nonrenewable resources, especially minerals.[17] In both works the threads of history are evident, interwoven through copious illustrations, producing a discursive and primitive macrohistorical geography of environmental adjustment and change through prolonged human occupation.[18] Physical geography had been, and would continue to be, a source of explanation in human patterns. William Morris Davis, a student of Shaler's at Harvard, was at this time developing a strongly historical approach to American landform study.

The growing interest shown in "man-land relations" rested not only on improved understanding of the American environment but also on a steady evolution in the historical interpretation of the national experience. A general shift in American culture during the nineteenth century from romanticism to realism brought with it a reorientation of historical writing from patrician to professional, and the rise by century's end of a scientific history based on a declared commitment to objectivity.[19] This kept history in a complementary position to geography, and the two

Büttner, ed., *Carl Ritter: Zur europäisch-amerikanischen Geographie an der Wende vom 18. zum 19. Jahrhundert* (Paderborn: Ferdinand Schöningh, 1980), pp. 201–219. See also Preston E. James and Geoffrey J. Martin, *All Possible Worlds: A History of Geographical Ideas*, 2d ed. (New York: John Wiley & Sons, 1981), pp. 126–131.

[15] See Willi Ule, "Darwins Bedeutung in der Geographie," *Deutsche Rundschau für Geographie und Statistik*, vol. 31 (1909), pp. 433–443; and especially David R. Stoddart, "Darwin's Influence on the Development of Geography in the United States, 1859–1914," in Blouet, *Origins of Academic Geography*, pp. 265–278 (see above, n. 9).

[16] On Marsh, see David Lowenthal, *George Perkins Marsh, Versatile Vermonter* (New York: Columbia University Press, 1958); on Shaler, see William A. Koelsch, "Nathaniel Southgate Shaler, 1841–1906," *Geographers: Biobibliographical Studies*, vol. 3 (1979), pp. 133–139.

[17] George Perkins Marsh, *Man and Nature; or, Physical Geography as Modified by Human Action* (New York: Charles Scribner & Sons, 1864), revised as *The Earth as Modified by Human Action* (New York: Charles Scribner's Sons, 1874; 3d ed., 1885); Nathaniel Southgate Shaler, *Nature and Man in America* (New York: Charles Scribner's Sons, 1891; 2d ed., 1900).

[18] Shaler had earlier contributed an essay, "The Effect of the Physiography of North America upon Men of European Origin," to Justin Winsor's *Narrative and Critical History of America*, vol. 4 (Boston: Houghton Mifflin & Co., 1885), pp. i–xxx, which two decades later a Harvard economist, Charles J. Bullock, considered appropriate to reprint in his *Selected Readings in Economics* (Boston: Ginn & Co., 1907), pp. 1–22. Shaler's claim as an early American historical geographer rests also on his historical study of *Kentucky: A Pioneer Commonwealth* (Boston: Houghton Mifflin & Co., 1884). Arranged chronologically, it gives explicit attention to the region's physical geography, and is perhaps one of the last formal state histories that could have been penned by a career geologist.

[19] John Higham, *History: Professional Scholarship in America* (Baltimore: Johns Hopkins University Press, rev. ed., 1989), pp. 3–5. This might be said to have paralleled a shift in national public policy, whereby leaders sought to define a new order through the reconceptualization of space: one based on the iden-

emerging disciplines made major inroads on the educational curriculum at all levels. Daniel Coit Gilman, who had once studied with Ritter in Berlin, staunchly promoted the dual study of history and geography, both as a lecturer at Yale University and later as president of Johns Hopkins University.[20] Francis W. Parker, called by John Dewey "the father of progressive education in America," made the first American academic statement on the interdependence of the two fields as director of the Cook County Normal School in Chicago. Paraphrasing what he saw as Ritter's view that "each and every characteristic area of the earth's surface has had a determining influence on the evolution of mankind," Parker nevertheless proposed three notable caveats: that territorial influences vary with stage of human development, and that they can be overcome both by human genes, and by the human spirit.[21] Though appearing in a prominent publication, these caveats seem to have attracted little immediate attention among American geographers of the time.

For all the ferment over the "new history" and the "new geography," however, the pursuit of scholarly problems in the two fields remained largely separate. For historians, geography offered the stage upon which the events of history unfolded, and whether personalities or institutions prevailed in historical explanation, the geographical factor was seen largely as a means of directing the traffic of history on the ground rather than as a means for its promulgation.[22] For geographers, history provided the required extension of time and the unfolding of specific events through which geographical conditions came into balance.

Where the two perspectives met in simple congeniality was in the history of exploration and discoveries. Johann Georg Kohl, "world traveler, geographer, cartographer, historian, and German savant extraordinaire," spent three and a half years (1854–1858) in America, documenting and interpreting the cartographic evidence for the increase in geographical knowledge about North America since the time of Columbus.[23] His map collection, now preserved in the Library of Congress, spurred

---

tification of homogeneous regions and highlighted through the growing use of thematic cartography for national ends. This is the argument made for example, in John Brinckerhoff Jackson, *American Space: The Centennial Years, 1865–1876* (New York: W. W. Norton & Co., 1972), pp. 14–18.

[20] John K. Wright, "Daniel Coit Gilman: Geographer and Historian," *Geographical Review*, vol. 51, 3 (1961), pp. 381–399.

[21] Francis W. Parker, "The Relations of Geography to History," *National Geographic Magazine*, vol. 5, 1 (1894), pp. 125–131. This address was delivered at the International Geographic Conference held in Chicago in 1893 in connection with the World's Columbian Exposition. Parker had studied at the University of Berlin during 1872–1875, and had taken some geography courses there from Kiepert, Ritter's successor. For a brief assessment of Parker's educational significance, see John Dewey, "In Memoriam: Colonel Francis Wayland Parker, Late Director of the School of Education, University of Chicago," *Elementary School Teacher*, vol. 2, 10 (1902), pp. 705–708.

[22] This can be seen clearly in those synthetic works which employed the term "historical geography" during this period. See, for example, Rev. Henry W. Hulbert, "The Historical Geography of the Christian Church," *Papers of the American Society of Church History*, vol. 3 (1891), pp. 135–142.

[23] Fergus J. Wood, "J. G. Kohl and the 'Lost Maps' of the American Coast," *American Cartographer*, vol. 3, 2 (1976), p. 107. See also Hermann A. Schumacher, "Kohls Amerikanische Studien," *Deutsche Geographische Blätter*, vol. 11, 2 (1888), pp. 105–221.

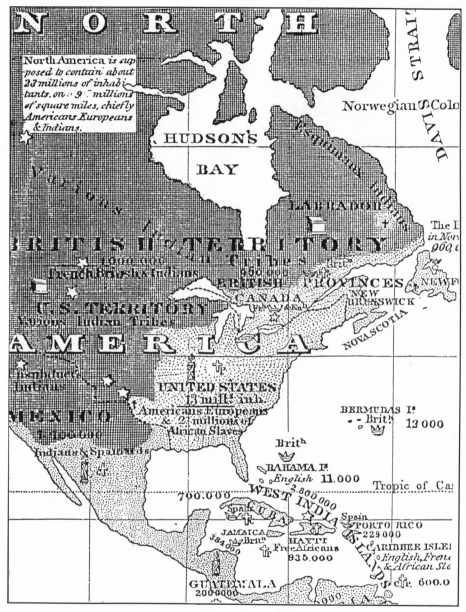

Fig. 1. Portions of "Moral and political chart of the inhabited world," in Woodbridge's School Atlas, copyrighted by William C. Woodbridge and Emma Willard in 1831. The map portrays American culture regions predicated on the notion of developmental stages of civilization, progressing from savagery to enlightenment.

major studies by historians and geographers during the following half century, notably those of Francis Parkman, Justin Winsor, and Walter B. Scaife.[24]

The substantive writing of the nineteenth century that would with today's outlook be considered historical geography fell into three groups: (1) interpretations of generalized human relations with the environment, offered at a broad scale for the most part by geographers and other natural scientists (e.g., Marsh and Shaler); (2) a small but lively literature on the ethnology of native Americans, with particular emphasis on those with fixed settlements, such as the pueblo cultures of the Southwest, by geographers and ethnologists;[25] and (3) accounts of exploration and discovery by historians and geographers, more often than not representing exercises in geographical history rather than historical geography.[26]

As the nineteenth century gave way to the twentieth, the historical impulse in geographical writing took two discernable forms. A controversial school of thought emerged that placed great emphasis on the role of "geographical influences" in human history, and at the same time a nascent but inchoate body of substantive study more or less self-consciously labeled "historical geography" began to emerge, gaining quiet acceptance for its solid contributions as the influences movement encountered increasing resistance. Both these developments, however, were made possible only through a number of larger trends in education and geography.

History, Geography, and Geology: The Ambiguity of Historical Geography

The winds of change that were advancing geography and history as formal fields of study in American school curricula were also blowing through the universities. Three developments held particular import for the historical perspective in geography. The first was the impact of educational reforms in German universities that established new, secular standards of academic freedom, accommodated the new sciences, and introduced new teaching methods, such as the graduate seminar. The German renaissance influenced the organization and curriculum of American higher education in two ways. It attracted many individuals to study there and obtain doctorates, sometimes in fields—such as geography—as yet unavailable in the

---

[24] See, for example, Francis Parkman, *The Discovery of the Great West* (Boston: Little, Brown & Co., 1869); Justin Winsor, *Cartier to Frontenac: Geographical Discovery in the Interior of North America in Its Historical Relations, 1534–1700, with Full Cartographical Illustrations from Contemporary Sources* (Boston: Houghton Mifflin and Co., 1894); and Walter B. Scaife, *America: Its Geographical History, 1492–1892* (Baltimore: Johns Hopkins Press, 1891). For an appreciation of the geographical thought of Justin Winsor, see William A. Koelsch, "'A Profound Though Special Erudition': Justin Winsor as Historian of Discovery," *Proceedings of the American Antiquarian Society*, vol. 93, 1 (1983), pp. 55–94.

[25] D. A. Robertson, "The Prehistoric Inhabitants of the Mississippi Valley, Part I: The Mound Builders," *Journal of the American Geographical Society*, vol. 5 (1874), pp. 256–272; and Cosmos Mindeleff, "Origin of the Cliff Dwellings," *Journal of the American Geographical Society*, vol. 30 (1890), pp. 111–126.

[26] Naming the features of the land followed logically upon "discovery," and a lively retrospective interest emerged during the 1880s in the derivation of place names; see, for example, David D. Field, "On the Nomenclature of Cities and Towns in the United States," *Journal of the American Geographical Society*, vol. 17 (1885), pp. 299–342; Robert T. Hill, "Descriptive Topographic Terms of Spanish America," *National Geographic Magazine*, vol. 7, 9 (1896), pp. 291–302.

United States, and it provided institutional models to be emulated in America in the founding of such institutions as the Johns Hopkins University and the University of Chicago, both designed to specialize in graduate training on a broad front.[27]

One such American who studied in Germany was Ellen Churchill Semple, a product of Vassar College who, after a master's degree in sociology, was attracted to Leipzig (1891–1892 and 1895) and into geography by the teaching there of Friedrich Ratzel. Semple then built an American career popularizing her understanding of Ratzel's ideas about environmental influence under the banner of anthropogeography.[28] Ratzel, the acknowledged European leader in the modern development of human geography, produced the two volumes of his most influential work, *Anthropogeographie*, a decade apart. Volume 1, published in 1882, emphasized the "application of geography to history" (*Grundzüge der Anwendung der Erdkunde auf die Geschichte*), as the subtitle put it, and explored the influence on human society of a host of external factors "in its environmental situation."[29] Only in 1891 did volume 2 appear, concerned with the geographical expansion of humankind (*Die geographische Verbreitung des Mensches*), in which the themes of migration and the reciprocal impact of humans on the environment were more fully developed.

While Ratzel throughout his writings was influenced, as one commentator has observed, "by the ecological emphasis on the totality and mutuality of environmental interaction," his formulations of the topic "were almost invariably vague and even mutually contradictory."[30] Though volume 2 had appeared by the time Semple took up study with Ratzel, she developed a lifelong concern with environmental influences derived much more obviously from the orientation of volume 1.[31] It is a sharp irony that Ratzel's views on human geography and the importance of migration in environmental relations, which were so fully treated in the second volume, apparently ignored by Semple, and which so influenced the growing sophistication of European geography by the turn of the century, had been shaped to a notable degree by his extensive travels in the United States and Mexico in 1873–1874.[32] The

---

[27] Martin, "Paradigm Change," p. 224 (see n. 8 above). It is in this period, 1890–1915, that geography as a whole became firmly established as a scholarly field in leading American universities. See Gary S. Dunbar, "Credentialism and Careerism in American Geography, 1890–1915," in Blouet, *Origins of Academic Geography*, pp. 71–88 (see n. 9, above).

[28] Ellen Churchill Semple, *Influences of Geographic Environment, on the Basis of Ratzel's System of Anthropogeography* (New York: Henry Holt & Co., 1911). Promotion of the term "anthropogeography" was so successful, it was canonized as a crucial key word for cross-indexing in the cataloging system of the Library of Congress, a usage that has remained frozen in time long after its loss of professional currency.

[29] Mark Bassin, "Friedrich Ratzel, 1844–1904," *Geographers: Biobibliographical Studies*, vol. 11 (1987), p. 126.

[30] Ibid., p. 127.

[31] Carl O. Sauer, "On the Background of Geography in the United States," in his *Collected Essays, 1963–1975* (Berkeley: Turtle Island Foundation, 1981), p. 259. "The second volume in which [Ratzel] considered cultural diffusion," notes Sauer drily, "did not attract her attention."

[32] Carl O. Sauer, "The Formative Years of Ratzel in the United States," *Annals of the Association of American Geographers*, vol. 61, 2 (1971), pp. 245–254; and Mark Bassin, "Friedrich Ratzel's Travels in the United States: A Study in the Genesis of His Anthropogeography," *History of Geography Newsletter*, no. 4 (1984), pp. 11–22.

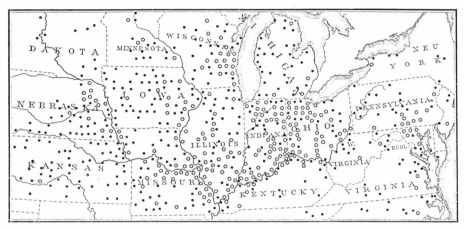

Fig. 2. *"Zones of densest German settlement in 1880," based on Engelbrecht, in Friedrich Ratzel's* Die Vereinigten Staaten von Amerika, *vol. 2, 2d ed., 1893. With symbols showing proportions of Germans to other immigrant groups at the county level (dots signify majority, circles a plurality), interest in the evolving geographical variability of ethnic settlement patterns at that time is well demonstrated.*

mature, two-volume work that emanated from that experience was published in Germany in 1878–1880 (fig. 2), and, as a synthetic treatment of their own culture, appears to have had little or no impact upon American human geographers in the decades that followed, even though many could read German and took considerable interest in German scholarship.[33]

A second development fostering the historical approach was the rise of geographical geology as a distinct field of interest within the natural sciences, and its vital role in creating autonomous departments of geography at American universities, a cause championed by the physiographer Davis. While Davis's own influential concept of the erosion cycle was fundamentally ahistorical, resting upon rigid notions of repetitive, cyclical change and equilibrium, the progress made in American physical geography was responsible for bringing many into the discipline at large with backgrounds in geology, and strengthened the interest in uniting concern for the evolution of the physiographic environment with that of its human occupation.[34] Through this lineage Albert Perry Brigham emerged to provide just such a unified approach, though in his case with a marked concern for history. Brigham started out

---

[33] A slightly earlier, lighter work detailing his travel observations has only recently been published in English: Friedrich Ratzel, *Sketches of Urban and Cultural Life in North America*, trans. and ed. Stewart A. Stehlin (New Brunswick, N.J.: Rutgers University Press, 1988).

[34] This is well reflected in Davis's own retrospective, partisan review of disciplinary growth. He stated that rapid progress in physiography had been a particularly American achievement and was responsible for the rise of domestic interest in its human implications, but, given the delayed progress in American human geography at the turn of the century, this was the sphere most dependent on the importation of European thought. See William M. Davis, "The Progress of Geography in the United States," *Annals of the Association of American Geographers*, vol. 14, 4 (1924), pp. 198–199.

as a Baptist minister but was drawn to study geology and physiography by encounters with Shaler and Davis at Harvard, where he gained a master's degree in 1892. A decade of teaching and writing on physical geography produced a shift in interest by 1902 toward the organic side of geography, stimulated by the facile way in which students of Davis claimed to see organic responses to the environment without accepting the burden of proof, a deficiency which drove Brigham into the human past for evidence.[35]

A third development was the alliance forged at the close of the nineteenth century between some progressive historians and a number of anthropogeographers. Chief among the new scientific historians was Frederick Jackson Turner, who went far beyond the more common regard for geography as a subsidiary aid to history to base his views regarding the character of the United States on a profoundly geographical premise—the significance of the settlement frontier in national cultural development.[36] For Turner, the frontier was a shifting zone at the margin of, and in sharp contrast to, the populated core, with which it interacted economically and socially in galvanic fashion. The frontier was above all a process, but also a generic place, which carried particular localities through a cultural transformation in an inexorable succession of stages. This special type of area, the frontier, continually reworked the central elements of American character and institutions more lastingly than any other source of national social change.[37]

In view of his graduate training, his deep fascination with maps as methodological tools, Turner's interest in the contemporary writings of geographers, and his interaction with them, Turner has been hailed as the "lineal forebearer . . . of historical geography in the United States," and "a cofounder of the American subdiscipline."[38] As a graduate student at Johns Hopkins University he heard Daniel Coit Gilman lecture on physical geography and, later, made extensive use of the statistical atlases of the U.S. Census prepared by Francis Walker and Henry Gannett. Early in his teaching career at Wisconsin, Turner developed an association with the distinguished geologist Thomas C. Chamberlin through his interest in physical regions of the United States, and Turner not only attended the American Historical Association meeting in Chicago in 1893 at which on July 12 he gave his now-famous paper on the frontier, but was also a delegate later that month to the special International Conference on Geographical Sciences held in conjunction with the World's Columbian Exposition, at which Chamberlin and Francis Parker both read papers. Five years later, in 1898, he was back in Chicago giving his first address before a geographical

---

[35] Preston E. James, "Albert Perry Brigham, 1855–1932," *Geographers: Biobibliographical Studies,* vol. 2 (1978), p. 14.

[36] Historical assessment of Turnerian thought in American history is legion. For authoritative treatments by historians, see Ray Allen Billington, *Frederick Jackson Turner: Historian, Scholar, Teacher* (New York: Oxford University Press, 1973); and Hofstadter, *Progressive Historians* (see n. 2, above).

[37] Frederick Jackson Turner, "The Significance of the Frontier in American History," *Proceedings of the State Historical Society of Wisconsin at Its Forty-first Annual Meeting, 1893* (Madison: State Printer, 1893), pp. 79–112.

[38] Robert H. Block, "Frederick Jackson Turner and American Geography," *Annals of the Association of American Geographers,* vol. 70, 1 (1980), pp. 31 and 41.

audience, on the "influence of geography upon the settlement of the United States."[39]

These separate developments converged to produce in the new century two decades or so of dramatic American debate about the extent and nature of geographical influence on human affairs.[40] It focused on the continuity of environmental influence upon history. It defined historical geography on a newly bold but narrow basis, namely, to use Carl Sauer's words, "the persistence of advantage or disadvantage of place, not one of change."[41] It offered geography a way of competing with history in accounting for large human patterns—a scheme that was timeless, but in time; accommodating of history and yet strangely ahistorical. The appeal of this concept thrust it to center stage within the young profession of geography. The debate drew vigorous reaction from historians but, more important, quite transformed the outlook of American geography.

The First School: Semple and "Geographic Influences" in History

The catalysts came with the simultaneous appearance in late 1903 of Semple's *American History and Its Geographic Conditions* and Brigham's *Geographic Influences in American History*,[42] and a new school of thought was launched.[43] The two books tackled a common theme but differed in approach. Brigham attempted "to combine the materials of American history and geography. One must invent a method as he can, for models in this field can scarcely be said to exist. The plan chosen is geographic, as might be expected from a student of earth science. Each division of the book deals with a region which is more or less distinct in its physical devel-

---

[39] Ibid., pp. 36–37.

[40] The earliest American use of the term "influence" appears to be in Semple's first scholarly paper, "The Influence of the Appalachian Barrier upon Colonial History," *Journal of School Geography*, vol. 1, 1 (1897), pp. 33–41. "Geographic influences" first appears in the title of Brigham's 1903 book.

[41] Sauer, "Background," p. 259 (see n. 31, above).

[42] (New York: Houghton Mifflin Co.) and (Boston: Ginn & Co.). Semple had prepared for her book with earlier studies on the Appalachian barrier and the hill folk of the Kentucky Mountains, both concerned with the isolating effects of mountains: "The Influence of the Appalachian Barrier upon Colonial History," and the influential article "The Anglo-Saxons of the Kentucky Mountains: A Study in Anthropogeography," *Geographical Journal*, vol. 17, 6 (1901), pp. 588–623. Brigham had covered similar ground with "The Eastern Gateway of the United States," *Geographical Journal*, vol. 13, 5 (1899), pp. 513–534, reprinted the following year in *Journal of School Geography*, vol. 4, 9 (1900), pp. 361–370.

[43] Recognizing schools in American historical geography implies a clear set of criteria by which to judge their existence. In this essay, for general purposes a school is recognized if a distinctive and consistent pattern of thought about objectives, themes, and methods has evolved over the course of time among sufficient scholars to sustain it for a significant period, and if such identity is acknowledged by at least a portion of the contributors to the field. Such a pattern is likely to arise from the imagination and drive of at least one leading thinker, through his or her own research and writing and the training of students, or the conversion of other scholars, who in turn become productive in the genre. A school is likely to be centered at a particular doctoral institution, given the heightened interactions and credentialling thereby made possible, and its growth can be influenced by recruitment of like-minded outside scholars to the faculty and the recall of promising students as colleagues for reinforcement, as well as by the dispersion of students to other institutions to spread the outlook of the school through teaching. These criteria better fit cases later in the twentieth century, when the discipline had become established in institutions of higher learning, but even the Sempelian school as defined here meets the minimum requirements.

opment, and which often shows in the end a good measure of historical unity."[44] Thus, Brigham wrote chapters on such themes as the "Eastern Gateway of the United States," "Shoreline and Hilltop in New England," "Prairie Country," "Where Little Rain Falls," though sometimes the regions were defined more by their staples ("Cotton, Rice, and Cane," "Mountain, Mine, and Forest"). The book also included chapters on the geography of the Civil War, American destiny, and government study of the national domain.

Semple, on the other hand, sought to "define the relationship between historical movements in the United States and the natural environment as the stage on which history unfolds."[45] Hence, her treatment offers much more room for human actors and their artifacts—exploration, immigrants, railroads, sea power, inland waterways, cities—and she offers chapters on the War of 1812 and the Civil War, ending with a consideration of the United States as a Pacific Ocean power. Both studies are richly larded with discussion of "geographical environment," "geographical influence," and occasionally "geographic control" of historical movements and events.

Both books were favorably received by geographers and historians alike, most noting the pioneering quality and the complementarity of both.[46] Ralph S. Tarr saw political overtones in both books, seeing Brigham's work as demonstrating the influence of geographic conditions on the development of "a great nation" and Semple's study as a grand argument for expansion. While recognizing that each book would find wide and appreciative audiences among geographers, schoolteachers, and a lay readership, he chided Semple for ignoring the Mormons, and chided Brigham, while noting that the latter was too savvy to think that geographic influences actually control, for nevertheless falling "into the use of the phrase 'geographic controls,' which comes so easily to some physiographers."[47]

Historians gave the two volumes prominent notice. Albert Bushnell Hart, for whom "geography is well known to be the handmaid of history," considered both to be fair contributions to geographical history. Turner, invited to review the books for the *Journal of Geography*, welcomed these synthetic works and was struck by the fact that they were written by geographers rather than historians, noting particularly that "Brigham's treatment admirably supplements and checks the work of Miss Semple."[48] In the view of both reviewers, Brigham, "an expert scientific man who

---

[44] Brigham, Preface to his *Geographic Influences in American History*, p. ix.

[45] Semple, Preface to the revised edition of *American History and Its Geographic Conditions* (1933), p. v. The first edition lacks a preface as well as any philosophical or methodological opening statement.

[46] The major exception was Ratzel, who, in a posthumously published pair of reviews in Germany, blithely praised his former pupil's work as suggestive of the value to be gained for North American geographical scholarship from German methodology, while dismissing Brigham's effort as poorly documented and written, and superficial, as evidenced by his disregard for nineteenth-century immigration—this last, a fair criticism. See Friedrich Ratzel, reviews of Semple and Brigham, *Geographischer Literatur-Bericht für 1905, Beilage zum 51. Band von Dr. A. Petermanns Geographische Mitteilungen* (1905), p. 73.

[47] Ralph S. Tarr, reviews of Semple and Brigham, *Bulletin of the American Geographical Society*, vol. 35, 5 (1903), pp. 566–570.

[48] Frederick Jackson Turner, joint review of *American History and Its Geographic Conditions*, and *Geographic Influences in American History*, in *Journal of Geography*, vol. 4, 1 (1905), p. 36.

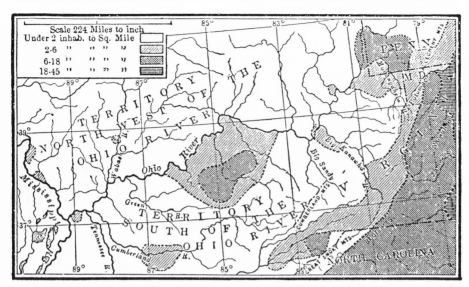

Fig. 3. "Trans-Allegheny Settlements in 1790," in Ellen Semple's American History and its Geographic Conditions *(1903). Generalized population density in relation to physiography was a
major theme in Semple's book, and the subject matter and scale of this map are typical of the illustrations in the work.*

loves the face of his country,"[49] undertook "to illustrate by facts of history and existing social and economic conditions the geographical influence of each province
upon its people," and in doing this "the geography, geology, and exposition of contemporaneous economic conditions leave the historical data rather in the background."[50] Semple, in Hart's view, patterned her "larger, more ambitious" work
"according to the historical advance of the frontier, rather than by a predetermined
geological system," and had "constantly in mind not so much the face of the country
as the movement of people across it"[51] (fig. 3).

But Turner, while sympathetic, also had subtle and important reservations:
Brigham offered too little historical evidence, while Semple "laid greater stress upon
the geographic influences as shown in exploration, early settlement and war, than in
those more enduring factors of natural resources, and conditions that are determining the social development of the American people of the present and of the future."
That is to say, Semple understated the role of human choice and social change.
Turner concluded that both books treated their topics in an introductory, popular
way "that must at some time be handled more deeply." Offering a glimpse of how
this might be done, he wrote, "When the American historian shall unfold the *com-*

---

[49] Albert Bushnell Hart, joint review of *Geographic Influences in American History* and *American History and Its Geographic Conditions,* in *American Historical Review,* vol. 9, 3 (1903–1904), p. 572.

[50] Turner, p. 37 (see n. 48, above).

[51] Hart, p. 572 (see n. 49, above).

bined influences of geography acting upon western expansion and shaping of society to the resources of these vast provinces, *and* of the ethnographic and social groupings, in explaining American development, we shall come nearer to an understanding of the meaning of the nation's history" [emphasis added]. [52]

The books were well written, and by all measures influential in geography. Their simultaneous publication heightened the impact of their essential message. One stemmed from a geological familiarity with landforms, the other from a sociological awareness of people moving through space, but both expounded a theme in which the broad character and layout of the physical landscape demonstrably affected the process by which the continent was peopled. This gave geographers the belief that they had as much to contribute to understanding American life as historians or other social scientists, but at the price, it seems, of accepting a pseudo-historical central paradigm. The influence of the physical environment on human patterns required the use of historical facts, though most interpretations treated time in a highly conflated fashion. Geographical influences came to be discovered and propounded with the frequency and imprecision of Davisian peneplains, and many studies of influence were flawed by overgeneralization and special pleading. At worst, such studies became outright arguments for "environmental determinism," a mechanical and passive model for human behavior.[53]

Some historians were certainly moved by the validity of geographical factors in history, though few were willing to accord them primacy, as many geographers urged. Turner brought historians and geographers together at conferences in 1907 and 1908 to explore their common ground further, but the stridency of Semple's presentations met forceful rebuttal in the person of George Lincoln Burr, a medieval historian who disparaged what he saw as a single-factor argument.[54] The fundamentally geographical basis of Turner's own frontier thesis gave him perhaps more sympathy than most historical colleagues for Semple's cause, but he was too rigorous a historian to rest easy with her often superficial and selective use of historical evidence.[55]

In geography, the geographic-influences persuasion gathered steam following the publication of Brigham's and Semple's books, and Semple's subsequent ap-

---

[52] Turner, p. 37 (see n. 48, above).

[53] Lawrence Gelfand has noted that Semple's early work on the Kentucky mountain people, carefully constructed and based on meticulous fieldwork, offered none of "the almost ridiculous extremes" to which she pushed her method in later writing. Lawrence Gelfand, "Ellen Churchill Semple: Her Geographical Approach to American History," *Journal of Geography*, vol. 53, 1 (1954), pp. 30–41.

[54] Block, "Frederick Jackson Turner," pp. 37–40 (see n. 38, above). Burr had credentials for taking the position he did, since he was arguably the first American historian to offer a university course in historical geography, at Cornell in 1902, having prepared for it by reading among others Marsh and Ratzel. See correspondence between Burr and his colleague J. Franklin Jameson, in Elizabeth Donnan and Leo F. Stock, eds., *An Historian's World: Selections from the Correspondence of John Franklin Jameson* (Philadelphia: American Philosophical Society, 1956), pp. 84–85. For Burr's general position, see George L. Burr, "The Place of Geography in the Teaching of History," *Annual Report of the New England History Teachers Association for 1907* (1908), pp. 1–13.

[55] See, for example, his listing of factual errors in Semple's American book, in Turner, review, p. 35 (see n. 48, above).

pointment to the University of Chicago, an association which lasted from 1904 to 1921.[56] Shortly some graduate theses began to employ the term, and between 1908 and 1918 a string of state-level interpretations appeared in articles, mostly midwestern and most appearing in the *Journal of Geography*, including two by Ray H. Whitbeck (called to the University of Wisconsin in 1909). Other large-scale applications emerged, such as geographic influences on slavery (Frederick V. Emerson), commerce (Emory R. Johnson), and political history (Turner). Later, town studies became popular as exemplars of successfully determined locations, including one by Nevin M. Fenneman on early Cincinnati, and a punchy one by Alexander N. Winchell asking "Why is Butte?"[57] It was a period in which, as Isaiah Bowman remarked approvingly, "the second stage of development of the historico-geographic field has now been entered. Students are working up the facts and laws of the evolution of the people of a small tract, with due attention to all the recognizable factors, before setting their hands to a continent."[58] An early bias toward landforms was extended to climate and climatic change through the work of Ellsworth Huntington.[59]

Despite rising criticism, the general concept of geographic influences maintained a certain popularity, appearing in theses and dissertation titles well into the 1940s, especially at Clark University, where Semple closed her career.[60] The last sustained use of the term in a publication (1962), however, belongs to Stephen S. Visher, a Semple disciple from her early Chicago days.[61]

[56] Rollin D. Salisbury engaged Semple to teach part-time (at her insistence) in the new geography department at the University of Chicago, attractive for its access to promising graduate students. Though Semple turned to other projects, the theme of her book spurred Harlan H. Barrows, newly appointed to the faculty there, to offer a course closely tied to Semple's book. See William A. Koelsch, ed., *Lectures on the Historical Geography of the United States as Given in 1933 by Harlan H. Barrows* (Chicago: University of Chicago Department of Geography, Research Paper no. 77, 1962), pp. v–vi.

[57] Ray H. Whitbeck, "Geographical Influences in the Development of New Jersey," *Journal of Geography*, vol. 6, 6 (1908), pp. 177–182; and "Geographical Influences in the Development of New York State," *Journal of Geography*, vol. 9, 5 (1911), pp. 119–124; Frederick V. Emerson, "Geographic Influences in American Slavery," *Bulletin of the American Geographical Society*, vol. 43, 1–3 (1911), pp. 13–26, 106–118, and 170–181; Emory R. Johnson, "Geographic Influences Affecting the Early Development of American Commerce," *Bulletin of the American Geographical Society*, vol. 40, 3 (1908), pp. 129–143; Frederick Jackson Turner, "Geographical Influences in American Political History," *Bulletin of the American Geographical Society*, vol. 46, 8 (1914), pp. 591–595; Nevin M. Fenneman, "Geographic Influences Affecting Early Cincinnati," *Journal of Geography*, vol. 9, 7 (1911), p. 192; and Alexander N. Winchell, "Why is Butte?" *Journal of Geography*, vol. 10, 3 (1911), pp. 86–88.

[58] In his review of Harlan Barrows's *Geography of the Middle Illinois Valley*, in *Bulletin of the American Geographical Society*, vol. 42, 9 (1910), p. 691.

[59] Ellsworth Huntington, *The Climatic Factor as Illustrated in Arid America* (Washington, D.C.: Carnegie Institution of Washington, Publication no. 192, 1914).

[60] Semple taught at Clark for ten years until her death in 1932. Continuing demand for copies of *American History and Its Geographic Conditions* spurred the preparation of a revised edition, enlarged and completed as her health failed with the assistance of Clarence F. Jones, a Clark colleague and one of Semple's most devoted former Chicago students. The volume was published posthumously in 1933.

[61] Stephen S. Visher, "Geographic Influences, Changes in Bloomington, Indiana," *Proceedings of the Indiana Academy of Science*, vol. 71 (1962), pp. 265–270. The term was used once more in print in 1984, but this appears to be an isolated throwback rather than any sign of revival: see Richard N. Pawling, "The Geographic Influences upon the Development and Decline of the Union Canal," *Pennsylvania Geographer*, vol. 22, 1–2 (1984), pp. 14–21.

An Independent "Historical Geography" becomes Respectable

It is clear that not all American geographers subscribed to environmental determinism during the early decades of this century. It was a theme with greatly varying degrees of acceptance, even in its heyday, but few at the time had the conviction to reject outright its more compelling attractions. There was criticism from the outset, from within and beyond the discipline.[62] As studies accumulated, the interpretive problems became obvious. Brigham himself, as early as 1905, voiced concern over standards of measurement for environmental influence, restated in his presidential address to the Association of American Geographers in 1914, though he did not abandon the axiom of environmental influences per se.[63] Added criticism arose from historians, who found geographers' use of historical sources unreliable,[64] and from new voices within geography, particularly after Huntington sought to link climate with levels of civilization.[65] As Guyot and Semple had labored to familiarize Americans with the writings of key German geographers, Isaiah Bowman sought to draw attention to those of the principal Frenchmen. A translation of Jean Brunhes's *Géographie humaine*, originally published in 1910, appeared in the United States in 1920, and in it Americans discovered a strong repudiation of geographical determinism, and in its place a viewpoint that came to be known as "possibilism."[66] In 1925 followed a translation of Lucien Febvre's *La terre et l'évolution humaine*, which helped further distance geographers from the determinist paradigm.[67]

---

[62] It must be noted that environmental determinism as a scientific paradigm was by no means peculiar to geography, and debate over the proper role of deterministic modes of explanation raged throughout history, philosophy, and the life sciences during this period. See Ernest Nage, "Determinism in History," *Philosophy and Phenomenological Research*, vol. 20, 3 (1960), pp. 291–317; and Sidney Hook, "Determinism," in *Encyclopaedia of the Social Sciences*, vol. 5 (New York: Macmillan Co., 1931), pp. 110–114.

[63] Albert Perry Brigham, "The Character and Limitations of Geographical Influence," *Minutes of the Third Annual Convention of the Association of History Teachers of the Middle States and Maryland, Held at New York University, March 10 and 11, 1905* (1905), pp. 43–55; and "Problems of Geographic Influence," *Annals of the Association of American Geographers*, vol. 5, 1 (1915), pp. 3–25.

[64] Semple's convictions, and her specialization in the Mediterranean world of antiquity, carried her fearlessly and frequently into the courts of historical opinion, a veritable activist as set against Brigham's more open-minded professional posture. In almost every encounter the reaction to her position was the same. Responding to a paper she gave at a historical meeting in 1916 on climatic and geographic influences upon ancient Mediterranean agriculture, discussion, it was reported, focused on "a general criticism of the methods of reasoning employed by historical geographers working in ancient history, though upon sound data, of the insufficiency of their training in those rigorous methods of criticism of sources which have been developed in ancient history, and of the failure to consider adequately the obvious variants from their general principles of the operation of constant geographic factors"; *American Historical Review*, vol. 22, 3 (1917), p. 518. Semple's scope for speculative study on a large scale was remarkable, but her work rested on perusal of largely secondary sources and a predisposition to select examples fitting her design while ignoring those that did not.

[65] Mark Jefferson, "Some Considerations on the Geographical Provinces of the United States," *Annals of the Association of American Geographers*, vol. 7, 1 (1917), p. 3; Ellsworth Huntington, *Climate and Civilization* (New Haven: Yale University Press, 1915).

[66] Jean Brunhes, *Human Geography: An Attempt at a Positive Classification, Principles and Examples*, transl. T. C. LeCompte (Chicago: Rand McNally & Co., 1920). Possibly, the difficulties of World War I, after which, in Geoffrey Martin's words, "relationships with German geographers were impaired," contributed to American interest in French geographers. Martin, "Paradigm," p. 230 (see n. 8, above).

[67] Lucien Febvre, *A Geographical Introduction to History* (New York: Alfred A. Knopf, 1925).

American geographers did not abandon historical study, however, for the record of publication on United States topics grew substantially during the decades of the teens and twenties. Two changes occurred. While old habits of learning lingered and new ideas filtered slowly through the academy, a moderation of terminology took place. There was less talk of geographical "control" and "influence," and more of "adjustment" and "response." These terms implied, at least, a larger role for human initiative.[68] In addition, there was a definite shift toward more localized regional studies in which geographic influences could be more closely considered against competing factors, and a number of substantial research efforts were completed. Notable among these were two works by Brigham, an early book on routeways through the Appalachian Mountains and a later study of Cape Cod.[69] Frederick V. Emerson made a double mark: he produced the first substantial investigation of evolutionary city-hinterland relations with his doctoral study of New York City, and he founded the specific study of Southern historical geography, with small but innovative works on slavery, Civil War campaigns, and the lower Mississippi Valley.[70]

In a quite independent vein, a remarkable study of Connecticut Valley towns was published in 1907 by Martha Krug Genthe, who had earned a doctorate under Alfred Hettner at Heidelberg and spent ten years (1901–1911) teaching school in the United States. In it, Genthe examined the periodic "transformation of geographical values" exhibited in the evolution of nucleated settlements and town growth in the region from European colonization to the industrial revolution. The study is interesting for its dissociation from the determinism of American geographers—and Ellen Semple in particular—at the time. Genthe saw her chosen study area as "an instructive example of how far man is from being helplessly dependent on his geographical environment."[71] The study is therefore conceptually advanced for the pe-

---

[68] Harlan H. Barrows, "Geography as Human Ecology," *Annals of the Association of American Geographers*, vol. 13, 1 (1923), pp. 1–14. This theme is treated at length in Gerhard Fuchs, *Der Wandel zum anthropogeographischen Denken in der amerikanischen Geographie: Strukturlinien der geographischen Wissenschaftstheorie; dargestellt an den vorliegenden wissenschaftlichen Veröffentlichungen, 1900–1930* (Marburg: Marburger Geographische Schriften, no. 32, 1966).

[69] Albert P. Brigham, *From Trail to Railway through the Appalachians* (Boston: Ginn & Co., 1907); and *Cape Cod and the Old Colony* (New York: G. P. Putnam's Sons, 1920).

[70] Frederick V. Emerson, *A Geographic Interpretation of New York City* (Chicago: University of Chicago, private edition, 1909), the first dissertation awarded a Ph.D. in an American department of geography (1907); and his "Geographic Influences in American Slavery" (see n. 57, above). Emerson had been drawn into geography through geology as an undergraduate at Colgate University by Brigham, and later taught at Louisiana State University until his death in 1919.

[71] Martha Krug Genthe, "Valley Towns of Connecticut," *Bulletin of the American Geographical Society*, vol. 39, 9 (1907), p. 515. Genthe had the distinction of earning the first doctorate ever awarded to a woman in geography, anywhere in the world, and was one of only two women founding members of the Association of American Geographers (established in 1904); Semple was the other. With a common exposure to German geographical teaching at the turn of the century, the philosophical contrast these two women offered is striking. Lacking access to a university position, however—excluded by nepotism rules from her spouse's college, she taught for eight years at the Beacon School in Hartford, Connecticut, and the Ethical Culture School in New York City—Genthe had far less opportunity to influence the course of American human geography. Some of the background information on Genthe is drawn from Allen D. Bushong, "Martha Krug Genthe and American Geography," paper presented at the Annual Meeting of the Associ-

riod, and is moreover a precocious dual investigation of American urban morphology and urban network analysis not surpassed for many years.

There was another trend that signaled change. Studies began appearing after 1911 specifically labeled as "historical geography."[72] Whether this was done in order to distinguish them from the broader studies of geographic influences is difficult to say, but the first two cases concerned state boundaries and are detailed reconstructions of the course of political events that determined the positioning of the boundary lines.[73] The third known case is that of Almon E. Parkins' celebrated *The Historical Geography of Detroit* (completed as a dissertation in 1914, published in 1918).[74] By the standards of the time, this work is voluminous (365 printed pages) and very well documented, employing a combination of primary as well as secondary sources. It followed Frederick Emerson's New York City study in basic concept, namely focusing on the city's changing locational significance over time, but concluded unequivocally that "geographic factors" had had only a relatively small role in Detroit's development.

Following Parkins's book, use of "historical geography" in the titles of works became relatively common, and the term gained sufficient favor to serve in one case as a label under which to offer old wine in a new bottle. Harlan H. Barrows's celebrated historical course at Chicago, offered from 1904 through the 1930s, began its run entitled "Influence of Geography on American History," but in 1923 it was changed to "Historical Geography of the United States."[75] One last Chicago dissertation of the period deserves mention, for while *The Geography of the Ozark Highland of Missouri*, completed in 1915 under Rollin D. Salisbury, betrays in its title no historical

---

ation of American Geographers, Miami, Florida, April 1991; see also "Karl Wilhelm Genthe, College Prof.," *Who Was Who in America*, vol. 5 (Chicago: A. N. Marquis & Co., 1973), p. 265.

[72] The only prior use of the term in substantive American work was for a historical school atlas (Townsend MacCoun, *An Historical Geography of the United States* [New York: The author, 1889, 1890, 1892, 1901]), and as used by historians; see nn. 22 and 54. MacCoun also published history textbooks in the 1880s.

[73] George J. Miller, "The Establishment of Michigan's Boundaries: A Study in Historical Geography," *Bulletin of the American Geographical Society*, vol. 43, 5 (1911), pp. 339–350; and Constance G. Eirich, "A Study in Historico-Geography: The Establishing of the Ohio-Michigan Boundary Line," *Journal of Geography*, vol. 12, 1 (1913), pp. 5–8.

[74] Private edition, University of Chicago Libraries, 1918; and Lansing: Michigan Historical Commission, University Series, no. 3, 1918.

[75] Similarly, shifts in student thesis nomenclature also reflected the move away from the term "influences." Mary Jean Lanier was listed in 1916 at work on a Chicago doctoral dissertation examining "Geographical Influence on the Development of the Atlantic Seaports," (*American Historical Review*, vol. 22, no. 3 [1917], p. 494); by 1921, the scope had been narrowed to "Geographical Influences on the Development of New England Seaports"; and so it continued until the year of its completion, at which point the actual title became "The Earlier Development of Boston as a Commercial Center" (Ph.D. diss., University of Chicago, 1924; *List of Doctoral Dissertations in History Now in Progress at the Chief American Universities, December 1921*, Washington, D.C., Carnegie Institution of Washington, Department of Historical Studies, 1922; idem, 1925). As for Harlan Barrows, the material of his popular lecture course, never published by him, nonetheless had a salutary impact on generations of geography students by presenting the historical perspective within a geographical setting. Transcribed notes from the mature 1933 course offering were ultimately edited and published as a memorial to Barrows. See Koelsch, *Lectures* (see n. 56, above).

orientation, its author, Carl Ortwin Sauer, would before long establish himself as a major scholar in the field.[76]

With the rise in the number of more careful investigations of the geographical evolution of places, there was a concomitant decline in the number of general and synthetic studies between 1915 and 1930. Agriculture replaced transportation as a preeminent focus of interest, and many specialized historical studies made their first appearance in urban and economic geography, as well as on questions of land use, manufacturing, and even perception.[77] Geographers at the University of Chicago, and later at the University of Wisconsin, though mainly preoccupied—as elsewhere—with defining the broad character of geography in such a way as to fully incorporate the human dimension, almost offhandedly trained a number of historically minded geographers before 1930 who went on to staff important teaching centers around the United States.[78]

The early interdisciplinary debates with historians had proved stimulating, for implicit in Semple's campaign was the search for general principles if history were to aspire to the status of a science.[79] "Scientific history" would eventually fail to capture the historical profession at large, but some historians did make particular use of geography in their research and teaching.[80] Besides Turner, others including Orin G. Libby (elections), Ulrich B. Phillips (slavery) and, later, Joseph Schafer (agricultural settlement) followed the Turnerian proclivity for cartographic analysis in shedding light on historical problems.[81] Maps had been valued in teaching American history since the days of Emma Willard, and Albert Hart, who had published general teaching atlases since 1891, kept his hand in with revised editions issued well into the

---

[76] Sauer's doctoral study drew a lengthy review essay by J. F. Unstead in the *Geographical Journal* (vol. 59, 1 [1922], pp. 55–59), convincing the reviewer that historical geography had, in the light of studies such as this, gained "independent existence as a science" separate from geography and history.

[77] Mark S. Jefferson, "How American Cities Grow," *Bulletin of the American Geographical Society*, vol. 48, 1 (1915), pp. 19–37; Ella M. Wilson, "The Aroostook Valley: A Study in Potatoes," *Geographical Review*, vol. 16, 2 (1926), pp. 196–205; James W. Goldthwait, "A Town That Has Gone Down Hill," *Geographical Review*, vol. 17, 4 (1927), pp. 527–552, focused on Lyme, New Hampshire, 1790–1925; Eric P. Jackson, "The Early Historical Geography of San Francisco," *Journal of Geography*, vol. 26, 1 (1927), pp. 12–22; Guy-Harold Smith, "The Populating of Wisconsin," *Geographical Review*, vol. 18, 3 (1928), pp. 402–421. A notably early "perception" study is Freeman Ward, "South Dakota and Some Misapprehensions," *Geographical Review*, vol. 17, 2 (1927), pp. 236–250.

[78] At Chicago, Barrows and Semple were the key figures who gave such support, though Salisbury (who directed Sauer) and J. Paul Goode (who directed Emerson) should also be noted; and at Wisconsin, Whitbeck.

[79] Higham, *History*, p. 108 (see n. 19, above).

[80] In the early methodological writing of Frederick J. Teggart, a proponent of scientific history, geography even represented half the "equation." See "The Geographical Factor in History" in his *The Processes of History* (New Haven: Yale University Press, 1918), pp. 41–78; reprinted in his *Theory and Processes of History* (Berkeley: University of California Press, 1941), pp. 247–267.

[81] See, for example, Orin G. Libby, *Geographical Distribution of the Vote of the Thirteen States on the Federal Constitution, 1787–8* (Madison: University of Wisconsin Bulletin; Economics, Political Science, and History Series, vol. 1, 1, 1894); Ulrich B. Phillips, "The Origin and Growth of the Southern Black Belts," *American Historical Review*, vol. 11, 4 (1906), pp. 798–816; and Joseph Schafer, *Wisconsin Domesday Book Town Studies*, vol. 1 (Madison: State Historical Society of Wisconsin, 1924).

1940s.[82] There was, however, one project that drew historians and geographers together in a particularly close and common interest, with spectacular results.

J. Franklin Jameson, a key figure in the early organization of the historical profession, began as early as 1902 when he was professor of history at the University of Chicago to lay the foundations for a major scholarly historical atlas for the United States.[83] It is not clear what gave him this specific idea, but Jameson had taken his doctorate in history at Johns Hopkins University, where he had been influenced among others by Daniel Coit Gilman, and as a teaching assistant there not only had conducted courses that included one on physical geography as a factor in ancient history, but also had taken on "arranging the bureau of maps" in the history department. It is reasonable to suppose that he would have been quite familiar with various European, especially German, historical atlases devoted to ancient and modern history. The newly created Carnegie Institution of Washington (headed by none other than Gilman), ultimately funded his proposal for an American atlas as part of the long-range activities of its Department of Historical Research, and from 1912 to 1927 Jameson (the department's director during that time) supervised the work on the project, which was coordinated by Charles O. Paullin (a former doctoral student of Jameson's at Chicago).[84] In 1929 the American Geographical Society was brought in to produce the maps and thus complete the project, and director Isaiah Bowman placed John Kirtland Wright in charge as editor.[85] Wright, to ensure that the atlas "be further strengthened geographically," revamped most sections and added many new maps with accompanying text, predicting that "unless one is much mistaken the *Atlas* will be a dynamic force in historical and geographical studies in this country for many years to come."[86] The *Atlas of the Historical Geography of the United States* was a publishing landmark for both fields. With 637 maps, many in color, covering eighteen themes (from environment, Indians, explorations, lands; through

---

[82] It was such involvement with maps and geography no doubt that drew Columbia University historian W. R. Shepherd (editor of *Shepherd's Historical Atlas*) to the First International Congress of Historical Geography, held in Brussels in 1930. Among the other four American participants, Edward L. Stevenson was also a geographical historian, interested in early maps. Significantly, though, while Clifford Darby, Gordon East, and Eva G. R. Taylor were there from Britain, and Henri Pirenne headed the host-country delegation, the European-oriented program failed to attract either the rising or the established historical geographers in the United States at the time. See "Liste des participants du congrès," in F. Quicke, ed. *Premier Congrès international de géographie historique*, vol. 1, *Compte-rendu des travaux du congrès 1930* (Brussels: Librairie Falk, for the Secrétariat Général, 1931), pp. 145–157.

[83] For a general account of his role, see John K. Wright, "J. Franklin Jameson and the Atlas of the Historical Geography of the United States," in Ruth Anna Fisher and William L. Fox, eds., *J. Franklin Jameson: A Tribute* (Washington, D.C.: Catholic University of American Press, 1965), pp. 66–79. Regarding the sources of his early interest in historical geography, see Waldo G. Leland, "Jameson, John Franklin," *Dictionary of American Biography*, vol. 22, suppl. 2 (New York: Charles Scribner's Sons, 1958), p. 340.

[84] Charles O. Paullin, "The Carnegie Institute's Atlas of the Historical Geography of the United States," *Journal of Geography*, vol. 14, 4 (1915), pp. 108-109.

[85] Among the host of consultants during the painstaking research phase, historians Frederick Jackson Turner, Herbert Bolton, and Orin Libby, geographers Ray Whitbeck and Lawrence Martin, and anthropologist Alfred Kroeber stand out. During Wright's editorial phase, additional help came from geographers such as Oliver E. Baker, Robert DeCourcy Ward, and Nevin Fenneman.

[86] John K. Wright, Introduction to *Atlas of the Historical Geography of the United States* (Washington: Carnegie Institution of Washington and the American Geographical Society of New York, 1932), p. xv.

settlement, population, and economic, social, political patterns; to military and urban topics) and 145 pages of commentary on sources, map construction, and interpretation, it offered in unprecedented depth and quality of historical research a grand
cartographic summary of the nation's development. Reviews were for the most part
in awe of the achievement, although historian Frederick Merk, student and colleague of Turner, paid it the best compliment with a fair but searching review in the
New England Quarterly.[87] In general, however, Wright's prediction was justified.[88]

The first quarter of the twentieth century had witnessed Promethean battles
over the scope and orientation of American geography, in which the historical perspective had played a critical role and produced a literature of brash generalization
balanced precariously upon fragmentary research. The Sempelian view waxed and
waned in this period though her influence lingered on, lodged in the synapses of a
generation, while the nonideological call of the past attracted attention from other
geographers, without fanfare but with small and comely results. The next quarter
century would see competition between new orthodoxies and a certain isolation of
historical studies in the field. As the general retreat from environmentalism took
refuge in small-area study and a near fixation with regional description, much of it
willfully contemporary, historically aware geographers responded in three ways. The
most outspoken and significant reaction came from Carl Sauer, whose broad intellectual outlook and teaching skill cultivated a sustained new historical tradition in
American geography of fully international stature. He was not the only champion of
the evolutionary approach in geography, however, and for those caught between culture history and regional geography Derwent S. Whittlesey's "sequent occupance"
approach to joining the past to the present held appeal. Beyond these lay a third research domain, focused with vigor on the past for its own sake and on the scrupulous examination of detailed historical sources. Each merits a closer look.

The Second School: Berkeley and Geographical Culture History

For American historical geography 1932 was a poignant year, for it saw the
deaths of all its established leaders, Semple, Brigham, and Turner. By then, however,

---

[87] Vol. 6, 3 (1933), pp. 620–625. The *Atlas* won the Loubat Prize for best publication in North American
history and geography. Aside from two short articles by John K. Wright based on data from the *Atlas* in
the *Geographical Review*, the atlas received only one independent assessment in an American geographical periodical, by Ralph H. Brown in the *Journal of Geography*, vol. 32, 4 (1933), pp. 177–178. By contrast, a
lengthy review article on it by Leopold Scheidl for a German audience appeared in *Mitteilungen der Geographischen Gesellschaft in Wien*, vol. 82 (1939), pp. 309–317.

[88] The year 1932 was also the bicentennial of George Washington's birth. To commemorate this event,
the federal government commissioned a separate scholarly atlas, prepared by the chief geographer at
the Library of Congress. See Lawrence Martin, ed., *The George Washington Atlas: A Collection of Eighty
Five Maps, Including Twenty-Eight Made by George Washington, Seven Used and Annotated by Him,
Eight Made at His Discretion, or for His Use, or Otherwise Associated with Him, and Forty-Two New
Maps Concerning His Activities in Peace and War and His Place in History* (Washington, D.C.: U.S.
George Washington Bicentennial Commission, 1932) 50 plates, 85 maps. Albert Hart was the project's historian, and advisers included Paullin and Wright, Albert Brigham, Ellen Semple, and Gilbert Grosvenor
of the National Geographic Society. This atlas, much simpler in purpose and preparation, was created in
less than a year. Among many interesting maps, it includes a locality series detailed enough to adjudicate
emphatically any and all claims that "George Washington slept here."

the changing of the guard had already taken place. Almost a decade before, in 1923, Carl Sauer had been called from the University of Michigan to head the department of geography at the University of California–Berkeley. Few at the time realized what this move presaged. It secured a stable venue for the long-term professional development of one of the most imaginative geographical thinkers in the United States in the twentieth century, and the emergence of a school of historical geography more scholastically robust and ultimately influential than the army of environmental-influence devotees once stimulated by Semple, and more conceptually focused than those who labored in the partial vacuum which followed that creed's decline.[89]

Sauer had taken courses from Semple and Barrows as a graduate student at the University of Chicago between 1909 and 1913, but he was not much impressed by Semple's environmental interpretations of human development. Born of Missouri German stock, Sauer had spent five years gaining a classical education in a German school at Calw, Württemberg, before attending college back in the Middle West. En route to his doctorate he worked in downtown Chicago for Rand McNally & Co. as a map editor, and, as he described later, "I read German geographers evenings who were doing what I wanted."[90] Equally important, he became a skilled observer in the field, which yielded evidence sharply at odds with the "rather simple mechanical behaviour in which human beings 'responded' in various but primarily economic ways to the qualities of their physical surroundings."[91] He spoke in later years of un-learning what the Chicago human geographers had taught, whereas his debt to the geomorphologist Rollin D. Salisbury and the botanist Henry C. Cowles at Chicago remained substantial.

There are signs of a growing interest in historical explanation in Sauer's early research, but its expression was then limited. His first monograph, a commissioned work for the Illinois Geological Survey on the upper Illinois Valley, provided a capsule overview of the area's human occupance as an appendage to a larger, geomorphological study.[92] His dissertation on the Missouri Ozarks is arranged topically, although the chapters on population, settlement, and livelihood are richly historical in content (fig. 4).[93] Sauer's preoccupations while in Michigan centered on land use

---

[89] The flow of scholarly assessments of Carl Sauer following his death has been likened to a cottage industry. Judging from the extended list included in the "Benchmark Scholars" section of the bibliography, including learned studies of such phases of his life as his teenage undergraduate experience, it might now be time to declare it a heavy industry.

[90] Quoted in Geoffrey J. Martin, Foreword to Martin S. Kenzer, ed., *Carl O. Sauer: A Tribute* (Corvallis: Oregon State University Press, 1987), p. ix.

[91] John B. Leighly, "Carl Ortwin Sauer, 1889–1975," *Geographers: Biobibliographical Studies*, vol. 2 (1978), p. 100.

[92] Carl O. Sauer, *Geography of the Upper Illinois Valley and History of Settlement* (Urbana: Illinois Geological Survey, Bulletin no. 27, 1916). Instigated by Harlan Barrows, this follows closely the organization of Barrows's own *Geography of the Middle Illinois Valley* (Urbana: Illinois State Geological Survey, Bulletin no. 15, 1910), which had spurred Isaiah Bowman in a highly favorable review to "earnestly hope for other papers of a like sort from the same source." See Isaiah Bowman, review of *Geography of the Middle Illinois Valley*, in *Bulletin of the American Geographical Society*, vol. 42, 9 (1910), p. 692.

[93] Carl O. Sauer, *The Geography of the Ozark Highland of Missouri* (Chicago: Geographic Society of Chicago, Bulletin no. 7, 1920).

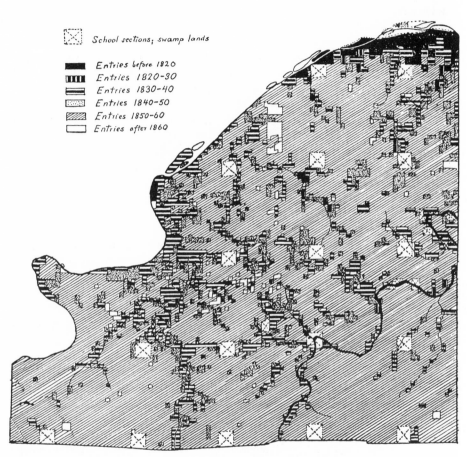

Fig. 4. "Order of land entries in Osage County," in Carl Sauer's The Geography of the Ozark Highland of Missouri *(1920). Prepared from the county land entry book, this diachronic map illustrates the use of original sources to portray a dynamic geographical process—the early spatial selectivity of land colonization by Euro-American settlers in a particular locale.*

and land planning, and it was not until he reached California that the call of the deep human past reached him. With the new luxury of free summers, he set out to explore neighboring regions, and in Mexico and the American Southwest acquired an abiding interest in the antiquity of cultures that knew no boundaries, intellectual or geographical.

Impatient not only with "environmental relations" but also with the orthodoxy of regional studies he had known in the Middle West, Sauer sought to outline a more satisfactory framework for research, and in *The Morphology of Landscape* (1925) drew especially on German writings and the concept of *Kulturlandschaft* to recommend to fellow Americans the "cultural landscape" as the proper object of geographical study: "The cultural landscape is fashioned out of a natural landscape by a culture group. Culture is the agent, the natural area is the medium, the cultural landscape is the result."[94] Historical time played a direct role, but the emphasis of the essay as a whole was on the cultural landscape as the present-day object of investigation for geographers. In this scheme, "Historical geography may be considered as the series of changes which the cultural landscapes have undergone and therefore involves the reconstruction of past cultural landscapes."[95] Sauer was to retreat in later years from the heavy landscape emphasis in this disciplinary manifesto, but it serves as a revealing benchmark in the evolution of his views on the proper conduct of geography, and his growing sympathy for an explicitly historical approach.

Well grounded in physical geography, but with a deepening commitment to culture as the key to human geography, Sauer developed close ties with anthropologist Alfred Kroeber and historian Herbert E. Bolton at Berkeley. They launched *Ibero-Americana*, a serial that would carry their work and that of their students to many corners of the world. Whatever might have been the competitive strengths of geographical centers in the East and the Middle West, Sauer soon attracted a string of outstanding doctoral students who would in time seed the training programs of other universities and promote what has come to be known as the Berkeley school of cultural-historical geography.[96]

The essence of Sauer's conceptual approach lay in clarifying what the Germans call the *Standortsproblem*, expressed by Sauer as the problem of understanding the "localization of ways of living."[97] This can be approached by studying the territorial spread of individual culture traits (or acquired habits), and identifying the culture complexes or culture areas that these traits in combination create. The richest source of evidence lies in the material content of the cultural landscape. "The whole task of human geography, therefore, is nothing less than comparative study of areally localized cultures." This demands historical inquiry: into the origins and changing functions, or modes of living, of the culture (those processes of living together as a group), and particularly into the distinction between those ways "discovered for themselves and those they acquired from other culture groups." Thus did Sauer define the logical basis for historical geography, a pursuit with fundamentally geographical objectives—the spatial differentiation of culture—as distinct from the history-serving orientation of Semple's geographical history. "The quality of understanding sought," argued Sauer, "is that of analysis of origins and processes. . . . Dealing with man and being genetic in its analysis, the subject is of necessity concerned with sequences in time."

---

94 Carl O. Sauer, *The Morphology of Landscape* (Berkeley: University of California Publications in Geography, vol. 2, 2, 1925), p. 46.

95 Ibid., p. 47.

96 See Joseph E. Spencer, "What's in a Name: 'The Berkeley School'?" *Historical Geography Newsletter*, vol. 6, 1 (1976), pp. 7–11; and William W. Speth, "Berkeley Geography: 1923–33," in Blouet, *Origins of Academic Geography*, pp. 221–244.

97 All the quotations in this paragraph are from Sauer, "Foreword," pp. 6–9.

This position placed culture history at the core of human geography, and stressed that cultural diffusion provided the key, most easily approached by measuring the morphology of cultural traits.[98] Not only was this a resounding dismissal of anthropogeography as practiced by American geographers during the first quarter of the century; it was also sharply at odds with the postenvironmentalist phase of what Sauer termed the "Great Retreat," the move from geology, through environmentalism, toward an even narrower "nongenetic description of the human content of areas."[99] As human geographers—led on by the functionalist *Weltanschauung* of the discipline's midwestern hearth—took refuge in seeing the world around them as an economic system that was "nothing but the temporarily equilibrated set of choices and customs of a particular group," Sauer in California strove during the 1930s to enrich, not simplify, the challenge of geography. When Richard Hartshorne published what Sauer caustically referred to as his "résumé" of American thought on the character and objectives of the field in 1939, consigning historical geography to the outer fringes of the subject, Sauer's response was nothing less than a *cri du coeur*. Citing Hartshorne's failure to "follow Hettner to his main position, namely that geography, in any of its branches, must be a genetic science," Sauer used his presidential address before the Association of American Geographers in late 1940 to insist that all geography must necessarily be historical in its broadest understanding, and sought thereby to rescue it from the tunnel vision condoned in the pursuit of "areal differentiation."[100]

Sauer's substantive work bore largely on Spanish America, particularly Mexico, concerned with cultural implantation and transfer, and the role cultivated plants played in this process. From time to time, local investigations led to bold syntheses on a grand scale, notably in his influential book *Agricultural Origins and Dispersals*.[101] Sauer maintained interest in research questions pertinent to regions within the United States, particularly the Southwest, and periodically wrote think pieces that commanded wide attention within and beyond the discipline.[102] As time passed,

---

[98]   Development of this argument can be traced in three programmatic articles by Sauer: "Recent Developments in Cultural Geography," in Edward C. Hayes, ed., *Recent Developments in the Social Sciences* (New York: Lippincott, 1927), pp. 154–212; "Historical Geography and the Western Frontier," in James F. Willard and Colin B. Goodykoontz, eds., *The Trans-Mississippi West* (Boulder: University of Colorado, 1930); and "Foreword" (see n. 3, above). For further discussion of this point, see William W. Speth, "Berkeley Geography" (see n. 96, above).

[99]   Sauer, "Foreword," pp. 2–3 (see n. 3, above).

[100]   Richard Hartshorne, *The Nature of Geography: A Critical Survey of Current Thought in the Light of the Past* (Lancaster, Pa.: Association of American Geographers, 1939), chapter 6: "The Relation of History to Geography," pp. 175–188. The quoted phrases are from Sauer, "Foreword," p. 2.

[101]   New York: American Geographical Society, 1952.

[102]   For example, see Carl O. Sauer, "Settlement of the Humid East," in *Climate and Man: Yearbook of Agriculture, 1941* (Washington, D.C.: Government Printing Office, 1942), pp. 157–166; "A Geographic Sketch of Early Man in America," *Geographical Review*, vol. 34 (1944), pp. 529–573; "Homestead and Community on the Middle Border," in Howard W. Ottoson, ed., *Land Use Policy in the United States* (Lincoln: University of Nebraska Press, 1963), pp. 65–85. Recently, a transcription of lectures he gave in this period on North America has been published, which reveals the keen insights he often had on evolutionary aspects of the United States, but also the heavy bias toward the humid East and early periods (coverage of the West and developments after 1850 was perfunctory). See Robert G. Bowman, *North*

it became clear how strongly his interests revolved around the central theme of human transformation of the earth, which bore fruit in his careful preparations for the epochal Symposium on Man's Role in Changing the Face of the Earth, held in Princeton, New Jersey, in 1955.[103] In later life, when arduous fieldwork was no longer practical, Sauer turned to a remarkable series of documentary studies of the landscape imagery and resource evaluations of Central and North America by the European colonists through the seventeenth century.[104] In all, Sauer's work was magisterial in its global reach, its anthropological depth, its historical insight, and its acuity in the field. And yet it should be noted that Sauer was perhaps too conscious of modern civilization's despoliation of the earth, too keenly aware of its awesome capacity to dissolve traditional ways of life, to take any serious analytical interest in the cultural currents that powered the great urban-industrial transformation of modern times.

Despite this limitation, Sauer's interests were catholic and contagious enough to stimulate similar studies by his students, principally in Latin America and the United States. Sauer's long tenure at Berkeley (1923-1957) and his fecundity as a teacher resulted in an unparalleled string of doctoral graduates who took academic positions throughout the country, but especially in California and the West, and through their own sound training and energy spread the influence of Sauerian cultural-historical geography in a period during the 1940s and 1950s when the discipline was not otherwise particularly open to the historical perspective.[105] The significance of this seeding is clearer when considered in the context of graduate training possibilities during the period. At the time the United States entered the Second World War only fifteen of its universities offered a doctorate in geography, and seven of those programs were younger than Berkeley's. While Berkeley was the eighth American university to offer the Ph.D. in geography, by 1946 it already ranked

---

America: Notes on Lectures by Professor Carl O. Sauer at the University of California, Berkeley, 1936 (Northridge: California State University–Northridge, Department of Geography, Occasional Paper no. 1, 1985), 49 pp. Comparison with Barrows's lectures on the same subject (also given in the mid-1930s, see footnote 56) is inviting, though the imbalance in the detail retained from the oral delivery of each series renders any firm conclusions hazardous.

[103] The proceedings were published in William L. Thomas, Jr., ed., *Man's Role in Changing the Face of the Earth* (Chicago: University of Chicago Press, 1956).

[104] Carl O. Sauer, *The Early Spanish Main* (Berkeley: University of California Press, 1966); *Northern Mists* (Berkeley: University of California Press, 1968); *Sixteenth Century North America: The Land and People as Seen by Europeans* (Berkeley: University of California Press, 1971); and *Seventeenth Century North America: Spanish and American Accounts* (Berkeley: Turtle Island Foundation, 1980).

[105] It is instructive that Hartshorne ultimately adopted a more charitable position regarding the place of historical geography in the discipline, thanks perhaps to the friendly persuasion of Andrew Clark, Hartshorne's departmental colleague and a Sauer student who, in his capacity as AAG monograph series editor, edited Hartshorne's important sequel to *The Nature of Geography*. See Richard Hartshorne, *Perspective on the Nature of Geography* (Chicago: Rand McNally & Co., for the Association of American Geographers, 1959), pp. 81–107. Clark's influence on Hartshorne in this regard is a point made in David Ward and Michael Solot, "Andrew Hill Clark, 1911–1975," *Geographers: Biobibliographical Studies*, vol. 14 (London: Mansell, 1992), pp. 16–17. For discussion of Sauer's reaction to Hartshorne's study, and of the unfashionable Berkeley historicism, see James J. Parsons, "Berkeley: The Later Sauer Years," *Annals of the Association of American Geographers*, vol. 69, 1 (1979), pp. 9–15.

fifth in number of doctorates awarded (twenty),[106] far ahead of the older programs at Harvard and Yale, and the great majority of the Berkeley dissertations were in cultural-historical geography.

While John Leighly was Sauer's first doctoral student and assistant in building the Berkeley department, and in the last years of his life made a number of contributions to American place-name geography, his more extensive work in climatology and on European topics muted his influence on research in American historical geography.[107] It was Fred B. Kniffen, Sauer's third doctoral recipient (Ph.D. 1930), who can fairly claim to have spearheaded the application of Sauerian thought to U.S. topics beyond the personal interests of Sauer himself. Kniffen's 1936 study of Louisiana house types marked the beginning of a long and deep interest in Louisiana culture and American folk landscapes in general, and, appointed to Louisiana State University, he built up a large student following over more than four decades there.[108] Following him, Lauren C. Post (Ph.D. 1937) wrote about the Acadian part of Louisiana from which he came, Hallock F. Raup (Ph.D. 1935) pioneered the indigenous geographical study of German settlements in America, with detailed studies in Pennsylvania and California, and Joseph E. Spencer (Ph.D. 1936) balanced his East Asian interests with early work on the settlements of southern Utah; Samuel N. Dicken (Ph.D. 1931), after a long career as a regional geographer, would in retirement coauthor with his wife Emily Dicken a fine synthesis of Oregon's historical geography.[109]

During the 1940s, as Sauer's ideas and training experience matured, three students appeared in quick succession who would leave their own mark on the historical geography of the United States. Leslie Hewes (Ph.D. 1940), George F. Carter (Ph.D. 1942), and Andrew H. Clark (Ph.D. 1944), all reflected Sauer's broad interest in indigenous peoples and human-induced vegetation change. Hewes elaborated on his doctoral study on the Cherokees of the central Great Plains, and went on to chronicle the European colonization of that region, establishing a tradition of historical study at the University of Nebraska. Carter scoured the Southwest for evidence of early human occupation, controversially pushing back the date for its appearance far into prehistory, and through such work attracted students at Johns Hopkins University

---

[106] Table 1 in Allen D. Bushong, "Geographers and Their Mentors: A Genealogical View of American Academic Geography," in Blouet, *Origins of Academic Geography*, p. 203.

[107] See John B. Leighly, "Town Names of Colonial New England in the West," *Annals of the Association of American Geographers*, vol. 68, 2 (1978), pp. 233–248. Leighly made an early contribution to American geographical perception studies, however; see his "John Muir's Image of the West," *Annals of the American Association of Geographers*, vol. 48, 4 (1958), pp. 309–318.

[108] Fred B. Kniffen, "Louisiana House Types," *Annals of the Association of American Geographers*, vol. 26, 4 (1936), pp. 179–193.

[109] Lauren C. Post, "Cultural Geography of the Prairies of Southwest Louisiana," Ph.D. diss., University of California–Berkeley, 1937, revised and published twenty-five years later as *Cajun Sketches: From the Prairies of Southwest Louisiana* (Baton Rouge: Louisiana State University Press, 1962); Hallock F. Raup, "Settlement and Settlement Forms of the Pennsylvania Dutch at the Forks of the Delaware, Northampton County, Pennsylvania," Ph.D. diss., University of California–Berkeley, 1935; and Joseph E. Spencer, "The Middle Virgin River Valley, Utah: A Study in Culture Growth and Change," Ph.D. diss., University of California–Berkeley, 1936; Samuel N. Dicken and Emily Dicken, *The Making of Oregon: A Study in Historical Geography* (Portland: Oregon Historical Society, 1979).

and later at Texas A & M University. Clark, a Canadian who worked first on New Zealand and later mostly on the Canadian Maritimes, emerged as a methodological spokesman for historical geography and tutored nearly a score of students on United States and Canadian themes at the University of Wisconsin.[110] James J. Parsons (Ph.D. 1948), primarily a Latin Americanist, developed a lively interest in United States topics throughout his career.[111] Right up to and beyond his own retirement in 1957, Sauer continued this pattern of training and influencing contributors to American historical geography. Edward T. Price (Ph.D. 1950), Wilbur Zelinsky (Ph.D. 1953), Homer Aschmann (Ph.D. 1954), and Marvin W. Mikesell (Ph.D. 1959) published on various American cultural and historical topics, and each has trained further students in the field at the universities of Oregon, Pennsylvania State, California–Riverside, and Chicago.[112]

As part of Sauer's program building at Berkeley, he brought a number of German geographers to California over the years, both as visitors and as permanent members of the faculty. Sauer sought to draw on the then richest tradition in the world in both physical and cultural geography in order to strengthen his own disciplinary initiatives in the United States. Among the cultural specialists who made a mark at Berkeley, Oskar Schmieder (1924–1929) and Gottfried Pfeifer (1931–1933) are the most notable, both for their influence on students and their studies in New World historical geography.[113] There were short-term visitors from other countries

---

[110] Leslie Hewes, "Geography of the Cherokee Country of Oklahoma," Ph.D. diss., University of California–Berkeley, 1940; George F. Carter, "Plant Geography and Culture History in the American Southwest," Ph.D. diss., University of California–Berkeley, 1942, published with the same title by the Viking Fund in their Publications in Anthropology, 1945; and Andrew H. Clark, "Suggestions for the Geographical Study of Agricultural Change in the United States, 1790–1840," *Agricultural History*, vol. 46, 1 (1972), pp. 155–172.

[111] See, for example, James J. Parsons, "The Uniqueness of California," *American Quarterly*, vol. 7, 1 (1955), pp. 45–55.

[112] Edward T. Price, "Mixed Blood Racial Islands of the Eastern United States as to Origin, Localization, and Persistence," Ph.D. diss., University of California–Berkeley, 1950; Wilbur Zelinsky, "Settlement Patterns of Georgia," Ph.D. diss., University of California–Berkeley, 1953; Homer Aschmann, "The Evolution of a Wild Landscape, and Its Persistence, in Southern California," *Annals of the Association of American Geographers*, vol. 49, 3, pt. 2 (1959), pp. 34–56; and Marvin W. Mikesell, "Franciscan Colonization at Santa Barbara," *Historical Society of Southern California Quarterly*, vol. 37, 3 (1955), pp. 211–222. Mikesell's article stemmed from his pre-Sauer UCLA master's work, but his later support of historical student work on the United States is a matter of record.

[113] Schmieder, two years Sauer's junior, was called to the chair of geography at Kiel in 1929, and arranged scholarship support for a Berkeley master's recipient, Edna Scofield, to pursue a doctorate under him there (no woman ever earned a doctorate with Sauer at Berkeley); the younger Pfeifer made substantial contributions to the historical geography of the United States, before and after he, too, returned to Germany. See, for example, Gottfried Pfeifer, "Die Bedeutung der 'Frontier' für die Ausbreitung der Vereinigten Staaten bis zum Mississippi," *Geographische Zeitschrift*, vol. 41, 4 (1935), pp. 138–158; and *Räumliche Gliederung der Landwirtschaft im nördlichen Kalifornien* (Leipzig: Wissenschaftliche Veröffentlichungen der Gesellschaft für Erdkunde zu Leipzig, vol. 10, 1936), 309 pp. A selection of Pfeifer's works on the United States is presented in Gerd Kohlhepp, ed., *Beiträge zur Kulturgeographie der Neuen Welt: Ausgewählte Arbeiten von Gottfried Pfeifer* (Berlin: Dietrich Reimer, 1981). Pfeifer also published a searching review of the intellectual development of American regional (and historical) geography for his German colleagues, quickly translated into English by John Leighly for American consumption, as well as a revealing survey of work by German geographers on North America during the interwar period. See Gottfried Pfeifer, "Entwicklungstendenzen in Theorie und Methode der regionalen Geographie in den Vereinigten Staaten nach dem Kriege," *Zeitschrift der Gesellschaft für Erdkunde zu Berlin 1938*, 3/4 (1938), pp. 93–125, published in English as *Regional Geography in the United States since the War: A Re-*

(Australia and Great Britain stand out), and from time to time foreign students were drawn to Berkeley for study, often completing doctoral work on historical California topics for their home universities.[114]

The Sauer legacy in American historical geography is by far the broadest and deepest in the discipline, and its intellectual heritage is still very much represented among leading scholars in the field today.[115] Its lineage is so long, in fact, that it runs parallel to most of the subsequent movements and schools that have appeared in the field in the last sixty years. One such movement emerged in the late 1920s not long after Sauer began building his program at Berkeley, but as a different kind of response to the pressures for change then felt in American human geography. In some ways it could be better described as methodological fashion than as movement, and, as is often so with fashions, it failed to transform the field. Known as the "sequent occupance" approach, it both flourished and largely subsided within a twenty-five-year period, and it would scarcely merit individual attention, perhaps, if it were not for the wide application and dogged longevity of its terminological and organizational appeal.

The Strange Career of Sequent Occupance

As studies in American historical geography became more devoted to localities and primary sources during the 1920s in reaction to the overgeneralizations of the geographic-influences school, attention focused increasingly upon the problem of how best to group and present evidence of human distributions over both space and time. Akin to the challenge of representing a round earth on flat paper, historically minded geographers faced the difficulty of discussing spatial patterns in constant

---

view of Trends in Theory and Method (New York: American Geographical Society, 1938); and "Arbeiten deutscher Geographen über Nordamerika seit dem Kriege," *Geographische Zeitschrift*, vol. 46, 9 (1940), pp. 322–334. There simply is no space here to examine the possible influence that research published on American topics in German outlets in this period had on American scholarship, nor to gauge what relation they bore to the methodological development of cultural geography in Germany. For an assessment of one research tradition, see Jürgen Bähr, Karlheinz Paffen, and Reinhard Stewig, "Entwicklung und Schwerpunkte der Amerika-Forschung am Kieler Geographischen Institut," in Karlheinz Paffen and Reinhard Stewig, eds., *Die Geographie an der Christian-Albrechts-Universität, 1879–1979: Festschrift aus Anlaß der Einrichtung des ersten Lehrstuhls für Geographie am 12. Juli 1879 an der Universität Kiel* (Kiel: Im Selbstverlag des geographischen Instituts der Universität Kiel, Kieler Geographische Schriften, vol. 50, 1979), pp. 431–447.

[114] Jan O. M. Broek, *The Santa Clara Valley, California: A Study in Landscape Change* (Utrecht: A. Oosthek's Uitgevers-Mij., 1932); Anton Wagner, *Los Angeles: Werden, Leben und Gestalt der Zweimillionenstadt in Südkalifornien* (Kiel: Schriften des Geographischen Instituts der Universität Kiel, no. 3, 1935); and Maurice E. Perret, *Les colonies tessinoises en Californie* (Lausanne: F. Rouge et Cie, 1950). Broek spent part of his Rockefeller Fellowship at Berkeley during 1930–1931 pursuing field and library work for this, his doctoral dissertation ("Broek, Jan Otto Marius: Geographer," *National Cyclopedia of American Biography*, vol. 59 [Clifton, N.J.: James T. White & Co., 1980], p. 135). Perret's study, submitted to the University of Lausanne, Switzerland, for the Ph.D. in 1950, grew out of a master's thesis ("The Italian Swiss Colonies in California") that he had completed at Berkeley in 1942.

[115] This legacy has become the subject of investigation in its own right—Sauerology. See Marvin W. Mikesell, "Sauer and 'Sauerology': A Student's Perspective," in Martin S. Kenzer, ed., *Carl O. Sauer: A Tribute* (Corvallis: Oregon State University Press, for the Association of Pacific Coast Geographers, 1987), pp. 144–150.

flux. Historians have often been wont to describe change as if it were geographically uniform, or practically so, and in such case a narrative style is well-suited to the task of verbalizing a sequence of events, causally linked through time. If areal differences are intimately bound up in the flow of, and rationale behind, change, however, the simultaneous handling of four dimensions of space and time then becomes more complicated. It was Derwent Whittlesey's contribution to give a distinctive name in 1929 to a presentational method already being tried by others, to which he appended a brief case study easy to simulate. "Sequent occupance" as a label received almost immediate currency and as a concept offered an idealized scheme of developmental stages through which regions might be seen to pass.[116]

Whittlesey, like Sauer, was a product of the University of Chicago, though his formal studies were first in history. Unlike Sauer, Whittlesey was influenced positively by Barrows and Semple, whose teaching aroused in him "an immediate enthusiasm for geography." While his major contributions were ultimately to lie in the sphere of political geography, his historian's feel for time, together with his "avid cultivation of field study" led him, not long after his eight years on the Chicago geography faculty, to propose a simple scheme by which to organize the facts of place across time.[117] For Whittlesey, "Human occupance of area, like other biotic phenomena, carries within itself the seed of its own transformation. . . . The view of geography as a succession of stages of human occupance establishes the genetics of each stage in terms of its predecessor. . . . The life history of each [generation of human occupance] discloses the inevitability of the transformation from stage to stage."[118]

Whittlesey noted that change could result both endogenously and exogenously, "from the inherent character of a particular mode of occupance" as well as from acts of God (expressed through natural causes) or the untoward machinations of humans. He regarded the identification in regions of sequential stages of occupance as a methodological advance over the ungeneralizability of detailed description per se, since "in nature relatively few sequence patterns have ever existed," and thus the few stages and their sequences from region to region would permit ready generalization, the absence of which in the practice of chorology—the study of individual regions—had till then bedeviled geographers. The attraction of this new scheme lay in

---

[116] Derwent S. Whittlesey, "Sequent Occupance," *Annals of the Association of American Geographers,* vol. 19, 3 (1929), pp. 162–165. This brief think piece, in light of its extended terminological success in American geography, must rank as the most effective four pages ever printed in the *Annals.*

[117] The quoted phrases are from Edward A. Ackerman, "Obituary: Derwent Stainthorpe Whittlesey," *Geographical Review,* vol. 47, 3 (1957), p. 443. Whittlesey is perhaps best known for his *The Earth and the State: A Study of Political Geography* (New York: Henry Holt & Co., 1939), chapter 16 of which ("The Geopolitical Structure of North America," pp. 503–555) offers a succinct historical political geography of the United States and Canada. Whittlesey's political interpretations influenced students of European history, like Norman Pounds and Edward Whiting Fox, more than students of American historical geography, whose preference for sequent occupance over geopolitics in the 1930s can certainly be claimed to have retarded adequate development of political historical geography.

[118] Whittlesey, "Sequent Occupance," pp. 162–163 (see n. 116, above). The similarity of this stage model to the frontier formulation of Turner has been noted by Donald W. Meinig. See his "Commentary on Walter Prescott Webb's 'Geographical-Historical Concepts in American History'," *Annals of the Association of American Geographers,* vol. 50, 1 (1960), pp. 95–96.

using as building blocks "the traits of the subject matter of chorology" rather than awkward taxonomies from "foreign disciplines."[119] Illustration was offered for an unidentified fifteen-square-mile region in northern New England which was said to have passed through three stages: a long first phase of virgin mixed forest through which wandered a few Indians gaining a livelihood from hunting and gathering; a second phase of "thoroughgoing subjection of the land to farming" at the hands of European settlers; and a third phase of pioneer second-growth forest partly grazed by calves and criss-crossed by an occasional grass-grown lane—very much a transitory phase as full forest was returning, ultimately (in a putative fourth stage) to be cut periodically by nonresident owners as a cash crop.[120]

Sequent occupance as an approach passed rather swiftly from novelty to relic and without, as a historian of the movement has observed, ever meeting serious critical review. The appeal lay perhaps in its character as an analogue model comparable in human geography to the erosion cycle in physiography and the plant succession concept in botany, not to mention the historian's concern for periodization. Its sequential and causally related stages offered the prospect, however, of substituting a form of historical determinism for the ultimately ahistorical Sempelian environmental determinism by then in serious disrepute. "The assumptions that landscape evolution could be described in terms of diagnostic stages, that the progression of these stages could be predicted, and that variations from predicted or normal sequences would result from exogenous forces," Mikesell has noted, "added up to a new generalization about landscape evolution and not merely a reiteration of what had already been verified."[121]

Some studies by Preston E. James appearing in the late 1920s are considered to prefigure the methodology Whittlesey advocated, and James's work on the Blackstone Valley, published in June 1929 three months before Whittlesey's manifesto, undoubtedly served at the time, notwithstanding its identification through the subtitle with chorography, as a prominent and suitable demonstration of how to go about studying sequent occupance.[122] It was quickly followed by Darrell H. Davis's study in the Kentucky Mountains, and Stanley D. Dodge's examination of an Illinois

[119] The quoted phrases appear in Whittlesey, "Sequent Occupance," p. 165 (n. 116, above).

[120] It is reasonable to assume that the area in question is centered on Ellsworth, Maine. Whittlesey had just moved from the University of Chicago to Harvard University in the fall of 1928, and the summer of 1929 was his first in New England. He cited 1930 faculty research funds as the basis for the work on Ellsworth presented in his "Coast Land and Interior Mountain Valley: A Geographical Study of Two Typical Localities in Northern New England," in John K. Wright, ed., New England's Prospect (New York: American Geographical Society, 1933), pp. 446–458.

[121] Marvin W. Mikesell, "The Rise and Decline of Sequent Occupance: A Chapter in the History of American Geography," in David Lowenthal and Martyn J. Bowden, eds., Geographies of the Mind: Essays in Historical Geosophy in Honor of John Kirtland Wright (New York: Oxford University Press, 1976), pp. 150 and 152–153.

[122] Preston E. James, "The Blackstone Valley: A Study in Chorography in Southern New England," Annals of the Association of American Geographers, vol. 19, 2 (1929), pp. 67–110. Chorography, and its explanatory counterpart, chorology, are ancient terms in geography, reaching back to Strabo. See "chorology," in The Dictionary of Human Geography, 2d ed., ed. Ronald J. Johnston et al. (Oxford: Basil Blackwell, 1986), pp. 52–53.

prairie (the first to use the precise term "sequent occupance" in the work's title).[123] Thereafter, the concept's popularity found expression in a long line of graduate dissertations and theses, beginning with Alfred H. Meyer's doctoral study of the Kankakee Marsh completed under Dodge's direction at Michigan in 1934, and a series of articles in major journals lasting through the mid-1950s.[124] Meyer's work on the Calumet region (Kankakee Marsh) is now considered the apogee of the genre, replete with sequential profiles and crowded stage maps of representative landscape features, constructed largely on the basis of secondary historical material, together with field reconnaissance and mapping for the contemporary stage. In such studies, real coverage ranged generally from sizable portions of states (northeastern Ohio, for example) to small river basins and townsites.[125]

Over the long term, the genre did not maintain vigor. There were problems internal to the method, and a broader disinterest among cultural and historical geographers attracted to alternative precepts. For one thing, no consensus developed over how to treat three aspects of the sequent-occupance approach: choice of criteria, periodization, and geographical scale. As Mikesell has shown, studies varied in the basis used for identifying occupance periods: sometimes it was ethnopolitical hegemony, sometimes land use or landscape features, sometimes transportation means. There was no consistency in periods chosen, ranging from a year to a century or more. There was no systematic basis for selecting the size of area to be studied, ranging from that of a neighborhood to that of a continent. And, ultimately, there was no explicit conceptual goal toward which individual findings could be directed, comparative or otherwise. These difficulties spurred comment and suggestions, but not outright rebuttal, though Richard E. Dodge did complain that geographers should not have to study occupance periods in the remote past from which no relics remain in

---

[123] Darrell H. Davis, "A Study of the Succession of Human Activities in the Kentucky Mountains: A Dissected Highland Area," *Journal of Geography*, vol. 29, 3 (1930), pp. 85–100; and Stanley D. Dodge, "Sequent Occupance of an Illinois Prairie," *Bulletin of the Geographic Society of Philadelphia*, vol. 29, 3 (1931), pp. 205–209 (Bureau Prairie, Bureau Co.). Davis's study went unnoticed in Mikesell's review, but its March 1930 publication (and title) must suggest the possibility that Davis prepared it before learning of Whittlesey's label; yet the study is organized, like that of James, according to general stages.

[124] Alfred H. Meyer, "The Kankakee Marsh of Northern Indiana and Illinois," Ph.D. diss., University of Michigan, 1934. Meyer would spend the next twenty-two years deriving publications from this research interest, culminating in his "Circulation and Settlement Patterns of the Calumet Region of Northwest Indiana and Northeast Illinois (The Second Stage of Occupancy: Pioneer Settlement and Subsistence Economy, 1830–1850)," *Annals of the Association of American Geographers*, vol. 46, 3 (1956), pp. 312–356. Explicit sequent occupance studies appeared during this period in *Economic Geography*, the *Annals of the Association of American Geographers*, and the *Journal of Geography*, but not in the *Geographical Review*. Doctoral dissertations in this genre were popular at Michigan during the 1930s, and at Chicago during the 1940s and 1950s.

[125] James S. Matthews, *Expressions of Urbanism in the Sequent Occupance of Northeastern Ohio* (Chicago: University of Chicago Department of Geography, Research Paper no. 5, 1949); Glenn T. Trewartha, "A Second Epoch of Destructive Occupance in the Driftless Hill Land (1760–1832): Period of British, Spanish, and Early American Control," *Annals of the Association of American Geographers*, vol. 30, 2 (1940), pp. 109–142; Lewis F. Thomas, "The Sequence of Areal Occupancy in a Section of St. Louis, Missouri," *Annals of the Association of American Geographers*, vol. 21, 1 (1931), pp. 75–90; Edward A. Ackerman, "Sequent Occupance of a Boston Suburban Community," *Economic Geography*, vol. 17, 1 (1941), pp. 61–74.

the contemporary landscape.[126] More broadly, students of culture history in geography, notably Sauer and his students, saw little advantage in adopting the formality of occupance periods, with their built-in bias toward stasis and inattention to the transforming forces that propelled society from one stage to the next.

As convenient snapshots of past conditions, occupance stages appealed more to contemporary geographers anxious to study safe geographical complexes, i.e., regions, rather than risk the charge of doing history, whereas historical geographers sought more direct means to uncover the complexities of almost continuous change over time. The Davisian premise that process is implicit in stage was insufficient, and, besides, too many stages overlapped hopelessly in the cultural components used to give them temporal definition.[127] More generally, however, the rise of ahistorical methodology following the publication of Richard Hartshorne's treatise on geographical praxis perhaps dampened the enthusiasm for this brand of historical explanation in geography, as did the undeniable difficulty of marshalling the requisite evidence for high-quality reconstructions of past landscape stages. Only Meyer's 1936 work stands as an impressive effort in this regard, as does the study of California's Santa Clara Valley by Jan O. M. Broek—which might better be seen as a skillful European-initiated attempt to combine stages with thorough discussion of the forces of change that produced them.[128] Remarkably, however, the concept of sequent occupance has displayed an extraordinary half-life in the United States: begun in the late 1920s, Mikesell may have declared it dead by the mid-1950s, but its allure remained alive in doctoral dissertation titles at least until 1972, and its use in article publications has been recorded as late as 1981, and in master's theses as recently as 1989—sixty years after its introduction.[129]

Muddy Boots Tramp to the Archives

The third developmental strand in the second quarter of the present century was colored less by the dominance of one scholar or guiding idea than by a growing interest among historical geographers in combining evidence from primary histori-

---

[126] Mikesell, "Rise and Decline," pp. 156–157 (see n. 120); Richard E. Dodge, "The Interpretation of Sequent Occupance," *Annals of the Association of American Geographers*, vol. 28, 4 (1938), pp. 233–237.

[127] Mikesell cites Kniffen's diagram of overlapping transport eras on the lower Mississippi to buttress this point. Mikesell, "Rise and Decline," p. 161 (see n. 120, above); Fred B. Kniffen, "Geography and the Past," *Journal of Geography*, vol. 50, 3 (1951), pp. 126-128.

[128] Jan O. M. Broek, *Santa Clara Valley* (see n. 114, above). The introduction relates the study to critical conceptual debates of the time in the German, French, and Dutch literature. Whittlesey's article is listed in the bibliography but not referred to in the text. Broek's method found later application in the organization of H. Clifford Darby's famous edited compendium, *A New Historical Geography of England* (London: Cambridge University Press, 1973). Nevertheless, it is clear that European, and specifically British, geographers found no reason to import the use of Whittlesey's American term to describe what they practiced.

[129] Roderick C. McKenzie, "The San Pasqual Grant: The Sequent Occupance of a Portion of the Mission San Gabriel Archangel Lands through Two Centuries," Ph.D. diss., University of California–Los Angeles, 1972; Joseph T. Manzo, "Sequent Occupance in Kansas City, Kansas: A Historical Geography of Strawberry Hill," *Kansas History*, vol. 4, 1 (1981), pp. 20–29; and Kay Boam, "A Sequent Occupance of the Clear Lake Basin," Master's thesis, California State University–Chico, 1989.

cal sources with that from traditional fieldwork and mapping. To be sure, a preeminent figure emerged in this respect, too—Ralph Hall Brown—but the movement was not strictly his invention, for Carl Sauer, Almon Parkins, and others had long before made use of local records. The spinning of this strand can be readily observed in the period between the publication of the *Atlas of the Historical Geography of the United States* in 1932 and the appearance in 1948 of Brown's second book, *Historical Geography of the United States*, arguably the first modern synthesis in American historical geography and certainly the first national summation since those of Semple and Brigham half a century before. This strand, however, was spun from fibers drawn as much from history as from geography.

Just as environmental determinism in geography produced a period of antithesis in which, as Mikesell has argued, regional geography and sequent-occupance study gained a footing, so Turner's frontier thesis had by the 1920s produced contest and reformulation among historians. Perhaps the boldest reformulation was that by Walter Prescott Webb, a geographical historian from Texas who published *The Great Plains* in 1931, a soon-to-be classic that would help build a reputation for a new group within the historical profession, the "sectional" or regional historians.

Webb had been a student of Lindley M. Keasbey, who had studied in Germany with the great settlement geographer August Meitzen and knew the work of other notable geographers—Friedrich Ratzel, Élisée Reclus, and Ellsworth Huntington—and what Webb drew from Keasbey was the emphatic importance of the relationship between environment and civilization.[130] The Great Plains environment, his home ground, "constitutes a geographic unity whose influences have been so powerful as to put a characteristic mark upon everything that survives within its borders. Particularly did it alter the American institutions and cultural complexes that came from a humid and timbered region."[131] It represented an insurmountable barrier to Spanish expansion from the southwest, and it stymied American pioneers coming later from the east, until rescued by the Industrial Revolution, most notably in the form of the railroad, the six-shooter, barbed wire fencing, and the windmill. Webb, as a neo-Turnerian, argued for the primacy of identifying change over continuity in institutions and life experience, but the geographical elements in his work, unlike Turner's, were truly environmental, not in the sense of having determinative influence—he was too acute a historian for that—but rather in that the specific environmental character of the plains was central to the argument.[132]

Some years later, Webb's lead would be followed by another plainsman, James C. Malin, but where the former succeeded through bold and masterful synthesis, the latter preferred demolishing myths and misconceptions, especially those perpetrated

---

[130] See Gary S. Dunbar, "Lindley Miller Keasbey (1867–1946)," *History of Geography Newsletter*, vol. 1 (1981), pp. 3–6. However, Keasbey, according to Dunbar, had repudiated any such ideas before publication of Webb's *Great Plains*, and was not pleased with what he had spawned. Personal communication, Gary S. Dunbar, June 25, 1992.

[131] Walter Prescott Webb, *The Great Plains* (Boston: Ginn & Co., 1931), p. vi.

[132] In this regard, for Turner, despite his great attention to the complex patterns of particular regions under study, one frontier conceptually was like any other.

by fellow historians, through extensive and often innovative use at the micro scale of manuscript censuses and other systematic local materials. Malin, too, appreciated the value of a thorough knowledge of the region's physical geography, and his *Grasslands of North America* shows deep familiarity with regional environmental research.[133]

Geographers paid some attention to the new geographical historians, but the significance of their accomplishments was slow to be recognized.[134] One who did recognize it was Ralph Brown, who taught at the University of Colorado from 1925 to 1929 before moving to Minnesota, where he was asked to institute a course in historical geography.[135] That last summer in Colorado, he attended a special conference there on "The History of the Trans-Mississippi West," at which several papers by geographical historians were read, including papers by Bolton and Schafer, and one by Webb entitled "The Great Plains and the Industrial Revolution."[136] Brown had studied economics and history at Pennsylvania's Wharton School before completing a doctorate in geography at Wisconsin under Vernor Finch. Brown's early work was regional and economic in character, exploring the significance of the setting in which he found himself—not unlike Sauer in his early career. Such work for Brown led easily to Colorado's mountain passes, a theme which begged retrospective treatment. Rejection of an article by the *Geographical Review* as too historical pushed him toward journals in that field, and by 1934 he was writing in *Minnesota History* about elements of that state's prehistory.[137] Thereafter all his work was historical in orientation, and soon he became the leading American exponent of historical—as distinct from cultural—geography. That distinction had little practical meaning for Sauer, who used the terms interchangeably, but Brown saw the value of a close study of historical documents for their geographical content and implications. Writing about western exploration was already a field well adjusted to the canons of historical scholarship, and his own experience in that sphere, together with the impressive display of documentary analysis apparent in the one geographer's book on the subject, by the Englishman Edmund W. Gilbert, perhaps spurred him in such a direction.[138] As Douglas McManis has put it,

---

133 James C. Malin, *The Grasslands of North America: Prolegomena to Its History* (Lawrence, Kans.: The author, 1947). For an informative review of Webb, Malin, and later scholars, see Allan G. Bogue, "The Heirs of James C. Malin: A Grassland Historiography," *Great Plains Quarterly*, vol. 1, 2 (1981), pp. 105–131.

134 It was not until 1960, thirty years after publication of *The Great Plains*, that Webb was invited to a special session at the annual meeting of the Association of American Geographers in order to discuss the geographical foundations of his major writings. Meinig, a commentator at the session, could only note with ill-concealed embarrassment that geographers simply had not responded to the interpretive challenges offered by Webb, Malin, and others. Meinig, "Commentary," p. 96 (see n. 117, above).

135 William A. Koelsch, "Ralph Hall Brown: Historical Geographer," *Dictionary of American Biography*, suppl. 4 (New York: Charles Scribner's Sons, 1974), p. 112.

136 Ralph H. Brown, "The History of the Trans-Mississippi West," Conference Report, *Geographical Review*, vol. 19, 4 (1929), pp. 672–673.

137 Ralph Hall Brown, "Some Aspects of Minnesota Prehistory," *Minnesota History*, vol. 15, 2 (1934), pp. 148–156.

138 Edmund W. Gilbert, *Exploration*. Gilbert's work grew out of his Oxford student thesis ("Geographical Influence on the Exploration of America West of the Mississippi, 1800–1850," B.Litt. thesis, University of

With the abandonment of the small-scale regional studies that had heretofore characterized his writings, Brown retained a focus on geographical content, but his methodological inspiration came from the contemporary practice of history rather than efforts of other geographers to deal with the past. The consequence was innovative in the development of American geography; Brown made research in historical geography synonymous with use of historical method. By adoption of crucial professional techniques from another discipline, Brown gave a new dimension of intellectual rigor and provided a precedent for later changes in American geography.[139]

Commitment to the study of original documents opened up for Brown the relationship between human perceptions, as distinct from actual knowledge, of environment and the limits they placed on human action, inaugurated with his 1936 study of "Fact and Fancy in Early Accounts of Minnesota's Climate."[140] He worked comfortably within the regionalist paradigm of the time; historical geography should "reconstruct the regional geography of antecedent periods. . . . Geography functions best in history," he wrote, "when relatively limited areas and periods of time are considered. Thus the flow of history must frequently be stopped in order to inspect the relatively static conditions of geography."[141] Brown, then, strongly championed pursuit of regional cross sections in time, but not those facile treatments accepted in the name of sequent-occupance study. For Brown, the availability and quality of original sources for single, critical eras in the early development of regions became an obsession, and ultimately a restriction for him. Unlike Sauer, who happily combined doc-

---

Oxford, 1928), and stands as a rare case of a substantial early British contribution to American historical geography, illustrating the close study of archival sources which has long been a hallmark of British work in the field. Gilbert's book was well received in the pages of American geographical journals. It also drew arch comment from one reviewer: "Considering the fact that 'The Exploration of Western America' was written entirely from manuscript sources, by a man who has never visited the region under discussion, it is impossible not to acknowledge its rather unusual merit"; Hershel Heath, review in *Economic Geography*, vol. 9, 3 [1933], p. 322.

There was in this period one other striking exemplar of British study of American archival sources, the unusual but seemingly little known study of wealth distribution in revolutionary North Carolina, based on detailed tax lists of the period, by Francis Grave Morris and Phyllis Mary Morris, "Economic Conditions in North Carolina about 1780: Part I—Landholdings; Part II—Ownership of Town Lots, Slaves, and Cattle," *North Carolina Historical Review*, vol. 16, 2 & 3 (1939), pp. 107–133, and 296–327. Both Morrises were at the time lecturers in geography at King's College, Newcastle upon Tyne, England, and had completed the research while on a six-month stay in the southeastern United States, of which, Grave Morris subsequently wrote, "I was privileged to make a tour lasting some four or five weeks [in the region] in the company of Dr. Carl O. Sauer [and others]"; *Geographical Journal*, vol. 90, 3 (1937), p. 369. It is doubtful that the tax-list study affected the course of American historical geography then or later, and it was perhaps too statistical, socioeconomic, and abstract to draw Ralph Brown's attention. Nonetheless, it stands as an early, thorough, geographical investigation of American official colonial records—thirty years ahead of its time as an exercise in large-scale quantitative analysis—published just at the time when Brown was finding his scholarly stride.

[139] Douglas R. McManis, "Prism to the Past: The Historical Geography of Ralph Hall Brown," *Social Science History*, vol. 3, 1 (1979), p. 73. The later changes McManis had in mind were the extradisciplinary borrowings of the quantitative/theoretical revolution in the 1960s.

[140] *Minnesota History*, vol. 17, 3 (1936), pp. 243–261.

[141] The quotations are given in Linda Miles Coppens, "Ralph Hall Brown, 1898–1948," *Geographers: Biobibliographical Studies*, vol. 9 (London: Mansell Publishing Co., 1985), p. 17.

umentary with relic material evidence, Brown insisted on abundance and diversity in the former as the only basis for sound historical geography (though his criteria for judging their actual sufficiency in any area were never elaborated).[142] This insistence drew him to the Atlantic regions of the country, and as a "regional reconstructionist" he produced a cross-sectional snapshot to end all snapshots, *Mirror for Americans: Likeness of the Eastern Seaboard, 1810*, published in 1943.[143] Based on numerous contemporary descriptions and commentaries, "the style and organization are both designed as composites of the geographical exposition of the time, and every thought and observation that is given here, although perhaps not enclosed in quotation marks, has its duplicate in the original sources. Because the contemporary writings failed to cover all problems and regions with equal penetration, this abridgement exhibits many lacunae."[144] One historical reviewer summed it up as "a description of economic activity without extended discussion or recreation of the Americans of 1810," although he was charmed by this "admirable and provocative book."[145] More recently, it has been hailed as a landmark in environmental perception.[146]

As early as 1935 Brown had signaled his desire to write a book on the historical geography of North America, and in 1944, the year following publication of *Mirror for Americans*, J. Russell Whitaker, his former roommate at Wisconsin and then geographical editor for Harcourt-Brace Publishing, persuaded him to prepare a college textbook in historical geography.[147] University and professional pressures at the close of World War II delayed the book, but *Historical Geography of the United States* was written essentially in the year before its publication in 1948.[148] The book is resolutely regional in structure, advancing through time up to about 1870 in order to focus on the phase of its first settlement by Europeans, the varying emphasis in turn contingent upon the richness of the surviving documentary evidence. "The past geography of a region is only *partly* told," he opined, with perhaps a dig at Sauer, "when account has been taken of the cultural landscape" [emphasis added]. It was

[142] Ralph Hall Brown, "Materials Bearing upon the Geography of the Atlantic Seaboard, 1790 to 1810," *Annals of the Association of American Geographers*, vol. 28, 3 (1938), pp. 201–231. A year's leave (1936–1937) spent in East Coast libraries, especially that of the American Geographical Society, resulted in a string of close examinations of such sources. Representative examples include his "The American Geographies of Jedidiah Morse," *Annals of the Association of American Geographers*, vol. 31, 3 (1941), pp. 145–217; and "The De Brahm Charts of the Atlantic Ocean, 1772–1776," *Geographical Review*, vol. 28, 1 (1938), pp. 124–132.

[143] Ralph Hall Brown, *Mirror for Americans: Likeness of the Eastern Seaboard, 1810* (New York: American Geographical Society, 1943).

[144] Ibid., p. x.

[145] Woodrow Borah, review of *Mirror for Americans*, in *William & Mary Quarterly*, 3d ser., vol. 3, 2 (1946), p. 297. For Whittlesey, it might be noted, Brown's cross-section approach acted as a suitable "corrective to the shallow, contemporaneous view of geography," but was to be seen as historical in only two senses: it employed techniques of historiography, and presented material of antiquarian interest. For Whittlesey, it omitted "the compelling time sequence of related events which is the vital spark of history." In other words, it failed to convey much sense of dynamism. Whittlesey, "The Horizon of Geography," *Annals of the Association of American Geographers*, vol. 35, 1 (1945), p. 32.

[146] McManis, "Prism to the Past," p. 79 (see n. 139, above).

[147] Coppens, "Brown," p. 17 (see n. 141, above).

[148] Ralph Hall Brown, *Historical Geography of the United States* (New York: Harcourt-Brace, 1948).

more important, Brown felt, to rely "on original, eyewitness accounts and contemporary maps"[149] (fig. 5). First, this precluded coverage prior to European intrusion, and that and other gaps justified on evidentiary grounds were quickly pounced upon by reviewers.[150] Even more problematic were the silences the writer bound himself to on subjects not noticed by contemporaries, such as the long-term ecological results of resource malappropriations. A sympathetic summary, however, was offered by William Koelsch: "The coverage is uneven, reflecting to a large degree what Brown himself had been able to accomplish in field and library work. Prominent themes were man's modification of the biotic environment and patterns of settlement, agriculture, and commerce, viewed from a strongly regional perspective," stressing "the role of concepts, true and false, about the land in each period."[151] Brown initiated no school of historical geography (he taught at colleges that lacked a doctoral program in geography and thus trained no advanced students), and died a week following publication of his text. However, for all its faults the book proved to be in itself a rich and enduring legacy—still in print at this writing; perhaps for lack of any subsequent single-authored, single-volume synthesis of American historical geography.

One general theme in the literature of American historical geography between 1930 and 1950 that demands recognition was the unmistakable emergence of an interest in settlement geography, that is, in both the physical and social morphology of rural settlement. With regard to settlement forms, this reflected in part the growing popularity of micro-scale study with the retreat from broad-scale environmentalism, in part a recognition of the value of such small-scale features in tracing diffusion patterns. It could be seen implicitly in Sauer's work, not so much in his empirical illustrations but certainly in his way of thinking; it was on sumptuous display in Brown's national synthesis (in which detailed maps of local settlement patterns abound); and it could be seen in a variety of specialist studies by cultural geographers of various persuasions. Of the Berkeley school, Kniffen has already been mentioned as an early contributor to American landscape study, and his 1936 article on Louisiana house types became a classic. In the same year Edna Lois Scofield, another Berkeley graduate, published a study of Tennessee house types, followed two years later by one on the morphogenesis of the New England town (fig. 6); Raup and Spencer published respectively on settlement forms of the Pennsylvania Dutch and the house types and

---

[149] Brown, *Historical Geography*, p. iii.

[150] See, in particular, Woodrow Borah's review in *William & Mary Quarterly*, 3d ser., vol. 7, 2 (1949), pp. 306-312. Andrew Clark, also, was quick to comment on Brown's self-imposed restriction: "If the very great amount of help which may be obtained by legitimate inference from field work in the areas considered, and from a great body of subsequent analysis, be added to the two types of source material [old maps and documents] which were paramount to Brown it appears that many other areas and many other times might have been as easy to justify." Clark went on to suggest, "Three words added to the title, 'Studies in the . . .' would have saved the situation (and greatly shortened this review)." These opinions were published, in German, in Andrew H. Clark, "Ralph Hall Browns Beitrag zur amerikanischen Historischen Geographie," *Erde*, vol. 5, 2 (1953), p. 150. The passages cited here are from the English manuscript version originally prepared by Clark ("The Contribution of Ralph Hall Brown to American Historical Geography," pp. 4–5, and 7). The writer is grateful to David Ward for a copy of the manuscript.

[151] Koelsch, "Brown," p. 114 (see n. 135, above). Brown's book won the Loubat Prize in American history and geography.

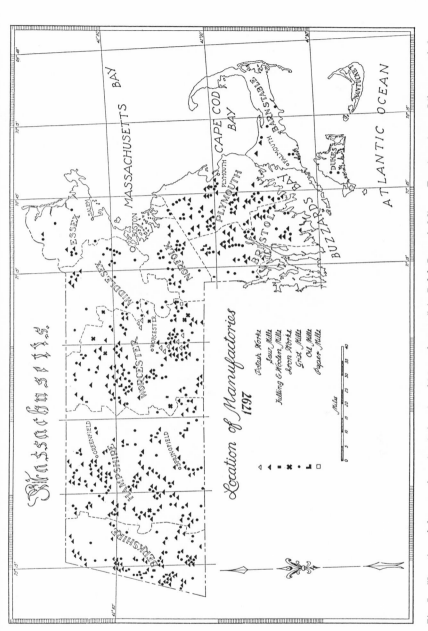

Fig. 5. "Location of the manufacturing industries of Massachusetts," in Ralph Brown's Mirror For Americans: Likeness of the Eastern Seaboard, 1810 (1943). This map, derived from Sotzmann's map of 1797, reflects, as does the book in which it appears, Brown's strong predilection for archival sources in historical geography.

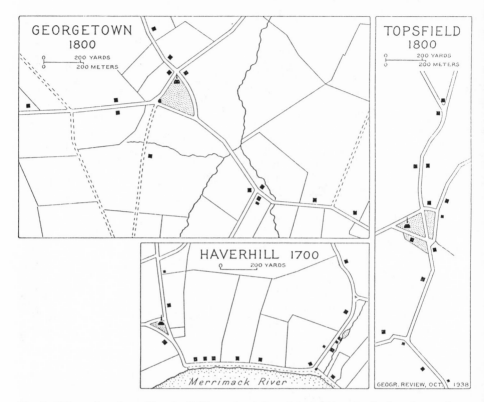

Fig. 6. Village plans from Edna Scofield's study of the origins of New England settlement forms in the Geographical Review *(1938). While derived from detailed early topographical surveys, these maps isolate the essential elements to be explained by systematic morphological analysis: property boundaries, roads, dwellings, meeting houses, "greens," and water courses.*

villages of southern Utah.[152] Innovative studies emanated from other centers as well: Trewartha at Wisconsin (during the phase when he was influenced by Sauer's ideas),[153] Darrell Davis at Minnesota, Dodge at Michigan; with parallel contributions from a few foreign geographers, mostly German.[154]

---

[152] Edna Lois Scofield, "The Evolution and Development of Tennessee Houses," *Journal of the Tennessee Academy of Science*, vol. 11, 4 (1936), pp. 229–240; "The Origin of Settlement Patterns in Rural New England," *Geographical Review*, vol. 28, 4 (1938), pp. 652–663. After earning a master's degree in Sauer's department, Scofield left Berkeley for a doctorate under Oscar Schmieder at Kiel University in Germany, where she absorbed the tradition of settlement studies reaching back to August Meitzen. Hallock F. Raup, "The Pennsylvania-Dutch of Northampton County: Settlement Forms and Culture Pattern," *Bulletin of the Geographical Society of Philadelphia*, vol. 36, 1 (1938), pp. 1–15; Joseph E. Spencer, "Development of Agricultural Villages of Southern Utah," *Agricultural History*, vol. 14, 4 (1940), pp. 181–189; and "House Types of Southern Utah," *Geographical Review*, vol. 35, 3 (1945), pp. 444–457.

[153] Glenn T. Trewartha, "The Prairie du Chien Terrace: Geography of a Confluence Site," *Annals of the Association of American Geographers*, vol. 22, 2 (1932), pp. 119–158; "The Unincorporated Hamlet: One Element in the American Settlement Fabric," *Annals of the Association of American Geographers*, vol. 33,

Closely allied with these studies were publications that showed an awakening interest in social aspects of the countryside, especially ethnic patterns. These ranged from the immigrant population mapping of Guy-Harold Smith, Max Hannemann, Hildegard Binder Johnson, and Maurice E. Perret to the "cultural island" studies of Walter M. Kollmorgen, and the ethnic syntheses of Helge M. O. Nelson.[155] In addition, study of the geographical structure of evolving rural neighborhoods and their service linkages to nearby villages and towns was pioneered during this period by the rural sociologist John H. Kolb, who immortalized Dane and Walworth Counties in Wisconsin for social scientists through his detailed, temporal mapping of their internal social and trading patterns between the mid-nineteenth century and 1948. Ironically, this work had little impact on American settlement geographers of the time, including Kolb's university colleague Trewartha, and went into rapid eclipse in rural sociology, although the British geographer Robert E. Dickinson quickly grasped its relevance for central place theory.[156]

1 (1943), pp. 32–81; "Types of Rural Settlement in Colonial America," *Geographical Review*, vol. 36, 4 (1946), pp. 568–596; and "Some Regional Characteristics of American Farmsteads," *Annals of the Association of American Geographers*, vol. 38, 3 (1948), pp. 169–225. Trewartha's flirtation with the Sauerian cultural-historical perspective, not common in the 1930s among those raised in the functionalist tradition of midwestern geography, is discussed by two pillars of that tradition in Richard Hartshorne and John R. Borchert, "In Memoriam: Glenn T. Trewartha, 1896–1984," *Annals of the Association of American Geographers*, vol. 78, 4 (1988), p. 732.

[154] Darrell H. Davis, "Amana: A Study in Occupance," *Economic Geography*, vol. 12, 3 (1936), pp. 217–230; and Stanley D. Dodge, "Bureau and the Princeton Community," *Annals of the Association of American Geographers*, vol. 22, 3 (1932), pp. 159–209. For German contributions, see especially the outstanding long article by Emil Meynen, "Das pennsylvaniendeutsche Bauernland," *Deutsches Archiv für Landes- und Volksforschung*, vol. 3 (1939), pp. 253–292; also his "Dorf und Farm: Das Schicksal altweltlicher Dörfer in Amerika," in Oskar Schmieder, ed., *Gegenwartsprobleme der Neuen Welt*, pt. 1, *Nordamerika* (Leipzig: Quelle & Meyer, 1943), pp. 565–615.

[155] See, for example, Guy-Harold Smith, "Notes on the Distribution of the Foreign-Born Scandinavian in Wisconsin in 1905," *Wisconsin Magazine of History*, vol. 14, 4 (1930–1931), pp. 419–436; Max Hannemann, *Das Deutschtum in den Vereinigten Staaten: Seine Verbreitung und Entwicklung seit der Mitte des 19. Jahrhunderts* (Gotha: Justus Perthes, Ergänzungsheft no. 224 zu Petermanns Mitteilungen, 1936); Hildegard Binder Johnson, "Der deutsche Amerika-Auswanderer des 18. Jahrhunderts im zeitgenössischen Urteil," *Deutsches Archiv für Landes- und Volksforschung*, vol. 4, 2 (1940), pp. 211–234, and "Factors Influencing the Distribution of the German Pioneer Population in Minnesota," *Agricultural History*, vol. 19, 1 (1945), pp. 39–57; Maurice E. Perret, *Les colonies tessinoises* (see n. 114, above); Walter M. Kollmorgen, *The German-Swiss in Franklin County, Tennessee: A Study of the Significance of Cultural Considerations in Farming Enterprises* (Washington, D.C.: Department of Agriculture, Bureau of Agricultural Economics, 1940); Helge M. O. Nelson, *The Swedes and the Swedish Settlements in North America*, vol. 1, *Text*; vol. 2, *Atlas* (Lund: C. W. K. Gleerup, 1943). For the unusual context in which Kollmorgen's research was conducted, see his personal recollections in "Kollmorgen as Bureaucrat," *Annals of the Association of American Geographers*, vol. 69, 1 (1979), pp. 77–89. For background on the fine American scholarship of the Swedish human geographer Nelson, see Karl-Erik Bergsten, "Helge Nelson, 1882–1966," *Geographers: Biobibliographical Studies*, vol. 8 (1984), pp. 69–75.

[156] See, for example, John H. Kolb, *Rural Primary Groups: A Study of Agricultural Neighborhoods* (Madison: University of Wisconsin Agricultural Experiment Station Research Bulletin no. 51, 1921)(Focus on Dane Co., c. 1840–1920); and John H. Kolb and LeRoy J. Day, *Interdependence in Town and Country Relations in Rural Society: A Study of Trends in Walworth County, Wisconsin, 1911–13 to 1947–48* (Madison: University of Wisconsin Agricultural Research Station Bulletin no. 172, 1950). On Kolb's research legacy, see A. F. Wileden, "In Memoriam: John H. Kolb (1888–1963)," *Rural Sociology*, vol. 29, 1 (1964), pp. 95–97. See also Robert E. Dickinson, *City Region and Regionalism: A Geographical Contribution to Human Ecology* (London: Kegan Paul, Trench, Trubner & Co., 1947), pp. 62–76.

A last notable feature of the period was the appearance of what British geographer John Paterson has felicitously called "regional sentinels," or local specialists—scholars who make it their business to study the evolution of a particular region and monitor change within it. Michigan-born Almon Parkins was appointed, within two years of receiving his doctorate from Chicago in 1914, to the chair of geography at George Peabody College for Teachers in Nashville, Tennessee, where he then spent the rest of his career and specialized in the American South. In 1931 he devoted his presidential address to the Association of American Geographers to the antebellum South, and by 1938 had written a major synthetic treatment of the region, focused mostly on its economic development but, nonetheless, the first book-length historical study by a geographer.[157] Another case of specializing in the historical geography of a region is that of Leslie Hewes, born in Oklahoma, who finished a doctorate under Sauer in 1940 and embarked on four decades of writing about the Great Plains.[158]

If the interwar years had witnessed lean times for general university support, they did not hinder the intellectual progress of the field, for major changes in the philosophical position and practice of historical geography had occurred. New methodological and substantive diversity had appeared, and environmentalism had largely disappeared. After World War II, the scales had somewhat shifted. Economic recovery from depression and war produced a long period of university expansion which lasted until the early 1970s, and unprecedented numbers of students were trained in historical geography (some drawn from Canada and Britain); but change in the theory and practice of historical geography was more evolutionary than revolutionary. The experience of the Depression had turned public policy debate to the economic and social viability of the rural domain as the nation's ultimate safety net, and perhaps this helps in part to explain the continuing focus, well into the postwar period, of historical-geographical work on agrarian topics. Liberal research support assisted individuals' productivity and imagination, and expanding teaching programs made them mobile. All this favored the proliferation and mixing of Berkeley-style cultural-historical geography with other modes, so that training programs became generally more eclectic. But within this general context, two developments deserve notice. Kniffen, as the earliest Sauer trainee to commit himself fully to research in United States cultural geography and a fixture in Baton Rouge since the 1930s, developed after the war a distinctive brand of historical geography—what might be termed the Louisiana school of landscape or settlement morphology. At the

[157] Parkins, Almon E., "The Antebellum South: A Geographic Interpretation," Annals of the Association of American Geographers, vol. 21, 1 (1931), pp. 1–35; and The South: Its Economic-Geographic Development (New York: John Wiley & Sons, 1938), revised 1949; reprinted Westport, Conn.: Greenwood Press, 1970. There exists an earlier monographic treatment of the subject, Hermann Gerhard's Die volkswirtschaftliche Entwicklung des Südens der Vereinigten Staaten von Amerika von 1860 bis 1900 (Halle: Gebauer-Schetschke Druckerei und Verlag, Angewandte Geographie: Hefte zur Verbreitung geographischer Kentnisse in ihrer Beziehung zum Kultur- und Wirtschaftsleben, 1st ser., vol. 12, 1904, 99 pp.), but there is no evidence that Parkins consulted it in the preparation of his study.

[158] More localized examples during this period were Edwin Foscue in Texas and the Southwest, Ruth Baugh in California, Stephen Visher in Indiana, Bert Hudgins in Michigan, Muriel Poggi in Illinois, Loyal Durand in Wisconsin, and Willard Miller in Pennsylvania. For the regional writings of these individuals, see the relevant sections of the bibliography.

same time, a later Sauer student, Andrew Clark, emerged in the 1950s to champion a firmly different and more detached variant of the Sauerian tradition, which he promoted through the concept of "geographical change" and which came to be known as the Wisconsin school.

Mid-Century: Settlement Morphology and the Louisiana Landscape School

Fred B. Kniffen's approach to cultural-historical geography perpetuated several hallmarks of Sauer's style. Chief among these were the affinity for cultural anthropology and acceptance of the man-land relationship as the conceptual starting point for geographical studies in cultural evolution, which kept a warm place for physical geography in the curriculum. Kniffen had local support for this from early on, for he taught in a joint department of geography and anthropology—a rare but stable arrangement—set within what came to be the School of Geoscience at Louisiana State University created with the help of Richard J. Russell, a Berkeley-trained geomorphologist, Kniffen's longtime colleague and long-serving dean.[159] (Robert West joined the faculty in 1948, reinforcing the local Sauerian outlook, complete with Latin American research orientation.) In addition, Kniffen replicated Sauer's preferences for research on rural topics, folkways, diffusionary processes, and examination of the cultural landscape, particularly through intensive fieldwork. What distinguished Kniffen from his mentor was his fascination for the artifacts of the landscape itself, habitations above all. Material culture held more interest than nonmaterial, although he did not slight the general importance of the latter.

Kniffen made a career of studying rural house types and in the process became something of an American Meitzen.[160] Indian tribes and Indian mounds, agricultural fairs, covered bridges, outdoor ovens, Spanish moss, and iron rock captured his attention from time to time, but no topic proved so absorbing as the multitudinous forms that folk housing could take. Whatever the object of study, his method was straightforward: choose a cultural form, identify the key elements, plot the distribution of different types, locate the probable hearth area from which it expanded, and trace the paths of diffusion. His work on folk housing and the processes that distinguished its many forms emphasized the contribution of ordinary people as opposed

---

[159] Merle C. Prunty, "Geography in the South," *Annals of the Association of American Geographers*, Special Issue: Seventy-Five Years of American Geography, vol. 69, 1 (1979), p. 55.

[160] Though Sauer had early pupils read German geographers (in German), including perhaps the works of the settlement geographer August Meitzen, Kniffen recalls that it was seminars and fieldwork with anthropologist Kroeber and his own later exploration of the Louisiana countryside that raised his interest in house types. Quickly he realized that it was the recurrent characteristics of the ubiquitous, humble dwellings of Louisiana rather than the more idiosyncratic plantation houses of the elite that captured his imagination. When on a sabbatical visit to Germany in 1938–1939, Kniffen did at last make a detailed study of Meitzen's classic work (*Siedelung und Agrarwesen der Westgermanen und Ostgermanen, der Kelten, Römer, Finnen und Slawen* [Berlin: W. Hertz, 1895], 3 vols. and atlas). See Fred B. Kniffen, "The Geographer's Craft—I: Why Folk Housing?" *Annals of the Association of American Geographers*, vol. 69, 1 (1979), pp. 59 and 62; and Robert C. West, ed., *Pioneers of Modern Geography: Translations Pertaining to German Geographers of the Late Nineteenth and Early Twentieth Centuries* (Baton Rouge: Louisiana State University, Geoscience & Man, vol. 28, 1990), pp. 1 and 8.

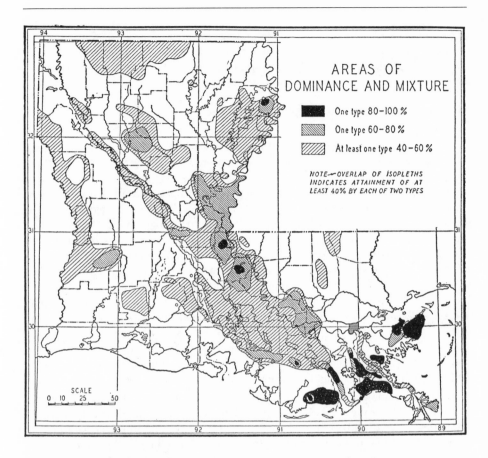

AREAS OF
DOMINANCE AND MIXTURE

■■■■ One type 80–100 %

▨▨▨ One type 60–80 %

▨▨▨ At least one type 40–60 %

*NOTE—OVERLAP OF ISOPLETHS
INDICATES ATTAINMENT OF AT
LEAST 40% BY EACH OF TWO TYPES*

SCALE
0 10 25   50

Fig. 7. Mapping culture traits to examine diffusion and regional differentiation is reflected in this summary map from Fred Kniffen's study of Louisiana folk housing types in the Annals of the Association of American Geographers *(1936). The types referred to include built-in porch, attached porch, porchless, open passage, oysterman, trapper, shotgun, and midwestern house forms. Their spatial exclusivity or admixture helps reveal patterns of multicultural colonization, competition, and isolation over time.*

to elites in the making and remaking of regional cultures and cultural landscapes. He established a new vocabulary in the study of landscape and material culture, beginning with his naming of the "I-house," that cipher for Pennsylvanian "Midland" culture that spread during the nineteenth century into the West and South.[161] With relict house forms as diagnostics to establish various cultural movements between and within regions (fig. 7), Kniffen felt content in pointing the way toward building

[161] Fred B. Kniffen, "Louisiana House Types" (see n. 108, above); and "Folk Housing: Key to Diffusion," *Annals of the Association of American Geographers*, vol. 55, 4 (1965), pp. 549–577.

up the corpus of systematic studies needed for the ultimate delineation and synthesis of true American culture regions.[162] His collaboration with Henry H. Glassie emboldened his generalizations, and the map of broad cultural diffusion throughout the eastern United States that he produced attracted notice from and improvement by others.[163] Never before had humble log-notchings, window placement, and chimney locations been given such scrupulous scholarly attention, and it stimulated a small army of recruits who today support the Pioneer America Society and its series of publications.

Kniffen's longevity at Louisiana State University produced a string of doctoral students who followed his penchant for field-based settlement morphology, providing grounds for recognizing an independent school within American historical geography. Most of his students completed dissertations in cultural-historical settlement topics, not a few of them in Louisiana. Among these individuals several were to gain positions at universities with doctoral programs,[164] and four have been especially productive in the Kniffen mold: Gary S. Dunbar on the Carolinas, Peter O. Wacker on New Jersey, Milton B. Newton on Louisiana and the Upland South, and Malcolm L. Comeaux on Acadian Louisiana.[165]

The character of study pursued by Kniffen and his Louisiana school falls squarely within the Sauerian tradition, sensu lato, and these scholars have made little effort to distance themselves from it. At the same time, there has been an almost undeviating focus by the Kniffen group upon issues concerned with settlement morphology, sensu stricto; a specialization within cultural geography far from characteristic of the Berkeley school at large. The chosen tool, following Sauer, was fresh-air field observation, so Brown's call to musty archives fell here on deaf ears.[166] But

---

[162] Only once did he venture a brief regional overview: "The Physiognomy of Rural Louisiana," *Louisiana History*, vol. 4, 4 (1963), pp. 291–299.

[163] Fred B. Kniffen and Henry H. Glassie, "Building in Wood in the Eastern United States: A Time-Place Perspective," *Geographical Review*, vol. 56, 1 (1966), pp. 40–66. The map was first offered in Kniffen, "Folk Housing," fig. 11 (see n. 162, above). See, especially, Peirce F. Lewis, "Common Houses, Cultural Spoor," *Landscape*, vol. 19, 2 (1975), pp. 1–22.

[164] Those with United States interests include Daniel Jacobson (Ph.D. 1954) at Michigan State University; Gary Dunbar (1956) at the University of California–Los Angeles; Peter Wacker (1966) at Rutgers University; Milton Newton (1967), appointed to the faculty at Louisiana State University; and Malcolm Comeaux (1969) at Arizona State University.

[165] Gary S. Dunbar, *Historical Geography of the North Carolina Outer Banks* (Baton Rouge: Louisiana State University Coastal Studies, no. 3, 1958); Peter O. Wacker, *The Musconetcong Valley of New Jersey: A Historical Geography* (New Brunswick: Rutgers University Press, 1968); "Traditional House and Barn Types in New Jersey: Keys to Acculturation, Past Culturogeographic Regions, and Settlement History," in H. Jesse Walker and William G. Haag, eds., *Man and Cultural Heritage: Papers in Honor of Fred B. Kniffen* (Baton Rouge: Louisiana State University School of Geoscience, Geoscience & Man, vol. 5, 1974), pp. 163–176; and "The Dutch Culture Area in the Northeast, 1609–1800," *New Jersey History*, vol. 104, 1 (1986), pp. 1–21; Milton B. Newton, Jr., "Cultural Preadaptation and the Upland South," in Walker and Haag, *Man and Cultural Heritage*: pp. 143–154; and Malcolm L. Comeaux, *Atchafalaya Swamp Life: Settlement and Folk Occupations* (Baton Rouge: Louisiana State University School of Geoscience, Geoscience & Man, vol. 2, 1972).

[166] Too many historical geographers have taken field and archive as mutually exclusive. Not surprisingly, Sauer saw them in a certain balance. Fieldwork, he felt, should be extensive while the body is young and vigorous, and later the library can supplant it—an approach exemplified in his own life.

as a result, a good deal of current understanding of the origins and transformations in American rural settlement patterns, particularly in the East and South, rests upon the spadework of this specialized school.[167] Thus, the study of vernacular architecture, so long denied and dismissed by architectural historians and folklorists and now so enthusiastically embraced, was given a firm foundation, and stands as an early reaction to the study of material history from the top down, with an unwavering view from the bottom up.

An assessment written several years after Kniffen's retirement (in 1970) noted that the Louisiana school had become firmly established in American historical geography, but noted that it is "limited in the kinds of questions it can address. Processes of social interaction and economic change are downplayed in favor of a more formal interpretation of culture areas."[168] One could even suggest that, if reconstructing cultural diffusion patterns is an ultimate goal of house-type research (an oft-stated goal when pressed for the implications of such work), it offers at best a circuitous method of establishing ethnocultural migration paths, since these can be less arduously established through historical population sources. Even on its own ground, however, the Louisiana school has been notably selective, for its commitment to the study of folk, ironically, has shown little interest in African American traditions—though, to be sure, no school of American historical geography has dealt adequately with such topics as slavery in particular and African American development in general. At the same time, if the dynamics of settlement as revealed through morphological change can yield new ideas concerning larger social change in particular geographical settings, such as perhaps Newton's concept of cultural "preadaptation" in its application to the Upland South, then the landscape perspective is likely to endure and broaden.[169]

Members of this school were not alone during the fifties and sixties in pursuing established aims in historical geography, and while several methodological avenues were open to scholars, there was an embarrassing surplus of questions to be asked— the unevenness of Brown's book made that clear—both old and unanswered as well as new and unexplored. How to square the ecological transition from Eastern woodlands to central grasslands and western deserts with the detailed record of settlement,

---

[167] Already by midcentury, Kniffen had established himself as one of the foremost authorities on rural settlement structure in America. He was one of four coauthors of the chapter "Settlement Geography" in Preston E. James and Clarence F. Jones, eds., *American Geography: Inventory and Prospect* (Syracuse, N.Y.: Syracuse University Press, for the Association of American Geographers, 1954), pp. 124–141, and the only one with substantive United States studies listed among the references.

[168] William K. Wyckoff, "On the Louisiana School of Cultural Geography and the Case of the Upland South," Syracuse University Department of Geography Discussion Paper no. 54 (1979). At least one member of this group has enlarged his realm of inquiry regarding the role of the landscape in the past and the types of evidence examined. See Peter O. Wacker, *Land and People: A Cultural Geography of Preindustrial New Jersey; Origins and Settlement Patterns* (New Brunswick: Rutgers University Press, 1975).

[169] See the debate between Mitchell and Newton on this issue in Robert D. Mitchell and Milton B. Newton, *The Appalachian Frontier: Views from the East and the Southwest* (London: Institute of British Geographers, Historical Geography Research Group, Historical Geography Research Series, no. 21, 1988), published shortly before Newton's untimely death.

prehistoric and European? How to relate the distribution of different population elements with the formation of culture regions and the rise of regional consciousness? How to interpret the record of institutions, governmental and social, in the formation of local communities and regional societies and their adjustment to the land? Woodrow Borah had chided Brown for not drawing out the implications of the relative cultural homogeneity of twentieth-century American society in the face of great historical variety in population origins and environmental conditions, the note on which Brown had closed his survey. This was to some extent a variation on the theme of declining regional distinctiveness, and while such large questions rarely served as explicit points of departure, studies in historical geography now began to attack these kinds of issues, albeit from fragmented bases and oblique angles.[170]

Publication in historical geography accelerated greatly between 1950 and 1970, and a large amount of work was done in the realm of agrarian settlement studies. Much of the energy came from scholars following Kniffen out of Berkeley: Leslie Hewes, George Carter, Andrew Clark, Edward Price, and Wilbur Zelinsky, each of whom had individual contributions to make. Hewes undertook studies of the settlement and agricultural development of the wet prairies separating the Great Lakes region from the Great Plains, fine case studies so obviously missing at the time Brown wrote his *Historical Geography* and richly documented in a fashion of which the latter would have approved, and Hewes followed them with examinations of the semiarid zone to the west, culminating in his overview of "sidewalk farming" as a way of life.[171] Carter, among the very few historical geographers with an interest in ancient American times, took on the anthropologists with work aimed at increasing both the antiquity of humankind in the Americas and the number and provenance of "discoveries" of the New World by the Old.[172] Price turned from his doctoral study of mixed-blood peoples in the East to root digging (for botanical drugs) in the Appalachians, and then to the diffusion of American courthouse square plans—a quintessential breadth of interest for a Berkeley-trained cultural geographer in the early 1950s.[173] Zelinsky, meanwhile, established a hectic, eclectic pace with numerous

---

[170] Borah, review, pp. 311–312 (see n. 150, above).

[171] Hewes spent the 1940s writing about his native Oklahoma and its Indians, the 1950s about Iowa and Nebraska and the wet prairies, and the following two decades about the dry plains. Representative studies are Leslie Hewes and Phillip E. Frandson, "Occupying the Wet Prairie: The Role of Artificial Drainage in Story County, Iowa," *Annals of the Association of American Geographers*, vol. 42, 1 (1952), pp. 24–50; Leslie Hewes and Arthur C. Schmieding, "Risk in the Central Great Plains: Geographical Patterns of Wheat Failure in Nebraska, 1931–52," *Geographical Review*, vol. 46, 3 (1956), pp. 375–387; and Leslie Hewes, *The Suitcase Farming Frontier: A Study in the Historical Geography of the Central Great Plains* (Lincoln: University of Nebraska Press, 1973).

[172] See George F. Carter, *Pleistocene Man at San Diego, California* (Baltimore: Johns Hopkins University Press, 1957); *Earlier Than You Think: A Personal View of Man in America* (College Station: Texas A & M University Press, 1980); and "Did China Discover America?" *Eastern Review*, vol. 4, 4 (1979), pp. 74–76. Carter's controversial positions closed some journals to him, so sympathetic ones, like the *Anthropological Journal of Canada*, came to carry much of his later writing. For the context of his work, see Stephen C. Jett, "George F. Carter and Cultural-Historical Geography," *Historical Geography*, vol. 15, 1 & 2 (1985), pp. 10-16.

[173] Edward T. Price, "The Central Courthouse Square in the American County Seat," *Geographical Review*, vol. 58, 1 (1968), pp. 29–60.

investigations of population composition and spread, building types, and even place names (to which he brought a conceptual sophistication rare in that branch of the field).[174] Carl Sauer continued his scholarship long after his retirement in 1957, and contributed several books on early European activities in the Americas, based on close study of selected published versions of mostly primary accounts, the best of which, it is generally agreed, was the first, *The Early Spanish Main*.[175]

And there were voices from other quarters, without Berkeley—or midwestern —roots. There was Hildegard Binder Johnson, who had earned a Ph.D. in geography at the University of Berlin in 1934, and who took a position at Macalester College in Minnesota in 1947 and built a distinguished list of publications on the social and agricultural historical geography of the Middle West.[176] Beginning with a series of innovative studies about social and cultural aspects of German settlement in the United States, ranging from Salzburger attitudes toward slavery in eighteenth century Georgia to interethnic marriage among mid-nineteenth century Germans in Minnesota, she turned her attention to wheat culture, the effect of land surveys on the rural settlement system, and the structure of artistic and literary perceptions of the land.[177] Kollmorgen, working at the micro scale, examined the historical basis for the long-term survival of ethnically distinctive farming throughout the South, drew early attention to sidewalk farming on the Northern Plains, and crafted a masterly presidential address to the Association of American Geographers in 1957 concerning the "Woodsman's Assaults on the Domain of the Cattleman."[178] Merle C. Prunty, Jr.,

---

[174] See, for example, Wilbur Zelinsky, "The Population Geography of the Free Negro in Ante-Bellum America," *Population Studies*, vol. 3, 4 (1950), pp. 386–401; "Where the South Begins: The Northern Limit of the Cis-Appalachian South in Terms of Settlement Landscape," *Social Forces*, vol. 30, 2 (1951), pp. 172–178; "Classical Town Names in the United States: The Historical Geography of an American Idea," *Geographical Review*, vol. 57, 4 (1967), pp. 463–495; and "The New England Connecting Barn," *Geographical Review*, vol. 48, 4 (1958), pp. 540–553.

[175] Carl O. Sauer, *The Early Spanish Main* (Berkeley: University of California Press, 1966); *Northern Mists* (Berkeley: University of California Press, 1968); *Sixteenth Century North America: The Land and the People as Seen by the Europeans* (Berkeley: University of California Press, 1971); and *Seventeenth Century North America* (Berkeley: Turtle Island Foundation, 1980). We can only speculate how Ralph Brown would have judged these efforts—as likewise Sauer's view of Brown's field skills. Notwithstanding their different approaches, it is said, there was mutual respect (Coppens, "Brown," p. 18; see n. 141, above).

[176] "Johnson, Hildegard Binder," *Contemporary Authors*, new revision ser., vol. 3 (Detroit: Gale Research Co., 1981), pp. 299–300.

[177] See, for example, Hildegard Binder Johnson, "Die Haltung der Salzburger in Georgia zur Sklaverei, 1734–1750," *Mitteilungen der Gesellschaft für Salzburger Landeskunde*, vol. 76 (1936), pp. 183–196; "Der deutsche Amerika-Auswanderer des 18. Jahrhunderts im zeitgenössischen Urteil," *Deutsches Archiv für Landes- und Volksforschung*, vol. 4, 2 (1940), pp. 211–234; "Intermarriages between German Pioneers and Other Nationalities in Minnesota in 1860 and 1870," *American Journal of Sociology*, vol. 51, 4 (1946), pp. 299–304; "The Location of German Immigrants in the Middle West," *Annals of the Association of American Geographers*, vol. 41, 1 (1951), pp. 1–41; and "Perceptions and Illustrations of the American Landscape in the Ohio Valley and the Midwest," in *This Land of Ours: The Acquisition and Disposition of the Public Domain* (Indianapolis: Indiana Historical Society, 1978), pp. 1–38.

[178] On agricultural islands, see Kollmorgen, *German-Swiss*. In addition, see Walter M. Kollmorgen and George F. Jenks, "Sidewalk Farming in Toole County, Montana, and Traill County, North Dakota," *Annals of the Association of American Geographers*, vol. 48, 3 (1958), pp. 209–231; and Walter M. Kollmorgen, "The Woodsman's Assaults on the Domain of the Cattleman," *Annals of the Association of American Geographers*, vol. 59, 2 (1969), pp. 215–239.

trained at Clark University in Massachusetts and founding geographer at the University of Georgia, wrote on many aspects of Southern agriculture, a number of which he treated historically; in particular, his study of the changing fortunes of the Southern plantation, which became a classic, and his examination of a case study for the light it could shed on questions about monoculture and soil exhaustion in the region.[179] And there was Donald W. Meinig, a Palouse native who became a fixture at Syracuse University by way of Washington, D.C., Seattle, Adelaide, and Salt Lake City, largely self-directed in becoming a historical geographer, whose writing early focused on the geographical shaping of regions that specific strategies of colonizing and settlement could achieve (fig. 8).[180]

If American agrarianism provided the general context for this collective burst of research activity, it also harbors two themes that at the time received close and almost coordinated attention. One was the basic system of demarcation and division by which land was given legal standing and transformed into parcels of property. Before, knowledge of such systems had been largely procedural, but their impact on the landscape and its shaping of the vital settlement pattern had been only intuitively grasped. Studies by William D. Pattison and Johnson in the fifties and Norman J. W. Thrower and Louis DeVorsey, Jr., in the sixties cast a good deal of light on these issues, and opened up a research domain much cultivated in the following decades.[181]

---

[179] Merle C. Prunty, Jr., "The Renaissance of the Southern Plantation," *Geographical Review*, vol. 45, 4 (1955), pp. 459–491; and "Land Management at Antebellum Hopeton Plantation in the Light of the Soil Exhaustion Thesis," *Memorandum Folio, Southeastern Division, Association of American Geographers*, vol. 11 (1959), pp. 97–101.

[180] See, for example, Donald W. Meinig, "The Growth of Agricultural Regions in the Far West, 1850–1910," *Journal of Geography*, vol. 54, 5 (1955), pp. 211–232; "The American Colonial Era: A Geographical Commentary," *Proceedings of the Royal Geographical Society of Australasia, South Australian Branch*, vol. 59 (1957–1958), pp. 1–22; "The Colonial Period," "Geography of Expansion," and "Elaboration and Change," in John H. Thompson, ed., *Geography of New York State* (Syracuse: Syracuse University Press, 1966), pp. 121–199; and "American Wests: Preface to a Geographical Introduction," *Annals of the Association of American Geographers*, vol. 62, 2 (1972), pp. 159–184. A personal account of Meinig's professional development is given in his address to the American Council of Learned Societies at the University of Chicago, May 1992, published as *A Life of Learning: The Charles Homer Haskins Lecture* (Philadelphia: American Council of Learned Societies, Occasional Paper no. 19, 1992), 20 pp.

[181] William D. Pattison, *Beginnings of the American Rectangular Land Survey System, 1784–1800* (Chicago: University of Chicago Department of Geography, Research Paper no. 50, 1957); and "The Survey of the Seven Ranges," *Ohio Historical Quarterly*, vol. 68, 2 (1959), pp. 115–140; Hildegard Binder Johnson, "Rational and Ecological Aspects of the Quarter Section: An Example from Minnesota," *Geographical Review*, vol. 47, 3 (1957), pp. 330–348; Norman J. W. Thrower, *Original Survey and Land Subdivision: A Comparative Study of the Form and Effect of Contrasting Cadastral Surveys* (Chicago: Rand McNally & Co., for the Association of American Geographers, Monograph no. 4, 1966); Louis DeVorsey, Jr., *The Indian Boundary in the Southern Colonies, 1763–1775* (Chapel Hill: University of North Carolina Press, 1966). It is striking the extent to which a British influence might be detected in these land division studies. By this time, rural settlement study, with its close attention to landownership and field systems, was an established interest in British geography, and in particular H. Clifford Darby was immersed in coordinating a massive research program on the Domesday geography of England, based at University College, London. Darby cherished a long-held notion that the American land surveyors' notes constituted a somewhat comparable American Domesday book, a grand baseline of the naive landscape against which, if it were fully reconstructed, all subsequent Euro-American development could be measured. Apart from Johnson, all the other three American scholars working on land survey issues had British connections. Thrower received his early education in England before attending college in the United States and pursuing this, his doctoral study at Wisconsin; Pattison studied with Darby at University College for two years (1952–

The other was the role of perception in evaluating environments and creating images of place. This theme, while not exactly new, received impetus from the writings of some environmental historians, including David Lowenthal, and from application to actual settlement processes in geographical studies by G. Malcolm Lewis from Britain (the semiarid Great Plains) and by Douglas R. McManis (prairie Illinois).[182]

Many of the preoccupations just discussed met at an unlikely crossroads created by the founding of a new periodical, *Landscape*. Launched and long sustained by John Brinckerhoff Jackson (Jr.), the son of a diplomat, a widely traveled, Harvard-educated, would-be rancher who settled in New Mexico, the magazine sought to stimulate "a far more effective appreciation of the countryside and its problems on the part of an increasingly urbanized society" than was evident in 1950.[183] Jackson, who considered himself a lay geographer and who wrote with the jargon-free, uncluttered verve and acuity of an inquisitive journalist, established his lively semiannual as a forum for description and interpretation of, and debate about, the nature of the human landscape.[184] Focused in the early years on the American Southwest and at one time subtitled *Magazine of Human Geography*, the journal quickly outgrew both the region and the exclusive alliance with geography. By the 1960s it espoused global scrutiny of issues—including urban as well as rural environments—and drew in interesting writers from such far-flung fields as "architecture, city and regional planning, landscape architecture, urban and regional planning, urban and rural history, conservation, historic preservation, environmental design and history, transportation and travel, landscape and the fine arts" as well as many from human and historical geography.[185] Jackson fused a "speculative interest" in contemporary landscape change with a predilection for its vernacular elements, and promoted

---

1954) before completing his doctoral dissertation at Chicago; and DeVorsey, following an M.A. at Indiana with Norman J. G. Pounds (a European-oriented historical geographer, himself a London graduate), earned his doctorate under Darby in London (1965) before returning to a career in the United States.

[182] Two challenging books by historians were Henry Nash Smith, *Virgin Land: The American West as Symbol and Myth* (Cambridge: Harvard University Press, 1950); and Roderick Nash, *Wilderness and the American Mind* (New Haven: Yale University Press, 1967). Essays by David Lowenthal were influential; see his "Is Wilderness 'Paradise Enow'?: Images of Nature in America," *Columbia University Forum*, vol. 7, 2 (1964), pp. 34–40; and "The American Scene," *Geographical Review*, vol. 58, 1 (1968), pp. 61–88. Geographical approaches to environmental perception in this period picked up momentum through such publications as G. Malcolm Lewis, "Changing Emphases in the Description of the Natural Environment of the American Great Plains Area," *Transactions of the Institute of British Geographers*, vol. 30 (1962), pp. 75–90; and Douglas R. McManis, *The Initial Evaluation and Utilization of the Illinois Prairies, 1815–1840* (Chicago: University of Chicago Department of Geography, Research Paper no. 94, 1964).

[183] On Jackson's parental background, see "Jackson, John Brinckerhoff, [Sr.]: Diplomat," in *Who Was Who in America*, vol. 1 (Chicago: A. N. Marquis Co., 1942), p. 624. The quoted phrase is from the elegant and perceptive examination of Jackson's aims and accomplishments by Donald W. Meinig, "Reading the Landscape: An Appreciation of W. G. Hoskins and J. B. Jackson," in his edited collection, *The Interpretation of Ordinary Landscapes: Geographical Essays* (New York: Oxford University Press, 1979), p. 212.

[184] The impetus for the magazine sprung not from any conviction that the earlier academic debates in geography concerning the analytical value of the term "landscape" should reach a broader public but rather that Americans at large should come to understand and enjoy the content and symbolic value of the visual settings they moved about in every day. Jackson himself, though, had read eclectically in the realm of human geography and believed the wisdom of the field should be better known.

[185] A 1976 broadsheet circulated by Jackson's editorial successor, in Meinig, "Reading," pp. 225–226.

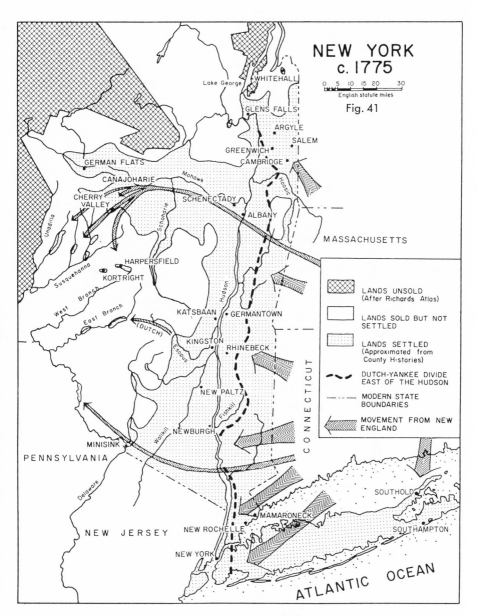

Fig. 8. "New York, c.1775," from Donald Meinig's contribution on the colonial period to Geography of New York State (1966). This depiction of regional economic patterns and arrow-borne cultural movements through space is a simple, early example of Meinig's trademark skill at diagrammatic generalization without losing real-world context.

a point of view that constantly stressed the importance of the life lived within the landscape, corroborated by vigorous observation and intuitive generalization. For the seventeen years that he edited the magazine (1951–1968) and as a general legacy, Jackson opened an avenue for the "intelligent layman" to "read" the workings of society in the material surroundings of daily life, and, for the professional, provided "an effective illustration of the continued value of landscape as an integrating concept in the social sciences."[186]

The Wisconsin School: Geographies of Change or Changing Geographies?

The cultural landscape received plenty of attention in the historical geography of the fifties and sixties, but it by no means served as the single organizing principle for work in the field. Sauer had long before veered away from landscape as the prime object of study for cultural geographers, and while some of his students clung to it as the most convenient approach to questions of cultural evolution, just as many did not. Brown meanwhile had quietly but effectively built up in American geography a new level of respect for and interest in the rigorous examination of historical sources and reconstruction of past geographies for their own sake as specialized, legitimate pursuits. Brown's work made it possible to recognize in geography for the first time a self-consciously historical approach to fundamental questions distinct from the cultural or cultural-historical approach of the Sauerian school.[187] Brown's early death produced a void in leadership along this path, into which, surprisingly enough, stepped Andrew H. Clark, an ambitious and independent-minded Sauer student.[188]

---

[186] Marvin W. Mikesell, "Landscape," in the *International Encyclopaedia of the Social Sciences*, vol. 8 (New York: Crowell-Collier and Macmillan, 1968), p. 579. Jackson, most comfortable as an essayist, was honored in 1970 with an anthology edited by Ervin H. Zube, *Landscapes: Selected Writings of J. B. Jackson* (Amherst: University of Massachusetts Press, 1970), but then did write one book: John Brinckerhoff Jackson, *American Space: The Centennial Years, 1865–1876* (New York: W. W. Norton, 1972). Subsequently his essays have been gathered in two further anthologies: see John Brinckerhoff Jackson, *The Necessity for Ruins, and Other Topics* (Amherst: University of Massachusetts Press, 1980); and *Discovering the Vernacular Landscape* (New Haven: Yale University Press, 1984).

[187] Earlier the term "historical" had carried diverse meanings, but it was rarely used by the Berkeley circle without the prefix "cultural-"; Sauer himself employed the term only twice, both in methodological excursions. See Sauer, "Western Frontier" (see n. 98, above); and "Foreword" (see n. 3, above).

[188] Andrew H. Clark, "The Whole is Greater Than the Sum of Its Parts: A Humanistic Element in Human Geography," in Donald R. Deskins et al., eds., *Geographic Humanism, Analysis, and Social Action: Proceedings of Symposia Celebrating a Half Century of Geography at Michigan* (Ann Arbor: University of Michigan Department of Geography, Michigan Geographical Publication no. 17, 1977), p. 19. Clark's speedy rise to prominence hinged on his selection in early 1949, following Brown's death, to chair the National Research Council's Committee on Historical Geography, charged with preparing a chapter for *American Geography: Inventory and Prospect*, which, when published, gave the subfield formal status and Clark general visibility. Brown, as secretary of the Association of American Geographers since 1942 and *Annals* editor since 1946, had been party to early preparations for the landmark project, and his position as well as his scholarly reputation doubtless explains in part why the volume contains a specific chapter on historical research, while the domain of cultural geography is represented in an oddly fragmented fashion. But then, too, the title of Carl Sauer's presidential address of 1940 still rang in the profession's ears. Clark's revised dissertation was about to appear as a full-blown book, perhaps the first detailed monograph in historical geography to be published on the basis of outside scholarly review by an independent university press, which must have brought him timely notice. Given the problematic organiza-

Throughout his life Clark's detailed, substantive research was devoted exclusively to regions, first in New Zealand, and then in Maritime Canada,[189] but for students of historical geography in the United States his importance lies in his methodological exhortations toward and tireless promotion of an "historical" historical geography, and his encouragement of like-minded research on American regions, particularly by—but by no means limited to—his students. His own doctoral study for Sauer had concerned the modification of the New Zealand habitat through biotic invasion, especially by people, and was conceived by Clark as the first in a series of studies "dealing with similar problems of the development of patterns and practices of land use in mid-latitude areas overseas which were settled by folk from the shores of the North Sea."[190] The study is structured by "vertical themes," tracing people, plants, and animals separately through time, a method in keeping with the Berkeley orientation toward process and time.[191] But ten years later, by which time he was securely established in the distinguished department at the University of Wisconsin, his next book, on Prince Edward Island in the Maritimes, employed a series of synthetic "cross-sections" linked by summaries of developments in between. His third book, a decade later, on neighboring Nova Scotia during the French period, offered a sequential discussion of three broad eras, within which topics were explored in turn, but without detailed cross-sectional treatment or temporal closure.[192]

This evolution in method in three richly detailed studies reveals at bottom a "Clarkian emphasis upon regional historical geography," Meinig has suggested; "none of his studies is focused on 'the making of the cultural landscape' in any general sense. . . . His main concern was 'area' and his main geographic method was to *map* populations, productions, and various elements in order to make a 'fine-grained analysis' of areal patterns and of changes in those patterns."[193]

---

tion of the prospective NRC-AAG book (from a cultural perspective), appointment of Sauer's ambitious pupil for this professional chore could not have displeased him.

[189] Work on New Zealand resulted from an opportunity for funded overseas research, while the Maritimes held ancestral roots for Clark himself. See the following essay by Graeme Wynn for further discussion of his substantive work.

[190] Andrew H. Clark, *The Invasion of New Zealand by People, Plants, and Animals: The South Island* (New Brunswick, N.J.: Rutgers University Press, 1949), p. iv.

[191] For a guide to various forms of possible analysis and presentation, see Robert M. Newcomb, "Twelve Working Approaches to Historical Geography," *Yearbook of the Association of Pacific Coast Geographers*, vol. 31 (1969), pp. 27–50.

[192] Andrew H. Clark, *Three Centuries and the Island: A Historical Geography of Settlement and Agriculture in Prince Edward Island* (Toronto: University of Toronto Press, 1959); and *Acadia: The Geography of Early Nova Scotia to 1760* (Madison: University of Wisconsin Press, 1968).

[193] Meinig, "Andrew Hill Clark, Historical Geographer," in James R. Gibson, ed., *European Settlement and Development in North America: Essays on Geographical Change in Honour and Memory of Andrew Hill Clark* (Toronto: University of Toronto Press, 1978), p. 13. Clark's maps came mostly in two general forms: detailed maps of small localities showing a plethora of settlement features for selected dates for which collation of sources was feasible, and choropleth maps of statistical change, most often of agricultural activity between two dates. Attempts to assay various types of change reach a speculative extreme in his study of "The Sheep/Swine Ratio as a Guide to a Century's Change in the Livestock Geography of Nova Scotia," *Economic Geography*, vol. 38, 1 (1962), pp. 38–55. Figure 10, for example, shows for the eighteen counties of the province between 1851 and 1951 the "adjusted rate-of-rate-of-rate of change in the

It is hard to ascribe this philosophical repositioning to any one influence, but it provided Clark with a certain mantle as Brown's spiritual successor—champion of an autonomous historical geography within the discipline—and as such some degree of intellectual independence from the powerful Berkeley persuasion. In a period when systematic studies were beginning to gain favor over strictly regional treatments, opting for this label offered him a way to strike out on his own, buoyed no doubt by the strong influence that Canadian economic historian Harold Innis had exerted on him when he was a teaching assistant for T. Griffith Taylor at the University of Toronto before going to Berkeley.[194] Central to Clark's general approach, it has been noted, were "a respect for source materials, a recognition of those historiographic issues which were capable of geographical analysis, and above all a keen sense of the appropriate regional or subcultural scale at which to conduct an investigation."[195] Clark developed strong ties to historians, particularly those economic, political, and cultural historians with interests in regionalism, and from this vantage point his enthusiasm for historiography distinguishes him most sharply from the more relaxed and anthropologically oriented ties of the Berkeley school.[196]

At the same time, Clark had limited patience for some of Brown's antiquarianisms: devotion to the literal pattern of a past delineated by the variable survival of preferred types of documents; the overvaluing of contemporary perceptions of geographical reality, even to the exclusion of interest in alternative measures; the willingness to confine attention to geographical portraits of single cross-sectional moments in the past; and the absent role for modern fieldwork in the research scheme. Clark admired Brown's results and his scholarly care, but he viewed the broader task of historical geography as more complex: it needed greater attention to the agencies and patterns of change, and greater methodological flexibility in arriving at conclusions that "showed a thorough familiarity with the larger patterns of geography and history relevant to the region under study."[197] Clark's program for this comprised a more resolute focus on "geographical change" as the central axiom for the field.[198]

---

sheep/swine ratio, in trios of twenty-year periods, by county" (p. 54); despite ingenious cartometry, meaning in the patterns remains opaque.

[194] Douglas R. McManis, "Andrew Hill Clark, 1911–1975," *Historical Geography*, vol. 6, 1 (1976), p. 14.

[195] David Ward, "Andrew H. Clark: A Memorial and Bibliography," *Annals of the Association of American Geographers*, vol. 67, 2 (1977), p. 146; a judgment the writer can endorse from personal memory of Clark's seminars.

[196] These included, besides Harold A. Innis at Toronto, his Madison colleagues Merle Curti, Merrill Jensen, Allan G. Bogue, Eric E. Lampard, and Morton Rothstein. On historians' interest in regional issues, see, e.g., Merrill Jensen, ed., *Regionalism in America* (Madison: University of Wisconsin Press, 1951).

[197] Meinig, "Clark," p. 12 (see n. 194, above).

[198] This is forcefully declared at the outset of Clark's 1954 review of the field, "Historical Geography," p. 71 (see n. 6, above), and repeated in "Geographical Change: A Theme for Economic History," *Journal of Economic History*, vol. 20, 4 (1960), pp. 607–616; and "Suggestions for the Geographical Study of Agricultural Change in the United States, 1790–1840," *Agricultural History*, vol. 46, 1 (1972), pp. 155–172. However, the provenance of the terminology is not made clear. While Clark cannot claim original authorship for the phrase as a technical term in English-language usage—it had been in sporadic use since the early part of the century at least—he was the first to endow it with systematic methodological value. As an example of prior use, see Robert L. Sherlock, "The Influence of Man as an Agent in Geographical Change," *Geographical Journal*, vol. 61, 4 (1923), pp. 258–273.

"He often applied the term very generally to a variety of studies," Meinig notes; "It was his way of emphasizing that the main purpose of historical geography was not to reconstruct the geography of an area at some particular time . . . but to see human geography as an ever-changing thing. But he also made clear in several careful expositions that he considered the most effective method for such study was to focus on 'the geographical structure of change' which revealed differences in the patterns of phenomena between one time and another."[199]

In the course of such proselytizing, Clark would often refer to "geographical change," "the geography of change," or "changing geography (or geographies)" as if the phrase employed stemmed more from stylistic choice than conceptual nicety. Yet distinctions can be observed among the terms, whether intended or not, and it is useful to specify which version best represents Clark's demonstrated position, the better to gauge the shape of his influence. "Geographical change" is the vaguest and most generic, as it would seem to accommodate both the other terms. "The geography of change" emphasizes a process—change—which itself exhibits an overall and corporate geography, however handled empirically; if anything is mapped it is an abstract quality (or quantity) of dynamism that is of prime interest, along with the fact that it is not uniformly distributed. "Changing geography (or geographies)," on the other hand, suggests a focus on areas and places undergoing alteration, far more in tune with traditional interest in the spatial structure of regions.[200] The record of Clark's substantive work suggests a steady drift in paradigmatic preference between the 1940s and the 1960s from that of Sauer to Brown, catching up, as it were, with his nominal declaration made early on in favor of Brown's historical (as distinct from cultural) geography, complete with its Brownian features of regional focus and commitment to documentary evidence. If Clark's own work is best described as the study of changing geographies, his endorsement of the geography of change might then be seen, rather differently, as a welcome—however intended—to specialized process studies in the field, which interestingly were to gain impetus from broad changes occurring in the social sciences during the 1960s. If Clark was in fact preaching more than he actually practiced, what effect did this have on those most likely to execute such proposals—his students?

Nineteen doctoral studies in historical geography at Wisconsin emerged from his tutelage, eleven of which were published in revised form as books, and many dissertations completed through other sponsors (inside and outside geography) bore the marks of his influence. Attention to those works focused on the United States will amply suffice to illuminate the flow of ideas and practice, and hint at some of the mutations that might be expected to occur.[201] The first three studies, directed by Clark through 1962, examined generally state-sized regions and were clearly concerned with their geographical content and arrangement. With David Ward's study

[199] Meinig, "Clark," p. 21 (see n. 194, above).

[200] These distinctions have been made in ibid., pp. 21–22.

[201] Lists of these dissertations are given in *Historical Geography*, vol. 6, 1 (1976), pp. 80–81; and in Gibson, *European Settlement*, pp. 229–230 (see n. 194, above).

of nineteenth-century Boston the following year two discontinuities with Clark's own predilections emerged: a sharp focus on social processes in space; and processes in urban space at that.[202] In the dozen years that followed, most studies undertook systematic investigations of one kind or another, though almost always set within a limited regional context. As with Sauer, Clark expected students to devise their own problems for study, though he likely took a larger role in shaping their methodology, committed as he was to the advancement of a coherent body of concepts and techniques in the field of historical geography.[203] Consequently, studies emerged on states such as North Carolina and Ohio, but more likely on portions of states such as New Jersey, Pennsylvania, Texas, Virginia, and Kansas, and in three cases on specific aspects of New England, the South, and the country as a whole; and topics ranged from improved cattle breeds to food supply, and frontier agriculture to immigrant farming. Many, if not most, can be described in Meinig's words, as "a form of geographic critique in which long-held general interpretations in history are replaced by detailed expositions of the complexities of processes and local circumstances. In each case . . . it is the geographer who provides the corrective."[204]

An illustration of this revisionist character can be found in a study by James T. Lemon, which in its published form, *The Best Poor Man's Country: A Geographical Study of Early Southeastern Pennsylvania*,[205] argues that historians in looking for the origins of the hard social realities of the nineteenth-century American republic should look not to New England or Virginia, usually regarded as founts of American mores, but instead to the middle colonies. There, weakening community, high geographical mobility, autonomous farms, palsied government, strong profit motive, religious diversity and ethnic pluralism emerged in their purest form, during the colonial period—a liberal reality that would later diffuse through the bulk of the nation's heartland. The study won the Beveridge Prize of the American Historical Association for best book in American history in 1972, became a fixture on reading lists in American social and political history, and formed the basis of an accelerating debate with some colonial historians over the modernity of early American society.[206] While the individuality of students and studies in historical

---

[202] David Ward, "Nineteenth Century Boston: A Study in the Role of Antecedent and Adjacent Conditions in the Spatial Aspects of Urban Growth," Ph.D. diss., University of Wisconsin–Madison, 1963.

[203] This capacity for taking the long view in an organizational sense was evident in his own research, noted earlier: "The very idea of projecting a coherent program of scholarly studies, of undertaking a lifetime of inquiry on a major topic, was virtually unheard of in American geography" (see Meinig, "Clark," p. 7; see n. 194, above).

[204] Ibid., p. 17.

[205] (Baltimore: Johns Hopkins University Press, 1972).

[206] For a representative and incisive historian's assessment, see John M. Murrin, review of *The Best Poor Man Man's Country*, in *American Historical Review*, vol. 78, 2 (1973), pp. 475–476. For orientation to the Lemon-Henretta debate over the modernity of early American farmers, see James T. Lemon, "Comment on James A. Henretta's 'Families and Farms: *Mentalité* in Pre-Industrial America,' with a Reply by James A. Henretta," *William & Mary Quarterly*, 3d ser., vol. 37, 4 (1980), pp. 688–700. Robert D. Mitchell continued the revisionist movement with his book, *Commercialism and Frontier: Perspectives on the Early Shenandoah Frontier* (Charlottesville: University Press of Virginia, 1977), as did D. Aidan McQuillan in the book that emerged from the last dissertation supervised by Clark, *Prevailing over Time: Ethnic*

geography at Wisconsin at that time is beyond question, the same quality of intellectual vigor and common assumptions that bound Sauer's progeny together could be found in that of Clark's—despite protests of ornery individualism entered in defense of the nonexistence of a school at both Berkeley and Madison.[207]

Fifteen of the nineteen who received doctorates under Clark secured employment between 1962 and 1974 at universities offering doctoral programs in geography, giving the group notable scope to be productive and influence the direction of the field. Eight now teach in Canada (four are native), and in the United States three teach in Texas and one each in Louisiana, Maryland, Tennessee, and Wisconsin. David Ward returned to Madison as a faculty member in 1966 to buttress Clark's program with urban expertise, Sam B. Hilliard was called to Louisiana State University to fill the gap left by Fred Kniffen's retirement, and more recently Terry G. Jordan was appointed to the University of Texas to fill the Walter Prescott Webb Chair of History and Ideas "in the Department of Geography."

Andrew Clark's legacy extends beyond the methodological statements he wrote and the advanced students he trained, for his organizational energies were called upon time and again.[208] Of interest here is the superb editorial help he gave his students in getting their studies revised for book publication, the planning and editorial stewardship he brought to the Historical Geography of North America series of books published by Oxford University Press between 1971 and 1977, and his founding coeditorship of an international serial, the *Journal of Historical Geography* (est. 1974–1975), which immediately became the premier journal in the field.[209] Substantively, however, the Clarkian tradition drew on strands from Innis, Sauer, and Brown to fashion a methodological approach distinct from what had gone before: explicitly historical, attentive to the economic basis of regions, devoted to field and archive, well integrated with professional history, analytically adventuresome, and book-oriented.[210] His scholarly standing ensured continuity in Madison after his

---

Adjustments on the Kansas Prairies, 1875–1925 (Lincoln: University of Nebraska Press, 1990), which won the Agricultural History Society's Theodore Saloutos Prize for best book in agricultural history in 1990.

[207] See Joseph E. Spencer, "What's in a Name: 'The Berkeley School'?" *Historical Geography Newsletter*, vol. 6, 1 (1976), pp. 7–11; and Ward, "Clark," p. 146 (see n. 196, above), in which he refers coyly to the "occasional murmurs that [Clark's] influence may have germinated a school of historical geography."

[208] His editorship of the monograph series of the Association of American Geographers, following Whittlesey's death, thrust him into preparations for publication of the inaugural volume, Richard Hartshorne's *Perspective on the Nature of Geography* (1959), which was followed by Donald W. Meinig's *On the Margins of the Good Earth* (1962).

[209] The Oxford series, produced in New York, grew to seven volumes: Donald W. Meinig, *Southwest: Three Peoples in Geographic Change* (1971); David Ward, *Cities and Immigrants: A Geography of Change in Nineteenth Century America* (1971); R. Cole Harris and John Warkentin, *Canada before Confederation: A Study in Historical Geography* (1974); Douglas R. McManis, *Colonial New England: A Historical Geography* (1975); James R. Gibson, *Imperial Russia in Frontier America: The Changing Geography of Supply of Russian America, 1784–1867* (1976); Hildegard Binder Johnson, *Order upon the Land: The U.S. Rectangular Land Survey and the Upper Mississippi Country* (1976); and John A. Jakle, *Images of the Ohio Valley: A Historical Geography of Travel, 1740 to 1860* (1977).

[210] On his early views of fieldwork, see Andrew H. Clark, "Field Research in Historical Geography," *Professional Geographer*, vol. 4 (1946), pp. 13–23. It appears to the writer that Clark's widely quoted devotion to fieldwork perhaps changed character over time. Certainly, he knew every mile of his own study areas,

death, and Ward's presence and growing reputation in his own right guaranteed the succession, strengthened by the addition of Robert C. Ostergren, who maintains the agrarian interests Clark held so dear.[211] Perhaps nowhere else in American historical geography has the passing of the torch in situ from one generation to another been effected with such relative ease.

Beyond the walls of Baton Rouge and Madison, the field of historical geography grew steadily—if one can measure the growth by the mere quantity of publication— and it was also treated to a series of partial efforts at synthesis the two schools had had little time for. In the 1930s and 1940s a fairly steady average of 60 articles per annum had been the rule; this rose to roughly 90 in the 1950s, and more than doubled thereafter to about 200 a year during the late sixties.[212] More encouraging still, the number of monograph-length studies in the field began to grow.[213] In the 1940s and early 1950s a number of doctoral dissertations were available as publications, the circulation of which represented virtually the only book-length printed material coming from scholars in the field, aside from the singular events of Brown's two books. Half a dozen such monographs appeared under the auspices of the University of Chicago Library dissertation private-edition series, later turned into the Department of Geography Research Papers series.[214]

But in the late 1950s Clark's lead in publishing his New Zealand study "postpartum," as it were, through an independent publisher (that is, unaffiliated with the author's doctoral institution) was at last followed.[215] George Carter was the first with a regular book from a university press in the field of American historical

---

an intense knowledge gained early and deepened with each visit. And as a canon of righteous training it was always proclaimed, but for many students it came to connote, it seems, visits to archives rather than intense reconnaissance of localities in the field. By the mid-sixties I recall no organized field excursions in human geography from Madison to nearby or distant locales as laboratory occasions to train and test students' observational powers. Such activity was the stuff of legend in the Sauer era, and was certainly routine in German programs at the time, as Clark would have known through his acquaintance with Gottfried Pfeifer and Helmut Jäger. But then, of course, in an era of documentary sources, a capacity to focus on the field of vision a few inches beyond one's nose may clearly suffice for certain types of topics.

[211] Ostergren's credentials have been burnished recently by publication of his award-winning book, *A Community Transplanted: The Trans-Atlantic Experience of a Swedish Immigrant Settlement in the Upper Middle West, 1835–1915* (Madison: University of Wisconsin Press, 1988), copublished at Uppsala, Sweden: Acta Universitatis Upsaliensis, Studia Multiethnica, no. 4, 1988.

[212] Calculations based on preliminary tabulations prepared from the data base from which the bibliography in this *Guide* has been created.

[213] Before 1940 geographical monographs with a historical dimension had been issued in the 1910s and 1920s almost exclusively courtesy of various state geological and natural history surveys—e.g., in Illinois, Wisconsin, Ohio, and Kentucky (the combined significance of which, as a chapter in the history of the discipline, has so far received but slight attention)—and the few during the 1930s in assorted university-wide scholarly and scientific bulletin series. The absence of commercial publishers indicates the specialized nature of the subject matter and the lack of a broad educational market.

[214] Berkeley's publication series in geography at this time featured extensive work on Latin American topics, and some North American work generally too brief to be considered monographic.

[215] The accounting that follows does not include Jean Gottmann's *Virginia at Mid-Century* (New York: Henry Holt & Co., 1955), reissued with a supplementary chapter as *Virginia in Our Century*, Charlottesville: University Press of Virginia, 1969), in which chapter 2, "Three and a Half Centuries of Change," represents a fine eighty-seven-page treatment of Virginia's historical geography, written by a French regionalist geographer of consummate skill.

geography (in 1957), followed by Lauren Post (1962), H. Roy Merrens (1964), Terry Jordan (1966), and Donald Meinig with three books in quick succession (1968, 1969, and 1971).[216] Carter's book gained wide notice among a specialized audience, but most of it was outside geography; more likely to influence historical geographers were the next six. Of these, Post's book was the least influential; based on a Berkeley dissertation completed twenty-five years before, it was a mature and engrossing evocation of the Cajun culture he knew from youth, historically rich, and engagingly written (with a title to match) for a general audience, not merely for academics. It gained status as a classic in the popular literature on Louisiana Cajuns, but garnered few notices among geographers.[217] The books by Merrens, Jordan, and Meinig, on the other hand, were written with a scholarly readership in mind, and all received extensive and favorable review in both national and international geographical and national historical journals. Merrens and Jordan had launched both their own careers and Clark's reputation as a director of dissertations in historical geography that become books, while Meinig, who claims no graduate mentor in the field, added briskly to his scholarly stature, drawing a long and appreciative review article about his Palouse book from Clark himself in the region's main journal of letters.[218] These books, carefully researched and challenging regional studies, opened the field during the 1960s to interdisciplinary notice and scrutiny as never before (for scholarly books get reviewed), and they laid the foundation for a more confident and rigorous level of scholarly performance that has been a hallmark of the field since.

Regional studies in historical geography are well adapted to examine cultural patterns over space, and this large theme was stirring thought about the geographical structure and origins of American culture areas. Already in the mid-sixties Meinig

---

[216] The full-length books of this period are: George F. Carter, *Pleistocene Man at San Diego, California* (Baltimore: Johns Hopkins University Press, 1957); Lauren C. Post, *Cajun Sketches from the Prairies of Southwest Louisiana* (Baton Rouge: Louisiana State University Press, 1962; reprinted 1974); H. Roy Merrens, *Colonial North Carolina in the Eighteenth Century: A Study in Historical Geography* (Chapel Hill: University of North Carolina Press, 1964); Terry G. Jordan, *German Seed in Texas Soil: Immigrant Farmers in Nineteenth Century Texas* (Austin: University of Texas Press, 1966); and Donald W. Meinig, *The Great Columbia Plain: A Historical Geography, 1805–1910* (Seattle: University of Washington Press, 1968); *Imperial Texas: An Interpretive Essay in Cultural Geography* (Austin: University of Texas Press, 1969); and *Southwest..*

[217] Only the *Professional Geographer* and the *Journal of Geography* carried brief reviews. William Knipmeyer, writing in the former, noted, "Post uses a style which is extremely well suited to convey a deep understanding of [the Acadian people's] culture and personality. *Cajun Sketches* is one of the uncommon examples of literary geographical exposition done by a geographer"; *Professional Geographer*, vol. 16, 1 (1964), p. 42. In one of the few historical reviews, W. Ramsey noted, "A professional geographer, [Post] has probed more deeply than the title of his book would suggest," *Journal of Southern History*, vol. 29, 3 (1963), p. 429. Post's book may not have reached every geographer's shelf, but it was reprinted in 1974, with a special foreword by the governor of Louisiana, testimony to its cultural role in the region, confirmed in a generous notice of the second edition by Malcolm Comeaux in *Revue de Louisiane.*

[218] Andrew H. Clark: "The Strategy and Ecology of Man's Occupation of the Intermontane Northwest: Review of D.W. Meinig, *The Great Columbia Plain,*" *Pacific Northwest Quarterly*, vol. 60, 2 (1969), pp. 98–102. Meinig's attraction to, and preparation in, historical geography was to a considerable extent through his own effort and reflection; such an avenue, he has opined, precludes the osmotic risk of adopting preconceived ideas. When he arrived in graduate school, however, the Australian-born Graham H. Lawton introduced him to the small literature of British and American historical geography. For details, see Donald W. Meinig, "A Life of Learning" (see n. 181, above).

had completed a study of the Mormon culture region, residing as he had near its heart and struck by its prominent demarcation on maps in recent national cultural studies.[219] The method and conceptual model displayed in this study invited elaboration and comparative work. Meinig himself next tackled the phenomenon of Texas: how to make sense of its regional and cultural parts and how to account for its peculiar place within American culture? Kniffen, Glassie, and others had worked on related questions of cultural influence and spread in the East. By the early 1970s major efforts at preliminary forms of synthesis were at hand. One result was *Regions of the United States*, edited by John Fraser Hart. As a contribution to the literature for participants in the 1972 International Geographical Congress in Montreal, the AAG authorized a nationwide collection of regional essays that, as it turned out, was overwhelmingly historical in general presentation.[220] While multiauthored and not complete in coverage, these essays together provided a fresh look at the mosaic of American regions, with many specific ideas about the origins and progress of particular regional traits. A year later, Zelinsky published *The Cultural Geography of the United States*, a slim volume in no way replacing Brown's aging survey, but a bold exploration of some core themes in American cultural and historical geography.[221] Imaginative, provocative, and schematic, Zelinsky's arguments were crammed into four crisp chapters: origins, identity, process, and structure. Among the few illustrations in the work is the "contemporary map of American culture areas," which its author almost diffidently suggested "is apparently the first attempt ever made to delimit cultural areas for the entirety of the coterminous United States" (fig. 9).[222] Key to its interpretation is the proposition that the delimited areas "can be explained in terms of the genesis, development, and expansion of the three principal colonial culture hearths located along the Atlantic Seaboard." Few maps of the cultural and historical geography of the United States have been so reproduced as this one. A strength of the book is Zelinsky's ability to draw creatively from research in all the flourishing traditions of cultural-historical geography and mold a cohesive argument regarding the geographical underpinnings of American character and social patterns.

Taken together, despite their dissimilarity, these two books mark a minor watershed in the evolution of American historical geography. They reflect a culmination of several long-running developments: research in largely regional and agrarian themes; a broadly achieved consensus over the aims and methods of investigation (notwithstanding the vitality and skirmishes among different schools—cultural ver-

---

[219] Donald W. Meinig, "The Mormon Culture Region: Strategies and Patterns in the Geography of the American West, 1847–1967," *Annals of the Association of American Geographers*, vol. 55, 2 (1965), pp. 191–220.

[220] (New York: Harper and Row, 1972), a reissue in book form of the March 1972 *Annals of the Association of American Geographers*, vol. 62, 1, aimed at wide college use in regional geography courses.

[221] Wilbur Zelinsky, *The Cultural Geography of the United States* (Englewood Cliffs, N.J.: Prentice-Hall, 1973).

[222] Ibid., p. 117.

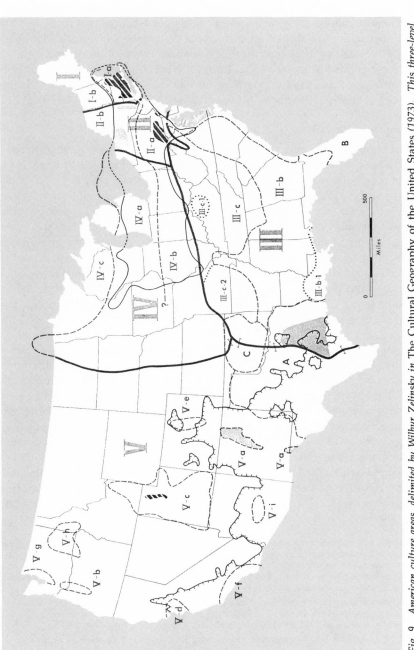

Fig. 9. *American culture areas, delimited by Wilbur Zelinsky in* The Cultural Geography of the United States *(1973). This three-level hierarchical classification of the country into cultural-genetic regions and subregions represents a major benchmark of synoptic mapping in American historical geography.*

sus historical, landscape versus economy, field versus library); and maturation as a subfield that expanded along with others during good educational times and now boasted high rates of published research, given the numbers involved, with a clear capacity for producing book-length original research that could hold its own in the review pages of history and the social sciences. What they do not show are signs of the methodological and ideological upheavals that were reshaping the discipline and the practice of historical geography between the 1960s and the early 1980s.[223]

Challenge and Pluralism

The changes that occurred in historical geography were part of broad trends in the discipline as a whole as well as in history and the social sciences at large.[224] The first was the challenge to regional geography raised by those who saw in it little of comparative value and who sought to derive general principles rather from systematic study, elevating the approach involved to the status of scientific method. Central to this was the study of process, in pursuit of generally abstract theories and model-building, but process predicated heavily upon economic assumptions of individual and group behavior. Changes also in the technology available for research, and the new sources opened up by this, all brought about a fundamental rethinking of scholarly practice and purpose. A conceptual and quantitative revolution rode through the social sciences during the late 1950s and 1960s that affected one discipline after another, filling geography and then history with heated debates over the kind of research that was appropriate and the way it should be done.[225] Somewhat later, the mechanistic workings of spatial theories popularized in this period brought reaction: from positivists seeking to improve explanation through better specification of actual human behavior; from Marxists concerned with the absence of structural explanations behind the patterns; and from cultural relativists unwilling to accept the universality of essentially economically driven models of behavior. This latter, phenomenological approach had its origins in earlier writing, and by the 1970s mounted a strong challenge to interpretations requiring assumptions of overwhelming rationality in human affairs. The fickleness of human nature, the oddities of chance, and the indeterminacies of action bulked large in such a view, and created a humanistic paradigm sensitive to human qualities in people and broad ethnocultural determinants of behavior.[226]

---

[223] The writer will resist the temptation to search for additional schools of thought or practice emerging in the most recent period of development. The record is too unfinished for any possible candidacy to be evaluated impartially. There is no doubt that there are some trends and notable individual achievements that, when placed in ultimate context, may presage recognition of further schools, but durability and the measure of lasting influence require time to pass for worthwhile assessments to be made.

[224] Discussions of these more recent developments are legion; useful overviews of debates carried on in English-language sources can be found in Ronald J. Johnston, *Geography and Geographers: Anglo-American Human Geography since 1945*, 2d ed. (London: Edward Arnold, 1983), pp. 50–93.

[225] Mark Billinge, Derek Gregory, and R. L. Martin, eds., *Recollections of a Revolution* (London: Macmillan, 1982).

[226] Early discussions of these perspectives in American geography appear in John K. Wright, *"Terrae Incognitae*: The Place of Imagination in Geography," *Annals of the Association of American Geography*, vol. 37, 1 (1947), pp. 1–15; and David Lowenthal, "Geography, Experience, and Imagination: Towards a

In history, consensus models of American social development were coming under challenge from those concerned with various overlooked and exploited segments of society, often, though not exclusively, through an appeal to Marxian perspectives. Using new means of measurement, a bottom-up approach to social history emerged to challenge what were seen as elite orientations, and this spread its assumptions to other branches of the discipline, and led ultimately and gave legitimacy to the history of everyday life (*Alltagsgeschichte*). At the same time, interest in the accumulated accomplishments of the French *Annales* school of *histoire totale*, stimulated especially by the works of Marc Bloch and Fernand Braudel, has led in the United States to the emergence of a strong brand of social science history, championed by such figures as Edward Whiting Fox, Charles Tilly, and Immanuel M. Wallerstein. These currents in history have found reflection in American historical geography, if rather faint so far, though interest in metatheoretical discourse is on the rise.[227]

In United States historical geography, the impact of these reevaluations lagged somewhat behind that in such other fields as economic and social geography, but was expressed when it came at two levels. One was a broad debate over area versus process, which was joined with William A. Koelsch's review of Clark's third book, *Acadia*. Seeing the study as a vast collation of ideographic detail with generalization almost indefinitely postponed, Koelsch bemoaned the inattention to geographical theories (those concerned, for example, with central places, location, and environmental perception) in a concluding chapter that took historians' concepts (about the frontier and metropolitanism) into account. Koelsch's concern was that historical geographers keep up with their own discipline by equipping themselves "with those conceptual frameworks, models, and techniques which have distinguished geography in the 1960s."[228]

The case was broadened substantially by a visiting British geographer, Hugh C. Prince, in a major review article that recognized a more catholic agenda for historical geography than that contained in the regional geographical-change or cultural-landscape paradigms he found being promoted among leading American practitioners.[229] Besides geographical change, argued Prince, there are valuable dimensions to explore through such other avenues as past geographies, processes of change, per-

Geographical Epistemology," *Annals of the Association of American Geography*, vol. 51, 3 (1961), pp. 241–260.

[227] A useful review of this movement is detailed in Carville V. Earle, Introduction to *Geographical Inquiry and American Historical Problems* (Stanford, Calif.: Stanford University Press, 1992), pp. 1–23.

[228] William A. Koelsch, review of *Acadia*, in *Economic Geography*, vol. 46, 2 (1970), p. 202. In agreement on the "immeasurable benefit" of the new positivist models in geography, not only for historical geographers but also for historians, was John A. Jakle in his methodological review, "Time, Space, and the Geographic Past: A Prospectus for Historical Geography," *American Historical Review*, vol. 76, 4 (1971), pp. 1084–1103, though he was "hesitant to suggest how interaction between the disciplines of academic history and geography might be cultivated" (p. 1103). Edward M. Cook, a historian, took up the point in his "Geography and History: Spatial Approaches to Early American History," *Historical Methods*, vol. 13, 1 (1980), pp. 19–28.

ceived landscapes and mental geographies, cultural appraisals, behavioral environments, models of interaction, counterfactual reconstructions, and probabilistic process simulations. Prince's smorgasbord opened the door to more experimentation with both method and substance than in the past, and his review might well be taken as the manifesto that cheered on a new pluralism.[230]

The second impact can be seen in fumbling efforts to accommodate quantitative analysis and model-building into the traditional tool kit of historical geography.[231] Numbers had been used as evidence in historical studies since time immemorial, but the discovery (and rediscovery) of systematic data sources in censuses (particularly manuscript schedules of old censuses opened for archival research), land records, tax lists, directories, and the like, together with the arrival of the electronic computer to aid in their large-scale analysis, served radically to alter the frequency and sophistication of their use. More significant, such sources proved attractive for studies exploring disaggregated populations for the more individually constructed bases of group behavior. This led to three prominent innovations in method. On a rudimentary level, traditionally conceptualized studies made far greater use of quantitative material as input, even if the output were simply in the form of percentages, cross-tabulations, and maps, and this change came to stay.[232] At a second level, some researchers were emboldened to incorporate advanced statistical techniques into their analyses and thereby added to the forms of proof, not to mention standards of technical comprehension, in the field. Notable efforts in this direction appear in the work of David Ward, Wilbur Zelinsky, and Peter G. Goheen, among others.[233] At a third level, there was a move to construct explicit process

[229] Hugh C. Prince, "Real, Imagined, and Abstract Worlds of the Past," in Christopher Board et al., eds., *Progress in Geography*, vol. 3 (London: Edward Arnold, 1971), pp. 1–86.

[230] David Ward, also commenting on "belated methodological stirrings," noted that the new issues "recall the humanistic interests of historical geography which only recently were dismissed as 'unscientific' and ideographic." See his "The Debate on Alternative Approaches in Historical Geography," *Historical Methods Newsletter*, vol. 8, 2 (1975), pp. 82–87.

[231] For a useful overview, see Peter G. Goheen, "Methodology in Historical Geography: The 1970s in Review," *Historical Methods*, vol. 16, 1 (1983), pp. 8–15.

[232] An early but overlooked case in point is provided by the remarkable North Carolina study noted earlier, Morris and Morris, "Economic Conditions" (see n. 138, above); Clark's Prince Edward Island study, "Sheep/Swine Ratio" (see n. 194, above) provides another. Perhaps the most prolific case is that of Pred, whose studies of nineteenth-century urbanization presented immense quantities of painstakingly reconstructed data series relating to industrial production and trade. See, for example, Allan R. Pred, *The Spatial Dynamics of U.S. Urban-Industrial Growth, 1800–1914* (Cambridge: MIT Press, 1966).

[233] See, for example, David Ward, "The Internal Spatial Structure of Immigrant Residential Districts in the Late Nineteenth Century," *Geographical Analysis*, vol. 1, 4 (1969), pp. 337–353, an early application of principal components analysis in historical geography. Trend surface analysis forms the basis of a 1966 study published a decade later: John W. Florin, *The Advance of Frontier Settlement in Pennsylvania, 1638–1850: A Geographical Interpretation* (University Park: Pennsylvania State University Department of Geography Paper no. 14, 1977). Zelinsky employed coefficients of similarity, numerical taxonomy, and factor analysis in his "Cultural Variation in Personal Name Patterns in the Eastern United States," *Annals of the Association of American Geographers*, vol. 60, 1 (1970), pp. 743–769. Goheen's study of Toronto, though a Canadian example, was undertaken at the University of Chicago under Brian J. L. Berry's direction and combined both principal components analysis and trend surface analysis for several discrete dates: see Peter G. Goheen, *Victorian Toronto, 1850 to 1900: Pattern and Process of Growth* (Chicago: University of Chicago Department of Geography, Research Paper no. 127, 1970). The use of multiple regression analy-

models, whether supported by advanced statistical analysis or not, and such efforts often brought into question the primary goals of the research: the advancement of ahistorical spatial theory or the explanation of historical change in the context of particular times. This is best illustrated by the work of Allan R. Pred, whose imaginative studies on American urbanization, sometimes inadvertently, raised this issue.[234] Occasionally, problem-oriented quantitative work in economic history influenced geographers, such as Robert W. Fogel's study that sought to explode the doctrine of indispensability that had come to dominate historians' assessment of the role of railroads in American economic growth.[235]

The advent of advanced quantitative analysis and model-building in American historical geography was greeted with little principled opposition; merely, perhaps, a reluctance to be drawn too naively into a venture that was onerous to mount and difficult to prove superior to conventional methods. The frequent lack of convenient quantitative, spatially disaggregated time series data for many areas and periods of the American past to answer geographically interesting questions has undoubtedly dampened enthusiasm for large, technically complex analyses, as has the need for thorough training in statistics to avoid the charge of dilettantism. But more telling is the failure of the early enthusiasts for statistical study to continue vigorous work in such a vein, suggesting that the payoff was not sufficiently great to repeat the investment of effort. Then there is the fluidity of methodological preferences: what constitutes interesting research changes complexion often enough to inhibit many from becoming tied too closely to particular analytical methods. The rise of behavioral and humanistic themes in historical geography drew many away from methods seen as the tools of logical positivism.[236] To be sure, the tradition of quantitative and statistical studies continues, but it represents only a small-to-moderate portion of the field, and must demonstrate greater sensitivity than in the past to questions about the ideological provenance and implications of data. Model-building, on the other

sis and the mapping of residuals is exemplified in Michael P. Conzen, *Frontier Farming in an Urban Shadow: The Influence of Madison's Proximity on the Agricultural Development of Blooming Grove, Wisconsin* (Madison: State Historical Society of Wisconsin, 1971); and in Edward K. Muller, "Selective Urban Growth in the Middle Ohio Valley, 1800–1860," *Geographical Review*, vol. 66, 2 (1976), pp. 178–199. A combination of principal components and regression analyses is offered in Michael P. Conzen, "A Transport Interpretation of the Growth of Urban Regions: An American Example," *Journal of Historical Geography*, vol. 1, 4 (1975), pp. 361–382. In a recent example, analysis of variance and assorted other statistical techniques are displayed in McQuillan, *Prevailing* (see n. 207, above).

[234] Pred, *Spatial Dynamics* (see n. 233, above). For an interesting, retrospective account of this work, albeit wrapped in the distracting jargon of "time-geography," see Allan R. Pred, "The Academic Past through a Time-Geographic Looking Glass," *Annals of the Association of American Geographers*, vol. 69, 1 (1979), pp. 175–180.

[235] Robert W. Fogel, *Railroads and American Economic Growth* (Baltimore: Johns Hopkins University Press, 1964).

[236] One scholar who has worried over the discrete spheres of explanation promoted by the "scientific explanation of spatial distributions" and the "social-historical perspective" is Bonnie Barton in her study, *The Comparability of Geographic Methodologies: A Study of New England Settlement* (Ann Arbor: University of Michigan Department of Geography Publications, no. 20, 1977), in which she examined the interrelation of the modes with respect to their accounting of settlement processes in New England between 1650 and 1800. She concluded that both are legitimate and cannot be combined, but can be accepted as complementary.

hand, has fared better, perhaps because there are so few rules about minimum logical structure and complexity, for it appears open to anyone able to link conceptual boxes with arrows or to sketch changing relationships in graphic form. As a mode by which to simplify untidy reality past and present for analytical ends, the use of models, however crude, is helpful, but there has been very little critical evaluation of the numerous models so produced, and they seem destined to play a limited, heuristic role, rather than a dominant and formal one, in historical geography.[237] A minute but noteworthy feature of the relationship between historical geography and those subfields focused resolutely on the present has been the small trade in adherents between the camps. Balancing those that started out in historical geography but made their careers on the strength of contemporary research are others who have forsaken relevant contemporary spatial analysis for the rewards of historical reflection.[238]

The shift to systematic and process-oriented study and the embrace of quantitative and theoretical model-building produced many variations among substantive interests in the field, and two cases will serve to illustrate changes that occurred. One is the realm of perceptual studies. This genre has been referred to earlier, but its progress requires a brief update. What distinguishes the earlier work from that which came later, during the 1970s and after, is the change in philosophical climate in geography in general and historical geography in particular. The earlier contributions were periodic and rather isolated and that pattern would perhaps have continued through the modern period had it not been for a reaction to the strength and dominance of the economic-functionalist-spatial paradigm in American human geography during the 1960s. Ralph Brown, John Leighly, Hildegard Johnson, and a few others wrote intermittently on the subjectivity of Americans in the past, mostly their general impressions of regions and environments, but it took more detailed studies, of a much wider range of primary sources (than even Brown had contemplated), representing more than the views of the famous and most literate, for the

---

[237] A rare evaluation of a process model in American historical geography is David R. Meyer, "A Critique of Pred's Model of Industrialization and Urban-Size Growth," *Proceedings of the New England–St. Lawrence Valley Division, Association of American Geographers*, vol. 5 (1975), pp. 6–10. Such vigilance, of course, invites return scrutiny: see William K. Wyckoff, "Revising the Meyer Model: Denver and the National Urban System, 1859–1879," *Urban Geography*, vol. 9, 1 (1988), pp. 1–18. Few American geographers seem willing to follow Canadian William Norton in his crusade on behalf of the abstract past: see his "Abstract Cultural Landscapes," *Journal of Cultural Geography*, vol. 8, 1 (1987), pp. 67-80.

[238] Among those whose early research in American historical geography was not sustained by later publication in the field are Elizabeth Burns, Edward Espenshade, Jerome Fellmann, Nevin Fenneman, John Florin, Roger Kasperson, Allen Philbrick, Marilyn Silberfein, Joseph Spencer, Warren Thornthwaite, Edward Ullman, and Bret Wallach; among those who qualify as later converts to the historical perspective are Samuel Dicken, John Hudson, Peirce Lewis, Barron McIntosh, David Meyer, James Vance, and Morton Winsberg. Hudson may be regarded as a renegade from the bruderbund of quantitative spatial analysts. Others might be regarded as occasional historical recreationists, such as Brian J. L. Berry, who recently published *Westward the American Shapleys* (Baltimore: Gateway Press, 1987), a 466-page family history well received by genealogists; but see his recent substantial historical investigations: *Long-Wave Rhythms in Economic Development and Political Behavior* (Baltimore: Johns Hopkins University Press, 1991); and *America's Utopian Experiments: Communal Havens from Long-Wave Crises* (Hanover, N.H.: University Press of New England, 1992).

perspective to show its potential.[239] In the 1960s G. Malcolm Lewis and Douglas R. McManis had began publishing several detailed cognitive studies of western environments, and by the 1970s they were joined by H. Roy Merrens, Kenneth Thompson, Martyn J. Bowden, John L. Allen, Terry Jordan, and John A. Jakle, sampling more regions but with the Great Plains still best covered.[240]

Much of the impetus for the more recent work came from scholars with either British backgrounds or ties to Nebraska, Chicago, and Clark, or both, but in an effort to separate and elevate the status of this emerging genre an effort was made to link it with the term once resurrected by John K. Wright (of the American Geographical Society): "geosophy, . . . the study of geographical knowledge from all points of view"; and, thanks to the subtitle of a memorial volume to Wright, the term has more or less stuck.[241] During the 1970s a substantial body of such work would lead Wisconsin historian Allan G. Bogue to note in relation to the Great Plains and the writings of geographical historian James Malin that "geographers rather than historians have

---

[239] These earlier works include Ward, "South Dakota" (see n. 77, above); Leighly, "Muir" (see n. 107); Brown, "Fact and Fancy" (see n. 140); "American Geographies" (see n. 142); and *Mirror* (see n. 143); and H. B. Johnson, 'Perceptions" (see n. 178). To them might be added four theses between 1933 and 1962 and three articles by Meinig and Rostlund: Walter M. Kollmorgen, "Some Geographic Misconceptions of the Climate of Nebraska and the Great Plains," Master's thesis, University of Nebraska; Nicholas J. Schmidt, Jr., "Evolving Geographic Concepts of the Kansas Area, with Emphasis on the Land Literature of the Santa Fe Railroad," Master's thesis, University of Kansas, 1949; Joseph B. Hoyt, "The Historical Geography of Berkshire County, Massachusetts: A Study of Man's Changing Evaluation of a Physical Setting," Ph.D. diss., Clark University, 1954; Michael R. C. Coulson, "Geographic Concepts of Kansas prior to 1803," Master's thesis, University of Kansas, 1962; Donald W. Meinig, "The Evolution of Understanding an Environment: Climates and Wheat Culture in the Columbia Plateau," *Yearbook of the Association of Pacific Coast Geographers*, vol. 16 (1954), pp. 25–34; and "Isaac J. Stevens, Practical Geographer of the Early Northwest," *Geographical Review*, vol. 45, 4 (1955), pp. 542–558; and Erhard Rostlund, "The Myth of a Natural Prairie Belt in Alabama: An Interpretation of Historical Records," *Annals of the Association of American Geographers*, vol. 47, 4 (1957), pp. 392–411.

[240] Lewis, "Changing Emphases," and McManis, *Initial Evaluation* (see n. 183, above); H. Roy Merrens, "The Physical Environment of Early America: Images and Image-Makers in Colonial South Carolina," *Geographical Review*, vol. 59, 4 (1969), pp. 530–556; Kenneth Thompson, "Insalubrious California: Perception and Reality," *Annals of the Association of American Geographers*, vol. 59, 1 (1969), pp. 50–64; Martyn J. Bowden, "The Perception of the Western Interior of the United States, 1800–1870: A Problem in Historical Geosophy," *Proceedings of the Association of American Geographers*, vol. 1 (1969), pp. 16–21; and "The Great American Desert and the American Frontier, 1800–1882: Popular Images of the Plains and Places in the Westward Movement," in Tamara K. Hareven, ed., *Anonymous Americans: Explorations in Nineteenth Century Social History* (Englewood Cliffs, N.J.: Prentice-Hall, 1971), pp. 48–79; Douglas R. McManis, *European Impressions of the New England Coast, 1497–1620* (Chicago: University of Chicago Department of Geography, Research Paper no. 139, 1972); Terry G. Jordan, "Pioneer Evaluation of Vegetation in Frontier Texas," *Southwestern Historical Quarterly*, vol. 76, 3 (1973), pp. 233–254; John L. Allen, *Passage through the Garden: Lewis and Clark and the Image of the Northwest* (Urbana: University of Illinois Press, 1975); John A. Jakle, *Images of the Ohio Valley* (New York: Oxford University Press, 1977); Bradley H. Baltensperger, "Newspaper Images of the Central Great Plains in the Late Nineteenth Century," *Journal of the West*, vol. 19, 2 (1980), pp. 64–70; and Robin W. Doughty, *At Home in Texas: Early Views of the Land* (College Station: Texas A & M University Press, 1987). For a perception of another order, see Sherry H. Olson, *The Depletion Myth: A History of Railroad Use of Timber* (Cambridge: Harvard University Press, 1971).

[241] Wright, "Terrae Incognitae" (see n. 227, above); Lowenthal and Bowden, *Geographies* (see n. 120, above). The term "geosophy" has been traced to a German geographer in 1877, but later use was extremely scattered before Wright's interest in it. See Dunbar, "Geosophy," pp. 3–4 (see n. 4, above). Of those instrumental in spurring perceptual studies between 1969 and 1975, half (Lewis, Merrens, Thompson, and Bowden) were British-born.

tended to pick up the challenges of [Malin's grassland] book. . . . in matters of environmental perception it is they who are truly Malin's heirs."[242] There are those who would insist that the geosophical persuasion in American historical geography represents another distinct school.[243] Such signs of recognition aside, critics have pointed to errors and omissions in the practice of geosophy. In the structuralist view of Robert W. Chambers, the sociology of knowledge has been practically ignored, in that ideas neither travel perfectly through society nor gain everyone's blithe acceptance, and further, studies in geosophy have been restricted largely to images of the physical environment and have generally failed to link image with act and consequence, since geographical behavior—such as migration—does not necessarily operate solely on the basis of environmental images.[244] There is no reason to believe that advocates of geosophical reconstruction will not respond with more comprehensive studies that meet such objections, for the theme has been a popular one and many unexploited sources remain, though the wave of domestic enthusiasm for this approach appears to have dipped in recent years.[245]

The second case in which substantive interests were profoundly affected by the quantitative and theoretical movement as it influenced historical geography was the

---

[242] Allan G. Bogue, "The Heirs of James C. Malin: A Grassland Historiography," *Great Plains Quarterly*, vol. 1, 2 (1981), pp. 105–131.

[243] The claim has been made for a "Clark University school of historical geography" by, among others, John Allen in a paper entitled "Geographical Cognition and Historical Geosophy: Inventory and Prospect," given at the Twentieth Annual Meeting of the Eastern Historical Geography Association, Clark University, Worcester, Massachusetts, 1989, p. 9. Trends in the last two decades have not sufficiently played through, in the writer's opinion, to identify with confidence the next generation of schools in the field, whether based on a cognitive or any other distinct approach, though some possibilities are certainly emerging. In the case of historical geosophy in the United States, the intellectual parentage claimed is remote (John K. Wright did not immediately inspire and train a string of followers and had no affiliation with Clark University); the first modern contributions came, almost simultaneously, from scholars with diverse (and often British) roots; and the corpus of work, heavily weighted to the American West and in particular the Great Plains, has yet to create a significant monographic publication record (Allen pointed to only three book-length studies on U.S. topics—those by himself, Jakle, and Merrens; to which he could have added a recent fourth, by Robin W. Doughty, another British-born scholar). Since the early 1970s, it should be noted that sustained graduate work in geosophy and a consequent flow of articles has emanated from Clark University under Martyn Bowden's vigorous stimulus—see, for example, the eight essays on geosophical topics in the *Journal of Historical Geography*, vol. 18, 1 (1992)—but aside from Allen's own study the books in the field have been emerging from other quarters.

[244] Robert W. Chambers, "Images, Acts, and Consequences: A Critical Review of Historical Geosophy," in Alan R. H. Baker and Mark Billinge, eds., *Period and Place: Research Methods in Historical Geography* (Cambridge: Cambridge University Press, 1982), pp. 197–204. "Geosophy has little value when removed from historical geography," Chambers concludes, "yet it is the most *human* level on which we can know the past—attitudes, values, and concepts are its data. Because of this geosophy could have a moderating and humanizing effect on historical geography. But to have this effect it must be integrated within, not kept separate from, historical geography" (p. 204).

[245] Historical perception studies dropped by one-third from 6 percent of all works in American historical geography during the 1970s to 4 percent during the 1980s, based on tabulations of the material presented in the bibliography of this work. But occasional contributions from France, cast from a rather different cultural and philosophical perspective, demonstrate the analytical possibilities of investigating geographical imagery embedded in one of the twentieth century's most potent mass media—the Western movie: see Michel Foucher, "Du désert, paysage du western," *Hérodote*, vol. 7 (1977), pp. 130–147; and the recent monograph by Jacques Mauduy and Gérard Henriet, *Géographies du western: Une nation en marche* (Paris: Éditions Nathan, 1989).

urban realm. The rising concern to understand deep changes in the human condition brought about by modern urbanization, which was quite evident in the pages of *Landscape* during the the the course of the 1960s, had its parallel in formal studies in American historical geography. As geography professionalized in the early twentieth century, efforts to comprehend the contemporary city did not notably lag far behind those given to the rural scene, but the historical dimension in urban patterns was slow to be addressed in any detail. Perhaps this reflects the preoccupation with pattern over process, and function over form, that seems to have characterized so much American urban geography between the World Wars.[246] Then, too, perhaps, the economic distress that affected the cities so visibly during the Great Depression had so focused minds on the supposed virtues of the agricultural life (at least in the folk memory of a self-sufficient past), that in the cities geographical minds stayed rooted in the problems of the moment. Whatever the case, in the long recovery after World War II the historical imagination remained largely devoted to questions of rural and regional evolution until the 1960s. By then, the march of industrial capitalism had so encumbered the northeast quadrant of the United States with large, factory-dependent cities that as they became vulnerable to countertrends of metropolitan and regional dispersion startling problems of geographical instability became apparent.

To come to terms with the forces producing such patterns, notable studies of industrial evolution in cities and of the regional dynamics of urban industrialization emerged.[247] Interdisciplinary research projects were undertaken, the most interesting to geographers involving study of long-term regional economic growth.[248] Soon, geographers' peculiar concern with the logic of spatial order brought forth historical studies of the evolving structure of the system of cities,[249] stimulated especially by

---

[246] For an overview of the major research themes of the period, see Harold M. Mayer, "A Half-Century of Urban Geography in the United States," *Urban Geography*, vol. 11, 4 (1990), pp. 418–421. On the relative neglect of urban form in American urban geography, see Michael P. Conzen, "Analytical Approaches to the Urban Landscape," in Karl W. Butzer, ed., *Dimensions of Human Geography: Essays on Some Neglected and Familiar Themes* (Chicago: University of Chicago Department of Geography, Research Paper no. 186, 1978), pp. 128–165.

[247] E. Willard Miller, "The Southern Anthracite Region: A Problem Region," *Economic Geography*, vol. 31, 4 (1955), pp. 331–350; Henry L. Hunker, *Industrial Evolution of Columbus, Ohio* (Columbus: Ohio State University, College of Commerce, Bureau of Business Research and Administration, 1958); Charles W. Boas, "Locational Patterns of American Automobile Assembly Plants, 1895–1958," *Economic Geography*, vol. 37, 3 (1961), pp. 218–230; Allan R. Pred, *The External Relations of Cities during Industrial Revolution* (Chicago: University of Chicago Department of Geography, Research Paper no. 76, 1962); John R. Borchert, *The Urbanization of the Upper Midwest, 1930–1960* (Minneapolis: Upper Midwest Research and Development Council, Upper Midwest Economic Study, Urban Report no. 2, 1963).

[248] Eric E. Lampard, "Regional Economic Development, 1870–1950," in Harvey S. Perloff, ed., *Regions, Resources, and Economic Growth* (Baltimore: Johns Hopkins University Press, 1960), pp. 109–292; Robert W. Fogel, *Railroads and American Economic Growth* (see above, n. 236).

[249] Fred E. Lukermann, "Empirical Expressions of Nodality and Hierarchy in a Circulation Manifold," *East Lakes Geographer*, vol. 2 (1966), pp. 17–44; John R. Borchert, "American Metropolitan Evolution," *Geographical Review*, vol. 57, 3 (1967), pp. 301–332; Eric E. Lampard, "The Evolving System of Cities in the United States: Urbanization and Economic Development," in Harvey S. Perloff and Lowden Wingo, Jr., eds., *Issues in Urban Economics* (Baltimore: Johns Hopkins University Press, 1968), pp. 81–138; and Michael P. Conzen, "The American Urban System in the Nineteenth Century," in David T. Herbert and Ronald J. Johnston, eds., *Geography and the Urban Environment: Research and Applications*, vol. 4 (New York: John Wiley & Sons, 1981), pp. 295–347.

the limited applicability in the United States of Christaller's central-place model, notwithstanding demonstrations in a few small regions of some spatial-hierarchical regularities.[250] James E. Vance, Jr., the first avowedly urban specialist ever appointed to the Berkeley department, studied the wholesale trade system and proposed a "mercantile model" of American urban development that has gained wide acceptance among geographers as the most plausible grand historical framework.[251] Allan Pred, Vance's younger colleague at Berkeley, explored the effects of industrialization on large American cities, especially those that had become prominent as commercial centers, and developed a "large-city industrial growth model" based on "initial advantage" and "circular and cumulative causation."[252] Pred's interpretation has also enjoyed wide currency. The flurry of conceptual studies encouraged at least a few applications of urban-systems thinking to the colonial period,[253] and to the late nineteenth century beyond the urban-industrial core of the nation.[254]

Eventually, conditions of congestion and decline inside large modern cities spurred inquiries into genesis and evolution, and fundamental studies appeared that laid the foundation for more specialized work to follow: on retail patterns, the central business district (CBD), inner residential districts occupied by successive waves of immigrants, and the work-residence link.[255] Much of this work was predicated on

---

[250] The earliest evolutionary empirical study based on an explicit application of Christallerian precepts to an American area was John A. Laska, "The Development of the Pattern of Retail Trade Centers in a Selected Area of Southwestern Iowa," Master's thesis, University of Chicago, 1958, summarized in Brian J. L. Berry, *The Geography of Market Centers and Retail Distribution* (Englewood Cliffs, N.J.: Prentice-Hall, 1967), pp. 5–9.

[251] James E. Vance, Jr., *The Merchant's World: The Geography of Wholesaling* (Englewood Cliffs, N.J.: Prentice-Hall, 1970). See also Andrew F. Burghardt, "A Hypothesis about Gateway Cities," *Annals of the Association of American Geographers*, vol. 61, 2 (1971), pp. 269–285, which examines several historical cases in the United States.

[252] Pred, *Spatial Dynamics* (see n. 233, above); and *Urban Growth and the Circulation of Information: The United States System of Cities, 1790–1840* (Cambridge: Harvard University Press, 1973); and *Urban Growth and City Systems in the United States: 1840–1860* (Cambridge: Harvard University Press, 1980). Overshadowed by the conceptual appeal of Pred's early work on the processes of regional industrialization, but still a fine study of regional industrialization built on extensive reconstruction from archival sources is Robert G. LeBlanc's *Location of Manufacturing in New England in the Nineteenth Century* (Hanover: Dartmouth University Geographical Publications, no. 7, 1969). Conceptual progress on the regional implications of industrial evolution is largely due to the work of David R. Meyer: see his "Emergence of the American Manufacturing Belt: An Interpretation," *Journal of Historical Geography*, vol. 9, 2 (1983), pp. 145–174, and later work. An unequaled study of the geographical development of a single industry is Kenneth Warren, *The American Steel Industry, 1850–1970: A Geographical Interpretation* (Oxford: Clarendon Press, 1973).

[253] James T. Lemon, "Urbanization and the Development of Eighteenth-Century Southeastern Pennsylvania and Adjacent Delaware," *William and Mary Quarterly*, 3d ser., vol. 24, 4 (1967), pp. 501–542; Carville V. Earle, "The First English Towns of North America," *Geographical Review*, vol. 67, 1 (1977), pp. 34–50; and James J. O'Mara, *An Historical Geography of Urban System Development: Tidewater Virginia in the Eighteenth Century* (Downsview, Ont.: York University Department of Geography, 1983).

[254] John C. Hudson, *Plains Country Towns* (Minneapolis: University of Minnesota Press, 1985); and J. Valerie Fifer, *American Progress: The Growth of the Transport, Tourist, and Information Industries in the Nineteenth Century West Seen through the Life and Times of George A. Crofutt, Pioneer Publicist of the Transcontinent Age* (Chester, Conn.: Globe Pequot Press, 1988).

[255] James E. Vance, Jr., "Emerging Patterns of Commercial Structure in American Cities," *Lund Studies in Geography*, ser. B, no. 24 (1962), pp. 485–518; David Ward, "The Industrial Revolution and the Emergence of Boston's Central Business District," *Economic Geography*, vol. 42, 2 (1966), pp. 152–171; and "The

showing that modern patterns had not always existed, that there was a specific period in which key elements of the city's geography emerged, and that these moments were generally older than cursory overviews had assumed. Hence, Ward pushed the emergence of the CBD back to the 1850s (fig. 10), and Edward K. Muller and Paul A. Groves that of specializing industrial districts to about the same period. Pred showed how the journey to work lengthened even before the arrival of mass transit, and Michael P. Conzen and Kathleen N. Conzen that retailing spread to noncentral clusters well before the end of the nineteenth century; and Ward countered the negative interpretations that social scientists had routinely applied to late nineteenth-century immigrant ghettoes.[256]

Ward summed up both external and internal economic and social forces in American urbanization during the period in a brief and masterly synthesis that proved to be influential among historians as well as geographers.[257] His *Cities and Immigrants* has probably been read by more social and urban historians during the 1970s and 1980s than any other single book by a geographer, and it built new bridges with historical and contemporary human geographers.

Aside from these functional dimensions, three studies tackled the morphological aspects of American cities: a collaborative effort between geographer Harold M. Mayer and historian Richard C. Wade describing with the aid of abundant historical photographs the physical building up of Chicago; a penetrating examination by Dutch geographer G. A. Wissink of the American style of urban fringe expansion (extensive and undisciplined); and a sprawling, sumptuously illustrated overview of the initial layout of American townsites across the continent by planner John Reps.[258] Informative syntheses of geographical forces shaping two very different cit-

Emergence of Central Immigrant Ghettos in American Cities: 1840–1920," *Annals of the Association of American Geographers*, vol. 58, 2 (1968), pp. 343–359; James E. Vance, Jr., "Labor-Shed, Employment Field, and Dynamic Analysis in Urban Geography," *Economic Geography*, vol. 36, 3 (1960), pp. 189–200.

[256] Ward, "Industrial Revolution"; Edward K. Muller and Paul A. Groves, "The Emergence of Industrial Districts in Mid-Nineteenth Century Baltimore," *Geographical Review*, vol. 69, 2 (1979), pp. 159–178; Pred, *Spatial Dynamics*, pp. 207–213 (see n. 233, above); Michael P. Conzen and Kathleen Neils Conzen, "Geographical Structure in Nineteenth-Century Urban Retailing: Milwaukee, 1836–90," *Journal of Historical Geography*, vol. 5, 1 (1979), pp. 45–66; David Ward, "Social Structure and Social Geography in Large Cities of the U.S. Urban-Industrial Heartland," in David Ward and John Radford, *North American Cities in the Victorian Age* (Norwich, England: Geo Books, Historical Geography Research Series, no. 12, 1983), pp. 1–31; and "Social Reform, Social Surveys, and the Discovery of the Modern City," *Annals of the Association of American Geography*, vol. 80, 4 (1990), pp. 491–503. For a detailed look at African-American residential history, see Donald R. Deskins, *Residential Mobility of Negroes in Detroit, 1837–1965* (Ann Arbor: University of Michigan, Department of Geography, Michigan Geographical Publications, no. 5, 1972); for an imaginative treatment of the evolution of urban neighborhood types in the more recent past, see Brian J. Godfrey, *Neighborhoods in Transition: The Making of San Francisco's Ethnic and Non-Conformist Communities* (Berkeley: University of California Publications in Geography, no. 27, 1988).

[257] David Ward, *Cities and Immigrants: A Geography of Change in Nineteenth-Century America* (New York: Oxford University Press, 1971).

[258] Harold M. Mayer and Richard C. Wade, *Chicago: Growth of a Metropolis* (Chicago: University of Chicago Press, 1969), best read in conjunction with Homer Hoyt's dated but classic *One Hundred Years of Land Values in Chicago: The Relationship of the Growth of Chicago to the Rise in Its Land Values, 1830–1933* (Chicago: University of Chicago Press, 1933); Gerardus A. Wissink, *America's Cities in Perspective: With Special Reference to the Development of Their Fringe Areas* (Assen: Van Gorcum, 1962); and John

ies have been provided in Peirce F. Lewis's succinct book on New Orleans and Sherry H. Olson's substantial one on Baltimore.[259] Interestingly, themes dealing with the social aspects of American urban development have gained more attention from historical geographers than economic themes since the early 1960s.

The rapid growth in historical-geographical writing since the 1970s can be measured in two ways: in its keeping pace with the growth of the profession as a whole, and success in its reaching new audiences both within and without geography; but these in turn resulted from the presence of several enabling factors residing in broad institutional developments. Communication among specialists was improved with the founding of the *Historical Geography Newsletter* in 1970 and the *Journal of Historical Geography* in 1975, the latter only the second journal created to cater to a subfield of American geography.[260] Major thematic conferences gave visibility to the field: the National Archives Conference on Historical Geography in 1971,[261] followed by a bidisciplinary meeting with historians known as the Historical Urbanization of North America Conference in 1973, at York University in Ontario. A regional group, the Eastern Historical Geography Association has flourished since 1967, and since 1979 there has been an international meeting of historical geographers, initially known as CUKANZUS, with consistently strong United States representation.[262] The Historical Geography Specialty Group organized within the Association of American Geographers (AAG) in 1979 is among the largest in the organization, and there has been an intermittently active Historical Geography Network within the Social Science History Association during the 1980s. The dramatic rise in books published by historical geographers with commercial and university presses since the early 1970s has been paralleled by an increasing number of book awards, principally from historians, but lately including also the AAG's Jackson Prize.[263] The National Geographic Society has published two outstanding cartographic projects in recent years, the *Making of America* map supplement series (1982–1988) and its *Historical Atlas of the United States* (1988), a publication marking the Society's centennial.[264]

W. Reps, *The Making of Urban America: A History of City Planning in the United States* (Princeton: Princeton University Press, 1965).

[259] Peirce F. Lewis, *New Orleans: The Making of an Urban Landscape* (Cambridge, Mass.: Ballinger, 1976); and Sherry H. Olson, *Baltimore: The Building of an American City* (Baltimore: Johns Hopkins University Press, 1980).

[260] The first was *Economic Geography*, established in 1925. In theory *Geographical Analysis*, begun in 1969, was to cater to any subfield, but in practice it favored those subfields which most aggressively adopted quantitative methods.

[261] Ralph E. Ehrenberg, ed., *Pattern and Process: Research in Historical Geography* (Washington, D.C.: Howard University Press, 1975).

[262] The acronym refers to participation from Canada, the United Kingdom, Australia and New Zealand, and the United States, but involvement has been since broadened further.

[263] John Hudson's *Plains Country Towns* was the first book to win the Jackson Prize, in 1985, and since then a disproportionate number of awards have gone to historical titles.

[264] These contributions are due in large measure to the society's appointment of John Garver as chief cartographer, who earned his Ph.D. in historical geography: John B. Garver, Jr., "The Role of the United States Army in the Colonization of the Trans-Missouri West: Kansas, 1804–1861," Ph.D. diss., Syracuse University, 1981.

With such a pattern of earnest communication established, it is hardly surprising to note that centers of graduate training in historical geography are fairly productive, though many colleagues fret over the limited scope for teaching historical courses in college geography curricula.[265] Looking to the established centers, it is clear that the Berkeley department has changed orientation fundamentally since the days of Sauer. The "Berkeley school" is an appellation belonging properly to those who directly experienced Sauer's influence, but the post-Sauer faculty has maintained strong interests in historical issues, as witnessed by the scholarship of Vance and Pred, and more recently Richard A. Walker. It might be suggested that the modern Berkeley program has been a staunch supporter of historical -isms: urbanism, behaviorism, Marxism, structurationism, and now postmodernism. The doctoral programs at Louisiana State University, the University of Wisconsin, and Syracuse University remain distinctly productive, as do a number of others where historical work has been to some significant degree maintained: Chicago, Clark, Illinois, Kansas, Maryland, Michigan State, Minnesota, Nebraska, Oklahoma, Oregon, Pennsylvania State, Rutgers, Tennessee, and Texas.

Big-Picture Historical Geography

The turn to process in modern times and the institutional developments in historical geography just described raise again the question of intellectual convergence and reintegration, both within the field and with the neighboring discipline of history. Building on advances in specialized undertakings reflected in the volumetric growth of doctoral research, monograph, and article production, what signs are there that a new round of synthesis may be under way? Here, again, the picture is one of significant activity. There have been a number of attempts to draw the threads of recent reinterpretations together—thematically, regionally, and generally.

In the field itself, several central themes have been addressed. Michael Williams has offered a monumental examination of the significance of forests to Americans throughout their history, a long-awaited response, as it were, to the Marsh symposium of 1955—at least in terms of a geographical assessment of the clearing (and unclearing) of the American woodlands.[266] Also extractive in focus is Wishart's brief but exemplary overview of the Western fur trade.[267] Altogether novel is a re-

---

[265] This worry led Meinig recently to review the accomplishments and status of historical geography within American academic geography, and to point out the discrepancy between pedagogical justification and scholarly achievement on the one hand and actual departmental representation on the other. See Donald W. Meinig, "The Historical Geography Imperative," *Annals of the Association of American Geographers*, vol. 79, 1 (1989), pp. 79–87.

[266] Michael Williams, *Americans and Their Forests: A Historical Geography* (New York: Cambridge University Press, 1989).

[267] David J. Wishart, *The Fur Trade of the American West, 1807–1840: A Geographical Synthesis* (Lincoln: University of Nebraska Press, 1979). The role of native peoples in the fur trade is well known, and a recent geographical anthology on American Indians is welcome: Thomas E. Ross and Tyrel G. Moore, eds., *A Cultural Geography of North American Indians* (Boulder: Westview Press, 1987), though the contributions make little use of the excellent work of Dietrich Fliedner: see his *Der Aufbau der vorspanischen Siedlungs- und Wirtschaftslandschaft im Kulturraum der Pueblo-Indianer: Eine historisch-geographische Interpretation wüstgefallener Ortsstellen und Feldflächen im Jemez-Gebiet, New Mexico*

cent cultural reinterpretation of the debts owed to ethnic pioneers who formed a viable clearing culture that moved across the eastern United States: according to Terry Jordan and Matti E. Kaups, Finns and Swedes from the Delaware River settlements, rather than English or Germans anywhere, combined their old-world experience with Indian borrowings to fashion a "pre-adapted" syncretic woodland culture ideal for taming the American backcountry.[268] Once people were well settled across the land, the question arises how a modern geographical state could emerge in America, and Zelinsky has attempted to examine this by studying the uses and misuses of nationalism.[269] The social consequences of industrial urbanization have been brought into sharper focus in David Ward's recent examination of the role of urban space in the reweaving of class, ethnicity, and deprivation during the rise of the large, modern American city.[270] Similarly wide in scope, landscape history in America, that composite reflection of changing impact of society on the land, has been given considerable treatment in recent years, building upon an upsurge of detailed work on the theme.[271] Two regional syntheses deserve mention, overlapping in area but quite different in treatment: a sound, well-illustrated historical-economic geography of the upper Middle West by John R. Borchert; and a brief, more social examination of the perceptual correlates of heartland regionalism by James R. Shortridge.[272]

Also in this vein of synthetic works, several volumes have appeared that show signs of finally retiring Ralph Brown's hardy perennial of 1948. In the absence of anything modern at the time, Ward edited an anthology of reprinted articles in 1979 that proved an attractive collection.[273] It was largely displaced by a recent, carefully constructed anthology of original material entitled *North America: The Historical Geography of a Changing Continent*.[274] Composed of chapters by eighteen authors covering the United States and Canada, this book ranks as the only modern one-volume

(Saarbrücken: Arbeiten aus dem Geographischen Institut der Universität des Saarlandes, vol. 19, 1974); and *Die Kolonisierung New Mexicos durch die Spanier: Ein Beitrag zum Problem der Entstehung von antropogenen Räumen* (Saarbrücken: Arbeiten aus dem Geographischen Institut der Universität des Saarlandes, vol. 21, 1975).

[268] Terry G. Jordan and Matti E. Kaups, *The American Backwoods Frontier: An Ethnic and Ecological Interpretation* (Baltimore: Johns Hopkins University Press, 1989).

[269] Wilbur Zelinsky, *Nation into State: The Shifting Symbolic Foundations of American Nationalism* (Chapel Hill: University of North Carolina Press, 1988).

[270] David Ward, *Poverty, Ethnicity, and the American City, 1840–1925: Changing Conceptions of the Slum and Ghetto* (New York: Cambridge University Press, 1989).

[271] John R. Stilgoe, *Common Landscape of America, 1580 to 1845* (New Haven: Yale University Press, 1982), covers the ground of J. B. Jackson's lecture courses given at Harvard and Berkeley during the 1970s. More comprehensive, and focused on broad historical forces in landscape-making, is the original anthology edited by Michael P. Conzen, *The Making of the American Landscape* (Boston: Unwin Hyman, 1990, now distributed by Routledge).

[272] John R. Borchert, *America's Northern Heartland: An Economic and Historical Geography of the Upper Midwest* (Minneapolis: University of Minnesota Press, 1987); and James R. Shortridge, *The Middle West: Its Meaning in American Culture* (Lawrence: University Press of Kansas, 1989).

[273] David Ward, ed., *Geographic Perspectives on America's Past: Readings on the Historical Geography of the United States* (New York: Oxford University Press, 1979).

[274] Robert D. Mitchell and Paul A. Groves, eds., *North America: The Historical Geography of a Changing Continent* (Totowa, N.J.: Rowman & Littlefield, 1987).

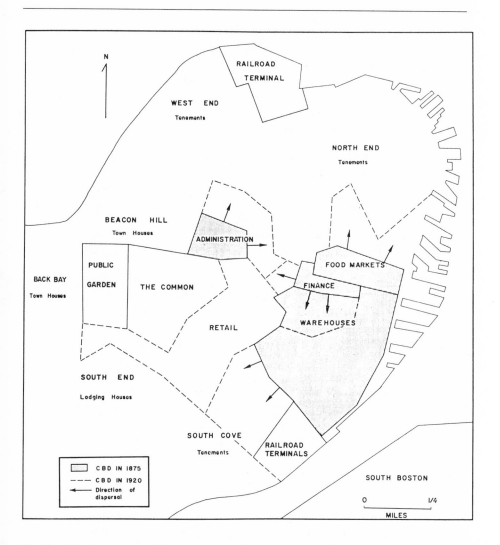

Fig. 10. "Immigrant residence and business expansion in Boston, 1875–1920," in David Ward's 1968 Annals *study of central immigrant ghettoes. Crucial to their interpretation is the evolving spatial differentiation of the expanding central business district into distinct but complementary functional zones during the period.*

treatment of the field; it is organized in a deft blend of chronological, regional, and topical chapters; while it lacks footnotes it does not lack heft. The contributions are serious efforts to distill modern research in American historical geography within a combinatorial framework of regions, topics, and periods. Understandably, there are limits to the intellectual coherence that can be wrung from so large a group of coauthors, although the unity of purpose and style achieved is impressive.

In a completely different realm of synthesis lies the recent work of Donald Meinig. The unquestioned dean of American historical geography since the passing of Sauer and Clark, Meinig has determined to crown his long and distinguished writing career by attempting what for the field is an unprecedented feat: a panoramic interpretation of the geographical evolution of the United States in North America to be known under the serial title of *The Shaping of America: A Geographical Perspective on 500 Years of History*, projected now to extend to at least four volumes.[275] No geographer before has had such ambition, or the discipline to carry such a project to completion. In 1986 the first volume appeared, entitled *Atlantic America, 1492–1800*, and it amply reveals the conceptual scope and polished style that will doubtless be the hallmark of the series as a whole.[276] Meinig's aim is to "view the United States as a gigantic geographic growth with a continually changing geographic character, structure, and system," resulting in "a new map of some important features of the American past."[277] This growth took place in the context of a European imperialism hinged on the Atlantic basin, a setting in which the "nation has been created by massive aggression against a long succession of peoples."[278] Seeking "not to allocate blame but to enlarge understanding," the book offers a sweeping interpretation of the geographical outcomes of this process, organized under four broad themes: "Outreach," in which the Atlantic world is created; "Implantations," an exploration of the regional foundations of American diversity; "Reorganizations," an examination of the geopolitical disruptions of trade, empire, and nation-forming; and lastly "Context," a review of the new nation in its regional and global circumstances around 1800.

Meinig's method is essentially that of a painter, using a brush dipped in the rich pigments of diverse, detailed, and distilled secondary sources, to delineate a broad, schematic "conspectus" showing the continual shaping of the peoples and their regions on a canvas so breathtakingly wide that the geographical context, coverage, scale, structure, tensions, and change involved are dynamically seen and consequential. By admission, the interpretation is biased toward political and social themes and treats lightly the ecological and economic bases of the nation's areal expansion and constant reformulation. The argument is crystalized at every turn with conceptual diagrams, cartograms, and artfully conceived maps full of movement, replete with thrusting arrows of all types describing the paths of progressive regional articulation.

Reaction to this first volume has been extensive. More widely reviewed in the scholarly and popular press than any geography book in living memory (well over fifty academic reviews have appeared), the book has been recognized for its boldness and creativity. "Eye-opening generalizations . . . a massive work of synthesis," noted

---

[275] First planned in three volumes (pre-1800; the nineteenth century; and the twentieth century), the middle period has already swollen to two volumes.

[276] New Haven: Yale University Press, 1986.

[277] Ibid., p. xv.

[278] Ibid., p. xviii.

the historian James Axtell in the *William & Mary Quarterly*; an "admirably ambitious and lavishly illustrated volume," wrote Jack P. Greene, who praised Meinig's "ability to produce a thoughtful and challenging synthesis."[279] Geographical reviewers have been equally appreciative, and the book has provoked particularly searching appraisals in two review essays by James T. Lemon and R. Cole Harris, specialists on the historical geography of the colonial era, both of whom explore the strengths and weaknesses of what they see as Meinig's stress on pattern at the expense of process.[280] The book's warm reception by historians has not been uncritical by any means, but understandably those who grasp its value as a "geographic complement to the work of historians" rather than as a substitute have more readily seen its groundbreaking qualities. Publication of volume 2, which will take the interpretation up to the Civil War, is expected before the close of 1992.

These developments suggest that historical geography in the United States has entered a signally new phase, one of mature research production, of rich and rising debate over concepts and substantive historical interpretations, and of renewed attempts at synthesis, grappling with levels of historiographical complexity undreamed of before—all of this through a significantly increased flow of monographic studies, an encouraging upturn in special-focus anthologies, and the appearance of masterful compositions of the most challenging ideas in the field.

What, then, of historical geography's relations with historians? After the days of Webb and Malin there followed a long period in which the historical profession was emphatically uninterested in the geographical and environmental basis of American society, and consequently exchange between the two fields was minimal. But by the 1970s the rise of such specialties as social, urban, rural, and environmental history made historians face up to the insinuating factor of space and its regional patterning, and geographers were invited to outline the potential they saw for fruitful cooperation. In 1971 Jakle sought to convey his personal view of research themes in historical geography, and gave particular emphasis to spatial and behavioral analysis, though he stopped short of laying out a prospectus for interdisciplinary cooperation.[281] Seven years later, Meinig met that challenge with a broad agenda congenial to historians.[282] At pains to stress that geography is no mere handmaiden to history—an assumption that many historians unfortunately still make, if they give geography any thought at all—Meinig offered "a tentative outline for an interpretive geographic study of [American] national experience," stressing the various ways geographers think about the evolution of and changing interrelations among areas

---

[279] James Axtell, review of *Atlantic America*, in *William & Mary Quarterly*, 3d ser., vol. 43, 2 (1988), pp. 173–175; Jack P. Greene, review of *Atlantic America*, in *Pennsylvania Magazine of History and Biography*, vol. 112, 2 (1988), pp. 281–282.

[280] James T. Lemon, "Atlantic Imperialism," *Reviews in American History*, vol. 15, 3 (1987), pp. 374–379; and R. Cole Harris, "Taking on a Continent," *Journal of Historical Geography*, vol. 14, 4 (1988), pp. 416–419.

[281] John A. Jakle, "Time, Space, and the Geographic Past: A Prospectus for Historical Geography," *American Historical Review*, vol. 76, 4 (1971), pp. 1084–1103.

[282] Donald W. Meinig, "The Continuous Shaping of America: A Prospectus for Geographers and Historians," *American Historical Review*, vol. 83, 5 (1978), pp. 1186–1205.

and regions as a crucial mediating element in national history.[283] Meinig's proposals drew favorable comment in the historians' conference session in which they were presented, but it is a measure of the "kin, but not close" nature of the two fields that whatever exchange benefit derives from such discussions and proposals is but subtly divined in the subsequent work of either field and more likely to flow from the published exemplars of each persuasion than from the pronouncements themselves.[284]

Summing Up and Looking On

It is time to consider the significance of past developments in American historical geography for present practice and future directions. While there is not space to be exhaustive, some suggestions can be made. The course of evolution as sketched here seems to yield several key inferences. First, the chief consequence of the protracted debate over environmental determinism, and the vehemence with which the "heresy" was ultimately disowned in the profession, appears to be the subsequent triumph of cultural determinism.[285] In the short term it was midwestern economic determinism that found favor among geographers, including historical geographers, but now that a more fully developed social determinism has settled in there is no immediate evidence to suggest that a good balance has been achieved between cultural and physical factors in most of the current explanations for historical change in geographical pattern and structure. Had there not been so wide a swing of the pendulum first toward and then away from physical determinism in the first half of this century, American historical geography, as the discipline at large, might even now harbor more sophisticated models of social-physical systems of change.[286] Second, regionalism held sway so long over human geography in the United States that it fed an appetite for regionalization, or delimitation, perhaps beyond a reasonable point. This did not in itself deter interest in interactions, but it may have conditioned acceptance of narrow spatial description as a general preoccupation, and of spatial units as more important than the movements within and between them.

---

[283] Ibid., p. 1188.

[284] This is exemplified in the work of historian Peter Simpson, who acknowledges his debt to Meinig's conceptual model of the West presented in his "American Wests" article (see note 181) as a basis for the analytical framework employed in his own study: see Peter K. Simpson, *The Community of Cattlemen: A Social History of the Cattle Industry in Southeastern Oregon, 1869–1912* (Moscow: University of Idaho Press, 1987), pp. 1–5.

[285] In the long run no one is more responsible for this than Sauer, who added to his dislike of environmental determinism a disinclination to give sufficient weight to economic processes in society, particularly in advanced regions—a bias which it took Clark and his students to correct.

[286] Testing this notion calls for comparison with other national experience in geographical development, beyond the scope of this essay. For a recent comment on the current deficiency, see D. Aidan McQuillan, "The Interface of Physical and Historical Geography: The Analysis of Farming Decisions in Response to Drought Hazards on the Margins of the Great Plains," in Alan R. H. Baker and Mark Billinge, eds., *Period and Process: Research Methods in Historical Geography* (London: Cambridge University Press, 1982), pp. 136–144. Michael Williams went so far as to assert recently that the "spectre of determinism" and "the tradition of denying the environment has frozen the critical mind" among historical geographers: see Michael Williams, "Time and the Environment: Environmental History and Historical Geography," paper given to the International Conference of Historical Geographers, Vancouver, British Columbia, August 1992, p. 14.

Third, the attention given visible landscapes in the middle part of the century without doubt focused heavy effort on recording outward forms, beneficial since the pressure for change always acts to reduce the surviving stock of traditional forms by which to read long-term cumulative development and change. But the difficulty in generalizing from studies of form to the workings of society and the specific agency of individuals and groups in creating patterns has yet to be successfully overcome. Had this been otherwise, then a fourth inference is that scholars could have proceeded more naturally with the integration of observations of direct human behavior in the larger structural models, such as those of land use, that were then in existence.

Fifth, a striking feature of the inordinate swings between research paradigms is the relative absence of politics and ideology, in any period, as a theme or component of investigation. By contrast, paradigmatic shifts in history and other social sciences have long been driven by debates over conflict, consensus, and the distribution of power, whether fueled by Marx, Weber, or others. Historically, the reason for this difference between geography and the other social sciences is not hard to identify, for geographers have by tradition framed their questions in terms of broad human-environment relationships and spatial patterns that reflect collective outcomes (shorn generally of the conflictual history that produced them). This may now be changing, but as a long-term consequence the protracted struggle among geographers to establish a suitable balance between environmental, economic, and sociocultural interpretations of the American past has been largely uninformed by the political dimension, and until recently little advantage has been taken of fruitful debates on the subject among historians. As a result, American historical geographers have been notably silent on such matters as slavery, the African American experience, labor history, and the roots and results of war.[287] As the field shifts away from the earlier aggregate study of the relations between land and people and probes more minutely the role of human agency, individual and collective, in that relation, the benefits of incorporating politics—not "correct," but suggestive—in the framework of American historical geography is becoming apparent. Then, perhaps, some of the startling silences may disappear.

Sixth, there has long been an uneasy dualism in geography between historical reconstruction as prelude to contemporary elucidation (in which the historical narrative always leads to the present, the real focus of explanation), and more historically specialized studies in which conditions in past periods are sufficient objects of study in their own right that their significance for contemporary geography remains undeclared (pending, of course, ultimate synthesis). As American historical geography gained respectability the growth of its literature necessarily brought more detailed work that related only to periods far in the past, making the link to contemporary issues harder to see and debate, and hence the very success of the field bred a

---

[287] The first volume of Meinig's grand synthesis deals at length with geopolitics, war, and slavery, and refreshingly so, but the lack of careful, focused studies on these issues by historical geographers has necessarily confined the search for the materials for synthesis to the literature of historians.

certain isolation and marginality. This long-standing dualism has only been exacerbated by the periodic arguments as to whether historical investigation in geography should be kept divided within each systematic division of the field or allowed to flourish as a self-consciously separate, but potentially remote, entity. It is clear that, as with other special fields within the discipline, the expertise needed to handle the specialized evidence of historical geography has warranted its development as an autonomous branch of investigation, yet the burden of remaining relevant to the discipline as a whole is not thereby diminished but rather increased.[288] Only recently does it seem that the old debates over studying a past segregated from the present have lapsed in favor of a more fluid view of process and pattern situated in a holistic flow of time.

Seventh, and related to the foregoing, it might be argued that the field is uniquely situated to profit from broader changes in the intellectual divisions of labor within the social sciences and humanities. Just as modernity brought with it a new alignment of emerging disciplines in the second half of the nineteenth century to cope with the new demands for knowledge in the industrial era—including, of course, geography—so in recent times (with the declared onset of postmodernity) we are seeing the rise of a new congeries of interstitial fields (cultural studies, international relations, American studies, popular culture, urban studies, political economy, and ethnic studies, to name a few) so that new and interesting problem domains come into being now not so much from within disciplines as at the margins. This is not to say that traditional disciplines are losing their raison d'être or that their particular intellectual perspective and training are devalued (quite the contrary), but that previously excluded spheres of inquiry now demand attention and can be accommodated when disciplinary drawbridges are laid down rather than drawn up. American historical geographers, given the history of their field, should be comparatively well prepared and nimble in responding to the challenges of the scholarly realignments that are taking place at the close of this century.

And, lastly, there is the question of linguistic parochialism. American geography has drawn at times significantly from non-English European thought, but the peculiar swings of interest toward and away from German and French literature at various moments left historical geographers with rather incomplete impressions of the conceptual developments occurring in the main European centers of historical-geographical activity (not to mention some further afield).[289] To be indebted mostly

---

[288] Today, as in the past, much excellent work in historical geography is done by those who would not consider themselves primarily (or at all) historical geographers. Perhaps because of its peculiar position in the discipline (it might be called a supra- or macrospecialty) historical geography is arguably the most permeable and welcoming of any of the discipline's recognized branches.

[289] Key statements regarding the nature and practice of historical geography beyond the confines of the English language can be found in Helmut Jäger, *Historische Geographie* (Braunschweig: Georg Westermann Verlag, 1969); Klaus Fehn and Helmut Jäger, eds., "Die Historische Dimension in der Geographie," *Erdkunde*, vol. 36, 2 (1982), pp. 65–123; Hubert Mücke, *Historische Geographie als lebensweltliche Umweltsanalyse* (Frankfurt am Main: Peter Lang, Geschichte und ihre Hilfswissenschaften, 1988); Dietrich Denecke and Klaus Fehn, eds., *Geographie in der Geschichte* (Stuttgart: Franz Steiner Verlag, Erdkundliches Wissen, vol. 96, 1989); Guus J. Borger, *Het werkterrein van de historische Geografie* (Assen, 1981); Paul Claval, "The Historical Dimension of French Geography," *Journal of Historical Geography*,

to Semple and then, forty years later, to Hartshorne for news of progress in German geographical thought represented a privation of sorts; worse could be said regarding news of French literature, particularly after the rise of the *annalistes*. Exhilarating though the debates among natives were on the best course for American geography to follow, on historical issues the debates doubtless would have benefited from more frequent cross-fertilization. The debt to actual foreign research on American topics in any period fell mostly to German works, though it is difficult to say what contribution, if any, they made at the time, as most publications were not in English.[290] In them, however, the modern eye can discern a similarity across space and time that suggests a relative coherence of method and aim, regardless of topic or locality.

Taken together, then, these consequences for modern American historical geography stemming from the main episodes of its history portray a field perhaps more faction-ridden and changeable than it might otherwise have been. Doubtless there are those who would wish it no other way, but as a consequence anachronisms and localisms have abounded when broader advances might have been made.

Turning our gaze forward, the immediate outlook for historical geography in the United States would appear to be one of continued pluralism and rising ferment. A point has been reached at which long-established research agendas have yielded a substantial body of improved knowledge that now demands bold synthesis. At the same time, quite new agendas are being articulated that call for wholly different lines of inquiry. Synthesis is apparent in the regionalist tradition, both at the national and regional levels, as exemplified by the latest work of Meinig and Borchert, as well as in other projects completed and in preparation.[291] Synthesis is also apparent with re-

---

vol. 10, 3 (1984), pp. 229-245; Lucio Gambi, *Una geografia per la storia* (Turin: Einaudi, 1973); Gaetano Ferro, *Società umane e natura nel tempo: Temi e problemi di geografia storica* (Milan: Cisalpino-Coliardica, 1974); Leos Jelecek, "Current Trends in the Development of Historical Geography in Czechoslovakia," *Historická geografie*, vol. 19 (1980), pp. 59–102; Theodore Shabad, ed., "The Nature of Historical Geography in the Soviet Union," *Soviet Geography: Review and Translation*, vol. 19, 3 (1978), pp. 160–195; Vladimir S. Zhekulin, *Istoricheskaia geografiia: Predmet i metody* (Leningrad: Nauka, Leningradskoe otd-nie, 1982); Toshio Kikuchi, *Rekishi-chirigaku hoho ron* (Tokyo: Daimeido, 1977); Masayuki Hattori, "Historical Geography in Japan," *Professional Geographer*, vol. 31, 3 (1979), pp. 321–326; and Hou Ren-Zhi, "The Study of Urban Historical Geography and City Planning," *Ti-li hsüeh-pao (Acta Geographica Sinica)*, vol. 34, 4 (1979), pp. 315–328. See also the small selection of regional literature summaries in Baker, *Progress in Historical Geography* (see n. 4, above).

[290] The recent exception is the work by Fliedner, who has published in both German and English, and consequently is better known among American geographers. German work on America has been ably indexed in several publications over the decades: for the period between the world wars, see Pfeifer, "Arbeiten deutscher Geographen" (see n. 113, above); for the period since 1945, see the excellent new compilation (published in English) by Andreas Dittmann and Hans Dieter Laux, eds., *German Geographical Research on North America: A Bibliography with Comments and Annotations* (Bonn: Ferd. Dümmlers Verlag, Bonner Geographische Abhandlungen, vol. 84, 1992). No equivalents exist for the much smaller amount of French work on North America. British contributions, like British immigrants to the United States, have blended in with the larger American corpus with little impediment or notoriety, but quantitatively have been meager. More consequential has been the transformation over the last thirty years or so of more than a dozen British natives with British first degrees in geography into highly productive resident North American career historical geographers through American graduate training. This phenomenon, and its impact on American historical geography, would amply merit closer scrutiny.

[291] Meinig, *Shaping of America* (see above, n. 277); Borchert, *Northern Heartland* (n. 273); Jordan and Kaups, *Backwoods Frontier* (see above, n. 269). The historical geography of the American West is for the

gard to various topical issues, most notably landscape-making[292] and environmental modification.[293] But as the seeds of one season sprout plants that flower in the next, so the cycle continues simultaneously with newly introduced species and altered nurture to change the composition over time. Before closure is reached on one cycle, the sprouts of a different crop appear. What of the new strains appearing in the field?

There is a growing interest to restore prestige in geography to a domain long conceded to, and often fumbled by, the historians: geographical history—and to do so within the context of the burgeoning social theory movement in the social sciences, and the return of macrohistory. An axiom that Andrew Clark fought so hard to establish—that geographers should engage in historical geography rather than geographical history, which should be left to historians—is coming under direct challenge. A new anthology by Carville V. Earle, *Geographical Inquiry and American Historical Problems*, seeks to define the theater of discourse.[294] His concern to apply geographical insights to questions central to American historiography was staked out well over a decade ago, when he distanced himself from Meinig's regionalist "prospectus" for cooperation between historians and geographers.[295] Earle's volume, containing both new essays and reprinted articles, some formerly coauthored, provides the first book-scale accumulation of substance to support his methodological position. It offers a dozen discrete case studies, "at once autonomous and interdependent," reexamining from a geographical viewpoint orthodox historical interpretations of such issues as urban retardation in the antebellum South, the profitability of slavery, the failure of American socialism, and the Southern soil-exhaustion thesis.[296] This form of geographical revisionism bears some resemblance to Andrew

---

first time to be the subject of an anthology of essays to be edited by Lary Dilsaver and William K. Wyckoff. The theme of exploration, so crucial to continental colonization, and so regional in its explication, is the focus of a forthcoming three-volume anthology under the editorship of John L. Allen.

[292] Conzen, *American Landscape* (see above, n. 272); Allen G. Noble, ed., *To Build in a New Land: Ethnic Landscapes in North America* (Baltimore: Johns Hopkins University Press, 1992). The rise in landscape-related interests is no statistical aberration: in the 1950s, with the Louisiana school hitting its stride, exactly 50 titles were recorded (about 5 percent of all historical geography output in the decade); by the 1980s a total of 278 titles were noted (over 10 percent of the total), and in calendar 1990 no fewer than 24 titles were counted, representing 15 percent of the total output for the field. The field has considerable application to preservation studies and public involvement, which perhaps is drawing added interest among geographers. There is likely in the future to be more attention given to the social and functional meanings behind forms, and a greater willingness to argue from process to form rather than the traditional reverse. Whatever the limitations of the recent collection on the making of the American landscape, the aim of that particular exercise was to suggest such a causal path and method both of investigation and presentation. Conzen, *American Landscape* (see n. 272, above).

[293] An anthology on the historical geography of the American environment is being prepared under the coeditorship of Craig Colten and Lary Dilsaver. Unlike landscape, this theme has produced no large and mature body of detailed modern work in the field, but in principle the planned collection represents less a new departure than a reawakening of ancient and somewhat dormant interests.

[294] Earle, *Geographical Inquiry* (see n. 228, above).

[295] Carville V. Earle, "Comments [on "The Continuous Shaping of America: A Prospectus for Geographers and Historians" by D. W. Meinig]," *American Historical Review*, vol. 83, 5 (1978), pp. 1206–1209.

[296] The analytical approach uniting these essays is based upon the following propositions: "That *where* something happened in the past deserves, indeed requires, interpretive consideration; that *when* it happened was conditioned by ecological (innovation) and locational (logistical spatial diffusion) considera-

Clark's earlier interest in engaging historians, though the ground chosen for battle with conventional historical wisdom now is demarcated ideologically with models of social conflict and defended methodologically with the weapons of econometrics. A greatly expanded tradition of macrohistorical geography may be in the making, in which the regional-imperialist framework developed by Meinig is linked to the process models of the Wallersteinian world system through sociological metatheory and economic contextualization.[297] An impetus was provided in this direction by Immanuel Wallerstein himself in a recent address to American geographers.[298] The rebirth of geographical history along these lines, genetically remote from its turn-of-the-century ancestor, promises a vision of purpose in American historical geography quite distinct from the broad consensus that has guided effort in recent times. And there are other intimations of change.

There is, for example, an emergent undertaking to "gender" the field. Whatever momentum this derives from social liberation movements mounted elsewhere in the past, its delayed arrival in American historical geography is notable.[299] The alarums of complaint concerning the pattern of disregard for the role of women in the geography of the American past recall the anguish displayed by early quantifiers who felt that their perspective was unappreciated by the discipline as a whole. The case for the discovery and insertion of women's historical experience into the theory and practice of historical geography has been put, and the writing of several notable practitioners scrutinized and found wanting.[300] Response has been predictable: the scale at which much geographical reconstruction takes place, considering how variable the specifically social coverage may be, presupposes—and usually delivers—joint consideration of both men and women. The rejoinder to such an argument is to stress that past orientation to male views of historic process has failed to recognize and recover the distinctiveness of the female contribution, regardless of topic. It remains to be seen how rapidly and fully the imbalance will be made up, and in what ways this will alter our understanding of past geographies and geographical change. The reinterpretation could well be substantial at certain scales

tions; and that *how and why* it happened depended very often upon the kinds of crops or other staples that were tended in that place or region." Earle, *Geographical Inquiry*, p. 23 (see n. 228, above).

[297] For another attempt to conceptualize geographical processes using this approach, see Peter J. Hugill, "The Macro-Landscape of the Wallerstein World Economy: King Cotton and the American South," in Richard L. Nostrand and Sam B. Hilliard, eds., *The American South* (Baton Rouge: Louisiana State University School of Geoscience, Geoscience & Man, vol. 25, 1988), pp. 77–84.

[298] Immanuel Wallerstein, "The TimeSpace [*sic*] of World-Systems Analysis: A Philosophical Essay," Distinguished Lecture in the Historical Geography of Social Change, Annual Meeting of the Association of American Geographers, San Diego, California, April 1992 (to be published by *Historical Geography*).

[299] American historical geography suffers an underrepresentation of women in its ranks, in common with most subfields of professional geography, though the problem does not appear to be as acute as in some specialties.

[300] An exchange on the relative position of gender in current writings in North American historical geography occurred recently: see Jeanne C. Kay, "On Articles by Meinig, Jordan, and Hornsby: The Future of Historical Geography in the United States," and replies by Meinig and Hornsby, *Annals of the Association of American Geographers*, vol. 80, 4 (1990), pp. 618–623; and also her "Landscapes of Women and Men: Rethinking the Regional Historical Geography of the United States and Canada," *Journal of Historical Geography*, vol. 17, 4 (1991), pp. 435–452.

and in certain contexts. The next step, it should be hoped, will bring substantive reinterpretations that demonstrate the margins of error now tolerated in the absence of a clear methodology and purpose for gendered analysis.[301] The scope of this project is immense, and its findings will be more valuable if the needed research is not left by default only to members of the slighted sex.[302]

A third major departure is the seepage into American historical geography of ideas gleaned from the debates in the humanities and social sciences over the meaning and timing of modernity, stimulated in large part by the writings of such European thinkers as Michel Foucault, Jürgen Habermas, and Anthony Giddens. This seepage constitutes but a whisper in several corners of the field, if it is felt at all, and it is hard yet to find much substantive work that has drawn power from these currents. But discussion is rising over the implications for historical geography both of theories of how social power has evolved in relation to space in the modern era, and of the critiques of rationality and privileged discourse that postmodernists regard as the key tyranny of the modern age.[303] In American writing, David Ward and Allan Pred have explored these issues most keenly to date. Ward's long-standing interest in modernity is reflected in his concern to place the Euro–North American Victorian city as artifact and social construct fairly precisely on the historical continuum from premodern to modern development.[304] Pred, whose interests took him on a long odyssey from spatial dynamics through behavioralism to structuralism, has now embraced the structurationist perspective of Giddens with more enthusiasm than anyone else. His study of Boston during the nineteenth century stands so far as one of the very few attempts to apply structuration theory to an empirical research problem in historical geography; so far there have been few imitators.[305] Perhaps Cole Harris put it best recently when saying, in relation to the writings of the key mod-

---

[301] At least one methodological signpost with historico-geographical relevance has already been offered: see Janice Monk, "Approaches to the Study of Women and Landscape," *Environmental Review*, vol. 8, 1 (1984), pp. 23–33.

[302] A significant effort has been made to include publications bearing on the historical geography of women in the bibliography of this work, as also of other minority classifications.

[303] A readable introduction to the former topic is provided by R. Cole Harris, "Power, Modernity, and Historical Geography," *Annals of the Association of American Geographers*, vol. 81, 4 (1991), pp. 671–683. A somewhat less readable general comment on postmodern incredulity, which extends to discussing the legitimacy of historical geography as a field of endeavor, is Michael Dear, "The Postmodern Challenge: Reconstructing Human Geography," *Transactions of the Institute of British Geographers*, new ser., vol. 13, 3 (1988), pp. 275–287. It is striking the extent to which discussions of modernity and postmodernity in North America have been fed with imported thought from British human and historical geographers: see, for example, Derek Gregory, "'Grand Maps of History': Structuration Theory and Social Change," in Jon Clark, Celia Modgil, and Sohan Modgil, eds., *Anthony Giddens: Consensus and Controversy* (London: Falmer Press, 1990), pp. 217–233. This general point has been made by Richard Dennis, "History, Geography, and Historical Geography," *Social Science History*, vol. 15, 2 (1991), p. 280.

[304] David Ward, "Victorian Cities: How Modern?" *Journal of Historical Geography*, vol. 1, 2 (1975), pp. 135–151; "The Place of Victorian Cities in Developmental Typologies of Urbanization," in John Patten, ed., *Urbanism and Urbanization* (London: Academic Press, 1983), pp. 355–379; and "Social Reform" (see n. 257, above).

[305] Allan R. Pred, "Structuration, Biography Formation, and Knowledge: Observations on Port Growth during the Late Mercantile Period," *Environment and Planning D: Society and Space*, vol. 2 (1984), pp. 251–275.

ernists, that their work offers "a diverse, much-disputed body of ideas that can be engaged in various ways," but are "least likely to be useful if fitted to formal research designs . . . their work is more likely to yield ideas that lurk, more or less influentially, in the background of research."[306]

And what of the current relations between history and geography in the United States? They share a relationship today, it seems, well within the extremes established in the past: not particularly close on most fronts, but neighborly on some. This is particularly so in economic and social history where the geographical scales of historical analysis have most often brought historians in contact with the tools geographers use to cope with spatial issues in detailed and intricate analyses. Numerous instances of close formal cooperation between the disciplines can be shown,[307] and certainly cases where specific and useful inspiration has been gained from geographical study and incorporated in the work of historians.[308] The reverse would in a sense be more difficult to show, because the borrowing is more pervasive, given the countless ways in which geographers rely on and take advantage of the outpouring of historical material of all kinds.

The historical impulse in geography remains as strong but as hard to control as ever, by those both in and out of sympathy with it. Yet it flourishes like a weed, perhaps indomitable, for even if we as geographers may think we are finished with the past, the past is not finished with us. And each season, each time a new geographical problem seems cleanly defined within contemporary terms of reference, this fourth dimension reasserts itself, a plant sprouting through cracks in the edifices of modern geographical thought, an entwining complication, a tendril that defies uprooting. Seeded in space, nurtured by environment, and pollinated by history, the historical imagination in geography is a creative and persistent force within the discipline. Its perennial and momentary preoccupations do not always reflect current fashions in human geography at large, but the gaps are often closed sooner or later and at times the historical impulse succeeds in blazing new interpretive trails, and almost always

---

[306] Harris, "Power," p. 678 (see n. 304, above).

[307] Notable examples of substantive interdisciplinary activity are Brian W. Blouet and Frederick C. Luebke, eds., *The Great Plains: Environment and Culture* (Lincoln: University of Nebraska Press, 1979); Theodore Herschberg, ed., *Philadelphia: Work Space, Family, and Group Experience in the Nineteenth Century* (New York: Oxford University Press, 1981); Frederick C. Luebke, Frances Kaye, and Gary E. Moulton, eds., *Mapping the North American Plains: Essays in the History of Cartography* (Norman: University of Oklahoma Press, 1987); Eugene D. Genovese and Leonard Hochberg, eds., *Geographic Perspectives in History: Essays in Honor of Edward Whiting Fox* (Oxford: Basil Blackwell, 1989); Robert D. Mitchell, ed., *Appalachian Frontiers: Settlement, Society, and Development in the Preindustrial Era* (Lexington: University of Kentucky Press, 1991); and Ira Katznelson, *Marxism and the City* (Oxford: Clarendon Press, 1992).

[308] Examples of historical works that show strong influence of modern geographical ideas and methods include Kathleen Neils Conzen, *Immigrant Milwaukee, 1836–1860: Accommodation and Community in a Frontier City* (Cambridge: Harvard University Press, 1976); Olivier Zunz, *The Changing Face of Inequality: Urbanization, Industrial Development, and Immigrants in Detroit, 1880–1920* (Chicago: University of Chicago Press, 1982); Simpson, *Community of Cattlemen* (see n. 235, above); and William J. Cronon, *Nature's Metropolis: Chicago and the Great West* (New York: W. W. Norton & Co., 1991), winner of the 1991 Beveridge Prize in American history.

contributes the most seasoned and durable syntheses in geography, whether in a regional or systematic vein.

In a discipline dedicated fundamentally to comparative work—because places differ—but in practice so compartmentalized by specialization and single-area case study, the historical impulse in geography offers perhaps the most instinctive form of comparative thought, comparisons over time in a more or less sequential system of explanation to account for the consequences of human action over space. This offers historical geography a constant challenge to situate interpretive developments in human geography within the full stream of time, in the process drawing on changing thought in history and the social sciences, while at the same time, by example, placing space at the core of many of the critical questions of social inquiry, and thereby demonstrating the time-honored inextricability of geography in human affairs.

Geographical Writing on the Canadian Past

Graeme Wynn

Imagine exploring a large and long-established graveyard on a dark and stormy night. Then contemplate the task of reviewing geographical writing on the Canadian past. The challenges are not dissimilar—although this is not to imply that historical geography is moribund. In each case, the general configuration of the terrain is more or less clear. Both scholarly field and hallowed ground have expanded with the years. Both show a semblance of order and coherence. Yet their bounds, in time and space, are far from obvious. Each exhibits a fabric crafted from many different materials. Even the casual reviewer/explorer can pick out a handful of shining monuments that stand above the rest. More careful investigation quickly reveals a bewildering range of stylistic changes (in scholarship and headstones) that beg questions about origins and inspiration. To whom, it must be asked, were these works addressed, and what did they say to them? Closer inquiry turns up many signs of familial connection; occasionally it is possible to trace elementary genealogies—of blood or intellect. But one also stumbles across apparently isolated individuals, and begins to wonder about evidence missed or lost, and about the nature of the congregation under examination. Was it warm, welcoming, confident, or preoccupied, defensive, and exclusive? The answers are invariably elusive. Analysis of the material evidence leads only so far. Texts are incomplete and allusive. The imagination runs all too quickly to ephemeral specters that owe more to current anxieties than to the past they seem to represent.

These challenges are far from unique, of course. Intellectual historians interested in the development of this or that academic discipline—including geography—have wrestled with them in various ways. Some have situated chronological accounts of particular disciplines in broad intellectual debates; others have seized a cerebral moment and explored the impact of a particular conjuncture upon several scholarly fields; yet others have made a few crucial practitioners the subjects of inquiry; and some have made windows of institutional structures—associations and journals—by using them to observe lines of intellectual development.[1]

---

[1] There are many examples of these approaches: for a chronological account of the discipline of geography see R. J. Johnston, *Geography and Geographers: Anglo-American Human Geography since 1945* (London: Edward Arnold, 1979). Marlene Shore, *The Science of Social Redemption: McGill, the Chicago School, and the Origins of Social Research in Canada* (Toronto: University of Toronto Press, 1987) provides an excellent example of a study tracing the emergence of a discipline and its place in the development of social science; although sociology is its subject, it also throws light on the development of historical and geographical scholarship in Canada. For an acclaimed study of a "cerebral moment" see Carl E. Schorske, *Fin-de-siècle Vienna: Politics and Culture* (New York: Knopf, 1979). Carl Berger, *The Writing of Canadian History: Aspects of English Canadian Historical Writing since 1900* (Toronto: University of Toronto Press, 1986) focuses on a handful of leading practitioners. Ian Cameron, *To the Farthest Ends of the Earth: The History of the Royal Geographical Society, 1830–1980* (London: Macdonald and Jane's,

In the end, most such inquiries fall into one of two broad categories.[2] The first—which incorporates much writing about the history of geography—encompasses studies with an essentially methodological focus. Here the emphasis is upon changes—in interpretation, approach, the conduct of inquiry, and the presentation of results—associated with the utilization of sources and the implementation of methods ignored by or unknown to earlier generations of scholars. Knowledge is regarded as cumulative. Interpretations of past and present work are inherently judgmental: that was amateurish, filiopietistic, polemical; this is wise and judicious. Disciplinary histories are generally presented in Whiggish terms. The significance of the story lies in its documentation of progress, of growth in the numbers of practitioners and publications, of increasing expertise and heightened utility.

The second approach—less common in assessments of geographical writing—relates disciplinary developments to prevailing climates of ideology and opinion. It sees knowledge as highly relative; in this view interpretations are not things to be judged true or false but artifacts that reflect their producers and their times. Thus this approach illuminates the social frameworks within which knowledge is shaped. It appreciates that scholarship has an audience. And it recognizes that knowledge may reinforce or challenge and change current political, social, and intellectual orthodoxies. From this perspective, intellectual byways and roads not taken can be as interesting and revealing as the main paths of development. The point is not to celebrate achievement but to appreciate why certain questions were asked and others were not. Silences and exclusions are as significant as enthusiasms and answers. In this view, understanding depends upon transcending the consensus that defines lines of inquiry and identifies "achievement" within a particular subject; it rests upon the accepted, self-referential canon of the discipline but requires that texts be read between the lines and that a critical ear be attuned to the everyday discourse of the field.[3]

If these distinctions oversimplify the realities of scholarly practice—because social frameworks influence epistemological preferences, just as methodologies and sources shape interpretations—they nonetheless provide a useful framework within which to consider the large and disparate compilation of geographical writing on the Canadian past assembled in the following pages. By any measure, the growth of the field has been striking. Although authors claimed coverage of both history and geography in works relating to parts of the present country from the eighteenth century onward, and a volume on Canada appeared as number 5 in Charles P. Lucas's early

---

1980); K. Peake-Jones, *The Branch without a Tree: The Centenary History of the Royal Geographical Society of Australasia (South Australian Branch)* (Adelaide: Royal Geographical Society of Australasia, 1985); and J. K. Wright, "British Geography and the American Geographical Society, 1851–1951" *Geographical Journal*, vol. 118, 2 (1952), pp. 153–167, exemplify the institution-as-window approach. The biographical perspective is well illustrated by T. W. Freeman, M. Oughton, and P. Pinchemel, eds., *Geographers: Biobibliographical Studies* (London: Mansell Information Publishing, 1977–present).

[2] This bipartite distinction is identified in historiography, for example, by R. A. Skotheim, *American Intellectual Histories and Historians* (Princeton: Princeton University Press, 1966), pp. 299–302.

[3] More on these points can be found in Georges Gurvitch, *The Social Frameworks of Knowledge*, trans. Margaret A. Thompson and Kenneth A. Thompson (New York: Harper and Row, 1971), pp. 10–17.

twentieth-century series, *Historical Geography of the British Colonies*, publications bearing the appellations "historical geography," "geographical history," or "history and geography" were strikingly few before 1914.[4] As in the United States, of course, there was a good deal of interest, through these early years of European exploration and settlement in New France, Rupert's Land, British North America, and Canada, in charting and describing the northern part of the continent and its resources.[5] Much of this work is now of great interest and value to historical geographers, but little of it was identified with the field when produced.[6] Even those works explicitly given to geographical description—such as Robert Rogers's *Concise Account of North America* (1765), Michael Smith's *Geographical View of the British Possessions in North America* (1814), and Joseph Bouchette's *Topographical Description of the Province of Lower Canada* (1815)—were heavily focused on the contemporary scene. The nineteenth century also yielded a large handful of school geographies encompassing all or part of the area north of the American border, but these, too, were invariably more descriptive than historical in emphasis.[7] Even with those late nineteenth- and early twentieth-century works that carry no explicit declaration of disciplinary affiliation in their titles yet warrant inclusion in this guide by virtue of the topics examined or approaches used, there was little historical geography (broadly

[4] Charles P. Lucas, *Historical Geography of the British Colonies*, vol. 5, *Canada* (Oxford: Clarendon Press, 1901–1911); Rev. H. B. George, "Canada," in his *A Historical Geography of the British Empire* (London: Methuen & Co., 1904), pp. 144–178; P. Vaillant, *A Geographical History of Nova Scotia* (London: Paul Vaillant, 1749); John G. Hodgins, *The Geography and History of British America, and of Other Colonies of the British Empire* (Toronto: McLear & Co., 1857).

[5] Among many possible examples the following are illustrative: J. J. Bigsby, "Notes on the Geography and Geology of Lake Huron," *Transactions of the Geological Society of London*, ser. 2, pt. 2 (1824), pp. 175–209; J. J. Bigsby, "On the Physical Geography, Geology, and Commercial Resources of Lake Superior," *Edinburgh New Philosophical Journal*, vol. 53 (1852), pp. 55–62; G. Barnston, "Remarks on the Geographical Distribution of Plants in the British Possessions of North America," *Canadian Naturalist and Geologist*, vol. 3, 1 (1858), pp. 28–32; J. Adams, "Sketches of the Tête de Boule Indians, River St. Maurice," *Transactions of the Literary and Historical Society of Quebec*, vol. 3 (1837), p. 25; W. E. Cormack, "Account of a Journey across the Island of Newfoundland," *Edinburgh Philosophical Journal*, vol. 10 (1823–1824), pp. 156–162; J. Franklin, *Journey to the Shores of the Polar Sea, in 1819–20–21–22, with a Brief Account of the Second Journey in 1825–26–27* (London: John Murray, 1829); James Cook, *Journals of Captain James Cook* (Stanford: Stanford University Press, 1974); Sir Joseph Banks, *Joseph Banks in Newfoundland and Labrador, 1766* (Berkeley: University of California Press, 1971). My own favorite, in light of Prime Minister Pierre Trudeau's observation that Canada's position alongside the United States in North America left it somewhat vulnerable to every stirring of the southern elephant, is T. Davies, "An Account of the Jumping Mouse of Canada," *Transactions of the Linnean Society*, vol. 4 (1798), pp. 155–157. None of this material falls within the criteria for inclusion in this guide. These brief comments depend upon Suzanne E. Zeller, "Nature's Gullivers and Crusoes," in John L. Allen, ed. *North American Exploration* (forthcoming: University of Nebraska Press), which offers a full and sensitive review of this material, and more; see also her *Inventing Canada: Early Victorian Science and the Idea of a Transcontinental Nation* (Toronto: University of Toronto Press, 1987).

[6] See A. H. Clark, "Titus Smith Junior and the Geography of Nova Scotia in 1801 and 1802," *Annals of the Association of American Geographers*, vol. 44, 4 (1954), pp. 291–314; J. Warkentin, ed., *The Western Interior of Canada* (Toronto: 1969); L. J. Burpee, "David Thompson: A Great Land Geographer," *Canadian Geographical Journal*, vol. 30, 5 (1945), pp. 238–239; M. Staveley, "Saskatchewan-by-the-Sea: The Topographic Work of Alexander Murray in Newfoundland," *Newfoundland Quarterly*, vol. 77 (1981), pp. 31–41.

[7] Although some, such as Zadock Thompson, *Geography and History of Lower Canada, Designed for the Use of Schools* (Sherbrooke, Quebec: Walton & Gaylord, 1835) covered both fields, albeit generally separately.

defined) published before 1920. Indeed, barely 170 of the Canadian entries in this volume bear pre-1950 imprints.

In the mid-1960s, when Cole Harris produced the first survey of geographical writing on the Canadian past, he observed that there were "few trained historical geographers in Canada," and that they had done little research.[8] Restricting attention, for the most part, to historical writing by geographers, he identified some fifty-seven graduate theses and fewer than a hundred publications in the field. Only a small fraction of these—less than 10 percent of the theses and barely 18 percent of the published items—had been completed before 1950. Taken as a whole, this was a markedly diffuse literature, much of it, in Harris's judgment, "under-researched and poorly written." Topical and regional coverage was highly uneven; early Ontario had received more consideration than other parts of the country; although historical writing on the western interior had "a larger and more penetrating geographical aspect" than that on any other Canadian region, geographers were only just beginning work on this area;[9] "the short past of British Columbia [had] received little historical and less geographical attention"; in forty years, since the 1920s, there had been "no geographical studies of early Canada as a whole." At best, there had been a "vigorous beginning" to work on the historical geography of Canada, but individual studies were insufficiently related to previous inquiries, and the main tasks lay ahead.[10]

Many of these assignments have been addressed in the quarter century since Harris wrote, to produce a literature that is—the Canadian pages of this guide attest—almost as broad as the country itself. The analysis of themes important in 1967—among them migration, settlement, cultural transfer, survey systems, landscapes, distributions, and locales—has been extended. New topics (including the geographies of native peoples, inner cities, urban systems, and environmental change) have been broached and, in some cases, explored in considerable depth.[11] Regional coverage is still uneven but the lacunae have contracted. Now Prince Edward Island, Labrador, and Yukon territory, rather than the Atlantic Region and the West, appear

---

[8] R. C. Harris, "Historical Geography in Canada," *Canadian Geographer*, vol. 11, 4 (1967), pp. 235–250.

[9] Work on the west was given this geographical aspect in substantial part by the Canadian Frontiers of Settlement project. Masterminded by Canadian-born Isaiah Bowman, founder and director of the American Geographical Society, the project turned on a detailed research plan developed by a committee of the American Geographical Society that included O. E. Baker and W. L. G. Joerg as well as historian Frederick Merk, sociologist Kimball Young, and W. J. Rutherford of the School of Agriculture at the University of Saskatchewan. In the end, eight books appeared from this collaborative venture, "all of which," the Pioneer Problems Committee stressed, were "not so much books on economics or agriculture as they were on frontier settlement." Political economist W. A. Mackintosh analyzed the geographical setting of prairie settlement; among historians involved in the project C. Martin wrote on land policy, A. W. Morton on the history of settlement, and H. A. Innis and A. R. M. Lower on settlement of the forest and mining frontiers. Sociologist C. A. Dawson wrote on the settlement of the Peace River area, immigrant groups, the social aspects of pioneering, and the development of metropolitan centers in the western interior. These developments are well treated in Shore, *Science of Social Redemption*, pp. 162–194.

[10] For the purposes of comparison it should be noted that by using somewhat more inclusive criteria than those adopted by Harris this guide identifies approximately 450 items with 1966 or earlier imprints.

[11] Further discussion of these developments can be found in the introduction to G. Wynn, ed., *People, Places, Patterns, Processes* (Toronto: Copp Clark Pitman, 1990), pp. 9–15.

relatively little studied from a geographical perspective. By the roughest of tallies, at least 120 professional geographers practicing their craft in Canada in the early 1990s have written on some aspect of the country's past.[12] The pages of this guide include over 1,000 articles published by Canadian geographers and more than 450 graduate theses completed in Canadian geography departments since 1967.[13] To the handful of monographs in print before that date, historical geographers have added a steady stream of new books over the years; several have been recognized as particularly important contributions to understanding the Canadian past.[14]

Taken alone, this impressive catalog of expansion suggests that geographical writing on the Canadian past has gathered remarkable momentum along a smooth, straight track. In detail, however, this growth has followed a narrow, winding, and often treacherous path across the intellectual landscape. It has been brought about through the efforts of a relatively small band of scholars scattered across a vast country. Language and distance have worked to divide and separate, as well as to inspire and challenge. As a result, many have worked in comparative isolation, more closely connected to local scholars with whom they share topical or regional interests than to a national community of historical geographers. Nor have these circumstances been markedly changed by the new freedom of movement afforded by air travel or the telecommunications revolution of the late twentieth century.[15] Moreover, historical geographers in Canada have been buffeted, like those elsewhere, by the crosscurrents of academic debate and epistemological fashion in geography, history, and related fields. If relatively little of the literature cataloged in these pages is given to methodological introspection, hardly any of it has escaped the imprint of its time—and place, for the particular contexts of Canadian scholarship have often, more or less subtly, influenced the ways in which winds of change blowing from beyond the country have worked their effects within it. Nor should it be forgotten that some Canadian geographers have made vigorous contributions to debates about the nature and legitimacy of historical inquiry within their discipline (see "Methodologi-

---

[12] Yet it is remarkable how few have made sustained contributions; of the nearly twelve hundred authors appearing in the Canadian section of this guide (not all of them formally geographers), barely a hundred geographers have five or more entries relating to Canada (though some with fewer entries have published on the United States and/or other parts of the world as well). Even more striking is that only twenty geographers have fifteen or more Canadian entries, and that only seven have more than twenty-five; it is also worth note that all but one of the latter group received their doctoral degrees in the 1970s.

[13] Although the bibliography in Wynn, People, Places, pp. 19–37, does not include all items on the Canadian past published by geographers between 1967 and 1987, it provides the fullest list for direct comparison with Harris's 1967 bibliography; the earlier inventory includes ninety-four items, the latter almost seven times as many.

[14] J. M. Bumsted, "Putting It on the Map," Beaver, vol. 68 (April-May 1988), p. 54.

[15] Thus there is no formal historical geography specialty group of the Canadian Association of Geographers; rarely are there substantial numbers of historical geographers at the annual meeting of the association. Buoyed by the larger-than-usual gathering of historical colleagues at the Halifax meeting of the CAG in 1988 (when numbers approached 20), and the transcontinental connections fostered by work on the Historical Atlas of Canada, Cole Harris and Graeme Wynn began the informal, biannual Newsletter for Canadian Historical Geographers/Bulletin des géographes historiques canadiens in November of that year. It was, however, intended to foster links rather than to reflect the existence of a regularly interacting community.

cal Statements" in the "General Sources" section of this guide) and their arguments have shaped research choices, influenced research strategies, and affected the ways in which research findings have been reported at home and abroad.

Diffuse Beginnings: Canadian Historical Geography to 1950

Location and filiation have shaped both Canada and its historical-geographical literature. French and British colonies in America, brought together in piecemeal and pragmatic manner to assume a pivotal place within the Pax Britannica, yet always closely implicated with, and influenced by, the states to the south, the territories of New France/British North America/Canada have been profoundly influenced by the interplay of old-world connections with new-world circumstances.[16] So, too, have efforts to understand the development of this northern realm, and to grasp the peculiar plight of its people.[17]

From the first, therefore, geographical writing in English and French applied prevailing conceptions of historical geography in Britain, the United States, and France to the task of understanding the Canadian past. Much of the earliest work focused on early mapping and on environmental influences on human activity. A substantial part of it was the work of European scholars, although a handful of Americans wrote on Canadian topics, and several items were published in American journals.[18] Canadian historians, economists, and sociologists also made valuable

---

[16] This tension is evident in many general accounts of Canadian development; it can be discerned, for example, in R. C. Harris, "The Pattern of Early Canada," in Wynn, People, Places, pp. 358–373; T. F. McIlwraith, Jr., "British North America, 1763–1867"; and G. Wynn, "Forging a Canadian Nation," both in R. D. Mitchell and P. A. Groves, eds., North America: The Historical Geography of a Changing Continent (Totowa, N.J.: Rowman & Littlefield, 1987), pp. 220–253 and 373–409.

[17] Perhaps the most powerful encapsulation of this theme is George M. Grant, "In Defence of North America," in his Technology and Empire: Perspectives on North America (Toronto: House of Anansi, 1969), pp. 13–40. For a different emphasis stressing the distinctive northernness of the Canadian experience see W. L. Morton, The Canadian Identity (Madison: University of Wisconsin Press, 1965); and T. J. Oleson and W. L. Morton, "The Northern Approaches to Canada," Dictionary of Canadian Biography, vol. 1 (Toronto: University of Toronto Press, 1966), pp. 16–21. C. C. Berger, The Sense of Power: Studies in the Ideas of Canadian Imperialism, 1867–1914 (Toronto: University of Toronto Press, 1970) treats the imperial enthusiasms of late nineteenth-century Canadians with sophistication and insight. In this context, it is not surprising that migration, settlement, and cultural transfer have been major themes in Canadian historical geography.

[18] Among the Europeans, M. I. Newbigin, Canada: The Great River, the Lands, and the Men (London: Christophers, 1926); W. Nederkorn, "Die Entdeckungs, Besiedlungs- und Entwicklungsgeschichte Canadas und seiner Grenzgebiete," Deutsche Geographische Blätter, vol. 22, 1 (1899), pp. 86–124; and 3, pp. 170–201; H. Nelson, Canada nybyggar landet (Stockholm: A. B. Magn. Bergvalls Forlag, 1922); H. Nelson, "Kolonisation och befolknings forskajatning inom kanadas prärieprovinser," Ymer, vol. 54 (1934), pp. 161–180; R. LeConte, "L'émigration allemande au Canada," Le mouvement géographique, vol. 33 (1920), pp. 424–432; C. Schott, Landnahme und Kolonisation in Kanada am Beispiel Sudontarios (Kiel: Schriften des Geographischen Instituts der Universität Kiel, vol. 6, 1936). Among the Americans: E. C. Semple, "The Influence of Geographic Environment on the Lower St. Lawrence," Bulletin of the American Geographical Society, vol. 36 (1904), pp. 449–466; R. H. Whitbeck, "The St. Lawrence River and Its Part in the Making of Canada," Bulletin of the American Geographical Society, vol. 47, 8 (1915), pp. 584–593; C. F. Jones, "Transportation Adjustments in the Railway Entrances and Terminal Facilities at Montreal," Bulletin of the Philadelphia Geographical Society, vol. 22, 3 (1924), pp. 98–110. In addition to the items in American journals noted above, E. N. Horsford published "John Cabot's Landfall: Site of Norumbega," and A. S. Packard published "The Geographical Evolution of Labrador," in Journal of the

contributions to the literature. Working in less discipline-bound days in a country that their contemporary, Prime Minister Mackenzie King, once described as possessed of "too much geography," they were explicit in recognizing the importance of "geographical" considerations (such as distance, space, climatic marginality) to their inquiries.[19] Formally trained geographers, most of whom began their careers in the 1940s, were responsible for a small fraction of the whole.[20]

Most turn-of-the-century work was relatively limited in conception and intellectual range. Few Canadian scholars were prepared to follow Emile Miller, a professor in Montreal's École des Arts et Manufactures, in his embrace of the teachings of France's Jean Brunhes (with their emphasis on the study of "material human works") and his endorsement of Victor Cousin's observation, "Donnez-moi la géographie d'un pays et je vous trouverai son histoire."[21] Even in Quebec, where scholars drew inspiration from French work that was generally cognizant of such geographical concerns as settlement and land use, and where the Société de Géographie du Québec (established in 1881) published the first issue of its *Bulletin* in 1886, early studies concentrated on such relatively circumscribed topics as political boundaries, place names, and early cartography.[22] Occasional articles dealt with topics such as shipbuilding, and in the 1930s, ethnologist and folklorist Marius Barbeau (who later taught a course on the geography of the Indians at Laval) wrote, in American journals, about an early French settlement on the St. Lawrence and on "French Survival

---

American Geographical Society, vol. 17 (1885), pp. 45–78, and vol. 20 (1888), pp. 208–230; C. Roland wrote "The Forest Resources of Canada," in *Economic Geography*, vol. 2, 3 (1926), pp. 394–413.

[19] See note 9 above and Wynn, *People, Places*, pp. 1–2.

[20] Established figures included T. G. Taylor, whose "Fundamental Factors in Canadian Geography" appeared in the *Canadian Geographical Journal*, vol. 12 (1936), pp. 161–171, a year after he became Foundation Professor of Geography at the University of Toronto at the age of fifty-four. "Newcomers" included J. W. Watson and W. A. D. Jackson. Watson completed the first doctoral thesis in historical geography granted by a Canadian institution at the University of Toronto in 1945, entitled "The Geography of the Niagara Peninsula." This work had a thoroughgoing historical cast, as revealed by the succession of articles drawn from it: "Urban Developments in the Niagara Peninsula," *Canadian Journal of Economics and Political Science*, vol. 9, 4 (1943), pp. 463–486; "The Changing Industrial Pattern of the Niagara Peninsula: A Study in Historical Geography," *Ontario Historical Society, Papers and Records*, vol. 37 (1945), pp. 49–58; "Mapping a Hundred Years of Change in the Niagara Peninsula," *Canadian Geographical Journal*, vol. 32, 6 (1946), pp. 266–283; "Rural Depopulation in Southwestern Ontario," *Annals of the Association of American Geographers*, vol. 3, 2 (1947), pp. 145–154; "The Influence of the Frontier on Niagara Settlements," *Geographical Review*, vol. 38, 1 (1948), pp. 113–119. Jackson completed "A Geographical Study of Early Settlement in Southern Ontario" as a master's thesis at the University of Toronto in 1948.

[21] E. Miller, "La géographie au service de l'histoire," *Revue trimestrielle canadienne*, vol. 1, 1 (1915), pp. 45–53.

[22] J. Bignell, "The Northern Boundary of the Province of Quebec," *Bulletin de la Société de géographie du Québec*, vol. 1 (1886), pp. 88–89, vol. 5 (1887), pp. 63–65; M. Gabriel "Cartographie de la Nouvelle-France," *Revue de géographie*, vol. 11 (1885), pp. 1–41; J.-E. Roy, "La cartographie et l'arpentage sous le Regime français," *Bulletin des recherches historiques*, vol. 1 (1895), pp. 33–45; B. Sulte, "La plus ancienne carte de la province de Québec," *Bulletin de la Société de géographie du Québec*, n.s. vol. 7 (1912), pp. 296–299; P. G. Roy, *Les noms géographiques de la province de Québec* (Levis, 1906); E. Rouillard, "Quelques noms géographiques," *Bulletin de la Société de géographie du Québec*, vol. 11 (1917), pp. 91–95; P. G. Roy, "D'où vient le nom de 'Nouvelle-France'?" *Bulletin de la Société de géographie du Québec*, vol. 12 (1918), pp. 79–80.

in Canada."[23] In this decade, too, French geographer Raoul Blanchard initiated his long and substantial contribution to the study of Quebec with a series of regional essays, almost all of which included significant historical discussions. Generally, these essays followed a familiar sequence, giving attention to the physical environment, the record of human occupance, and the pattern of human adjustments to physical circumstances.[24] Marked by a firm sense of the connections between modes of production and ways of life, and turning on the concept of genre de vie, this work was modeled on that done by Jean Brunhes and Vidal de la Blache in France.[25] Despite the appointment of Benoit Brouillette to the École des Hautes Études Commerciales in Montreal after he became the first French-Canadian to receive a doctoral degree in geography, however, it was not until the establishment of geography departments at Laval (1946) and Montreal (1947) that French-Canadian scholars begin to address, in print and in any number, the historical geography of Quebec by exploring such themes as "la marche du peuplement," "le rang," and "utilisation du sol."[26]

In English Canada, early studies in historical geography were equally narrowly conceived. So botanist and local historian W. F. Ganong—a historical geographer by avocation—followed late nineteenth-century convention (exemplified by E. A. Freeman's *The Historical Geography of Europe*, which traced the extent of various states at different times with painstaking care) in his early twentieth-century studies of boundary changes in New Brunswick.[27] Other parts of Ganong's work reflected con-

---

[23] N. LeVasseur, "La construction des navires à Québec," *Bulletin de la Société de géographie du Québec*, vol. 11, 4 (1917), pp. 187–201; M. Barbeau, "An Early French Settlement on the St. Lawrence," *Bulletin of the Philadelphia Geographical Society*, vol. 30, 2 (1932), pp. 79–87; M. Barbeau, "French Survival in Canada," *Journal of the Washington Academy of Sciences*, vol. 23, 8 (1933), pp. 365–378. For a fuller account of these developments see L.-E. Hamelin, "Petite histoire de la géographie dans le Québec et à l'Université Laval," *Cahiers de géographie du Québec*, vol. 7, 13 (1962–1963), pp. 1–16.

[24] R. Blanchard, "Le peuplement," and "Les genres de vie anciens," in his "La presqu'île de Gaspé," *Revue de géographie alpine*, vol. 18 (1930), pp. 56–66 and 67–76; "Le côte nord, 1: Les genres de vie et leur évolution," in his "Le rebord nord de l'estuaire et du golfe du Saint-Laurent," *Revue de géographie alpine*, vol. 20 (1932), pp. 444–500; "Les étapes de mise en valeur," in his "Le Saguenay et le lac Saint-Jean," *Revue de géographie alpine*, vol. 21 (1933), pp. 64–94; "Le peuplement," in his "Les cantons de l'est," *Revue de géographie alpine*, vol. 25 (1937), pp. 155–204; "Les étapes de la mise en valeur et du peuplement," in his "Les Laurentides," *Revue de géographie alpine*, vol. 26 (1938), pp. 59–115; "Le peuplement de la plaine," in his "La plaine de Montréal," *Revue de géographie alpine*, vol. 27 (1939), pp. 302–333; "Les étapes et les modalités de la colonisation," in his "l'Abitibi-Témiscamingue," *Revue de géographie alpine*, vol. 37 (1949), pp. 472–500. See also the entry regarding Blanchard in the "Benchmark Scholars" section of this guide.

[25] See Anne Buttimer, *Society and Milieu in the French Geographic Tradition* (Chicago: Rand McNally for the Association of American Geographers, 1971); and Howard F. Andrews, "L'oeuvre de Paul Vidal de la Blache: Notes bibliographiques," *Canadian Geographer*, vol. 28, 1 (1984), pp. 1–18.

[26] Brouillette obtained his doctorate from the University of Paris in 1931; he spent 1941–1942 in the social sciences division at Laval University, and was first professor of Geography in the Institut de Géographie at the University of Montreal. L.-E. Hamelin, "La marche du peuplement à l'intérieur du diocèse de Joliette," *Société canadienne d'histoire de l'église catholique* (1949–1950), pp. 13–21; L.-E. Hamelin, "Le rang d'habitat: Étude pluridisciplinaire de signification," Master's thesis, Université Laval, 1949; B. Prud'homme, "Étude du peuplement du comté de Vaudreuil," Master's thesis, Clark University, 1949.

[27] E. A. Freeman, *The Historical Geography of Europe* (London: Longmans, Green and Co., 1881). For more on Ganong's intellectual connections see G. Wynn, "W. F. Ganong, A. H. Clark, and the Historical Geography of Maritime Canada," *Acadiensis*, vol. 10, 2 (1981), pp. 5–28.

temporary interests in exploration and cartography, and these themes were also pursued by R. Douglas and Matthias Thordarson, who examined early maps of Nova Scotia and the Vinland voyages.[28]

Slightly later, Scottish geographer Marion Newbigin (whose *Canada: The Great River, the Lands, and the Men* was published in 1926) and the peripatetic Griffith Taylor (a graduate of the universities of Sydney and Cambridge who came to the University of Toronto to found the geography department via Chicago, Sydney, and Scott's Antarctic expedition) followed contemporaries on both sides of the Atlantic in giving great weight to the influence of environment on people. Indeed, the very subject of Newbigin's book paralleled that of earlier papers by Ellen Churchill Semple and Ray Hughes Whitbeck, and the theme was revisited at a larger scale in a study of the Ile d' Orléans completed at Clark University in the 1940s.[29] Writing from a "possibilist" rather than a strictly determinist position, Newbigin outlined the ways in which the St. Lawrence River and the Canadian Shield had affected the discovery, exploration, settlement, and military defeat of New France.[30]

In a similar vein, several members of the first generation of professional historians in Canada—among them H. A. Innis, A. R. M. Lower, and Walter Sage—were influenced by the view, particularly strong in the United States, that the environment determined human destiny. Whether subscribers to Frederick Jackson Turner's views about the transformative powers of the frontier, or simply pioneering scholars writing about pioneering settlers who were impressed by the achievements of their forbears, they gave the land—geography and the environment—a significant place in their interpretations of Canadian development.[31] Indeed, Harold Innis's now

---

[28] W. F. Ganong, "A Monograph of the Cartography of the Province of New Brunswick," *Transactions of the Royal Society of Canada*, vol. 3 (1897), sec. 2, pp. 313–427; W. F. Ganong, "Cartography of the St. Lawrence from Cartier to Champlain," *Transactions of the Royal Society of Canada*, ser. 1, vol. 7 (1889), pp. 17–58; W. F. Ganong, "Champlain in Acadia," *Bulletin de la Société de géographie du Québec*, vol. 3, 2 (1908), pp. 17–24; R. Douglas, "An Early Map of Nova Scotia," *Canadian Geographical Magazine*, vol. 5 (1932), pp. 21–25; M. Thordarson, *The Vinland Voyages* (New York: American Geographical Society, Research Series, no. 18, 1930); H. Palmer, "Early Explorations in British Columbia for the Canadian Pacific Railway," *Bulletin of the Philadelphia Geographical Society*, vol. 16, 3 (1918), pp. 75–91; T. Lloyd, "Mapping Western Canada: The Red River Valley," *Canadian Geographical Journal*, vol. 26, 5 (1943), pp. 230–239.

[29] Semple, "The Influence of Geographic Environment on the Lower St. Lawrence"; Whitbeck, "The St. Lawrence River"; M. B. Banks, "The Isle of Orleans: A Study of the Influences of a River Island Environment on the Life of a People, 1648–1948," Master's thesis, Clark University, 1944. Other examples of work in this vein include C. F. Jones, "Geographic Influences in the Routes and Railway Traffic of the Atlantic Railway Connections at Montreal," *Bulletin of the Philadelphia Geographical Society*, vol. 23, 1 (1925), pp. 1–12; A. S. Gaught, "Geographical factors in the Development of the Maritime Provinces," Master's thesis, King's College, London, 1932; T. G. Taylor, "Topographic Control in the Toronto Region," *Canadian Journal of Economics and Political Science*, vol. 2, 4 (1936), pp. 493–511; W. B. Merriam, "Some Environmental Influences in the Cultural Development of the Haida," *Yearbook of the Association of Pacific Coast Geographers*, vol. 8 (1942), pp. 23–26; and G. E. Loft, "Geographical Influences in the Development of Manitoba," Ph.D. diss., University of Wisconsin, 1925.

[30] "Man can modify the lands in which he dwells," wrote Newbigin, but "in other respects he must follow where nature leads."

[31] More on this point can be found in the introduction to Wynn, *People, Places*, pp. 1–2. Settlement studies were also relatively common in the 1930s and 1940s; see for example J. R. Randall, "Settlement of the Great Clay Belt of Northern Ontario and Quebec," *Bulletin of the Philadelphia Geographical Society*,

classic discussions of the trades in beaver and cod, and their roles in shaping Canada, are highly revealing of the contexts in which much contemporary work was written. Both books reflect the impact of American economic historians upon Innis's thinking during his graduate school days at the University of Chicago. Each is imbued with Innis's strong sense of the vastness and relative inhospitableness of much of the northern half of the continent. Each was underpinned, to some degree, by Innis's familiarity with the writings of Vidal de la Blache and Ellsworth Huntington. And the first, in particular, owed much to Marion Newbigin's examination of the geography of the St. Lawrence and its effect upon the history of New France, although Innis regarded her treatment of the fur trade as superficial and accorded economics, technology, and geography more determinant power than she had done: Canada he observed, in what has become perhaps his most famous phrase, "emerged not in spite of geography but because of it."[32]

The diversity of approach and emphasis suggested by these examples was hardly surprising. Historical geography was an ill-defined domain in the first half of the twentieth century. Scholars in England, France, and North America perceived its parameters and purposes rather differently, and debated among themselves about its place in the discipline. Reviewing a landmark English work in the field in 1937, French historian Marc Bloch observed, "Our vocabulary is so imperfect that to entitle a book 'An historical geography' is to risk not giving in advance a very precise idea of its content."[33] A dozen years later, debate about the content of historical geography showed few signs of waning.[34] In France, history and geography were so closely allied—geography so infused with a retrospective sense and history so permeated by an awareness of setting—that historical geography held no distinctive niche: it was, at once, "both everywhere and nowhere."[35] In Britain, the prevailing view of the subject, articulated by J. F. Unstead in 1907, Halford Mackinder in 1928, and a growing

---

vol. 35, 3 & 4 (1937), pp. 53–66; D. W. Kirk, "Settlement Pattern of the Listowel Region, Southwestern Ontario," *Economic Geography*, vol. 23, 1 (1947), pp. 67–71; Jackson, "A Geographical Study of Early Settlement in Southern Ontario."

[32] H. A. Innis, *The Fur Trade of Canada: An Introduction to Canadian Economic History* (Toronto: Oxford University Press, 1927); and *The Cod Fisheries: The History of an International Economy* (Toronto: University of Toronto Press, 1954). Berger expands on some of these matters in "Harold Innis: The Search for Limits," pp. 85–111 of his *The Writing of Canadian History*; pp. 112–136 of this work discuss A. R. M. Lower. That the fur trade (and the St. Lawrence axis along which it ran) held a pivotal place in the minds of scholars seeking to understand the pattern of Canada in the 1930s is further suggested by the appearance of B. Brouillette, *La chasse des animaux à fourrure au Canada* (Paris: Gallimard, 1934). The trade itself has continued to receive a good deal of attention from Canadian historians, anthropologists, and historical geographers (especially A. J. Ray, C. Heidenreich, and W. Moodie). Cole Harris has refocused attention on some of the wider implications of Innis's arguments in recent years: see "The Pattern of Early Canada" and the preface to the *Historical Atlas of Canada*, vol. 1, ed. R. C. Harris (Toronto: University of Toronto Press, 1987), n.p.

[33] M. Bloch, "En Angleterre: L'histoire et le terrain," *Annales d'histoire économique et sociale*, vol. 9 (1937), p. 208.

[34] Review of N. J. G. Pounds, *A Historical and Political Geography of Europe*, by E. M. J. Campbell in *Geographical Journal*, vol. 112, 3 (1948), pp. 95–96.

[35] Xavier de Planhol, "Historical Geography in France," in A. R. H. Baker, ed., *Progress in Historical Geography* (Newton Abbott: David and Charles, 1972), pp. 29–44, quotation on p. 40.

number of scholars in the 1930s, had its origins in the writings of German geographer Alfred Hettner.[36] Historical geography was defined as the reconstruction of past geographies, no more and no less. Yet others embraced a more genetic approach, urging examination of the effects of past processes on the present, of "vertical themes" of landscape change (clearing, draining), and of the growth and development of geographical phenomena.[37]

Similar differences of opinion were also evident in the United States. With his 1939 essay *The Nature of Geography*, Wisconsin geographer Richard Hartshorne codified the subject for a generation. Drawing his arguments from the works of German scholars, especially Kant and Hettner, he maintained that geography was concerned with "spatial arrangement[s] on the surface of the earth." Sharing with history the task of integrating knowledge, it remained quite separate from that discipline because it studied associations in space, not time. The historian's task was to identify and to understand the character of historical periods; to geographers fell the challenges of distinguishing regions and describing the differences between areas and places. History was chronology, geography chorology, a subject in which "time in general steps into the background." In this view, the only appropriate course for geographers with a historical bent was to examine the geography of past periods. Patterns, rather than processes, were to be the focal points of their inquiries. Historical geographical studies did not "begin, proceed and end, according to a time sequence." They were "essentially different in character" from the work that "any historian could or would . . . [produce]."[38]

Others dissented. Among them, Carl Sauer of the University of California–Berkeley, agreed that human geography examined "the areal differentiation of human activities," but insisted that a knowledge of origins as well as distributions was essential to understanding the location of geographical phenomena. Focusing his interests upon the landscape—which he conceptualized as early as 1925 by reference to the work of German geographers as a complex combination of patterns and features, some of them remnants of earlier times—he charged historical geography with the task of deciphering the "catalytic relation" between people and place. This was to be addressed, in particular, by investigation of the material features that successive episodes of human occupance inscribed in the landscape. After strong initial resistance to Hartshorne's attempt to circumscribe the geographical canon, however, the

---

[36] A. R. H. Baker, "Historical Geography in Britain," in Baker, ed., *Progress in Historical Geography*, pp. 90–110; J. N. L. Baker, "The Development of Historical Geography in Britain during the Last Hundred Years," *Advancement of Science*, vol. 8 (1952), pp. 406–412.

[37] More on these views can be found in H. C. Darby, "The Problem of Geographical Description," *Transactions of the Institute of British Geographers*, vol. 30 (1962), pp. 1–14; H. C. Darby, "On the Relations of Geography and History," *Transactions of the Institute of British Geographers*, vol. 19 (1954), pp. 1–11; H. C. Darby, "Historical Geography," in H. P. R. Finberg, ed., *Approaches to History* (London: Routledge and Kegan Paul, 1962); and H. C. Darby, "Historical Geography in Britain, 1920–1980: Continuity and Change," *Transactions of the Institute of British Geographers*, n.s. vol. 8 (1983), pp. 421–428.

[38] R. Hartshorne, *The Nature of Geography: A Critical Survey of Current Thought in Light of the Past* (Lancaster, Pa.: Association of American Geographers, 1939).

interests of Sauer and his students turned away from historical study per se to pursue more broadly cultural-anthropological interests beyond North America.[39]

Between Space and Time: Canadian Historical Geography, 1950–1970

The expansion of Canadian historical geography after 1950 reflected these circumstances, as students in American, British, and German universities embarked on studies of the Canadian past. Over two dozen significant works came from these countries in the twenty years after midcentury, many written by Canadians who had gone abroad for advanced degrees. Most of those who enrolled in graduate programs at American institutions to study aspects of the Canadian past attended universities relatively close to the forty-ninth parallel. At Michigan, between 1947 and 1963, George Rumney, Robert Hodgson, Burke Vanderhill, and George Rae completed doctoral dissertations bearing on Canada; at Wisconsin, George McDermott wrote on the settlement of the Great Clay belt of Quebec and Ontario (1959), Bert Farley examined the early cartography of British Columbia (1960), and Cole Harris produced a geography of the seigneurial system during the French Regime (1964); at Minnesota in the early 1960s, Robert LeBlanc charted the expulsion of the Acadians from Nova Scotia, John Marshall explored central places in the Queen's Bush, and Denis Fitzgerald examined pioneer settlement in northern Saskatchewan. Ralph Krueger wrote on the Niagara fruit belt from Indiana, and a few years later, Lorne Russwurm investigated urbanization in the Hamilton-London corridor for an Illinois doctorate.[40]

Chicago, Ohio State, Syracuse, and SUNY-Buffalo were also centers for Canadian work in the 1960s, and on the west coast three theses on British Columbia were submitted to universities in Washington and Oregon.[41] Further afield, Maryland ac-

---

[39] C. O. Sauer, "The Morphology of Landscape," in J. Leighly, ed., *Land and Life: A Selection from the Writings of Carl Ortwin Sauer* (Berkeley: University of California Press, 1967), pp. 315–350; Sauer's 1941 presidential address to the Association of American Geographers expresses his concern at the "pernicious anemia" of the "but-is-this-geography" mentality that he saw in the discipline's embrace of Hartshorne's ideas; after this date he rarely if ever used the term "historical geography." See C. O. Sauer, "Foreword to Historical Geography," in Leighly, ed., *Land and Life*, pp. 351–388.

[40] G. R. Rumney, "Settlement of the Nipissing Passageway," Ph.D. diss., University of Michigan, 1947; Robert D. Hodgson, "Champlain-Richelieu Lowland: A Study in Historical Geography," Ph.D. diss., University of Michigan, 1951; B. G. Vanderhill, "Settlement in the Forest Lands of Manitoba, Saskatchewan, and Alberta: A Geographic Analysis," Ph.D. diss., University of Michigan, 1956; G. R. Rae, "The Settlement of the Great Slave Lake Frontier, Northwest Territories, from the Eighteenth to the Twentieth Centuries," Ph.D. diss., University of Michigan, 1963; G. L. McDermott, "Frontier Settlement in the Great Canadian Clay Belt," Ph.D. diss., University of Wisconsin–Madison, 1959; A. L. Farley, "Historical Cartography of British Columbia, with a Separate Appendix of Maps," Ph.D. diss., University of Wisconsin–Madison, 1960; R. C. Harris, "A Geography of the Seigneurial System in Canada during the French Regime," Ph.D. diss., University of Wisconsin–Madison, 1964; R. G. LeBlanc, "The Acadian Migrations," Master's thesis, University of Minnesota, 1962; J. U. Marshall, "Central Places in the Queen's Bush: A Study of Service Centers and Their Evolution in Bruce and Grey Counties, Ontario," Master's thesis, University of Minnesota, 1964; D. P. Fitzgerald, "Pioneer Settlement in Northern Saskatchewan," Ph.D. diss., University of Minnesota, 1965; R. R. Krueger, "Changing Land Use Patterns in the Niagara Fruit Belt," Ph.D. diss., Indiana University, 1958; L. H. Russwurm, "Expanding Urbanization in the London to Hamilton Area of Western Ontario: 1941–1961," Ph.D. diss., University of Illinois, 1964.

[41] R. S. Corkran, "Rail Route Selection in the Northern Rocky Mountains, 1853–1890," Master's thesis, University of Chicago, 1968; J. P. Weller, "The Evolution of Toronto: A Geographic Study," Master's thesis,

cepted Louis Gentilcore's 1950 dissertation on Antigonish, Nova Scotia, and W. A. D. Jackson's study of the lands along the St. Lawrence River in the nineteenth century.[42] Georgia awarded R. G. Putnam a master's degree for his work on land-use changes in part of Ontario, and Berkeley saw completion of Joan Sunderland's M.A. on that most favored topic of the period, the settlement of the Great Clay Belt.[43] Much of this work applied broadly familiar approaches to well-accepted themes: frontier settlement and land-use patterns were the dominant motifs, with a suggestion of sequent occupance and, in the 1960s, a touch of geographical theory added in. Taken as a group, however, these studies form an important taproot of historical geography in Canada, because several of their authors were appointed to faculty positions in expanding Canadian universities during the late 1960s and early 1970s.[44]

Frontier settlement, land-use patterns, and urban growth were also the central interests of the half dozen or so German scholars—including Eckhert Ehlers, Carl Schott, and Karl Lenz—who turned attention to the Great Clay Belt and the Prairies, in particular, after the Second World War.[45] In Britain, however, students at the

Ohio State University, 1963; A. A. Schneider, "The Historical Geography of the Erie Triangle," Ph.D. diss., Ohio State University, 1963; L. R. G. Martin, "A Comparative Study of the Development of Settlement and Agriculture in the Quinte Region of Eastern Ontario and the St. Lawrence Region of Northern New York," Master's thesis, Syracuse University, 1965; C. K. Duguemin, "Sequent Occupance in the Lower Valley of the Twenty Mile Creek, Lough Township, Lincoln County, Ontario; 1800–1905," Master's thesis, State University of New York–Buffalo, 1968; J. B. Koszuta, "An Interpretation of the Sequent Patterns of Trails, Roads, and Highways in the Niagara Frontier to 1950," Master's thesis, State University of New York–Buffalo, 1969; J. Lotzkar, "The Boundary County of Southern British Columbia: A Study of Resources and Human Occupance, "Master's thesis, University of Washington, 1953; L. M. Yakimovitch, "An Historical Interpretation of the Land Utilization and Tenure Pattern in the Vernon Rural Area of the Okanagan Valley, British Columbia," Master's thesis, University of Oregon, 1966; H. W. Bockemuehl, "Doukhobor Impact on the British Columbia Landscape: An Historical Geographical Study," Master's thesis, Western Washington State College, 1968.

[42] R. L. Gentilcore, "Land-Use and Agricultural Production in Antigonish County, Nova Scotia," Ph.D. diss., University of Maryland, 1950; this work began from an interest in the contemporary cooperative movement (the "Antigonish Movement") but it led Gentilcore into specifically historical inquiry after a chance encounter and discussion of the thesis with A. H. Clark; see Wynn, "W. F. Ganong, A. H. Clark," for further detail. The derivative study is R. L. Gentilcore, "The Agricultural Background of Settlement in Eastern Nova Scotia," Annals of the Association of American Geographers, vol. 46, 3 (1956), pp. 378–404. W. A. D. Jackson, "The Lands along the Upper St. Lawrence: Canadian American Development during the Nineteenth Century," Ph.D. diss., University of Maryland, 1952.

[43] R. G. Putnam, "Three Decades of Land Use Changes on the Central Lake Ontario Plain," Master's thesis, University of Georgia, 1961. J. R. Sunderland, "Settlement of the Clay Belt of Northern Ontario and Quebec," Master's thesis, University of California–Berkeley, 1955.

[44] Farley (University of British Columbia), Gentilcore (McMaster), Harris (Toronto, later University of British Columbia), Krueger (Waterloo), and Marshall (York) among them; the pattern is only strengthened by inclusion of Paul Koroscil ("The Changing Landscape of the Yukon Territory and the Settlement of Whitehorse," Ph.D. diss., University of Michigan, 1970) appointed at Simon Fraser; Jim Richtik ("The Historical Geography of Southern Manitoba, 1870–1886," Ph.D. diss., University of Minnesota, 1971) at Winnipeg; Arthur J. Ray ("Indian Exploitation of the Forest-Grassland Transition Zone in Western Canada, 1650–1860: A Geographical View of Two Centuries of Change," Ph.D. diss., University of Wisconsin–Madison, 1971) at York; T. F. McIlwraith ("The Logistical Geography of the Great Lakes Grain Trade 1820–1850," Ph.D. diss., University of Wisconsin–Madison, 1973) at Toronto (Erindale), in 1971.

[45] e.g., E. Ehlers, Die agraren Siedlungsgrenzen der Erde: Gedanken zu ihrer Genese und Typologie am Beispiel des Kanadischen Waldlandes (Wiesbaden: Franz Steiner Verlag, Erdkundliches Wissen, vol. 69, 1984); H. Hottenroth, The Great Clay Belts in Ontario and Québec: Struktur und Genese eines Pionier-

universities of London, Oxford, and Edinburgh worked to rather different lasts. Historical cartography was the subject of two theses at the University of London: Marilyn Olsen's M.A. on the mapping of pre-Confederation Ontario, and Richard Ruggles's earlier Ph.D., the first step in a career-long exploration of the cartographic record of the Canadian West from the department of geography at Queen's University.[46] At Oxford and Edinburgh, W. H. Parker and Eric Ross adopted rigid cross-sectional templates for their studies of Lower Canada in 1837 and the Canadian Northwest in 1811; both yielded important publications, among which Ross's carefully crafted *Beyond the River and the Bay* stands as a splendid example of writing "in the style of the times."[47] Both Ross and his fellow Canadian and Edinburgh contemporary John Stager (who wrote on the historical geography of the Mackenzie River valley) returned to university positions in Canada, Stager to the University of British Columbia and Ross to Victoria, Bishop's, and Mount Allison.[48]

In Quebec, by contrast, scholars continued to draw approaches and inspiration from the work of French geographers and historians. Pierre Deffontaines, like Raoul

raumes an der nördlichen Siedlungsgrenze Ost-kanada (Marburg: Marburger Geographische Schriften, no. 39, 1968); K. Lenz, "Entwicklung und Stand der Urbanisierung in Kanada: Eine statistische Analyse," in C. Schott, ed., *Beiträge zur Kulturgeographie von Kanada* (Marburg: Marburger Geographische Schriften, no. 50, 1971); K. Lenz, *Die Prärieprovinzen Kanadas: Der Wandel der Kulturlandschaft von der Kolonisation bis zur Gegenwart unter dem Einfluss der Industrie* (Marburg: Marburger Geographische Schriften, no. 21, 1965); K. Lenz, "Die Grossstädte im Mittleren Westen Kanadas: Ihre Entwicklung und Stellung innerhalb der provinzen, *Geographische Zeitschrift*, vol. 51, 4 (1963) pp. 301–323; C. Schott, *Die kanadischen Marschen* (Kiel: Schriften des Geographischen Instituts der Universität Kiel, vol. 15, 2, 1955); C. Schott, "Wandlungen der landwirtschaft in den Kanadischen Prärieprovinzen," *Tagungsberichte und Wissenschafflichen Abhandlungen des Deutschen Geographentages Essen 1953* (Wiesbaden: Franz Steiner Verlag, 1955). E. Winkler, "Die canadischen Prärieprovinzen in industriellen Umbruch," *Geographica Helvetica*, vol. 7 (1952), pp. 235–249, might also be included here.

[46] M. I. Olsen, "Aspects of the Mapping of Southern Ontario, 1783–1867," Master's thesis, University of London, 1968; R. I. Ruggles, "The Historical Geography and Historical Cartography of the Canadian West, 1670–1795," Ph.D. diss., University of London, 1958. A brief assessment of the culminating achievement of Ruggles's career, *A Country So Interesting: The Hudson's Bay Company and Two Centuries of Mapping, 1670–1870* (Montreal: McGill-Queen's University Press, 1991) is offered in a review by G. Wynn in *B.C. Studies*, no. 94 (1992), pp. 82–85.

[47] W. H. Parker, "The Geography of the Province of Lower Canada in 1837," Ph.D. diss., Oxford University, 1958; E. D. Ross, "The Canadian Northwest in 1811: A Study in the Historical Geography of the Old Northwest of the Fur Trade on the Eve of the First Agricultural Settlement," Ph.D. diss., University of Edinburgh, 1962; E. D. Ross, *Beyond the River and the Bay* (Toronto: University of Toronto Press, 1970).

[48] J. K. Stager, "Historical Geography of the Mackenzie River Valley, 1750–1850," Ph.D. diss., University of Edinburgh, 1962. Both Stager's and Ross's theses were completed under the supervision of J. W. Watson, who had joined the Edinburgh department after working with the Canadian Geographical Branch and establishing the departments of geography at McMaster and Carleton universities. Also at Edinburgh in these years was J. D. Wood, who completed a cross-sectional study of a Scottish region ("The Geography of the Nithsdale-Annandale Region, Dumfriesshire, 1813–1816," Ph.D. diss., University of Edinburgh, 1962) before turning to work on Ontario from Atkinson College, York University. Two other students who embarked on doctoral dissertations on Canadian topics at British universities during the 1960s held university appointments in Canada: J. L. Tyman, who founded the Department of Geography at Brandon University in 1962, completed a study entitled "Historical Geography: The Disposition of Farm Lands in Manitoba," Ph.D. diss., Oxford University, 1971; and W. G. Ross, "Hudson Bay Whaling, 1860–1915," Ph.D. diss., Cambridge University, 1971 (at Bishop's University). G. M. Stubbs completed "Geography of Cultural assimilation in the Prairie Provinces," Ph.D. diss., Oxford University, 1965, but appears to have made no further contribution to the historical literature on Canada.

Blanchard, was born and trained in France but became a frequent sojourner in Quebec; between 1948 and 1952 he was the first professor of geography in the Institute of History and Geography at Laval. Deffontaines played a vital role in developing a distinctive strand of Canadian geography. Writing (as Blanchard had done), in the wake of the great regional monographs contrasting traditional and modern ways of living that were produced by French geographers in the first half of the century, Deffontaines clearly revealed his intellectual debt to Paul Vidal de la Blache with his "Hiver et genres de vie au Canada français," and his larger, later study, *L'homme et l'hiver au Canada.*[49] With the examples of Blanchard and Deffontaines before them, a small number of younger French-Canadian scholars—among them L.-E. Hamelin and L. Beauregard—began to explore aspects of the social geography of, and the spread of settlement in, several parts of early Quebec during the 1950s and 1960s.[50] Yet they did so in a discipline intent upon adapting its French roots to American soil; new emphases, in periglacial studies and upon the North, were being pursued in the classroom and the field. For all the achievements of the first half of the century, the 1960s yielded remarkably few studies of the Quebec past in French; by the end of the next decade, even Louis-Edmond Hamelin was more widely known for his work on the concept of Nordicity than for his numerous studies in historical geography.

New work also began to emerge from the universities of English Canada as geography secured a place in the curriculum alongside other, newly emergent social sciences. In the fifteen years between the establishment of an autonomous department at Toronto and the middle of the century, geographers were appointed in their own, or joint, departments at McMaster (1942), McGill (1945), British Columbia (1946), Western Ontario (1949), and Carleton (1950).[51] Manitoba and Alberta followed

---

[49] P. Deffontaines, "Hiver et genres de vie au Canada français," *Revue canadienne de géographie,* vol. 9, 2 & 3 (1955), pp. 73–91; *L'homme et l'hiver au Canada* (Paris: Gallimard, 1957).

[50] See note 24 above and L.-E. Hamelin, "Émigration rurale à l'échelon paroissial," *Canadian Geographer,* vol. 5 (1955), pp. 53–61; L.-E. Hamelin, "Le population totale de Canada dupuis 1600," *Cahiers de géographie du Québec,* vol. 9, 18 (1965), pp. 159–168; L. Beauregard, "Le peuplement du Richelieu," *Revue de géographie de Montréal,* vol. 19, 182 (1965), pp. 43–74; L. Beauregard, "Les étapes de la mise en valeur agricole de la vallée du Richelieu," *Cahiers de géographie du Québec,* vol. 19, 48 (1970), pp. 171–214; G. Boileau, "Études de peuplement du comté des Deux-Montagnes," Master's thesis, University of Montreal, 1954; G. Boileau, "Évolution démographique de la population rurale dans soixante paroisses de la province de Québec depuis le début du siècle," *Canadian Geographer,* vol. 9, 2 (1957), pp. 49–54; M.-A. Lefebvre, "La genèse et l'évolution du terroir de l'ancienne seigneurie de Nicolet," Ph.D. diss., University of Montreal, 1956.

[51] Dating the beginnings of geography in Canadian universities is a tricky business; single courses were offered before departments were formally established, and geologists, economists, and others inserted the words "geography" or "geographical" into their course descriptions. The dates given here are for the establishment of autonomous departments and/or the appointment of trained geographers. Note that there was a professorship in economic geography at the University of Montreal in 1910, and a joint department of geology and geography existed at the University of British Columbia from 1922. Single courses in commercial or economic geography were taught at Toronto after 1906, and at several universities in the 1920s. H. A. Innis held the title of associate professor of economic geography at the University of Toronto for four years before T. G. Taylor arrived to found the department of geography in 1935. The complexities are further illustrated by the career of J. W. Watson, who graduated with a degree in geography from Edinburgh in 1935, was appointed assistant lecturer in geography at Sheffield, and moved to McMaster as an instructor in 1938. Enrolling concurrently in the Ph.D. program at Toronto under Taylor, he was appointed first professor of geography at McMaster on completion of his doctorate in 1945. Three

suit early in the 1950s, and by 1965 most universities west of the Ottawa River, as well as Memorial University of Newfoundland (1960) had geographers on their faculties. Departments were small by modern-day standards, and especially in the early years faculty members characteristically found themselves teaching a broad spectrum of material. But growing numbers pursued historical-geographical research, and as departments added graduate—initially mainly masters—programs to their curricula, a trickle of historical theses and dissertations grew into a small, steady stream.

Much of this work took its place in a discipline firmly focused on spatial patterns. Little attention was given to the mechanisms of, or reasons for, change. Geographers produced virtually no analyses of human impacts upon the natural environment or of European-Indian contacts. They were little interested in the intellectual contexts out of which patterns and landscapes were created. Through the 1950s, cross-sectional studies were common. So too were articles and theses devoted to discussions of population distributions and settlement patterns, land-use changes, and past and present patterns of regional economic activity.[52] To be sure, there were distinctions to be made between departments in the ways in which historical geography was conceived and in the types of work undertaken in different parts of the country. Settlement studies, in the vein of those produced by Blanchard, began to appear from the University of Montreal early in the 1950s. At McGill, most students worked at the regional scale, producing historical geographies of the St. Maurice and Saguenay valleys, of Brome County, of Southeastern Quebec, and the Lesser Slave Lake area, among others.[53] A strong local emphasis marked work at the universities of Alberta, British Columbia, Manitoba, and Western Ontario as the first generation of graduate students in geography set out to chart the basic lineaments of development in their regions. Indeed the handful of historical theses completed at the University of Manitoba before 1967 well exemplify the wider pattern; topics included the relationships between settlement and the physical environment of the West Lake area; population and economic activity in the Red River valley; an analysis of the areal growth and functional development of Winnipeg; historical geographies of the Red River set-

---

years later he moved to Carleton, where his wife, Jessie, also an Edinburgh graduate, had been appointed the first full-time lecturer in geography. The details of the development of geography at Toronto can be found in the Cody, Falconer, and Mavor Papers in the University Archives and Rare Books Collections. The Falconer Papers (box 118) reveal that Innes advocated the appointment of Taylor in March 1929. These developments are also treated in M. Sanderson, *Griffith Taylor: Antarctic Scientist and Pioneer Geographer* (Ottawa: Carleton University Press, 1988), pp. 118, 128–143, 145–173.

[52] See for examples T. L. Hills, "The St. Francis to Chaudière, 1830," *Canadian Geographer*, vol. 1, 6 (1955), pp. 27–38; J. D. Wood, "The Stage is Set: Dumfries Township 1816," *Waterloo Historical Society Annual Volume*, vol. 48 (1960), pp. 40–50; W. H. Parker, "Quebec City in the 1830s," *Cahiers de géographie du Québec*, vol. 6 (1959), pp. 261–273; J. H. Warkentin, "Western Canada in 1886," *Papers Read before the Historical and Scientific Society of Manitoba*, sec. 3, vol. 20 (1963–1964), pp. 85–116; J. H. Warkentin, "Late Nineteenth Century Geographic Patterns on the Canadian Prairies," *Monograph*, vol. 3 (1965–1966), pp. 14–29.

[53] P. E. Uren, "The Historical Geography of the St. Maurice Valley," Master's thesis, McGill University, 1949; M. Johnston, "The Historical Geography of the Saguenay River Valley," Master's thesis, McGill University, 1950; J. D. Booth, "An Historical Geography of Brome County, 1800–1911," Master's thesis, McGill University 1966; G. C. Merrill, "The Human Geography of the Lesser Slave Lake Area of Central Alberta," Master's thesis, McGill University, 1953; Hills, "The St. Francis to the Chaudière."

tlement and the Interlake area; and a study of Manitoba agriculture.[54] At the University of Toronto, work in historical geography had ranged more widely in space, scale, and approach in the two decades since Wreford Watson's study of the Niagara peninsula. Studies of Edmonton, of the Dauphin and Fort Smith areas, and of Mennonite settlement in Manitoba had been completed alongside cross-sectional and crop-distribution studies of parts of Ontario, and a tightly focused analysis of accessibility and rural land use along Yonge Street, an important route into the Toronto backcountry.[55] From British Columbia to McGill, however, there was growing recognition of the importance of original documents to historical geographical enquiry, and a clear sense of the potential inherent in geographical approaches to the past.

Ironically enough, these signs of a growing commitment to careful, archivally based study among geographers interested in the Canadian past came just as English-Canadian historians began to abandon the broad, essentially economic and geographic conceptualizations that had given the natural environment so significant a place in their works. Instead, they turned to biography and political history, in part because these topics (and the "great men" approach to the past that they encouraged) seemed particularly germane in the context of the Cold War, and in part specifically to differentiate their work from that of the political economists in fear that not to do so would undermine the autonomy of their discipline.[56] By the late 1950s, the natural environment seemed irrelevant to most of the work of Canadian historians. Disciplinary specialization and the growing fragmentation of academic inquiry had set history and geography further asunder than ever.

---

[54] W. J. Carlyle, "The Relationship between Settlement and the Physical Environment in Part of the West Lake Area of Manitoba from 1878 to 1963," Master's thesis, University of Manitoba, 1965; J. Clarke, "Population and Economic Activity: A Geographical and Historical Analysis, Based upon Selected Censuses of the Red River Valley in the Period 1832 to 1856," Master's thesis, University of Manitoba, 1967; H. A. Hosse, "Areal Growth and Functional Development of Winnipeg 1870–1913," Master's thesis, University of Manitoba, 1956; B. Kaye, "Some Aspects of the Historical Geography of the Red River Settlement from 1812 to 1870," Master's thesis, University of Manitoba, 1967; J. M. Richtik, "A Historical Geography of the Interlake Area of Manitoba from 1870 to 1921," Master's thesis, University of Manitoba, 1964; R. C. Fordham, "The Structure of Manitoba's Agricultural Geography 1951–1964," Master's thesis, University of Manitoba, 1966.

[55] O. D. Jones, "The Historical Geography of Edmonton, Alberta," Master's thesis, University of Toronto, 1963; J. H. Warkentin, "The Geography of the Dauphin Area," Master's thesis, University of Toronto, 1954; J. G. McConnell, "The Fort Smith Area 1780 to 1961: A Historical Geography," Master's thesis, University of Toronto, 1966; J. H. Warkentin, "The Mennonite Settlements of Southern Manitoba," Ph.D. diss., University of Toronto, 1960; Jackson, "Geographical Study of Early Settlement in Ontario"; J. D. Wood, "The Historical Geography of Dumfries Township, Upper Canada, 1816–1852," Master's thesis, University of Toronto, 1958; J. Retallack, "The Changing Distribution of Wheat in Southern Ontario, 1850–1880," Master's thesis, University of Toronto, 1966; J. H. Horner, "Changing Spatial Patterns in the Production and Utilization of Milk in Southern Ontario, 1910–1961," Master's thesis, University of Toronto, 1967; T. F. McIlwraith, Jr., "Accessibility and Rural Land Utilization in the Yonge Street Area of Upper Canada," Master's thesis, University of Toronto, 1966.

[56] P. Novick, *That Noble Dream: The "Objectivity Question" and the American Historical Profession* (New York: Cambridge University Press, 1988); D. G. Creighton, "Presidential Address," *Canadian Historical Association, Annual Report* (1957), p. 3. I thank Marlene Shore for insightful comments that led me to this point. For the political economy approach, see R. Whitaker, " 'Confused Alarms of Struggle and Flight': English Canadian Political Science in the 1970s," *Canadian Historical Review*, vol. 60, 1 (1979), pp. 1–18.

The roots, intellectual tensions, and conceptual limitations of English-Canadian historical geography during these years are remarkably well illustrated in the work of its leading practitioner, Andrew H. Clark.[57] Born in Manitoba, of migrant Maritime stock, Clark came to geography by a circuitous, but quintessentially Canadian path. Educated at Brandon Collegiate Institute and Brandon College (where he completed the course work for a McMaster University B.A. in 1930), he was employed during the depression as an actuarial assistant with a Toronto insurance company. In 1935 he joined the newly established geography department of the University of Toronto as "student, instructor and general factotum." There he encountered Harold Adams Innis, and worked closely with Griffith Taylor. From them he heard that physical environments defined and shaped patterns of human existence, and learned the value of field study; a summer of field reconnaissance in western Europe and North Africa with Taylor in 1938 was the culmination of his geographical apprenticeship.

Clark then entered the doctoral program at Berkeley under the supervision of Carl Sauer. His plans for a study of Nova Scotia were derailed by the offer of a faculty position in the newly established department of geography at the University of Canterbury, New Zealand, and it was there that Clark completed his first substantial work in historical geography. This account of cultural transfer and landscape modification clearly reflected Sauer's interests in diffusion and environmental change.[58] It was a remarkable piece of work—for the speed with which it was completed, and the landmark contribution that it made to New Zealand scholarship, as well as for its embrace of change and its clear argument (essentially contrary to the teachings of Griffith Taylor) that people had an enormous capacity to transform places. It was also likely the focus of considerable discussion between Clark and his colleagues in the small New Zealand geographical fraternity. Although an adequate history of these formative years in New Zealand geography remains to be written, the growing purchase of Hartshorne's definition of the subject in that country seems clear enough. Kenneth B. Cumberland, a British-trained scholar, and colleague of Clark's at Canterbury, for example, turned from work on the transition from natural to cultural vegetation and soil erosion in New Zealand in the early 1940s to espouse a view of geography as areal differentiation by 1946. Similarly, a student in the Canterbury department in the mid-1940s recalls the relief with which he and his peers found a "true" definition of geography in Hartshorne's work.[59]

---

[57] The fullest appraisal of Clark's career is D. W. Meinig, "Prologue: Andrew Hill Clark, Historical Geographer," in J. R. Gibson, ed., *European Settlement and North American Development* (Toronto: University of Toronto Press, 1978), pp. 3–26.

[58] "The South Island of New Zealand: A Geographical Study of the Introduction and Modification of British Rural Patterns and Practices Associated with the Exotic Plants and Animals of the Island," Ph.D. diss., University of California–Berkeley, 1944; this was published as *The Invasion of New Zealand by People, Plants, and Animals* (New Brunswick, N.J.: Rutgers University Press, 1949).

[59] Cumberland's changing views can be inferred from his "A Century's Change: Natural to Cultural Vegetation in New Zealand," *Geographical Review*, vol. 31 (1941), pp. 529–554; *Soil Erosion in New Zealand: A Geographical Reconnaissance* (Wellington: Soil Conservation and Rivers Control Council, 1944); "The Geographer's Point of View," an inaugural lecture delivered on 2 April 1946 at Auckland Uni-

Returning to North America to lecture air force cadets in meteorology and to work for the U.S. State Department before taking up a faculty position at Rutgers University in 1946, Clark soon began again to probe the Maritime past. In retrospect, his initial efforts seem halting and uncertain. Shortly after his appointment at Rutgers, he drew upon his earlier interest in the Canadian Maritime provinces to reflect on the effects of insularity on Prince Edward Island and New Zealand.[60] Then he turned back to Nova Scotia. In addresses to historians and others he began to outline his views of historical geography. Initially, he presented it as a retrospective enterprise and justified his study of the past as a key to the present. Working on what he described as "the origins and development of patterns and practices of land use in Maritime Canada," he saw his enquiries elucidating the nature of the present cultural rural landscape. His role was to decide where techniques and patterns originated and to offer "explanations . . . of the present situation."[61] He stressed his interest in the "transference of agricultural and pastoral patterns and practices" from old world to new, and later described his aspiration to understand "changes in regional character, viewed geographically," associated with European settlement overseas.[62] Periodically, as in presentations to the Association of American Geographers, and the history department in the University of Toronto, he drew examples from the record of settlement in the Maritime provinces to exorcise the old demon of environmental determinism.[63] Then, after moving to the University of Wisconsin in the early 1950s, he turned to the notebooks of an extraordinary botanist and surveyor to draw a picture (in essence a cross section) of Nova Scotia at the beginning of the nineteenth century.[64] Five years later, Prince Edward Island was the focus of Clark's second book—the first, and for five years the only, English-language monograph in Canadian historical geography written by a Canadian.[65]

Three Centuries and the Island was as much a methodological tract as a study of Prince Edward Island. It was, quite simply, Clark's attempt to reconcile his interest in

---

versity College, Auckland; and "American Geography: Review and Commentary," *New Zealand Geographer*, vol. 11 (1955), pp. 184–185. The student of the 1940s was Murray McCaskill. See his "Growing Up in New Zealand Geography," in P. G. Holland and W. B. Johnston, eds., *Southern Approaches: Geography in New Zealand* (Christchurch: New Zealand Geographical Society, 1987), pp. 25–32. M. M. Roche, "Andrew Clark and Soil Conservation in New Zealand," *Historical Geography*, vol. 21, 1 (1991), pp. 7–8, throws additional light on Clark's initial intentions, which seem to have turned on an assessment of land use and productivity "from Maori times to the present."

[60] A. H. Clark, "South Island, New Zealand, and Prince Edward Island, Canada: A Study in Insularity," *New Zealand Geographer*, vol. 3, 2 (1947), pp. 137–150.

[61] A. H. Clark, "The Origins and Development of Pattern and Practices of Land Use in Maritime Canada," Typescript with emendations, late 1948, Clark Papers MG1, vol. 1517, no. 7, Public Archives of Nova Scotia (PANS).

[62] A. H. Clark, "The Rationale of Historical Geography," Address to the University of Toronto History Department, 1951(?), Clark Papers, MG1, vol. 1517, no. 10, Public Archives of Nova Scotia.

[63] A. H. Clark, "Legend and Fact in Historical Geography: An Illustration from Nova Scotia," abstract in *Annals of the Association of American Geographers*, vol. 38, 1 (1948), pp. 85–88.

[64] Clark, "Titus Smith Junior."

[65] A. H. Clark, *Three Centuries and the Island: A Historical Geography of Settlement and Agriculture in Prince Edward Island, Canada* (Toronto: University of Toronto Press, 1959).

change with Hartshorne's narrow view of historical geography as thin sections of the past. The solution presented in *Three Centuries* had already been outlined in abstract terms when Clark enjoined historical geographers to see geographies as "continually changing entities" and to study "the past circumstances of, or . . . changes in, phenomena of concern to geography."[66] Now it was elaborated in a book heavy with maps that summarized the spatial patterns of phenomena and provided "skeletonized frameworks" of "instantaneous cross-sections of area." These confirmed the work's geographical pedigree. But additional maps and discussions of change added an interpretive element, and allowed Clark to claim that the changing distributions of people, crops, and livestock on the island had been "studied as dynamic rather than static entities."

As *Three Centuries* appeared, Hartshorne conceded Clark's point. In his *Perspective on the Nature of Geography*, also published in 1959, he recognized that he had drawn the boundaries between history and geography too categorically in 1939. The distinction between the two fields was not absolute, but they showed clear "difference[s] in purpose and emphasis." Although the difficulties of presenting change over space and time were large, the challenge might be met "by selecting a relatively small region of restricted variation in area and affected by a limited number of factors producing historical change."[67]

Through the 1960s, Clark's work, and that of most other historical geographers writing on Canadian topics in English, fell within the niche opened by the debates of the 1950s. In retrospect this was a considerable opening, at least in terms of the numbers of practicing historical geographers and the range of geographical publications on the Canadian past.[68] By 1970, several universities ran large and productive graduate programs in historical geography. Counting faculty and students from the University of Toronto and York University together, Toronto may have had the largest single concentration of historical geographers in North America.[69]

---

[66] A. H. Clark, "Historical Geography," in P. F. James and C. F. Jones, eds., *American Geography: Inventory and Prospect* (Syracuse: Syracuse University Press for the Association of American Geographers, 1954), pp. 72–73; and "Geographical Change: A Theme for Economic History," *Journal of Economic History*, vol. 20, 4 (1960), pp. 607–616.

[67] R. Hartshorne, *Perspective on the Nature of Geography* (Chicago: Rand McNally and Co. for the Association of American Geographers, 1959).

[68] This guide identifies some 300 items published in the 1950s and 1960s; not all were by formally trained geographers, but most were, and the total is almost double that for work published before 1950. There were also several score graduate theses.

[69] The mark of Wisconsin was well evident in these two universities, with Cole Harris, Jim Lemon, and Tom McIlwraith at Toronto, and Roy Merrens, Jim Gibson, and Skip Ray (all students of Andrew Clark) at York. Harris would soon move to the University of British Columbia, but his position was filled by Aidan McQuillan, another Wisconsin graduate. Grant Head, the eighth student of Clark's to hold a faculty position in Canada, was at Waterloo Lutheran (later Wilfrid Laurier) University; other historical geographers at York and Toronto were: at York, John Warkentin (Ph.D. Toronto, 1960), Jim Cameron (Ph.D. Glasgow, 1971), David Wood (Ph.D. Edinburgh, 1962), Conrad Heidenreich (Ph.D. McMaster, 1970), and John Radford (Ph.D. Clark, with interests in U.S. cities); Roy Wolfe (Ph.D. Toronto, 1956) and J. U. Marshall (Ph.D. Toronto, 1968) may not have described themselves thus but they also produced several historical items listed in the guide; so, too, at Toronto, where Don Kerr (Ph.D. Toronto, 1950) and Jacob

Taken as a whole, the much-expanded corpus of work produced by this small battalion of scholars was overwhelmingly regional, heavily empirical, and largely devoted to the elucidation of spatial patterns (especially of economic activity). It was also, generally, quite distinct from the work produced by historians, in that it paid little attention to individuals, ideas, and the complexities of human societies. Quite typically, Clark's monumental study of early Acadia, which appeared in 1968, was replete with detail and rich in information about settlement patterns and techniques of dyke-building, but conspicuously failed to raise questions about the connections between labor requirements, landholding patterns, and kin ties.[70]

That Clark considered such questions to lie beyond the pale of legitimate geographical inquiry surely owed something to his training and temperament; but it also reflected the straitjacket of Hartshornian orthodoxy. In Innis's empiricism and suspicion of broad generalization, Clark found support for his own inclination toward "scholarly prudence." And neither Innis's view of the past ("filled," according to one commentator, "with beaver and cod rather than people") nor the static "superorganic" conception of culture that Clark encountered at Berkeley encouraged him to recognize the shifting nuances and complexities of ideas, groups, and societies.[71]

But the tenor of geographical inquiry in the 1950s and 1960s was set by the quest for legitimacy within the pantheon of social science and all that flowed from it, including a desire to establish the distinctiveness of geography by claiming a unique subject matter, identifying a characteristic methodology, and patrolling the perimeters of the discipline. In consequence, Clark's work, like most historical geographical writing on Canada during these years, was more evidently geographical than historical. Struggling to hold a place for their subject in a discipline focused on the study of areal differentiation, distance and space, its authors largely ignored the fact, recognized by generations of historians, that the essential task and fascination of historical scholarship lay in telling the story of people struggling with their circumstances.[72] Although Clark had made the study of change a central tenet of historical geography,

---

Spelt (Ph.D. Utrecht, 1955) had broadly historical interests and Jock Galloway (Ph.D. London, 1965) pursued work in Latin America. Among graduate students in these programs who made continuing contributions to historical geography in Canada during the 1970s were, at Toronto, Peter Ennals, Gunter Gad, Leonard Guelke, Graeme Wynn; at York, Michael Doucet. Others at Toronto at this period included Denis Cosgrove, Helen Parson, and Cecil Houston (then working on the Soviet Union); John Mannion, whose thesis was defended in 1971, had earlier left Toronto for a position at Memorial University.

[70] A. H. Clark, *Acadia: The Geography of Early Nova Scotia to 1760* (Madison, Wis.: University of Wisconsin Press, 1968).

[71] Whitaker, "'Confused Alarms of Struggle and Flight,'" p. 3; J. S. Duncan, "The Superorganic in American Cultural Geography," *Annals of the Association of American Geographers*, vol. 70, 2 (1980), pp. 181–198.

[72] Even J. W. Watson, poet and most historically, socially, and culturally inclined geographer of his time in Canada, echoed the disciplinary pressures of the 1950s; see his "Geography: A Discipline in Distance," *Scottish Geographical Magazine*, vol. 71, 1 (1955), pp. 1–13. Among many examples of historians arguing the importance of the latter point, see B. Bailyn, "The Challenge of Modern Historiography," *American Historical Review*, vol. 87, 1 (1982), pp. 1–24; and M. Bloch, *The Historian's Craft* (New York: Vintage Books, 1953), p. 26.

most of its practitioners were content simply to embrace the passage of time, and rarely grappled with the processes that transformed societies and environments.

Ironically, the characteristic concerns of historical geographers rapidly came to appear dated and divorced from the preoccupations of most of their colleagues in the 1960s. As the philosophical tenets of logical positivism took hold across the social sciences, many geographers turned away from the regional studies that Hartshorne had regarded as the capstones of the discipline to pursue the development and identification of distinctive spatial laws. In these tumultuous times, Clark's *Acadia* became a lightning rod in a gathering storm of criticism directed at historical geography. Although the American Historical Association recognized it as the best historical study on Canada published in 1968, both the book, and the field that its author had done so much to establish, were savaged in some geographical reviews. One especially acerbic critic indicted Clark's work for its failure to offer more than "the clearest possible record of what had happened." With the much-heralded quantitative and behavioral revolutions pointing the way to a brave new world of scientific geography, the study of geographical change was dismissed as a cul-de-sac. As the old classificatory tradition of geography was swept aside by a "model-based" paradigm, "orthodox doctrines . . . ceased to carry conviction." Inductive methodologies and the principles of historical scholarship were declared irrelevant to the task of understanding geographical change. Narrative accounts were derided for offering no more than "loose, weakly explanatory, non-rigorous modes of temporal explanation." By failing to adopt the conceptual frameworks and techniques embraced by other geographers, historical geography was on the verge of becoming, in the exuberant metaphor of one of its most vigorous detractors, a beast with the familial expectations of a mule.[73]

Mule or Phoenix? Canadian Historical Geography since 1970

Amid the widespread ensuing meditations on, and reconsiderations of, the place of the past in geography, heralds read the banns of a new union between historical geography and (quantitative) theory. From this liaison, they anticipated, would come dynamic, stochastic models of spatial development over time, a past illuminated by the "retrogressive application of concepts and theories," and studies of "imagined worlds of the past"—of the ways in which people had perceived earlier environments—that would allow historical geography to "find a secure and relevant place in contemporary developments in the subject as a whole."[74] Within Canada,

[73] W. A. Koelsch, "Review of Acadia," *Economic Geography*, vol. 46 (1970), pp. 201–202; M. J. Bowden, "Review of C. T. Smith, *An Historical Geography of Western Europe before 1800* (New York: Frederick A. Praeger, 1967)," in *Economic Geography*, vol. 46 (1970), pp. 202–203; A. R. H. Baker et al., "The Future of the Past," *Area* (1969); A. R. H. Baker, "Rethinking Historical Geography," in *Progress in Historical Geography*, pp. 11–28.

[74] J. H. C. Patten, "The Past and Geography Reconsidered," *Area*, vol. 3 (1970), pp. 37–39; P. M. Koroscil, "Historical Geography: A Resurrection," *Journal of Geography*, vol. 70, 7 (1971), pp. 415–420; Baker, "Rethinking Historical Geography"; R. J. Chorley, "The Role and Relations of Physical Geography," *Progress in Geography*, vol. 3 (1971), p. 97.

the first examples of work in this vein began to appear in the mid-1960s and found their most notable champion in William Norton during the following decade.[75]

In *Historical Analysis in Geography*, an extended commentary on the field published in 1984, Norton identified work on the evolution of spatial form as one of three significant strands of historical geographical inquiry, alongside studies of geographical change (identified with Andrew Clark) and investigations of landscape development (associated with Carl Sauer). In this exegesis, the quantitative, logical-positivist emphases of spatial form analysis are conspicuous, as they are in the cluster of articles and theses devoted to "the temporal . . . analysis of process to form relationships," making up the Canadian segment of this literature (to which Norton himself has made several substantive contributions). In most of this work, the specification and formal testing of hypotheses, the explicit use of theoretical constructs, and the application of mathematical techniques to simulate (or to generate models of) spatial forms are characteristic.[76] Among examplars of the genre might be recognized Norton's simulation analysis of agricultural settlement patterns in Upper Canada, Peter Goheen's study of Victorian Toronto, and Randy Smith's study of the urban system of Southern Ontario.[77] Enquiry in this vein continues in the 1990s, but it has never assumed the dominance anticipated by its advocates of two decades ago.

Far from carrying the day, the new prescriptions for historical geography formulated to meet criticisms of the field in the 1960s prompted introspection and vigorous counterargument. Early in the 1970s, two geographers from the University of

[75] For early examples see C. J. B. Wood, "Human Settlement in the Long Point Region, 1790–1825," Master's thesis, McMaster University, 1966; C. F. J. Whebell, "Corridors: A Theory of Urban Systems, "*Annals of the Association of American Geographers*, vol. 59, 1 (1969), pp. 1–26; D. W. Moodie, "Content Analysis: A Method for Historical Geography," *Area*, vol. 4 (1969), pp. 146–149; R. I. Ruggles, "The West of Canada in 1763: Imagination and Reality," *Canadian Geographer*, vol. 15, 3 (1971), pp. 235–261; J. Clarke, "Spatial Variations in Population Density: Southwestern Ontario in 1851," in W. P Adams and F. M. Helleiner, eds., *International Geography* (Toronto: University of Toronto Press, 1972); R. Hayward, "Content Analysis in Historical Geography: A Case Study in Immigration in Toronto to 1847," Master's thesis, Queen's University, 1972; D. Janelle, "Scale Components in the Descriptive Analysis of Urban Land Use Change: London, Ontario, 1850–1960," *Ontario Geography*, vol. 7 (1972), pp. 66–68.

[76] Examples are J. D. Wood, "Simulating Pre-Census Population Distribution," *Canadian Geographer*, vol. 18, 3 (1974), pp. 250–264; W. Norton, "The Process of Rural Land Occupation in Upper Canada," *Scottish Geographical Magazine*, vol. 91, 3 (1975), pp. 145–152; W. Norton, "Process and Form Relationships: An Example from Historical Geography," *Professional Geographer*, vol. 30, 2 (1978), pp. 128–134; W. Norton, "Constructing Abstract Worlds of the Past," *Geographical Analysis*, vol. 8, 3 (1976), pp. 269–288; W. Norton, "Some Comments on Late Nineteenth Century Agriculture in Areas of European Overseas Expansion," *Ontario History*, vol. 74, 2 (1982), pp. 113–117; W. Norton and E. C. Conkling, "Land-Use Theory and the Pioneering Economy," *Geografiska annaler*, vol. 56B (1974), pp. 44–56; L. H. Russwurm and B. Thakur, "Hierarchical and Functional Stability and Change in a Strongly Urbanizing Area of Southwestern Ontario, 1871–1971," *Canadian Geographer*, vol. 25, 2 (1981), pp. 149–166; M. H. Yeates, "The Core/Periphery Model and Urban Development in Central Canada," *Urban Geography*, vol. 6, 2 (1985), pp. 101–121; J. P. Wiesinger, "Modelling the Agricultural Settlement Process of Southern Manitoba, 1872–1891: Some Implications for Settlement Theory," *Prairie Forum*, vol. 10, 1 (1985), pp. 83–104.

[77] W. Norton, "Agricultural Settlement Patterns in Upper Canada, 1782–1851: A Simulation Analysis," Ph.D. diss., McMaster University, 1973; P. G. Goheen, *Victorian Toronto, 1850 to 1900: Pattern and Process of Growth* (Chicago: University of Chicago Department of Geography Research Paper no. 127, 1970); R. W. Smith, *Aspects of Growth in a Regional Urban System: Southern Ontario, 1851–1921* (North York: York University, Atkinson College Geographical Monographs, no. 12, 1982).

Toronto took issue with current arguments—forcefully put in a department at the forefront of the quantitative and logical positivist "revolutions" in Canada—for the development of a theoretical geography devoted to the study of spatial relations. Graduate student Leonard Guelke, pursuing doctoral research on early Dutch settlement in South Africa, argued that human geography's "much vaunted" theoretical turn had promised far more than it could deliver. Although it adopted a deductive-nomological definition of explanation (or the probabilistic form thereof), its methods were but "a pale shadow of the scientific procedure employed in the physical sciences." Its models and theories were not generally capable of empirical verification. Human behavior could not be reduced to sets of laws. In their haste to distance themselves from traditional, subjective—and admittedly not always compelling—regional geography, advocates of the new approaches had achieved internal consistency but lost their grip on reality. The geographer's essential task, maintained Guelke, was to describe and understand the real world.[78]

At the same time, Cole Harris worried that definitions of geography as a formal deductive science might so discount the value of geographical synthesis as to cut the subject off from the valuable insights to be drawn from intelligent reflection on the relationships between people and place, culture and environment. Arguing, with philosopher Louis Mink, that understanding was not dependent on an explicit positivist methodology, but that it could come "from a form of thinking dependent on wide experience, memory, imagination, on the habit of seeing things together, of reflecting on experience," Harris insisted on the value of studies directed to the development of a "synthesizing understanding [of particular regions, places, landscapes, or themes] analogous to that in history." Rather than concede ground to critics of the field, he insisted on the stubbornness of the historical geographical mule, and expressed optimism that the future would "reveal its fertility to even the most skeptical."[79]

In the two decades since, geographical writing on the Canadian past has flourished. As a new generation of geographers conceived their subject in more "humanistic" terms than those offered by the orthodoxies of areal differentiation and spatial science, geography became a strikingly pluralistic discipline. Methods and

[78] L. Guelke, "Problems of Scientific Explanation in Geography," *Canadian Geographer*, vol. 15, 1 (1971), pp. 38–53. Guelke has continued to extend, elaborate, and refine his position through the years: see especially his "An Idealist Alternative in Historical Geography," *Annals of the Association of American Geographers*, vol. 64, 2 (1974), pp. 193–202; "On Rethinking Historical Geography," *Area*, vol. 7, 2 (1975), pp. 135–138; *Historical Understanding in Geography: An Idealist Approach* (Cambridge: Cambridge University Press, 1982).

[79] C. Harris, "Reflections on the Fertility of the Historical Geographical Mule," University of Toronto Discussion Paper no. 10 (November 1970); the central arguments of this paper appeared in "Theory and Synthesis in Historical Geography," *Canadian Geographer*, vol. 15, 3 (1971), pp. 157–172. Harris, too, continued to defend the essence of this position: see his "The Historical Mind and the Practice of Geography," in D. Ley and M. Samuels, eds., *Humanistic Geography: Problems and Prospects* (Chicago: Maroufa Press, 1978). Other contributions to this debate by Canadian historical geographers include D. W. Moodie and J. C. Lehr, "Fact and Theory in Historical Geography," *Professional Geographer*, vol. 28, 2 (1976), pp. 132–135.

philosophies were borrowed from many sources. Interests proliferated and spread. To some the subject now seems diffuse and unbound. Earlier concerns about identity and definition have largely disappeared. Few currently question the "geographical-ness" (or ungeographicalness) of particular pieces of work. Geography has become what geographers do.

In this context, there is far more openness to contextual studies and interpretive, hermeneutic methodologies than there was twenty years ago. Historical geographers in Canada have responded to these circumstances by adopting a wide spectrum of approaches to the task of understanding a strikingly diverse range of topics and data. One consequence has been a blurring of the distinctions between historical geography and a significant amount of historical writing in other fields. As their discipline turned to address more social questions, some historical geographers began to incorporate the ideas of historical sociologists into their work. One expression of this, drawing inspiration also from the literature on British cities and the Marxist tradition in Western scholarship, has been a stronger interest in questions of social and economic class and its manifestations than is perhaps characteristic of the historical-geographical literature on the United States.[80]

As geographers left behind the rigid orthodoxy of spatial science, historians—whose own field had bifurcated far beyond its political-biographical core to encompass a wide range of specializations (such as social, labor, urban, and recently even environmental history)—found their work more familiar and more interesting. Thus there has been a considerable degree of cross-fertilization between the two scholarly communities—a fact attested by the appreciable number of works by Canadian historians that find a place in this guide.

In Quebec, too, a new generation of historians and historical geographers began to examine their society's past through new, and often shared, lenses in the 1970s. Raised during Quebec's "Quiet Revolution"—when the old alliance of church and state was swept aside by the forces of modernization and secularization unleashed by the prosperity that came from the sale of natural resources to American markets after World War II—they generally rejected earlier identifications of Catholicism and

---

[80] Examples of work explicitly addressed to questions of class include R. D. Lewis, *The Segregated City: Residential Differentiation by Class and Occupation in Montreal, 1861–1901* (Montreal: McGill University Department of Geography, Shared Spaces/Partage de l'espace, no. 3, 1986); Q. T. Thach, *Social Class and Residential Mobility: The Case of the Irish in Montreal, 1851 to 1871* (Montreal: McGill University Department of Geography, Shared Spaces/Partage de l'espace, no. 1, 1985); R. D. Lewis "The Segregated City: Class, Residential Patterns, and the Development of Industrial Districts in Montreal, 1861 and 1901," *Journal of Urban History*, vol. 17, 1 (1991), pp. 123–152; R. Harris, B. Osborne, and G. Levine, "Housing Tenure and Social Classes in Kingston, Ontario, 1881–1901," *Journal of Historical Geography*, vol. 7, 3 (1981), pp. 271–289; G. J. Levine, "Class, Ethnicity, and Property Transfers in Montreal, 1907–1909," *Journal of Historical Geography*, vol. 14, 4 (1988), pp. 360–380; R. Harris, "Working-Class Home Ownership and Housing Affordability across Canada in 1931," *Histoire sociale/Social History*, vol. 19, 37 (1986), pp. 121–138; R. Harris, "Residential Segregation and Class Formation in Canadian Cities: A Critical Review," *Canadian Geographer*, vol. 28, 2 (1984), pp. 186–196; R. S. Harris, "A Political Chameleon: Class Segregation in Kingston, Ontario, 1961–1976," *Annals of the Association of American Geographers*, vol. 74, 3 (1984), pp. 454–476; D. Hiebert, "The Geography of Jewish Immigrants and the Garment Industry in Toronto, 1908–1913: A Study of Ethnic and Class Relations," Ph.D. diss., University of Toronto, 1987.

rural life, or what historian Michel Brunet termed *messianisme, anti-étatisme, and agriculturalisme*, as the foundations of Quebec's distinctiveness.[81] Instead they turned attention to economic, political, and social structures, downplayed the importance of such events as the English conquest of New France in 1760, and found in nineteenth- and twentieth-century Quebec an urbanizing, industrializing, class-divided society, rather like others of the time. Even its rural dwellers were far from the devout, homogeneous, backward peasants of earlier interpretations; capitalism had reached into the countryside, farmers were connected to distant markets, and there were clear differences in their material circumstances.[82] Much of this work draws upon European models, especially those offered by the French *Annales* school, and the Marxian theoretical tradition, and this has tended to differentiate it from most English Canadian historical geography. It is also distinctive for the close relationships it has fostered between history and geography. Several prominent Quebec historians have active links with the vigorous center of historical geographical research developed by Serge Courville at Laval University in the 1980s, and some excellent studies by historians might be considered historical geographies in all but name.[83]

Taken as a whole, however, the Canadian literature in historical geography is far from amorphous. It has grown between the mainstreams of historical and geographical writing about Canada and has developed a handful of characteristic concerns: the organization of space; the modification of environments; the look of the land; the ways in which people have made sense of their settings and conducted themselves within them; the development of community, region, and nation. More than this it remains close to the ground. Its most common scales of inquiry are close to those at which lives were lived, and the majority of its most productive practitioners are clearly identified with particular regions of the country that they have "made their own" through sustained, intensive investigation.[84]

---

[81] Michel Brunet, "Trois dominantes de la pensée canadienne-française: l'agriculturalisme, l'anti-étatisme, et le messianisme" in his *La présence anglaise et les Canadiens* (Montreal: Beauchemin, 1958), pp. 113–166. The essential argument of this paragraph rests upon Ronald Rudin, "Revisionism and the Search for a Normal Society: A Critique of Recent Quebec Historical Writing," *Canadian Historical Review*, vol. 73, 1 (1992), pp. 30–57.

[82] N. Seguin and S. Courville, *Rural Life in Nineteenth Century Quebec* (Ottawa: Canadian Historical Association, 1989); S. Courville, *Entre ville et campagne: L'essor du village dans les seigneuries du Bas-Canada* (Quebec: Presses de l'Université Laval, 1990); L. Dechêne, *Habitants et marchands de Montréal au XVIIe siècle* (Paris: Plon, 1974); Allan Greer, *Peasant, Lord, and Merchant: Rural Society in Three Quebec Parishes, 1740–1840* (Toronto: University of Toronto Press, 1985).

[83] Serge Courville continues to work closely with historians Jean-Claude Robert, Normand Seguin, and others: see for example the collaboration of the first three on "La vallée du Saint-Laurent à l'époque du rapport Durham: Économie et société," *Journal of Canadian Studies*, vol. 25, 1 (1990), pp. 78–95; for a fine example of a "historical geography" written by historians see R. Hardy and N. Seguin, *Forêt et société en Mauricie* (Montreal: Éditions du Boréal Express, 1984).

[84] So in alphabetical order, and without pretense at completeness, Alan Brunger might be associated with ethnic settlement patterns in Ontario and the Peterborough region; John Clarke has written extensively on Essex County, Ontario; Serge Courville can be identified with the St. Lawrence valley in the nineteenth century; Conrad Heidenreich with Huronia and early Canadian cartography; and Jock Lehr with Ukrainian settlement on the Prairies. John Mannion's particular turf is Irish Newfoundland; Wayne

Most of these distinctive characteristics were evident—at least in bud—in *Canada before Confederation*, which Andrew Clark described as a "new kind of study of geographical change." Published in 1974, it reflected its genesis in the late 1960s and early 1970s, as well as the interests and concerns of its joint authors, Cole Harris and John Warkentin. A native of British Columbia, and a graduate of the joint honors program in history and geography at the University of British Columbia, Harris completed a Ph.D. on the seigneurial regime in early Canada with Andrew Clark at Wisconsin in the early 1960s and taught at the University of Toronto through the remainder of that decade before returning to British Columbia. Born in Manitoba, Warkentin completed M.A. (1954) and Ph.D. (1960) theses on his native province at the University of Toronto and pursued research interests in the exploration and settlement of the western interior (while maintaining a broad concern with the development of Canada as a whole) from York University in Toronto. Arguing that history and geography shared a common interest in synthesis, Harris and Warkentin insisted that historical geographers had the same interests as other geographers "except that they tend[ed] to ask questions about the past." They were interested in "the regions and landscapes of human life," and the processes of their creation by people. They were, perforce, considerably concerned with social and economic history, but they emphasized their inquiries in ways that historians did not because they were interested in the imprint of people on the surface of the earth and the description, analysis, and explanation of unlike places.[85]

Intended as a "deliberately provocative synthesis" that ventured a reasonably comprehensive interpretation of the northern part of the continent before 1867, the bulk of *Canada before Confederation* was given to broadly chronological treatments of each of the country's major regions. Within this template the authors treated the spread of settlement, the emergence of distinctive subregions, the bases of economic development, networks of communication and commerce, patterns (of survey, village growth, ethnic groups) on the land, and the material fabric of towns, villages, and countrysides. The result firmly signaled the diversity and uniqueness of Canada's component parts, and presented a historical geography that was "empirical, descriptive and resolutely regional in focus"; in the eyes of several historians and geographers it was also "the finest survey of early Canada."[86]

No comparable treatment of late nineteenth- and twentieth-century Canada seemed feasible to Harris and Warkentin in 1973. Prudence impelled them to end their study at Confederation because neither of them had worked on the processes of urbanization and industrialization that largely shaped the country after 1867, and "the geographical literature of this period of Canadian development [was] still al-

Moodie's interests are in the Prairies; Brian Osborne has written extensively on Ontario; Skip Ray has explored the meeting of Native and European worlds in the fur trade; and Graeme Wynn has made the Maritime provinces the main focus of his Canadian research.

[85] Cole Harris and John Warkentin, *Canada before Confederation* (New York: Oxford University Press, 1974), preface. J. Warkentin, ed., *Canada: A Geographical Interpretation* (Toronto: Methuen, 1968), p. viii.

[86] Berger, *The Writing of Canadian History*, 2d ed. (Toronto: University of Toronto Press, 1986), p. 283.

most non-existent." In Canada, as in the United States and beyond, "traditional historical geography [had] dealt reluctantly with cities."[87] But circumstances changed rapidly in the late 1970s and 1980s. Following the turn to urban studies in history and contemporary geography, new generations of graduate students focused their inquiries on the cities in which they studied, and from which many of them came.

With sizable graduate programs in both of its universities, Toronto benefited most from these developments; the two decades after 1970 saw completion of well over two dozen theses and dissertations on the city and its suburbs, many of which later yielded publications or led into further work. But there were similar developments in other centers. In Vancouver, where students drew inspiration from, and were supervised by, both historical and contemporary urban geographers, a good deal of attention was directed to investigations of the city's distinctive residential fabric, the impact of "social belief" and ideology on the landscape, and the social geographies of elites and immigrants in the west coast metropolis.[88] In Montreal, the "Shared Spaces/Partage de l'espace" project under the leadership of Sherry Olson at McGill University, and her associates David Hanna (McGill), Patricia Thornton (Concordia), and Robert Lewis (McGill) has produced approximately twenty-five items on the social geography of the city (ranging from B.A. essays through Ph.D. dissertations to discussion papers and journal articles), since the early 1980s. Many smaller centers, from Edmonton—where the work of Peter Smith has encouraged an interest in the planning process—through Ottawa to Hamilton, have also been the focus of relatively intense inquiry.[89] Together, these works have filled in many formerly sketchy details of urban expansion. Developed in tandem with a growing interest in the post-Confederation period among Canadian historians, and taking their place alongside new geographical work on the late nineteenth- and early twentieth-century countryside, they allowed the first sketch of a sweeping geographical interpretation of Canada between Confederation and the Great Depression.[90]

The same literature also underpinned a substantial part of volume 3 of *The Historical Atlas of Canada* published in 1990. This ambitious work (volume 1, *From the Beginning to 1800,* was published in 1987 and treats the northern part of North America; volume 2 is anticipated in the early 1990s) stands as a major achievement

---

[87] Michael P. Conzen, "Historical Geography: Changing Spatial Structure and Social Patterns of Western Cities," *Progress in Human Geography,* vol. 7, 1 (1983), p. 88.

[88] The critical figures here during the early 1970s were W. G. Hardwick, D. F. Ley, and R. C. Harris. For all its richness, this work on Vancouver, like most similar assemblages of theses and dissertations, forms a fragmented and disparate cluster of inquiries, and most of it remains unpublished. Still, it provided essential building blocks for a recent synthesis and interpretation of the development of the city: Graeme Wynn, "The Rise of Vancouver," in G. Wynn and T. R. Oke, eds., *Vancouver and Its Region* (Vancouver: University of British Columbia Press, 1992), pp. 69–148.

[89] Particularly notable has been the collaboration between geographer Michael Doucet and historian John Weaver in the analysis of Hamilton's development; the fruits of their labors have been brought together in M. Doucet and J. Weaver, *Housing the North American City* (Montreal: McGill-Queen's University Press, 1991).

[90] Wynn, "Forging a Canadian Nation."

of, and substantial tribute to, the work of Canadian historical geographers. Bold, comprehensive, integrative, informative, and indubitably geographical, *The Historical Atlas* offers a full and fascinating picture of Canadian development over several centuries. It is also remarkable in combining rich local detail with wider, albeit cautious, interpretations of regional and subcontinental development in a manner relatively uncharacteristic of, although not unknown in, geographical writing on the Canadian past during the last two decades.

Yet several gaps remain. Working, effectively, in the lee of the theoretical impulse that promised to remake geography in the 1960s, most Canadian historical geographers have been highly dubious of the value of covering laws, shy of explicit theorization, and surprisingly reluctant to recognize the potential value of loosely theoretical constructs (big interpretive ideas) to their inquiries. Generally studies have been more admired for the "sheer power of their factual substantiality" than for their purchase on wide interpretive horizons.[91]

In addition, and for all the achievements of the last two decades, many important topics warrant further attention. Although a few theses have broached the topic in recent years, very little geographical writing on the Canadian past has grappled with the gendered nature of human experience or acknowledged that women and men may have differed in the ways in which they used, shaped, or regarded the spaces and places of the past.[92] If somewhat more attention has been given to the impact of Canadians upon their environment, to the themes of ecological and environmental change, these topics also appear remarkably neglected, given the magnitude of the transformations involved, the long-standing claim that geographers are interested in human modifications of the natural environment, the rise in public awareness of environmental issues in the last two decades, and the rich harvest that some historians have begun to reap from the field of environmental history.[93]

For all the recent intensification of interest in urban and industrial life in Canada, questions of class and power have remained very much in the background

---

[91] The phrase is from C. Geertz, *Works and Lives: The Anthropologist as Author* (Stanford: Stanford University Press, 1988), p. 3.

[92] But see S. Mackenzie, "Reproduction of Labour in the Industrial City: A Study of the Position of Women with Reference to Nineteenth-Century Toronto," Master's thesis, University of Toronto, 1978; P. M. White, "Restructuring the Domestic Sphere: Prairie Indian Women on Reserves; Image, Ideology, and State Policy, 1880–1930," Ph.D. diss., McGill University, 1987; J. Momsen, "Gender, Class, and Ethnicity in Western Canadian Mining Towns," *Journal of Women and Gender Studies*, vol. 1 (1990), pp. 119–134; Catherine G. Pickles, "The Lives of Girls and Women in Mid-Nineteenth Century Pictou County, Nova Scotia," Master's thesis, University of British Columbia, 1992.

[93] The "Environmental Change" sections of the national and regional divisions of the bibliography list a good part of the most clearly ecological of this work; because many have been cognizant, at least in passing, of the impact of settlement on the environment, several other items bear on the topic. Still, there has been relatively little direct concern. Two items completed too late for inclusion in the guide are Yasmeen Qureshi, "Environmental Issues in British Columbia: An Historical Geographical Perspective," Master's thesis, University of British Columbia, 1991; and Wynn and Oke, *Vancouver and Its Region*, in which ecological and environmental change is a major theme. For an outstanding example of work in environmental history that transcends any putative boundaries between this field and historical geography, see W. Cronon, *Nature's Metropolis: Chicago and the Great West* (New York: W. W. Norton and Co., 1991).

of the rural and more general literature in historical geography, and there has been surprisingly little connection with either the vigorous "new labor history" that has drawn inspiration from the work of E. P. Thompson and Herbert Gutman, among others, or the vital debate about the capitalist penetration of the countryside that has engaged many American historians (and a few geographers) since the 1970s.[94]

Perhaps this owes something to the argument derived initially and rather loosely from Frederick Jackson Turner, but advanced most clearly and penetratingly by Cole Harris in the 1970s, that small populations and abundant resources in the new world dramatically revised the terms of access to land in these areas by comparison with Europe, and effectively pared extremes of wealth and poverty from the early Canadian countryside.[95] Resting, in part, on Harris's recognition that Andrew Clark's often-proclaimed ambition to compare the settlement of Europeans in mid-latitude lands across the oceans foundered for want of a clear analytical focus, the argument for the "simplification of Europe overseas" focuses on the most extreme circumstances of isolated new world settlement to lay bare the basic factors effecting the transformation of immigrant societies.

Where land was cheap and markets for agricultural products were poor, Harris wrote, rural landscapes were "enormously simplified. Gone were the extremes of wealth and squalor of the European countryside. . . . In their place rose farmhouse after farmhouse, most of them set amid their own fields, one house much like another, one farm much like the next." These were the settings of everyday life in "remarkably homogeneous societies," in which material circumstances differed little and "opportunities for domination" were "relatively slight," except within the family. This was a striking idea, cogently asserted. Its basic premises and conclusions significantly sharpened debate about the evolution of frontier societies. But like many such arresting formulations it promises to become a springboard for revisionist interpretations as well as a penetrating interpretive tool.[96]

---

[94] For a summary of this debate see Allan Kulikoff, "The Transition to Capitalism in Rural America," *William and Mary Quarterly*, ser. 3, vol. 46 (1989), pp. 120–144. A pivotal set of case studies is S. Hahn and J. Prude, eds., *The Countryside in the Age of Capitalist Transformation: Essays in the Social History of Rural America* (Chapel Hill: University of North Carolina Press, 1985). These matters are explored in Nova Scotia in R. Bitterman, R. Mackinnon, and G. Wynn, "Of Inequality and Interdependence in the Nova Scotian Countryside, 1850–1870," *Canadian Historical Review* (forthcoming).

[95] See R. C. Harris and L. T. Guelke, "Land and Society in Early Canada and South Africa," *Journal of Historical Geography*, vol. 3, 2 (1977), pp. 135–153; R. C. Harris, "The Extension of France into Rural Canada," in Gibson ed., *European Settlement and Development in North America*, pp. 27–45; R. C. Harris, "The Simplification of Europe Overseas," *Annals of the Association of American Geographers*, vol. 67, 4 (1977), pp. 468–482; R. C. Harris, "European Beginnings in the Northwest Atlantic: A Comparative View," in D. D. Hall and D. G. Allen eds., *Seventeenth Century New England* (Boston: Colonial Society of Massachusetts, 1985), pp. 119–153.

[96] Indeed, a new generation of historians has already begun to argue the existence of considerable inequality among the *censitaires* of eighteenth-century rural Canada, despite their ease of access to land. See Thomas Wien, "Peasant Accumulation in a Context of Colonization: Rivière du Sud, Canada, 1720–1773," Ph.D. diss., McGill University, 1988; Sylvie Dépatie, "L'Évolution d'une société rurale: L'île Jésus au XVIIIe siècle," Ph.D. diss., McGill University 1988; Christian Dessureault, "L'égalitarianisme paysan dans l'ancienne société rurale de la Vallée du Saint-Laurent," *Revue d'histoire de l'Amérique française*, vol. 40, 3 (1987), pp. 373–407. The issues and the literature are thoughtfully reviewed by Catherine Desbarats,

On another tack, although the scholarly work of Canadian historical geographers over the last two or three decades makes it clear that the Canadian landscape is a complex repository of artifacts, aspirations, ideas, successes, failures, and unanticipated consequences that can be interpreted both literally and symbolically, there has been relatively little attention to the dialectic of structure and agency in much of this literature.[97] If anything, this omission has been pointed up only by recent work from Quebec, which illuminates the dysfunction between orderly official designs for remote and poorly understood colonial territories and the often diffuse grass-roots responses of ordinary settlers to local circumstances.[98]

And so it goes. The challenge of providing a satisfactory understanding of the Canadian past from a geographical perspective will never be met—for long. Changing circumstances generate new questions about the past as the producers and consumers of historical writing seek new perspectives on, and understanding of, themselves and their societies. Yet one thing seems clear. Many of the old convictions that anchored and oriented scholarship in the humanities and social sciences in the past are being reexamined in the 1990s. If historical geographers rejected the possibility of developing universal laws of spatial behavior in the 1960s, and appreciated, with historians, that each generation would see the past through rather different lenses, they could still believe that they were reporting "the facts." Without laws or general theories to help them, historical geographers had to exercise judgment in constructing their accounts of the past. Unable to deal with everything, they selected those "attributes of the landscape that most warrant[ed] attention," and decided which "actions were most important in shaping th[ose] characteristics." Too thin a knowledge of area and context might lead scholars to offer interpretations that others, more informed, "could show to be erroneous or simplistic." But hard work, growing familiarity with the subject of their inquiries, and increasing acuity would allow able researchers to "describe and explain the landscape in ways that other[s] . . . found plausible and enlightening." Far from being personal and idiosyncratic, the choices implicit in interpretation were weighed and valued in the marketplace of informed scholarly opinion; their legitimacy depended upon their relation to established un-

---

"Agriculture within the Seigneurial Regime of Eighteenth Century Canada: Some Thoughts on the Recent Literature," *Canadian Historical Review*, vol. 73, 1 (1992), pp. 1–29; see also the discussion of Quebec historical geography since 1970, above.

[97] Paul Simpson-Housley and Glen Norcliffe, *A Few Acres of Snow: Literary and Artistic Images of Canada* (Toronto: Dundurn Press, 1992) offers several case studies exploring ways in which the landscape has been "socially constructed."

[98] e.g., S. Courville, "Espace, territoire, et culture en Nouvelle-France: Une vision géographique," *Revue d'histoire de l'Amérique française*, vol. 37, 3 (1983), pp. 417–429. On this point also see historian Jean Blain, "La frontière en Nouvelle-France," *Revue d'histoire de l'Amérique française*, vol. 35, 3 (1971), p. 400, translated in S. Gagnon, *Man and His Past* (Montreal: Harvest House, 1982), p. 20, as follows: "By French-Canadian historians' near-absolute dependence on a kind of source that tends to reveal much more about an ideal of colonization than about colonial reality . . . our historians have been insidiously led to write the history of New France that should have been in the view of those who directed it, rather than the New France that actually was."

derstandings and the larger body of evidence (in field or archive) from which they had been extracted.[99]

Similar assumptions and principles held sway in many fields of inquiry. Historians characteristically claimed to provide their readers with accurate knowledge of the past. Ethnographers sought verisimilitude in their texts—warranting the truth of their accounts of distant lands and peoples by establishing the strong sense that they had (as Clifford Geertz expressed it) "been there." Indeed, the rise of "social science" rested in substantial part on the contention that its practitioners—detached Olympian formulators of hypotheses about and interpretations of the world around them—offered their readers objective, factual accounts, not fictions, romances, or subjective perceptions. "Cultural anthropology," insisted Bronislaw Malinowski, in a preface to Raymond Firth's *We, the Tikopia* that framed a refrain common in many fields of intellectual endeavor through the middle years of the twentieth century, "need not be . . . a factory of impressionistic short-cuts or guess-work reconstructions"; it could take its proud place as a "social *science*" (emphasis added). Social scientists left impressionistic, idiosyncratic portrayals of the human condition to others. They were careful cartographers, not exuberant, individualistic painters of the social world.[100]

In academic discipline after academic discipline, however, these comforting verities have been thrown into question. Prompted by reflections on the nature of discourse and the character of authorial authority, by Roland Barthes, Michel Foucault, Hayden White, and others, social scientists of the 1980s have begun to reexamine the very ground upon which their disciplinary endeavors stand.[101] Introspection—and doubt—have followed. Many wonder whether they are, as Barthes has suggested, "professional intellectual[s] caught between wanting to create a bewitching verbal structure . . . and wanting to communicate facts and ideas, to merchandise information; and indulging fitfully the one desire or the other."[102] With the end of colonialism and the development of strong feelings of national, ethnic, and racial identity among peoples in all quarters of the globe, some question their capacity (and right) to explain and interpret others.

At the same time, the audience of scholarship has been diversified and fragmented by modern communications and the widespread movement of people around the world; for whom, then, several writers wonder, do they write? In many eyes it is no longer appropriate—perhaps indeed it is no longer even possible—to

---

[99] The quotations are from Harris, "Theory and Synthesis," but they represent a far wider consensus.

[100] Much of the argument of this paragraph rests upon Geertz, *Works and Lives*, pp. 5–17, from which the Malinowski quotation is drawn.

[101] M. Foucault, "What is an Author," in J. V. Harari, ed., *Textual Strategies: Perspectives in Post-Structuralist Criticism* (Ithaca, N.Y.: Cornell University Press, 1979), pp. 141–160; R. Barthes, "Authors and Writers," in S. Sontag, ed., *A Barthes Reader* (New York: Hill and Wang, 1972), pp. 185–193; H. White, *The Content of the Form* (Baltimore: Johns Hopkins University Press, 1987); and *Tropics of Discourse* (Baltimore: Johns Hopkins University Press, 1978); J. Clifford and G. E. Marcus, eds., *Writing Culture: The Poetics and Politics of Ethnography* (Berkeley: 1986); Geertz, *Works and Lives*.

pretend to "tell it like it is" (or was). Representation—description, comparison, classification, generalization—is a delusion. The "whole visualist ideology of referential discourse" is an emperor without clothes.[103] All texts are—to borrow another memorable encapsulation from the current introspective mood of ethnography—evocations.

If the influence of this self-conscious anxiety upon geographical writing on the Canadian past remains limited in the early 1990s, its impact seems bound to spread. Modern geography, like much of modern social science, is absorbed with that diffuse body of ideas about society known as social theory, and the relativistic, "heteroglossial" impulse of postmodernism is being felt across the academic enterprise.[104] Indeed, Cole Harris has provided a clear portent of one possible future for historical geography in his recent reflection upon the pertinence of social theorists Foucault, Habermas, and others to the field. Convinced that their ideas warrant careful attention, that they have the potential to provide historical geography with "some new interpretive edges," and that engagement with them could yield new interdisciplinary links and bring historical geography to the center of "an intellectually reinvigorated and reintegrated human geography," Harris is nonetheless led to wonder about the legitimacy of his recent work on native-European contact in early British Columbia. Conscious that he explores these matters while debate about native land claims and their very place in Canadian society simmers (and erupts, periodically), he asks: "Am I, in a sense, living off the avails, somewhat like the archeologist Harlan Smith who came in the 1890s to study the Thompson Indians and shipped to New York every important artefact he could find? Are my texts, like those of ethnographers who assumed natives were becoming Europeans, making it harder for people to be what they are or want to be? If they might be, then have I the right to write?"[105]

From the the wider intellectual moment out of which such concerns grow, geographical writing about the Canadian past is likely to become much more con-

---

[102] The quotation is Clifford Geertz's summary of Barthes position in *Works and Lives*, p. 20.

[103] S. Tyler, "Post-modern Ethnography," in Clifford and Marcus, eds., *Writing Culture*, pp. 130–131.

[104] The recent engagement of these ideas in Canadian historical geography stems in considerable part from two sources: the evident tendency among some of the most enthusiastic advocates of "postmodern" perspectives in contemporary geography to engross the past (and more or less explicitly to dismiss the existence of historical geography as a distinct field), and the stimulus provided by Derek Gregory at the University of British Columbia and a new generation of graduate students entering Canadian programs (mainly from Britain) thoroughly familiar with the key literature. Daniel Clayton, "Geographies of the Lower Skeena, 1830–1920," Master's thesis, University of British Columbia, 1989 (reported in part as "Geographies of the Lower Skeena," in *B.C. Studies*, no. 94 [1992], pp. 29–58), exemplifies the capacity of these perspectives to refocus existing historical interpretations. For another, lesser, example of the impact of these ideas on historical geographical writing, see Graeme Wynn, "Ideology, Society, and State in the Maritime Colonies of British North America, 1840–1860," in Allan Greer and Ian Radforth, eds., *Colonial Leviathan: State Formation in Mid-Nineteenth-Century Canada* (Toronto: University of Toronto Press, 1992), pp. 284–328.

[105] C. Harris, "Power, Modernity, and Historical Geography," *Annals of the Association of American Geographers*, vol. 81, 4 (1991), pp. 671–683. For more on recent work on British Columbia by Harris, see his "The Fraser Canyon Encountered," *B.C. Studies*, no. 94 (1992), pp. 5–28.

cerned with such hitherto largely ignored matters as the burden of authorship, the nature of authorial assumptions, textual strategies, and the asymmetries of authority and power. But historical geographers will still be called upon first and foremost to illuminate the different settings and circumstances in which lives have been lived. In the process, their work will continue to mark the achievements of the past, reveal the power of people to shape their worlds, provide perspective on the present, and help to sustain discourse across the cleavages of societies that are, simultaneously and paradoxically, both more fragmented and more integrated than ever before. If it does so in ways that reflect the introspection and sensitivities of the late twentieth century, it may well contribute significantly to the emergence of a humbler, wiser enterprise, one that encourages humanistic reflection on our world as well as the more formal analysis of modern social science.

Organizational Framework
of the Bibliography

Michael P. Conzen, Thomas A. Rumney, and Graeme Wynn

Content

The bibliography employs a rather inclusive definition of what research and writing constitutes "historical geography." Succinctly put, it embraces all published writing of a geographical nature that deals with past periods and change over time. The main elements of this definition deserve immediate elaboration, but it is important to stress that the selections do not cover all source material that conceivably might be relevant to the historical geography of a given topic, but rather they cover all such interpretive writing on a topic that has been undertaken with a clearly detectable perspective rooted in the imaginative realm of historical geography.

Geographical Character

Works that address in an essential way some aspect of the evolution of human settlement on the continent in relation to space and environment are deemed to fall within the scope of the definition. Geographical writing, as with any other field, reflects changing conceptual and methodological fashions, and the definition employed attempts to accommodate as many of these as possible. Any preferences for particular approaches are better exercised by the users than presumptively asserted by the compilers of works such as this. Thus, a strong attempt has been made to include studies regardless of conceptual orientation in the interest of a full record of the subject matter and interpretive history of the field of North American historical geography.

Many professional geographers in the United States and Canada regard themselves explicitly as historical geographers, and if their publications have dealt with North America they should be found in this bibliography. Membership in this guild, however, is not a prerequisite. Geographers with diverse thematic interests have often taken up historical questions or treated their subjects in a historical manner, and such works, when found, have likewise been included.[1] Scholars in fields other than geography sometimes cultivate the borderlands between their disciplines and historical geography, and, where such work relates overtly to the themes and approaches of historical geography, such items, when found, have also been included. Similarly, the boundary between professional scholars in geography and a broader

---

[1] Many studies exemplifying the various approaches of cultural geography, for example, will be found here—if they give explicit and substantial attention to development over time. While the aims and methods of cultural geography and historical geography can often be distinguished (and mental effort indeed has been expended from time to time in declaring them separate), in practice such divisions more likely inhibit than augment the desired flow of ideas.

community of writers with marked geographical curiosity and insight is, for the present project, difficult to draw and dubious in value. Thus, works here and there by "geographers at heart," regardless of educational background, will also be found. To confine the bibliography within practical limits, however, works of an essentially journalistic nature have been disregarded in favor of writing adhering more or less to accepted canons of scholarship.

Treatment of Time

The bibliography contains material addressing time periods found within the whole chronological span of human presence in North America, from the original peopling of the continent up to the very recent past. Some caveats are in order. Characteristically, far more work on early, pre-European-contact peoples has been done by anthropologists and archaeologists than by geographers. Since this compilation focuses on geographical contributions to the literature about the past, its relatively light coverage of precontact subjects mirrors the proportionate attention given them by the geographical community. Similarly, historical geographers in the United States have done less work on the colonial period of European occupation than on the nineteenth century—the era of national expansion and accelerated growth in population and economy. In Canada, however, where nationhood came later, the imbalance between pre- and post-Confederation work is less marked. All in all, though, work on nineteenth-century topics bulks the largest of any chronological period in this bibliography.

It was common until fairly recently to regard periods in the twentieth century as too recent to merit examination from the particular perspective of historical geography. Human processes and places needed to be studied in the sufficiently distant past to ensure adequate analytical detachment. While perspectives doubtless change with the passage of time, we felt it appropriate, in 1990, to include a good deal of twentieth-century material. Hence, a distinctive feature of the bibliography is its coverage of topics after 1900, including studies that follow conditions into the 1970s and 1980s. There is a qualification, however. To be included, works dealing with twentieth-century conditions need to cover a period of twenty years or more.[2] The proviso separates studies focusing on significant forces of change with long-term consequences from those dealing primarily with contemporary situations and short-term fluctuations. Many studies by geographers intended as contributions to contemporary understanding have incorporated evidence stretching over several years, or have presented data from two consecutive censuses, for example, but few would seriously contend that they are contributions to historical geography in any apparent sense.[3]

---

[2] Exempted are studies of moments or short periods in the early twentieth century that are offered explicitly as studies in historical geography.

[3] It can be argued that ultimately such works might become suitable source material for the pursuit of historical geography. Indeed, for several years Michael Conzen has offered, as historical geography, a course at the University of Chicago on twentieth-century North America for which the reading material includes many geographical articles published during the periods under review, regarded now as relevant witness to the times.

As the number of professional journals in American geography expanded after the second decade of this century, contemporary works multiplied, none of which belong in this bibliography unless they pay serious attention to significant periods of change. Many have done so, in varying degrees, and a mechanism was needed to distinguish those included from those omitted. A work (article, pamphlet, or book) has been included if one or more of the following criteria are satisfied: (1) the study is framed in the context of long-term change; (2) evidence is presented that covers at least a twenty-year span; (3) at least half of the interpretive discussion employs the past tense in referring to phenomena examined; or (4) the sequence of discussion is essentially chronological, or organized into historical or evolutionary phases. These last two measures proved immensely valuable in promptly assessing the historicity of the material. These guidelines served well to draw within the orbit of this bibliography many studies that would not be considered conventional historical geography—not least by the authors themselves—but that nevertheless offer explicit insights and evidence about temporal processes in space highly pertinent to the aims and purpose of historical geography writ large.

Materials appear in this bibliography because they offer interpretations about substantive questions dealing with change over time. For the most part, presentist material concerned with conditions at the time of writing are disregarded; the writer must in effect be seen to be writing "historically." Otherwise, the compilation would reach no limit. To stress the key point, this listing attempts not to present all material of conceivable interest to historical geographers, but rather to record all studies purporting to offer insights about geographical change in North American localities.

Treatment of Space and Scale

The issue of localities is straightforward. We have attempted to collect material dealing with all regions and places within Canada and the continental United States, at all geographical scales (see Appendix 1). This includes studies of national or continentwide phenomena, as well as studies of individual places, even down to the level of a single settlement or other cultural landscape artifact. In the latter cases, however, broader regional issues of process and typology need to be explicit in the discussion to qualify for inclusion. There is, for example, a vast literature dealing with the peculiarities of individual houses and other singular landscape features (stemming from research in cultural geography, folk-life studies, landscape architecture, and related fields), most of which this bibliography cannot hope to cover. Thus, while included material relates to all geographical scales, the emphasis is placed on collectivities of phenomena in space and on regional associations, however defined.

Sources Consulted

A wide range of published sources have been examined, within and beyond the formal arena of geographical publications. A serious attempt has been made to extend the search for relevant material to international publications in geography, with notable results. Sufficient interest in the historical geography of North America has been evidenced in writing by British, German, and French geographers over the decades in particular to reveal the limitations imposed on the McManis bibliography by its restriction to a search of domestic publications.[4] Contributions have also been found in the journals and occasional monographs of geographers from many other countries, reflecting no doubt the long history of specific cultural ties between those regions and these two immigrant nations of North America. We believe the bibliography is significantly enriched by such scholarly infusions.

A multiple strategy was followed in collecting the material that appears in this work. The kernel of the collection was formed by a consolidation of the personal research card and computer files that each collaborator brought to the project. Since these resources reflected considerable prior experience in publishing bibliographic reviews in the field, the files provided a solid basis for enlargement.[5]

The next step was to consult a variety of standard reference works in geography and history to acquire additional listings, chief among them being *The Research Catalog of the American Geographical Society, Current Geographical Publications, Geo Abstracts, Bibliographie géographique internationale, Writings on American History: A Subject Bibliography of Articles*, and *America: History and Life*. This was augmented by a search through the review sections of the major North American geographical journals to enlarge the representation of books and monographs. Listings of graduate theses and dissertations on historical topics in geography were culled from various sources: two classic dissertation compilations in the *Annals of the Association of American Geographers* published in 1935 and 1946;[6] two special compilations;[7] the *Comprehensive Dissertation Index, 1861–1972*, vol. 1, *Geography and Geology* (and subsequent editions);[8] the AAG *Guide to Departments of Geography in the United States and Canada* (1979/80 to 1990/91 editions); and selected in-house listings requested directly from departments.[9]

A third stage was commenced with a systematic search of major geographical and historical journals in the United States and Canada, and geographical journals

---

[4] Douglas R. McManis, *Historical Geography of the United States: A Bibliography, Excluding Alaska and Hawaii* (Ypsilanti: Eastern Michigan University Press, 1965).

[5] The earlier bibliographic publications of the compilers can be found in the bibliographic sections of the appropriate regional units of the bibliography.

[6] Derwent Whittlesey, "Dissertations in Geography Accepted by Universities in the United States for the Degree of Ph.D. as of May 1935," *Annals of the Association of American Geographers*, vol. 25, 4 (1935), pp. 211–237; and Leslie Hewes, "Dissertations in Geography Accepted by Universities in the United States and Canada for the Degree of Ph.D., June 1935 to June 1946, and Those Currently in Progress," *Annals of the Association of American Geographers*, vol. 36, 4 (1946), pp. 215–238.

[7] Clyde E. Browning, *A Bibliography of Dissertations in Geography: 1901 to 1969* (Chapel Hill: University of North Carolina Department of Geography, Studies in Geography no. 1, 1970); and Merrill M. Stuart, *A Bibliography of Master's Theses in Geography: American and Canadian Universities* (Tualatin, Ore.: Geographic and Area Study Publications, 1973).

[8] Ann Arbor, Mich.: Xerox University Microfilms, 1973.

[9] Reporting thesis titles in the past has sorely taxed the profession's commitment to bibliographic accuracy. These sources vary considerably in the reliability of their entries, the 1935 and 1946 *Annals* lists and the *Dissertation Index* being the most consistent, and the *Professional Geographer* annual listings the least. The centralization of reporting through the microfilm network has much improved the situation in recent years. Despite our considerable efforts at cross-checking titles for accuracy, discrepancies undoubtedly remain, particularly for somewhat older material.

overseas.[10] In the geographical journals, effort was made to extract all material that satisfied the criteria for content discussed above. Material written by geographers dealing significantly with conditions in the past and with a concern for change over time was routinely extracted. Contributions by nongeographers, if they satisfied these content criteria, were also included, particularly those by historians. If a historian, for example, passed the editorial review process for publication of a historically oriented piece in a geographical outlet, then we deemed the material to be, prima facie, of geographical interest. This was less automatic for invited collections of interdisciplinary scope, even where geographers served as editors; in such cases individual items had to meet the content criteria rigidly applied to each.

In the case of historical journals, monographs, and collections, a rather different perspective was needed. A few pieces by historians qualified for extraction because their geographical approach was explicit and sustained. One straightforward measure was the presence of thematic maps in the work, coupled with their centrality to the author's interpretation. When this was self-evident, such items were extracted. Not all books and articles illustrated with maps, however, qualified. Many regional historical journals over the last decade or so have become heavily illustrated with graphic devices, including maps.[11] Generally, it proved easy to spot cases where maps contributed mere decoration to the pages of an article, and as such added no extra punch to the ideas in the work. When the texts of such cases did not meet the standard criteria of geographical interest and approach, they were not included. Articles in historical journals by geographers, however, were nearly always extracted. Most such items have been written by professional historical geographers, writing historical geography. Even when maps are absent and the topic may seem more mainstream-historical in caste, most such cases were extracted on the grounds that a geographical intelligence informed the conceptualization and perspective of the writer. In practice, few geographers have published material in historical journals that does not amply display a clearly geographical approach.

A "distance decay" function exists in the interdisciplinary and international literature surrounding the historical geography of North America. Domestic geographical publications, understandably, yield the most abundant material; they are followed in importance by domestic historical journals, especially state and provincial organs. Thereafter, a fairly steep drop-off occurs in the incidence of relevant material in domestic journals of the other social sciences and in the humanities. Overseas, geographical serials proved the most likely to yield material of interest, particularly in Britain, because of the common language and historical ties, and in Germany, because of long-standing commitments to overseas comparative fieldwork and the system of university monographic publications in geography. French geographers have

---

[10] See Appendix 2: List of Serials Consulted. The entire run of each journal listed was searched, thanks to the combined resources of the five principal university libraries canvassed (see Preface).

[11] Whether this reflects a yearning for broader audiences, the altered economics of printing pictures, or capitulation to diminished tolerance for dense text in a television age cannot, of course, be examined here. The changed appearance of history journals, nonetheless, has been dramatic.

shown some interest in French Canadian historical geography, but much less in United States or Canadian topics outside Quebec. Other European interest is even more sporadic, generally related to regionally localized ethnic ties. Beyond foreign geographical journals, very little relevant material appeared in spot-checks of historical and interdisciplinary journals, and there were no indications from any other sources (e.g., footnotes in literature of any kind) that major additional sources of foreign writing on the historical geography of North America have been overlooked.

A fourth stage was initiated with an effort to secure personal lists of publications from professional historical geographers. Given how resourceful many have proven to be over the years in placing their research in a wide variety of publications, this move was aimed at discovering articles and monographs published under auspices not well known to us. All members of the Association of American Geographers (AAG) who signify submembership in the association's Historical Geography Specialty Group—about 490 individuals—received a request to forward their lists of publications to the compilers, annotated to show which items they considered eligible for inclusion in the bibliography. A similar approach was made to the 100 or so historical geographers on the mailing list of the *Newsletter for Canadian Historical Geographers/Bulletin des géographes historiques canadiens*. Given this opportunity, a very healthy proportion of the professionally active members responded, and these lists yielded a virtual avalanche of additional material, much of it scattered in publications that would have been difficult, if not impossible, to predict. In addition, supplementary groups of geographers were contacted for the same purpose. One such list was drawn from faculty rosters (individuals listing historical geography as an interest) published in the AAG *Guide to Departments of Geography in the United States and Canada, 1990–91*; and another list picked up yet other individuals from the preliminary alphabetical printouts of our own, growing bibliography.

All told, we heard from over 300 professional geographers, giving details of material relevant to the project.[12] An important, though incidental, by-product of this process was the ability in these cases to cross-check the accuracy of information secured from the various sources. While doubtless we have contributed unwitting errors of our own in a work of this complexity and character, it was dismaying to discover the relatively high frequency of small errors in people's own resumes (when checked, where possible, against the actual printed items in the library). We have endeavored throughout the course of the project to check the accuracy of entries regardless of source, but a small percentage of the material of necessity is presented substantially as received from authors.

Lastly, we consulted published publication lists of deceased geographers for relevant material. These sources include obituaries from the *Annals of the Association*

---

[12] A total of about seven hundred requests were mailed to individuals on the combined lists. A little investigating confirmed that most of the nonrespondents appeared to be graduate students with as yet no publications to their names, or other geographers with few or no publications in this particular field. All things considered, we regard the level of response to our inquiries to have been exceedingly high.

of American Geographers, listings in various *Festschriften* and memorial volumes, and several compilations appearing in *Geographers: Biobibliographical Studies.*

Other Criteria and Problematic Issues

This is a fully retrospective bibliography, presenting all discovered material published between the mid–nineteenth century and the end of calendar 1990.[13] The sole exceptions to this rule are the unpublished graduate theses and dissertations, which we believe important to include, considering the quantity of scholarly research they represent. Interlibrary loan services available to most scholars make such material at least as accessible as many a fugitive journal or out-of-print book.

Not systematically included are so-called working papers and discussion papers, which many regard as semi-publications and as editorially immature works. They are also notoriously fugitive, even on the scholarly circuit. Some have been included in cases where no mature version of the paper appeared in print later, but we have made no effort to gain comprehensive coverage. Also covered in spotty fashion are studies that were published as technical reports for public and private agencies. The range of professional treatment given these studies as publications by their sponsors varies widely, as does the distribution effort to place them in scholarly libraries. Those that have come to our attention and that meet our criteria for content have been included. Surely, titles have been missed.

The bibliography does not include book reviews, review essays, or editorials, in keeping with our focus on material that deals directly with substantive problems. Reviews and review essays, while important in shaping intellectual debate over interpretive issues and research practice, represent nevertheless a stage of scholarly activity once-removed from primary sources.[14] It also made sense to steer clear of pieces in which opinion looms large. Besides, a line needed to be drawn on quantitative grounds alone.

Two categories of methodological interest, however, have been included: core statements of philosophy and practice written by historical geographers resident in North America, and assessments of the contributions made to North American historical geography by acknowledged leaders in the field (see the "Benchmark Scholars" portion of the "General Sources" section). The first offers a concise but fairly comprehensive, chronologically arranged list of statements on the nature, purpose, and approaches of the field, representing the evolution of ideas about the subject in the two countries. Clearly this literature over the years owes something to the interaction with British thought on the subject, given the shared language (and occasionally to writings in German and French), but this particular listing helps isolate the

---

[13] "Published" with respect to 1990 periodical literature also means available in major research libraries by the end of January 1991. In a few cases, notice of relevant material in journal issues delayed in issuance was obtained directly from editors. A few books published in early 1991 that came to our attention have been included, but the arduous task of tracing journal articles was closed at the end of 1990 to avoid further delay in completing this work.

[14] A few review essays have been included where the list of references is so large as to constitute a small bibliography in its own right. These items appear in the regionally appropriate bibliographic subsections.

North American experience.[15] We included the second category on the grounds that in any field one looks sooner or later for a personal sense of the structure of knowledge underlying the myriad facts and interpretations about the phenomena examined. A simple and concise way of providing some landmarks by which to navigate this terrain is to examine the record of master scholars who have gone before. Their imagination, predilections, and silences offer a stimulating guide to the subject matter of the field and how it has been approached.

There remain five problematic questions of inclusion in the bibliography. First, we found no easy way to determine how much coverage there should be of physical geography. Even if entries are restricted to works explicitly linking physical conditions to issues of human settlement, the corpus of work recognized might be considerably larger than that presented. One practical characteristic helped distinguish the material we were convinced should be included: a similarity to studies on the cultural side in the way concept and evidence are presented in published form. A substantial proportion of research in physical geography appears in what, for cultural geographers, are an austere and clipped technical-scientific format and style. While not wishing to trigger needless dispute over the healthy diversity in modes of knowing and communicating, or to question the primacy of intellectual substance over presentational form, we have nevertheless favored a select set of studies in the physical geography of the continent that is simply more accessible to nonspecialists than are others.

A second problem concerns the coverage of the history of North American cartography. Since many historical geographers have written about aspects of mapping history as a key dimension in the advance of geographical knowledge, the topic has a secure place within our conceptual scheme. On the other hand, as with physical geography, a vigorous pursuit of relevant literature would take us quite far afield and into some narrowly technical domains. The bibliography does not attempt to double as a comprehensive guide to cartographic history on the continent. What it best reflects is the pattern of particular interests exhibited by geographers in the subject. Emphasis has been given to useful interpretive works, and, for good measure, a reasonable sampling of works that are well illustrated with facsimile reproductions of old maps. Cartobibliographies and map catalogs generally have been omitted, although useful interpretive introductions to some works of that type have been included. Thematic atlases dealing specifically with historical themes have been fully researched for inclusion, provided that they contain maps specifically designed to illustrate historical events and processes.

A third difficulty lies in the sphere of historical travel literature. As with the history of cartography, travel accounts document evolving patterns of geographical knowledge, with particular relevance to the perceptual dimension, and their examination belongs firmly within the compass of historical geography. The vast hoard of travel accounts per se was excluded as representing basically primary source material,

---

[15] Due regard for the influence of European methodological writings on American and Canadian thought can be found in the historiographic essays by Conzen and Wynn elsewhere in this volume.

for which, in any case, useful bibliographic guides exist.[16] Lately, historians, geographers, literature specialists, and others have been interpreting such material with rising conceptual sophistication, and this scholarly genre is notable in the fields of history and American studies. How much to include, and where to draw the line? Again, we have opted to hew fairly closely to studies done by geographers themselves. A few forays outside this slender orbit were made over terrain geographers have been slow to cultivate, even though the geographical relevance of the subject matter and its scholarly treatment are self-evident. One example is the now booming interpretive field of women's travel accounts, a few exemplars of which, by historians and others, are included in an attempt to help rectify a currently perceived imbalance of coverage.

The fourth problematical issue concerns place names. Geographers and others have long been interested in the place-name cover of North American regions. At its best, the onomastic literature deals with broad principles of name origins and distributions; at another level, writing about place names barely goes beyond descriptions of the idiosyncratic facts behind the naming of countless individual places. The bibliography contains some place-name studies, gleaned mostly from material supplied by cooperating geographers, as well as searches of one or two main journals in the field and the leading bibliography,[17] but the coverage is not comprehensive.

Finally, a problem arose in how to treat the subject of historic preservation. The phenomenon is at once an aesthetic movement, a real-estate pursuit, a set of construction practices, a form of social engineering, and a political arena. It also has its historical geography. Clearly, only a small fraction of the broad literature on historic preservation qualifies for inclusion in this bibliography, and only some of the writing by geographers qualifies. Thus, studies of historic preservation as a social force and landscape factor over time qualify; discussions of the topic framed in terms of contemporary public policy do not.

The content of the bibliography, then, is designed to present an inclusive view of the existing body of scholarly work devoted to the historical geography of North America.[18] At its core lies the research and writing of geographers who consider themselves to be historical geographers, but surrounding that is a broad penumbra of writing by geographers who are not necessarily so identified but whose concern for their subject led them to frame their research nonetheless in something of a historical context. Beyond that is a periphery that is populated with the works of scholars in neighboring fields and writers with other backgrounds, represented in this bibliography by pieces displaying a clear sensitivity to geographical processes over time and to

---

[16] See, e.g., the bibliographies listed under "Narrative Sources" in Ronald E. Grim, *Historical Geography of the United States: A Guide to Information Sources* (Detroit: Gale Research Co., 1982), pp. 87–89.

[17] Richard B. Sealock, Margaret M. Sealock, and Margaret S. Powell, comps., *Bibliography of Place-Name Literature: United States and Canada*, 3d ed. (Chicago: Special Libraries Association, 1982).

[18] Some well-known geographers with broadly historical credentials do not, or but barely, appear in the listings because the bulk of their writings address universal themes and are couched in such sweepingly normative or comparative terms as to offer no specific or particular focus on the United States or Canada, or their regions.

their expression in the cultural landscapes of the continent. This annular conceptual structure of the literature is not, however, the basis for the bibliography's arrangement. That dimension was designed to implement a number of more practical purposes.

Arrangement

The arrangement of material in this bibliography follows three simple but interlocking principles. The fundamental divisions are regional, ordered by large territorial units and smaller ones within them. The second principle is a separation according to broad topical groupings of subject matter. These topical subdivisions appear within each of the various scales of regional differentiation. To this—conventional—system we have added a third ordering principle. Within regional and topical groupings, entries have been arranged chronologically by their dates of publication.

To arrange material topically within regional sections provides basic access to detailed work from the national to the very local level. We have chosen to employ McManis's regional categories, where appropriate, for the United States, and to add to them where desirable. This preserves some basis for comparing the growth of geographical literature in any particular sphere of interest over the quarter century since his compendium was published.[19] By extending coverage to the twentieth century and to all of Canada, however, we have had to modify the classification system in places. This is most evident in the greatly expanded set of topical categories used here, necessitated by changing interests and conceptual developments since the mid-1960s.

Within these categories, there seemed no compelling reason to list items alphabetically by author. We felt an additional practical dimension could be provided by arranging material chronologically within sections.[20] This offers an immediate picture of the timing and historical sequence by which particular topics and intellectual concerns made their appearance in the scholarly literature. Earliest dates for the appearance of work in a given category signal timeliness or tardiness in the awakening of curiosity in that subject, while the longevity or transience of interest reflected in the density or paucity of work at particular times can be equally revealing. The view is necessarily fragmented by the numerous regional subdivisions in the work. Tracing the emergence of geographical concern with cities or ethnic groups, for example, requires cross-reference among all regional sections of relevance. But this chore

---

[19] The growth of geographical scholarship has been dramatic. McManis chose to include numerous works by historians in his compilation because, in 1965, there was often no suitable writing by geographers on the topics and localities defined by the project. We have made no such substitutions here; if coverage by geographers of certain topics in some regions is thin or lacking, then it is simply apparent (see Appendix 3). We consider that to be a certain advantage, in that it may act as a stimulus to further research and writing.

[20] Chronology by date of publication was chosen for its lack of ambiguity and for its utility. Chronology by temporal span of subject matter would have been quite impractical to determine and arrange in a simple, sequential manner, given the great variation in time periods covered in individual works and the way such periods are treated by each author.

notwithstanding, organization by date of publication draws immediate attention to the antiquity (or otherwise) of scholarly concern with particular topics and issues. For researchers striking out into fields of investigation new to them, this feature, we hope, will prove novel and useful.

To augment the practicality of the bibliography, two indexes at the end of the work provide immediate entrée to individual authors and to highly specific subject matter. Since the bibliography is too large to permit duplicate entries, users will likely find these indexes essential to their efficient use of the work.

Style

Some standardization of elements within entries has been made for the sake of consistency. The titles of all monographs and separate publications (including booklets, pamphlets, etc.) are italicized, even when part of a publication series. This draws attention to their self-standing nature. A study of 150 pages, for instance, when issued as a separate item, is the functional equivalent of a book, even if it appears as part of a series which includes other volumes that are collections of independent articles. Hence, in a few cases the styling of some publication series may appear to present them as the functional equivalent of journals in one context, and in another as the title of a publisher's series of which an individual book may be a part.

Where personal names are given in full in the original publication (i.e., given name, middle name or initial, last name, and, in some instances of historic male vanity, bloodline sequence—Jr., III, etc.), they are included here as such and, furthermore, have been extended to all entries under those authors' names. This eased computerized cross-checking and bibliographic control during the compilation of the work, and its retention helps lessen potential confusion between different authors with similar name forms.

If ensuring that Waldo Smith IV receives credit for all his publications, even when an item of his appears in some plebeian journal under the less regal "W. Smith," we have been less successful in guaranteeing that Winnie Hofnagel is kept whole in this bibliography through all of life's nominal changes. In the Author Index we have made an attempt to match maiden, married, and (?) postmarried last names for women authors, when known to us, but we are confident only in the conviction that we have doubtless missed some connections. Changing preferences in the styling of last names, the sometimes careening calculus of marital relations, and the absence of a universal lifetime name register all make it difficult to eliminate the possibility that some decidedly singular individuals may appear in this work with unfathomably multiple identities. This is regrettable, but, for any given publication entry, at least, a woman's name form has been transcribed from the source without significant alteration, subject to the minor streamlining mentioned above.[21]

---

[21] Winnie Hofnagel, for instance, would appear in all her separate nominal incarnations spread through the Author Index (with cross-references), while any of her books or articles would be listed in the bibliography itself only under the name she sanctioned at the time of its publication.

Final caveats

It should be needless to say, but no compilation procedures, even those de-
voutly dedicated to Logic, can outsmart the mischief of Human Error, however in-
nocent and playful the latter may be. Without doubt this work, owing to its size and
complexity, contains errors and challengeable judgments—of omission, inclusion,
and placement. The compilers have worked hard to harmonize their approach to the
raw material from which this guide is fashioned, and to systematize citation forms
for entries drawn from many different sources. But they know in their hearts that
Perfection remains, as usual, aloof; guarding her dignity, perhaps, behind a sardonic
smile cast upon this finite and foibled effort.

Appendix 1

Regions, Provinces, and States
of the United States and Canada

Additional regions recognized
in the bibliography (not shown on map)

RUPERT'S LAND	APPALACHIA	SOUTHWEST
EAST (U.S.)	EASTERN INTERIOR	MOUNTAIN WEST
NORTHEAST (U.S.)	MISSISSIPPI VALLEY	PACIFIC NORTHWEST
District of Columbia	GREAT PLAINS	

Subregions

Quebec	a	Southern Quebec
	b	Northern Quebec
Ontario	a	Eastern Ontario
	b	Central Ontario
	c	Southwestern Ontario
	d	Northern Ontario

0   500   1,000
Miles

MPC

Appendix 2

List of Serials Consulted

Complete runs of the following journals and monograph series have been consulted for this bibliography.

UNITED STATES
GEOGRAPHICAL
SERIALS

Alaska Geographic
Annals of the Association of American Geographers
Annals of Tourism Research
Antipode
Bulletin of the Philadelphia Geographical Society
Bulletin of the American Geographical Society (*later* Journal, *then* Geographical Review)
Bulletin of the Illinois Geographical Society
California Geographer
East Lakes Geographer
Economic Geography
Ecumene
Florida Geographer
Geographical Bulletin
Geographical Perspectives
Geographical Review
Geographical Survey
Geoscience and Man
Great Plains–Rocky Mountains Geographical Journal
Historical Geography
Journal of Cultural Geography
Journal of Geography
Journal of the American Geographical Society (*formerly* Bulletin)
Kansas Geographer
Landscape
Material Culture (*formerly* Pioneer America)
Mississippi Geographer
Names
National Geographic Magazine
North American Culture
Northwestern University Studies in Geography
Ohio Geographers

Pennsylvania Geographer
Physical Geography
Pioneer America (*later* Material Culture)
Pioneer America Society Transactions
Proceedings of the Association of American Geographers
Proceedings of the New England–St. Lawrence Valley Division of the Association of American Geographers
Professional Geographer
Southeastern Geographer
Sport Place
Terra Incognita
Texas Geographic Magazine
University of California Publications in Geography
University of Chicago Geography Research Papers
Urban Geography
Vermont Geographer
Virginia Geographer
Wisconsin Geographer
Yearbook of the Association of Pacific Coast Geographers

UNITED STATES
HISTORICAL SERIALS

Agricultural History
Alabama Historical Quarterly
Alabama Review
Alaska History
American Historical Review
Annals of Iowa
Annals of Wyoming
Arizona and the West (*later* Journal of the Southwest)
Arkansas Historical Quarterly
California Historical Society Quarterly (*later* California History)
California History
Chicago History

Chronicles of Oklahoma
Connecticut Historical Bulletin
Connecticut Historical Society Bulletin
Connecticut History
Delaware History
East Tennessee Historical Society Publications
Essex Institute Historical Collections
Ethnohistory
Explorations in Economic History
Filson Club History Quarterly
Florida Historical Quarterly
Forest History (*later* Journal of Forest History)
Georgia Historical Quarterly
Great Lakes Review (*later* Michigan Historical Review)
Hawaiian Journal of History
Historical Methods
Historical New Hampshire
Idaho Yesterdays
Illinois Historical Journal
Indiana Magazine of History
Journal of American Ethnic History
Journal of American History
Journal of Arizona History
Journal of Economic History
Journal of Forest History
Journal of Interdisciplinary History
Journal of Mississippi History
Journal of Negro History
Journal of Social History
Journal of Southern History
Journal of the Early Republic
Journal of the Southwest
Journal of the West
Journal of Urban History
Kansas Historical Quarterly (*later* Kansas History)
Kansas History

Kentucky Historical Society
Register
Louisiana History
Maine Historical Society
Quarterly
Maryland Historical Magazine
Michigan History
Michigan Historical Review
Minnesota History
Mississippi Valley Historical
Review (later Journal of
American History)
Missouri Historical Review
Montana
Nebraska History
Nevada Historical Quarterly
New Jersey History
New Mexico Historical Review
New York Historical Society
Quarterly
New York History
North Carolina Historical Review
North Dakota History
Northern Louisiana Historical
Society Journal
Ohio History
Old Northwest
Oregon Historical Quarterly
Pacific Historical Review
Pennsylvania History
Pennsylvania Magazine of
History and Biography
Pittsburgh History
Prologue
Rhode Island History
Social Science History
South Carolina Historical
Magazine
South Dakota History
Southern California Quarterly
Southwestern Historical
Quarterly
Tennessee Historical Quarterly
Upper Midwest History
Utah Historical Quarterly
Vermont History
Virginia Magazine of History &
Biography
West Virginia History
Western Historical Quarterly
Western Pennsylvania Historical
Magazine (later Pittsburgh
History)

William & Mary Quarterly
Wisconsin Magazine of History

UNITED STATES
INTERDISCIPLINARY
SERIALS

American Quarterly
American Review of Canadian
Studies
Bulletin of the Southern
California Academy of
Sciences
Climatic Change
Environmental Review
Great Plains Journal
Great Plains Quarterly
Journal of American Culture
Journal of the Tennessee
Academy of Science
Journal of the Washington
Academy of Science
Kiva
Palacio
Papers of the Michigan Academy
of Science, Arts, and Letters
(later Michigan Academician)
Plateau
Proceedings of the California
Academy of Sciences
Proceedings of the Colorado
Scientific Society
Proceedings of the Indiana
Academy of Science
Proceedings of the Iowa
Academy of Science
Proceedings of the Minnesota
Academy of Science
Proceedings of the Montana
Academy of Sciences
Proceedings of the North Dakota
Academy of Science
Proceedings of the Ohio
Academy of Science
Proceedings of the Oklahoma
Academy of Science
Proceedings of the Pennsylvania
Academy of Science
Proceedings of the Utah
Academy of Science, Arts, and
Letters
Proceedings of the West Virginia
Academy of Science
Quarterly Journal of the Florida
Academy of Science

Revue de Louisiane/Louisiana
Review
Rocky Mountain Social Science
Journal (later Social Science
Journal)
Social Science Journal
Transactions of the Connecticut
Academy of Arts and Sciences
Transactions of the Illinois State
Academy of Science
Transactions of the Kansas
Academy of Science
Transactions of the Wisconsin
Academy of Science, Arts, and
Letters
United States Yearbook of
Agriculture
Urbanism Past & Present
Western Illinois Regional Studies
Winterthur Portfolio

CANADIAN
GEOGRAPHICAL
SERIALS

Albertan Geographer
B.C. Geographical Studies (later
Western Geography)
Bulletin of the Association of
Canadian Map Libraries and
Archives
Cahiers de géographie du
Québec
Canadian Cartographer (later
Cartographica)
Canadian Geographer
Canadian Geographic
Canadian Geographical Journal
(later Canadian Geographic)
Geographical Bulletin (Ottawa)
Ontario Geography
Plan Canada
Regina Geographical Studies
Revue de géographie de
Montréal
Western Geography

CANADIAN NON-
GEOGRAPHICAL AND
INTERDISCIPLINARY
SERIALS

Acadiensis
Alberta Historical Review
Alberta History
Archivaria

Arts Canada
B.C. Studies
Beaver
Bulletin of Canadian Studies
Bulletin of the Society for the Study of Architecture in Canada
Canadian Historical Association Historical Papers (*later* Journal of the Canadian Historical Association)
Canadian Ethnic Studies/Études ethniques du Canada
Canadian Historical Review
Canadian Journal of History and Social Science
Canadian Journal of Irish Studies
Canadian Papers in Rural History
Histoire sociale (see Social History)
History and Social Science Teacher
Island Magazine
Journal of Canadian Studies
Manitoba History
Material History Bulletin
Newfoundland Quarterly
Newfoundland Studies
Nova Scotia Historical Quarterly
Nova Scotia Historical Review
Ontario History
Plains Anthropologist
Prairie Forum
Québec Studies
Revue d'histoire de l'Amérique française
Saskatchewan History
Social History/Histoire sociale
Urban History Review

OVERSEAS GEOGRAPHICAL SERIALS

Abhandlungen des Geographischen Instituts der Freien Universität Berlin
Annales de géographie
Arbeiten aus dem Geographischen Institut der Universität des Saarlandes

Bonner Geographische Abhandlungen
Bulletin de l'Association de géographie français
Bulletin de la Société belge d'études géographiques
Cahiers d'outre mer
Colloquium geographicum
Deutsches Archiv für Landes- und Volkskunde
Erde
Erdkunde
Erdkundliches Wissen
Estudios geograficos
Frankfurter Geographische Hefte
Fränkische Geographische Gesellschaft, Mitteilungen
Freiburger Geographische Hefte
Geographische Gesellschaft in München, Mitteilungen
Geografiska annaler
Geographica helvetica
Geographical
Geographical Journal
Geographical Magazine (*later* Geographical)
Geography
Geographische Gesellschaft Hamburg, Mitteilungen
Geographische Gesellschaft Lübeck, Mitteilungen
Göttinger Geographische Abhandlungen
Hamburger Geographische Studien
Heidelberger Geographische Arbeiten
Imago Mundi
Information géographique
Irish Geography
Jahrbuch der Geographische Gesellschaft von Bern
Jahrbuch der Geographische Gesellschaft zu Hannover
Journal of Historical Geography
Karlsruher Geographische Hefte
Kieler Geographische Schriften
Kölner Geographische Arbeiten
Lund Studies in Geography, Series B

Mainzer Geographische Studien
Marburger Geographische Schriften
Mosella
Münchener Geographische Hefte
Münstersche Geographische Arbeiten
Norois
Pacific Viewpoint
Petermanns Geographische Mitteilungen
Petermanns Mitteilungen, Ergänzungshefte
Proceedings of the International Geographical Congresses
Revue belge de géographie
Rivista geografica italiana
Schriften des Geographisches Institut der Universität Kiel (*later* Kieler Geographische Schriften)
Scottish Geographical Magazine
Stuttgarter Geographische Studien
Transactions of the Institute of British Geographers
Tübinger Geographische Studien
Umeå University Geographical Reports
Verhandlungen der Deutscher Geographentag
Volksforschung
Westfälische Geographische Studien
Wiener Geographische Schriften
Wissenschaftliche Verhandlungen der Gesellschaft für Erdkunde zu Leipzig
Würzburger Geographische Arbeiten

OVERSEAS NONGEOGRAPHICAL SERIALS

British Journal of Canadian Studies
Journal of American Studies
Journal of Pacific History

Appendix 3

Gaps in the Bibliographical Record of Canadian and United States Historical Geography

(as reflected through missing categories in the bibliography)

The tables presented here show gaps in the research record of historical geography for the two countries, but they should not be interpreted too literally, as there are several forms of possible dual coverage in the topical treatment of regions not obvious in such tabulation. First, many topical categories can overlap significantly; see "Organization of the Topical Sections" (p. 134) for clarification. Second, individual works, particularly books, of a more general nature may cover many topics simultaneously and in depth. The gaps shown below reflect primarily the absence of work focused explicitly, by title, on topics that form the core of those categories.

Topical categories:

1	General	13	Extractive activity
2	Environmental change	14	Agriculture
3	Native peoples & white relations	15	Landscape
4	Exploration & mapping	16	Communications & trade
5	Popular images & evaluation	17	Manufacturing & industrialization
6	Regional settlement	18	Urban networks & urbanization
7	Population	19	Town growth
8	Rural & regional social geography	20	Urban economic structure
9	Political & administrative geography	21	Urban social structure
10	Economic development	22	Townscape
11	Resource management	23	Recreation & tourism
12	Land & land use	24	Planning
		25	Place names

CANADA

Region/Province	1	2	3	4	5	6	7	8	9	10	11	12	13	14	15	16	17	18	19	20	21	22	23	24	25
MULTIPLE REGIONS				•					•										•				•		
ATLANTIC PROVINCES		•					•		•	•				•	•		•	•	•				•		
Newfoundland & Labrador												•					•	•		•		•			•
Prince Edward Island	•		•	•			•	•	•		•	•	•		•	•	•	•	•	•	•		•	•	•
Nova Scotia	•		•						•								•						•		
New Brunswick	•				•				•								•	•		•			•		
Quebec as a whole									•				•				•	•	•			•		•	
Southern Quebec		•							•																
Northern & Eastern Quebec	•		•		•				•		•			•	•	•	•		•			•	•		•
Ontario as a whole									•									•	•			•			
Eastern Ontario				•					•														•		
Central Ontario							•		•		•				•										•
Southwestern Ontario																									
Northern Ontario	•					•	•							•				•		•					•
PRAIRIE PROVINCES									•								•		•				•	•	
Manitoba									•										•				•		
Saskatchewan		•		•				•									•	•				•	•	•	
Alberta				•			•	•									•			•					
British Columbia																									
Yukon Territory	•	•		•			•	•	•		•			•	•		•	•		•	•	•			
NORTH												•	•		•	•		•	•		•	•	•	•	
RUPERT'S LAND						•	•		•		•			•		•	•	•	•		•	•			
Northwest Territories	•				•		•	•	•		•		•	•		•	•		•	•		•		•	

UNITED STATES

Region/State	1	2	3	4	5	6	7	8	9	10	11	12	13	14	15	16	17	18	19	20	21	22	23	24	25
EAST											•						•	•	•	•	•		•	•	•
NORTHEAST		•										•					•		•		•				
NEW ENGLAND										•	•						•	•			•			•	
Maine			•		•					•	•					•	•				•		•		
New Hampshire	•	•	•	•	•		•	•	•	•	•	•		•	•	•	•	•	•		•	•		•	
Vermont													•							•		•	•		
Massachusetts													•					•							
Rhode Island		•	•	•	•			•			•	•		•	•			•		•	•				
Connecticut			•	•							•	•	•									•		•	•
MIDDLE ATLANTIC											•														
New York											•														
New Jersey		•						•			•					•				•					•
Pennsylvania	•										•														
Delaware	•			•	•	•	•	•	•	•	•	•	•	•	•		•		•			•	•	•	
Maryland				•				•	•	•				•							•				
District of Columbia	•	•		•	•	•		•	•	•	•					•	•	•		•					•
APPALACHIA	•		•	•		•		•		•	•	•	•	•	•	•	•	•					•	•	
SOUTH											•							•	•	•					
Virginia		•											•				•						•	•	
West Virginia	•	•	•		•	•		•			•		•	•	•	•	•	•	•		•	•	•		
North Carolina			•	•						•	•											•			
South Carolina		•							•							•					•	•			
Georgia										•	•										•	•			
Florida							•			•											•				
Alabama	•	•						•	•	•					•	•	•	•	•		•	•			
Mississippi			•					•	•	•	•					•				•	•	•	•	•	•
Tennessee			•			•					•					•			•		•	•			
Kentucky	•	•						•			•		•			•		•			•	•	•		
Missouri		•									•											•	•		
Arkansas		•		•			•				•					•			•			•	•		
Louisiana			•							•						•	•								
Texas																			•						
EASTERN INTERIOR	•	•	•			•		•			•			•			•		•	•	•		•	•	
MISSISSIPPI VALLEY				•				•			•	•					•			•		•			
MIDDLE WEST											•									•		•			
Ohio	•	•																			•				
Indiana								•	•																
Illinois																									
Michigan								•												•					
Wisconsin																									
Minnesota																									
Iowa		•	•				•	•	•			•		•				•			•	•	•		
WEST										•	•						•		•	•	•			•	•
GREAT PLAINS											•					•		•	•	•	•			•	•
North Dakota	•	•	•			•	•	•		•	•				•		•		•	•	•				
South Dakota			•					•	•				•	•	•	•		•	•			•	•		
Nebraska							•		•	•			•		•		•		•			•	•		
Kansas									•							•		•			•	•			
Oklahoma				•					•						•		•			•	•	•	•		
SOUTHWEST								•			•		•				•		•	•	•	•			
MOUNTAIN WEST	•	•				•			•	•					•		•		•	•		•			
New Mexico			•				•		•						•		•			•	•	•	•		
Arizona				•	•		•	•							•		•					•	•		
Colorado			•			•									•		•						•	•	
Utah						•					•		•			•				•	•	•	•		
Nevada			•	•		•	•		•	•	•	•	•	•	•		•	•		•	•	•	•		
Wyoming	•	•		•			•	•	•	•	•	•	•	•	•	•	•	•	•	•	•	•	•		
Montana			•		•	•	•							•			•		•	•	•	'	•	•	
Idaho	•	•	•	•	•	•			•				•			•	•		•	•	•	•	•	•	
PACIFIC NORTHWEST					•							•			•				•	•	•		•	•	
Washington		•								•	•	•		•							•		•	•	
Oregon																							•	•	
California																								•	
Alaska									•			•		•		•			•	•	•	•	•		
Hawaii									•		•		•				•								

PART II

GENERAL SOURCES

BIBLIOGRAPHIES

GENERAL FINDING AIDS

Published works

[Note: The sequence of listing in this subsection (only) is from comprehensive to specialized coverage.]

Bibliographie géographique internationale (Paris: Centre national de la recherche scientifique, Laboratoire d'information et de documentation en géographie, 1891–), quarterly. **1**

Current Geographical Publications: Additions to the Research Catalogue of the American Geographical Society Collection of the University of Wisconsin–Milwaukee Library (Milwaukee: University of Wisconsin–Milwaukee, American Geographical Society Collection, Golda Meir Library, 1– , 1938–), 10 issues per annum. **2**

Geo Abstracts, Series D, *Social and Historical Geography* (Norwich, England: Geo Abstracts, 1966–1988), bimonthly. **3**

American Geographical Society, *Research Catalogue of the American Geographical Society* (Boston: G. K. Hall, 1962), 15 vols., 10,453 pp. **4**

American Geographical Society, *Research Catalogue of the American Geographical Society: First Supplement* (Boston: G. K. Hall, 1972–1974), 4 vols.: *Regional* (1972), 2 vols.; *Topical* (1974), 2 vols. **5**

American Geographical Society, *Research Catalogue of the American Geographical Society: Second Supplement* (Boston: G. K. Hall, 1978), 2 vols.: *Regional Catalog*, 614 pp.; *Topical Catalog*, 686 pp. **6**

Writings on American History: A Subject Bibliography of Articles (Washington, D.C.: American Historical Association, various series, 1902–). **7**

America: History and Life (Santa Barbara: American Bibliographical Center–CLIO, 1964–). **8**

Bibliographia Cartographica (New York: K. G. Saur, 1974–). **9**

Harris, Chauncy D., et al., eds., *A Geographical Bibliography for American Libraries* (Washington, D.C.: Association of American Geographers and the National Geographic Society, 1985), 437 pp. **10**

Kish, George, ed., *Bibliography of International Geographical Congresses, 1871–1976* (Boston: G. K. Hall, 1979), 540 pp. **11**

Dunbar, Gary S., *The History of Modern Geography: An Annotated Bibliography of Selected Works* (New York: Garland Publishing, 1985), 386 pp. Also *The History of Modern Geography: Corrigenda and Addenda* (n.p.: The author, 1987), 57 pp. **12**

Brown, Catherine L., and James O. Wheeler, *A Bibliography of Geographic Thought* (New York: Greenwood Press, 1989), 520 pp. **13**

Steiner, Michael C., and Clarence Mondale, *Region and Regionalism in the United States: A Sourcebook for the Humanities and Social Sciences* (New York: Garland Publishing Co., 1988), 495 pp. **14**

Pfeiffer, Gottfried, "Arbeiten deutscher Geographen über Nordamerika seit dem Kriege," *Geographische Zeitschrift*, vol. 46, 9 (1940), pp. 322–334. **15**

Lee, David R., *Women and Geography: A Comprehensive Bibliography* (Boca Raton: Florida Atlantic University, 1988), 63 pp. Also annual supplements, 1988–1991. **16**

Carlson, Alvar W., "A Bibliography of the Geographical Literature on the American Indian, 1920–1971," *Professional Geographer*, vol. 24, 3 (1972), pp. 258–263. **17**

Sutton, Imre, *Indian Land Tenure: Bibliographical Essays and a Guide to the Literature* (New York: Clearwater Publishing Co., 1975), 290 pp. **18**

Jakle, John A., *Ethnic and Racial Minorities in North America: A Selected Bibliography of the Geographical Literature* (Monticello, Ill.: Council of Planning Librarians Exchange Bibliography, nos. 459–460, 1973), 71 pp. **19**

Ernst, Robert T., *The Geographical Literature of Black America, 1949–1972: A Selected Bibliography of Journal Articles, Serial Publications, Theses, and Dissertations* (Monticello, Ill.: Council of Planning Librarians Exchange Bibliography, no. 492, 1973), 29 pp. **20**

Parsons, James J., and Natalia Vonnegut, eds., *Sixty Years of Berkeley Geography, 1923–1983: Biobibliographies of 159 PhDs Granted by the University of California, Berkeley, since the Establishment of a Doctoral Program in Geography in 1923* (Berkeley: University of California Department of Geography, Supplement to *Itinerant Geographer*, Nov. 1983), 162 pp. **21**

Theses & dissertations

Whittlesey, Derwent S., "Dissertations in Geography Accepted by Universities in the United States for the Degree of Ph.D. as of May 1935," *Annals of the Association of American Geographers*, vol. 25, 4 (1935), pp. 211–237.   22

Hewes, Leslie, "Dissertations in Geography Accepted by Universities in the United States and Canada for the Degree of Ph.D., June 1935, to June 1946, and Those Currently in Progress," *Annals of the Association of American Geographers*, vol. 36, 4 (1946), pp. 215–238.   23

Browning, Clyde E., *A Bibliography of Dissertations in Geography: 1901 to 1969; American and Canadian Universities* (Chapel Hill: University of North Carolina Department of Geography, Studies in Geography no. 1, 1970), 1,582 entries, 96 pp.   24

Fraser, J. Keith, and Mary C. Hynes, *List of Theses and Dissertations on Canadian Geography* (Ottawa: Department of Environment, Lands Directorate, Geographical Paper no. 51, 1972), 114 pp.   25

Comprehensive Dissertation Index, 1861–1972, vol. 16, *Geography and Geology*, and later annual supplements (Ann Arbor, Mich.: University Microfilms International, 1973–).   26

Stuart, Merrill M., *A Bibliography of Master's Theses in Geography: American and Canadian Universities* (Tualatin, Oreg.: Geographic and Area Study Publications, 1973), 5,050 entries, 275 pp.   27

Hodson, Dean R., *A Bibliography of Dissertations and Theses in Geography on Anglo-America, 1960–1972* (Monticello, Ill.: Council of Planning Librarians Exchange Bibliography, nos. 583–584, 1974), 202 pp.   28

Association of American Geographers, *Guide to Departments of Geography in the United States and Canada*, various editions (Washington, D.C.: The Association, 1979–1990).   29

Browning, Clyde E., *A Bibliography of Dissertations in Geography: 1969 to 1982; American and Canadian Universities* (Chapel Hill: University of North Carolina Department of Geography, Studies in Geography no. 18, 1983), 145 pp.   30

NORTH AMERICA

General works

Rumney, Thomas A., *The Practice of Historical Geography in the U.S. and Canada: A Bibliography, 1978–1988* (Oxford: Miami University, for the Ohio Department of Geography and Association of American Geographers Historical

Geography Specialty Group, Paper no. 1, 1988), 63 pp.   31

Topical works

Meynen, Emil, *Bibliography on German Settlement in Colonial North America* (Leipzig: O. Harrassowitz, 1937), 636 pp.   32

Merrens, H. Roy, *Urban Waterfront Redevelopment in North America: An Annotated Bibliography* (Toronto: University of Toronto/York University Joint Program in Transportation, Research Report no. 66, 1980), 104 pp.   33

Sealock, Richard B., Margaret M. Sealock, and Margaret S. Powell, *Bibliography of Place-Name Literature: United States and Canada*, 3d ed. (Chicago: American Library Association, 1982), 435 pp.   34

CANADA

General works

Ehlers, Eckart, "Deutsche Beiträge zur geographischen Kanada-Forschung: Möglichkeiten und Grenzen komparativer Forschung," *Zeitschrift der Gesellschaft für Kanada-Studien*, vol. 2 (1983), pp. 35–47.   35

Rumney, Thomas A., *The Historical Geography of Canada: A Selected Bibliography* (Monticello, Ill.: Vance Bibliographies, 1985), 34 pp. Revised 1988, 44 pp.   36

Regional works

Wood, J. David, "Historical Geography in Alberta," *Albertan Geographer*, vol. 1 (1964–1965), pp. 17–19.   37

Durocher, René, and Paul-André Linteau, *Histoire du Québec: Bibliographie selective, 1867–1970* (Trois-Rivières: Éditions Boréal Express, 1970), 1,897 entries, 189 pp.   38

Ross, Eric, "The Atlantic Provinces in Recent Studies in Canadian Historical Geography," *Acadiensis*, vol. 5, 1 (1975), pp. 108–117.   39

Crochetière, Jacques, and Louis Dupont, "Genèse des structures d'habitat dans les seigneuries du Québec: Une bibliographie selective," *Cahiers de géographie du Québec*, vol. 28, 73–74 (1984), pp. 317–327.   40

Topical works

Hayward, Robert J., "Sources for Urban Historical Research: Insurance Plans and Land Use Atlases," *Urban History Review*, vol. 1–73 (1973), pp. 2–9.   41

Marshall, John U., "Geography's Contribution to the Historical Study of Urban Canada," *Urban History Review*, no. 1–73 (1973), pp. 15–23. 42

Winearls, Joan, *Mapping Upper Canada, 1784–1867: An Annotated Bibliography of Manuscript and Printed Maps* (Toronto: University of Toronto Press, 1991), 986 pp. 43

UNITED STATES

General works

Hanchey, Marguerite, "Geographical Information in the Serial Publications of Selected State Historical Associations: An Annotated Bibliography," Master's thesis, Louisiana State University, 1962. 44

McManis, Douglas R., *Historical Geography of the United States: A Bibliography, Excluding Alaska and Hawaii* (Ypsilanti: Eastern Michigan University Press, 1965), 249 pp. 45

Murray, Mary R. C., "Geography in the Nineteenth Century Agricultural Publications of the U.S. Patent Office and the U.S. Department of Agriculture, 1845–1899: A Selected, Annotated Bibliography," Master's thesis, Louisiana State University, 1969. 46

Janiskee, Robert L., and Ary J. Lamme III, *Applied Historical Geography: An Annotated Bibliography* (Columbia: University of South Carolina, Department of Geography, 1977), 12 pp. 47

Jakle, John A., *Past Landscapes: A Bibliography for Historic Preservationists; A Revised Edition* (Monticello, Ill.: Vance Bibliographies, A–314, 1980), 68 pp. 48

Conzen, Michael P., *New Geographies of the Past: A Register of Research Interest in and Recent Publications on American and Related Historical Geography* (Chicago: University of Chicago, Department of Geography, for the Historical Geography Specialty Group, Association of American Geographers, 1981), 56 pp. 49

Grim, Ronald E., *Historical Geography of the United States: A Guide to Information Sources* (Detroit: Gale Research Co., 1982), 291 pp. 50

Regional works

The North

Pillsbury, Richard R., *Field Guide to Folk Architecture of the Northern United States* (Hanover: Dartmouth College Publications in Geography, no. 8, 1970). 51

Conzen, Michael P., and Kay J. Carr, eds., *The Illinois & Michigan Canal National Heritage Corridor: A Guide to Its History and Sources*

(Dekalb, Ill.: Northern Illinois University Press, 1988), 337 pp. 52

The South

Gritzner, Janet H., "Historical Archeology of the Colonial Southeast: A Bibliography," *Florida Journal of Anthropology*, vol. 5 (1980), pp. 26–28. 53

Stoddard, Ellwyn R., Richard L. Nostrand, and Jonathan P. West, *Borderlands Sourcebook: A Guide to the Literature on Northern Mexico and the American Southwest* (Norman: University of Oklahoma Press, 1983), 445 pp. 54

The West

Durrenberger, Robert W., "A Selected California Bibliography: Explorations and Settlement: The Spanish and Mexican Period," *California Geographer*, vol. 6 (1965), pp. 73–86. 55

Durrenberger, Robert W., "A Selected California Bibliography: Exploration and Settlement: The American Period," *California Geographer*, vol. 7 (1966), pp. 55–81. 56

Conroy, William B., "Studies in Historical Geography on the Dry Lands of the U.S.," in Otis W. Templer, ed., *Social Science Research in the Drylands: Frontiers of the Semi-Arid World, An International Symposium* (Lubbock: Texas Tech University International Center for Arid and Semi-Arid Studies, 1976), pp. 5–13. 57

Carney, George O., *Oklahoma's Folk Music Traditions: A Resource Guide* (Stillwater: Oklahoma State University Publishing, 1979), 104 pp. 58

Topical works

The Environment

Colten, Craig E., *Industrial Waste Management Practices, 1890–1950: A Bibliography* (Monticello, Ill.: Vance Bibliographies, 1986), 25 pp. 59

Cartography

Karrow, Robert W., ed., *Checklist of Maps of the Middle West Printed before 1900*, 13 vols. (Boston: G. K. Hall, 1981); vol. 14: *Index* (Chicago: Newberry Library, 1983). 60

Ehrenberg, Ralph E., *Scholar's Guide to Washington, D.C. for Cartography and Remote Sensing* (Washington: Smithsonian Institute, 1987), 420 pp. 61

Political geography

Sable, Martin H., "The Northwest Ordinance of 1787: An Interdisciplinary Bibliography," *Bulletin of the Special Libraries Association Geog-*

raphy and Map Division, no. 149 (Sept. 1987), pp. 16–43.   **62**

Landscape

Noble, Allen G., "A Preliminary Annotated Bibliography on Silos," *Historic Schaefferstown Record*, vol. 10, 1 (1976), pp. 2–12.   **63**

Meyer, Douglas K., John A. Jakle, and Robert W. Bastian, *American Common Houses: A Selected Bibliography of Vernacular Architecture* (Monticello, Ill.: Vance Bibliographies, no. A–574, 1981), 29 pp.   **64**

Noble, Allen G., "The Farm Silo: An Annotated Bibliography," *Journal of Cultural Geography*, vol. 1, 2 (1981), pp. 118–126.   **65**

Noble, Allen G., "Sod Houses and Similar Structures: A Brief Evaluation of the Literature," *Pioneer America*, vol. 13, 2 (1981), pp. 61–66.   **66**

Noble, Allen G., and Jean Danis, "The Literature on Fences, Walls, and Hedges as Cultural Landscape Features," *Pennsylvania Folklore*, vol. 33, 1 (1983), pp. 41–47.   **67**

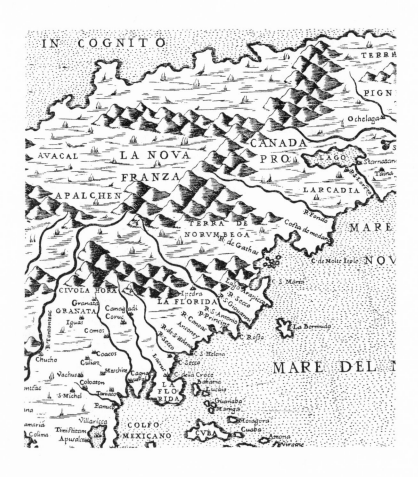

METHODOLOGICAL
STATEMENTS

Includes works focused specifically on the practice of historical geography in the United States and Canada, and also more general reflections on the flow of ideas in the field by scholars resident in the two countries.

NORTH AMERICA

Substantive works

Clark, Andrew Hill, "Historical Geography in North America," in Alan R. H. Baker, ed., *Progress in Historical Geography* (Newton Abbot: David & Charles, 1972), pp. 129–143. **68**

Harris, R. Cole, "The Historical Geography of North American Regions," *American Behavioral Scientist*, vol. 22, 1 (1978), pp. 115–130. **69**

Conzen, Michael P., "Historical Geography: North American Progress during the 1970s," *Progress in Human Geography*, vol. 4, 4 (1980), pp. 549–559. **70**

Earle, Carville V., et al., "Historical Geography," in Gary L. Gaile and Cort J. Willmott, eds., *Geography in America* (Columbus: Merrill Publishing Co., 1989), pp. 156–191. **71**

Methodological works

Goheen, Peter G., "Methodology in Historical Geography: The 1970s in Review," *Historical Methods*, vol. 16, 1 (1983), pp. 8–15. **72**

Mitchell, Robert D., "The North American Past: Retrospect and Prospect," in Robert D. Mitchell and Paul A. Groves, eds., *North America: The Historical Geography of a Changing Continent* (Totowa, N.J.: Rowman & Littlefield, 1987), pp. 3–21. **73**

Green, D. Brooks, ed., *Historical Geography: A Methodological Portrayal* (Totowa, N. J.: Rowman & Littlefield, 1991, 400 pp. **74**

Kay, Jeanne C., "Landscapes of Women and Men: Rethinking the Regional Historical Geography of the United States and Canada," *Journal of Historical Geography*, vol. 17, 4 (1991), pp. 435–452. **75**

CANADA

Substantive works

Harris, R. Cole, "Historical Geography in Canada," *Canadian Geographer*, vol. 11, 4 (1967), pp. 235–250. **76**

Meinig, Donald W., "Interpreting Canada: An American View," in Graeme Wynn, ed., *Interpreting Canada: Four Essays*, (Vancouver: Tantalus Research, B.C. Geographical Series, no. 43, 1986), pp. 27–42. **77**

Ruggles, Richard I., "The Next Step Forward: A Further Review of Research on the History of Cartography and Historical Cartography in Canada," in Barbara Farrell and Aileen Desbarats, eds., *Explorations in the History of Canadian Mapping: A Collection of Essays* (Ottawa: Association of Canadian Map Libraries and Archives, 1988), pp. 1–19. **78**

Wynn, Graeme, Introduction to his *People, Places, Patterns, Processes: Geographical Perspectives on the Canadian Past* (Toronto: Copp Clark Pitman, 1990), pp. 1–37. **79**

Methodological works

Miller, Émile, "La géographie au service de l'histoire," *Revue trimestrielle canadienne*, vol. 1, 1 (1915), pp. 45–53. **80**

Lowther, G. R., "Idealist History and Historical Geography," *Canadian Geography*, vol. 14 (1959), pp. 30–36. **81**

Clark, Andrew Hill, "Honing the Edge of Curiosity: The Challenge of Historical Geography in Canada," Canadian Association of Geographers, British Columbia Division, *Occasional Papers*, vol. 4 (1963), pp. 1–8. **82**

Fieguth, Wolfgang, "Historical Geography and the Concept of the Authentic Past as a Regional Resource," *Ontario Geographer*, vol. 1 (1967), pp. 55–59. **83**

Harris, R. Cole, "Reflections on the Fertility of the Historical Geographical Mule," University of Toronto Department of Geography Discussion Paper no. 10 (1970). **84**

Moodie, D. Wayne, and John C. Lehr, "Fact and Theory in Historical Geography," *Professional Geographer*, vol. 28, 2 (1970), pp. 132–135. **85**

Gentilcore, R. Louis, "The Use of Maps in Historical Geography," *Proceedings of the Annual Conference of the Association of Canadian Map*

Libraries, vol. 5 (1971), pp. 41–48. Reprinted in Barbara Farrell and Aileen Desbarats, eds., *Explorations in the History of Canadian Mapping: A Collection of Essays* (Ottawa: Association of Canadian Map Libraries and Archives, 1988), pp. 21–31.   86

Guelke, Leonard T., "Problems of Scientific Explanation in Geography," *Canadian Geographer*, vol. 15, 1 (1971), pp. 38–53.   87

Harris, R. Cole, "Theory and Synthesis in Historical Geography," *Canadian Geographer*, vol. 15, 2 (1971), pp. 157–172. Reprinted in D. Brooks Green, ed., *Historical Geography: A Methodological Portrayal* (Savage, Md.: Rowman & Littlefield Publishers, 1991), pp. 147–164.   88

Koroscil, Paul M., "An Introduction to Historical Geography," Indiana State University Department of Geography, Discussion Paper no. 4 (1971).   89

Koroscil, Paul M., "Historical Geography: A Resurrection," *Journal of Geography*, vol. 70, 7 (1971), pp. 415–420.   90

Johnston, Judith A., "The Use of Perception in Historical Geography," Master's thesis, University of Toronto, 1972.   91

Warkentin, John H., "Nineteenth and Twentieth Century Maps and the Teaching of Canadian Studies," *Proceedings of the Sixth Annual Conference of the Association of Canadian Map Libraries* (1972), pp. 36–45.   92

Lemon, James T., "Approaches to the Study of the Urban Past: Geography," *Urban History Review*, vol. 2–73 (1973), pp. 13–19.   93

Lemon, James T., "Study of the Urban Past: Approaches by Geographers," in *Canadian Historical Papers 1973* (Ottawa: Canadian Historical Association, 1973), pp. 179–190.   94

Guelke, Leonard, "An Idealist Alternative in Historical Geography," *Annals of the Association of American Geographers*, vol. 64, 2 (1974), pp. 193–202.   95

Moodie, D. Wayne, John C. Lehr, and John A. Alwin, "Zelinsky's Pursuit: Wild Goose or Canard?" *Historical Geography Newsletter*, vol. 4, 2 (1974), pp. 18–21. Reprinted in D. Brooks Green, ed., *Historical Geography: A Methodological Portrayal* (Savage, Md.: Rowman & Littlefield Publishers, 1991), pp. 194–197.   96

Zubrzycki, Andrée Gendreau, "Réflexions sur la géographie historique," *Cahiers de géographie du Québec*, vol. 18, 44 (1974), pp. 353–356.   97

Guelke, Leonard, "On Rethinking Historical Geography," *Area*, vol. 7, 2 (1975), pp. 135–138.   98

Lovell, W. George, "The Place of Synthesis in Geographical Investigation and Study of Historical Geography," *Albertan Geographer*, vol. 12 (1976), pp. 71–81.   99

Moodie, D. Wayne, and John C. Lehr, "Fact and Theory in Historical Geography," *Professional Geographer*, vol. 28, 2 (1976), pp. 132–135. Reprinted in D. Brooks Green, ed., *Historical Geography: A Methodological Portrayal* (Savage, Md.: Rowman & Littlefield Publishers, 1991), pp. 212–216.   100

Harris, R. Cole, "The Historical Mind and the Practice of Geography," in David Ley and Marwyn Samuels, eds., *Humanistic Geography: Problems and Prospects* (Chicago: Maroufa Press, 1978), pp. 123–137. Reprinted in D. Brooks Green, ed., *Historical Geography: A Methodological Portrayal* (Savage, Md.: Rowman & Littlefield Publishers, 1991), pp. 285–298.   101

Mannion, John J., "Multidisciplinary Dimensions in Material History," *Material History Bulletin*, vol. 8 (Mar. 1979), pp. 11–20. Reprinted in Barbara Reily, ed., *Canada's Material History: A Forum* (Ottawa: National Museum of Man, 1980), pp. 21–25.   102

Norton, William, "Current Trends of Historical Approach in Geographical Research," in *Historical Geography*, vol. 19 (Prague: Institute of Czechoslovak and World History of the Czechoslovak Academy of Sciences, 1980), pp. 37–57.   103

Norton, William, "The Analysis of Progress in Historical Geography," *South African Geographical Journal*, vol. 63, 1 (1981), pp. 24–34.   104

Chambers, Robert W., "Images, Acts, and Consequences: A Critical Review of Historical Geosophy," in Alan R. H. Baker and Mark Billinge, eds., *Period and Place: Research Methods in Historical Geography* (Cambridge: Cambridge University Press, 1982), pp. 197–204.   105

Guelke, Leonard, *Historical Understanding in Geography: An Idealist Approach* (Cambridge: University of Cambridge, 1982), 109 pp.   106

Norton, William, "Historical Geography as the Evolution of Spatial Form," in Alan R. H. Baker and Mark Billinge, eds., *Period and Place: Research Methods in Historical Geography* (Cambridge: Cambridge University Press, 1982), pp. 251–257. Reprinted in D. Brooks Green, ed., *Historical Geography: A Methodological Portrayal* (Savage, Md.: Rowman & Littlefield Publishers, 1991), pp. 363–370.   107

Norton, William, "The Cultural Landscape of the Historical Frontier," *Journal of Cultural Geography*, vol. 3, 2 (1983), pp. 115–120.   108

Wynn, Graeme, "Settler Societies in Geographical Focus," *Historical Studies*, vol. 20, 3 (1983), 353–366. **109**

Norton, William, *Historical Analysis in Geography* (New York: Longman, 1984), 231 pp. **110**

Wiesinger, Judith P., "Simulation Modeling in Historical Settlement Geography," *Modeling and Simulation*, vol. 15 (1984), pp. 195–199. **111**

Norton, William, "Historical Geography, Spatial Analysis, and the New Economic History," *National Geographical Journal of India*, vol. 33, 2 (1987), pp. 97–109. **112**

Norton, William, "Abstract Cultural Landscapes," *Journal of Cultural Geography*, vol. 8, 1 (1987), pp. 67–80. **114**

Kidd, Betty, "Maps as Sources of Historical Evidence," in Barbara Farrell and Eileen Desbarats, eds., *Explorations in the History of Canadian Mapping: A Collection of Essays* (Ottawa: Association of Canadian Map Libraries, 1988), pp. 33–46. **113**

Warkentin, John H., "Historical Geography," *Canadian Encyclopedia*, vol. 2 (Edmonton: Hurtig Publishers, 1988), p. 991. **115**

Norton, William, *Explorations in the Understanding of Landscape: A Cultural Geography* (Westport, Conn.: Greenwood Press, 1989), 201 pp. **116**

UNITED STATES

Substantive works

Clark, Andrew Hill (chairman, editorial committee; and principal author), "Historical Geography," in Preston E. James and Clarence F. Jones, eds., *American Geography: Inventory and Prospect* (Syracuse: Syracuse University Press for the Association of American Geographers, 1954), pp. 70–105. **117**

Bumsted, John, and James T. Lemon, "New Approaches in Early American Studies: The Local Community in New England," *Social History/Histoire Sociale*, vol. 2 (1968), pp. 98–112. **118**

Trindell, Roger T., "American Folklore Studies and Geography," *Southern Folklore Quarterly*, vol. 34, 1 (1970), pp. 1–11. **119**

Dunbar, Gary S., "Illustrations of the American Earth: A Bibliographical Essay on the Cultural Geography of the United States," *American Studies*, vol. 12, 1 (1973), pp. 3–15. **120**

Meinig, Donald W., "The Continuous Shaping of America: A Prospectus for Geographers and Historians," *American Historical Review*, vol. 83, 5 (1978), pp. 1186–1217. **121**

Lewis, Peirce F., "Learning from Looking: Geographic and Other Writing about the American Cultural Landscape," *American Quarterly*, vol. 35, 3 (1983), pp. 242–261. **122**

Methodological works

Early pedagogical statements

Hillard, George S., "On the Connection between Geography and History," *Lectures Delivered before the American Institute of Instruction, 1845*, vol. 16 (1846), pp. 269–307. Also published separately: *On the Connection between Geography and History* (Boston: William D. Ticknor & Co., 1846), 43 pp. **123**

Hinsdale, Burke A., "History and Geography," *Teacher* (New York), vol. 5, 1 (1892), pp. 15–18. **124**

Parker, Francis W., "The Relations of Geography to History," *National Geographic Magazine*, vol. 5, 1 (1894), pp. 125–131. **125**

Channing, Edward, "The Relation of Geography to History," *Proceedings of the National Educational Association*, vol. 34 (1895), pp. 192–196. **126**

Russell, James E., "History and Geography in the Higher Schools of Germany," *School Review*, vol. 5, 5 (1897), pp. 257–268, 539–547. **127**

Redway, Jacques W., "Influence of Environment on the Development of United States History," *Proceedings of the National Educational Association*, vol. 37 (1898), pp. 139–149, 160–162. **128**

Professional statements

Turner, Frederick Jackson, "Influence of Geography upon the Settlement of the United States," paper delivered to the Geographic Society of Chicago, c. 1898 (invited by Rollin D. Salisbury). While unpublished, it merits inclusion as seemingly the first discussion by a professional historian or geographer of the relations between geography and history applied to the American setting. MS in the Frederick Jackson Turner Papers, Henry E. Huntington Library, San Marino, California, File Drawer 14–A. **129**

Brigham, Albert Perry, "The Character and Limitations of Geographic Influence," *Proceedings of the Third Annual Convention of the Association of History Teachers, Middle States and Maryland Division* (1905), 13 pp. **130**

Brigham, Albert Perry, "Geography and History in the United States," *Journal of Geography*, vol. 3, 8 (1904), pp. 359–366. Also published in *Report of the Eighth International Geographical Congress, Held in the United States, 1904* (Washington, D.C.: Government Printing Office, House Document no. 460, 1905), pp. 958–965. **131**

Hubbard, George D., "Geographic Influence: A Field for Investigation" in *Report of the Eighth International Geographical Congress, Held in the United States, 1904* (Washington, D.C.: Government Printing Office, House Document no. 460, 1905), pp. 992–996.   132

Semple, Ellen Churchill, "Emphasis upon Anthropogeography in School" in *Report of the Eighth International Geographical Congress, Held in the United States, 1904* (Washington, D.C.: Government Printing Office, House Document no. 460, 1905), pp. 657–663.   133

Burr, George Lincoln, "The Place of Geography in the Teaching of History," *Annual Report of the New England History Teachers Association for 1907* (1908), pp. 1–13.   134

Turner, Frederick Jackson, "Report of the Conference on the Relations of Geography and History," *Annual Report of the American Historical Association for 1907*, vol. 1 (1908), pp. 45–48.   135

Semple, Ellen Churchill, "The Operation of Geographic Factors in History," *Report of the Ohio Valley Historical Association*, vol. 2 (1909), pp. 26–41. Also published in *Bulletin of the American Geographical Society*, vol. 41 (1909), pp. 422–439.   136

Sparks, Edwin E., "Report on the Conference on the Relations of Geography and History," *American Historical Association, Annual Report, 1908* (Washington, D.C.: 1909), pp. 57–61.   137

Huntington, Ellsworth, "The Geographer and History," *Geographical Journal*, vol. 43, 1 (1914), pp. 19–32.   138

Brigham, Albert Perry, "Problems of Geographic Influence," *Annals of the Association of American Geographers*, vol. 5 (1915), pp. 3–25. Also published in *Science*, n.s. vol. 41, 1051 (1915), pp. 261–280; and excerpted in *Scientific American* suppl. no. 2061 (July 1915), pp. 10–11.   139

Bone, Hugh A., "Geographic Problems in American History," *Proceedings of the Mississippi Valley Historical Association for the Year 1917–1918*, vol. 9 (1919), pp. 450–453.   140

Barnes, Harry E., "The Relation of Geography to the Writing and Interpretation of History," *Journal of Geography*, vol. 20, 9 (1921), pp. 321–337.   141

Brigham, Albert Perry, "Environment in the History of American Agriculture," *Journal of Geography*, vol. 21, 2 (1922), pp. 41–49.   142

Barrows, Harlan H., "Geography as Human Ecology," *Annals of the Association of American Geography*, vol. 13, 1 (1923), pp. 1–14.   143

Sauer, Carl Ortwin, "Recent Developments in Cultural Geography," in Harry E. Barnes et al., *Recent Developments in the Social Sciences* (Philadelphia: J. B. Lippincott Co., 1927), pp. 154–212.   144

Whittlesey, Derwent S., "Sequent Occupance," *Annals of the Association of American Geographers*, vol. 19, 3 (1929), pp. 162–165.   145

Sauer, Carl O., "Historical Geography and the Western Frontier," in James F. Willard and Colin B. Goodykoontz, eds., *The Trans-Mississippi West: Papers Presented at a Conference Held at the University of Colorado, June 18–21, 1929* (Boulder: University of Colorado, 1930), pp. 267–289. Reprinted in part in John Leighly, ed., *Land and Life: A Selection from the Writings of Carl Ortwin Sauer* (Berkeley: University of California Press, 1963), pp. 45–52.   146

Sauer, Carl O., "Geography, Cultural," *Encyclopaedia of the Social Sciences*, vol. 6 (New York: Macmillan Co., 1931), pp. 621–624. Reprinted in Philip L. Wagner and Marvin W. Mikesell, eds., *Readings in Cultural Geography* (Chicago: University of Chicago Press, 1962), pp. 30–34.   147

Vance, Rupert B., "Frontier: Geographical and Social Aspects," *Encyclopaedia of the Social Sciences*, vol. 6 (New York: Macmillan Co., 1931), pp. 503–506.   148

Dodge, Stanley D., et al., "Round Table on Problems in Cultural Geography," *Annals of the Association of American Geographers*, vol. 27, 3 (1937), pp. 155–175. [Sizeable contributions by Fred B. Kniffen, Derwent S. Whittlesey, Ralph Brown, and Preston James]   149

Huntington, Ellsworth, "Geography and History," *Canadian Journal of Economics and Political Science*, vol. 3, 4 (1937), pp. 565–572.   150

Dodge, Richard E., "The Interpretation of Sequent Occupance," *Annals of the Association of American Geographers*, 28, 4 (1938), pp. 233–237.   151

Odum, Howard W., and Harry E. Moore, "Exploring the Region: The Geographers," in their *American Regionalism: A Cultural-Historical Approach to National Integration* (New York: Henry Holt & Co., 1938), pp. 277–302.   152

Hartshorne, Richard, "The Relation of History to Geography," in his *The Nature of Geography: A Critical Survey of Current Thought in the Light of the Past* (Lancaster, Pa.: Association of American Geographers, 1939), pp. 175–188. Reprinted in D. Brooks Green, ed., *Historical Geography: A Methodological Portrayal* (Savage, Md.: Rowman & Littlefield Publishers, 1991), pp. 17–28.   153

Broek, Jan O. M., "The Relations between History and Geography," *Pacific History Review*, vol. 10, 3 (1941), pp. 321–325. Reprinted in D. Brooks Green, ed., *Historical Geography: A Methodological Portrayal* (Savage, Md.: Rowman & Littlefield Publishers, 1991), pp. 29–33.   **154**

Sauer, Carl O., "Foreword to Historical Geography," *Annals of the Association of American Geographers*, vol. 31, 1 (1941), pp. 1–24. Reprinted in John Leighly, ed., *Land and Life: A Selection from the Writings of Carl Ortwin Sauer* (Berkeley: University of California Press, 1963), pp. 351–379.   **155**

Whitaker, J. Russell, "Human Forces Remaking the Face of the Earth," *Social Education*, vol. 7, 7 (1943), pp. 301–306.   **156**

Steward, Julian H., "Cultural Geography and the Social Sciences," *Bulletin of the American Society for Professional Geographers*, vol. 2, 5 (1944), pp. 1–2.   **157**

Whittlesey, Derwent S., "The Horizon of Geography," *Annals of the Association of Geographers*, vol. 35, 1 (1945), pp. 1–36.   **158**

Clark, Andrew Hill, "Field Research in Historical Geography," *Professional Geographer*, vol. 4 (1946), pp. 13–23.   **159**

Brown, Ralph Hall, "The Treatment of Geographic Knowledge and Understanding in History Courses, with Special Reference to American History," in Clyde F. Kohn, ed., *Geographic Approaches to Social Education* (Washington, D.C.: National Council for the Social Studies, Nineteenth Yearbook, 1948), pp. 261–272. Summary version also published in *Journal of Geography*, vol. 47, 3 (1948), pp. 103–105.   **160**

Whitaker, J. Russell, "Historical Geography in School and College," *Peabody Journal of Education*, vol. 27 (1949), pp. 3–15.   **161**

Brown, Ralph H., "A Plea for Geography, 1813 Style," *Annals of the Association of American Geographers*, vol. 41, 3 (1951), pp. 233–236.   **162**

Kniffen, Fred B., "Geography and the Past," *Journal of Geography*, vol. 50, 3 (1951), pp. 126–129.   **163**

Mood, Fulmer, "The Origin, Evolution, and Application of the Sectional Concept: 1750–1900," in Merrill Jensen, ed., *Regionalism in America* (Madison: University of Wisconsin Press, 1951), pp. 5–98.   **164**

Platt, Robert S., "The Rise of Cultural Geography of America," *Proceedings of the Eighth General Assembly and Seventeenth International Congress, International Geographical Union, Washington, D.C.* (Washington: National Academy of Sciences–National Research Council, 1952), pp.

485–490. Reprinted in Philip L. Wagner and Marvin W. Mikesell, eds., *Readings in Cultural Geography* (Chicago: University of Chicago Press, 1962), pp. 35–43.   **165**

Malin, James C., "Historians and Geography," in his *On the Nature of History: Essays about History and Dissidence* (Lawrence, Kans.: The author, 1955), pp. 90–127.   **166**

Bacon, H. Phillip, "An Approach to Social Studies through Historical Geography," in Preston E. James, ed., *New Viewpoints in Geography* (Washington, D.C.: National Council for the Social Studies, Twenty-Ninth Yearbook, 1959), pp. 144–161.   **167**

Hartshorne, Richard, "Time and Genesis in Geography," in his *Perspectives on the Nature of Geography* (Chicago: Rand McNally, for the Association of American Geographers, 1959), pp. 81–107. Reprinted in D. Brooks Green, ed., *Historical Geography: A Methodological Portrayal* (Savage, Md.: Rowman & Littlefield Publishers, 1991), pp. 98–107.   **168**

Koelsch, William A., "Historical Geography: Perspective on the Past," Master's thesis, Clark University, 1959.   **169**

Clark, Andrew Hill, "Geographical Change: A Theme for Economic History," *Journal of Economic History*, vol. 20, 4 (1960), pp. 607–613.   **170**

Kniffen, Fred B., "To Know the Land and Its People," *Landscape*, vol. 9, 3 (1960), pp. 20–23.   **171**

Webb, Walter Prescott, "Geographical-Historical Concepts in American History and Comments," *Annals of the Association of American Geographers*, vol. 50, 2 (1960), pp. 85–97.   **172**

Wright, John K., "Geography and History Cross Classified," *Professional Geographer*, vol. 12, 5 (1960), pp. 7–10.   **173**

Wagner, Philip, and Marvin W. Mikesell, "The Themes of Cultural Geography," in Philip L. Wagner and Marvin W. Mikesell, eds., *Readings in Cultural Geography* (Chicago: University of Chicago Press, 1962), pp. 1–24.   **174**

Zobler, Leonard, "An Economic-Historical View of Natural Resource Use and Conservation," *Economic Geography*, vol. 38, 3 (1962), pp. 189–194.   **175**

Jackson, John Brinckerhoff, "The Meanings of 'Landscape'," *Kulturgeografi*, vol. 16, 88 (1964), pp. 47–51.   **176**

Ackermann, Edward, et al., "Studies in Cultural Geography," in *The Science of Geography*, Report of the Ad Hoc Committee on Geography, Earth Sciences Division, National Academy of

Sciences—National Research Council, Publication 1277 (Washington, D.C.: Government Printing Office, 1965), pp. 23–31.   177

Aschmann, Homer, "Cultural Geography: Applied and Theoretical," *Annals of the Association of American Geography*, vol. 55, 4 (1965), p. 604.
                                                             178

Broek, Jan O. M., "The Historical Dimension," in his *Geography: Its Scope and Spirit* (Columbus, Ohio: Charles E. Merrill Books, 1965), pp. 27–30.
                                                             179

Jacobson, Daniel, "The Role of Historical Geography in the American School," *Journal of Geography*, vol. 64, 3 (1965), pp. 99–105.   180

Merrens, Harry Roy, "Historical Geography and Early American History," *William & Mary Quarterly*, 3d ser., vol. 22, 4 (1965), pp. 529–548.
                                                             181

Newcomb, Robert M., *An Introduction to Historical Geography and Its Methods: A Compendium* (Aarhus, Denmark: University of Aarhus Geographical Institute, 1965), 28 pp.   182

Pitts, Forrest R., "A Graph-Theoretic Approach to Historical Geography," *Professional Geographer*, vol. 17, 5 (1965), pp. 15–20.   183

Stone, Kirk H., "The Development of a Focus for the Geography of Settlement," *Economic Geography*, vol. 41, 4 (1965), pp. 346–355.   184

Zelinsky, Wilbur, "Of Time and the Geographer," *Landscape*, vol. 15, 2 (1965–1966), pp. 21–22.   185

Gritzner, Charles F., Jr., "The Scope of Cultural Geography," *Journal of Geography*, vol. 65, 1 (1966), pp. 4–11.   186

Jordan, Terry G., "On the Nature of Settlement Geography," *Professional Geographer*, vol. 18, 1 (1966), pp. 26–28.   187

Stone, Kirk H., "Further Development of a Focus for the Geography of Settlement," *Professional Geographer*, vol. 18, 4 (1966), pp. 208–209.   188

Ward, David, "The Changing Dimensions of Historical Geography," in *Geographical Dialogue: University Viewpoints for Teachers* (Vancouver: Tantalus Research, B. C. Geographical Series, vol. 3, 1966), pp. 35–39.   189

Newcomb, Robert M., "The Persistence of Place," *Landscape*, vol. 17, 1 (1967), pp. 24–26.   190

Jacobson, Daniel, "Historical Geography," in John W. Morris, ed. *Methods of Geographic Instruction* (Waltham, Mass.: Blaisdell Publishing Co., 1968), pp. 276–285.   191

Mikesell, Marvin W., "Landscape," *International Encyclopedia of the Social Sciences*, vol. 8 (New

York: Macmillan Co. and the Free Press, 1968), pp. 575–580.   192

Price, Edward T., "Cultural Geography," *International Encyclopedia of the Social Sciences*, vol. 6 (New York: Macmillan Co. and the Free Press, 1968), pp. 129–134.   193

Trindell, Roger T. , "The Geographer, the Archives, and American Colonial History," *Professional Geographer*, vol. 20, 2 (1968), pp. 98–102.   194

Whitaker, J. Russell, "Recurrent Themes in the Historical Geography of the United States," *Peabody Journal of Education*, vol. 46, 1 (1968), pp. 9–13.   195

Newcomb, Robert M., "Twelve Working Approaches to Historical Geography," *Yearbook of the Association of Pacific Coast Geographers*, vol. 31 (1969), pp. 27–50. Reprinted in D. Brooks Green, ed., *Historical Geography: A Methodological Portrayal* (Savage, Md.: Rowman & Littlefield Publishers, 1991), pp. 106–125.   196

Seig, Louis, "The Challenge of Historical Geography," *Journal of the Minnesota Academy of Science*, vol. 36, 2–3 (1969–1970), pp. 110–112.   197

Newcomb, Robert M., "An Example of the Applicability of Remote Sensing: Historical Geography," *Geoforum*, vol. 2 (1970), pp. 89–92.   198

Henry, J. T., and Om Dikshit, "The Temporal Process in Geographic Thought," *Deccan Geographer*, vol. 9, 2 (1971), pp. 217–230.   199

Jakle, John A., "Time, Space, and the Geographic Past: A Prospectus for Historical Geography," *American Historical Review*, vol. 76, 4 (1971), pp. 1084–1103. Reprinted in D. Brooks Green, ed., *Historical Geography: A Methodological Portrayal* (Savage, Md.: Rowman & Littlefield Publishers, 1991), pp. 165–187.   200

Miller, Vincent P., Jr., "Some Observations on the Science of Cultural Geography," *Journal of Geography*, vol. 70, 1 (1971), pp. 27–35.   201

Clark, Andrew Hill, "Suggestions for the Geographical Study of Agricultural Change in the United States, 1790–1840," *Agricultural History*, vol. 46, 1 (1972), pp. 155–172. Reprinted, with omissions, in David Ward, ed., *Geographic Perspectives on America's Past: Readings on the Historical Geography of the United States* (New York: Oxford University Press, 1979), pp. 179–187.   202

Hornbeck, David, "Processes of Change and the Concept of Acculturation in Historical Geography," *Geographical Survey*, vol. 1, 2 (1972), pp. 24–33.   203

Zelinsky, Wilbur, "In Pursuit of Historical Geography and Other Wild Geese," *Historical Ge-*

ography Newsletter, vol. 3, 2 (1973), pp. 1–5. Reprinted in D. Brooks Green, ed., *Historical Geography: A Methodological Portrayal* (Savage, Md.: Rowman & Littlefield Publishers, 1991), pp. 188–193.   204

Jakle, John A., "A Historical Perspective on Rural Settlement: Comment," *Agricultural History*, vol. 48, 1 (1974), pp. 26–30.   205

Jakle, John A., "In Pursuit of a Wild Goose: Historical Geography and the Geographic Past," *Historical Geography Newsletter*, vol. 4, 1 (1974), pp. 13–16.   206

Sauer, Carl O., "The Fourth Dimension of Geography," *Annals of the Association of American Geographers*, vol. 64, 2 (1974), pp. 189–192. Reprinted in Carl O. Sauer, *Selected Essays, 1963–1975*, ed. Bob Callahan (Berkeley, Calif.: Turtle Island Foundation, for the Netzahaulcoyotl Historical Society, 1981), pp. 279–286.   207

Ullman, Edward L., "Space and/or Time: Opportunity for Substitution and Prediction," *Transactions of the Institute of British Geographers*, vol. 63 (1974), pp. 125–139. Reprinted in his *Geography as Spatial Interaction* (Seattle: University of Washington Press, 1980), pp. 41–63.   208

Ballas, Donald J., "Time and Place: An Introduction to Historical Geography," *Places*, vol. 2, 2 (1975), pp. 5–9.   209

Clark, Andrew Hill, "First Things First," in Ralph E. Ehrenberg, ed., *Pattern and Process: Research in Historical Geography* (Washington: Howard University Press, 1975), pp. 9–21.   210

Lowenthal, David, "Past Time, Present Place: Landscape and Memory," *Geographical Review*, vol. 65, 1 (1975), pp. 1–36.   211

Piellusch, Frederick, "Applied Historical Geography," *Pennsylvania Geographer*, vol. 13, 1 (1975), pp. 7–11. Reprinted in D. Brooks Green, ed., *Historical Geography: A Methodological Portrayal* (Savage, Md.: Rowman & Littlefield Publishers, 1991), pp. 206–211.   212

Pitzl, Gerald R., "A Note on the Element of Persistence," *Professional Geographer*, vol. 27, 1 (1975), pp. 113–115.   213

Wagner, Philip L., "The Themes of Cultural Geography Rethought," *Yearbook of the Association of Pacific Coast Geographers*, vol. 37 (1975), pp. 7–14.   214

Ward, David, "The Debate on Alternative Approaches in Historical Geography," *Historical Methods Newsletter*, vol. 8, 2 (1975), pp. 82–87. Reprinted in D. Brooks Green, ed., *Historical Geography: A Methodological Portrayal* (Savage, Md.: Rowman & Littlefield Publishers, 1991), pp. 198–205.   215

Dunbar, Gary S., "Historical Geography: Its Status and Concerns," *Environmental History Newsletter*, vol. 3, 1 (1976), pp. 15–17.   216

Gade, Daniel W., "L'optique culturelle dans la géographie américaine," *Annales de Géographie*, vol. 85, no. 472 (1976), pp. 672–693.   217

Clark, Andrew H., "The Whole Is Greater Than the Sum of Its Parts: A Humanistic Element in Human Geography," in Donald R. Deskins et al., eds., *Geographic Humanism, Analysis, and Social Action: A Half Century of Geography at Michigan* (Ann Arbor: University of Michigan, Michigan Geographical Publications, no. 17, 1977), pp. 3–26.   218

Kovacik, Charles F., "Applied Historical Geography and Landscape Studies," in Harold A. Winters and Marjorie K. Winters, eds., *Applications of Geographic Research: Viewpoints from Michigan State University* (East Lansing: Michigan State University Department of Geography, 1977), pp. 51–59.   219

Wagner, Philip L., "The Concept of Environmental Determinism in Cultural Evolution," in Charles A. Reed, ed., *Origins of Agriculture* (The Hague: Mouton, 1977), pp. 49–74.   220

Ernst, Joseph A., and H. Roy Merrens, "Praxis and Theory in the Writing of American Historical Geography," *Journal of Historical Geography*, vol. 4, 3 (1978), pp. 277–290.   221

Mikesell, Marvin W., "Tradition and Innovation in Cultural Geography," *Annals of the Association of American Geographers*, vol. 68, 1 (1978), pp. 1–16.   222

Spencer, Joseph E., "The Growth of Cultural Geography," *American Behavioral Scientist*, vol. 22, 1 (1978), pp. 79–92.   223

Vicero, Ralph D., "The Organizing of Historical Geography," *Historical Geography*, vol. 8, 2 (1978), pp. 20–21, 41.   224

Kniffen, Fred B., "Why Folk Housing?" *Annals of the Association of American Geographers*, vol. 69, 1 (1979), pp. 59–63.   225

Vanderhill, Burke G., and Rashey A. Malik, "Historical Perspective on Rural Settlement Geography," *Pakistan Geographical Review*, vol. 34, 1–2 (1979), pp. 11–32.   226

Wyckoff, William K., "On the Louisiana School of Cultural Geography and the Case of the Upland South," Syracuse University Department of Geography Discussion Paper no. 54 (1979), 34 pp.   227

Bastian, Robert W., "Urban Housetypes as a Research Focus in Historical Geograpy," *Environmental Review*, vol. 4, 2 (1980), pp. 27–34.   228

Cook, Edward M., Jr., "Geography and History: Spatial Approaches to Early American History," *Historical Methods*, vol. 13, 1 (1980), pp. 19–28.
229

Dunbar, Gary S., "Geosophy, Geohistory, and Historical Geography: A Study in Terminology," *Historical Geography*, vol. 10, 2 (1980), pp. 1–8.
230

Duncan, James S., "The Superorganic in American Cultural Geography," *Annals of the Association of American Geographers*, vol. 70, 2 (1980), pp. 181–198.
231

Jakle, John A., "Historical Geography: Focus on the Geographic Past and Historical Place," *Environmental Review*, vol. 4, 2 (1980), pp. 2–5.
232

Janiskee, Robert L., "Socially and Ecologically Responsible Historical Geography," *Environmental Review*, vol. 4, 2 (1980), pp. 35–40.
233

Ryan, K. Bruce, "Oral Historical Geography," in J. N. Jennings and G. J. R. Linge, eds., *Of Time and Place: Essays in Honour of O. H. K. Spate* (Canberra: Australian National University Press, 1980), pp. 95–115.
234

James, Preston E., and Geoffrey J. Martin, "The New Geography of the United States—World War I to Midcentury: Historical Geography," in their *All Possible Worlds: A History of Geographical Ideas* (New York: John Wiley & Sons, 1981), pp. 324–330.
235

Seager, Joni, and Michael Steinitz, "Preserving the Past: Some Recent Contributions in Applied Historical Geography," *Monadnock*, vol. 54–55 (1981–1982), pp. 27–42.
236

Denevan, William M., "Adaptation, Variation, and Cultural Geography," *Professional Geography*, vol. 35, 4 (1983), pp. 399–406.
237

McLennan, Marshall S., "New Opportunities in Historical Geography," *Geographical Bulletin*, vol. 26 (1984), pp. 5–9.
238

Monk, Janice, "Approaches to the Study of Women and Landscape," *Environmental Review*, vol. 8, 1 (1984), pp. 23–33.
239

Speth, William W., "On the Discrimination of Anthropo-Geographies," *Canadian Geographer*, vol. 31, 1 (1987), pp. 72–74.
240

Tímár, Lajos, "Some Special Directions of Research in U.S. Historical Geography from an East-Central European Point of View," *Historical Geography*, vol. 17, 2 (1987), pp. 1–11.
241

Meinig, Donald W., "The Historical Geography Imperative," *Annals of the Association of American Geographers*, vol. 79, 1 (1989), pp. 79–87.
242

Estaville, Lawrence, "Organizing Time in Historical Geography," in D. Brooks Green, ed., *Historical Geography: A Methodological Portrayal* (Savage, Md.: Rowman & Littlefield Publishers, 1991), pp. 310–324.
243

Jordan, Terry G., "Settlement Geography," in Gary S. Dunbar, ed., *Modern Geography: An Encyclopedic Survey* (New York: Garland Publishing, 1991), pp. 159–160.
244

Mitchell, Robert D., "Historical Geography," in Gary S. Dunbar, ed., *Modern Geography: An Encyclopedic Survey* (New York: Garland Publishing, 1991), pp. 77–78.
245

BENCHMARK
SCHOLARS

Includes works focusing on individuals who have made significant contributions to the historical geography of the United States and Canada, and who are deceased. Includes some individuals whose contributions to North American historical geography are embedded within larger effort in other subfields, marked (*), or beyond the discipline (**).

All material found relating to scholars specializing in historical geography has been included. Material on those whose historical contributions were less central to their own body of work has been included only selectively, favoring extended treatments and key statements.

CANADA

Johann Georg Kohl (*)
(1808–1878)

See UNITED STATES

William Francis Ganong (**)
(1864–1941)

Early student of Maritime settlement history and place names

"Ganong, William Francis, Botanist," *Who Was Who in America*, vol. 1 (Chicago: A. N. Marquis Co., 1942), p. 438.   **246**

Webster, John C., "William Francis Ganong (1864–1941)," *Transactions of the Royal Society of Canada*, 3d ser., vol. 36 (1942), pp. 90–91.   **247**

"Ganong, William Francis (1864–1941), Botanist and Historian," *Macmillan Dictionary of Canadian Biography* (London: Macmillan, 1963), p. 257.   **248**

"Ganong, William Francis, Botanist and Historian," *Encyclopedia Canadiana*, vol. 4 (Toronto: Grolier of Canada, [1975]), p. 318.   **249**

Bell, John B., and Gary T. Whiteford, "Exploring New Brunswick with W. F. Ganong," *Canadian Geographic*, vol. 99, 1 (1979), pp. 38–43.   **250**

Wynn, Graeme, "W. F. Ganong, A. H. Clark, and the Historical Geography of Maritime Canada," *Acadiensis*, vol. 10, 2 (1981), pp. 5–28.   **251**

McCallum, Margaret E., "Ganong, William Francis, Regional Historian, Cartographer, Botanist, Linguist," *Canadian Encyclopedia*, 2d ed., vol. 2 (Edmonton: Hurtig publishers, 1988), p. 873.   **252**

Marion Isabel Newbigin (*)
(1869–1934)

British geographer with interests in the broad historical geography of the St. Lawrence River basin

"Dr. Marion I. Newbigin," *Geographical Review*, vol. 24, 4 (1934), p. 676.   **253**

"Marion Isabel Newbigin," *Scottish Geographical Magazine*, vol. 50, 5 (1934), pp. 331–333.   **254**

Taylor, Eva G. R., "Dr. Marion I. Newbigin," *Geographical Journal*, vol. 84, 4 (1934), p. 367.   **255**

Freeman, T. Walter, "Two Ladies," *Geographical Magazine*, vol. 49, 3 (1976), p. 208.   **256**

Lawrence Johnston Burpee
(1873–1946)

Librarian-scholar, founding editor of the Canadian Geographical Journal, *who published the first historical atlas of Canada*

Read, John E., "Lawrence J. Burpee," *Canadian Geographical Journal*, vol. 33, 5 (1946), p. 240.   **257**

"Necrologie: Dr. L. J. Burpee," *Revue canadienne de géographie*, vol. 1, 1 (1947), p. 32.   **258**

Pelham, Edgar, "Lawrence J. Burpee," *Proceedings of the Royal Society of Canada*, 3d ser., vol. 41 (1947), pp. 115–117.   **259**

"Burpee, Lawrence Johnston (1873–1946)," *Macmillan Dictionary of Canadian Biography*, 3d ed. (Toronto: Macmillan Co., 1963), p. 95.   **260**

Raoul Blanchard (*)
(1877–1965)

French geographer who studied the "genre de vie" of Quebec in great detail

Dagenais, Pierre, "M. Raoul Blanchard," *Revue canadienne de géographie*, vol. 13, 1–2 (1959), pp. 80–82.   261

Institut de géographie de l'Université Laval, "Biographie" et "Liste des travers," *Mélanges géographiques canadiens offerts à Raoul Blanchard* (Québec: Presses de l'Université Laval, 1959), pp. 13–27, 35–45.   262

Hamelin, Louis-Edmond, "Homage à Monsieur Raoul Blanchard," *Revue canadienne de géographie*, vol. 14, 1–4 (1960), pp. 81–86.   263

Blanchard, Raoul, *Ma jeunesse sous l'aile de Péguy* (Paris: Fayard, 1961), 243 pp.   264

Hamelin, Louis-Edmond, "La géographie de Raoul Blanchard," *Canadian Geographer*, vol. 5, 1 (1961), pp. 1–9.   265

Blanchard, Raoul, *Je découvre l'université* (Paris: Fayard, 1963), 215 pp.   266

Dagenais, Pierre, "Hommage à la mémoire de Raoul Blanchard," *Revue de géographie de Montréal*, vol. 18, 2 (1964), pp. 133–135.   267

Blache, Jules, "Raoul Blanchard (1877–1965)," *Revue de géographie alpine*, vol. 53, 3 (1965), 361–370.   268

Crist, Raymond E., "Raoul Blanchard," *Geographical Review*, vol. 55, 4 (1965), pp. 602–603.   269

Faucher, Daniel, "Raoul Blanchard (1877–1965)," *Revue de géographie des Pyrénées et du sud-ouest*, vol. 36, 2 (1965), pp. 159–160.   270

Grenier, Fernand, "Raoul Blanchard (1877–1965)," *Canadian Geographer*, vol. 9, 2 (1965), pp. 101–104.   271

Perpillou, Aimé V., "Raoul Blanchard," *Acta geographica* (Paris), vol. 57, 3 (1965), p. 1.   272

Dresch, Jean, and Pierre George, "Raoul Blanchard (1877–1965)," *Annales de géographie*, vol. 75, 407 (1966), pp. 1–25.   273

In memoriam Raoul Blanchard (1877–1965) (Grenoble: Association des amis de l'université de Grenoble, 1966), 123 pp.   274

Dickinson, Robert E., "Raoul Blanchard," in his *The Makers of Modern Geography* (London: Routledge & Kegan Paul, 1969), pp. 234–236.   275

Taton, Juliette, "Blanchard, Raoul," *Dictionary of Scientific Biography*, vol. 2 (New York: Charles Scribner's Sons, 1970), pp. 190–191.   276

Hamelin, Louis-Edmond, "Connaissance de Raoul Blanchard," *Cahiers de géographie du Québec*, vol. 17, 42 (1973), pp. 483–488.   277

Beauregard, Ludger, "Raoul Blanchard à travers sa géographie de Montréal," *Cahiers de géographie du Québec*, vol. 30, 80 (1986), pp. 271–279.   278

Courville, Serge, and Normand Séguin, "Spatialité et temporalité chez Blanchard: propos d'heuristique," *Cahiers de géographie du Québec*, vol. 30, 80 (1986), pp. 293–298.   279

DeKoninck, Rodolphe, "L'oeuvre de Raoul Blanchard: Un heritage à investir," *Cahiers de géographie du Québec*, vol. 30, 80 (1986), pp. 133–136.   280

Dugas, Clermont, "Région et régionalisation au Québec depuis Raoul Blanchard," *Cahiers de géographie du Québec*, vol. 30, no. 80 (1986), pp. 189–202.   281

Hamelin, Louis-Edmond, and Collette Hamelin, "Les carrières canadiennes de Raoul Blanchard et Pierre Deffontaines," *Cahiers de géographie du Québec*, vol. 30, 80 (1986), pp. 137–150.   282

Nash, Peter H., "Mark I Role Model and Inspiring Catalyst: Some Characteristics from a Perspective of Four Decades," *Cahiers de géographie du Québec*, vol. 30, 80 (1986), pp. 151–161.   283

Sanguin, André-Louis, "Le paradigme régional, la pensée géographique, et l'oeuvre québécois de Raoul Blanchard," *Cahiers de géographie du Québec*, vol. 30, 80 (1986), pp. 175–188.   284

Villeneuve, Paul, "Étudier Québec un demi-siècle après Raoul Blanchard," *Cahiers de géographie du Québec*, vol. 30, 80 (1986), pp. 281–291.   285

Nash, Peter H., "A Still Revered "Tomodachi" after Half a Century: Reflections on Raoul Blanchard and Epistomological Changes in Canada," in Richard Preston and Bruce Mitchell, eds., *Reflections and Visions: Twenty-five Years of Geography at Waterloo* (Waterloo: University of Waterloo Department of Geography Publication Series, no. 33, 1990), pp. 61–75.   286

Thomas Griffith Taylor (*)
(1880–1963)

Proponent of an environmentalist interpretation of the Canadian settlement experience

Taylor, T. Griffith, *Journeyman Taylor: The Education of a Scientist* (New York: Transatlantic, 1959), 352 pp.   287

Putnam, Donald F., "Griffith Taylor, 1880–1963," *Canadian Geographer*, vol. 7, 4 (1963), pp. 197–200.   288

Andrews, John, "Griffith Taylor, 1880–1963," *Australian Geographical Studies*, vol. 2, 1 (1964), pp. 1–9. 289

Arousseau, M., "Obituary: Griffith Taylor, 1880–1963," *Australian Geographer*, vol. 9, 2 (1964), pp. 131–133. 290

Browne, William R., "Thomas Griffith Taylor," *Yearbook of the Australian Academy of Sciences*, Canberra (1964), pp. 41–53. 291

Crone, Gerald R., "Obituary: Thomas Griffith Taylor," *Geographical Journal*, vol. 130, 1 (1964), pp. 189–191. 292

Marshall, Ann, "Griffith Taylor, 1880–1963," *Geographical Review*, vol. 54, 3 (1964), pp. 427–429. 293

Niland, D'Arcy, "Griffith Taylor: A Man for All Seasons," *Walkabout*, vol. 30 (1964), pp. 17–30. 294

Rose, John Kerr, "Griffith Taylor," *Annals of the Association of American Geographers*, vol. 54, 4 (1964), pp. 622–629. 295

Singh, S. M., "Griffith Taylor (1880–1963)," *National Geographical Journal of India*, vol. 10, 1 (1964), p. 63. 296

Tomkins, George S., "Griffith Taylor and Canadian Geography," Ph.D. diss., University of Washington, 1967. 297

Tomkins, George S., *Griffith Taylor and Canadian Geography* (Ann Arbor: University Microfilms, 1968), 540 pp. 298

Fisher, Eric, Robert D. Campbell, and Eldon S. Miller, "Griffith Taylor (1880–1963)," in their *A Question of Place: The Development of Geographic Thought* (Arlington, Va.: R. W. Beatty, 1969), pp. 267–277. 299

Powell, Joseph M., "The Bowman, Huntington, and Taylor Correspondence, 1928," *Australian Geographer*, vol. 14, 2 (1978), pp. 123–125. 300

Powell, Joseph M., "Thomas Griffith Taylor, 1880–1963," *Geographers: Biobibliographical Studies*, vol. 3 (London: Mansell Publishing Co., 1979), pp. 141–153. 301

Hanley, W. S., "Griffith Taylor's Antarctic Achievements: A Geographical Foundation," *Australian Geographical Studies*, vol. 18, 1 (1980), pp. 22–36. 302

Marshall, Ann, "Griffith Taylor's Correlative Science," *Australian Geographical Studies*, vol. 18, 2 (1980), pp. 184–193. 303

Powell, Joseph M., "The Cyclist on Ice: Griffith Taylor as Explorer," *Proceed-ings of the Royal Geographical Society of Australasia, South Australia Branch, 1979*, vol. 80 (1981), pp. 1–28. 304

Sanderson, Marie, "Griffith Taylor: A Geographer to Remember," *Canadian Geographer*, vol. 26, 4 (1982), pp. 293–299. 305

Sanderson, Marie, *Griffith Taylor: Antarctic Scientist and Pioneer Geographer* (Ottawa: Carleton University Press, 1987), 218 pp. 306

Sanderson, Marie, "Taylor, Thomas Griffith, Geographer, Educator, Explorer," *Canadian Encyclopedia*, 2d ed., vol. 4 (Edmonton: Hurtig Publishers, 1988), p. 2115. 307

Sanderson, Marie, "Griffith Taylor and Geography in Canada," in Richard Preston and Bruce Mitchell, eds., *Reflections and Visions: Twenty-five Years of Geography at Waterloo* (Waterloo: University of Waterloo Department of Geography Publication Series, no. 33, 1990), pp. 37–49. 308

Helge M. O. Nelson
(1882–1966)

See UNITED STATES

Émile Miller
(1885–1926)

Laval geographer who was the first Canadian to write about the relation between geography and history

Brouillette, Benoît, "Un pionnier de la géographie au Canada français: Émile Miller," *Revue canadienne de géographie*, vol. 4, 1–2 (1950), pp. 94–96. 309

Samuel Eliot Morison
(1887–1976)

See UNITED STATES

Harold Adams Innis (**)
(1894–1952)

Eminent historian concerned with the great staple trades and their shaping of the Canadian economy and settlement pattern

Creighton, Donald G., "Harold Adams Innis (1894–1952)," *Canadian Historical Review*, vol. 33, 4 (1952), pp. 405–406. 310

Bladen, Vincent W., W. T. Easterbrook, and Joseph H. Willits, "Harold Adams Innis, 1894–1952," *American Economic Review*, vol. 43, 1 (1953), pp. 1–25. 311

Clark, Andrew Hill, "Harold Adams Innis," *Geographical Review*, vol. 43, 2 (1953), p. 282. 312

"Harold Adams Innis (1894–1952)," *Proceedings of the Royal Society of Canada*, 3d ser., vol. 47 (1953), pp. 89–92.   313

Creighton, Donald G., *Harold Adams Innis: Portrait of a Scholar* (Toronto: University of Toronto Press, 1957), 146 pp.   314

"Innis, Harold Adams," *Encyclopedia Canadiana*, vol. 5 (Ottawa: Canadiana Co., 1958), pp. 278–279.   315

"Innis, Harold Adams (1894–1952), economist and historian," *Macmillan Dictionary of Canadian Biography* (Toronto: Macmillan Co., 1963), p. 339.   316

"Innis, Harold Adams (1894–1952)," in Nora Story, ed., *Oxford Companion to Canadian History and Literature* (Toronto: Oxford University Press, 1967, pp. 380–381.   317

Neill, Robin F., *A New Theory of Value: The Canadian Economics of H. A. Innis* (Toronto: University of Toronto Press, 1972), 159 pp.   318

Eccles, William J., "A Belated Review of Harold Adams Innis' 'The Fur Trade in Canada,'" *Canadian Historical Review*, vol. 60, 4 (1979), pp. 419–441.   319

Patterson, Graeme, "Harold Innis and the Writing of History," *Canadian Literature*, vol. 83 (1979), pp. 118–130.   320

Carey, J., "Culture, Geography, and Communications: The Work of Harold Innis in an American Context," in W. H. Melody, L. Salter, and P. Heyer, eds., *Culture, Communications, and Dependency: The Tradition of H. A. Innis* (Norwood, N.J.: Ablex Publishing Corp., 1981), pp. 73–91.   321

Havelock, Eric A., *Harold A. Innis: A Memoir* (Toronto: Harold Innis Foundation, Publication no. 2, 1982), 43 pp.   322

Watson, A. John, "Marginal Man: Harold Innis' Communications Works in Context," Ph.D. diss., University of Toronto, 1982.   323

Kroker, Arthur, "Technological Realism: Harold Innis' Empire of Communications," in Arthur Kroker, ed., *Technology and the Canadian Mind* (Montreal: New World Perspectives, 1984), pp. 87–124.   324

Chapman, Louis, "Harold Adams Innis and Geography: His Work and Its Potential for Modern Geography," Master's thesis, University of Ottawa, 1985.   325

Dunbar, Gary S., "Harold Innis and Canadian Geography," *Canadian Geographer*, vol. 29, 2 (1985), pp. 159–164.   326

Berger, Carl, "Harold Innis: The Search for the Limits," in his *The Writing of Canadian History: Aspects of English-Canadian Historical Writing since 1900*, 2d ed. (Toronto: University of Toronto Press, 1986), pp. 85–111.   327

Berdoulay, Vincent, and R. Louis Chapman, "Le possibilisme de Harold Innis," *Canadian Geographer*, vol. 31, 1 (1987), pp. 2–11.   328

Christian, William, "Innis, Harold Adams, Political Economist, and Pioneer in Communications Studies," *Canadian Encyclopedia*, vol. 2 (Edmonton: Hurtig Publishers, 1988), p. 1069.   329

Parker, I., "Harold Innis as a Canadian Geographer," *Canadian Geographer*, vol. 32, 1 (1988), pp. 63–69.   330

Christian, William. "Harold Adams Innis," *Dictionary of Literary Biography*, vol. 88 (Detroit: Gale Research, 1989), pp. 124–132.   331

Berdoulay, Vincent, "Harold Innis and Canadian Geography: Discursive Impediments to an Original School of Thought," in Richard Preston and Bruce Mitchell, eds., *Reflections and Visions: Twenty-five Years of Geography at Waterloo* (Waterloo: University of Waterloo Department of Geography Publication Series, no. 33, 1990), pp. 51–60.   332

Patterson, Graeme, *History and Communications: Harold Innis, Marshall McLuhan, and the Interpretation of History* (Toronto: University of Toronto Press, 1990), 251 pp.   333

Pierre Deffontaines (*)
(1894–1978)

French geographer interested in climate and cadaster in Quebec

Dickinson, Robert E., "Pierre Deffontaines," in his *The Makers of Modern Geography* (London: Routledge & Kegan Paul, 1969), pp. 241–243.   334

Raveneau, Jean et al., "Hommage à Pierre Deffontaines (1894–1978)," *Cahiers de géographie du Québec*, vol. 22, 57 (1978), pp. 437–444.   335

"Hommage à Pierre Deffontaines," *Acta Geographica*, 3d ser., no. 38 (Apr. 1979), pp. 4–24.   336

Migliorini, Paolo, "Pierre Deffontaines," *Bollettino della Società geografica italiana*, ser. 10, vol. 8 (1979), pp. 401–406.   337

1986—see Raoul Blanchard

William Archibald Mackintosh (**)
(1895–1970)

Political economist with interests in the history of Canadian settlement frontiers

"Mackintosh, William Archibald, Principal of Queen's University," *Encyclopedia Canadiana*, vol. 6 (Toronto: Grolier of Canada, 1957), p. 284. 338

Knox, Frank A., "William Archibald Mackintosh, 1895–1970," *Proceedings of the Royal Society of Canada*, 4th ser., vol. 9 (1971), pp. 67–72. 339

"Mackintosh, William Archibald, University Administrator," *Who Was Who in America*, vol. 5 (Chicago: Marquis, 1973), p. 450. 340

Owram, Douglas, "Mackintosh, William Archibald," *Canadian Encyclopedia*, vol. 2 (Edmonton: Hurtig Publishers, 1988), p. 1274. 341

Benoît Brouillette (*)
(1904–1979)

Economic geographer interested in historical industrial patterns in Quebec

Lapierre, Richard, "Benoît Brouillette," *Revue canadienne de géographie*, vol. 9, 1 (1955), pp. 3–7. 342

Falaise, Noël, "Biographie et bibliographie de Benoît Brouillette," *Cahiers de géographie du Québec* vol. 17, 40 (1973), pp. 5–34. 343

Beauregard, Ludger, "Hommage et reconnaissance à Benoît Brouillette et Pierre Dagenais," *Revue de géographie de Montréal*, vol. 29, 3 (1975), pp. 189–190. 344

Camu, Pierre, "Benoît Brouillette, 1904–1979," *Proceedings of the Royal Society of Canada*, 4th ser., vol. 19 (1981), pp. 55–58. 345

Dagenais, Pierre, "Benoît Brouillette (1904–1979)," *Canadian Geographer*, vol. 25, 4 (1981), pp. 388–389. 346

Carl Schott (*)
(1905–1990)

German geographer interested in Canadian colonization processes

Meynen, Emil, "Carl Schott zum 65. Geburtstag," *Berichte zur deutschen Landeskunde*, vol. 43, 2 (1969), pp. 221–232. 347

Niemeier, G., "Carl Schott und die deutschen Landeskunde," *Berichte zur deutsche Landeskunde*, vol. 48 (1974), pp. 7–16. 348

Burghardt, Andrew F., "The Settling of Southern Ontario: An Appreciation of the Work of Carl Schott," *Canadian Geographer* vol. 25, 1 (1981), pp. 75–93. 349

Lenz, Karl, "Carl Schott zum 80. Geburtstag," *Berichte zu deutsche Landeskunde*, vol. 59, 1 (1985), pp. 7–9. 350

Lenz, Karl, "Die Kanada-Forschungen Carl Schotts," in Karl Lenz und Alfred Pletsch, eds., *Kanada: Wirtschafts- und siedlungsgeographische Entwicklungen und Probleme von Carl Schott* (Berlin: Dietrich Reimer Verlag, 1985), pp. 9–18. 351

Raleigh Ashlin Skelton
(1906–1970)

British cartographic historian who studied the mapping history of North America

Koeman, Cornelis, "Introduction to Volume 25, Being the R. A. Skelton Memorial Volume of *Imago Mundi*," *Imago Mundi*, vol. 25 (1971), pp. 9–11. 352

Quinn, David B., "Raleigh Ashlin Skelton: His Contributions to the History of Discovery," *Imago Mundi*, vol. 25 (1971), pp. 13–15. 353

Wallis, Helen, "Obituary: Raleigh Ashlin Skelton," *Transactions of the Institute of British Geographers*, vol. 58 (1973), pp. 139–148. 354

Quinn, David B., "Skelton, Raleigh Ashlin (1906–1970), Cartographical Historian," in E. T. Williams and C. S. Nicholls, eds. *Dictionary of National Biography, 1961–1970* (Oxford: Oxford University Press, 1981), pp. 953–955. 355

Andrew Hill Clark
(1911–1975)

1981—*see* W. F. Ganong

See also under UNITED STATES

James Wreford Watson
(1915–1990)

British geographer who studied the historical geography of southern Ontario and the role of myths in settlement history

"Watson, James Wreford," *Contemporary Authors*, new rev. ser., vol. 19 (1987), pp. 463–464. 356

Robinson, Guy M., "Wreford Watson's Social Geography and a Social Geography of Canada," and "James Wreford Watson: An Appreciation, with a Bibliography of His Work," in Guy M. Robinson, ed., *A Social Geography of Canada: Essays in Honour of J. Wreford Watson* (Edinburgh: North British Publishing, 1988), pp. 1–18, 374–384. 357

Collins, Lyndhurst, "Obituary: James Wreford Watson, 1915–1990," *Transactions of the Institute of British Geographers*, n.s. vol. 16, 2 (1991), pp. 227–232. 358

Crosbie, A. J., "Obituary: Professor James Wreford Watson," *Scottish Geographical Magazine*, vol. 107, 1 (1991), p. 72.   **359**

Reeds, Lloyd, "James Wreford Watson, 1915–1990," *Canadian Geographer*, vol. 35, 2 (1991), pp. 187–188.   **360**

Coolie Verner (*)
(1917–1979)

Student of the early mapping history of North America

Dahl, Edward H., "Coolie Verner's Contribution in the Field of Maps," *Bulletin of the Association of Canadian Map Libraries*, vol. 33 (1979), pp. 32–33.   **361**

Wallis, Helen, "Obituary: Coolie Verner," *Map Collector*, no. 12, (1979), p. 38.   **362**

Woodward, Frances M., "Coolie Verner's Publications Relating to the History of Cartography and Cartobibliography," *Bulletin of the Association of Canadian Map Libraries*, vol. 33 (1979), pp. 33–35.   **363**

Wallis, Helen, "Obituary: Coolie Verner (1917–1979)," *Imago Mundi*, vol. 33 (1981), pp. 99–102.   **364**

"Verner, Coolie, 1917–1979," *Contemporary Authors*, new rev. ser., vol. 7 (Detroit: Gale Research Co., 1990–1992), pp. 509–510.   **365**

Norman Leon Nicholson (*)
(1920–1984)

Contributed to the political boundary and settlement history of Canada

"Nicholson, Norman Leon," *Writer's Directory 1982–1984* (New York: St. Martin's Press, 1981), p. 696.   **366**

"Nicholson, Norman Leon, 1919– [*sic*]," *Contemporary Authors*, new rev. ser., vol. 3 (1981), pp. 396–397.   **367**

Pleva, Edward G., "Norman L. Nicholson, 1920–1984," *Canadian Geographer*, vol. 29, 2 (1985), pp. 98–99.   **368**

UNITED STATES

Emma Hart Willard (**)
(1787–1870)

New England–born educator who pioneered the study of American history with the aid of maps

Fowler, Henry, "The Educational Services of Miss Emma Willard," *American Journal of Education*, vol. 6 (1859), pp. 125–168.   **369**

Lord, John, *The Life of Emma Willard* (New York: D. Appleton & Co., 1873), 351 pp.   **370**

"Willard, Mrs. Emma," in Frances E. Willard and Mary A. Livermore, eds., *A Woman of the Century: Fourteen Hundred–Seventy Biographical Sketches Accompanied by Portraits of Leading American Women in All Walks of Life* (Buffalo: Charles Wells Moulton, 1893), p. 777.   **371**

Fairbanks, Mrs. A. W., ed., *Emma Willard and Her Pupils, or Fifty Years of Troy Female Seminary, 1822–1872* (New York: Mrs. Russell Sage, 1898), 895 pp.   **372**

Lutz, Alma, *Emma Willard: Daughter of Democracy* (Boston: Houghton Mifflin, 1929), 291 pp.   **373**

Lutz, Alma, "Willard, Emma Hart, Educator," *Dictionary of American Biography*, vol. 20 (New York: Charles Scribner's Sons, 1936), pp. 231–233.   **374**

Calhoun, Daniel H., "Eyes for the Jacksonian World: William C. Woodbridge and Emma Willard," *Journal of the Early Republic*, vol. 4, 1 (1984), pp. 1–26.   **375**

Nelson, Murry R., "Emma Willard: Pioneer in Social Studies Education," *Theory and Research in Social Education*, vol. 15, 4 (1987), pp. 245–256.
                                                            376

George Perkins Marsh (**)
(1801–1882)

Early American scholar who examined the historical relation of humans to their environment, and their exploitation of it

Marsh, Mrs. Caroline Crane, *Life and Letters of George Perkins Marsh* (New York: Charles Scribner's Sons, 1888), 479 pp.   **377**

Lowenthal, David, "George Perkins Marsh and the American Geographical Tradition," *Geographical Review*, vol. 43, 2 (1953), pp. 207–213.   **378**

Lowenthal, David, *George Perkins Marsh: Versatile Vermonter* (New York: Columbia University Press, 1958), 442 pp.   **379**

Lowenthal, David, "Marsh, George Perkins," *International Encyclopedia of the Social Sciences*, vol. 10 (New York: Macmillan Co. and the Free Press, 1968), pp. 23–25.   **380**

Fisher, Eric, Robert D. Campbell, and Eldon S. Miller, "George Perkins Marsh (1801–1882)," in their *A Question of Place: The Development of*

Geographic Thought (Arlington, Va.: R. W. Beatty, 1969), pp. 370–379. **381**

Olwig, Kenneth R., "Historical Geography and the Society/Nature 'Problematic': The Perspective of J. F. Schouw, G. P. Marsh, and E. Reclus," *Journal of Historical Geography*, vol. 6, 1 (1980), pp. 29–45. **382**

James, Preston E., and Geoffrey J. Martin, "George Perkins Marsh," in their *All Possible Worlds: A History of Geographical Ideas* (New York: John Wiley & Sons, 1981), pp. 149–150. **383**

Foster, Richard H., "Congressman George Perkins Marsh and the Man-Nature Theme," *Bulletin of the Association of North Dakota Geographers*, vol. 32, 1 (1982), pp. 34–41. **384**

Gade, Daniel W., "The Growing Recognition of George Perkins Marsh," *Geographical Review*, vol. 73, 3 (1983), pp. 341–344. **385**

George Stillman Hillard (**)
(1808–1879)

First American to examine the formal links between history and geography

Palfrey, Francis Winthrop, "Memoir of George Stillman Hillard," *Proceedings of the Massachusetts Historical Society*, vol. 19 (1882), pp. 339–348. **386**

Genzmer, George H., "Hillard, George Stillman, Lawyer, Man of Letters," *Dictionary of American Biography* (New York: Charles Scribner's Sons, 1932), pp. 49–50. **387**

Manheim, Frank J., "George Stillman Hillard—An Early American Apostle of Human Geography," *Bulletin of the Geographical Society of Philadelphia*, vol. 35, 1 (1937), pp. 1–7. **388**

Johann Georg Kohl (*)
(1808–1878)

Visiting German scholar who offered the first systematic examination of the cartographic record of North American discoveries by Europeans

Deane, Charles, ["Tribute to Dr. Kohl"], *Proceedings of the Massachusetts Historical Society*, vol. 16 (Dec. 1878), pp. 381–385. **389**

Wolkenhauer, W., "Johann Georg Kohl, bedeutender Reiseschriftsteller und Geograph," *Allgemeine Deutsche Biographie*, vol. 16 (Leipzig: Duncker & Humbolt, 1882), pp. 425–428. **390**

Schumacher, Hermann A., "Kohls amerikanische Studien," *Deutsche Geographische Blätter*, vol. 11, 2 (1888), pp. 105–221. **391**

Cammaerts, Emmanuel, "J. G. Kohl et la géographie des communications," *Bulletin de la Société royale Belge de géographie*, vol. 28 (1904), pp. 36–61. **392**

Alexander, Anneli, "J. G. Kohl und seine Bedeutung für die deutsche Landes- und Volksforschung," *Deutsche Geographische Blätter*, vol. 43, 1–2 (1940), pp. 7–126. **393**

Peucker, Thomas K., "Johann Georg Kohl: A Theoretical Geographer of the Nineteenth Century," *Professional Geographer*, vol. 20, 4 (1968), pp. 247–250. **394**

Pfeifer, Gottfried, ". . . Man sollte J. G. Kohl nicht vergessen," in Karl-Friedrich Schreiber and Peter Weber, eds., *Mensch und Erde: Festschrift für Wilhelm Müller-Wille* (Münster: Institut für Geographie und Länderkunde der Universität Münster, Westfälische Geographische Studien, vol. 33, 1976), pp. 221–236. **395**

Wood, Fergus J., "J. G. Kohl and the 'Lost Maps' of the American Coast," *American Cartographer*, vol. 3, 2 (1976), pp. 107–115. **396**

Wolter, John A., "Johann Georg Kohl and America," *Map Collector*, no. 17 (1981), pp. 10–14. **397**

Bieder, Robert E., Introduction to Johann Georg Kohl, *Kitchi-Gami: Life among the Lake Superior Ojibway*, trans. Lascelles Wraxall (St. Paul: Minnesota Historical Society Press, 1985), pp. xiii–xxxix. **398**

Rufus Blanchard (**)
(1821–1904)

Early author and publisher of American historical maps and atlases

"Rufus Blanchard," in Rufus Blanchard, *History of DuPage County, Illinois* (Chicago: O. L. Baskin & Co., 1882), pp. 48–49. **399**

"Blanchard, Rufus, Cartographer, Author," *Who Was Who in America*, vol. 1 (Chicago: A. N. Marquis Co., 1942), p. 105. **400**

Selmer, Marsha L., "Rufus Blanchard: Early Chicago Map Publisher," in Michael P. Conzen, ed., *Chicago Mapmakers: Essays on the Rise of the City's Map Trade* (Chicago: Chicago Historical Society, for the Chicago Map Society, 1984), pp. 23–31. Copublished in *Chicago History*, vol. 13, 1 (1984), pp. 23–31. **401**

Daniel Coit Gilman (**)
(1831–1908)

First American university educator to promote the joint study of American history and geography

Fabian, Franklin, *The Life of Daniel Coit Gilman* (New York: Dodd, Mead & Co., 1910), 446 pp.   **402**

Mitchell, Samuel Chiles, "Gilman, Daniel Coit, University President, Author, and Publicist," *Dictionary of American Biography* (New York: Charles Scribner's Sons, 1931), pp. 299–303.   **403**

Flexner, Abraham, *Daniel Coit Gilman: Creator of the American Type of University* (New York: Harcourt Brace & Co., 1946), 173 pp.   **404**

Wright, John K., "Daniel Coit Gilman: Geographer and Historian" *Geographical Review*, vol. 51, 3 (1961), pp. 381–399. Reprinted in John K. Wright, *Human Nature in Geography: Fourteen Essays, 1925–1965* (Cambridge, Mass.: Harvard University Press, 1966), pp. 168–187.   **405**

Justin Winsor (**)
(1831–1897)

American historian of European discoveries and exploration of North America

Channing, Edward, "Justin Winsor," *American Historical Review*, vol. 3, 1 (1898), pp. 197–202.   **406**

Markham, Sir Clements R., "Justin Winsor," *Geographical Journal*, vol. 11, 1 (Jan. 1898), pp. 77–78.   **407**

Scudder, Horace E., "Memoir of Justin Winsor," *Proceedings of the Massachusetts Historical Society*, 2d ser., vol. 12 (1899), pp. 457–482.   **408**

Yust, William F., *A Bibliography of Justin Winsor* (Cambridge: Harvard University Library, 1902), 32 pp.   **409**

Adams, James Truslow, "Winsor, Justin (Jan. 2, 1831–Oct. 22, 1897), Historian, Librarian," *Dictionary of American Biography*, vol. 20 (New York: Charles Scribner's Sons, 1936), pp. 403–404.   **410**

Borome, Joseph A., "The Life and Letters of Justin Winsor," Ph.D. diss., Columbia University, 1950.   **411**

Borome, Joseph A., "Winsor's History of America," *Boston Public Library Quarterly*, vol. 5 (1953), pp. 119–139.   **412**

Cutler, Wayne, and Michael H. Harris, eds., *Justin Winsor: Scholar-Librarian* (Littleton, Colo.: Libraries Unlimited, 1980), 196 pp.   **413**

Koelsch, William A., "A Profound Though Special Erudition: Justin Winsor as Historian of Discovery," *Proceedings of the American Antiquarian Society*, vol. 39, 1 (1983), pp. 55–94.   **414**

Simms, L. Moody, Jr., "Justin Winsor," *Dictionary of Literary Biography*, vol. 47 (Detroit: Gale Research, 1986), pp. 358–364.   **415**

John Wesley Powell (**)
(1834–1902)

Explorer, geologist, geographer, and ethnographer of American Indians

Gilbert, Grove Karl, "John Wesley Powell," *Science*, n.s., vol. 16 (1902), pp. 561–567.   **416**

Gilbert, Grove Karl, ed., "John Wesley Powell: A Memorial to an American Explorer and Scholar," a series of articles that appeared in *Open Court*, vol. 16, 12 (1902), pp. 705–716; vol. 17, 1 (1903), pp. 14–25; 2, pp. 86–94; 3, pp. 162–174; 4, pp. 228–239; 5, pp. 281–290; and 6, pp. 342–351. Also published as a collection under this title (Chicago: Open Court Publishing Co., 1903), 75 pp.   **417**

Merrill, George P., "John Wesley Powell," *American Geologist*, vol. 31 (1903), pp. 327–333.   **418**

Wolcott, Charles D., "John Wesley Powell," *U.S. Geological Survey Annual Report* (1903), pp. 271–287.   **419**

Darrah, William C., *Powell of the Colorado* (Princeton: Princeton University Press, 1951), 426 pp.   **420**

Meadows, Paul, *John Wesley Powell: Frontiersman of Science* (Lincoln: University of Nebraska Studies, n.s. no. 10, 1952), 106 pp.   **421**

Stegner, Wallace, *Beyond the Hundredth Meridian: John Wesley Powell and the Second Opening of the American West* (Boston: Houghton Mifflin, 1954), 438 pp.   **422**

Darrah, William C., "Powell, John Wesley," *International Encyclopedia of the Social Sciences*, vol. 12 (New York: Macmillan Co. and the Free Press, 1968), pp. 404–405.   **423**

James, Preston E., "John Wesley Powell, 1834–1902," *Geographers: Biobibliographical Studies*, vol. 3 (London: Mansell Publishing Co., 1979), pp. 117–124.   **424**

James, Preston E., and Geoffrey J. Martin, "John Wesley Powell," in their *All Possible Worlds: A History of Geographical Ideas* (New York: John Wiley & Sons, 1981), pp. 158–160.   **425**

Francis Wayland Parker (**)
(1837–1902)

First educator to incorporate historical geography into a teacher-training curriculum

Parker, Francis W., "Autobiographical Sketch," in William M. Giffin, *School Days in the Fifties* (Chicago: A. Flanagan Co., 1906), appendix, pp. 110–137.   **426**

Judd, Charles H., "The Development of Colonel Parker's Ideas," in "Francis Wayland Parker Memorial," *University of Chicago Record*, n.s. vol. 3, 1 (1917), pp. 61–65.   **427**

Judd, Charles H., "Parker, Francis Wayland, Educator," *Dictionary of American Biography*, vol. 14 (New York: Charles Scribner's Sons, 1934), p. 221.   **428**

Heffron, Ida Cassa, *Francis Wayland Parker: An Interpretive Biography* (Los Angeles: I. Deach, Jr., 1934), 127 pp.   **429**

Campbell, Jack K., *Colonel Francis W. Parker: The Children's Crusader* (New York: Teachers College Press, 1967), 283 pp.   **430**

Nathaniel Southgate Shaler (**)
(1841–1906)

Geologist, naturalist, and geographer who interpreted American regional history from an environmental perspective

Shaler, Nathaniel Southgate, *The Autobiography of Nathaniel Southgate Shaler, with a Supplementary Memoir by His Wife* (Boston and New York: Houghton Mifflin & Co., 1909), 481 pp.   **431**

Malin, James C., "N. S. Shaler on the Frontier Concept and the Grassland," in his *Essays on Historiography* (Lawrence, Kans.: The author, 1946), pp. 45–92.   **432**

Berg, Walter L., "Nathaniel Southgate Shaler: A Critical Study of an Earth Scientist," Ph.D. diss., University of Washington, 1957.   **433**

Berg, Walter L., "Shaler, Nathaniel Southgate," *Dictionary of Scientific Biography*, vol. 12 (New York: Charles Scribner's Sons, 1975), pp. 343–344.   **434**

Koelsch, William A., "Nathaniel Southgate Shaler," *Geographers: Biobibliographical Studies*, vol. 3 (London: Mansell Publishing Co., 1979), pp. 133–137.   **435**

Livingstone, David N., "Nature and Man in America: Nathaniel Southgate Shaler and the Conservation of Natural Resources," *Transactions, Institute of British Geographers*, n.s. vol. 5, 3 (1980), pp. 369–382.   **436**

Livingstone, David N., "Environment and Inheritance: Nathaniel Southgate Shaler and the American Frontier," in Brian W. Blouet, ed., *The Origins of Academic Geography in the United*

States (Hamden, Conn.: Shoestring Press, 1981), pp. 123–138.   **437**

Zabilka, Ivan L., "Nathaniel Shaler and the Kentucky Geological Survey," *Register of the Kentucky Historical Society*, vol. 80 (1982), pp. 408–431.   **438**

Bladen, Wilford A., "Nathaniel Southgate Shaler and Early American Geography," in Wilford A. Bladen and Pradyumna P. Karan, eds., *The Evolution of Geographic Thought in America: A Kentucky Root* (Dubuque: Kendall Hunt Publishing Co., 1983), pp. 13–27.   **439**

Livingstone, David N., *Nathaniel Southgate Shaler and the Culture of American Science* (Tuscaloosa: University of Alabama Press, 1987), 395 pp.   **440**

Friedrich Ratzel
(1844–1904)

Visiting German geographer who perceived American national development in broad cultural-historical terms

Genthe, Martha Krug, and Ellen Churchill Semple, "Tributes to Friedrich Ratzel," *Bulletin of the American Geographical Society*, vol. 36 (1904), pp. 550–553.   **441**

Ravenstein, Ernest George, "Obituary: Friedrich Ratzel," *Geographical Journal*, vol. 24, 4 (1904), pp. 485–487.   **442**

Genthe, Martha Krug, "An Appreciation of Friedrich Ratzel," in *Report of the Eighth International Geographic Congress, Held in the United States, 1904* (Washington, D.C.: Government Printing Office, House Document no. 460, 1905), pp. 1053–1055.   **443**

Sauer, Carl O., "Ratzel, Friedrich," *Encyclopaedia of the Social Sciences*, vol. 13 (New York: Macmillan Co., 1934), pp. 120–121.   **444**

Broek, Jan O. M., "Friedrich Ratzel in Retrospect," *Annals of the Association of American Geographers*, vol. 44, 2 (1954), p. 207.   **445**

Steinmetzler, Johannes, *Die Anthropogeographie Friedrich Ratzels und ihre ideengeschichtlichen Wurzeln* (Bonn: Selbstverlag des Geographischen Instituts der Universität Bonn, 1956), 151 pp.   **446**

Wanklyn, Harriet, *Friedrich Ratzel: A Biographical Memoir and Bibliography* (Cambridge: Cambridge University Press, 1961), 96 pp.   **447**

Mikesell, Marvin W., "Ratzel, Friedrich," *International Encyclopedia of the Social Sciences*, vol. 13 (New York: Macmillan Co. and the Free Press, 1968), pp. 327–329.   **448**

Dickinson, Robert E., "Leaders of the First Generation: Friedrich Ratzel (1844–1904)," in his *The Makers of Modern Geography* (New York: Frederick A. Praeger, 1969), pp. 62–76.   449

Fisher, Eric, Robert D. Campbell, and Eldon S. Miller, "Friedrich Ratzel (1844–1904)," in their *A Question of Place: The Development of Geographic Thought* (Arlington, Va.: R. W. Beatty, 1969), pp. 95–99.   450

Sauer, Carl O., "The Formative Years of Ratzel in the United States," *Annals of the Association of American Geographers*, vol. 61, 2 (1971), pp. 245–254. Reprinted in Carl O. Sauer, *Selected Essays, 1963–1975*, ed. Bob Callahan (Berkeley, Calif.: Turtle Island Foundation, for the Netzahaulcoyotl Historical Society, 1981), pp.   451

Beckinsale, Robert P., "Ratzel, Friedrich," *Dictionary of Scientific Biography*, vol. 11 (New York: Charles Scribner's Sons, 1975), pp. 308–310.   452

Buttmann, Günter, *Friedrich Ratzel: Leben und Werk eines deutschen Geographen, 1844–1904* (Stuttgart: Wissenschaftliche Verlagsgesellschaft, 1977), 152 pp.   453

James, Preston E., and Geoffrey J. Martin, "Friedrich Ratzel," in their *All Possible Worlds: A History of Geographical Ideas* (New York: John Wiley & Sons, 1981), pp. 168–171.   454

Hunter, James M., *Perspectives on Ratzel's Political Geography* (Lanham, Md.: University Press of America, 1983), 544 pp.   455

Bassin, Mark, "Friedrich Ratzel's Travels in the United States: A Study in the Genesis of His Anthropogeography," *History of Geography Newsletter*, vol. 4 (1984), pp. 11–22.   456

Stehlin, Stewart A., Introduction to Friedrich Ratzel, *Sketches of Urban and Cultural Life in North America*, trans. and ed. Stewart A. Stehlin (New Brunswick: Rutgers University Press, 1988), pp. xiii–xxix.   457

Bergevin, Jean, "À propos de la géographie politique: La parole est à Friedrich Ratzel," *Cahiers de géographie du Québec*, vol. 33, 88 (1989), pp. 59–66.   458

Townsend MacCoun (**)
(1845–1932)

Historical cartographer and publisher who authored the first 'historical geography' atlas of the United States

"Townsend MacCoun," *Bulletin of the Geographical Society of Philadelphia*, vol. 30, 4 (1932), pp. 234–235.   459

"MacCoun, Townsend, Cartographer," *Who Was Who in America*, vol. 4 (Chicago: A. N. Marquis Co., 1968), p. 597.   460

Albert Perry Brigham
(1855–1932)

Geomorphologist and human geographer who wrote an early environmental interpretation of American regional development

"Brigham, Albert Perry, Clergyman, Geologist, and Educator," *National Cyclopedia of American Biography*, vol. 17 (New York: James T. White & Co., 1920), p. 287.   461

Dodge, Richard E., "Albert Perry Brigham," *Annals of the Association of American Geographers*, vol. 20, 2 (1930), pp. 55–62. [Introduction to an anniversary issue of the *Annals* on the occasion of Brigham's seventy-fifth birthday]   462

Other tributes in that issue relevant to Brigham as a historical geographer:

Brown, Robert M., "[Brigham as] Educator," pp. 91–98.   463

Whitbeck, Ray H., "[Brigham as] Human Geographer," pp. 73–81.   464

Davis, William Morris," Albert Perry Brigham," *Journal of Geography*, vol. 31, 6 (1932), pp. 265–266.   465

Martin, Lawrence, "Albert Perry Brigham," *Geographical Review*, vol. 22, 3 (1932), pp. 499–500.   466

Baker, Oliver E., "Memoir of Albert Perry Brigham," *Annals of the Association of American Geographers*, vol. 23, 1 (1933), pp. 27–32.   467

Keith, Arthur, "Memorial of Albert Perry Brigham," *Bulletin of the Geological Society of America*, vol. 44 (1933), pp. 307–311.   468

"Brigham, Albert Perry, Geographer," *National Cyclopedia of American Biography*, vol. 24 (New York: James T. White & Co., 1935), p. 281.   469

"Brigham, Albert Perry, Geologist," *Who Was Who in America*, vol. 1 (Chicago: A. N. Marquis Co., 1942), p. 138.   470

Dodge, Richard E., "Brigham, Albert Perry, Geographer," *Dictionary of American Biography*, vol. 21, suppl. 1 (New York: Charles Scribner's Sons, 1944), pp. 119–120.   471

Burdick, Alger E., "The Contributions of Albert Perry Brigham to Geographic Education," Ph.D. diss., George Peabody College for Teachers, 1951.   472

Fisher, Eric, Robert D. Campbell, and Eldon S. Miller, "Albert Perry Brigham (1855–1932)," in their *A Question of Place: The Development of Geographic Thought* (Arlington, Va.: R. W. Beatty, 1969), pp. 410–418.   **473**

James, Preston E., "Albert Perry Brigham, 1855–1932," *Geographers: Biobibliographical Studies*, vol. 2 (London: Mansell Publishing Co., 1978), pp. 13–20.   **474**

James, Preston E., and Geoffrey J. Martin, "Albert Perry Brigham," in their *All Possible Worlds: A History of Geographical Ideas* (New York: John Wiley & Sons, 1981), pp. 307–308.   **475**

John Franklin Jameson (**)
(1859–1937)

Historian who conceived the idea for an atlas of American historical geography

Donnan, Elizabeth and Leo F. Stock, eds., *An Historian's World: Selections from the Correspondence of John Franklin Jameson* (Philadelphia: American Philosophical Society, 1956), 382 pp.   **476**

Leland, Waldo G., "Jameson, John Franklin (Sept. 19, 1859–Sept. 28, 1937), Historian, Teacher, Editor," *Dictionary of American Biography*, vol. 22, suppl. 2 (New York: Charles Scribner's Sons, 1958), pp. 339–344.   **477**

Van Tassel, David B., "John Franklin Jameson," in Clifford L. Lord, ed., *Keepers of the Past* (Chapel Hill: University of North Carolina Press, 1965), pp. 81–96.   **478**

Wright, John K., "J. Franklin Jameson and the 'Atlas of the Historical Geography of the United States,'" in Ruth Anna Fisher and William L. Fox, eds., *J. Franklin Jameson: A Tribute* (Washington, D.C.: Catholic University of America Press, 1965), pp. 66–79.   **479**

Shrader, Richard A., "J. Franklin Jameson," *Dictionary of Literary Biography*, vol. 17 (Detroit: Gale Research, 1983), pp. 230–235.   **480**

Frederick Jackson Turner (**)
(1861–1932)

Eminent historian of the frontier thesis, and promoter of geographical approaches to American history

"Frederick Jackson Turner," *Geographical Review*, vol. 22, 3 (1932), p. 499.   **481**

Malin, James C., "Space and History: Reflections on the Closed-Space Doctrines of Turner and Mackinder and the Challenge of These Ideas by the Air Age," *Agricultural History*, vol. 18, 1 (1944), pp. 65–74. Reprinted, in expanded form, as "Turner-Mackinder Space Concept of His-

tory," in his *Essays on Historiography* (Lawrence, Kans.: The author, 1946), pp. 1–44.   **482**

Gulley, J. L. M., "The Turner Frontier: A Study in the Migration of Ideas," *Tijdschrift voor economische en sociale geografie*, vol. 50, 3 (1959), pp. 65–72; and 4 (1959), pp. 81–91.   **483**

Mikesell, Marvin W., "Comparative Studies in Frontier History," *Annals of the Association of American Geographers*, vol. 50, 1 (1960), pp. 62–74. Reprinted in Richard Hofstadter and Seymour M. Lipset, eds., *Turner and the Sociology of the Frontier* (New York: Basic Books, 1968), pp. 152–171.   **484**

Billington, Ray A., "Turner, Frederick Jackson," *International Encyclopedia of the Social Sciences*, vol. 16 (New York: Macmillan Co. and the Free Press, 1968), pp. 168–170.   **485**

Jacobs, Wilbur R., ed., *The Historical World of Frederick Jackson Turner; With Selections from His Correspondence* (New Haven: Yale University Press, 1968), 289 pp.   **486**

Billington, Ray A., *Frederick Jackson Turner: Historian, Scholar, Teacher* (New York: Oxford University Press, 1973), 599 pp.   **487**

Eigenheer, Richard A., "The Frontier Hypothesis and Related Spatial Concepts," *California Geographer*, vol. 14 (1973–1974), pp. 55–69.   **488**

Holtgrieve, Donald G., "Frederick Jackson Turner as a Regionalist," *Professional Geographer*, vol. 26 (1974), pp. 159–165.   **489**

Holtgrieve, Donald G., "Frederick Jackson Turner Map Collection: An Annotated Bibliography," *Historical Geography Newsletter*, vol. 5, 1 (1975), pp. 25–28.   **490**

Steiner, Michael C., "The Significance of Turner's Sectional Thesis," *Western Historical Quarterly*, vol. 10, 4 (1979), pp. 437–466.   **491**

Block, Robert H., "Frederick Jackson Turner and American Geography," *Annals of the Association of American Geographers*, vol. 70, 1 (1980), pp. 31–42.   **492**

Faulk, Odie B., "Frederick Jackson Turner," *Dictionary of Literary Biography*, vol. 17 (Detroit: Gale Research, 1983), pp. 407–417.   **493**

Kearns, Gerard, "Closed Space and Political Practice: Frederick Jackson Turner and Halford Mackinder," *Environment and Planning D: Society and Space*, vol. 2, 1 (1984), pp. 23–34.   **494**

Billington, Ray A., *Frederick Jackson Turner: Wisconsin's Historian of the Frontier* (Madison: State Historical Society of Wisconsin, 1986), 71 pp.   **495**

Ellen Churchill Semple
(1863–1932)

Human geographer, promoter of Ratzel and of an environmentalist anthropogeography

Chisholm, George G., "Miss Semple on the Influences of Geographical Environment," *Geographical Journal*, vol. 39, 1 (1912), pp. 31–37. **496**

Atwood, Wallace W., "An Appreciation of Ellen Churchill Semple" *Journal of Geography*, vol. 31, 6 (1932), p. 267. **497**

Bingham, Millicent Todd, "Ellen C. Semple, Geographer," *Vassar Quarterly*, vol. 60 (1932), pp. 236–240. **498**

Whitbeck, Ray H., "Ellen Churchill Semple," *Geographical Review*, vol. 22, 3 (1932), pp. 500–501. **499**

Colby, Charles C., "Ellen Churchill Semple," *Annals of the Association of American Geographers*, vol. 23, 4 (1934), pp. 229–240. **500**

Sauer, Carl O., "Semple, Ellen Churchill," *Encyclopedia of the Social Sciences*, vol. 13 (1934), pp. 661–662. **501**

Garrison, Hazel Shields, "Semple, Ellen Churchill, Anthropogeographer," *Dictionary of American Biography*, vol. 16 (New York: Charles Scribner's Sons, 1935), p. 583. **502**

"Semple, Ellen Churchill (Deceased)," in Wallace W. Atwood, comp., *The Graduate School of Geography: Our First Twenty-Five Years: 1921–1946* (Worcester, Mass.: Clark University, 1946), p. 83. **503**

"Semple, Ellen Churchill, anthropo-geographer," *National Cyclopedia of American Biography*, vol. 35 (New York: James T. White & Co., 1949), p. 139. **504**

Gelfand, Lawrence, "Ellen Churchill Semple: Her Geographical Approach to American History," *Journal of Geography*, vol. 53, 1 (1954), pp. 30–41. **505**

Wright, John K., "Miss Semple's 'Influences of Geographic Environment': Notes Toward a Bibliography," *Geographical Review*, vol. 52, 3 (1962), pp. 346–361. **506**

Hawley, Arthur J., "Environmental Perception: Nature and Ellen Churchill Semple," *Southeastern Geographer*, vol. 8 (1968), pp. 54–59. **507**

Fisher, Eric, Robert D. Campbell, and Eldon S. Miller, "Ellen Churchill Semple (1863–1932)," in their *A Question of Place: The Development of Geographic Thought* (Arlington, Va.: R. W. Beatty, 1969), pp. 399–407. **508**

"Semple, Ellen Churchill, geographer," in Edward T. James, Janet Wilson James, and Paul S. Boyer, eds., *Notable American Women, 1607–1950*, vol. 3 (Cambridge: Belknap Press of Harvard University Press, 1971), pp. 260–262. **509**

Bronson, Judith A. Conoyer, "Ellen Semple: Contributions to the History of American Geography," Ph.D. diss., St. Louis University, 1973. **510**

Berman, Mildred, "Sex Discrimination and Geography: The Case of Ellen Churchill Semple," *Professional Geographer*, vol. 26, 1 (1974), pp. 8–11. **511**

Bronson, Judith A. Conoyer, "A Further Note on Sex Discrimination and Geography: The Case of Ellen Churchill Semple," *Professional Geographer*, vol. 27, 1 (1975), pp. 111–112. **512**

Bushong, Allen D., "Women as Geographers: Some Thoughts of Ellen Churchill Semple," *Southeastern Geographer*, vol. 15, 2 (1975), pp. 102–109. **513**

Schegetz, Linda S., "Ellen Churchill Semple in Retrospect," *Ohio Geographers: Recent Research Themes*, vol. 4 (1976), pp. 94–101. **514**

Bushong, Allen D., "Ellen Churchill Semple," *Encyclopedia of Southern History* (Baton Rouge: Louisiana State University Press, 1979), p. 1092. **515**

Elliott, Harold M., "Mental Maps and Ethnocentrism: Geographic Characterizations in the Past," *Journal of Geography*, vol. 78, 7 (1979), pp. 250–265. [Includes Semple] **516**

Lewis, C. B., "The Biography of a Neglected Classic: Ellen Churchill Semple's 'The Geography of the Mediterranean Region,'" Master's thesis, University of South Carolina, 1979. **517**

Broc, Numa, "Les classiques de Miss Semple: Essai sur les sources des 'Influences of Geographic Environment,'" *Annales de géographie*, vol. 90, 497 (1981), pp. 87–102. **518**

James, Preston E., and Geoffrey J. Martin, "Ellen Churchill Semple," in their *All Possible Worlds: A History of Geographical Ideas* (New York: John Wiley & Sons, 1981), pp. 304–307 **519**

James, Preston E., Wilford A. Bladen, and Pradyumna P. Karan, "Ellen Churchill Semple and the Development of a Research Paradigm," in Wilford A. Bladen and Pradyumna P. Karan, eds., *The Evolution of Geographic Thought in America: A Kentucky Root* (Dubuque: Kendall Hunt Publishing Co., 1983), pp. 28–57. **520**

Bushong, Allen D., "Ellen Churchill Semple, 1863–1932," *Geographers: Biobibliographical Studies*, vol. 8 (London: Mansell Publishing Co., 1984), pp. 87–94. **521**

Ogilvie, Marilyn Bailey, "Semple, Ellen Churchill (1863–1932), U.S. Geographer," *Women in Science, Antiquity through the Nineteenth Century: A Biographical Dictionary with Annotated Bibliography* (Cambridge, Mass.: MIT Press, 1986), pp. 59–60.   522

Bushong, Allen D., "Unpublished Sources in Biographical Research: Ellen Churchill Semple," *Canadian Geographer*, vol. 31, 1 (1987), pp. 79–81.   523

Joseph Schafer (**)
(1867–1941)

Historian who mapped past social patterns in Wisconsin at the micro scale

Hicks, John D., "Joseph Schafer," *Mississippi Valley Historical Review*, vol. 27, 4 (1941), pp. 726–728. Also published, slightly shortened, in *American Historical Review*, vol. 46, 3 (1941), pp. 758–759.   524

Kellogg, Louise Phelps, and Clarence B. Lester, *Joseph Schafer: Student of Agriculture* (Madison: State Historical Society of Wisconsin, 1942), 30 pp.   525

"Schafer, Joseph, Historian," *Who Was Who in America*, vol. 1 (Chicago: Marquis Co., 1942), p. 1085.   526

Smith, Alice E., "A Dedication to the Memory of Joseph Schafer, 1867–1941," *Arizona and the West*, vol. 9, 2 (1967), pp. 102–108.   527

Nash, Gerald D., "Schafer, Joseph, Historian," in Howard R. Lamar, ed., *Reader's Encyclopedia of the American West* (New York: Thomas Y. Crowell Co., 1977), p. 1089.   528

Charles Oscar Paullin (**)
(1868–1944)

Historian and chief compiler of the Atlas of the Historical Geography of the United States

"Paullin, Charles Oscar, Author," *Who Was Who in America*, vol. 2 (Chicago: A. N. Marquis Co., 1950), p. 416.   529

Frederick Valentine Emerson
(1871–1919)

First historical geographer of the American South

Brigham, Albert Perry, "Memoir of Frederick Valentine Emerson," *Annals of the Association of American Geographers*, vol. 10, 4 (1920), pp. 149–152.   530

Martha Krug Genthe (*)
(1871–1945)

German-trained historical settlement geographer who taught in Connecticut

Bushong, Allen D., "Martha Krug Genthe and American Geography," Paper presented at the Annual Meeting of the Association of American Geographers, Miami, Apr. 1991.   531

Ray Hughes Whitbeck (*)
(1871–1939)

Wisconsin human geographer who popularized regional geographies with a historical component

"Whitbeck, Ray Hughes, Geographer," *National Cyclopedia of American Biography*, vol. E (New York: James T. White & Co., 1938), pp. 452–453.   532

Finch, Vernor C., "Ray Hughes Whitbeck, 1871–1939," *Journal of Geography*, vol. 38, 6 (1939), pp. 252–253.   533

Williams, Frank E., "Ray Hughes Whitbeck: Geographer, Teacher, and Man," *Annals of the Association of American Geographers*, vol. 30, 3 (1940), pp. 211–218.   534

Ellsworth Huntington (*)
(1876–1947)

Human geographer who explored American climatic history for its influence on human settlement change, particularly in the Southwest

Visher, Stephen S., "Memoir to Ellsworth Huntington, 1876–1947," *Annals of the Association of American Geographers*, vol. 38, 1 (1948), pp. 39–50.   535

Spate, Oscar H. K., "Toynbee and Huntington: A Study in Determinism," *Geographical Journal*, vol. 118, 4 (1952), pp. 406–424.   536

Akatiff, Clark A., "An Evaluation of Some Geographical Concepts of Ellsworth Huntington," Master's thesis, University of California–Los Angeles, 1963.   537

Chappell, John E., Jr., "Huntington and His Critics: The Influence of Climate on Civilization," Ph.D. diss., University of Kansas, 1968.   538

Spate, Oscar H. K., "Huntington, Ellsworth," *International Encyclopedia of the Social Sciences*, vol. 7 (New York: Macmillan Co. and the Free Press, 1968), pp. 26–27.   539

Martin, Geoffrey J., *Ellsworth Huntington: His Life and Thought* (Hamden, Conn.: Archon Books, 1973), 315 pp.   540

Harlan Harland Barrows
(1877–1960)

Chicago human geographer who offered the longest-running university course on American historical geography

Colby, Charles C., and Gilbert F. White, "Harlan H. Barrows, 1877–1960," *Annals of the Association of American Geographers*, vol. 51, 4 (1961), pp. 395–400.   **541**

Platt, Robert S., "Harlan H. Barrows," *Geographical Review*, vol. 51, 1 (1961), pp. 139–141.   **542**

"Barrows, Harlan Hiram [sic], geographer," *National Cyclopedia of American Biography*, vol. 45 (New York: James T. White & Co., 1962), pp. 298–299. [Middle name in error; should be Harland]
                                                                    543

"Barrows, Harlan H., Geographer," *Who Was Who in America*, vol. 4 (Chicago: A. N. Marquis Co., 1968), pp. 59–60.   **544**

Fisher, Eric, Robert D. Campbell, and Eldon S. Miller, "Harlan Harland Barrows (1877–1960)," in their *A Question of Place: The Development of Geographic Thought* (Arlington, Va.: R. W. Beatty, 1969), pp. 421–424.   **545**

Koelsch, William A., "The Historical Geography of Harlan H. Barrows," *Annals of the Association of American Geographers*, vol. 59, 4 (1969), pp. 632–651.   **546**

Chappell, John E., "Harlan Barrows and Environmentalism," *Annals of the Association of American Geographers*, vol. 61, 1 (1971), pp. 198–201.
                                                                    547

Isaiah Bowman (*)
(1878–1950)

Geographical student of the pioneer fringe, including the American West

Carter, George F., "Isaiah Bowman, 1878–1950," *Annals of the Association of American Geographers*, vol. 40, 4 (1950), pp. 335–350.   **548**

Stefansson, Vilhjalmur, "Isaiah Bowman, 1878–1950," *Yearbook of the American Philosophical Society* (1951), Philadelphia, 1952, pp. 291–294.
                                                                    549

Wright, John K., and George F. Carter, "Isaiah Bowman, December 26, 1878–January 6, 1950," National Academy of Sciences, *Biographical Memoirs*, vol. 33 (Washington, D.C.: Government Printing Office, 1959), pp. 39–64.   **550**

Knadler, George A., "Bowman, Isaiah," *International Encyclopedia of the Social Sciences*, vol. 2 (New York: Macmillan Co. and Free Press, 1968), pp. 137–138.   **551**

Martin, Geoffrey J., "Bowman, Isaiah, geographer and university president," *Dictionary of American Biography*, Supplement Four (New York: Charles Scribner's Sons, 1974), pp. 98–100.   **552**

Martin, Geoffrey J., *The Life and Thought of Isaiah Bowman* (Hamden, Conn.: Archon Books, 1980), 272 pp.   **553**

Roland McMillan Harper (*)
(1878–1966)

Geographer and naturalist with historical interests in the American Southeast

Ewan, Joseph, "Roland M. Harper," *Bulletin of the Torrey Botanical Club*, vol. 95 (1968), pp. 390–393.   **554**

Ewan, Joseph, "Harper, Roland McMillan, Botany, Geography, Demography," *Dictionary of Scientific Biography* (New York: Charles Scribner's Sons, 1972), pp. 122–123.   **555**

Delacourt, Hazel R., "Roland McMillan Harper: Recorder of Early Twentieth-Century Landscapes of the South," *Pioneer America*, vol. 10, 2 (1978), pp. 36–50.   **556**

Louis Charles Karpinski (**)
(1878–1956)

Historian of Great Lakes cartography

"Karpinski, Louis Charles, Educator," *Who Was Who in America*, vol. 3 (Chicago: Marquis, 1960), p. 462.   **557**

Jones, Phillip S., "Louis Charles Karpinski, Historian of Mathematics and Cartography," *Historia Mathematica*, vol. 3 (1976), pp. 185-202.   **558**

Jones, Phillip S., "Karpinski, Louis Charles, History of Mathematics, Cartography," *Dictionary of Scientific Biography*, vol. 15, supplement 1 (New York: Charles Scribner's Sons, 1978), pp. 255-257.   **559**

Darrell Haug Davis
(1879–1962)

Early specialist in the historical geography of the Middle West

"Davis, Darrell Haug, Geographer," *Who Was Who in America*, vol. 4 (Chicago: Marquis Co., 1968), p. 232.   **560**

"Davis, Darrell Haug," *Encyclopedia of American Biography*, n.s. vol. 39 (West Palm Beach, Fla.: American Historical Co., 1969), pp. 213–215. **561**

Almon Ernest Parkins
(1879–1940)

Preeminent early interpreter of the historical geography of the American South

"Almon Ernest Parkins," *Geographical Review*, vol. 30, 2 (1940), p. 332. **562**

Whitaker, J. Russell, "Almon Ernest Parkins, 1879–1940," *Journal of Geography*, vol. 39, 4 (1940), pp. 167–168. **563**

Whitaker, J. Russell, "Almon Ernest Parkins," *Annals of the Association of American Geographers*, vol. 31, 1 (1941), pp. 46–50. **564**

"Parkins, Almon Ernest, Geographer," *National Cyclopedia of American Biography*, vol. 38 (New York: James T. White & Co., 1953), pp. 469–470. **565**

James Walter Goldthwait (*)
(1880–1948)

Geomorphologist who contributed a classic microstudy of New England settlement history

Wrigley, Gladys M., "James Walter Goldthwait," *Geographical Review* vol. 38, 3 (1948), pp. 504–505. **566**

"Goldthwait, James Walter, Prof. Geology," *Who Was Who in America*, vol. 2 (Chicago: Marquis Co., 1950), p. 213. **567**

Lawrence Martin (*)
(1880–1955)

Cartographer of George Washington's great deeds

Wright, John K., and William O. Field, "Lawrence Martin," *Geographical Review*, vol. 45, 4 (1955), pp. 587–588. **568**

Williams, Frank E., "Lawrence Martin, 1880–1955," *Annals of the Association of American Geographers*, vol. 46, 3 (1956), pp. 357–358. **569**

"Martin, Lawrence, Geographer," *National Cyclopedia of American Biography*, vol. 44 (New York: James T. White & Co., 1962), pp. 42–43. **570**

Helge M. O. Nelson
(1882–1966)

Swedish geographer with special interest in the historical geography of Scandinavian settlement in North America

Bergsten, Karl-Erik, "Helge Nelson," *Svensk geografisk årsbok*, vol. 42 (1966), pp. 109–120. **571**

Tuneld, John, "Helge Nelson," *Kungliga Gustav Adolfs akademiens minnesbok 1957–1972*, vol. 2 (1981), pp. 89–131. **572**

Hägerstrand, Torsten, "Proclamations about Geography from the Pioneering Years in Sweden," *Geografiska annaler*, vol. 64B, 2 (1982), pp. 119–125. **573**

Bergsten, Karl-Erik, "Helge Nelson, 1882–1966," *Geographers: Biobibliographical Studies*, vol. 8 (1984), pp. 69–75. **574**

Oliver Edwin Baker (*)
(1883–1949)

Agricultural geographer who contributed historically informed studies of American agricultural regions

Holden, Arline, "Oliver Edwin Baker," *Geographical Review*, vol. 40, 2 (1950), pp. 333–334. **575**

"Baker, Oliver E.," in Wallace W. Atwood, comp., *The Graduate School of Geography: Our First Twenty-Five Years: 1921–1946* (Worcester, Mass.: Clark University, 1946), p. 85. **576**

Visher, Stephen S., and Charles Y. Hu, "Oliver Edwin Baker, 1883–1949," *Annals of the Association of American Geographers*, vol. 40, 4 (1950), pp. 328–334. **577**

"Baker, Oliver Edwin, Agricultural Economist," *National Cyclopedia of American Biography*, vol. 37 (New York: James T. White & Co., 1951), pp. 166–167. **578**

Kirkendall, Richard S., "Baker, Oliver Edwin, Agricultural and Economic Geographer," *Dictionary of American Biography*, suppl. 4 (New York: Charles Scribner's Sons, 1974), pp. 44–46. **579**

Charles Carlyle Colby (*)
(1884–1965)

Economic geographer who early studied the agricultural historical geography of the upper Middle West

Harper, Robert A., "Charles Carlyle Colby (1884–1965)," *Geographical Review*, vol. 56, 2 (1966), pp. 296–297. **580**

Harris, Chauncy D., "Charles Carlyle Colby, 1884–1965," *Annals of the Association of American Geographers*, vol. 56, 2 (1966), pp. 378–382. **581**

"Colby, Charles Carlyle, Educator and Geographer," *National Cyclopedia of American Biography*, vol. 51 (New York: James T. White & Co., 1969), pp. 590–591. **582**

Calef, Wesley, "Charles Carlyle Colby, 1884–1965," *Geographers: Biobibliographical Studies*, vol. 6

(London: Mansell Publishing Co., 1982), pp. 17–
22.   583

William Oscar Blanchard (*)
(1886–1952)

Regional geographer who studied the
geographical evolution of southwest Wisconsin

Page, John L. "William Oscar Blanchard," *Annals*
of the Association of American Geographers,
vol. 42, 4 (1952), pp. 324–326.   584

Lewis Francis Thomas (*)
(1886–1950)

Urban historical geographer of St. Louis

Crisler, Robert M., "Lewis F. Thomas," *Annals of*
the Association of American Geographers, vol.
40, 4 (1950), pp. 351–353.   585

"Thomas, Lewis Francis, Educator," *Who Was*
Who in America, vol. 3 (Chicago: Marquis Co.,
1960), p. 849.   586

Bert F. Hudgins (*)
(1887–1978)

Student of Michigan historical geography

"Hudgins, Bert," in Wallace W. Atwood, comp.,
The Graduate School of Geography: Our First
Twenty-Five Years: 1921–1946 (Worcester,
Mass.: Clark University, 1946), p. 108   587

Samuel Eliot Morison (**)
(1887–1976)

Historian of North American discoveries
and exploration

Allen, John L., "Samuel Eliot Morison and the European Discovery of America," *Journal of His-*
torical Geography Newsletter, vol. 2, 2 (1976), pp.
184–187.   588

Whitehill, Walter M., "In Memoriam: Samuel
Eliot Morison (1887–1976)," *New England Quar-*
terly, vol. 49, 3 (1976), pp. 459–463.   589

Taylor, Philip A. M., "Samuel Eliot Morison: Historian," *Journal of American Studies,* vol. 11, 1
(1977), pp. 13–26.   590

Metzger, Linda, "Morison, Samuel Eliot, 1887–
1976," *Contemporary Authors,* new rev. ser., vol.
4 (1981), pp. 432–434.   591

Bargar, Bradley D., "Samuel Eliot Morison," *Dic-*
tionary of Literary Biography, vol. 17 (Detroit:
Gale Research, 1983), pp. 296–307.   592

Eugene Van Cleef (*)
(1887–1973)

Ohio geographer who studied the Finns
in America

"Van Cleef, Eugene," in Wallace W. Atwood,
comp., *The Graduate School of Geography: Our*
First Twenty-Five Years: 1921–1946 (Worcester,
Mass.: Clark University, 1946), p. 97.   593

Van Cleef, Eugene, "My Reminiscences Concerned with American Geography," *Geographical*
Bulletin, vol. 1 (1970), pp. 7–13.   594

"Van Cleef, Eugene, Geographer, Author," *Who*
Was Who in America, vol. 6 (Chicago: A. N. Marquis Co., 1976), p. 414.   595

Martin, Geoffrey J., ed., "Autobiography of Eugene
Van Cleef (1887–1973)," *History of Geography*
Newsletter, vol. 3 (1983), pp. 13–20.   596

"Van Cleef, Eugene, 1887–1973," *Contemporary*
Authors, vol. 107 (Detroit: Gale Research Co.,
1983), p. 532.   597

Brown, Earl S., "Eugene Van Cleef, 1887–1973,"
Geographers: Biobibliographical Studies, vol. 9
(1985), pp. 137–143.   598

Stephen Sargent Visher (*)
(1887–1967)

Contributed early work on the historical
geography of the northern Great Plains and
Indiana, from the perspective of "geographic
influences" and sequent occupance

Harris, Chauncy D., "Stephen Sargent Visher,"
Journal of Geography, vol. 67, 6 (1968), pp. 378–
379.   599

Rose, John Kerr, "Stephen Sargent Visher, 1887–
1967," *Annals of the Association of American*
Geographers, vol. 61, 2 (1971), pp. 394–406.   600

"Visher, Stephen Sargent, Educator and Geographer," *National Cyclopedia of American Biog-*
raphy, vol. 53 (New York: James T. White & Co.,
1971), pp. 493–494.   601

John Harrison Kolb (**)
(1888–1963)

Rural sociologist who first studied the spatial
structure of Wisconsin rural communities
over time

Wileden, A. F., "John H. Kolb (1888–1963)," *Rural*
Sociology, vol. 29, 1 (1964), pp. 95–97.   602

"Kolb, John Harrison, Educator," *Who Was Who in America*, vol. 4 (Chicago: Marquis Co., 1968), p. 540.   **603**

Walter Prescott Webb (**)
(1888–1963)

Historian who wrote extensively on the meaning of the environment in the settlement of the Great Plains

Shannon, Fred A., *An Appraisal of Walter Prescott Webb's "The Great Plains"* (New York: Social Science Research Council, Bulletin no. 36, 1940), 254 pp.   **604**

Meinig, Donald W., "Commentary on Walter Prescott Webb's Geographical-Historical Concepts in American History," *Annals of the Association of American Geographers*, vol. 50, 1 (1960), pp. 95–96.   **605**

"Walter Prescott Webb," *American Historical Review*, vol. 68, 4 (1963), pp. 1211–1212.   **606**

Frantz, Joe B., et al., eds., *Essays on Walter Prescott Webb* (Austin: University of Texas Press, 1976), 123 pp.   **607**

Furman, Necah S., *Walter Prescott Webb: His Life and Impact* (Albuquerque: University of New Mexico Press, 1976), 222 pp.   **608**

Tobin, Gregory M., *The Making of a History: Walter Prescott Webb and the Great Plains* (Austin: University of Texas Press, 1976), 184 pp.   **609**

Rundell, Walter, Jr., "Webb, Walter Prescott, Historian," *Dictionary of American Biography*, suppl. 7 (New York: Charles Scribner's Sons, 1981), pp. 770–772.   **610**

Connelly, Thomas L., "Walter Prescott Webb," *Dictionary of Literary Biography*, vol. 17 (Detroit: Gale Research, 1983), pp. 418–423.   **611**

"Webb, Walter Prescott, 1888–1963," *Contemporary Authors*, vol. 113 (1985), p. 506.   **612**

Ruth Emily Baugh (*)
(1889–1973)

Early specialist on the historical geography of southern California

"Baugh, Ruth E.," in Wallace W. Atwood, comp., *The Graduate School of Geography: Our First Twenty-Five Years: 1921–1946* (Worcester, Mass.: Clark University, 1946), p. 104.   **613**

Trussell, Margaret E., "Five Western Woman Pioneer Geographers," *Yearbook of the Association of Pacific Coast Geographers*, 49 (1987), pp. 7–34.   **614**

Bushong, Allen D., "Ruth Emily Baugh (1889–1973): A Centennial Assessment," Paper presented to the Annual Meeting of the Association of American Geographers, Baltimore, 1989.   **615**

Otis Willard Freeman (*)
(1889–1964)

Economic geographer who contributed evolutionary studies of resource extraction in the Pacific Northwest

"Freeman, Otis W.," in Wallace W. Atwood, comp., *The Graduate School of Geography: Our First Twenty-Five Years: 1921–1946* (Worcester, Mass.: Clark University, 1946), p. 104–105.   **616**

[Martin, Howard H.], "Otis Willard Freeman Receives the Distinguished Service Award for 1958," *Journal of Geography*, vol. 58, 5 (1959), pp. 255–257.   **617**

Martin, Howard H., "Obituary: Otis Willard Freeman, 1889–1964," *Journal of Geography*, vol. 63, 7 (1964), p. 332.   **618**

Anderson, Jeremy, "Otis Willard Freeman: A Preliminary Bibliography," *Yearbook of the Association of Pacific Coast Geographers*, vol. 47 (1985), pp. 105–114.   **619**

"Freeman, Otis Willard, College President Emeritus, Educator," *Who Was Who in America*, vol. 8 (Chciago: Marquis, 1985), pp. 143–144.   **620**

George Henry Primmer (*)
(1889–1946)

Economic geographer who contributed evolutionary studies of agricultural commodities and of the development of Minnesota

Burgy, J. Herbert, "George Henry Primmer," *Annals of the Association of American Geographers*, vol. 37, 2 (1947), pp. 120–121.   **621**

Carl Ortwin Sauer
(1889–1975)

Most influential American historical geographer of the twentieth century, proponent of culture history as the basis for a genetic human geography

Sauer, Carl O., "The Education of a Geographer," *Annals of the Association of American Geographers*, vol. 46, 3 (1956), pp. 287–299. Reprinted in John Leighly, ed., *Land and Life: A Selection from the Writings of Carl Ortwin Sauer* (Berkeley: University of California Press, 1963), pp. 389–404.   **622**

Davies, Lawrence, "Personality Portrait–XIV: Professor of Human Geography, Dr. Sauer Maps People First, Land Is Merely a Setting," *Saturday Review*, vol. 40 (May 4, 1957), p. 64. **623**

Chaunu, Pierre, "Une histoire hispano-américaniste pilote: En marge de l'oeuvre de l'école de Berkeley," *Revue historique*, vol. 224 (1960), pp. 339–368. [Discusses Sauer, Borah, Cook, Parsons, West, and others] **624**

Leighly, John B., ed., Introduction to *Land and Life: A Selection from the Writings of Carl Ortwin Sauer* (Berkeley: University of California Press, 1963; repr. 1974), pp. 1–8. **625**

Pfeifer, Gottfried, "Carl Ortwin Sauer zum 75. Geburtstage am 24.xii.1964," *Geographische Zeitschrift*, vol. 53, 1 (1965), pp. 1–9. **626**

Parsons, James J., "Sauer, Carl O.," *International Encyclopedia of the Social Sciences*, vol. 14 (New York: Macmillan Co. and Free Press, 1968), pp. 17–19. **627**

Fisher, Eric, Robert D. Campbell, and Eldon S. Miller, "Carl O. Sauer (1889–)," in their *A Question of Place: The Development of Geographic Thought* (Arlington, Va.: R. W. Beatty, 1969), pp. 424–435. **628**

Speth, William W., "Historicist Anthropogeography: Environment and Culture in American Anthropological Thought from 1890 to 1950," Ph.D. diss., University of Oregon, 1972. **629**

Ballas, Donald J., "Carl Ortwin Sauer's Life and Work," *Places*, vol. 26, 3 (1975), pp. 24–31. **630**

"Carl Ortwin Sauer," *Geographical Journal*, vol. 141, 3 (1975), pp. 516–517. **631**

"Carl Ortwin Sauer, 1889–1975, Geographer," *New York Times*, July 21, 1975), p. 24. **632**

Humlum, Johannes, "Carl Ortwin Sauer, 24 December 1889–18 Juli 1975," *Kulturgeografi*, vol. 26, 125 (1975), pp. 236–237. **633**

Janke, James, "Some Thoughts on the Impact of Sauer's 'Morphology of Landscape'," *Kansas Geographer*, vol. 10 (1975), pp. 21–27. **634**

Kramer, Fritz L., "Carl Ortwin Sauer, Geographer (1889–1975)," *Geopub Review*, vol. 1, 11 (1975), pp. 337–347. **635**

"Milestones—Died: Carl O. Sauer, 85, American Geographer," *Time*, vol. 106, 5 (Aug. 4, 1975), p. 53. **636**

Pfeifer, Gottfried, "Carl Ortwin Sauer (24.12.1889–18.7.1975)," *Geographische Zeitschrift*, vol. 63, 3 (1975), pp. 161–169. **637**

Spencer, Joseph E., "Carl Sauer: Memories of a Teacher," *California Geographer*, vol. 15 (1975), pp. 83–84. **638**

Stanislawski, Dan, "Carl Ortwin Sauer, 1889–1975," *Journal of Geography*, vol. 74, 9 (1975), pp. 548–554. **639**

Bruman, Henry J., "In Memory of Carl Sauer: Remarks Made at a Commemorative Convocation in Berkeley on October 5, 1975," *Historical Geography Newsletter*, vol. 6, 1 (1976), pp. 5–6. **640**

Leighly, John B., "Carl Ortwin Sauer, 1889–1975," *Annals of the Association of American Geographers*, vol. 66, 3 (1976), pp. 337–348. **641**

Leighly, John B., "Carl Ortwin Sauer, 1889–1975," *Historical Geography Newsletter*, vol. 6, 1 (1976), pp. 3–4. **642**

Newcomb, Robert M., "Carl O. Sauer, Teacher," *Historical Geography Newsletter*, vol. 6, 1 (1976), pp. 21–30. **643**

Parsons, James J., "Carl Ortwin Sauer, 1889–1975," *Geographical Review*, vol. 66, 1 (1976), pp. 83–89. **644**

Parsons, James J., "Carl Ortwin Sauer (1889–1975)," *Yearbook of the American Philosophical Society (1975)*, Philadelphia, 1976, pp. 163–167. **645**

Riess, Richard O., "Some Notes on Salem Normal School and Carl Sauer, 1914," *Proceedings of the New England–St. Lawrence Valley Division of the Association of American Geographers*, vol. 6 (1976), pp. 63–67. **646**

Sauer, Carl O., "Casual Remarks," Offered at the Special Session in Honor of Carl O. Sauer: Fifty Years at Berkeley, Association of Pacific Coast Geographers, San Diego, 1973, ed. David Hornbeck, *Historical Geography Newsletter*, vol. 6, 1 (1976), pp. 70–76. **647**

"Sauer, Carl Ortwin, 1889–1975," *Contemporary Authors*, vols. 61–64 (1976), pp. 483–484. **648**

"Sauer, Carl (Ortwin), Geographer," *Who Was Who in America*, vol. 6 (Chicago: Marquis Co., 1976), p. 359. **649**

Sestini, Aldo, "Carl Ortwin Sauer," *Rivista geografica italiana*, vol. 83, 1 (1976), pp. 123–124. **650**

Spencer, Joseph E., "What's in a Name: 'The Berkeley School'?" *Historical Geography Newsletter*, vol. 6, 1 (1976), pp. 7–11. **651**

Speth, William W., "Carl Ortwin Sauer on Destructive Exploitation," *Biological Exploitation*, vol. 11, 2 (1977), pp. 145–160. **652**

Leighly, John B., "Carl Ortwin Sauer, 1889–1975," in T. Walter Freeman and P. Pinchemel, eds., *Geographers: Biobibliographical Studies*, vol. 2

(London: Mansell Publishing Co., 1978), pp. 99–108.   **653**

Leighly, John B., "Scholar and Colleague: Homage to Carl Sauer," *Yearbook of the Association of Pacific Coast Geographers*, vol. 40 (1978), pp. 117–133.   **654**

Parsons, James J., "The Later Sauer Years," *Annals of the Association of American Geographers*, vol. 69, 1 (1979), pp. 9–15.   **655**

West, Robert C., *Carl Sauer's Fieldwork in Latin America* (Ann Arbor: University Microfilms International, Dellplain Latin American Studies, vol. 3, 1979), 165 pp.   **656**

Hooson, David J. M., "Carl O. Sauer," in Brian W. Blouet, ed., *The Origins of Academic Geography in the United States* (Hamden, Conn.: Shoestring Press, 1981), pp. 165–174.   **657**

Sauer, Carl O., *Selected Essays, 1963–1975* (Berkeley: Turtle Island Foundation, 1981), 391 pp.   **658**

Speth, William W., "Berkeley Geography: 1923–33," in Brian W. Blouet, ed., *The Origins of Academic Geography in the United States* (Hamden, Conn.: Shoestring Press, 1981), pp. 221–244.   **659**

West, Robert C., "The Contribution of Carl Sauer to Latin American Geography," in Tom L. Martinson and Gary S. Elbow, eds., *Geographic Research on Latin America: Benchmark 1980* (Muncie, Ind.: Proceedings of the Conference of Latin Americanist Geographers, vol. 8, 1981), pp. 8–21.   **660**

Entrikin, J. Nicholas, "Sauer on Social Science: Howard Odum's Institute for Research in Social Science," *History of Geography Newsletter*, vol. 2 (1982), pp. 35–38.   **661**

Kersten, Earl W. Jr., "Carl Sauer and 'Geographic Influences'," *Yearbook of the Association of Pacific Coast Geographers*, vol. 44 (1982), pp. 47–73.   **662**

West, Robert C., *Andean Reflections: Letters from Carl O. Sauer While on a South American Trip under a Grant from the Rockefeller Foundation* (Boulder, Colo.: Westview Press, Dellplain Latin American Studies, vol. 11, 1982), 139 pp.   **663**

Belil, Mireia, and Isabel Clos, "Notes a l'entorn del pensament de Carl O. Sauer (1889–1975)," (in Catalan) *Documents d'analisi geografica*, Universitat Autonoma de Barcelona, vol. 2 (1983), pp. 177–188.   **664**

Dow, Maynard W., "Geographers on Film: The First Interview—Carl O. Sauer Interviewed by Preston James," *History of Geography Newsletter*, no. 3 (1983), pp. 8–12.   **665**

Hart, John Fraser, "Hart on Sauer," in Wilford A. Bladen and Pradyumna P. Karan, eds., *The Evolution of Geographic Thought in America: A Kentucky Root* (Dubuque: Kendall Hunt Publishing Co., 1983), pp. 113–114.   **666**

Hewes, Leslie, "Carl Sauer: A Personal View," *Journal of Geography*, vol. 82, 4 (1983), pp. 140–147.   **667**

Parsons, James J., and Natalia Vonnegut, "Biographical Sketch: Carl Ortwin Sauer (1889–1975)," in their *Sixty Years of Berkeley Geography, 1923–1983: Biobibliographies of 159 PhDs Granted by the University of California, Berkeley, since the Establishment of a Doctoral Program in Geography in 1923* (Berkeley: University of California Department of Geography, Supplement to *Itinerant Geographer*, Nov. 1983), pp. 157–160.   **668**

Williams, Michael, "The Apple of My Eye: Carl Sauer and Historical Geography," *Journal of Historical Geography*, vol. 9, 1 (1983), pp. 1–28.   **669**

Entrikin, J. Nicholas, "Carl O. Sauer, Philosopher in Spite of Himself," *Geographical Review*, vol. 74, 4 (1984), pp. 387–408.   **670**

Kenzer, Martin S., "Carl O. Sauer: Nascent Human Geographer at Northwestern," *California Geographer*, vol. 25 (1985), pp. 1–11.   **671**

Kenzer, Martin S., "Milieu and the 'Intellectual Landscape': Carl O. Sauer's Undergraduate Heritage," *Annals of the Association of American Geographers*, vol. 75, 2 (1985), pp. 258–270.   **672**

Pederson, Leland R., "A Dedication to the Memory of Carl Ortwin Sauer, 1889–1975," *Arizona and the West*, vol. 27, 4 (1985), pp. 305–308.   **673**

Kenzer, Martin S., "Carl Sauer and the Carl Ortwin Sauer Papers," *History of Geography Newsletter*, no. 5 (1986), pp. 1–9.   **674**

Kenzer, Martin S., "The Making of Carl O. Sauer and the Berkeley School of Historical Geography," Ph.D. diss., McMaster University, 1986.   **675**

Pfeifer, Gottfried, "Carl Ortwin Sauer: Die Berkeleyer Schule und das 'Morale' der Geographie," in *Festschrift zur 150-Jahrfeier der Frankfurter Geographischen Gesellschaft, 1839–1986* (Frankfort: Frankfurter Geographische Hefte, vol. 55, 1986), pp. 423–437.   **676**

Solot, Michael, "Carl Sauer and Cultural Evolution," *Annals of the Association of American Geographers*, vol. 76, 4 (1986), pp. 508–520.   **677**

Entrikin, J. Nicholas, "Archival Research: Carl O. Sauer and Chorology," *Canadian Geographer*, vol. 31, 1 (1987), pp. 77–79. **678**

Kenzer, Martin S., "Tracking Sauer across Sour Terrain," *Annals of the Association of American Geographers*, vol. 77, 3 (1987), pp. 469–474. **679**

Kenzer, Martin S., ed., *Carl O. Sauer: A Tribute* (Corvallis: Oregon State University Press for the Association of Pacific Coast Geographers, 1987). **680**

Chapters include:

Aschmann, Homer, "Carl Sauer, A Self-Directed Career," pp. 137–143; **681**

Bruman, Henry J., "Carl Sauer in Mid-Career: A Personal View by One of His Students," pp. 125–136; **682**

Kenzer, Martin S., "Like Father, Like Son: William Albert and Carl Ortwin Sauer," pp. 40–65; **683**

Macpherson, Anne, "Preparing for the National Stage: Carl Sauer's First Ten Years at Berkeley," pp. 69–89; **684**

Mathewson, Kent, "Sauer South by Southwest: Antimodernism and the Austral Impulse," pp. 90–111; **685**

Mikesell, Marvin W., "Sauer and 'Sauerology': A Student's Perspective," pp. 144–150; **686**

Speth, William W., "Historicism: The Disciplinary World View of Carl O. Sauer," pp. 11–39 **687**

Urquhart, Alvin W., "Carl Sauer: Explorer of the Far Sides of Frontiers," pp. 217–224. **688**

Leighly, John B., "Ecology as Metaphor: Carl Sauer and Human Ecology," *Professional Geographer*, vol. 39, 4 (1987), pp. 405–412. **689**

Mathewson, Kent, "Humane Ecologist: Carl Sauer as Metaphor?" *Professional Geographer*, vol. 39, 4 (1987), pp. 412–413. **690**

Porter, Philip W., "Ecology as Metaphor: Sauer and Human Ecology," *Professional Geographer*, vol. 39, 4 (1987), p. 414. **691**

Turner, Billie Lee, II, "Comment on Leighly [regarding Sauer]," *Professional Geographer*, vol. 39, 4 (1987), pp. 415–416. **692**

Williams, Michael, "Sauer and 'Man's Role in Changing the Face of the Earth,'" *Geographical Review*, vol. 77, 2 (1987), pp. 218–226. **693**

Kenzer, Martin S., "Commentary on Carl O. Sauer," *Professional Geographer*, vol. 40, 3 (1988), pp. 333–336. **694**

Rucinque, Héctor F., "Carl O. Sauer: Geógrafo y maestro *par excellence*," *Trimestre Geografico*

(Association of Colombian Geographers), vol. 14 (May 1990), pp. 3–19. **695**

Derwent Stainthorpe Whittlesey
(1890–1956)

Exponent of sequent occupance as a methodological approach to human geography

Ackerman, Edward A., "Derwent Stainthorpe Whittlesey," *Geographical Review*, vol. 47, 3 (1957), pp. 443–445. **696**

"Whittlesey, Derwent Stainthorpe, Geographer and Author," *National Cyclopedia of American Biography*, vol. 42 (New York: James T. White & Co., 1958), pp. 467–468. **697**

Mikesell, Marvin W., "The Rise and Decline of Sequent Occupance: A Chapter in the History of American Geography," in David Lowenthal and Martyn Bowden, eds., *Geographies of the Mind: Essays in Historical Geosophy in Honor of John Kirtland Wright* (New York: Oxford University Press, 1976), pp. 149–169. Reprinted in Brian J. L. Berry, ed., *The Nature of Change in Geographical Ideas* (DeKalb: Northern Illinois University Press, 1979), pp. 3–15. **698**

Nash, Peter H., "Injection of Topophilia via Historical Geography: Reflections on Harvard's 'The Boston Region' Field Course as Taught by Derwent Whittlesey," *Proceedings of the New England–St. Lawrence Valley Geographical Society*, vol. 6 (1976), pp. 59–63. **699**

Nash, Peter H., "Versatile Whittlesey: Influences on and from a Sisyphean Synthesizer," *History of Geography Newsletter*, no. 1 (Dec. 1981), pp. 15–20. **700**

Martin, Geoffrey J., "On Whittlesey, Bowman, and Harvard," *Annals of the Association of American Geographers*, vol. 78, 1 (1987), pp. 152–158. **701**

Oskar Schmieder (*)
(1891–1980)

German cultural geographer with interests in North American colonization processes and patterns

Lauer, Wilhelm, "Oskar Schmieder zu seinem 70. Geburtstag," in *Beiträge zur Geographie der Neuen Welt* (Kiel: Schriften des Geographischen Instituts der Universität Kiel, vol. 20, 1961), pp. 9–13. **702**

Dickinson, Robert E., "Oskar Schmieder," in his *The Makers of Modern Geography* (London: Routledge & Kegan Paul, 1969), pp. 157–160. **703**

Schmieder, Oskar, *Lebenserinnerungen und Taschenbuchblätter eines Geographen* (Kiel: Schriften des Geographischen Instituts der Universität Kiel, vol. 40, 1972), 181 pp. Also as separate book, Kiel: Verlag Ferdinand Hirt, 1972, 186 pp. **704**

Bähr, Jürgen, "Oskar Schmieders länderkundliches Lebenswerk," *Kieler Geographische Schriften*, vol. 52 (1981), pp. 1–10. **705**

Bähr, Jürgen, and E. Dillner, "Oskar Schmieder, un geógrafo hispanista y americanista," *Revista de geografía* (Barcelona), vol. 15, 1–2 (1981), pp. 35–43. **706**

John Kirtland Wright (*)
(1891–1969)

Eclectic geographer with special interest in the significance of human nature in American historical geography

Kahn, Ely J., Jr., "Profiles: Big Geographer," *New Yorker*, vol. 17, 24 (1941), pp. 20–24, 26–28. **707**

Light, Richard U., "John Kirtland Wright," *Geographical Review*, vol. 40, 1 (1950), pp. 3–4. **708**

Wright, John K., Introduction to his *Human Nature in Geography: Fourteen Papers, 1925–1965* (Cambridge: Harvard University Press, 1966), pp. 1–10. **709**

Lowenthal, David, "John Kirtland Wright, 1891–1969," *Geographical Review*, vol. 59, 4 (1969), pp. 598–604. **710**

Bowden, Martyn J., "John Kirtland Wright, 1891–1969," *Annals of the Association of American Geographers*, vol. 60, 2 (1970), pp. 394–403. **711**

"Wright, John Kirtland, Educator," *Who Was Who in America*, vol. 5 (Chicago: Marquis Co., 1973), p. 800. **712**

Edna Fay Campbell
(1892–1969)

Student of the historical geography of the lower Mississippi Valley

"Campbell, Edna Fay," in Wallace W. Atwood, comp., *The Graduate School of Geography: Our First Twenty-Five Years: 1921–1946* (Worcester, Mass.: Clark University, 1946), p. 108. **713**

"Campbell, Edna Fay, Author, Lecturer," *Who's Who of American Women*, vol. 1 (Chicago: A. N. Marquis Co., 1958), p. 205. **714**

John Wesley Coulter (*)
(1893–1967)

Student of the historical geography of Hawaii

"Coulter, John Wesley, Educator," *National Cyclopedia of American Biography*, vol. 55 (Clifton, N.J.: James T. White & Co., 1974), pp. 281–282. **715**

Alfred Herman Meyer
(1893–1988)

Contributed exhaustive sequent-occupance studies that made the bistate Kankakee Marsh a region famous among geographers

"Meyer, Alfred Herman," *Contemporary Authors*, permanent ser., vol. 1 (1975), p. 443. **716**

Harris, Chauncy D., "Alfred H. Meyer 1893–1988," *Journal of Geography*, vol. 87, 6 (1988), p. 236. **717**

James Claude Malin (**)
(1893–1979)

Historian whose environmental studies of the American grasslands built on the findings of geographers and other earth scientists

LeDuc, Thomas H., "An Ecological Interpretation of Grassland History: The Work of James C. Malin as Historian and as Critic of Historians," *Nebraska History*, vol. 31 (1950), pp. 226–233. **718**

Nichols, Roy F., "Kansas Historiography: The Technique of Cultural Analysis," *American Quarterly*, vol. 9, 1 (1957), pp. 85–91. **719**

Bell, Robert G., "James C. Malin: A Study in American Historiography," Ph.D. diss., University of California–Los Angeles, 1968. **720**

Bell, Robert G., "James C. Malin and the Grasslands of North America," *Agricultural History*, vol. 46, 3 (1972), pp. 414–424. **721**

Bogue, Allan G., "Recent Deaths: James C. Malin," *American Historical Review*, vol. 84, 3 (1979), pp. 915–916. **722**

Bogue, Allan G., "The Heirs of James C. Malin: A Grassland Historiography," *Great Plains Quarterly*, vol. 1, 2 (1981), pp. 105–131. **723**

LaForte, Robert S., "James C. Malin, Optimist: The Basis of His Philosophy of History," *Kansas History*, vol. 6, 2 (1983), pp. 110–119. **724**

"Malin, James Claude, 1893–1979," *Contemporary Authors*, vol. 113 (1985), p. 303. **725**

Swierenga, Robert P., "The Malin Thesis of Grassland Acculturation and the New Rural History (North America)," in Donald H. Akenson, ed., *Canadian Papers in Rural History*, vol. 5 (Gananoque: Langdale Press, 1986), pp. 11–22. **726**

John Barger Leighly (*)
(1895–1986)

Berkeley cultural-historical geographer whose later work advanced American place-name geography

Leighly, John B., "Drifting into Geography in the Twenties" *Annals of the Association of American Geographers*, vol. 69, 1 (1979), pp. 4–9. **727**

Singh, Rana P. B., "Obituary: John Barger Leighly (1895–1986)," *National Geographical Journal of India*, vol. 32, 3 (1986), pp. 276–277. **728**

Miller, David H. "John Leighly, 1895–1986," *Annals of the Association of American Geographers*, vol. 78, 2 (1988), pp. 347–357. **729**

Parsons, James J., "John Leighly, 1895–1986," *Geographers: Biobibliographical Studies*, vol. 12 (London: Mansell Publishing Co., 1988), pp. 113–119. **730**

Guy-Harold Smith (*)
(1895–1976)

Population geographer who made innovative historical maps of Wisconsin population and ethnic patterns, and of George Washington's Ohio Valley campaigns

Brown, Earle S., "Guy-Harold Smith, 1895–1976)," *Annals of the Association of American Geographers*, vol. 68, 1 (1978), pp. 115–118. **731**

"Smith, Guy-Harold," *Contemporary Authors*, permanent ser., vol. 2 (1978), p. 481. **732**

Glenn Thomas Trewartha (*)
(1896–1984)

Major contributor to the genetic study of American settlement morphology, and the historical geography of the upper Mississippi Valley

Hartshorne, Richard, and John R. Borchert, "Glenn T. Trewartha, 1896–1984," *Annals of the Association of American Geographers*, vol. 78, 4 (1988), pp. 728–735. **733**

Stanley Dalton Dodge
(1897–1966)

Contributed to the historical geography of American population, and of Illinois and New England

"Dodge, Stanley Dalton, Geographer and Educator," *National Cyclopedia of American Biography*, vol. 54 (Clifton, N.J.: James T. White & Co., 1973), pp. 22–23. **734**

Charles Langdon White (*)
(1897–1989)

Student of Western historical geography

"White, (Charles) Langdon," in Wallace W. Atwood, comp., *The Graduate School of Geography: Our First Twenty-Five Years: 1921–1946* (Worcester, Mass.: Clark University, 1946), p. 95. **735**

Ralph Hall Brown
(1898–1948)

Published the first synthetic historical geography of the United States based on documentary sources, and was the first geographical specialist in the American colonial period

Dodge, Stanley D., "Ralph Hall Brown, 1898–1948," *Annals of the Association of American Geographers*, vol. 38, 4 (1948), pp. 305–309. **736**

Visher, Stephen S., "Ralph H. Brown," *Journal of Geography*, vol. 47, 5 (1948), pp. 206. **737**

[Wrigley, Gladys M.], "Ralph Hall Brown," *Geographical Review*, vol. 38, 3 (1948), pp. 505–506. **738**

"Brown, Ralph Hall, University Professor," *Who Was Who in America*, vol. 2 (Chciago: A. N. Marquis Co., 1950), p. 85. **739**

Clark, Andrew Hill, "Ralph Browns Beitrag zur amerikanischen historischen Geographie," *Erde*, vol. 5, 2 (1953), pp. 148–152. **740**

Darby, H. Clifford, "Brown, Ralph H.," *International Encyclopedia of the Social Sciences*, vol. 2 (New York: Macmillan Co. and Free Press, 1968), pp. 155–156. **741**

Koelsch, William A., "Ralph Hall Brown, Historical Geographer," *Dictionary of American Biography*, suppl. 4 (New York: Charles Scribner's Sons, 1974), pp. 112–113. **742**

Runyan, Christine L., "A Comment on the Contributions of Ralph H. Brown," *Ohio Geographers: Recent Research Themes*, vol. 4 (1976), pp. 85–93. **743**

McManis, Douglas R., "Prism to the Past: The Historical Geography of Ralph Hall Brown," *Social Science History*, vol. 3, 1 (1979), pp. 279–285. **744**

Miles, Linda J., "Ralph Hall Brown: Gentlescholar of Historical Geography," Ph.D. diss., University of Oklahoma, 1982. **745**

Coppens, Linda Miles, "Ralph Hall Brown, 1898–1948," *Geographers: Biobibliographic Studies*, vol. 9 (London: Mansell Publishing Co., 1985), pp. 15–20. **746**

Edwin Jay Foscue
(1899–1972)

Contributed to the historical geography of agriculture in Texas and the American southwest

"Foscue, Edwin J.,"in Wallace W. Atwood, comp., *The Graduate School of Geography: Our First Twenty-Five Years: 1921–1946* (Worcester, Mass.: Clark University, 1946), p. 110.   747

"Foscue, Edwin Jay," *Contemporary Authors*, 1st rev., vols. 1–4 (1967), p. 326.   748

"Foscue, Edwin J., Geographer," *Who Was Who in America*, vol. 5 (Chicago: Marquis, 1973), p. 242.   749

Preston Everett James (*)
(1899–1986)

Contributed an early classic study in the sequent occupance of the Blackstone Valley in southern New England

"James, Preston E.," in Wallace W. Atwood, comp., *The Graduate School of Geography: Our First Twenty-Five Years: 1921–1946* (Worcester, Mass.: Clark University, 1946), p. 93.   750

Hartshorne, Richard, Introduction to Donald W. Meinig, ed., *On Geography: Selected Writings of Preston E. James* (Syracuse: Syracuse University Press, 1971), pp. ix-xiv.   751

Jensen, Robert G., "Preston Everett James, 1899–1986," *Journal of Geography*, vol. 85, 6 (1986), pp. 273–274.   752

Singh, Rana P. B., "Obituary: Preston James (1899–1986)," *National Geographical Journal of India*, vol. 32, 3 (1986), pp. 275–276.   753

Martin, Geoffrey J., "Preston Everett James, 1899–1986," *Geographers: Biobibliographical Studies*, vol. 11 (London: Mansell Publishing Co., 1987), pp. 63–70.   754

Martin, Geoffrey J., "Preston E. James, 1899–1986," *Annals of the Association of American Geographers*, vol. 78, 1 (1988), pp. 164–175.   755

"James, Preston Everett, 1899–1986," *Contemporary Authors*, new rev. ser., vol. 29 (1990), pp. 216–217.   756

Francis Grave Morris
(1899–1952)

British student of early American historical geography, particularly of North Carolina

Jervis, Walter W., "Francis Grave Morris," *Geography*, vol. 37, 1 (1952), pp. 36–37.   757

Lauren Chester Post
(1899–1976)

Specialist in the cultural-historical geography of Louisiana

Comeaux, Malcolm C., "Lauren Chester Post," *California Geographer*, vol. 16 (1976), pp. 85–88.   758

"Post, Lauren Chester, Educator," *National Cyclopedia of American Biography*, vol. 59 (1980), pp. 357–358.   759

Charles Warren Thornthwaite (*)
(1899–1963)

Interpreted Great Plains settlement history in climatic terms, based on his famed global climate classification scheme

Hare, F. Kenneth, "Charles Warren Thornthwaite, 1899–1963," *Geographical Review*, vol. 53, 4 (1963), pp. 595–597.   760

Leighly, John B., "Charles Warren Thornthwaite, 1899–1963," *Annals of the Association of American Geographers*, vol. 54, 4 (1964), pp. 615–621.   761

"Thornthwaite, Charles Warren, Consulting Climatologist," *Who Was Who in America*, vol. 4 (Chicago: Marquis Co., 1968), p. 941.   762

Lester Jesse Cappon (**)
(1900–1981)

Historian who coordinated development of the Atlas of Early American History

Washburn, Wilcomb E., "Dedication," *William & Mary Quarterly*, 3d ser., vol. 26, 3 (1969), pp. 322–326.   763

"Cappon, Lester Jesse, American History," *Directory of American Scholars*, 7th ed., vol. 1 (1978), p. 101.   764

"Cappon, Lester Jesse, 1900–1981," *Contemporary Authors*, vol. 106 (1982), pp. 97–98.   765

Tate, Thad W., "Lester Jesse Cappon," *Proceedings of the American Antiquarian Society*, vol. 92, 1 (1982), pp. 23–25.   766

William Patterson Cumming
(1900–1989)

Cartographic historian of the Atlantic Coast

"Cumming, William Patterson," *Contemporary Authors*, vols. 33–36 (1978), p. 222.   767

DeVorsey, Louis, Jr., "Obituary: William Patterson Cumming, 1900–1989," *Map Collector*, no. 49 (1989), pp. 44–45.   **768**

Ristow, Walter W., "William P. Cumming Awarded Honorary Degree," *Map Collector*, no. 49 (1989), pp. 38.   **769**

Quinn, David B., "William Patterson Cumming, 1900–1989," *Geographical Journal*, vol. 156, 1 (1990), p. 116.   **770**

Wallis, Helen, "William Patterson Cumming," *Imago Mundi*, vol. 42 (1990), pp. 114–116.   **771**

Edmund William Gilbert
(1900–1973)

British historical geographer with an interest in the European exploration of the American West

"Edmund William Gilbert," *Geographical Journal*, vol. 140, 1 (1974), pp. 176–177.   **772**

Freeman, T. Walter, "E. W. Gilbert, 1900–1973," *Geography*, vol. 59, 1 (1974), p. 68.   **773**

"Gilbert, Edmund William, 1900–1973," *Contemporary Authors*, vols. 65–68 (1977), p. 248.   **774**

Freeman, T. Walter, "Edmund William Gilbert, 1900–1973," *Geographers: Biobibliographical Studies*, vol. 3 (London: Mansell Publishing Co., 1979), pp. 63–71.   **775**

Robinson, Guy M., and John Patten, "Edmund W. Gilbert and the Development of Historical Geography, with a Bibliography of His Work" *Journal of Historical Geography*, vol. 6, 4 (1980), pp. 409–419.   **776**

Erhard Rostlund
(1900–1961)

Student of native American ecological relation to food resources

Leighly, John B., "Erhard Rostlund," *University of California in Memoriam* (Apr. 1962), pp. 78–81.   **777**

Sauer, Carl O., "Erhard Rostlund," *Geographical Review*, vol. 52, 1 (1962), pp. 133–135.   **778**

Samuel Newton Dicken (*)
(1901–1989)

Late contributor to the historical geography of Oregon and the Pacific Northwest

Dicken, Samuel N., *The Education of a Hillbilly, Sixty Years in Six Colleges: The Memoirs of Samuel Newton Dicken* (Eugene, Oreg.: University of Oregon Department of Geography, for

the Lane County Geographical Society, 1988), 93 pp.   **779**

Pitts, Forrest R., "Samuel N. Dicken, 1901–1989," *Geographers: Biobibliographical Studies*, vol. 13 (London: Mansell Publishing Co., 1991), pp. 17–22.   **780**

Gottfried Pfeifer
(1901–1985)

German historical geographer interested in the political and economic development of the United States, and of the Southeast

Overbeck, Hermann, "Gottfried Pfeifer zum 65. Geburtstag," *Heidelberger Geographische Arbeiten*, vol. 15 (1966), pp. 1–28.   **781**

Kohlhepp, Gerd, "Der Beitrag Gottfried Pfeifers zur kulturgeographischen Lateinamerika Forschung," *Geographische Zeitschrift*, vol. 64, 1 (1976), pp. 1–12.   **782**

Kohlhepp, Gerd, "Die Forschungen Gottfried Pfeifers zur Kulturgeographie der Neuen Welt," in Gerd Kohlhepp, ed., *Beiträge zur Kulturgeographie der Neuen Welt: Ausgewählte Arbeiten von Gottfried Pfeifer* (Berlin: Dietrich Reimer Verlag, 1981), pp. 7–17.   **783**

Kilchenmann, A., "Interview mit Gottfried Pfeifer," *Karlsruher Manuskripte zur mathematischen und theoretischen Wirtschafts- und Sozialgeographie*, vol. 72 (1985), 27 pp.   **784**

Sandner, Gerhard, "Zum Tode Gottfried Pfeifers," *Geographische Zeitschrift*, vol. 74, 1 (1986), pp. 1–2.   **785**

Kohlhepp, Gerd, "Gottfried Pfeifer (20.1. 1901–6.7.1985)" *Geographisches Taschenbuch 1987/1988* (1987), pp. 133–157.   **786**

Hallock Floyd Raup
(1901–1985)

Contributed to the historical and ethnic geography of Pennsylvania and California

"Raup, Hallock Floyd," *Contemporary Authors*, vols. 37–40, 1st rev. (1979), pp. 450–451.   **787**

Loyal Durand (*)
(1902–1970)

Contributed to the historical geography of dairying, particularly in Wisconsin

"Durand, Loyal, Jr., Former Educator," *Who Was Who in America*, vol. 5 (Chicago: Marquis Co., 1973), p. 202.   **788**

"Durand, Loyal, Jr., 1902–1970," *Contemporary Authors,* permanent ser., vol. 2 (Detroit: Gale Research Co., 1978), p. 173.   789

Lester Earl Klimm (*)
(1902–1960)

Developed a special interest in the historical carrying capacity of land in relation to population

Russell, Joseph A., "Lester E. Klimm," *Geographical Review,* vol. 51, 3 (1961), pp. 424–426.   790

Starkey, Otis P., "Lester Earl Klimm, 1902–1960," *Annals of the Association of American Geographers,* vol. 52, 1 (1962), pp. 115–117.   791

Adelbert K. Botts (*)
(1903–1983)

Student of New England historical geography

"Botts, Adelbert K.,"in Wallace W. Atwood, comp., *The Graduate School of Geography: Our First Twenty-Five Years: 1921–1946* (Worcester, Mass.: Clark University, 1946), p. 113.   792

Jan Otto Marius Broek
(1904–1974)

Contributed a classic methodological study of landscape change in the Santa Clara Valley, California

Ormerling, Ferdinand Jan, Sr., "In Memoriam Prof. Dr. Jan O. M. Broek," *Geografisch Tijdschrift,* vol. 8, 5 (1974), pp. 403–406.   793

"Broek, Jan Otto Marius, Geographer," *Who Was Who in America,* vol. 6 (Chicago: Marquis Co., 1976), p. 54.   794

"Broek, Jan Otto Marius, 1904–1974," *Contemporary Authors,* permanent ser., vol. 2 (1978), p. 86.   795

"Broek, Jan Otto Marius, Geographer," *National Cyclopedia of American Biography,* vol. 59 (Clifton, N.J.: James T. White & Co., 1980), pp. 135–136.   796

Emyr Estyn Evans
(1905–1989)

British cultural geographer with an interest in the Celtic presence in North America

Buchanan, R. H., "Emyr Estyn Evans, 1905–1989: An Appreciation," *Irish Geography,* vol. 22, 2 (1989), pp. 117–119.   797

Jones, Emrys, "Emyr Estyn Evans, 1905–1989," *Geographical Journal,* vol. 156, 1 (1990), pp. 116–117.   798

Glasscock, Robin E., "E. Estyn Evans, 1905–1989," *Journal of Historical Geography,* vol. 17, 1 (1991), pp. 87–91.   799

Herman Ralph Friis
(1905–1989)

Contributed authoritative population maps of colonial America, and studies on the role of the federal government in mapping the West

"Friis, Herman Ralph," *Directory of American Scholars,* 7th ed., vol. 1 (1978), pp. 226–227.   800

Joseph Earle Spencer (*)
(1907–1984)

Early work included contributions to the settlement morphology of southern Utah

"Spencer, Joseph Earle," *Contemporary Authors,* vols. 45–48 (1974), p. 545.   801

Nelson, Howard, "J. E. Spencer, 1907–1984," *Annals of the Association of American Geographers,* vol. 75, 4 (1985), pp. 595–603.   802

"Joseph Earle Spencer (1907–1984)," *National Geographical Journal of India,* vol. 32, 2 (1986), p. 178.   803

Newcomb, Robert M., "Joseph Spencer, Teacher and Orientalist," *Historical Geography,* vol. 20, 2 (1990), pp. 8–15.   804

Thomas, William L., Jr., and Herbert M. Eder, "Joseph E. Spencer, 1907–1984," *Geographers: Biobibliographical Studies,* vol. 13 (London: Mansell Publishing Co., 1991), pp. 81–92.   805

Andrew Hill Clark
(1911–1975)

Proponent of "geographical change" as the theme for North American historical geography, and student of the Canadian Maritimes

Clark, Andrew Hill, "Praemia Geographiae: The Incidental Rewards of a Professional Career," *Annals of the Association of American Geographers,* vol. 52, 2 (1962), pp. 229–241.   806

Perry, Peter J., "Andrew H. Clark," *New Zealand Geographer,* vol. 31, 2 (1975), p. 188.   807

Harris, R. Cole, "Andrew Hill Clark, 1911–1975: An Obituary," *Journal of Historical Geography,* vol. 2, 1 (1976), pp. 1–2.   808

McManis, Douglas R., "Andrew Hill Clark, 1911–1975," *Historical Geography Newsletter*, vol. 6, 1 (1976), pp. 13–20.   **809**

Ward, David, "Andrew Hill Clark, 1911–1975," *Annals of the Association of American Geographers*, vol. 67, 1 (1977), 145–148.   **810**

"Clark, Andrew Hill, 1911–1975," *Contemporary Authors*, permanent ser., vol. 2 (1978), pp. 116–117.   **811**

Meinig, Donald W., "Prologue: Andrew Hill Clark, Historical Geographer," in James R. Gibson, ed., *European Settlement and Development in North America: Essays on Geographical Change in Honour and Memory of Andrew Hill Clark* (Toronto: University of Toronto Press, 1978), pp. 3–26.   **812**

Harris, Cole, "Clark, Andrew Hill, Historical Geographer," *Canadian Encyclopedia*, 2nd ed., vol. 1 (Edmonton: Hurtig Publishers, 1988), p. 432.   **813**

Ward, David, and Michael Solot, "Andrew Hill Clark, 1911–1975," *Geographers: Biobibliographic Studies*, vol. 14 (London: Mansell Publishing Co., 1992), 13–26.   **814**

Merle Charles Prunty, Jr. (*)
(1917–1982)

Contributed to the historical geography of agriculture and settlement in the American South

"Prunty, Merle Charles," *Contemporary Authors*, vols. 37–40, 1st rev. (1979), p. 444.   **815**

Aiken, Charles S., "Merle Charles Prunty, Jr.," *Southeastern Geographer*, vol. 23, 1 (1983), pp. 1–9.   **816**

"Prunty, Merle Charles, Educator," *Who Was Who in America*, vol. 8 (Chicago: Marquis Co., 1983), p. 328.   **817**

Milton Birchard Newton, Jr.
(1936–1989)

Proponent of cultural "preadaptation" in the folk migrations of the American South

Richardson, Miles, and Earnest S. Easterly III, "Eulogy for a Pioneer American: Milton B. Newton, Jr.," *Material Culture*, vol. 21, 3 (1989), pp. 45–50.   **818**

John Brian Harley
(1932–1991)

Student of early American cartography, particularly of the Revolutionary period

Scott, Valerie G., "Profile: Brian Harley," *Map Collector*, no. 38 (1987), pp. 40–41.   **819**

Woodward, David, "Obituary: J. B. Harley (1932–1991)" *Imago Mundi*, vol. 44 (1992), pp. 120–125.   **820**

Lawton, Richard, "Obituary: J. B. Harley, 1932–1991," *Journal of Historical Geography*, vol. 18, 2 (1992), pp. 210–212.   **821**

HISTORICAL ATLASES AND
—————— MAP SERIES ——————

Includes secondary, interpretive atlases, and collections of facsimile map reproductions.

Works in "historical geography" are those that treat a broad range of interpretive themes considered central to inquiry in cultural and historical geography. Works in "geographical history" are those that cover cartographic themes of prime interest to historians, traditionally those of territorial evolution, politics, wars, and very general socioeconomic patterns.*

NORTH AMERICA

*Historical geography

Rooney, John F., Wilbur Zelinsky, and Dean Louder, eds., *This Remarkable Continent: An Atlas of United States and Canadian Society and Culture* (College Station: Texas A & M University Press, 1982), 361 pp.   **822**

*Geographical history

Bennet, Roelof G., and J. Van Wijk Roelandszoon, *Verhandeling over de Nederlandsche ontdekkingen in Amerika* . . . (Utrecht: J. Altheer, 1827), 8 maps.   **823**

Bradford, Thomas G., *An Illustrated Atlas, Geographical, Statistical, and Historical, of the United States and the Adjacent Countries* (Boston: Weeks, Jordan & Co., 1838), 170 pp.   **824**

Lange, Henry, ed., *Kartenwerk zu Dr. Karl Andree's Nordamerika nach den neuesten Materialien, mit Besonderer Rücksicht auf physikalische Verhältnisse und genauer Angabe der County-Einteilung, der Eisenbahnen, Canäle, Poststraßen und Dampfschiffahrt* (Braunschweig: Georg Westermann, 1854), 18 maps, 28 pp.   **825**

Pinart, Alphonse L., *Recueil des cartes, plans, et vues relatifs aux États-Unis et au Canada, New York, Boston, Montréal, Québec, Louisbourg, 1651–1731. Reproduits d'après les originaux manuscrits et inedits, etc., exposés a la Bibliotèque Nationale a l'occasion du quatrième centenaire de la découverte de l'Amérique* (Paris: E. Dufosse, 1893), 16 pp.   **826**

Bartholomew, John G., *A Literary and Historical Atlas of America* (New York: E. P. Dutton, 1911, 1918, 1930), 91 maps, 231 pp.   **827**

Crockett, Thomas, and Bertie C. Wallis, *North America during the Eighteenth Century: A Geographical History* (Cambridge: Cambridge University Press, 1915), 116 pp.   **828**

Clurg, George, *Open-Air and Wide Horizons: Graphic American History, Historical Atlas and Touring Guide. A History of the United States and Adjoining Regions, Emphasizing the Locale and Background of Events in Their Outdoor Setting* (Watsonville, Ca.: Goodrich Stationery Co., 1939), 163 pp.   **829**

Gray, Henry, *Historical Atlas of Colonial North America from Prehistoric Times to 1823: Exploration, Conquest, and Settlement* (Washington, D.C.: Educational Research Bureau, 1942), 9 maps, 16 pp.   **830**

Johnson, Adrian, *America Explored: A Cartographic History of the Exploration of North America* (New York: Viking Press, 1974), 264 pp.   **831**

Waldman, Carl, *Atlas of the North American Indian* (New York: Facts on File, 1985), 276 pp.   **832**

Portinaro, Pierluigi, and Franco Knirsch, *The Cartography of North America, 1500–1800* (New York: Facts on File, 1987), 319 pp.   **833**

Buisseret, David, ed., *From Sea Charts to Satellite Images: Interpreting North American History through Maps* (Chicago: University of Chicago Press, 1990), 324 pp.   **834**

Goss, John, *The Mapping of North America: Three Centuries of Map-Making, 1500–1860* (Secaucus, N.J.: Wellfleet Press, 1990), 85 map facsimiles.   **835**

CANADA

Historical geography

Harris, R. Cole, ed., *Historical Atlas of Canada,* vol. 1, *Canada before 1800* (Toronto: University of Toronto Press, 1987), 69 plates, 198 pp.   **836**

Kerr, Donald G., and Deryck W. Holdsworth, eds., *Historical Atlas of Canada,* vol. 3, *Addressing the Twentieth Century, 1891-1961* (Toronto: University of Toronto Press, 1990), 212 pp.   **837**

Gentilcore, R. Louis, ed., *Historical Atlas of Cana-da*, vol. 2, *The Nineteenth Century* (Toronto: University of Toronto Press, forthcoming).   838

Geographical history

Burpee, Laurence J., ed., *An Historical Atlas of Canada* (Toronto: Thomas Nelson & Sons, 1927), 48 pp. [32 pp. of maps]   839

Morrison, Olin D., *Canada and the Provinces: New Historical Atlas, Economic, Social, Political*, vol. 2, *Maps* (Athens, Ohio: O. D. Morrison, 1958).   840

Kerr, Donald Gordon Grady, *Historical Atlas of Canada* (Don Mills, Ontario: T. Nelson & Sons, 1960, 1966, 1975), 100 pp.   841

Chalmers, John W., William J. Eccles, and Harold Fullard, *Philips' Historical Atlas of Canada* (London: George Philip and Son, 1966), 48 pp.   842

Canadian Department of Energy, Mines, and Re-sources, *The National Atlas of Canada*, 14th ed. (Ottawa: Macmillan Co. of Canada, 1974). [His-torical map section, pp. 71–94]   843

Verner, Coolie, and Basil Stuart-Stubbs, *The Northpart of America: An Atlas of Facsimile Maps* (Toronto: Academic Press, 1979), 292 pp.   844

Atlas of Canada (Montreal: Reader's Digest Asso-ciation [Canada], 1980), 220 pp.   845

Dahl, Edward H., and Conrad E. Heidenreich, "A Critical Analysis of 'The Northpart of America': A Facsimile Atlas of Early Canadian Maps," *Cartographica*, vol. 17, 1 (1980), pp. 1–23.   846

Armstrong, Joe C. W., *From Sea unto Sea: Art and Discovery Maps of Canada* (Scarborough, Ont.: Fleet, 1982), 76 pp.   847

Saint-Yves, Maurice, *Atlas de géographie histo-rique du Canada* (Boucherville: Éditions Fran-çaises, 1982), 96 pp.   848

Dahl, Edward H., *Historical Maps of Canada*, Fo-lios 1–3 (Ottawa: Association of Canadian Map Librarians, 1986), 125 pp.   849

Topical works

Oppen, William A., *The Riel Rebellions: A Carto-graphic History* (Toronto: University of Toronto Press, Cartographica Monograph nos. 21–22, 1978), 109 pp.   850

Luciuk, Lubomyr Y., and Bohdan S. Kordan, *Creat-ing a Landscape: A Geography of Ukrainians in Canada* (Toronto: University of Toronto Press, 1989), 66 pp.   851

Alberta

University of Alberta Department of Geography, "History," *Atlas of Alberta* (Edmonton: Univer-sity of Alberta Press, 1969), pp. 43–49.   852

"Alberta Report," *The Atlas of Alberta* (Edmonton: Interwest Publications, 1984), pp. 8–23. [Histori-cal map section]   853

The Atlantic Provinces

Ganong, William F., *Crucial Maps in the Early Cartography and Place-Nomenclature of the Atlantic Coast of Canada* (Toronto: University of Toronto Press, 1964), 511 pp.   854

Arseneault, Samuel P., et al., *Atlas de l'Acadie: Petit atlas des francophones des maritimes* (Moncton: Éditions d'Acadie, 1978), 31 pp.   855

British Columbia

Farley, Albert L., *Atlas of British Columbia: People, Environment, and Resource Use* (Vancouver: University of British Columbia Press, 1979), 135 pp.   856

Eastern Canada

Zaborski, Bogdan, *Atlas des paysages et de l'habi-tat du Canada de l'est* (Montreal: Sir George Williams University, 1972), 200 pp.   857

Manitoba

Weir, Thomas R., *Economic Atlas of Manitoba* (Winnipeg: University of Manitoba Press, 1960). [Includes historical section]   858

Ruggles, Richard I., and John H. Warkentin, *His-torical Atlas of Manitoba: A Selection of Fac-simile Maps, Plans, and Sketches from 1612 to 1969* (Winnipeg: Historical and Scientific Soci-ety of Manitoba, 1970), 585 pp. [Reproductions]   859

Artibise, Alan F. J., and Edward H. Dahl, "Maps in the Study of Winnipeg's Urban Development," in A. R. McCormack and Ian Macpherson, eds., *Cities in the West: Papers of the Western Canada Urban History Conference* (Ottawa: National Museum of Man, 1975), pp. 139–157.   860

Artibise, Alan F. J., and Edward H. Dahl, *Winnipeg in Maps, 1816–1972* (Ottawa: Public Archives of Canada, National Map Collection, 1975), 80 pp.   861

Weir, Thomas R., *Atlas of Winnipeg* (Toronto: University of Toronto Press, 1978), 67 leaves.   862

Nova Scotia

Dawson, Joan, *The Mapmaker's Eye: Nova Scotia through Early Maps* (Halifax: Nimbus Publishing for Nova Scotia Museum, 1988), 156 pp.   863

Ontario

Nagy, Thomas L., *Ottawa in Maps: A Brief Cartographic History of Ottawa, 1825–1973* (Ottawa: Public Archives of Canada, National Map Collection, 1974), 87 pp.   864

Head, C. Grant, and R. Louis Gentilcore, *Ontario's History in Maps* (Toronto: University of Toronto Press, 1984), 284 pp. [Facsimile atlas]   865

Quebec

Bourdon, Jean, *Plans of the First French Settlements on the St. Lawrence, 1635–1642* (Montreal: McGill University Library, 1958), 9 plates. [Reproductions]   866

Trudel, Marcel, *Atlas historique du Canada français, des origines à 1867* (Quebec: Presses de l'Université Laval, 1961), 93 pp. [Reproductions]   867

Letarle, Jacques, *Atlas d'histoire économique et sociale du Québec, 1851–1901* (Montreal: Fides, 1971), 44 foldout maps, 13 pp.   868

Trudel, Marcel, *An Atlas of New France* (Quebec: Presses de l'Université Laval, 1973), 219 pp.   869

Gathier, Majella, and Louis Marie Bouchard, *Atlas régional du Saguenay-Lac-Saint-Jean: Àla découverte de la Sagamie* (Chicoutimi: Gaetan Morin et Associés, pour Laboratoires de géographie de l'Université du Québec à Chicoutimi avec la collaboration de l'Office de planification et de développement du Québec, 1981), 228 pp.   870

Courville, Serge, et al., *Paroisses et municipalités de la région de Montréal au XIXe siècle (1825–1861): Répertoire documentaire et cartographique* (Quebec: Presses de l'Université Laval, 1988), 350 pp.   871

Saskatchewan

Richards, J. Howard B., ed., "Historical Geography," *Atlas of Saskatchewan* (Saskatoon: University of Saskatchewan, 1969), pp. 6–26.   872

UNITED STATES

Historical geography

Paullin, Charles O., and John K. Wright, *Atlas of the Historical Geography of the United States* (New York: Carnegie Institute of Washington and the American Geographical Society, 1932), 688 maps, 162 pp.   873

Lord, Clifford L., and Elizabeth H. Lord, *Historical Atlas of the United States* (New York: H. Holt & Co., 1944), 312 maps, 253 pp. Reprinted 1953, 238 pp. Revised 1972, 238 pp.   874

Meinig, Donald W., et al., eds., *The Making of America: A Series of Seventeen Maps* (Washington, D.C.: National Geographic Society, Cartography Division, 1982–1988). Issued as folded maps with the *National Geographic Magazine: The Southwest* (Nov. 1982); *Atlantic Gateways* (Mar. 1983); *Deep South* (Aug. 1983); *Hawaii* (Nov. 1983); *Alaska* (Jan. 1984); *Far West* (Apr. 1984); *Central Rockies* (Aug. 1984); *Northern Approaches* (Feb. 1985); *Central Plains* (Sept. 1985); *Ohio Valley* (Dec. 1985); *Texas* (Mar. 1986); *Pacific Northwest* (Aug. 1986); *Northern Plains* (Dec. 1986); *New England* (Feb. 1987); *Great Lakes* (July 1987); *Tidewater* (June 1988).   875

National Geographic Society, *Historical Atlas of the United States* (Washington, D.C.: National Geographic Society, 1988), 289 pp.   876

Geographical history

Willard, Emma H., *A Series of Maps to Willard's History of the United States, or Republic of America. Designed for Schools and Private Libraries* (New York: White, Gallaher and White, 1828; various later editions to 1833), 12 maps.   877

Holgate, Jerome B., *Atlas of American History on a Novel Plan, Comprising a Complete Synopsis of Events from the Discovery of the American Continent by Columbus in 1492* (Cambridge, Mass.: n.p., 1842), 6 maps.   878

Blanchard, Rufus, *Historical Map of the United States, Showing Early Spanish, French, and English Discoveries and Explorations, Also Forts, Towns, and Battlefields of Historic Interest* (Chicago: Rufus Blanchard, 1876), 1 folded map.   879

Smith, Lucien H., *Historical and Chronological Atlas of the United States* (Washington, D.C.: National Republican Printing and Publishing Co., 1881), 8 maps, 19 pp.   880

Hardesty, Hiram H., *Hardesty's Historical and Geographical Encyclopedia* (Chicago and Toledo: H. H. Hardesty & Co., 1883), 56 maps.   881

MacCoun, Townsend, *An Historical Geography of the United States* (New York: Townsend MacCoun, 1889; repr. 1890, 1892, 1901; Silver, Burdett & Co., 1911), 44 maps, 46 pp.   882

Hart, Albert B., *Epoch Maps Illustrating American History* (New York: Longmans, Green & Co., 1891, 1893, 1899, 1904, 1910), 14 maps.   883

Blanchard, Rufus, *Historical Atlas of the United States* (Chicago: T. Kane, 1893), 20 maps.   884

Van Campen, Savillion, *Our Country, from 1800 to 1900: An Atlas Showing the Growth of the United States of America during the Nineteenth Century* (Washington, D.C.: Washington Times, 1900), 12 maps.   885

Austin, Oscar P., *Territorial Expansion of the United States. The Additions Made to the Territory of the Thirteen Colonies and Its Transformation into Territories and States* (Washington, D.C.: United States Bureau of Statistics, 1901), 35 maps.   886

Cram, George F., *Handy Historical, Statistical and Chronological Atlas of the United States, AD 901–1901* (Chicago: G. F. Cram, 1901).   887

Hodder, Frank H., *Outline Maps for an Historical Atlas of the United States, Illustrating Territory Growth and Development* (Boston: Ginn & Co., 1901; repr. 1902, 1903, 1904; rev. eds., 1913, 1921), 21–24 maps.   888

Foster, Eli G., *The Illustrative Historical Maps: Territorial, Administrative, Political, Discoveries, Military Campaigns* (Topeka, Kans.: Historical Publishing Co., 1904, 1905; rev. ed., Chicago: Rand McNally & Co., 1910), 32 maps, 35 pp.   889

Bond, Frank, and I. P. Berthrong, *United States, Showing Routes of Principal Explorers and Early Roads and Highways* (Washington, D.C.: United States General Land Office, 1908), 1 folded map.   890

Croscup, George E., *History Made Visible: United States History with Synchronic Charts, Maps, and Statistical Diagrams* (New York: Windsor Publishing Co., 1910, 1911, 1912, 1915), 127 pp.   891

Baker, Marion M., *Baker's Historical Geography Maps of the United States* (Philadelphia: McConnell School Supply Co., 1914), 44 maps.   892

Bone, Hugh A., *Geographic Factors in American History: A Laboratory Manual to Accompany the Study of United States History* (Sioux City, Iowa: Print Shop Ye Highe Schools, 1917), 83 pp.   893

Hart, Albert B., and Herbert E. Bolton, *American History Atlas: Reductions from Large Wall Maps* (Chicago: Denoyer-Geppert Co., 1918, 1924; rev. eds., 1930, 1940, 1942, 1945), 24–62 maps.   894

Fox, Dixon R., *Harper's Atlas of American History, Selected from "The American Nation" Series, with Map Studies* (New York: Harper & Brothers, 1920), 115 maps.   895

Newton, Lewis S., and Peyten Irving, *Victory Historical Maps and Outline Book: American History* (Dallas: Southern Publishing Company, 1921, 1922), 27 maps, 86 pp.   896

Atlas no. 1: United States History (Philadelphia: McKinley Publishing Co., 1922, 1933), 25 maps.   897

Rand-McNally Historical Development Atlas of the U.S.A., 1650–1926 (Chicago and New York: Rand McNally & Co., 1926), 19 maps, 32 pp.   898

Jones, Clarence F., *Manual to Accompany American History and Its Geographic Conditions* (New York: Houghton Mifflin Co., 1933), 46 pp. of maps.   899

Adams, James Truslow, *Atlas of American History* (New York: C. Scribner's Sons, 1943), 147 maps, 360 pp.   900

Morrison, Olin D., and Erwin J. Raisz, *The Comprehensive Series: Social Studies Maps of the United States* (Goshen, Ind.: Modern School Supply, 1947, 1948; rev. ed., ed. Franklin D. Scott and Erwin J. Raisz, 1952), 36 maps, 38 pp.   901

Hammond, C. S., & Co., *Hammond's American History Atlas* (New York: C. S. Hammond & Co., 1948), 34 maps, 36 pp.   902

Wesley, Edgar B., *Denoyer-Geppert Atlas of American History* (Chicago: Denoyer-Geppert, 1957, 1965), 32 pp.   903

Wesley, Edgar B., *Our United States: Its History in Maps* (Chicago: Denoyer-Geppert, 1957, 1961, 1965), 96 pp.   904

Sale, Randall D., and Edwin D. Karn, *American Expansion: A Book of Maps* (Lincoln: University of Nebraska Press, 1962; repr. 1979), 27 pp.   905

Fox, Edward W., *Atlas of American History* (New York: Oxford University Press, 1964), 48 pp.   906

Kagon, Hilde H., ed., *The American Heritage Pictorial Atlas of United States History* (New York: American Heritage Co., 1966), 424 pp.   907

Cole, Donald B., *Atlas of American History* (Boston: Ginn & Co., 1967), 151 pp.   908

Gilbert, Martin J., *American History Atlas* (New York: Macmillan, 1969), 119 pp.   909

Miller, Theodore R., *Graphic History of the Americas* (New York: John Wiley, 1969), 61 pp.   910

U.S. Geological Survey, *The National Atlas of the United States of America*, ed. Arch Gerlach (Washington, D.C.: Government Printing Office, 1970), 417 pp.   911

United States History Atlas (Maplewood, N.J.: Hammond, 1971), 192 pp.   912

These United States: Atlas of American History (Chicago: Rand McNally, 1974), 64 pp.   913

Kirkham, E. Kay, A Genealogical and Historical Atlas of the United States of America (Logan, Utah: Everton Publishers, 1976), 328 pp.   914

Klemp, Egon, America in Maps Dating from 1500 to 1856 (New York: Holmes and Meier, 1976), 239 pp.   915

United States History Atlas (Maplewood, N.J.: Hammond, 1977), 64 pp.   916

Jackson, Kenneth T., and James Truslow Adams, eds., Atlas of American History, rev. ed. (New York: Charles Scribner's Sons, 1978), 294 pp.   917

Tooley, Ronald V., The Mapping of America (New York: Holland Press, 1980), 519 pp.   918

Ferrell, Robert H., and Richard Natkiel, Atlas of American History (New York: Facts on File, 1987), 192 pp.   919

Ancient Times, European Contact, and Native Peoples

Royce, Charles, Indian Land Cessions in the United States (Washington, D.C.: Government Printing Office, 1899), 67 plates.   920

Hilliard, Sam B., "Map of Indian Land Cessions," Annals of the Association of American Geographers, map suppl. no. 15, vol. 62, 2 (1972).   921

Ferguson, Thomas J., and E. Richard Hart, A Zuni Atlas (Norman: University of Oklahoma Press, 1985), 164 pp.   922

Coe, Michael, Dean Snow, and Elizabeth Benson, Atlas of Ancient America (New York: Facts on File Publications, 1986), 240 pp.   923

Tanner, Helen H., ed., Atlas of Great Lakes Indian History (Norman: University of Oklahoma Press, 1987), 230 pp.   924

Harley, J. Brian, Maps and the Columbian Encounter: An Interpretive Guide to the Travelling Exhibition (Milwaukee: Golda Meir Library, 1990), 160 pp.   925

Prucha, Francis P., Atlas of American Indian Affairs (Lincoln: University of Nebraska Press, 1990), 191 pp.   926

Colonial Period

Fite, Emerson D., and Archibald Freeman, A Book of Old Maps, Delineating American History from the Earliest Days Down to the Close of the Revolutionary War (Cambridge: Harvard University Press, 1926), 299 pp.   927

Friis, Herman R., A Series of Population Maps of the Colonies and the United States, 1623–1790

(New York: American Geographical Series; rev. ed., 1968), 10 maps, 52 pp.   928

Cummings, William P., ed., British Maps of Colonial America (Chicago: University of Chicago Press, 1974), 114 pp.   929

Revolutionary Period

Marshall, John, Life of George Washington: Maps and Subscribers' Names (Philadelphia: C. P. Wayne, 1807), 10 maps, 22 pp.   930

Wilkinson, James, Diagrams and Plans, Illustrative of the Principal Battles and Military Affairs, Treated of in Memoires of My Own Times (Philadelphia: A. Small, 1816), 19 maps.   931

LeBoucher, Odet Julien [Atlas pour servir à l'histoire de la guerre de l'independence des États-Unis] (Paris: Anselin, 1830), 7 maps.   932

Marshall, John, Atlas to Marshall's Life of Washington (Philadelphia: J. Crissy, 1832, 1833, 1850), 10 folded maps.   933

Guizot, François P. G., Vie, correspondence, et écrits de Washington, publiés d'après l'édition américaine et précédés d'une introduction sur l'influence et le caractère de Washington dans la Révolution des États-Unis d'Amérique . . . Atlas (Paris: C. Gosselin, 1840), 165 maps.   934

Faden, William, Atlas of Battles of the American Revolution, Together with Maps Showing the Routes of the British and American Armies, Plans of Cities, Surveys of Harbors, etc., Taken during That Eventful Period by Officers Attached to the Royal Army (New York: Bartlett and Welford, 1845), 36 maps, 56 pp.   935

Carrington, Henry B., Battle Maps and Charts of the American Revolution, with Explanatory Notes and School History References (New York and Chicago: A. S. Barnes & Co., 1881), 33 maps, 88 pp.   936

Martin, Lawrence, ed., The George Washington Atlas: A Collection of Eighty-Five Maps, Including Twenty-Eight Made by George Washington, Seven Used and Annotated by Him, Eight Made at His Discretion, or For His Use, or Otherwise Associated with Him, and Forty-Two New Maps Concerning His Activities in Peace and War and His Place in History (Washington, D.C.: U.S. George Washington Bicentennial Commission, 1932) 50 plates, 85 maps.   937

Guthorn, Peter J., American Maps and Map Makers of the Revolution (Monmouth Beach, N.J.: Philip Freneau Press, 1966), 48 pp.   938

Greenwood, W. Bart, comp., The American Revolution, 1775–1783: An Atlas of Eighteenth Century Maps and Charts, introduction by Louis DeVorsey, Jr. (Washington, D.C.: U.S. Department of the Navy, Naval History Division, 1972), 20 maps, 85 pp.   **939**

Nebenzahl, Kenneth, *Atlas of the American Revolution* (Chicago: Rand McNally & Co., 1974), 50 maps, 216 pp.   **940**

Cappon, Lester J., Barbara Bartz Petchenik, and John H. Long, eds., *Atlas of Early American History: The Revolutionary Era, 1760–1790* (Princeton: Princeton University Press, for the Newberry Library and the Institute of Early American History and Culture, 1976), 157 pp. **941**

Marshall, Douglas W., and Howard M. Peckham, *Campaigns of the American Revolution: An Atlas of Manuscript Maps* (Ann Arbor: University of Michigan Press, and Maplewood, N.J.: Hammond, 1976), 138 pp.   **942**

Symonds, Craig, *A Battlefield Atlas of the American Revolution* (Annapolis, Md.: Nautical and Aviation Publication Co. of America, 1986), 110 pp.   **943**

Antebellum Period

Latour, Arsene L., *Atlas to the Historical Memoir of the War in West Florida and Louisiana* (Philadelphia: J. Conrad & Co., 1816), 8 maps. **944**

Lewis, Meriwether, and William Clark, *Atlas Accompanying the Original Journals of the Lewis and Clark Expedition, 1804–1806, Being Facsimile Reproductions of Maps Chiefly by William Clark, Illustrating the Route of the Expedition . . .* ed. Reuben Gold Thwaites (New York: Dodd, Mead & Co., 1905), 56 maps, 62 pp.   **945**

Martin, Lawrence, *Constitution Sesquicentennial Atlas* (Washington: U.S. Constitution Sesquicentennial Commission, 1944), 19 maps.   **946**

Colles, Christopher, *A Survey of the Roads of the United States, 1789,* ed. Walter W. Ristow (Cambridge: Harvard University Press, 1961), 227 pp. **947**

Guthorn, Peter J., *United States Coastal Charts, 1783–1861* (Exton, Pa.: Schiffer Publishing Co., 1984), 224 pp. facsimile maps.   **948**

Civil War

Bechler, Gustavus R., *Atlas Showing Battles, Engagements, and Important Localities Connected with the Campaigns in Virginia, Completing the Campaign Map Designed, Engraved, and Published by Gustavus Bechler* (Philadelphia, 1864), 16 maps.   **949**

Paris, Louis Philippe A. d'Orléans, Comte de, *[Histoire de la guerre civile en Amérique] Atlas* (Paris: M. Lévy, 1874–1890), 30 maps.   **950**

Van Horne, Thomas B., *History of the Army of the Cumberland: Its Organization, Campaigns, and Battles, Written at the Request of Major-General George H. Thomas . . . Illustrated with Campaign and Battle Maps, compiled by Edward Ruger . . . Atlas* (Cincinnati: R. Clarke & Co., 1875), 22 maps.   **951**

Whitney, William H., *Union and Confederate Campaigns in the Lower Shenandoah Valley Illustrated: Twenty Years After—at the First Reunion of Sheridan's Veterans on the Fields and in the Camps of the Valley* (Boston: W. H. Whitney, 1883), 25 maps, 66 pp.   **952**

U.S. War Department, *Atlas to Accompany the Official Records of the Union and Confederate Armies,* 2 vols. (Washington, D.C.: U.S. Government Printing Office, 1891–1895), 178 plates. Reprinted New York: Arno Press, Crown Publishers, 1978.   **953**

Formby, John, *The American Civil War: A Concise History of the Causes, Progress, and Results* (New York: Charles Scribner's Sons, 1910), 68 maps.   **954**

Fiebeger, Gustav J., *Campaigns of the American Civil War* (West Point, N.Y.: U.S. Military Academy Printing Office, 1914), 46 pp. of maps.   **955**

Other American Wars

Steele, Matthew F., *American Campaigns,* vol. 2, *Maps* (Washington: B. S. Adams, 1909), 311 maps.   **956**

Esposito, Vincent J., ed., *The West Point Atlas of American Wars,* vol. 1, *1689–1900;* vol. 2, *1900–1953* (New York: Frederick A. Praeger, 1959), 774 pp.   **957**

The War of 1812 in the Northwest in Maps and Pictures (Columbus, Ohio: Anthony-Wayne Parkway Board, 1961), 30 pp., incl. 14 maps. **958**

Natkiel, Richard, John G. Kirk, and John Westwood, *Atlas of American Wars* (Arch Cape Press, 1986), 160 pp.   **959**

Natkiel, Richard, *Atlas of American Military History* (New York: Barnes & Noble, 1990), 160 pp. **960**

Political Geography

Territorial boundaries

U.S. Treasury Department, Bureau of Statistics, *Territorial Development of the United States, Compiled 1901* (Washington, D.C.: Government Printing Office 1901), 35 maps.   **961**

Van Zandt, Franklin K., *Boundaries of the United States and the Several States* (Washington,

D.C.: U.S. Geological Survey Professional Paper no. 909, 1976), 191 pp. 962

Parson, Stanley B., et al., *United States Congressional Districts, 1788–1841* (Westport, Conn.: Greenwood Press, 1978), 416 pp. 963

Earle, Carville V., ed., *Historical U.S. County Outline Maps, 1840–1980* (Baltimore: University of Maryland Baltimore County, Department of Geography, 1984). 964

Long, John H., *Historical Atlas and Chronology of County Boundaries, 1788–1980*, 5 vols. (Boston: G. K. Hall, 1984). 965

Historical geography of voting

Lord, Clifford L., ed., *The Atlas of Congressional Roll Calls for the Continental Congresses, 1777–1781* (Cooperstown: New York State Historical Association, 1943), 116 pp. 966

Lord, Clifford L., ed., *The Atlas of Congressional Roll Calls for the Continental Congresses, 1777–1789* (Cooperstown: New York State Historical Association, 1943), 267 pp. 967

Martis, Kenneth C., *The Historical Atlas of United States Congressional Districts, 1789–1983* (New York: Macmillan, 1982), 302 pp. 968

Martis, Kenneth C., *The Historical Atlas of Political Parties in the United States Congress, 1789–1989* (New York: Macmillan, 1989), 518 pp. 969

Social and Economic Geography

Gaustad, Edwin S., *Historical Atlas of Religion in America*, 2 vols. (New York: Harper & Row, 1962, 1976), 189 pp. 970

Elliott, Harold M., "Historical Atlas of the Domestic Trunk Airlines of the United States," Master's thesis, California State University–San Francisco, 1970. 971

Kloss, Heinz, *Atlas of Nineteenth and Early Twentieth Century German-American Settlements* (Marburg: N. G. Elwert Verlag, 1974), 108 plates. 972

Bennett, Sari, and Carville, V. Earle, *The Geography of American Labor and Industrialization, 1865–1908: An Atlas* (Catonsville, Md.: University of Maryland–Baltimore County, Department of Geography, GALI Working Paper no. 2, 1980), 82 pp. 973

Allen, James P., and Eugene J. Turner, *We the People: An Atlas of America's Ethnic Diversity* (New York: Macmillan, 1987), 315 pp. 974

Asante, Molefi, and Mark T. Mattson, *Historical and Cultural Atlas of African Americans* (New York: Macmillan, 1990), 192 pp. 975

The East

Kurath, Hans, *Linguistic Atlas of New England* (Providence: Brown University, 1941), 240 pp. 976

Kurath, Hans, *Handbook of the Linguistic Geography of New England* (Providence: Brown University Press, 1939), 240 pp. 977

Kurath, Hans, *A Word-Geography of the Eastern United States* (Ann Arbor: University of Michigan Press, 1949), 163 maps, 88 pp. 978

Atwood, Elmer B., *A Survey of Verb Forms in the Eastern United States* (Ann Arbor: University of Michigan Press, 1953), 31 maps, 53 pp. 979

Kurath, Hans, and Raven I. McDavid, *The Pronunciation of English in the Atlantic States* (Ann Arbor: University of Michigan Press, 1961), 180 plates, 182 pp. 980

DeVorsey, Louis, Jr., ed., *The Atlantic Pilot by William de Brahm* (Gainesville: University of Florida Press, 1974; repr. from 1772 and annotated), 25 + 6 pp. 981

Baer, Christopher T., *Canals and Railroads of the Mid-Atlantic States, 1800–1860* (Wilmington, Del.: Eleutherian Mills–Hagley Foundation, Regional Economic History Center, 1981), 5 maps, 80 pp. 982

The South

Cumming, William P., *The Southeast in Early Maps* (Chapel Hill: University of North Carolina Press, 1962), 284 pp. 983

Birdsall, Stephen S., and John W. Florin, *A Series of County Outline Maps of the Southeastern United States for the Period 1790–1860* (Chapel Hill: University of North Carolina Department of Geography, Map Study no. 2, 1973), 8 maps and 27 pp. 984

Hilliard, Sam B., *Atlas of Antebellum Southern Agriculture* (Baton Rouge: Louisiana State University Press, 1984), 77 pp. 985

Clay, James, et al., *Land of the South* (Birmingham, Ala.: Oxmoor House, 1989), 214 pp. 986

The Middle West

Brown, Lloyd A., *Early Maps of the Ohio Valley: A Selection of Maps, Plans, and Views Made by Indians and Colonials from 1673–1783* (Pittsburgh: University of Pittsburgh Press, 1959), 132 pp. 987

Allen, Harold B., *The Linguistic Atlas of the Upper Midwest*, 3 vols. (Minneapolis: University of Minnesota Press, 1973–1976). 988

Karrow, Robert W., ed., *Checklist of Maps of the Middle West Printed before 1900*, 11 vols. (Boston: G. K. Hall, 1981).   989

Wood, W. Raymond, *An Atlas of Early Maps of the American Midwest* (Springfield: Illinois State Museum, Scientific Papers, vol. 18, Facsimile Reproductions, with commentary, 1983), 52 plates, 14 pp.   990

The West

Wagner, Henry R., *The Cartography of the Northwest Coast of America to the Year 1800*, 2 vols. (Berkeley: University of California Press, 1937), 543 pp.   991

Highsmith, Richard M., Jr., ed., *Atlas of the Pacific Northwest: Resources and Development*, 3d ed. (Corvallis: Oregon State University Press, 1953), 72 maps, 118 pp. Frequent later editions.   992

Morgan, Dale L., and Carl S. Wheat, *Jedediah Smith and His Maps of the American West* (San Francisco: California Historical Society, 1954), 86 pp.   993

Wheat, Carl I., *Mapping the Transmississippi West, 1540–1861*, 5 vols. (San Francisco: Institute of Historical Cartography, 1957–1963), 1,641 pp.   994

Beck, Warren A., and Ynez D. Haase, *Historical Atlas of the American West* (Norman: University of Oklahoma Press, 1974; 2d ed., 1989), 240 pp.   995

Franzwa, Gregory M., *Maps of the Oregon Trail* (Gerald, Mo.: Patrice Press, 1982), 292 pp.   996

Patterson, Richard, *Historical Atlas of the Outlaw West* (Boulder: Johnson Books, 1984), 250 pp.   997

Franzwa, Gregory M., *Maps of the Santa Fe Trail* (St. Louis, Patrice Press, 1989), 196 pp.   998

Alabama

Dodd, Donald B., *Historical Atlas of Alabama* (University, Ala.: University of Alabama Press, 1974), 160 pp.   999

Alaska

Marshall, Philip S., comp., *Alaska Exploration Map Series* (Fairbanks: University of Alaska Press, for the University of Alaska Arctic Environmental Information and Data Center, 1987), 4 maps: 1. *Europe Discovers Alaska, 1728–1794*; 2. *Russian Alaska, 1794–1867*; 3. *America Explores Alaska, 1867–1897*; 4. *Last Frontiers in Alaska, 1897–1941*.   1000

Arizona

Baker, Simon, and Thomas J. McCleneghan, *An Arizona Economic and Historic Atlas* (Tucson: University of Arizona, Division of Economic and Business Research, 1966), 40 pp.   1001

Walker, Henry P., and Donald F. Bufkin, *Historical Atlas of Arizona* (Norman: University of Oklahoma Press, 1979), 152 pp. Revised, 1986.   1002

Arkansas

Hanson, Gerald T., and Carl H. Moneyhon, *Historical Atlas of Arkansas* (Norman: University of Oklahoma Press, 1989), 192 pp.   1003

California

Giffen, Guy J., *Historic California in Maps* (La Canada, Calif.: G. J. Giffen, 1938), 9 maps.   1004

Wheat, Carl I., *The Maps of the California Gold Region, 1848–1857* (San Francisco: Grabhorn Press, 1942), 152 pp.   1005

Harlow, Neal, *The Maps of San Francisco Bay from the Spanish Discovery in 1769 to the American Revolution* (San Francisco: Book Club of California, 1950), 140 pp. [Reproductions and commentary]   1006

Durrenberger, Robert W., *Patterns on the Land: Geographical, Historical, and Political Maps of California*, 2d ed. (Northridge: Roberts Publishing Co., 1960; 4th ed., Palo Alto: Mayfield Publishing Co., 1972), 102 pp.   1007

Johnson, Robert N., *California-Nevada Ghost Town Atlas* (Susanville, Calif.: Cy Johnson, 1967), 48 pp.   1008

Becker, Robert H., *Designs on the Land: Diseños of California Ranchos and Their Makers* (San Francisco: Book Club of California, 1969), 161 pp.   1009

Beck, Warren A., and Ynez D. Haase, *Historical Atlas of California* (Norman: University of Oklahoma Press, 1974), 227 pp. Revised 1989, 240 pp.   1010

Preston, Ralph N., *Early California: Northern Edition* (Portland, Oreg.: Binford & Mort Publishers, 1974), 76 pp.   1011

Preston, Ralph N., *Early California: Southern Edition* (Portland, Oreg.: Binford & Mort Publishers, 1974), 76 pp.   1012

Harlow, Neal, *Maps and Surveys of the Pueblo Lands of Los Angeles* (Los Angeles: Dawson's Book Shop, 1976), 169 pp.   1013

Donley, Michael W., et al., *Atlas of California* (Culver City, Calif.: Pacific Book Center, 1979), 191 pp. [Historical sections, pp. 4–28]   1014

Hornbeck, David, Jr., "Diseños of California," *Yearbook of the Association of Pacific Coast Geographers*, map suppl. no. 6 (1980). 1015

Hornbeck, David, Jr., *California Patterns: A Geographical and Historical Study* (Palo Alto: Mayfield Publishing Co., 1983), 117 pp. 1016

Leon-Portilla, Miguel, *Cartografia y cronicas de la antiqua California* (Coyoacán, Mexico: Fundación de investigaciones sociales, 1989), 207 pp. 1017

Colorado

Basic Maps of Colorado and History of Changes in County Boundaries (Denver: Colorado Water Conservation Board, 1939), 16 pp. 1018

Erickson, Kenneth A., and Albert W. Smith, *Atlas of Colorado* (Boulder: Colorado Associated University Press, 1985), 73 pp. [Includes several historical maps] 1019

Connecticut

Sherer, Thomas E., "The Connecticut Atlas: A Graphic Guide to the Land, People, and History of Connecticut," Master's thesis, Central Connecticut State University, 1990. 1020

Florida

Fernauld, Edward A., "History and Culture," in *Atlas of Florida* (Tallahassee: Florida State University Foundation, 1981), 114–151. 1021

Georgia

Bryant, Pat, comp., *Georgia's Counties: Their Changing Boundaries* (Atlanta: State Printing Office, 1977), 19 maps, 162 pp. 1022

Georgia's Maps through the Years ([Atlanta]: Georgia Department of Transportation, 1983), 14 maps, 16 pp. [Early trails, state highway maps, 1920–1983] 1023

Hodler, Thomas W., and Howard A. Schretter, "Settlement and Conflict," in *The Atlas of Georgia* (Athens: University of Georgia, Institute of Community and Area Development, 1986), pp. 63–87. 1024

Hawaii

University of Hawaii Department of Geography, "History" section, *Atlas of Hawaii* (Honolulu: University of Hawaii Press, 1973), pp. 97–106. Revised 1983. 1025

Idaho

Preston, Ralph N., *Early Idaho Atlas* (Portland, Oreg.: Binford and Mort, 1978), 60 pp. 1026

Illinois

Tucker, Sara J., *Indian Villages of the Illinois Country, Part 1: Atlas* (Springfield: Illinois State Museum, Scientific Papers, vol. 2, 1942), 54 plates. [Reproductions] 1027

Illinois Secretary of State, *Counties of Illinois: Their Origin and Evolution* (Springfield: State Printer, 1972), 23 maps, 65 pp. 1028

Long, John H., "Studying George Rogers Clark's Illinois Campaign with Maps," in *The French, The Indians, and George Rogers Clark in the Illinois Country* (Indianapolis: Indiana Historical Society, 1977), pp. 67–91. 1029

Indiana

Illustrated Historical Atlas of the State of Indiana (Chicago: Baskin, Forster & Co., 1876), 149 maps, 462 pp. 1030

Dull, Daniel F., *Lake County, Indiana, in Maps* (Bloomington: Indiana University Department of Geography, Occasional Paper no. 6, 1971), 52 pp. 1031

Bergen, John V., *Atlas of Johnson County, Indiana, 1820 to 1900: Featuring Maps, Pictures, Text, and Statistics from County Atlases (1866, 1881, and 1900), County Histories (1881, 1888, and 1913), and Many Other Sources* (Franklin, Ind.: Johnson County Historical Society, 1984), 400 pp. 1032

Iowa

Andreas, Alfred T., *Illustrated Historical Atlas of the State of Iowa* (Chicago, 1875), 139 maps, 440 pp. 1033

Kansas

Baughman, Robert W., *Kansas in Maps* (Topeka: Kansas State Historical Society, 1961), 104 pp. [Facsimile reproductions] 1034

Carman, Justice N., *Foreign-Language Units of Kansas*, vol. 1, *Historical Atlas and Statistics* (Lawrence: University of Kansas Press, 1962), 330 pp. 1035

Socolofsky, Homer E., and Huber Self, *Historical Atlas of Kansas* (Norman: University of Oklahoma Press, 1972), 140 pp. Revised 1988, 192 pp. 1036

Kentucky

Karan, Pradyumna P., and Eugene Cotton Mather, eds., *Atlas of Kentucky* (Lexington: University Press of Kentucky, 1977), 182 pp. 1037

Clark, Thomas D., *Historic Maps of Kentucky* (Lexington: University of Kentucky Press, 1979), 90 pp.   1038

Louisiana

Newton, Milton B., *Atlas of Louisiana: A Guide for Students* (Baton Rouge: Louisiana State University, School of Geoscience, 1972), 196 pp.   1039

West, Robert C., *An Atlas of Louisiana Surnames of French and Spanish Origin* (Baton Rouge: Louisiana State University, Geoscience Publications, 1986), 217 pp.   1040

Maine

Morris, Gerald E., and Richard D. Kelly, Jr., eds., *The Maine Bicentennial Atlas: An Historical Survey* (Portland: Maine Historical Society, 1976), 69 plates, 20 pp.   1041

Maryland

Maryland Historical Atlas (Annapolis: State of Maryland Department of Economic and Community Development, 1973), 61 pp.   1042

Papenfuse, Edward C., and Joseph M. Cook, *The Hammond-Hanrood House Atlas of Historical Maps of Maryland, 1608–1908* (Baltimore: Johns Hopkins University Press, 1982), 128 pp.   1043

Massachusetts

Dexter, Lincoln A., *Maps of Early Massachusetts: Pre-History through the Seventeenth Century* (Brookfield, Mass.: Lincoln A. Dexter, 1979), 123 pp. Revised 1984.   1044

Wilkie, Richard W., and Jack Tager, eds., *Historical Atlas of Massachusetts* (Amherst: University of Massachusetts Press, 1991), 160 pp.   1045

Michigan

Hinsdale, Wilbert B., *Archeological Atlas of Michigan* (Ann Arbor: University of Michigan Press, 1931), 38 pp.   1046

Karpinski, Louis C., *Bibliography of the Printed Maps of Michigan, 1804–1880, with a Series of over One Hundred Reproductions of Maps Constituting an Historical Atlas of the Great Lakes and Michigan* (Lansing: Michigan Historical Commission, 1931), 539 pp.   1047

Veatch, Jethro O., *Pre-Settlement Forest in Michigan* (East Lansing: Michigan State University, Department of Resource Development, 1959), 2 sheets.   1048

Welch, Richard W., *County Evolution in Michigan, 1790–1897* (Lansing: Michigan Department of Education, State Library Services Occasional Paper no. 2, 1972), 22 maps, 44 pp.   1049

Sommers, Lawrence A., "History and Culture," in his *Atlas of Michigan* (East Lansing: Michigan State University Press, 1977), pp. 99–134.   1050

Hodler, Thomas W., et al., *Pre-Settlement Vegetation of Kalamazoo County, Michigan* (Kalamazoo: Western Michigan University, 1981), 1 map.   1051

Henry A. Raup, Thomas W. Hodler, and Lawrence G. Brewer, "The Presettlement Vegetation of Southwestern Michigan," *East Lakes Geographer*, map suppl., vol. 22 (1987), pp. 216–217.   1052

Minnesota

Andreas, Alfred T., *An Illustrated Historical Atlas of the State of Minnesota* (Chicago, 1874), 76 maps, 272 pp.   1053

Borchert, John R., *A Reconnaissance Atlas of Minnesota Agriculture* (Minneapolis: University of Minnesota Department of Geography and Minnesota Council for Geographic Education, 1955), 60 maps and 22 pp. Revised 1958, 100 maps and 30 pp.   1054

Borchert, John R., and Donald P. Yeager, *Atlas of Minnesota Resources and Settlement* (St. Paul: Minnesota State Planning Agency, 1969), 262 pp.   1055

Marschner, Francis J., *The Original Vegetation of Minnesota, Compiled from U.S. General Land Office Survey Notes* (St. Paul: U.S. Department of Agriculture, Forest Service, North Central Forest Experiment Station, 1974; original mapping 1930). [Color map, 54" x 48" 1:500,000]   1056

Ostergren, Robert C., "Nineteen Statistical Maps," in June D. Holmquist, ed., *They Chose Minnesota: A Survey of the State's Ethnic Groups* (St. Paul: Minnesota Historical Society Press, 1981).   1057

Dooley, Mary T., Perry S. Wood, and Philip S. Kelley, *Railroad Grants, 1864–1894: Blue Earth County, Minnesota* (Mankato, Minn.: Mankato State University Bureau of Planning and Department of Geography Cartographic Services, 1982). [Color map, 40 x 53 cm, 1:125,000]   1058

Dooley, Mary T., Perry S. Wood, and Philip S. Kelley, *Vegetation, 1854–55: Blue Earth County, Minnesota* (Mankato, Minn.: Mankato State University Bureau of Planning and Department of Geography Cartographic Services, 1982). [Color map, 40.5 x 50 cm. 1:125,000]   1059

Dooley, Mary T., Perry S. Wood, and Philip S. Kelley, *Ethnic Background, 1880: Resident Rural Landowners, Blue Earth County, Minnesota* (Mankato, Minn.: Mankato State University Bureau of Planning and Department of Geography

Cartographic Services, 1984). [Color map, 42.2 x 53.1 cm, 1:119,000]   1060

Dooley, Mary T., Phil Kelley, and John Aongstad, *Original Land Alienation: Land Transfers from the Federal Government to Individuals, States, Towns, and Railroads, Blue Earth County, Minnesota* (Mankato, Minn.: Mankato State University Bureau of Planning and Department of Geography Cartographic Services, 1988). [Color map, 42 x 53.5 cm, 1:121,500]   1061

Mississippi

Cross, Ralph D., Robert Wales, and Charles Taylor, "History," *Atlas of Mississippi* (Jackson: University Press of Mississippi, 1974), pp. 23–60.
1062

Missouri

Rafferty, Milton D., *Historical Atlas of Missouri* (Norman: University of Oklahoma Press, 1982), 256 pp.   1063

Montana

Waldron, Ellis, *Montana Politics since 1864: An Atlas of Elections* (Missoula: Montana State University Press, 1958), 428 pp.   1064

Waldron, Ellis, and Paul B. Wilson, *Atlas of Montana Elections, 1889–1976* (Missoula: University of Montana, Publications in History, 1978), 335 pp.   1065

Nebraska

Searcy, N. D., and A. R. Longwell, "History and Government," in *Nebraska Atlas* (Kearney: Nebraska Atlas Publishing Co., 1964), pp. 16–22.
1066

Nimmo, Sylvia, *Maps Showing County Boundaries, Nebraska, 1854–1925* (Papillion, Neb.: The author, 1978), 34 maps, 38 pp.   1067

Nevada

1980—*see* California

New Jersey

Rose, Theodore F., H. C. Woolman, and T. T. Price, *Historical and Biographical Atlas of the New Jersey Coast* (Philadelphia: Woolman and Rose, 1878), 45 maps, 372 pp.   1068

Snyder, John P., *The Story of New Jersey's Civil Boundaries, 1606–1968* (Trenton: Bureau of Geology and Topography, 1969), 37 maps, 294 pp.
1069

New Jersey Road Maps of the Eighteenth Century (Princeton, N.J.: Princeton University Library, 1970), 48 pp.   1070

New Mexico

Beck, Warren A., and Ynez D. Haase, *Historical Atlas of New Mexico* (Norman: University of Oklahoma Press, 1969), 145 pp.   1071

Williams, Jerry L., "Historical Landscapes," in *New Mexico in Maps* (Albuquerque: University of New Mexico Press, 1981), pp. 74–147. Revised 1986.   1072

New York

White, William P., *Maps Showing Indian Possessions and Settled Areas 1775–1790 and 1820 in New York State* (Utica, N.Y., 1927), 6 maps, 7 pp.
1073

Munger, William P., ed., *Historical Atlas of New York State* (Phoenix, N.Y.: Frank E. Richards, 1941), 194 maps, 195 pp.   1074

Kantrowitz, Nathan, *Negro and Puerto Rican Populations of New York City in the Twentieth Century*, (New York: American Geographical Society, Studies in Urban Geography, no. 1, 1969), 5 plates. [Two-color map folio]   1075

Palazzo, Nicholas A., *Urban Development of the City of New York, 1625–1988* (New York: City of New York Department of City Planning, 1988), 1 map, 1:63,360.   1076

North Carolina

Cumming, William P., *North Carolina in Maps* (Raleigh: North Carolina Department of Cultural Resources, Division of Archives and History, 1966), 15 maps, 36 pp. [Reproductions and commentary]   1077

Lonsdale, Richard E., *Atlas of North Carolina* (Chapel Hill: University of North Carolina Press, 1967) [Historical sections, pp. 33–53.]   1078

Corbitt, David L., *Formation of North Carolina Counties, 1663–1943* (Raleigh: North Carolina State Department of Archives and History, 1969), 12 maps, 323 pp.   1079

North Dakota

Andreas, Alfred T., *Andreas' Historical Atlas of Dakota* (Chicago: A. T. Andreas, 1884), 69 maps, 257 pp.   1080

Sherman, William C., *Prairie Mosaic: An Ethnic Atlas of Rural North Dakota* (Fargo: North Dakota Institute for Regional Studies, 1983), 152 pp.   1081

Ohio

Clagg, Sam, *Ohio Atlas* (Huntington, W.Va.: The author, 1959), 42 pp.   1082

Gordon, Robert B., *Natural Vegetation of Ohio at the Time of the Earliest Land Surveys*, Cartography by Hal Flint (Columbus: Ohio Biological Survey and Ohio State University Natural Resources Institute, 1961; repr. 1966), 1 map.   1083

Smith, Thomas, *The Mapping of Ohio* (Kent, Ohio: Kent State University Press, 1977), 252 pp.   1084

Oklahoma

Rutherford, James C., and John W. Morris, *Oklahoma History and Geography Maps* (Durant, Okla.: J. M. Thompson and W. H. Innerarity, 1950), 10 maps.   1085

Morris, John W., and Edwin C. McReynolds, *Historical Atlas of Oklahoma* (Norman: University of Oklahoma Press, 1965), 166 pp. Revised 1976, 166 pp.; 3d ed., with Charles Goins, 1986, 208 pp.   1086

Oregon

Loy, William G., ed., *Atlas of Oregon* (Eugene: University of Oregon Department of Geography, 1972), 215 pp. [Includes historical maps]   1087

Preston, Ralph N., *Maps of Historical Oregon* (Corvallis, Oreg.: Western Guide Publishers, 1972), 64 pp. [17 reproductions and commentary]   1088

Farmer, Judith A., and Kenneth L. Holmes, *An Historical Atlas of Early Oregon* (Portland: Historical Cartographic Publications, 1973), 63 pp.   1089

Bowen, William A., "Mapping an American Frontier: Oregon in 1850," *Annals of the Association of American Geographers*, map suppl. 18 (Mar. 1975).   1090

1988—*see* Washington

Pennsylvania

Muller, Edward K., ed., *A Concise Historical Atlas of Pennsylvania* (Philadelphia: Temple University Press, 1989), 41 pp. A separate publication of pp. 73–115 of David J. Cuff et al., eds., *The Atlas of Pennsylvania* (Philadelphia: Temple University Press, 1989), 288 pp.   1091

Rhode Island

Cady, John H., *Rhode Island Boundaries, 1636–1936* (Providence: Rhode Island Tercentenary Commission, 1936), 6 maps, 31 pp.   1092

Wright, Marion I., and Robert J. Sullivan, *The Rhode Island Atlas* (Providence: Rhode Island Publications Society, 1982), 239 pp. [Includes historical maps]   1093

South Carolina

Mills, Robert, *Mills' Atlas of South Carolina: An Atlas of the Districts of South Carolina in 1825*. Facsimile reproduction, introd. by Charles E. Lee (Columbia, S.C.: Wilkins & Keels, 1965), 32 pp.   1094

South Dakota

1884—*see* North Dakota

Peterson, E. Frank, *Historical Atlas of South Dakota* (Vermillion, S.D.: E. F. Peterson, 1904), 82 maps, 215 pp.   1095

Texas

Fulmore, Zachary T., *History of the Geography of Texas* (Chicago: Caston Co., 1897), 5 maps on one sheet.   1096

Ransey, George D., *Atlas of Texas History* (Chicago: Union School Furnishing Co., 1914), 24 maps, 33 pp.   1097

Ransey, George D., *Atlas of Texas History for Texas and United States Histories* (Chicago: Union School Furnishing Co., 1917), 30 maps, 39 pp. Revised Houston, 1925.   1098

Hotchkiss, David S., *Spanish Missions of Texas, from 1776, Including the Battle of the Alamo, 1835* (Corpus Christi, Tex.: The author, 1966), 11 maps.   1099

Jordan, Terry G., "Population Origin Groups in Rural Texas," *Annals of the Association of American Geographers*, vol. 60, 3 (1970), pp. 404–405, and map suppl. no. 13.   1100

Gilbert, Glen G., *Linguistic Atlas of Texas German* (Austin: University of Texas Press, 1973), 148 pp.   1101

Pool, William C., *A Historical Atlas of Texas* (Austin: Encino Press, 1975), 190 pp.   1102

Arbingast, Stanley A., et al., "Culture and History," in *Atlas of Texas* (Austin: Bureau of Business and Economic Research, 5th ed., 1976), pp. 29–56.   1103

Martin, James C., and Robert S. Martin, *Maps of Texas and the Southwest, 1513–1900* (Albuquerque: University of New Mexico Press, for Amon Carter Museum, 1984), 173 pp.   1104

Stephens, A. Ray, and William H. Holmes, *Historical Atlas of Texas* (Norman: University of Oklahoma Press, 1989), 160 pp.   1105

Utah

Miller, David E., *Utah History Atlas*, 2d ed. (Salt Lake City: Smith Secretarial Service, 1968), 47 maps, 100 pp.   1106

Grear, Deon C., et al., eds., *Atlas of Utah* (Provo: Brigham Young University Press for Weber State College, 1981), 300 pp. [Historical section] 1107

Vermont

Burgett, H. W. & Co., *Illustrated Topographical and Historical Atlas of the State of Vermont* (New York: H. W. Burgett, 1876), 24 maps, 163 pp. 1108

Virginia

Hale, John S., *Historical Atlas of Colonial Virginia* (Staunton, Va.: Old Dominion Publications, 1978), 100 pp. 1109

Stephenson, Richard W., *The Cartography of Northern Virginia: Facsimile Reproductions of Maps Dating from 1608 to 1915* (Fairfax, Va.: Fairfax County Office of Comprehensive Planning, History and Archeology Section, 1981), 145 pp. 1110

Pontius, Stephen K., ed., *An Atlas of Virginia: Seventeenth, Eighteenth, and Early Nineteenth Centuries* (Dubuque: Kendall/Hunt Publishing Co., for the Virginia Geographic Alliance, 1989), 33 pp. 1111

Washington

Abbott, Newton C., and Fred E. Carver, *The Evolution of Washington Counties*, comp. J. W. Helm (Yakima, Wash.: Yakima Valley Genealogical Society and Klickitat County Historical Society, 1978), 169 pp. 1112

Preston, Ralph N., *Early Washington Atlas*, 2d ed. (Portland, Oreg.: Binford and Mont, 1981), 68 pp. [18 reproductions and commentary] 1113

Scott, James W., and Daniel E. Turbeville III, *Whatcom County in Maps: 1832–1937* (Belling-

ham: Western Washington University Center for Pacific Northwest Studies, 1983), 70 pp. 1114

Parker, Martha B., *Washington and Oregon: A Map History of the Oregon Country* (Fairfield, Wash.: Ye Galleon Press, 1988), 138 pp. 1115

Scott, James W., and Ronald L. Delorme, *Historical Atlas of Washington* (Norman: University of Oklahoma Press, 1988), 77 pp. 1116

Scott, James W., *Washington: A Centennial Atlas* (Bellingham: Western Washington University Center for Pacific Northwest Studies, 1989), 155 pp. 1117

West Virginia

Clagg, Sam, *West Virginia Conceptual Atlas* (Chicago: Rand McNally & Co., 1972), 32 pp. 1118

Wisconsin

Historical Atlas of Wisconsin (Milwaukee: Snyder, Van Vechten & Co., 1878), 108 maps, 322 pp. 1119

Page, Herbert R., & Co., *Illustrated Historical Atlas of Wisconsin* (Chicago: H. R. Page & Co., 1881), 104 maps, 221 pp. 1120

Hill, George W., "The People of Wisconsin According to Ethnic Stocks, 1940," Cartography by E. Mayland. Map to Accompany George W. Hill, *Wisconsin's Changing Population* (Madison: Bulletin of the University of Wisconsin, Serial no. 2642, gen. ser. no. 2426, 1942), 90 pp. 1121

Finley, Robert W., *Original Vegetation Cover of Wisconsin, Compiled from United States General Land Office Notes* (St. Paul, Minn.: U.S. Department of Agriculture, Forest Service, North Central Forest Experimental Station, 1976). 1122

PART III

NORTH AMERICA

The continent as a whole, or parts of it that cover both the United States and Canada; also comparisons between regions in North America and elsewhere

GENERAL

Andree, Karl T., *Nord-Amerika in geographischen und geschichtlichen Umrissen. Mit besonderer Berücksichtigung der Eingeborenen und der indianischen Alterthümer, der Einwanderung und der Ansiedlungen, des Ackerbaues, der Gewerbe, der Schiffahrt, und des Handels* (Braunschweig: Georg Westermann, 1851), 810 pp.
1123

Crockett, Thomas, and Bertie C. Wallis, *North America during the Eighteenth Century: A Geographical History* (Cambridge: Cambridge University Press, 1915), 116 pp.
1124

Jones, L. Rodwell, and Patrick W. Bryan, "Part I—Historical Geography," in their *North America: An Historical, Economic, and Regional Geography* (New York: Dial Press, 1924), pp. 1–134.
1125

[Sauer, Carl O.], *North America: Notes on Lectures by Professor Carl O. Sauer of the University of California, Berkeley, 1936* (Northridge: California State University at Northridge, Department of Geography, Occasional Paper no. 1, 1985), 49 pp.
1126

Pfeifer, Gottfried, *Die Kolonisierung Nordamerikas durch die europäischen Staaten* (Bonn: Verlag Gebrüder Scheur, 1942), 67 pp.
1127

Sauer, Carl O., "Time and Place in Ancient America," *Landscape*, vol. 6, 2 (1956–1957), pp. 8–13.
1128

Sauer, Carl O., *The Early Spanish Main* (Berkeley: University of California Press, 1966), 306 pp.
1129

Sauer, Carl O., *Sixteenth Century North America: The Land and the People as Seen by the Europeans* (Berkeley: University of California Press, 1971), 319 pp.
1130

Sauer, Carl O., *Northern Mists* (Berkeley: University of California Press, 1968), 204 pp.
1131

Clark, Andrew Hill, "The Conceptions of 'Empires' of the St. Lawrence and the Mississippi: An Historico-Geographical View with Some Quizzical Comments on Environmental Determinism," *American Review of Canadian Studies*, vol. 5, 2 (1975), pp. 4–27.
1132

Gibson, James R., ed., *European Settlement and Development in North America: Essays on Geographical Change in Honour and Memory of*

Andrew Hill Clark (Toronto: University of Toronto Press, 1978), 231 pp.
1133

Wynn, Graeme, "Essays on European Settlement and North American Development," *Acadiensis*, vol. 9, 1 (1979), pp. 104–113.
1134

Sauer, Carl O., *Seventeenth Century North America* (Berkeley: Turtle Island Foundation, 1980), 295 pp.
1135

Kohlhepp, Gerd, ed., *Beiträge zur Kulturgeographie der Neuen Welt: Ausgewählte Arbeiten von Gottfried Pfeifer* (Berlin: Dietrich Reimer, 1981), 326 pp.
1136

Mitchell, Robert D., and Paul A. Groves, eds., *North America: The Historical Geography of a Changing Continent* (Totowa, N.J.: Rowman & Littlefield, 1987), 468 pp.
1137

Mitchell, Robert D., "The Colonial Origins of Anglo-America," in Robert D. Mitchell and Paul A. Groves, eds., *North America: The Historical Geography of a Changing Continent* (Totowa, N.J.: Rowman & Littlefield, 1987), pp. 93–120.
1138

Vance, James E., Jr., "Revolution in American Space since 1945, and a Canadian Contrast," in Robert D. Mitchell and Paul A. Groves, eds., *North America: The Historical Geography of a Changing Continent* (Totowa, N.J.: Rowman & Littlefield, 1987), pp. 438–459.
1139

Claval, Paul, *La conquête de l'espace américain: du Mayflower au Disneyworld* (Paris: Flammarion, 1989), 320 pp.
1140

Meinig, Donald W., "A Geographical Transect of the Atlantic World, ca.1750," in Eugene D. Genovese and Leonard Hochberg, eds., *Geographic Perspectives in History: Essays in Honor of Edward Whiting Fox* (Oxford: Basil Blackwell, 1989), pp. 185–204.
1141

Canadian–United States comparisons & border areas

Oppel, Alwin, "Der Obere See in Nordamerica: I—Geographische Grundzüge; II—Entdeckung, Besiedlung und wirtschaftliche Ausnutzung," *Globus*, vol. 88, 15 (1905), pp. 229–233; 16, pp. 245–248; 18, pp. 277–281; and 19, pp. 297–304.
1142

Sauer, Carl O., "The Role of Niagara Falls in History," *Historical Outlook*, vol. 10, 2 (1919), pp. 57–65.   **1143**

Mackintosh, William A., "Canada and Vermont: A Study in Historical Geography," *Canadian Historical Review*, vol. 8, 1 (1927), pp. 9–30.
1144

Jackson, Eric P., "The Early Geography of the Champlain Lowland," Ph.D. diss., University of Chicago, 1929.   **1145**

Hodgson, Robert D., "The Champlain-Richelieu Lowland: A Study in Historical Geography," Ph.D. diss., University of Michigan, 1951.   **1146**

Deutsch, Herman, "Geographic Setting for the Recent History of the Inland Empire," *Pacific Northwest Quarterly*, vol. 49, 4 (1958), pp. 150–161; vol. 50, 1 (1959), pp. 14–25. [Spokane's hinterland, including southeast British Columbia]
1147

Thomas, William L., Jr., "The Pacific Coast of North America: As Viewed from the Pacific," *Yearbook of the Association of Pacific Coast Geographers*, vol. 41 (1979), pp. 7–28.   **1148**

Wynn, Graeme, "Atlantic Perspectives," *Canadian Historical Review*, vol. 64 (1988), pp. 340–351.   **1149**

Jacobson, Daniel, "Michigan-Ontario Connections," *Michigan Social Studies* (Spring 1988), pp. 77–85.   **1150**

Hornsby, Stephen J., Victor A. Konrad and James J. Herlon, eds., *The Northeastern Borderlands: Four Centuries of Interaction* (Fredericton, N.B.: Acadiensis Press, 1989), 160 pp.   **1151**

North American comparisons with other areas

Gibson, James R., "The Canadian and Russian Northlands: Critical Contrasts," York University Department of Geography Discussion Paper no. 2, 1972. Reprinted in *North/Nord*, vol. 2, 2 (1973), pp. 11–22.   **1152**

Harris, R. Cole, "The Simplification of Europe Overseas," *Annals of the Association of American Geographers*, vol. 67, 4 (1977), pp. 468–482.
1153

ENVIRONMENTAL CHANGE

General

Ingersoll, Ernest, "How the Settlement of North America Has Affected Its Wild Animals," *Journal of the American Geographical Society*, vol. 17 (1885), pp. 17–44.   **1154**

Adams, Charles C., "The Post-Glacial Dispersal of the North American Biota," in *Report of the Eighth International Geographic Congress, Held in the United States, 1904* (Washington, D.C.: Government Printing Office, House Document no. 460, 1905), pp. 623–637.   **1155**

Cronon, William J., "Boundaries and Ecosystems in U.S. and Canadian History," *Appalachia*, vol. 180 (Summer 1985), pp. 9–28.   **1156**

Climate

Borchert, John R., "The Climate of the Central North American Grasslands," *Annals of the Association of American Geographers*, vol. 40, 1 (1950), pp. 1–49.   **1157**

Griffin, James B., "Some Correlations of Climatic and Cultural Change in Eastern North American Prehistory," *Annals of the New York Academy of Sciences*, vol. 95, 1 (1961), pp. 710–717.
1158

Alford, John, "A Geographical Appraisal of Pleistocene Overkill in North America," *Proceedings of the Association of American Geographers*, vol. 3 (1971), pp. 10–15.   **1159**

McGuirk, James P., "A Century of Precipitation Variability along the Pacific Coast of North America and Its Impact," *Climatic Change*, vol. 4, 1 (1982), pp. 41–56.   **1160**

Fritts, H. C., and J. M. Lough, "An Estimate of Average Annual Temperature Variations for North America, 1602 to 1961," *Climatic Change*, vol. 7, 2 (1985), pp. 203–224.   **1161**

Karl, Thomas R., "Perspective of Climatic Change in North America during the Twentieth Century," *Physical Geography*, vol. 6, 3 (1985), pp. 207–229.   **1162**

Lough, J. M., and H. C. Fritts, "An Assessment of the Possible Effects of Volcanic Eruptions on North American Climate Using Tree-Ring Data, 1602 to 1900 AD," *Climatic Change*, vol. 10, 3 (1987), pp. 219–239.   **1163**

Grove, Jean M., "The Little Ice Age in North America and Greenland," in her *The Little Ice Age* (London: Methuen, 1988), pp. 231–262.
1164

Sanderson, Marie, "Effects of Climate Change on the Great Lakes," *Transactions of the Royal Society of Canada*, 5th ser., vol. 3 (1988), pp. 33–46. [Focus on 1880–1980]   **1165**

Physiography

Roe, Frank G., "Some Historical Evidence on the Earlier Physiography of the North American Prairies," *Transactions of the Royal Society of*

Canada, 3d ser., vol. 55, sec. 2 (1961), pp. 9–35.
1166

Flora

Harshberger, John W., "Methods of Determining the Age of the Different Floristic Elements of Eastern North America" in *Report of the Eighth International Geographic Congress, Held in the United States, 1904* (Washington, D.C.: Government Printing Office, House Document no. 460, 1905), pp. 601–607.
1167

Schott, Carl, "Die Erschließung des nordamerikanischen Waldlandes," *Zeitschrift für Erdkunde*, vol. 5 (1937), pp. 554–563.
1168

Malin, James C., *The Grasslands of North America: Prolegomena to Its History* (Lawrence, Kans.: By the author, 1947), 398 pp.
1169

Malin, James C., "Man, the State of Nature, and Climax: As Illustrated by Some Problems of the North American Grassland," *Scientific Monthly* 74, 1 (1952), pp. 1–8.
1170

Clark, Andrew Hill, "The Impact of Exotic Invasion on the Remaining New World Mid-Latitude Grasslands," in William L. Thomas, ed., *Man's Role in Changing the Face of the Earth* (Chicago: University of Chicago Press, 1956), pp. 737–762.
1171

Wedel, Waldo R., "The Central North American Grassland: Man-Made or Natural?" in *Studies in Human Ecology: A Series of Lectures Given at the Anthropological Society of Washington* (Washington, D.C.: Pan American Union, Department of Cultural Affairs, Social Science Division, 1960), pp. 39–69.
1172

Nelson, J. Gordon, and Robert E. England, "Some Comments on the Causes and Effects of Fire in the Northern Grasslands Area of Canada and the Nearby United States, c.1750–1900," *Canadian Geographer*, vol. 15, 3 (1971), pp. 295–306. Reprinted in J. Gordon Nelson, *Man's Impact on the Western Canadian Landscape* (Toronto: McClelland & Stewart, Carleton Library Series, no. 90, 1976), pp. 33–43.
1173

Moore, Conrad T., "Man and Fire in the Central North American Grassland, 1535–1890: A Documentary Historical Geography," Ph.D. diss., University of California–Los Angeles, 1972.
1174

Fauna

Turner, John P., "The Story of the Buffalo," *Geographical Magazine*, vol. 3, 4 (1936), pp. 221–234. [Focus on the United States and Canada; map of extinction of the bison]
1175

Carter, George F., "Pre-Columbian Chickens in America," in Carroll L. Riley, Charles J. Kelley,

Campbell W. Pennington, and Robert L. Rands, eds., *Man across the Sea: Problems of Pre-Columbian Contacts* (Austin: University of Texas Press, 1971), pp. 178–218.
1176

McDonald, Jerry, "The Reordered North American Selection Regime and Late Quaternary Megafaunal Extinction," in P. S. Martin and R. G. Klein, eds., *Quaternary Extinctions* (Tucson: University of Arizona Press, 1984), pp. 404–439.
1177

NATIVE PEOPLES & WHITE RELATIONS

General

Powell, John Wesley, "A Discourse on the Philosophy of the North American Indians," *Journal of the American Geographical Society*, vol. 8 (1876), pp. 251–265. [Evolved world belief systems of native Americans]
1178

Wissler, Clark O. *The Relation of Nature to Man in Aboriginal America* (New York: Oxford University Press, 1926), 248 pp.
1179

Early human colonization

Krause, Fritz, "Wanderungen nordamerikanischer Indianer: Ein Beitrag zur Methode der Wanderforschung," *Verhandlungen des neunzehnten Deutschen Geographentages zu Strassburg, 1914* (Berlin: Dietrich Reimer, 1915), pp. 213–226. [Migrations during the nineteenth century]
1180

Waterman, Thomas T., "North American Indian Dwellings," *Geographical Review*, vol. 14, 1 (1924), pp. 1–25.
1181

LeConte, René, "Le peuplement de l'Amérique avant Colomb," *Bulletin de la Société de géographie de Québec*, vol. 19, 3 (1925), pp. 163–167; 4, pp. 241–245.
1182

Antevs, Ernst, "The Spread of Aboriginal Man to North America," *Geographical Review*, vol. 25, 2 (1935), pp. 302–309.
1183

Sauer, Carl O., "American Agricultural Origins: A Consideration of Nature and Culture," in *Essays in Anthropology Presented to A. L. Kroeber in Celebration of His Sixtieth Birthday, June 11, 1936* (Berkeley: University of California Press, 1936), pp. 278–297. Reprinted in John Leighly, ed., *Land and Life: A Selection from the Writings of Carl Ortwin Sauer* (Berkeley: University of California Press, 1963), pp. 121–144.
1184

Brand, Donald D., "The Origin and Early Distribution of New World Cultivated Plants," *Agricultural History*, vol. 13, 2 (1939), pp. 109–117.
1185

Sauer, Carl O., "A Geographic Sketch of Early Man in America," *Geographical Review*, vol. 34 (1944), pp. 529–573. Reprinted in John Leighly, ed., *Land and Life: A Selection from the Writings of Carl Ortwin Sauer* (Berkeley: University of California Press, 1963), pp. 197–245.　　1186

Carter, George F., "Géographie des plantes, géographie humaine, et ethnologie en Amérique du Nord: Culture du maïs et civilisations des Indiens," *Revue de géographie humaine et d'ethnologie*, vol. 2 (Apr.-June 1948), pp. 5–16.　　1187

Rostlund, Erhard, "The Evidence for the Use of Fish as Fertilizer in Aboriginal North America," *Journal of Geography*, vol. 56, 5 (1957), pp. 222–228.　　1188

Fogel, Ira L., "The Disposal of Copper Artifacts of the Archaic Tradition in Prehistoric North America," Master's thesis, University of Chicago, 1962.　　1189

Jett, Stephen C., "Diffusion versus Independent Development: The Bases of Controversy," in Carroll L. Riley, et al., eds., *Man across the Sea: Problems of Pre-Columbian Contacts* (Austin: University of Texas Press, 1971), pp. 5–59.　　1190

Walters, Michael, "Early Man Distribution in the Western Hemisphere: 38,000 B.P. to 9,000 B.P.," Master's thesis, Western Illinois University, 1972.　　1191

Denevan, William M., ed., *The Native Population of the Americas in 1492* (Madison: University of Wisconsin Press, 1976), 353 pp.　　1192

Post-contact period

Douglas, James, "The Consolidation of the Iroquois Confederacy: Or, What Happened on the St. Lawrence between Cartier and Champlain," *Journal of the American Geographical Society*, vol. 29 (1897), pp. 41–54.　　1193

Price, A. Grenfell, *White Settlers and Native Peoples: A Historical Survey of Racial Contacts between English-Speaking Whites and Aboriginal Peoples in the United States, Canada, Australia and New Zealand* (Melbourne: Georgian House, 1949), 232 pp.　　1194

Rostlund, Erhard, "Three Early Historical Reports of North American Fresh Water Fishes," *Copeia*, no. 4 (1951), pp. 295–296.　　1195

Moodie, D. Wayne, and Barry Kaye, "The Northern Limit of Indian Agriculture in North America," *Geographical Review*, vol. 59, 4 (1969), pp. 513–529.　　1196

Ross, Thomas E., and Tyrel G. Moore, eds., *A Cultural Geography of North American Indians* (Boulder: Westview, 1987), 331 pp.　　1197

Konrad, Victor A., "The Iroquois Return to Their Homeland: Military Retreat or Cultural Adjustment?" in Thomas E. Ross and Tyrel G. Moore,

eds., *A Cultural Geography of North American Indians* (Boulder: Westview, 1987), pp. 191–212.　　1198

Intercontinental comparisons

Mills, James, "Spiritual Landscapes: A Comparative Study of Burial Mound Sites in the Upper Mississippi River Basin and the Practice of Feng Shui in East Asia," Ph.D. diss., University of Minnesota, 1990.　　1199

EXPLORATION & MAPPING

Amerindian mapping

DeVorsey, Louis, Jr., "Amerindian Contributions to the Mapping of North America: A Preliminary View," *Imago Mundi*, vol. 30 (1978), pp. 71–78.　　1200

Lewis, G. Malcolm, "The Indigenous Maps and Mapping of North American Indians," *Map Collector*, vol. 9 (1979), pp. 25–32.　　1201

Vollmar, Rainer, *Indianische Karten Nordamerikas: Beiträge zur historischen Kartographie vom 16. bis zum 19. Jahrhundert* (Berlin: Dietrich Reimer Verlag, 1981), 179 pp.　　1202

Lewis, G. Malcolm, "Indicators of Unacknowledged Assimilations from Amerindian Maps on Euro-American Maps of North America: Some General Principles Arising from a Study of La Verendrye's Composite Map, 1728–29," *Imago Mundi*, vol. 38 (1986), pp. 9–34.　　1203

Rundstrom, Robert A., "A Cultural Interpretation of Inuit Map Accuracy," *Geographical Review*, vol. 80, 2 (1990), pp. 155–168.　　1204

Who "discovered" America?

Kohl, Johann Georg, "Substance of a Lecture Delivered at the Smithsonian Institution on a Collection of the Charts and Maps of America," *Annual Report of the Smithsonian Institution, 1856* (Washington, 1857), pp. 93–146.　　1205

Rahn, C. C., "Northmen in America," *Journal of the American Geographical and Statistical Society*, vol. 1, 6 (1859), pp. 178–179.　　1206

Kohl, Johann Georg, *Die beiden ältesten General-Karten von Amerika. Ausgeführt in den Jahren 1527 und 1529 auf Befehl Kaiser Karl's v. Im besitz der großherzoglichen Bibliothek zu Weimar* (Weimar: Geographisches Institut, 1860), 185 pp.　　1207

Kohl, Johann Georg, *Geschichte der Entdeckung Amerikas von Columbus bis Franklin* (Bremen: H. Strack, 1861). English edition, London: Chapman & Hall, 1862, 1864, and 1865. Revised Leipzig: Schulze & Co., 1885.　　1208

DeCosta, Benjamin F., "The Northmen in America," *Journal of the American Geographical and Statistical Society*, vol. 2, 2 (1870), pp. 40–54. **1209**

Kohl, Johann Georg, "Sir Martin Frobishers Seefahrten und Entdeckungsreisen zum Norden Amerikas in den Jahren 1576 bis 1578," *Das Ausland*, vol. 51, 22 (1878), pp. 421–423; 23, pp. 454–457; 24, pp. 464–468; 25, pp. 488–491. **1210**

Moos, Ferdinand, "Zur Geschichte der Geographie Amerikas," *Das Ausland*, vol. 57, 22 (1884), pp. 434–437. [Focus on the European exploration of North America] **1211**

Harrisse, Henry, *The Discovery of North America: A Critical, Documentary, and Historic Investigation, with an Essay on the Early Cartography of the New World* (London: H. Stevens, 1892), 802 pp. Reprinted Amsterdam: N. Israel, 1961. **1212**

Taylor, W. A., "The Discovery of America," *Scottish Geographical Magazine*, vol. 8, 8 (1892), pp. 425–430. **1213**

Murray, John, "The Discovery of America by Columbus," *Scottish Geographical Magazine*, vol. 9, 11 (1893), pp. 561–586. **1214**

Masters, F. J., "Did a Chinaman Discover America?" *Bulletin of the Geographical Society of California*, vol. 2 (1894), pp. 59–76. **1215**

Oldham, Henry Y., "A Pre-Columbian Discovery of America," *Geographical Journal*, vol. 5, 3 (1895), pp. 221–233. **1216**

Nansen, Fridtjof, "The Norsemen in America," *Scottish Geographical Magazine*, vol. 27, 12 (1911), pp. 617–632. **1217**

Kohl, Johann Georg, "Asia and America: An Historical Disquisition Concerning the Ideas Which Former Geographers Had about the Geographical Relations and Connection of the Old and New World," *Proceedings of the American Antiquarian Society*, n.s. vol. 21 (1911), pp. 285–338. **1218**

Almagia, Roberto, "La scoperta dell'America da parte dei Normanni," *Rivista geografia italiana*, vol. 20 (1913), pp. 496–500. **1219**

Almagia, Roberto, "Ancore sulla scoperta dell' America da parte dei Normanni," *Rivista Geografia Italiana*, vol. 21, 3 (1914), pp. 531–534. **1220**

Kolischer, Karl A., "Die Normannen in Amerika vor Columbus," *Mitteilungen der Geographischen Gesellschaft in Wien*, vol. 57 (1914), pp. 239–249. **1221**

Nunn, George E., *The Geographical Conceptions of Columbus: A Critical Consideration of Four Problems* (Ph.D. diss., University of California–Berkeley, 1924; published under same title, New York: American Geographical Society Research Series, no. 14, 1924), 148 pp. **1222**

Gould, Rupert T., "The Landfall of Columbus: An Old Problem Restated," *Geographical Journal*, vol. 49, 4 (1927), pp. 403–429. **1223**

Burpee, Lawrence J., *The Discovery of Canada* (Ottawa: Graphic Publishers, 1929), 96 pp. Revised 1944, 280 pp. **1224**

Thórdarson, Matthias, *The Vinland Voyages* (New York: American Geographical Society, Research Series, no. 18, 1930), 76 pp. **1225**

Karpinski, Louis C., "The First Map with the Name America," *Geographical Review*, vol. 20, 4 (1930), pp. 664–668. **1226**

Kallbrunner, Annemarie, "Zur Frage der vorcolumbischen Entdeckung Amerikas durch die Portugiesen," *Mitteilungen der Geographischen Gesellschaft in Wien*, vol. 80 (1937), pp. 298–301. **1227**

Morison, Samuel Eliot, *Admiral of the Ocean Sea: A Life of Christopher Columbus*, maps by Erwin Raisz (Boston: Little, Brown & Co., 1942), 680 pp. **1228**

Almagia, Roberto, "A proposito di un recente libro e di altri scritti su Amerigo Vespucci," *Rivista geografia italiana*, vol. 63, 1 (1956), pp. 1–14. **1229**

Quinn, David B., "The Argument for the English Discovery of America between 1480 and 1494," *Geographical Journal*, vol. 127, 3 (1961), pp. 277–285. **1230**

Marston, Thomas E., "The Vinland Map: Dating the Manuscript," *Canadian Cartographer*, vol. 3, 1 (1966), pp. 1–5. **1231**

McManis, Douglas R., "The Traditions of Vinland," *Annals of the Association of American Geographers*, vol. 59, 4 (1969), pp. 797–814. **1232**

Edwards, Clinton R., "Mapping by Questionnaire: An Early Spanish Attempt to Determine New World Geographical Positions," *Imago Mundi*, vol. 23 (1969), pp. 17–28. **1233**

Morison, Samuel Eliot, *The European Discovery of America* (New York: Oxford University Press, 1971–1974), 2 vols. **1234**

Fuson, Robert H., and Walter H. Treftz, "A Theoretical Reconstruction of the First Atlantic Crossing of Christopher Columbus," *Proceedings of the Association of American Geographers*, vol. 8 (1976), pp. 155-159. **1235**

Carter, George F., "Did China Discover America?" *Eastern Review*, vol. 4, 4 (1979), pp. 74–76. **1236**

Kaups, Matti E., "Shifting Vinland: Tradition and Myth," *Terrae Incognitae*, vol. 10, 3 (1979), pp. 29–60. **1237**

Kaups, Matti E., "Leifr Eiricksson," in Helen Delpar, ed., *The Discoverers: An Encyclopedia of Explorers and Exploration* (New York: McGraw-Hill, 1980), pp. 149–150. **1238**

Kaups, Matti E., "Norse Maritime Discoveries," in Helen Delpar, ed., *The Discoverers: An Encyclopedia of Explorers and Exploration* (New York: McGraw-Hill, 1980), pp. 288–297. **1239**

Kaups, Matti E., "Vinland," in Helen Delpar, ed., *The Discoverers: An Encyclopedia of Explorers and Exploration* (New York: McGraw-Hill, 1980), pp. 437–440. **1240**

Carter, George F., "Saga America," *Historical Diffusionism*, vol. 31 (1981), pp. 31–58. **1241**

Carter, George F., "On Pre-Columbian Discoveries of America," *Anthropological Journal of Canada*, vol. 19 (1981), pp. 10–17. **1242**

Fuson, Robert H., "The *Diario de Colón*: A Legacy of Poor Transcription, Translation, and Interpretation," *Terrae Incognitae*, vol. 15 (1983), pp. 51–75. **1243**

Davies, Arthur, "Prince Madoc and the Discovery of America in 1477," *Geographical Journal*, vol. 150, 3 (1984), pp. 363–372. **1244**

DeVorsey, Louis, Jr., and John T. Parker, eds., *In the Wake of Columbus: Islands and Controversy* (Detroit: Wayne State University Press, 1985), 231 pp. **1245**

Fuson, Robert H., transl., *The Log of Christopher Columbus* (Camden, Maine: International Marine Publishing, 1987), 252 pp. **1246**

Harley, J. Brian, *Maps and the Columbian Encounter: An Interpretive Guide to the Travelling Exhibition* (Milwaukee: Golda Meir Library, 1990), 160 pp. **1247**

Continental exploration & mapping

Winsor, Justin, *The Anticipations of Cartier's Voyages, 1492–1534* (Cambridge, Mass.: J. Wilson and Son, 1893), 14 pp. **1248**

Winsor, Justin, *Cartier to Frontenac: Geographical Discovery in the Interior of North America in Its Historical Relations, 1534–1700; With Full Cartographical Illustrations from Contemporary Sources* (Boston and New York: Houghton Mifflin & Co., 1894), 379 pp. **1249**

Harrisse, Henry, *Découverte et évolution cartographique de Terre Neuve et des pays circonvoisons, 1497–1501–1769: Essais de géographie historique et documentaire* (Paris: H. Welter,

1900), 420 pp. Reprinted Amsterdam: N. Israel, 1968. **1250**

Pelletier, Fr., "Un épisode des explorations françaises dans l'Amérique septentrionale pour la découverte de la mer de l'Ouest," *Bulletin de géographie historique et descriptive*, vol. 17 (1902), pp. 187–206. **1251**

Burpee, Lawrence J., *The Search for the Western Sea: The Story of the Exploration of North-Western America* (Toronto: Musson Book Co., 1908), 651 pp. Revised Macmillan Co., 1935, 2 vols. **1252**

Friederici, Georg, "Der Grad der Durchdringbarkeit Nordamerikas im Zeitalter der Entdeckungen und ersten Durchforschung des Kontinents durch die Europäer," *Petermanns Geographische Mitteilungen, Ergänzungsheft*, no. 209 (1930), pp. 216–229. **1253**

Hobbs, William H., "The Progress of Discovery and Exploration within the Arctic Region," *Annals of the Association of American Geographers*, vol. 27, 1/1 (1937), pp. 1–22. **1254**

Hoffman, Bernard G., *Cabot to Cartier: Sources for a Historical Ethnography of Northeastern North America, 1497–1550* (Toronto: University of Toronto Press, 1961), 287 pp. **1255**

Sauer, Carl O., "Terra Firma: Orbis Novus," in Adolph Leidlmair, ed., *Hermann von Wissmann—Festschrift* (Tübingen: Geographisches Institut der Universität Tübingen, 1962), pp. 258–270. **1256**

Skelton, Raleigh A., *The European Image and Mapping of America, AD 1000–1600* (Minneapolis: Associates of the James Ford Bell Collection, James Ford Bell Lectures, 1, 1964), 28 pp. **1257**

Lambert, A. F., "Maintaining the Canadian–United States Boundary," *Canadian Cartographer*, vol. 2, 2 (1965), pp. 67–71. **1258**

Allen, John L., "Pyramidal Height of Land: A Persistent Myth in the Exploration of Western Anglo-America," in W. P. Adams and F. M. Helleiner, eds., *International Geography, 1972*, vol. 1, sec. 5, *Historical Geography* (Toronto: University of Toronto Press, for the International Geographical Union, 1972), pp. 395–396. **1259**

Harley, J. Brian, "Specifications for Military Survey in British North America, 1750–75," in W. P. Adams and F. M. Helleiner, eds., *International Geography, 1972*, vol. 1, sec. 5, *Historical Geography* (Toronto: University of Toronto Press, for the International Geographical Union, 1972), pp. 424–425. **1260**

Cumming, William P., et al., *The Exploration of North America, 1630–1776* (New York: G. P. Putnam's, 1974), 272 pp. **1261**

Johnson, Adrian, *America Explored: A Cartographical History of the Exploration of North America* (New York: Viking Press, 1974), 252 pp. **1262**

Thrower, Norman J. W., "New Geographical Horizons: Maps," in Fredi Chiappelli, ed., *First Images of America: The Impact of the New World on the Old* (Berkeley: University of California Press, 1975), vol. 2, pp. 659–674. **1263**

Harley, J. Brian, "The Map User in Eighteenth-Century North America," in Brian S. Osborne, ed., *The Settlement of Canada: Origins and Transfer* (Kingston, Ont.: Proceedings of the 1975 British-Canadian Symposium on Historical Geography, 1976), pp. 47–69. **1264**

Lockman, Ronald F., "North America in the Cartography of Guillaume Delisle," *Bulletin of the Western Association of Map Libraries*, vol. 10, 1 (1978), pp. 20–31. **1265**

Kish, George, *The Discovery and Settlement of North America, 1500–1865: A Cartographic Perspective* (New York: Harper and Row, 1979), 61 pp. **1266**

Heidenreich, Conrad E., and Edward H. Dahl, "The French Mapping of North America in the Seventeenth Century," *Map Collector*, vol. 13 (1980), pp. 2–11. **1267**

Schwartz, Seymour I., and Ralph E. Ehrenberg, *The Mapping of North America* (New York: Harry M. Abrams, 1980), 363 pp. **1268**

Ristow, Walter W., "The Ebeling-Sotzman Atlas von Nordamerika," *Map Collector* 14 (1981), pp. 2–9. **1269**

Heidenreich, Conrad E., and Edward H. Dahl, "The French Mapping of North America, 1600–1760," *Map Collector*, vol. 19 (1982), pp. 1–20. [Reprint of two previous articles on this topic in this serial] **1270**

Dahl, Edward H., "The Original Beaver Map: De-Fer's 1698 Wall Map of America," *Map Collector*, vol. 29 (1984), pp. 22–26. **1271**

Quinn, David B., "Artists and Illustrators in the Early Mapping of North America," *Mariner's Mirror*, vol. 72, 3 (1986), pp. 244–273. **1272**

Wolter, John A., "Nordamerika," in Ingrid Kretschmer, Johannes Dörflinger and Franz Wawrick, eds., *Lexicon zur Geschichte der Kartographie: Von den Anfängen bis zum Ersten Weltkrieg*, vol. 1 (Vienna: Franz Deuticke, 1986), pp. 536–541. **1273**

DeVorsey, Louis, Jr., "The New Land: The Discovery and Exploration of Eastern North America," in Robert D. Mitchell and Paul A. Groves, eds., *North America: The Historical Geography of a Changing Continent* (Totowa, N.J.: Rowman & Littlefield, 1987), pp. 25–47. **1274**

Great Lakes

Gravier, Gabriel, *Carte des Grands Lacs de l'Amérique du Nord dressée en 1670 par Brehan de Galinée Missionaire Sulpicien* (Rouen: Imprimerie E. Cagniard, 1895). Reprinted in *Acta Cartographica*, vol. 2 (1968), pp. 199–223. **1275**

Fleming, R. F., "Charting the Great Lakes," *Canadian Geographical Magazine*, vol. 12 (1936), pp. 69–77. **1276**

Rogers, Richard R., "Historical Cartography of the Great Lakes," *Papers of the Michigan Academy of Science, Arts, and Letters*, vol. 34 (1948), pp. 175–184. **1277**

Krenn, Ernst, "Wer hat Amerika zuerst entdeckt? Die Großen Seen und Entdeckungsfahrten des irischen Mönches Brendan im 6. Jahrhundert," *Petermanns Geographische Mitteilungen*, vol. 94, 4 (1950), pp. 207–211. **1278**

Harley, J. Brian, "Mapping the Great Lakes," *Journal of Historical Geography*, vol. 4 (1978), pp. 228–230. **1279**

Heidenreich, Conrad E., "Seventeenth Century Maps of the Great Lakes: An Overview and Procedures for Analysis," *Archivaria*, vol. 6 (1978), pp. 83–112. **1280**

Heidenreich, Conrad E., "Mapping the Great Lakes: The Period of Exploration, 1603–1700," *Cartographica*, vol. 17, 3 (1980), pp. 32–64. **1281**

Lewis, G. Malcolm, "Changing National Perspectives and the Mapping of the Great Lakes Between 1755 and 1975," *Cartographica*, vol. 17, 3 (1980), pp. 1–31. **1282**

Heidenreich, Conrad E., "Mapping the Great Lakes: The Period of Imperial Rivalries, 1700–1760," *Cartographica*, vol. 18, 3 (1981), pp. 74–109. **1283**

Heidenreich, Conrad E., "The Fictitious Islands of Lake Superior," *Inland Seas*, vol. 43, 3 (1987), pp. 168–177. **1284**

Pacific & Northwest

Wagner, Henry R., *The Cartography of the Northwest Coast of America to the Year 1800*, 2 vols. (Berkeley: University of California Press, 1937), 543 pp. **1285**

Wagner, Philip L., "Russian Exploration in North America," Master's thesis, University of California–Berkeley, 1950. **1286**

Farley, Albert L., "Fact and Fancy in Mapping Northwest America to 1800," *Occasional Papers*

of the British Columbia Division of the Canadian Association of Geographers, vol. 3 (1962),
pp. 27–36.   1287

Friis, Herman R., ed., The Pacific Basin: A History
of Its Geographical Exploration (New York:
American Geographical Society Special Publication no. 38, 1967), 457 pp.   1288

Cannon, Christine J., "Mapping Western North
America and Puget Sound," Master's thesis,
University of Washington, 1969.   1289

Thematic maps

Hebert, John E., Introduction to Panoramic Maps
of Cities in the United States and Canada
(Washington, D.C.: Library of Congress, 1984),
pp. 1–12.   1290

Modelski, Andrew M., Railroad Maps of North
America: The First Hundred Years (Washington: Government Printing Office, 1984), 186 pp.
                                              1291

Reps, John W., "The Making and Selling of Urban
Views," in his Views and Viewmakers of America: Lithographs of Towns and Cities in the
United States and Canada, Notes on the Artists
and Publishers, and a Union Catalogue of Their
Work, 1825–1925 (Columbia: University of Missouri Press, 1984), pp. 3–94.
                                              1292

Monmonier, Mark S., "Maps in The Times (of
London) and The New York Times, 1870–1980: A
Cross-National Study in Journalistic Cartography," Proceedings of the Pennsylvania Academy of Science, vol. 59, 1 (1985), pp. 61–66.   1293

Monmonier, Mark, "The Rise of Map Use by Elite
Newspapers in England, Canada, and the
United States," Imago Mundi, vol. 38 (1986), pp.
46–60.   1294

Conzen, Michael P., "North American County
Maps and Atlases," in David Buisseret, ed.,
From Sea Charts to Satellite Images: Interpret-
ing North American History through Maps
(Chicago: University of Chicago Press, 1990), pp.
186–211.   1295

Pedley, Mary, "Land Company Mapping in North
America: Fiefdom in the New Republic," Imago
Mundi, vol. 42 (1990), pp. 106–113.   1296

POPULAR IMAGES & EVALUATION

Early regional & environmental perceptions

Crouse, Nellis M., "Contributions of the Canadian
Jesuits to the Geographical Knowledge of New
France, 1632–1675," Ph.D. diss., Cornell Univer-
sity, 1924.   1297

Watson, J. Wreford, "Mental Images and Geo-
graphical Reality in the Settlement of North
America," Cust Foundation Lectures, University
of Nottingham, no. 3 (1967), pp. 3–24. Revised as
"Role of Illusion in North American Geography:
A Note on the Geography of North American
Settlement," Canadian Geographer, vol. 13, 1
(1969), pp. 10–27.   1298

McManis, Douglas R., "English Evaluation of
North American Iron during the Late Sixteenth
and Early Seventeenth Centuries," Professional
Geographer, vol. 21, 2 (1969), pp. 93–96.   1299

Aiken, S. Robert, "The New-Found-Land Perceived: An Exploration of Environmental Attitudes in Colonial British America," Ph.D. diss.,
Pennsylvania State University, 1971.   1300

McManis, Douglas R., "In Search of a Rational
World: The Encyclopedists' Image of Northern
and Western North America," Historical Geography, vol. 5, 2 (1975), pp. 18–29.   1301

Johnson, Hildegard Binder, "New Geographical
Horizons: Concepts," in Fredi Chiappalli, ed.,
First Images of America: The Impact of the New
World on the Old, vol. 2 (Berkeley: University of
California Press, 1975), pp. 615–633.   1302

Quinn, David B., "New Geographical Horizons:
Literature," in Fredi Chiappalli, ed., First Images of America: The Impact of the New World
on the Old (Berkeley: University of California
Press, 1975), vol. 2, pp. 635–658.   1303

Perez-Alejos, P., "The Interpretation of the Human and Natural Resources of the New World
by the Sixteenth Century Spaniard," Master's
thesis, University of Alberta, 1976.   1304

Canadian–United States border regions

Arthur, Elizabeth, "The Disregarded Border:
Rainy River in the Nineteenth Century," Upper
Midwest History, vol. 2 (1982), pp. 31–43.   1305

Richtik, James M., "The Western Canadian Per-
ception of North Dakota in the Late Nineteenth
Century," Bulletin of the Association of North
Dakota Geographers, vol. 32 (1982), pp. 48–55.
                                              1306

Mather, Eugene Cotton, "O Canada! Reality and
the Image in America," Journal of Geography,
vol. 83, 5 (1984), pp. 195–198.   1307

Louder, Dean R., "Le Québec et la Franco-
Américanie: A Mother Country in the Making,"
in Stephen J. Hornsby, Victor A. Konrad, and
James J. Herlon, eds., The Northeastern Borderlands: Four Centuries of Interaction (Fredericton, N.B.: Acadiensis Press, 1989), pp. 127–136.
                                              1308

Niagara Falls

McGreevy, Patrick V., "Visions at the Brink: Imagination and the Geography of Niagara Falls," Ph.D. diss., University of Minnesota, 1984. 1309

McGreevy, Patrick V., "Niagara as Jerusalem," *Landscape*, vol. 28, 2 (1985), pp. 26–32. 1310

McGreevy, Patrick V., "Imagining the Future at Niagara Falls," *Annals of the Association of American Geographers*, vol. 77, 1 (1987), pp. 48–62. 1311

McGreevy, Patrick V., "The End of America: The Beginning of Canada," *Canadian Geographer*, vol. 32, 4 (1988), pp. 307–318. 1312

McGreevy, Patrick V., "Visions of the Future at Niagara Falls," *Earthwatch*, vol. 8, 2 (1989), pp. 14–16. 1313

Intercontinental urban imagery

Ford, Larry R., "The Highrise in City Structure and Urban Images: A Cross-Cultural Comparison between Argentina and the American Midwest," *Geographical Survey*, vol. 1, 2 (1972), pp. 1–23. 1314

REGIONAL SETTLEMENT

General

Shaler, Nathaniel Southgate, "Effects of the Physiography of North America on Men of European Origin," in Justin Winsor, ed., *Narrative and Critical History of America* (Boston: Houghton Mifflin & Co., 1885), vol. 4, pp. i–xxx. Reprinted in Charles J. Bullock, ed., *Selected Readings in Economics* (Boston: Ginn & Co., 1907), pp. 1–22. 1315

Wright, John K., "Altitude and Settlement in North America," *Geographical Review*, vol. 16 (1926), p. 136. 1316

Colonization & pioneering

Günter, Otto, "Die Anfänge der Besiedlung Nordamerikas," *Jahresbericht Württembergischer Verein für Handelsgeographie*, vols. 11 & 12 (1893), pp. 81–82. 1317

Tuckermann, Walther, "Der französische Siedlungsraum in Nordamerika," *Verhandlungen des 22. Deutschen Geographentages zu Karlsruhe* (Breslau: Ferdinand Hirt, 1928), pp. 99–112. 1318

Malin, James C., "The Grasslands of North America: Its Occupance and the Challenge of Continuous Reappraisal," in William L. Thomas, ed., *Man's Role in Changing the Face of the Earth* (Chicago: University of Chicago Press, 1956), pp. 350–366. Reprinted in Barbara Gutmann Rosen-

krantz and William A. Koelsch, eds., *American Habitat: A Historical Perspective* (New York: Free Press, 1973), pp. 218–134. 1319

Johnson, Hildegard Binder, "French Canada and the Ohio Country: A Study in Early Spatial Relationships," *Canadian Geographer*, vol. 3 (1958), pp. 1–10. 1320

Landing, James E., "Amish Settlement in North America: A Geographical Brief," *Bulletin of the Illinois Geographical Society*, vol. 12, 3 (1970), pp. 65–69. 1321

Preston, Richard E., "Audit Bureau of Circulation Daily Newspaper Records as a Source in Studies of Post-1915 Settlement Patterns in the United States and Canada," *Historical Geography Newsletter*, vol. 7, 1–2 (1977), pp. 1–12. 1322

Gibson, James R., "Bostonians and Muscovites on the Northwest Coast, 1788–1841," in Thomas Vaughan, ed., *The Western Shore: Oregon Country Essays Honoring the American Revolution* (Portland: Oregon Historical Society, 1975), pp. 81–119. Reprinted in W. Peter Ward and Robert A. J. McDonald, eds., *British Columbia: Historical Readings* (Vancouver: Douglas and McIntyre, 1981), pp. 66–95. 1323

Lyon, Eugene, "Spain's Sixteenth-Century North American Settlement Attempts: A Neglected Aspect," *Florida Historical Quarterly*, vol. 59, 3 (1981), pp. 275–291. 1324

Becker, Hans, "The Settlement Process in the Klondike and Alaska Gold Fields," in Alfred Hecht, ed., *Regional Development in the Peripheries of Canada and Europe* (Winnipeg: University of Manitoba Department of Geography, Manitoba Geographical Studies no. 8, 1983), pp. 81–98. 1325

Harris, R. Cole, "European Beginnings in the Northwest Atlantic: A Comparative View," in D. Hall and D. G. Allen, eds., *Seventeenth Century Massachusetts* (Boston: Massachusetts Colonial Society, 1985), pp. 119–152. 1326

Harris, R. Cole, "France in North America," in Robert D. Mitchell and Paul A. Groves, eds., *North America: The Historical Geography of a Changing Continent* (Totowa, N.J.: Rowman & Littlefield, 1987), pp. 65–92. 1327

Jordan, Terry G., "Preadaptation and European Colonization in Rural North America," *Annals of the Association of American Geographers*, vol. 79, 4 (1989), pp. 489–500. 1328

Rural settlement morphology

Meynen, Emil, "Dorf und Farm: Das Schicksal altweltlicher Dörfer in Amerika," in Oskar Schmieder, ed., *Lebensraumfragen europäischer Völker*, vol. 3, *Gegenwartsprobleme der*

Neuen Welt—Part 1: Nordamerika (Leipzig: Quelle & Meyer, 1943), pp. 565–615.   **1329**

Morton, William L., "The Significance of Site in the Settlement of the American and Canadian West," *Agricultural History*, vol. 25 (1951), pp. 97–104.

1330

Bartz, Fritz, "Französische Einflüsse im Bilde der Kulturlandschaft Nordamerikas: Hufensiedlungen und Marschpolder in Kanada und in Louisiana," *Erdkunde*, vol. 9 (1955), pp. 286–305.

1331

Martin, Larry R. G., "A Comparative Study of the Development of Settlement and Agriculture in the Quinte Region of Eastern Ontario and the St. Lawrence Region of Northern New York," Master's thesis, Syracuse University, 1965.   **1332**

Denecke, Dietrich, "Tradition und Anpassung der agraren Raumorganisation und Siedlungsgestaltung im Landnahmeprozeß des östlichen Nordamerikas im 17. und 18. Jahrhundert," in *Tagungsbericht und wissenschaftliche Abhandlungen 40. Deutscher Geographentag Innsbruck* (Wiesbaden: Franz Steiner Verlag, 1976), pp. 228–255.   **1333**

Lenz, Karl, "Die Konzentration der Versorgung im ländlichen Bereich: Untersuchungen in den nördlichen Präriegebieten von Nordamerika," in Carl Schott, ed., *Beiträge zur Geographie Nordamerikas* (Marburg: Marburger Geographische Schriften, vol. 66, 1976), pp. 9–48. [Focus on Alberta and North Dakota, 1940–1974]   **1334**

Lenz, Karl, "Die Siedlungen der Hutterer in Nordamerika: Ausdruck einer sozialgeographischen Gruppe," *Geographische Zeitschrift*, vol. 65, 3 (1977), pp. 216–238. [Focus on 1918–1972]   **1335**

Overseas comparisons

Meinig, Donald W., "Colonization of Wheatlands: Some Australian and American Comparisons," *Australian Geographer*, vol. 7 (1959), pp. 205–213.   **1336**

Sauer, Carl O., "European Backgrounds of American Agricultural Settlement," *Historical Geography*, vol. 6, 1 (1976), pp. 35–57. Reprinted in Carl O. Sauer, *Selected Essays, 1963–1975*, ed. Bob Callahan (Berkeley, Calif.: Turtle Island Foundation, for the Netzahaulcoyotl Historical Society, 1981), pp. 45–56.   **1337**

Gibson, James R., "Russian Expansion in Siberia and America," *Geographical Review*, vol. 70, 2 (1980), pp. 127–136.   **1338**

Gibson, James R., "Russian Expansion in Siberia and America: Critical Contrasts," *Kennan Insti-tute for Advanced Russian Studies*, Occasional Paper no. 72 (1980), 17 pp. Reprinted in S. Frederick Starr, ed., *Russia's American Colony* (Durham: Duke University Press, 1987), pp. 32–40.   **1339**

Norton, William, "A Comparative Analysis of Frontier Settlement in the Cape Province, South Africa, and Southern Ontario, Canada," *South African Geographer*, vol. 12 (1984), pp. 43–55.

1340

Wyckoff, William K., and Gary J. Hausladen, "Settling the Russian Frontier, with Comparisons to North America," *Soviet Geography*, vol. 30 (1989), pp. 179–188.   **1341**

POPULATION

General

Schott, Carl, "Zur Bevölkerungsentwicklung in Nordamerika," in Oskar Schmieder, ed., *Gegenwartsprobleme der Neuen Welt*, pt. 1, *Nordamerika* (Leipzig: Quelle & Meyer, 1943), pp. 435–512.   **1342**

Geddes, Arthur, "Variability of Population in the United States and Canada, 1900–1951," *Geographical Review*, vol. 44 (1954), pp. 88–100.

1343

Brookes, Alan A., "The Exodus: Migration from the Maritime Provinces to Boston during the Second Half of the Nineteenth Century," Ph.D. diss., University of New Brunswick, 1979.   **1344**

Richtik, James M., "Competition for Settlers: The Canadian Viewpoint," *Great Plains Quarterly*, vol. 3, 1 (1983), pp. 39–49.   **1345**

Richtik, James M., "Running the Gauntlet: American Agents and Canadian Settlers in the Nineteenth Century," *Regina Geographical Studies*, no. 4 (1984), pp. 67–78.   **1346**

Zelinsky, Wilbur, *The Historical Geography of Season of Marriage: North America, 1844–1974* (University Park: Pennsylvania State University Population Issues Research Center, Working Paper no. 1984–15, 1984), 43 pp.   **1347**

Widdis, Randy W., "Tracing Eastern Ontarian Emigrants to New York State, 1880–1910," *Ontario History*, vol. 81, 3 (1989), pp. 201–233.   **1348**

Ethnic groups

LeConte, René, "Colonisation et émigration Allemandes en Amérique, avant 1815," *Bulletin de la Société de géographie de Québec*, vol. 17, 2 (1923), pp. 80–89; 3, pp. 164–176.   **1349**

Tuckerman, Walther, "Der französische Siedlungsraum in Nordamerika," in Edwin Fels, ed., *Verhandlungen des 22. Deutschen Geograph-*

entages 1927 Karlsruhe (Breslau: Perdimand Hirt, 1928), pp. 99–112. 1350

Pakstas, Kazys, "Lithuanians in North America," Geografiski Raksti, vol. 1 (1928), pp. 146–147. 1351

LeBlanc, Robert G., "The Acadian Migrations," Master's thesis, University of Minnesota, 1962. 1352

Paquet, Gilles, "L'émigration des Canadiens français vers le Nouvelle-Angleterre, 1870–1910: Prises du vue quantitatives," Recherche sociographiques, vol. 5 (1964), pp. 319–370. 1353

Lewthwaite, Gordon R., Christiane Mainzer, and Patrick J. Holland, "From Polynesia to California: Samoan Migration and its Sequel," Journal of Pacific History, vol. 8 (1973), pp. 133–157. 1354

Raitz, Karl B., "North American Ethnic Maps," Geographical Review, vol. 68, 3 (1978), pp. 335–350. 1355

LaVoie, Yolande, L'émigration de Québécois aux États-Unis de 1840 à 1930 (Quebec: Editeur Officiel, 1979), 57 pp. 1356

Lane, Mara Melia, "The Migration of Hawaiians to Coastal British Columbia, 1810 to 1869," Master's thesis, University of Hawaii, 1985. 1357

Ostergren, Robert C., "Swedish Migration to North America in Transatlantic Perspective," in Ira Glazier and Luigi de Rosa, eds., Migration across Time and Nations (New York: Holmes & Meier, 1986), pp. 125–147. 1358

Waddell, Eric, "Les revenants: Une dimension cachée des rapports entre la Québec et les diasporas canadienne-française et acadienne en Amérique du Nord," Études canadiennes, vol. 21, 1 (1986), pp. 97–103. 1359

Regional comparisons

Innes, Frank C., "Differential Regional Mortalities: Some Canadian and American South Contrasts in the Nineteenth Century," Geoscience and Man, vol. 25 (1988), pp. 41–56. 1360

Nash, Alan, "Demographic Regions in the American South and Caribbean, 1620–1820," in Richard L. Nostrand and Sam B. Hilliard, eds., The American South (Baton Rouge: Louisiana State University School of Geoscience, Geoscience and Man, vol. 25, 1988), pp. 25–40. 1361

RURAL & REGIONAL SOCIAL GEOGRAPHY

Ratzel, Friedrich, "Zur Geschichte des Deutschtums in Nordamerika," Die Grenzboten: Zeitschrift für Politik, Literatur und Kunst, vol. 56 (1897), pp. 519–522. 1362

Nelson, Helge M. O., "Nagra svenskbygder: Nordamerika," Sydsvenska geografiska sallskapet årsbok, ser. C, no. 1 (1925), pp. 13–48. 1363

Nelson, Helge M. O., "Svenskar och svensk bygder i Nordamerika: Deras geografiska utbredning," in Karl Hildebrand and Axel Fredenholm, eds., Svenskarna: Amerika (Stockholm: Historiska Förlag, 1925), pp. 346–360. 1364

Nelson, Helge M. O., Nordamerika: Natur, bydg, och svenskbygd, 2 vols. (Stockholm: A. B. M. Bergvalls, 1926), 523 pp. [Regional and historical; emphasis on Swedish colonization] 1365

Meynen, Emil, "Das Deutschtum in Nordamerika," in Paul Gauss, ed., Das Buch vom deutschen Volkstum: Wesen, Lebensraum, Schicksal (Leipzig: F. A. Brockhaus, 1935), pp. 332–339. 1366

Schmieder, Oskar and Heinrich Schmitthenner, eds., Lebensraumfragen europäischer Völker, vol. 2, Europas koloniale Ergänzungsräume (Leipzig: Quelle & Meyer, 1941), pp. 271–353. 1367

Nelson, Helge M. O., "Svensk gruppkolonisation och svenskarnas deltagande i erövringen av Nordamerikas väster," Svensk geografisk årsbok, vol. 19 (1943), pp. 155–161. 1368

Nelson, Helge M. O., The Swedes and the Swedish Settlements in North America, vol. 1, Text; vol. 2, Atlas (Lund: C. W. K. Gleerup, 1943), 73 maps, 418 pp. 1369

Nelson, Helge M. O., "Den svenska folkstammen i Nordamerika," Svensk geografisk årsbok, vol. 24 (1948), pp. 7–30. [English summary] 1370

Totten, Don E., "Patterns of Group Occupance in the Manitoba–North Dakota Border Area," Master's thesis, University of Chicago, 1950. 1371

Evans, E. Estyn, "The Scotch-Irish in the New World: An Atlantic Heritage," Journal of the Royal Society of Antiquaries of Ireland, vol. 95 (1965), pp. 39–49. 1372

Evans, E. Estyn, "Cultural Relics of the Ulster-Scots in the Old West of North America," Ulster Folklife, vol. 12 (1965), pp. 33–38. 1373

Evans, E. Estyn, "Culture and Land Use in the Old West of North America," Heidelberger Geographische Arbeiten, vol. 15 (1966), pp. 72–80. 1374

Rosenvall, Lynn A., "Mormon Fortifications in Western North America," in Ronald M. Getty and Knut R. Fladmark, eds., Historical Archaeology in North-Western North America (Calgary: University of Calgary, Archaeology Association, 1973), pp. 195–212. 1375

Vance, James E., Jr., "The Classical Revival and
Urban-Rural Conflict in Nineteenth Century
North America," *Canadian Review of American
Studies*, vol. 4, 2 (1973), pp. 149–168.
                                                    1376

Gibson, James R., "Russian Sources for the Ethnohistory of the Pacific Coast of North America in
the Eighteenth and Nineteenth Centuries,"
Western Canadian Journal of Anthropology, vol.
6, 1 (1976), pp. 91–115.   1377

Gibson, James R., "Smallpox on the Northwest
Coast, 1835–1838," *B.C. Studies*, vol. 56 (1982–
1983), pp. 61–81.   1378

Hunter, John M., Gary W. Shannon, and Stephanie L. Sambrook, "Rings of Madness: Service
Areas of Nineteenth Century Asylums in North
America," *Social Science and Medicine*, vol. 23,
10 (1986), pp. 1033–1050.   1379

LeBlanc, Robert G., "A French-Canadian Education and the Persistence of La Franco-
Américanie," *Journal of Cultural Geography*,
vol. 8, 2 (1988), pp. 49–64.   1380

Canadian–United States comparisons

Foster, Richard H., Jr., "Changing Uses of Rural
Churches: Examples from Minnesota and
Manitoba," *Yearbook of the Association of Pacific Coast Geographers*, vol. 45 (1983), pp. 55–
70.   1381

Houston, Cecil J., and William J. Smyth, "Trans-
ferred Loyalties: Orangeism in the United States
and Canada," *American Review of Canadian
Studies*, vol. 14, 2 (1984), pp. 193–212.   1382

Overseas comparisons

Heimonen, Henry S., "Finnish Rural Culture in
South Ostrobothnia (Finland) and the Lake Superior Region (United States)," Ph.D. diss., University of Wisconsin–Madison, 1941.   1383

Pfeifer, Gottfried, "Deutsche bäuerliche Kolonisation in den Vereinigten Staaten und Brasilien:
Konvergenzen und Kontraste," in *Im Dienste
der Geographie und Kartographie: Symposium
Emil Meynen* (Cologne: Kölner Geographische
Arbeiten, vol. 30, 1973), pp. 37–54. Reprinted in
Kohlhepp, Gerd, ed., *Beiträge zur Kulturgeographie der Neuen Welt: Ausgewählte Arbeiten
von Gottfried Pfeifer* (Berlin: Dietrich Reimer,
1981), pp. 310–325.   1384

Harris, R. Cole, and Leonard T. Guelke, "Land and
Society in Early Canada and South Africa," *Journal of Historical Geography*, vol. 3, 2 (1977), pp.
135–154.   1385

Norton, William, "Comparative Cultural Analysis
on Nineteenth-Century Frontiers: Rationale and
Prospects," *National Geographical Journal of
India*, vol. 32 (1986), pp. 85–92. [Cape Province,
South Africa, and Southern Ontario]   1386

POLITICAL & ADMINISTRATIVE
GEOGRAPHY

The Canada–United States border

Winsor, Justin, *The Cartographical History of the
Northeastern Boundary Controversy between
the United States and Great Britain* (Cambridge: John Wilson and Son, 1887), 24 pp.   1387

Davis, John W., "The Unguarded Boundary,"
Geographical Review, vol. 12, 4 (1922), pp. 585–
601.   1388

Jones, Stephen B., "The Forty-Ninth Parallel in the
Great Plains: The Historical Geography of a
Boundary," *Journal of Geography*, vol. 31, 9
(1932), pp. 357–368. Reprinted in George J.
Miller, ed., *Human Geography Studies: The
United States* (Bloomington, Ill.: McKnight &
McKnight, Geographic Education Series, 1935),
pp. 180–191.   1389

Jones, Stephen B., "The Cordilleran Section of the
Canada-U.S. Borderland," *Geographical Journal*, vol. 89 (1937), pp. 439–450.   1390

DeVorsey, Louis, Jr., and Megan DeVorsey, "The
World Court Decision in the Canada–United
States Gulf of Maine Seaward Boundary Dis-
pute: A Perspective from Historical Geography,"
*Case Western Reserve Journal of International
Law*, vol. 18, 3 (1986), pp. 415–442.   1391

DeVorsey, Louis, Jr., "Historical Geography and
the Canada–United States Seaward Boundary
on Georges Bank," in Gerald Blake, ed., *Maritime Boundaries and Ocean Resources* (London: Croom-Helm, 1987), pp. 182–207.   1392

Other themes

Johnson, Hildegard Binder, "Zur historischen und
rechtlichen Problematik von Grenze und Fluß-
gebiet in Nordamerika," *Forschungen zu Staat
und Verfassung*, Festgabe für Fritz Hartung
(Berlin: Duncker and Humblot, 1958), pp. 307–
324.   1393

Juricek, John T., "English Territorial Claims in
North America under Elizabeth and the Early
Stuarts," *Terrae Incognitae*, vol. 7 (1976), pp. 7–
22.   1394

Gibson, James R., "Old Russia in the New World:
Adversaries and Adversities in Russian America," in James R. Gibson, ed., *European Settle-*

ment and Development in North America: Essays on Geographical Change in Honour and Memory of Andrew Hill Clark (Toronto: University of Toronto Press, 1978), pp. 46–65.
1395

Gibson, James R., "The Significance of Cook's Third Voyage to Russian Tenure in the North Pacific," Pacific Studies, vol. 1, 2 (1978), pp. 119–146.
1396

Chardon, Roland E., "The Linear League in North America," Annals of the Association of American Geographers, vol. 70, 2 (1980), pp. 129–153.
1397

Fletcher, Roy J., "Military Radar Defence Lines of Northern North America: An Historical Geography," Polar Record, vol. 26, 159 (1990), pp. 265–276.
1398

ECONOMIC DEVELOPMENT

General

Deckert, Emil, "Die Ströme im nordamerikanischen Wirtschaftsleben," in Georg Kollm, ed., Verhandlungen des vierzehnten Deutschen Geographentages zu Cöln, 1903 (Berlin: Dietrich Reimer, 1903), pp. 126–141.
1399

Windhorst, Hans-Wilhelm, "Wandlungen in der wirtschaftlichen Inwertsetzung der nordamerikanischen Prärien und Great Plains," Zeitschrift für Wirtschaftsgeographie, vol. 21, 1 (1977), pp. 4–16.
1400

Canada–United States comparisons & borderlands

Jackson, W. A. Douglas, "The Lands along the Upper St. Lawrence: Canadian-American Development during the Nineteenth Century," Ph.D. diss., University of Maryland, 1952.
1401

Kellogg, James E., "The Impact of the Railroad upon a Frontier Region: The Case of Alaska and the Yukon," Ph.D. diss., Indiana State University, 1975.
1402

Gough, Barry, "Canadian and American Frontiers: Some Comments, Comparisons, and a Case Study (British Columbia and California in the Mid-1800s)," in M. C. Brown and Graeme Wynn, eds., The Bellingham Collection of Geographical Studies (Vancouver: Tantalus Research, B.C. Geographical Series, no. 27, 1979), pp. 7–17.
1403

Craig, Beatrice, "Agriculture and the Lumberman's Frontier in the Upper St. John Valley, 1800–1870," Journal of Forest History, vol. 32 (1988), pp. 125–137.
1404

RESOURCE MANAGEMENT

Lee, Lawrence, "The Canadian-American Irrigation Frontier, 1884–1914," Agricultural History, vol. 40 (1966), pp. 271–284.
1405

Williams, Michael, "Thinking about the Forest: A Comparative View from Three Continents," in Susan Flader, ed., The Great Lakes Forest: An Environmental and Social History (Minneapolis: University of Minnesota Press, 1983), pp. 253–273.
1406

Wynn, Graeme, "New Views of the Great Forest," Canadian Geographer, vol. 34, 2 (1990), pp. 175–185.
1407

EXTRACTIVE ACTIVITY

Fisheries

Bartz, Fritz, Fischgründe und Fischereiwirtschaft an der Westküste Nordamerikas: Werdegang, Lebens- und Siedlungsformen eines jungen Wirtschaftsraumes (Kiel: Schriften des Geographischen Instituts der Universität Kiel, no. 12, 1942), 175 pp. [Focus on 1864–1940]
1408

Rostlund, Erhard, Freshwater Fish and Fishing in Native North America (Berkeley: University of California Publications in Geography, vol. 9, 1952), 314 pp.
1409

Bartz, Fritz, "Das Fischereigebiet der Grossen Seen Nordamerikas," Geographica Helvetica, vol. 8 (1953), pp. 303–316.
1410

Fur trade

Gibson, James R., "The Russian Fur Trade," in Carol M. Judd and Arthur J. Ray, eds., Old Trails and New Directions: Papers of the Third North American Fur Trade Conference (Toronto: University of Toronto Press, 1980), pp. 217–230.
1411

Ray, Arthur J., "The Fur Trade in North America: An Overview from an Historical and Geographical Perspective" in Resource Management and the North American Fur Trade (Toronto: Ontario Ministry of National Resources; Wildlife Branch, 1987), pp. 13–21.
1412

Gibson, James R., "Furs and Food: Russian America and the Hudson's Bay Company," Columbia: The Magazine of Northwest History, vol. 4, 2 (1990), 3–9. Reprinted in Barbara Sweetland Smith and Redmond J. Barnett, eds., Russian America: The Forgotten Frontier (Tacoma: Washington State Historical Society, 1990), pp. 41–53.
1413

AGRICULTURE

Brigham, Albert P., "The Development of Wheat Culture in North America," *Geographical Journal*, vol. 35 (1910), pp. 42–55.   1414

Baker, Oliver E., "Agricultural Regions of North America," an eleven-part work which appeared serially in *Economic Geography*, from 1926 to 1932; most parts deal with regions defined wholly within the United States (and are individually listed in the UNITED STATES section), but one part includes significant portions of the prairie provinces of Canada: "Part VI: The Spring Wheat Region," vol. 4, 4 (1928), pp. 399–433.   1415

Sauer, Carl O., "The March of Agriculture across the Western World," Abstract published in *Proceedings of the Eighth American Scientific Congress* (1942), pp. 63–65; full paper first published in Carl O. Sauer, *Selected Essays, 1963–1975*, ed. Bob Callahan (Berkeley, Calif.: Turtle Island Foundation, for the Netzahaulcoyotl Historical Society, 1981), pp. 45–56.   1416

Gibson, James R., "Food for the Fur Traders: The First Farmers in the Pacific Northwest, 1805–1846," *Journal of the West*, vol. 7, 1 (1968), pp. 18–30.   1417

Gibson, James R., *Farming the Frontier: The Agricultural Opening of the Oregon Country, 1786–1846* (Vancouver: University of British Columbia Press, 1985), 265 pp.   1418

Smith, David C., et al., "Salt Marshes as a Factor in the Agriculture of Northeastern North America," *Agricultural History*, vol. 63, 2 (1989), pp. 270–294.   1419

Overseas comparisons

Lewthwaite, Gordon R., "Wisconsin and the Waikato: A Comparative Study of Dairy Farming in the United States and New Zealand," *Annals of the Association of American Geographers* vol. 54, 1 (1964), pp. 59–87.   1420

Heller, Charles F., "The Role of Wheat in Nineteenth Century Middle-Latitude Settlement: Examples from Canterbury and Michigan," *Australian Geographical Studies*, vol. 4, 2 (1966), pp. 96–118.   1421

Gibson, James R., *Imperial Russia in Frontier America: The Changing Geography of Supply of Russian America, 1784–1867* (New York: Oxford University Press, 1976), 257 pp.   1422

LANDSCAPE

Norris, Darrell A., "Ontario Fences and the American Scene," *American Review of Canadian Studies*, vol. 12, 2 (1982), pp. 37–50.   1423

Noble, Allen G., *Wood, Brick, and Stone: The North American Settlement Landscape*, vol. 1, *Houses*; vol. 2, *Barns and Farm Structures* (Amherst: University of Massachusetts Press, 1984), 160 and 186 pp.   1424

Harris, R. Cole, "French Landscapes in North America," in Michael P. Conzen, ed., *The Making of the American Landscape* (Boston: Unwin Hyman, 1990), pp. 63–79.   1425

Overseas comparisons

Wilson, Eugene M., "Some Similarities between American and European Folk Houses," *Pioneer America*, vol. 3, 2 (1976), pp. 8–14.   1426

Ennals, Peter M., "The Vernacular Revolution in Architecture: A Cross Cultural Comparison [Canada-Japan]," *Annual Studies*, Kwansei Gakuin University, vol. 36 (1987), pp. 85–95.   1427

COMMUNICATIONS

Blum, I., "Geographie und Geschichte im Verkehrs- und Siedlungswesen Nordamerikas," *Archiv für Eisenbahnwesen*, vol. 2 (Mar.-Apr. 1934), pp. 241–286; vol. 3 (May-June 1934), pp. 553–616.   1428

McIlwraith, Thomas F., Jr., "The Logistical Geography of the Great Lakes Grain Trade, 1820–1850," Ph.D. diss., University of Wisconsin-Madison, 1973.   1429

Hurst, Michael E., "The Railway Epoch and the North American Landscape," in J. Wreford Watson and Timothy O'Riordan, eds., *The American Environment: Perceptions and Policies* (New York: Wiley, 1976), pp. 183–206.   1430

McIlwraith, Thomas F., Jr., "Freight Capacity and Utilization of the Erie and Great Lakes Canals before 1850," *Journal of Economic History*, vol. 36, 4 (1976), pp. 852–877.   1431

Kaye, Barry, "The Trade in Livestock between the Red River Settlement and the American Frontier, 1812–1870," *Prairie Forum*, vol. 6, 2 (1981), pp. 163–182.   1432

Jackson, John N., "The Erie and Welland Canals: A Comparative Evaluation," in *Publication no. 4*, St. Catherines Historical Museum (1984), pp. 51–71.   1433

External trade & overseas comparisons

Meinig, Donald W., "A Comparative Historical Geography of Two Railnets: Columbia Basin and South Australia," *Annals of the Association of American Geographers*, vol. 52, 3 (1962), pp. 394–413.   1434

Abler, Ronald F., and Thomas Falk, "Development and Diffusion of Communications Technologies in Sweden and the United States," in Bjorn Fjaestad, ed., *Planera Numera* (Stockholm: Riksbankens Jubileumsfond, 1979), pp. 20–24.   1435

Gibson, James R., "The Maritime Trade of the North Pacific Coast," in Wilcomb E. Washburn, ed., *History of Indian-White Relations* (Washington, D.C.: Smithsonion Institution, Handbook of North American Indians, vol. 4, 1988), pp. 375–390.   1436

MANUFACTURING & INDUSTRIALIZATION

Clark, Ivan S., "An Isolated Industry: Pottery of North America," *Journal of Geography*, vol. 25, 9 (1926), pp. 222–228.   1437

Lukermann, Fred E., "The Changing Pattern of Cement Mill Location in North America," *Przeglad Geograficzny*, vol. 32, 4 (1960), pp. 537–559.   1438

URBAN NETWORKS & URBANIZATION

Gley, Werner, *Die Großstädte Nordamerikas und die Ursachen ihrer Entwicklung* (Frankfort: Frankfurter Geographische Hefte, vol. 1, 2, 1927), 96 pp.   1439

Bobek, Hans, "Die nordamerikanischen Kleinstädte und ihre Entwicklung," *Mitteilungen der Geographische Gesellschaft in Wien*, vol. 73 (1930), pp. 60–64.   1440

Krim, Arthur J. "The Innovation and Diffusion of the Street Railway in North America," Master's thesis, University of Chicago, 1967.   1441

Hofmeister, Burkhard, *Stadt und Kulturraum Angloamerika* (Braunschweig: Friedrich Vieweg und Sohn, 1971), 341 pp.   1442

Muller, Edward K., "Regional Urbanization and the Selective Growth of Towns in North American Regions," *Journal of Historical Geography*, vol. 3, 1 (1977), pp. 21–40.   1443

Denecke, Dietrich, "Die multifunktionale Siedlung mit überörtlichen funktionalen Beziehungsfeldern im östlichen Nordamerika des 18. und 19. Jahrhunderts: Entstehung, Planung und Entwicklung in Abhängigkeit von der Art und dem Entwicklungsstand räumlicher Siedlungsmuster," *Frankfurter Wirtschafts- und Sozialgeographische Schriften*, vol. 28 (1978), pp. 141–169.   1444

Ward, David, "The Place of Victorian Cities in Developmental Typologies of Urbanization," in John Patten, ed., *Urbanism and Urbanization* (London: Academic Press, 1983), pp. 355–379.   1445

Radford, John P., "Regional Ideologies and Urban Growth on the Victorian Periphery: Southern Ontario and the U.S. South," in David Ward and John Radford, *North American Cities in the Victorian Age* (Norwich, England: Geo Books, Historical Geography Research Series, no. 12, 1983), pp. 32–57.   1446

URBAN ECONOMIC STRUCTURE

Sharpless, John B., "The Economic Structure of Port Cities in the Mid-Nineteenth Century: Boston and Liverpool, 1840–1860," *Journal of Historical Geography*, vol. 2, 2 (1976), pp. 131–144.   1447

Doucet, Michael J., "Urban Land Development in Nineteenth-Century North America," *Journal of Urban History*, vol. 8, 3 (1982), pp. 299–342.   1448

URBAN SOCIAL STRUCTURE

General

Ward, David, "Victorian Cities: How Modern?" *Journal of Historical Geography*, vol. 1, 2 (1975), pp. 135–151.   1449

Ward, David, and John P. Radford, *North American Cities in the Victorian Age* (Norwich, England: Geo Books, Historical Geography Research Series, no. 12, 1983), 57 pp.   1450

Selected themes

Astles, Allen R., "The Evolution and Role of Historic and Architectural Preservation in the North American City," Master's thesis, Simon Fraser University, 1972.   1451

Ward, David, "The North American Ghetto," *Geographical Magazine*, vol. 54, 7 (1982), pp. 376–380.   1452

Southall, Humphrey, "British Artisan Unions in the New World," *Journal of Historical Geography*, vol. 15, 2 (1989), pp. 163–182.   1453

Overseas comparisons

Ward, David, "The Victorian Slum: An Enduring Myth?" *Annals of the Association of American Geographers*, vol. 66, 2 (1976), pp. 323–336.   1454

Ward, David, "The Early Victorian City in England and America: On the Parallel Development of an Urban Image," in James R. Gibson, ed., *European Settlement and Development in North America: Essays in Geographical Change in Honour and Memory of Andrew Hill Clark* (Toronto: University of Toronto Press, 1978), pp. 170–189.   1455

Bouman, Mark J., "City Lights and City Life: A Study of Technology and Urbanity," Ph.D. diss.,

University of Minnesota, 1984. [Focus on Minneapolis; Sheffield, England; and Bochum, Germany, in the nineteenth century]   **1456**

Bouman, Mark J., "Luxury and Control: The Urbanity of Street Lighting in Three Nineteenth Century Cities," *Journal of Urban History*, vol. 14, 1 (1987), pp. 7–37. [Focus on Minneapolis; Sheffield, England; and Bochum, Germany]   **1457**

Ward, David, "The Progressives and the Urban Questions: British and American Responses to the Inner City Slums, 1880–1920," *Transactions of the Institute of British Geographers*, n.s. vol. 9 (1984), pp. 299–314.   **1458**

Harris, Richard S., and Chris Hamnett, "The Myth of the Promised Land: The Social Diffusion of Home Ownership in Britain and North America," *Annals of the Association of American Geographers*, vol. 77, 2 (1987), pp. 173–190.   **1459**

TOWNSCAPE

Boesch, Hans, "Schachbrett-Texturen nordamerikanischer Siedlungen," in Herbert Wilhelmy, ed., *Hermann Lautensach-Festschrift* (Stuttgart: Stuttgarter Geographische Studien, no. 69, 1957), pp. 337–344.   **1460**

Louder, Dean R., "Vieux-carré et vieux Québec: Vestiges urbaines de l'Amérique française," *Cahiers de géographie de Québec*, vol. 23, 59 (1979), pp. 303–316.   **1461**

Doucet, Michael J., and John C. Weaver, "Material Culture and the North American House: The Era of the Common Man, 1870–1920," *Journal of American History*, vol. 72 (1985), pp. 560–587.   **1462**

Hall, Nigel, "The Development of Street Form in North America from 1880 to 1930," Master's thesis, University of Toronto, 1986.   **1463**

Lai, David Chuen-yan, "Cityscape of Old Chinatowns in North America," in Paul Groth, ed., *Vision, Culture, and Landscape: Working Papers from the Berkeley Symposium on Cultural Landscape Interpretation* (Berkeley: Department of Landscape Architecture, University of California–Berkeley, 1990), pp. 77–97.   **1464**

Linteau, Paul-André, "Canadian Suburbanization in a North American Context: Does the Border Make a Difference?" in Gilbert A. Stelter, ed., *Cities and Urbanization: Canadian Historical Perspective* (Toronto: Copp Clark Pitman, 1990), pp. 208–224.   **1465**

Overseas comparisons

Ward, David, "A Comparative Historical Geography of Streetcar Suburbs in Boston, Massachusetts, and Leeds, England: 1850–1920," *Annals of the Association of American Geographers*, vol. 54, 4 (1964), pp. 477–489.   **1466**

RECREATION & TOURISM

Innes, Frank C., "On the Relevance of an Accurate Reconstruction of Pioneer America," *Proceedings of the Pioneer America Society*, vol. 1 (1973), pp. 130–132.   **1467**

Demars, Stanford E., "Morphology of North American Seaside Resorts: The British Connection," *Proceedings of the New England–St. Lawrence Valley Division, Association of American Geographers*, vol. 8 (1978), pp. 23–29.   **1468**

Jakle, John A., *The Tourist: Travel in Twentieth Century North America* (Lincoln: University of Nebraska Press, 1985), 382 pp.   **1469**

PLACE NAMES

Russell, Israel C., "The Names of the Larger Geographical Features of North America," *Bulletin of the Geographical Society of Philadelphia*, vol. 2 (1899), pp. 55–59.   **1470**

Ganong, William F., "The Origin of the Place-Names Acadia and Norumbega," *Proceedings and Transactions of the Royal Society of Canada*, 3d ser., vol. 11, sec. 2 (1917), pp. 105–111.   **1471**

Holmer, Nils M., *Indian Place Names in North America* (Upsala: Lundequistka Bokhandeln; and Cambridge, Mass.: Harvard University Press, for the American Institute in the University of Upsala, Essays and Studies on American Language and Literature, no. 7, 1948), 44 pp.   **1472**

Phillips, James W., *Alaska-Yukon Place Names* (Seattle: University of Washington Press, 1973), 149 pp.   **1473**

Diament, Henri, "La toponymis français de l'Amérique du Nord," *Proceedings of the French Colonial Historical Society*, vol. 11, 1 (1985), pp. 3–11.   **1474**

Poirier, Jean, "Vers un répertoire des noms de lieux français en Amérique du Nord," *Proceedings of the French Colonial Historical Society*, vol. 11, 1 (1985), pp. 13–17.   **1475**

Landelius, Otto R., *Swedish Place Names in North America* (Carbondale: Southern Illinois University Press, 1985), 372 pp.   **1476**

Jackson, John N., "Canadian and American Names across the Niagara Boundary," *Canoma*, vol. 16, 1 (1990), pp. 33–41.   **1477**

Mackintosh, Anne, "The Thousand Islands and Their Canadian and American Toponymy," *Canoma*, vol. 16, 1 (1990), pp. 28–32.   **1478**

PART IV

CANADA

——————— CANADA AS A WHOLE ———————

GENERAL

See also 1144

Synthetic treatments

Hodgins, John G., *The Geography and History of British America, and of the Other Colonies of the British Empire* (Toronto and Montreal: Mc-Lear & Co., 1857), 129 pp. Revised 1858, 1866. **1479**

Nederkorn, W., "Die Entdeckungs, Besiedlungs-und Entwicklungsgeschichte Canadas und seiner Grenzgebiete," *Deutsche Geographische Blätter*, vol. 22, 1 (1899), pp. 1–30; 2, pp. 86–124; and 3, pp. 170–201. **1480**

Lucas, Charles P., ed. *Historical Geography of the British Colonies*, vol. 5, *Canada* (Oxford: Clarendon Press, 1901–1911), 302 pp.; pt. 1, "New France," by Charles P. Lucas (1901); pt. 2, "Historical," by Hugh E. Edgerton (1908); pt. 3, "Geographical," by J. D. Rogers (1911); pt. 4, "Newfoundland," by J. D. Rogers (1911). **1481**

George, Rev. Hereford B., "Canada," in his *A Historical Geography of the British Empire* (London: Methuen & Co., 1904), pp. 144–178. **1482**

Newbigin, Marian I., *Canada: The Great River, the Lands, and the Men* (London: Christophers, 1926), 308 pp. [Focus on the period up to 1763] **1483**

Taylor, T. Griffith, "Fundamental Factors in Canadian Geography," *Canadian Geographical Journal*, vol. 12 (1936), pp. 161–171. **1484**

Taylor, T. Griffith, *Canada: A Study of Cool Continental Environments and Their Effects on British and French Settlement* (New York: E. P. Dutton, 1947), 526 pp. **1485**

Clark, Andrew Hill, "Geographical Diversity and the Personality of Canada," in M. McCaskill, ed., *Land and Livelihood: Geographical Essays in Honour of George Jobberns* (Christchurch, N.Z.: New Zealand Geographical Society, 1962), pp. 23–47. Reprinted in Robert M. Irving, ed., *Readings in Canadian Geography* (Toronto: Holt, Rinehart and Winston, 1972), pp. 3–16. **1486**

Gentilcore, R. Louis, ed., *Canada's Changing Geography: A Selection of Readings* (Scarborough, Ont.: Prentice-Hall Canada, 1967), 224 pp. **1487**

Nicholson, Norman L., "Human Geography and the Development of the Canadian Nation," in José A. Sporck, ed. *Mélanges de géographie*

physique, humaine, économique, appliqué offerts à M. Omer Tulippe, vol. 1 (Gembloux, Belgium: Éditions J. Duculot, 1967), pp. 589–596. **1488**

Clark, Andrew Hill, and Donald Q. Innis, "The Roots of Canada's Geography," in John H. Warkentin, ed., *Canada: A Geographical Interpretation* (Toronto: Methuen, 1968), pp. 13–53. **1489**

Woodcock, George, "Canada: The Demanding Land," *Geographical Magazine*, vol. 42, 2 (1969), pp. 105–114. **1490**

McCann, Larry D., ed., *Heartland and Hinterland: A Geography of Canada* (Toronto: Prentice-Hall, 1982), 500 pp. Revised 1987. **1491**

Lenz, Karl, *Kanada: Eine geographische Landeskunde* (Darmstadt: Wissenschaftliche Buchgesellschaft, 1988), 489 pp. **1492**

Courville, Serge, "Note critique: A mari usque ad mare: La grande saga canadienne," *Revue d'histoire de l'Amérique française*, vol. 42, 3 (1989), pp. 429–439. **1493**

Wynn, Graeme, ed., *People, Places, Patterns, Processes: Geographical Perspectives on the Canadian Past* (Toronto: Copp Clark Pitman, 1990), 373 pp. **1494**

Pre-Confederation period

Harris, R. Cole, and John H. Warkentin, *Canada before Confederation: A Study in Historical Geography* (New York: Oxford University Press, 1974), 338 pp. Reprinted Ottawa: Carleton University Press, 1991. **1495**

Harris, R. Cole, "The Pattern of Early Canada," *Canadian Geographer*, vol. 31, 4 (1987), pp. 290–298. Reprinted in revised form in Graeme Wynn, ed., *People, Places, Patterns, Processes: Geographical Perspectives on the Canadian Past* (Toronto: Copp Clark Pitman, 1990), pp. 358–373. **1496**

McIlwraith, Thomas F., Jr., "British North America, 1763–1867," in Robert D. Mitchell and Paul A. Groves, eds., *North America: The Historical Geography of a Changing Continent* (Totowa, N.J.: Rowman & Littlefield, 1987), pp. 220–253. **1497**

Wynn, Graeme, "On the Margins of Empire (1760–1840)," in Craig Brown, ed., *The Illustrated History of Canada* (Toronto: Lester and Orpen Dennys, 1987), pp. 189–278. Translated and revised as "Aux confins de l'empire, 1760–1860," in

Histoire générale du Canada, by L. A. Linteau (Montreal: Éditions du Boreal, 1988 and 1990), pp. 223–331. Paper ed. Toronto: Lester Publishing, 1991.   **1498**

Post-Confederation period

Wynn, Graeme, "Forging a Canadian Nation," in Robert D. Mitchell and Paul A. Groves, eds., *North America: The Historical Geography of a Changing Continent* (Totowa, N.J.: Rowman & Littlefield, 1987), pp. 373–409.   **1499**

Selected themes

Whitbeck, Ray H., "The St. Lawrence River and Its Part in the Making of Canada," *Bulletin of the American Geographical Society*, vol. 47, 8 (1915), pp. 584–593.   **1500**

Deffontaines, Pierre, *L'homme et l'hiver au Canada* (Paris: Gallimard, 1957), 293 pp.   **1501**

Burghardt, Andrew F., "Canada and the World," in John H. Warkentin, ed., *Canada: A Geographical Interpretation* (Toronto: Methuen, 1968), pp. 569–582.   **1502**

Clark, Andrew Hill, "The Canadian Habitat," in R. H. Buchanan, Emrys Jones, and Desmond McCourt, eds., *Man and His Habitat: Essays Presented to E. Estyn Evans* (London: Routledge and Kegan Paul Press, 1971), pp. 218–246.   **1503**

Warkentin, John H., "The Shape of Canada," *Arts Canada*, vol. 31, 1 (1974), pp. 17–35.   **1504**

Clark, Andrew Hill, "The Look of Canada," *Historical Geography*, vol. 6, 1 (1976), pp. 59–68.   **1505**

Faucher, Albert, "Les politiques nationales et l'espace transcontinental dans l'histoire canadienne," *Transactions of the Royal Society of Canada*, 4th ser., vol. 14 (1976), pp. 149–161.   **1506**

Tremblay, Marc-Adélard, "Espaces géographiques et distance culturelle: Essai de définition du fondement des mentalités régionales au Québec," *Transactions of the Royal Society of Canada*, 4th ser., vol. 14 (1976), pp. 131–147.   **1507**

Careless, J. Maurice S., "Metropolis and Region: The Interplay between City and Region in Canadian History before 1914," *Urban History Review*, no. 3–78 (1978), pp. 99–118.   **1508**

Harris, R. Cole, "Regionalism and the Canadian Archipelago," in Larry D. McCann, ed., *Heartland and Hinterland: A Geography of Canada* (Scarborough: Prentice-Hall Canada, 1982), pp. 459–484; Revised ed. 1987, pp. 532–559. Reprinted in James M. Bumsted, ed., *Interpreting Canada's Past*, vol. 2, *After Confederation* (Toronto: Oxford University Press, 1986), pp. 453–471.   **1509**

Holdsworth, Deryck W., "Dependence, Diversity, and the Canadian Identity," *Journal of Geography*, vol. 83, 4 (1984), pp. 199–204.   **1510**

Harris, Richard S., "Home Ownership and Class in Modern Canada," *International Journal of Urban and Regional Research*, vol. 10, 1 (1986), pp. 67–86.   **1511**

Wynn, Graeme, ed., *Interpreting Canada: Four Essays* (Vancouver: Tantalus Research, B.C. Geographical Series, no. 43, 1986), 94 pp.   **1512**

Waddell, Eric W., "La grande famille canadienne-française: Divorce et réconciliation," in J. Tessier and P. L. Vaillancourt, eds., *Les autres littératures d'expression française en Amérique du Nord* (Ottawa: Université d'Ottawa, 1987), pp. 9–18.   **1513**

Bernier, Jacques, "Pluralism and National Unity," in Guy M. Robinson, ed., *A Social Geography of Canada: Essays in Honour of J. Wreford Watson* (Edinburgh: North British Publishing, 1988), pp. 29–46. Also Toronto: Durdurn Press, 1991, pp. 61–81.   **1514**

Careless, J. Maurice S., *Frontier and Metropolis: Regions, Cities, and Identities in Canada before 1914* (Toronto: University of Toronto Press, 1989), 132 pp.   **1515**

NATIVE PEOPLES & WHITE RELATIONS

General

Müller-Wille, Ludger, "Indianer und Land im Expansions- und Integrationsbestreben des Staates Kanada," in Alfred Pletsch and Carl Schott, eds., *Kanada: Naturraum und Entwicklungspotential* (Marburg: Marburger Geographische Schriften, vol. 79, 1979), pp. 57–76.   **1516**

Ray, Arthur J., "When Two Worlds Met," in C. Brown, ed., *The Illustrated History of Canada* (Toronto: Lester and Orpen Dennys, 1987), pp. 17–104.   **1517**

Native cartography

Moodie, D. Wayne, "Native Mapmaking," *New Canadian Encyclopedia*, vol. 1 (Edmonton: Hurtig, 1985), p. 294.   **1518**

Geographical distribution

Heidenreich, Conrad E., "Mapping the Location of Native Groups, 1600–1760," *Mapping History*, vol. 2 (1981), pp. 6–13.   **1519**

Selected themes

Ray, Arthur J., "Indians as Consumers in the Eighteenth Century," in Carol M. Judd and Arthur J. Ray, eds., *Old Trails and New Directions: Papers of the Third North American Fur Trade Confer-*

ence (Toronto: University of Toronto Press, 1980), pp. 255–271. **1520**

Ray, Arthur J., "Native Economic Dependency: Searching for the Evidence," in *Overcoming Economic Dependency: Papers and Comments from the First Newberry Library Conference on Themes in American Indian History* (Chicago: Newberry Library, Center for the History of the American Indian, Occasional Papers in Curriculum, no. 9, 1988), pp. 95–100. **1521**

Moodie, D. Wayne, "Manomin: Historical Geographical Perspectives on the Ojibway Production of Wild Rice," in Jean Friesen and Kerry Abel, eds., *Aboriginal Resource Use in Canada: Historical and Legal Aspects* (Winnipeg: University of Manitoba Press, 1991), pp. 71–79. **1522**

EXPLORATION & MAPPING

All entries dealing with the early discoveries of "America" (including the territory of present-day Canada) will be found under NORTH AMERICA

General

Morison, Samuel Eliot, *Samuel de Champlain: Father of New France* (Boston: Little, Brown & Co., 1972), 299 pp. **1523**

Heidenreich, Conrad E., "Measures of Distance Employed on Seventeenth and Early Eighteenth Century Maps of Canada," *Canadian Cartographer*, vol. 12, 2 (1976), pp. 121–137. **1524**

Heidenreich, Conrad E., "Some General Observations on Canadian Seventeenth Century Maps as Travel Literature," *University of Ottawa Quarterly*, vol. 48, 1–2 (1978), pp. 6–11. **1525**

Gentilcore, R. Louis, "The Use of Maps in the Historical Geography of Canada," in Barbara Farrell and Aileen Desbarats, eds., *Explorations in the History of Canadian Mapping: A Collection of Essays* (Ottawa: Association of Canadian Map Libraries and Archives, 1988), pp. 21–32. **1526**

General history of Canadian cartography

Marcel, Gabriel, "Cartographie de la Nouvelle France," *Revue de géographie*, vol. 11 (1885), pp. 1–41. Reprinted in *Acta cartographica*, vol. 4 (1969), pp. 349–388. **1527**

Hay, J. C., and R. D. Davidson, "A Brief History of Mapping in Canada," *Canadian Surveyor*, vol. 10 (1951), pp. 24–29. **1528**

Layng, Theodore E., "Highlights in the Mapping of Canada," *Canadian Library*, vol. 16, 6 (1960), pp. 283–288. **1529**

Layng, Theodore E., "The First Line in the Cartography of Canada," *Canadian Surveyor*, vol. 18, 1 (1964), pp. 67–75. **1530**

Thomson, Don W., *Men and Meridians: The History of Surveying and Mapping in Canada*, 3 vols. (Ottawa: Queen's Printer, 1966), 1057 pp. **1531**

Ruggles, Richard I., "Research on the History of Cartography and Historical Cartography of Canada: Retrospect and Prospect," *Proceedings of the Annual Conference of the Association of Canadian Map Libraries*, vol. 10 (1976), pp. 15–23. Reprinted in *Canadian Surveyor*, vol. 31, 1 (1977), pp. 25–33. **1532**

Wilson, A. Virginia, and D. S. C. Mackay, "Mapping Canada's History," *Canadian Cartographer*, vol. 15, 1 (1978), pp. 13–22. **1533**

Fahmy, Jean, "The Birth of Canadian Cartography," *Bulletin of the Association of Canadian Map Libraries*, vol. 46 (1983), pp. 27–39. **1534**

Fillmore, Stanley, and R. W. Sandilands, *The Chartmakers: A History of Nautical Surveying in Canada* (Toronto: NC Press, 1983), 255 pp. **1535**

Farrell, Barbara, and Aileen Desbarats, eds. *Explorations in the History of Canadian Mapping: A Collection of Essays* (Ottawa: Association of Canadian Map Libraries and Archives, 1988), 274 pp. **1536**

Development of government mapping

Evans, Geraint N. D., *Uncommon Obdurate: The Several Public Careers of J. F. W. DesBarres* (Toronto: University of Toronto Press, 1969), 130 pp. **1537**

Sebert, Lou M., *Every Square Inch: The Story of Canadian Topographic Mapping* (Ottawa: Department of Energy, Mines, and Resources, 1970), 25 pp. **1538**

Sebert, Lou M., "The History of the 1:250,000 Map of Canada," *Canadian Cartographer*, vol. 7, 1 (1970), pp. 15–26. **1539**

Winearls, Joan, "Federal Electoral Maps of Canada, 1867–1970," *Canadian Cartographer*, vol. 9, 1 (1972), pp. 1–24. **1540**

Nicholson, Norman L., "The Evolving Nature of National and Regional Atlases," *Bulletin of the Special Libraries Association Geography and Map Division*, no. 94 (1973), pp. 20–25. **1541**

Military cartography

Marshall, Douglas W., "The British Military Engineers, 1741–1783: A Study of Organization, Social Origin, and Cartography," Ph.D. diss., University of Michigan, 1976. **1542**

Commercial mapmaking

Verner, Coolie, "The Arrowsmith Firm and the Cartography of Canada," *Proceedings of the Annual Conference of the Association of Cana-*

dian Map Libraries, vol. 4 (1970), pp. 16–21. Reprinted in Barbara Farrell and Aileen Desbarats, eds., *Explorations in the History of Canadian Mapping: A Collection of Essays* (Ottawa: Association of Canadian Map Libraries and Archives, 1988), pp. 47–54.   **1543**

Rural landownership mapping

Sitwell, O. F. George, "County Maps of the Nineteenth Century as Historical Documents," *Proceedings of the Second Annual Conference of the Association of Canadian Map Libraries* (1968), pp. 49–70.   **1544**

Layng, Theodore, Introduction to Betty May, comp., *County Atlases of Canada: A Descriptive Catalogue* (Ottawa: Public Archives of Canada, National Map Collection, 1970), pp. i-iv.   **1545**

Sitwell, O. F. George, "County Maps of the Nineteenth Century as Historical Documents: A New Use," *Canadian Cartographer*, vol. 7, 1 (1970), pp. 27–41.   **1546**

Corbett, B., "County Atlases," *Canadian Antiques Collector*, vol. 6, 3 (1971), pp. 6–9.   **1547**

Winearls, D. Joan, "Nineteenth Century County Land Ownership Maps of Canada: An Introductory Essay," in Heather Maddick, comp., *County Maps: Land Ownership Maps of Canada in the Nineteenth Century* (Ottawa: Public Archives of Canada, National Map Collection, 1976), pp. 1–16.   **1548**

Urban cartography

Hayward, Robert J., "Insurance Plans and Land Use Atlases: Sources for Urban Historical Research," *Urban History Review*, vol. 1 (1973), pp. 2–9.   **1549**

Hayward, Robert J., "Charles E. Goad and Fire Insurance Cartography," *Proceedings of the Annual Conference of the Association of Canadian Map Libraries*, vol. 8 (1974), pp. 51–72. Reprinted in Barbara Farrell and Eileen Desbarats, eds., *Explorations in the History of Canadian Mapping: A Collection of Essays* (Ottawa: Association of Canadian Map Libraries and Archives, 1988), pp. 179–192.   **1550**

Bloomfield, Gerald T., "Canadian Fire Insurance Plans and Industrial Archeology," *IA: The Journal of the Society for Industrial Archeology*, vol. 8, 1 (1982), pp. 67–80.   **1551**

POPULAR IMAGES & EVALUATION

Watson, J. Wreford, "Canadian Regionalism in Life and Letters," *Geographical Journal*, vol. 131, 1 (1965), pp. 21–33. Reprinted in R. Louis Gentilcore, ed., *Canada's Changing Geography* (Scar-

borough, Ont.: Prentice-Hall of Canada, 1967), pp. 213–224.   **1552**

Brouillette, Benoît, "Paysages d'autrefois," *Revue de géographie de Montréal*, vol. 20, 1–2 (1966), pp. 47–58.   **1553**

Harris, R. Cole, "The Myth of the Land in Canadian Nationalism," in Peter Russell, ed., *Nationalism in Canada* (Toronto: McGraw-Hill, 1966), pp. 27–43.   **1554**

Merrill, Gordon C., "Regionalism and Nationalism," in John H. Warkentin, ed., *Canada: A Geographical Interpretation* (Toronto: Methuen, 1968), pp. 556–568.   **1555**

Watson, J. Wreford, "The Image of Canada," *Bulletin of Canadian Studies*, vol. 1, 1 (1977), pp. 1–14.   **1556**

Harris, R. Cole, "The Emotional Structure of Canadian Regionalism," in *The Challenge of Canada's Regional Diversity* (Toronto: Canada Studies Foundation, Walter L. Gordon Lecture Series, vol. 5, 1980–1981), pp. 9–30.   **1557**

McCann, Larry D., "The Myth of the Metropolis: The Role of the City in Canadian Regionalism," *Urban History Review*, vol. 9, 3 (1981), pp. 52–58.   **1558**

Morrison, Carolyn, "Perception of the City: The Urban Image in Canadian Fiction," Master's thesis, University of British Columbia, 1981.   **1559**

Armour, L., "Canada and the Idea of Nature: An Interpretation," in Graeme Wynn, ed., *Interpreting Canada: Four Essays* (Vancouver: Tantalus Research, B.C. Geographical Series, no. 43, 1986), pp. 43–66.   **1560**

Meinig, Donald W., "Interpreting Canada: An American View" in Graeme Wynn, ed., *Interpreting Canada: Four Essays* (Vancouver: Tantalus Research, B.C. Geographical Series, no. 43, 1986), pp. 27–42.   **1561**

Osborne, Brian S., "The Iconography of Nationhood in Canadian Art," in Dennis Cosgrove and Stephen Daniels, eds., *The Iconography of Landscape* (Cambridge: Cambridge University Press, 1988), pp. 162–178.   **1562**

Walker, Paul, "C. W. Jeffreys and Images of Canadian Identity in School Textbooks," Master's thesis, Queen's University, 1990.   **1563**

REGIONAL SETTLEMENT

Nelson, Helge O. M., *Canada nybyggar landet* (Stockholm: A.B. Magn. Bergvalls Förlag, 1922), 180 pp. [Emphasis on resources and colonization]   **1564**

Innis, Harold A., "Canadian Frontiers of Settlement: A Review," *Geographical Review*, vol. 25, 1 (1935), pp. 92–106.　　　1565

Ehlers, Eckart, "Die Ausweitung der Siedlungsgrenze in Kanada: Ein Beitrag zum nordamerikanischen Frontierproblem," *Geographische Rundschau*, vol. 18, 9 (1966), pp. 327–337.　　1566

Gentilcore, R. Louis, "Change in Settlement (Canada), 1800–50: A Correlative Analysis of Historical Source Materials," in W. P. Adams and F. M. Helleiner, eds., *International Geography, 1972*, vol. 1, sec. 5, *Historical Geography* (Toronto: University of Toronto Press, for the International Geographical Union, 1972), pp. 418–419.　1567

Hamelin, Louis-Edmond, "Evolution of the Settlement Pattern," in his *Canada: A Geographical Perspective* (Toronto: Wiley Publishers of Canada, 1973), pp. 94–101.　　　1568

Lenz, Karl, "Agrarkolonisation in Prärie und Waldland in Kanada: Ein räumlicher und historischer Vergleich," in Hans-Jurgen Nitz, ed., *Landerschließung und Kulturlandschaftswandel an den Siedlungsgrenzen der Erde* (Göttingen: Göttinger Geographische Abhandlungen, vol. 66, 1976), pp. 119–135.　　1569

Osborne, Brian S., ed., *The Settlement of Canada: Origins and Transfer* (Kingston: Queen's University, 1976), 239 pp.　　　1570

Robinson, J. Lewis, *The Physical Environment of Canada and the Evolution of Settlement Patterns* (Vancouver: Talon, 1982), 43 pp. Also in his *Concepts and Themes in the Regional Geography of Canada* (Vancouver: Talonbooks, 1983), pp. 31–68.　　　1571

Wonders, William C., "The Influence of the Surveyor on Rural Settlement Patterns in Canada," *Terravue*, vol. 1 (1982), pp. 15–26.　　1572

Ehlers, Eckart, *Die agraren Siedlungsgrenzen der Erde: Gedanken zu ihrer Genese und Typologie am Beispiel des kanadischen Waldlandes* (Wiesbaden: Franz Steiner Verlag, Erdkunliches Wissen, vol. 69 (1984), 82 pp.　1573

Butzin, Bernhard, "'Counterurbanization,' räumliche Arbeitsteilung und regionaler Lebenszyklus in Kanada," *Verhandlungen des Deutschen Geographentages, 1985*, vol. 45 (Stuttgart: Franz Steiner Verlag, 1987), pp. 392–401.　　　1574

POPULATION

General

Weir, Thomas R., "Population Changes in Canada, 1867–1967," *Canadian Geographer*, vol. 11, 4 (1967), pp. 197–215. Reprinted in R. Louis Gentilcore, ed., *Geographical Approaches to Canadian*

Problems (Scarborough: Prentice-Hall, 1971), pp. 4–18.　　　1575

Weir, Thomas R., "The People," in John H. Warkentin, ed., *Canada: A Geographical Interpretation* (Toronto: Methuen, 1968), pp. 137–176.　　　1576

Anderson, Isabel B., "Population Growth and Distribution in Canada, 1921–1961," in Robert M. Irving, ed., *Readings in Canadian Geography* (Toronto: Holt, Rinehart and Winston, 1972), pp. 81–90.　　　1577

Hamelin, Louis-Edmond, "The Origin and Development of Canadian Demographic Characteristics," in his *Canada: A Geographical Perspective* (Toronto: Wiley Publishers of Canada, 1973), pp. 47–55.　　　1578

Weir, Thomas R., "Road Back from the Prairie," *Geographical Magazine*, vol. 45, 7 (1973), pp. 506–510. [Focus on Canadian population history, 1871–1970s]　　　1579

Migrations

LeConte, René, "L'émigration allemand au Canada," *Mouvement géographique*, vol. 33 (1920), pp. 424–432.　　　1580

Wilson, Roland, "Migration Movements in Canada, 1868–1925," *Canadian Historical Review*, vol. 13, 2 (1932), pp. 157–182.　　　1581

Lamoureux, Pierre, "Les premières années de l'immigration chinoise au Canada," *Revue canadienne de géographie*, vol. 9, 1 (1955), pp. 9–28.　　　1582

McArthur, Neil, and Martin E. Gerland, "The Spread and Migration of French Canadians," *Tijdschrift voor economische en sociale geografie*, vol. 52 (1961), pp. 141–147.　　1583

Kokich, George J. V., "Interprovincial Migration in Canada between 1931 and 1941 with Special Reference to Ontario," Master's thesis, University of Western Ontario, 1966.　　　1584

Lai, David Chuen-yan, "Home County and Clan Origins of Overseas Chinese in Canada in the Early 1880s," *B.C. Studies*, vol. 27 (1975), pp. 3–29.　　　1585

Lai, David Chuen-yan, "An Analysis of Data on Home Journeys by Chinese Immigrants in Canada, 1892–1915," *Professional Geographer*, vol. 29, 4 (1977), pp. 359–365.　　1586

Cameron, James M., "The Role of Shipping from Scottish Ports in Emigration to the Canadas, 1815–55," in Donald H. Akenson, ed., *Canadian Papers in Rural History*, vol. 2 (Gananoque, Ont.: Langdale Press, 1980), pp. 135–154.　　1587

Bumsted, James M., *The People's Clearance: Highland Emigration to British North America, 1770–1815* (Winnipeg: University of Manitoba Press, 1982), 305 pp.   **1588**

Mundende, D. C., "African Immigration to Canada since World War II," Master's thesis, University of Alberta, 1982.   **1589**

Luciuk, Lubomyr Y., "Searching for Place: Ukrainian Refugee Migration to Canada after World War II," Ph.D. diss., University of Alberta, 1984.
                                                          1590

Lehr, John C., "From Russia with Faith," *Horizon Canada*, vol. 2, 17 (1985), pp. 398–403.   **1591**

Dreiszinger, N. F., "Immigration and Re-migration: The Changing Urban-Rural Distribution of Hungarian Canadians, 1886–1986," *Hungarian Studies Review*, vol. 13, 2 (1986), pp. 20–41.   **1592**

Kobayashi, Audrey L., "Regional Backgrounds of Japanese Emigrants to Canada, and the Social Consequences of Regional Diversity for Japanese Canadians," Albatross Discussion Paper, ser. 1 (1986).   **1593**

Houston, Cecil J., and William J. Smyth, "The Geography of Irish Emigration to Canada," *Familia*, vol. 2, 4 (1988), pp. 7–20.   **1594**

Houston, Cecil J., and William J. Smyth, "Irish Emigrants to Canada: Whence They Came," in R. O'Driscoll and Lorna Reynolds, eds., *The Untold Story: The Irish in Canada*, vol. 1 (Toronto: Celtic Arts of Canada, 1988), pp. 27–35.   **1595**

Kobayashi, Audrey L., "Regional and Demographic Aspects of Japanese Migration to Canada," *Canadian Geographer*, vol. 32, 4 (1988), pp. 356–360.   **1596**

Vibert, Dermot W., "Asian Migration to Canada in Historical Context," *Canadian Geographer*, vol. 32, 4 (1988), pp. 352–354.   **1597**

Widdis, Randy W., "Scale and Context: Approaches to the Study of Canadian Migration Patterns in the Nineteenth Century," *Social Science History*, vol. 12, 3 (1988), pp. 269–304. **1598**

Houston, Cecil J., and William J. Smyth, *Irish Emigration and Canadian Settlement: Patterns, Links, and Letters* (Toronto: University of Toronto Press, 1990), 370 pp.   **1599**

Ethnic distributions

Duncan, M., "The French Canadian Population: Its Distribution and Development," Master's thesis, University of Aberdeen, 1944.   **1600**

Van Cleef, Eugene, "Finnish Settlement in Canada," *Geographical Review*, vol. 42, 2 (1952), pp. 253–266.   **1601**

Rosenberg, Louis, *A Gazetteer of Jewish Communities in Canada, Showing the Jewish Population in Each of the Cities, Towns, and Villages in Canada, 1851–1951* (Montreal: Canadian Jewish Congress, Bureau of Social and Economic Research, Canadian Jewish Population Studies, Canadian Jewish Community Series, no. 7, 1957), 46 pp.   **1602**

Rosenberg, Louis, *A Study of the Changes in the Population Characteristics of the Jewish Community in Canada, 1931–1961* (Montreal: Canadian Jewish Congress, Bureau of Social and Economic Research, Canadian Jewish Population Studies, Canadian Jewish Community Series, no. 2, 1965), 16 pp.   **1603**

Saarinen, Oiva W., "The Pattern and Impact of Finnish Settlement in Canada," *Terra*, vol. 79, 4 (1967), pp. 113–120.   **1604**

Wood, J. David, "Scandinavian Settlers in Canada Revisited," *Geografiska annaler B*, vol. 49B, 1 (1967), pp. 1–9.   **1605**

Houston, Cecil J., and William J. Smyth, "The Irish Abroad: Better Questions through a Better Source, the Canadian Census," *Irish Geography*, vol. 13 (1980), pp. 1–19.   **1606**

Lai, David Chuen-yan, "A 'Prison' for Chinese Immigrants," *Asianadian*, vol. 2, 4 (1980), pp. 16–19.
                                                          1607

Age groups

Bekkering, Mark H., "Patterns of Change in the Spatial Distribution of the Elderly in Canada, 1966 to 1986," Master's thesis, Queen's University, 1990.   **1608**

RURAL & REGIONAL SOCIAL GEOGRAPHY

Rosenberg, Louis, *Canada's Jewish Coummunity: A Brief Survey of Its History, Growth, and Characteristics* (Montreal: Canadian Jewish Congress, Bureau of Social and Economic Research, Canadian Jewish Population Studies, Canadian Jewish Community Series, no. 1, 1954), 16 pp.
                                                          1609

Whebell, Charles F. J., "The Bicultural Problem: An 1839 View," *Journal of Canadian Studies*, vol. 2, 3 (1967), pp. 11–23.   **1610**

Hamelin, Louis-Edmond, "Cultural Groups and the Growth of Canada," in his *Canada: A Geographical Perspective* (Toronto: Wiley Publishers of Canada, 1973), pp. 101–121.   **1611**

Houston, Cecil J., and William J. Smyth, "The Ulster Legacy," *Multiculturalism*, vol. 1, 4 (1978), pp. 9–12.   **1612**

Houston, Cecil J., and William J. Smyth, *The Sash Canada Wore: A Historical Geography of the Orange Order in Canada* (Toronto: University of Toronto Press, 1980), 215 pp.   **1613**

Koroscil, Paul M., "Canada, a Multi-Cultural Society: The Portuguese Experience," *North Dakota Quarterly*, vol. 52, 3 (1984), pp. 236–256.   **1614**

Marburg, Sandra Lin, "Women and Environment: Subsistence Paradigms, 1850–1950," *Environmental Review*, vol. 8, 1 (1984), pp. 7–22. [Focus in part on the Inuit]   **1615**

Kobayashi, Audrey L., "Le déracinement des Canadiens-Japonais après 1941: De la tyrannie à la justice," *Tribune juive*, vol. 5, 1 (1987), pp. 4–11 and 28–35.   **1616**

Houston, Cecil J., and William J. Smyth, "Orangemen in Canada," in R. O'Driscoll and Lorna Reynolds, eds., *The Untold Story: The Irish in Canada*, vol. 2 (Toronto: Celtic Arts of Canada, 1988), pp. 743–752.   **1617**

Kobayashi, Audrey L., "The Early Japanese Canadian Community," in C. Kobayashi and R. Miki, eds., *Spirit of Redress: Japanese Canadians in Conference* (Vancouver: National Association of Japanese Canadians, JC Publications, 1989), pp. 81–88.   **1618**

Luciuk, Lubomyr Y., "Trouble All Around: Ukrainian Canadians and Their Encounter with the Ukrainian Refugees of Europe, 1943–51," *Canadian Ethnic Studies*, vol. 21, 3 (1989), pp. 37–54.   **1619**

Kobayashi, Audrey L., "The Historical Context of Japanese-Canadian Uprooting," in Ludger Müller-Wille, ed., *Social Change and Space: Indigenous Nations and Ethnic Communities in Canada and Finland*, 2d ed. (Montreal: McGill University Department of Geography, Northern Studies Program, 1990), pp. 69–82.   **1620**

Moore, Susan Kathleen, "Diffusion du phénomène d'immersion au Canada, 1965–1987," Master's thesis, Université Laval, 1990.   **1621**

POLITICAL & ADMINISTRATIVE GEOGRAPHY

General

Trudel, Marcel, "Projet d'invasion du Canada au début de 1778," *Revue d'histoire de l'Amérique française*, vol. 2 (1948), pp. 163–184.   **1622**

Nicholson, Norman L., "The Confederation of Canada," in W. Gordon East and E. A. Moodie, eds., *The Changing World: Studies in Political Geography* (Yonkers-on-Hudson: World Book Co., 1956), pp. 312–329.   **1623**

Gibson, James R., "Russia on the Pacific: The Role of the Amur," *Canadian Geographer*, vol. 12, 1 (1968), pp. 15–27.   **1624**

Knight, David B., and Susan Burrows, "Centrality by Degrees: A Nineteenth Century Canadian's Measurement for Central Location," *Canadian Cartographer*, vol. 12, 2 (1975), pp. 109–120. **1625**

Knight, David B., *A Capital for Canada: Conflict and Compromise in the Nineteenth Century* (Chicago: University of Chicago Department of Geography, Research Paper no. 182, 1977), 341 pp.   **1626**

Waddell, Eric W., "State, Language, and Society: The Vicissitudes of French in Quebec and Canada," in A. Cairns and C. Williams, eds., *The Politics of Gender, Ethnicity, and Language in Canada* (Toronto: University of Toronto, Royal Commission on the Economic Union and Development Prospects for Canada, 1986), pp. 67–110.   **1627**

Kobayashi, Audrey L., "Racism and the Law in Canada: A Geographical Perspective," *Urban Geography*, vol. 11, 5 (1990), pp. 447–473.   **1628**

Waddell, Eric W., "Language, Community, and National Identity: Some Reflections in French-English Relations in Canada," in A. G. Gagnon and J. P. Bickerton, eds., *Canadian Politics: An Introduction to the Discipline* (Petersborough: Bookview Press, 1990), pp. 609–622.   **1629**

Boundaries

Nicholson, Norman L., "A Dissertation on Canadian Boundaries: Their Evolution, Establishment, and Significance," Ph.D. diss., University of Ottawa, 1951.   **1630**

Nicholson, Norman L., *The Boundaries of the Canadian Confederation* (Toronto: McClelland and Stewart, 1979), 252 pp.   **1631**

Government policies

Nicholson, Norman L., "The National Government and Development," in John H. Warkentin, ed., *Canada: A Geographical Interpretation* (Toronto: Methuen, 1968), pp. 177–186.   **1632**

Lehr, John C., "The Role of Clifford Sifton in Ukrainian Immigration to Canada, 1896–1905," *Studia ucrainica*, vol. 2 (1984), pp. 225–236. **1633**

Struthers, J., "Canadian Unemployment Policy in the 1930s," in *Cultural Dimensions of Canada's Geography: Proceedings of the German-Canadian Symposium, August 28–September 11, 1983* (Peterborough: Trent University, Department of Geography, Occasional Paper no. 10, 1984), pp. 2–20.   **1634**

Antler, James, "Federal Unemployment Policy under the Conservative Government of R. B. Bennett, 1930–1935," Master's thesis, University of Toronto, 1988.　　　　　1635

Vibert, Dermot W., "Canada's Chinese Immigration Policy and Immigration Security, 1947–1953," Master's thesis, McGill University, 1988.　　　　　1636

Administration

Brydon, Dianne P., "Wanting the Rights of Men and All the Privileges of Their Sex: Women in the Canadian Civil Service, 1895–1907," Ph.D. diss., Queen's University, 1987.　　　　　1637

ECONOMIC DEVELOPMENT

Wolfe, Roy I., "Economic Development," in John H. Warkentin, ed., *Canada: A Geographical Interpretation* (Toronto: Methuen, 1968), pp. 187–228.　　　　　1638

Code, William R., "The Spatial Dynamics of Financial Intermediaries: An Interpretation of the Distribution of Financial Decision-Making in Canada," Ph.D. diss., University of California–Berkeley, 1971.　　　　　1639

Brickman, Barry, "The Evolution of Electric Power Capacity in Canada: A Geographical Analysis," Master's thesis, Carleton University, 1975.　1640

Code, William R., "The Spatial Evolution of Financial Communities in Canada," *International Geography '76*, sec. 9, *Historical Geography* (Moscow: Twenty-third International Geographical Union, 1976), pp. 46–50.　　　　　1641

Sitwell, O. F. George, and Neil R. M. Seifried, *The Regional Structure of the Canadian Economy* (Toronto: Methuen, 1984), 192 pp.　　　　　1642

Acheson, T. William, "Understanding Canada: A View from the Maritimes," in Graeme Wynn, ed., *Interpreting Canada: Four Essays* (Vancouver: Tantalus Research, B.C. Geographical Series, no. 43, 1986), pp. 67–74.　　　　　1643

Quigley, Neil C., "Bank Credit and the Structure of the Canadian Space Economy, c.1890–1935," Ph.D. diss., University of Toronto, 1986.　1644

Pletsch, Alfred, "Zentrum-Peripheriestrukturen in Kanada: Allgemeine Kennzeichen und Problemstellung," *Zeitschrift der Gesellschaft für Kanada-Studien*, vol. 8, 1 (1988), pp. 7–21.　1645

Ceh, S. Brian, "The Changing Canadian Inventive Spatial Economic Pattern: An Urban and Regional Analysis between 1881 and 1986," Mas-

ter's thesis, Wilfrid Laurier University, 1989.　　　　　1646

RESOURCE MANAGEMENT

Nelson, J. Gordon, "Canada's National Parks: Past, Present, and Future," *Canadian Geographical Journal*, vol. 86, 3 (1973), pp. 68–89. Reprinted in his *Man's Impact on the Western Canadian Landscape* (Toronto: McClelland and Stewart, Carleton Library Series, no. 90, 1976), pp. 78–101, and in Geoffrey Wall and John S. Marsh, eds., *Recreational Land Use: Perspectives on Its Evolution in Canada* (Ottawa: Carleton University Press, 1982), pp. 41–61.　　　　　1647

Ray, Arthur J., "Some Conservation Schemes of the Hudson's Bay Company, 1821–50: An Examination of the Problems of Resource Management in the Fur Trade," *Journal of Historical Geography*, vol. 1, 1 (1975), pp. 49–68.　　1648

Brown, Douglas L., "Origins of Resource Management and Conservation in Canada: A Cultural-Historical Interpretation," Master's thesis, Simon Fraser University, 1979.　　　　　1649

Johnson, Ronald C. A., "Resource Management in Canada's National Parks, 1885–1911," *Albertan Geographer*, vol. 15 (1979), pp. 19–36.　　1650

EXTRACTIVE ACTIVITY

Fur trade

Heidenreich, Conrad E., and Arthur J. Ray, *The Early Fur Trade: A Study in Cultural Interaction* (Toronto: McClelland and Stewart, 1976), 95 pp.　　　　　1651

Moodie, D. Wayne, "Agriculture and the Fur Trade," in Carol M. Judd and Arthur J. Ray, eds., *Old Trails and New Directions: Papers of the Third North American Fur Trade Conference* (Toronto: University of Toronto Press, 1980), pp. 272–290.　　　　　1652

Ray, Arthur J., "Reflections on Fur Trade Social History and Métis History in Canada," *American Indian Culture and Research Journal*, vol. 6 (1982), pp. 91–107.　　　　　1653

McEachran, Ure, "The Reorganization of the Fur Trade after the 'Merger' of the Hudson's Bay Company and the North West Company, 1821–1826," York University Department of Geography Discussion Paper no. 39 (1989).　　　　1654

Ray, Arthur J., *The Canadian Fur Trade in the Industrial Age* (Toronto: University of Toronto Press, 1990), 283 pp.　　　　　1655

Ray, Arthur J., "Rivals for Fur," *Beaver*, vol. 70, 2 (1990), pp. 30–43. **1656**

Forestry

Craig, Roland C., "The Forest Resources of Canada," *Economic Geography*, vol. 2, 3 (1926), pp. 394–413. **1657**

Mining

Innis, Harold A., "Settlement and the Mining Frontier," in W. A. Mackintosh and W. L. G. Joerg, ed., *Canadian Frontiers of Settlement*, vol. 9 (Toronto: Macmillan Co. of Canada, 1936), pp. 167–412. **1658**

AGRICULTURE

Bishop, Avard L., "Development of Wheat Production in Canada," *Bulletin of the American Geographical Society*, vol. 44, 1 (1912), pp. 10–17. **1659**

Ruddick, J. A., "The Dairying and Fruit Industries in Canada," *Journal of Geography*, vol. 11, 8 (1913), pp. 243–245. **1660**

Krueger, Ralph R., "The Geography of the Orchard Industry of Canada," *Geographical Bulletin* (Ottawa), vol. 7 (1965), pp. 27–71. Reprinted with modifications in Robert M. Irving, ed., *Readings in Canadian Geography* (Toronto: Holt, Rinehart and Winston, 1972), pp. 216–241. **1661**

Sitwell, O. F. George, "Difficulties in the Interpretation of the Agricultural Statistics in the Canadian Census of the Nineteenth Century," *Canadian Geographer*, vol. 13, 1 (1969), pp. 72–76. **1662**

Furniss, I. F., "Post-War Productivity Gains in Canadian Agriculture," In Robert M. Irving, ed., *Readings in Canadian Geography* (Toronto: Holt, Rinehart and Winston, 1972), pp. 200–215. **1663**

McInnis, Marvin, "The Changing Structure of Canadian Agriculture, 1867–1897," *Journal of Economic History*, vol. 42, 1 (1982), pp. 191–198. **1664**

Schott, Carl, "Strukturwandel der kanadischen Landwirtschaft seit dem Zweiten Weltkrieg," *Zeitschrift der Gesellschaft für Kanada-Studien*, vol. 4 (1984), pp. 5–18. **1665**

LANDSCAPE

Wonders, William C., "Log Dwellings in Canadian Folk Architecture," *Annals of the Association of American Geographers*, vol. 69, 2 (1979), pp. 187–207. **1666**

COMMUNICATIONS & TRADE

General

Wolfe, Roy I., "Transportation and Politics: The Example of Canada," *Annals of the Association of American Geographers*, vol. 52, 2 (1962), pp. 176–190. **1667**

Schmidt, Raymond G., "Transportation Expansion and Development in Canada to 1927: A Political Economy Approach," Master's thesis, Queen's University, 1976. **1668**

Everitt, John C., and D. S. Everitt, "American Influences in the Canadian Grain Trade: An Overview," *Bulletin of the Association of North Dakota Geographers*, vol. 34 (1984), pp. 1–9. **1669**

Railways

Parkin, George R., "The Railway Development of Canada," *Scottish Geographical Magazine*, vol. 25, 5 (1909), pp. 225–250. **1670**

Lowe, J. Norman, "Canada's Third Transcontinental Railway: The Grand Trunk Pacific/National Transcontinental Railways," *Journal of the West*, vol. 17, 4 (1978), pp. 52–61. **1671**

Airways

Garry, Robert, "Le développement de la ligne aérienne trans-Canada," *Cahiers de géographie du Québec*, vol. 3, 6 (1959), pp. 367–392. **1672**

Newspapers

Wilks, Joseph G., "Geographical Trends of Content in Historical Newspapers," Master's thesis, McMaster University, 1976. **1673**

Goheen, Peter G., "The Changing Bias of Inter-Urban Communications in Nineteenth-Century Canada," *Journal of Historical Geography*, vol. 16, 2 (1990), pp. 177–196. **1674**

Telephone

Norris, Darrell A., "The Bell Telephone Historical Collection and Late Nineteenth Century Canadian Urban History: A Preliminary Report," *Urban History Review*, vol. 10, 3 (1982), pp. 47–54. **1675**

Postal system

Osborne, Brian S., and Robert Pike, "The Postal Service and Canadian Social History, Part 1: Petitions, Inspector's Report, and the Postal Archives," *Postal History Society of Canada Journal*, vol. 35 (1983), pp. 37–42. **1676**

Osborne, Brian S., "The Canadian National Postal System, 1852–1914: An Examination of a Regional Communication System," in R. Berry and J. Acheson, eds., *Regionalism and National Iden-*

tity (Christchurch, N.Z.: ACSANZ, 1985), pp. 227–240.   **1677**

Osborne, Brian S., and Robert Pike, "The Postal Service and Canadian Social History, Part 2: The Locational Decision," *Postal History Society of Canada Journal*, vol. 41 (1985), pp. 11–14.   **1678**

Osborne, Brian S., and Robert Pike, "The Postal Service and Canadian Social History, Part 3: L'encouragement aux habitudes d'économie," *Postal History Society of Canada Journal*, vol. 42 (1985), pp. 21–27.   **1679**

Osborne, Brian S., and Robert Pike, "The Postal Service and Canadian Social History, Part 4: The Human Dimension," *Postal History Society of Canada Journal*, vol. 43 (1986), pp. 13–18.   **1680**

Osborne, Brian S., and Robert M. Pike, "From a Cornerstone of Canada's Social Structure to Financial Self-Suffiency: The Transformation of the Canadian Postal Service, 1852–1987," *Canadian Journal of Communications*, vol. 13, 1 (1987), pp. 1–26.   **1681**

MANUFACTURING & INDUSTRIALIZATION

McGuire, B. J., "Aluminium: The Story of Fifty Years of Growth by the Canadian Industry," *Canadian Geographical Journal*, vol. 43, 4 (1951), pp. 144–163.   **1682**

Kerr, Donald G., "The Spatial Organization of the Iron and Steel Industry in Canada," in R. Louis Gentilcore, ed., *Canada's Changing Geography* (Scarborough, Ont.: Prentice-Hall of Canada, 1967), pp. 139–148.   **1683**

Vogelsang, Roland R., "Changes in Canadian Manufacturing: Restructuring Rather Than Deindustrialization," *Erde*, vol. 121, 2 (1990), pp. 105–118. [Focus on 1961–1985]   **1684**

URBAN NETWORKS & URBANIZATION

General

Brittain, Isabel G., "Geographical Influences in the Location of Leading Canadian Cities," *Journal of Geography*, vol. 11, 8 (1913), pp. 256–260.   **1685**

Whitaker, J. Russell, "Regional Contrasts in the Growth of Canadian Cities," *Scottish Geographical Magazine*, vol. 53 (1937), pp. 373–379. [Focus on 1881–1931]   **1686**

Kerr, Donald G., "Metropolitan Dominance in Canada," in John H. Warkentin, ed., *Canada: A Geographical Perspective* (Toronto: Methuen, 1968), pp. 531–555.   **1687**

Oster, C. F., "The Process of Urbanization in Canada, 1600–1961," Master's thesis, Simon Fraser University, 1968.   **1688**

Lenz, Karl, "Entwicklung und Stand der Urbanisierung in Kanada: Eine statistische Analyse," in Carl Schott, ed., *Beiträge zur Kulturgeographie von Kanada* (Marburg: Marburger Geographische Schriften, no. 50, 1971), pp. 43–69. [Focus on 1851–1966]   **1689**

Lithwick, N. H., "The Process of Urbanization in Canada," In Robert M. Irving, ed., *Readings in Canadian Geography* (Toronto: Holt, Rinehart and Winston, 1972), pp. 130–145.   **1690**

Deshaies, Laurent, "La croissance des villes minières canadiennes: Essai d'explication," *Cahiers de géographie du Québec*, vol. 19, 46 (1975), pp. 61–86. [Focus on 1941–1971]   **1691**

Preston, Richard E., "The Evolution of Urban Canada: The Post-Confederation Period," in Robert M. Irving, ed., *Readings in Canadian Geography*, 3d ed. (Toronto: Holt, Rinehart & Winston of Canada, 1978), pp. 19–46.   **1692**

Goheen, Peter G., "Some Aspects of Canadian Urbanization from 1850–1920," in Woodrow Borah, Jorge Hardoy, and Gilbert A. Stelter, eds., *Urbanization in the Americas* (Ottawa: History Division, National Museum of Man, 1980), pp. 77–84. Also issued as a special number of the *Urban History Review* (1980).   **1693**

Juniper, Paul, "Metropolitan Dominance in Canada, 1867–1980," Master's thesis, York University, 1981.   **1694**

Watson, J. Wreford, "Centre and Periphery: The Transfer of Urban Ideas from Britain to Canada," in John H. C. Patten, ed., *The Expanding City: Essays in Honour of Professor Jean Gottmann* (London: Academic Press, 1983), pp. 381–411.   **1695**

Collins, Lyndhurst, "Canadian Cities: Recent Developments and the Changing Image," in Guy M. Robinson, ed., *A Social Geography of Canada: Essays in Honour of J. Wreford Watson* (Edinburgh: North British Publishing, 1988), pp. 105–117. Also Toronto: Dundurn Press, 1991. [Focus on 1951–1981]   **1696**

McCann, Lawrence D., and Peter J. Smith, "Canada Becomes Urban: Cities and Urbanization in Historical Perspective," in Trudy Bunting and Pierre Filion, eds., *Canadian Cities in Transition* (Toronto: Oxford University Press, 1991), pp. 69–99.   **1697**

Evolution of the system of cities

Simmons, James W., *The Growth of the Canadian Urban System* (Toronto: University of Toronto,

Centre for Urban and Community Studies, Paper no. 65, 1974), 28 pp. **1698**

Simmons, James W., "The Evolution of the Canadian Urban System," in Alan F. J. Artibise and Gilbert A. Stelter, eds., *The Usable Urban Past: Planning and Politics in the Modern Canadian City* (Toronto: Macmillan, 1979), pp. 9–33. **1699**

Simmons, James W., "The Impact of the Public Sector on the Canadian Urban System," in Gilbert A. Stelter and Alan F. J. Artibise, eds., *Power and Place: Canadian Urban Developments in the North American Context* (Vancouver: University of British Columbia Press, 1986), pp. 21–50. **1700**

Marshall, John U., "Structural Change in the Canadian Urban System: An Analysis of Employment Profiles and Industrial Diversification, 1951–1981," *London Journal of Canadian Studies*, vol. 4 (1987), pp. 51–67. **1701**

Green, Milton B., and Rod B. McNaughton, "Canadian Interurban Merger Activity, 1962–1984," *Canadian Geographer*, vol. 33, 3 (1989), pp. 253–264. **1702**

Stelter, Gilbert A., "The Changing Imperial Context of Early Canadian Urban Development," in Gilbert A. Stelter, ed., *Cities and Urbanization: Canadian Historical Perspectives* (Toronto: Copp, Clark, Pittman, 1990), pp. 16–38. **1703**

Special-function towns

Artibise, Alan F. J., and Gilbert A. Stelter, "Canadian Resource Towns in Historical Perspective," in Gilbert A. Stelter and Alan F. J. Artibise, eds., *Shaping the Urban Landscape: Aspects of the Canadian City-Building Process* (Ottawa: Carleton University Press, 1982), pp. 413–434. **1704**

Forward, Charles N., "The Development of Canada's Five Leading National Ports," *Urban History Review*, vol. 10, 3 (1982), pp. 25–45. **1705**

TOWN GROWTH

Knight, David B., "'Boosterism' and Locational Analysis; or One Man's Swan is Another Man's Goose," *Urban History Review*, vol. 3 (1973), pp. 10–16. **1706**

URBAN ECONOMIC STRUCTURE

Williams, Keith G., "Income Changes and Urban Economic Growth in Selected Canadian Cities, 1941 and 1961," Master's thesis, University of Toronto, 1966. **1707**

Hamilton, William, "Economic Base Analysis for Canadian Cities, 1931–1961," Master's thesis, Waterloo Lutheran University, 1970. **1708**

Forward, Charles N., "Changes in the Functional Structure of Canadian Cities, 1951–1981," in Edgar L. Jackson, ed., *Current Research by Western Canadian Geographers: The Simon Fraser University Papers, 1987* (Vancouver: Tantalus Research, B.C. Geographical Series, no. 45, 1987), pp. 33–50. **1709**

Norris, Darrell A., "Flightless Phoenix: Fire Risk and Fire Insurance in Urban Canada, 1882–1886," *Urban History Review*, vol. 16, 1 (1987), pp. 61–68. **1710**

URBAN SOCIAL STRUCTURE

General

Forward, Charles N., "The Elderly Population in Canadian Metropolitan Areas," (Vancouver: Tantalus Research, 1979), pp. 41–61. [Focus on 1881–1971] **1711**

Lai, David Chuen-yan, *Chinatowns: Towns within Cities in Canada* (Vancouver: University of British Columbia Press, 1988), 347 pp. **1712**

Goheen, Peter G., "Symbols in the Streets: Parades in Victorian Urban Canada," *Urban History Review*, vol. 18, 3 (1990), pp. 237–243. **1713**

Housing and residence

McAfee, Ann, "Four Decades of Geographical Impact by Canadian Social Housing Policies," in Barr, Brenton M., ed., *Studies in Canadian Regional Geography: Essays in Honor of J. Lewis Robinson* (Vancouver: Tantalus Research, B.C. Geographical Series, no. 17, 1984), pp. 92–108. **1714**

Harris, Richard S., "Residential Segregation and Class Formation in Canadian Cities: A Critical Review," *Canadian Geographer*, vol. 28, 2 (1984), pp. 186–196. **1715**

Harris, Richard S., "Housing in Canadian Cities: An Agenda and Review of Sources," *Urban History Review*, vol. 14, 3 (1986), pp. 259–266. **1716**

Harris, Richard S., "Working-Class Home Ownership and Housing Affordability across Canada in 1931," *Histoire sociale/Social History*, vol. 19, 37 (1986), pp. 121–138. **1717**

Linteau, Paul-André, "Canadian Suburbanization in a North American Context—Does the Border Make a Difference?" in G. A. Stelter, ed., *Cities and Urbanization: Canadian Historical Perspectives* (Toronto: Copp Clark Pitman, 1990), pp. 16–38. **1718**

Political reform

Harris, Richard S., "A Social Movement in Urban Politics: A Reinterpretation of Urban Reform in Canada," *International Journal of Urban and*

Regional Research, vol. 11, 3 (1987), pp. 363–381.
1719

Harris, Richard S., "A Defense of Urban 'Reform'," *Urban History Review*, vol. 17, 3 (1989), pp. 209–210. **1720**

Olson, Sherry H., "Paternalism and Urban Reform: An Introduction," *Urban History Review*, vol. 17, 3 (1989), pp. 143–147. **1721**

TOWNSCAPE

McFarland, E., "The Beginning of Municipal Park Systems," in Geoffrey Wall and John S. Marsh, eds., *Recreational Land Use: Perspectives on Its Evolution in Canada* (Ottawa: Carleton University Press, 1982), pp. 257–271. **1722**

Stelter, Gilbert A., and Alan F. J. Artibise, eds., *Shaping the Urban Landscape: Aspects of the Canadian City-Building Process* (Ottawa: Carleton University Press, 1982), 436 pp. **1723**

Wood, J. David, "Grand Design on the Fringes of Empire: New Towns for British North America," *Canadian Geographer*, vol. 26, 3 (1982), pp. 243–255. **1724**

Bloomfield, Gerald T., "Albert Kahn and Canadian Industrial Architecture, 1908–1938," *Bulletin of the Society for the Study of Architecture in Canada*, vol. 10, 4 (1985), pp. 4–10. **1725**

Isin, Engin F., "The Birth of the Modern City in British North America," Ph.D. diss., University of Toronto, 1990. **1726**

Lai, David Chuen-yan, "The Visual Character of Chinatowns," *Places*, vol. 7, 1 (1990), pp. 28–31. **1727**

Olson, Sherry, "The Evolution of Metropolitan Form," in Trudy Bunting and Pierre Filion, eds., *Canadian Cities in Transition* (Toronto: Oxford University Press, 1991), pp. 240–262. **1728**

RECREATION & TOURISM

Holdsworth, Deryck W., "Built Forms and Social Realities: A Review Essay of Recent Work on Canadian Heritage Structures," *Urban History Review*, vol. 9, 2 (1980), pp. 123–138. **1729**

Benidickson, Jamie, "Paddling for Pleasure: Recreational Canoeing as a Canadian Way of Life," in Geoffrey Wall and John S. Marsh, eds., *Recreational Land Use: Perspectives on Its Evolution in Canada* (Ottawa: Carleton University Press, 1982), pp. 323–340. **1730**

Wall, Geoffrey, "Changing Views of the Land as a Recreational Resource," in Geoffrey Wall and

John S. Marsh, eds., *Recreational Land Use: Perspectives on Its Evolution in Canada* (Ottawa: Carleton University Press, 1982), pp. 15–25. **1731**

PLANNING

Saarinen, Oiva W. "The Influence of Thomas Adams and the British New Towns Movement in the Planning of Canadian Resource Communities," in Alan F. J. Artibise and Gilbert A. Stelter, eds., *The Usable Urban Past: Planning and Politics in the Modern Canadian City* (Toronto: Macmillan, 1979), pp. 268–292. **1732**

Smith, Peter J., "John Arthur Roebuck: A Canadian Influence on the Development of Planning Thought in the Early Nineteenth Century," *Plan Canada*, vol. 19, 4 (1979), pp. 200–210. **1733**

Hatchard, R. D., "Horace L. Seymour and Early Canadian Town Planning, 1900–1940," Master's thesis, University of Western Ontario, 1985. **1734**

Smith, Peter J., "Theory and Practice of Urban Renewal Planning in Canada," in Peter J. Smith and E. L. Jackson, eds., *A World of Real Places: Essays in Honour of William C. Wonders* (Edmonton: University of Alberta, Department of Geography, 1990), pp. 191–206. **1735**

PLACE NAMES

Douglas, Robert, "The Place-Names of Canada," *Scottish Geographical Magazine*, vol. 36, 3 (1920), pp. 154–157. **1736**

Armstrong, G. H., *The Origin and Meaning of Place Names in Canada* (Toronto: Macmillan Co. of Canada, 1930), 312 pp. **1737**

Barbeau, Marius, "Les noms les plus anciens sur la carte du Canada," *Revue trimestrielle canadienne*, vol. 35 (1949), pp. 243–255. **1738**

Rudnyckyi, Jaroslav Bohdan, "Canadian Place Names of Ukrainian Origin," Ukrainian Free Academy of Sciences, *Onomastica*, vol. 2 (1957), pp. 1–88. **1739**

Hamelin, Louis-Edmond, "Classement des noms de lieux du Canada," in José A. Sporck, ed., *Mélanges de géographie physique, humaine, économique, appliquée offerts à M. Omer Tulippe*, vol. 1 (Gembloux, Belgium: Éditions J. Duculot, 1967), pp. 617–627. **1740**

Rayburn, J. Alan, "Geographical Names of Amerindian Origin in Canada, Part I," *Names*, vol. 15, 3 (1967), pp. 203–215; "Part 2," vol. 17, 2 (1969), pp. 149–158. **1741**

MATERIAL COVERING MULTIPLE
——————— REGIONS ———————

GENERAL

See also 1151

Bruce, E. L., "The Canadian Shield and Its Geographic Effects," *Geographical Journal*, vol. 93, 3 (1939), pp. 230–239.   **1742**

ENVIRONMENTAL CHANGE

Moodie, D. Wayne, and Alan J. W. Catchpole, *Environmental Data from Historical Documents by Content Analysis* (Winnipeg: University of Manitoba Department of Geography, Manitoba Geographical Studies, vol. 5, 1975), 119 pp.   **1743**

Ball, Timothy F., and Roger A. Kingsley, "Instrumental Temperature Records at Two Sites in Central Canada: 1768 to 1910," *Climatic Change*, vol. 6, 1 (1984), pp. 39–56.   **1744**

Ball, Timothy F., "Historical Evidence and Climatic Implications of a Shift in the Boreal Forest Tundra Transition in Central Canada," *Climatic Change*, vol. 8, 2 (1986), pp. 121–134. [1721–1851] **1745**

NATIVE PEOPLES & WHITE RELATIONS

See also 1193, 1198

Pentland, David H., "Cartographic Concepts of the Northern Algonquians," *Canadian Cartographer*, vol. 12, 2 (1975), pp. 149–160.   **1746**

Moodie, D. Wayne, and Barry Kaye, "The Ac-ko-mok-ki Map," *Beaver*, Outfit 307, 4 (1977), pp. 4–15.   **1747**

Van Voorhis, Eugene P., "The Hydrographic Factor in Ottawa Culture and History, 1615–1836," Master's thesis, Bowling Green State University, 1983.   **1748**

Moodie, D. Wayne, "Indian Map-Making: Two Examples from the Fur Trade West," *Bulletin of the Association of Canadian Map Libraries*, no. 55 (1985), pp. 32–43.   **1749**

Ray, Arthur J., "The Hudson's Bay Company and Native People," in Wilcomb E. Washburn, ed., *The Handbook of North American Indians*, vol. 4, *History of Indian-White Relations* (Washington D.C.: Smithsonian Institution, 1988), pp. 335–350.   **1750**

EXPLORATION & MAPPING

St. Jean D'Ars, Sister Marie de, "La carte des Jésuites," *Revue d'histoire de l'Amérique française*, vol. 4, 2 (1950), pp. 249–267.   **1751**

Wroth, Lawrence C., "An Unknown Champlain Map of 1616," *Imago Mundi*, vol. 11 (1955), pp. 85–94.   **1752**

Caron, Fabien, "Exploration et géographie: Albert Peter Low dans l'Ungava-Labrador," Master's thesis, Université Laval, 1965.   **1753**

Caron, Fabien, "Albert Peter Low et l'exploration du Québec-Labrador," *Cahiers de géographie du Québec*, vol. 9, 18 (1965), pp. 169–182.   **1754**

Sebert, Lou M., "The Map That Opened the West," *Canadian Cartographer*, vol. 4, 2 (1967), pp. 105–115.   **1755**

Warkentin, John H., "David Thompson's Geology: A Document," *Journal of the West*, vol. 6, 3 (1967), pp. 468–490.   **1756**

Ruggles, Richard I., "Westward Thrust in a New World," *Geographical Magazine*, vol. 45, 2 (1972), pp. 116–125.   **1757**

Hopwood, Victor G., "David Thompson and His Maps," *Proceedings of the Annual Conference of the Association of Canadian Map Libraries*, vol. 7 (1973), pp. 45–52. Reprinted in Barbara Farrell and Eileen Desbarats, eds., *Explorations in the History of Canadian Mapping: A Collection of Essays* (Ottawa: Association of Canadian Map Libraries and Archives, 1988), pp. 205–210.   **1758**

Heidenreich, Conrad E., *Explorations and Mapping of Samuel de Champlain, 1603–1632* (Toronto: Cartographica Monograph no. 17, 1976), 140 pp.   **1759**

Heidenreich, Conrad E., "Seventeenth Century Maps of the Great Lakes and St. Lawrence Area as Ethno-Historical Material," *Western Canadian Journal of Anthropology*, vol. 6, 1 (1976), pp. 12–29.   **1760**

Heidenreich, Conrad E., "Champlain's Undated Carte Géographique: A Recent Discovery and Some Thoughts on Its Printing History," *Canadian Cartographer*, vol. 15, 2 (1978), pp. 186–188.   **1761**

Wheeler, J. O., "The Wheeler Family in the Mapping of the Canadian Cordillera," *Proceedings of the Association of Canadian Map Libraries*, vol. 28 (1978), pp. 18–34. Reprinted in part, with modifications, as "A. O. Wheeler and Mapping in the Canadian Cordillera," in Barbara Farrell and Eileen Desbarats, eds., *Explorations in the History of Canadian Mapping: A Collection of Essays* (Ottawa: Association of Canadian Map Libraries and Archives, 1988), pp. 211–222. **1762**

Heidenreich, Conrad E., and Edward H. Dahl, "The Two States of Champlain's Carte Géographique," *Canadian Cartographer*, vol. 16, 1 (1979), pp. 1–16. **1763**

Pritchard, J. S., "French Charting of the East Coast of Canada," in Derek Howse, ed., *Five Hundred Years of Nautical Science, 1400–1900* (Greenwich, England: National Maritime Museum, 1981), pp. 119–129. **1764**

Heidenreich, Conrad E., "The Fictitious Island of Lake Superior," *Map Collector*, vol. 27 (1984), pp. 21–25. **1765**

Heidenreich, Conrad E., "An Analysis of the Seventeenth Century Map 'Nouvelle France'," *Cartographica*, vol. 25, 3 (1988), pp. 67–111. **1766**

Gilmartin, Patricia P., "Mary Jobe Akeley's Explorations in the Canadian Rockies," *Geographical Journal*, vol. 156, 3 (1990), pp. 297–303. **1767**

REGIONAL SETTLEMENT

Innis, Harold A., "Industrialism and Settlement in Western Canada," *International Geographical Congress, Cambridge, 1928 Report of the Proceedings* (Cambridge: Cambridge University Press, 1930), pp. 369–376. **1768**

Randall, John R., "Settlement of the Great Clay Belt of Northern Ontario and Quebec," *Bulletin of the Philadelphia Geographical Society*, vol. 35, 3 & 4 (1937), pp. 53–66. **1769**

Sunderland, Joan R., "Settlement of the Clay Belt of Northern Ontario and Quebec," Master's thesis, University of California–Berkeley, 1955. **1770**

McDermott, George L., "Frontier Settlement in the Great Canadian Clay Belt," Ph.D. diss., University of Wisconsin–Madison, 1959. **1771**

McDermott, George L., "Frontiers of Settlement in the Great Clay Belt, Ontario and Quebec," *Annals of the Association of American Geographers*, vol. 51 (1961), pp. 261–273. Reprinted in Robert M. Irving, ed., *Readings in Canadian Geography* (Toronto: Holt, Rinehart and Winston, 1972), pp. 41–55. **1772**

Hottenroth, Helmut, *The Great Clay Belts in Ontario and Québec: Struktur und Genese eines Pionierraumes an der nördlichen Siedlungs-*grenze Ost-kanada (Marburg: Marburger Geographische Schriften, no. 39, 1968), 167 pp. **1773**

Green, Jerry E., "A Functional Analysis of the Populated Places in Canada's Yukon Territory and the Mackenzie District of the Northwest Territories, 1898–1971: A Study in Settlement Persistence," Ph.D. diss., University of North Carolina, 1976. **1774**

Burghardt, Andrew F., "The Role of Ontario in the Settlement of the Canadian West," *Bamberger Geographische Schriften*, vol. 4 (1982), pp. 225–231. **1775**

Burghardt, Andrew F., "Ontario as a Springboard to the Prairie West," in Thomas F. McIlwraith, Jr., ed., *By River, Road, and Rail: Transportation in Old Ontario* (Toronto: Ontario Museum Association, 1984), pp. 97–104. **1776**

Sinclair, Peter, "Agricultural Colonization in Ontario and Quebec: Some Evidence from the Great Clay Belt, 1900–45," in Donald H. Akenson, ed., *Canadian Papers in Rural History*, vol. 5 (Gananoque, Ont.: Langdale Press, 1986), pp. 104–120. **1777**

Ross, Eric, *Full of Hope and Promise: The Canadas in 1841* (Montreal: McGill-Queen's University Press, 1991), 165 pp. **1778**

POPULATION

Talman, James, "Migration from Ontario to Manitoba in 1871," *Ontario History*, vol. 43 (1951), pp. 35–41. **1779**

RURAL & REGIONAL SOCIAL GEOGRAPHY

Gilbert, Anne, and André Langlois, "Les pays de l'Ottawa depuis Blanchard jusqu'à aujourd'hui: La confirmation d'une régionalisation ethnolinguistique," *Cahiers de géographie du Québec*, vol. 30, 80 (1986), pp. 235–247. **1780**

Momsen, Janet D., "Gender, Class, and Ethnicity in Western Canadian Mining Towns," *Journal of Women and Gender Studies*, vol. 1 (1990), pp. 119–134. **1781**

POLITICAL & ADMINISTRATIVE GEOGRAPHY

See also 1387–1388, 1390

Nicholson, Norman L., "Boundary Adjustments in the Gulf of St. Lawrence Region," *Newfoundland Quarterly*, vol. 53, 1 (1954), pp. 13–17. **1782**

ECONOMIC DEVELOPMENT

Mackintosh, William A., "The Laurentian Plateau in Canadian Economic Development," *Economic Geography*, vol. 2, 4 (1926), pp. 537–549.
1783

Isbister, John, "Agriculture, Balanced Growth, and Social Change in Central Canada since 1850: An Interpretation," *Economic Development and Cultural Change*, vol. 25, 4 (1976–1977), pp. 673–697.
1784

Kerr, Donald G., and William J. Smith, "Agriculture, Balanced Growth, and Social Change in Central Canada since 1850: Some Comments toward a More Complete Explanation," *Economic Development and Cultural Change*, vol. 28, 3 (1980), pp. 615–622.
1785

Hecht, Alfred, and Karl Lenz, "Die Entwicklung einer neuen wirtschaftlichen Kernregion in Kanada," *Erde*, vol. 113, 3–4 (1982), pp. 273–289. [Focus on Alberta and British Columbia, 1960–1981]
1786

Kerr, Donald G., "The Emergence of the Industrial Heartland, c.1750–1950," in Larry D. McCann, ed., *Heartland and Hinterland: A Geography of Canada* (Toronto: Prentice-Hall, 1982), pp. 64–99. Revised ed. 1987, pp. 70–107.
1787

Ommer, Rosemary E., *Merchant Credit and Labour Strategies in Historical Perspective* (Fredericton, N.B.: Acadiensis Press, 1990), 376 pp.
1788

LAND & LAND USE

Schott, Carl, *Die kanadischen Marschen* (Kiel: Schriften des Geographischen Instituts der Universität Kiel, vol. 15, 2, 1955), 69 pp. Reprinted in Karl Lenz and Alfred Pletsch, eds., *Kanada: Wirtschafts- und siedlungsgeographische Entwicklungen und Probleme von Carl Schott* (Berlin: Dietrich Reimer Verlag, 1985), pp. 91–142.
1789

Bryant, Christopher R., Lorne H. Russwurm, and S. Y. Wong, "Census Farmland Change in Canadian Urban Fields, 1941–1976," *Ontario Geography*, vol. 18 (1981), pp. 7–24.
1790

Pletsch, Alfred, "Township and Range: Some Deliberation on Their Origin, Mutual Influence, and Land Tenure in Québec and Ontario before 1791," in *Cultural Dimensions of Canada's Geography: Proceedings of the German-Canadian Symposium, August 28–September 11, 1983* (Peterborough: Trent University, Department of Geography, Occasional Paper no. 10 (1984), pp. 347–357.
1791

EXTRACTIVE ACTIVITY

Lower, Arthur R. M., "Settlement and the Forest Frontier in Eastern Canada," in W. A. Mackin-tosh and W. L. G. Joerg, eds., *Canadian Frontiers of Settlement*, vol. 9 (Toronto: Macmillan Co. of Canada, 1936), pp. 1–166.
1792

Ommer, Rosemary E., "From Outpost to Outport: The Jersey Merchant Triangle in the Nineteenth Century," Ph.D. diss., McGill University, 1979.
1793

Bradbury, John H., "The Impact of Industrial Cycles in the Mining Sector: The Case of the Quebec-Labrador Region of Canada," *International Journal of Urban and Regional Research*, vol. 8, 3 (1984), pp. 311–331.
1794

Bradbury, John H., "The Rise and Fall of the 'Fourth Empire of the St. Lawrence': The Quebec-Labrador Iron-ore Mining Region," *Cahiers de géographie du Québec*, vol. 29, 78 (1985), pp. 351–364. [1950–1984]
1795

Wynn, Graeme, "Hail the Pine!" *Horizon Canada*, vol. 4, 37 (1985), pp. 872–877.
1796

Ommer, Rosemary E., *From Outpost to Outport: A Structural Analysis of the Jersey-Gaspé Cod Fishery, 1767–1886* (Montreal: McGill-Queen's University Press, 1991), 245 pp.
1797

AGRICULTURE

Schott, Carl, "Die Auswirkungen der technischen Revolution in der Landwirtschaft nach 1945 auf die ländlichen Siedlungen Ostkanadas," in Carl Schott, ed., *Beiträge zur Kulturgeographie von Kanada* (Marburg: Marburger Geographische Schriften, vol. 66, 1978), pp. 89–110.
1798

Vanderhill, Burke G., "Agriculture's Struggle for Survival in the Great Clay Belt of Ontario and Quebec," *American Review of Canadian Studies*, vol. 18, 4 (1988), pp. 455–464.
1799

LANDSCAPE

Mannion, John J., "Irish Imprints on the Landscape of Eastern Canada in the Nineteenth Century: A Study of Cultural Transfer and Adaptation," Ph.D. diss., University of Toronto, 1971.
1800

Mannion, John J., *Irish Settlements in Eastern Canada: A Study of Cultural Transfer and Adaptation* (Toronto: University of Toronto Department of Geography Research Publication no. 12, 1974), 219 pp.
1801

Holdsworth, Deryck W., and E. Mills, "The B.C. Mills Prefabricated System: The Emergence of Ready-Made Buildings in Western Canada," *Occasional Papers in Archeology and History*, Canadian Historical Sites, no. 14 (1976), pp. 127–169.
1802

Dahms, Frederic A., *The Heart of the Country: From the Great Lakes to the Atlantic Coast: Re-*

discovering the Towns and Countryside of Canada (Toronto: Deneau, 1988), 191 pp.   **1803**

COMMUNICATIONS & TRADE

Kerfoot, Denis E., "The Western Grain Route," *Occasional Papers of the Canadian Association of Geographers, British Columbia Division,* vol. 6 (1964), pp. 4–19. [Focus on 1922–1963]   **1804**

Willis, G. A., "Development of Transportation in the Peace River Region of Alberta and British Columbia," Master's thesis, University of Alberta, 1966.   **1805**

Corkran, R. S., "Rail Route Selection in the Northern Rocky Mountains, 1853–1890," Master's thesis, University of Chicago, 1968.   **1806**

Simpson, J. Keith, "A Geographical Analysis of Grain Flows through Eastern Canada," Master's thesis, Queen's University, 1968.   **1807**

Clairet, G., et al., "Évolution du transport dans la région d'Ottawa-Hull," *Géoscope,* vol. 5, 2 (1974), pp. 7–11.   **1808**

Wonders, William C., "Athabasca Pass: Gateway to the Pacific," *Canadian Geographical Journal,* vol. 88, 2 (1974), pp. 20–29.   **1809**

Lenz, Karl, "Der St. Lorenz-Seeweg: 25 Jahre nach seiner Eröffnung," *Zeitschrift der Gesellschaft für Kanada-Studien,* vol. 4 (1984), pp. 56–64. **1810**

Ommer, Rosemary E., "The Decline of the Eastern Canadian Shipping Industry, 1880–1895," *Journal of Transport History,* 3d ser., vol. 5, 1 (1984), pp. 25–44.   **1811**

Osborne, Brian S., and Robert Pike, "Lowering the Walls of Oblivion: The Revolution in Postal Communication in Central Canada, 1851–1911," in Donald H. Akenson, ed., *Canadian Papers in Rural History,* vol. 4 (Gananoque, Ont.: Langdale Press, 1984), pp. 200–225.   **1812**

Kaczwowski, Viktor, "The Development of the Canadian Great Lakes Drybulk Shipping Fleet, 1945–1984," Master's thesis, York University, 1986.   **1813**

Goheen, Peter G., "Canadian Communications circa 1845," *Geographical Review,* vol. 77, 1 (1987), pp. 35–51.   **1814**

Osborne, Brian S., and Robert Pike, "The Postal Revolution in Central Canada, 1851–1911," in Lorne Tepperman and James Curtis, eds., *Readings in Sociology: An Introduction* (Toronto: McGraw-Hill Ryerson, 1988), pp. 232–244.   **1815**

Goheen, Peter G., "The Impact of the Telegraph on the Newspaper in Mid-Nineteenth Century British North America," *Urban Geography,* vol. 11, 2 (1990), pp. 107–129.   **1816**

MANUFACTURING & INDUSTRIALIZATION

Agbemenu, W. C. K., "The Glass-Container Industry of Western Canada: Past, Present, and Future," Master's thesis, University of Alberta, 1969.   **1817**

Roberge, Roger A., "The Timing, Type, and Location of Adaptive Inventive Activity in the Eastern Canadian Pulp and Paper Industry, 1806–1840," Ph.D. diss., Clark University, 1972.   **1818**

Gilmour, James M., and K. Murricane, "Structural Divergence in Canada's Manufacturing Belt," *Canadian Geographer,* vol. 17, 1 (1973), pp. 1–18.   **1819**

Steed, Guy P. F., *An Historical Geography of the Canadian Clothing Industries: 1800–1930s* (Ottawa: University of Ottawa Department of Geography and Regional Planning, Research Note no. 11, 1976), 52 pp.   **1820**

Gillis, Peter, "Ottawa and Hull, 1870–1930: A Description and Analysis of Their Industrial Structure," in Rolf Welsche and Marianne Kugler-Gagnon, eds., *Ottawa-Hull: Spatial Perspectives and Planning* (Ottawa: University of Ottawa, Department of Geography, Occasional Paper no. 4, 1978), pp. 13–20.   **1821**

URBAN NETWORKS & URBANIZATION

Yeates, Maurice H., "Urbanization in the Windsor–Quebec City Axis, 1921–1981," *Urban Geography,* vol. 5, 1 (1984), pp. 2–24.   **1822**

Yeates, Maurice H., "The Core/Periphery Model and Urban Development in Central Canada," *Urban Geography,* vol. 6, 2 (1985), pp. 101–121.   **1823**

Goheen, Peter G., "Communications and Urban Systems in Mid-Nineteenth Century Canada," *Urban History Review,* vol. 14, 3 (1986), pp. 235–246.   **1824**

URBAN ECONOMIC STRUCTURE

Steed, Guy P. F., "Centrality and Locational Change: Printing, Publishing, and Clothing in Montreal and Toronto," *Economic Geography,* vol. 52, 3 (1976), pp. 193–205.   **1825**

Steed, Guy P. F., "Standardization, Scale, Incubation, and Inertia: Montreal and Toronto Clothing Industries," *Canadian Geographer,* vol. 20, 3 (1976), pp. 298–309.   **1826**

Buse, G., "The Growth and Development of Single-Enterprise Communities: The Case of Yellowknife and Whitehorse," Master's thesis, University of Alberta, 1985.　　　　**1827**

URBAN SOCIAL STRUCTURE

Harris, Richard S., and Marc Choko, *The Evolution of Housing Tenure in Montreal and Toronto since the Mid-Nineteenth Century* (Toronto: University of Toronto, Centre for Urban and Community Studies, 1988), 126 pp.　　　　**1828**

Taylor, D. R. Fraser, "Mapping the Socio-Economic Landscape of Ottawa-Hull," in Guy M. Robinson, ed., *A Social Geography of Canada: Essays in Honour of J. Wreford Watson* (Edinburgh: North British Publishing, 1988), pp. 118–138. [Focus on 1951–1981]　　　**1829**

Choko, Marc, and Richard Harris, "The Local Culture of Property: A Comparative History of Housing Tenure in Montreal and Toronto," *Annals of the Association of American Geographers*, vol. 80, 1 (1990), pp. 73–95.　　　**1830**

TOWNSCAPE

Whitzman, Carolyn, "Landscape and Street Names: A Comparison of Montreal and Toronto, 1825 to 1914," *Proceedings of the New England–St. Lawrence Valley Division, Association of American Geographers*, vol. 16 (1986), pp. 27–33.　　　　**1831**

RECREATION & TOURISM

Hadley, Margery, "Photography, Tourism, and the CPR: Western Canada, 1884–1914," in Lynn A.

Rosenvall and Simon M. Evans, eds., *Essays on the Historical Geography of the Canadian West: Regional Perspectives on the Settlement Process* (Calgary: University of Calgary Department of Geography, 1987), pp. 48–69.　　**1832**

PLACE NAMES

White, James, "Place-Names in the Rocky Mountains between the 49th Parallel and the Athabaska River," *Proceedings and Transactions of the Royal Society of Canada*, 3d ser., vol. 10 (1917), sec. 2, pp. 501–535.　　　**1833**

Rand, S. Tertius, *Micmac Place-Names in the Maritime Provinces and Gaspé Peninsula* (Ottawa: Geographic Board of Canada, 1919), 116 pp.　　　　**1834**

Robinson, Percy J., "Some of Cartier's Place-Names, 1535–1536," *Canadian Historical Review*, vol. 26, 4 (1945), pp. 401–405.　　**1835**

Barbeau, Marius, "Les plus anciens noms du Saint-Laurent," *Revue de l'Université Laval*, vol. 3 (1949), pp. 649–657.　　　　**1836**

Barbeau, Marius, "Legend and History in the Oldest Geographical Names of the St. Lawrence," *Canadian Geographical Journal*, vol. 61 (1960), pp. 2–9.　　　　**1837**

Morissonneau, Christian, *Le langue géographique de Cartier et de Champlain: Choronymie, vocabulaire, et perception* (Quebec: Presses de l'Université Laval, 1978), 230 pp.　　**1838**

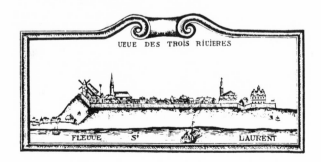

UEUE DES TROIS RIUIERES

FLEUUE Sᵗ LAURENT

ATLANTIC PROVINCES

GENERAL

See also 1149

Gaught, A. S., "Geographical Factors in the Development of the Maritime Provinces," Master's thesis, King's College, London, 1932.   **1839**

Clark, Andrew Hill, "Acadia and the Acadians: The Creation of a Geographical Entity," in John Andrews, ed., *Frontiers and Men: A Volume in Memory of Griffith Taylor (1880–1963)* (Melbourne: F. W. Cheshire, 1966), pp. 90–119.   **1840**

Erskine, David, "The Atlantic Region," in John H. Warkentin, ed., *Canada: A Geographical Interpretation* (Toronto: Methuen, 1968), pp. 231–280.
                                                          1841

Schott, Carl, "Das atlantische Kanada: Ein Notstandsgebiet Nordamerikas," in Carl Schott, ed., *Beiträge zur Kulturgeographie von Kanada* (Marburg: Marburger Geographische Schriften, vol. 50, 1971), pp. 117–149. Reprinted in Karl Lenz and Alfred Pletsch, eds., *Kanada: Wirtschafts- und siedlungsgeographische Entwicklungen und Probleme von Carl Schott* (Berlin: Dietrich Reimer Verlag, 1985), pp. 171–216. **1842**

Clark, Andrew Hill, "Acadian Heritage in Maritime New France," *Geographical Magazine*, vol. 45 (1972), pp. 219–227.   **1843**

Arseneault, Samuel P., "Geography and the Acadians," in J. Daigle, ed., *The Acadians of the Maritimes* (Moncton: Université de Moncton, Centre d'études acadiennes, 1982), pp. 87–124.
                                                          1844

Wynn, Graeme, "The Maritimes: The Geography of Fragmentation and Underdevelopment," in Larry D. McCann, ed., *Heartland and Hinterland: A Geography of Canada* (Scarborough, Ont.: Prentice-Hall Canada, 1982), pp. 156–213. Revised ed. 1987, pp. 174–245.   **1845**

Wynn, Graeme, "A Province Too Much Dependent on New England," *Canadian Geographer*, vol. 31, 2 (1987), pp. 98–113. [Greater Nova Scotia, including New Brunswick and Prince Edward Island]   **1846**

Wynn, Graeme, "A Region of Scattered Settlements and Bounded Possibilities: Northeastern America, 1775–1800," *Canadian Geographer*, vol. 31, 4 (1987), pp. 319–338. Reprinted in abbreviated form in Graeme Wynn, ed., *People, Places, Patterns, Processes: Geographical Per-*

spectives on the Canadian Past (Toronto: Copp Clark Pitman, 1990), pp. 329–357.   **1847**

Wynn, Graeme, "The Geography of the Maritime Provinces in 1800: Patterns and Questions," in Margaret Conrad, ed., *They Planted Well: New England Planters in Maritime Canada* (Fredericton, N.B.: Acadiensis Press, 1988), pp. 138–150.   **1848**

Wynn, Graeme, "New England's Outpost in the Nineteenth Century," in Stephen J. Hornsby, Victor A. Konrad, and James J. Herlan, eds., *The Northeastern Borderlands: Four Centuries of Interaction* (Fredericton, N.B.: Acadiensis Press, 1989), pp. 64–90.   **1849**

ENVIRONMENTAL CHANGE

Wynn, Graeme, "Beyond Capes and Bays," in P. A. Buckner, ed., *Teaching Maritime Studies* (Fredericton, N.B.: Acadiensis Press, 1986), pp. 37–47.   **1850**

EXPLORATION & MAPPING

Horsford, E. N., "John Cabot's Landfall, Site of Norumbega," *Journal of the American Geographical Society*, vol. 17 (1885), pp. 45–78.   **1851**

Ganong, William F., "Champlain in Acadia," *Bulletin de la Société de géographie du Québec*, vol. 3, 2 (1908), pp. 17–24.   **1852**

Ganong, William F., *Crucial Maps in the Early Cartography and Place-Nomenclature of the Atlantic Coast of Canada* (Toronto: University of Toronto Press, 1964), 511 pp.   **1853**

Taylor, Eva G. R., "The Fishermen's Story, 1354," *Geographical Magazine*, vol. 37, 9 (1965), pp. 709–712.   **1854**

Jost, Thaddeus P., "Voyages of Discovery: Hugh Say Alias John Day, the Men of Bristol, and Joao Fernandes," *Canadian Cartographer*, vol. 4, 1 (1967), pp. 1–12.   **1855**

Malinski, Richard M., "The Importance of the 'Map of Cabotia' in the Early Nineteenth Century Mapping Sequence of Eastern Canada," Master's thesis, University of Alberta, 1973.
                                                          1856

Morrison, Walter K., "The Other Revolution in 1775," in *Proceedings of the Annual Conference of the Association of Canadian Map Libraries*, vol. 9 (1975), pp. 59–79. Reprinted, with modifications, as "The Cartographical Revolution of 1775," in Barbara Farrell and Aileen Desbarats, eds., *Explorations in the History of Canadian Mapping: A Collection of Essays* (Ottawa: Association of Canadian Map Libraries and Archives, 1988), pp. 75–88.   **1857**

Dawson, Joan, "Putting Acadia on the Map: The Transitional Cartography of Nova Scotia, 1600–1755," *Cartographica*, vol. 22, 2 (1985), pp. 79–91.
1858

Garlock, Gayle, "Cartographic Journal of the 1684 Voyage of the Marianne: A Note," in Barbara Farrell and Aileen Desbarats, eds., *Explorations in the History of Canadian Mapping: A Collection of Essays* (Ottawa: Association of Canadian Map Libraries and Archives, 1988), pp. 71–74.
1859

O'Dea, Fabian, "Cabot's Landfall—Yet Again," in Barbara Farrell and Aileen Desbarats, eds., *Explorations in the History of Canadian Mapping: A Collection of Essays* (Ottawa: Association of Canadian Map Libraries and Archives, 1988), pp. 55–69.   **1860**

POPULAR IMAGES & EVALUATION

Wynn, Graeme, "The Mark of the Maritimes," in R. Berry and J. Acheson, eds., *Regionalism and National Identity* (Christchurch, N.Z.: Association for Canadian Studies in Australia and New Zealand, 1985), pp. 555–568.   **1861**

REGIONAL SETTLEMENT

Bird, J. Brian, "Settlement Patterns in Maritime Canada, 1687–1786," *Geographical Review*, vol. 45 (1955), pp. 385–404.   **1862**

Hugo-Brunt, Michael, "The Origin of Colonial Settlements in the Maritimes," *Plan*, vol. 1, 2 (1960), pp. 78–114.   **1863**

Ommer, Rosemary E., "Scots Kinship, Migration, and Early Settlement in Southwestern Newfoundland," Master's thesis, Memorial University of Newfoundland, 1974.   **1864**

Wynn, Graeme, "Paradise North," *Horizon Canada*, vol. 3, 33 (1985), pp. 769–775.   **1865**

POPULATION

See also 1344

LeBlanc, Robert G., "The Acadian Migrations," Master's thesis, University of Minnesota, 1962.
1866

LeBlanc, Robert G., "The Acadian Migrations," *Proceedings of the Minnesota Academy of Science*, vol. 30, 1 (1962), pp. 55–59. Reprinted, with minor modifications, in *Canadian Geographical*

Journal, vol. 81, 1 (1970), pp. 10–19; as "Les migrations acadiennes," in *Cahiers de géographie du Québec*, vol. 11, 24 (1967), pp. 523–541; in the same journal, vol. 23, 60 (1979), pp. 99–124; and in Dean R. Louder and Eric Wadell, eds., *Du continent perdu à l'archipel retrouvé: Le Québec et l'Amérique française* (Quebec: Presses de l'Université Laval, 1983), pp. 137–162.   **1867**

Ommer, Rosemary E., "Highland Scots Migration to Southwestern Newfoundland: A Study of Kinship," in John J. Mannion, ed., *The Peopling of Newfoundland: Essays in Historical Geography* (St. Johns: Memorial University of Newfoundland, Institute of Social and Economic Research, Publication no. 8, 1977), pp. 212–233.   **1868**

Thornton, Patricia A., "Some Preliminary Comments on the Extent and Consequences of Out-Migration from the Atlantic Region, 1870–1920," in L. R. Fischer and E. W. Sager, eds., *Merchant Shipping and Economic Development in Atlantic Canada* (St. John's: Memorial University of Newfoundland Maritime History Group, 1982), pp. 185–218.   **1869**

Thornton, Patricia A., "The Problem of Out-Migration from Atlantic Canada, 1871–1921: A New Look," *Acadiensis*, vol. 15, 1 (1985), pp. 3–34.   **1870**

Thornton, Patricia A., and David B. Frost, *County Level Net Migration in Atlantic Canada, 1871–1921* (Montreal: Concordia University, Department of Geography, Occasional Papers in Geography, no. 2, 1986), 123 pp.   **1871**

Wynn, Graeme, "Ethnic Migrations and Atlantic Canada: Geographical Perspectives," *Canadian Ethnic Studies*, vol. 18, 1 (1986), pp. 1–15.   **1872**

LeBlanc, Robert G., "Émigration, colonisation, et rapatriement: The Acadian Perspective," *Cahiers de la Société historique acadienne*, vol. 19, 3 (1988), pp. 71–104.   **1873**

RURAL & REGIONAL SOCIAL GEOGRAPHY

Ommer, Rosemary E., "Primitive Accumulation and the Scottish *Clann* in the Old World and the New," *Journal of Historical Geography*, vol. 12, 2 (1986), pp. 121–141.   **1874**

Williams, Alan F., ed., *Father Baudoin's War: D'Iberville's Campaigns in Acadia and Newfoundland, 1696, 1697* (St. John's: Memorial University Department of Geography, 1987), 191 pp.
1875

ECONOMIC DEVELOPMENT

Clark, Andrew Hill, "Contributions of Its Southern Neighbors to the Underdevelopment of the Maritime Provinces Area of Present Canada, 1710–1867," in R. A. Preston, ed., *The Influences of the United States on Canadian Development: Eleven Case Studies* (Durham: Duke University Press, 1972), pp. 164–184. **1876**

Alexander, David, "Economic Growth in the Atlantic Region, 1880 to 1940," *Acadiensis*, vol. 8, 1 (1978), pp. 47–76. **1877**

McCann, Larry D., "Living a Double Life: Town and Country in the Industrialization of the Maritimes," in Douglas Day, ed., *Geographical Perspectives on the Maritime Provinces* (Halifax: St. Mary's University, 1988), pp. 93–113. **1878**

Wynn, Graeme, "A Share of the Necessaries of Life: Remarks on Migration Development and Dependency in Atlantic Canada," in B. Fleming, ed., *Beyond Anger and Longing: Community and Development in Atlantic Canada* (Fredericton, N.B.: Acadiensis Press, 1988), pp. 17–55. **1879**

LAND & LAND USE

Wynn, Graeme, "The Utilization of the Chignecto Marshlands of Nova Scotia and New Brunswick, 1750–1800," Master's thesis, University of Toronto, 1969. **1880**

AGRICULTURE

Wynn, Graeme, "Late Eighteenth-Century Agriculture on the Bay of Fundy Marshlands," *Acadiensis*, vol. 8, 2 (1979), pp. 80–89. **1881**

Troughton, Michael J., "From Nodes to Nodes: The Rise and Fall of Agricultural Activity in the Maritime Provinces," in Douglas Day, ed., *Geographical Perspectives on the Maritime Provinces* (Halifax: St. Mary's University, 1988), pp. 25–46. **1882**

LANDSCAPE

Ennals, Peter M., and Deryck W. Holdsworth, "Vernacular Architecture and the Cultural Landscape of the Maritime Provinces—A Reconnaissance," *Acadiensis*, vol. 10, 2 (1981), pp. 86–106. Reprinted with revisions in Graeme Wynn, ed., *People, Places, Patterns, Processes: Geographical Perspectives on the Canadian Past* (Toronto: Copp Clark Pitman, 1990), pp. 177–195. **1883**

Ennals, Peter M., "The Folk Legacy in Acadian Domestic Architecture: A Study in Mislaid Self-Images," in Shane O'Dea, ed., *Dimensions of Canadian Architecture* (Ottawa: Society for the

Study of Architecture in Canada, Selected Papers, no. 6, 1984), pp. 8–12. **1884**

Ennals, Peter M., "Inside the Front Door: Recent Approaches and Themes for Interpreting Past Housing," in P. A. Buckner, ed., *Teaching Maritime Studies* (Fredericton, N.B.: Acadiensis Press, 1986), pp. 235–240. **1885**

Ennals, Peter M., and Deryck W. Holdsworth, "The Cultural Landscape of the Maritime Provinces," in Douglas Day, ed., *Geographical Perspectives on the Maritime Provinces* (Halifax: St. Mary's University, 1988), pp. 1–14. **1886**

URBAN NETWORKS & URBANIZATION

McCann, Larry D., "Metropolitanism and Branch Businesses in the Maritimes, 1881–1931," *Acadiensis*, vol. 8, 1 (1983), pp. 112–125. Reprinted in Graeme Wynn, ed., *People, Places, Patterns, Processes: Geographical Perspectives on the Canadian Past* (Toronto: Copp Clark Pitman, 1990), pp. 233–246. **1887**

Macowan, Brian H., "The Evolution of a Regional Urban Network: New Brunswick and Nova Scotia, 1871–1971," Ph.D. diss., University of Waterloo, 1986. **1888**

TOWNSCAPE

Ennals, Peter M., "The Main Streets of Maritime Canada," *Bulletin of the Society for the Study of Architecture in Canada*, vol. 11, 3 (1986), pp. 11–13. **1889**

McCalla, Robert, "Land Use Development in Cityport Waterfronts: A Model," in Douglas Day, ed., *Geographical Perspectives on the Maritime Provinces* (Halifax: St. Mary's University, 1988), pp. 131–143. **1890**

RECREATION & TOURISM

Wynn, Graeme, and Stephen Hornsby, "Walking through the Past," *Acadiensis*, vol. 10, 2 (1981), pp. 152–159. **1891**

PLACE NAMES

Rayburn, J. Alan, "Acadia: The Origin of the Name and Its Geographical and Historical Utilization," *Canadian Cartographer*, vol. 10, 1 (1973), pp. 26–43. Translated without illustrations as "Acadie: L'origine du nom et son usage géographique et historique," *Canoma*, vol. 2 (1976), pp. 1–5. **1892**

NEWFOUNDLAND & LABRADOR

GENERAL

Packard, A. S., "The Geographical Evolution of Labrador," *Journal of the American Geographical Society*, vol. 20 (1888), pp. 208–230.   **1893**

Head, C. Grant, "The Changing Geography of Newfoundland in the Eighteenth Century," Ph.D. diss., University of Wisconsin–Madison, 1971.   **1894**

Head, C. Grant, *Eighteenth Century Newfoundland: A Geographer's Perspective* (Toronto: McClelland and Stewart, 1976), 296 pp.   **1895**

Brown, H., "The Impact of Modernization on a Traditional Regional System: The Case of Inner Placentia Bay, Newfoundland, 1911–1966," Master's thesis, Memorial University of Newfoundland, 1985.   **1896**

ENVIRONMENTAL CHANGE

Mednis, Robert J., "Forest Fires on Fogo Island," *Newfoundland Quarterly*, vol. 74, 2 (Summer 1978), pp. 25–26.   **1897**

NATIVE PEOPLES & WHITE RELATIONS

Marshall, Ingeborg, "An Unpublished Map Made by John Cartwright between 1768 and 1773 Showing Beothuck Indian Settlements and Artifacts and Allowing a New Population Estimate," *Ethnohistory*, vol. 24, 3 (1977), pp. 223–250.   **1898**

Trudel, François, "Les Inuit du Labrador meridional face à l'exploitation canadienne et française des pêcheries (1700–1760)," *Revue d'histoire de l'Amérique française*, vol. 31, 4 (1978), pp. 481–500.   **1899**

Pastore, Ralph, "The Collapse of the Beothuk World," *Acadiensis*, vol. 19, 1 (1989), pp. 52–71.   **1900**

EXPLORATION & MAPPING

Skelton, Raleigh A., *James Cook: Surveyor of Newfoundland, Being a Collection of Charts of the Coasts of Newfoundland and Labrador &c, Drawn . . . by James Cook and Michael Lane*

(San Francisco: David Magee, 1965), 31 pp. [First published London: T. Jeffreys, 1769–1770]   **1901**

Ross, W. Gillies, "Exploration of the Unknown River in the Labrador," *Beaver*, Outfit 296, 2 (1965), pp. 30–35. Reprinted in *Among the Deep Sea Fishers* (National Grenfell Association), vol. 65, 3 (1967), pp. 72–79.   **1902**

O'Dea, Fabian, *The Seventeenth Century Cartography of Newfoundland* (Toronto: B. V. Gutsell, Cartographica Monograph no. 1, 1971), 47 pp.   **1903**

Barkham, Selma, "First Will and Testament on the Labrador Coast," *Geographical Magazine*, vol. 49, 9 (1977), pp. 574–581.   **1904**

Barkham, Selma, "The Identification of Labrador Ports in Spanish Sixteenth Century Documents," *Canadian Cartographer*, vol. 14, 1 (1977), pp. 1–9.   **1905**

Staveley, Michael, "Saskatchewan-by-the-Sea: The Topographic Work of Alexander Murray in Newfoundland," *Newfoundland Quarterly*, vol. 77, 2–3 (1981), pp. 31–41.   **1906**

Staveley, Michael, "The Topographical Work of Alexander Murray in Newfoundland," *Bulletin of the Association of Canadian Map Libraries*, vol. 40 (1981), pp. 1–19. Reprinted in Barbara Farrell and Eileen Desbarats, eds., *Explorations in the History of Canadian Mapping: A Collection of Essays* (Ottawa: Association of Canadian Map Libraries and Archives, 1988), pp. 239–250.   **1907**

Williams, Alan F., "With D'Iberville in the Bays of the Avalon Peninsula, Newfoundland, 1697," *Bulletin of Canadian Studies*, vol. 8, 1 (1984), pp. 50–70.   **1908**

Handcock, W. Gordon, "State-of-the-Art French Cartography in Eighteenth Century Newfoundland: The Work of Marc Antoine Sicre de Cinq-Mars," *Newfoundland Studies*, vol. 4, 2 (1988), pp. 145–162.   **1909**

POPULAR IMAGES & EVALUATION

Williams, Susan, "Images of Newfoundland in Promotional Literature, 1890–1914," Master's thesis, McGill University, 1980.   **1910**

REGIONAL SETTLEMENT

Head, C. Grant, "Settlement Migration in Central Bonavista Bay, Newfoundland," Master's thesis, McMaster University, 1964. 1911

Head, C. Grant, "Settlement Migration in Central Bonavista Bay, Newfoundland," in R. Louis Gentilcore, ed., *Canada's Changing Geography* (Scarborough, Ont.: Prentice-Hall of Canada, 1967), pp. 92–110. 1912

Handcock, W. Gordon, "The Origin and Evolution of the Commission of Government (Newfoundland) Land Settlements, 1934–1969," Master's thesis, Memorial University of Newfoundland, 1970. 1913

Head, C. Grant, "The Establishment of Year-Round Settlement in Newfoundland," in W. P. Adams and F. M. Helleiner, eds., *International Geography, 1972*, vol. 1, sec. 5, *Historical Geography* (Toronto: University of Toronto Press, for the International Geographical Union, 1972), pp. 425–427. 1914

Treude, Erhard, *Nordlabrador: Entwicklung und Struktur von Siedlung und Wirtschaft in einem polarem Grenzraum der Ökumene* (Münster: Westfälische Geographische Studien, no. 29, 1974), 300 pp. 1915

Macpherson, Alan G., "A Model Sequence in the Peopling of Central Bonavista Bay, 1676–1857," in John J. Mannion, ed., *The Peopling of Newfoundland: Essays in Historical Geography* (St. Johns: Memorial University of Newfoundland, Institute of Social and Economic Research, Publication no. 8, 1977), pp. 102–135. 1916

Mannion, John J., ed., *The Peopling of Newfoundland: Essays in Historical Geography* (St. Johns: Memorial University of Newfoundland, Institute of Social and Economic Research, Publication no. 8, 1977), 289 pp. 1917

Mannion, John J., "Settlers and Traders in Western Newfoundland," in John J. Mannion, ed., *The Peopling of Newfoundland: Essays in Historical Geography* (St. John's: Memorial University of Newfoundland, Institute of Social and Economic Research, Publication no. 8, 1977), pp. 234–275. 1918

Thornton, Patricia A., "The Demographic and Mercantile Bases of Initial Permanent Settlement in the Strait of Belle Isle," in John J. Mannion, ed., *The Peopling of Newfoundland: Essays in Historical Geography* (St. Johns: Memorial University of Newfoundland, Institute of Social and Economic Research, Publication no. 8, 1977), pp. 152–183. 1919

Thornton, Patricia A., "Dynamic Equilibrium: Settlement, Population, and Ecology in the Strait of Belle Isle, Newfoundland, 1840–1940," Ph.D. diss., University of Aberdeen, 1978. 1920

Anderson, David, "The Development of Settlement in Southern Coastal Labrador, with particular reference to Sandwich Bay," *Bulletin of Canadian Studies*, vol. 8, 1 (1984), pp. 23–49. 1921

POPULATION

Williamson, H. Anthony, "Population Movement and the Food Gathering Economy of Northern Labrador," Master's thesis, McGill University, 1964. 1922

Staveley, Michael, "Migration and Mobility in Newfoundland and Labrador: A Study in Population Geography," Ph.D. diss., University of Alberta, 1973. 1923

Adams, J. Gordon L., "Newfoundland Population Movements with Particular Reference to the Post-War Period," Ph.D. diss., McGill University, 1976. 1924

Handcock, W. Gordon, "Spatial Patterns in a Trans-Atlantic Migration Field: The British Isles and Newfoundland during the Eighteenth and Nineteenth Centuries," in Brian S. Osborne, ed., *The Settlement of Canada: Origins and Transfers* (Kingston: Queen's University, 1976), pp. 13–40. 1925

Handcock, W. Gordon, "English Migration to Newfoundland," in John J. Mannion, ed., *The Peopling of Newfoundland: Essays in Historical Geography* (St. Johns: Memorial University of Newfoundland, Institute of Social and Economic Research, Publication no. 8, 1977), pp. 15–48. 1926

Staveley, Michael, "Population Dynamics in Newfoundland: The Regional Patterns," in John J. Mannion, ed., *The Peopling of Newfoundland: Essays in Historical Geography* (St. Johns: Memorial University of Newfoundland, Institute of Social and Economic Research, Publication no. 8, 1977), pp. 49–76. 1927

Handcock, W. Gordon, "Historical Geography of the Origins of English Settlement in Newfoundland: A Study of the Migration Process," Ph.D. diss., University of Birmingham (England), 1979. 1928

Handcock, W. Gordon, "The West Country Migrations to Newfoundland," *Bulletin of Canadian Studies*, vol. 5, 1 (1981), pp. 5–24. 1929

Thornton, Patricia A., "Newfoundland's Frontier Demographic Experience: The World We Have

Not Lost," *Newfoundland Studies,* vol. 1, 2 (1985), pp. 141–162.　　　　　　　　**1930**

Mannion, John J., "Patrick Morris and Newfoundland Irish Immigration," in C. J. Byrne and M. Harry, eds., *Talamh an EISC: Canadian and Irish Essays* (Halifax: Numbus Publishers, 1986), pp. 180–202.　　　　　　　　**1931**

Mannion, John J., "Kilkenneymen in Newfoundland," *Old Kilkenney Review,* vol. 3, 4 (1987), pp. 358–363.　　　　　　　　**1932**

Macpherson, Alan G., "The People of Newfoundland: A Longue Durée in Historical Geography," in Guy M. Robinson, ed., *A Social Geography of Canada: Essays in Honour of J. Wreford Watson* (Edinburgh: North British Publishing, 1988), pp. 280–294. Also Toronto: Dundurn Press, 1991, pp. 373–392.　　　　　　　　**1933**

Handcock, W. Gordon, *Soe Longe as There Comes Noe Women: Origins of English Settlement in Newfoundland* (St. Johns: Breakwater Books, Newfoundland History Series, no. 6, 1989), 343 pp.　　　　　　　　**1934**

RURAL & REGIONAL SOCIAL GEOGRAPHY

Waddell, Eric, and Claire Doran, "Les Franco-Terre-Neuviens: Survie et renaissance équivoques," *Cahiers de géographie du Québec,* vol. 23, 58 (1979), pp. 143–156.　　**1935**

Mannion, John J., "Migration and Upward Mobility: The Meagher Family in Ireland and Newfoundland, 1780–1830," *Irish Economic and Social History,* vol. 15 (1988), pp. 54–70.　　**1936**

Mannion, John J., "Old World Antecedents: New World Adaptations: Instioge (Co. Kilkenny) Immigrants in Newfoundland," *Newfoundland Studies,* vol. 5, 2 (1989), pp. 103–176.　　**1937**

POLITICAL & ADMINISTRATIVE GEOGRAPHY

See also 1391

Sharpe, Christopher A., "The Race of Honour: A Regional Analysis of Enlistments and Casualties in the Armed Forces of Newfoundland, 1914–1918," *Newfoundland Studies,* vol. 4, 1 (1988), pp. 27–55.　　　　　　　　**1938**

ECONOMIC DEVELOPMENT

Le Messurier, H. W., "The Early Relations between Newfoundland and the Channel Islands," *Geographical Review,* vol. 2, 6 (1916), pp. 449–457.　　　　　　　　**1939**

Mannion, John J., *Point Lance in Transition: The Transformation of a Newfoundland Outport* (Toronto: McClelland and Stewart, 1976), 64 pp.

Reprinted in abbreviated form in Graeme Wynn, ed., *People, Places, Patterns, Processes: Geographical Perspectives on the Canadian Past* (Toronto: Copp Clark Pitman, 1990), pp. 301–328.　　　　　　　　**1940**

Sanger, Chesley W., "The Evolution of Sealing and the Spread of Settlement in Northeastern Newfoundland," in John J. Mannion, ed., *The Peopling of Newfoundland: Essays in Historical Geography* (St. Johns: Memorial University of Newfoundland, Institute of Social and Economic Research, Publication no. 8, 1977), pp. 136–151.　　　　　　　　**1941**

Pinsent, Charles, "The Impact of Confederation on a Newfoundland Outport: A Microgeographical Study," Master's thesis, York University, 1978.　　　　　　　　**1942**

Handcock, W. Gordon, "The Poole Mercantile Community and Growth of Trinity, 1700–1839," *Newfoundland Quarterly,* vol. 80, 3 (1985), pp. 19–30.　　　　　　　　**1943**

Young, Andrea Margaret Kent, "Organizational Change and Economic Development in Rural Newfoundland," Master's thesis, Carleton University, 1985. [Focus on 1949–1980]　　**1944**

LAND & LAND USE

Treude, Erhard, "Eighteenth Century Eskimo Land Cessions in Northern Labrador," *Musk-Ox,* vol. 26 (1980), pp. 3–12.　　　　　　**1945**

McEwen, A., "The Township System of Surveys in Newfoundland," *Canadian Surveyor,* vol. 37, 2 (1983), pp. 39–50.　　　　　　　　**1946**

EXTRACTIVE ACTIVITY

Fisheries

Sanger, Chesley W., "Technological and Spatial Adaptation in the Newfoundland Seal Industry during the Nineteenth Century," Master's thesis, Memorial University of Newfoundland, 1973.　　　　　　　　**1947**

Sanger, Chesley W., "The Nineteenth Century Newfoundland Seal Fishery and the Influence of Scottish Whalemen," *Polar Record,* vol. 20, 126 (1980), pp. 231–252.　　　　　　**1948**

Brire, Jean-François, and S. Dale Standen, "Géographie historique de la pêche terre-neuvière française dans la première moitié du XVIIIe siècle," *Proceedings of the Annual Meeting of the French Colonial Historical Society,* vol. 10 (1984), pp. 95–112.　　　　　　　　**1949**

Sanger, Chesley W., "The Dundee–St. John's Connection: Nineteenth Century Interlinkages between Scottish Arctic Whaling and the Newfoundland Seal Fishery," *Newfoundland Studies*, vol. 4, 1 (1988), pp. 1–26.   **1950**

Sanger, Chesley W., and A. B. Dickinson, "The Origins of Modern Shore Based Whaling in Newfoundland and Labrador: The Cabot Steam Whaling Company, Ltd., 1896–1898," *International Journal of Maritime History*, vol. 1, 1 (1989), pp. 129–157.   **1951**

Sanger, Chesley W., and A. B. Dickinson, "Modern Shore-Based Whaling in Newfoundland and Labrador: Expansion and Consolidation, 1898–1902," *International Journal of Maritime History*, vol. 2, 1 (1990), pp. 83–116.   **1952**

Thornton, Patricia A., "The Transition from the Migratory to the Resident Fishery in the Strait of Belle Isle," *Acadiensis*, vol. 19, 2 (1990), pp. 92–120. Reprinted in Rosemary E. Ommer, ed., *Merchant Credit and Labour Strategies in Historical Perspective* (Fredericton, N.B.: Acadiensis Press, 1990), pp. 138–166.   **1953**

Lumbering

Cokes, E., "The Spatial Pattern of Log Cutting in Bay D'Espoir, 1895–1922," Master's thesis, Memorial University of Newfoundland, 1973.
1954

Fur trade

Hastings, Clifford, "Mercantilism and Laissez-Faire Capitalism in the Ungava Peninsula, 1670–1940: The Economic Geography of the Fur Trade," Master's thesis, McGill University, 1985.
1955

AGRICULTURE

Mackinnon, Robert A., "The Growth of Commercial Agriculture around St. John's, 1800–1935: A Study of Local Trade in Response to Urban Demand," Master's thesis, Memorial University of Newfoundland, 1981.   **1956**

Mackinnon, Robert A., "Farming the Rock: The Evolution of Commercial Agriculture around St. John's, Newfoundland, to 1945," *Acadiensis*, vol. 20, 2 (1991), pp. 32–61.   **1957**

LANDSCAPE

Jett, Stephen C., "A French Origin for the 'Beehive' Structures of Ungava?" *Anthropological Journal of Canada*, vol. 7, 2 (1969), pp. 16–21.
1958

Mills, David B., "The Evolution of Folk Architecture in Trinity Bay," *Newfoundland Quarterly*, vol. 69, 3 (1972), pp. 17–23.   **1959**

Mills, David B., "The Evolution of Folk House Forms in Trinity Bay, Newfoundland," Master's

thesis, Memorial University of Newfoundland, 1975.   **1960**

Mills, David B., "The Development of Folk Architecture in Trinity Bay," in John J. Mannion, ed., *The Peopling of Newfoundland: Essays in Historical Geography* (St. Johns: Memorial University of Newfoundland, Institute of Social and Economic Research, Publication no. 8, 1977), pp. 77–101.   **1961**

Houston, Cecil J., and William J. Smyth, "The Impact of Fraternalism on the Landscape of Newfoundland," *Canadian Geographer*, vol. 29, 1 (1985), pp. 59–65.   **1962**

COMMUNICATIONS & TRADE

Barr, William, "S. S. Nascopie: Newfoundland Sealing Steamer," *Newfoundland Quarterly*, vol. 74, 3 (1978), pp. 19–28.   **1963**

Mannion, John J., "The Waterford Merchants and the Irish-Newfoundland Provisions Trade, 1770–1820," in L. M. Cilen and Paul Butel, eds., *Négoce et industrie en France et en Irlande aux XVIIIe et XIXe siècles* (Paris: Centre National de la Recherche Scientifique, 1980), pp. 27–43. Reprinted in Donald H. Akenson, ed., *Canadian Papers of Rural History*, vol. 3 (Gananoque, Ont.: Langdale Press, 1982), pp. 178–203.   **1964**

Mannion, John J., "Irish Merchants Abroad: The Newfoundland Experience, 1750–1850," *Newfoundland Studies*, vol. 2, 2 (1986), pp. 127–190.
1965

Orr, J. A., "Scottish Merchants in the Newfoundland Trade, 1800–1835: A Colonial Community in Transition," Master's thesis, Memorial University of Newfoundland, 1987.   **1966**

Mannion, John J., "Henry Shea (1767–1830): A Tipperary Trader in Newfoundland," *Tipperary Journal*, vol. 1 (1988), pp. 182–191.   **1967**

URBAN ECONOMIC STRUCTURE

Koh, Ngiap-Puoy, "Modelling Retail System Dynamics: An Application to the System of Major Retail Centres in St. John's, Newfoundland, 1960–1980," Master's thesis, Memorial University of Newfoundland, 1990.   **1968**

TOWNSCAPE

Oliver, Elizabeth D., "The Rebuilding of the City of St. John's after the Great Fire of 1892: A Study in Urban Morphogenesis," Master's thesis, Memorial University of Newfoundland, 1983.
1969

RECREATION & TOURISM

Overton, J., "Tourism Development, Conservation, and Conflict: Game Laws for Caribou Protection in Newfoundland," in Geoffrey Wall and John S. Marsh, eds., *Recreational Land Use: Perspectives on Its Evolution in Canada* (Ottawa: Carleton University Press, 1982), pp. 354–364.   **1970**

PLACE NAMES

Rouillard, Eugène, "Toponymie de la côte nord du Saint-Laurent et du Labrador canadien," *Bulletin de la Société de géographie du Québec*, vol. 7 (1913), pp. 208–212.   **1971**

Seary, Edgar R., "Linguistic Variety in the Place Names of Newfoundland," *Canadian Geographical Journal*, vol. 65, 5 (1962), pp. 146–155.   **1972**

Ross, W. Gillies, "Exploration and Toponymy on the Unknown River, Labrador," *Cahiers de géographie du Québec*, vol. 10, 20 (1966), pp. 291–299.   **1973**

Seary, Edgar R., *Place Names of the Avalon Peninsula of the Island of Newfoundland* (Toronto: University of Toronto Press, for Memorial University of Newfoundland, Memorial University Series, no. 2, 1971), 383 pp.   **1974**

Handcock, W. Gordon, "The View from Mount Janus: J. Cartwright's 1768 Exploits River Toponymy," *Canoma*, vol. 14, 1 (1988), pp. 6–11. Reprinted, in expanded form, in *Newfoundland Quarterly*, vol. 85, 1 (1989), pp. 17–31.   **1975**

Macpherson, Alan G., "A Name in Search of a Place," *Canoma*, vol. 15, 1 (1989), pp. 30–33. [Parkhurst]   **1976**

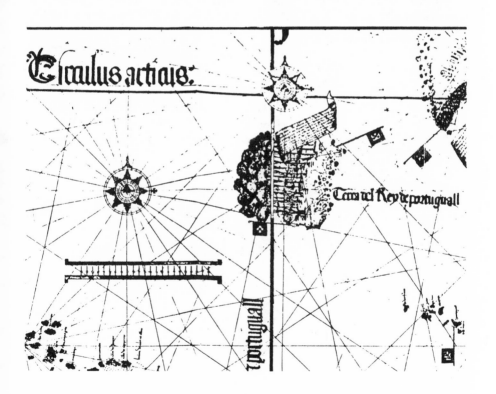

——— PRINCE EDWARD ISLAND ———

GENERAL

Clark, Andrew Hill, "South Island, New Zealand, and Prince Edward Island, Canada: A Study of 'Insularity'," *New Zealand Geographer*, vol. 3, 2 (1947), pp. 137–150.   **1977**

Clark, Andrew Hill, *Three Centuries and the Island: A Historical Geography of Settlement and Agriculture in Prince Edward Island, Canada* (Toronto: University of Toronto Press, 1959), 287 pp.   **1978**

POPULAR IMAGES & EVALUATION

Squire, Shelagh J., "L. M. Montgomery's Prince Edward Island: A Study of Literary Landscapes and Tourist Development," Master's thesis, Carleton University, 1988.   **1979**

REGIONAL SETTLEMENT

Greenhill, Basil, and A. Gifford, *Westcountrymen in Prince Edward's Isle: A Fragment of the Great Migration* (Toronto: University of Toronto Press, 1967).   **1980**

Bumsted, James M., *Land, Settlement, and Politics on Eighteenth-Century Prince Edward Island* (Kingston: McGill-Queen's University Press, 1987), 238 pp.   **1981**

RURAL & REGIONAL SOCIAL GEOGRAPHY

Robertson, I. R., "Highlanders, Irishmen, and the Land Question in Nineteenth-Century Prince Edward Island," in L. M. Cullen and T. C. Smout, eds., *Comparative Aspects of Scottish and Irish Economic and Social History, 1600–1900* (Edinburgh: John Donald Publishers, 1977), pp. 227–240.   **1982**

Bumsted, James M., "The Origins of the Land Question on Prince Edward Island, 1767–1805," *Acadiensis*, vol. 11, 1 (1981), pp. 65–85.   **1983**

Bittermann, Rusty, "Escheat!: Rural Protest on Prince Edward Island, 1832–1842," Ph.D. diss., University of New Brunswick, 1991.   **1984**

Bittermann, Rusty, "Agrarian Protest and Cultural Transfer: Irish Emigrants and the Escheat Movement on Prince Edward Island," in Tom Power, ed., *The Irish in Atlantic Canada* (Fredericton, N.B.: New Ireland Press, 1991, pp. 96–106.   **1985**

LAND & LAND USE

Raymond, Charles W., and J. Alan Rayburn, "Land Abandonment in Prince Edward Island," *Geographical Bulletin* (Ottawa), vol. 19 (1963), pp. 78–86.   **1986**

PLACE NAMES

Rayburn, J. Alan, *Geographical Names of Prince Edward Island* (Ottawa: Department of Energy, Mines, and Resources, Surveys and Mapping Branch, for the Canadian Permanent Committee on Geographical Names, Toponymy Study no. 1, 1973), 135 pp.   **1987**

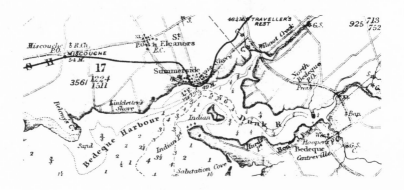

NOVA SCOTIA

GENERAL

Vaillant, Paul, *A Geographical History of Nova Scotia, Containing an Account of the Situation, Extent, and Limits Thereof; As Also of the Various Struggles between the Two Crowns of England and France for the Possession of that Province, Wherein Is Shewn, the Importance of It, as Well with Regard to Our Trade, as to the Securing of Our Other Settlements in North America; To Which Is Added, an Accurate Description of the Bays, Harbours, Lakes, and Rivers, the Nature of the Soil, and the Produce of the Country, Together with the Manners and Customs of the Indian Inhabitants* (London: Printed for Paul Vaillant, 1749), 110 pp. Translated by Etienne de LaFargue as *Histoire géographique de la Nouvelle Ecosse . . .* [Paris, 1755?], 164 pp.   **1988**

Clark, Andrew Hill, *Acadia: The Geography of Early Nova Scotia to 1760* (Madison: University of Wisconsin Press, 1968), 450 pp.   **1989**

Hornsby, Stephen J., "An Historical Geography of Cape Breton Island in the Nineteenth Century," Ph.D. diss., University of British Columbia, 1986.   **1990**

EXPLORATION & MAPPING

Douglas, R., "An Early Map of Nova Scotia," *Canadian Geographical Magazine*, vol. 5 (1932), pp. 21–25.   **1991**

Clark, Andrew Hill, "Titus Smith, Junior, and the Geography of Nova Scotia in 1801 and 1802," *Annals of the Association of American Geographers*, vol. 44, 4 (1954), pp. 291–314.   **1992**

Shipton, Nathaniel N., "Samuel Holland's Plan of Cape Breton," *Canadian Cartographer*, vol. 5, 2 (1968), pp. 81–89.   **1993**

Robinson, Arthur H., "Nathaniel Blackmore's Plaine Chart of Nova Scotia: Isobaths in the Open Sea?" *Imago Mundi*, vol. 2 (1976), pp. 137–141.   **1994**

Morrison, Walter K., "The 'Modern Mapping' of Nova Scotia," *Map Collector*, vol. 18 (1982), pp. 28–34.   **1995**

POPULAR IMAGES & EVALUATION

Wynn, Graeme, "Images of the Acadian Valley: The Photographs of Amos Lawson Hardy," *Acadiensis*, vol. 15, 1 (1985), pp. 59–83.   **1996**

REGIONAL SETTLEMENT

Robinson, B. E., "Grand Pré of the Acadians," *Canadian Geographical Journal*, vol. 11, 2 (1935), pp. 76–84.   **1997**

Hobson, Peggie M., "Population and Settlement in Nova Scotia," *Scottish Geographical Magazine*, vol. 70, 2 (1954), pp. 49–63.   **1998**

Gentilcore, R. Louis, "The Agricultural Background of Settlement in Eastern Nova Scotia," *Annals of the Association of American Geographers*, vol. 46, 3 (1956), pp. 378–404. Reprinted in R. Louis Gentilcore, ed., *Canada's Changing Geography* (Scarborough, Ont.: Prentice-Hall of Canada, 1967), pp. 34–55.   **1999**

McNabb, Debra, "Land and Families in Horton Township, Nova Scotia, 1760–1830," Master's thesis, University of British Columbia, 1986.   **2000**

Hornsby, Stephen J., "Scottish Emigration and Settlement in Early Nineteenth Century Cape Breton," in Graeme Wynn, ed., *People, Places, Patterns, Processes: Geographical Perspectives on the Canadian Past* (Toronto: Copp Clark Pitman, 1990), pp. 110–138.   **2001**

POPULATION

Brookes, Alan A., "The Golden Age and the Exodus: the Case of Canning, King's County (Nova Scotia)," *Acadiensis*, vol. 11, 1 (1981), pp. 57–82.   **2002**

Hornsby, Stephen J., "Migration and Settlement: The Scots of Cape Breton," in Douglas Day, ed., *Geographical Perspectives on the Maritime Provinces* (Halifax: St. Mary's University, 1988), pp. 15–24.   **2003**

RURAL & REGIONAL SOCIAL GEOGRAPHY

Clark, Andrew Hill, "Old World Origins and Religious Adherence in Nova Scotia," *Geographical Review*, vol. 50 (1960), pp. 317–344.   **2004**

Livingstone, Roger, "Ethnic Response of Acadians and Scots to the Credit Union Movement in Nova Scotia, 1933–1940," Ph.D. diss., Syracuse University, 1973.   **2005**

Wynn, Graeme, "This Dark Vale of Sorrow," *Nova Scotia Historical Review*, vol. 6, 2 (1986), pp. 55–62.   **2006**

Bitterman, Rusty, "Economic Stratification and Agrarian Settlement: Middle River in the Early Nineteenth Century," in K. Donovan, ed., *The Island: New Perspectives on Cape Breton History, 1713–1975* (Sydney and Fredericton: University College of Cape Breton and Acadiensis Press, 1990), pp. 71–87.   2007

POLITICAL & ADMINISTRATIVE GEOGRAPHY

Menger, Garry L., "Spatial and Temporal Variations in Government Expenditures: Nova Scotia Highway Expenditures, 1940–1980," Master's thesis, University of Toronto, 1983.   2008

ECONOMIC DEVELOPMENT

Clark, Andrew Hill, "New England's Role in the Underdevelopment of Cape Breton Island during the French Regime, 1713–1758," *Canadian Geographer*, vol. 9, 1 (1965), pp. 1–12.   2009

Sitwell, O. F. George, "The Relationship of the Agricultural Revolution to Economic Development: The Case of Nova Scotia," *Albertan Geographer*, vol. 2 (1965–1966), pp. 41–44.   2010

Ross, Eric D., "The Rise and Fall of Pictou Island," in Larry D. McCann, ed., *People and Place: Studies of Small Town Life in the Maritimes* (Fredericton, N.B.: Acadiensis Press, 1987), pp. 161–190.   2011

Ross, Eric D., "Growth and Decay in the Rural Maritimes: The Example of Pictou Island," in Guy M. Robinson, ed., *A Social Geography of Canada: Essays in Honour of J. Wreford Watson* (Edinburgh: North British Publishing, 1988), pp. 268–279. Also Toronto: Dundurn Press, 1991, pp. 359–372.   2012

Hornsby, Stephen J., "Staple Trades, Subsistence Agriculture, and Nineteenth-Century Cape Breton Island," *Annals of the Association of American Geographers*, vol. 79, 3 (1989), pp. 411–434.   2013

LAND & LAND USE

Gentilcore, R. Louis, "Land-Use and Agricultural Production in Antigonish County, Nova Scotia," Ph.D. diss., University of Maryland, 1950.   2014

Gentilcore, R. Louis, "Land Use and the Dairy Industry in Antigonish County, Nova Scotia," *Canadian Geographer*, vol. 2 (1952), pp. 43–50.
                                                   2015

Nicholson, Norman L., "Rural Settlement and Land Use in the New Glasgow Region," *Geographical Bulletin* (Ottawa), no. 7 (1955), pp. 38–64.   2016

Cornwall, Brooke, "A Land-Use Reconnaissance of the Annapolis-Cornwallis Valley, Nova Scotia," *Geographical Bulletin* (Ottawa), no. 9 (1958), pp. 22–51.   2017

Sitwell, O. F. George, "Land Use and Settlement Patterns in Pictou County, Nova Scotia," Ph.D. diss., University of Toronto, 1968.   2018

Eaton, Ernest L., "The Survey Plan of Cornwallis Township, Kings County," *Nova Scotia Historical Review*, vol. 1, 2 (1981), pp. 16–33.   2019

McNabb, Debra, "The Role of the Land in the Development of Horton Township, 1760–1775," in Margaret Conrad, ed., *They Planted Well: New England Planters in Maritime Canada* (Fredericton, N.B.: Acadiensis Press, 1988), pp. 151–160.   2020

EXTRACTIVE ACTIVITY

Millward, Hugh A., "The Development, Decline, and Revival of Mining on the Sydney Coalfield," *Canadian Geographer*, vol. 28, 2 (1984), pp. 180–185.   2021

Millward, Hugh A., "Mine Locations and the Sequence of Coal Exploitation on the Sydney Coalfields, 1720–1980," in K. Donovan, ed., *Cape Breton at 200: Historical Essays in Honor of the Island's Bicentennial, 1785–1985* (Sydney: University College of Cape Breton Press, 1985), pp. 183–202.   2022

Millward, Hugh A., "A Model of Coalfield Development: Six Stages Exemplified by the Sydney Field," *Canadian Geographer*, vol. 29, 3 (1985), pp. 234–248.   2023

Sandberg, L. Anders, "Swedish Forestry Legislation in Nova Scotia: The Rise and Fall of the Forest Improvement Act, 1965–1986," in Douglas Day, ed., *Geographical Perspectives on the Maritime Provinces* (Halifax: Saint Mary's University, 1988), pp. 179–196.   2024

AGRICULTURE

Clark, Andrew Hill, "The Sheep/Swine Ratio as a Guide to a Century's Change in the Livestock Geography of Nova Scotia," *Economic Geography*, vol. 38, 1 (1962), pp. 38–55.   2025

Bittermann, Rusty, "The Hierarchy of the Soil: Land and Labour in a Nineteenth-Century Cape Breton Community," *Acadiensis*, vol. 18, 1 (1988), pp. 33–55.   2026

Mackinnon, Robert A., and Graeme Wynn, "Nova Scotian Agriculture in the 'Golden Age': A New Look," in Douglas Day, ed., *Geographical Perspectives on the Maritime Provinces* (Halifax: St. Mary's University, 1988), pp. 47–59.   2027

Wynn, Graeme, "Exciting a Spirit of Emulation among the Plod-Holes: Agricultural Reform in Pre-Confederation Nova Scotia," *Acadiensis*, vol. 20, 1 (1990), pp. 5–51.   **2028**

Mackinnon, Robert A., "The Historical Geography of Agriculture in Nova Scotia, 1851–1951," Ph.D. diss., University of British Columbia, 1991.   **2029**

LANDSCAPE

Ennals, Peter M., "The Yankee Origins of Bluenose Vernacular Architecture," *American Review of Canadian Studies*, vol. 12, 2 (1982), pp. 5–21.   **2030**

Trask, Deborah, and Debra McNabb, "Carved in Stone: Material Evidence in the Graveyards of King's County, Nova Scotia," *Material History Bulletin*, no. 23 (1986), pp. 35–42.   **2031**

COMMUNICATIONS & TRADE

Ommer, Rosemary E., "Anticipating the Trend: The Pictou Ship Register, 1840–1889," *Acadiensis*, vol. 10, 1 (1980), pp. 67–89.   **2032**

MANUFACTURING & INDUSTRIALIZATION

McCann, Larry D., "The Mercantile-Industrial Transition in the Metal Towns of Pictou County, 1857–1931," *Acadiensis*, vol. 10, 2 (1981), pp. 29–64. Reprinted in Gilbert A. Stelter ed., *Cities and Urbanization: Canadian Historical Perspectives* (Toronto: Copp Clark Pitman, 1990), pp. 87–123.   **2033**

Sandberg, L. Anders, "The Deindustrialization of Pictou County, Nova Scotia: Capital, Labour, and the Process of Regional Decline, 1881–1921," Ph.D. diss., McGill University, 1986.   **2034**

TOWN GROWTH

McCann, Larry D., "Staples and the New Industrialism in the Growth of Post-Confederation Halifax," *Acadiensis*, vol. 8, 2 (1979), pp. 47–79. Reprinted in Gilbert A. Stelter and Alan F. J. Artibise, eds., *Shaping the Urban Landscape: Aspects of the Canadian City-Building Process* (Toronto: Oxford University Press, 1982), pp. 84–115.   **2035**

URBAN SOCIAL STRUCTURE

McCann, Larry D., and Jill Burnett, "Social Mobil-

ity and the Ironmasters of Late Nineteenth Century New Glasgow," in Larry D. McCann, ed., *People and Place: Studies of Small Towns in the Maritimes* (Fredericton, N.B.: Acadiensis Press, 1987), pp. 59–77.   **2036**

McCann, Larry D., "Class, Ethnicity, and Residential Differentiation in Mid-Victorian Halifax," in Richard Preston and Bruce Mitchell, eds., *Reflections and Visions: Twenty-five Years of Geography at Waterloo* (Waterloo: University of Waterloo Department of Geography Publication Series, no. 33, 1990), pp. 239–265.   **2037**

TOWNSCAPE

Watson, J. Wreford, "Relict Geography in an Urban Community," in Ronald Miller and J. Wreford Watson, eds., *Geographical Essays in Memory of Alan G. Ogilvie* (London: Thomas Nelson and Sons, 1959), pp. 110–143. [Halifax]   **2038**

Buggey, Susan, "Building Halifax, 1841–1871," in Gilbert A. Stelter and Alan F. J. Artibise, eds., *Shaping the Urban Landscape: Aspects of the Canadian City-Building Process* (Ottawa: Carleton University Press, 1982), pp. 232–255.   **2039**

McCann, Larry D., "Of Sleighs, Trains, and Jeeps: Three Landscapes in the Evolution of Halifax," in P. Thomas, ed., *The Red Jeep and Other Landscapes* (Fredericton, N.B.: Goose Lane Editions, 1987), pp. 45–52.   **2040**

Muise, Del, "'The Great Transformation': Changing the Urban Face of Nova Scotia, 1871–1921," *Nova Scotia Historical Review*, vol. 11, 2 (1991), pp. 1–42.   **2041**

RECREATION & TOURISM

Moffatt, C. A., "The Development of Tourism in Nova Scotia," in Geoffrey Wall and John S. Marsh, eds., *Recreational Land Use: Perspectives on Its Evolution in Canada* (Ottawa: Carleton University Press, 1982), pp. 123–132.   **2042**

PLACE NAMES

Public Archives of Canada, *Place-Names and Places of Nova Scotia* (Halifax: Nova Scotia Series, no. 3, 1967), 751 pp.   **2043**

Fraser, Ian A., "Placenames of Scottish Origin in Nova Scotia," *Names*, vol. 34, 4 (1986), pp. 364–372.   **2044**

-------------------- NEW BRUNSWICK --------------------

GENERAL

Ganong, William F., "A Monograph of the Historic Sites of the Province of New Brunswick," *Transactions of the Royal Society of Canada*, vol. 5 (1899), sec. 2, pp. 213–357.   2045

Ganong, William F., "Additions and Corrections to Monographs on the Place-Nomenclature, Cartography, Historic Sites, Boundaries, and Settlement Origins of the Province of New Brunswick," *Transactions of the Royal Society of Canada*, vol. 12 (1906) sec. 2 , pp. 3–157.   2046

NATIVE PEOPLES & WHITE RELATIONS

Hamilton, W. D., "Indian Lands in New Brunswick: The Case of the Little South West Reserve," *Acadiensis*, vol. 13, 2 (1984), pp. 3–28.   2047

EXPLORATION & MAPPING

Ganong, William F., "A Monograph of the Cartography of the Province of New Brunswick," *Transactions of the Royal Society of Canada*, vol. 3 (1897), sec. 2, pp. 313–427.   2048

Malinski, Richard M., "Purdy's 'Map of Cabotia' and the Mapping Sequence of New Brunswick," *Proceedings of the Annual Conference of the Association of Canadian Map Libraries*, vol. 9 (1975), pp. 32–58. Reprinted, with slight modifications, in Barbara Farrell and Aileen Desbarats, eds., *Explorations in the History of Canadian Mapping: A Collection of Essays* (Ottawa: Association of Canadian Map Libraries and Archives, 1988), pp. 133–145.   2049

REGIONAL SETTLEMENT

Ganong, William F., "A Monograph of the Origins of Settlements of the Province of New Brunswick," *Transactions of the Royal Society of Canada*, vol. 10 (1904), sec. 2, pp. 3–185.   2050

Ganong, William F., "Historical-Geographical Documents Relating to New Brunswick, 7: The Foundations of Modern Settlement of the Miramichi," *Collections of the New Brunswick Historical Society*, vol. 3, 9 (1909), pp. 307–343.   2051

POPULATION

Wynn, Graeme, "Population Patterns in Pre-Confederation New Brunswick," *Acadiensis*, vol. 10, 2 (1981), pp. 124–138.   2052

Toner, Peter M., "The Irish of New Brunswick at Mid-Century: The 1851 Census," in P. M. Toner, ed., *New Ireland Remembered: Historical Essays on the Irish in New Brunswick* (Fredericton: New Ireland Press, 1988), pp. 63–70.   2053

Toner, Peter M., "The Origins of the New Brunswick Irish, 1851," *Journal of Canadian Studies*, vol. 23, 1 & 2 (1988), pp. 104–119.   2054

RURAL & REGIONAL SOCIAL GEOGRAPHY

Vernex, Jean-Claude, "La survivance acadienne au Nouveau-Brunswick: Quelques interrogations sur son devenir," *Le globe*, vol. 115 (1975), pp. 15–58.   2055

Vernex, Jean-Claude, "Espace et appartenance: L'exemple des Acadiens au Nouveau-Brunswick," *Cahiers de géographie du Québec*, vol. 23, 60 (1979), pp. 125–142.   2056

Wynn, Graeme, "Deplorably Dark and Demoralized Lumberers? Rhetoric and Reality in Early Nineteenth-Century New Brunswick," *Journal of Forest History*, vol. 24, 4 (1980), pp. 168–187.   2057

Arseneault, Samuel, "'On est venu, c'est pour rester': Caraquet, the Development of an Acadian Identity," Ph.D. diss., Queen's University, 1988.   2058

POLITICAL & ADMINISTRATIVE GEOGRAPHY

Ganong, William F., "A Monograph of the Evolution of the Boundaries of the Province of New Brunswick," *Transactions of the Royal Society of Canada*, vol. 7 (1901), sec. 2, pp. 137–449.   2059

Wynn, Graeme, "Administration in Adversity: The Deputy Surveyors and Control of the New Brunswick Crown Forest before 1844," *Acadiensis*, vol. 6, 1 (1977), pp. 49–65.   2060

Wynn, Graeme, "New Brunswick Parish Boundaries in the Pre-1861 Census Years," *Acadiensis*, vol. 7, 2 (1977), pp. 95–105.   2061

Arseneault, Samuel P., et al., "Les paroisses civiles du Nord-Est 1788–1986," *Revue d'histoire de la Société historique Nicolas-Denys*, vol. 13, 2 (1985), pp. 58–68.   2062

ECONOMIC DEVELOPMENT

Young, R. A., "Development, Planning, and Participation in New Brunswick, 1945–1975," Ph.D. diss., University of Oxford, 1979.　　2063

Wynn, Graeme, *Timber Colony: A Historical Geography of Early Nineteenth Century New Brunswick* (Toronto: University of Toronto Press, 1981), 224 pp.　　2064

Wieger, Axel, "Die erste Wüstungsphase in der atlantischen Provinz New Brunswick (Kanada): 1871 bis ca.1930," *Geographische Zeitschrift*, vol. 70, 3 (1982), pp. 201–222.　　2065

Wieger, Axel, "Wüstungsvorgänge an der Peripherie Kanadas: Das Beispiel New Brunswick," *Geographische Rundschau*, vol. 35 (1983), pp. 386–391.　　2066

LAND & LAND USE

Raymond, Charles W., "Agricultural Land Use in the Upper Saint John River Valley, New Brunswick," *Geographical Bulletin* (Ottawa), vol. 16 (1961), pp. 65–83.　　2067

Wieger, Axel, *Agrarkolonisation, Landnutzung und Kulturlandschaftsverfall in der Provinz New Brunswick (Kanada)* (Aachen: Aachener Geographische Arbeiten, vol. 22, 1990), 510 pp. [Summaries in English, pp. 429–439, and French, pp. 440–453]　　2068

EXTRACTIVE ACTIVITY

Wynn, Graeme, "The Assault on the New Brunswick Forest, 1780–1850," Ph.D. diss., University of Toronto, 1974.　　2069

Wynn, Graeme, "Industrialism, Entrepreneurship, and Opportunity in the New Brunswick Timber Trade," in L. R. Fischer and E. W. Sager, eds., *The Enterprising Canadians: Entrepreneurs and Economic Development in Eastern Canada, 1820–1914* (St. John's: Memorial University of Newfoundland, 1979), pp. 5–22.　　2070

AGRICULTURE

Putnam, Donald F., "Distribution of Agriculture in New Brunswick," *Public Affairs*, vol. 3, 1 (1939), pp. 8–11.　　2071

Wieger, Axel, "Das mittlere St. John River Gebiet (N.B.) als hoch-spezialisierter agrarischer Sonderraum in den atlantischen Provinzen Kanadas," in F. Ahnert and R. Zschocke, eds., *Festschrift für Felix Monheim* (Aachen: Aachener

Geographische Arbeiten, vol. 14, 1, 1981), pp. 321–344.　　2072

LANDSCAPE

Konrad, Victor A., and Michael Chaney, "Madawaska Twin Barn," *Journal of Cultural Geography*, vol. 3, 1 (1982), pp. 64–75.　　2073

COMMUNICATIONS & TRADE

Wynn, Graeme, "Moving Goods and People in Mid Nineteenth-Century New Brunswick," in Donald H. Akenson, ed., *Canadian Papers in Rural History*, vol. 6 (Gananoque, Ont.: Langdale Press, 1988), pp. 226–239.　　2074

MANUFACTURING & INDUSTRIALIZATION

Houston, Cecil J., and William J. Smyth, "New Brunswick Shipbuilding and Irish Shipping: The Commissioning of the *Londonderry*, 1838," *Acadiensis*, vol. 16, 2 (1987), pp. 95–106.　　2075

URBAN SOCIAL STRUCTURE

Northrup, David A., "Saint John, New Brunswick, 1871–1891: The Changing Residential Structure of a Slow Growth City," Master's thesis, York University, 1979.　　2076

PLACE NAMES

Ganong, William F., "A Monograph of the Place-Nomenclature of the Province of New Brunswick," *Transactions of the Royal Society of Canada*, vol. 2 (1896), sec. 2, pp. 175–289.　　2077

Rouillard, Eugène, "À travers le Nouveau-Brunswick, quelques vocables géographiques," *Bulletin de la Société de géographie du Québec*, vol. 14 (1920), pp. 275–292.　　2078

Ganong, William F., "The Origin of the Major Canadian Place-Names of Fundy and Miramichi," *Transactions of the Royal Society of Canada*, vol. 20 (1926), sec. 2, pp. 15–35.　　2079

Rayburn, J. Alan, *Geographical Names of New Brunswick* (Ottawa: Canadian Department of Energy, Mines, and Resources, Survey and Mapping Branch, for the Canadian Permanent Committee on Geographical Names, Toponymy Study no. 2, 1965), 304 pp.　　2080

Rayburn, J. Alan, "Characteristics of Toponymic Generics in New Brunswick," *Cahiers de géographie du Québec*, vol. 16, 38 (1972), pp. 285–311.　　2081

QUEBEC AS A WHOLE

GENERAL

See also 1145

Thompson, Zadock, *Geography and History of Lower Canada, Designed for the Use of Schools* (Stanstead: Walton & Gaylord, 1835), 114 pp.   2082

Odell, Clarence B., "Some Remarks on Rural French Canada," *Journal of Geography*, vol. 39, 9 (1940), pp. 344–351. [Focus on 1871–1931]   2083

Deffontaines, Pierre, "Hiver et genres de vie au Canada français," *Revue canadienne de géographie*, vol. 9, 2 & 3 (1955), pp. 73–91.   2084

Parker, William H., "The Geography of the Province of Lower Canada in 1837," Ph.D. diss., Oxford University, 1958.   2085

Harris, R. Cole, "The St. Lawrence: River and Sea," *Cahiers de géographie du Québec*, vol. 11, 23 (1967), pp. 171–180.   2086

Innes, Frank C., "Heartbreak of Former New France," *Geographical Magazine*, vol. 45, 4 (1973), pp. 277–283.   2087

Claval, Paul, "Architecture sociale, culture, et géographie au Québec: Un essai d'interprétation historique," *Annales de géographie*, vol. 83, 458 (1974), pp. 394–419.   2088

Dechêne, Louise, *Habitants et marchands de Montréal au XVIIe siècle* (Paris: Plon, 1974), 588 pp.   2089

Morissonneau, Christian, "Mobilité et identité québécoise," *Cahiers de géographie du Québec*, vol. 23, 60 (1979), pp. 29–38.   2090

Morissonneau, Christian, and Maurice Asselin, "La colonisation au Québec: Une décolonisation manquée," *Cahiers de géographie du Québec*, vol. 24, 61 (1980), pp. 145–156.   2091

Waddell, Eric W., "Cultural Hearth, Continental Diaspora: The Place of Quebec in North America," in Larry D. McCann, ed., *Heartland and Hinterland: A Geography of Canada* (Scarborough, Ont.: Prentice-Hall of Canada, 1982), pp. 133–154. Revised ed. 1987, pp. 148–172.   2092

Courville, Serge, "Espace, territoire, et culture en Nouvelle-France: Une vision géographique," *Revue d'histoire de l'Amérique française*, vol. 37, 3 (1983), pp. 417–429. Translated as "Space, Territory, and Culture in New France: A Geo-

graphical Perspective," in Graeme Wynn, ed., *People, Places, Patterns, Processes: Geographical Perspectives on the Canadian Past* (Toronto: Copp Clark Pitman, 1990), pp. 165–176.   2093

Louder, Dean R., Christian Morissonneau, and Eric Waddell, "Picking Up the Pieces of a Shattered Dream: Quebec and French America," *Journal of Cultural Geography*, vol. 4, 1 (1983), pp. 44–56.   2094

Louder, Dean R., and Eric Waddell, eds., *Du continent perdu à l'archipel retrouvé: Le Québec et l'Amérique française* (Quebec: Presses de l'Université Laval, 1983), 292 pp.   2095

Courville, Serge, "Espace, territoire, et culture au Québec: Perspectives géo-historiques," *Rapports et mémoires de recherche du Centre d'études sur la langue, les arts, et les traditions populaires des francophones en Amérique du Nord* (Laval University) vol. 5 (1984), pp. 49–52.
2096

Courville, Serge, "Une territorialité oubliée," *Cahiers de géographie du Québec*, vol. 28, 73–74 (1984), pp. 5–7.   2097

Harris, R. Cole, "Towards a Conclusion," *Cahiers de géographie du Québec*, vol. 28, 73–74 (1984), pp. 329–332. [On the historical-geographical character of Quebec, closing a special issue on "Rangs et villages du Québec: Perspectives géo-historiques"]   2098

Courville, Serge, "Le développement québécois: De l'ère pionnière conquêtes post-industrielles," *Le Québec statistique* [1985–1986] (Quebec: Publications du Québec, 1985), pp. 37–55.
2099

Bernier, Jacques, "Social Cohesion and Conflicts in Quebec," in Guy M. Robinson, ed., *A Social Geography of Canada* (Edinburgh: North British Publishing, 1988), pp. 47–54. Also Toronto: Dundurn Press, 1991, pp. 82–91.   2100

ENVIRONMENTAL CHANGE

Brouillette, Benoît, "Quelques observations climatiques en Nouvelle-France au dix-huitième siècle," *Transactions of the Royal Society of Canada*, 4th ser., vol. 8 (1970), pp. 93–99.   2101

NATIVE PEOPLES & WHITE RELATIONS

Gaumond, Michel, "Premiers résultats de l'exploration d'un site archéologique à Sillery," *Cahiers de géographie du Québec*, vol. 5, 9 (1961), pp. 63–72. [Site associated with the Abenaquis and Huron peoples]   **2102**

Clermont, Norman, "L'hiver et les Indiens nomades du Québec à la fin de la préhistoire," *Revue de géographie de Montréal*, vol. 28, 4 (1974), pp. 447–452.   **2103**

EXPLORATION & MAPPING

Ganong, William F., "Cartography of the St. Lawrence from Cartier to Champlain," *Transactions of the Royal Society of Canada*, ser. 1, vol. 7 (1889), pp. 17–58.   **2104**

POPULAR IMAGES & EVALUATION

See also 1309

Barbeau, Marius, "Notre géographie en peinture," *Bulletin des Sociétés de géographie du Québec et de Montréal*, vol. 1, 5 (1942), pp. 33–44.   **2105**

LeBlanc, Robert G., "The Francophone 'Conquest' of New England: Geopolitical Conceptions and Imperial Ambition of French Canadian Nationalists in the Nineteenth Century," *American Review of Canadian Studies*, vol. 15, 3 (1985), pp. 288–310.   **2106**

REGIONAL SETTLEMENT

Kemp, Harold S., "New Colonies in Old Quebec," *Economic Geography*, vol. 12, 1 (1936), pp. 54–60.   **2107**

Hamelin, Louis-Edmond, "Le rang d'habitat: Étude pluridisciplinaire de signification," Master's thesis, Université Laval, 1949.   **2108**

Tyman, John L., "Man and the North Shore: A Study in Environmental Response," Master's thesis, McGill University, 1961.   **2109**

Schroeder-Lanz, Helmut, "Kulturgeographische Folgeerscheinungen der Besiedlung und Erschließung Québecs: Ein historisch-geographischer kulturmorphologischer Überblick," in Hans-Josef Niederehe and Hellmut Schroeder-Lanz, eds., *Beiträge zur landeskundlich-linguistischen Kenntnis von Québec* (Trier: Geographische Gesellschaft Trier, Trierer Geographische Schriften, special issue no. 1, 1977), pp. 24–58.   **2110**

Hamelin, Louis-Edmond, "Essai d'évaluation du nombre de rangs au Québec," *Cahiers de géographie du Québec*, vol. 34, 91 (1990), pp. 5–20. [Focus on 1660–1980]   **2111**

POPULATION

See also 1353, 1356, 1359

Barbeau, Marius, "French Survival in Canada," *Journal of the Washington Academy of Sciences*, vol. 23, 8 (1933), pp. 365–378.   **2112**

Lewis, H. Harry, "Population of Quebec Province: Its Distribution and National Origins," *Economic Geography*, vol. 16, 1 (1940), pp. 59–68.   **2113**

Hamelin, Louis-Edmond, "Émigration rurale à l'échelon paroissial," *Canadian Geographer*, vol. 5 (1955), pp. 53–61.   **2114**

Boileau, Gilles, "Évolution démographique de la population rurale dans soixante paroisses de la province de Québec depuis le début du siècle," *Canadian Geographer*, vol. 9, 2 (1957), pp. 49–54.   **2115**

Flatrès, Pierre, "Bretagne et Canada: Quelques aspects de l'émigration bretonne au Canada," *Cahiers de géographie du Québec*, vol. 3, 6 (1959), pp. 103–113. [Focus on 1763–1958]   **2116**

Hamelin, Louis-Edmond, "La population totale de Canada depuis 1600," *Cahiers de géographie du Québec*, vol. 9, 18 (1965), pp. 159–168.   **2117**

Robert, Bernard, "L'influence des migrations intérieures sur la répartition géographique des effectifs de la population: Province de Québec, 1941–1966," Université Laval, 1970.   **2118**

Louder, Dean R., Michel Bisson, and Pierre La Rochelle, "Analyse centrographique de la population du Québec de 1951 à 1971," *Cahiers de géographie du Québec*, vol. 18, 45 (1974), pp. 421–444.   **2119**

Bisson, Michel, "Méthodes d'études de la structure spatiale des fluctuations de la natalité au Québec (1926–1971)," *Cahiers de géographie du Québec*, vol. 19, 46 (1975), pp. 229–241.   **2120**

LaRochelle, Pierre, Dean Louder, and Jean Raveneau, "Description graphique des caractéristiques de l'évolution de la population des municipalités du Québec, 1951–1971," *Cahiers de géographie du Québec*, vol. 19, 46 (1975), pp. 147–166.   **2121**

Kirouac, René, "Les caprices du vieillissement de la population québécoise de 1931 à 1971," Master's thesis, Université Laval, 1977.   **2122**

Saint Maurice, Denis, "Perspective géographique de la natalité générale au Québec, de 1894 à 1973," Master's thesis, Université Laval, 1977.   **2123**

LeBlanc, Robert G., "Regional Competition for Franco-American Repatriates, 1870–1930," *Québec Studies*, vol. 1 (1983), pp. 110–129.   **2124**

Weisz, George, "The Geographical Origins and Destinations of Medical Graduates in Quebec, 1834–1939," *Histoire sociale/Social History*, vol. 19, 37 (1986), pp. 93–120.   2125

RURAL & REGIONAL SOCIAL GEOGRAPHY

Veyret, P., "Un cas d'isolement: Les Canadiens français," in *Mélanges géographiques offerts à Ph. Arbas*, vol. 2 (Paris: Société d'édition "Les Belles Lettres," for the Institut de géographie de l'Université Clermont-Ferrand, 1953), pp. 293–299.   2126

Hamelin, Louis-Edmond, "Contribution aux recherches sociales du Québec par une étude des variations régionales du nombre des vocations sacerdotales," *Cahiers de géographie du Québec*, vol. 2, 3 (1957), pp. 5–36. [Focus on 1850–1950]   2127

Barbeau, Marius, "La géographie de notre folklore," *Cahiers de géographie du Québec*, vol. 3, 6 (1959), pp. 115–122.   2128

Hamelin, Louis-Edmond, "Nombre annuel des nouveaux prêtres, Canada-français (1660–1933)," *Bulletin des recherches historiques*, vol. 65, 2 (1959), pp. 35–44.   2129

Parker, William H., "A New Look at Unrest in Lower Canada in the 1830s," *Canadian Historical Review*, vol. 40, 3 (1959), pp. 209–217.   2130

Hamelin, Louis-Edmond, "Évolution numérique séculaire du clergé catholique dans le Québec," *Recherches sociographiques*, vol. 2, 2 (1961), pp. 189–242.   2131

Harris, R. Cole, *Two Societies: Life in Mid–Nineteenth Century Quebec* (Toronto: McClelland and Stewart, 1976), 63 pp.   2132

Tremblay, Marc-Adelard, "Existe-t-il des cultures régionales au Québec?" *Transactions of the Royal Society of Canada*, 4th ser., vol. 15 (1977), pp. 137–144.   2133

Harris, R. Cole, "The Extension of France into Rural Canada," in James R. Gibson, ed., *European Settlement and Development in North America: Essays on Geographical Change in Honour and Memory of Andrew Hill Clark* (Toronto: University of Toronto Press, 1978), pp. 27–45. Reprinted in Graeme Wynn, ed., *People, Places, Patterns, Processes: Geographical Perspectives on the Canadian Past* (Toronto: Copp Clark Pitman, 1990), pp. 94–109.   2134

Ravault, René-Jean, "L'amorce du redressement des francophones hors-Québec: Analyse critique des héritiers de Lord Durham et de deux

poids, deux mesures," *Cahiers de géographie du Québec*, vol. 23, 58 (1979), pp. 15–28.   2135

Müller-Wille, Ludger, and Alfred Pletsch, "Ethnizitätskonflikt sozioökonomischer Wandel und Territorialentwicklung in Québec/Kanada," *Erde*, vol. 112, 1 (1981), pp. 61–89.   2136

DeKoninck, Rodolphe, "Pourquoi les paysans? Interrogations sur la territorialité de l'agriculture familiale et notes sur le cas québécois," *Cahiers de géographie du Québec*, vol. 28, 73–74 (1984), pp. 261–274.   2137

Dugas, Clemont, "Évolution du monde rurale québécois," *Cahiers de géographie du Québec*, vol. 28, 73–74 (1984), pp. 183–204.   2138

Waddell, Eric W., "On Being 'English' in Quebec," in G. L. Gold, ed., *Minorities and Mother Country Imagery* (St. John's: Memorial University of Newfoundland, Institute of Social and Economic Research, Publication no. 13, 1984), pp. 97–111.   2139

Waddell, Eric W., "Les Québécois et le continent, ou la transformation progressive d'une identité construite en identité réelle," in Alfred Pletsch, ed., *Ethnicity in Canada* (Marburg: Marburger Geographische Schriften, vol. 96, 1985), pp. 155–163.   2140

Klein, Juan-Luis, "Des genres de vie aux modes de vie: Splendeur et déclin de la géographie régionale au Québec," *Cahiers de géographie du Québec*, vol. 30, 80 (1986), pp. 203–216.   2141

Dugas, Clemont, "Marginalité économique et mobilité géographique dans l'espace rural québécois," *Recherches sociographiques*, vol. 29, 2–3 (1988), pp. 431–444.   2142

Bischoff, Peter, "Des forges du Saint-Maurice aux fonderies de Montréal: Mobilité géographique, solidarité communautaire, et action syndicale des mouleurs, 1829–1881," *Revue d'histoire de l'Amérique française*, vol. 43, 1 (1989), pp. 3–30.   2143

Cohen, Yolande, "Le déploiement géographique des cercles de fermières au Québec, 1915–1949," *Éspaces, population, sociétés*, vol. 1 (1989), pp. 87–98.   2144

Courville, Serge, and Normand Seguin, *Le monde rural québécois au XIXe siècle: Rural Life in Nineteenth Century Quebec* (Ottawa: Canadian Historical Association, Brochure no. 47, 1989), 29 pp.   2145

Greer, Allen, and Leon Robichaud, "La rébellion de 1837–1838 au Bas-Canada: Une approche géographique," *Cahiers de géographie du Québec*, vol. 33, 90 (1989), pp. 345–377.   2146

Hamelin, Louis-Edmond, "Rang, côte, et concession au sens de peuplement aligné au Québec depuis le XVIIe siècle," *Revue de l'histoire de l'Amérique française*, vol. 42, 4 (1989), pp. 519–544.   **2147**

POLITICAL & ADMINISTRATIVE GEOGRAPHY

See also **5060**

Bignell, John, "The Northern Boundary of the Province of Québec," *Bulletin de la Société de géographie du Quebec*, 1 (1886), pp. 88–89; no. 5 (1887), pp. 63–65.   **2148**

Hamelin, Jean, Jacques Letarte, and Marcel Hamelin, "Les élections provinciales dans le Québec," *Cahiers de géographie du Québec*, vol. 4, 7 (1960), pp. 5–207. [Focus on 1867–1956]   **2149**

Frenette, Jean-Vianney, "La recherche d'un cadre régionale au Québec méridional: Quelques étapes, de 1932 à 1966," *Cahiers de géographie du Québec*, vol. 17, 40 (1973), pp. 69–84.   **2150**

Cestre, Gilbert, "Québec: Évolution des limites municipales depuis 1831–1832," *Cahiers de géographie du Québec*, vol. 20, 51 (1976), pp. 561–568.   **2151**

ECONOMIC DEVELOPMENT

LeVasseur, N., "La construction des navires à Québec," *Bulletin de la Société de géographie du Québec*, vol. 11, 4 (1917), pp. 187–201.   **2152**

Brouillette, Benoît, *La chasse des animaux à fourrure au Canada* (Paris: Gallimard, 1934), 205 pp.   **2153**

Rousseau, Jacques, "La forêt mixte du Québec dans la perspective historique," *Cahiers de géographie du Québec*, vol. 7, 13 (1962–1963), pp. 111–120.   **2154**

Marchand, Claude, "Quebec and the Continental Economy: Spatio-Temporal Change, 1957–1975," Ph.D. diss., University of Toronto, 1979.   **2155**

Boucher, Louis-J., "Idéologies de développement chez une élite régionale: Le cas du projet de chemin de fer Montréal-Occidental (1867–1897)," Master's thesis, Université Laval, 1985.   **2156**

Courville, Serge, "Un monde rural en mutation: Le Bas-Canada dans la première moitié du XIXe siècle," *Histoire sociale/Social History*, vol. 20, 40 (1987), pp. 237–258.   **2157**

LAND & LAND USE

Rousseau, L. Z., "Surveys and Land-Use Planning in the Province of Quebec," *Canadian Surveyor*

(Special Proceedings of the Thirty-fourth Annual Meeting, 1941), pp. 24–29.   **2158**

Barette, Gérald, "Contribution de l'arpenteur-géomètre à la géographie du Québec," *Canadian Geographer*, vol. 1, 2 (1952), pp. 67–71.   **2159**

Brouillette, Benoît, "Rien que la terre," *Cahiers de l'Académie canadienne-française*, vol. 8 (1964), pp. 11–20; and a continuation of the same article under the title, "Paysages d'autrefois," in *Revue de géographie de Montréal*, vol. 20, 1 & 2 (1966), pp. 47–58.   **2160**

DeKoninck, Rodolphe, Anne-Marie Turcot, et André G. Zubrzycki, "Les pâturages communaux du lac Saint-Pierre: De leur histoire et de leur actualité," *Cahiers de géographie du Québec*, vol. 17, 41 (1973), pp. 317–329.   **2161**

Sanguin, André-L., "Les origines normandes du rang canadien-français: Quelques éléments de géographie historiques," *Études normandes*, vol. 27, 1–2 (1978), pp. 7–20.   **2162**

Bureau, Luc, "Et dieu créa le Rang," *Cahiers de géographie du Québec*, vol. 28, 73–74 (1984), pp. 235–240.   **2163**

Eberle, Ingo, "Townships in Quebec: Land Survey, Spatial Orientation, and Development of Land Division since the British Conquest of New France," in *Cultural Dimensions of Canada's Geography: Proceedings of the German-Canadian Symposium, August 28–September 11, 1983* (Peterborough: Trent University, Department of Geography, Occasional Paper no. 10 (1984), pp. 328–345.   **2164**

Courville, Serge, "L'origine du rang au Québec: La politique territoriale de la France dans la première moitié du 17e siècle," in E. P. Fitzgerald, ed., *Proceedings of the Eighth Annual Meeting of the French Colonial Historical Society* (Lanham, Md.: University Press of America, 1985), pp. 201–223.   **2165**

Noël, Françoise, "Seigneurial Survey and Land Granting Policies," in Donald H. Akenson, ed., *Canadian Papers in Rural History*, vol. 5 (Gananoque, Ont.: Langdale Press, 1986), pp. 150–180.   **2166**

Hamelin, Louis-Edmond, "Le rang d'arrière-fleuve en Nouvelle France," *Canadian Geographer*, vol. 34, 2 (1990), pp. 110–119.   **2167**

AGRICULTURE

Parker, William H., "A Revolution in the Agricultural Geography of Lower Canada, 1833–1838," *Revue canadienne de géographie*, vol. 11, 4 (1957), pp. 189–194.   **2168**

Lavertue, Robert, "L'histoire de l'agriculture québécoise au XIXe siècle: Une schématisation des faits et des interprétations," *Cahiers de géographie du Québec*, vol. 28, 73–74 (1984), pp. 275–287. **2169**

Hamelin, Louis-Edmond, "Structures agraires du Québec," in Raquel Soeiro de Brito, ed., *Estudos em Homenagem a Mariano Feio* (Lisbon: Instituto Nacional de Investgeao Cientifica, 1986), pp. 301–318. **2170**

LANDSCAPE

Deffontaines, Pierre, "Évolution du type d'habitation rurale au Canada français," *Cahiers de géographie du Québec*, vol. 11, 24 (1967), pp. 497–522. **2171**

COMMUNICATIONS & TRADE

Normand, France, "La navigation intérieure à Québec au dernier quart du XIXe siècle," *Revue d'histoire de l'Amérique française*, vol. 43, 3 (1990), pp. 323–352. **2172**

MANUFACTURING & INDUSTRIALIZATION

Girard, Jacques, "Les industries de transformation de la Nouvelle France," *Cahiers de géographie du Québec*, vol. 3, 6 (1959), pp. 305–320. [Focus on 1608–1760] **2173**

Girard, Jacques, "Les industries de transformation de la province de Québec, 1841–1914," *Revue canadienne de géographie*, vol. 14, 1–4 (1960), pp. 63–66. **2174**

Lavertue, Robert, "Le rôle de l'agriculture dans le procès de développement industriel: L'exemple historique du Québec," Ph.D. diss., Université Laval, 1988. **2175**

URBAN NETWORKS & URBANIZATION

Manseau, Hubert, "La petite ville et le gros village du Québec," Master's thesis, Université de Montréal, 1974. **2176**

Morin, Denis, "La croissance allométrique des 62 principales agglomérations du Québec," Master's thesis, Université Laval, 1974. **2177**

Manseau, Hubert, "La croissance récente des petites agglomerations du Québec (1951–1971)," *Cahiers de géographie du Québec*, vol. 19, 46 (1975), pp. 39–59. **2178**

Morin, Denis, "Allométrie du système urbain du Québec, 1941–1971," *Cahiers de géographie du Québec*, vol. 19, 46 (1975), pp. 17–37. **2179**

Martin, Jean-Pierre A., "La croissance selective des lieux centraux de la province du Québec, 1850–1914," *Recherches géographiques à Strasbourg*, vol. 6 (1977), pp. 13–49. **2180**

Rudin, Ronald, "Montreal Banks and the Urban Development of Quebec, 1840–1914," in Gilbert A. Stelter and Alan F. J. Artibise, eds., *Shaping the Urban Landscape: Aspects of the Canadian City-Building Process* (Ottawa: Carleton University Press, 1982), pp. 65–83. **2181**

TOWNSCAPE

Camu, Pierre, "Le paysage urbain de Québec," *Geographical Bulletin*, vol. 10 (1957), pp. 22–35. **2182**

Paré, Yves, "Morphogénèse d'une banlieue: Orsainville," Master's thesis, Université Laval, 1983. **2183**

Guay, Lorraine, "Le cimetière vide," Master's thesis, Université Laval, 1989. **2184**

Thibault, Nathalie, "Formes architecturales et idéologiques à Québec: 1960–1990," Master's thesis, Université Laval, 1990. **2185**

PLACE NAMES

Roy, Pierre G., *Les noms géographiques de la province de Québec* (n.p.: Lévis, 1906), 514 pp. **2186**

Rouillard, Eugène, "Quelques noms géographiques," *Bulletin de la Société de géographie du Québec*, vol. 11 (1917), pp. 91–95. **2187**

Roy, Pierre G., "D'où vient le nom de 'Nouvelle France'?" *Bulletin de la Société de géographie du Québec*, vol. 12 (1918), pp. 79–80. **2188**

Carrière, Gaston, "Essai de toponymie oblate canadienne, I: Dans la province de Québec," *Revue canadienne de géographie*, vol. 11, 1 (1957), pp. 31–45. **2189**

Dorion, Henri, and Louis-Edmond Hamelin, "De la toponymie traditionelle à une choronymie totale," *Cahiers de géographie du Québec*, vol. 20 (1966), pp. 195–211. **2190**

Dorion, Henri, *Contribution à la connaissance de choronymie aborigène de la Côte-Nord: Les noms de lieux montagnais des environs de Mingan* (Québec: Presses de l'Université Laval, 1967), 214 pp. **2191**

Langevin, Jean, "Notes choronymiques sur l'île de Grâce ou le témoignage d'un territoire nommé," *Cahiers de géographie du Québec*, vol. 28, 73–74 (1984), pp. 241–259. **2192**

Courville, Serge, and Serge Labrecque, *Seigneuries et fiefs du Québec: Nomenclature et cartographie* (Quebec: Université Laval, Centre d'études sur la langue, les arts, et les traditions populaire des francophones en Amérique du Nord et Commission de toponymie, Outil de recherche no. 3, 1988), 202 pp. **2193**

Desy, Claude, "Lecture de paysage par les noms de rues: Exemples de Québec," Master's thesis, McGill University, 1988. **2194**

Hamelin, Louis-Edmond, "L'élément *rang* dans la toponymie de langue française," *Onomastica Canadiana*, vol. 71, 2 (1989), pp. 53–66. **2195**

Poirier, Jean, "Toponymie des États-Unis au Québec," *Canoma*, vol. 16, 1 (1990), pp. 22–24. **2196**

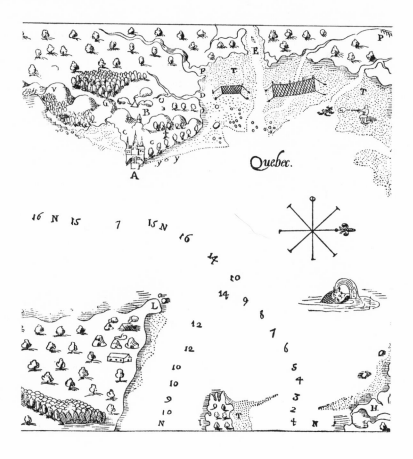

SOUTHERN QUEBEC

(INCLUDING THE EASTERN TOWNSHIPS)

GENERAL

Semple, Ellen Churchill, "The Influence of Geographic Environment on the Lower St. Lawrence," *Bulletin of the American Geographical Society*, vol. 36 (1904), pp. 449–466.   2197

Dresser, John A., "The Eastern Townships of Quebec: A Study in Human Geography," *Transactions of the Royal Society of Canada*, 3d ser., vol. 29 (1935), sec. 2, pp. 89–100.   2198

Banks, Marion B., "The Isle of Orleans: A Study of the Influences of a River Island Environment on the Life of a People, 1648–1948," Master's thesis, Clark University, 1944.   2199

Cobban, Aileen, and Robert M. Lithgow, "A Regional Study of the Richelieu Valley," Master's thesis, McGill University, 1952.   2200

Hills, Theo L., "The St. Francis to the Chaudière, 1830: A Study in the Historical Geography of Southeastern Quebec," *Canadian Geographer*, vol. 1, 6 (1955), pp. 25–36.   2201

Mingasson, Christian, "Évolution récente de l'île d'Orléans," *Cahiers de géographie du Québec*, vol. 1, 1 (1956), pp. 55–84. [Focus on 1851–1951]   2202

Martin, Yves, "L'île-aux-Coudres: Population et économie," *Cahiers de géographie du Québec*, vol. 1, 2 (1957), pp. 167–195. [Focus on 1720–1954]   2203

Bernard, E.-Mercier, "De paroisse rurale à paroisse urbaine: Notre Dame-des-Anges de Cartierville, 1910–1956; Essai géographique et démographique," *Revue canadienne de géographie*, vol. 12, 3–4 (1958), pp. 99–115.   2204

Booth, J. Derek, "An Historical Geography of Brome County, 1800–1911," Master's thesis, McGill University, 1966.   2205

DeKoninck, Rodolphe, "Les Cent-Iles du lac St.-Pierre: Études de géographie historique et ethnographique," Master's thesis, Université Laval, 1967.   2206

Ross, W. Gillies, *A Century of Change in Selected Eastern Township Villages: Barnston, Huntingville, Hatley, Massawippi* (Lenoxville, Que.: Bishop's University Department of Geography, 1967), 64 pp.   2207

Biays, Pierre, "Southern Quebec," in John H. Warkentin, ed., *Canada: A Geographical Interpretation* (Toronto: Methuen, 1968), pp. 281–333.   2208

Clibbon, Peter B., "The Nature, Evolution, and Present Extension of the Ecumene in the Shield Section of the Saint-Maurice Valley (Québec)," *Cahiers de géographie du Québec*, vol. 13, 28 (1969), pp. 5–33.   2209

Clibbon, Peter B., "Evolution and Present Patterns of the Ecumene of Southern Quebec," in F. Grenier, ed., *Études sur la géographie de Québec* (Toronto: University of Toronto Press, 1972), pp. 13–30.   2210

Courville, Serge, "Origine et évolution des campagnes dans le comté des Deux-Montagnes, 1755–1971," Master's thesis, Université de Montréal, 1973.   2211

Beauregard, Ludger, "Géographie historique des côtes de l'île de Montréal," *Cahiers de géographie du Québec*, vol. 28, 73–74 (1984), pp. 47–62.   2212

Hardy, René and Normand Seguin, *Forêt et société en Mauricie* (Montréal: Éditions du Borcel express, 1984), 222 pp.   2213

Brouillette, Normand, Laurent Deshaies, and Armand Séguin, "De la Mauricie de Blanchard à la Mauricie actuelle: Continuités et changements," *Cahiers de géographie du Québec*, vol. 30, 80 (1986), pp. 217–233. [Focus on 1947–1980]   2214

Courville, Serge, "Villages and Agriculture in the Seigneuries of Lower Canada: Conditions of a Comprehensive Study of Rural Quebec in the First Half of the Nineteenth Century," in Donald H. Akenson, ed., *Canadian Papers in Rural History*, vol. 5 (Gananoque, Ont.: Langdale Press, 1986), pp. 121–149.   2215

Gilbert, Anne, and André Langlois, "Les pays de l'Ottawa depuis Blanchard jusqu'à aujourd'hui: La confirmation d'une régionalisation ethnolinguistique," *Cahiers de géographie du Québec*, vol. 30, 80 (1986), pp. 235–247. [Focus on 1941–1980]   2216

Morin, Denis, et al., "Des cantons-de-l'est à l'Estrie," *Cahiers de géographie du Québec*, vol. 30, 80 (1986), pp. 249–269.   2217

Courville, Serge, Jean C. Robert, and Normand Seguin, "La vallée du Saint-Laurent à l'époque du rapport Durham: Économie et société," *Journal of Canadian Studies*, vol. 25, 1 (1990), pp. 78–95.　　　　　　　　　　　　2218

NATIVE PEOPLES & WHITE RELATIONS

Gaumond, Michel, "Premiers résultats de l'exploration d'un site archéologique à Sillery," *Cahiers de géographie du Québec*, vol. 5, 9 (1960–1961), pp. 63–72. [Site associated with the Abenaquis and Huron peoples]　　　　　　2219

EXPLORATION & MAPPING

Roy, Joseph-Edmond, "La cartographie et l'arpentage sous le régime français," *Bulletin des recherches historiques*, vol. 1 (Mar. 1895), pp. 33–45.　　　　　　　　　　　　2220

Sulte, B., "La plus ancienne carte de la Province de Québec," *Bulletin de la Société de géographie du Québec*, n.s. vol. 7 (1912), pp. 296–299. 　　　　　　　　　　　　2221

Roy, Pierre-Georges, "Un hydrographe du roy à Québec: Jean-Baptiste-Louis Franquelin," *Mémoires et comptes rendus de la Société royale du Canada*, ser. 3, vol. 13 (1919), sec. 1, pp. 47–60. 　　　　　　　　　　　　2222

Shipton, Nathaniel N., "General James Murray's Map of the St. Lawrence," *Canadian Cartographer*, vol. 4, 2 (1967), pp. 93–101.　　　2223

Charbonneau, André, "Un cartographe de Québec au XVIIe siècle: Jean-Baptiste-Louis Franquelin," Master's thesis, Université de Montréal, 1972.　　　　　　　　　2224

Dahl, Edward H., et al., "Maps and the Study of the Urban Development of Québec City in the Nineteenth Century," *Proceedings of the Annual Conference of the Association of Canadian Map Libraries*, vol. 6 (1972), pp. 95–116.　2225

Charbonneau, Hubert, and Yolande LaVoie, "Cartographie du premier découpage territorial des paroisses du Québec, 1721–1722," *Revue de géographie de Montréal*, vol. 27, 1 (1973), pp. 81–87.　　　　　　　　　　　　2226

Garant, Jean-Marc, "Jacques-Nicolas, 1703–1772, cartographe, hydrographe, ingénieur du Ministère de la Marine: Sa vie, son oeuvre, sa valeur historique," Master's thesis, Université de Montréal, 1973.　　　　　　　　2227

Hudson, H. P., "The Original Reconnaissance Map for the Battle of Québec," *British Library Journal*, vol. 1, 1 (1975), pp. 22–24.　　2228

Tessier, Ives, "Quelques cartes anciennes du Québec, pour l'étude de l'histoire locale," *Bulletin*

de l'Association des professeurs d'histoire locale du Québec, vol. 4, 1 (1978), pp. 14–22.　2229

Pritchard, J. S., "Early French Hydrographic Surveys in the St. Lawrence River," *International Hydrographic Review*, vol. 56, 1 (1979), pp. 125–142.　　　　　　　　　　　　2230

Shields, J. Gordon, "The Murray Map Cartographically Considered: A Study of General James Murray's Survey of the St. Lawrence Valley in 1761," Master's thesis, Queen's University, 1980.　　　　　　　　　　　　2231

Courville, Serge, "La carte de Bouchette rééditée," *Cahiers de géographie du Québec*, vol. 25, 65 (1981), pp. 283–290.　　　　　　　2232

Shields, J. Gordon, "General James Murray's Map of the St. Lawrence River Valley in 1761: A Cartographic Commentary," *Bulletin of the Association of Canadian Map Libraries*, vol. 48 (1983), pp. 30–35.　　　　　　　　　　　2233

POPULAR IMAGES & EVALUATION

Parson, Helen E., "Settlement Policy and Land Evaluation at the Turn of the Twentieth Century in Quebec," *Area*, vol. 9, 4 (1977), pp. 290–292. 　　　　　　　　　　　　2234

Rousseau, Guido, and Jean Laprise, "Le discours du sol dans le roman mauricien de 1850 à 1950," *Cahiers de géographie du Québec*, vol. 26, 67 (1982), pp. 121–137.　　　　　　2235

Brosseau, Marc, "Un lieu du discours géographique québécois: Le manuel scolaire de 1804–1957," Master's thesis, University of Ottawa, 1988.　　　　　　　　　　　　2236

Brosseau, Marc, "Régions et régionalisation dans les manuels de géographie: L'exemple de l'Outaouais, 1804–1957," *Cahiers de géographie du Québec*, vol. 33, 89 (1989), pp. 179–196.　2237

REGIONAL SETTLEMENT

Barbeau, Marius, "An Early French Settlement on the St. Lawrence," *Bulletin of the Philadelphia Geographical Society*, vol. 30, 2 (1932), pp. 79–87.　　　　　　　　　　　　2238

Tuckermann, W., "Die Orleansinsel im Lorenzstrom: Eines der ältesten Siedlungszentren in Kanada," *Koloniale Rundschau*, vol. 27 (1936), p. 123.　　　　　　　　　　　　2239

Banks, Marion S., "The Isle of Orleans: A Study of the Influence of a River Island Environment on the Life of a People," Master's thesis, Clark University, 1944.　　　　　　　　2240

Prud'homme, B., "Étude du peuplement du comté de Vaudreuil," Master's thesis, Université de Montréal, 1949.   **2241**

Boileau, Gilles, "Études de peuplement du comté des Deux-Montagnes," Master's thesis, Université de Montréal, 1954.   **2242**

Bailey, P. J. M., "The Geography of Settlement in Stanstead Township, Province of Québec," *Geography*, vol. 41, 1 (1956), pp. 39–48.   **2243**

Beauregard, Ludger, "Le peuplement du Richelieu," *Revue de géographie de Montréal*, vol. 19, 1 & 2 (1965), pp. 43–74.   **2244**

Gibson, Pauline Margaret, "Settlement and Abandonment of Land in the Rouge River Valley, Laurentides, Quebec: An Historical Geography," Master's thesis, McGill University, 1967.
2245

Turay, Harry, "The Process of Settlement and Land Clearance in Papineau County, Quebec (1800–1967)," Master's thesis, University of Ottawa, 1969.   **2246**

McCardell, Nora E., "Lawrence Colony: A Study of Settlement in Quebec," Master's thesis, Waterloo Lutheran University, 1970.   **2247**

Thompson, Robert P., "Cultural Sequences in an Eastern Townships County: Missisquoi County, Quebec," Master's thesis, University of Vermont, 1973.   **2248**

DeKoninck, Rodolphe, and Jean Langevin, "La pérennité des peuplements insulaires laurentiens: Le cas de l'île Saint-Ignace et de l'île Dupas," *Cahiers de géographie du Québec*, vol. 18, 44 (1974), pp. 317–336. [Focus on 1861–1971]
2249

Courville, Serge, "Les caractères originaux de la conquête du sol dans les seigneuries de la Rivière-du-Chêne et du Lac-des-Deux-Montagnes, Québec," *Revue de géographie de Montréal*, vol. 29, 1 (1975), pp. 41–60.   **2250**

Harris, R. Cole, "Brief Interlude with New France," *Geographical Magazine*, vol. 52 (1979), pp. 274–280.   **2251**

Pletsch, Alfred, "Die Eastern Townships von Québec (Kanada): Kolonisationsphasen und Kulturlandschaftsentwicklung," in Gerhard Sandner and Helmut Nun, eds. *Verhandlungen des Deutschen Geographentages, 1979*, vol. 42 (Wiesbaden: Franz Steiner Verlag, 1980), pp. 369–371.   **2252**

Eberle, Ingo, "Einzelhofwüstung und Siedlungskonzentration im ländlichen Raum des Outaouais (Qué): Jüngere Siedlungsveränderungen als Konsequenz des Strukturwandels in der Holz- und Landwirtschaft einer peripheren Waldbauernregion Ostkanadas," *Geogra-*

phische Zeitschrift, vol. 70 (1982), pp. 81–105.
2253

Pletsch, Alfred, "Les cantons de l'est canadien: Colonisation et abandon d'une région marginale," *Norois*, vol. 29, 114 (1982), pp. 185–204.
2254

Bélanger, Marcel, "Le réseau de Léa," *Cahiers de géographie du Québec*, vol. 28, 73–74 (1984), pp. 289–302.   **2255**

Jarnoux, Philippe, "La colonisation de la seigneurie de Bastican aux XVIIe et XVIIIe siècles: L'espace et les hommes," *Revue d'histoire de l'Amérique française*, vol. 40, 2 (1986), pp. 163–192.   **2256**

McQuillan, D. Aidan, "Beaurivage: The Development of an Irish Ethnic Identity in Quebec, 1820–1860," in Robert O'Driscoll and Lorna Reynolds, eds., *The Untold Story: The Irish in Canada*, vol. 1 (Toronto: Celtic Arts of Canada, 1988), pp. 263–270.   **2257**

POPULATION

Blanchard, Raoul, "Le peuplement," in his "Les cantons de l'est," *Revue de géographie alpine*, vol. 25 (1937), pp. 155–204.   **2258**

Blanchard, Raoul, "Les étapes de la mise en valeur et du peuplement," in his "Les Laurentides," *Revue de géographie alpine*, vol. 26 (1938), pp. 59–115.   **2259**

Blanchard, Raoul, "Le peuplement de la plaine," in his "La plaine de Montréal," *Revue de géographie alpine*, vol. 27 (1939), pp. 302–333.   **2260**

Schaeffer, Danièlle, "Évolution de la population dans trois paroisses de la Côte de Beaupré: Boischatel, L'Ange Gardien, et Château-Richer," Master's thesis, Université Laval, 1970.
2261

Harris, R. Cole, "The French Background of Immigrants to Canada before 1700," *Cahiers de géographie du Québec*, vol. 16, 38 (1972), pp. 313–324. Reprinted in James M. Bumsted, ed., *Interpreting Canada's Past*, vol. 1, *Before Confederation* (Toronto: Oxford University Press, 1986), pp. 52–62.   **2262**

Bellavance, Marcel, "La mobilité démographique et immobilière à Compton au tournant du siècle," *Cahiers de géographie du Québec*, vol. 28, 73–74 (1984), pp. 89–105.   **2263**

Gagnon, François, "Parenté et migration: Le cas des Canadiens français à Montréal entre 1845 et 1875," *Historical Papers, Canadian Historical Association* (1988), pp. 63–85.   **2264**

RURAL & REGIONAL SOCIAL GEOGRAPHY

Blanchard, Raoul, "Le côte nord, I: Les genres de vies et leur évolution," in his "Le rebord nord de l'estuaire et du golfe du Saint Laurent," *Revue de géographie alpine*, vol. 20 (1932), pp. 444–500.
2265

Harris, R. Cole, "Of Poverty and Helplessness in Petite-Nation," *Canadian Historical Review*, vol. 52 (1971), pp. 23–50.
2266

Lépine, Yolande, "Forces sociales et forces de production dans les terres noires de Napierville-Châteauguay," *Cahiers de géographie du Québec*, vol. 17, 42 (1973), pp. 389–414. [Focus on 1945–1972]
2267

Ross, W. Gillies, *Three Eastern Townships: Mining Villages since 1863: Albert Mines, Capelton, and Eustis, Quebec* (Lennoxville: Bishop's University, Department of Geography, 1974), 187 pp. Excerpts reprinted in I. Abella and D. Miller, eds., *The Canadian Worker in the Twentieth Century* (Toronto: Oxford University Press, 1978), pp. 20–22 and 89–93.
2268

Courville, Serge, "L'habitant canadien et le système seigneurial de 1627 à 1854," Ph.D. diss., Université de Montréal, 1979.
2269

Hardy, René, Jean Roy, and Normand Seguin, "Une recherche en cours: Le monde rural mauricien au 19e siècle," *Cahiers de géographie du Québec*, vol. 26, 67 (1982), pp. 145–154.
2270

Mercier, Guy, "Essai sur la notion de propriété: Le témoignage de l'habitat artisan-ouvrier à Beauport (1840–1920)," Master's thesis, Université Laval, 1984.
2271

Monette, Michel, "Groupes dominants et structure locale de pouvoir à Deschambault et Saint-Casimir, comté de Portneuf (1829–1870)," *Cahiers de géographie du Québec*, vol. 28, 73–74 (1984), pp. 73–88.
2272

Robert, Jean-Claude, "Aperçu sur les structures socio-professionelles des villages de la région nord de Montréal durant la première moitié du XIXe siècle," *Cahiers de géographie du Québec*, vol. 28, 73–74 (1984), pp. 63–72.
2273

Courville, Serge, "Minorités ethniques et recherches d'appartenance: Propos d'étape sur la présence étrangère dans le village québécois des années 1830," *Province historique*, vol. 35, 142 (1985), pp. 377–400.
2274

Pletsch, Alfred, "French and English Settlement in the Eastern Townships (Québec): Conflict or Coexistence?" *Marburger Geographische Schriften*, vol. 96 (1985), pp. 164–183.
2275

Courville, Serge, "L'habitant canadien dans la première moitié du XIXe siècle: Survie ou survivance?" *Recherches sociographiques*, vol. 27, 2 (1986), pp. 177–193.
2276

Courville, Serge, Jean C. Robert, and Normand Seguin, "La vie de relation dans l'axe laurentien au XIXe siècle: L'exemple du lac Saint-Pierre," *Annales de Bretagne et des pays de l'ouest*, vol. 95, 4 (1988), pp. 347–359.
2277

Little, J. I., *Nationalism, Capitalism, and Colonization in Nineteenth Century Quebec: The Upper St. Frances District* (Montreal: McGill-Queen's University Press, 1989), 306 pp.
2278

Crochetière, André, "Hiérarchie socio-professionnelle des villages au Bas-Canada durant la première moitié du XIXe siècle: Le cas de l'aire seigneuriale," Master's thesis, Université Laval, 1990.
2279

Little, J. I., *Crofters and Habitants: Settler Society, Economy, and Culture in a Quebec Township, 1848–1881* (Montreal: McGill-Queen's University Press, 1991), 368 pp.
2280

POLITICAL & ADMINISTRATIVE GEOGRAPHY

Bonenfant, Jean-Charles, "Les douze circonscriptions électorales 'privilégiées' du Québec," *Cahiers de géographie du Québec*, vol. 6, 11 (1962), pp. 161–166. [Focus on 1867–1960]
2281

Bellavance, Marcel, "Quelques éléments spatiaux de la conjoncture politique québécoise en 1867," *Cahiers de géographie du Québec*, vol. 24, 62 (1980), pp. 225–248.
2282

Verrault-Roy, Louise, "La reconstitution du périmètre des paroisses: L'exemple mauricien de trois paroisses seigneuriales," *Cahiers de géographie du Québec*, vol. 26, 67 (1982), pp. 155–162.
2283

Desaulnier, Philippe, "La cartographie des découpages administratifs anciens du territoire québécois: Méthodologie d'une recherche; La région de Montréal (1825–1861)," Master's thesis, Université Laval, 1987.
2284

Courville, Serge, et al., "Les découpages administratifs anciens de la région de Montréal au XIXe siècle (1825–1861): Méthodologie d'une recherche," *Canadian Geographer*, vol. 33, 4 (1989), pp. 342–352.
2285

ECONOMIC DEVELOPMENT

See also **1404**

Blanchard, Raoul, "La region d'Ottawa: Les étapes de l'occupation," in his "Les pays d'Ottawa," *Revue de géographie alpine*, vol. 37 (1949), pp. 179–219.
2286

Scarlett, Maurice J., "The Rural Economy of Part of the Montreal Economic Region from 1940 to the Present: Counties of Beauharnois, Chateauguay, Huntingdon, Soulanges, and Vaudreuil," Ph.D. diss., Université de Montréal, 1967.　**2287**

Rudin, Ronald, "Saint-Hyacinthe and the Development of a Regional Economy, 1840–1895" (Downsview: York University Department of Geography Discussion Paper no. 15, 1977), 25 pp.　**2288**

MacGregor, Louise M., "Les transformations de la seigneurie et de la propriété au XVIIIe siècle: L'exemple de L'Ange-Gardien et du Chateau-Richer," Master's thesis, McMaster University, 1978.　**2289**

Courville, Serge, "La crise agricole du Bas-Canada: Éléments d'une réflexion géographique, Part I," *Cahiers de géographie du Québec*, vol. 24, 62 (1980), pp. 193–224; "Part II," 63 (1980), pp. 385–428.　**2290**

Courville, Serge, "Rente declarée payée sur la censive de 90 arpents au recensement nominatif de 1831: Méthodologie d'une recherche," *Cahiers de géographie du Québec*, vol. 27, 70 (1983), pp. 43–61.　**2291**

Courville, Serge, "Esquisse du développement villageois au Québec: Le cas de l'aire seigneuriale entre 1760 et 1854," *Cahiers de géographie du Québec*, vol. 28, 73–74 (1984), pp. 9–46.　**2292**

Courville, Serge, *Entre ville et campagne: L'essor du village dans les seigneuries du Bas-Canada* (Québec: Presses de Université Laval, 1990), 350 pp.　**2293**

LAND & LAND USE

Deffontaines, Pierre, *Le rang: Type de peuplement rural du Canada français* (Québec: Presses Universitaires Laval, Institut d'histoire et de géographie, Cahiers de géographie, no. 5, 1953), 32 pp. Translated as "The Rang—Pattern of Rural Settlement in French Canada," in M. Rioux and Y. Martin, eds., *French Canadian Society*, vol. 1 (Toronto: McClelland and Stewart, 1964), pp. 3–19; and in Robert M. Irving, ed., *Readings in Canadian Geography* (Toronto: Holt, Rinehart and Winston, 1972), pp. 70–80.　**2294**

Derruau, Max, "A l'origine du 'rang' canadien," *Cahiers de géographie du Québec*, vol. 1, 1 (1956), pp. 39–47.　**2295**

Lefebvre, M.-A., "La genèse et l'évolution du terroir de l'ancienne seigneurie de Nicolet," Ph.D. diss., Université de Montréal, 1956.　**2296**

Clibbon, Peter B., "The Evolution and Present Pattern of Land Use in Terrebonne County, Que-

bec," Master's thesis, Université de Montréal, 1962.　**2297**

Clibbon, Peter B., "Changing Land Use in Terrebonne County, Quebec," *Cahiers de géographie du Québec*, vol. 15, 8 (1964), pp. 5–40.　**2298**

Harris, R. Cole, "A Geography of the Seigneurial System in Canada during the French Regime," Ph.D. diss., University of Wisconsin–Madison, 1964.　**2299**

Harris, R. Cole, *The Seigneurial System in Early Canada: A Geographical Study* (Madison: University of Wisconsin Press; and Québec: Laval University Press, 1966). Revised ed. Montreal: McGill-Queen's University Press, 1984, 247 pp.　**2300**

Harris, R. Cole, "Some Remarks on the Seigneurial Geography of Early Canada," in R. Louis Gentilcore, ed., *Canada's Changing Geography* (Toronto: Prentice-Hall, 1967), pp. 30–33.　**2301**

Courville, Serge, "Contribution à l'étude de l'origine du rang au Québec: La politique spatiale des Cent-Associés," *Cahiers de géographie du Québec*, vol. 25, 65 (1981), pp. 197–236.　**2302**

EXTRACTIVE ACTIVITY

Hills, Theo L., "The Canadian Asbestos Industry," *Geographical Studies*, vol. 2, 1 (1955), pp. 27–38.　**2303**

St-Amand, Roland, "Montauban-Les-Mines: Vicissitudes d'un centre minier," *Cahiers de géographie du Québec*, vol. 13, 28 (1969), pp. 91–108. [Focus on 1913–1961]　**2304**

Booth, J. Derek, "Changing Forest Utilization Patterns in the Eastern Townships of Québec," Ph.D. diss., McGill University, 1972.　**2305**

AGRICULTURE

Peattie, Roderick, "Farms and Farming in the Lower St. Lawrence Valley," *Journal of Geography*, vol. 21, 5 (1922), pp. 174–179.　**2306**

Jones, Robert L., "French-Canadian Agriculture in the St. Lawrence Valley, 1815–1850," *Agricultural History*, vol. 16, 3 (1942), pp. 137–148.　**2307**

Jones, Robert L., "The Agricultural Development of Lower Canada, 1850–1867," *Agricultural History*, vol. 19, 4 (1945), pp. 212–224.　**2308**

Pelletier, Raymond, "Évolution agricole de l'île Jésus," *Revue canadienne de géographie*, vol. 16, 1–4 (1962), pp. 31–48.　**2309**

Beauregard, Ludger, "Les étapes de la mise en valeur agricole de la vallée du Richelieu,"

Cahiers de géographie du Québec, vol. 14, 32 (1970), pp. 171–214. **2310**

Parson, Helen E., "The Rise and Fall of Farming in a Marginal Area: The Gatineau Valley, Québec," *Cahiers de géographie du Québec*, vol. 19, 48 (1975), pp. 573–582. **2311**

Courville, Serge, "Le marche des 'subsistances': L'exemple de la plaine de Montréal au début des années 1830; Une perspective géographique," *Revue d'histoire de l'Amérique française*, vol. 42, 2 (1988), pp. 193–239. **2312**

Poudrier, Maryse, "Les transformations de l'agriculture au Bas-Canada dans la première moitié du XIXe siècle: L'exemple de Sainte-Thérèse-de-Blainville, Master's thesis, Université Laval, 1990. **2313**

LANDSCAPE

Guérin, Marc-Aimé, "La maison de chaume des basses-terres du Saint Laurent," *Revue canadienne de géographie*, vol. 11, 1 (1957), pp. 47–50. **2314**

Guérin, Marc-Aimé, "Une classification des maisons rurales du Comté de Naperville-Laprairie (centre du Canada français)," *Cahiers de géographie du Québec*, vol. 3, 6 (1959), pp. 203–207. **2315**

Frost, Pauline M., "Cultural Landscapes of the Rouge River Valley, Quebec," *Cahiers de géographie du Québec*, vol. 13, 28 (1969), pp. 77–89. **2316**

Courville, Serge, "Les constructions de pierre dans le comté des Deux-Montagnes (notes historiques)," in C. Laverdière and P. Guimond, eds., *La roche en place: Rapport préliminaire*, no. 12 (Montreal: Centre de recherches écologiques de Montréal, 1973), pp. 95–109. **2317**

McKinnon, Sarah M., *Traditional Rural Architecture in Quebec, 1600–1800* (Toronto: University of Toronto Centre for Urban and Community Studies, Research Paper no. 9, 1977), 108 pp. **2318**

Pletsch, Alfred, "Kolonisationsphasen und Kulturlandschaftswandel im Südosten der Provinz Québec (Kanada)," *Erdkunde*, vol. 34, 1 (1980), pp. 61–73. **2319**

Mathieu, Jacques, and Réal Brisson, "La vallée Laurentienne au XVIIIe siècle: Un paysage à connaître," *Cahiers de géographie du Québec*, vol. 28, 73–74 (1984), pp. 107–124. **2320**

COMMUNICATIONS & TRADE

Jones, Clarence F., "Transportation Adjustments in the Railway Entrances and Terminal Facilities at Montreal," *Bulletin of the Philadelphia Geographical Society*, vol. 22, 3 (1924), pp. 98–110. **2321**

Jones, Clarence F., "Geographic Influences in the Routes and Traffic of the Atlantic Railway Connections at Montreal," *Bulletin of the Philadelphia Geographical Society*, vol. 23, 1 (1925), pp. 1–12. **2322**

Corley, Nora T., "The Montreal Ship Channel, 1805–1865," Master's thesis, McGill University, 1961. **2323**

Corley, Nora T., "The St. Lawrence Ship Channel, 1805–1865," *Cahiers de géographie du Québec*, vol. 11, 23 (1967), pp. 277–306. **2324**

Hamelin, Jean, and Jean Provencher, "La vie des relations sur le Saint Laurent entre Québec et Montréal, au milieu de XVIIIe siècle," *Cahiers de géographie du Québec*, vol. 11, 23 (1967), pp. 243–252. **2325**

Hoekstra, Anna E., and W. Gillies Ross, "The Craig and Gosford Roads: Early Colonization Routes in the Eastern Townships of Quebec," *Canadian Geographical Journal*, vol. 79, 2 (1969), pp. 52–57. **2326**

Soltész, Joseph-A., and Rodolphe de Koninck, "Les transports aux Cent-îles du lac Saint-Pierre: L'équilibre ou l'éclatement d'un pays," *Cahiers de géographie du Québec*, vol. 17, 42 (1973), pp. 449–464. **2327**

Courville, Serge, Jean-Claude Robert, and Normand Seguin, "Le Saint-Laurent, artère de vie: Réseau routier et métiers de la navigation au XIXe siècle," *Cahiers de géographie du Québec*, vol. 34, 92 (1990), pp. 181–196. **2328**

MANUFACTURING & INDUSTRIALIZATION

Brouillette, Normand, "Le déclin industriel de Shawinigan: Ses conséquences sur l'organisation de la vie urbaine," Master's thesis, Université Laval, 1972. **2329**

Brouillette, Normand, "Le développement industriel d'une région du proche hinterland québécois: La Mauricie, 1900–1975," Ph.D. diss., McGill University, 1983. **2330**

Courville, Serge, "Croissance villageoise et industries rurales dans les seigneuries du Québec, 1815–1851," in Norman Seguin and François Lebrun, eds., *Sociétés villageoises et rapports villes-campagnes au Québec et dans la France de l'ouest, XVIIe-XXe siècle: Actes du colloque franco-québécois de Québec, 1985* (Trois-Rivières: Centre de recherches en études québécois, 1987), pp. 205–219. **2331**

Lanthier, Pierre, and Normand Brouillette, "Shawinigan Falls de 1895 à 1930: L'émergence d'une ville industrielle au sein du monde rural," *Urban History Review*, vol. 19, 1 (1990), pp. 42–55. 2332

URBAN NETWORKS & URBANIZATION

Uren, Philip E., "A Historical Geography of the St. Maurice Valley, with Special Reference to Urban Occupance," Master's thesis, McGill University, 1949. 2333

Camu, Pierre, "Le port et l'arrière-pays de Trois-Rivières," *Geographical Bulletin*, vol. 1 (1951), pp. 30–51. 2334

Ballabon, Maurice B., "A Regional Study of the Richelieu Valley: The Urban Centres," Master's thesis, McGill University, 1952. 2335

Routaboule, Danièle, "Villes moyennes du Québec," *La vie urbaine*, n.s. (Oct.-Dec., 1966), pt. 4, pp. 281–316. 2336

Kestelman, Paula S., "The Evolution of an Urban Culture Core: A Study of French Canadian Institutions and Commerce in Central East Montreal," Master's thesis, Carleton University, 1984. [Focus on 1818–1982] 2337

TOWN GROWTH

Blanchard, Raoul, "L'évolution de Québec," in his "Québec: Esquisse de géographie urbaine," *Revue de géographie alpine*, vol. 22 (1934), pp. 294–351. 2338

Blanchard, Raoul, "L'évolution urbaine," in his "Montréal: Esquisse de géographie urbaine," *Revue de géographie alpine*, vol. 35 (1947), pp. 164–246. 2339

Blanchard, Raoul, "Montréal: Equisse de géographie urbaine," *Revue canadienne de géographie*, vol. 4, 1–2 (1950), pp. 31–46. 2340

Parker, William H., "Québec City in the 1830s," *Cahiers de géographie du Québec*, vol. 3, 6 (1959), pp. 261–273. 2341

Kayser, Edmond, "Industry in Hull: Its Origins and Development," Master's thesis, University of Ottawa, 1967. 2342

O'Brien, Raymond J., "Fulford, Québec: The Changing Geography of a Canadian Village," Master's thesis, McGill University, 1968. 2343

Smith, Willard V., "The Evolution of a Fall Line Settlement: Buckingham, Quebec," Master's thesis, University of Ottawa, 1968. 2344

Pampalon, Robert, "L'analyse de la dynamique spatiale à Charlesbourg: Un exemple de la spécialisation de l'espace intra-urbain," *Cahiers de*

géographie du Québec, vol. 19, 46 (1975), pp. 119–145. [Focus on 1954–1974] 2345

Hulbert, François, "Pouvoir municipal et développement urbain: Le cas de Sainte-Foy en banlieue de Québec," *Cahiers de géographie du Québec*, vol. 25, 66 (1981), pp. 361–402. [Focus on 1958–1980] 2346

Dechêne, Louise, "Quelques aspects de la ville de Québec au XVIIIe siècle d'après les dénombrements paroissiaux," *Cahiers de géographie du Québec*, vol. 28, 75 (1984), pp. 485–505. 2347

Olson, Sherry H., *The Tip of the Iceberg: Strategy for Research on Nineteenth-Century Montreal* (Montreal: McGill University Department of Geography, Shared Spaces/Partage de l'espace, no. 5, 1986), 43 pp. 2348

Salois, Johanne, "Étude de la structuration d'un village: Le cas de Bourg Saint-Louis, 1767–1828," Master's thesis, Université Laval, 1987. 2349

Chénier, Rémi, *Québec: Ville coloniale française en Amérique, 1660 à 1690* (Ottawa: Lieux historiques nationaux, Service des parcs, 1991), 293 pp. Translated as *Québec: A French Colonial Town in America, 1660–1690* (Ottawa: National Historic Sites Parks Service, Environment Canada, Studies in Archeology, Architecture, and History, 1991), 279 pp. 2350

Desloges, Yvon, *Une ville de locataires: Québec au XVIIIe siècle* (Ottawa: Lieux historiques nationaux, Service des parcs, 1991), 313 pp. Translated as *A Tenants' Town: Quebec in the Eighteenth Century* (Ottawa: National Historic Sites Parks Service, Environment Canada, Studies in Archeology, Architecture, and History, 1991), 299 pp. 2351

URBAN ECONOMIC STRUCTURE

Camu, Pierre, *Étude du port de Québec* (Ottawa: Ministère des mines et des relevés techniques, Direction de la géographie, Étude géographique no. 17, 1958), 79 pp. [Focus on 1935–1955] 2352

Bouchard, Diana C., "Location Patterns of Selected Retail Activities in the Urban Environment: Montreal, 1950–1970," *Revue de géographie de Montréal*, vol. 27, 3 (1973), pp. 319–327. 2353

Boisvert, Michel, "Spatio-dynamique bancaire en milieu urbanisé: L'île de Montréal (1945–1972)," *Revue de géographie de Montréal*, vol. 29, 3 (1975), pp. 243–252. 2354

Steed, Guy P. F., "Locational Factors and Dynamics of Montreal's Large Garment Complex," *Tijdschrift voor economische en sociale geografie*, vol. 67, 3 (1976), pp. 151–168. 2355

Beauregard, Ludger, and Normand Dupont, "La réorganisation du commerce dans la région métropolitaine de Montréal," *Cahiers de géographie du Québec,* vol. 27, 71 (1983), pp. 277–305. [Focus on 1951–1971] **2356**

Levine, Gregory J., "Criticizing the Assessment: Views of the Property Evaluation Process in Montreal, 1870–1920, and Their Implications for Historical Geography," *Canadian Geographer,* vol. 28, 3 (1984), pp. 276–284. **2357**

Hoskins, Ralph F. H., *Original Acquisition of Land in Montreal by the Grand Trunk Railway of Canada* (Montreal: McGill University Department of Geography, Shared Spaces/Partage de l'espace, no. 7, 1987), 12 pp. **2358**

Lewis, Robert D., "The Development of an Early Suburban Industrial District: The Montreal Ward of Saint-Ann, 1851–71," *Urban History Review,* vol. 19, 3 (1991), pp. 166–180. **2359**

URBAN SOCIAL STRUCTURE

Montreal

Population

Rosenberg, Louis, *A Study of the Growth and Changes in the Distribution of the Jewish Population of Montreal* (Montreal: Canadian Jewish Congress, Bureau of Social and Economic Research, Canadian Jewish Population Studies, Canadian Jewish Community Series, no. 4, 1955), 51 pp. **2360**

Rosenberg, Louis, *Population Characteristics of the Jewish Community of Montreal* (Montreal: Canadian Jewish Congress, Bureau of Social and Economic Research, Canadian Jewish Population Studies, Canadian Jewish Community Series, no. 6, 1956), 58 pp. **2361**

Thach, Q. Thuy, "Socio-Spatial Patterns of Infant Survival in Montreal, 1859–1860," Master's thesis, McGill University, 1988. **2362**

Thornton, Patricia A., Sherry H. Olson, and Quoc Thuy Thach, *A Geography of Little Children in Nineteenth-Century Montreal* (Montreal: McGill University Department of Geography, Shared Spaces/Partage de l'espace, no. 10, 1988), 30 pp. **2363**

Thornton, Patricia, Sherry H. Olson, and Quoc Thuy Thach, *Infant Mortality in Montreal in 1860: The Roles of Culture, Class, and Habitat* (Montreal: McGill University Department of Geography, Shared Spaces/Partage de l'espace, no. 9, 1988), 35 pp. **2364**

Olson, Sherry H., Patricia Thornton, and Quoc Thuy Thach, "Dimensions sociales de la mortal

ité infantile à Montréal au milieu du XIXe siècle," *Annales de démographie historique* 1988 (1989), pp. 299–325. **2365**

Thornton, Patricia A., and Sherry Olson, "Family Contexts of Fertility and Infant Survival in Nineteenth Century Montreal," *Journal of Family History,* vol. 16, 4 (1990), pp. 401–417. **2366**

Property & property relations

Bellavance, Marcel, and Jean-Daniel Gronoff, "Les structures de l'espace Montréalais a l'époque de la Confédération," *Cahiers de géographie du Québec,* vol. 24, 63 (1980), pp. 363–384. **2367**

Hertzog, Stephen, *A City of Tenants: Homeownership and Social Class in Montreal, 1847–1881* (Montreal: McGill University Department of Geography, Shared Spaces/Partage de l'espace, no. 2, 1985), 59 pp. **2368**

Hertzog, Stephen, "A Stake in the System: Domestic Property Ownership and Social Class in Montreal, 1847–1881," Master's thesis, McGill University, 1985. **2369**

Hanna, David B., *The Layered City: A Revolution in Housing in Mid-Nineteenth-Century Montreal* (Montreal: McGill University Department of Geography, Shared Spaces/Partage de l'espace, no. 6, 1986), 25 pp. **2370**

Hertzog, Stephen, and Robert D. Lewis, "A City of Tenants: Homeownership and Social Class in Montreal, 1847–1881," *Canadian Geographer,* vol. 30, 4 (1986), pp. 316–323. **2371**

Levine, Gregory J., "Class, Ethnicity, and Property Transfers in Montreal, 1907–1909," *Journal of Historical Geography,* vol. 14, 4 (1988), pp. 360–380. **2372**

Lewis, Robert D., "Homeownership Reassessed for Montreal in the 1840s," *Canadian Geographer,* vol. 34, 2 (1990), pp. 150–152. **2373**

Occupations

Hanna, David B., and Sherry Olson, "Métiers, loyers, et bout de rue: L'armature de la société Montréalaise, 1881 à 1901," *Cahiers de géographie du Québec,* vol. 27, 71 (1983), pp. 255–275. **2374**

Olson, Sherry H., *Occupations as Cues to Social Structure in Nineteenth-Century Montreal* (Montreal: McGill University Department of Geography, Shared Spaces/Partage de l'espace, no. 4, 1986), 52 pp. **2375**

Hoskins, Ralph F. H., *An Analysis of the Payrolls of the Grand Trunk Railway, 1880–1918* (Montreal: McGill University Department of Geography,

Shared Spaces/Partage de l'espace, no. 8, 1987), 23 pp. **2376**

Hoskins, Ralph F. H., "An Analysis of the Payrolls of the Point St. Charles Shops of the Grand Trunk Railway," *Cahiers de géographie du Québec*, vol. 33, 90 (1989), pp. 323–344. **2377**

Duchesne, André, *A Study of the Garrison Families in Montréal and Québec City, 1855–1865* (Montreal: McGill University Department of Geography, Shared Spaces/Partage de l'espace, no. 11, 1990), 31 pp. **2378**

Residential patterns

Chichekian, Garo, "Armenian Immigrants in Canada and Their Distribution in Montreal," *Cahiers de géographie du Québec*, vol. 21, 52 (1977), pp. 65–82. [Focus on 1900–1966] **2379**

Ruddick, Susan M., "The Movement for Public Housing in Montreal, 1930–1958," Master's thesis, McGill University, 1979. **2380**

Langlois, André, "Évolution de la répartition spatiale des groupes ethniques dans l'espace résidentiel Montréalais 1931–1971," *Cahiers de géographie du Québec*, vol. 29, 76 (1985), pp. 49–65. **2381**

Lewis, Robert D., "The Segregated City: Residential Differentiation, Rent, and Income in Montreal, 1861–1901," Master's thesis, McGill University, 1985. **2382**

Thach, Q. Thuy, *Social Class and Residential Mobility: The Case of the Irish in Montreal, 1851 to 1871* (Montreal: McGill University Department of Geography, Shared Spaces/Partage de l'espace, no. 1, 1985), 30 pp. **2383**

Lewis, Robert D., *The Segregated City: Residential Differentiation by Class and Occupation in Montreal, 1861–1901* (Montreal: McGill University Department of Geography, Shared Spaces/Partage de l'espace, no. 3, 1986), 46 pp. **2384**

Behiels, Michael, "Neo-Canadians and Schools in Montreal, 1900–1970," *Journal of Cultural Geography*, vol. 8, 2 (1988), pp. 5–16. **2385**

Olson, Sherry H., "Occupations and Residential Spaces in Nineteenth-Century Montreal," *Historical Methods*, vol. 22, 3 (1989), pp. 81–96. **2386**

Lewis, Robert D., "The Segregated City: Class Residential Patterns and the Development of Industrial Districts in Montreal, 1861 and 1901," *Journal of Urban History*, vol. 17, 2 (1991), pp. 123–152. **2387**

Quebec

Grenier, Manon, Maurice Roy, and Louis Bouchard, "L'évolution de la population des enfants au centre de la ville de Québec et en banlieue,

1951–1971," *Cahiers de géographie du Québec,* vol. 18, 45 (1974), pp. 541–552. **2388**

Roy, Aimé, "Capital immobilier, propriétaires fonciers, et aménagement de la ville: La cas du quartier Saint-Jean-Baptiste à Québec," *Cahiers de géographie du Québec*, vol. 25, 64 (1981), pp. 133–148. **2389**

Lafrance, Marc, and T. Ruddel, "Physical Expansion and Socio-Cultural Segregation in Quebec City, 1765–1840," in Gilbert A. Stelter and Alan F. J. Artibise, eds., *Shaping the Urban Landscape: Aspects of the Canadian City-Building Process* (Ottawa: Carleton University Press, 1982), pp. 148–172. **2390**

TOWNSCAPE

See also 1461

Montreal

Routaboule, Danièle, "Aux sources de la morphologie urbaine au Québec," *Revue de géographie de Montréal*, vol. 23, 1 (1969), pp. 88–97. **2391**

Hanna, David B., "The New Town of Montreal: Creation of an Upper Middle Class Suburb on the Slope of Mount Royal in the Mid-Nineteenth Century," Master's thesis, University of Toronto, 1977. **2392**

Aiken, S. Robert, and Lawrence P. Kredl, "Monreal's Upper Peel Street: How Fast the Past Has Gone," *Canadian Geographical Journal*, vol. 98, 2 (1979), pp. 38–43. **2393**

Hanna, David B., "Creation of an Early Victorian Suburb in Montreal," *Urban History Review*, vol. 9, 2 (1980), pp. 38–64. Reprinted in G. A. Stelter, ed., *Cities and Urbanization: Canadian Historical Perspectives* (Toronto: Copp Clark Pitman, 1990), pp. 39–65. **2394**

Linteau, Paul-André, *Maisonneuve, ou comment des promoteurs fabriquent une ville, 1883–1918* (Montreal: Boreal Express, 1981), 280 pp. Translated as *The Promoter's City: Building the Industrial Town of Maisonneuve, 1883–1918* (Toronto: Lorimer, 1985), 225 pp. **2395**

Linteau, Paul-André, "The Development and Beautification of an Industrial City: Maisonneuve, 1883–1918," in Gilbert A. Stelter and Alan F. J. Artibise, eds., *Shaping the Urban Landscape: Aspects of the Canadian City-Building Process* (Ottawa: Carleton University Press, 1982), pp. 304–320. **2396**

Linteau, Paul-André, "Le contrôle de l'espace et du bâti dans la banlieue montréalaise, 1840–1914," in M. Garden et Y. Lequin, eds., *Habiter la ville, XV-XX siècles* (Lyon: Presses Universitaires de Lyon, 1984), pp. 153–174. **2397**

Hanna, David B., "Montreal: A City Built by Small Builders, 1867–1880," Ph.D. diss., McGill University, 1986. **2398**

Hanna, David B., "L'abitazione e la rivolutione industriale: Montréal nella seconda metà dell' 1800," *Storia urbana*, vol. 11, 38 (1987), pp. 33–59. **2399**

Quebec

LaMontagne, Gilles, "Contribution à l'étude de la rue St. Jean," Master's thesis, Université Laval, 1965. **2400**

Lebel, Aline, "Les propriétés foncières des Ursulines et le développement de Québec, 1854–1940," *Cahiers de géographie du Québec*, vol. 25, 64 (1981), pp. 119–132. **2401**

Bervin, George, "Espace physique et culture matérielle du marchand-négociant à Québec au début du XIXe siècle, 1820–1830," *Material History Bulletin* (Canada), no. 14 (1982), pp. 1–18. **2402**

Shawinigan

Dupont, Louis, "Morphogénèse du milieu construit du centreville du Shawinigan," *Cahiers de géographie du Québec*, vol. 26, 67 (1982), pp. 103–119. **2403**

Brouillette, Normand, "Le rôle de la Shawinigan Water and Power Company dans la structuration de l'espace urbain shawiniganais, 1898–1921," *Cahiers de géographie du Québec*, vol. 34, 92 (1990), pp. 197–208. **2404**

Other centers

Ross, W. Gillies, "Encroachment of the Jeffrey Mine on the Town of Asbestos, Quebec," *Geographical Review*, vol. 57, 4 (1967), pp. 523–537. **2405**

Rudin, Ronald, "Land Ownership and Urban Growth: The Experience of Two Quebec Towns, 1840–1914," *Urban History Review*, vol. 8, 2 (1979), pp. 23–46. [Sherbrooke and Sorel] **2406**

Delisle, Jacques, "Morphologie urbaine et tenures foncières à Ste. Foy-Sillery," Master's thesis, Université Laval, 1981. **2407**

RECREATION & TOURISM

Gazillo, Stephen, "The Evolution of Restaurants and Bars in Vieux-Québec since 1900," *Cahiers de géographie du Québec*, vol. 25, 64 (1981), pp. 101–118. **2408**

Marceau, Renée and Richard Pelletier, "La restauration patrimoniale de la Vieille ville de Québec: Le rôle des petits propriétaires," *Cahiers de géographie du Québec*, vol. 25, 64 (1981), pp. 87–100. **2409**

Lundgren, Jan O. J., "The Development of Tourist Accommodation in the Montreal Laurentians," in Geoffrey Wall and John S. Marsh, eds., *Recreational Land Use: Perspectives on Its Evolution in Canada* (Ottawa: Carleton University Press, 1982), pp. 175–189. **2410**

Lundgren, Jan O. J., "Development Patterns and Lessons in the Montreal Laurentians," in Peter J. Murphy, ed., *Tourism in Canada: Selected Issues and Options* (Victoria: University of Victoria Department of Geography, Western Geographical Series no. 21, 1983), pp. 95–126. [Focus on 1890–1980] **2411**

PLANNING

Kredl, Lawrence P., "The Origin and Development of Mount Royal Park, Montreal, 1870–1900: Ideal vs. Reality," Master's thesis, York University, 1984. **2412**

PLACE NAMES

Poirier, Jean, "La toponymie historique et actuelle de l'île d'Orléans," Master's thesis, Université Laval, 1961. **2413**

Poirier, Jean, "La toponymie de l'île d'Orléans," *Cahiers de géographie du Québec*, vol. 6, 12 (1962), pp. 183–199. **2414**

Poirier, Jean, "Le toponyme Ile au Ruau," *Revue de géographie de Montréal*, vol. 23, 1 (1969), pp. 21–26. **2415**

Arseneault, Yves, "La choronymie de la Côte de Beaupré," Master's thesis, Université Laval, 1970. **2416**

Bonnelly, Christian, Jean-Marc Nicole, and Judith Roy, "La processus de formation et d'évolution des hagionymes: Exemples tirés de trois inventaires chrononymiques dans l'est du Québec," *Cahiers de géographie du Québec*, vol. 16, 437 (1972), pp. 99–112. **2417**

Taylor, Charlotte A., "Cultural Sequent Occupance and the Impact on Nomenclature in the Eastern Townships, Quebec," Master's thesis, University of Vermont, 1978. **2418**

Paquet, Christiane, *Itinéraire toponymique du Saint-Laurent: Ses rives et ses îles* (Quebec: Gouvernement du Québec, Commission de Toponymie, 1984), 451 pp. **2419**

Dugas, Jean-Yves, "L'espace québécois et son expression toponymique," *Cahiers de géographie du Québec*, vol. 28, 75 (1984), pp. 435–455. **2420**

Poirier, Jean, "Le nom de la ville d'Ottawa," *Canoma*, vol. 14, 1 (1988), pp. 12–14. **2421**

Poirier, Jean, "Les noms de lieux du Québec ayant une origine anthroponymique," *Canoma*, vol. 15, 2 (1989), pp. 15–16. **2422**

NORTHERN & EASTERN
QUEBEC

GENERAL

Blanchard, Raoul, "Les étapes de mise en valeur," in his "Le Saguenay et le lac Saint-Jean," *Revue de géographie alpine*, vol. 21 (1933), pp. 64–94.
2423

Glendinning, R. M., "The Lake Saint Jean Lowland, Province of Quebec," *Papers of the Michigan Academy of Science, Arts, and Letters*, vol. 20 (1934), pp. 313–341.
2424

Johnston, Claire M., "The Historical Geography of the Saguenay Valley," Master's thesis, McGill University, 1950.
2425

Bouchard, Gérard, "Introduction à l'étude de la société saguenayenne aux XIXe et XXe siècles," *Revue d'histoire de l'Amérique française*, vol. 31, 1 (1977), pp. 3–28.
2426

Hamelin, Louis-Edmond, "L'ère française Menier de 1895 à 1926 a l'île d'Anticosti (Canada)," *Annales de géographie*, vol. 89, 492 (1980), pp. 157–177.
2427

Martin, Jean, "De l'agriculture à l'industrie: Les communautés de scieurs au Saguenay, 1839–1871," Master's thesis, Université Laval, 1990.
2428

EXPLORATION & MAPPING

Rousseau, Jacques, "La cartographie de la région du lac Mistassini," *Revue d'histoire de l'Amérique française*, vol. 3, 2 (1949), pp. 298–312.
2429

Rousseau, Jacques, "Les concepts cartographiques du lac Mistassini avant l'ère de l'arpentage," *Revue de géographie de Montréal*, vol. 24, 4 (1970), pp. 403–416.
2430

REGIONAL SETTLEMENT

Caron, L'Abbé Ivanhoe, "La colonisation du Témiscamingue," *Bulletin de la Société de géographie du Québec*, vol. 4, 5 (1910), pp. 337–346.
2431

Blanchard, Raoul, "Les étapes et les modalités de la colonisation," in his "L'Abitibi—Témiscamingue," *Revue de géographie alpine*, vol. 37 (1949), pp. 472–500.
2432

Hamelin, Louis-Edmond, "La marche du peuplement à l'intérieur du diocèse de Joliette," *Rap-port du congrès de la Société canadienne d'histoire de l'Eglise catholique* (Hull, P.Q.: The Society, 1951), pp. 5–14.
2433

Falaise, Noël, "L'habitat aux îles de la Madeleine," *Cahiers de géographie du Québec*, vol. 3, 6 (1959), pp. 209–211. [Focus on 1792–1959]
2434

Bussières, Paul, "La population de la côte–nord," *Cahiers de géographie du Québec*, vol. 7, 14 (1963), pp. 157–192; and 8, 15 (1964), pp. 41–93. [Focus from the eleventh century to 1961]
2435

Biays, Pierre, *Les marges de l'eokoumène dans l'est du Canada: Partie orientale du Bouclier canadien et île de Terre-Neuve* (Quebec: Presses de l'Université Laval, Travaux et documents du Centre d'études nordiques, no. 2, 1964), 760 pp.
2436

Clibbon, Peter B., "Utilisation du sol et colonisation de la région des Laurentides centrales," *Geographical Bulletin* (Ottawa), no. 21 (1964), pp. 5–20.
2437

Malaurie, Jean, and Jacques Rousseau, eds., *Le Nouveau-Québec; Contribution à l'étude de l'occupation humaine* (Paris: Mouton, 1964), 464 pp. [Quebec-Labrador]
2438

Hamelin, Louis-Edmond, "Bilan statistique des lots de colonisation en Abitibi et au Témiscamingue (Québec)," *Cahiers de géographie du Québec*, vol. 11, 24 (1967), pp. 479–496.
2439

Hamelin, Louis-Edmond, "Évolution rurale et choronymie à Saint-Didace de Maskinongé, Québec, Canada," *Cahiers de géographie du Québec*, vol. 13, 28 (1969), pp. 55–76.
2440

Gaudreau, Guy, and Normand Guilbait, "L'habitat rural de la fin du XIXe siècle et du début du XXe siècle aux Iles-de-la-Madeleine, Québec," *Revue de géographie de Montréal*, vol. 30, 4 (1976), pp. 393–396.
2441

Hamelin, Louis-Edmond and Benoit Dumont, "Anticosti: L'aspect régional du peuplement," *Cahiers de géographie du Québec*, vol. 23, 60 (1979), pp. 435–450.
2442

Pouyez, C., R. Roy, and Gérard Bouchard, "La mobilité géographique en milieu rural: Le Saguenay, 1852–1861," *Histoire sociale/Social History*, vol. 14, 27 (1981), pp. 123–155.
2443

Asselin, Maurice, "Aspects géologiques de la colonisation de l'Abitibi," Master's thesis, Université Laval, 1982.   **2444**

Remiggi, Frank W., "Nineteenth-Century Settlement and Colonization on the Gaspé North Coast: An Historical-Geographical Interpretation," Ph.D. diss., McGill University, 1983. **2445**

LeBlanc, Robert G., "Colonisation et repatriement au Lac Saint-Jean (1895–1905)," *Revue d'histoire de l'Amérique française*, vol. 38, 3 (1985), pp. 379–408.   **2446**

Gauvreau, Danielle, "Mouvements migratoires et familles: Le peuplement du Saguenay avant 1911," *Revue d'histoire de l'Amérique française*, vol. 42, 2 (1988), pp. 167–192.   **2447**

POPULATION

Bouchard, Gérard, "Family Structures and Geographic Mobility at Laterrière, 1851–1935," *Journal of Family History*, vol. 2, 4 (1977), pp. 350–369.   **2448**

Bouchard, Gérard, and Jeannette Larouche, "Dynamique des populations locales: La formation des paroisses rurales au Saguenay (1840–1911)," *Revue d'histoire de l'Amérique française*, vol. 41, 3 (1988), pp. 363–388.   **2449**

St-Hilaire, Marc, "Origines et destins des familles pionnières d'une paroisse saguenayenne au XIXe siècle," *Cahiers de géographie du Québec*, vol. 32, 85 (1988), pp. 27–47.   **2450**

RURAL & REGIONAL SOCIAL GEOGRAPHY

Blanchard, Raoul, "Le peuplement," and "Les genres de vie anciens," in his "La presqu'île de Gaspé," *Revue de géographie alpine*, vol. 18 (1930), pp. 56–66 and 67–76.   **2451**

Hamelin, Louis-Edmond, "Le rang à Saint-Didace de Maskinongé," *Notes de géographie*, vol. 3 (Quebec: Université Laval, 1953), pp. 1–7. **2452**

Remiggi, Frank W., "Persistence of Ethnicity: A Study of Social and Spatial Boundaries on the Eastern Lower North Shore: 1820–1970," Master's thesis, Memorial University of Newfoundland, 1975.   **2453**

Remiggi, Frank W., "Ethnic Diversity and Settler Location on the Eastern Lower North Shore of Quebec," in John J. Mannion, ed., *The Peopling of Newfoundland: Essays in Historical Geography* (St. Johns: Memorial University of Newfoundland, Institute of Social and Economic Research, Publication no. 8, 1977), pp. 184–211. **2454**

Remiggi, Frank W., "Quelques origines spatiales du présent conflit francophone-anglophone au

Québec: Exemple de la Basse-Côte-Nord," *Cahiers de géographie du Québec*, vol. 24, 61 (1980), pp. 157–166.   **2455**

Rouffignat, Joël, "Espace matrimonial et espace social d'un village québécois: Le cas de Saint-Jean-Port-Joli," *Cahiers de géographie du Québec*, vol. 28, 73–74 (1984), pp. 163–182. **2456**

Bouchard, Gérard, "Évolution de l'alphabétisation (masculine) au Saguenay: Les variables géographiques, 1842–1971," *Historical Papers, Canadian Historical Association* (1989), pp. 13–35.
                    2457

ECONOMIC DEVELOPMENT

Bradbury, John H., "State Corporations and Resource Based Regional Development in Quebec, Canada, 1960–1980," *Economic Geography*, vol. 58, 1 (1982), pp. 45–61.   **2458**

Grandbois, Maryse, "Le développement des disparités régionales en Gaspésie, 1760–1960," *Revue d'histoire de l'Amérique française*, vol. 36, 4 (1983), pp. 483–506.   **2459**

Samson, Roch, "La Gaspésie au XIXe siècle: Espace maritime, espace marchand," *Cahiers de géographie du Québec*, vol. 28, 73–74 (1984), pp. 205–221.   **2460**

Willis, John, "Urbanization, Colonization, and Underdevelopment in the Bas-Saint-Laurent: Fraserville and the Temiscouata in the Late Nineteenth Century," *Cahiers de géographie du Québec*, vol. 28, 73–74 (1984), pp. 125–161. **2461**

Ommer, Rosemary E., "The Truck System in Gaspé, 1822–1877," *Acadiensis*, vol. 19, 1 (1989), pp. 91–114. Reprinted in Rosemary E. Ommer, *Merchant Credit and Labour Strategies in Historical Perspective* (Fredericton, N.B.: Acadiensis Press, 1990), pp. 49–72.   **2462**

LAND & LAND USE

Innes, Frank C., "The Land Use and Settlement of the Quebec Clay Belts: A Pilot Study in the Historical Geography of Québec, with Particular Reference to Man's Role in Changing the Face of the Earth," Master's thesis, McGill University, 1960.   **2463**

EXTRACTIVE ACTIVITY

Brouillette, Benoît, "L'expansion minière vers le nord du Québec," *Annales de géographie*, vol. 59 (1950), pp. 38–43. [Focus on 1912–1946] **2464**

Clarke, Roger, "In Them Days: The Breakdown of a Traditional Fishing Economy in an English Village on the Gaspé Coast," Ph.D. diss., McGill University, 1973. **2465**

Bradbury, John H., "The Rise of the 'Fourth Empire of the St. Lawrence': The Quebec-Labrador Iron Ore Mining Region," *Cahiers de géographie du Québec*, vol. 29, 78 (1985), pp. 351–364. [Focus on 1950–1984] **2466**

AGRICULTURE

Bouchard, Gérard, "L'agriculture saguenayenne entre 1840 et 1950: L'évolution de la technologie," *Revue d'histoire de l'Amérique française*, vol. 43, 3 (1990), pp. 353–380. **2467**

TOWN GROWTH

Ouellet, M. F., "Évolution des fonctions urbaines de Chicoutimi," *Canadian Geographer*, vol. 1 (1950), pp. 25–30. **2468**

Laverdière, Camille, "Oskélanéo: Village du haut Saint-Maurice," *Cahiers de géographie du Québec*, vol. 3, 6 (1959), pp. 223–235. [Focus on 1914–1959] **2469**

Harvey, Jacquelin, "Havre-Saint-Pierre: Le plus ancien des ports miniers Québécois," *Cahiers de géographie du Québec*, vol. 18, 44 (1974), pp. 357–365. [Focus on 1948–1974] **2470**

Currie-Mills, Russell, "Mining and the Emergence of Val d'Or as a Gateway City: A Study in Historical Geography," Master's thesis, University of Vermont, 1975. **2471**

PLACE NAMES

Hamelin, Louis-Edmond, "Aspects d'une histoire du peuplement par les choronymes d'habitat à Saint-Didace, Québec," *Revue d'histoire sociale*, vol. 2 (1968), pp. 115–122. **2472**

———— ONTARIO AS A WHOLE ————

GENERAL

See also 1150

Synthetic treatments

Spelt, Jacob, "Southern Ontario," in John Warkentin, ed., *Canada: A Geographical Interpretation* (Toronto: Methuen, 1968), pp. 334–395. **2473**

Gentilcore, R. Louis, "Ontario Emerges from the Trees," *Geographical Magazine*, vol. 45, 5 (1973), pp. 383–391. **2474**

Wood, J. David, ed., *Perspectives on Landscape and Settlement in Nineteenth Century Ontario* (Toronto: McClelland and Stewart, 1975), 220 pp. **2475**

Gentilcore, R. Louis, "The Making of a Province: Ontario to 1850," *American Review of Canadian Studies*, vol. 14, 2 (1984), pp. 137–156. **2476**

Selected themes

Dahms, Frederic A., "Small Town and Village Ontario," *Ontario Geography*, vol. 16 (1980), pp. 19–32. **2477**

Osborne, Brian S., "The Hinterland: Rural Place or Urban Process?" in David Gagan, ed., *New Directions for the Study of Ontario's Past* (Hamilton: McMaster University Press, 1988), pp. 267–283. **2478**

ENVIRONMENTAL CHANGE

Kelly, Kenneth, "Damaged and Efficient Landscapes in Rural and Southern Ontario, 1880–1900," *Ontario History*, vol. 66, 1 (1974), pp. 1–14. Reprinted in Graeme Wynn, ed., *People, Places, Patterns, Processes: Geographical Perspectives on the Canadian Past* (Toronto: Copp Clark Pitman, 1990), pp. 213–227. **2479**

Kelly, Kenneth, "The Artificial Drainage of Land in Nineteenth Century Southern Ontario," *Canadian Geographer*, vol. 19, 3 (1975), pp. 279–298. **2480**

Kelly, Kenneth, "The Impact of Nineteenth Century Settlement on the Land," in J. David Wood, ed., *Perspectives on Landscape and Settlement in Nineteenth Century Ontario* (Toronto: McClelland and Stewart, 1975), pp. 64–77. **2481**

Fecteau, Rodolphe, "The Introduction and Diffusion of Cultivated Plants in Southern Ontario," Master's thesis, York University, 1985. **2482**

McLaughlin, John, "The Lost Lands: The Draining of Ontario, 1781–1900," Master's thesis, Queen's University, 1991. **2483**

NATIVE PEOPLES & WHITE RELATIONS

Ross, William A., "The Petun: A Micromigration Pattern within the Late Ontario Iroquois," Master's thesis, York University, 1976. **2484**

Hamalainen, Peter, "Patterns of Faunal Exploitation by the Petun Indians," Master's thesis, York University, 1981. **2485**

Konrad, Victor A., "An Iroquois Frontier: The North Shore of Lake Ontario during the Late Seventeenth Century," *Journal of Historical Geography*, vol. 7, 2 (1981), pp. 129–144. **2486**

Roberts, Arthur C., "Preceramic Occupations along the North Shore of Lake Ontario," Ph.D. diss., York University, 1982. **2487**

Burgar, Robert, "Points to Ponder: A Regional Analysis of the Batten Kill Phase in Southern Ontario," Master's thesis, York University, 1985. **2488**

EXPLORATION & MAPPING

See also 1275–1284

Whebell, Charles F. J., "Printed Maps of Upper Canada, 1800–1864," *Ontario History*, vol. 49, 3 (1957), pp. 139–144. **2489**

Heidenreich, Conrad E., "Maps Relating to the First Half of the Seventeenth Century and Their Use in Determining the Location of Jesuit Missions in Huronia," *Canadian Cartographer*, vol. 3, 2 (1966), pp. 103–126. **2490**

Olsen, Marilyn J. M., "Aspects of the Mapping of Southern Ontario, 1783–1867," Master's thesis, University of London (England), 1968. **2491**

Olsen, Marilyn J. M., "Aspects of the Mapping of Southern Ontario, 1783–1867," *Proceedings of the Annual Conference of the Association of Canadian Map Libraries*, vol. 5 (1971), pp. 30–40. Reprinted in Barbara Farrell and Aileen Desbarats, eds., *Explorations in the History of Canadian Mapping: A Collection of Essays* (Ottawa: Association of Canadian Map Libraries and Archives, 1988), pp. 147–162. **2492**

White, James J., "Aspects of the Map Publishing Trade with Special Reference to Upper Canada and Canada West to 1867," Master's thesis, University of Western Ontario, 1973. **2493**

Phelps, Edward, "Facsimile Atlases, II: The Business of Their Production," *Proceedings of the Association of Canadian Map Libraries*, vol. 10 (1976), pp. 18–35. [Focus on nineteenth-century county atlases] **2494**

Thomson, Don W., "The Survey Story: Rideau Canal," *Geos*, vol. 11, 4 (1982), pp. 9–11. **2495**

Harding, Kathryn M. M., "Three Hundred Years of Ontario's Evolution in Maps," in Nick and Helma Mika, eds., *The Shaping of Ontario* (Belleville, Ont.: Mika Publishing Co., 1985), pp. 248–275. **2496**

Phelps, Edward, "The County Atlases of Ontario, 1875–1982," in Barbara Farrell and Eileen Desbarats, eds., *Explorations in the History of Canadian Mapping: A Collection of Essays* (Ottawa: Association of Canadian Map Libraries and Archives, 1988), pp. 163–177. **2497**

POPULAR IMAGES & EVALUATION

Warkentin, John H., "Southern Ontario: A View from the West," *Canadian Geographer*, vol. 10 (1966), pp. 157–171. Reprinted in a special issue of *Geographical Bulletin*, Selected Geographical Papers of Canada, Twenty-first International Geographical Congress, 1968. **2498**

Walker, Ian L., "The Evaluation of Upper Canada by European Visitors and Settlers from 1816–1867," Master's thesis, University of Toronto, 1969. **2499**

Kelly, Kenneth, "The Changing Attitude of Farmers to Forest in Nineteenth Century Ontario," *Ontario Geography*, vol. 8 (1974), pp. 64–77. **2500**

Bouchier, Michele, "Impact of the Northern Railroad on Sense of Place in Canada West, 1850–1865," Master's thesis, York University, 1979. **2501**

Hall, Cheryl J., "The Image of the Small Ontario Town in Fiction, 1900–1918: A Case Study in Humanistic Geography," Master's thesis, Queen's University, 1979. **2502**

Parson, Helen E., "An Overview of Landscape Assessment and Settlement Policy on the Southern Ontario Section of the Canadian Shield in the Nineteenth Century," *Ontario Geography*, vol. 22 (1983), pp. 15–28. **2503**

Dilley, Robert S., "British Travellers in Early Upper Canada: A Content Analysis of Itineraries and Images," in Donald H. Akenson, ed., *Canadian Papers in Rural History*, vol. 5 (Gananoque, Ont.: Langdale Press, 1986), pp. 198–223. **2504**

REGIONAL SETTLEMENT

Schott, Carl, *Landnahme und Kolonisation in Kanada am Beispiel Südontarios* (Kiel: Schriften des Geographischen Instituts der Universität Kiel, vol. 6, 1936), 330 pp. [Focus on 1800–1930s] **2505**

Jackson, W. A. Douglas, "A Geographical Study of Early Settlement in Southern Ontario," Master's thesis, University of Toronto, 1948. **2506**

Wood, J. David, "The Woodland Oak Plains Transition Zone in the Settlement of Western Upper Canada," *Canadian Geographer*, vol. 5, 1 (1961), pp. 43–47. **2507**

Brunger, Alan G., "Analysis of Site Factors in Nineteenth Century Ontario Settlement," in W. P. Adams and F. M. Helleiner, eds., *International Geography, 1972*, vol. 1, sec. 5, *Historical Geography* (Toronto: University of Toronto Press, for the International Geographical Union, 1972), pp. 400–402. **2508**

Gentilcore, R. Louis, "Settlement," in R. Louis Gentilcore, ed., *Ontario: Studies in Canadian Geography* (Toronto: University of Toronto Press, 1972), pp. 23–44. **2509**

Norton, William, "Agricultural Settlement Patterns in Upper Canada, 1782–1851: A Simulation Analysis," Ph.D. diss., McMaster University, 1973. **2510**

Gentilcore, R. Louis, and J. David Wood, "A Military Colony in a Wilderness: The Upper Canada Frontier," in J. David Wood, ed., *Perspectives on Landscape and Settlement in Nineteenth Century Ontario* (Toronto: McClelland and Stewart, 1975), pp. 32–50. **2511**

Norton, William, "The Process of Rural Land Occupation in Upper Canada," *Scottish Geographical Magazine*, vol. 91, 3 (1975), pp. 145–152. **2512**

Norton, William, "Constructing Abstract Worlds of the Past," *Geographical Analysis*, vol. 8, 3 (1976), pp. 269–288. [Southern Ontario] **2513**

Norton, William, "Process and Form Relationships: An Example from Historical Geography," *Professional Geographer*, vol. 30, 2 (1978), pp. 128–134. [Focus on southern Ontario, 1782–1851] **2514**

Wynn, Graeme, "Notes on Society and Environment in Old Ontario," *Journal of Social History*, vol. 13, 1 (1979), pp. 49–65. **2515**

Brunger, Alan G., "Geographical Propinquity among Pre-Famine Catholic Irish Settlers in Upper Canada," *Journal of Historical Geography*, vol. 8, 3 (1982), pp. 265–282. **2516**

POPULATION

See also 5322–5323, 5544

Migration

Cameron, James M., "A Study of the Factors That Assisted and Directed Scottish Emigration to Upper Canada, 1815–1855," Ph.D. diss., University of Glasgow, 1971. **2517**

Cameron, James M., "Scottish Emigration to Upper Canada, 1815–1855: A Study of Process," in W. P. Adams and F. M. Helleiner, eds., *International Geography, 1972*, vol. 1, sec. 5, *Historical Geography* (Toronto: University of Toronto Press, for the International Geographical Union, 1972), pp. 404–406. **2518**

Hovinen, Elizabeth L., "Migration of Quakers from Pennsylvania to Upper Canada, 1800–1820," Master's thesis, York University, 1976. **2519**

Mika, Nick, and Helma Mika, "The Arrival of the Loyalists," in N. Mika and H. Mika, eds., *The Shaping of Ontario: From Exploration to Confederation* (Belleville, Ont.: Mika, 1985), pp. 37–50. **2520**

McLean, Marianne, *The People of Glengarry: Highlanders in Transition, 1745–1820* (Montreal: McGill-Queen's University Press, 1991), 285 pp. **2521**

Population change

Taylor, Iain C., "Components of Population Change, Ontario: 1850–1940," Master's thesis, University of Toronto, 1967. **2522**

Brozowski, R., "Population Changes in Ontario Towns and Villages, 1941–1966," Ph.D. diss., University of Windsor, 1971. **2523**

Wood, J. David, "Simulating Pre-Census Population Distribution," *Canadian Geographer*, vol. 18, 3 (1974), pp. 250–264. **2524**

Bannister, Geoffrey, "Population Change in Southern Ontario," *Annals of the Association of American Geographers*, vol. 65, 2 (1975), pp. 177–188. **2525**

Clarke, John L., Harry W. Taylor, and W. Robert Wightman, "Areal Patterns of Population Change in Southern Ontario, 1831–1891: Core, Frontier, and Intervening Space," *Ontario Geography*, vol. 12 (1978), pp. 27–48. **2526**

Innes, Frank C., and K. Pryke, "Dimensions of Disease and Death for 1870–71: An Insight into Quality of Life," in D. B. Honor, ed., *In the Footsteps of the Habitants* (Toronto: Ontario Genealogical Society, 1986), pp. 141–151. **2527**

Wood, J. David, "Population Change on an Agricultural Frontier: Upper Canada, 1796 to 1841," in R. Hall, W. Westfall, and L. S. MacDowell, eds., *Patterns of the Past: Interpreting Ontario's History* (Toronto: Dundurn Press, 1988), pp. 55–77. **2528**

Wood, J. David, "The Population of Ontario: A Study of the Foundation of a Social Geography," in Guy M. Robinson, ed., *A Social Geography of Canada: Essays in Honour of J. Wreford Watson* (Edinburgh: North British Publishing, 1988), pp. 55–94. Also Toronto: Dundurn Press, 1991, pp. 92–140. **2529**

Ethnic distributions

MacLeod, Peter U., "Gualainn Ri Gualainn: A Study of Concentrations of Scottish Settlement in Nineteenth Century Ontario," Master's thesis, Carleton University, 1972. **2530**

Clarke, John, and Peter U. Macleod, "Concentration of Scots in Rural Southern Ontario, 1851–1901," *Canadian Cartographer*, vol. 11, 2 (1974), pp. 107–113. **2531**

Brunger, Alan G., "Geographical Patterns of Settlement of English People in Mid-Nineteenth Century Ontario," in *Cultural Dimensions of Canada's Geography: Proceedings of the German-Canadian Symposium, August 28–September 11, 1983* (Peterborough: Trent University, Department of Geography, Occasional Paper no. 10 (1984), pp. 198–211. **2532**

Brunger, Alan G., "The Distribution of English in Upper Canada, 1851–1871," *Canadian Geographer*, vol. 30, 4 (1986), pp. 337–343. **2533**

Elliott, Bruce S., "Regionalized Migration and Settlement Patterns of the Irish in Upper Canada," in Robert O'Driscoll and Lorna Reynolds, eds., *The Untold Story: The Irish in Canada* (Toronto: Celtic Arts of Canada, 1988), pp. 309–318. **2534**

Elliott, Bruce S., *Irish Migrants in the Canadas: A New Approach* (Montreal: McGill-Queen's University Press, 1988), 371 pp. **2535**

Brunger, Alan G., "The Distribution of Scots and Irish in Upper Canada, 1851–71," *Canadian Geographer*, vol. 34, 3 (1990), pp. 250–258. **2536**

RURAL & REGIONAL SOCIAL GEOGRAPHY

Walker, Gerald E., "Social Networks in Rural Space: A Comparison of Two Southern Ontario Localities," *East Lakes Geographer*, vol. 10 (1974), pp. 68–77. **2537**

Houston, Cecil J., and William J. Smyth, *The Orange Order in Nineteenth-Century Ontario: A Study in Institutional Cultural Transfer* (Toronto: University of Toronto Department of Geography Discussion Paper no. 22, 1977). **2538**

Houston, Cecil J., and William J. Smyth, "The Orange Order and the Expansion of the Frontier in Ontario, 1830–1900," *Journal of Historical Geography*, vol. 4, 3 (1978), pp. 251–264.   **2539**

Carew, Lois M., "John C. Clark: A Man, His Life, His Space; A Case Study in Historical Geography, 1832–1862," Master's thesis, Queen's University, 1979.   **2540**

Brunger, Alan G., "Geographical Patterns of Early Settlement: Social Institutions on the Frontier of Upper Canada," *Bamberger Geographische Schriften*, vol. 4 (1982), pp. 267–284.   **2541**

Akenson, Donald H., *The Irish in Ontario: A Study in Rural History* (Montreal: McGill-Queen's University Press, 1984), 404 pp.   **2542**

Arnold, Richard, "The Geography of Colonial Unrest in Upper Canada, 1820–1840," Master's thesis, York University, 1986.   **2543**

Hoelscher, Steven D., "The German Element of Two Townships in Southern Ontario: Settlement, Landscape, and Language," Master's thesis, University of Toronto, 1989.   **2544**

Park, Deborah, "Changing Shadows: The Huronia Regional Centre, 1876–1934," Master's thesis, York University, 1990.   **2545**

POLITICAL & ADMINISTRATIVE GEOGRAPHY

Jackson, W. A. Douglas, "The Regressive Effects of Late Eighteenth Century British Colonial Policy on Land Development along the Upper St. Lawrence River," *Annals of the Association of American Geographers*, vol. 45, 3 (1955), pp. 258–268.   **2546**

Richards, J. Howard B. "Lands and Policies: Attitudes and Controls in the Alienation of Lands in Ontario during the First Century of Settlement," *Ontario History*, vol. 50, 4 (1958), pp. 193–209.   **2547**

Whebell, Charles F. J., "Core Areas in Intrastate Political Organization," *Canadian Geographer*, vol. 12, 2 (1968), pp. 99–112.   **2548**

Grossman, Lawrence, "Settlement Policy in Upper Canada: The William Berczy Affair," Master's thesis, York University, 1974.   **2549**

Whebell, Charles F. J., "Robert Baldwin and Decentralization, 1841–1849," in F. H. Armstrong, H. A. Stevenson, and J. D. Wilson, eds., *Aspects of Nineteenth Century Ontario: Essays Presented to James J. Talman* (Toronto: University of Toronto Press, 1974), pp. 65–79.   **2550**

Cartwright, Donald G., "Ecclesiastical Territorial Organization and Institutional Conflict in Eastern and Northern Ontario, 1840–1910," *Histori-*

cal Papers, Canadian Historical Association (1978), pp. 176–199.   **2551**

Hicks, Elisabeth A., "The Measurement of Electoral Bias and Ontario Provincial Elections, 1934–1987," Master's thesis, University of Toronto, 1988.   **2552**

Whebell, Charles F. J., "The Upper Canada District Councils Act of 1841 and British Colonial Policy," *Journal of Imperial and Commonwealth History*, vol. 17, 2 (1989), pp. 185–209.   **2553**

ECONOMIC DEVELOPMENT

Lee, Judith M., "Inventive Activity and Its Relations to Industrial Development in Southern Ontario, 1881–1911," Master's thesis, University of Waterloo, 1972.   **2554**

Lee, Judith M., "Inventive Activity in Southern Ontario, 1881–1911," in David F. Walker and James H. Bater, eds., *Industrial Development in Southern Ontario* (Waterloo: University of Waterloo Department of Geography, [Publication] no. 3, 1974), pp. 1–39.   **2555**

Norton, William, and Edgar C. Conkling, "Land Use Theory and the Pioneering Economy," *Geografiska annaler*, vol. 56B (1974), pp. 44–56. [Southern Ontario]   **2556**

Gentilcore, R. Louis, "The Planting of a Province: Economic Geography and Settlement Beginnings in Ontario, Canada, 1792–1796," *International Geography '76*, sec. 9, *Historical Geography* (Moscow: Twenty-third International Geographical Union, 1976), pp. 50–53.   **2557**

McCalla, Douglas, "The Wheat Staple and Upper Canadian Development," *Historical Papers, Canadian Historical Association* (1978), pp. 34–45.   **2558**

McCalla, Douglas, "The 'Loyalist' Economy of Upper Canada, 1784–1806," *Histoire sociale/Social History*, vol. 16, 32 (1983), pp. 279–304.   **2559**

McCalla, Douglas, "The Internal Economy of Upper Canada: New Evidence on Agricultural Marketing before 1850," *Agricultural History*, vol. 54 (1985), pp. 389–416. Reprinted in J. K. Johnson and B. G. Wilson, eds., *Historical Essays on Upper Canada: New Perspectives* (Ottawa: Carleton University Press, 1989), pp. 237–260.   **2560**

McCalla, Douglas, "Rural Credit and Rural Development in Upper Canada, 1790–1850," in R. Hall, W. Westfall, and L. S. MacDowell, eds., *Patterns of the Past: Interpreting Ontario's History* (Ottawa: Carlton University Press, 1988), pp. 37–54.   **2561**

LAND & LAND USE

Land survey

Taylor, T. Griffith, "Towns and Townships in Southern Ontario," *Economic Geography*, vol. 21, 2 (1945), pp. 88–96.   **2562**

Gentilcore, R. Louis, "Lines on the Land: Crown Surveys and Settlement in Upper Canada," *Ontario History*, vol. 61, 2 (1969), pp. 57–73.   **2563**

Gentilcore, R. Louis, and Margaret Kate Donkin, *Land Surveys of Southern Ontario: An Introduction and Index to the Field Notebooks of the Ontario Land Surveyors, 1784–1859* (Toronto: Cartographica Monograph no. 8, 1973), 116 pp.   **2564**

Wightman, W. Robert, "A Survey of Ontario Land Records: Sources, Nature, and Location," *The London Project Report* (London: University of Western Ontario, 1977), 68 pp.   **2565**

Whebell, Charles F. J., "Two Polygonal Settlement Schemes from Upper Canada," *Ontario Geography*, vol. 12 (1978), pp. 85–92.   **2566**

Sebert, Lou M., "The Surveying of Township no. 1," *Ontario Land Surveyor*, vol. 22, 1 (1979), pp. 21–22.   **2567**

Sebert, Lou M., "The Land Surveys of Ontario, 1750–1980," *Canadian Cartographer*, vol. 17, 3 (1980), pp. 65–106.   **2568**

Land tenure

Parson, Helen E., "An Analysis of Farmland Abandonment Trends," *Ontario Geography*, vol. 14 (1979), pp. 41–57.   **2569**

Widdis, Randy W., "Motivation and Scale: A Method of Identifying Land Speculators in Upper Canada," *Canadian Geographer*, vol. 23, 4 (1979), pp. 337–351.   **2570**

Widdis, Randy W., "Tracing Property Ownership in Nineteenth Century Ontario: A Guide to the Archival Sources," in Donald H. Akenson, ed., *Canadian Papers in Rural History*, vol. 2 (Gananoque, Ont.: Langdale Press, 1980), pp. 83–102.   **2571**

Widdis, Randy W., "Speculation and the Surveyor: An Analysis of the Role Played by the Surveyors in the Settlement of Upper Canada," *Histoire sociale/Social History*, vol. 15, 30 (1982), pp. 443–458.   **2572**

Land use

Richards, J. Howard B., "Land Use and Settlement Patterns on the Fringe of the Shield of Southern Ontario," Ph.D. diss., University of Toronto, 1954.   **2573**

Reeds, Lloyd G., "Agricultural Regions of Southern Ontario, 1880 and 1951," *Economic Geography*, vol. 35, 2 (1959), pp. 219–227. Reprinted in R. Louis Gentilcore, ed., *Canada's Changing Geography* (Scarborough, Ont.: Prentice-Hall of Canada, 1967), pp. 84–91.   **2574**

Putnam, Robert G., "Three Decades of Land Use Changes on the Central Lake Ontario Plain," Master's thesis, University of Georgia, 1961.   **2575**

Norton, William, "Rural Land Value and Land Use Patterns in Mid-Nineteenth Century Southern Ontario," Master's thesis, Queen's University, 1969.   **2576**

Khan, Jafar Reza, "Agricultural Land Use Changes in Southern Ontario, 1867–1951," *Geographical Review of India*, vol. 42, 4 (1980), pp. 342–354.   **2577**

Taylor, Harry W., John Clarke, and W. Robert Wightman, "Contrasting Land Development Rates in Southern Ontario to 1891," in Donald H. Akenson, ed., *Canadian Papers in Rural History*, vol. 2 (Gananoque, Ont.: Langdale Press, 1986), pp. 50–72.   **2578**

EXTRACTIVE ACTIVITY

See also **1410**

Head, C. Grant, "An Introduction to Forest Exploitation in Nineteenth Century Ontario," in J. David Wood, ed., *Perspectives on Landscape and Settlement in Nineteenth Century Ontario* (Toronto: McClelland and Stewart, 1975), pp. 78–112.   **2579**

McCalla, Douglas, "Forest Products and Upper Canadian Development, 1815–46," *Canadian Historical Review*, vol. 68, 2 (1987), pp. 159–198.   **2580**

AGRICULTURE

Whitaker, J. Russell, "Distribution of Dairy Farming in Peninsular Ontario," *Economic Geography*, vol. 16, 1 (1940), pp. 69–78.   **2581**

Richards, J. Howard B., "Agricultural Patterns in the Pre-Cambrian Area of Southern Ontario," *Canadian Geographer*, vol. 5 (1955), pp. 63–70.   **2582**

Retallack, Joan, "The Changing Distribution of Wheat in Southern Ontario, 1850–1880," Master's thesis, University of Toronto, 1966.   **2583**

Forester, Joseph E., "Fur Farming in Ontario," Master's thesis, University of Western Ontario, 1967.
                                                                                2584

Horner, John H., "Changing Spatial Patterns in the Production and Utilization of Milk in Southern Ontario, 1910–1961," Master's thesis, University of Toronto, 1967.   2585

Crothall, W. Robert, "French Canadian Agriculture in Ontario, 1861–1871," Master's thesis, University of Toronto, 1968.   2586

Kelly, Kenneth, "The Transfer of British Ideas on Improved Farming to Ontario during the First Half of the Nineteenth Century," Ontario History, vol. 63, 2 (1971), pp. 103–111.   2587

Kelly, Kenneth, "Notes on a Type of Mixed Farming Practised in Ontario during the Early Nineteenth Century," Canadian Geographer, vol. 17, 2 (1973), pp. 205–219.   2588

Kelly, Kenneth, "The Transfer of British Ideas on Agriculture to Nineteenth Century Ontario," in Brian S. Osborne, ed., The Settlement of Canada: Origins and Transfer (Kingston: Queen's University, 1976), pp. 70–93.   2589

Pomfret, Richard, "The Mechanization of Reaping in Nineteenth Century Ontario: A Case Study of the Pace and Causes of Embodied Technical Change," Journal of Economic History, vol. 36, 2 (1976), pp. 399–415.   2590

O'Mara, James J., "The Seasonal Round of Gentry Farmers in Early Ontario: A Preliminary Analysis," in Donald H. Akenson, ed., Canadian Papers in Rural History, vol. 2 (Gananoque, Ont.: Langdale Press, 1980), pp. 103–112.   2591

Norton, William, "Some Comments on Late Nineteenth Century Agriculture in Areas of European Overseas Expansion," Ontario History, vol. 74, 2 (1982), pp. 113–117.   2592

McKay, Ian A., "A Note on Ontario Agriculture: The Development of Soybeans, 1893–1952," Ontario History, vol. 75, 2 (1983), pp. 175–186.   2593

Norton, William, "Agricultural Evolution on the Frontier," Professional Geographer, vol. 36, 1 (1984), pp. 18–27.   2594

McInnis, Marvin, "Ontario Agriculture, 1851–1901: A Cartographic Overview," in Donald H. Akenson, ed., Canadian Papers in Rural History, vol. 5 (Gananoque, Ont.: Langdale Press, 1986), pp. 290–301.   2595

Marr, William L., "The Distribution of Tenant Agriculture in Ontario, Canada, 1871," Social Science History, vol. 11, 2 (1987), pp. 169–186.
                                                                                2596

LANDSCAPE

See also 1423

Ennals, Peter M., "The Development of Farm Barn Types in Southern Ontario during the Nineteenth Century," Master's thesis, University of Toronto, 1968.   2597

Ennals, Peter M., "Nineteenth Century Barns in Southern Ontario," Canadian Geographer, vol. 16, 3 (1972), pp. 256–270.   2598

Wightman, W. Robert, "Construction Trends in Colonial Ontario, 1831–1861," Proceedings of the Association of American Geographers, vol. 5 (1973), pp. 298–302.   2599

Knight, David B., Cemeteries as Living Landscapes (Ottawa: Ontario Genealogical Society, Publication no. 73–8, 1973), 55 pp. Reprinted 1978.   2600

Wightman, W. Robert, "Construction Materials in Colonial Ontario, 1831–61," in F. H. Armstrong, H. A. Stevenson, and J. Wilson, eds., Aspects of Nineteenth Century Ontario: Essays Presented to James J. Talman (Toronto: University of Toronto Press, 1974), pp. 114–134.   2601

McIlwraith, Thomas F., Jr. , "The Diamond Cross: An Enigmatic Sign in the Rural Ontario Landscape," Pioneer America, vol. 12 (1981), pp. 25–38.   2602

Coffey, Brian, "The Pioneer House in Southern Ontario, Canada: Construction Material Use and Resistant Forms to 1850," Ph.D. diss., University of Oregon, 1982.   2603

Norris, Darrell A., "Vetting the Vernacular: Local Variations in Ontario's Housing," Ontario History, vol. 74, 2 (1982), pp. 66–94.   2604

McIlwraith, Thomas F., Jr., "Altered Buildings: Another Way of Looking at the Ontario Landscape," Ontario History, vol. 75, 2 (1983), pp. 110–134.   2605

Coffey, Brian, "The Canadian Inventory of Historic Buildings as a Basis for House Type Classification: An Example from Southern Ontario," Canadian Geographer, vol. 28, 1 (1984), pp. 83–89.   2606

Coffey, Brian, "From Shanty to House: Log Construction in Nineteenth-Century Ontario," Material Culture, vol. 16, 2 (1984), pp. 66–76.   2607

McIlwraith, Thomas F., Jr., "Ontario's Ordinary Countryside," Journal of Geography, vol. 83, 5 (1984), pp. 234–239.   2608

Coffey, Brian, "Factors Affecting the Use of Construction Materials in Early Ontario," Ontario History, vol. 77, 4 (1985), pp. 301–318.   2609

Norris, Darrell A., "Ontario Gravestones," *Markers*, vol. 5 (1988), pp. 122–149. **2610**

COMMUNICATIONS & TRADE

See also **1429, 1431, 1433**

General

McIlwraith, Thomas F., Jr., "Transportation in the Landscape of Early Upper Canada," in J. David Wood, ed., *Perspectives on Landscape and Settlement in Nineteenth Century Ontario* (Toronto: McClelland and Stewart, 1975), pp. 51–63. **2611**

Doucet, Michael J., "Space, Sound, Culture, and Politics: Radio Broadcasting in Southern Ontario," *Canadian Geographer*, vol. 27, 2 (1983), pp. 109–127. **2612**

McIlwraith, Thomas F., Jr., *By River, Road, and Rail: Transportation in Old Ontario* (Toronto: Ontario Museum Association, 1984), 106 pp. **2613**

McIlwraith, Thomas F., Jr., "Transportation in Old Ontario," *American Review of Canadian Studies*, vol. 14, 2 (1984), pp. 177–192. **2614**

Burghardt, Andrew F., "Transportation in Early Canada," in N. Mika and H. Mika, eds., *The Shaping of Ontario: From Exploration to Confederation* (Belleville, Ont.: Mika, 1985), pp. 210–219. **2615**

Burghardt, Andrew F., "Some Economic Constraints on Land Transportation in Upper Canada/Canada West," *Urban History Review*, vol. 18, 3 (1990), pp. 232–236. **2616**

Roads

Spragge, George W., "Colonization Roads in Canada West, 1850–1867," *Ontario History*, vol. 49, 1 (1957), pp. 1–17. **2617**

McIlwraith, Thomas, F., Jr., "The Adequacy of Rural Roads in the Era before Railways: An Illustration from Upper Canada," *Canadian Geographer*, vol. 14, 4 (1970), pp. 344–360. Reprinted in Graeme Wynn, ed., *People, Places, Patterns, Processes: Geographical Perspectives on the Canadian Past* (Toronto: Copp Clark Pitman, 1990), pp. 196–212. **2618**

Railways

Waters, N. M., "The Growth of the Southern Ontario Railway System: A Network Analysis," Master's thesis, University of Western Ontario, 1973. **2619**

Stoddard, P. J., "The Development of the Southern Ontario Steam Railway Network under Competition Conditions, 1830–1914," Master's thesis, University of Guelph, 1976. **2620**

Commerce

Walker, David F., "Transportation of Coal into Southern Ontario, 1871–1921," *Ontario History*, vol. 63, 1 (1971), pp. 15–30. **2621**

Norris, Darrell A., "The Micro-Geography of Micro-Places: Late Nineteenth Century Business Activity and Rural Society," in Brian S. Osborne, ed., *The Settlement of Canada: Origins and Transfer* (Kingston: Queen's University, 1976), pp. 139–161. **2622**

Osborne, Brian S., "Trading on a Frontier: The Function of Peddlers, Markets, and Fairs in Nineteenth Century Ontario," in Donald H. Akenson, ed., *Canadian Papers in Rural History*, vol. 2 (Gananoque, Ont.: Langdale Press, 1980), pp. 59–81. **2623**

Media

Bolton, John, "The Spread and Growth of Newspapers in Ontario, 1780–1977," Master's thesis, Wilfrid Laurier University, 1977. **2624**

MANUFACTURING & INDUSTRIALIZATION

General

Walker, David F., "The Role of Coal as a Location Factor in the Development of Manufacturing Industry in Southern Ontario, 1871–1921," Master's thesis, University of Toronto, 1967. **2625**

Bland, Warren R., "The Changing Locational Pattern of Manufacturing in Southern Ontario for 1881 to 1932," Ph.D. diss., Indiana University, 1970. **2626**

Gilmour, James M., "Structural and Spatial Change in Manufacturing Industry: Southern Ontario, 1850–1890," Ph.D. diss., University of Toronto, 1970. **2627**

Walker, David F., "The Energy Sources of Manufacturing Industry in Southern Ontario, 1871–1921," *Ontario Geography*, vol. 6 (1971), pp. 56–66. **2628**

Gilmour, James M., *Spatial Evolution of Manufacturing: Southern Ontario, 1851–1891* (Toronto: University of Toronto Press, 1972), 214 pp. **2629**

Bland, Warren R., "The Location of Manufacturing in Southern Ontario in 1881," *Ontario Geography*, vol. 8 (1974), pp. 9–39. **2630**

Walker, David F., "Energy and Industrial Location in Southern Ontario, 1871–1921," in David F. Walker and James H. Bater, eds., *Industrial Development in Southern Ontario* (Waterloo:

University of Waterloo Department of Geography, no. 3, 1974), pp. 41–68. **2631**

Warrian, Peter, "Sons of Toil: The Impact of Industrialization on Craft Workers in Late Nineteenth Century Ontario," in David F. Walker and James H. Bater, eds., *Industrial Development in Southern Ontario* (Waterloo: University of Waterloo Department of Geography, no. 3, 1974), pp. 69–99. **2632**

Bloomfield, Gerald T., and Elizabeth Bloomfield, "Mills, Factories, and Craftshops of Ontario, 1870: A Machine-Readable Source for Material Historians," *Material History Bulletin,* vol. 25 (1987), pp. 35–47. **2633**

Selected industries

Silva, W. P. T., "Some Aspects of the Development of the Fruit and Vegetable Canning Industry in Southern Ontario," Master's thesis, University of Toronto, 1962. **2634**

Mackay, Daniel S. C., "The Influence of Government Policy and Technological Change on Mill Development in Upper Canada, 1783–1850," Master's thesis, Carleton University, 1974. **2635**

Bland, Warren R., "The Changing Location of Metal-Fabricating and Clothing Industries in Southern Ontario: 1881–1932," *Ontario Geography,* vol. 9 (1975), pp. 34–57. **2636**

McBridge, Norine J., "The Mining Machinery and Equipment Sector in Ontario: Location and Structure, 1961–1981," Master's thesis, University of Toronto, 1985. **2637**

Bloomfield, Gerald T., and Elizabeth Bloomfield, "Waterwheels and Steam Engines in Ontario: Industrial Power Reported in the 1871 Manuscript Census," *Scientia canadensis,* vol. 13, 1 (1989), pp. 3–38. **2638**

URBAN NETWORKS & URBANIZATION

See also **1446**

Spelt, Jacob, *The Urban Development in South-Central Ontario* (Assen: Koninklyke Van Gorcum & Co., 1955), 241 pp. Also Toronto: McClelland and Stewart, 1972, 300 pp. **2639**

Whebell, Charles F. J., "Corridors: A Theory of Urban Systems," *Annals of the Association of American Geographers,* vol. 59, 1 (1969), pp. 1–26. **2640**

Smith, W. Randy, "Rail Network Development and Changes in Ontario's Urban System, 1850–1890," Master's thesis, York University, 1975. **2641**

Marshall, John U., and W. Randy Smith, "The Dynamics of Growth in a Regional Urban System: Southern Ontario, 1851–1971," *Canadian Geographer,* vol. 22, 1 (1978), pp. 22–40. **2642**

Smith, W. Randy, "Transport Improvements and Urban Network Evolution: Southern Ontario, 1851–1921," Ph.D. diss., York University, 1978. **2643**

Dahms, Frederic A., "The Evolving Spatial Organization of Settlements in the Countryside: An Ontario Example," *Tijdschrift voor economische en sociale Geografie,* vol. 71, 5 (1980), pp. 295–306. **2644**

Stelter, Gilbert A., "Urban Planning and Development in Upper Canada before 1850," in Woodrow Borah, Jorge Hardoy, and Gilbert A. Stelter, eds., *Urbanization in the Americas* (Ottawa: History Division, National Museum of man, 1980), pp. 143–155. **2645**

Dahms, Frederic A., "The Evolution of Settlement Systems: A Canadian Example, 1851–1970," *Journal of Urban History,* vol. 7, 2 (1981), pp. 189–204. Reprinted in Gilbert A. Stelter, ed., *Cities and Urbanization: Canadian Historical Perspectives* (Toronto: Copp Clark Pitman, 1990), pp. 177–207. **2646**

Smith, W. Randy, *Aspects of Growth in a Regional Urban System: Southern Ontario, 1851–1921* (North York: York University, Atkinson College Geographical Monographs, no. 12, 1982), 191 pp. **2647**

Dahms, Frederic A., "Regional Urban History: Small Towns and Their Hinterlands," *Urban History Review,* vol. 15, 2 (1986), pp. 172–174. **2648**

TOWN GROWTH

Dahms, Frederic A., "Residential and Commercial Renaissance: Another Look at Small Town Ontario," *Small Town,* vol. 17, 1 (1986), pp. 10–15. **2649**

TOWNSCAPE

Doucet, Michael J., and John C. Weaver, "The North American Shelter Business, 1860–1920: A Study of a Canadian Real Estate and Property Management Agency," *Business History Review,* vol. 58 (1984), pp. 234–262. Reprinted in Gilbert A. Stelter, ed., *Cities and Urbanization: Canadian Historical Perspectives* (Toronto: Copp Clark Pitman, 1990), pp. 152–176. **2650**

RECREATION & TOURISM

Wolfe, Roy I., "The Summer Resorts of Ontario in the Nineteenth Century," *Ontario History,* vol. 54 (1962), pp. 149–160. **2651**

Konrad, Victor A., "Historical Artifacts as Recreational Resources," in Geoffrey Wall and John S. Marsh, eds., *Recreational Land Use: Perspectives on Its Evolution in Canada* (Ottawa: Carleton University Press, 1982), pp. 393–416.   **2652**

Morrison, K., "The Evolution of the Ontario Provincial Park System," in Geoffrey Wall and John S. Marsh, eds., *Recreational Land Use: Perspectives on Its Evolution in Canada* (Ottawa: Carleton University Press, 1982), pp. 102–121.   **2653**

Wall, Geoffrey, and N. Zalkind, "The Canadian National Exhibition: Mirror of Canadian Society," in Geoffrey Wall and John S. Marsh, eds., *Recreational Land Use: Perspectives on Its Evolution in Canada* (Ottawa: Carleton University Press, 1982), pp. 311–321.   **2654**

Wolfe, Roy I., "The Changing Patterns of Tourism in Ontario," in Geoffrey Wall and John S. Marsh, eds., *Recreational Land Use: Perspectives on Its Evolution in Canada* (Ottawa: Carleton University Press, 1982), pp. 133–138.   **2655**

Brunger, Alan G., "Historic Landscape Regions: Recreation, Tourism, and Interpretation," *Recreation Research Review*, vol. 14, 4 (1989), pp. 24–34.   **2656**

PLACE NAMES

Moore, William F., *Indian Place Names in Ontario* (Toronto: Macmillan Co. of Canada, 1930), 48 pp.   **2657**

Cameron, James M., "An Introduction to the Study of Scottish Settlement of Southern Ontario: A Comparison of Place Names," *Ontario History*, vol. 61, 3 (1969), pp. 167–172.   **2658**

Carter, Floreen E., *Place Names of Ontario*, 2 vols. (London, Ont.: Phelps Publishing Co., 1984), 1,531 pp.   **2659**

EASTERN ONTARIO

GENERAL

O'Neil, Lynne E., ed., *Studies in the Historical Geography of the Peterborough Area* (Peterborough: Trent Student Geographer, Trent University Geographical Society, vol. 6, 1977), 90 pp.
2660

Ennals, Peter M., "Land and Society in Hamilton Township, Upper Canada, 1797–1861," Ph.D. diss., University of Toronto, 1978.   **2661**

Brunger, Alan G., ed., *By Lake and Lock* (Peterborough, Ont.: Heritage Press, 1987), 41 pp.   **2662**

ENVIRONMENTAL CHANGE

Harshman, Robert P., "The Process of Forest Clearance in Oxford-on-Rideau Township from 1821 to 1850," Master's thesis, York University, 1972.   **2663**

Adams, Peter, "The Climate: Past and Present," in Peter Adams and Colin Taylor, eds., *Peterborough and the Kawarthas* (Peterborough: Heritage Press, 1985), pp. 29–47.   **2664**

Casteran, Nicole, "Écologie et agriculture préindustrielle dans l'Est Ontario," Master's thesis, University of Ottawa, 1985.   **2665**

NATIVE PEOPLES & WHITE RELATIONS

Taylor, Gordon G., "The Mississauga Indians of Eastern Ontario, 1634–1881," Master's thesis, Queen's University, 1981.   **2666**

POPULAR IMAGES & EVALUATION

Wagner, Michael J., "Gentry Perception and Land Utilization in the Peterborough–Kawartha Lake Region, 1818–1851," Master's thesis, University of Toronto, 1968.   **2667**

Osborne, Brian S., "Frontier Settlement in Eastern Ontario in the Nineteenth Century: A Study in Changing Perceptions of Land and Opportunity," in David H. Miller and Jerome O. Steffen, eds., *The Frontier: Comparative Studies* (Norman: University of Oklahoma Press, 1977), pp. 201–226.   **2668**

Finnegan, Gregory F., "Cognizance of Land Quality: Surveyor, Speculator, and Settler in Fitzroy

Township, Ontario, 1822–1861," Master's thesis, Carleton University, 1985.   **2669**

REGIONAL SETTLEMENT

See also **1332**

Cumberland, R. W., "The United Empire Loyalist Settlements between Kingston and Adolphustown," *Queen's Quarterly*, vol. 30, 4 (1923), pp. 395–419.   **2670**

Cartwright, Donald G., "French Canadian Colonization in Eastern Ontario to 1910: A Study of Process and Pattern," Ph.D. diss., University of Western Ontario, 1973.   **2671**

Brunger, Alan G., "Early Settlement in Contrasting Areas of Peterborough County, Ontario," in J. David Wood, ed., *Perspectives on Landscape and Settlement in Nineteenth Century Ontario* (Toronto: McClelland and Stewart, 1975), pp. 117–140.   **2672**

Osborne, Brian S., "The Settlement of Kingston's Hinterland," in Gerald J. Tulchinsky, ed., *To Preserve and Defend: Essays on Kingston in the Nineteenth Century* (Montreal: McGill-Queen's University Press, 1976), pp. 63–79.   **2673**

Ferguson, G. R., "The Peter Robinson Settlers in Emily Township, 1825 to 1861," Master's thesis, Queen's University, 1979.   **2774**

Weldon, Jessie T., "The Salient Factors Contributing to the Earliest Settlement Pattern in East and West Hawkesbury Townships, Upper Canada, 1788–1846," Master's thesis, Carleton University, 1980.   **2675**

Gordanier, Deborah Ann, "The Settlement of Augusta Township, Upper Canada, 1783–1840," Master's thesis, Carleton University, 1982.   **2676**

Lockwood, Glenn, "Irish Immigrants and the 'Critical Years' in Eastern Ontario: The Case of Montague Township, 1821–1881," in Donald H. Akenson, ed., *Canadian Papers in Rural History*, vol. 4 (Gananoque, Ont.: Langdale Press, 1984), pp. 153–178. Reprinted in J. K. Johnson and B. G. Wilson, eds., *Historical Essays on Upper Canada: New Perspectives* (Ottawa: Carleton University Press, 1989), pp. 203–236.   **2677**

Parson, Helen E., "The Colonization of the Southern Canadian Shield in Ontario: Hastings

Road," *Ontario History*, vol. 79, 3 (1987), pp. 263–274.   **2678**

POPULATION

See also **1348**

Ray, D. Michael, "Settlement and Rural Out-Migration in Easternmost Ontario, 1783–1956," Master's thesis, University of Ottawa, 1961.
2679

Lindsay, Virginia, "The Perth Military Settlement: Characteristics of Its Permanent and Transitory Settlers, 1816–1822," Master's thesis, Carleton University, 1972.   **2680**

Osborne, Brian S., "The Cemeteries of the Midland District of Upper Canada: A Note on Mortality in a Frontier Society," *Pioneer America*, vol. 6, 1 (1974), pp. 46–55.   **2681**

Norris, Darrell A., "Household and Transiency in a Loyalist Township: The People of Adolphustown, 1784–1822," *Histoire sociale/Social History*, vol. 13, 26 (1980), pp. 399–415.   **2682**

Widdis, Randy W., "Pioneer Life on the Bay of Quinte: An Evaluation of Genealogical Source Data in the Study of Migration," *Canadian Geographer*, vol. 26, 3 (1982), pp. 273–282.   **2683**

Flear, Margaret, "The Occupational and Geographic Mobility of the Irish in Kingston, 1861–1881," Master's thesis, Queen's University, 1986.
2684

Moore, Eric G., and Brian S. Osborne, "Marital Fertility in Kingston, 1861–1881: A Study of Socio-Economic Differentials," *Histoire sociale/Social History*, vol. 20, 39 (1987), pp. 9–27.   **2685**

RURAL & REGIONAL SOCIAL GEOGRAPHY

Cartwright, Donald G., "Institutions on the Frontier: French-Canadian Settlement in Eastern Ontario in the Nineteenth Century," *Canadian Geographer*, vol. 21, 1 (1977), pp. 1–21.   **2686**

Anderson, Richard, "Respectability Versus Rowdyism: Non-Material Culture, Ideology, and Geography in Victoria County, Ontario, 1860–1880," Master's thesis, York University, 1985.
2687

Code, George L., "Social and Spatial Mobility in a Nineteenth-Century Ontario Intermediate Urban Centre: The Case of Belleville, 1861–1881," Master's thesis, York University, 1985.   **2688**

Lockwood, Glenn J., "Success and the Doubtful Image of Irish Immigrants in Upper Canada: The Case of Montague Township, 1820–1900," in Robert Driscoll and Lorna Reynolds, eds., *The*

Untold Story: The Irish in Canada (Tornot: Celtic Arts of Canada, 1988), pp. 319–334.   **2689**

Parkinson, Grenville, "Birthplace, Religion, and Agricultural Production in Peterborough County, 1851–1861," Master's thesis, McMaster University, 1988.   **2690**

POLITICAL & ADMINISTRATIVE GEOGRAPHY

Knight, David B., "The Persistence of an Idea amid Divergent Regional Forces: How Ottawa Became Capital," in Rolf Welsche and Marianne Kugler-Gagnon, eds., *Ottawa-Hull: Spatial Perspectives and Planning* (Ottawa: University of Ottawa Department of Geography Occasional Paper no. 4, 1978), pp. 3–12.   **2691**

Knight, David B., "The Ottawa Valley and the Selection of Canada's Capital City," in Vrenia Ivonoffski, ed., *Exploring Our Heritage: The Ottawa Valley Experience* (Arnprior: Historical Society and the Ontario Heritage Foundation, 1980), pp. 105–114.   **2692**

Whebell, Charles F. J., "Why Pembroke? The Politics of Selecting a County Capital in the Mid-Nineteenth Century," *Ontario History*, vol. 78, 2 (1986), pp. 127–156.   **2693**

ECONOMIC DEVELOPMENT

See also **1401**

Richards, J. Howard, "Population and the Economic Base in Northern Hastings County, Ontario," *Canadian Geographer*, vol. 11 (1958), pp. 23–33.   **2694**

George, V. Alan, "The Rideau Corridor: The Effect of a Canal System on a Frontier System, 1832–1895," Master's thesis, Queen's University, 1972.
2695

Tosine, Tonu Peep, "Cheese Factories in the Quinte–Upper St. Lawrence Area of Ontario, 1865–1905," Master's thesis, York University, 1974.   **2696**

Osborne, Brian S., "The Farmer and the Land," in Bryan Rollason, ed., *County of a Thousand Lakes: The History of the County of Frontenac, 1673–1973* (Kingston: Frontenac County Council, 1982), pp. 81–94.   **2697**

LAND & LAND USE

Delisle, David, "An Analysis of the Layout of the Agricultural Holdings in Four Townships of Eastern Ontario," Master's thesis, University of Toronto, 1968.   **2698**

Hesselink, Herm, "Settlement Pattern and Land Use Changes in Belmont Township, Ontario," in W. P. Adams and F. M. Helleiner, eds., *International Geography, 1972*, vol. 1, sec. 5, *Historical Geography* (Toronto: University of Toronto Press, for the International Geographical Union, 1972), pp. 430–432. [Durham Co.]   2699

Neugebauer, P. J., "Land Use History, Landscape Change, and Resource Conflict in the Sandbanks Provincial Park Area, Prince Edward County, Ontario," Master's thesis, University of Western Ontario, 1974.   2700

Widdis, Randy W., "A Perspective on Land Tenure in Upper Canada: A Study of Elizabethtown Township, 1790–1840," Master's thesis, McMaster University, 1977.   2701

Khan, Jafar R., "Changing Patterns of Agricultural Land Use in Renfrew County, 1951–1971," Master's thesis, Carleton University, 1977.   2702

Parson, Helen E., "Assessment of Land Capability Past and Present: The Example of McNab Township," *Journal of Geography*, vol. 83, 3 (1984), pp. 126–129.   2703

EXTRACTIVE ACTIVITY

Ellsworth, Joan L., "The Eastern Lake Ontario Commercial Fishery, 1673–1900: A Cultural Heritage, a Forgotten Staple," Master's thesis, Queen's University, 1983.   2704

LeFeuvre, Susan E., "Of Mica and Miners: A Survey of Southeastern Ontario's Mica Mining Economy," Master's thesis, Queen's University, 1988.   2705

Osborne, Brian S., "Organizing the Lake Fisheries: Landscapes and Waterscapes," *Historic Kingston*, vol. 38 (1990), pp. 81–94.   2706

AGRICULTURE

Dix, Ernest, "United States Influences on the Agriculture of Prince Edward County, Ontario," *Economic Geography*, vol. 26, 2 (1950), pp. 179–182.   2707

Casteran, Nicole, "Les stratégies agricoles du paysan canadien-français de l'est ontarien (1870)," *Revue l'histoire de l'Amérique française*, vol. 41, 1 (1987), pp. 23–52.   2708

Skof, Karl J., "Agriculture in a Forest Setting: Lanark County, 1851–1871," Master's thesis, Carleton University, 1988.   2709

LANDSCAPE

Mooney, Patrick B., "Landscape and Culture in North Easthope Township, Southern Ontario,

1829–1856," Master's thesis, York University, 1970.   2710

Brunger, Alan G., "The Development of the Cultural Landscape of Peterborough and the Kawarthas," in Peter Adams and Colin Taylor, eds., *Peterborough and the Kawarthas* (Peterborough: Heritage Press, 1985), pp. 95–116. 2711

Brunger, Alan G., Frederick M. Helleiner, and D. McKenzie, "A Selection of Field Trips," in Peter Adams and Colin Taylor, eds., *Peterborough and the Kawarthas* (Peterborough: Heritage Press, 1985), pp. 145–157.   2712

Coffey, Brian, "Building Materials in Early Ontario: The Example of Augusta Township," *Canadian Geographer*, vol. 32, 2 (1988), pp. 150–159.   2713

COMMUNICATIONS & TRADE

Chiotte, Quentin, "The Evolving Food Distribution Network: An Analysis of Conflicting Agrarian, Commercial, and Municipal Interest in Kingston, Ontario, 1879–1906," Master's thesis, Queen's University, 1984.   2714

MANUFACTURING & INDUSTRIALIZATION

Price, Elizabeth, "The Changing Geography of the Woolen Industry in Lanark, Renfrew, and Carleton Counties, 1830–1911," Master's thesis, University of Toronto, 1979.   2715

Degenova, Donald, "Ottawa's Manufacturing Geography 1958–1979; with a Case Study of the Region's High Technology Industry," Master's thesis, University of Ottawa, 1984.   2716

URBAN NETWORKS & URBANIZATION

Cramm, Earl W. R., "An Analysis of the Urban Process in Pickering Township," Master's thesis, University of Toronto, 1962.   2717

Ashcroft, Robert J., "Intrametropolitan Branch Banking: Ottawa, 1930–1979," Master's thesis, Carleton University, 1980.   2718

Ashcroft, Robert J., "Intrametropolitan Branch Banking: Ottawa, 1930–1979," *Ontario Geography*, vol. 17 (1981), pp. 1–18.   2719

TOWN GROWTH

Holder, Brian G., "The Importance of Site in Urban Development: A Synopsis of the Economic Geography of Kingston," *Southern Quarterly*, vol. 4, 3 (1966), pp. 319–330.   2720

Osborne, Brian S., "The Site of Kingston," in G. Betts, ed., *Kingston 300: A Social Snapshot*

(Kingston: Editorial Committee, 1973), pp. 8–13.
2721

Ennals, Peter M., "Cobourg and Port Hope: The Struggle for the Control of the Back Country," in J. David Wood, ed., *Perspectives on Landscapes and Settlement in Nineteenth Century Ontario* (Toronto: McClelland and Stewart, 1975), pp. 183–196.
2722

Osborne, Brian S., "Kingston in the Nineteenth Century: A Study in Urban Decline," in J. David Wood, ed., *Perspectives on Landscape and Settlement in Nineteenth Century Ontario* (Toronto: McClelland and Stewart, 1975), pp. 159–182.
2723

Drummond, Sarah J., "Kingston as the Foot-of-the-Great-Lakes Terminus: A Study in Urban Boosterism," Master's thesis, Queen's University, 1986.
2724

Osborne, Brian S., and Donald Swainson, *Kingston: Building on the Past* (Westport, Ont.: Butternut Press, 1988), 381 pp.
2725

Osborne, Brian S., "The Long and Short of It: Kingston as the Foot-of-the-Great-Lakes Terminus," *Freshwater*, vol. 4 (1989), pp. 1–19.
2726

URBAN ECONOMIC STRUCTURE

Fox, Michael F., "The Analysis of Office Distributional Patterns in Central Ottawa, 1940–1970," Master's thesis, Carleton University, 1973.
2727

Purdy, Michael, "An Inquiry into the Functions of a Ribbon Road: A Case Study of Bank Street, Ottawa, Ontario, 1891–1972." Master's thesis, Carleton University, 1974.
2728

Trotman, D. James, "Ottawa in 1878: Land Use Patterns in a Canadian City," Master's thesis, Carleton University, 1977.
2729

Osborne, Brian S., Gregory Levine, and Richard S. Harris, *The Housing Question in Kingston, Ontario, 1881–1901: Report on an Investigation* (Kingston: Queen's University Department of Geography, 1982), 142 pp.
2730

McDonald, John F., "An Examination of the Forces Affecting the Locational Decisions of Physicians in Ottawa, 1875–1915," Master's thesis, Carleton University, 1983.
2731

URBAN SOCIAL STRUCTURE

Cross, L. Doreen, "Locating Selected Occupations: Ottawa, 1871," *Urban History Review*, no. 2–74 (1974), pp. 5–14.
2732

Levine, Gregory J., "Residential Mobility in Kingston, 1860–1861," Master's thesis, Queen's University, 1975.
2733

Tunbridge, John E., "Separation of Residence from Workplace: A Kingston Example," *Urban History Review*, no. 3–78 (1978), pp. 23–32.
2734

Luciuk, Lubomyr Y., "Ukrainians in the Making: Their Kingston Story," Master's thesis, Queen's University, 1979.
2735

Levine, Gregory J., "In God's Service: The Role of the Anglican, Methodist, Presbyterian, and Roman Catholic Churches in the Cultural Geography of Late Nineteenth-Century Kingston," Ph.D. diss., Queen's University, 1980.
2736

Harris, Richard S., Gregory Levine, and Brian S. Osborne, "Housing Tenure and Social Classes in Kingston, Ontario, 1881–1901," *Journal of Historical Geography*, vol. 7, 3 (1981), pp. 271–289.
2737

Tunbridge, John E., "Home-Workplace Separation in Kingston: The Legal and Medical Professions; Past, Present, and Future," *Urban History Review*, vol. 11, 1 (1982), pp. 11–16.
2738

Harris, Richard S., "A Political Chameleon: Class Segregation in Kingston, Ontario, 1961–1976," *Annals of the Association of American Geographers*, vol. 74, 3 (1984), pp. 454–476.
2739

TOWNSCAPE

Sabourin, Joanne, "The Evolution of the Ottawa Central Area," in Rolf Welsche and Marianne Kugler-Gagnon, eds., *Ottawa-Hull: Spatial Perspectives and Planning* (Ottawa: University of Ottawa, Department of Geography, Occasional Paper no. 4, 1978), pp. 53–63.
2740

Rice, Jeanette J., "From Crown to City: The Urban Land Development Process, Kingston, Ontario, 1800–1900," Master's thesis, Queen's University, 1980.
2741

Green, Philip A., "The Land Development Process in Charlesville, Kingston, 1881–1891," Master's thesis, Queen's University, 1984.
2742

Tunbridge, John E., "Clarence Street, Ottawa: Contemporary Change in an Inner City 'Zone of Discard,'" *Urban History Review*, vol. 14, 3 (1986), pp. 247–258.
2743

RECREATION & TOURISM

Marsh, John S., and C. Moffatt, "The Historical Development of Resorts and Cottages in the Kawartha Lakes Area, Ontario," in John S. Marsh, ed., *Water Based Recreation Problems and Progress* (Peterborough: Trent University,

Department of Geography, Occasional Paper
no. 8, 1979), pp. 27–49.   **2744**

Helleiner, Frederick M., "A History of Recreation
on the Trent-Severn Waterway," in Geoffrey
Wall and John S. Marsh, eds., *Recreational
Land Use: Perspectives on Its Evolution in
Canada* (Ottawa: Carleton University Press,
1982), pp. 190–200.   **2745**

Dewar, R. Keith, "Resort Development in the
Rideau Lakes Region of Eastern Ontario, 1826–
1955," Master's thesis, Carleton University,
1983.   **2746**

PLACE NAMES

See also **1478**

Rayburn, J. Alan, *Geographical Names of Renfrew
County* (Ottawa: Department of Energy, Mines,
and Resources, Geographical Branch, Geographical Paper no. 40, 1967), 74 pp.   **2747**

Mackintosh, Anne, "Place Names in the Thousand Islands," *Canoma*, vol. 13, 1 (1987), pp. 5–8.
2748

CENTRAL ONTARIO

GENERAL

Taylor, T. Griffith, "Topographic Control in the Toronto Region," *Canadian Journal of Economics and Political Science*, vol. 2, 4 (1936), pp. 493–511. **2749**

ENVIRONMENTAL CHANGE

Konrad, Victor A., "The Effects of Past Human Habitation on the Soils of Two Huron Villages," Master's thesis, York University, 1973. **2750**

Wilson, John P., "The Problems of Accelerated Soil Erosion, Cultural Eutrophication, and Their Management in the Lake Simcoe–Couchiching Basin, Canada, 1800–1983," Ph.D. diss., University of Toronto, 1986. **2751**

Wilson, John P., and Christine M. Ryan, "Landscape Change in the Lake Simcoe–Couchiching Basin, 1800–1983," *Canadian Geographer*, vol. 32, 3 (1988), pp. 206–222. **2752**

NATIVE PEOPLES & WHITE RELATIONS

Heidenreich, Conrad E., "The Huron Occupance of Simcoe County," *Canadian Geographer*, vol. 7, 2 (1963), pp. 131–144. Revised as "The Indian Occupance of Huronia, 1600–1650," in R. Louis Gentilcore, ed., *Canada's Changing Geography* (Scarborough, Ont.: Prentice-Hall of Canada, 1967), pp. 15–29. **2753**

Cruickshank, James G., and Conrad E. Heidenreich, "Pedological Investigations at the Huron Village of Cahiague," *Canadian Geographer*, vol. 13, 1 (1969), pp. 34–46. **2754**

Heidenreich, Conrad E., "The Historical Geography of Huronia in the First Half of the Seventeenth Century," Ph.D. diss., McMaster University, 1970. **2755**

Heidenreich, Conrad E., *Huronia: A History and Geography of the Huron Indians, 1600–1650* (Toronto: McClelland and Stewart, 1971), 337 pp. **2756**

Heidenreich, Conrad E., "The Natural Environment of Huronia and Huron Seasonal Activities," in Carl Schott, ed., *Beiträge zur Kulturgeographie von Kanada* (Marburg: Marburger Geographische Hefte, 1971), pp. 103–116. Reprinted with revisions in Graeme Wynn, ed., *People, Places, Patterns, Processes: Geographical Perspectives in the Canadian Past* (Toronto: Copp Clark Pitman, 1990), pp. 42–55. **2757**

Heidenreich, Conrad E., and S. Navratil, "Soil Analysis at the Robitaille Site: Determining the Perimeter of the Village," *Ontario Archeology*, vol. 20 (1973), pp. 25–32. **2758**

Konrad, Victor A., "The Archeological Resources of the Metropolitan Toronto Planning Area: Inventory and Prospect" (Downsview: York University Department of Geography Discussion Paper no. 10, 1973), 166 pp. **2759**

Heidenreich, Conrad E., "A Relict Indian Corn Field near Creemore, Ontario," *Canadian Geographer*, vol. 18, 4 (1974), pp. 379–394. **2760**

Konrad, Victor A., "Distribution, Site, and Morphology of Prehistorical Settlements in the Toronto Area," in J. David Wood, ed., *Perspectives on Landscape and Settlement in Nineteenth Century Ontario* (Toronto: McClelland and Steward, 1975), pp. 6–31. **2761**

EXPLORATION & MAPPING

Riddell, W. R., "Toronto in Cartography," *Papers and Records of the Ontario Historical Society*, vol. 28 (1932), pp. 143–145. **2762**

Robinson, Percy J., "Cartography of the Toronto Region from 1600 to 1816," in his *Toronto during the French Regime: A History of the Toronto Region from Brule to Simcoe, 1615–1793* (Toronto: Ryerson, 1933), pp. 226–232. **2763**

POPULAR IMAGES & EVALUATION

Hayward, Robert J., "Content Analysis in Historical Geography: A Case Study in Immigration in Toronto to 1847," Master's thesis, Queen's University, 1972. **2764**

Hayward, Robert J., and Brian S. Osborne, "The *British Colonist* and the Immigration to Toronto of 1847: A Content Analysis Approach to Newspaper Research in Historical Geography," *Canadian Geographer*, vol. 17, 4 (1973), pp. 391–402. **2765**

Konrad, Victor A., "Orientation toward the Past in the Environment of the Present: Retrospect in Metropolitan Toronto," Ph.D. diss., McMaster University, 1978. **2766**

Konrad, Victor A., and S. Martin Taylor, "Retrospective Orientation in Metropolitan Toronto,"

Urban History Review, vol. 9, 2 (1980), pp. 65–90.
2767

REGIONAL SETTLEMENT

Schwar, Helmut S., "Settlement in Markham Township, 1794–1861," Master's thesis, York University, 1976.
2768

POPULATION

Blair, James W., "Components of Population Change in the Toronto Region, 1951–1971," Master's thesis, York University, 1975.
2769

Gagan, David, "Geographical and Social Mobility in Nineteenth-Century Ontario: A Microstudy," *Canadian Review of Sociology and Anthropology*, vol. 13, 2 (1976), pp. 152–164.
2770

Hovinen, Elizabeth L., "Quakers of Yonge Street," *Canadian Geographical Journal*, vol. 92, 1 (1976), pp. 52–57.
2771

Hovinen, Elizabeth L. "The Quakers of Yonge Street" (Downsview: York University Department of Geography Discussion Paper no. 17, 1978), 39 pp.
2772

RURAL & REGIONAL SOCIAL GEOGRAPHY

Harris, R. Cole, Pauline J. Roulston, and Chris de Freitas, "The Settlement of Mono Township," *Canadian Geographer*, vol. 19, 1 (1975), pp. 1–17.
2773

Gagan, David, *Hopeful Travellers: Families, Land, and Social Change in Mid-Victorian Peel County, Canada West* (Toronto: University of Toronto Press, 1981), 197 pp.
2774

ECONOMIC DEVELOPMENT

Silva, W. P. T., "The Economic Geography of the Southern Georgian Bay Area: A Study of Change from 1855 to 1961," Ph.D. diss., University of Toronto, 1966.
2775

Kelly, Kenneth, "The Development of Farm Produce Marketing Agencies and Competition between Market Centres in Eastern Simcoe County, 1850–1875," in Donald H. Akenson, ed., *Canadian Papers in Rural History*, vol. 1 (Gananoque, Ont.: Langdale Press, 1978), pp. 67–86.
2776

LAND & LAND USE

Putnam, R. G., "Changes in Rural Land Use Patterns on the Central Lake Ontario Plain," *Canadian Geographer*, vol. 6, 2 (1962), pp. 60–68.
2777

Crewson, Daryll M., "Study of Farmland Loss in Central Ontario, 1951–1971," Master's thesis, McMaster University, 1977.
2778

AGRICULTURE

Hallman, D. E., "Orchard Resources in the Toronto-Hamilton Area, 1931–1965," Master's thesis, University of Waterloo, 1967.
2779

Kelly, Kenneth, "The Agricultural Geography of Simcoe County, Ontario, 1820–1880," Ph.D. diss., University of Toronto, 1968.
2780

Kelly, Kenneth, "Wheat Farming in Simcoe County in the Mid-Nineteenth Century," *Canadian Geographer*, vol. 15, 1 (1971), pp. 95–112.
2781

LANDSCAPE

Punter, John V., "Urbanites in the Countryside: Case Studies of the Impact of Exurban Development on the Landscape in the Toronto-Centred Region, 1954–1971," Ph.D. diss., University of Toronto, 1974.
2782

COMMUNICATIONS & TRADE

Burbidge, Allison A., "The Changing Role of Transportation in Simcoe County from 1800 to 1866," Master's thesis, McMaster University, 1961.
2783

McIlwraith, Thomas F., Jr., "Accessibility and Rural Land Utilization in the Yonge Street Area of Upper Canada," Master's thesis, University of Toronto, 1966.
2784

URBAN NETWORKS & URBANIZATION

Wretham, B., "Functional Analysis of Settlements and Metropolitan Dominance: Toronto and York County, 1921–1961," Master's thesis, University of Waterloo, 1970.
2785

TOWN GROWTH

Toronto

Weller, James P., "The Evolution of Toronto: A Geographic Study," Master's thesis, Ohio State University, 1963.
2786

Spelt, Jacob, "The Development of the Toronto Conurbation," *Buffalo Law Review*, vol. 13, 3 (1964), pp. 557–573.
2787

Kerr, Donald G., and Jacob Spelt, *The Changing Face of Toronto* (Ottawa: Queen's Printer, 1965), 163 pp.
2788

Armstrong, Frederick H., "Toronto in 1834," *Canadian Geographer*, vol. 10, 3 (1966), pp. 172–183.
2789

Goheen, Peter G., *Victorian Toronto, 1850 to 1900: Pattern and Process of Growth* (Chicago: University of Chicago Department of Geography, Research Paper no. 127, 1970), 278 pp.   2790

Thomas, Stephen M., "Railway Satellite: West Toronto Junction 1884–1909," Master's thesis, York University, 1973.   2791

Lemon, James T., "Toronto among North American Cities: A Historical Perspective on the Present," in V. L. Russell, ed., *Forging a Consensus: Historical Essays on Toronto* (Toronto: University of Toronto Press, 1984), pp. 323–351.   2792

Threlfall, Rosemary J., "Toronto Annexation, 1883 to 1893," Master's thesis, University of Toronto, 1984.   2793

Lemon, James T., *Toronto since 1918: An Illustrated History* (Toronto: Lorimer, 1985), 224 pp.
2794

Lemon, James T., *The Annex: A Brief Historical Geography* (Toronto: Annex Residents Association, 1986), 30 pp.   2795

Bryant, Christopher R., "L'évolution de la ville régionale en Amérique du Nord: Le cas de Toronto," *Annals de géographie*, vol. 95, 1 (1986), pp. 26–42.   2796

Luymes, Martin, "The Building of Greater Toronto: Annexation, 1903 to 1914," Master's thesis, University of Toronto, 1986.   2797

Harris, Richard S., and Martin Luymes, "The Growth of Toronto, 1861–1941: A Cartographic Essay," *Urban History Review*, vol. 18, 3 (1990), pp. 244–255.   2798

Other centers

Roulston, Pauline J., "The Urbanization of Nineteenth-Century Orangeville, Ontario: Some Historical and Geographical Aspects," Master's thesis, University of Toronto, 1974.   2799

Smith, W. Randy, "The Early Development of Three Upper Canadian Towns: Barrie, Hollow Landing and Newmarket" (Downsview: York University Department of Geography Discussion Paper, no. 16, 1977), 54 pp.   2800

Noble, E. J., "Entrepreneurship and Nineteenth Century Urban Growth: A Case Study of Orillia, Ontario, 1867–1898," *Urban History Review*, vol. 9, 1 (1980), pp. 64–89.   2801

URBAN ECONOMIC STRUCTURE

Toronto

Cosgrove, Denis E., "Dry and Fancy Goods Wholesaling in Nineteenth Century Toronto," Master's thesis, University of Toronto, 1971. 2802

Mellen, Frances N., "The Development of the Toronto Waterfront during the Railway Expansion Era, 1850–1912," Ph.D. diss., University of Toronto, 1974.   2803

Smith, John Duncan, "Branch Banking in Metropolitan Toronto, 1946–1971: A Spatial Examination," Master's thesis, York University, 1974.
2804

Lemon, James T., ed., "Internal Relationships within the Nineteenth Century City" (Downsview: York University Department of Geography, Discussion Paper no. 11, 1975), 30 pp.   2805

Gad, Gunter H. K., "Toronto's Central Office Complex: Growth, Structure, and Linkages," Ph.D. diss., University of Toronto, 1976.   2806

O'Mara, James J., "'The Mart of Ontario': Wholesaling in Toronto's Central Business District, 1850–1900," Master's thesis, York University, 1976.   2807

Doucet, Michael J., "Mass Transit and the Failure of Private Ownership: The Case of Toronto," *Urban History Review*, no. 3–77 (1977), pp. 3–33.
2808

Doucet, Michael J., "Politics, Space, and Trolleys: Mass Transit in Early Twentieth Century Toronto," in Gilbert A. Stelter and Alan F. J. Artibise, eds., *Shaping the Urban Landscape: Aspects of the Canadian City-Building Process* (Ottawa: Carleton University Press, 1982), pp. 356–381.
2809

Gad, Gunter H. K., and Deryck W. Holdsworth, "Building for City, Region, and Nation: Office Development in Toronto, 1834–1984," in V. L. Russell, ed., *Forging a Consensus: Historical Essays on Toronto* (Toronto: University of Toronto Press, 1984), pp. 272–319.   2810

Gad, Gunter H. K., and Deryck W. Holdsworth, "Large Office Buildings and Changing Occupancy, Toronto, 1880–1950," *Bulletin of the Society for the Study of Architecture in Canada*, vol. 10, 4 (1985), pp. 19–26.   2811

Dennis, Richard, *Landlords and Rented Housing in Toronto, 1885–1914* (Toronto: University of Toronto, Centre for Urban and Community Studies, Research Paper no. 162, 1987), 57 pp.
2812

Hiebert, Daniel J., "Discontinuity and the Emergence of Flexible Production: Garment Production in Toronto, 1901–1931," *Economic Geography*, vol. 65, 3 (1990), pp. 229–253. **2813**

Young, Deborah, "The Link between Urban Industrial History and Soil Quality in Toronto," Master's thesis, York University, 1990. **2814**

URBAN SOCIAL STRUCTURE

Toronto

Population

Rosenberg, Louis, *A Study of the Changes in the Geographic Distribution of the Jewish Population in the Metropolitan Area of Toronto, 1851–1951* (Montreal: Canadian Jewish Congress, Bureau of Social and Economic Research, Canadian Jewish Population Studies, Canadian Jewish Community Series, no. 2, 1954), 27 pp. **2815**

Rosenberg, Louis, *Population Characteristics of the Jewish Community of Toronto* (Canadian Jewish Population Studies, Canadian Jewish Community Series, no. 3, 2, 1955), 58 pp. **2816**

Njau, Gilbert J., "The Change in Population Distribution in Metropolitan Toronto: 1941–1961," Master's thesis, University of Toronto, 1967. **2817**

Property & property relations

Harris, Richard S., "The Unremarked Home Ownership Boom in Toronto," *Histoire sociale/Social History*, vol. 18, 36 (1985), pp. 433–437. **2818**

Harris, Richard S., *The Family Home in Working Class Life* (Toronto: University of Toronto Centre for Urban and Community Studies, Research Paper no. 171, 1989), 27 pp. **2819**

Harris, Richard S., "Household Work Strategies and Suburban Home Ownership in Toronto, 1899–1913," *Environment and Planning D: Society and Space*, vol. 8, 1 (1990), pp. 97–121. **2820**

Harris, Richard S., "Self-Building and the Social Geography of Toronto, 1901–1913: A Challenge for Urban Theory," *Transactions of the Institute of British Geographers*, n.s. vol. 15, 4 (1990), pp. 387–402. **2821**

Occupations

Mackenzie, Suzanne, "Reproduction of Labour in the Industrial City: A Study of the Position of Women with Reference to Nineteenth-Century Toronto," Master's thesis, University of Toronto, 1978. **2822**

Mackenzie, Suzanne, *Women and the Reproduction of Labour Power in the Industrial City: A*

Case Study (Brighton [U.K.]: University of Sussex, Urban & Regional Studies Working Paper no. 23, 1980). **2823**

Residential patterns

Campbell, Kenneth M., "The Changing Residential Patterns in Toronto, 1880–1910," Master's thesis, University of Toronto, 1971. **2824**

Doucet, Michael J., "Urban Residential Mobility: Magnitude and Spatial Patterns for Late Nineteenth Century Toronto," Master's thesis, York University, 1971. **2825**

Maher, Christopher A., "Residential Change and Filtering Process: Central Toronto, 1953–1971," Ph.D. diss., University of Toronto, 1972. **2826**

Doucet, Michael J., "Nineteenth Century Residential Mobility: Some Preliminary Comments" (Downsview: York University Department of Geography Discussion Paper no. 4, 1972), 64 pp. **2827**

Friedman, Susan W., "Public Schools and Residential Areas in Toronto, 1871–1921," Master's thesis, University of Toronto, 1980. **2828**

Kalbach, Warren, *Historical and Generational Perspectives of Ethnic Residential Segregation in Toronto, Canada, 1851–1971* (Toronto: University of Toronto Centre for Urban and Community Studies, Research Paper no. 118, 1980), 32 pp. **2829**

Harney, Robert F., ed., *Gathering Place: Peoples and Neighbourhoods of Toronto, 1834–1945* (Toronto: Multicultural History Society of Ontario, 1985), 304 pp. **2830**

Sanford, Barbara, "The Origins of Residential Differentiation: Capitalist Industrialization, Toronto, Ontario, 1851–1881," Ph.D. diss., University of Toronto, 1985. **2831**

Ethnicity & welfare

Wertepny, Michael, "The Distribution of Ukrainian Settlement in Toronto: 1903–1976," Master's thesis, York University, 1978. **2832**

Simone, Nick, "Italian Immigrants in Toronto, 1890–1930" (Downsview: York University Geography Department Discussion Paper no. 26, 1981), 35 pp. **2833**

Gorys, Paul K., "The Pisterzani in Toronto: A Case Study in the Adjustment of an Ethnic Group," Master's thesis, York University, 1984. **2834**

Jones, Simon R., "A Legitimate Charge on the Municipality? The City of Toronto and the Relief of Unemployment, 1890–1940," Master's thesis, University of Toronto, 1986. **2835**

Hiebert, Daniel J., "The Geography of Jewish Immigrants and the Garment Industry in Toronto,

1900–1913: A Study of Ethnic and Class Relations," Ph.D. diss., University of Toronto, 1987. **2836**

TOWNSCAPE

Toronto

Reitsma, Hendrik-Jan A., "North York: The Development of a Suburb," Master's thesis, University of Toronto, 1962. **2837**

Morrison, Philip S., "Residential Property Conversion Subdivision, Merger, and Quality Change in the Inner City Housing Stock, Metropolitan Toronto, 1958–1973," Ph.D. diss., University of Toronto, 1978. **2838**

Moore, Peter W., "Measuring Residential Environment Quality," *Historical Methods*, vol. 13, 4 (1980), pp. 193–203. **2839**

Bordessa, Karina, "A Corporate Suburb for Toronto: Lawrence Park, 1905–1930," Master's thesis, York University, 1981. **2840**

Ganton, Isobel, "The Subdivision Process in Toronto, 1851–1883," in Gilbert A. Stelter and Alan F. J. Artibise, eds., *Shaping the Urban Landscape: Aspects of the Canadian City-Building Process* (Ottawa: Carleton University Press, 1982), pp. 200–231. **2841**

Paterson, Ross, "Kingsway Park, Etobicoke: An Analysis of the Development of an Early Twentieth-Century Suburb," Master's thesis, York University, 1982. **2842**

McIlwraith, Thomas F., Jr., "The Influence of Street Railways upon City Street Engineering: The Toronto Experience, 1860–1890," in Richard A. Jarrell and Arnold E. Roos, eds., *Critical Issues in the History of Canadian Science, Technology and Medicine* (Thornhill, Ont.: HSTC Publications, 1983), pp. 218–227. **2843**

Paterson, Ross, "The Development of an Interwar Suburb: Kingsway Park, Etobicoke," *Urban History Review*, vol. 13, 3 (1985), pp. 225–235. **2844**

Gad, Gunter H. K., and Deryck W. Holdsworth, "Corporate Capitalism and the Emergence of the High Rise Office Building," *Urban Geography*, vol. 8, 3 (1987), pp. 212–231. Reprinted with revisions in Graeme Wynn, ed., *People, Places, Patterns, Processes: Geographical Perspectives on the Canadian Past* (Toronto: Copp Clark Pitman, 1990), pp. 247–266. **2845**

Gad, Gunter H. K., and Deryck W. Holdsworth, "Looking Inside the Skyscraper: Size and Occupancy of Toronto Office Buildings, 1890–1950," *Urban History Review*, vol. 16, 2 (1987), pp. 176–189. **2846**

Sanford, Barbara, "The Political Economy of Land Development in Nineteenth Century Toronto," *Urban History Review*, vol. 16, 1 (1987), pp. 17–33. **2847**

Desfor, Gene, H. Roy Merrens, and Michael Goldrick, "Redevelopment on the North American Water-Frontier: The Case of Toronto," in B. S. Hoyle, D. A. Pinder, and M. S. Husain, eds., *Revitalising the Waterfront: International Dimensions of Dockland Redevelopment* (London: Belhaven Press, 1988), pp. 92–113. **2848**

Gad, Gunter H. K., and Deryck W. Holdsworth, "Streetscape and Society: The Changing Built Environment of King Street, Toronto," in Roger Hall, William Westfall, and Laurel S. MacDowell, eds., *Patterns of the Past: Interpreting Ontario's History* (Toronto: Dundurn Press, 1988), pp. 174–205. **2849**

Merrens, H. Roy, "Port Authorities as Urban Land Developers: The Case of the Toronto Harbour Commissioners and Their Outer Harbour Project, 1912–1968," *Urban History Review*, vol. 17 (1988), pp. 92–105. **2850**

Paterson, Ross, "Creating Suburbia: Processes of Housing Production and Consumption in Toronto, 1911–1941," Ph.D. diss., York University, 1989. **2851**

Matheson, R. Neil, "A Toronto Portrait, 1857," *Beaver*, vol. 70, 3 (1990), pp. 27–37. **2852**

RECREATION & TOURISM

Wolfe, Roy I., "Wasaga Beach: The Divorce from the Geographic Environment," *Canadian Geographer*, vol. 2 (1952), pp. 57–65. **2853**

Norris, Darrell A., "Preserving Main Street: Some Lessons of Leacock's Mariposa," *Journal of Canadian Studies*, vol. 17, 2 (1982), pp. 128–136. **2854**

McIlwraith, Thomas F., Jr., "Mississauga: Heritage Management in an Ordinary Place," *Urban History Review*, vol. 13, 3 (1985), pp. 237–244. **2855**

PLANNING

Knappe, Charles F., "Development of Planning in Toronto, 1893–1922: A Survey," Master's thesis, University of Toronto, 1974. **2856**

Moore, Peter W., "Zoning and Neighborhood Change in the Annex in Toronto, 1900–1970," Ph.D. diss., University of Toronto, 1978. **2857**

Moore, Peter W., "Zoning and Planning: The Toronto Experience, 1904–1970," in Alan F. J. Artibise and Gilbert A. Stelter, eds., *The Useable Urban Past: Planning and Politics in the Modern*

Canadian City (Toronto: Macmillan, 1979), pp. 316–342.   **2858**

Weaver, John C., "The Modern City Realized: Toronto Civic Affairs, 1880–1915," in Alan F. J. Artibise and Gilbert A. Stelter, eds., *The Usable Urban Past: Planning and Politics in the Modern Canadian City* (Toronto: Macmillan, 1979), pp. 39–72.   **2859**

Moore, Peter W., "Zoning and Neighborhood Change: The Annex in Toronto, 1900–1970," *Canadian Geographer*, vol. 26, 1 (1982), pp. 21–36.   **2860**

Moore, Peter W., "Public Services and Residential Development in a Toronto Neighborhood, 1880–1915," *Journal of Urban History*, vol. 9, 4 (1983), pp. 445–472.   **2861**

Lemon, James T., "Tracy Deavin LeMay: Toronto's First Planning Commissioner, 1930–1954," *City Planning*, vol. 1, 4 (1984), pp. 4–7, 36.   **2862**

Desfor, Gene, H. Roy Merrens, and Michael Goldrick, "A Political Economy of the Water Frontier: Planning and Development in Toronto," *Geoforum*, vol. 20, 4 (1989), pp. 487–501.   **2863**

Lemon, James T., "Plans for Early Twentieth-Century Toronto: Lost in Management," *Urban History Review*, vol. 18, 1 (1989), pp. 11–31.   **2864**

Craig, Anne Marie, "The Genesis of Housing Policy in Toronto: 1930 to 1940," Master's thesis, University of Toronto, 1990.   **2865**

Goldrick, Michael, and H. Roy Merrens, "Waterfront Changes and Institutional Status: The Role of the Toronto Harbour Commission, 1911–1989," in B. S. Hoyle, ed., *Port Cities in Context: The Impact of Waterfront Regeneration* (Southampton, U.K.: Transport Geography Study Group, Institute of British Geographers, 1990), pp. 119–153.   **2866**

MILLS & RES. OF JOHN DALZIEL, ESQ. GRANDBEND, ONT.

─── SOUTHWESTERN ONTARIO ───

GENERAL

See also 1143

Watson, J. Wreford, "The Geography of the Niagara Peninsula," Ph.D. diss., University of Toronto, 1945.　　　　　　　　　2867

Haldane, Elizabeth Ann, "Historical Geography of Waterloo Township," Master's thesis, McMaster University, 1963.　　　　　　2868

Schneider, A. A., "The Historical Geography of the Erie Triangle," Ph.D. diss., Ohio State University, 1963.　　　　　　　　　2869

Wightman, W. Robert, "The Historical Sector," in Victor Sim, ed., *Erie Project Report* (London: University of Western Ontario Department of Geography, 1970), pp. 81–95.　　　2870

Kureth, Elwood J. C., "Geographic, Historic, Political Factors Affecting Canada's Chemical Valley," Ph.D. diss., University of Michigan, 1972.　　　　　　　　　　　　2871

Waterston, Elizabeth, and Douglas Hoffman, eds., *On Middle Ground: Landscapes and Life in Wellington County, 1841–1891* (Guelph: University of Guelph, 1974), 80 pp.　　　2872

Dahms, Frederic A., "How Ontario's Guelph District Developed," *Canadian Geographical Journal*, vol. 94, 1 (1977), pp. 48–55.　　　2873

Brown, David L., and John Clarke, "Foci of Human Activity, Essex County, Ontario, 1825–1852: Archival Sources and Research Strategies," *Archivaria*, vol. 12 (Summer 1981), pp. 31–57.　　2874

Dahms, Frederic A., "Regional Urban History: A Statistical and Cartographic Survey of Huron and Southern Bruce Counties, 1864–1981," *Urban History Review*, vol. 15, 3 (1987), pp. 254–268.　　　　　　　　　　　　2875

ENVIRONMENTAL CHANGE

Clark, Lloyd J., "The Baldoon Settlement Lands: The Effects of Changing Drainage Technology, 1804–1967," Master's thesis, University of Western Ontario, 1970.　　　2876

Clarke, John, and G. F. Finnegan, "Colonial Survey Records and the Vegetation of Essex County, Ontario," *Journal of Historical Geography*, vol. 10, 2 (1984), pp. 119–138.　　2877

NATIVE PEOPLES & WHITE RELATIONS

Sample, K. A., "Changes in Agriculture on the Six Nations Indian Reservation," Master's thesis, McMaster University, 1971.　　　2878

Ferris, Neal, "Southwestern Ontario Ojibwa Cultural Continuity, A.D. 1780–1861," Master's thesis, York University, 1990.　　　2879

EXPLORATION & MAPPING

Clarke, John, "Mapping the Lands Supervised by Colonel the Honourable Thomas Talbot in the Western District of Upper Canada, 1811–1849," *Canadian Cartographer*, vol. 8, 1 (1971), pp. 8–18.　　　　　　　　　　　　2880

POPULAR IMAGES & EVALUATION

See also 1310

Gentilcore, R. Louis, "The Niagara District of Robert Gourlay," *Ontario History*, vol. 54, 4 (1962), pp. 229–236.　　　　　2881

Alexander, William R., "Colonial Land Appraisal for Land-Use Hazards: The Case of Drainage in South Western Ontario, 1788–1855," Master's thesis, University of Western Ontario, 1974. 2882

Hilts, Stewart G., "In Praise of Progress: Attitudes to Urbanization in Southwestern Ontario, 1850–1900," Ph.D. diss., University of Toronto, 1981.　　　　　　　　　　　　2883

Winchester, A. J. L., "Scratching along Amongst the Stumps: Letters from Thomas Priestman, a Settler in the Niagara Peninsula, 1811–1839," *Ontario History*, vol. 81, 1 (1989), pp. 41–58.　2884

REGIONAL SETTLEMENT

See also 1340

Watson, J. Wreford, "Mapping a Hundred Years of Change in the Niagara Peninsula," *Canadian Geographical Journal*, vol. 32, 6 (1946), pp. 266–283.　　　　　　　　　　　　2885

Kirk, Donald W., "Settlement Pattern of the Listowel Region, Southwestern Ontario," *Economic Geography*, vol. 23, 1 (1947), pp. 67–71. [Focus on 1871–1940]　　　　　　　　　2886

Watson, J. Wreford, "The Influence of the Frontier on Niagara Settlements," *Geographical Review*, vol. 38, 1 (1948), pp. 113–119.　　2887

Nicholson, Norman L., "The Establishment of Settlement Patterns in the Ausable Watershed, Ontario," *Geographical Bulletin* (Ottawa), 1 (1953), pp. 1–13.　　　　　　　2888

Wood, J. David, "The Historical Geography of Dumfries Township, Upper Canada, 1816–1852," Master's thesis, University of Toronto, 1958. **2889**

Wood, J. David, "The Stage is Set: Dumfries Township, 1816," *Waterloo Historical Society Annual Volume*, no. 48 (1960), pp. 40–50. **2890**

Johnson, Charles M., "An Outline of Early Settlement in the Grand River Valley," *Ontario History*, vol. 54, 1 (1962), pp. 43–68. **2891**

Gentilcore, R. Louis, "The Beginnings of Settlement in the Niagara Peninsula, 1782–1792," *Canadian Geographer*, vol. 7, 1 (1963), pp. 72–82. **2892**

Wood, Leslie J., "Settlements at the Mount Elgin Ridges," Master's thesis, University of Western Ontario, 1965. **2893**

Cameron, James M., "Guelph and the Canada Company, 1827–1851: An Approach to Resource Development," Master's thesis, University of Guelph, 1966. **2894**

Wood, Colin J. B., "Human Settlement in the Long Point Region, 1790–1825," Master's thesis, McMaster University, 1966. **2895**

Duquemin, Colin K., "Sequent Occupance in the Lower Valley of the Twenty Mile Creek, Lough Township, Lincoln County, Ontario: 1800–1905," Master's thesis, State University of New York–Buffalo, 1968. **2896**

Clarke, John, "A Geographical Analysis of Colonial Settlement in the Western District of Upper Canada, 1788–1850," Ph.D. diss., University of Western Ontario, 1970. **2897**

Officer, E. Roy, "Waterloo County: Some Aspects of Settlement and Economy before 1900," in A. G. McLellan, ed., *The Waterloo County Area: Selected Geographical Essays* (Waterloo: University of Waterloo Department of Geography, 1971), pp. 11–19. **2898**

Brunger, Alan G. "A Spatial Analysis of Individual Settlement in Southern London District, Upper Canada, 1800–1836," Ph.D. diss., University of Western Ontario, 1974. **2899**

Cameron, James M., "The Canada Company and Land Settlement as Resource Development in the Guelph Block," in J. David Wood, ed., *Perspectives on Landscape and Settlement in Nineteenth Century Ontario* (Toronto: McClelland and Stewart, 1975), pp. 141–158. **2900**

POPULATION

Watson, J. Wreford, "Rural Depopulation in Southwestern Ontario," *Annals of the Association of American Geographers*, vol. 37, 2 (1947), pp. 145–154. [Focus on 1861–1941] **2901**

Johnston, H. J., "Immigration to the Five Eastern Townships of the Huron Tract," *Ontario History*, vol. 54, 3 (1962), pp. 207–224. **2902**

Skinner, J. G., "Demographic Aspects of the Huron Upland of Southwestern Ontario," Master's thesis, University of Western Ontario, 1964. **2903**

Clarke, John, "Spatial Variations in Population Density: Southwestern Ontario in 1851," in W. P. Adams and F. M. Helleiner, eds., *International Geography, 1972*, vol. 1, sec. 5, *Historical Geography* (Toronto: University of Toronto Press, for the International Geographical Union, 1972), pp. 408–411. **2904**

Clarke, John, "Military and United Empire Loyalists in the Western District of Upper Canada in 1836," *Canadian Cartographer*, vol. 11, 2 (1974), pp. 186–190. **2905**

Walker, Gerald E., "Migrants and Places of Birth: A Methodological Note," *Professional Geographer*, vol. 27, 1 (1975), pp. 58–64. **2906**

Dahms, Frederic A., *Historical Background, Population Change, and Agriculture: Wellington County, 1840–1976* (Guelph: University of Guelph Centre for Resources Development, no. 89, 1978), 75 pp. **2907**

Dilley, Robert S., "Migration and the Mennonites: Nineteenth-Century Waterloo County, Ontario," in Donald H. Akenson, ed., *Canadian Papers in Rural History*, vol. 4 (Gananoque, Ont.: Langdale Press, 1984), pp. 108–129. **2908**

Norris, Darrell A., "Migration, Pioneer Settlement, and the Life Course: The First Families of an Ontario Township," in Donald H. Akenson, ed., *Canadian Papers in Rural History*, vol. 4 (Gananoque, Ont.: Langdale Press, 1984), pp. 130–152. Reprinted in J. K. Johnson and B. G. Wilson, eds., *Historical Essays on Upper Canada: New Perspectives* (Ottawa: Carleton University Press, 1989), pp. 175–202. **2909**

RURAL & REGIONAL SOCIAL GEOGRAPHY

Nitkin, David A., "Negro Colonization as a Response to Racism: An Historical Geography of a Southwestern Ontario Experience, 1830 to 1860," Master's thesis, York University, 1973. **2910**

McPherson, Murdo, "The Geography of Itinerancy: A Case Study of Methodist Circuit Organization in Bruce and Grey Counties, 1845–1855," Master's thesis, University of Toronto, 1980. **2911**

Sills, Elizabeth Ann, "Belonging: Kinship and Permanence on the North Shore of Lake Huron, 1870–1909," Master's thesis, McMaster University, 1983. **2912**

Clarke, John, and Karl Skof, "Social Dimensions of an Ontario County, 1851–52," in David B.

Knight, ed., *Our Geographical Mosaic: Research Essays in Honour of G. C. Merrill* (Ottawa: Carleton University Press, 1985), pp. 107–136.　**2913**

Buchanan, Elizabeth Ann, "Belonging: Kinship and Permanence on the North Shore of Lake Huron, 1870–1909," Ph.D. diss., McMaster University, 1990.　**2914**

POLITICAL & ADMINISTRATIVE GEOGRAPHY

Whebell, Charles F. J., "The Fragmentation of the Western District, 1830–1860: A Study in Local Separatism," in K. G. Pryke and L. L. Kiisek, eds., *The Western District: Papers from the Western District Conference* (Windsor: Essex County Historical Society, 1983), pp. 168–190.　**2915**

ECONOMIC DEVELOPMENT

Wells, W. Douglas, "The Hamilton Region, 1800–1882: The Interrelationships between Transportation and Industrial Development," Master's thesis, University of Waterloo, 1973.　**2916**

Dahms, Frederic A., "The Changing Functions of Villages and Hamlets in Wellington County, 1881–1971," *Urban History Review*, vol. 8, 3 (1980), pp. 3–19.　**2917**

Dahms, Frederic A., "The Role of the Country Town in Ontario, Yesterday and Today: The Case of Wellington and Huron Counties," in A. A. Brookes, ed., *The Country Town in Rural Ontario's Past* (Guelph: University of Guelph School of Part-Time Studies and Continuing Education, 1982), pp. 58–78.　**2918**

Dahms, Frederic A., *The Changing Functions of Rural Settlements in Huron and Southern Bruce Counties: Historical Background and Major Trends* (Guelph: University of Guelph School of Rural Planning and Development, no. 110, 1982), 66 pp.　**2919**

Dahms, Frederic A., *The Changing Functions of Settlements in Bruce County: Historical Background and Major Trends* (Guelph: University of Guelph School of Rural Planning and Development, no. 116, 1983), 54 pp.　**2920**

Dahms, Frederic A., *Functions of Settlements in the Waterloo Region, 1851–1985, with Historical Background and Comparative Data for the Counties of Bruce, Huron, and Wellington* (Guelph: University of Guelph, Department of Geography, Occasional Paper no. 8, 1986), 88 pp.　**2921**

Burghardt, Andrew F., "The Move from County to Region," in Michael J. Dear, J. J. Drake, and L. G. Leeds, eds., *The Steel City: Hamilton and Region* (Toronto: University of Toronto Press, 1987), pp. 156–169.　**2922**

RESOURCE MANAGEMENT

Battin, James G., and J. Gordon Nelson, "Recreation and Conservation: The Struggle for Balance in Point Pelee National Park, 1918–1978," *Laurentian Review*, vol. 11, 2 (1979), pp. 43–69. Reprinted in Geoffrey Wall and John S. Marsh, eds., *Recreational Land Use: Perspectives on Its Evolution in Canada* (Ottawa: Carleton University Press, 1982), pp. 77–101.　**2923**

LAND & LAND USE

General

Clarke, John, "Documentary and Map Sources for Reconstructing the History of the Reserved Lands in the Western District of Upper Canada," *Canadian Cartographer*, vol. 8, 2 (1971), pp. 75–83.　**2924**

Land tenure

Clarke, John, "Military, Loyalist, and Other Land Grants in the Western District, 1836," *Ontario Register*, vol. 4, 3 (1971), pp. 129–144.　**2925**

Clarke, John, "The Role of Political Position and Family and Economic Linkage in Land Speculation in the Western District of Upper Canada, 1788–1815," *Canadian Geographer*, vol. 19, 1 (1975), pp. 18–34.　**2926**

Clarke, John, "Land Acquisition in Essex County, 1788–1900," in Brian S. Osborne, ed., *The Settlement of Canada: Origins and Transfer* (Kingston: Proceedings of the British-Canadian Symposium in Historical Geography, Queen's University, 1976), pp. 214–216.　**2927**

Clarke, John, "Nineteenth Century Land Acquisition Slopes: Essex County, Ontario," *International Geography '76*, sec. 9, *Historical Geography* (Moscow: Twenty-third International Geographical Union, 1976), pp. 43–46.　**2928**

Clarke, John, "Aspects of Land Acquisition in Essex County, Ontario, 1790–1900," *Histoire sociale/Social History*, vol. 11, 21 (1978), pp. 98–119.　**2929**

Clarke, John, "Land and Law in Essex County: Malden Township and the Abstract Index to Deeds," *Histoire sociale/Social History*, vol. 11, 22 (1978), pp. 475–493.　**2930**

Clarke, John, "William McCormick's Land Holding in Essex County, 1805–1839," in R. A. Douglas, ed., *A Sketch of the Western District of Upper Canada, Being the Southern Extremity of That Interesting Province, by William McCormick* (Windsor: University of Windsor Press and the Essex County Historical Society, Occasional Paper no. 1, 1980), pp. 42–45.　**2931**

Clarke, John, "The Activity of an Early Canadian Land Speculator in Essex County, Ontario: Would the Real John Askin Please Stand Up?"

in Donald H. Akenson, ed., *Canadian Papers of Rural History*, vol. 3 (Gananoque, Ont.: Langdale Press, 1982), pp. 84–109.   **2932**

MacAuley, Robert W., "The Land Dispute in Norwich Township in the London District of Upper Canada, 1811–1840," Master's thesis, University of Toronto, 1982.   **2933**

Clarke, John, "Geographical Aspects of Land Speculation in Essex County in 1825: The Strategy of Particular Individuals," in K. Pryke and L. Kiisek, eds., *The Western District* (Windsor: University of Windsor Press and the Essex County Historical Society, 1983), pp. 69–112. Reprinted in J. K. Johnston and B. G. Wilson, eds., *Historical Essays on Upper Canada* (Ottawa: Carleton University Press, 1989), pp. 81–129.   **2934**

Land use

Krueger, Ralph R., "Changing Land Use Patterns in the Niagara Fruit Belt," Ph.D. diss., Indiana University, 1958.   **2935**

Krueger, Ralph R., "Changing Land Uses in the Niagara Fruit Belt," *Geographical Bulletin* (Ottawa), vol. 14 (1960), pp. 5–24.   **2936**

Battin, James G., "Land Use History and Landscape Change, Point Pelee National Park, Ontario," Master's thesis, University of Western Ontario, 1975.   **2937**

Leverette, C. E., "Land-Use History of the Canadian Detroit River Islands," Master's thesis, University of Western Ontario, 1976.   **2938**

Van der Wal, Hylke T., "Agricultural Settlement and Land Use Changes in Bosanquet Township, Ontario, 1829–1977," Master's thesis, Eastern Michigan University, 1977.   **2939**

Reid, Deborah R., "Land-Use Change in a Selected Area of the Niagara Fruit Belt," Master's thesis, McMaster University, 1980.   **2940**

Land value

Clarke, John, and David L. Brown, "Land Prices in Essex County, Ontario, 1798 to 1852," *Canadian Geographer*, vol. 26, 4 (1982), pp. 300–317.   **2941**

Clarke, John, and David L. Brown, "Pricing Decisions for Ontario Land: The Farm Community and the Speculator in Essex County during the First Half of the Nineteenth Century," *Canadian Geographer*, vol. 31, 2 (1987), pp. 169–176.   **2942**

EXTRACTIVE ACTIVITY

Hilborn, W. H., "Forest and Forestry of the Norfolk Sand Plain," Master's thesis, University of Western Ontario, 1971.   **2943**

Peters, J. H., "Commercial Fishing in Lake Huron, 1800 to 1915: The Exploitation and Decline of

Whitefish and Lake Trout," Master's thesis, University of Western Ontario, 1981.   **2944**

AGRICULTURE

Hudgins, Bert, "Tobacco Growing in Southwestern Ontario," *Economic Geography*, vol. 14, 3 (1938), pp. 223–232.   **2945**

Krueger, Ralph R., "Changing Land-Use Patterns in the Niagara Fruit Belt," *Transactions of the Royal Canadian Institute*, vol. 32, 67, pt. 2 (1959), pp. 38–140.   **2946**

Helleiner, Frederick M., "Changing Orchard Distribution in the London Region since 1920," Master's thesis, University of Western Ontario, 1966.   **2947**

Sheldon, Samuel R., "Ontario's Flue-Cured Tobacco Industry: The Southern United States Legacy," *American Review of Canadian Studies*, vol. 18, 2 (1988), pp. 195–212.   **2948**

LANDSCAPE

Subins, Gunars, "The Evolution of the Landscape of the Huron-Erie Lowlands," Master's thesis, University of Western Ontario, 1964.   **2949**

Whebell, Charles F. J., "Pre-Confederation Houses in Norfolk County, Ontario," *Ontario History*, vol. 58, 4 (1966), pp. 225–235.   **2950**

Norris, Darrell A., and Victor A. Konrad, "Time, Context, and House Type Validation: Euphrasia Township, Ontario," in Donald H. Akenson, ed., *Canadian Papers in Rural History*, vol. 3 (Gananoque, Ont.: Langdale Press, 1982), pp. 50–83.   **2951**

Dahms, Frederic A., "Wroxeter, Huron Co., Ontario: The Anatomy of a 'Dying' Village," *Small Town*, vol. 14, 2 (1984), pp. 17–23.   **2952**

Jackson, John N., "The Niagara Peninsula: The Progressive Creation of Landscape," in N. Mika and H. Mika, eds., *The Shaping of Ontario: From Exploration to Confederation* (Belleville: Mika, 1985), pp. 94–101.   **2953**

Davis, Linda Strath, "Evolving Landscape Productivities in Four Rural Townships of Southern Ontario, 1810–1980," Ph.D. diss., University of Waterloo, 1986.   **2954**

COMMUNICATIONS & TRADE

Hamil, Fred C., "Early Shipping and Land Transportation on the Lower Thames," *Ontario History*, vol. 34 (1942), pp. 46–62.   **2955**

Burghardt, Andrew F., "The Origin and Development of the Road Network of the Niagara Peninsula, Ontario, 1770–1851," *Annals of the Association of American Geographers*, vol. 59, 3 (1969), pp. 417–440.   **2956**

Koszuta, Joanna B., "An Interpretation of the Sequent Patterns of Trails, Roads, and Highways on the Niagara Frontier to 1950," Master's thesis, State University of New York–Buffalo, 1969. 2957

Markovich, Robert, "The Evolution of Public Transport Networks in Windsor, Ontario, and London, Ontario, 1872–1968," Master's thesis, University of Windsor, 1971. 2958

Norris, Darrell A., "Business Location and Consumer Behavior, 1882–1910: Eastern Grey County, Ontario," Master's thesis, McMaster University, 1976. 2959

Jackson, John N., and John Burtniak, *Railways in the Niagara Peninsula* (Belleville: Mika, 1978), 240 pp. 2960

Jackson, John N., and Fred A. Addis, *The Welland Canals: A Comprehensive Guide* (St. Catherines: Welland Canals Foundation, 1982), 141 pp. 2961

Jackson, John N., *The Four Welland Canals: A Journal of Discovery in St. Catherines and Thorold* (St. Catherines: Vanwell, 1988), 76 pp. 2962

MANUFACTURING & INDUSTRIALIZATION

Watson, J. Wreford, "The Changing Industrial Pattern of the Niagara Peninsula: A Study in Historical Geography," *Ontario Historical Society Papers and Records*, vol. 37 (1945), pp. 49–58. 2963

Whebell, Charles F. J., "The Industrial Development of Haldimand County," Master's thesis, University of Western Ontario, 1955. 2964

Cartwright, Donald G., "Cheese Production in Southwestern Ontario," Master's thesis, University of Western Ontario, 1965. 2965

Middleton, Diana J., and David F. Walker, "Manufacturers and Industrial Development Policy in Hamilton, 1890–1910," *Urban History Review*, vol. 8, 3 (1980), pp. 20–46. 2966

Weaver, John C., "The Location of Manufacturing Enterprises: The Case of Hamilton's Attraction of Foundries, 1830–1890," in Richard A. Jarrell and Arnold E. Roos, eds., *Critical Issues in the History of Canadian Science, Technology, and Medicine* (Thornhill, Ont.: HSTC Publications, 1983), pp. 197–217. 2967

Jackson, John N., "Industrial Niagara," in M. Fram, ed., *Niagara* (Toronto: Ontario Society for Industrial Archeology, 1984), pp. 86–98. 2968

URBAN NETWORKS & URBANIZATION

Watson, J. Wreford, "Urban Developments in the Niagara Peninsula," *Canadian Journal of Economics and Political Science*, vol. 9, 4 (1943), pp. 463–486. 2969

Kirk, Donald W., "Southwestern Ontario: The Areal Pattern of Urban Settlements in 1850," Ph.D. diss., Northwestern University, 1949. 2970

Woods, John K., "Ports and Harbours of the Lake Erie North Shore," Master's thesis, University of Western Ontario, 1955. 2971

Gibson, Edward M., "A Sequent Occupance Study of the Norfolk Sand Plain with Special Reference to Urbanism," Master's thesis, University of Western Ontario, 1963. 2972

Marshall, John U., "Central Places in the Queen's Bush: A Study of Service Centers and Their Evolution in Bruce and Grey Counties, Ontario," Master's thesis, University of Minnesota, 1964. 2973

Russwurm, Lorne H., "Expanding Urbanization in the London to Hamilton Area of Western Ontario: 1941–1961," Ph.D. diss., University of Illinois, 1964. 2974

Overton, D. J. B., "An Examination of Models of Port Development: Lake Erie North Shore, 1784–1870," Master's thesis, University of Western Ontario, 1970. 2975

Thakur, Baleshwar, "The Changing Functional Makeup of Central Place Hierarchies in South Western Ontario between 1871 and 1971," Master's thesis, University of Waterloo, 1972. 2976

Dahms, Frederic A., "Some Quantitative Approaches to the Study of Central Places in the Guelph Area: 1851–1970," *Urban History Review*, no. 2–75 (1975), pp. 9–30. 2977

Norris, Darrell A., "Theory and Observation: A Perspective on Consumer Trip Behavior and the Decline of the Ontario Hamlet," *Urban History Review*, vol. 10, 2 (1981), pp. 1–12. 2978

Russwurm, Lorne H., and B. Thakur, "Hierarchical and Functional Stability and Change in a Strongly Urbanizing Area of Southwestern Ontario, 1871–1971," *Canadian Geographer*, vol. 25, 2 (1981), pp. 149–166. 2979

Dahms, Frederic A., "The Process of 'Urbanization' in the Countryside: A Study of Huron and Bruce Counties, Ontario, 1891–1981," *Urban History Review*, vol. 12, 3 (1984), pp. 1–18. 2980

TOWN GROWTH
Guelph

Johnson, Leo, "Ideology and Political Economy in Urban Growth: Guelph, 1827–1927," in Gilbert A. Stelter and Alan F. J. Artibise, eds., *Shaping the Urban Landscape: Aspects of the Canadian City-Building Process* (Ottawa: Carleton University Press, 1982), pp. 30–64. 2981

Hamilton

Doucet, Michael J., Michael B. Katz, and Mark Stern, "Population Persistence and Early Industrialization in a Canadian City: Hamilton, Ontario, 1851–1871," *Social Science History*, vol. 2, 2 (1978), pp. 208–229.   **2982**

Gentilcore, R. Louis, "The Beginnings: Hamilton in the Nineteenth Century," in Michael J. Dear, J. J. Drake, and L. G. Reeds, eds., *The Steel City: Hamilton and Region* (Toronto: University of Toronto Press, 1987), pp. 99–118.   **2983**

Wood, Harold A., "Emergence of the Modern City: Hamilton, 1891–1950," in Michael J. Dear, J. J. Drake, and L. G. Reeds, eds., *The Steel City: Hamilton and Region* (Toronto: University of Toronto Press, 1987), pp. 119–137.   **2984**

Niagara-on-the-Lake

Whitfield, Faye V., "The Origin of the Settlement of Niagara-on-the-Lake," Master's thesis, McMaster University, 1986.   **2985**

St. Catherines

Tweed, Edwin, "The Evolution of St. Catherines, Ontario," Master's thesis, McMaster University, 1960.   **2986**

Jackson, John N., *St. Catherines, Ontario: Its Early Years* (Belleville: Mika, 1976), 416 pp.   **2987**

Jackson, John N., *St. Catherines: The Contribution of the City to Two Hundred Years of Ontario Life* (St. Catherines: Historical Society of St. Catherines, 1984), 415 pp.   **2988**

URBAN ECONOMIC STRUCTURE

Hamilton

Roberts, R. D., "The Changing Patterns in Distribution and Composition of Manufacturing Activity in Hamilton between 1861 and 1921," Master's thesis, McMaster University, 1964.   **2989**

Cowell, Gregory T., "Functional Change in Hamilton's Central Business District, 1853–1921," Master's thesis, McMaster University, 1974.
                                                      2990

Black, Laura, "Public Transit and Industry: Hamilton, Ontario, 1871–1974," Master's thesis, University of Waterloo, 1980.   **2991**

London

Janelle, Donald, "Scale Components in the Descriptive Analysis of Urban Land Use Change: London, Ontario, 1850–1960," *Ontario Geography*, vol. 7 (1972), pp. 66–86.   **2992**

Parker, W. J. C., "The Evolution of a Retail Strip: A Case Study of Richmond Street in London, Ontario, 1880–1980," Master's thesis, University of Western Ontario, 1984.   **2993**

Other centers

Donkin, Margaret Kate, "An Analysis of the Changing Land-Use Morphology of Waterdown, 1795–1960," Master's thesis, McMaster University, 1969.   **2994**

Melville, Douglas, "Inter-City Pattern of Office Development and Location in Kitchener-Waterloo, 1952–1972," Master's thesis, University of Waterloo, 1977.   **2995**

URBAN SOCIAL STRUCTURE

Hamilton

Doucet, Michael J., "Spatial Differentiation in a Commercial City: Hamilton, 1851–52," in Michael B. Katz, ed., *The Canadian Social History Project: Fourth Interim Report* (Toronto: Department of History and Philosophy of Education, Ontario Institute for Studies in Education, 1973), pp. 251–279.   **2996**

Davey, Ian, and Michael J. Doucet, "The Social Geography of a Commercial City ca. 1855," in Michael Katz, ed., *The People of Hamilton, Canada West* (Cambridge: Harvard University Press, 1975), pp. 319–342.   **2997**

Bird, Timothy R., "Cultural Conflict and Crime among Irish Immigrants in Hamilton, Ontario in 1891," Master's thesis, Queen's University, 1977.   **2998**

Doucet, Michael J., "Discriminant Analysis and the Delineation of Household Structure: Toward a Solution to the Boarder/Relative Problem on the 1871 Canadian Census," *Historical Methods Newsletter*, vol. 10, 4 (1977), pp. 149–157.   **2999**

Caussy, Devianne, "Residential Mobility of Italian Immigrants in Hamilton," Master's thesis, McMaster University, 1980.   **3000**

Katz, Michael B., Michael J. Doucet and Mark J. Stern, *The Social Organization of Early Industrial Capitalism* (Cambridge, Mass.: Harvard University Press, 1982), 444 pp.   **3001**

Pollard, Jane, "Restructuring, Gender and Female Participation Rates in Hamilton, 1951–1986," Master's thesis, McMaster University, 1987.
                                                      3002

Other centers

Clarke, Kenneth L., "Social Relations and Urban Change in a Late Nineteenth Century Southwestern Ontario Railway City: St. Thomas, 1868 to 1890," Master's thesis, York University, 1976.
                                                      3003

Orr, Patricia, "The Wrong Side of the Canal: Social Connections and Residential Land Use Patterns in Nineteenth-Century Thorold," Master's thesis, York University, 1985.   **3004**

Parr, Joy, *The Gender of Breadwinners: Women, Men, and Change in Two Industrial Towns, 1880–1950* (Toronto: University of Toronto Press, 1990), 314 pp. [Hanover and Paris] **3005**

TOWNSCAPE

Hamilton

Doucet, Michael J., "Working Class Housing in a Small Nineteenth Century Canadian City: Hamilton, Ontario, 1852 to 1881," in G. S. Kealey and Peter Warrian, eds., *Essays in Canadian Working Class History, 1850–1925* (Toronto: McClelland and Stewart, 1976), pp. 83–105. **3006**

Doucet, Michael J., "Building the Victorian City: The Process of Land Development in Hamilton, Ontario, 1847–1881," Ph.D. diss., University of Toronto, 1977. **3007**

Doucet, Michael J., "The Role of the *Spectator* in Shaping Attitudes towards Land in Hamilton, Ontario, 1847–1881," *Histoire sociale/Social History*, vol. 12, 24 (1979), pp. 431–443. **3008**

Doucet, Michael J., "Speculation and the Physical Expansion of Mid–Nineteenth Century Hamilton," in Gilbert A. Stelter and Alan F. J. Artibise, eds., *Shaping the Urban Landscape: Aspects of the Canadian City-Building Process* (Ottawa: Carleton University Press, 1982), pp. 173–199. **3009**

Weaver, John C., "From Land Assembly to Social Maturity: The Suburban Life of Westdale (Hamilton), Ontario, 1911–1951," in Gilbert A. Stelter and Alan F. J. Artibise, eds., *Shaping the Urban Landscape: Aspects of the Canadian City-Building Process* (Ottawa: Carleton University Press, 1982), pp. 321–355. **3010**

Doucet, Michael J., and John C. Weaver, "Town Fathers and Urban Continuity: The Roots of Community Power and Physical Form in Hamilton, Upper Canada, in the 1830s," *Urban History Review*, vol. 13, 2 (1986), pp. 75–90. Reprinted in J. K. Johnson and B. G. Wilson, eds., *Historical Essays on Upper Canada: New Perspectives* (Ottawa: Carleton University Press, 1989), pp. 425–459. **3011**

London

Jackson, John T., "The House as a Visual Indicator of Social Status Change: The Example of London, Ontario, 1861–1915," Master's thesis, University of Western Ontario, 1973. **3012**

Jackson, John T., "Houses as Urban Artifacts: A Case Study of London, Ontario, 1845–1915," *Ontario Geography*, vol. 12 (1978), pp. 49–68. **3013**

Pompilio, Sergio E., "Suburbanization in London, Ontario, 1927–1977: A Study in Changing Morphology," Master's thesis, University of Western Ontario, 1982. **3014**

Bloomfield, Gerald T., "No Parking Here to Corner: London Reshaped by the Automobile, 1911–1961," *Urban History Review*, vol. 18, 2 (1989), pp. 139–158. **3015**

RECREATION & TOURISM

Killan, Gerald, "Mowat and a Park Policy for Niagara Falls, 1873–1887," in Geoffrey Wall and John S. Marsh, eds., *Recreational Land Use: Perspectives on Its Evolution in Canada* (Ottawa: Carleton University Press, 1982), pp. 220–238. **3016**

Norris, Darrell A., "Reaching the Sublime: Niagara Falls Visitor Origins, 1831–1854," *Journal of American Culture*, vol. 9, 1 (1986), pp. 53–60. **3017**

PLANNING

Bloomfield, Elizabeth, "Reshaping the Urban Landscape: Town Planning Efforts in Kitchener-Waterloo, 1912–1926," in Gilbert A. Stelter and Alan F. J. Artibise, eds., *Shaping the Urban Landscape: Aspects of the Canadian City-Building Process* (Ottawa: Carleton University Press, 1982), pp. 256–303. **3018**

Stelter, Gilbert A., "Guelph and the Early Canadian Town Planning Tradition," *Ontario History*, vol. 77, 2 (1985), pp. 83–106. **3019**

PLACE NAMES

See also **1477**

Jackson, John N., "Names along Ontario's Niagara River Parkway," *Canoma*, vol. 11, 2 (1985), pp. 1–5. **3020**

Jackson, John N., *Names across Niagara* (St. Catherines: Vanwell, 1989), 113 pp. **3021**

NORTHERN ONTARIO

GENERAL

Wonders, William C., "The Penetanguishene Peninsula," *Canadian Geographical Journal*, vol. 37, 3 (1948), pp. 118–129. **3022**

Dean, William G., "Human Geography of the Lower Albany River Basin," *Geographical Bulletin* (Ottawa), vol. 10 (1957), pp. 54–75. **3023**

Usher, Anthony, "Northwestern Ontario in 1900," Master's thesis, University of Toronto, 1973. **3024**

Wightman, W. Robert, *Forever on the Fringe: Six Studies on the Development of Manitoulin Island* (Toronto: University of Toronto Press, 1982), 293 pp. **3025**

Hutchison, Ina E., "The Formation of North Western Ontario, 1791–1912," Master's thesis, Carleton University, 1986. **3026**

NATIVE PEOPLES & WHITE RELATIONS

Harington, C. J., "The Influence of Location on the Development of an Indian Community at the Rapids of the St. Mary's River," Master's thesis, University of Western Ontario, 1979. **3027**

Hoyle, Allan, "Ojibwa Adjustment to Changing Conditions in the Boundary Waters Area: 1763–1873," Master's thesis, York University, 1986. **3028**

Haywood, Norman A., "Palaeo-Indians and the Palaeoenvironments of the Rainy River District, Northwestern Ontario," Master's thesis, University of Manitoba, 1987. **3029**

EXPLORATION & MAPPING

Hennig, Richard, "Das Wikingergrab von Beardmore (Ontario)," *Petermanns Geographische Mitteilungen*, vol. 85, 11–12 (1939), pp. 355–356. **3030**

Sebert, Lou M., "The Mapping of Northern Ontario," *Bulletin of the Association of Canadian Map Libraries*, vol. 47 (1983), pp. 1–17. **3031**

POPULAR IMAGES & EVALUATION

See also **1306**

Laskin, Susan L., "The Myth of a Northern Agricultural Frontier in Nineteenth-Century Ontario," Master's thesis, University of Toronto, 1979. **3032**

REGIONAL SETTLEMENT

Rumney, George R., "Settlement of the Nipissing Passageway," Ph.D. diss., University of Michigan, 1947. **3033**

Baine, Richard P., "The Settlement of the Sudbury Region," Master's thesis, University of Toronto, 1952. **3034**

Wall, Geoffrey, "Pioneer Settlement in Muskoka," *Agricultural History*, vol. 44, 4 (1970), pp. 393–400. **3035**

Watson, Denis M., "Frontier Movement and Economic Development in Northeastern Ontario, 1850–1914," Master's thesis, University of British Columbia, 1971. **3036**

Pugh, Donald E., "Ontario's Great Clay Belt Hoax," *Canadian Geographical Journal*, vol. 90, 1 (1975), pp. 19–24. **3037**

Rasmussen, M. A., "The Geographic Impact of Finnish Settlement on the Thunder Bay Area of Northern Ontario," Master's thesis, University of Alberta, 1978. **3038**

Harvey, S. J., "The Role of Agriculture in the Settlement of Rural Northern Ontario: The Algoma Case Study," Master's thesis, University of Western Ontario, 1985. **3039**

Wightman, Nancy M., and W. Robert Wightman, "Agricultural Settlements in Northwestern Ontario to 1930," *Papers and Records of the Thunder Bay Historical Museum Society*, vol. 17 (1989), pp. 44–63. **3040**

ECONOMIC DEVELOPMENT

Nuttall, Alan J., "The Success of Government Settlement Policy on the Ottawa Huron Territory, 1853–1898," Master's thesis, Queen's University, 1981. **3041**

Wallace, Iain, "The Canadian Shield: The Development of a Resource Frontier," in Larry D. McCann, ed., *Heartland and Hinterland: A Geography of Canada* (Scarborough, Ont.: Prentice-Hall Canada, 1982), pp. 373–409. Revised ed. 1989, pp. 442–481. **3042**

Troughton, Michael J., "The Failure of Agricultural Settlement in Northern Ontario," *Nordia*, vol. 17, 1 (1983), pp. 141–151. **3043**

RESOURCE MANAGEMENT

Lytwyn, Victor P., T. E. Holzkamn, and L. G. Waisberg, "Rainy River Sturgeon: An Ojibway Resource in the Fur Trade Economy," *Canadian Geographer*, vol. 32, 3 (1988), pp. 194–205. **3044**

LAND & LAND USE

Wall, Geoffrey, "Land Use Interrelationships in Nineteenth Century Muskoka," Master's thesis, University of Toronto, 1968. **3045**

Wall, Geoffrey, "Nineteenth-Century Land Use and Settlement on the Canadian Shield Frontier," in David H. Miller and Jerome O. Steffen, eds., *The Frontier: Comparative Studies* (Norman: University of Oklahoma Press, 1977), pp. 227–242. **3046**

EXTRACTIVE ACTIVITY

Wright, Phillip C., "A Historical Geography of Silver and Gold Mining in the Cobalt, the Porcupine, and the Kirkland/Larder Lake Camps of Ontario, with Implications for an Interpretive Program," Master's thesis, Wilfrid Laurier University, 1979. **3047**

Goodier, J. L., "The Nineteenth Century Fisheries of the Hudson's Bay Company Trading Posts on Lake Superior: A Biogeographical Study," *Canadian Geographer*, vol. 28, 4 (1984), pp. 341–357. **3048**

AGRICULTURE

Troughton, Michael J., and Stephen J. Harvey, "The Changing Role of Agriculture in the Algoma District, Northern Ontario," *Nordia*, vol. 20, 1 (1988), pp. 95–104. **3049**

Bonneville, Marc J., "An Integrated Approach to the Study of Agricultural Change on Manitoulin Island," Ph.D. diss., Carleton University, 1989. [1951–1986] **3050**

COMMUNICATIONS & TRADE

Rumney, George R., "The Ottawa-Nipissing Canoe Route in Early Western Travel," *Canadian Geographical Journal*, vol. 42, 1 (1951), pp. 26–33. **3051**

Konarek, Joseph, "Algoma Central and Hudson Bay Railway: The Beginnings," *Ontario History*, vol. 62, 2 (1970), pp. 71–81. **3052**

Wall, Geoffrey, "Transportation in a Pioneer Area: A Note on Muskoka," *Transport History*, vol. 5, 1 (1972), pp. 54–66. **3053**

Osborne, Brian S., and Donald Swainson, *The Sault Ste. Marie Canal: A Chapter in the History of Great Lakes Transport* (Ottawa: Parks Canada, 1986), 148 pp. Also French ed. **3054**

MANUFACTURING & INDUSTRIALIZATION

Barton, Thomas F., "Saxicultural District of the Sudbury Area," *Transactions of the Illinois State Academy of Science*, vol. 35 (1942), pp. 108–110. **3055**

URBAN NETWORKS & URBANIZATION

Dahms, Frederic A., and Carol Hoover, "The Evolution of Settlement Functions in the Southeastern Parry Sound District, 1871–1976," *Canadian Geographer*, vol. 23, 4 (1979), pp. 352–360. **3056**

TOWN GROWTH

Torlone, Joe G., "The Evolution of the City of Timmins: A Single-Industry Community," Master's thesis, Wilfrid Laurier University, 1979. **3057**

Saarinen, Oiva W., "Single Sector Communities in Northern Ontario: The Creation and Planning of Dependent Towns," in Gilbert A. Stelter and Alan F. J. Artibise, eds., *Power and Place: Canadian Urban Development in the North American Context* (Vancouver: University of British Columbia Press, 1986), pp. 219–264. **3058**

Saarinen, Oiva W., "Sudbury: A Historical Case Study of Multiple Urban-Economic Transformation," *Ontario History*, vol. 82, 1 (1990), pp. 53–81. **3059**

URBAN SOCIAL STRUCTURE

Stelter, Gilbert A., "Community Development in Toronto's Commercial Empire: The Industrial Towns of the Nickel Belt, 1883–1931," *Laurentian University Review*, vol. 6, 3 (1974), pp. 3–54. **3060**

Goltz, Eileen A., "A Corporate View of Housing and Community in a Company Town: Copper Cliff, 1886–1920," *Ontario History*, vol. 82, 1 (1990), pp. 29–52. **3061**

RECREATION & TOURISM

Wolfe, Roy I., "The Summer Resorts of Ontario in the Nineteenth Century," *Ontario History*, vol. 54 (1962), pp. 149–160. **3062**

Wall, Geoffrey, "Recreational Land Use in Muskoka," *Ontario Geography*, vol. 11 (1977), pp. 11–28. Reprinted in Geoffrey Wall and John Marsh, eds., *Recreational Land Use: Perspectives on Its*

Evolution in Canada (Ottawa: Carleton University Press, 1982), pp. 139–154.   **3963**

Benidickson, Jamie, "Northern Ontario's Tourist Frontier," in Geoffrey Wall and John S. Marsh, eds., *Recreational Land Use: Perspectives on Its Evolution in Canada* (Ottawa: Carleton University Press, 1982), pp. 155–174.   **3064**

Johnston, M., "Historical Recreation Geography of Tourist Lodges: The Example of Algonquin Park,

Ontario," *Recreation Research Review*, vol. 10, 3 (1983), pp. 22–33.   **3065**

PLANNING

Saarinen, Oiva W., "Provincial Land Use Planning Initiatives in the Town of Kapuskasing," *Urban History Review*, vol. 10, 1 (1981), pp. 1–16.   **3066**

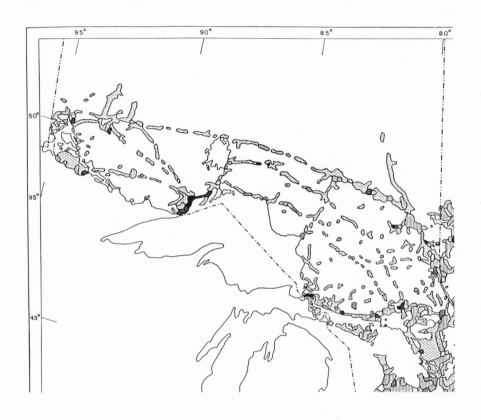

PRAIRIE PROVINCES

GENERAL

Morice, A. G., "L'ouest canadien: Esquisse géographique, ethnographique, historique, et demographique," *Bulletin de la Société Neuchateloise de géographie*, vol. 37 (1928), pp. 5–58; 38 (1929), pp. 1–44.   3067

Lenz, Karl, *Die Prärieprovinzen Kanadas: Der Wandel der Kulturlandschaft von der Kolonisation bis zur Gegenwart unter dem Einfluß der Industrie* (Marburg: Marburger Geographische Schriften, no. 21, 1965), 256 pp.   3068

Warkentin, John H., "Western Canada in 1886," *Papers Read before the Historical and Scientific Society of Manitoba*, ser. 3, vol. 20 (1963–1964), pp. 85–116. Reprinted in R. Louis Gentilcore, ed., *Canada's Changing Geography* (Scarborough, Ont.: Prentice-Hall of Canada, 1967), pp. 56–82.   3069

Warkentin, John H., "Late Nineteenth Century Geographic Patterns on the Canadian Prairies," *Monograph*, vol. 3 (1965–1966), pp. 14–29.   3070

Richards, J. Howard B., "The Prairie Region," in John H. Warkentin, ed., *Canada: A Geographical Interpretation* (Toronto: Methuen, 1968), pp. 396–437.   3071

Clark, Andrew Hill, "Historical and Geographical Perspectives," in David K. Elton, ed., *One Prairie Province? A Question for Canada* (Lethbridge: University of Lethbridge, 1970), pp. 325–336.   3072

Warkentin, John H., "Time and Place in the Western Interior," *Arts Canada*, vol. 29, 3 (1972), pp. 20–37.   3073

Kaye, Barry, and D. Wayne Moodie, "Geographical Perspectives on the Canadian Plains," in Richard Allen, ed., *A Region of the Mind: Interpreting the Western Canadian Plains* (Regina: University of Regina, Canadian Plains Research Centre, 1973), pp. 17–46.   3074

Palmer, Howard, and Donald Smith, eds., *The New Provinces: Alberta and Saskatchewan, 1905–1980* (Vancouver: Tantalus Research, Proceedings of the Twelfth Western Canada Studies Conference, B.C. Geographical Series, no. 30, 1980), 227 pp.   3075

Rosenvall, Lynn A., and Simon M. Evans, eds., *Essays on the Historical Geography of the Canadian West: Regional Perspectives on the Settle-* *ment Process* (Calgary: University of Calgary Department of Geography, 1987), 195 pp.   3076

Rees, Ronald, *New and Naked Land: Making the Prairies Home* (Saskatoon: Western Producer Prairie Books, 1988), 188 pp.   3077

ENVIRONMENTAL CHANGE

See also 1157, 1166, 1169–1174

Watts, F. B., "The Natural Vegetation of the Southern Great Plains of Canada," *Geographical Bulletin* (Ottawa), no. 14 (1960), pp. 25–43.   3078

Nelson, J. Gordon, "Man and Landscape in the Western Plains of Canada," *Canadian Geographer*, vol. 11, 4 (1967), pp. 251–264. Reprinted in J. Gordon Nelson, *Man's Impact on the Western Canadian Landscape* (Toronto: McClelland and Stewart, Carleton Library Series, no. 90, 1976), pp. 19–32.   3079

Catchpole, Alan J. W., D. Wayne Moodie, and Barry Kaye, "Content Analysis: A Method for Identification of Dates of First Freezing and First Breaking from Descriptive Accounts," *Professional Geographer*, vol. 22, 5 (1970), pp. 252–257.   3080

Nelson, J. Gordon, "Some Reflections on Man's Impact on the Landscape of the Canadian Prairies and Nearby Areas," in Peter J. Smith, ed., *The Prairie Provinces* (Toronto: University of Toronto Press, 1972), pp. 33–50.   3081

Nelson, J. Gordon, "Animals, Fire, and Landscape in the Northwestern Plains of North America in Pre- and Early-European Days," in Anthony W. Rasporich and H. C. Klassen, eds., *Prairie Perspectives 2: Selected Papers of the Western Canadian Studies Conferences, 1970, 71* (Toronto: Holt, Rinehart and Winston, 1973), pp. 63–79.   3082

Nelson, J. Gordon, *The Last Refuge* (Montreal: Harvest House, 1973), 230 pp. [Focus on Indians in Saskatchewan and Alberta, 1750–1885]   3083

Moodie, D. Wayne, and Arthur J. Ray, "Buffalo Migrations in the Canadian Plains," *Plains Anthropologist*, vol. 21, 71 (1976), pp. 45–52.   3084

Nelson, J. Gordon, *Man's Impact on the Western Canadian Landscape* (Toronto: McClelland and Stewart, 1976), 205 pp.   3085

Rinn, Dennis L., "The Acquisition, Diffusion, and Distribution of the European Horse among the Blackfeet Tribes in Western Canada," Master's thesis, University of Manitoba, 1976. **3086**

Hildebrand, David V., and Geoffrey A. J. Scott, "Relationships between Moisture Deficiency and Amount of Tree Cover on the Pre-Agricultural Canadian Prairies," *Prairie Forum*, vol. 12, 2 (1987), pp. 203–216. **3087**

NATIVE PEOPLES & WHITE RELATIONS

Ray, Arthur J., "Indian Exploitation of the Forest-Grassland Transition Zone in Western Canada, 1650–1860: A Geographical View of Two Centuries of Change," Ph.D. diss., University of Wisconsin–Madison, 1971. **3088**

Ray, Arthur J., "Indian Adaptations to the Forest-Grassland Boundary of Manitoba and Saskatchewan, 1650–1821: Some Implications for Interregional Migration," *Canadian Geographer*, vol. 16, 1 (1972), pp. 103–118. **3089**

Martel, Gilles, "Quand une majorité devient une minorité: Les métis francophones de l'ouest canadien," *Cahiers de géographie du Québec*, vol. 23, 60 (1979), pp. 73–98. **3090**

McQuillan, D. Aidan, "Creation of Indian Reserves on the Canadian Prairies, 1870–1885," *Geographical Review*, vol. 70, 4 (1980), pp. 379–396. **3091**

Moodie, D. Wayne, "Historic Indian Gardens," *Prairie Gardener*, no. 48 (1987), pp. 122–125. **3092**

White, Pamela M., "Restructuring the Domestic Sphere: Prairie Indian Women on Reserves: Image, Ideology, and State Policy, 1880–1930," Ph.D. diss., McGill University, 1987. **3093**

Decker, Jody F., "Tracing Historical Diffusion Patterns: The Case of the 1780–82 Smallpox Epidemic among the Indians of Western Canada," *Native Studies Review*, vol. 4 (1988), pp. 1–24. **3094**

Doige, Gary B., "Warfare Patterns of the Assiniboine to 1809," Master's thesis, University of Manitoba, 1989. **3095**

Decker, Jody F., "The Diffusion and Cumulative Impact of Acute Infectious Diseases Affecting the Natives on the Northern Plains of the Western Interior of Canada, 1774–1839," Ph.D. diss., York University, 1990. **3096**

EXPLORATION & MAPPING

Exploration

Spry, Irene, "Captain John Palliser and the Exploration of Western Canada," *Geographical Journal*, vol. 125, 2 (1959), pp. 149–184. **3097**

Warkentin, John H., *The Western Interior of Canada: A Record of Geographical Discovery, 1612–1917* (Toronto: McClelland and Stewart, 1964), 304 pp. **3098**

Goldsmith, Ronald, "The Palliser and Hind Expedition, 1857–1860: Application of a Content Analysis Technique," Master's thesis, York University, 1972. **3099**

Spry, Irene, "The Palliser Expedition," in Richard C. Davis, ed., *Rupert's Land: A Cultural Tapestry* (Waterloo: Wilfried Laurier University Press, 1988), pp. 195–212. **3100**

Mapping

Sebert, Lou M., "The Three-Mile Sectional Maps of the Canadian West," *Canadian Cartographer*, vol. 4, 2 (1967), pp. 112–119. **3101**

Ray, Arthur J., "Early French Mapping of the Western Interior of Canada: A View from Hudson Bay," *Canadian Cartographer*, vol. 9, 2 (1972), pp. 85–98. **3102**

Richtik, James M., "Mapping the Quality of Land for Agriculture in Western Canada," *Great Plains Quarterly*, vol. 5, 4 (1985), pp. 236–248. Reprinted in Frederick C. Luebke, Frances Kaye, and Gary E. Moulton, eds., *Mapping the North American Plains: Essays in the History of Cartography* (Normon: University of Oklahoma Press, 1987), pp. 161–171. **3103**

Murray, Jeffrey S., "The Map-Makers," *Beaver*, vol. 69, 1 (1989), pp. 14–27. **3104**

POPULAR IMAGES & EVALUATION

See also 1307

Ruggles, Richard I., "The West of Canada in 1763: Imagination and Reality," *Canadian Geographer*, vol. 15, 3 (1971), pp. 235–261. **3105**

Dunbar, Gary S., "Isotherms and Politics: Perception of the Northwest in the 1850s," in Anthony W. Rasporich and H. C. Klassen, eds., *Prairie Perspectives 2: Selected Papers of the Western Canadian Studies Conferences 1970, 71* (Toronto: Holt, Rinehart and Winston, 1973), pp. 80–101. **3106**

Warkentin, John H., "Steppe, Desert, and Empire," in Anthony W. Rasporich and H. C. Klassen, eds., *Prairie Perspectives 2: Selected Papers of the Western Canadian Studies Conferences, 1970, 71* (Toronto: Holt, Rinehart and Winston, 1973), pp. 102–136. **3107**

Spry, Irene, "Early Visitors to the Canadian Prairies," in Brian W. Blouet and Merlin P. Lawson, eds., *Images of the Plains: The Role of Human Nature in Settlement* (Lincoln: University of Nebraska Press, 1975), pp. 165–180. **3108**

Tyman, John L., "Subjective Surveyors: The Appraisal of Farm Lands in Western Canada, 1870–1930," in Brian W. Blouet and Merlin P. Lawson, eds., *Images of the Plains: The Role of Human Nature in Settlement* (Lincoln: University of Nebraska Press, 1975), pp. 75–100. **3109**

Warkentin, John H., "The Desert Goes North," in Brian W. Blouet and Merlin P. Lawson, eds., *Image of the Plains: The Role of Human Nature in Settlement* (Lincoln: University of Nebraska Press, 1975), pp. 149–164. **3110**

Rees, Ronald, "Images of the Prairie: Landscape Painting and Perception in the Western Interior of Canada," *Canadian Geographer*, vol. 20, 3 (1976), pp. 259–278. **3111**

Jankunis, Frank J., "Perception, Innovation and Adaptation: The Palliser Triangle of Western Canada," *Yearbook of the Association of Pacific Coast Geographers*, vol. 39 (1977), pp. 63–76. **3112**

Lehr, John C., and D. Wayne Moodie, "The Polemics of Pioneer Settlement: Ukrainian Immigration and the Winnipeg Press," *Canadian Ethnic Studies*, vol. 12, 2 (1980), pp. 88–101. **3113**

Rees, Ronald, "Painting, Place, and Identity: A Prairie View," *Western Geographical Series*, vol. 20 (Victoria: University of Victoria Department of Geography, 1982), pp. 117–142. **3114**

Lehr, John C., "Propaganda and Belief: Ukrainian Immigrant Views of the Canadian West," in J. Rosumnyj, ed., *The Ukrainian Experience in Canada* (Winnipeg: University of Manitoba Press and Ukrainian Academy of Arts and Sciences in Canada, 1983), pp. 1–17. **3115**

Rees, Ronald, *Land of Earth and Sky: Landscape Painting of Western Canada* (Saskatoon: Western Producer Prairie Books, 1984), 148 pp. **3116**

Lehr, John C., "Government Perceptions of Ukrainian Immigrants to Western Canada, 1896–1902," *Canadian Ethnic Studies*, vol. 19, 2 (1987), pp. 1–12. **3117**

Warkentin, John H., "Boundary Lines in the Prairie Geographical Imagination," *Western Geography*, vol. 1, 1 (1990), pp. 1–6. **3118**

REGIONAL SETTLEMENT

See also **1320, 1334**

Mackintosh, William A., and W. L. G. Joerg, eds., *Canadian Frontiers of Settlement: Prairie Settlement, the Geographical Setting* (Toronto: Macmillan Co. of Canada, 1934), 242 pp. **3119**

Nelson, Helge M. O., "Kolonisation och befolknings forskjatning inom kanadas prarieprovinser," *Ymer*, vol. 54 (1934), pp. 161–180. **3120**

England, Robert E., *The Colonization of Western Canada: A Study of Contemporary Land Settlement, 1896–1934* (London: P. S. King, 1936), 341 pp. **3121**

Vanderhill, Burke G., "Settlement in the Forest Lands of Manitoba, Saskatchewan, and Alberta: A Geographic Analysis," Ph.D. diss., University of Michigan, 1956. **3122**

Tyman, John L., "Patterns of Western Land Settlement," *Transactions of the Historical and Scientific Society of Manitoba*, ser. 3, no. 28 (1971–1972), pp. 117–136. **3123**

Warkentin, John H., "Water and Adaptive Strategies in Settling the Canadian West," *Transactions of the Historical and Scientific Society of Manitoba*, ser. 3, no. 28 (1971–1972), pp. 59–74. **3124**

Tyman, John L., *By Section Township and Range: Studies in Prairie Settlement* (Brandon: Assiniboine Historical Society, 1972), 250 pp. **3125**

Lehr, John C., "The Rural Settlement Behavior of Ukrainian Pioneers in Western Canada, 1891–1914," in Brenton M. Barr, ed., *Western Canadian Research in Geography: The Lethbridge Papers*(Vancouver: Tantalus Research, B.C. Geographical Series, no. 21, 1975), pp. 51–66. **3126**

Norrie, Kenneth H., "The Rate of Settlement of the Canadian Prairies, 1870–1911," *Journal of Economic History*, vol. 35, 2 (1975), pp. 410–427. **3127**

Rees, Ronald, "Eccentric Settlements in the Canadian West, 1882–1900," *History Today*, vol. 27, 9 (1977), pp. 607–614. **3128**

Schlichtmann, Hansgeorg, "Rural Settlements in the Prairie Region of Canada," *Proceedings of the Royal Geographical Society of Australia, South Australian Branch*, vol. 78 (1977), pp. 29–49. **3129**

Lehr, John C., "Pattern and Process of Ukrainian Rural Settlement in Western Canada, 1892–1914," Ph.D. diss., University of Manitoba, 1978. **3130**

Vanderhill, Burke G., "The Passing of the Pioneer Fringe in Western Canada," *Geographical Review*, vol. 72, 2 (1982), pp. 200–217. **3131**

Rees, Ronald, "Wascana Centre: A Metaphor for Prairie Settlement," *Journal of Garden History*, vol. 3, 3 (1983), pp. 219–232. **3132**

Carlyle, William J., "Rural Change in the Prairies," in Guy M. Robinson, ed., *A Social Geography of Canada: Essays in Honour of J. Wreford Watson* (Edinburgh: North British Publishing, 1988), pp. 243–267. Also Toronto: Dundurn Press, 1991, pp. 332–358. [Focus on 1901–1983] **3133**

Lewry, Marilyn L., "The Invisible Partner: The Influence of the Financial Sponsor on the Development of Three Nineteenth Century Hebridean Colonies in Western Canada," *Regina Geographical Studies*, no. 5 (1988), pp. 1–23. **3134**

POPULATION

Merrill, Lesly I., "Population Distribution in the Riding Mountains, Duck Mountains, and Adjacent Plains in Manitoba and Saskatchewan, 1870–1946," Master's thesis, McGill University, 1953. **3135**

Bjork, K. O., "Scandinavian Migration to the Canadian Prairie Provinces, 1893–1914," *North American Studies*, vol. 26 (1974), pp. 3–30. **3136**

Evans, Simon M., "Some Developments in the Diffusion Patterns of Hutterite Colonies," *Canadian Geographer*, vol. 29, 4 (1985), pp. 327–339. **3137**

Widdis, Randy W., "An Evaluation of Canadian Border Crossing Records in the Study of American Migration to the Canadian West," *Proceedings of the Combined Meeting of the Canadian Association of Geographers–Prairie Division and the Association of North Dakota Geographers*, vol. 39 (1989), pp. 18–35. **3138**

RURAL & REGIONAL SOCIAL GEOGRAPHY

Common, S., "The Economics of the Settlement of the Prairie Provinces of Canada, 1900–1931," Ph.D. diss., University of London, 1933. **3139**

Dawson, C. A., *Group Settlement: Ethnic Communities in Western Canada*, vol. 7 of W. A. Mackintosh and W. L. G. Joerg, eds., *Canadian Frontiers of Settlement*, 9 vols. (Toronto: Macmillan Co. of Canada, 1936), 395 pp. **3140**

Lehmann, Heinz, "Zur Karte des Deutschtums in den kanadischen Prärieprovinzen," *Deutsches Archiv für Landes- und Volkforschung*, vol. 2 (1938), pp. 859–866. **3141**

Stubbs, G. M., "Geography of Cultural Assimilation in the Prairie Provinces," Ph.D. diss., University of Oxford, 1965. **3142**

Wise, M., "An Areal Analysis of French-Canadian Settlement and Linguistic Assimilation in the Prairie Provinces," Master's thesis, University of British Columbia, 1969. **3143**

Tracie, Carl J., "Ethnicity and the Prairie Environment: Patterns of Old Colony Mennonite and Doukhobor Settlement," in R. Allen, ed., *Man and Nature on the Prairies* (Regina: University of Regina, Canadian Plains Research Centre, no. 6, 1976), pp. 46–65. **3144**

Schlichtmann, Hansgeorg, "Ethnic Themes in Geographical Research in Western Canada," *Canadian Ethnic Studies*, vol. 9, 2 (1977), pp. 9–41. **3145**

Lehr, John C., "The Canadian Ukraine," *Canadian Golden West*, vol. 13, 3 (1978), pp. 8–12. **3146**

Lehr, John C., "The Ukrainian Presence on the Prairies," *Canadian Geographical Journal*, vol. 97, 2 (1978), pp. 28–33. **3147**

Hufferd, James L., "Pioneering: Cultural Integration on the Canadian Prairie in the Pioneer Period," Ph.D. diss., University of Minnesota, 1979. **3148**

Rees, Ronald, "In a Strange Land: Homesick Pioneers on the Canadian Prairie," *Landscape*, vol. 26, 3 (1982), pp. 1–9. [Focus on 1920–1980] **3149**

Lehr, John C., "Kinship and Society in the Ukrainian Pioneer Settlement of the Canadian West," *Canadian Geographer*, vol. 29, 3 (1985), pp. 207–219. Reprinted in Graeme Wynn, ed., *People, Places, Patterns, Processes: Geographical Perspectives on the Canadian Past* (Toronto: Copp Clark Pitman, 1990), pp. 139–160. **3150**

Lehr, John C., "Wrestlers of the Spirit," *Horizon Canada*, vol. 6, 64 (1986), pp. 1526–1531. **3151**

POLITICAL & ADMINISTRATIVE GEOGRAPHY

See also **1389**

Richtik, James M., "The Policy Framework for Settling the Canadian West, 1870–1880," *Agricultural History*, vol. 49, 4 (1975), pp. 613–628. **3152**

Lehr, John C., "The Government and the Immigrant: Perspectives on Ukrainian Block Settlement in the Canadian West," *Canadian Ethnic Studies*, vol. 9, 2 (1977), pp. 42–52. **3153**

Lehr, John C., "Government Coercion in the Settlement of Ukrainian Immigrants in Western Canada," *Prairie Forum*, vol. 8, 2 (1983), pp. 179–194. **3154**

Carlyle, William J., "The Changing Geography of Administrative Units for Rural Schooling and Local Government on the Canadian Prairies," *Prairie Forum*, vol. 12, 1 (1987), pp. 5–35. **3155**

ECONOMIC DEVELOPMENT

See also **1400**

Winkler, Ernst, "Die canadischen Prärieprovinzen im industriellen Umbruch," *Geographica Helvetica*, vol. 7 (1952), pp. 235–249. [Focus on 1910–1950] **3156**

Rivizzigno, Victoria L., "The Evolving Dimensions of a Canadian Prairie Regionalization: A Factor Analysis of Canadian Census Data, 1901 to 1961," Master's thesis, State University of New York–Buffalo, 1972. **3157**

Barr, Brenton M., and John C. Lehr, "The Western Interior: The Transformation of a Hinterland Region," in Larry D. McCann, ed., *Heartland and Hinterland: A Geography of Canada* (Scarborough, Ont.: Prentice-Hall Canada, 1982), pp. 251–293. Revised ed. 1987, pp. 287–349. **3158**

Ray, Arthur J., "The Northern Great Plains: Pantry of the Northwestern Fur Trade, 1774–1885," *Prairie Forum*, vol. 9, 2 (1984), pp. 263–280. **3159**

Eagle, John A., *The Canadian Pacific Railroad and the Development of Western Canada, 1896–1914* (Montreal: McGill-Queen's University Press, 1989), 325 pp. **3160**

RESOURCE MANAGEMENT

See also **1405**

Norbeck, C., and J. Gordon Nelson, "Canadian Conservation and the Cypress Hills," *Prairie Forum*, vol. 1, 1 (1976), pp. 47–58. **3161**

Spry, Irene, "The Great Transformation: The Disappearance of the Commons in Western Canada," in R. Allen, ed., *Man and Nature on the Prairies* (Regina: University of Regina, Canadian Plains Resource Centre, no. 6, 1976), pp. 21–45. **3162**

Kaye, Barry, and D. Wayne Moodie, "The Psoralea Food Resource of the Northern Plains," *Plains Anthropologist*, vol. 23, 82, pt. 1 (1978), pp. 329–336. **3163**

Kaye, Barry, and D. Wayne Moodie, "Rooting for the Truth: A Reply to Reid on the Importance and Distribution of Psoralea Esculenta," *Plains Anthropologist*, vol. 26, 91 (1981), pp. 81–83. **3164**

LAND & LAND USE

Sebert, Lou M., "The History of the Rectangular Township of the Canadian Prairies," *Canadian Surveyor*, vol. 17, 5 (1963), pp. 380–389. **3165**

Lehr, John C., "Land's Sakes," *Horizon Canada*, vol. 3, 36 (1985), pp. 854–859. **3166**

EXTRACTIVE ACTIVITY

Judd, Carol M., and Arthur J. Ray, eds., *Old Trails and New Directions: Papers of the Third North American Fur Trade Conference* (Toronto: University of Toronto Press, 1980), 337 pp. **3167**

Freeman, Donald B., and Frances L. Dungey, "A Spatial Duopoly: Competition in the Western Canadian Fur Trade, 1770–1835," *Journal of His-* *torical Geography*, vol. 7, 3 (1981), pp. 252–270. **3168**

AGRICULTURE

See also **1415**

Baker, Oliver E., "Agricultural Regions of North America," an eleven-part work which appeared serially in *Economic Geography*, from 1926 to 1932; most parts deal with regions defined wholly within the United States (and are individually listed in the UNITED STATES section), but one part includes significant portions of the prairie provinces of Canada: "Part VI: The Spring Wheat Region," vol. 4, 4 (1928), pp. 399–433. **3169**

Brayer, Herbert O., "British Cattle Ranches in America," *Geographical Magazine*, vol. 20, 4 (1947), pp. 125–131. **3170**

Johnson, Charles W., "Relative Decline of Wheat in the Prairie Provinces of Canada," *Economic Geography*, vol. 24, 3 (1948), pp. 209–216. **3171**

Schott, Carl, "Wandlungen der Landwirtschaft in den kanadischen Prärieprovinzen," *Tagungsberichte und Wissenschaftlichen Abhandlungen des Deutschen Geographentages Essen 1953* (Wiesbaden: Franz Steiner Verlag, 1955), pp. 83–95. Reprinted in Karl Lenz and Alfred Pletsch, eds., *Kanada: Wirtschafts- und siedlungsgeographische Entwicklungen und Probleme von Carl Schott* (Berlin: Dietrich Reimer Verlag, 1985), pp. 53–74. **3172**

Warkentin, John H., "Dry Farmers on the Canadian Plains," *Geographical Magazine*, vol. 45, 6 (1973), pp. 443–450. **3173**

Evans, Simon M., "American Cattlemen on the Canadian Range, 1874 to 1914," *Prairie Forum*, vol. 4, 1 (1974), pp. 121–135. **3174**

Evans, Simon M., "The Passing of a Frontier: Ranching in the Canadian West, 1882–1912," Ph.D. diss., University of Calgary, 1976. **3175**

Evans, Simon M., "Stocking the Canadian Range," *Alberta History*, vol. 26, 3 (1978), pp. 1–8. **3176**

Evans, Simon M., "Canadian Beef for Victorian Britain," *Agricultural History*, vol. 53, 4 (1979), pp. 748–762. **3177**

Evans, Simon M., "The Origin of Ranching in Western Canada: American Diffusion or Victorian Transplant?" *Great Plains Quarterly*, vol. 3, 2 (1983), pp. 79–91. Reprinted in Lynn A. Rosenvall and Simon M. Evans, eds., *Essays on the Historical Geography of the Canadian West: Regional Perspectives on the Settlement Process* (Calgary: University of Calgary Department of Geography, 1987), pp. 70–94. **3178**

Evans, Simon M., "The End of the Open Range Era in Western Canada," *Prairie Forum*, vol. 8, 1 (1983), pp. 71–87. **3179**

Sundstrom, Marvin, "Geographical Aspects of Dominion Government Creameries in the Northwest Territories, 1897–1905," *Prairie Forum*, vol. 10, 1 (1985), pp. 129–146. **3180**

Keddie, Philip D., "The Changing Varietal Composition of Prairie Wheat Production, 1941–1985," *Prairie Forum*, vol. 15, 1 (1990), pp. 103–122. **3181**

LANDSCAPE

General

Moodie, D. Wayne, "The Prairie Landscape," *Beaver*, Outfit 309, 3 (1978), pp. 4–8. **3182**

Rees, Ronald, "Nostalgic Reaction and the Canadian Prairie Landscape," *Great Plains Quarterly*, vol. 2, 3 (1982), pp. 157–167. **3183**

Holdsworth, Deryck W., and John C. Everitt, "Bank Branches and Elevators: Expressions of Big Corporations in Small Prairie Towns," *Prairie Forum*, vol. 13, 2 (1988), pp. 173–190.
3184

Burley, David, and Gayle Horsfall, "Vernacular Houses and Farmsteads of the Canadian Métis," *Journal of Cultural Geography*, vol. 10, 1 (1989), pp. 19–34. **3185**

Ethnic signatures

Lehr, John C., "Changing Ukrainian House Styles," *Alberta History*, vol. 23, 1 (1975), pp. 25–29. **3186**

Schlichtmann, Hansgeorg, "The 'Ethnic Architecture in the Prairies' Conference: A Report and a Geographer's Reflections," *Prairie Forum*, vol. 1 (1976), pp. 69–75. **3187**

Lehr, John C., "The Log Buildings of Ukrainian Settlers in Western Canada," *Prairie Forum*, vol. 5, 2 (1980), pp. 183–196. **3188**

Lehr, John C., "Colour Preferences and Building Decoration among Ukrainians in Western Canada," *Prairie Forum*, vol. 6, 2 (1981), pp. 203–206. **3189**

Lehr, John C., "Ukrainian Vernacular Architecture in Western Canada," *Papers and Proceedings of the Society for the Study of Architecture in Canada* (Ottawa: SSAC, 1981), pp. 8–21. **3190**

Lehr, John C., "The Landscape of Ukrainian Settlement in the Canadian West," *Great Plains Quarterly*, vol. 2, 2 (1982), pp. 94–105. **3191**

Lehr, John C., "Ukrainians," in Dell Upton, ed., *America's Architectural Roots: Ethnic Groups That Built America* (Washington: Preservation Press, National Trust for Historic Preservation, 1986), pp. 160–165. **3192**

Lehr, John C., "The Ukrainian Sacred Landscape: A Metaphor of Survival and Acculturation," *Material History Bulletin*, vol. 29 (1989), pp. 3–11.
3193

COMMUNICATIONS & TRADE

See also **1432**

Mason, R. G., "Transport Changes and Settlement Growth in the Canadian Northwest," Master's thesis, University of Western Ontario, 1974.
3194

Kerr, Donald G., "Wholesale Trade on the Canadian Plains in the Late Nineteenth Century: Winnipeg and Its Competition," in Howard Palmer, ed., *The Settlement of the West* (Calgary: University of Calgary Press, 1977), pp. 130–152. **3195**

Kaye, Barry, and John A. Alwin, "The Beginnings of Wheeled Transport in Western Canada," *Great Plains Quarterly*, vol. 4, 2 (1984), pp. 121–134. **3196**

Darby, Peter A., "From River Boats to Rail Lines: Circulation Patterns in the Canadian West during the Last Quarter of the Nineteenth Century," in Lynn A. Rosenvall and Simon M. Evans, eds., *Essays on the Historical Geography of the Canadian West: Regional Perspectives on the Settlement Process* (Calgary: University of Calgary Department of Geography, 1987), pp. 7–26.
3197

Everitt, John C., "The End of the Line: The Brandon, Saskatchewan, and Hudson's Bay Railway," in R. Keith Semple and Lawrence Martz, eds., *Prairie Geography, Saskatchewan Geography* (Saskatoon: University of Saskatchewan, Department of Geography, Publication no. 2, 1989), pp. 1–22. **3198**

Everitt, John C., Roberta Kempthorne, and Charles Schafer, "Controlled Aggression: James J. Hill and the Brandon, Saskatchewan, and Hudson's Bay Railway," *North Dakota History*, vol. 56, 2 (1989), pp. 3–19. **3199**

URBAN NETWORKS & URBANIZATION

Lenz, Karl, "Die Großstädte im Mittleren Westen Kanadas: Ihre Entwicklung und Stellung innerhalb der Provinzen," *Geographische Zeitschrift*, vol. 51, 4 (1963), pp. 301–323. Revised and translated as "Large Urban Places in the Prairie Provinces: Their Development and Location," in R. Louis Gentilcore, ed., *Canada's Changing Geography* (Scarborough, Ont.: Prentice-Hall of Canada, 1967), pp. 199–211. **3200**

McCann, Larry D., "Urban Growth in Western Canada, 1881–1961," *Albertan Geographer*, 5 (1969), pp. 65–74.   **3201**

White-Lobsinger, Teresa, "Statistical Correlates of Urban Growth in the Canadian Prairie Region, 1941–1971," Master's thesis, Carleton University, 1978.   **3202**

Selwood, H. John, and Evelyn Baril, "The Hudson's Bay Company and Prairie Town Development, 1870–1888," in Alan F. J. Artibise, ed., *Town and City: Aspects of Western Canadian Urban Development* (Regina: University of Regina, Canadian Plains Research Centre, Canadian Plains Studies, no. 10, 1981), pp. 61–94.   **3203**

Artibise, Alan F. J., "The Urban West: The Evolution of Prairie Towns and Cities to 1930," in Gilbert A. Stelter and Alan F. J. Artibise, eds., *The Canadian City: Essays in Urban History* (Ottawa: Carleton University Press, 1984), pp. 138–164.   **3204**

Smith, Peter J., "Urban Development Trends in the Prairie Provinces," in Anthony W. Rasporich, ed., *The Making of the Modern West: Western Canada since 1945* (Calgary: University of Calgary Press, 1984), pp. 133–144.   **3205**

Wiesinger, Judith P., "Towards a Study of Prairie Urbanization," *Western Canadiana Newsletter*, no. 16 (1984), pp. 4–5.   **3206**

TOWN GROWTH

Forward, Charles N., "Regina and Saskatoon as Retirement Centres," *Urban History Review*, no. 1–78 (1978), pp. 9–17.   **3207**

URBAN SOCIAL STRUCTURE

Careless, J. Maurice S., "Aspects of Urban Life in the West, 1870–1914," in A. W. Rasporich and H. C. Klassen, eds., *Prairie Perspectives 2: Selected Papers of the Western Canadian Studies Conferences, 1970, 71* (Toronto: Holt, Rinehart and Winstone, 1973), pp. 25–40.   **3208**

TOWNSCAPE

Smith, Peter J., "Changing Forms and Patterns in the Cities," in Peter J. Smith, ed., *The Prairie Provinces* (Toronto: University of Toronto Press, 1972), pp. 99–117.   **3209**

Artibise, Alan F. J., "Continuity and Change: Elites and Prairie Urban Development, 1914–1950," in Alan F. J. Artibise and Gilbert A. Stelter, eds., *The Usable Urban Past: Planning and Politics in the Modern Canadian City* (Toronto: Macmillan, 1979), pp. 130–154.   **3210**

Artibise, Alan F. J., "In Pursuit of Growth: Municipal Boosterism and Urban Development in the Canadian Prairie West, 1871–1913," in Gilbert A. Stelter and Alan F. J. Artibise, eds., *Shaping the Urban Landscape: Aspects of the Canadian City-Building Process* (Ottawa: Carleton University Press, 1982), pp. 116–147.   **3211**

RECREATION & TOURISM

Lehr, John C., "Preservation of the Ethnic Landscape in Western Canada," *Prairie Forum*, vol. 15, 2 (1990), pp. 263–276.   **3212**

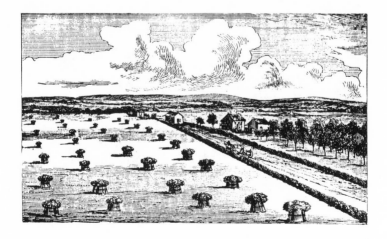

MANITOBA

GENERAL

Loft, Genivera E., "Geographical Influences in the Development of Manitoba," Ph.D. diss., University of Wisconsin, 1925.   **3213**

Warkentin, John H., "The Geography of the Dauphin Area," Master's thesis, University of Toronto, 1954.   **3214**

Richtik, James M., "A Historical Geography of the Interlake Area of Manitoba from 1870 to 1921," Master's thesis, University of Manitoba, 1964.
                                                                                                            3215

Kaye, Barry, "Some Aspects of the Historical Geography of the Red River Settlement from 1812 to 1870," Master's thesis, University of Manitoba, 1967.   **3216**

Warkentin, John H., "Human History of the Glacial Lake Agassiz Region in the Nineteenth Century," in William J. Mayer-Oakes, eds., *Life, Land, and Water: Proceedings of the 1966 Conference on Environmental Studies of the Glacial Lake Agassiz Region* (Winnipeg: University of Manitoba Press, University of Manitoba Department of Anthropology Occasional Paper no. 2, 1967), pp. 325–337.   **3217**

Windsor, D. C., and W. Carlyle, "A Geographical Study of a Township in the Pembina Valley, Manitoba," *Bulletin of the Association of North Dakota Geographers*, vol. 36, 1 (1987), pp. 113–131.   **3218**

ENVIRONMENTAL CHANGE

Bryson, Reid A., and Wayne M. Wendland, "Tentative Climatic Patterns for Some Late Glacial and Post-Glacial Episodes in Central North America," in William J. Mayer-Oakes, eds., *Life, Land, and Water: Proceedings of the 1966 Conference on Environmental Studies of the Glacial Lake Agassiz Region* (Winnipeg: University of Manitoba Press, University of Manitoba Department of Anthropology Occasional Paper no. 2, 1967), pp. 271–298.   **3219**

McDowell, David J., "Settlement and Arboreal Vegetation Change in the Carman-Morden Area of Southern Manitoba," Master's thesis, University of Manitoba, 1981.   **3220**

Suggett, Glen, "Environment and Man in Delta Marsh, Manitoba," in John Rogge, ed., *The Prairies and the Plains: Prospects for the '80s; Proceedings of the Prairie Division of the Cana-*
dian Association of Geographers Annual Meeting, Delta Marsh, Manitoba, September 1980* (Winnipeg: University of Manitoba Department of Geography, Manitoba Geographical Studies, no. 7, 1981), pp. 127–139.   **3221**

Rannie, W. F., "Breakup and Freezeup of the Red River at Winnipeg, Manitoba, Canada, in the Nineteenth Century and Some Climatic Implications," *Climatic Change*, vol. 5, 3 (1983), pp. 283–296.   **3222**

NATIVE PEOPLES & WHITE RELATIONS

Cataudella, Mario, "Le minoranze etniche in America: Il caso degli Indiani del Manitoba," *Rivista geografica italiana*, vol. 80, 1 (1973), pp. 1–27.   **3223**

Ens, Gerhard, "Dispossesion or Adaptation: Migration and Persistence of the Red River Métis, 1835–1890," *Historical Papers, Canadian Historical Association* (1988), pp. 120–144.   **3224**

Tough, Frank, "Economic Aspects of Aboriginal Title in Northern Manitoba: Treaty 5 Adhesions and Métis Scrip," *Manitoba History*, no. 15 (1988), pp. 3–16.   **3225**

Lore, Patricia, "Territory, Subsistence, and the Emergence of a Trading Post Band: Case Study of the Little Red River Cree, 1700–1899," Master's thesis, York University, 1990.   **3226**

Tough, Frank, "Indian Economic Behavior, Exchange and Profits in Northern Manitoba during the Decline of Monopoly, 1870–1930," *Journal of Historical Geography*, vol. 16, 4 (1990), pp. 385–401.   **3227**

EXPLORATION & MAPPING

Lloyd, Trevor, "Mapping Western Canada: The Red River Valley," *Canadian Geographical Journal*, vol. 26, 5 (1943), pp. 230–239.   **3228**

Artibise, Alan F. J., and Edward H. Dahl, *Winnipeg in Maps, 1816–1972* (Ottawa: Public Archives of Canada, National Map Collection, 1975), 80 pp.
                                                                                                            3229

POPULAR IMAGES & EVALUATION

Richtik, James M., "Trees or Grass: Manitoba Settlers' Choices in the 1870s," *Regina Geographical Studies*, no. 3 (1980), pp. 12–21.   **3230**

Richtik, James M., "The Agricultural Frontier in Manitoba: Changing Perceptions of the Resource Value of Prairie and Woodland," *Upper Midwest History*, vol. 3 (1983), pp. 55–61. **3231**

Loewen, Brad, and Gregory G. Monks, "Visual Depictions of Upper Fort Garry," *Prairie Forum*, vol. 13, 1 (1988), pp. 1–24. **3232**

REGIONAL SETTLEMENT

Weir, Thomas R., "Settlement in Southwest Manitoba, 1870–1891," *Papers Read before the Historical and Scientific Society of Manitoba*, ser. 3, vol. 17 (1960–1961), pp. 54–64. **3233**

Vanderhill, Burke G., and David E. Christensen, "The Settlement of New Iceland," *Annals of the Association of American Geographers*, vol. 53, 3 (1963), pp. 350–363. **3234**

Friesen, John, "Expansion of Settlement in Manitoba, 1870–1890," *Papers Read before the Historical and Scientific Society of Manitoba*, ser. 3, vol. 20 (1963–1964), pp. 35–48. **3235**

Weir, Thomas R., "Pioneer Settlement of Southwest Manitoba, 1879–1901," *Canadian Geographer*, vol. 8, 1 (1964), pp. 64–71. **3236**

Carlyle, William J., "The Relationship between Settlement and the Physical Environment in Part of the West Lake Area of Manitoba from 1878 to 1963," Master's thesis, University of Manitoba, 1965. **3237**

Lamb, James E., "Some Aspects of the Settlement Geography of Southern Manitoba," Master's thesis, University of Manitoba, 1970. **3238**

Rogge, John R., and D. Wayne Moodie, "Luftbild Selkirk, Manitoba," *Erde*, vol. 101, 2 (1970), pp. 87–91. **3239**

Richtik, James M., "The Historical Geography of Southern Manitoba, 1870 to 1886," Ph.D. diss., University of Minnesota, 1971. **3240**

Richtik, James M., "Manitoba: Population and Settlement in 1870," in Alexander Paul, ed., *International Geographical Congress, Southern Prairies Field Excursion Background Papers* (Regina: University of Saskatchewan–Regina Campus, 1972), pp. 29–44. **3241**

Tyman, John L., "The Landscape of Early Group Settlements in Western Manitoba," in W. P. Adams and F. M. Helleiner, eds., *International Geography, 1972*, vol. 1, sec. 5, *Historical Geography* (Toronto: University of Toronto Press, for the International Geographical Union, 1972), pp. 1348–1350. **3242**

Warkentin, John H., "Manitoba Settlement Patterns," in Robert M. Irving, ed., *Readings in Canadian Geography* (Toronto: Holt, Rinehart and Winston, 1972), pp. 56–69. **3243**

Richtik, James M., "Prairie Woodland and the Manitoba Escarpment: Settlement and Agricultural Development in Carlton Municipality to 1887," *Red River Valley Historian* (Summer 1976), pp. 16–26. **3244**

Richtik, James M., and Danny Hutch, "When Jewish Settlers Farmed in Manitoba's Interlake Area," *Canadian Geographical Journal*, vol. 95, 1 (1977), pp. 32–35. **3245**

Richtik, James M., and Frank Tough, "Settlement and Development on the Prairie-Woodland Margin: Township 15–2E in Manitoba," *Great Plains–Rocky Mountain Geographical Journal*, vol. 8 (1979), pp. 31–40. **3246**

Kaye, Barry, "Birsay Village on the Assiniboine," *Beaver*, Outfit 312, 3 (1981), pp. 18–21. **3247**

Wiesinger, Judith P., "Agricultural Settlement in Southern Manitoba, 1872 to 1891: A Process-Form Approach," Master's thesis, University of Manitoba, 1981. **3248**

Lehr, John C., "The Peculiar People: Ukrainian Settlement of Marginal Lands in Southeastern Manitoba," in David C. Jones and Ian MacPherson, eds., *Building beyond the Homestead: Rural History on the Prairies* (Calgary: University of Calgary Press, 1985), pp. 29–46. **3249**

Richtik, James M., "Settlement in the 1870s: An Example from Manitoba's Pembina Mountain," in D. C. Jones and Ian MacPherson, eds., *Building beyond the Homestead: Rural History on the Prairies* (Calgary: University of Calgary Press, 1985), pp. 7–28. **3250**

Wiesinger, Judith P., "Modelling the Agricultural Settlement Process of Southern Manitoba, 1872–1891: Some Implications for Settlement Theory," *Prairie Forum*, vol. 10, 1 (1985), pp. 83–104. **3251**

Kaye, Barry, "The Red River Settlement: Lord Selkirk's Isolated Colony in the Wilderness," *Prairie Forum*, vol. 11, 1 (1986), pp. 1–20. **3252**

Richtik, James M., "Settlement of the Riding Mountain Area: 1874–1895," in H. John Selwood and John C. Lehr, eds., *Prairie and Northern Perspectives: Geographical Essays* (Winnipeg: University of Winnipeg Department of Geography, 1989), pp. 59–78. **3253**

Williams, Allison, and John C. Everitt, "An Analysis of Settlement Development in Southwest Manitoba: The Lenore Extension, 1902–1982," in H. John Selwood and John C. Lehr, eds., *Prairie and Northern Perspectives: Geographical Essays* (Winnipeg: University of Winnipeg Department of Geography, 1989), pp. 87–106. **3254**

POPULATION

Hopkinson, M. F., "An Investigation into the Reasons for, and Characteristics of, Population Change in the Area South of Riding Mountain between 1941–1961," Master's thesis, University of Manitoba, 1969.   3255

Evans, Brian M., "Migration into Manitoba, ca.1885–ca.1920, and Some Problems and Questions Which It Raises," in T. J. Kuz, ed., *Winnipeg, 1874–1974: Progress and Prospects* (Winnipeg: Manitoba Department of Industry and Commerce, 1974), pp. 21–26.   3256

Richtik, James M., "Bound for Manitoba," *Horizon Canada*, vol. 6, 68 (1985), pp. 1609–1615.   3257

Richtik, James M., "Chain Migration among Icelandic Settlers in Canada to 1891," *Scandinavian-Canadian Studies*, vol. 2 (1986), pp. 73–88.   3258

Werschler, Timothy J., "An Examination of the Seasonal Birth Pattern in Manitoba: 1920 to the Present," Master's thesis, University of Manitoba, 1990.   3259

RURAL & REGIONAL SOCIAL GEOGRAPHY

See also 1371, 1381

Warkentin, John H., "Mennonite Agricultural Settlements of Southern Manitoba," *Geographical Review*, vol. 49, 3 (1959), pp. 342–368.   3260

Warkentin, John H., "The Mennonite Settlements of Southern Manitoba," Ph.D. diss., University of Toronto, 1960.   3261

Sawatzky, H. Leonhard, "Viability of Ethnic Group Settlement, with Reference to Mennonites in Manitoba," *Canadian Ethnic Studies*, vol. 2, 2 (1970), pp. 147–160.   3262

Ross, Kathleen J., "Studies in Belgian Settlement in Manitoba, 1870–1985," Master's thesis, University of Manitoba, 1987.   3263

POLITICAL & ADMINISTRATIVE GEOGRAPHY

Selwood, H. John, and Evelyn Baril, "Land Policies of the Hudson's Bay Company at Upper Fort Garry, 1869–1879," *Prairie Forum*, vol. 2, 2 (1977), pp. 101–119.   3264

ECONOMIC DEVELOPMENT

Clarke, John, "Population and Economic Activity: A Geographical and Historical Analysis, Based upon Selected Censuses, of the Red River Valley in the Period 1832 to 1856," Master's thesis, University of Manitoba, 1967.   3265

LAND & LAND USE

Tyman, John L., "Historical Geography: The Disposition of Farm Lands in Manitoba," Ph.D. diss., University of Oxford, 1971.   3266

Richtik, James M., et al., "Land Claims in Southwestern Manitoba during the 1880s Boom Period," *Bulletin of the Association of North Dakota Geographers*, vol. 36, 2 (1986), pp. 88–101.   3267

EXTRACTIVE ACTIVITY

Tough, Frank, "Manitoba's Commercial Fisheries: A Study in Development," Master's thesis, McGill University, 1980.   3268

Tough, Frank, "Native People and the Regional Economy of Northern Manitoba, 1870–1930s," Ph.D. diss., York University, 1987.   3269

AGRICULTURE

Fordham, Richard C., "The Structure of Manitoba's Agricultural Geography, 1951–1964: Its Significance in Relation to Projected Future Trends," Master's thesis, University of Manitoba, 1966.   3270

Guertin, Edward G., "A Geographical Study of Farm Depopulation in the Municipality of Eriksdale, 1941–1961," Master's thesis, University of Manitoba, 1968.   3271

Kaye, Barry, "The Settlers' Grand Difficulty: Haying in the Economy of the Red River Settlement," *Prairie Forum*, vol. 9, 1 (1984), pp. 1–12.   3272

LANDSCAPE

Wonders, William C., "Scandinavian Homesteaders," *Alberta History*, vol. 24, 3 (1976), pp. 1–4.   3273

Lehr, John C., "Folk Architecture in Manitoba: Mennonites and Ukrainians," *Bulletin of the Society for the Study of Architecture in Canada*, vol. 11, 2 (1986), pp. 3–5.   3274

COMMUNICATIONS & TRADE

Transport

Russell, William J., "Geography of Roads West of Lake Winnipeg Inter Lake Area," Master's thesis, McGill University, 1951.   3275

Alwin, John A., "The Historic Winnipeg River," *Canadian Geographical Journal*, vol. 92, 1 (1976), pp. 44–51.   3276

Barr, William, "On to the Bay," *Beaver*, Outfit 316, 2 (1985), pp. 43–53. [Hudson Bay Railway]   3277

Trade

Everitt, John C., "The Manitoba Elevator Commission: An Historical Geography," *Proceedings of the Canadian Association of Geographers* (1985), pp. 117–150. **3278**

Everitt, John C., "A 'Tragic Muddle' and a 'Cooperative Success': An Account of Two Elevator Experiments in Manitoba, 1906–1928," *Manitoba History*, vol. 18 (1989), pp. 12–24. **3279**

MANUFACTURING & INDUSTRIALIZATION

Kaye, Barry, "Flour Milling at Red River: Wind, Water, and Steam," *Manitoba History*, vol. 2 (1981), pp. 12–20. **3280**

Selwood, H. John, "Mr. Brydges' Bridges: The Red River and Assiniboine Bridge Company," *Beaver*, Outfit 312, 1 (1981), pp. 14–21. **3281**

URBAN NETWORKS & URBANIZATION

Warkentin, John H., "The Development of Trading Centres in the Mennonite East Reserve of Manitoba," *Shield*, vol. 7 (1956), pp. 24–39. **3282**

Richtik, James M., "Manitoba Service Centers in the Early Settlement Period," *Journal of the Minnesota Academy of Science*, vol. 34, 1 (1967), pp. 17–21. **3283**

Sarbit, Lawrence, "Central Place Structure and Change in Southern Manitoba Communities, 1911–1971," Master's thesis, York University, 1977. **3284**

Wiesinger, Judith P., "The Evolving Urban System in the Canadian Prairies: Manitoba, 1870–1901," Ph.D. diss., Queen's University, 1989. **3285**

TOWN GROWTH

Shrode, Ida May, "The Development and Functioning of the Port of Churchill," *Journal of Geography*, vol. 36, 2 (1937), pp. 54–60. **3286**

Hossé, Hans A., "Areal Growth and Functional Development of Winnipeg, 1870–1913," Master's thesis, University of Manitoba, 1956. **3287**

Weir, Thomas R., "Winnipeg: A City in the Making," in Tony J. Kuz, ed., *Winnipeg 1874–1974: Progress and Prospects* (Winnipeg: Manitoba Department of Industry and Commerce, 1974), pp. 43–63. **3288**

Parsons, G. F., "Winnipeg as a Financial Centre," in Tony J. Kuz, ed., *Winnipeg 1874–1974: Progress and Prospects* (Winnipeg: Manitoba Department of Industry and Commerce, 1974), pp. 189–210. **3289**

Hiebert, Daniel J., "Winnipeg and Its North End, 1895–1935," Master's thesis, University of Toronto, 1980. **3290**

Eaton, Leonard K., "Winnipeg: The Northern Anchor of the Wholesale Trade," *Urban History Review*, vol. 11, 2 (1982), pp. 17–30. **3291**

Everitt, John C., and Christoph Stadel, "Spatial Dimensions of the Urban Growth of Brandon, Manitoba, 1882–1982," *Bulletin of the Association of North Dakota Geographers*, vol. 35 (1985), pp. 1–32. **3292**

Welsted, John, John Everitt, and Christoph Stadel, eds., *Brandon: Geographical Perspectives on the Wheat City* (Regina: University of Regina, Canadian Plains Research Centre, 1988), 224 pp. **3293**

Munski, Douglas C., "Using Hinges, Gateways, and Bridges to Teach Aspects of Winnipeg's Urban Historical Geography," in H. John Selwood and John C. Lehr, eds., *Prairie and Northern Perspectives: Geographical Essays* (Winnipeg: University of Winnipeg Department of Geography, 1989), pp. 107–112. **3294**

Selwood, John, and James M. Richtik, "Dauphin: Emergence of the Urban Cadastre to 1908," in J. Welsted and J. Everitt, eds., *The Dauphin Papers: Research by Prairie Geographers* (Brandon: Department of Geography, Brandon Geographical Studies, no. 1, 1991), pp. 69–78. **3295**

URBAN SOCIAL STRUCTURE

Carlyle, William J., "Growth, Ethnic Groups, and Socio-Economic Areas of Winnipeg," in Tony J. Kuz, ed., *Winnipeg 1874–1974: Progress and Prospects* (Winnipeg: Manitoba Department of Industry and Commerce, 1974), pp. 27–42. **3296**

Artibise, Alan F. J., "Divided City: The Immigrant in Winnipeg Society, 1874–1921," in Gilbert A. Stelter and Alan F. J. Artibise, eds., *The Canadian City: Essays in Urban History* (Toronto: McClelland and Stewart, 1977), pp. 300–336. **3297**

Swales, Stephen J., "The Population, Social, and Spatial Structures of a Frontier City: Winnipeg, 1881," Master's thesis, University of Calgary, 1982. **3298**

Everitt, John C., Marian Westenberger, and Christoph Stadel, "The Development of Brandon's Social Areas, 1881–1919," *Albertan Geographer*, vol. 21 (1985), pp. 79–95. **3299**

TOWNSCAPE

Selwood, H. John, "Urban Development and the Streetcar: Winnipeg, 1881–1914," *Urban History Review*, no. 3–77 (1977), pp. 34–41. **3300**

Selwood, H. John, "Invisible Landscape: Premature Urban Subdivision in the Winnipeg Region," *Regina Geographical Studies*, no. 4 (1984), pp. 41–58.   3301

Selwood, H. John, "A Process Model of Urban Growth and Form," *History and Social Science Teacher*, vol. 19, 4 (1984), pp. 215–222.   3302

Selwood, H. John, "Lots, Plots, and Blocks: Some Winnipeg Examples of Subdivision Design," *Bulletin of the Society for the Study of Architecture in Canada*, vol. 2 (1986), pp. 6–8.   3303

RECREATION & TOURISM

Cavett, M., H. John Selwood, and John C. Lehr, "Social Philosophy and the Early Development of Winnipeg's Parks," *Urban History Review*, vol. 11, 1 (1982), pp. 27–39.   3304

Selwood, H. John, "A Note on the Destruction of Upper Fort Garry," *Manitoba History*, vol. 4 (1982), p. 28.   3305

Lehr, John C., M. Schultz, and H. John Selwood, "An Investment in Health: Children's Summer Camps in the Winnipeg Region," *Recreation Research Review*, vol. 10, 3 (1983), pp. 51–56.
3306

Selwood, H. John, E. Badiuk, and John C. Lehr, "Victoria Beach: Company Resort Town," *Bulletin of the Association of North Dakota Geographers*, vol. 33 (1983), pp. 31–37.   3307

PLACE NAMES

Board on Geographic Names, *Place Names of Manitoba* (Ottawa: J. O. Paternaude, 1933), 95 pp.   3308

Rudnyckyi, Jaroslav Bohdan, *Manitoba: Mosaic of Place Names* (Winnipeg: Canadian Institute of Onomastic Sciences, 1970), 221 pp.   3309

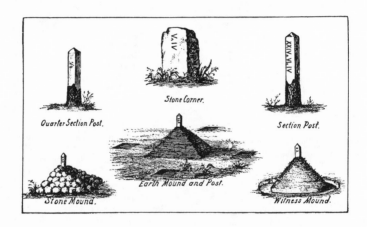

SASKATCHEWAN

GENERAL

McCormick, Patricia L., "An Historical Geography of the District of Assiniboia, Saskatchewan, 1903–1904," Master's thesis, University of Saskatchewan, 1977. 3310

NATIVE PEOPLES & WHITE RELATIONS

Raby, Stewart, "Indian Treaty no. 5 and the Pas Agency, Saskatchewan, Northwest Territories," *Saskatchewan History*, vol. 25, 3 (1972), pp. 92–114. 3311

Raby, Stewart, "Indian Land Surrenders in Southern Saskatchewan," *Canadian Geographer*, vol. 17, 1 (1973), pp. 36–52. 3312

POPULAR IMAGES & EVALUATION

Kadaali, Stephen J., "The *Leader-Post* and the Natural Hazards of 1929–1939: A Content Analysis," Master's thesis, University of Regina, 1977. 3313

REGIONAL SETTLEMENT

Fitzgerald, Denis P., "Pioneer Settlement in Northern Saskatchewan," Ph.D. diss., University of Minnesota, 1965. 3314

King, Gillian M., "A Geographical Analysis of the Settlement of La Ronge, Saskatchewan," Master's thesis, University of Saskatchewan, 1968. 3315

Tracie, Carl J., "Ethnicity and Settlement in Western Canada: Doukhobor Village Settlement in Saskatchewan," in Brenton M. Barr, ed., *Western Canadian Research in Geography: The Lethbridge Papers* (Vancouver: Tantalus Research, B.C. Geographical Series, no. 21, 1975), pp. 67–76. 3316

Powell, T. J., "Northern Settlement, 1929–1935," *Saskatchewan History*, vol. 30, 3 (1977), pp. 81–98. 3317

Grismer, Glen, "Early Squatter Holdings in Saskatchewan, 1878–1886," *Regina Geographical Studies*, no. 3 (1980), pp. 22–30. 3318

McCormick, Patricia L., "Transportation and Settlement: Problems in the Expansion of the Frontier of Saskatchewan and Assiniboia in 1904," *Prairie Forum*, vol. 5, 1 (1980), pp. 1–18. 3319

Vogelsang, Roland R., *Nichtagrarische Pioniersiedlungen in Kanada: Untersuchungen zu* einem Siedlungstyp an Beispielen aus Mittel- und Nordsaskatchewan (Marburg: Marburger Geographische Schriften, no. 82, 1980), 294 pp. 3320

Grismer, Glen B., "Squatter Settlement in Saskatchewan, 1878–1886," Master's thesis, University of Saskatchewan, 1981. 3321

McDonald, John, "Soldier Settlement and Depression Settlement in the Forest Fringe of Saskatchewan," *Prairie Forum*, vol. 6, 1 (1981), pp. 35–56. 3322

Schlichtmann, Hansgeorg, "Saskatchewan Rural Settlements after 1930: Problems and Observations," in John Rogge, ed., *The Prairies and the Plains: Prospects for the '80s: Proceedings of the Prairie Division of the Canadian Association of Geographers Annual Meeting, Delta Marsh, Manitoba, September 1980*(Winnipeg: University of Manitoba Department of Geography, Manitoba Geographical Studies no. 7, 1981), pp. 45–64. 3323

Dick, Lyle, "Factors Affecting Prairie Settlement: A Case Study of Abernathy, Saskatchewan, in the 1890s," *Historical Papers, Canadian Historical Association* (1985), pp. 11–28. 3324

POPULATION

Paul, Alexander H., "Depopulation and Spatial Change in Southern Saskatchewan," in Joseph E. Spencer, ed., *Saskatchewan Rural Themes* (Regina: University of Regina Department of Geograpy, Regina Geographical Studies, no. 1, 1977), pp. 65–86. 3325

Qureshi, Anwar S., "Local Variation in Rural Farm Depopulation in Southwestern Saskatchewan, 1931–1965," Master's thesis, University of Regina, 1977. 3326

Lewry, Marilyn L., "A Study of the Locational Changes among Hebridean Immigrants in Southwest Saskatchewan, 1883–1926," Master's thesis, University of Regina, 1986. 3327

Marauskas, G. Thomas, Milford B. Green, and Robert M. Bone, "Modeling Changes in the In-Migration Patterns of Northern Saskatchewan Communities: A Log-Linear Approach," *Cahiers de géographie du Québec*, vol. 30, 79 (1986), pp. 5367. 3328

Boyd, Stephen, "Prairie Bound: A Geographical Analysis of Migration and Settlement in the Luseland and Hyas-Norquay Areas of Saskatchewan, 1902–1930," Master's thesis, University of Regina, 1989. **3329**

RURAL & REGIONAL SOCIAL GEOGRAPHY

Baker, W. B., "Changing Community Patterns in Saskatchewan," *Canadian Geographical Journal*, vol. 56, 2 (1958), pp. 44–56. Reprinted in Robert M. Irving, ed., *Readings in Canadian Geography* (Toronto: Holt, Rinehart and Winston, 1972), pp. 90–99. **3330**

McQuillan, D. Aidan, "The Importance of Ethnicity among Homesteaders in Central Saskatchewan," *Proceedings of the Canadian Association of Geographers* (1970), pp. 225–232. **3331**

Friesen, Richard J., "Old Colony Mennonite Settlements in Saskatchewan: A Study in Settlement Change," Master's thesis, University of Alberta, 1975. **3332**

Friesen, Richard J., "Saskatchewan Mennonite Settlements: The Modification of an Old World Settlement Pattern," *Canadian Ethnic Studies*, vol. 9, 2 (1977), pp. 72–90. **3333**

POLITICAL & ADMINISTRATIVE GEOGRAPHY

Glenn, John E., "The Role of Government Legislation, Policy and Agency Activity in Irrigation Development: The Cypress Hills Area, 1888–1968," Master's thesis, University of Calgary, 1968.
3334

RESOURCE MANAGEMENT

Turner, Allan R., "How Saskatchewan Dealt with Her Dust Bowl," *Geographical Magazine*, vol. 28, 4 (1955), pp. 182–192. [Focus on 1905–1955]
3335

Blackwell, Ronald Lee, "The Geography of Irrigation Diffusion in the South Saskatchewan River Irrigation District Number 1," Master's thesis, University of Regina, 1989. **3336**

LAND & LAND USE

Stutt, R. A., "Changes in Land Use and Farm Organization in the Prairie Area of Saskatchewan, 1951 to 1966," in Robert M. Irving, ed., *Readings in Canadian Geography* (Toronto: Holt, Rinehart and Winston, 1972), pp. 241–251. **3337**

Schlichtmann, Hansgeorg, "More Farmsteads on Even-Numbered Sections? Observations from Saskatchewan," *Perspectives*, vol. 10, 2 (1975), pp. 5–17. **3338**

Laut, Peter, "The Development of Community Pastures in Saskatchewan: A Case Study in the

Development of Land Policy," in Brenton M. Barr, ed., *New Themes in Western Canadian Geography: The Langara Papers* (Vancouver: Tantalus Research, B.C. Geographical Series, no. 22, 1976), pp. 119–142. [Focus on 1907–1969]
3339

Schlichtmann, Hansgeorg, "Land Disposal and Patterns of Farmstead Distribution in Southern Saskatchewan," in Joseph E. Spencer, ed., *Saskatchewan Rural Themes* (Regina: University of Regina Department of Geograpy, Regina Geographical Studies, no. 1, 1977), pp. 1–24. [Focus on 1920s–1970s] **3340**

EXTRACTIVE ACTIVITY

Freedman, Michael, "A Geographical Analysis of the Estevan (Saskatchewan) Coalfield, 1880–1966," Master's thesis, University of Saskatchewan, 1968. **3341**

COMMUNICATIONS & TRADE

Bloomfield, Gerald T., "I Can See a Car in That Crop: Motorization in Saskatchewan, 1906–1934," *Saskatchewan History*, vol. 37, 1 (1984), pp. 3–24. **3342**

Bloomfield, Gerald T., "Motorization of the New Frontier: The Case of Saskatchewan, Canada, 1906–1934," in Theo Barker, ed., *The Economic and Social Effects of the Spread of Motor Vehicles* (London: Macmillan, 1987), pp. 165–193. **3343**

URBAN NETWORKS & URBANIZATION

Rees, Ronald, "The Small Towns of Saskatchewan," *Landscape*, vol. 18, 3 (1969), pp. 29–33.
3344

TOWN GROWTH

Selwood, H. John, "The Hudson's Bay Company and Fort Qu'Appelle Townsite Development up to 1918," *Regina Geographical Studies*, vol. 3 (1980), pp. 1–11. **3345**

TOWNSCAPE

Mose, John L., "City Council's Decisions in the Morphological Development of Regina, 1903–1930," Master's thesis, University of Regina, 1977. **3346**

Gross, Timothy D., "Infill Housing in Regina: The Roles of the Actors in the Implementation Process," Master's thesis, University of Regina, 1984. **3347**

ALBERTA

GENERAL

Merrill, Gordon C., "The Human Geography of the Lesser Slave Lake Area of Central Alberta," Master's thesis, McGill University, 1951.　　**3348**

Lake, David W., "The Historical Geography of the Coal Branch," Master's thesis, University of Alberta, 1967.　　**3349**

McPherson, Harold J., "Historical Development of the Lower Red Deer Valley, Alberta," *Canadian Geographer*, vol. 12, 3 (1968), pp. 227–240.　　**3350**

Smith, Peter J., "Alberta since 1945: The Maturing Settlement System," in Larry D. McCann, ed., *Heartland and Hinterland: A Geography of Canada* (Scarborough: Prentice-Hall of Canada, 1982), pp. 295–337. Revised ed. 1987, pp. 350–399.　　**3351**

ENVIRONMENTAL CHANGE

Byrne, A. Roger, "Man and Landscape Change in the Banff National Park Area before 1911," Master's thesis, University of Calgary, 1964.　　**3352**

Nelson, J. Gordon, and A. Roger Byrne, "Man as an Instrument of Landscape Change: Fires, Floods, and National Parks in the Bow Valley, Alberta," *Geographical Review*, vol. 56, 2 (1966), pp. 226–238.　　**3353**

Byrne, A. Roger, *Man and Landscape Change in the Banff National Park Area before 1911* (Calgary: University of Calgary, Department of Geography, National Park Series no. 2, Studies in Land Use and Landscape Change, 1968), 173 pp.　　**3354**

Nelson, J. Gordon, "The Effects of European Invasion on Animal Life and Certain Aspects of Landscape in the Bow Valley Area, Alberta: 1750–1885," in J. Gordon Nelson and M. J. Chambers, eds., *Vegetation, Soils, and Wildlife* (Toronto: Methuen, 1969), pp. 219–238.　　**3355**

Noble, L. B., "A Study of the Cultural-Geographic Relationships of the Grizzly Bear and Man in Banff National Park, since c1800," Master's thesis, University of Calgary, 1969.　　**3356**

Nelson, J. Gordon, "Man and Landscape Change in Banff National Park: A National Park Problem in Perspective," in J. Gordon Nelson, ed., *Canadian Parks in Perspective* (Montreal: Harvest House, 1970), pp. 63–98.　　**3357**

NATIVE PEOPLES & WHITE RELATIONS

Ugarenko, Leonard, "The Beaver Indians and the Fur Trade on the Peace River, 1700–1850," Master's thesis, York University, 1979.　　**3358**

Notzke, Claudia, "Indian Land in Southern Alberta," in Thomas E. Ross and Tyrel G. Moore, eds., *A Cultural Geography of North American Indians* (Boulder: Westview, 1987), pp. 107–126.　　**3359**

Notzke, Claudia, "The Past in the Present: Spatial and Land Use Change on Two Indian Reserves," in Lynn A. Rosenvall and Simon M. Evans, eds., *Essays on the Historical Geography of the Canadian West: Regional Perspectives on the Settlement Process* (Calgary: University of Calgary Department of Geography, 1987), pp. 95–121.　　**3360**

Myers, Kenneth M., "The Struggle for a Way of Life: The History of the Lubicon Lake Cree Land Claim, 1899–1989," Master's thesis, Trent University, 1990.　　**3361**

POPULAR IMAGES & EVALUATION

Tracie, Carl J., "Land of Plenty or Poor Man's Land: Environmental Perception and Appraisal Respecting Agricultural Settlement in the Peace River Country, Canada," in Brian W. Blouet and Merlin P. Lawson, eds., *Images of the Plains: The Role of Human Nature in Settlement* (Lincoln: University of Nebraska Press, 1975), pp. 115–124.　　**3362**

Sitwell, O. F. George, "Pioneer Attitudes as Revealed by the Townscape of Strathcona, Alberta," in Brian S. Osborne, ed., *The Settlement of Canada: Origins and Transfers* (Kingston: Queen's University Press, 1976), pp. 236–237.　　**3363**

REGIONAL SETTLEMENT

Jones, Stephen B., "Human Occupance of the Bow-Kicking Horse Region, Canadian Rocky Mountains," Ph.D. diss., Harvard University, 1934.　　**3364**

Leppard, Henry M., "The Settlement of the Peace River Country," *Geographical Review*, vol. 25, 1 (1935), pp. 62–78.　　**3365**

Moodie, D. Wayne, "The St. Albert Settlement: A Study in Historical Geography," Master's thesis, University of Alberta, 1965.   3366

Ehlers, Eckart, *Das nördliche Peace River Country, Alberta, Kanada: Genese und Struktur eines Pionierraumes im borealen Waldland Nordamerikas* (Tübingen: Tübinger Geographische Studien, no. 18, 1965), 246 pp.   3367

Boileau, Gilles, "L'homme et le sol chez les canadiens français de Rivière-la-Paix (Alberta)," *Revue de géographie de Montréal*, vol. 20, 1–2 (1966), pp. 3–26.   3368

Common, Robert, "Early Settlement about Medicine Hat, Alberta," *Geographical Bulletin*, vol. 9, 3 (1967), pp. 284–293.   3369

Tracie, Carl J., "Agricultural Settlement in the South Peace River Area," Master's thesis, University of Alberta, 1967.   3370

Stone, Donald N. G., "The Process of Rural Settlement in the Athabasca Area, Alberta," Master's thesis, University of Alberta, 1970.   3371

Tracie, Carl J., "An Analysis of Three Variables Affecting Farm Location in the Process of Agricultural Settlement: The South Peace River Area," Ph.D. diss., University of Alberta, 1970.   3372

Lehr, John C., "Mormon Settlements in Southern Alberta," Master's thesis, University of Alberta, 1971.   3373

Vogelsang, Roland R., "The Initial Agricultural Settlement of the Morinville-Westlock Area, Alberta," Master's thesis, University of Alberta, 1972.   3374

Proudfoot, Bruce, "Agricultural Settlement in Alberta North of Edmonton," in Anthony W. Rasporich and H. C. Klassen, eds., *Prairie Perspectives 2: Selected Papers of the Western Canadian Studies Conferences, 1970, 71* (Toronto: Holt, Rinehart and Winston, 1973), pp. 142–153.   3375

Ironside, Robert G., et al., eds., *Frontier Settlement* (Edmonton: University of Alberta, Department of Geography, 1974), 283 pp.   3376

Lehr, John C., "The Sequence of Mormon Settlement in Southern Alberta," *Albertan Geographer*, vol. 10 (1974), pp. 20–29.   3377

Bedford, E., "An Historical Geography of Settlement in the North Saskatchewan River Valley, Edmonton," Master's thesis, University of Alberta, 1976.   3378

Ironside, Robert G., and E. Tomasky, "Agriculture and River Lot Settlement in Western Canada: The Case of Pakan (Victoria), Alberta," *Prairie Forum*, vol. 1, 1 (1976), pp. 3–18.   3379

Ironside, Robert G., and K. J. Fairbairn, "The Peace River Region: An Evaluation of a Frontier

Economy," *Geoforum*, vol. 8, 1 (1977), pp. 39–49.   3380

Wonders, William C., "Far Corner of the Strange Empire: Central Alberta on the Eve of Homestead Settlement," *Great Plains Quarterly*, vol. 3, 2 (1983), pp. 92–108.   3381

Wonders, William C., "Mot Kanadas Nordvast: Pioneer Settlement by Scandinavians in Central Alberta," *Geografiska annaler*, vol. 65B, 2 (1983), pp. 129–152.   3382

Evans, Simon M., "The Hutterites in Alberta: Past and Present Settlement Patterns," in Lynn A. Rosenvall and Simon M. Evans, eds., *Essays on the Historical Geography of the Canadian West: Regional Perspectives on the Settlement Process* (Calgary: University of Calgary Department of Geography, 1987), pp. 145–171.   3383

POPULATION

Crawford, Margaret E., "A Geographic Study of the Distribution of Population Change in Alberta, 1931–61," Master's thesis, University of Alberta, 1962.   3384

Marriott, Peter J., "Migration of People to and within the County of Grande Prairie, Alberta, 1956–67," Master's thesis, University of Alberta, 1969.   3385

Lamont, G. R., "Migrants and Migration in Part of the South Peace River Region, Alberta," Master's thesis, University of Alberta, 1970.   3386

King, M. S., "Some Aspects of Post-War Migration to Edmonton, Alberta," Master's thesis, University of Alberta, 1971.   3387

Laatsch, William G., "Hutterite Colonization in Alberta," *Journal of Geography*, vol. 70, 6 (1971), pp. 347–359.   3388

Wonders, William C., "Scandinavian Homesteaders in Central Alberta," in H. B. Palmer and D. B. Smith, eds., *The New Provinces: Alberta and Saskatchewan, 1905–1980* (Vancouver: Tantalus Research Ltd., Proceedings of the Twelfth Western Canada Studies Conference, B.C. Geographical Series, no. 30, 1980) pp. 131–171. [Focus on 1867–1971]   3389

Lehr, John C., "The Mormons," *Horizon Canada*, vol. 3, 32 (1985), pp. 728–733. Reprinted as "Religions," in L. Stutz, ed., *Chief Mountain Country*, vol. 2 (Cardston: Cardston Local History Society, 1987), pp. 139–141.   3390

RURAL & REGIONAL SOCIAL GEOGRAPHY

Jackson, W. H., "Ethnicity and Areal Organization among French Canadians in the Peace River

Region, Alberta," Master's thesis, University of Alberta, 1970. **3391**

Evans, Simon M., "The Dispersal of Hutterite Colonies in Alberta, 1918–71: The Spatial Expression of Cultural Identity," Master's thesis, University of Calgary, 1973. **3392**

Evans, Simon M., "Spatial Bias in the Incidence of Nativism: Opposition to Hutterite Expansion in Alberta," *Canadian Ethnic Studies*, vol. 6 (1974), pp. 1–16. **3393**

Evans, Simon M., "The Spatial Expression of Cultural Identity: The Hutterites in Alberta," in Brenton M. Barr, ed., *The Kootenay Collection of Research Studeis in Geography* (Vancouver: Tantalus Research, B.C. Geographical Series, no. 18, 1974), pp. 9–20. [Focus on 1880–1972] **3394**

Rosenvall, Lynn A., "The Transfer of Mormon Culture to Alberta," *American Review of Canadian Studies*, vol. 12, 2 (1982), pp. 51–63. Reprinted in Lynn A. Rosenvall and Simon M. Evans, eds., *Essays on the Historical Geography of the Canadian West: Regional Perspectives on the Settlement Process* (Calgary: University of Calgary Department of Geography, 1987), pp. 122–144. **3395**

Lehr, John C., "Polygamy, Patrimony, and Prophecy: The Mormon Colonization of Cardston," *Dialogue: A Journal of Mormon Thought*, vol. 21, 4 (1988), pp. 114–121. **3396**

ECONOMIC DEVELOPMENT

Vanderhill, Burke G., "Trends in the Peace River Country," *Canadian Geographer*, vol. 7, 1 (1963), pp. 33–41. **3397**

Darby, Peter A., "The Integration of Southern Alberta with Canada, 1700–1885: An Historical Geography," Master's thesis, University of Calgary, 1977. **3398**

LAND & LAND USE

Moodie, D. Wayne, "Alberta Settlement Surveys," *Alberta Historical Review*, vol. 12, 4 (1964), pp. 1–7. **3399**

Gibson, John S., "An Evaluation of the Role of Physical Factors in the Evolution of Land Use in the Bow River Valley in Calgary," Master's thesis, University of Alberta, 1965. **3400**

Singh, J., "Land Use Changes in the Eastern Irrigation District of Alberta," Master's thesis, University of Alberta, 1968. **3401**

Nelson, J. Gordon, "Land Use History, Landscape Change, and Planning Problems in Banff National Park," *IUCN Bulletin* (International

Union for the Conservation of Nature), n.s. 2 (1969), pp. 80–82. **3402**

Brown, Sheila A., "The Impact of the Great Slave Lake Railway on Agricultural Land Use in the North Peace, Alberta," Master's thesis, University of Alberta, 1971. **3403**

Mallett, R. B., "Settlement Process and Land Use Change in the Lethbridge–Medicine Hat Area," Master's thesis, University of Alberta, 1971. **3404**

Paterson, John H., "Unit Size as a Factor in Land Disposal Policy," in Robert G. Ironside et al., eds., *Frontier Settlement* (Edmonton: University of Alberta Department of Geography, 1974), pp. 151–163. **3405**

Haden, A. J., "Farmer's Attitudes and Agricultural Land Expansion in Improvement District 23, Alberta," Master's thesis, University of Alberta, 1990. **3406**

EXTRACTIVE ACTIVITY

Hamilton, Sally Ann, "An Historical Geography of Coal Mining in the Edmonton Area," Master's thesis, University of Alberta, 1971. **3407**

Ironside, Robert G., and Sally Ann Hamilton, "Historical Geography of Coal Mining in the Edmonton District," *Alberta Historical Review*, vol. 20, 3 (1972), pp. 6–16. **3408**

AGRICULTURE

Lupton, Austin A., "Cattle Ranching in Alberta, 1874–1910: Its Evolution and Migration," *Albertan Geographer*, vol. 3 (1966–1967), pp. 48–58. **3409**

Batchelor, Bruce E., "The Agrarian Frontier near Red Deer and Lacombe, Alberta, 1882–1914," Ph.D. diss., Simon Fraser University, 1978. **3410**

Breen, David H., *The Canadian Prairie West and the Ranching Frontier, 1874–1924* (Toronto: University of Toronto Press, 1983), 302 pp. **3411**

LANDSCAPE

Hull, Virginia L., "A Geographical Study of the Impact of Two Ethnic Groups on the Rural Landscape in Central Alberta," Master's thesis, University of Alberta, 1965. **3412**

Lehr, John C., "Mormon Settlement Morphology in Southern Alberta," *Albertan Geographer*, vol. 8 (1972), pp. 6–13. **3413**

Lehr, John C., "The Mormon Cultural Landscape in Alberta," in Robert Leigh, ed., *Malaspina Papers: Studies in Human and Physical Geography* (Vancouver: Tantalus Research, B.C. Geographical Series, no. 17, 1973), pp. 25–33. [Focus on the period after 1887]   **3414**

Lehr, John C., "Ukrainian Houses in Alberta," *Alberta Historical Review*, vol. 21, 4 (1973), pp. 9–15.   **3415**

Lehr, John C., "Ukrainian Vernacular Architecture," *Canadian Collector*, vol. 11, 1 (1976), pp. 66–70.   **3416**

Lehr, John C., *Ukrainian Vernacular Architecture in Alberta* (Edmonton: Alberta Culture, Historical Resources Division, Historic Sites Service, Occasional Paper no. 1, 1976), 43 pp.   **3417**

Rees, Ronald, and Carl J. Tracie, "The Prairie House," *Landscape*, vol. 22, 3 (1978), pp. 3–8. [Focus on Alberta during the twentieth century]   **3418**

Wonders, William C., and M. Rasmussen, "Log Buildings of West Central Alberta," *Prairie Forum*, vol. 5, 2 (1980), pp. 197–218.   **3419**

COMMUNICATIONS & TRADE

Wonders, William C., "The Toast at the Punch Bowl," *Alberta Historical Review*, vol. 22, 4 (1974), pp. 26–30. [Athabasca Pass]   **3420**

Garrett, D. F. A., "The Northern Alberta Railway: A Geographical Analysis," Master's thesis, University of Alberta, 1980.   **3421**

Holmes, John D. R., "The Canmore Corridor, 1880–1914: A Case Study of the Selection and Development of a Pass Site," in Lynn A. Rosenvall and Simon M. Evans, eds., *Essays on the Historical Geography of the Canadian West: Regional Perspectives on the Settlement Process* (Calgary: University of Calgary Department of Geography, 1987), pp. 27–47.   **3422**

MANUFACTURING & INDUSTRIALIZATION

Mullins, Gary E., "The Spatial Behavior of Alberta's Electricity Industry, 1888–1965: The Impact of Economies of Scale," Master's thesis, University of British Columbia, 1970.   **3423**

Crowston, M. A., "The Growth of the Metal Industries in Edmonton," Master's thesis, University of Alberta, 1971.   **3424**

URBAN NETWORKS & URBANIZATION

Anderson, J., "Change in a Central Place System: Trade Centres and Rural Service in Central Alberta," Master's thesis, University of Alberta, 1967.   **3425**

Keys, C. L., "Spatial Reorganization in a Central Place System: An Alberta Case," Ph.D. diss., University of Alberta, 1975.   **3426**

Smith, Peter J., "The Changing Structure of the Settlement System," in Brenton M. Barr and Peter J. Smith, eds., *Environment and Economy: Essays on the Human Geography of Alberta* (Edmonton: Pica Pica Press, 1984), pp. 16–35.   **3427**

TOWN GROWTH

Calgary

Smith, Peter J., "Calgary: A Study in Urban Pattern," *Economic Geography*, vol. 38, 4 (1962), pp. 315–329.   **3428**

Smith, Peter J., "Change in a Youthful City: The Case of Calgary, Alberta," *Geography*, vol. 56, 1 (1971), pp. 1–14.   **3429**

Edmonton

Jones, Owen D., "The Historical Geography of Edmonton, Alberta," Master's thesis, University of Toronto, 1963.   **3430**

Ward, R. G., "Country Residential Development in the Edmonton Area to 1973: A Case Study of Exurban Residential Growth," Master's thesis, University of Alberta, 1977.   **3431**

Graham, W. M., "Construction of Large-Scale Structural Base Maps of Central Edmonton for 1907, 1911, and 1914," Master's thesis, University of Alberta, 1984.   **3432**

Other centers

Ironside, Robert G., and E. Tomasky, "Development of Victoria Settlement," *Alberta Historical Review*, vol. 19, 2 (1971), pp. 20–29.   **3433**

Scace, Robert C., "Banff Townsite: An Historical-Geographical View of Urban Development in a Canadian National Park," in Geoffrey Wall and John Marsh, eds., *Recreational Land Use: Perspectives on Its Evolution in Canada* (Ottawa: Carleton University Press, 1982), pp. 203–219.   **3434**

URBAN ECONOMIC STRUCTURE

Lai, Hermia K., "Evolution of the Railway Network of Edmonton and Its Land Use Effects," Master's thesis, University of Alberta, 1967.   **3435**

Woo, H. M., "Relationship between Stores and Population over Time in Northwest Calgary, 1948–1968," Master's thesis, University of Calgary, 1969.   **3436**

Chow, N., "The Evolution and the Changing Functions of a Commercial Ribbon: A Case Study," Master's thesis, University of Alberta, 1970. 3437

Smith, Peter J., and M. J. Bannon, "The Dimensions of Change in the Central Area of Edmonton, 1946–1966," in W. R. D. Sewell and H. D. Foster, eds., *The Geographer and Society* (Victoria: University of Victoria, Western Geographical Series, vol. 1, 1970), pp. 202–217. 3438

Zieber, George H., "Inter- and Intra-City Location Patterns of Oil Offices for Calgary and Edmonton, 1950–1970," Ph.D. diss., University of Alberta, 1971. 3439

Smith, Peter J., and H. L. Diemer, "Equity and the Annexation Process: Edmonton's Bid for the Strathcona Industrial Corridor," in Peter J. Smith, ed., *Edmonton: The Emerging Metropolitan Pattern* (Victoria: University of Victoria, Western Geographical Series, vol. 15, 1978), pp. 263–289. 3440

TOWNSCAPE

Bannon, M. J., "The Evolution of the Central Area of Edmonton, Alberta, 1946–1966," Master's thesis, University of Alberta, 1967. 3441

McCann, Larry D., "Processes of Change in Residential Areas in Transition," Master's thesis, University of Alberta, 1969. 3442

McCann, Larry D., "Changing Morphology of Residential Areas in Transition," Ph.D. diss., University of Alberta, 1972. 3443

Diemer, H., "Annexation and Amalgamation in the Territorial Expansion of Edmonton and Calgary," Master's thesis, University of Alberta, 1975. 3444

Smith, Peter J., and Larry D. McCann, "The Sequence of Physical Change in Apartment Redevelopment Areas in Edmonton," *Plan Canada*, vol. 15, 1 (1975), pp. 30–37. 3445

McCann, Larry D., and Peter J. Smith, "The Residential Development Cycle in Space and Time," in Peter J. Smith, ed., *Edmonton: The Emerging Metropolitan Pattern* (Victoria: University of Victoria, Western Geographical Series, vol. 15, 1978), pp. 119–159. 3446

Foran, Max, "Land Development Patterns in Calgary, 1884–1945," in Alan F. J. Artibise and Gilbert A. Stelter, eds., *The Usable Urban Past: Planning and Politics in the Modern Canadian City* (Toronto: Macmillan, 1979), pp. 293–315. 3447

Smith, Peter J., and Larry D. McCann, "Residential Land Use Change in Inner Edmonton," *Annals of the Association of American Geographers*, vol. 71, 4 (1981), pp. 536–551. [Focus on 1921–1971] 3448

Holtz, A., "'Small Town Alberta': A Geographical Study of the Development of Urban Form," Master's thesis, University of Alberta, 1987. 3449

Smith, Peter J., "Community Aspirations, Territorial Justice, and the Metropolitan Form of Edmonton and Calgary," in Guy M. Robinson, ed., *A Social Geography of Canada: Essays in Honour of J. Wreford Watson* (Edinburgh: North British Publishing, 1988), pp. 179–196. Also Toronto: Dundurn Press, 1991, pp. 245–266. 3450

RECREATION & TOURISM

Scace, Robert C., "Banff: A Cultural-Historical Study of Land Use and Management in a National Park Community, to 1945," Master's thesis, University of Calgary, 1968. 3451

Scace, Robert C., *A Cultural-Historical Study of Land Use and Management in a National Park Community to 1945* (Calgary: University of Calgary, National Park Series, no. 2, Studies in Land Use History and Landscape Change, 1968), 154 pp. 3452

Todhunter, Rodger, "Banff and the Canadian National Park Idea," *Landscape*, vol. 25, 2 (1981), pp. 33–39. [Focus on 1885–1980] 3453

Rasmussen, M. A., "The Heritage Boom: Evolution of Historical Resource Conservation in Alberta," *Prairie Forum*, vol. 15, 2 (1990), pp. 235–262. 3454

PLANNING

Chan, W. M. W., "The Impact of the Technical Planning Board on the Morphology of Edmonton," Master's thesis, University of Alberta, 1969. 3455

Dale, Edmund H., "The Role of Successive Town and City Councils in the Evolution of Edmonton, Alberta, 1892 to 1966," Ph.D. diss., University of Alberta, 1969. 3456

Dale, Edmund H., "Decision-Making in Edmonton: Planning without a Plan, 1913–1945," *Plan Canada*, vol. 11, 2 (1971), pp. 134–145. 3457

Harasym, D. G., "The Planning of New Residential Areas in Calgary, 1944–1973," Master's thesis, University of Alberta, 1975. 3458

Smith, Peter J., and D. G. Harasym, "Planning for Retail Services in New Residential Areas since 1944," in Brenton M. Barr, ed., *Calgary: Metropolitan Structure and Influence* (Victoria: University of Victoria, Western Geographical Series, vol. 11, 1975), pp. 157–191. 3459

Graden, R. R., "The Planning of New Residential Areas in Edmonton, 1950–1976," Master's thesis, University of Alberta, 1979.   3460

Smith, Peter J., "The Principle of Utility and the Origins of Planning Legislation in Alberta, 1912–1975," in Alan F. J. Artibise and Gilbert A. Stelter, eds., *The Usable Urban Past: Planning and Politics in the Modern Canadian City* (Toronto: Macmillan, 1979), pp. 196–225.   3461

Smith, Peter J., "Municipal Conflicts over Territory and the Effectiveness of the Regional Planning System in the Edmonton Metropolitan Area," in H. Becker, ed., *Kulturgeographische Prozeßforschung in Kanada* (Bamberg: Bamberger Geographische Schriften, vol. 4, 1982), pp. 207–233.   3462

Smith, Peter J., "American Influences and Local Needs: Adaptations to the Alberta Planning System in 1928–1929," in Gilbert A. Stelter and Alan F. J. Artibise, eds, *Power and Place: Canadian Urban Development in the North American Context* (Vancouver: University of British Columbia Press, 1986), pp. 109–132.   3463

PLACE NAMES

Dempsey, Hugh A., *Indian Names for Alberta Communities* (Calgary: Glenbow-Alberta Institute, 1969), 19 pp.   3464

Karamitsanis, Aphrodite, *Place Names of Alberta* (Edmonton: Alberta Culture and Multiculturalism and the University of Calgary Press, 1990), 292 pp.   3465

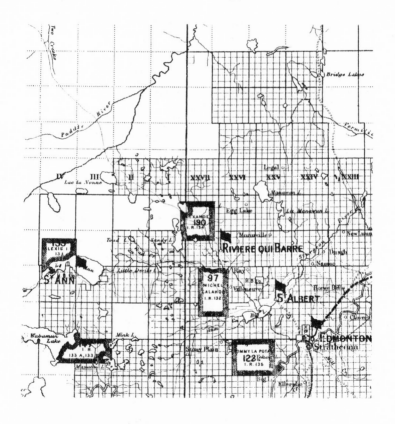

BRITISH COLUMBIA

GENERAL

See also 1147–1148

Begg, Alexander, "Notes on Vancouver Island," *Scottish Geographical Magazine*, vol. 11, 12 (1895), pp. 625–635.   **3466**

Thorington, J. Munroe, "The Historical Geography of the Columbia-Kootenay Valley," *Bulletin of the Philadelphia Geographical Society*, vol. 31, 1 (1933), pp. 10–26.   **3467**

Taylor, T. Griffith, "British Columbia: A Study in Topographic Control," *Geographical Review*, vol. 32, 3 (1942), pp. 372–402.   **3468**

Robinson, J. Lewis, and Walter G. Hardwick, "The Canadian Cordillera," in John H. Warkentin, ed., *Canada: A Geographical Interpretation* (Toronto: Methuen, 1968), pp. 438–472. Also published as *British Columbia: 100 Years of Geographical Change* (Vancouver: Talon Books, 1973), 63 pp.   **3469**

Floyd, P., "The Human Geography of Southeastern Vancouver Island," Master's thesis, University of Victoria, 1969.   **3470**

Brown, John A., "The Historical Geography of South Surrey, British Columbia," Master's thesis, Western Washington State College, 1971.   **3471**

Forward, Charles N., "Evolution of Regional Character," in Charles N. Forward, ed., *British Columbia: Its Resources and People* (Victoria: University of Victoria Western Geographical Series, vol. 22, 1987), pp. 1–22.   **3472**

Clayton, Daniel W., "Geographies of the Lower Skeena, 1830–1920," Master's thesis, University of British Columbia, 1989.   **3473**

ENVIRONMENTAL CHANGE

See also 1160

Pogue, Basil G., "Some Aspects of Settlement, Land-Use, and Vegetation Change in the Revelstoke Area, B.C. 1885–1962," Master's thesis, University of Calgary, 1970.   **3474**

Lake, David, "A Study of Landscape Evolution in the Crowsnest Pass Region, 1898–1971," Ph.D. diss., University of Oklahoma, 1972.   **3475**

Roe, N. A., and J. Gordon Nelson, "Man, Birds, and Mammals of Pacific Rim National Park,

B.C.: Past, Present, and Future," in J. Gordon Nelson and L. D. Cordes, eds., *Pacific Rim: An Ecological Approach to a New Canadian National Park* (Calgary: University of Calgary, Studies in Land Use History and Landscape Change, no. 4, 1972), unpaginated. Reprinted in J. Gordon Nelson, *Man's Impact on the Western Canadian Landscape* (Toronto: McClelland and Stewart, Carleton Library Series, no. 90, 1976), pp. 102–139.   **3476**

Kahrer, Anna Gabrielle, "Logging and Landscape Change on the North Shore of Burrard Inlet, British Columbia, 1860s to 1930s," Master's thesis, University of British Columbia, 1988.   **3477**

NATIVE PEOPLES & WHITE RELATIONS

Boas, Franz, "The Indians of British Columbia," *Journal of the American Geographical Society*, vol. 28 (1896), pp. 229–243.   **3478**

Merriam, Willis B., "Some Environmental Influences in the Cultural Development of the Haida," *Yearbook of the Association of Pacific Coast Geographers*, vol. 8 (1942), pp. 23–26.   **3479**

Borden, Charles E., "Prehistory of the Lower Mainland," in Alfred H. Siemens, ed., *Lower Fraser Valley: Evolution of a Cultural Landscape* (Vancouver: Tantalus Research, B.C. Geographical Series, no. 9 (1968), pp. 9–26.   **3480**

Aziz, S. A., "Selected Aspects of Cultural Change among Amerindians: A Case Study of Southeast Vancouver Island," Master's thesis, University of Victoria, 1970.   **3481**

Henderson, John R., "The Changing Settlement Pattern of the Haida," in Roger Leigh, ed., *Contemporary Geography: Research Trends* (Vancouver: Tantalus Research, B.C. Geographical Series, no. 16, 1972), pp. 63–72. [Focus on 1774–1897]   **3482**

Wagner, Philip L., "The Persistence of Native Settlement in Coastal British Columbia," in Julian V. Minghi, ed., *Peoples of the Living Land: Geography of Cultural Diversity in British Columbia* (Vancouver: Tantalus Research, B.C. Geographical Series, no. 15, 1972), pp. 15–27.   **3483**

Blake, T. Michael, "The Exploration of Late Prehistoric Settlement Pattern Variation in the Thompson and Fraser River Valleys, British Columbia," *B.C. Perspectives*, vol. 5 (1974), pp. 1–18.   **3484**

EXPLORATION & MAPPING

See also **1285–1289**

Palmer, Howard, "Early Explorations in British Columbia for the Canadian Pacific Railway," *Bulletin of the Philadelphia Geographical Society*, vol. 16, 3 (1918), pp. 75–91.   **3485**

Taylor, Doreen M., "Early Mapping of British Columbia, 1566–1858," *British Columbia Library Quarterly*, vol. 22, 1 (1958), pp. 9–14.   **3486**

Farley, Albert L., "Historical Cartography of British Columbia, with a Separate Appendix of Maps," Ph.D. diss., University of Wisconsin, 1960.   **3487**

Farley, Albert L., "Thoughts on the Historical Cartography of British Columbia," *Occasional Papers of the Canadian Association of Geographers, British Columbia Division*, vol. 2 (1961), pp. 39–44.   **3488**

Farley, Albert L., "Fact and Fancy in Mapping Northwest America to 1800," *Occasional Papers, Canadian Association of Geographers, British Columbia Division*, vol. 3 (1962), pp. 27–36.   **3489**

Sandilands, Robert W., "The History of Hydrographic Surveying in British Columbia," *Canadian Cartographer*, vol. 7, 2 (1970), pp. 105–115.   **3490**

Sandilands, Robert W., "The History of Hydrographic Surveying in British Columbia," *Proceedings of the Annual Conference of the Association of Canadian Map Libraries*, vol. 4 (1970), pp. 22–34. Also published, with modifications, in *Canadian Cartographer*, vol. 7, 2 (1970), pp. 105–115; and reprinted in Barbara Farrell and Aileen Desbarats, eds., *Explorations in the History of Canadian Mapping: A Collection of Essays* (Ottawa: Association of Canadian Map Libraries and Archives, 1988), pp. 113–131.   **3491**

Phillips, B. F., "Filling in the Map: Maps and Mapping in British Columbia since 1850," *British Columbia Library Quarterly*, vol. 35, 2 (1971), pp. 17–29.   **3492**

Sandilands, Robert W., "Hydrographic Charting and Oceanography on the West Coast of Canada from the Eighteenth Century to the Present Day," *Proceedings of the Royal Society of Edinburgh (B)*, vol. 73, 9 (1971–1972), pp. 75–83.   **3493**

Spittle, John, *Early Printed Maps of British Columbia* (North Vancouver: The author, 1973).   **3494**

Spittle, John S., "Early Printed Maps of British Columbia: Maps Printed and Published in New Westminster, 1861–1866," *Proceedings of the Annual Conference of the Association of Canadian Map Libraries*, vol. 7 (1973), pp. 16–30. Reprinted in Barbara Farrell and Eileen Desbarats, eds., *Explorations in the History of Canadian Mapping: A Collection of Essays* (Ottawa: Association of Canadian Map Libraries and Archives, 1988), pp. 193–204.   **3495**

Pearson, Donald F., "An Historical Outline of Mapping in British Columbia," *Canadian Cartographer*, vol. 11, 2 (1974), pp. 114–124.   **3496**

Woodward, Frances M., "The Influence of the Royal Engineers on the Development of British Columbia," *B.C. Studies*, vol. 24 (1974), pp. 3–52.   **3497**

Woodward, Frances M., "The Royal Engineers' Mapping of British Columbia, 1845–1906," *Information Bulletin of the Western Association of Map Libraries*, vol. 7, 3 (1976), pp. 28–42.   **3498**

North, Margaret E. A., Deryck W. Holdsworth, and Jan Teversham, "A Brief Guide to the Use of Land Surveyors' Notebooks in the Lower Fraser Valley, British Columbia, 1859–1890," *B.C. Studies*, vol. 34 (1977), pp. 45–60.   **3499**

Lamb, W. Kaye, "Maps Relating to the Vancouver Expedition," *Bulletin of the Association of Canadian Map Libraries*, vol. 28 (1978), pp. 8–18. Reprinted, with modifications, as "Vancouver's Charts of the Northwest Coast," in Barbara Farrell and Aileen Desbarats, eds., *Explorations in the History of Canadian Mapping: A Collection of Essays* (Ottawa: Association of Canadian Map Libraries and Archives, 1988), pp. 99–111.   **3500**

Verner, Coolie, "Maps Relating to Cook's age," *Bulletin of the Association of Canadian Map Libraries*, vol. 28 (1978), pp. 2–8. Reprinted in Barbara Farrell and Aileen Desbarats, eds., *Explorations in the History of Canadian Mapping: A Collection of Essays* (Ottawa: Association of Canadian Map Libraries and Archives, 1988), pp. 89–98.   **3501**

Woodward, Frances M., "Exploration and Survey of the Kootenay District," *Bulletin of the Association of Canadian Map Libraries*, vol. 38 (1981), pp. 2–26. Reprinted, with minor modifications, as "Exploration and Survey of the Kootenay District, 1800–1918," in Barbara Farrell and Eileen Desbarats, eds., *Explorations in the History of Canadian Mapping: A Collection of Essays* (Ottawa: Association of Canadian Map Libraries and Archives, 1988), pp. 223–238.   **3502**

Gilmartin, Patricia P., "Key Maps of British Columbia's Past," in Charles N. Forward, ed., *British Columbia: Its Resources and People* (Victoria: University of Victoria, Western Geographical Series, vol. 22, 1987), pp. 25–41.   **3503**

POPULAR IMAGES & EVALUATION

Jackson, C. Ian, "A Territory of Little Value: The Wind of Change on the Northwest Coast, 1861–67," *Beaver*, Outfit 298, 1 (1967), pp. 40–45.   **3504**

Reimer, Derek L., "Travel Literature as a Source for Historical Geography: A Case Study from Early British Columbia, 1841–1871," Master's thesis, Queen's University, 1973. **3505**

Forward, Charles N., "The Physical Geography of Victoria, circa 1860, as Perceived by Colonists, Mapmakers, and Visitors," in H. D. Foster, ed., *Victoria: Physical Environment and Development* (Victoria: University of Victoria Western Geographical Series, vol. 12, 1976), pp. 1–43. **3506**

Schwartz, Joan M., "Images of Early British Columbia: Landscape Photography, 1858–1888," Master's thesis, University of British Columbia, 1977. **3507**

Schwartz, Joan M., "The Photographic Record of Pre-Confederation British Columbia," *Archivaria*, vol. 5 (1977–1978), pp. 17–44. **3508**

Kobayashi, Audrey L., "Landscape and the Poetic Act: The Role of Haiku Clubs for the Issei," *Landscape*, vol. 24, 1 (1980), pp. 42–47. **3509**

Schwartz, Joan M., "The Past in Focus: Photography and British Columbia, 1958–1914," *B.C. Studies*, vol. 52 (1981–1982), pp. 5–15. **3510**

Schwartz, Joan M., and L. Koltun, "A Visual Cliché: Five Views of Yale," *B.C. Studies*, vol. 52 (1981–1982), pp. 113–128. **3511**

Meredith, Thomas C., "The Upper Columbia Valley, 1900–20: An Assessment of 'Boosterism' and the Biography of Landscape," *Canadian Geographer*, vol. 29, 1 (1985), pp. 44–55. **3512**

REGIONAL SETTLEMENT

See also **1324, 1338–1339**

Wright, John M., "The Settlement of the Victoria Region, British Columbia," Master's thesis, McGill University, 1956. **3513**

Siemens, Alfred H., "Mennonite Settlement in the Lower Fraser Valley," Master's thesis, University of British Columbia, 1960. **3514**

Krenzlin, Anneliese, *Die Agrarlandschaft an der Nordgrenze der Besiedlung im intermontanen British Columbia* (Frankfort: Frankfurter Geographische Hefte, no. 40, 1965), 66 pp. **3515**

Gunn, Angus M., "Gold and the Early Settlement of British Columbia, 1858–1885," Master's thesis, University of British Columbia, 1966. **3516**

Howell-Jones, Gerald I., "A Century of Settlement Change: A Study of the Evolution of Settlement Patterns in the Lower Mainland of British Columbia," Master's thesis, University of British Columbia, 1966. **3517**

Siemens, Alfred H., "The Process of Settlement in the Lower Fraser Valley in Its Provincial Context," in Alfred H. Siemens, ed., *Lower Fraser Valley: Evolution of a Cultural Landscape* (Vancouver: Tantalus Research, B.C. Geographical Series, no. 9, 1968), pp. 27–49. **3518**

McCann, Larry D., and Norman A. Cook, "The Process of Agricultural Settlement in British Columbia," *Albertan Geographer*, vol. 6 (1970), pp. 4–10. **3519**

Riis, Nelson A., "Settlement Abandonment: A Case Study of Walhachin: Myth and Reality," Master's thesis, University of British Columbia, 1970. **3520**

Jüngst, Peter, "Siedlungen des Erzbergbaus in den kanadischen Kordilleren," in Carl Schott, ed., *Beiträge zur Kulturgeographie von Kanada* (Marburg: Marburger Geographische Schriften, no. 50, 1971), pp. 151–188. **3521**

Neave, Ronald, "A History of Settlement in the Lac Du Bois Basin, 1840–1970: A Study in Sequent Occupancy," *B.C. Perspectives*, vol. 1 (1972), pp. 4–23. **3522**

Siemens, Alfred H., "Settlement," in J. Lewis Robinson, ed., *British Columbia* (Toronto: University of Toronto Press, 1972), pp. 9–31. **3523**

White, Brian P., "The Morphology of Settlement in the Nootka Sound Region of Vancouver Island's West Coast, 1900–1970," in Roger Leigh, ed., *Contemporary Geography: Research Trends* (Vancouver: Tantalus Research, B.C. Geographical Series, no. 16, 1972), pp. 73–86. **3524**

White, Brian P., "The Settlement of Nootka Sound: Its Distributional Morphology, 1900–1970," Master's thesis, Simon Fraser University, 1972. **3525**

Riis, Nelson A., "The Walhachin Myth: A Study in Settlement Abandonment," *B.C. Studies*, no. 17 (1973), pp. 3–25. **3526**

Reeves, Colin M., "The Establishment of the Kelowna Orcharding Area: A Study of Accommodation to Site and Situation," Master's thesis, University of British Columbia, 1973. **3527**

Cook, Donna, "Early Settlement in the Chilliwack Valley," Master's thesis, University of British Columbia, 1979. **3528**

Koroscil, Paul M., "Soldier Settlement in British Columbia, 1915–1930: A Synchronic Analysis," in Alan R. H. Baker and Mark Billinge, eds., *Period and Place: Research Methods in Historical Geography* (Cambridge: Cambridge University Press, 1982), pp. 51–68. **3529**

Koroscil, Paul M., "Soldiers, Settlement, and Development in British Columbia, 1915–1930," *B.C. Studies*, vol. 54 (1982), pp. 63–87.　　3530

Koroscil, Paul M., "Boosterism and the Settlement Process in the Okanagan Valley, British Columbia, 1890–1914," in Donald H. Akenson, ed., *Canadian Papers in Rural History*, vol. 5 (Gananoque, Ont.: Langdale Press, 1986), pp. 73–103.　　3531

Wisenthal, Christine B., "Insiders and Outsiders: Two Waves of Jewish Settlement in British Columbia, 1858–1914," Master's thesis, University of British Columbia, 1987.　　3532

POPULATION

See also 1358

Robinson, J. Lewis, "Population Trends and Distribution in British Columbia," *Canadian Geographer*, vol. 4 (1954), pp. 27–32.　　3533

Lai, David Chuen-yan, "Chinese Attempts to Discourage Emigration to Canada: Some Findings from the Chinese Archives in Victoria," *B.C. Studies*, vol. 18 (1973), pp. 33–49.　　3534

Lai, David Chuen-yan, "Chinese Immigrants into British Columbia and Their Distribution, 1858–1970," *Pacific Viewpoint*, vol. 14, 1 (1973), pp. 102–108.　　3535

Lai, David Chuen-yan, "Imprints of the Chinese in British Columbia," *Proceedings of the Asian Canadian Symposium* (Fredericton: University of New Brunswick, 1977), pp. 20–27.　　3536

Lai, David Chuen-yan, "Chinese Imprints in British Columbia," *B.C. Studies*, vol. 39 (1978), pp. 20–29.　　3537

Galois, Robert M., "Mapping the British Columbia Census, 1881," *Bulletin of the Association of Canadian Map Libraries*, no. 47 (June 1983), pp. 26–36.　　3538

Kobayashi, Audrey L., "Emigration to Canada and the Development of the Residential Landscape in a Japanese Village: The Paradox of the Sojourner," *Canadian Ethnic Studies*, vol. 16, 3 (1984), pp. 111–131.　　3539

Lane, M. Melita, "The Migration of Hawaiians to Coastal British Columbia to 1870," Master's thesis, University of Hawaii, 1984.　　3540

Kobayashi, Audrey L., "Emigration to Canada, Landholding, and Social Networks in a Japanese Village, 1885–1950," in M. Soga and B. Saint-Jacques, eds., *Japanese Studies in Canada* (Ottawa: Canadian Asian Studies Association, 1985), pp. 162–186.　　3541

RURAL & REGIONAL SOCIAL GEOGRAPHY

See also 1377–1378

Ginn, Edith Margaret, "Rural Dutch Immigrants in the Lower Fraser Valley," Master's thesis, University of British Columbia, 1967.　　3542

Ginn, Edith Margaret, "The Dutch and Dairying," in Alfred H. Siemens, ed., *Lower Fraser Valley: Evolution of a Cultural Landscape* (Vancouver: Tantalus Research, B.C. Geographical Series, no. 9, 1968), pp. 117–137. [Focus on the lower Fraser Valley, 1945–1965]　　3543

Sandhu, Kernial S., "Indian Immigration and Racial Prejudice in British Columbia: Some Preliminary Observations," in Julian Minghi, ed., *Peoples of the Living Land: Geography of Cultural Diversity in British Columbia* (Vancouver: Tantalus, B.C. Geographical Series, no. 15, 1972), pp. 29–39.　　3544

Irby, Charles, "The Black Settlers on Saltspring Island, Canada, in the Nineteenth Century," *Yearbook of the Association of Pacific Coast Geographers*, vol. 36 (1974), pp. 35–44.　　3545

Read, John M., "The Pre-War Japanese Canadians of Maple Ridge: Landownership and the Ken Tie," Master's thesis, University of British Columbia, 1975.　　3546

Siemens, Alfred H., "Ethnische Gruppen und der Gang der Besiedlung in British-Columbien," *Geographische Rundschau*, vol. 28, 2 (1976), pp. 58–64.　　3547

Gale, Donald T., and Paul M. Koroscil, "Doukhobor Settlements: Experiments in Idealism," *Canadian Ethnic Studies*, vol. 9, 2 (1977), pp. 53–71.　　3548

Kobayashi, Audrey L., "Transition and Change: The Culture of the Issei in the Okanagan Valley," in Garrick Chu et al., eds., *Inalienable Rice: A Chinese and Japanese Canadian Anthology* (Vancouver: Powell Street Review and the Chinese Canadian Writers Workshop, 1979), pp. 17–20.　　3549

Crossley-Kershaw, Adrian, "Ideological Conflict, Assimilation, and the Cultural Landscape: A Case Study of the Doukhobors in Canada," in Nigel M. Waters, ed., *Aspects of Human Geography: The Kelowna Papers, 1981* (Vancouver: Tantalus Research, B.C. Geographical Series, no. 34, 1982), pp. 9–26.　　3550

Harris, R. Cole, and Elizabeth Phillips, eds., *Letters from Windermere, 1912–1914* (Vancouver: University of British Columbia Press, 1984), 243 pp.　　3551

Bagshaw, Roberta Lee, "Settlement and the Church of England in the Bishopric of British

Columbia: 1859–1863," Master's thesis, Simon Fraser University, 1987. **3552**

Koroscil, Paul M., "A Gentleman Farmer in British Columbia's Garden of Eden," in Paul M. Koroscil, ed., *British Columbia: Geographical Essays in Honour of A. Macpherson* (Burnaby, B.C.: Department of Geography, Simon Fraser University, 1991), pp. 87–112. **3553**

POLITICAL & ADMINISTRATIVE GEOGRAPHY

See also **1395**

Minghi, Julian V., "The Evolution of a Border Region: The Pacific Coast Section of the Canada–United States Boundary," *Scottish Geographical Magazine*, vol. 80, 1 (1964), pp. 37–52. **3554**

Halsey-Brandt, Gregory C., "An Analysis of the Changing Function and Contemporary Impact of the Alaska–British Columbia Boundary," Master's thesis, University of British Columbia, 1969. **3555**

Gibson, James R., "The Russian Contract: The Agreement of 1838 [*sic*, for 1839] between the Hudson's Bay and Russian-American Companies," in Richard A. Pierce, ed., *Russia in North America: Proceedings of the Second International Conference on Russian America* (Kingston: Limestone Press, 1990), pp. 157–180. **3556**

ECONOMIC DEVELOPMENT

See also **1403**

Lotzkar, J., "The Boundary Country of Southern British Columbia: A Study of Resources and Human Occupance," Master's thesis, University of Washington, 1953. **3557**

Akrigg, Helen B., "History and Economic Development of the Shuswap Area," Master's thesis, University of British Columbia, 1964. **3558**

Taylor, Mary D., "Development of the Electricity Industry in British Columbia," Master's thesis, University of British Columbia, 1965. **3559**

Begg, Hugh M., "Resource Endowment and Economic Development: The Case of the Gulf Islands of British Columbia," *Scottish Geographical Magazine*, vol. 89, 2 (1973), pp. 119–130. **3560**

Harris, R. Cole, "Locating the University of British Columbia," *B.C. Studies*, vol. 32 (1976–1977), pp. 106–125. **3561**

Wilson, J. W., "Electric Power Development in British Columbia: A Case of Metropolitan Dominance," in Len J. Evenden, ed., *Vancouver:*

Western Metropolis (Victoria: Western Geographical Series, no. 16, 1978), pp. 79–94. **3562**

Malzahn, Manfred R., "Merchants and the Evolution of the North Cariboo, British Columbia, 1908–1933," Master's thesis, McGill University, 1979. **3563**

RESOURCE MANAGEMENT

Davies, Eric O., "The Wilderness Myth: Wilderness in British Columbia," Master's thesis, University of British Columbia, 1972. **3564**

Draper, Diane, "Eco-Activism: Issues and Strategies of Environmental Interest Groups in British Columbia," Master's thesis, University of Victoria, 1972. **3565**

Wynn, Graeme, "Wilderness, Forestry, and Environmental History in British Columbia," *Journal of Forest History*, vol. 32 (1988), pp. 159–160. **3566**

Kahrer, Anna Gabrielle, *From Speculative to Spectacular: The Seymour Rural Valley, 1870s to 1980s; A History of Resource Use* (Burnaby, B.C.: Greater Vancouver Regional District Parks, 1989), 81 pp. **3567**

LAND & LAND USE

Aitken, George G., "The Progress of Survey and Settlement in British Columbia," *Geographical Review*, vol. 15 (1925), pp. 399–410. **3568**

Yakimovitch, Larry M., "An Historical Interpretation of the Land Utilization and Tenure Pattern in the Vernon Rural Area of the Okanagan Valley, British Columbia," Master's thesis, University of Oregon, 1966. **3569**

Bagshaw, Roberta Lee, "Church of England Land Policy in Colonial British Columbia," in Paul M. Koroscil, ed., *British Columbia: Geographical Essays in Honour of A. Macpherson* (Burnaby, B.C.: Department of Geography, Simon Fraser University, 1991), pp. 41–66. **3570**

EXTRACTIVE ACTIVITY

See also **1408, 1411, 1413**

Forestry

Hardwick, Walter G., "Changing Logging and Sawmill Sites in Coastal British Columbia," *Occasional Papers of the Canadian Association of Geographers, British Columbia Division*, vol. 2 (1961), pp. 1–7. [Focus on 1860–1956] **3571**

Hardwick, Walter G., *Geography of the Forest Industry of Coastal British Columbia* (Vancouver:

Tantalus, Occasional Papers in Geography, no. 5, 1963), 98 pp. **3572**

Mullins, Doreen K., "Changes in Location and Structure in the Forest Industry of North Central British Columbia, 1909–1966," Master's thesis, University of British Columbia, 1967. **3573**

Hardwick, Walter G., "The Forest Industry in Coastal British Columbia, 1870–1970," in Robert M. Irving, ed., *Readings in Canadian Geography* (Toronto: Holt, Rinehart and Winston, 1972), pp. 318–324. **3574**

Vance, Eric C., "The Impact of the Forest Industry on Economic Development in the Central Interior of British Columbia," Master's thesis, University of British Columbia, 1981. **3575**

Wagner, William, "Privateering in the Public Forest? A Study of the Expanding Role of the Forest Industry in the Management of Public Forest Land in British Columbia," Master's thesis, University of Victoria, 1987. **3576**

Fisheries

Dean, Leslie J., "The Eastern Pacific Halibut Fishery, 1888–1972: An Evolutionary Study of the Spatial Structure of a Resource-Based Complex," Master's thesis, University of British Columbia, 1973. **3577**

Sandberg, L. Anders, "A Study in Canadian Political Economy: The Case of the British Columbia Salmon Canning Industry, 1870–1914," Master's thesis, University of Victoria, 1979. **3578**

Lee, Helen, "Corporate Strategy in the British Columbia Fish-Processing Sector," Master's thesis, Simon Fraser University, 1983. **3579**

Newell, Dianne, "Dispersal and Concentration: The Slowly Changing Spatial Pattern of the British Columbia Salmon Canning Industry," *Journal of Historical Geography*, vol. 14, 1 (1988), pp. 22–36. **3580**

Higginbottom, Edward N., "The Changing Geography of Salmon Canning in British Columbia, 1870–1931," Master's thesis, Simon Fraser University, 1989. **3581**

Roberts, Arthur, and Edward Higginbottom, "Aerial Archeology of Historic Period Salmon Cannery Sites," in Paul M. Koroscil, ed., *British Columbia: Geographical Essays in Honour of A. Macpherson* (Burnaby, B.C.: Department of Geography, Simon Fraser University, 1991), pp. 113–36. **3582**

Mining

Nicol, Douglas J., "Changing Spatial Patterns in the Lode-Metal Mining Industry of British Co-

lumbia, 1887–1945," Master's thesis, University of British Columbia, 1972. **3583**

Jüngst, Peter, *Erzbergbau in den kanadischen Kordilleren: Strukturwandlungen und Standortveränderungen* (Marburg: Marburger Geographische Schriften, no. 57, 1973), 128 pp. **3584**

Carter, Norman M., "Johnny Harris of Sandon," *Beaver*, Outfit 306, 4 (1976), pp. 42–49. **3585**

Harris, R. Cole, "Industry and the Good Life around Idaho Peak," *Canadian Historical Review*, vol. 66, 3 (1985), pp. 315–343. **3586**

AGRICULTURE

See also 1417–1418, 1422

Weir, Thomas R., *Ranching in the Southern Interior Plateau of British Columbia* (Ottawa: Queen's Printer, 1955), 124 pp. Revised 1964, 165 pp. **3587**

Winter, George R., "Agricultural Development in the Lower Fraser Valley," in Alfred H. Siemens, ed., *Lower Fraser Valley: Evolution of a Cultural Landscape* (Vancouver: Tantalus Research, B.C. Geographical Series, no. 9, 1968), pp. 101–115. **3688**

Wilson, K. Wayne, "Irrigating the Okanagan: 1860–1920," Master's thesis, University of British Columbia, 1989. **3589**

LANDSCAPE

Bockemuehl, Harold W., "Doukhobor Impact on the British Columbia Landscape: An Historical Geographical Study," Master's thesis, Western Washington State College, 1968. **3590**

Gale, Donald T., "Belief and the Landscape of Religion: The Case of the Doukhobors," Master's thesis, Simon Fraser University, 1974. **3591**

Philpot, Mary E., "In This Neglected Spot: The Rural Cemetery Landscape in Southern British Columbia," Master's thesis, University of British Columbia, 1976. **3592**

Sommer, Warren F., "Upon Thy Holy Hill: A Historical Geography of the Early Vernacular Church Architecture of the Southern Interior of British Columbia," Master's thesis, University of British Columbia, 1977. **3593**

Sommer, Warren F., "Mission Church Architecture on the Industrial Frontier," in John Veillette and Gary White, eds., *Early Indian Village Churches: Wooden Frontier Architecture in British Columbia* (Vancouver: University of British Columbia Press, 1977), pp. 12–23. **3594**

Bunny, Gary, "Log Buildings in Southern British Columbia: Pioneer Adaptation to Housing Need in the Kettle Valley and Chilcotin," Master's thesis, University of Victoria, 1980. **3595**

Holdsworth, Deryck W., "Regional Distinctiveness in an Industrial Age: Some California Influences on British Columbia Housing," *American Review of Canadian Studies*, vol. 12, 2 (1982), pp. 64–81. **3596**

Koroscil, Paul M., "The Transformation of the Okanagan Valley Landscape," in J. Peltre, ed., *Transformations historiques du parcellaire et de l'habitat rural* (Nancy: Presses de l'Université de Nancy, 1985), pp. 515–545. **3597**

Coates, Colin M., "Monuments and Memories: The Evolution of British Columbian Cemeteries, 1850–1950," *Material History Bulletin*, no. 25 (1987), pp. 11–21. **3598**

COMMUNICATIONS & TRADE

See also **1436**

Weir, Thomas R., "Early Trails of Burrard Peninsula," *British Columbia Historical Quarterly*, vol. 9, 4 (1945), pp. 273–275. **3599**

Clemson, Donovan, "The Cariboo Road," *Canadian Geographical Journal*, vol. 64, 4 (1962), pp. 114–123. **3600**

Kerfoot, Denis E., "The Martime Foreign Trade of British Columbia," Master's thesis, University of British Columbia, 1964. **3601**

Kerfoot, Denis E., *Port of British Columbia: Development and Trading Patterns* (Vancouver: Tantalus Research, B.C. Geographical Series, no. 2, 1966), 120 pp. **3602**

Meyer, Ronald H., "The Evolution of Roads in the Lower Fraser Valley," in Alfred H. Siemens, ed., *Lower Fraser Valley: Evolution of a Cultural Landscape* (Vancouver: Tantalus Research, B.C. Geographical Series, no. 9, 1968), pp. 68–88. **3603**

Roy, Patricia E., "The Changing Role of Railways in the Lower Fraser Valley, 1895–1965," in Alfred H. Siemens, ed., *Lower Fraser Valley: Evolution of a Cultural Landscape* (Vancouver: Tantalus Research, B.C. Geographical Series, no. 9, 1968), pp. 50–67. **3604**

Meyer, Ronald H., "The Evolution of Railways in the Kootenay's," Master's thesis, University of British Columbia, 1970. **3605**

Wills, Michael J., "Development of the Highway Network, Traffic Flow, and the Growth of Settlements in the Interior of British Columbia," Master's thesis, University of British Columbia, 1971. **3606**

Rheumer, George A., "Nineteenth Century Trails of the Similkameen Valley of Southern British Columbia," in M. C. Brown and Graeme Wynn, eds., *The Bellingham Collection of Geographical Studies* (Vancouver: Tantalus Research, B.C. Geographical Series, no. 27, 1979), pp. 19–40. [Focus on the period after 1811] **3607**

Harris, R. Cole, "Moving amid the Mountains, 1870–1930," *B.C. Studies*, vol. 58 (1983), pp. 3–39. **3608**

Ndaba, Doris, "Development of the Air Transportation Industry in British Columbia, 1900–1980," Master's thesis, Simon Fraser University, 1986. **3609**

MANUFACTURING & INDUSTRIALIZATION

Hardwick, Walter G., "The Persistence of Vancouver as the Focus for Wood Processing in Coastal British Columbia," *Canadian Geographer*, vol. 9, 2 (1965), pp. 92–96. **3610**

URBAN NETWORKS & URBANIZATION

Forrester, Elizabeth A. M., "The Urban Development of Central Vancouver Island," Master's thesis, University of British Columbia, 1966. **3611**

Howell-Jones, Glynn I., "The Urbanization of the Fraser Valley," in Alfred H. Siemens, ed., *Lower Fraser Valley: Evolution of a Cultural Landscape* (Vancouver: Tantalus Research, B.C. Geographical Series, no. 9, 1968), pp. 139–162. [Focus on 1850s–1961] **3612**

McCann, Larry D., "Urban Growth in a Staple Economy: The Emergence of Vancouver as a Regional Metropolis, 1886–1914," in L. J. Evenden, ed., *Vancouver: Western Metropolis* (Victoria: University of Victoria, Western Geographical Series, vol. 16, 1978), pp. 17–41. **3613**

Bradbury, John H., "Instant Resource Towns Policy in British Columbia, 1965–1972," *Plan Canada*, vol. 20, 1 (1980), pp. 19–38. **3614**

Forward, Charles N., "The Functional Structure of the British Columbia System of Ports and the Interactions with the Primate Port, Vancouver," in Nigel M. Waters, ed., *Geographical Research in the 1980s: The Nanaimo Papers* (Vancouver: Tantalus Research, B.C. Geographical Series, no. 31, 1981), pp. 75–92. **3615**

TOWN GROWTH

Vancouver

Jüngst, Peter, "Vancouver, eine stadtgeographische Skizze," in Carl Schott, ed., *Beiträge zur Kul-*

turgeographie von Kanada (Marburg: Marburger Geographische Schriften, vol. 50, 1971), pp. 71–102.   **3616**

Hardwick, Walter G., *Vancouver* (Toronto: Collier-Macmillan, 1974), 214 pp.   **3617**

Robinson, J. Lewis, "How Vancouver Has Grown and Changed," *Canadian Geographical Journal*, vol. 89, 4 (1974), pp. 40–48.   **3618**

Evenden, Len J., ed., *Vancouver: Western Metropolis* (Victoria: Western Geographical Series, no. 16, 1978), 277 pp.   **3619**

MacDonald, Norbert, "CPR Town: The Building Process in Vancouver, 1860–1914," in Gilbert A. Stelter and Alan F. J. Artibise, eds., *Shaping the Urban Landscape: Aspects of the Canadian City-Building Process* (Ottawa: Carleton University Press, 1982), pp. 382–412.   **3620**

Other centers

Weir, Thomas R., "A Geographic Study of New Westminster and Its Regional Relationships," Ph.D. diss., Syracuse University, 1944.   **3621**

Crerar, Alistair D., "The Development of the Port of Prince Rupert, British Columbia," *Yearbook of the Association of Pacific Coast Geographers*, vol. 11 (1949), pp. 23–26.   **3622**

Forward, Charles N., "The Port of Prince Rupert: Always a Bridesmaid," in Brenton M. Barr and M. C. Brown, eds., *Geographical Perspective on Western Canada: The Prince George Papers* (Vancouver: Tantalus Research, B.C. Geographical Series, no. 28, 1979), pp. 7–19.   **3623**

Rheumer, George A., "Princeton: The First Twenty-Five Years," in James W. Scott, ed., *The Pacific Northwest and Beyond: Essays in Honor of Howard J. Critchfield* (Bellingham: Western Washington State University Center for Northwest Studies, 1980), pp. 89–98.   **3624**

Forward, Charles N., "The Development of Victoria as a Retirement Centre," *Urban History Review*, vol. 13, 2 (1984), pp. 117–120.   **3625**

Meredith, Thomas C., "Boosting in British Columbia: the Creation and Rise of Invermere," *Urban History Review*, vol. 16, 3 (1988), pp. 271–279.
3626

URBAN ECONOMIC STRUCTURE

Stevens, Leah, "Rise of the Port of Vancouver, British Columbia," *Economic Geography*, vol. 12, 1 (1936), pp. 61–70.   **3627**

Ivanisko, Henry I., "Changing Patterns of Residential Land Use in the Municipality of Maple Ridge, 1930–1960," Master's thesis, University of British Columbia, 1964.   **3628**

Ulmer, Arno L., "A Comparison of Land Use Changes in Richmond, British Columbia," Master's thesis, University of British Columbia, 1964.   **3629**

Forward, Charles N., "The Functional Characteristics of the Geographic Port of Vancouver," in L. J. Evenden, ed., *Vancouver: Western Metropolis* (Victoria: Western Geographical Series, vol. 16, 1978), pp. 57–77.   **3630**

Forward, Charles N., "The Evolution of Victoria's Functional Character," in Alan F. J. Artibise, ed., *Town and City: Aspects of Western Canadian Urban Development, 1870–1888* (Regina: University of Regina, Canadian Plains Research Centre, Canadian Plains Studies, no. 10, 1981), pp. 347–370.   **3631**

URBAN SOCIAL STRUCTURE

Vancouver

Glyn-Jones, Vivian, "Changing Patterns in School Location, Vancouver School District," Master's thesis, University of British Columbia, 1964.
3632

Cho, George, and Roger Leigh, "Patterns of Residence of the Chinese in Vancouver," in Julian Minghi, ed., *Peoples of the Living Land: Geography of Cultural Diversity in British Columbia* (Vancouver: Tantalus, B.C. Geographical Series, no. 15, 1972), pp. 67–84.   **3633**

McAfee, Ann, "Evolving Inner-City Residential Environments: The Case of Vancouver's West End," in Julian Minghi, ed., *Peoples of the Living Land: Geography of Cultural Diversity in British Columbia* (Vancouver: Tantalus, B.C. Geographical Series, no. 15, 1972), pp. 163–181.   **3634**

Robertson, Angus E., "The Pursuit of Power, Profit, and Privacy: A Study of Vancouver's West End Elite, 1886–1914," Master's thesis, University of British Columbia, 1977.   **3635**

Carr, Adrianne J., "The Development of Neighborhood in Kitsilano: Ideas, Actors, and the Landscape," Master's thesis, University of British Columbia, 1980.   **3636**

Galois, Robert M., "Social Structure in Space: The Making of Vancouver, 1886–1901," Master's thesis, Simon Fraser University, 1980.   **3637**

Collett, Christopher W., "The Congregation of Italians in Vancouver," Master's thesis, Simon Fraser University, 1983.   **3638**

Jackson, Bradley G., "Social Worlds in Transition: Neighborhood Change in Grandview-Woodland, Vancouver," Master's thesis, University of British Columbia, 1984.   **3639**

Anderson, Kay J., "East as West: Place, State, and the Institutionalization of Myth in Vancouver's

Chinatown, 1880–1980," Ph.D. diss., University of British Columbia, 1987. **3640**

Anderson, Kay J., "The Idea of Chinatown: The Power of Place and Institutional Practice in the Making of a Racial Category," *Annals of the Association of American Geographers*, vol. 77, 7 (1987), pp. 580–598. **3641**

Anderson, Kay J., "Community Formation in Official Context: Residential Segregation and the 'Chinese' in Early Vancouver," *Canadian Geographer*, vol. 32, 4 (1988), pp. 354–356. **3642**

Anderson, Kay J., "Cultural Hegemony and the Race-Definition Process in Chinatown, Vancouver: 1880–1980," *Environment and Planning D: Society and Space*, vol. 6, 2 (1988), pp. 127–150. **3643**

Robinson, J. Lewis, "Vancouver: Changing Geographical Aspects of a Multicultural City," *B.C. Studies*, vol. 79 (1988), pp. 59–80. **3644**

Anderson, Kay J., *Vancouver's Chinatown: Racial Discourse in Canada, 1875–1980* (Montreal: McGill-Queen's University Press, 1991), 323 pp. **3645**

Victoria

Lai, David Chuen-yan, "The Chinese Consolidated Benevolent Association in Victoria: Its Origins and Functions," *B.C. Studies*, vol. 15 (1972), pp. 53–67. **3646**

Lai, David Chuen-yan, "The Demographic Structure of a Canadian Chinatown in the Mid-Twentieth Century," *Canadian Ethnic Studies*, vol. 11, 2 (1979), pp. 49–62. [Victoria] **3647**

Lai, David Chuen-yan, "The Issue of Discrimination in Education in Victoria, 1901–1923," *Canadian Ethnic Studies*, vol. 19, 3 (1987), pp. 47–67. **3648**

Lai, David Chuen-yan, "From Self-Segregation to Integration: The Vicissitudes of Victoria's Chinese Hospital," *B.C. Studies*, vol. 80 (1988–1989), pp. 52–68. **3649**

Other centers

Moffat, Benjamin L., "A Community of Working Men: The Residential Environment of Early Nanaimo, British Columbia, 1875–1891," Master's thesis, University of British Columbia, 1981. **3650**

Ripmeester, Michael R., "Everyday Life in the Golden City: A Historical Geography of Rossland, B.C." Master's thesis, University of British Columbia, 1990. **3651**

TOWNSCAPE

Gibson, Edward M., "Industrial Captains and Their Castles in British Columbia, 1886–1917," in

Paul M. Koroscil, ed., *British Columbia: Geographical Essays in Honour of A. Macpherson* (Burnaby, B.C.: Department of Geography, Simon Fraser University, 1991), pp. 67–86. **3652**

Vancouver

Hardwick, Walter G., "Vancouver: The Emergence of a Core-Ring Urban Pattern," in R. Louis Gentilcore, ed., *Geographical Approaches to Canadian Problems* (Scarborough: Prentice-Hall, 1971), pp. 112–118. **3653**

Holdsworth, Deryck W., "Vernacular Form in an Urban Context: A Preliminary Investigation of Facade Elements in Vancouver Housing," Master's thesis, University of British Columbia, 1971. **3654**

Astles, Allen R., "The Role of Historical and Architectural Preservation in the Vancouver Townscape," in Julian Minghi, ed., *Peoples of the Living Land: Geography of Cultural Diversity in British Columbia* (Vancouver: Tantalus, B.C. Geographical Series, no. 15, 1972), pp. 145–162. **3655**

Gale, Donald T., "The Impact of Canadian Italians on Retail Functions and Façades in Vancouver, 1921–1961," in Julian Minghi, ed., *Peoples of the Living Land: Geography of Cultural Diversity in British Columbia* (Vancouver: Tantalus, B.C. Geographical Series, no. 15, 1972), pp. 107–124. **3656**

Gibson, Edward M., "The Impact of Social Belief on Landscape Change: A Geographical Study of Vancouver," Ph.D. diss., University of British Columbia, 1972. **3657**

Gibson, Edward M., "Lotus Eaters, Loggers, and the Vancouver Landscape," in Len Evenden and Frank Cunningham, eds., *Cultural Discord in the Modern World* (Vancouver: Tantalus Research, B.C. Geographical Series, no. 20, 1974), pp. 57–74. **3658**

Holdsworth, Deryck W., "House and Home in Vancouver: Images of West Coast Urbanism, 1886–1929," in Gilbert A. Stelter and Alan F. J. Artibise, eds., *The Canadian City: Essays in Urban History* (Toronto: McClelland and Stewart, 1977), pp. 186–211. **3659**

Holdsworth, Deryck W., "House and Home in Vancouver: The Emergence of a West Coast Urban Landscape, 1886–1929," Ph.D. diss., University of British Columbia, 1981. **3660**

McCririck, Donna, "Opportunity and the Workingman: A Study of Land Accessibility and the Growth of Blue Collar Suburbs in Early Vancouver," Master's thesis, University of British Columbia, 1981. **3661**

McKee, W. C., "The Vancouver Park System, 1886–1929: A Product of Local Business," in

Geoffrey Wall and John S. Marsh, eds., *Recreational Land Use: Perspectives on Its Evolution in Canada* (Ottawa: Carleton University Press, 1982), pp. 299–310.   3662

Holdsworth, Deryck W., "Cottages and Castles for Vancouver Home-Seekers," *B.C. Studies*, vol. 69–70 (1986), pp. 11–32; and in Robert A. J. McDonald and Jean Barman, eds., *Vancouver Past: Essays in Social History* (Vancouver: University of British Columbia Press, 1986), pp. 11–32. 3663

Ley, David J., "Styles of the Times: Liberal and Neo-Conservative Landscapes in Inner Vancouver, 1968–1986," *Journal of Historical Geography*, vol. 13, 1 (1987), pp. 40–56.   3664

McCririck, Donna, and Graeme Wynn, "Building 'Self-Respect and Hopefulness': The Development of Blue-Collar Suburbs in Early Vancouver," in Graeme Wynn, ed., *People, Places, Patterns, Processes: Geographical Perspectives on the Canadian Past* (Toronto: Copp Clark Pitman, 1990), pp. 267–284.   3665

Victoria

Forward, Charles N., "The Immortality of a Fashionable Residential District: The Uplands," in Charles N. Forward, ed., *Residential and Neighborhood Studies in Victoria* (Victoria: University of Victoria Western Geographical Series, vol. 5, 1973), pp. 1–39.   3666

Goid, C., "Wartime Housing in Victoria, British Columbia," Master's thesis, University of Victoria, 1977.   3667

Lai, David Chuen-yan, "The History and Architecture of Victoria's Chinatown," *West Coast Review*, vol. 15, 4 (1981), pp. 36–41.   3668

Lai, David Chuen-yan, "The Chinese Cemetery in Victoria," *B.C. Studies*, vol. 75 (1987), pp. 24–42.   3669

RECREATION & TOURISM

Marsh, John S., "Man, Landscape, and Recreation in Glacier National Park, British Columbia, 1880 to Present," Ph.D. diss., University of Calgary, 1972.   3670

Leonard, Eric M., "Parks and Resource Policy: The Role of British Columbia's Provincial Parks,

1911–1945," Master's thesis, Simon Fraser University, 1974.   3671

Marsh, John, "The Evolution of Recreation in Glacier National Park: British Columbia, 1880 to Present," in Geoffrey Wall and John Marsh, eds., *Recreational Land Use: Perspectives on Its Evolution in Canada* (Ottawa: Carleton University Press, 1982), pp. 62–76.   3672

Marsh, John, "The Rocky and Selkirk Mountains and the Swiss Connection, 1885–1914," *Annals of Tourism Research*, vol. 12, 3 (1985), pp. 417–433.   3673

Wightman, Deborah, and Geoffrey Wall, "The Spa Experience at Radium Hot Springs," *Annals of Tourism Research*, vol. 12, 3 (1985), pp. 393–415. [Focus on 1910–1985]   3674

PLANNING

Lee, Christopher L., "The Effect of Planning Controls on the Morphology of the City of Victoria," Master's thesis, University of Victoria, 1970.   3675

Bottomley, John, "Ideology, Planning, and the Landscape: The Business Community, Urban Reform, and the Establishment of Town Planning in Vancouver, British Columbia, 1900–1940," Ph.D. diss., University of British Columbia, 1977.   3676

Scott, Laura E., "Imposition of British Culture as Portrayed in the New Westminster Capital Plan of 1859 to 1862," Master's thesis, Simon Fraser University, 1985.   3677

PLACE NAMES

Walbran, John T., *British Columbia Coast Names, 1592–1906: Their Origin and History* (Ottawa: Government Printing Bureau, 1909), 546 pp.   3678

Boas, Franz, *Geographical Names of the Kwakiutl Indians* (New York: Columbia University Press, 1934), 83 pp. Reprinted AMS Press, 1969. 3679

Akrigg, George P. V., and Helen B. Akrigg, *1001 British Columbia Place Names* (Vancouver: Discovery Press, 1970), 195 pp.   3680

YUKON TERRITORY

NATIVE PEOPLES & WHITE RELATIONS

Leechman, Douglas, "Prehistoric Migration Routes through the Yukon," *Canadian Historical Review*, vol. 27, 4 (1946), pp. 383–390. 3681

McSkimming, Robert J., "Territory, Territoriality, and Cultural Change in an Indigenous Society: Old Crow, Yukon Territory," Master's thesis, University of British Columbia, 1975. 3682

REGIONAL SETTLEMENT

Duerden, Frank, "The Evolution and Nature of the Contemporary Settlement Pattern in a Selected Area of the Yukon Territory," Master's thesis, University of Manitoba, 1969. 3683

Koroscil, Paul M., "The Changing Landscape of the Yukon Territory and the Settlements of Whitehorse," Ph.D. diss., University of Michigan, 1970. 3684

Becker, Hans, "Siedlungsgründungen des ausgehenden 19. Jahrhunderts an der kanadischen Bergbaufrontier im Klondike-Goldfeld," *Erde*, vol. 111, 4 (1980), pp. 329–352. 3685

Becker, Hans, "Ausbildung und Verfall eines zentralörtlich organisierten Siedlungssystems an der kanadischen Bergbaufrontier: Das Beispiel des Klondike-Goldfeldes," in Hans Becker, ed., *Kulturgeographische Prozessforschung in Kanada* (Bamberg: Bamberger Geographische Schriften, vol. 4, 1982), pp. 305–325. 3686

ECONOMIC DEVELOPMENT

See also 1402

EXTRACTIVE ACTIVITY

Laatsch, William G., "Yukon Mining Settlement: An Examination of Three Communities," Ph.D. diss., University of Alberta, 1972. 3687

COMMUNICATIONS & TRADE

Clibbon, Peter B., "Skagway, Whitehorse, and the White Pass and Yukon Route Railway," *Cahiers de géographie du Québec*, vol. 34, 91 (1990), pp. 45–79. 3688

TOWN GROWTH

Denis, Paul-Yves, "Les facteurs géographiques de la situation et du site de Whitehorse," *Revue canadienne de géographie*, vol. 9, 4 (1955), pp. 161–178. 3689

Doogen, Mike, "Dawson City," *Alaska Geographic*, vol. 15, 2 (1988), pp. 7–74. 3690

Koroscil, Paul M., "The Historical Development of Whitehorse: 1898–1945," *American Review of Canadian Studies*, vol. 18, 3 (1988), pp. 271–294. 3691

Clibbon, Peter B., "The Evolution and Present Land Use Patterns of Whitehorse, Yukon Territory," *Cahiers du Centre de recherches en aménagement et en dévelopment*, vol. 12, 2 (1989), 61 pp. 3692

TOWNSCAPE

Koroscil, Paul M., "The Changing Landscape of Whitehorse, Yukon Territory: A Historical Perspective," in Julian V. Minghi, ed., *Peoples of the Living Land: Geography of Cultural Diversity in British Columbia* (Vancouver: Tantalus Research, B.C. Geographical Series, no. 15, 1972), pp. 183–211. 3693

PLANNING

Koroscil, Paul M., "Planning and Development in Whitehorse, Yukon Territory," *Plan Canada*, vol. 18, 1 (1978), pp. 30–45. 3694

Mackinnon, C. S., "The Rise and Decline of Agriculture and Horticulture in the Mackenzie District and the Yukon," *Musk-Ox*, vol. 30 (1982), pp. 48–63. 3695

PLACE NAMES

See 1473

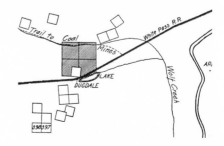

THE NORTH

GENERAL

See also 1152

Botts, Adelbert K., "Geographic Backgrounds of Hudson Bay History," *Social Education*, vol. 11, 8 (1947), pp. 343–345.   **3696**

Taylor, Andrew, "An Introduction to the Northern Islands Region of the Canadian Arctic Archipelago: Its Historical and Geographical Setting," Master's thesis, Université de Montréal, 1950.
3697

Stager, John K., "Historical Geography of the Mackenzie River Valley, 1750–1850," Ph.D. diss., University of Ediburgh, 1962.   **3698**

McConnell, John G., "The Fort Smith Area, 1780 to 1961: A Historical Geography," Master's thesis, University of Toronto, 1966.   **3699**

Ross, W. Gillies, "On the Barrens, 1934," *Beaver*, Outfit 299, 2 (1968), pp. 48–53.   **3700**

Wonders, William C., "The Forest Frontier and Subarctic," in John H. Warkentin, ed., *Canada: A Geographical Interpretation* (Toronto: Methuen, 1968), pp. 473–507.   **3701**

Zaslow, M., *The Opening of the Canadian North 1870–1914* (Toronto: McClelland and Stewart, 1971), 339 pp.   **3702**

Jensen, Kenneth D., "A Cultural Historical Study of Domination, Exploitation, and Cooperation in the Canadian Arctic," Ph.D. diss., Michigan State University, 1975.   **3703**

Lloyd, Trevor, "Canada and the Circumpolar World-Comparisons and Challenges," in Morris Zaslow, ed., *A Century of Canada's Arctic Islands, 1880–1980* (Ottawa: Royal Society of Canada, 1981), pp. 309–318.   **3704**

ENVIRONMENTAL CHANGE

Harrington, Richard, "History, Distribution, and Ecology of the Muskoxen," Master's thesis, McGill University, 1961.   **3705**

Catchpole, Alan J. W., and D. Wayne Moodie, "Multiple Reflection in Arctic Regions," *Weather*, vol. 26, 4 (1971), pp. 157–163.   **3706**

Plumet, Patrick, "L'archéologie et le relèvement glacio-isostatique de la région de Poste-de-la-Baleine, Nouveau-Québec," *Revue de géographie de Montréal*, vol. 28, 4 (1974), pp. 443–447.
3707

Ross, W. Gillies, "Distribution, Migration, and Depletion of Bowhead Whales in Hudson Bay, 1860–1915," *Arctic and Alpine Research*, vol. 6, 1 (1974), pp. 85–98.   **3708**

Teillet, John V., "A Reconstruction of Summer Sea Ice Conditions in the Labrador Sea Using Hudson's Bay Company Log-Books, 1751 to 1870," Master's thesis, University of Manitoba, 1988.
3709

Catchpole, Alan J. W., and Irene Hanuta, "Severe Summer Ice in Hudson Strait and Hudson Bay Following Major Volcanic Eruptions, 1751 to 1889 A.D.," *Climatic Change*, vol. 14, 1 (1989), pp. 61–79.   **3710**

Hanuta, Irene, "Reconstruction of Sea Ice and Weather Conditions in the Hudson Bay Region for the Summer of 1836," in H. John Selwood and John C. Lehr, eds., *Prairie and Northern Perspectives: Geographical Essays* (Winnipeg: University of Winnipeg Department of Geography, 1989), pp. 9–22.   **3711**

NATIVE PEOPLES & WHITE RELATIONS

Jenness, Diamond, "The Cultural Transformation of the Copper Eskimo," *Geographical Review*, vol. 11, 4 (1921), pp. 541–550. [Coronation Gulf]
3712

Collins, Henry B., "Prehistoric Eskimo Culture on St. Lawrence Island," *Geographical Review*, vol. 22, 1 (1932), pp. 107–119.   **3713**

Hargrave, M. R., "Changing Settlement Patterns amongst the Mackenzie Eskimos of the Canadian Northwestern Arctic," *Albertan Geographer*, vol. 2 (1965), pp. 25–30. Reprinted in Robert M. Irving, ed., *Readings in Canadian Geography* (Toronto: Holt, Rinehart and Winston, 1972), pp. 99–106.   **3714**

Morris, Margaret W., "Great Bear Lake Indians: A Historical Demography and Ecology," Master's thesis, University of Saskatchewan, 1972.   **3715**

Morris, Margaret W., "Great Bear Lake Indians; A Historical Demography and Human Ecology: Part I—The Situation Prior to European Contact"; "Part II—European Influences," *Musk-Ox*, vol. 11 (1972), pp. 3–27; vol. 12 (1973), pp. 58–80.   **3716**

Ross, W. Gillies, *Whaling and Eskimos: Hudson's Bay 1860–1915* (Ottawa: National Museum of

Man, Publications in Ethnology, 1975), 164 pp.
3717

Ross, W. Gillies, "Inuit and the Land in the Nineteenth Century," in Milton M. R. Freeman, *Inuit Land Use and Occupancy Project*, vol. 2 (Ottawa: Department of Indian and Northern Affairs, 1976), pp. 123–139. **3718**

Ross, W. Gillies, "Whaling and the Decline of Native Populations," *Arctic Anthropology*, vol. 14, 2 (1977), pp. 1–8. **3719**

Ross, W. Gillies, "Commercial Whaling and Eskimos in the Eastern Canadian Arctic, 1819–1920," in Allen P. McCartney, ed., *Thule Eskimo Culture: An Anthropological Retrospective* (Ottawa: National Museum of Man, Mercury Series, Archeological Survey of Canada Paper no. 88, 1979), pp. 242–266. **3720**

Ross, W. Gillies, "Whaling, Eskimos, and the Arctic Islands," in Morris Zaslow, ed., *A Century of Canada's Arctic Islands, 1880–1980* (Ottawa: Royal Society of Canada, 1981), pp. 33–50. **3721**

Julig, Patrick J., "Human Use of the Albany River from Preceramic Times to the Late Eighteenth Century," Master's thesis, York University, 1982.
3722

Ross, W. Gillies, "The Earliest Sound Recordings among North American Inuit," *Arctic*, vol. 37, 3 (1984), pp. 291–292. **3723**

Ross, W. Gillies, "George Comer, Franz Boas, and the American Museum of Natural History," *Études/Inuit/Studies*, vol. 8, 1 (1984), pp. 145–164. **3724**

Ross, W. Gillies, "The Sound of Eskimo Music," *Beaver*, Outfit 315, 3 (1984), pp. 28–36. **3725**

EXPLORATION & MAPPING

Hennig, Richard, "Normanen des 11. Jahrhunderts in der Hudson-Bai und auf den Großen Seen," *Petermanns Geographische Mitteilungen*, vol. 85, 2 (1939), pp. 58–60. **3726**

Fraser, J. Keith, "Tracing Ross across Boothia," *Canadian Geographer*, no. 10 (1957), pp. 40–60.
3727

Ross, W. Gillies, "Parry's Second Voyage," *History Today*, vol. 5, 2 (1960), pp. 100–105. **3728**

Lotz, James R., "Northern Ellesmere Island: A Study in the History of Geographical Discovery," *Canadian Geographer*, vol. 6, 2 (1962), pp. 151–161. **3729**

Layng, Theodore E., "Early Geographical Concepts of the Northwest Passages," *Canadian Cartographer*, vol. 2, 2 (1965), pp. 81–91. **3730**

Stager, John K., "Alexander Mackenzie's Exploration of the Grand River," *Geographical Bulletin* (Ottawa), vol. 7, 3 & 4 (1965), pp. 213–242.
3731

Wonders, William C., "Search for Franklin," *Canadian Geographical Journal*, vol. 76, 4 (1968), pp. 116–127. **3732**

Spink, John, "Eskimo Maps from the Canadian Eastern Arctic," Master's thesis, University of Manitoba, 1969. **3733**

Ross, W. Gillies, and William Barr, "Voyages in Northwestern Hudson Bay, 1720–1772, and Discovery of the Knight Relics on Marble Island," *Musk-Ox*, no. 11 (1972), pp. 28–33. **3734**

Spink, John, and D. Wayne Moodie, *Eskimo Maps from the Canadian Eastern Arctic* (Toronto: B. V. Gutsell, Cartographica Monograph no. 5, 1972), 98 pp. **3735**

Verner, Coolie, and Frances Woodward, *Explorers' Maps of the Canadian Arctic, 1818–1860* (Toronto: B. V. Gutsell, Cartographica Monograph no. 6, 1972), 84 pp. **3736**

DeReyes, Urte E., "Mercator's Changing Concept of the North Pole," Master's thesis, University of Manitoba, 1973. **3737**

Spink, John, and D. Wayne Moodie, "Inuit Maps from the Canadian Eastern Arctic," in Milton Freeman, ed., *Inuit Land Use and Occupancy Project Report*, vol. 2 (Ottawa: Department of Indian and Northern Affairs, 1976), pp. 39–46.
3738

Wallace, Hugh, "Geographical Explorations to 1880," in Morris Zaslow, ed., *A Century of Canada's Arctic Islands, 1880–1980* (Ottawa: Royal Society of Canada, 1981), pp. 15–32. **3739**

Wonders, William C., "Unrolling the Map of Canada's Arctic," in Morris Zaslow, ed., *A Century of Canada's Arctic Islands, 1880–1980* (Ottawa: Royal Society of Canada, 1981), pp. 1–14. **3740**

Alagon, Simonetta Ballo, "Emile Petitot: Missionatio-esploratore nel Nord-Ouest del Canada," *Rivista geografia italiana*, vol. 89, 3 (1982), pp. 419–433. **3741**

Barr, William, and Chuck Tolley, "The German Expedition at Clearwater Fiord, 1882–83," *Beaver*, Outfit 313, 2 (1982), pp. 36–45. **3742**

Wonders, William C., "Geographical Mapping of Canada's Arctic Islands, 1880–1980," *Information Bulletin of the Western Association of Map Libraries*, vol. 13, 3 (1982), pp. 257–273. **3743**

Harding, Kathryn M. M., "Discovery Maps of the Canadian Northwest: The Hudson's Bay Company, the Royal Navy, and the British Map Trade, 1819–1857," Master's thesis, Queen's University, 1987. **3744**

POPULAR IMAGES AND EVALUATION

Spink, John, "Historic Eskimo Awareness of Past Changes in Sea Level," *Musk-Ox*, vol. 5 (1969), pp. 37–40.   3745

REGIONAL SETTLEMENT

Treude, Erhard, "Studien zur Siedlungs und Wirtschaftsentwicklung in der östlichen kanadischen Zentralarktis," *Erde*, vol. 104, 3 (1973), pp. 247–276. Translated as "Studies in Settlement Development and Evolution of the Economy in the Eastern Central Canadian Artic," *Musk-Ox*, vol. 16 (1975), pp. 53–66. [Focus on 1920–1972]
3746

POPULATION

Bird, J. Brian, "The Arctic," in John H. Warkentin, ed., *Canada: A Geographical Interpretation* (Toronto: Methuen, 1968), pp. 508–528.   3747

RURAL & REGIONAL SOCIAL GEOGRAPHY

Cole, Leslie. "The Southernization of Food Habits on Baffin Island, 1955–1985," Master's thesis, University of Ottawa, 1988.   3748

Stager, John K., "Co-operatives as Instruments of Social Change for the Inuit of Canada," in Guy M. Robinson, ed., *A Social Geography of Canada* (Edinburgh: North British Publishing, 1988), pp. 295–306. Also Toronto: Dundurn Press, 1991, pp. 393–407.   3749

POLITICAL & ADMINISTRATIVE GEOGRAPHY

Ross, W. Gillies, "Canadian Sovereignty in the Arctic: The Neptune Expedition of 1903–04," *Arctic*, vol. 29, 2 (1976), pp. 87–104.   3750

Taylor, M. J., "The Development of Mineral Policy for the Eastern Arctic, 1953–1985," Master's thesis, Carleton University, 1985.   3751

ECONOMIC DEVELOPMENT

Patton, Harold S., "Canada's Advance to Hudson Bay," *Economic Geography*, vol. 5, 3 (1929), pp. 215–235.   3752

EXTRACTIVE ACTIVITY

Trapping and fur trade

Van Stone, James W., "Changing Patterns of Indian Trapping in the Canadian Subarctic," *Arctic*, vol. 16, 3 (1963), pp. 158–174. Reprinted in Robert M. Irving, ed., *Readings in Canadian Geography* (Toronto: Holt, Rinehart and Winston, 1972), pp. 107–118.   3753

Stager, John K., "Fur Trading Posts in the Mackenzie Region up to 1850," *Occasional Papers in Geography*, Canadian Association of Geographers, British Columbia Division, no. 1–4 (1965), pp. 37–46.   3754

Usher, Peter, "The Growth and Decay of the Trading and Trapping Frontiers in the Western Canadian Arctic," *Canadian Geographer*, vol. 19, 3 (1975), pp. 308–320.   3755

Ray, Arthur J., "The Decline of Paternalism in the Hudson's Bay Company Fur Trade, 1870–1945," in Rosemary F. Ommer, ed., *Merchant Credit and Labour Strategies in Historical Perspective* (Fredericton: Acadiensis Press, 1990), pp. 188–202.   3756

Fisheries

Ross, W. Gillies, "American Whaling in Hudson Bay: The Voyage of the *Black Eagle*, 1866–67," *Canadian Geographical Journal*, vol. 75, 6 (1967), pp. 198–205.   3757

Cooke, Alan, and W. Gillies Ross, "The Drift of the Whaler *Viewforth* in Davis Strait, 1835–36, from William Elder's Journal," *Polar Record*, vol. 14, 92 (1969), pp. 581–591.   3758

Ross, W. Gillies, "The Nature and Distribution of Bowhead Whaling in Hudson Bay, 1860–1915," in *Études d'histoire maritime présentées au XIIIe Congrès international des sciences historiques par la Commission internationale d'histoire maritime à l'occasion de son XIIIe colloque* (Moscow, 16–23 Aug. 1970), pp. 181–198.
3759

Ross, W. Gillies, "Hudson Bay Whaling, 1860–1915," Ph.D. diss., University of Cambridge, 1971.   3760

Ross, W. Gillies, "Whaling in Hudson Bay (Part 1)," *Beaver*, Outfit 303, 4 (1973), pp. 4–11; "Part 2," Outfit 304, 1 (1973), pp. 40–47; "Part 3," Outfit 304, 2 (1973), pp. 52–59.   3761

Ross, W. Gillies, "The Annual Catch of Greenland (Bowhead) Whales in Waters North of Canada 1719–1915: A Preliminary Compilation," *Arctic*, vol. 32, 2 (1979), pp. 91–121.   3762

Ross, W. Gillies, ed., *An Arctic Whaling Diary: The Journal of Captain George Comer in Hudson Bay, 1903–1905* (Toronto: University of Toronto Press, 1984), 271pp.   3763

Ross, W. Gillies, *Arctic Whalers, Icy Seas: Narratives of the Davis Strait Whale Fishery* (Toronto: Irwin Publishing, 1985), 263pp.   3764

COMMUNICATIONS & TRADE

Stager, John K., "Fort Anderson: The First Post for Trade in the Western Arctic," *Geographical Bulletin* (Ottawa), vol. 9, 1 (1967), pp. 45–56. **3765**

TOWN GROWTH

Miller, Roscoe R., "Hudson Bay and Its Ports," *Bulletin of the Philadelphia Geographical Society*, vol. 30, 4 (1932), pp. 207–213. **3766**

Huber, A., "Churchill, ein Außenposten an der Hudson Bay," *Geographica Helvetica*, vol. 9 (1954), pp. 16–39. **3767**

MacBain, Sheila Keith, "The Evolution of Frobisher Bay as a Major Settlement in the Canadian Eastern Arctic," Master's thesis, McGill University, 1970. **3768**

Vogelsang, Roland R., "Generationen von Bergbausiedlungen im Norden Kanadas: Die Beispiele Goldfields, Eldorado, Uranium City und Rabbit Lake Mine," *Erde*, vol. 110, 79 (1980), pp. 275–298. **3769**

PLACE NAMES

White, James, "Place Names in Northern Canada," *Proceedings and Transactions of the Royal Society of Canada*, 3d ser., vol. 4 (1910), sec. 4, pp. 37–40. **3770**

Müller-Wille, Ludger, "Inuit Toponymy and Cultural Sovereignty," in Ludger Müller-Wille, ed., *Beiträge zum Entwicklungskonflikt in Nouveau-Québec* (Marburg: Marburger Geographische Schriften, no. 89, 1983), pp. 131–150. Also published as Ludger Müller-Wille, ed., *Conflict in Development: Nouveau-Québec* (Montreal: McGill University Centre for Northern Studies and Research, Subarctic Research Paper no. 37, 1983). [Evolution of place-name systems, 1800–1982] **3771**

Müller-Wille, Ludger, "Une méthodologie pour les enquêtes toponymiques autochtones: Le répertoire inuit de la région de Kativik et de sa zone côtière," *Études/Inuit/Studies*, vol. 9, 1 (1985), pp. 51–66. **3772**

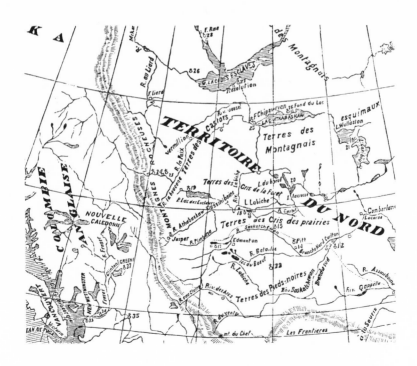

RUPERT'S LAND

(SEE ALSO PRAIRIE PROVINCES AND NORTHWEST TERRITORIES)

GENERAL

Ellis, George E., "Hudson Bay Company, 1670–1870," *Journal of the American Geographical Society*, vol. 18 (1886), pp. 127–136.   3773

Ross, Eric D., "The Canadian Northwest in 1811: A Study in the Historical Geography of the Old Northwest of the Fur Trade on the Eve of the First Agricultural Settlement," Ph.D. diss., University of Edinburgh, 1962.   3774

Ross, Eric D., *Beyond the River and the Bay* (Toronto: University of Toronto Press, 1970), 190 pp.   3775

Moodie, D. Wayne, "The Hudson's Bay Company and Its Geographical Impress, 1670–1870," *International Geography '76*, sec. 9, *Historical Geography* (Moscow: Twenty-third International Geographical Union, 1976), pp. 71–74.   3776

Yerbury, J. C., "Lake Athabasca Region before 1765," *Alberta History*, vol. 29, 1 (1981), pp. 31–35.   3777

Davis, Richard C., ed., *Rupert's Land: A Cultural Tapestry* (Waterloo: Wilfrid Laurier University Press, 1988), 314 pp.   3778

ENVIRONMENTAL CHANGE

General

Simpson, Samuel J., "The York Factory Area, Hudson Bay: An Account of the Environment and the Evolution of the Tract of Land between the Mouths of the Nelson and Hayes Rivers," Ph.D. diss., University of Manitoba, 1972.   3779

Moodie, D. Wayne, and Barry Kaye, "Taming and Domesticating the Wild Animals of Rupert's Land," *Beaver*, Outfit 307, 3 (1976), pp. 10–19.   3780

Climatic change and ice conditions

Minns, Robert, "An Air Mass Climatology of Canada during the Early Nineteenth Century: An Analysis of the Weather Records of Certain Hudson's Bay Company Forts," Master's thesis, University of British Columbia, 1970.   3781

Catchpole, Alan J. W., D. Wayne Moodie, and D. Milton, "Freeze-up and Break-up of Estuaries on Hudson Bay in the Eighteenth and Nine-

teenth Centuries," *Canadian Geographer*, vol. 20, 3 (1976), pp. 279–297.   3782

Moodie, D. Wayne, and Alan J. W. Catchpole, "Valid Climatological Data from Historical Sources by Content Analysis," *Science*, vol. 193, 4247 (1976), pp. 51–53.   3783

Catchpole, Alan J. W., D. Milton, and D. Wayne Moodie, "Spring Break-up of Estuaries on Hudson Bay," *Weather*, vol. 32, 10 (1977), pp. 364–372.   3784

Faurer, Marcia Anne, "Evidence of Sea Ice Conditions in Hudson Strait, 1750–1870, Using Ships' Logs," Master's thesis, University of Manitoba, 1981.   3785

Madison, Gerry N., "Reconstruction and Testing of Historical Dates of First Frost and First Snow, James Bay, Ontario, 1705–1870," Master's thesis, University of Manitoba, 1981.   3786

Magne, Mary A., "Two Centuries of River Ice Dates in Hudson Bay Region from Historical Sources," Master's thesis, University of Manitoba, 1981.   3787

Ball, Timothy F., "The Migration of Geese as an Indicator of Climatic Changes in the Southern Hudson Bay Region between 1715 and 1851," *Climatic Change*, vol. 5, 1 (1983), pp. 85–94.   3788

Catchpole, Alan J. W., and Marcia-Anne Faurer, "Summer Sea Ice Severity in Hudson Strait, 1751–1870," *Climatic Change*, vol. 5, 2 (1983), pp. 115–140.   3789

Catchpole, Alan J. W., and Janet Halpin, "Measuring Summer Sea Ice Severity in Eastern Hudson Bay, 1751–1870," *Canadian Geographer*, vol. 31, 3 (1987), pp. 233–244.   3790

NATIVE PEOPLES & WHITE RELATIONS

Ray, Arthur J., *Indians in the Fur Trade: Their Role as Trappers, Hunters, and Middlemen in the Lands Southwest of Hudson Bay, 1660–1870* (Toronto: University of Toronto Press, 1974), 249 pp.   3791

Ray, Arthur J., "Smallpox: The Epidemic of 1837–38," *Beaver*, Outfit 306, 2 (1975), pp. 8–13.   3792

Ray, Arthur J., "Diffusion of Diseases in the Western Interior of Canada, 1830–1850," *Geographi-*

cal Review, vol. 66, 2 (1976), pp. 139–157. Reprinted in abbreviated form in Graeme Wynn, ed., People, Places, Patterns, Processes: Geographical Perspectives on the Canadian Past (Toronto: Copp Clark Pitman, 1990), pp. 68–87. **3793**

Lewer, Else, "The Dispersal and Impact of Church of England Missions in Rupert's Land and the Indian Territories, 1822–1868: A Geography of Religion," Master's thesis, Carleton University, 1977. **3794**

Ray, Arthur J., and Donald Freeman, Give Us Good Measure: An Economic Analysis of Relations between the Indians and the Hudson's Bay Company before 1763 (Toronto: University of Toronto Press, 1978), 298 pp. **3795**

Moodie, D. Wayne, and Barry Kaye, "Indian Agriculture in the Fur Trade Northwest," Prairie Forum, vol. 11, 2 (1986), pp. 171–184. **3796**

Tough, Frank, "Research on Fur Trade and Native Economies in the Post-1870 Period: An Historical Geography Approach to the Daily Journals of the Hudson's Bay Company," Native Studies Review, vol. 3 (1987), pp. 129–146. **3797**

EXPLORATION & MAPPING

Ruggles, Richard I., "The Historical Geography and Historical Cartography of the Canadian West, 1670–1795: The Discovery, Exploration, Geographical Description, and Cartographic Delineation of Western Canada to 1795," Ph.D. diss., University of London, 1958. **3798**

Williams, Glyndwyr, "A Remarkable Map," Beaver, Outfit 293 (1962), pp. 30–36. [R. W. Seale, map of North America, 1748] **3799**

Williams, Glyndwyr, "Captain Coats and Exploration along the East Main," Beaver, Outfit 294 (1963), pp. 4–13. **3800**

Ruggles, Richard I., "Hospital Boys of the Bay: The Hudson's Bay Company Surveying and Mapping Apprentices," Beaver, Outfit 308, 2 (1977), pp. 4–11. **3801**

Ruggles, Richard I., "Hudson's Bay Company Mapping," in Carol M. Judd and Arthur J. Ray, eds., Old Trails and New Directions: Papers of the Third North American Fur Trade Conference (Toronto: University of Toronto Press, 1980), pp. 24–36. **3802**

Ball, Timothy, and David Dyck, "Observations of the Transit of Venus at Prince of Wales' Fort in 1769," Beaver, Outfit 315, 2 (1984), pp. 51–56. **3803**

Ruggles, Richard I., "Mapping the Interior Plains of Rupert's Land by the Hudson's Bay Company to 1870," Great Plains Quarterly, vol. 4, 3 (1984),

pp. 152–165. Reprinted in Frederick C. Luebke, Frances Kaye, and Gary E. Moulton, eds., Mapping the North American Plains: Essays in the History of Cartography (Norman: University of Oklahoma Press, 1987), pp. 145–160. **3804**

Ruggles, Richard I., "Canada's First 'National' Map Agency: The Hudson's Bay Company," Bulletin of the Association of Canadian Map Libraries, no. 55 (1985), pp. 1–18. **3805**

Ruggles, Richard I., "Beyond the Furious over Fall: Map Images of Rupert's Land and the Northwest," in Richard Davis, ed., Rupert's Land: A Cultural Tapestry (Waterloo: Wilfrid Laurier University Press, 1988), pp. 13–50. **3806**

Ruggles, Richard I., A Country So Interesting: The Hudson's Bay Company and Two Centuries of Mapping, 1670–1870 (Montreal: McGill-Queen's University Press, 1991), 304 pp. **3807**

POPULAR IMAGES & EVALUATION

Young, Greg A., "Changes in Geographical Knowledge of the Interior as Seen through Fort Albany by Hudson's Bay Men in the Eighteenth Century," Master's thesis, York University, 1974. **3808**

Moodie, D. Wayne, "Early British Images of Rupert's Land," in R. Allen, ed., Man and Nature on the Prairies (Regina: University of Regina, Canadian Plains Research Centre, no. 6, 1976), pp. 1–20. **3809**

Moodie, D. Wayne, "Science and Reality: Arthur Dobbs and the Eighteenth Century Geography of Rupert's Land," Journal of Historical Geography, vol. 2, 4 (1976), pp. 293–309. **3810**

Kemp, David, "Attitudes to Winter in the Northwest Fur Trade," Canadian Geographer, vol. 31, 1 (1987), pp. 49–57. **3811**

Allen, John L., "To Unite the Discoveries: The American Response to the Early Exploration of Rupert's Land," in Richard Davis, ed., Rupert's Land: A Cultural Tapestry (Waterloo: Wilfrid Laurier University Press, 1988), pp. 79–96. **3812**

REGIONAL SETTLEMENT

Moodie, D. Wayne, "The Trading Post Settlement of the Canadian Northwest, 1774–1821," Journal of Historical Geography, vol. 13, 4 (1987), pp. 360–374. **3813**

POLITICAL & ADMINISTRATIVE GEOGRAPHY

Ruggles, Richard I., "Governor Samuel Wegg: The Winds of Change," Beaver, Outfit 307, 2 (1976), pp. 10–20. **3814**

Ruggles, Richard I., "Governor Samuel Wegg: Intelligent Layman of the Royal Society, 1753–1802," *Notes and Records of the Royal Society of London*, vol. 32, 2 (1978), pp. 181–199. **3815**

RESOURCE MANAGEMENT

Ray, Arthur J., "Competition and Conservation in the Early Subarctic Fur Trade," *Ethnohistory*, vol. 25, 4 (1978), pp. 347–358. **3816**

EXTRACTIVE ACTIVITY

Fur trade

Merriam, Willis B., "The Role of Pemmican in the Canadian Northwest Fur Trade," *Yearbook of the Association of Pacific Coast Geographers*, vol. 17 (1955), pp. 34–38. **3817**

Ray, Arthur J., "History and Archeology of the Northern Fur Trade," *American Antiquity*, vol. 43, 1 (1976), pp. 26–34. **3818**

Ray, Arthur J., "The Hudson's Bay Company Fur Trade in the Eighteenth Century: A Comparative Economic Study," in James R. Gibson, ed., *European Settlement and Development: Essays in Geographical Change in Honour and Memory of Andrew Hill Clark* (Toronto: University of Toronto Press, 1978), pp. 116–135. **3819**

Lytwyn, Victor P., "The Historical Geography of the Fur Trade of the Little North and Its Expansion into the East Winnipeg Country to 1821," Master's thesis, University of Manitoba, 1981. **3820**

Moodie, D. Wayne, and John C. Lehr, "Macro-Historical Geography and the Great Chartered Companies: The Case of the Hudson's Bay Company," *Canadian Geographer*, vol. 25, 3 (1981), pp. 267–271. **3821**

Lytwyn, Victor P., "Geographical Situation and the Early Fur Trade of the East Winnipeg Country," *Regina Geographical Studies*, no. 4 (1984), pp. 33–40. **3822**

Ray, Arthur J., "Periodic Shortages, Native Welfare, and the Hudson's Bay Company, 1670–1930," in Shepard Krech, ed., *The Subarctic Fur Trade: Native Social and Economic Adaptations* (Vancouver: University of British Columbia Press, 1984), pp. 1–20. **3823**

Ray, Arthur J., "William Todd: Doctor and Trader for the Hudson's Bay Company," *Prairie Forum*, vol. 9, 1 (1984), pp. 13–26. **3824**

Schwoerer, Ute, "Reorganization of the Hudson's Bay Company Fur Trade between 1821 and 1826," Master's thesis, York University, 1987. **3825**

Decker, Jody F., "Scurvy at York," *Beaver*, vol. 69, 1 (1989), pp. 42–48. **3826**

AGRICULTURE

Moodie, D. Wayne, "An Historical Geography of Agricultural Patterns and Resource Appraisals in Rupert's Land, 1670–1774," Ph.D. diss., University of Alberta, 1972. **3827**

Moodie, D. Wayne, "Gardening on Hudson Bay: the First Century," *Beaver*, Outfit 309, 1 (1978), pp. 54–57. **3828**

COMMUNICATIONS & TRADE

Alwin, John A., "The Uncelebrated Boats of the Albany," *Beaver*, Outfit 305, 4 (1975), pp. 47–53. **3829**

Ray, Arthur J., *The Factor and the Trading Captain in the Hudson's Bay Company Fur Trade before 1763* (Ottawa: National Museum of Man, Ethnology Service, Mercury Series, Paper no. 28, 1975), 46 pp. **3830**

Ray, Arthur J., "The Early Hudson's Bay Company Account Books as Sources for Historical Research: An Analysis and Assessment," *Archivaria*, vol. 1, 1 (1975–1976), pp. 3–38. **3831**

Alwin, John A., "Mode, Pattern, and Pulse: Hudson's Bay Company Transport 1670–1821," Ph.D. diss., University of Manitoba, 1977. **3832**

Ray, Arthur J., "Higgling and Haggling at Ye Bay," *Beaver*, Outfit 308, 1 (1977), pp. 38–46. **3833**

Alwin, John A., "Colony and Company Sharing the York Mainline," *Beaver*, Outfit 310, 1 (1979), pp. 4–11. **3834**

Ray, Arthur J., "Buying and Selling Hudson's Bay Company Furs in the Eighteenth Century," in D. Cameron, ed., *Explorations in Canadian Economic History: Essays in Honour of Irene M. Spry* (Ottawa: University of Ottawa Press, 1985), pp. 95–115. **3835**

Ray, Arthur J., "Adventurers at the Crossroads," *Beaver*, vol. 66, 2 (1986), pp. 4–12. [Hudson's Bay, 1871] **3836**

PLACE NAMES

Freeman, Randolph S., "Geographical Naming in the Old North-West: A Study of the Naming of Geographical Features by Fur Traders in the Western Interior of British North America, 1780–1820," Master's thesis, University of Alberta, 1985. **3837**

Freeman, Randolph S., *Geographical Naming in Western British North America, 1780–1820* (Edmonton: Alberta Culture, Historic Sites Service, Occasional Paper no. 15, 1985), 97 pp. **3838**

NORTHWEST TERRITORIES

(SEE ALSO RUPERT'S LAND AND PRAIRIE PROVINCES)

GENERAL

Crowe, Keith J., "A Cultural Geography of Northern Foxe Basin, Northwest Territories," Master's thesis, University of British Columbia, 1969. 3839

NATIVE PEOPLES & WHITE RELATIONS

Vesty, Jennifer, "Igloolik Eskimo Settlement and Migration, 1900–1970," Master's thesis, McGill University, 1973. 3840

Flouquet, Anne, "Géographie historique des sociétés autochtones du Mackenzie au contact des Occidentaux," *Bulletin de l'Association de géographes français*, vol. 57, 473–474 (1980), pp. 385–392. [Focus on 1845–1930] 3841

EXPLORATION & MAPPING

Baird, P. D., and J. Lewis Robinson, "A Brief History of Exploration and Research in the Canadian Eastern Arctic," *Canadian Geographical Journal*, vol. 30, 3 (1945), pp. 137–157. 3842

Robinson, M. J., and J. Lewis Robinson, "Exploration and Settlement of Mackenzie District, Northwest Territories," *Canadian Geographical Journal*, "Part 1," vol. 32, 6 (1946), pp. 246–255; "Part 2," vol. 33, 1 (1946), pp. 42–49. 3843

Kershaw, G. P., "The Canol Project and Its Role in the Evolution of Maps of the Mackenzie Mountains, N.W.T., Canada," *Bulletin of the Association of Canadian Map Libraries*, vol. 39 (1981), pp. 1–18. Reprinted in Barbara Farrell and Eileen Desbarats, eds., *Explorations in the History of Canadian Mapping: A Collection of Essays* (Ottawa: Association of Canadian Map Libraries and Archives, 1988), pp. 251–268. 3844

REGIONAL SETTLEMENT

Adams, John Q., "Settlements of the Northeastern Canadian Arctic," *Geographical Review*, vol. 31, 1 (1941), pp. 112–126. 3845

Giraud, Marcel, "Métis Settlement in the Northwest Territories," *Saskatchewan History*, vol. 7, 1 (1954), pp. 1–16. 3846

Rae, George R., "The Settlement of the Great Slave Lake Frontier, Northwest Territories, from the Eighteenth to the Twentieth Centuries," Ph.D. diss., University of Michigan, 1963. 3847

Zarchikoff, William W., "The Development of Settlement Patterns in Hay River, Northwest Territories, 1892–1971," Master's thesis, Simon Fraser University, 1976. 3848

ECONOMIC DEVELOPMENT

Wonders, William C., "Economic Change in the Mackenzie Valley Area," *Canadian Geographical Journal*, vol. 63, 4 (1961), pp. 138–147. 3849

Bradbury, John H., "Living with Boom and Bust Cycles: New Towns on the Resource Fontier: Canada, 1945–1986," in T. B. Brealey, C. C. Neil, and P. W. Newton, eds., *Resource Communities: Settlement and Workforce Issues* (Canberra: Commonwealth Scientific and Industrial Research Organization, 1988), pp. 3–20. 3850

Dathan, Patricia W., "The Reindeer Years: Contribution of A. Erling Porsild to the Continental Northwest, 1926–1935," Master's thesis, McGill University, 1988. 3851

EXTRACTIVE ACTIVITY

Usher, Peter, *Fur Trade Posts of the Northwest Territories, 1870–1970* (Ottawa: Northern Science Research Group, Department of Indian Affairs and Northern Development, 1971), 180 pp. 3852

COMMUNICATIONS & TRADE

Alcock, Frederick J., "Past and Present Trade Routes to the Canadian Northwest," *Geographical Review*, vol. 10, 2 (1920), pp. 57–83. 3853

TOWN GROWTH

Wallace, J. C., "Hay River, N.W.T.," Master's thesis, University of Alberta, 1966. 3854

Weir, D. A., "A Study of Three Northern Settlements: Fort Norman, Fort Franklin, and Norman Wells," Master's thesis, University of Alberta, 1967. 3855

Koroscil, Paul M., "Urbanization in the Canadian North: Yellowknife, Northwest Territories," in Paul M. Koroscil and Stanley E. McMullin, eds.,

Canadian Issues: The Canadian Urban Experience (Waterloo: University of Waterloo Press, 1975), pp. 115–135.   **3856**

Ray, Arthur J., "York Factory: The Crises of Transition, 1870–1880," *Beaver*, Outfit 313, 2 (1982), pp. 26–31.   **3857**

Harrison, D. H., "Hay River, Northwest Territories, 1800–1950: A Geographical Study of Site and Situation," Ph.D. diss., University of Alberta, 1984.
                                                   3858

Wonders, William C., and H. Black, "Aklavik, Northwest Territories: The Town That Did Not

Die," in R. Olson, R. Hastings, and F. Geddes, eds., *Northern Ecology and Resource Management* (Edmonton: University of Alberta Press, 1984), pp. 405–424.   **3859**

RECREATION & TOURISM

Keller, C. P., "Stages of Peripheral Tourism Development: Canada's Northwest Territories," *Tourism Management*, vol. 8, 1 (1987), pp. 20–32.
                                                   3860

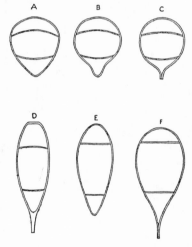

LES RAQUETTES

PART V

UNITED STATES

UNITED STATES
AS A WHOLE

GENERAL

Synthetic treatments

Geographical history &
proto-historical geography

Willard, Emma Hart, *History of the United States;
or Republic of America Exhibited in Connexion
with Its Chronology and Progressive Geography,
by Means of a Series of Maps* (New York:
White, Gallaher & White, 1828), 426 pp.   3861

Marsh, George Perkins, *Man and Nature; or Physical Geography as Modified by Human Action*
(New York: Charles Scribner, 1864), 577 pp. Revised as *The Earth as Modified by Human Action* (New York: Charles Scribner, 1874), 656 pp.
3862

Ratzel, Friedrich, *Die Vereinigten Staaten von
Nordamerika*, vol. 2, *Kulturgeographie der Vereinigten Staaten von Nordamerika unter besonderer Berücksichtigung der wirtschaftlichen
Verhältnisse* (Munich: R. Oldenbourg, 1880), 762
pp.   3863

Shaler, Nathaniel Southgate, *Nature and Man in
America* (New York: Charles Scribner's Sons,
1891), 240 pp.   3864

Turner, Frederick Jackson, "The Significance of
the Frontier in American History," *Proceedings
of the State Historical Society of Wisconsin at
Its Forty-first Annual Meeting, 1893* (Madison:
State Printer, 1893), pp. 79–112. Reprinted in *Report of the American Historical Association for
1893* (Washington, 1894), pp. 199–227; in Frederick Jackson Turner, *The Frontier in American
History* (New York: Henry Holt & Co., 1920), pp.
1–38; in Roger E. Kasperson and Julian V. Minghi, eds., *The Structure of Political Geography*
(Chicago: Aldine Publishing Co., 1969), pp. 132–
139; and in numerous other publications.   3865

Turner, Frederick Jackson, "Is Sectionalism in
America Dying Away?" *American Journal of
Sociology*, vol. 8, 5 (1908), pp. 661–675. Reprinted
in Frederick Jackson Turner, *The Significance of
Sections in American History* (New York: Henry
Holt & Co., 1932), pp. 287–314.   3866

Turner, Frederick Jackson, *The Frontier in American History* (New York: Henry Holt & Co., 1920),
375 pp.   3867

Turner, Frederick Jackson, "The Significance of
the Section in American History," *Wisconsin
Magazine of History*, vol. 8, 3 (1925), pp. 255–280.
Reprinted in Frederick Jackson Turner, *The
Significance of Sections in American History*
(New York: Henry Holt & Co., 1932), pp. 22–51.
3868

Turner, Frederick Jackson, *The Significance of
Sections in American History* (New York: Henry
Holt & Co., 1932), 347 pp.   3869

Muelder, Hermann R., and David M. Delo, *Years
of the Land: A Geographical History of the United States* (New York: D. Appleton-Century,
1943), 243 pp.   3870

Perkins, Dexter, "Geographical Influences in
American History," *Geographical Journal*, vol.
109, 1–3 (1947), pp. 26–38.   3871

Billington, Ray A., *Westward Expansion: A History
of the American Frontier* (New York: Macmillan
Co., 1949), 873 pp.   3872

Historical geography

Brigham, Albert Perry, *Geographic Influences in
American History* (Boston: Ginn & Co., 1903),
366 pp.   3873

Semple, Ellen Churchill, *American History and Its
Geographic Conditions* (New York: Houghton
Mifflin, 1903), 466 pp. Revised, in collaboration
with Clarence F. Jones, 1933; reissued New York:
Russell and Russell 1968), 541 pp.   3874

Genthe, Martha Krug, "Die geographischen
Grundlagen der amerikanischen Geschichte.
Nach E. C. Semple," *Geographische Zeitschrift*,
vol. 15, 7 (1909), pp. 386–408, 450–463.   3875

Wright, John K., Introduction to Charles O. Paullin, ed., *Atlas of the Historical Geography of the
United States* (Washington, D.C.: Carnegie Institute and American Geographical Society,
1932), pp. xi–xv.   3876

Barrows, Harlan H., *Lectures on the Historical
Geography of the United States: Interpretive Essays, 1933*, edited by William Koelsch (Chicago:
University of Chicago Department of Geography, Research Paper no. 77, 1962), 248 pp.   3877

Fleure, Herbert J., "United States: A Study of Unity
in Diversity," *Scottish Geographical Magazine*,
vol. 62, 1 (1946), pp. 1–7.   3878

Brown, Ralph Hall, *Historical Geography of the United States* (New York: Harcourt Brace and World, 1948), 596 pp.   3879

Gottmann, Jean, "Changements de structure dans la géographie humaine des États-Unis," *Annales de géographie*, vol. 57 (1948), pp. 131–145. [Focus on the 1930s and 1940s]   3880

Boesch, Hans H., *USA: Die Erschließung eines Kontinents* (Bern: Kümmerly & Frey, 1956), 272 pp. Revised as *USA: Werden und Wandel eines kontinentalen Wirtschaftsraumes* (Bern: Kümmerly & Frey, 1973), 255 pp.   3881

Watson, J. Wreford, "Geography and the Development of the U.S.A.," in Dennis Welland, ed., *The United States: A Companion to American Studies* (London: Methuen & Co., 1974), pp. 13–58.   3882

Meinig, Donald W., "The Continuous Shaping of America: A Prospectus for Geographers and Historians," *American Historical Review*, vol. 83, 5 (1978), pp. 1186–1217.   3883

Ward, David, ed., *Geographic Perspectives on America's Past: Readings on the Historical Geography of the United States* (New York: Oxford University Press, 1979), 364 pp.   3884

Meinig, Donald W., *The Shaping of America: A Geographical Perspective on 500 Years of History*, vol. 1, *Atlantic America, 1491–1800* (New Haven: Yale University Press, 1986), 500 pp. 3885

Claval, Paul, *La conquête de l'espace Américain: Du Mayflower au Disneyworld* (Paris: Flammarion, 1989), 320 pp.   3886

Colonial era

Meinig, Donald W., "The American Colonial Era: A Geographical Commentary," *Proceedings of the Royal Geographical Society of Australasia, South Australian Branch*, vol. 59 (1957–1958), pp. 1–22.   3887

Lemon, James T., "Colonial America in the Eighteenth Century," in Robert D. Mitchell and Paul A. Groves, eds., *North America: The Historical Geography of a Changing Continent* (Totowa, N.J.: Rowman & Littlefield, 1987), pp. 121–146.   3888

Early national period

Pfeifer, Gottfried, "Die Bedeutung der 'Frontier' für die Ausbreitung der Vereinigten Staaten bis zum Mississippi," *Geographische Zeitschrift*, vol. 41, 4 (1935), pp. 138–158. Reprinted in Gerd Kohlhepp, ed., *Beiträge zur Kulturgeographie der Neuen Welt: Ausgewählte Arbeiten von Gottfried Pfeifer* (Berlin: Dietrich Reimer, 1981), pp. 47–68.   3889

Anderson, Olga A., "Some Significant Geographic Factors Related to the Early Period of American History," Master's thesis, University of Nebraska, 1941.   3890

Brown, Ralph Hall, *Mirror for Americans: Likeness of the Eastern Seaboard, 1810* (New York: American Geographical Society, 1943), 312 pp.   3891

Era of expansion

Meinig, Donald W., "Continental America, 1800–1915: The View of an Historical Geographer," *History Teacher*, vol. 22, 2 (1989), pp. 189–203.
3892

Early twentieth century

Lewis, Peirce F., "America between the Wars: The Engineering of a New Geography," in Robert D. Mitchell and Paul A. Groves, eds., *North America: The Historical Geography of a Changing Continent* (Totowa, N.J.: Rowman & Littlefield, 1987), pp. 410–437.   3893

Modern period

Stewart, George R., *U.S. 40: Cross-Section of the United States of America* (Boston: Houghton Mifflin, 1953), 311 pp.   3894

Hart, John Fraser, *Regions of the United States* (New York: Harper and Row, 1972), 219 pp. 3895

Zelinsky, Wilbur, *The Cultural Geography of the United States* (Englewood Cliffs, N.J.: Prentice-Hall, 1973), 164 pp. Revised ed.1992, 226 pp. 3896

Gastil, Raymond D., *Cultural Regions of the United States* (Seattle: University of Washington Press, 1975), 366 pp.   3897

Selected themes

Walker, Francis A., Supt., *Tenth Census of the United States* (Washington, D.C.: Government Printing Office, 1883–1888). Numerous reports presenting historical and geographical interpretation of specific aspects of the nation's economic and social development. Reports with the strongest historico-geographical flavor include vol. 1, *Population:* Francis A. Walker and Henry Gannett, "Progress of the Nation, 1790–1880" (pp. xi–xx); vol. 2, *Manufactures:* Carroll D. Wright, "Factory System" (pp. 529–610); James M. Swank, "Iron and Steel Production" (pp. 729–900); William C. Wyckoff, "Silk Manufacturing Industry" (pp. 901–935); William L. Roland, "Manufacture of Chemical Products and Salt" (pp. 985–1028); Joseph D. Weeks, "History of Glass-Making in the United States" (pp. 1115–1137); vol. 3, *Agriculture:* J. B. Killebrew, "Culture and Curing of Tobacco" (pp. 583–880); vol. 8, *Special Reports:* S. N. D. North, "Newspaper and Periodical Press" (446 pp.); Ivan Petroff,

"Alaska" (189 pp.); Henry Hall, "Ship-building" (276 pp.); vols. 18 & 19, *Social Statistics of Cities*, comp. George E. Waring, Jr.   **3898**

Lillard, Richard G., "Some Factors Which Enabled Europeans Successfully to Settle the American Forests," *Proceedings of the Indiana Academy of Science*, vol. 55 (1946), pp. 92–95.   **3899**

Brown, Ralph Hall, "The Land and the Sea: Their Larger Traits," *Annals of the Association of American Geographers*, vol. 41, 3 (1951), pp. 199–216.   **3900**

Broek, Jan O. M., "National Character in the Perspective of Cultural Geography," *Annals of the American Academy of Political and Social Science*, vol. 370 (1967), pp. 8–15.   **3901**

Brook, Anthony, "Spatial Systems in American History," *Area*, vol. 8, 1 (1976), pp. 47–52.   **3902**

Hochholzer, Hans, "Zweihundert Jahre U.S.A.: Grundzüge einer historisch-genetischen Wirtschafts- und Sozialgeographie," *Zeitschrift für Wirtschaftsgeographie*, vol. 20, 4 (1976), pp. 97–102.   **3903**

Lenz, Karl, "Entwicklung und Ausprägung des Nord-Süd-Gegensatzes in den USA," *Geographische Rundschau*, vol. 28, 12 (1976), pp. 497–506.   **3904**

Meinig, Donald W., "Spatial Models of a Sequence of Trans-Atlantic Interactions," *International Geography '76, sec. 9, Historical Geography* (Moscow: Twenty-third International Geographical Union, 1976), pp. 30–35.   **3905**

Gritzner, Charles F., "Chickens, Worms, and a Little Bull: Some Animated Perspectives on American History," *Journal of Geography*, vol. 76, 3 (1977), pp. 111–112.   **3906**

Niemz, Günter, "200 Jahre USA: Beharrung und Wandel in einem Großraum," *Frankfurter Geographische Hefte*, vol. 53 (1980), pp. 113–121.   **3907**

Williams, Michael, "Clearing the United States Forests: Pivotal Years, 1810–1860," *Journal of Historical Geography*, vol. 8, 1 (1982), pp. 12–28.   **3908**

Williams, Michael, *Americans and Their Forests: A Historical Geography* (New York: Cambridge University Press, 1989), 599 pp.   **3909**

Divers collections

Wright, John K., *Human Nature in Geography: Fourteen Papers, 1925–1965* (Cambridge: Harvard University Press, 1966), 361 pp.   **3910**

Ehrenberg, Ralph E., ed., *Pattern and Process: Research in Historical Geography* (Washington,

D.C.: Howard University Press, 1975), 360 pp.   **3911**

Miller, David H., and Jerome O. Steffen, eds., *The Frontier: Comparative Studies* (Norman: University of Oklahoma Press, 1977), 327 pp.   **3912**

ENVIRONMENTAL CHANGE

General

Trimble, Stanley W., "Nature's Continent," in Michael P. Conzen, ed., *The Making of the American Landscape* (Boston: Unwin Hyman, 1990), pp. 9–26.   **3913**

Physiography

Goode, J. Paul, "The Influence of Physiographic Factors upon the Occupations and Economic Development in the United States," Ph.D. diss., University of Pennsylvania, 1901.   **3914**

Climate

Lacy, Walter N., "Some Climatic Influences in American History," *Monthly Weather Review*, vol. 36 (1908), pp. 169–173.   **3915**

Huntington, Ellsworth, *The Climatic Factor as Illustrated in Arid America* (Washington, D.C.: Carnegie Institution of Washington, Publication no. 192, 1914), 341 pp.   **3916**

Bruckner, Eduard, "The Settlement of the United States as Controlled by Climate and Climatic Oscillations," *Memorial Volume of the Transcontinental Excursion of 1912 of the American Geographical Society of New York* (New York: American Geographical Society, 1915), pp. 125–139.   **3917**

Brown, Ralph Hall, "The First Century of Meteorological Data in America," *Monthly Weather Review*, vol. 8 (1940), pp. 130–133.   **3918**

Hoyt, William G., and Walter B. Langbein, "The Yield of Streams as a Measure of Climatic Fluctuations," *Geographical Review*, vol. 34, 2 (1944), pp. 218–234. [Covers 1910–1942]   **3919**

Hoyt, Joseph B., "The Cold Summer of 1816," *Annals of the Association of American Geographers*, vol. 48, 2 (1958), pp. 118–131.   **3920**

Hunt, Richard L., "The Agricultural Drought of 1894," Master's thesis, Southern Connecticut State College, 1969.   **3921**

Thompson, Kenneth, "Forests and Climatic Change in America: Some Early Views," *Climatic Change*, vol. 3, 1 (1981), pp. 47–64.   **3922**

Thompson, Kenneth, "The Question of Climatic Stability in America before 1900," *Climatic Change*, vol. 3, 3 (1981), pp. 227–242.   **3923**

Balling, Robert C., Jr., and Merlin P. Lawson, "Twentieth Century Changes in Winter Climatic Regions," *Climatic Change*, vol. 4, 1 (1982), pp. 57–70. [1940–1965] **3924**

Kupperman, Karen Ordahl, "The Puzzle of the American Climate in the Early Colonial Period," *American Historical Review*, vol. 87, 5 (1982), pp. 1262–1289. **3925**

Soil

Hulbert, Archer B., *Soil: Its Influence on the History of the United States, with Special Reference to Migration and the Scientific Study of Local History* (New Haven: Yale University Press, 1930), 227 pp. **3926**

Flora

Cottam, Walter P., and George Stewart, "Plant Succession as a Result of Grazing and of Meadow Desiccation by Erosion since Settlement in 1862," *Journal of Forestry*, vol. 38, 8 (1940), pp. 613–626. **3927**

Stewart, Omer C., "Burning and Natural Vegetation in the United States," *Geographical Review*, vol. 41, 2 (1951), pp. 317–329. **3928**

Fauna

Shaler, Nathaniel Southgate, *Domesticated Animals: Their Relation to Man and to His Advancement in Civilization* (New York: Charles Scribner's Sons, 1895), 267 pp. **3929**

Carter, George F., "The Chicken in America," *Anthropological Journal of Canada*, vol. 13, 1 (1975), pp. 25–26. **3930**

Doughty, Robin W., "Sparrows for America: A Case of Mistaken Identity," *Journal of Popular Culture*, vol. 14, 2 (1980), pp. 212–228. **3931**

Human impact

Doerr, Arthur H., and Lee Guernsey, "Man as a Geomorphological Agent: The Example of Coal Mining," *Annals of the Association of American Geographers*, vol. 46, 2 (1956), pp. 197–210. [Focus on 1915–1950] **3932**

Colten, Craig E., "Historical Questions in Hazardous Waste Management," *Public Historian*, vol. 10 (1988), pp. 7–20. **3933**

Colten, Craig E., "Historical Development of Waste Minimization," *Environmental Professional*, vol. 11 (1989), pp. 94–99. **3934**

Colten, Craig E., "Historical Hazards: The Geography of Relict Industrial Wastes," *Professional Geographer*, vol. 42, 2 (1990), pp. 143–156. **3935**

NATIVE PEOPLES & WHITE RELATIONS

General

Parry, Francis, "The Sacred Symbols and Numbers of Aboriginal Americans in Ancient and Modern Times," *Journal of the American Geographical Society*, vol. 26 (1894), pp. 163–207. **3936**

Huntington, Ellsworth, "The First Americans," *Harper's Magazine*, vol. 122, 729 (Feb. 1911), pp. 451–462. [Focus on the Hohokam people] **3937**

Huntington, Ellsworth, *The Red Man's Continent: A Chronicle of Aboriginal America* (New Haven: Yale University Press, 1919), 183 pp. **3938**

Seig, Louis, *Tobacco, Peacepipes, and Indians* (Palmer Lake, Colo.: Filter Press, 1971), 43 pp. **3939**

Jackson, Richard H., "The American Indian: A Neglected Area of Geographical Study," *Great Plains–Rocky Mountain Geographical Journal*, vol. 1 (1972), pp. 46–53. **3940**

Jett, Stephen C., "Pre-Columbian Transoceanic Contacts," in Jesse Jennings, ed., *Ancient Native Americans* (San Francisco: W. H. Freeman, 1978), pp. 592–650. **3941**

Butzer, Karl W., "This is Indian Country," *Geographical Magazine*, vol. 52, 2 (1979), pp. 140–148. **3942**

Ballas, Donald J., "Historical Geography and American Indian Development," in Thomas E. Ross and Tyrel G. Moore, eds., *A Cultural Geography of North American Indians* (Boulder: Westview Press, 1987), pp. 15–31. **3943**

Butzer, Karl W., "The Indian Legacy in the American Landscape," in Michael P. Conzen, ed., *The Making of the American Landscape* (Boston: Unwin Hyman, 1990), pp. 27–50. **3944**

Population origins & history

Dethier, Bernard E., "The Problem of Early Man's Entry into the New World," Ph.D. diss., Johns Hopkins University, 1958. **3945**

Carter, George F., "Early Man in America," *Anthropological Journal of Canada*, vol. 10, 3 (1972), pp. 2–9. **3946**

Todd, John B., "Distributional Changes in Early Man Sites in Response to a Changing Environment in the Coterminous United States: 9000 B.P. to 2000 B.P.," Master's thesis, Western Illinois University, 1972. **3947**

Carter, George F., "An American Lower Paleolithic," *Anthropological Journal of Canada*, vol. 16, 1 (1978), pp. 2–37. **3948**

Carter, George F., *Earlier Than You Think: A Personal View of Man in America* (College Station, Tex.: Texas A & M University Press, 1980), 348 pp. **3949**

Agriculture

Carter, George F., "Origins of American Indian Agriculture," *American Anthropologist*, vol. 48, 1 (1946), pp. 1–21. **3950**

Carter, George F., "Sweet Corn among the Indians," *Geographical Review*, vol. 38, 2 (1948), pp. 206–221. **3951**

Buildings and architecture

Mindeleff, Cosmos, "Aboriginal Architecture in the United States," *Journal of the American Geographical Society*, vol. 30 (1898), pp. 414–427. **3952**

Indian-White relations

Ewers, John C., *The Role of the Indian in National Expansion* (Washington, D.C.: United States Department of the Interior, National Park Service, 1938), 190 pp. **3953**

Wills, Berndt L., "Native Americans and Early Explorers," *Bulletin of the Association of North Dakota Geographers*, vol. 27 (1977), pp. 1–12. **3954**

Jacobs, Wilbur R., "The Indian and the Frontier in American History: A Need for Revision," *Western Historical Quarterly*, vol. 4, 1 (1973), pp. 43–56. Reprinted, with omissions, in David Ward, ed., *Geographic Perspectives on America's Past: Readings on the Historical Geography of the United States* (New York: Oxford University Press, 1979), pp. 70–76. **3955**

Kay, Jeanne C., "The Fur Trade and Native American Population Growth," *Ethnohistory*, vol. 31, 4 (1984), pp. 265–287. **3956**

Manzo, Joseph T., "Economic Aspects of Indian Removal," *Southeastern Geographer*, vol. 24, 2 (1984), pp. 115–125. **3957**

Manzo, Joseph T., "Women in Indian Removal," in Thomas E. Ross and Tyrel G. Moore, eds., *A Cultural Geography of North American Indians* (Boulder: Westview Press, 1987), pp. 213–226. **3958**

White, Richard, and William J. Cronon, "Ecological Change and Indian-White Relations," in Wilcomb E. Washburn, ed., *Handbook of North American Indians*, vol. 4, *Indian-White Relations* (Washington, D.C.: Smithsonian Institution, 1988), pp. 417–429. **3959**

Communications

Manzo, Joseph T., "The Indian Pre-Removal Information Network," *Journal of Cultural Geography*, vol. 2, 2 (1982), pp. 72–83. **3960**

Hickey, Joseph V., and Charles E. Webb, *The Lyons Serpent: Speculations on the Indian as Geographer* (Emporia: Emporia State University, Emporia Kansas State Research Studies, Research Studies, vol. 33, no. 4, 1985), 52 pp. **3961**

Lewis, G. Malcolm, "Indian Delimitations of Primary Biogeographic Regions," in Thomas E. Ross and Tyrel G. Moore, eds., *A Cultural Geography of North American Indians* (Boulder: Westview Press, 1987), pp. 93–104. **3962**

Reservations

Janke, Robert A., "The Development and Persistence of Land Tenure Problems on Indian Reservations in the United States," Master's thesis, University of Wisconsin–Milwaukee, 1967. **3963**

Hofmeister, Burkhard, "Indianerreservationen in den USA: Territoriale Entwicklung und wirtschaftliche Eignung," *Geographische Rundschau*, vol. 28, 12 (1976), pp. 507–519. **3964**

Wishart, David J., "Education, Geography, and Indian Assimilation, 1887–1933," *Journal of Geography*, vol. 81, 6 (1982), pp. 204–210. **3965**

Janke, Robert A., "The Loss of Indian Lands in Wisconsin, Montana, and Arizona," in Thomas E. Ross and Tyrel G. Moore, eds., *A Cultural Geography of North American Indians* (Boulder: Westview Press, 1987), pp. 127–148. **3966**

Weil, Richard H., "The Loss of Lands inside Indian Reservations," in Thomas E. Ross and Tyrel G. Moore, eds., *A Cultural Geography of North American Indians* (Boulder: Westview Press, 1987), pp. 149–171. [Focus on Minnesota, North and South Dakota] **3967**

Frantz, Klaus, "Zur Frage der territorialen Entwicklung und Souveränität der US: Amerikanischen Indianerreservationen," *Mitteilungen der Österreichischen Geographischen Gesellschaft*, vol. 131 (1989), pp. 27–46. **3968**

EXPLORATION & MAPPING

All entries treating the early discoveries of America' will be found under NORTH AMERICA

Early continental exploration and mapping

Gravier, Gabriel, "Étude sur une carte inconnue: La première dressée par Louis Jolliet en 1674, après son exploration du Mississippi," *Revue de géographie*, vol. 6 (1880), pp. 81–101. **3969**

Scaife, Walter B., *America: Its Geographical History, 1492–1892: Six Lectures Delivered to Graduate Students of the Johns Hopkins University* (Baltimore: Johns Hopkins University Press, 1892), 176 pp. **3970**

Krug, Martha, "Die Kartographie der Meeresströmungen in ihren Beziehungen zur Entwicklung der Meereskunde," *Deutsche Geographische Blätter*, vol. 24, 3–4 (1901), pp. 96–174. 3971

Krug, Martha, "Ein Beitrag zur Geschichte und Methodik der Seekarten, dargestellt am Beispiel des Golfstroms," Ph.D. diss., Universität Heidelberg, 1901. 3972

Strengers, J., "Hennepin et la découverte du Mississippi," *Bulletin de la société royale Belge de géographie*, vol. 67, 2 (1945), pp. 61–82. 3973

Melón Ruiz de Gordejuela, Amando, "Las exploraciones españoles en América del Norte, alentadas por la obra misional de Fray Junipero Serra," *Estudios geograficos*, vol. 7, 22 (1946), pp. 29–46. 3974

Cappon, Lester J., "Geographers and Map-Makers, British and American, from about 1750–1789," *Proceedings of the American Antiquarian Society*, vol. 81, 2 (1971), pp. 243–271. 3975

DeVorsey, Louis, Jr., "Hydrography: A Note on the Equipage of Eighteenth-Century Survey Vessels," *Mariner's Mirror*, vol. 58 (1972), pp. 173–178. 3976

Allen, John L., "Lands of Myths, Waters of Wonder: The Place of the Imagination in the History of Geographical Exploration," in David Lowenthal and Martyn J. Bowden, eds., *Geographies of the Mind: Essays in Historical Geosophy in Honor of John Kirtland Wright* (New York: Oxford University Press, 1976), pp. 41–61. 3977

DeVorsey, Louis, Jr., "Pioneer Charting of the Gulf Stream: The Contributions of Benjamin Franklin and William Gerard de Brahm," *Imago Mundi*, vol. 28 (1976), pp. 105–120. 3978

DeVorsey, Louis, Jr., "The Gulf Stream on Eighteenth-Century Maps and Charts," *Map Collector*, no. 15 (1981), pp. 2–10. 3979

DeVorsey, Louis, Jr., "Yankee Whaler Wisdom and Benjamin Franklin's Gulf Stream Maps," *Bloomsbury Geographer*, vol. 10 (1981), pp. 62–75. 3980

DeVorsey, Louis, Jr., "William Gerard de Brahm," *Geographers: Biobibliographic Studies*, vol. 10 (1986), pp. 41–47. 3981

General history of American cartography

Raisz, Erwin O., "Outline of the History of American Cartography," *Isis*, vol. 26 (1937), pp. 373–391. 3982

Attanayake, Sri Chandra, "The Development of Thematic Mapping in the United States of America: A Critical Analysis of Special Purpose

Cartography Published in Geography and by the Federal Government," Master's thesis, University of Wisconsin–Milwaukee, 1968. 3983

Woodward, David, "Cerotyping and the Rise of Modern American Commercial Cartography: A Case Study of the Influence of Printing Technology on Cartographic Style," Ph.D. diss., University of Wisconsin–Madison, 1970. 3984

Woodward, David, and Arthur H. Robinson, "Notes on a 'Genealogical Chart' of Some American Commercial Map and Atlas Producers," *Bulletin of the Special Libraries Association, Geography and Map Division*, vol. 79 (1970), pp. 2–6. 3985

Wolter, John A., "Source Materials for the History of American Cartography," in Robert H. Walker, ed., *American Studies: Topics and Sources* (Westport, Conn.: Greenwood Press, 1976), pp. 81–95. 3986

Woodward, David, *The All-American Map: Wax-Engraving and Its Influence on Cartography* (Chicago: University of Chicago Press, 1977), 168 pp. 3987

Tooley, Ronald V., *The Mapping of America* (New York: Holland Press, 1980), 519 pp. 3988

Ristow, Walter W., "U.S. amerikanische Kartographie," in Ingrid Kretschmer, ed., *Lexikon zur Geschichte der Kartographie von den Anfängen bis zum ersten Weltkrieg*, vol. 2 (Vienna: Johannes Dörflinger und Franz Wawrich, 1986), pp. 838–843. 3989

Hudson, Alice C., "Pre–Twentieth Century Women Mapmakers," *Meridian: Journal of the Map & Geography Round Table of the American Library Association*, vol. 1 (1989), pp. 29–33. 3990

Amerindian cartography

Burland, Coffie A., "American Indian Map Makers," *Geographical Magazine*, vol. 20, 7 (1947), pp. 285–292. 3991

Lewis, G. Malcolm, "Misinterpretation of Amerindian Information as a Source of Error on Euro-American Maps," *Annals of the Association of American Geographers*, vol. 77, 4 (1987), pp. 542–563. 3992

Development of federal government mapping

Friis, Herman R., "Highlights in the First Hundred Years of Surveying and Mapping and Geographical Exploration of the United States by the Federal Government, 1775–1880," *Surveying and Mapping*, vol. 18, 2 (1958), pp. 186–206. 3993

Friis, Herman R., "A Brief Review of the Development and Status of Geographical and Cartographical Activities of the United States Government, 1776–1818," *Imago Mundi*, vol. 19 (1965), pp. 68–80. **3994**

Friis, Herman R., "Highlights of the Geographical and Cartographical Contributions of Graduates of West Point with a Specialization as Topographical Engineers prior to 1800," *Proceedings of the Middle States Division, Association of American Geographers*, vol. 1 (1968), pp. 10–29. **3995**

Edwards, A. Cherie, "Walker's 1870 Statistical Atlas and the Development of American Cartography," Master's thesis, University of Wisconsin–Madison, 1969. **3996**

Stephenson, Richard W., *Federal Government Map Collecting: A Brief History* (Washington, D.C.: Special Libraries Association, Washington, D.C., Chapter, 1969), 60 pp. **3997**

Friis, Herman R., "Statistical Cartography in the United States prior to 1870 and the Role of Joseph C. G. Kennedy and the U.S. Census Office," *American Cartographer*, vol. 1, 2 (1974), pp. 131–157. **3998**

Friis, Herman R., "Original and Published Sources in Research in Historical Geography: A Comparison," in Ralph E. Ehrenberg, ed., *Pattern and Process: Research in Historical Geography* (Washington, D.C.: Howard University Press, 1975), pp. 139–159. **3999**

Ehrenberg, Ralph E., "Mapping Land, Sea, and Sky: Federal Cartography from 1775 to 1950," *Government Publications Review*, vol. 10 (1983), pp. 361–374. **4000**

Friis, Herman R., "Archivist's Perspective: Charting a New Land: Mapmaking and the Congress, 1774–1861," *Prologue: The Journal of the National Archives*, vol. 16, 3 (1984), pp. 191–198. **4001**

Edney, Matthew B., "Politics, Science, and Government Mapping in the United States, 1800 to 1925," Master's thesis, University of Wisconsin–Madison, 1985. **4002**

Grim, Ronald E., "Maps of the Township and Range System," in David Buisseret, ed., *From Sea Charts to Satellite Images: Interpreting North American History through Maps* (Chicago: University of Chicago Press, 1990), pp. 89–109. **4003**

Karrow, Robert W., "Topographic Surveys of the United States," in David Buisseret, ed., *From Sea Charts to Satellite Images: Interpreting North American History through Maps* (Chicago: University of Chicago Press, 1990), pp. 238–259. **4004**

Mapping the Revolution

Guthorn, Peter J., *American Maps and Map Makers of the Revolution* (Monmouth Beach, N.J.: Philip Freneau Press, 1966), 48 pp. **4005**

Harley, J. Brian, "The American Revolution Maps of William Faden," *American Philosophical Society Yearbook* (1966), pp. 346–349. **4006**

Ristow, Walter W., "Maps of the American Revolution: A Preliminary Survey," *Quarterly Journal of the Library of Congress*, vol. 28, 3 (1971), pp. 196–215. **4007**

DeVorsey, Louis, Jr., "A Background to Surveying and Mapping at the Time of the American Revolution: An Essay on the State of the Art," in *The American Revolution, 1775–1783: An Atlas of Eighteenth Century Maps and Charts* (Washington, D.C.: Naval History Division, Department of the Navy, 1972), pp. 1–16. **4008**

Guthorn, Peter J., *British Maps of the American Revolution* (Monmouth Beach, N.J.: Philip Freneau Press, 1972), 79 pp. **4009**

Guthorn, Peter J., "A Hessian Map from the American Revolution: Its Origin and Purpose," *Quarterly Journal of the Library of Congress*, vol. 33, 3 (1976), pp. 219–231. **4010**

Guthorn, Peter J., "Kosciuszko as Military Cartographer and Engineer in America," *Imago Mundi*, vol. 29 (1977), pp. 49–53. **4011**

Guthorn, Peter J., "Revolutionary War Mapmakers," *Prologue: The Journal of the National Archives*, vol. 9, 2 (1977), pp. 171–177. **4012**

Guthorn, Peter J., "Military Mapping during the American Revolution," *Map Collector*, no. 2 (1978), pp. 8–21. **4013**

Harley, J. Brian, Barbara Bartz Petchenik, and Lawrence W. Towner, eds., *Mapping the American Revolutionary War* (Chicago: University of Chicago Press, 1978), 187 pp. **4014**

Ristow, Walter W., "Cartography of the Battle of Bunker Hill," *Revista da Universidade de Coimbra*, vol. 27 (1979), pp. 263–279. **4015**

Mapping the Civil War

Muntz, Alfred P., "Union Mapping in the American Civil War," *Imago Mundi*, vol. 17 (1963), pp. 90–94. **4016**

Stephenson, Richard W., "Mapping the Atlanta Campaign," *Bulletin of the Special Libraries Association Geography and Map Division*, no. 127 (1982), pp. 7–17. **4017**

Stephenson, Richard W., Introduction to *Civil War Maps: An Annotated List of Maps and At-*

lases in the Library of Congress, 2d ed. (Washington, D.C.: Library of Congress, 1989), pp. 1–26. Reprinted, with modifications, as "Mapping the Civil War," in Frances H. Kennedy, The Civil War Battlefield Guide (Boston: Houghton Mifflin Co., 1990), pp. 41–43.   4018

Stephenson, Richard W., "Mapping the Civil War," Professional Surveyor, vol. 9 (1989), pp. 10–13.   4019

Commercial mapmaking

Ristow, Walter W., "Early American Atlases," Surveying and Mapping, vol. 22, 4 (1962), pp. 569–574.   4020

Verner, Coolie, "The Fry and Jefferson Map," Imago Mundi, vol. 21 (1967), pp. 70–94.   4021

Woodward, David, "The Foster Woodcut Map Controversy: A Further Examination of the Evidence," Imago Mundi, no. 21 (1967), pp. 52–61.   4022

Klinefelter, Walter, Lewis Evans and His Maps (Philadelphia: Transactions of the American Philosophical Society, n.s. vol. 61, 7, 1971), 65 pp.   4023

Carpenter, Stefanie A., "Lettering Characteristics in Commercial American Atlases Produced by Copper Engraving, Lithography, and Wax Engraving, 1850–1972," Master's thesis, University of Wisconsin–Madison, 1975.   4024

Harley, J. Brian, "Atlas Maker for Independent America," Geographical Magazine, vol. 49 (1977), pp. 766–771. [Focus on Mathew Carey]   4025

Ristow, Walter W., Maps for an Emerging Nation: Commercial Cartography in Nineteenth Century America (Washington, D.C.: Library of Congress Catalog, 1977), 66 pp.   4026

Ristow, Walter W., "The First Maps of the United States of America," in La cartographie au XVIIIe siècle et l'oeuvre du Comté de Ferraris—1726–1814: Coloque International, Spa, 8–11 Sept. 1976 (Brussels: Crédit communal de Belgique, 1978), pp. 179–190.   4027

Ristow, Walter W., "Aborted American Atlases," Quarterly Journal of the Library of Congress, vol. 36, 3 (1979), pp. 320–335.   4028

Ristow, Walter W., American Maps and Mapmakers: Commercial Cartography in the Nineteenth Century (Detroit: Wayne State University Press, 1985), 488 pp.   4029

Stephenson, Richard W., "Henry Harrisse," Lexikon zur Geschichte der Kartographie, vol. C-1 (Vienna: Franz Deuticke, 1986), pp. 286–287. 4030

Stephenson, Richard W., "John Melish," Lexikon zur Geschichte der Kartographie, vol. C-2 (Vienna: Franz Deuticke, 1986), pp. 483–484.   4031

DeVorsey, Louis, Jr., "Eighteenth-Century Large Scale Maps," in David Buisseret, ed., From Sea Charts to Satellite Images: Interpreting North American History through Maps (Chicago: University of Chicago Press, 1990), pp. 67–87.   4032

Rural landownership mapping

Thrower, Norman J. W., "The County Atlas of the United States," California Geographer, vol. 1 (1960), pp. 7–16. Reprinted in Surveying and Mapping, vol. 21, 3 (1961), pp. 365–373.   4033

Stephenson, Richard W., Introduction to Land Ownership Maps: A Checklist of Nineteenth Century United States County Maps in the Library of Congress (Washington, D.C.: Library of Congress, 1967), pp. vii-xxv.   4034

Thrower, Norman J. W., "Cadastral Survey and County Atlases of the United States," Cartographic Journal, vol. 9, 1 (1972), pp. 43–51.   4035

Swenson, Russell G., "Illustrations of Material Culture in Nineteenth-Century County and State Atlases," Pioneer America Society Transactions, vol. 5 (1982), pp. 63–70.   4036

Conzen, Michael P., "The County Landownership Map in America: Its Commercial Development and Social Transformation, 1814–1939," Imago Mundi, vol. 36 (1984), pp. 9–31.   4037

Conzen, Michael P., "Landownership Maps and County Atlases," Agricultural History, vol. 58, 2 (1984), pp. 118–122.   4038

Conzen, Michael P., "County Mapping and Mass Markets in America: Early Lessons in the Success of Targeting?" Meridian: Journal of the Map & Geography Round Table of the American Library Association, vol. 5 (1990), pp. 37–38.   4039

Urban cartography

Ristow, Walter W., "United States Insurance and Underwriters' Maps, 1852–1968," Quarterly Journal of the Library of Congress, vol. 25, 3 (1968), pp. 194–218.   4040

Ristow, Walter W., Introduction to Fire Insurance Maps in the Library of Congress; Plans of North American Cities and Towns Produced by the Sanborn Map Company: A Checklist (Washington, D.C.: Library of Congress, 1981), pp. 1–9.   4041

Bevington, Dierdre, "Perspective and Accuracy in the Nineteenth Century Panoramic Map: Methodological Derivations of Cartographic and Art

Historical Theory," Master's thesis, University of Maryland, 1986. 4042

Danzer, Gerald A., "Bird's-Eye Views of Towns and Cities," in David Buisseret, ed., *From Sea Charts to Satellite Images: Interpreting North American History through Maps* (Chicago: University of Chicago Press, 1990), pp. 143–163. 4043

Danzer, Gerald A., "City Maps and Plans," in David Buisseret, ed., *From Sea Charts to Satellite Images: Interpreting North American History through Maps* (Chicago: University of Chicago Press, 1990), pp. 165–185. 4044

Karrow, Robert, and Ronald E. Grim, "Two Examples of Thematic Maps: Civil War and Fire Insurance Maps," in David Buisseret, ed., *From Sea Charts to Satellite Images: Interpreting North American History through Maps* (Chicago: University of Chicago Press, 1990), pp. 213–237. 4045

Highway maps

Ristow, Walter W., "American Road Maps and Guides," *Scientific Monthly*, vol. 62 (May 1946), pp. 397–406. 4046

Ristow, Walter W., "A Half Century of Oil-Company Road Maps," *Surveying and Mapping*, vol. 24, 4 (1964), pp. 617–637. 4047

Schlereth, Thomas J., "Twentieth-Century Highway Maps," in David Buisseret, ed., *From Sea Charts to Satellite Images: Interpreting North American History through Maps* (Chicago: University of Chicago Press, 1990), pp. 260–281. 4048

Scholarly cartography

Paullin, Charles O., "The Carnegie Institute's Atlas of the Historical Geography of the United States," *Journal of Geography*, vol. 14, 4 (1915), pp. 108–109. 4049

Wright, John K., "Sections and National Growth: An Atlas of the Historical Geography of the United States," *Geographical Review*, vol. 22, 3 (1932), pp. 353–360. 4050

Cappon, Lester J., "The Historical Map in American Atlases," *Annals of the Association of American Geographers*, vol. 69, 4 (1979), pp. 622–634. 4051

POPULAR IMAGES & EVALUATION

General

Stein, Gertrude, *The Geographical History of America; or the Relation of Human Nature to the Human Mind* (New York: Vintage Books, 1936), 243 pp. Reprinted 1973. [Vintage Stein, too] 4052

Lowenthal, David, "Is Wilderness 'Paradise Enow'? Images of Nature in America," *Columbia University Forum*, vol. 7, 2 (1964), pp. 34–40. 4053

Nash, Roderick, *Wilderness and the American Mind* (New Haven: Yale University Press, 1967), 256 pp. Reprinted 1973 and 1982. 4054

Watson, J. Wreford, "Image Geography: The Myth of America in the American Scene," *British Association for the Advancement of Science*, vol. 27 (1970), pp. 1–9. 4055

Johnson, Hildegard Binder, "New Geographical Horizons: Concepts," in Fred Chiapelli, ed., *First Images of America*, vol. 2 (Berkeley: University of California Press, 1976), pp. 715–733. 4056

Lowenthal, David, and Martyn J. Bowden, eds., *Geographies of the Mind: Essays in Historical Geosophy in Honor of John Kirtland Wright* (New York: Oxford University Press, 1976), 263 pp. 4057

Rosenkrantz, Barbara G., and William A. Koelsch, comps., *American Habitat: A Historical Perspective* (New York: Free Press, 1973), 372 pp. 4058

Powell, Joseph M., *Mirrors of the New World: Images and Image-makers in the Settlement Process* (Hamden, Conn.: Archon Books, 1977), 207 pp. 4059

Early geographies

Baker, Marcus, "A Century of Geography in the United States," *Science*, n.s. vol. 7, 173 (1898), pp. 541–551. 4060

Storms, Walter W., "Geography Then and Now," *Inland Educator*, vol. 8, 2 (1899), pp. 77–78. [Focus on Morse's geographies] 4061

Johnson, Clifton, "The First American Geography," *New England Magazine*, n.s. vol. 28, 5 (1903), pp. 516–524; and *Journal of Geography*, vol. 3, 7 (1904), pp. 311–322; and as chap. 12 in his *Old-Time Schools and School-Books* (New York: Macmillan Co., 1904), pp. 318–336. 4062

Johnson, Clifton, "Geographies of Our Forefathers," *New England Magazine*, n.s. vol. 29, 1 (1903), pp. 61–72; and as "Later Geographies" in *Journal of Geography*, vol. 3, 10 (1904), pp. 467–485; and as chap. 13 in his *Old-Time Schools and School-Books* (New York: Macmillan Co., 1904), pp. 337–362. 4063

Earley, Albert, "Geographies of the Eighteenth Century," *Journal of Geography*, vol. 16, 1 (1917), pp. 17–18. 4064

Chamberlain, James F., "Early American Geographies," *Yearbook of the Association of Pacific Coast Geographers*, vol. 5 (1939), pp. 23–29. 4065

Morse, James King, *Jedidiah Morse: A Champion of New England Orthodoxy* (New York: Columbia University Press, 1939), 179 pp. **4066**

Brown, Ralph Hall, "The American Geographies of Jedidiah Morse," *Annals of the Association of American Geographers,* vol. 31, 3 (1941), pp. 145–217. **4067**

Mood, Fulmer, "The English Geographers and the Anglo-American Frontier in the Seventeenth Century," *University of California Publications in Geography,* vol. 6 (1944), pp. 363–395. **4068**

Landy, Dorothy, "Geographies Then and Now," *Journal of Geography,* vol. 48, 9 (1949), pp. 373–380. **4069**

Brown, Ralph Hall, "A Letter to the Reverend Jedidiah Morse, Author of the American Universal Geography," *Annals of the Association of American Geographers,* vol. 41, 3 (1951), pp. 188–198. **4070**

Antonelli, Michael F., "The Role of Maps in Early American Geographies, 1784–1890," Master's thesis, Syracuse University, 1969. **4071**

Antonelli, Michael F., "The Role of Maps in Early American Geographies," *Proceedings of the Middle States Division of the Association of American Geographers,* vol. 2 (1969), pp. 63–78. **4072**

Fries, Sylvia Doughty, "The Slavery Issue in Northern School Readers, Geographies, and Histories, 1850–1875," *Internationales Jahrbuch für Geschichts- und Geographie-Unterricht,* vol. 13 (1970–1971), pp. 214–222. **4073**

Travel literature

Bredeson, Robert C., "Landscape Description in Nineteenth-Century American Travel Literature," *American Quarterly,* vol. 20, 1 (1968), pp. 864–894. **4074**

Jett, Stephen C., "The Journals of George C. Fraser '95: Early Twentieth Century Travels in the South and Southwest," *Princeton University Library Chronicle,* vol. 35, 3 (1975), pp. 290–308. **4075**

Worley, Linda Kraus, "Through Others' Eyes: Narratives of German Women Travelling in Nineteenth-Century America," *Yearbook of German-American Studies,* vol. 21 (1986), pp. 39–50. **4076**

Landscape imagery

McManis, Douglas R., "The Perception of the Seaboard Environment," in J. Wreford Watson and Timothy O'Riordan, eds., *The American Environment: Perception and Policies* (New York: John Wiley & Sons, 1976), pp. 29–36. **4077**

Johnson, Hildegard Binder, *The Orderly Landscape: Landscape Tastes and the United States Survey* (Minneapolis: James Ford Bell Lecture no. 15, Bell Library, University of Minnesota, 1977), 19 pp. **4078**

Rubin, Barry L., "Hudson River Landscape Art: Perspectives on American Attitudes towards Nature, 1820–1870," Master's thesis, University of Maryland, 1978. **4079**

Lowenthal, David, "The Pioneer Landscape: An American Dream," *Great Plains Quarterly,* vol. 2, 1 (1982), pp. 5–19. **4080**

Brown, Jacqueline, "The American Frontier Landscape in Tall Tales, 1800–1925," Master's thesis, California State University–Fullerton, 1987. **4081**

Buisseret, David, "Nineteenth-Century Landscape Views," in David Buisseret, ed., *From Sea Charts to Satellite Images: Interpreting North American History through Maps* (Chicago: University of Chicago Press, 1990), pp. 111–141. **4082**

Urban imagery

Krim, Arthur J., "Photographic Imagery of the American City, 1840–1860," *Professional Geographer,* vol. 25, 2 (1973), pp. 136–139. **4083**

Francaviglia, Richard V., "Main Street U.S.A.: The Creation of a Popular Image," *Landscape,* vol. 21, 3 (1977), pp. 18–22. **4084**

Lloyd, William J., "Images of Late Nineteenth Century Urban Landscapes," Ph.D. diss., University of California–Los Angeles, 1977. **4085**

Jakle, John A., *The American Small Town: Twentieth-Century Place Images* (Hamden, Conn.: Archon Books, 1982), 195 pp. **4086**

Fiction

Nolan, Olive, "The Influence of Geography and History on Washington Irving's Writings," *Education,* vol. 50, 10 (1930), pp. 598–605. **4087**

Salter, Christopher L., "John Steinbeck's *The Grapes of Wrath* as a Primer for Cultural Geography," in Douglas C. D. Pocock, ed., *Humanistic Geography and Literature: Essays on the Experience of Place* (Totowa, N.J.: Barnes & Noble, 1981), pp. 142–158. **4088**

Fryer, Judith, "Women and Space: The Flowering of Desire," in Jack Salzman, ed., *Prospects: An Annual of American Cultural Studies,* vol. 9 (New York: Cambridge University Press, 1984), pp. 187–230. **4089**

Jeans, Dennis N., "Fiction and the Small Town in the United States: A Contribution to the Study of Urbanization," *Australian Geographical Studies,* vol. 22, 2 (1984), pp. 261–274. **4090**

Kolodny, Annette, *The Land Before Her: Fantasy and Experience of the American Frontiers, 1630–1860* (Chapel Hill: University of North Carolina Press, 1984), 293 pp.   4091

Hayward, Mark, "Mark Twain: An Original Geographer," *Geographical Magazine*, vol. 57, 11 (1985), pp. 612–615. {Focus on Samuel Clemens]   4092

Fryer, Judith, *Felicitous Space: The Imaginative Structures of Edith Wharton and Willa Cather* (Chapel Hill: University of North Carolina Press, 1986), 403 pp.   4093

Dixon, Melvin, *Ride Out the Wilderness: Geography and Identity in Afro-American Literature* (Urbana: University of Illinois Press, 1987), 182 pp.   4094

Other themes

Travis, Richard W., *Regional Components of the Recognition of Historic Places* (Urbana: University of Illinois Department of Geography Occasional Paper no. 3, 1972), 15 pp.   4095

Kay, Jeanne C., and Craig J. Brown, "Mormon Beliefs about Land and Natural Resources, 1847–1877," *Journal of Historical Geography*, vol. 11, 3 (1985), pp. 253–267.   4096

Cutter, Susan L., "Changes in Interstate Ranking, 1931–1980," *Geographical Review*, vol. 76, 3 (1986), pp. 276–287.   4097

McConnaughy, Robert D., "Medical Landscapes: Perceived Links between Environment, Health, and Disease in Pre-Twentieth Century America," Ph.D. diss., University of North Carolina, 1986.   4098

Lewis, Peirce F., "Taking Down the Velvet Rope: Cultural Geography and the Human Landscape," in Jo Blatti, ed., *Past Meets Present: Essays about Historical Interpretation and Public Audiences* (Washington, D.C.: Smithsonian Institution Press, 1987), pp. 23–29.   4099

Meyer, William B., "Everyman His Own Location Theorist: Spatial Generalization in Early American Thought," Ph.D. diss., Clark University, 1990.   4100

REGIONAL SETTLEMENT

Colonization, pioneering, & frontier settling

Günter, Otto, "Die Anfänge der Besiedlung Nordamerikas," *Jahresbericht des Württembergischen Vereins für Handelsgeographie*, vols. 11 & 12 (1893), pp. 81–82.   4101

Bowman, Isaiah, *The Pioneer Fringe* (New York: American Geographical Society, 1931), 361 pp.   4102

Mitchell, Robert D., "The Presbyterian Church as an Indicator of Westward Expansion in Eighteenth Century America," *Professional Geographer*, vol. 18, 5 (1966), pp. 293–299.   4103

Jordan, Terry G., "Evolution of American Backwoods Pioneer Culture: The Role of the Delaware Finns," in Noel Polk, ed., *Mississippi's Piney Woods: A Human Perspective* (Jackson: University Press of Mississippi, 1986), pp. 25–39.   4104

Jordan, Terry G., and Matti E. Kaups, *The American Backwoods Frontier: An Ethnic and Ecological Interpretation* (Baltimore: Johns Hopkins University Press, 1989), 340 pp.   4105

Jordan, Terry G., "New Sweden's Role on the American Frontier: A Study in Cultural Preadaptation," *Geografiska annaler B*, vol. 71B, 2 (1989), pp. 71–83.   4106

Broad settlement patterns

Leighly, John B., "Settlement and Cultivation in the Summer-Dry Climate," in *Climate and Man: 1941 Yearbook of Agriculture* (Washington, D.C.: Government Printing Office, 1941), pp. 197–204.   4107

Wagner, Philip L., "America Emerging," *Landscape*, vol. 13, 1 (1963), pp. 22–26. [Focus on the settlement pattern between 1930 and 1960] 4108

Davis, John F., "Transportation and American Settlement Patterns," in J. Wreford Watson and Timothy O'Riordan, eds., *The American Environment: Perceptions and Policies* (New York: John Wiley & Sons, 1976), pp. 169–182.   4109

Piellusch, Frederick B., "Historical Geography of Rural Areas," *Pennsylvania Geographer*, vol. 15, 4 (1977), pp. 55–62. [Focus on eastern Nebraska and Pennsylvania]   4110

Fisher, James S., and Ronald L. Mitchelson, "Forces of Change in the American Settlement Pattern," *Geographical Review*, vol. 71, 3 (1981), pp. 298–310. [Focus on 1950–1980]   4111

Rural settlement morphology

Trewartha, Glenn T., "The Unincorporated Hamlet: An Analysis of Data Sources," *Rural Sociology*, vol. 6 (1941), pp. 35–42.   4112

Meynen, Emil, "Dorf und Farm: Das Schicksal altweltlicher Dörfer in Amerika," in Oskar Schmieder, ed., *Gegenwartsprobleme der Neuen Welt*, pt. 1, *Nordamerika* (Leipzig: Quelle & Meyer, 1943), pp. 565–615.   4113

Trewartha, Glenn T., "The Unincorporated Hamlet: One Element in the American Settlement Fabric," *Annals of the Association of American Geographers*, vol. 33, 1 (1943), pp. 32–81.   4114

Trewartha, Glenn T., "Types of Rural Settlement in Colonial America," *Geographical Review*, vol. 36, 4 (1946), pp. 568–596. Reprinted in Philip L. Wagner and Marvin W. Mikesell, eds., *Readings in Cultural Geography* (Chicago: University of Chicago Press, 1962), pp. 517–538. 4115

Jordan, Terry G., "Abandonment of Farm-Village Tradition in New Land Settlement: The Example of Anglo-America," in *Geographic Dimensions of Rural Settlements* (Varanasi, India: Proceedings of the International Geographical Union, Varanasi Symposium, 1976), pp. 84–88. 4116

POPULATION

General distribution patterns & trends

Lüddecke, Richard, "Entwicklung der Besiedlung der Vereinigten Staaten," *Petermanns Geographische Mitteilungen*, vol. 34, 5 (1888), pp. 129–136. [Focus on 1790–1880] 4117

Gannett, Henry, "Movements of Our Population," *National Geographic Magazine*, vol. 5, 2 (Apr. 20, 1894), pp. 21–44. 4118

Blum, Richard, *Die Entwicklung der Vereinigten Staaten von Nordamerika: Nach den amtlichen Berichten über die Volkszählungen der Vereinigten Staaten von 1880, 1890 und 1900 und zum Teil zurück bis 1790* (Gotha: Justus Perthes, Ergänzungsheft no. 142 zu Petermanns Mitteilungen, 1903), 105 pp. 4119

Harper, Roland M., "Some Movements of State Centers of Population and Their Significance," *Journal of Geography*, vol. 15, 7 (1917), pp. 227–231. [Focus on 1880–1910] 4120

Sutherland, Stella H., *Population Distribution in Colonial America* (New York: Columbia University Press, 1933), 353 pp. Reprinted New York: AMS Press, 1966. 4121

Dodge, Stanley D., "Population Regions of the United States," *Papers of the Michigan Academy of Science, Arts, and Letters*, vol. 21 (1935), pp. 343–353. [Focus on 1790–1930] 4122

Friis, Herman R., "A Series of Population Maps of the Colonies and the United States, 1625–1790," *Geographical Review*, vol. 30, 3 (1940), pp. 463–470. 4123

Dodge, Stanley D., "Periods in the Population History of the United States," *Papers of the Michigan Academy of Science, Arts, and Letters*, vol. 32 (1946), pp. 253–260. 4124

Zelinsky, Wilbur, "Changes in the Geographic Patterns of Rural Population in the United States, 1790–1960," *Geographical Review*, vol. 52, 4 (1962), pp. 492–524. 4125

Van Royen, William, and Victor Roterus, "Thirty Years of Population Changes in the United States," *Tijdschrift van het Koninklijk Nederlandsch Aardrijkskundig Genootschap*, vol. 83, 4 (1966), pp. 389–399. [Focus on 1930–1960] 4126

Warntz, William, "Macroscopic Analysis and Some Patterns of the Geographical Distribution of Population in the United States, 1790–1950," *Northwestern University Studies in Geography*, no. 13 (1967), pp. 191–218. 4127

Ward, David, "Population Growth, Migration, and Urbanization, 1860–1920," in Robert D. Mitchell and Paul A. Groves, eds., *North America: The Historical Geography of a Changing Continent* (Totowa, N.J.: Rowman & Littlefield, 1987), pp. 299–320. 4128

Comparative local studies

Joy, Barnard, "Population Studies in Three American Communities," *Economic Geography*, vol. 15, 1 (1939), pp. 11–26. [Focus on Pope Co., Ark.; Marshall Co., Iowa; Clackamas Co., Oreg., 1880–1930] 4129

Immigration & emigration (to the United States)

LeConte, René, "Un siècle d'émigration allemande aux États-Unis, 1819–1919," *Mouvement géographique*, vol. 34 (1921), pp. 318–322, 329–331. 4130

Dureau, Agnès, "L'immigration aux États-Unis," *Annales de géographie*, vol. 45 (1936), pp. 286–302. 4131

Johnson, Hildegard Binder, "Der deutsche Amerika-Auswanderer des 18. Jahrhunderts im zeitgenössischen Urteil," *Deutsches Archiv für Landes- und Volksforschung*, vol. 4, 2 (1940), pp. 211–234. 4132

Meynen, Emil, and Gottfried Pfeifer, "Die Ausbreitung des europäischen Lebensraumes auf die Neue Welt: Die Vereinigten Staaten," in Karl H. Dietzel, Oskar Schmieder, and Heinrich Schmitthenner, eds., *Lebensraumfragen europäischer Völker*, vol. 2 (Leipzig: Quelle & Meyer, 1941), pp. 271–353; and in Oskar Schmieder, ed., *Gegenwartsprobleme der Neuen Welt*, pt. 1, *Nordamerika* (Leipzig: Quelle and Meyer, 1943), pp. 351–433. 4133

Textor, L. A., "Amerikas Bevölkerung und ihre Ursprünge: Kulturströmungen aus aller Welt prägen das heutige Bild der Vereinigten Staaten," *Zeitschrift für Wirtschaftsgeographie*, vol. 12, 3 (1968), pp. 84–86. 4134

Raffestin, Claude, "L'évolution de l'immigration allemande aux États-Unis," *Globe*, vol. 109 (1969), pp. 31–45. 4135

MacDonagh, Oliver, "The Irish Famine Emigration to the United States," *Perspectives in American History*, vol. 10 (1976), pp. 355–446.   **4136**

Muller, Edward K., "Introduction: A National Overview of Immigration," in Warren C. Born, ed., *Language and Culture: Heritage and Horizons* (Montpelier, Vt.: Capital City Press, 1976), pp. 15–31.   **4137**

Kortum, Gerhard, "Untersuchungen zur Integration und Rückwanderung nordfriesisches Amerikaauswanderer," *Nordfriesisches Jahrbuch*, n.s. vol. 14 (1978), pp. 45–91.   **4138**

Brayshay, Mark, "Using American Records to Study Nineteenth-Century Emigrants from Britain," *Area*, vol. 11, 2 (1979), pp. 156–160.   **4139**

Thomas, David, "Welsh Emigration to the United States: A Note on Surname Evidence," *Cambria*, vol. 6, 1 (1979), pp. 1–12.   **4140**

Ward, David, "Immigration: Settlement Patterns and Spatial Characteristics," in Stephen B. Thernstrom, ed., *Harvard Encyclopedia of American Ethnic Groups* (Cambridge: Harvard University Press, 1980), pp. 496–508.   **4141**

Kortum, Gerhard, "Migrationstheoretische und bevölkerungsgeographische Probleme der nordfriesischen Amerikarückwanderung," in Kai D. Sievers, ed., *Die deutsche und skandinavische Amerikaauswanderung im 19. und 20. Jahrhundert: Forschungsstand, Methoden, Quellen, mit Fallstudien aus Schleswig-Holstein und Hamburg* (Neumünster: Wachholtz, Studien zur Wirtschafts- und Sozialgeschichte Schleswig-Holsteins, vol. 3, 1981), pp. 111–201.   **4142**

Parsons, James J., "The Migration of Canary Islanders to the Americas: An Unbroken Current since Columbus," *The Americas*, vol. 39 (1983), pp. 447–481.   **4143**

Widdis, Randy W., "With Scarcely a Ripple: English Canadian Migration to the United States at the Turn of the Century," Ph.D. diss., Queens University, 1984.   **4144**

Carlson, Alvar W., "One Century of Foreign Immigration to the United States: 1880–1980," *International Migration*, vol. 23, 3 (1985), pp. 309–334.   **4145**

Constantinou, Stavros T., and Nicholas D. Diamantides, "Modeling International Migration: Determinants of Emigration from Greece to the United States, 1820–1980," *Annals of the Association of American Geographers*, vol. 75, 3 (1985), pp. 352–369.   **4146**

Schreuder, Yda, "Municipal Records in Nineteenth Century Dutch Emigration Research," *International Migration Review*, vol. 21, 1 (1987), pp. 114–122.   **4147**

Internal migration

Siebert, Wilbur H., "Light on the Underground Railroad," *American Historical Review*, vol. 1, 3 (1895), pp. 455–463.   **4148**

Brandon, Donald G., "Migration of Negroes in the United States, 1910–1947," Ph.D. diss., Columbia Teachers College, 1949.   **4149**

Farrell, Walter C., and James H. Johnson, "Black Migration as a Response to Social-Psychological Stress: A Note on Migrant Letters, 1916–1918," *Proceedings of the New England–St. Lawrence Valley Geographical Society*, vol. 6 (1976), pp. 42–46. Reprinted in *Geographical Survey*, vol. 7, 1 (1978), pp. 22–27.   **4150**

Allen, James P., "Changes in the American Propensity to Migrate," *Annals of the Association of American Geographers*, vol. 67, 4 (1977), pp. 577–587.   **4151**

Schwartz, Ulrich, "Binnenwanderung in den USA, 1915–1975," *Zeitschrift für Wirtschaftsgeographie*, vol. 21, 2 (1977), pp. 53–55.   **4152**

Hudson, Tim W., "Health Migration in America's Nineteenth Century Westward Movement," *Ecumene*, vol. 13 (1981), pp. 50–58.   **4153**

Berry, Brian J. L., *Westward the American Shapleys: The Family and Descendants of David Shapley, A Seventeenth Century Marblehead Fisherman* (Baltimore: Gateway Press, 1987), 466 pp.   **4154**

Ethnic & racial distribution patterns

Kiaer, A. N., "Den norsk-amerikanske Befolknings geografiske Udbredelse i de Forenede Stater," *Norske geografiske selskab aarbok*, vol. 17 (1906), pp. 17–64.   **4155**

Kloss, Heinz, "Rußlanddeutsche in den Vereinigten Staaten: Beiträge zur Siedlungsgeographie des Nordamerika-Deutschtums," *Petermanns Geographische Mitteilungen*, vol. 77, 7/8 (1931), pp. 171–178.   **4156**

Hannemann, Max, *Das Deutschtum in den Vereinigten Staaten: Seine Verbreitung und Entwicklung seit der Mitte des 19. Jahrhunderts* (Gotha: Justus Perthes, Ergänzungsheft no. 224 zu Petermanns Mitteilungen, 1936), 62 pp.   **4157**

Hannemann, Max, "Das Vordringen der 'German Frontier' im Präriegebiet der Vereinigten Staaten," *Zeitschrift für Geopolitik*, vol. 14, 10 (1937), pp. 824–836.   **4158**

Zelinsky, Wilbur, "The Population Geography of the Free Negro in Ante-Bellum America," *Population Studies*, vol. 3, 4 (1950), pp. 386–401.   **4159**

Sedlmeyer, Karl A., "Die Neger und ihre geographische Verbreitung," *Geographische Rundschau*, vol. 6, 10 (1954), pp. 374–378.   **4160**

Hart, John Fraser, "The Changing Distribution of the American Negro," *Annals of the Association of American Geographers*, vol. 50, 3 (1960), pp. 242–266. [Focus on 1880–1950]   **4161**

Kaups, Matti E., "Some Observations on the Distribution of Finnish Immigrants in America," *Hajy* (Helsinki), no. 3 (1965), pp. 8–10.   **4162**

Mehan, Christine Judy, "Polish Migration to and Settlement in the United States: A Geographical Interpretation," Master's thesis, Syracuse University, 1965.   **4163**

Duhaime, Paul F., "Puerto Rican Migration to the United States, 1900–1960," Master's thesis, Pennsylvania State University, 1972.   **4164**

McKee, Jesse O., "A Geographical Analysis of the Origin, Diffusion, and Spatial Distribution of the Black American in the United States," *Southern Quarterly*, vol. 12, 3 (1974), pp. 203–216. [Focus on 1790–1970]   **4165**

Bowen, William A., "American Ethnic Regions, 1880," *Proceedings of the Association of American Geographers*, vol. 8 (1976), pp. 44–46.   **4166**

Schneider, Mark, "Ethnic Regions of the United States, 1890–1970," *Polity*, vol. 12, 2 (1979), pp. 273–290.   **4167**

Blanton, Patricia, "Chinese Americans: The Spatial Dynamics of a Politically Constrained Population, 1870 to 1980," Master's thesis, University of North Carolina, 1983.   **4168**

Winsberg, Morton D., "The Relative Location of the British and Irish in the United States between 1850 and 1980," *Geography*, vol. 69, 4 (1984), pp. 342–345.   **4169**

Winsberg, Morton D., "Irish Settlement in the United States, 1850–1980," *Eire-Ireland*, vol. 20, 1 (1985), pp. 7–14.   **4170**

Winsberg, Morton D., "Patterns of Dutch Settlement in the U.S. between 1845 and 1980," *Dutch International Society Magazine*, vol. 16, 4 (1986), pp. 18–20.   **4171**

Haverluk, Terrance W., "The Changing Distribution of Hispanics in the United States, 1598 to 1980," Master's thesis, University of Minnesota, 1987.   **4172**

Winsberg, Morton D., "The Changing Relative Location of the Swedish-Born in the United States, 1850–1980," *Swedish-American Historical Quarterly*, vol. 38, 4 (1987), pp. 160–166.   **4173**

Age-related patterns

Peterson, Donald D., "Regional Variations in the Age Structure of the United States: 1870–1970," Master's thesis, University of Northern Iowa, 1975.   **4174**

Graff, Thomas O., and Robert F. Wiseman, "Changing Concentrations of Older Americans," *Geographical Review*, vol. 68, 4 (1978), pp. 379–393. [Focus on 1950–1970]   **4175**

Population dynamics

Schnell, George A., and Mark S. Monmonier, "The Mortality-Fertility Ratio: A Useful Measure for Describing Demographic Change in the United States, 1940–1975," *Geographical Survey*, vol. 8, 2 (1979), pp. 21–30.   **4176**

Labor force

Fitzsimmons, James D., "Growth in U.S. Female Labor Force Participation, 1950–1980," Ph.D. diss., University of Minnesota, 1990.   **4177**

RURAL & REGIONAL SOCIAL GEOGRAPHY

Social environment & ideology

Huntington, Ellsworth, "A Geographer's View of America's Queerness," *Education*, vol. 52, 5 (1932), pp. 254–257.   **4178**

Wright, John K., "Notes on Early American Geopiety," *Human Nature in Geography: Fourteen Papers, 1925–1965* (Cambridge: Harvard University Press, 1966), pp. 250–285.   **4179**

Lemon, James T., "Early Americans and Their Social Environment," *Journal of Historical Geography*, vol. 6, 2 (1980), pp. 115–132.   **4180**

Vance, James E., Jr., "Utopia on the American Earth," *Geographical Magazine*, vol. 52, 8 (1980), pp. 555–560.   **4181**

Lemon, James T., "Spatial Order: Households in Local Communities and Regions," in Jack P. Greene and J. R. Pole, eds., *Colonial British America: Essays in the New History of the Early Modern Era* (Baltimore: Johns Hopkins University Press, 1984), pp. 86–122.   **4182**

Vance, James E., Jr., "Democratic Utopia and the American Landscape," in Michael P. Conzen, ed., *The Making of the American Landscape* (Boston: Unwin Hyman, 1990), pp. 204–220.   **4183**

Regional cultures

Strong, Helen M., "Regionalism: Its Cultural Significance," *Economic Geography*, vol. 12, 4 (1936), pp. 392–410.   **4184**

Mitchell, Robert D., "The Formation of Early American Cultural Regions: An Interpretation," in James R. Gibson, ed., *European Settlement and Development in North America: Essays in Geographical Change in Honour and Memory of Andrew Hill Clark* (Toronto: University of Toronto Press, 1978), pp. 66–90.   **4185**

Nationality, ethnicity, race, & slavery

Ratzel, Friedrich, "Sklavenbefreiung in Amerika," *Meyers Konversationslexicon*, 3d ed. vol. 17 (1880), pp. 812–816. **4186**

Emerson, Frederick V., "Geographic Influences in American Slavery," *Bulletin of the American Geographical Society*, vol. 43, 1–3 (1911), pp. 13–26, 106–118, and 170–181. **4187**

Dietrich, Bruno, "Volkstum und Rasse in den Vereinigten Staaten von Amerika," *Mitteilungen der Geographischen Gesellschaft in Wien*, vol. 73 (1930), pp. 253–269. **4188**

Tauschnitz, Bernhard, "Die Entwicklung des Negerproblems in den Vereinigten Staaten von Amerika," *Geographische Wochenschrift*, vol. 3 (1935), pp. 109–114. **4189**

Ethnic communities

African Americans

Morrill, Richard L., and O. Fred Donaldson, "Geographical Perspectives on the History of Black America," *Economic Geography*, vol. 48, 1 (1972), pp. 1–23. Reprinted, with omissions, in David Ward, ed., *Geographic Perspectives on America's Past: Readings on the Historical Geography of the United States* (New York: Oxford University Press, 1979), pp. 77–93. **4190**

Davis, George A., and O. Fred Donaldson, *Blacks in the United States: A Geographic Perspective* (Boston: Houghton Mifflin Co., 1975), 270 pp. **4191**

Ihde, H., *Von der Plantage zum schwarzen Ghetto: Geschichte und Kultur der Afroamerikaner in den USA* (Leipzig: Urania-Verlag, 1975), 167 pp. **4192**

Jordan, Terry G., "Cowboys," in R. M. Miller and J. D. Smith, eds., *Dictionary of Afro-American Slavery* (New York: Greenwood Press, 1988), pp. 152–153. **4193**

Amish & Mennonite

Landing, James E., "Geographic Model of Old Order Amish Settlements," *Professional Geographer*, vol. 21, 4 (1969), pp. 238–243. **4194**

Landing, James E., "The Buggy Cultures," *Mennonite Historical Bulletin*, vol. 31, 4 (1970), pp. 3–4. **4195**

Landing, James E., "The Failure of Amish Settlements in the United States: An Appeal for Inquiry," *Mennonite Quarterly Review*, vol. 44, 4 (1970), pp. 376–388. **4196**

Landing, James E., "Old Order Amish Population," *Mennonite Historical Bulletin*, vol. 31, 4 (1970), p. 3. **4197**

Landing, James E., "Landscape Perception and Minority Group Viability: Some Insight into Cultural Group Extinction," *Geographical Perspectives*, vol. 29 (1972), pp. 30–32. **4198**

Landing, James E., "The Old Order Amish: Problem Solving through Migration," *Bulletin of the Illinois Geographical Society*, vol. 17, 2 (1975), pp. 36–48. **4199**

Crowley, William K., "Old Order Amish Settlement: Diffusion and Growth," *Annals of the Association of American Geographers*, vol. 68, 2 (1978), pp. 249–264. **4200**

Purvis, Thomas L., "The Pennsylvania Dutch and the German-American Diaspora in 1790," *Journal of Cultural Geography*, vol. 6, 2 (1986), pp. 81–99. **4201**

Trinonoff, Karen M., "Amish Culture as Preserved in Quilts," *Journal of Cultural Geography*, vol. 10, 1 (1990), pp. 63–73. **4202**

Assyrians

Smith, Gary N., "From Urmia to Stanislaus: A Cultural-Historical Geography of Assyrian Christians in the Middle East and America," Ph.D. diss., University of California–Davis, 1981. **4203**

Chinese and Japanese

Vogelsang, Roland, "Die chinesische Minderheit in den USA—oder An der Behandlung der Minderheiten sollt Ihr sie erkennen!" *Praxis Geographie*, vol. 15, 1 (1985), pp. 34–39. **4204**

Vogelsang, Roland, "Die chinesische und japanische Minorität in den USA: Gegensätze und Gemeinsamkeiten in Geschichte und Gegenwart," in Hans-Wilhelm Windhorst and William H. Berentsen, eds., *Beiträge zur räumlichen Prozeßforschung in den USA* (Vechta: Vechtaer Arbeiten zur Geographie und Regionalwissenschaft, vol. 2, 1986), pp. 83–98. **4205**

Dutch

Van Heite, J., "Nederlandse nederzettingen in de Verenigde Staten van Amerika, 1847–1947," *Tijdschrift van het Koninklijk Nederlandsch Aardrijkskundig Genootschap*, vol. 64 (1947), pp. 411–429. [Michigan, Iowa, the West] **4206**

Finns

Van Cleef, Eugene, "The Finn in America," *Geographical Review*, vol. 6, 3 (1918), pp. 185–214. **4207**

Alanen, Arnold R., "In Search of the Pioneer Finnish Homesteader in America," *Finnish America*, vol. 4 (1981), pp. 72–92. **4208**

Jordan, Terry G., and Matti E. Kaups, "Finns and the Cultural Legacy of the New Sweden Colony,"

Scandinavian Review, vol. 75 (1987), pp. 117–123.
                                                    4209

Germans

LeConte, René, "Pangermanisme et germanisme aux États-Unis," *Mouvement géographique*, vol. 34 (July 1921), pp. 436–442.   4210

LeConte, René, "Le rôle des Allemands aux États-Unis au XIXe siècle," *Mouvement géographique*, vol. 34 (July 1921), pp. 361–367.   4211

Kloss, Heinz, "Über die mittelbare kartographische Erfassung der jüngeren deutschen Volksinseln in den Vereinigten Staaten," *Deutsches Archiv für Landes- und Volksforschung*, vol. 3 (1939), pp. 453–474.   4212

Johnson, Hildegard Binder, "Adjustment to the United States," in A. E. Zucker, ed., *The Forty-Eighters* (New York: Columbia University Press, 1950), pp. 43–78.   4213

Jordan, Terry G., "Germans in the Making of America," *Humanities*, vol. 4 (1983), pp. 18–20.
                                                    4214

Kampfhoefner, Walter D., "300 Jahre Deutsche in den USA," *Geographische Rundschau*, vol. 35, 4 (1983), pp. 169–173.   4215

Vollmar, Rainer, "Weltanschauung und Siedlungsplan: Theorie und Beispiele religiöskommunitärer und säkularer deutscher Siedlungen in den USA," in Hans-Wilhelm Windhorst and William H. Berentsen, eds., *Beiträge zur räumlichen Prozeßforschung in den USA* (Vechta: Vechta Druckerei und Verlag, Zentralverband der Deutschen Geographen, Arbeitskreis USA, Vechtaer Arbeiten zur Geographie und Regionalwissenschaft, vol. 2, 1986), pp. 11–30.   4216

Greeks

Balk, Helen H., "Economic Contributions of the Greeks to the United States," *Economic Geography*, vol. 19, 3 (1943), pp. 270–275.   4217

Jews

Mesinger, Jonathan S., and Ary J. Lamme III, "American Jewish Ethnicity," in Jesse O. McKee, ed., *Ethnicity in Contemporary America* (Dubuque: Kendall/Hunt, 1985), pp. 145–168.
                                                    4218

Mexicans

Nostrand, Richard L., "Mexican American and Chicano: Emerging Terms for a People Coming of Age," *Pacific Historical Review*, vol. 42, 3 (1973), pp. 389–406.   4219

Religious affiliation

General

Sernett, Milton C., "Geographic Considerations in Afro-American Religious History: Past Performance, Present Problems, and Future Hopes," Syracuse University Department of Geography Discussion Paper no. 69 (1981), 29 pp.   4220

Stump, Roger W., "Changing Regional Patterns of White Protestantism in the United States, 1906–1971," Ph.D. diss., University of Kansas, 1981.
                                                    4221

Stump, Roger W., "National Parishes as an Index of Catholic Ethnicity," *Proceedings of the Middle States Division, Association of American Geographers*, vol. 17 (1983), pp. 87–96.   4222

Stump, Roger W., "Regional Divergence in Religious Affiliations in the United States," *Sociological Analysis*, vol. 45 (1984), pp. 283–299.   4223

Stump, Roger W., "Regional Migration and Religious Commitments in the United States," *Journal for the Scientific Study of Religion*, vol. 23, 3 (1984), pp. 292–303.   4224

Comparative studies

Raitz, Karl B., "Theology on the Landscape: A Comparison of Mormon and Amish-Mennonite Land Use," *Utah Historical Quarterly*, vol. 41, 1 (1973), pp. 23–34. [Utah and Lancaster Co., Pa.]
                                                    4225

Lifchez, Raymond, "Inspired Planning: Mormon and Fourierist Communities in the Nineteenth Century," *Landscape*, vol. 20, 3 (1976), pp. 29–35.
                                                    4226

Individual denominations & sects

Meyer, Judith W., "The Historical Geography of the Lutheran Church: Missouri Synod, 1847–1967: A Case Study in Religious Geography," Master's thesis, Southern Illinois University, 1967.   4227

Lamme, Ary J., III, "From Boston in One Hundred Years: Christian Science," *Professional Geographer*, vol. 23, 4 (1971), pp. 329–332.   4228

Mooers, Richard E., "Origin and Dispersion of Unitarianism in America," Master's thesis, Syracuse University, 1971.   4229

Tatum, Charles E., "The Christian Methodist Episcopal Church in America, with Emphasis on Negroes in Texas, 1870 to 1970," Ph.D. diss., Michigan State University, 1971.   4230

Lamme, Ary J., III, "Christian Science in the U.S.A., 1900–1910: A Distributional Study," Syracuse University Department of Geography Discussion Paper no. 3 (1975), 29 pp.   4231

Meyer, Judith W., "Ethnicity, Theology, and Immigrant Church Expansion," *Geographical Review*, vol. 65, 2 (1975), pp. 180–197. **4232**

Tatum, Charles E., and Lawrence M. Sommers, "The Spread of the Black Christian Methodist Episcopal Church in the United States, 1870 to 1970," *Journal of Geography*, vol. 74, 6 (1975), pp. 343–357. **4233**

Peffers, Diane D., "The Diffusion and Dispersion of the Reorganized Church of Jesus Christ of the Latter Day Saints: An Overview," Master's thesis, Brigham Young University, 1980. **4234**

Caldwell, John M., "The Methodist Organization of the United States, 1784–1844: An Historical Geography of the Methodist Episcopal Church from Its Formation to Its Division," Ph.D. diss., University of Oklahoma, 1982. **4235**

Stump, Roger W., "Patterns of Survival among Catholic National Parishes, 1940–1980," *Journal of Cultural Geography*, vol. 7, 1 (1986), pp. 77–97. **4236**

Utopian communities

Porter, Philip W., and Fred E. Lukermann, "The Geography of Utopia," in David Lowenthal and Martyn J. Bowden, eds., *Geographies of the Mind: Essays in Historical Geosophy in Honor of John Kirtland Wright* (New York: Oxford University Press, 1976), pp. 197–223. [Focus on frontier settings] **4237**

Social class

Vogeler, Ingolf K., "American Peasantry," *Anthropological Quarterly*, vol. 48, 4 (1975), pp. 223–235. **4238**

Hugill, Peter J., "Home and Class among an American Landed Elite," in John Agnew and James S. Duncan, eds., *The Power of Place: Bringing Together Geographical and Sociological Imaginations* (Boston: Unwin Hyman, 1989), pp. 66–80. **4239**

Social laws & customs

Jones, Mary Somerville, "An Historical Geography of Changing Divorce Law in the United States," Ph.D. diss., University of North Carolina, 1978. **4240**

Jones, Mary Somerville, *An Historical Geography of Changing Divorce Law in the United States, 1867–1972* (New York: Garland Publishing Co., 1987), 227 pp. **4241**

McGreevy, Patrick V., "Place in the American Christmas," *Geographical Review*, vol. 80, 1 (1990), pp. 32–42. **4242**

Social movements

Brown, Lawrence A., and S. G. Philliber, "The Diffusion of a Population-Related Innovation: The Planned Parenthood Affiliate," *Social Science Quarterly*, vol. 58 (1977), pp. 215–228. [Focus on 1916–1973] **4243**

Sechrist, Robert P., "A Comparative Analysis of Multi-Dimensional Diffusion Models: The Diffusion of the Prohibition Movement in the United States of America, 1876–1919," Ph.D. diss., Louisiana State University, 1986. **4244**

Social terms of labor

Earle, Carville V., "A Staple Interpretation of Slavery and Free Labor," *Geographical Review*, vol. 68, 1 (1978), pp. 51–65. **4245**

Earle, Carville V., and Ronald A. Hoffman, "The Foundation of the Modern Economy: Agriculture and the Costs of Labor in the United States and England, 1800–60," *American Historical Review*, vol. 85, 5 (1980), pp. 1055–1094. **4246**

Spiker, J. Scott, "A Geographic Analysis of Unemployment in the United States, 1965–1987," Master's thesis, West Virginia University, 1990. **4247**

Education

Dryer, Charles R., "A Century of Geographic Education in the United States," *Annals of the Association of American Geographers*, vol. 14 (1924), pp. 117–149. **4248**

Wright, John K., "Notes on Measuring and Counting in Early American Geography," *Human Nature in Geography: Fourteen Papers, 1925–1965* (Cambridge: Harvard University Press, 1966), pp. 205–249. **4249**

Hart, John Fraser, and Janet S. Cyr-Henderson, "The Development and Spatial Patterns of Black Colleges," *Southeastern Geographer*, vol. 11, 2 (1971), pp. 133–138. **4250**

Sublett, Michael D., "Geographic Patterns of American Church Colleges," *Virginia Geographer*, vol. 8, 1 (1973), pp. 8–15. **4251**

Schofer, Jerry P., "Presbyterian and Congregational Colleges in the United States," *Proceedings of the Middle States Division, Association of American Geographers*, vol. 14 (1980), pp. 66–70. [Focus on 1636–1861] **4252**

Dorschner, Donald L., and Robert O. Marten, "The Spatial Evolution of Academic Geography in the United States," *Journal of Geography*, vol. 89, 3 (1990), pp. 101–108. **4253**

Pathologies & their containment

McBryde, Felix W., "Influenza in America during the Sixteenth Century," *Bulletin of the History of Medicine*, vol. 8 (1940), pp. 296–302. **4254**

Pyle, Gerald F., "The Diffusion of Cholera in the United States in the Nineteenth Century," *Geographical Analysis*, vol. 1, 1 (1968), pp. 59–75. Reprinted in Paul W. English and Robert C. Mayfield, eds., *Man, Space, and Environment: Concepts in Contemporary Human Geography* (New York: Oxford University Press, 1972), pp. 410–422; and in David A. Lanegran and Risa Palm, eds., *An Invitation to Geography* (New York: McGraw-Hill Book Co., 1973), pp. 71–86.   **4255**

Harries, Keith D., "The Historical Geography of Homicide in the U.S.: 1935–1980," *Geoforum*, vol. 16, 1 (1985), pp. 73–83.   **4256**

Hunter, John M., and Gary W. Shannon, "Jarvis Revisited: Distance Decay in Service Areas of Mid-Nineteenth Century Asylums," *Professional Geographer*, vol. 37, 3 (1985), pp. 296–302.   **4257**

Foster, Stuart A., "Analyses of the Changing Geographic Distribution of Physicians in the United States from 1950 through 1985," Ph.D. diss., Ohio State University, 1988.   **4258**

Husband, Elizabeth, "A Geographical Perspective on U.S. Capital Punishment, 1801–1960," Ph.D. diss., Louisiana State University, 1990.   **4259**

Voluntary associations

Schein, Richard H., "A Geographical and Historical Account of the American Benevolent Fraternal Order," Master's thesis, Pennsylvania State University, 1983.   **4260**

Consumption

Shortridge, James R., and Barbara G. Shortridge, "Patterns of American Rice Consumption, 1955 and 1980," *Geographical Review*, vol. 73, 4 (1983), pp. 417–429.   **4261**

Pillsbury, Richard R., *From Boarding House to Bistro: The American Restaurant in a Time-Place Perspective* (Boston: Unwin Hyman, 1990), 247 pp.   **4262**

Fairs

Kniffen, Fred B., "The American Agricultural Fair: The Pattern," *Annals of the Association of American Geographers*, vol. 39 (1949), pp. 264–282.   **4263**

Kniffen, Fred B., "The American Agricultural Fair: Time and Place," *Annals of the Association of American Geographers*, vol. 41, 1 (1951), pp. 42–57.   **4264**

Popular music

Gordon, Jeffrey J., "Rock-and-Roll Music: A Diffusion Study," Master's thesis, Pennsylvania State University, 1970.   **4265**

Ford, Larry R., "Geographic Factors in the Origin, Evolution, and Diffusion of Rock and Roll Music," *Journal of Geography*, vol. 70, 8 (1971), pp. 455–464.   **4266**

Carney, George O., "Bluegrass Grows All Around: The Spatial Dimensions of a Country Music Style," *Journal of Geography*, vol. 73, 1 (1974), pp. 34–55.   **4267**

Carney, George O., "T for Texas, T for Tennessee: The Origins of American Country Music Notables," *Journal of Geography*, vol. 78, 6 (1979), pp. 218–225.   **4268**

Carney, George O., ed., *The Sounds of People and Places: Readings in the Geography of Music* (Washington, D.C.: University Press of America, 1987), 336 pp.   **4269**

Fouts, Elliot D., "A Geographical Analysis of Competitive Drum and Bugle Corps in the United States," Master's thesis, Oklahoma State University, 1990.   **4270**

POLITICAL & ADMINISTRATIVE GEOGRAPHY

General

Turner, Frederick Jackson, "Geographical Influences in American Political History," *Bulletin of the American Geographical Society*, vol. 46, 8 (1914), pp. 591–595. Reprinted in Frederick Jackson Turner, *The Significance of Sections in American History* (New York: Henry Holt & Co., 1932), pp. 183–192.   **4271**

Whittlesey, Derwent S., "The United States: The Origin of a Federal State," and "The United States: Expansion and Consolidation," in W. Gordon East and E. A. Moodie, eds., *The Changing World: Studies in Political Geography* (Yonkers-on-Hudson: World Book Co., 1956), pp. 239–260, 261–284.   **4272**

Zelinsky, Wilbur, *Nation into State: The Shifting Symbolic Foundations of American Nationalism* (Chapel Hill: University of North Carolina Press, 1988), 350 pp.   **4273**

Territorial evolution

Gannett, Henry, "A Graphic History of the United States," *Journal of the American Geographical Society*, vol. 28 (1896), pp. 251–272. [Focus on the evolution of state boundaries, to 1896]   **4274**

Viallate, Achille, "Le développement territorial des États-Unis (1783–1899): Essai de géographie historique," *Revue de géographie*, vol. 50 (1902), pp. 127–140, 201–217.   **4275**

Regionalism and sectionalism

Turner, Frederick Jackson, "Geographic Sectionalism in American History," *Annals of the Associ-*

ation of American Geographers, vol. 16, 2 (1926), pp. 85–93. Reprinted in Frederick Jackson Turner, *The Significance of Sections in American History* (New York: Henry Holt & Co., 1932), pp. 193–206. **4276**

Wright, John K., "Geographical Sections and American Political History as Illustrated by Certain Maps in the Atlas of the Historical Geography of the United States," *Comptes rendus du Congress international de géographie, Varsovie 1934*, vol. 4 (Varsovie: Département général, 1938), pp. 103–107. **4277**

Steiner, Michael C., "Regionalism in the Great Depression," *Geographical Review*, vol. 73, 4 (1983), pp. 430–446. **4278**

Martis, Kenneth C., "Sectionalism and the United States Congress," *Political Geography Quarterly*, vol. 7, 2 (1988), pp. 99–109. **4279**

Wade, Larry, "The Influence of Sections and Periods on Economic Voting in American Presidential Elections: 1828–1964," *Political Geography Quarterly*, vol. 8, 3 (1989), pp. 271–288. **4280**

Building federation & state

Libby, Orin G., *Geographical Distribution of the Vote of the Thirteen States on the Federal Constitution, 1787–8* (Madison: University of Wisconsin Bulletin; Economics, Political Science, and History Series, vol. 1, 1, 1894). 116 pp. **4281**

Turner, Frederick Jackson, "Western State Making in the Revolutionary Era," *American Historical Review*, vol. 1, 1 (1895), pp. 70–87, and 2 (1896), pp. 251–269. Reprinted in Frederick Jackson Turner, *The Significance of Sections in American History* (New York: Henry Holt & Co., 1932), pp. 86–138. **4282**

Dauer, Manning J., *The Adams Federalists* (Baltimore: Johns Hopkins University Press, 1953), 292 pp. Revised 1968. **4283**

Vance, James E., Jr., "Areal Political Structure and Its Influence on Urban Patterns," *Yearbook of the Association of Pacific Coast Geographers*, vol. 22 (1960), pp. 40–49. [Focus on the development of the American county] **4284**

Fifer, J. Valerie, "Unity by Inclusion: Core Area and Federal State at American Independence," *Geographical Journal*, vol. 142, 3 (1976), pp. 462–470. **4285**

Hannah, Matthew G., "The Mid to Late Nineteenth Century United States Census as a Focus for Positivist Geographic Thought," Master's thesis, Pennsylvania State University, 1988. **4286**

Marston, Sallie A., "Who are 'The People'?: Gender, Citizenship, and the Making of the Ameri-

can Nation," *Environment and Planning D: Society and Space*, vol. 8, 4 (1990), pp. 449–458. **4287**

Geopolitics

Ryan, Jerry B., "Geographic Rationalization in American Expansion and Territorial Aggression: 1775–1920," Ph.D. diss., University of Kansas, 1972. **4288**

Fifer, J. Valerie, "Transcontinental: The Political Word," *Geographical Journal*, vol. 144, 3 (1978), pp. 438–449. **4289**

Hoffman, George W., "Nineteenth Century Roots of American World Power Relations: A Study in Historical Political Geography," *Political Geography Quarterly*, vol. 1, 3 (1982), pp. 279–282. **4290**

Elections & voting patterns

Garst, Ronald D., "Parallelism in American Presidential Elections, 1896–1964: A Geographic Analysis," Master's thesis, Arizona State University, 1967. **4291**

Archer, J. Clark, and Peter J. Taylor, *Section and Party: A Political Geography of American Presidential Elections, from Andrew Jackson to Ronald Reagan* (Chichester, England: Research Studies Press, 1981), 271 pp. **4292**

Martis, Kenneth C., and Ruth A. Rowles, "Mapping Congress: Developing a Geographic Understanding of American Political History," *Prologue: Journal of the National Archives*, vol. 16, 1 (1984), pp. 5–21. **4293**

Military organization

Showalter, William J., "America's New Soldier Cities: The Geographical and Historical Environment of the National Army Cantonments and National Guard Camps," *National Geographic Magazine*, vol. 32, 5 (1917), pp. 439–476. **4294**

Rhyne, David, "Army Posts in American Culture: A Historical and Cultural Geography of Army Posts in the United States," Master's thesis, Pennsylvania State University, 1979. **4295**

Gulley, Harold E., "Maps in the Civil War: An Examination of Map Use during the Peninsular Campaign," Master's thesis, University of Georgia, 1985. **4296**

Gulley, Harold E., and Louis DeVorsey, Jr., "Lost in Battle: Deficient Maps in the American Civil War," *Geographical Magazine*, vol. 58, 6 (1986), pp. 288–293. **4297**

Kreger, Robert D., "The Making of an Institutional Landscape: Case Studies of Air Force Bases, World War I to the Present," Ph.D. diss., University of Illinois, 1988. [Nebraska, Ohio, Washington, D.C., Illinois] **4298**

Laws, policies, & justice

Sawvell, Robert D., "The Influence of Government Policy on the Amount of Land Devoted to Sugar Production in the Continental United States, 1890 to the Present," Ph.D. diss., University of Oklahoma, 1973. **4299**

Bal Kumar, K. C., "The Spatial Diffusion of Public Policy Innovations and the Role of Modernization in the United States, 1870–1970," Ph.D. diss., University of Texas, 1977. **4300**

Malakoff, Harry S., "Sunday Closing Laws: Their History and Their Current Impact on Retail Facilities," Master's thesis, Columbia University, 1979. **4301**

DeVorsey, Louis, Jr., "The Use of Historical Maps in Litigation," *Technical Papers of the American Congress on Surveying and Mapping* (1981), pp. 41–51. **4302**

DeVorsey, Louis, Jr., "Historical Maps before the United States Supreme Court," *Map Collector*, vol. 19 (1982), pp. 24–31. **4303**

Haynes, Kingsley E., K. C. Bal Kumar, and Ronald Briggs, "Regional Patterns in the Spatial Diffusion of Public Policy Innovations in the U.S., 1870–1970," *Political Geography Quarterly*, vol. 2, 4 (1983), pp. 289–308. **4304**

Lutz, James M., "The Spatial and Temporal Diffusion of Selected Licensing Laws in the United States," *Political Geography Quarterly*, vol. 5, 2 (1986), pp. 141–159. **4305**

Lamme, Ary J., III, "Spatial Criteria in Supreme Court Decisions on Preservation Studies," *Geographical Review*, vol. 80, 4 (1990), pp. 343–354. **4306**

Political parties & movements

Luria, Daniel, "Suburbanization, Ethnicity, and Party Base: Spatial Aspects of the Decline of American Socialism," *Antipode*, vol. 11, 3 (1979), pp. 76–80. **4307**

Bennett, Sari J., "The Geography of American Socialism: Continuity and Change, 1900–1912," *Social Science History*, vol. 7, 3 (1983), pp. 267–288. **4308**

Earle, Carville V., and Sari J. Bennett, "Socialism in America: A Geographical Interpretation of Its Failure," *Political Geography Quarterly*, vol. 2, 1 (1983), pp. 31–55. **4309**

ECONOMIC DEVELOPMENT

General

McGee, William J., "The Growth of the United States," *National Geographic Magazine*, vol. 9, 9 (1898), pp. 377–386. **4310**

Huntington, Ellsworth, "The Handicap of Poor Land," *Economic Geography*, vol. 2, 3 (1926), pp. 335–357. **4311**

Morris, Francis Grave, "Environment and Regional Development in the Colonial Period," *Social Forces*, vol. 16, 1 (1937), pp. 12–23. **4312**

Lampard, Eric E., "Regional Economic Development, 1870–1950," in Harvey S. Perloff, ed., *Regions, Resources, and Economic Growth* (Baltimore: Johns Hopkins University Press, 1960), pp. 109–292. **4313**

Fogel, Robert W., *Railroads and American Economic Growth* (Baltimore: Johns Hopkins University Press, 1964), 296 pp. **4314**

Lankford, Philip M., *Regional Incomes in the United States, 1929–1967: Level, Distribution, Stability, and Growth* (Chicago: University of Chicago Department of Geography, Research Paper no. 145, 1972), 137 pp. **4315**

Zimon, Henry A., "U.S. Regional Inequalities, 1950–1978: A Multi-Scale/Multi-Regional Inquiry into the Patterns and Processes," Ph.D. diss., Ohio State University, 1979. **4316**

Estall, Robert C., "The Changing Balance of the Northern and Southern Regions of the United States," *Journal of American Studies*, vol. 14, 3 (1980), pp. 365–386. [Focus on 1950–1977] **4317**

Schnell, George A., "Economic Development and Fertility: The States and Territories in 1850," *Proceedings of the Pennsylvania Academy of Science*, vol. 54 (1980), pp. 67–72. **4318**

Briggs, Ronald, "The Role of Transportation and Environmental Amenity Resources in the Development of Nonmetropolitan America, 1950 to 1980," in John S. Adams, Werner Fricke, and Wolfgang Herden, eds., *American German International Seminar* (Heidelberg: Geographisches Institut der Universität Heidelberg, Heidelberger Geographische Arbeiten, vol. 73, 1983), pp. 146–166. **4319**

Meyer, David R., "The National Integration of Regional Economies, 1860–1920," in Robert D. Mitchell and Paul A. Groves, eds., *North America: The Historical Geography of a Changing Continent* (Totowa, N.J.: Rowman & Littlefield, 1987), pp. 321–346. **4320**

Staples

Dudley, Jonas G., "A Paper on the Growth, Trade, and Manufactures of Cotton," *Bulletin of the American Geographical and Statistical Society*, vol. 1, 2 (1853), pp. 105–194. **4321**

Engelbrecht, Thiess H., *Die geographische Verteilung der Getreidepreise in den Vereinigten Staaten von 1862 bis 1900* (Berlin: P. Parey, 1903), 108 pp. **4322**

Earle, Carville V., "The Significance of Staples in American History," *Ohio Geographers: Recent Research Themes*, vol. 13 (1985), pp. 54–69. **4323**

Earle, Carville V., and Ronald A. Hoffman, "Regional Staples and Urban Systems in the Antebellum United States," in Jeane Chase, ed., *Géographie du capital marchand aux Ameriques, 1760–1860* (Paris: Éditions de L'école des hautes études en sciences sociales, 1987), pp. 151–181. **4324**

Financial & commercial intermediaries

Girling, Peter D., "The Diffusion of Banks in the United States from 1781 to 1861," Master's thesis, Pennsylvania State University, 1968. **4325**

Conzen, Michael P., "State Business Directories in Historical and Geographical Research," *Historical Geography*, vol. 2, 2 (1972), pp. 1–14. **4326**

Wheeler, James O., "The U.S. Metropolitan Corporate and Population Hierarchies, 1960–1980," *Geografiska Annaler B*, vol. 67B, 2 (1985), pp. 89–97. **4327**

Economic sectors

Kirn, Thomas J., "Growth and Change in the Service Sector of the United States: A Spatial Perspective," *Annals of the Association of American Geographers*, vol. 77, 3 (1988), pp. 353–372. [Focus on 1958–1977] **4328**

Perturbations

Burghardt, Andrew F., "The Economic Impact of War: The Case of the U.S. Civil War," *Journal of Geography*, vol. 72, 6 (1973), pp. 7–10. **4329**

Alston, Lee J., "Farm Foreclosures in the United States during the Interwar Period," *Journal of Economic History*, vol. 43, 4 (1983), pp. 885–903. **4330**

Berry, Brian J. L., *Long-Wave Rhythms in Economic Development and Political Behavior* (Baltimore: Johns Hopkins University Press, 1991), 241 pp. [Focus on the United States] **4331**

RESOURCE MANAGEMENT

Forests

Whitaker, J. Russell, "Our Forests, Past and Present," in Almon E. Parkins and J. Russell Whit-aker, *Our Natural Resources and Their Conservation* (New York: J. Wiley & Sons, 1936), pp. 229–250. **4332**

Olson, Sherry H., "Commerce and Conservation: A History of Railway Timber," Ph.D. diss., Johns Hopkins University, 1965. **4333**

Olson, Sherry H., "Commerce and Conservation: The Railroad Experience," *Forest History*, vol. 9, 4 (1966), pp. 2–15. **4334**

Olson, Sherry H., "Resource Utilization: The Case of Railway Timber," *Proceedings of the Pennsylvania Academy of Science*, vol. 39, 2 (1966), pp. 240–243. [Focus on 1870–1960] **4335**

Olson, Sherry H., *The Depletion Myth: A History of Railroad Use of Timber* (Cambridge: Harvard University Press, 1971), 228 pp. **4336**

Fauna

Doughty, Robin W., "Concern for Fashionable Feathers," *Forest History*, vol. 16, 2 (1972), pp. 4–11. **4337**

Doughty, Robin W., *Feather Fashions and Bird Preservation: A Study in Nature Protection* (Berkeley: University of California Press, 1975), 184 pp. **4338**

Doughty, Robin W., *The English Sparrow in the American Landscape: A Paradox in Nineteenth Century Wildlife Conservation* (Oxford: University of Oxford, School of Geography, Research Paper no. 19, 1978), 36 pp. **4339**

Doughty, Robin W., *The Return of the Whooping Crane* (Austin: University of Texas Press, 1989), 182 pp. **4340**

Energy sources

Fels, Edwin, "Die Stauseen der Vereinigten Staaten von Amerika," *Erde*, vol. 95, 1 (1964), pp. 36–52. [Focus on 1884–1964] **4341**

Ottum, Margaret G., "Changing Patterns in the Production and Consumption of Residual Fuel Oil in the United States, 1940–1972," Ph.D. diss., Oregon State University, 1976. **4342**

Howard, Robert B., and Debra Shiroma, "Windmill Sites in Mountainous Areas," *California Geographer*, vol. 18 (1978), pp. 85–93. **4343**

Fitzsimmons, A. K., "The Changing United States Energy Situation," *Geography*, vol. 64, 2 (1979), pp. 126–129. [Focus on 1950–1975] **4344**

Hanham, Robert Q., and Frank J. Calzonetti, "Regional and Temporal Trends in Power Plant Unit Siting, 1912–1978," *Professional Geographer*, vol. 35, 4 (1983), pp. 416–426. **4345**

Waste disposal

Sicular, Daniel T., "Currents in the Waste Stream: A History of Refuse Management and Resource

Recovery in America," Master's thesis, University of California–Berkeley, 1984.　4346

Environmental quality

Kay, Jeanne C., "Preconditions of Natural Resource Conservation," *Agricultural History*, vol. 59, 2 (1985), pp. 124–135.　4347

Kay, Jeanne C., "Restoration of American Wilderness: A Humanistic Perspective," in Z. Dubinsky and Y. Steinberger, eds., *Environmental Quality and Ecosystem Stability*, vol. 3, *Proceedings of the Third International Conference of the Israel Society for Ecology and Environmental Quality Sciences* (Ramat Gan, Israel: Bar-Ilan University Press, 1986), pp. 385–394.　4348

LAND & LAND USE

Land survey

Pratt, Joseph H., "American Prime Meridians," *Geographical Review*, vol. 32, 2 (1942), pp. 233–244.　4349

Pattison, William D., *Beginnings of the American Rectangular Land Survey System, 1784–1800* (Chicago: University of Chicago Department of Geography, Research Paper no. 50, 1957), 248 pp.　4350

Pattison, William D., "The Original Plan for an American Rectangular Land Survey," *Surveying and Mapping*, vol. 21, 3 (1961), pp. 339–345.　4351

Johnson, Hildegard Binder, "Man, Rectangularity and Landscape," in W. P. Adams and F. M. Helleiner, eds., *International Geography, 1972*, vol. 1, sec. 5, *Historical Geography* (Toronto: University of Toronto Press, for the International Geographical Union, 1972), pp. 436–437.　4352

Johnson, Hildegard Binder, "The United States Land Survey as a Principle of Order," in Ralph E. Ehrenberg, ed., *Pattern and Process: Research in Historical Geography* (Washington, D.C.: Howard University Press, 1975), pp. 114–130. 4353

Pattison, William D., "Reflections on the American Rectangular Land Survey System," in Ralph E. Ehrenberg, ed., *Pattern and Process: Research in Historical Geography* (Washington, D.C.: Howard University Press, 1975), pp. 131–138. 4354

Carstensen, Vernon, "Patterns on the American Land," *Proceedings of the American Congress on Surveying and Mapping, Fall Convention, Seattle* (1976), pp. 8–14.　4355

Grim, Ronald E., "How Old Surveys Shaped Today's Landscapes," in *Our American Land: 1987 Yearbook of Agriculture* (Washington, D.C.: U.S. Department of Agriculture, 1987), pp. 43–47. 4356

Johnson, Hildegard Binder, "Toward a National Landscape," in Michael P. Conzen, ed., *The Making of the American Landscape* (Boston: Unwin Hyman, 1990), pp. 123–145.　4357

Land tenure

Stewart, Charles L., "Farm Realty Changes in Eastern and Western United States," *Economic Geography*, vol. 19, 2 (1943), pp. 196–205.　4358

Harris, Marshall D., *Origin of the Land Tenure System in the United States* (Ames: Iowa State College Press, 1953), 445 pp.　4359

Paterson, John H., "Unit Size as a Factor in Land Disposal Policy," in Robert G. Ironside et al., eds., *Frontier Settlement* (Edmonton: University of Alberta, Department of Geography, 1974), pp. 151–163.　4360

Holtgrieve, Donald G., "Land Speculation and Other Processes in American Historical Geography," *Journal of Geography*, vol. 75, 1 (1976), pp. 53–64.　4361

Ehrenberg, Ralph E., "Taking the Measure of the Land," *Prologue: Journal of the National Archives*, vol. 9, 3 (1977), pp. 129–150.　4362

Conzen, Michael P., "The Woodland Clearances," *Geographical Magazine*, vol. 52, 7 (1980), pp. 483–491. [Focus on landholding]　4363

Albers, Patricia, and Jeanne C. Kay, "Sharing the Land: A Study in American Indian Territoriality," in Thomas E. Ross and Tyrel G. Moore, eds., *A Cultural Geography of North American Indians* (Boulder: Westview Press, 1987), pp. 47–92.　4364

Curry-Roper, Janel M., "Nineteenth Century Land Law and Current Landownership Patterns," *Geographical Review*, vol. 77, 3 (1987), pp. 261–278.　4365

Land improvement

Hewes, Leslie, "Drained Land in the United States in the Light of the Drainage Census," *Professional Geographer*, vol. 5, 6 (1953), pp. 6–12. 4366

Land use

Hart, John Fraser, "Urban Encroachment on Rural Areas," *Geographical Review*, vol. 66, 1 (1976), pp. 1–17. [Focus on 1950–1970]　4367

Clawson, Marion, "Competitive Land Use in American Forestry and Agriculture," *Journal of Forestry History*, vol. 25, 4 (1981), pp. 222–227.　4368

EXTRACTIVE ACTIVITY

Fur trade

Kay, Jeanne C., "Native Americans in the Fur Trade and Wildlife Depletion," *Environmental Review*, vol. 9, 2 (1985), pp. 118–130.　4369

Mining

Hubbard, George D., "Gold and Silver Mining as a Geographic Factor in the Development of the United States," Ph.D. diss., Cornell University, 1905. **4370**

DePaepe, Duane, and Carol A. Hill, "Historical Geography of the United States Saltpeter Caves," *N.S.S. (National Speleological Society) Bulletin*, vol. 43, 4 (1981), pp. 88–93. **4371**

Forestry

Miller, Joseph A., "The Changing Forest: Recent Research in the Historical Geography of American Forests," *Forest History*, vol. 9, 1 (1965), pp. 18–24. **4372**

Williams, Michael, "Products of the Forest: Mapping the Census of 1840," *Journal of Forest History*, vol. 24, 1 (1980), pp. 4–23. **4373**

Williams, Michael, "Industrial Impacts on the Forests of the United States, 1860–1920," *Journal of Forest History*, vol. 31, 3 (1987), pp. 108–121. **4374**

Fisheries

Tower, Walter S., *A History of the American Whale Fishery* (Philadelphia: Publications of the University of Pennsylvania, Series in Political Economy and Public Law, no. 20, 1907), 145 pp. **4375**

Comeaux, Malcolm L., "Historical Development of the Crawfish Industry in the United States," in James W. Arault, ed., *Freshwater Crawfish* (Baton Rouge: Lousiana State University Press, 1975), pp. 609–619. **4376**

AGRICULTURE

See also 3950–3951

General

Brigham, Albert Perry, "Environment in the History of American Agriculture," *Journal of Geography*, vol. 21, 2 (1922), pp. 41–49. **4377**

Baker, Oliver E., "Agricultural Regions of North America: Part I—The Basis of Classification," *Economic Geography*, vol. 2, 4 (1926), pp. 459–493. **4378**

Grotewold, Andreas, *Regional Changes in Crop Production in the United States from 1909 to 1949* (Chicago: University of Chicago, Department of Geography Research Paper no. 40, 1955), 78 pp. **4379**

Harris, Chauncy D., "Agricultural Production in the United States: The Past Fifty Years and the Next," *Geographical Review*, vol. 47, 2 (1957), pp. 175–193. **4380**

Warntz, William, "An Historical Consideration of the Terms 'Corn' and 'Corn Belt' in the United States," *Agricultural History*, vol. 31 (1957), pp. 40–45. **4381**

Spencer, Joseph E., and Ronald J. Horvath, "How Does an Agricultural Region Originate?" *Annals of the Association of American Geographers*, vol. 53, 1 (1963), pp. 74–92. Reprinted in Fred E. Dohrs and Lawrence M. Sommers, eds., *Cultural Geography: Selected Readings* (New York: Thomas Y. Crowell Co., 1967), pp. 487–514. [Contains a section "The Origin and Evolution of the American Corn Belt," pp. 489–499] **4382**

Gregor, Howard F., "The Changing Plantation," *Annals of the Association of American Geographers*, 55, 2 (1965), pp. 221–238. **4383**

Paterson, John H., "American Agriculture and the Decline of the Agrarian Ideal," in José A. Sporck, ed., *Mélanges de géographie physique, humaine, économique, appliquée offerts à M. Omer Tulippe*, vol. 1 (Gembloux, Belgium: Éditions J. Duculot, 1967), pp. 344–351. **4384**

Peet, J. Richard, "The Spatial Expansion of Commercial Agriculture in the Nineteenth Century: A Theoretical Analysis of British Import Zones and the Movement of Farming into the Interior United States," Ph.D. diss., University of California–Berkeley, 1968. **4385**

Peet, J. Richard, "The Spatial Expansion of Commercial Agriculture in the Nineteenth Century: A Von Thünen Interpretation," *Economic Geography*, vol. 45, 4 (1969), pp. 283–301. **4386**

Clark, Andrew Hill, "Suggestions for the Geographical Study of Agricultural Change in the United States, 1790–1840," *Agricultural History*, vol. 46, 1 (1972), pp. 155–172. Reprinted, with omissions, in David Ward, ed., *Geographic Perspectives on America's Past: Readings on the Historical Geography of the United States* (New York: Oxford University Press, 1979), pp. 179–187. **4387**

Prunty, Merle C., Jr., "Persistence of the Plantation and National Agricultural Problems," *Proceedings of the Tall Timbers Ecology and Management Conference*, vol. 16 (1979), pp. 89–110. **4388**

Gregor, Howard F., *Industrialization of U.S. Agriculture: An Interpretive Atlas* (Boulder: Westview Press, 1982), 259 pp. **4389**

Winsberg, Morton D., "Agricultural Specialization in the United States since World War II," *Agricultural History*, vol. 56, 4 (1982), pp. 692–701. **4390**

Hart, John Fraser, "Cropland Change in the United States, 1944–78," in Julian L. Simon and Herman Kahn, eds., *The Resourceful Earth* (Oxford: Basil Blackwell, 1984), pp. 224–249. **4391**

Lemon, James T., "Agriculture and Society in Early America," *Agricultural History Review*, vol. 35, 1 (1987), pp. 76–94.   **4392**

Hart, John Fraser, *The Land That Feeds Us* (New York: W. W. Norton & Co., 1991), 398 pp.   **4393**

Mechanization

Pfeifer, Gottfried, "Zur Geographie der Technisierung der USA-Landwirtschaft," *Technik und Wissenschaft*, vol. 1, 3 (1939), pp. 49–50.   **4394**

Patterson, Ethel Simkins, "A Geographical Study of Power Farming in the United States, 1925–1945," Ph.D. diss., University College of the South West (England), 1953.   **4395**

Hilliard, Sam B., "The Dynamics of Power: Recent Trends in Mechanization on the American Farm," *Technology and Culture*, vol. 13, 1 (1972), pp. 1–24.   **4396**

Major staple crops

Landon, Charles E., "The Westward Movement of Cotton Growing in the United States," *Journal of Geography*, vol. 29, 5 (1930), pp. 215–219. [Focus on 1900–1928]   **4397**

Seig, Louis, "The Spread of Tobacco: A Study in Cultural Diffusion," *Professional Geographer*, vol. 15, 1 (1963), pp. 17–21.   **4398**

Grains

Weaver, John C., "American Barley Production: A Study in Agricultural Geography," Ph.D. diss., University of Wisconsin, 1942.   **4399**

Weaver, John C., "Barley in the United States: A Historical Sketch," *Geographical Review*, vol. 33, 1 (1943), pp. 56–73.   **4400**

Assiff, Lee, "Regional Changes in Oat Distribution in the United States, 1850–1954," Master's thesis, Illinois State University, 1960.   **4401**

Beans

Primmer, George H., "The United States Soybean Industry," *Economic Geography*, vol. 15, 2 (1939), pp. 205–211.   **4402**

Munn, Alvin A., "Production and Utilization of the Soybean in the United States," *Economic Geography*, vol. 26, 3 (1950), pp. 223–234. [Focus on 1924–1945]   **4403**

Scott, Steven L., "The Spatial Distribution of Dry Edible Bean Production in the United States, 1879–1959," Master's thesis, Western Illinois University, 1968.   **4404**

Sugar & syrup

Winberry, John J., "The Sorghum Syrup Industry, 1854–1975," *Agricultural History*, vol. 54 (1980), pp. 343–352.   **4405**

Galloway, Jock H., "Tradition and Innovation in the American Sugar Industry, c1500–1800: An Explanation," *Annals of the Association of American Geographers*, vol. 75, 3 (1985), pp. 334–351.   **4406**

Other field crops

Primmer, George H., "The United States Flax Industry," *Economic Geography*, vol. 17, 1 (1941), pp. 24–30.   **4407**

Jackson, Richard H., et al., "The Historical Diffusion of Alfalfa," *Journal of Agronomic Education*, vol. 6 (1977), pp. 13–19.   **4408**

Dairying

Durand, Loyal, Jr., "The Migration of Cheese Manufacture in the United States," *Annals of the Association of American Geographers*, vol. 42, 4 (1952), pp. 263–282.   **4409**

Durand, Loyal, Jr., "Historische Geographie und Westwanderung der Käse-Erzeugung im amerikanischen Milchwirtschaftgebiet," *Die Erde*, vol. 5, 2 (1953), pp. 122–135.   **4410**

Cattle

Brinkman, Leonard W., "The Historical Geography of Improved Cattle in the United States to 1870," Ph.D. diss., University of Wisconsin–Madison, 1964.   **4411**

Wilhelm, Eugene J., "Animal Drives: A Case Study in Historical Geography," *Journal of Geography*, vol. 66, 6 (1967), pp. 327–334.   **4412**

Jordan, Terry G., "The Origins and Distribution of Open-Range Ranching," *Social Science Quarterly*, vol. 53 (1972), pp. 105–121.   **4413**

Vineyards & orchards

Gumprecht, Thaddäus E., "Der Weinbau in den Vereinigten Staaten von Nord-Amerika," *Petermanns Geographische Mitteilungen*, vol. 2, 6 (1856), pp. 222–229.   **4414**

Olmstead, Clarence W., "American Orchard and Vineyard Regions," *Economic Geography*, vol. 32, 3 (1956), pp. 189–236.   **4415**

Durrenberger, Robert W., "The Evolution of the American Lemon Growing Industry," *California Geographer*, vol. 8 (1967), pp. 103–113.   **4416**

Specialty farming

Peterson, Arthur G., "Peanuts: Prices, Production, and Foreign Trade since the Civil War," *Economic Geography*, vol. 7, 1 (1931), pp. 59–68.   **4417**

Landing, James E., "The Cultivation of Peppermint and Spearmint," *Southeastern Geographer*, vol. 3 (1963), pp. 28–33.   **4418**

Landing, James E., "Peppermint and Spearmint in the United States," *Journal of Geography,* vol. 67, 9 (1968), pp. 548–553.   **4419**

Landing, James E., *American Essence: A History of the Peppermint and Spearmint Industry in the United States* (Kalamazoo: Michigan Public Museum, 1969), 244 pp.   **4420**

Doughty, Robin W., "Ostrich Farming American Style," *Agricultural History,* vol. 47, 2 (1973), pp. 133–145.   **4421**

Agricultural practices & pests

Harding, George E., "Distribution of the Mexican Bean Beetle," *Economic Geography,* vol. 9, 3 (1933), pp. 273–278. [Focus on 1850–1929]   **4422**

Shaw, Earl B., "Geography of Mast Feeding," *Economic Geography,* vol. 16, 3 (1940), pp. 233–249.   **4423**

LANDSCAPE

See also **3952**

Synthetic treatments

Boesch, Hans, *Amerikanische Landschaft* (Zurich: Kommissionverlag Gebrüder Fretz, Naturforschende Gesellschaft in Zürich, Neujahrsblatt 157, 1955. Reprinted in *Arbeiten,* ser. A, no. 69, Geographisches Institut der Universität Zürich, 1955), 66 pp.   **4424**

Jackson, John Brinckerhoff, *American Space: The Centennial Years, 1865–1876* (New York: W. W. Norton, 1972), 254 pp.   **4425**

Hart, John Fraser, *The Look of the Land* (Englewood Cliffs, N.J.: Prentice-Hall, 1975), 210 pp.   **4426**

Stilgoe, John R., *Common Landscape of America, 1580 to 1845* (New Haven: Yale University Press, 1982), 429 pp.   **4427**

Conzen, Michael P., ed., *The Making of the American Landscape* (Boston: Unwin Hyman, 1990), 433 pp.   **4428**

General

Shaler, Nathaniel Southgate, "The Landscape as a Means of Culture," *Atlantic Monthly,* vol. 82 (1898), pp. 777–785.   **4429**

Hart, John Fraser, "The Changing American Countryside," in Saul B. Cohen, ed., *Problems and Trends in American Geography* (New York: Basic Books, 1967), pp. 64–74.   **4430**

Lowenthal, David, "The American Scene," *Geographical Review,* vol. 58, 1 (1968), pp. 61–88. Reprinted, with omissions, in David Ward, ed., *Geographic Perspectives on America's Past:*

Readings on the Historical Geography of the United States (New York: Oxford University Press, 1979), pp. 17–32.   **4431**

Zube, Ervin H., ed., *Landscapes: Selected Writings of J. B. Jackson* (Amherst: University of Massachusetts Press, 1970), 160 pp.   **4432**

Ballas, Donald J., "American Landscapes: A Geographic Perspective," *Places,* vol. 3, 2 (1976), pp. 5–11, 50–51.   **4433**

Lowenthal, David, "The Place of the Past in the American Landscape," in David Lowenthal and Martyn J. Bowden, eds., *Geographies of the Mind: Essays in Historical Geosophy in Honor of John Kirtland Wright* (New York: Oxford University Press, 1976), pp. 89–117.   **4434**

Jackson, John Brinckerhoff, "The Order of a Landscape: Reason and Religion in Newtonian America," in Donald W. Meinig, ed., *The Interpretation of Ordinary Landscapes: Geographical Essays* (New York: Oxford University Press, 1979), pp. 153–163.   **4435**

Lewis, Peirce F., "Axioms for Reading the Landscape: Some Guides to the American Scene," in Donald W. Meinig, ed., *The Interpretation of Ordinary Landscapes: Geographical Essays* (New York: Oxford University Press, 1979), pp. 11–32. Reprinted, with omissions, in Thomas J. Schlereth, ed., *Material Culture Studies in America* (Nashville: American Association for State and Local History, 1982), pp. 174–182.   **4436**

Meinig, Donald W., "Symbolic Landscapes: Models of American Community," in Donald W. Meinig, ed., *The Interpretation of Ordinary Landscapes: Geographical Essays* (New York: Oxford University Press, 1979), pp. 164–192.   **4437**

Jackson, John Brinckerhoff, *The Necessity for Ruins, and Other Topics* (Amherst: University of Massachusetts Press, 1980), 129 pp.   **4438**

Conzen, Michael P., "What Makes the American Landscape," *Geographical Magazine,* vol. 53, 1 (1980), pp. 36–41.   **4439**

Cosgrove, Denis E., "America as Landscape," chap. 6 in his *Social Formation and Symbolic Landscape* (London: Croom Helm, 1984), pp. 161–188.   **4440**

Jackson, John Brinckerhoff, *Discovering the Vernacular Landscape* (New Haven: Yale University Press, 1984), 165 pp.   **4441**

Zelinsky, Wilbur, "Oh Say, Can You See? Nationalistic Emblems in the Landscape," *Winterthur Portfolio,* vol. 19, 4 (1984), pp. 277–286.   **4442**

Zelinsky, Wilbur, "The Changing Face of Nationalism in the American Landscape," *Canadian Geographer,* vol. 30, 2 (1986), pp. 171–175.   **4443**

Flad, Harvey K., "Meaning (and Morality) in Preserved Landscapes," *North American Culture*, vol. 4, 2 (1988), pp. 4–21.   4444

Jakle, John A., "Abandonment in America: Lessons from the Cloverleaf Line," *Pioneer America Society Transactions*, vol. 11 (1988), pp. 1–8.   4445

Alanen, Arnold R., "Grounded in Reality: The Importance of Vernacular Landscapes," *Courier: Newsmagazine of the National Park Service*, vol. 34 (1989), pp. 10–13.   4446

Extractive & industrial landscapes

Muller, Edward K., "The Legacy of Industrial Rivers," *Pittsburgh History*, vol. 72, 2 (1989), pp. 64–75.   4447

Williams, Michael, "The Clearing of the Forests," in Michael P. Conzen, ed., *The Making of the American Landscape* (Boston: Unwin Hyman, 1990), pp. 146–168.   4448

Francaviglia, Richard V., *Hard Places: Reading the Landscape of America's Historic Mining Districts* (Iowa City: University of Iowa Press, 1991), 237 pp.   4449

Ethnic signatures

Schmieder, Oskar, "Spuren spanischer Kolonisation in U.S.-amerikanischen Landschaften," in Karl H. Dretzel and Hans Rudolphi, eds., *Koloniale Studien: Hans Meyer zum siebzigsten Geburtstag* (Berlin: D. Reimer and E. Vohsen, 1928), pp. 272–282.   4450

Nostrand, Richard L., "Spanish Roots in the Borderlands," *Geographical Magazine*, vol. 52, 3 (1979), pp. 203–209.   4451

Lewis, Peirce F., "When America Was English," *Geographical Magazine*, vol. 53, 5 (1980), pp. 342–348.   4452

Ainsley, W. Frank, Jr., "Folk Architecture in Early Twentieth Century Ethnic Agricultural Colonies," *SEASA 83: Design, Pattern, Style: Proceedings of the Southeastern American Studies Association* (1983), pp. 12–15.   4453

Hugill, Peter J., "English Landscape Tastes in the United States," *Geographical Review*, vol. 76, 4 (1986), pp. 408–423.   4454

Conzen, Michael P., "Ethnicity on the Land," in Michael P. Conzen, ed., *The Making of the American Landscape* (Boston: Unwin Hyman, 1990), pp. 221–248.   4455

Other collective imprints

Mook, Maurice A., and John A. Hostettler, "The Amish and Their Land," *Landscape*, vol. 6, 3 (1957), pp. 21–29.   4456

Hayden, Dolores, "Communal Idealism and the American Landscape," *Landscape*, vol. 20, 2 (1976), pp. 20–32.   4457

Zelinsky, Wilbur, "Lasting Impact of the Prestigious Gentry," *Geographical Magazine*, vol. 52, 12 (1980), pp. 817–824.   4458

Kuhar, Jane E., "Physical Form and Social Process in Nineteenth-Century American Utopian Settlement," Master's thesis, University of Chicago, 1981.   4459

Heatwole, Charles A., "Sectarian Ideology and Church Architecture," *Geographical Review*, vol. 79, 1 (1989), pp. 63–78.   4460

Wyckoff, William K., "Landscapes of Private Power and Wealth," in Michael P. Conzen, ed., *The Making of the American Landscape* (Boston: Unwin Hyman, 1990), pp. 335–354.   4461

Zelinsky, Wilbur, "The Imprint of Central Authority," in Michael P. Conzen, ed., *The Making of the American Landscape* (Boston: Unwin Hyman, 1990), pp. 311–334.   4462

Houses, farmsteads, & architecture

Scott, Clare, "Geographic Influence Affecting Early American Homes," Master's thesis, Clark University, 1939.   4463

Trewartha, Glenn T., "Some Regional Characteristics of American Farmsteads," *Annals of the Association of American Geographers*, vol. 38, 3 (1948), pp. 169–225.   4464

Newcomb, Rexford, "Regionalism in American Architecture," in Merrill Jensen, ed., *Regionalism in America* (Madison: University of Wisconsin Press, 1951), pp. 273–295.   4465

Jackson, John Brinckerhoff, "The Westward-Moving House: Three American Houses and the People Who Lived in Them," *Landscape*, vol. 2, 3 (1953), pp. 8–21.   4466

Price, Edward T., "The Matter of Housing: Notes on the Longevity of American Dwellings," *Landscape*, vol. 5, 2 (Winter 1955–1956), pp. 31–37.   4467

Wright, Martin, "The Antecedents of the Double Pen House Type," *Annals of the Association of American Geographers*, vol. 48, 2 (1958), pp. 109–117.   4468

Kniffen, Fred B., "Folk Housing: Key to Diffusion," *Annals of the Association of American Geographers*, vol. 55, 4 (1965), pp. 549–577. Reprinted in H. Jesse Walker and Milton B. Newton, Jr., eds., *Environment and Culture* (Baton Rouge: Louisiana State University, Department of Geography and Anthropology, 1978), pp. 175–191; in Dell Upton and John Michael Vlach, eds., *Common Places: Readings in American Vernacular Archi-*

tecture (Athens: University of Georgia Press, 1986), pp. 3–26; and in H. Jesse Walker and Randall A. Detro, eds., *Cultural Diffusion and Landscapes: Selections by Fred B. Kniffen* (Baton Rouge: Louisiana State University, Geoscience Publications, Geoscience & Man, vol. 27, 1990), pp. 49–68. **4469**

Trindell, Roger T., "Building in Brick in Early America," *Geographical Review*, vol. 58, 3 (1968), pp. 484–487. **4470**

Wilson, Eugene M., "Form Changes in Folk Houses," in H. Jesse Walker and William G. Haag, eds., *Man and Cultural Heritage: Papers in Honor of Fred B. Kniffen* (Baton Rouge: Louisiana State University School of Geoscience, Geoscience & Man, vol. 5, 1974), pp. 65–71. **4471**

Lewis, Peirce F., "Common Houses, Cultural Spoor," *Landscape*, vol. 19, 2 (1975), pp. 1–22. **4472**

Harvey, Thomas W., "Mail-Order Architecture in the Twenties," *Landscape*, vol. 25, 3 (1981), pp. 1–9. **4473**

Stump, Roger W., "The Dutch Colonial House and the Colonial Revival," *Journal of Cultural Geography*, vol. 1, 2 (1981), pp. 44–55. **4474**

Wood, Joseph S., "Cultural Meaning in a Common House," *North American Culture*, vol. 2, 2 (1986), pp. 77–86. **4475**

Darlington, James W., "A Home for All: Orson Fowler and the Domestic Octagon," *North American Culture*, vol. 3, 2 (1987), pp. 19–29. **4476**

Jordan, Terry G., and Matti E. Kaups, "Folk Architecture in Cultural and Ecological Context," *Geographical Review*, vol. 77, 1 (1987), pp. 52–75. **4477**

Edwards, Jay D., "The Complex Origins of the American Domestic Piazza-Veranda-Gallery," *Material Culture*, vol. 21, 2 (1989), pp. 3–58. **4478**

Jackson, John Brinckerhoff, "The House in the Vernacular Landscape," in Michael P. Conzen, ed., *The Making of the American Landscape* (Boston: Unwin Hyman, 1990), pp. 355–369. **4479**

Kniffen, Fred B., "The Study of Folk Architecture: Geographical Perspectives," in H. Jesse Walker and Randall A. Detro, eds., *Cultural Diffusion and Landscapes: Selections by Fred B. Kniffen* (Baton Rouge: Louisiana State University Geoscience Publications, Geoscience & Man, vol. 27, 1990), pp. 35–48. **4480**

Log buildings and construction

Kniffen, Fred B., "On Corner-Timbering," *Pioneer America*, vol. 1, 1 (1969), pp. 1–8. **4481**

Newton, Milton B., Jr., and Linda Pulliam-DiNapoli, "Log Houses as Public Occasions: A Historical Theory," *Annals of the Association of American Geographers*, vol. 67, 3 (1977), pp. 360–383. **4482**

Jordan, Terry G., "Alpine, Alemannic, and American Log Architecture," *Annals of the Association of American Geographers*, vol. 70, 2 (1980), pp. 154–180. **4483**

Kaups, Matti E., "Log Architecture in America: European Antecedents in a Finnish Context," *Journal of Cultural Geography*, vol. 2, 1 (1981), pp. 131–153. **4484**

Jordan, Terry G., "Log Construction," in R. C. Davis, ed., *Encyclopedia of American Forest and Conservation History*, vol. 1 (New York: Macmillan, 1983), pp. 344–347. **4485**

Jordan, Terry G., "A Reappraisal of Fenno-Scandian Antecedents for Midland American Log Construction," *Geographical Review*, vol. 73, 1 (1983), pp. 58–94. **4486**

Jordan, Terry G., "Moravian, Schwenkfelder, and American Log Construction," *Pennsylvania Folklife*, vol. 33 (1983–1984), pp. 98–124. **4487**

Jordan, Terry G., *American Log Buildings: An Old World Heritage* (Chapel Hill: University of North Carolina Press, 1985), 193 pp. **4488**

Jordan, Terry G., Matti E. Kaups, and Richard Lieffort, "New Evidence on the European Origin of Pennsylvania V Notching," *Pennsylvania Folklife*, vol. 36 (1986–1987), pp. 20–31. **4489**

Jordan, Terry G., Matti E. Kaups, and Richard Lieffort, "Diamond Notching in America and Europe," *Pennsylvania Folklife*, vol. 36, 2 (1986–1987), pp. 70–78. **4490**

Jordan, Terry G., and Jon T. Kilpinen, "Square Notching in the Log Carpentry Tradition of Pennsylvania Extended," *Pennsylvania Folklife*, vol. 40 (1990–1991), pp. 2–18. **4491**

Barns

Hart, John Fraser, and Eugene Cotton Mather, "The Character of Tobacco Barns and Their Role in the Tobacco Economy of the United States," *Annals of the Association of American Geographers*, vol. 51, 3 (1961), pp. 274–293. **4492**

Gildea, Ray Y., Jr., "The Legacy of Early American Barns," *Virginia Geographer*, vol. 9, 1 (1974), pp. 10–12. **4493**

Jordan, Terry G., "Some Neglected Swiss Literature on the Forebay Bank Barn," *Pennsylvania Folklife*, vol. 37 (1987–1988), pp. 75–80. **4494**

Fences

Raup, Hallock F., "The Fence in the Cultural Landscape," *Western Folklore*, vol. 6, 1 (1947), pp. 1–12.   **4495**

Mather, Eugene Cotton, and John Fraser Hart, "Fences and Farms," *Geographical Review*, vol. 44, 2 (1954), pp. 301–323.   **4496**

Hart, John Fraser, and Eugene Cotton Mather, "The American Fence," *Landscape*, vol. 6, 3 (1957), pp. 4–8.   **4497**

Zelinsky, Wilbur, "Walls and Fences," *Landscape*, vol. 8, 3 (1959), pp. 14–18.   **4498**

Winberry, John J., "The Osage Orange: A Botanical Artifact," *Pioneer America*, vol. 11, 3 (1979), pp. 134–141.   **4499**

Highways and automobiles

Kniffen, Fred B., "The American Covered Bridge," *Geographical Review*, vol. 41, 1 (1951), pp. 114–123. Reprinted in H. Jesse Walker and Milton B. Newton, Jr., eds., *Environment and Culture* (Baton Rouge: Louisiana State University, Department of Geography and Anthropology, 1978), pp. 193–198.   **4500**

Jackson, John Brinckerhoff, "The Domestication of the Garage," *Landscape*, vol. 20, 2 (1976), pp. 10–19.   **4501**

Vale, Thomas R., and Geraldine R. Vale, *U.S. 40 Today: Thirty Years of Landscape Change* (Madison: University of Wisconsin Press, 1983), 198 pp.   **4502**

Schlereth, Thomas J., *U.S. 40: A Roadscape of the American Experience* (Indianapolis: Indiana Historical Society, 1985), 150 pp.   **4503**

Norris, Darrell A., "Roadside America: A Twilight Landscape," *Pioneer America Society Transactions*, vol. 9 (1986), pp. 39–44.   **4504**

Zeigler, Donald J., "Covered Bridges and the Customization of the American Landscape," *Pioneer America Society Transactions*, vol. 9 (1986), pp. 9–15.   **4505**

Puzo, Rita, "Route 66: A Ghost Road Geography," Master's thesis, California State University–Fullerton, 1988.   **4506**

Jakle, John A., "Landscapes Redesigned for the Automobile," in Michael P. Conzen, ed., *The Making of the American Landscape* (Boston: Unwin Hyman, 1990), pp. 293–310.   **4507**

Krim, Arthur J., "Mapping Route 66: A Cultural Cartography," in Jan Jennings, ed., *Roadside America: The Automobile in Design and Culture* (Ames: Iowa State University Press, 1990), pp. 198–208.   **4508**

Other features

Francaviglia, Richard V., "The Cemetery as an Evolving Cultural Landscape," *Annals of the Association of American Geographers*, vol. 61, 3 (1971), pp. 501–509.   **4509**

Jordan, Terry G., "Evolution of the American Windmill: A Study in Diffusion and Modification," *Pioneer America*, vol. 5, 2 (1973), pp. 3–12.   **4510**

Watson, Daryl G., "An Historical Geography of Shade and Ornamental Trees of Nineteenth Century America," Ph.D. diss., University of Illinois, 1978.   **4511**

Noble, Allen G., "The Evolution of American Farm Silos," *Journal of Cultural Geography*, vol. 1, 1 (1980), pp. 138–148.   **4512**

Noble, Allen G., "The Diffusion of Silos," *Landscape*, vol. 25, 1 (1981), pp. 11–14. [Focus on 1862–1886]   **4513**

Lawrence, Henry W., "The Geography of the U.S. Nursery Industry: Locational Change and Regional Specialization in the Production of Woody Ornamental Plants," Ph.D. diss., University of Oregon, 1985.   **4514**

Walters, William D., "The American Shale Paver: Its Origin, Evolution, and Role in Landscape Preservation," *Pioneer America Society Transactions*, vol. 10 (1987), pp. 59–65.   **4515**

COMMUNICATIONS & TRADE

Transport

General

Holdsworth, John T., "Transportation, Part I—An Outline: The Canal Era, 1825–1837"; "Part II—Contest between Canal and Railway"; "Part III—The Railroad Era"; "Part IV—Combination Period, 1870–1898"; "Part V—The Merger Period"; "Part VI—Financial Control," *Journal of Geography*, vol. 3 (1904), pp. 112–121, 150–162, 413–420; 4 (1905), pp. 74–80, 168–173, and 227–238.   **4516**

Vance, James E., Jr., *Capturing the Horizon: The Historical Geography of Transportation since the Transportation Revolution of the Sixteenth Century* (New York: Harper & Row, 1986), 660 pp. Reprinted Baltimore: Johns Hopkins University Press, 1990.   **4517**

Vance, James E., Jr., "Geography and Human Mobility: The Perpetual Revolution in Transportation," in *Earth '88: Changing Geographic Perspectives; Proceedings of the Centennial Conference* (Washington, D.C.: National Geographic Society, 1988), pp. 144–159. [Focus on the nineteenth and twentieth centuries]   **4518**

Roads

Jakle, John A., "Motel by the Roadside: America's Room for the Night," *Journal of Cultural Geography*, vol. 1, 1 (1981), pp. 34–39.　　　4519

Hugill, Peter J., "Good Roads and the Automobile in the United States, 1880–1929," *Geographical Review*, vol. 72, 3 (1982), pp. 327–349.　　4520

Jakle, John A., "Roadside Restaurants: The Evolution of Place-Product-Packaging," *Journal of Cultural Geography*, vol. 3, 1 (1982), pp. 76–93.
　　　4521

Huh, Wookung, "Commuting and Nonmetropolitan Changes: A Case Study of Ohio, Georgia, and Texas, 1960–1980," Ph.D. diss., Ohio State University, 1983.　　　4522

Hollingshead, Craig A., "Now Joining the North and the South: A History of the Mason & Dixon Line's Marketing and Operations Management, 1932–1982," Ph.D. diss., University of Tennessee, 1985.　　　4523

Water transport

Friese, Heinz W., "Die Bedeutung der Binnenwasserwege für die Besiedlung und Erschließung der USA," *Jahrbuch für Amerikastudien*, vol. 5 (1960), pp. 185–214.　　　4524

Taylor, James, "The Effect of the Clipper Ship on American Shipping," *Kansas Geographer*, vol. 6 (1971), pp. 16–22.　　　4525

Railroads & interurbans

Miller, E. Willard, "Some Economic Aspects of the Early Transportation of Crude," *Producers Monthly*, vol. 5 (1941), pp. 8–18.　　　4526

Pardé, Maurice, "Les chemins de fer des États-Unis," *Annales de géographie*, vol. 56 (1947), pp. 274–294.　　　4527

Meinig, Donald W., "Railroad Archives and the Historical Geographer," *Professional Geographer*, vol. 7, 3 (1955), pp. 6–10.　　　4528

Meinig, Donald W., "Research in Railroad Archives," *Pacific Northwest Quarterly*, vol. 47, 1 (1956), pp. 20–22.　　　4529

Walmsley, Mildred M., "The Bygone Electric Interurban Railway System," *Professional Geographer*, vol. 17, 3 (1965), pp. 1–6.　　　4530

Quastler, Imre E., "Interrailroad Territorial Nonaggression Agreements in the Nineteenth Century United States," *Proceedings of the Association of American Geographers*, vol. 8 (1976), pp. 65–70.　　　4531

Mayer, Harold M., "The Changing American Railroad Pattern," in John D. Eyre, ed., *A Man for All Regions: The Contribution of Edward L. Ullman to Geography* (Chapel Hill: University of North

Carolina, Studies in Geography, no. 11 1978), pp. 108–143. [Focus on 1939–1975]　　　4532

Quastler, Imre E., "Some Major Unanswered Questions about the Historical Geography of American Railroads," *Historical Geography Newsletter*, vol. 8, 1 (1978), pp. 1–9.　　4533

Loetterle, Francis E., "The Evolution of the American Railroad Network: A Cartographic Analysis," Master's thesis, State University of New York–Binghamton, 1982.　　　4534

Airways

Barry, W. S., "Air Transport in the United States: A Study in the Economic Geography of the Growth and Function of Selected Airlines," Ph.D. diss., University of London, 1954.　　　4535

Fairweather, Malcolm, "The Spatial Development of the American Airlines Route Network," *Proceedings of the Middle States Division, Association of American Geographers*, vol. 15 (1981), pp. 15–24.　　　4536

Fairweather, Malcolm, "The Historical Development of Delta Airlines," *Geographical Bulletin*, vol. 22, 2 (1982), pp. 22–34.　　　4537

Schofield, Peter, "Developments in U.S. Domestic Air Passenger Flows between Twenty-Five Cities Located in the Sunbelt and Core Regions from 1960 to 1980," Master's thesis, State University of New York–Buffalo, 1983.　　　4538

Communications

Newspapers & periodicals

Raitz, Karl B., and Stanley D. Brunn, "Geographic Processes in the Historical Development of Farm Publications," *Journalism History*, vol. 6, 1 (1979), pp. 14–15 and 31–32.　　　4539

Brooker-Gross, Susan R., "Timeliness: Interpretations from a Sample of Nineteenth Century Newspapers," *Journalism Quarterly*, vol. 58, 4 (1981), pp. 594–598.　　　4540

Telegraph & telephone

Lefferts, Marshall, "The Electric Telegraph: Its Influence and Geographical Distribution," *Bulletin of the American Geographical and Statistical Society*, vol. 2 (1857), pp. 242–264.　　　4541

Abler, Ronald F., "The Telephone and the Evolution of the American Metropolitan System," in Ithiel De Sola Pool, ed., *The Social Impact of the Telephone* (Cambridge: MIT Press, 1977), pp. 318–341.　　　4542

Langdale, John V., "The Growth of Long-Distance Telephony in the Bell System: 1875–1907," *Journal of Historical Geography*, vol. 4, 2 (1978), pp. 145–159.　　　4543

Fischer, Carl S., and G. R. Carroll, "Telephone and Automobile Diffusion in the United States, 1902–1937," *American Journal of Sociology*, vol. 93, 5 (1988), pp. 1153–1178.   4544

Radio & television

Bell, William, "The Diffusion of Radio and Television Broadcasting in the United States," Master's thesis, Pennsylvania State University, 1965.   4545

Carney, George O., "Country Music and the Radio: A Historical Geographic Assessment," *Rocky Mountain Social Science Journal*, vol. 11, 2 (1974), pp. 19–32.   4546

Carney, George O., "From Down Home to Uptown: The Diffusion of Country-Music Radio Stations in the United States," *Journal of Geography*, vol. 76, 3 (1977), pp. 104–110.   4547

News dissemination

Brooker-Gross, Susan R., "Spatial Organization of News Wire-Services in the Nineteenth Century United States," Ph.D. diss., University of Illinois, 1977.   4548

Brooker-Gross, Susan R., "News Wire Services in the Nineteenth Century United States," *Journal of Historical Geography*, vol. 7, 2 (1981), pp. 167–179.   4549

Brooker-Gross, Susan R., "Nineteenth Century News Definitions and Wire Service Usage," *Journalism Quarterly*, vol. 60, 1 (1983), pp. 24–27, 40.   4550

Brooker-Gross, Susan R., "The Changing Concept of Place in the News," in Jacqueline E. Burgess and John R. Gold, eds., *Geography: The Media and Popular Culture* (Kent, U.K.: Croom Helm, 1985), pp. 63–85.   4551

Monmonier, Mark S., "Telegraphy, Iconography and the Weather Map: Cartographic Weather Reports by the United States Weather Bureau, 1870–1935," *Imago Mundi*, vol. 40 (1988), pp. 15–31.   4552

Monmonier, Mark S., *Maps with the News: The Development of American Journalistic Cartography* (Chicago: University of Chicago Press, 1989), 331 pp.   4553

Trade

Johnson, Emory R., "Geographic Influences Affecting the Early Development of American Commerce," *Bulletin of the American Geographical Society*, vol. 40, 3 (1908), pp. 129–143.   4554

Johnson, Emory R., and Thurman W. Van Metre, *History of Domestic and Foreign Commerce in the United States*, vol. 1 (Washington, D.C.:

Carnegie Institution of Washington, 1915), 363 pp.   4555

Markham, Charles H., "The Development, Strategy, and Traffic of the Illinois Central System," *Economic Geography*, vol. 2, 1 (1926), pp. 1–18.   4556

Rothstein, Morton, "Antebellum Wheat and Cotton Exports: Contrast in Marketing Organization and Economic Development," *Agricultural History*, vol. 40, 2 (1966), pp. 91–100.   4557

Sivakuma, Venkataraman, "Spatial Dynamics of U.S. Wholesale Trade, 1948–1972," Master's thesis, University of South Carolina, 1977.   4558

Carlson, Alvar W., "Ginseng: America's Botanical Drug Connection to the Orient," *Economic Botany*, vol. 40, 2 (1986), pp. 233–249.   4559

MANUFACTURING & INDUSTRIALIZATION

Aggregate locational patterns

Wright, Alfred J., "Manufacturing Districts of the United States," *Economic Geography*, vol. 14, 2 (1938), pp. 195–200.   4560

Dietrich, Bruno, "Die Verlagerung der Industrien in den Vereinigten Staaten von Amerika," in Oskar Schmieder, ed., *Gegenwartsprobleme der Neuen Welt* (Leipzig: Quelle & Meyer, 1943), pp. 727–774.   4561

Fuchs, Victor R., *Changes in the Location of Manufacturing in the United States since 1929* (New Haven: Yale University Press, 1962), 566 pp. [Focus on 1929–1954]   4562

Goheen, Peter G., "Industrialization and the Growth of Cities in Nineteenth Century America," *American Studies*, vol. 14, 1 (1973), pp. 49–65.   4563

Meyer, David R., "Industrious Entrepreneurs Make Their Mark," *Geographical Magazine*, vol. 52 (1980), pp. 647–654. [Focus on the American industrial revolution]   4564

Mueller, Paul, "Locational Behavior of Manufacturing Establishments, 1947–1979," Master's thesis, University of Wisconsin–Milwaukee, 1980.   4565

Meyer, David R., "Emergence of the American Manufacturing Belt: An Interpretation," *Journal of Historical Geography*, vol. 9, 2 (1983), pp. 145–174.   4566

Glasgow, Jon A., "Innovation on the Frontier of the American Manufacturing Belt," *Pennsylvania History*, vol. 52, 1 (1985), pp. 1–21.   4567

Graham, Julie, Katherine D. Gibson, Ronald J. Horvath, and Don M. Shakow, "Restructuring in United States Manufacturing: The Decline of Monopoly Capitalism," *Annals of the Association of American Geographers*, vol. 78, 3 (1988), pp. 473–490. [Focus on 1958–1977]   4568

Meyer, David R., "The Division of Labor and the Market Areas of Manufacturing Firms," *Sociological Forum*, vol. 3 (1988), pp. 433–453.   4569

Meyer, David R., "The New Industrial Order," in Michael P. Conzen, ed., *The Making of the American Landscape* (Boston: Unwin Hyman, 1990), pp. 249–268.   4570

Processing industries

Meatpacking

Egan, Esther, "The Meat Packing Industry," *Journal of Geography*, vol. 26, 12 (1927), pp. 342–350.   4571

Logan, R. Deborah, "Changes in the Spatial Distribution of Meat Packing Plants in the United States, 1939–1965," Master's thesis, Indiana University, 1971.   4572

Broadway, Michael J., and Terry Ward, "Recent Changes in the Structure and Localization of the U.S. Meatpacking Industry," *Geography*, vol. 75, 1 (1990), pp. 76–79. [Focus on 1959–1986]   4573

Brewing

Bechtol, Bruce E., and Jerry R. Williams, "Locational Trends in the American Brewing Industry," *Yearbook of the Association of Pacific Coast Geographers*, vol. 40 (1978), pp. 29–38. [Focus on 1935–1975]   4574

Gebhardt, Mary, "A Geography of Beer in the United States, 1933–1977," Master's thesis, Oklahoma State University, 1979.   4575

Smith, Michael L., "The Historical Geography of the United States Brewing Industry," Master's thesis, University of Vermont, 1990.   4576

Other

Deasy, George F., "Geography of the United States Flaxseed Industry," *Journal of Geography*, vol. 39, 6 (1940), pp. 226–231.   4577

Lukermann, Fred E., "The Geography of Cement," *Professional Geographer*, vol. 12, 4 (1960), pp. 1–6.   4578

Gundrun, Paul, "The Charcoal Iron Industry in Eighteenth Century America: An Expression of Regional Economic Variation," Master's thesis, University of Wisconsin–Madison, 1973.   4579

Fabricating industries

Textiles

Brown, Robert M., "Cotton Manufacturing: North and South," *Economic Geography*, vol. 4, 1 (1928), pp. 74–87.   4580

Hayden, Marilyn A., "Locational Trends of the Textile Industries in the United States," Master's thesis, Clark University, 1960.   4581

Feller, Irwin, "The Diffusion and Location of Technological Change in the American Cotton-Textile Industry, 1890–1970," *Technology and Culture*, vol. 15, 4 (1974), pp. 569–593.   4582

Iron & steel

Jacobson, Daniel, "Taconite and the American Iron and Steel Industry," *Kentucky Engineer*, vol. 17 (Nov. 1954), pp. 23–24, 36.   4583

Warren, Kenneth, *The American Steel Industry, 1850–1970: A Geographical Interpretation* (Oxford: Clarendon Press, 1973), 337 pp.   4584

Automobiles

Boas, Charles W., "Locational Patterns of American Automobile Assembly Plants, 1895–1958," *Economic Geography*, vol. 37, 3 (1961), pp. 218–230.   4585

Rubinstein, James M., "Changing Distribution of the American Automobile Industry," *Geographical Review*, vol. 76, 3 (1986), pp. 288–300. [Focus on 1945–1986]   4586

Bloomfield, Gerald T., "Coils of the Commercial Serpent: A Geography of the Ford Branch Distribution System, 1904–1933," in Jan Jennings, ed., *Roadside America: The Automobile in Design and Culture* (Ames: Iowa State University Press, 1990), pp. 40–51.   4587

Hugill, Peter J., "Technology and Geography in the Emergence of the American Automobile Industry, 1895–1915," in Jan Jennings, ed., *Roadside America: The Automobile in Design and Culture* (Ames: Iowa State University Press, 1990), pp. 29–39.   4588

Other

Kreuger, L. B., "Shipbuilding in the United States, Past and Present," *Journal of Geography*, vol. 15, 8 (1916), pp. 251–258.   4589

Stewart, Harold E., "The Development of the White Ware Industry: A Geographic Interpretation," Ph.D. diss., Ohio State University, 1937.   4590

Hammond, Edwin H., "The Localization of the Aircraft Industry in the United States," *Yearbook of the Association of Pacific Coast Geogra-*

phers, vol. 7 (1941), pp. 33–40. [Focus on 1920s–1941]   4591

Paul, Robert A., "The Location and Intensity of the American Shoe Manufacturing Industry to 1958," Master's thesis, Clark University, 1966.   4592

Peterson, Merrill, "The Changing Geography of the Locomotive Manufacturing Industry in the United States: 1830–1970," Master's thesis, Western Illinois University, 1974.   4593

Hwang, Manik, "Geographical and Structural Change in the Mobile Home Industry in the United States, 1960–1980," Ph.D. diss., University of Tennessee, 1982.   4594

Winberry, John J., "Shake and Shingle Industry," in Richard C. Davis, ed., *Encyclopedia of American Forest and Conservation History*, vol. 2 (New York: Macmillan, 1983), pp. 596–598.   4595

Pudup, Mary Beth, "From Farm to Factory: Structuring and Location of the U.S. Farm Machinery Industry," *Economic Geography*, vol. 63, 3 (1987), pp. 203–222.   4596

URBAN NETWORKS & URBANIZATION

General

Tower, Walter S., "The Geography of American Cities," *Bulletin of the American Geographical Society*, vol. 37, 10 (1905) pp. 577–588.   4597

Jefferson, Mark S., "How American Cities Grow," *Bulletin of the American Geographical Society*, vol. 48, 1 (1915), pp. 19–37. [Focus on 1790–1910]   4598

Roth, Lawrence V., "The Growth of American Cities," *Geographical Review*, vol. 5, 5 (1918), pp. 384–398. [Focus on 1790–1910]   4599

Northam, Ray, "Declining Urban Centers in the United States, 1940–1960," *Annals of the Association of American Geographers*, vol. 53, 1 (1963), pp. 50–59.   4600

Ward, David, *Cities and Immigrants: A Geography of Change in Nineteenth-Century America* (New York: Oxford University Press, 1971), 164 pp.   4601

Goheen, Peter G., "Interpreting the American City: Some Historical Perspectives," *Geographical Review*, vol. 64, 3 (1974), pp. 362–384.   4602

Harvey, David W., "The Political Economy of Urbanization in Advanced Capitalist Countries: The Case of the United States," in G. Gappert and Harold M. Rose, eds., *The Social Economy of Cities* (Beverly Hills, Calif.: Sage Publications, Urban Affairs Annual, 1975), pp. 119–163.   4603

Earle, Carville V., "The First English Towns of North America," *Geographical Review*, vol. 67, 1 (1977), pp. 34–50.   4604

Vance, James E., Jr., "Metropolitan America: Evolution of an Ideal," in Gyorgy Enyedi, ed., *Urban Development in the U.S.A. and Hungary* (Budapest: Akademiai Kiado, 1978), pp. 15–44.   4605

Conzen, Michael P., "The Progress of American Urbanism, 1860–1930," in Robert D. Mitchell and Paul A. Groves, eds, *North America: The Historical Geography of a Changing Continent* (Totowa, N.J.: Rowman & Littlefield, 1987), pp. 347–370.   4606

Muller, Edward K., "From Waterfront to Metropolitan Region: The Geographical Development of American Cities," in Howard Gillette and Zane Miller, eds., *American Urbanism: A Historiographical Review* (Westport, Conn.: Greenwood Press, 1987), pp. 105–133.   4607

Eysberg, Cees D., "The Origins of the American Urban System: Historical Accident and Initial Advantage," *Journal of Urban History*, vol. 15, 2 (1989), pp. 185–195.   4608

Berry, Brian J. L., "Long Waves in American Urban Evolution," in John Fraser Hart, ed., *Our Changing Cities* (Baltimore: Johns Hopkins University Press, 1991), pp. 31–50.   4609

Urban definitions

Blodgett, James H., "'Free Burghs' in the United States," *National Geographic Magazine*, vol. 7, 3 (1896), pp. 116–122. [Municipal history]   4610

Muller, Edward K., "Town Population in the Early United States Censuses: An Aid to Research," *Historical Methods Newsletter*, vol. 3, 2 (1970), pp. 2–8.   4611

Helbock, Richard W., "Postal Records as an Aid to Urbanization Studies," *Historical Methods Newsletter*, vol. 3, 2 (1976), pp. 9–14.   4612

Colonial towns

Earle, Carville V., "Reflections on the Colonial City," *Historical Geography*, vol. 4 (1974), pp. 1–15.   4613

Commercial networks

Sears, Alfred F., "Commercial Cities: The Law of Their Birth and Growth," *Transactions of the American Society of Civil Engineers*, vol. 14 (Jan. 1885), pp. 19–27. [Focus on U.S. cities]   4614

Smith, J. Russell, "The Development of Commercial Centers," *Bulletin of the American Geographical Society*, vol. 42, 5 (1910), pp. 346–355.   4615

Vance, James E., Jr., *The Merchant's World: The Geography of Wholesaling* (Englewood Cliffs, N.J.: Prentice-Hall, 1970), 167 pp.　　**4616**

Burghardt, Andrew F., "A Hypothesis about Gateway Cities," *Annals of the Association of American Geographers*, vol. 61, 2 (1971), pp. 269–285.　　**4617**

Industrialization of cities

Pred, Allan R., *The External Relations of Cities during Industrial Revolution* (Chicago: University of Chicago Department of Geography, Research Paper no. 76, 1962), 113 pp.　　**4618**

Pred, Allan R., "Industrialization, Initial Advantage, and American Metropolitan Growth," *Geographical Review*, vol. 55, 2 (1965), pp. 158–185. Reprinted, with omissions, in David Ward, ed., *Geographic Perspectives on America's Past: Readings on the Historical Geography of the United States* (New York: Oxford University Press, 1979), pp. 275–290.　　**4619**

Meyer, David R., "A Critique of Pred's Model of Industrialization and Urban-Size Growth," *Proceedings of the New England–St. Lawrence Valley Division, Association of American Geographers*, vol. 5 (1975), pp. 6–10.　　**4620**

Evolution of the system of cities

Lukermann, Fred E., "Empirical Expressions of Nodality and Hierarchy in a Circulation Manifold," *East Lakes Geographer*, vol. 2 (1966), pp. 17–44.　　**4621**

Pred, Allan R., *The Spatial Dynamics of U.S. Urban-Industrial Growth, 1800–1914* (Cambridge: MIT Press, 1966), 225 pp.　　**4622**

Borchert, John R., "American Metropolitan Evolution," *Geographical Review*, vol. 57, 3 (1967), pp. 301–332.　　**4623**

Lampard, Eric E., "The Evolving System of Cities in the United States: Urbanization and Economic Development," in Harvey S. Perloff and Lowden Wingo, Jr., eds., *Issues in Urban Economics* (Baltimore: Johns Hopkins University Press, 1968), pp. 81–138.　　**4624**

Borchert, John R., "America's Changing Metropolitan Regions," *Annals of the Association of American Geographers*, vol. 62, 2 (1972), pp. 352–373.　　**4625**

Conzen, Michael P., "The Maturing Urban System in the United States, 1840–1910," *Annals of the Association of American Geographers*, vol. 67, 1 (1977), pp. 88–108. Reprinted, with omissions, in David Ward, ed., *Geographic Perspectives on America's Past: Readings on the Historical Ge-*

ography of the United States (New York: Oxford University Press, 1979), pp. 253–274.　　**4626**

Borchert, John R., "Major Control Points in American Economic Geography," *Annals of the Association of American Geographers*, vol. 68, 2 (1978), pp. 214–232.　　**4627**

Dunn, Edgar S., Jr., *The Development of the U.S. Urban System*, vol. 1, *Concepts, Structures, Regional Shifts* (Baltimore: Johns Hopkins University Press for Resources for the Future, 1980), 205 pp.　　**4628**

Conzen, Michael P., "The American Urban System in the Nineteenth Century," in David T. Herbert and Ronald J. Johnston, eds., *Geography and the Urban Environment: Research and Applications*, vol. 4 (New York: John Wiley & Sons, 1981), pp. 295–347.　　**4629**

Borchert, John R., "Instability in American Metropolitan Growth," *Geographical Review*, vol. 73, 2 (1983), pp. 127–149. [Focus on 1920–1980]　　**4630**

Conzen, Michael P., "American Cities in Profound Transition: The New City Geography of the 1980s," *Journal of Geography*, vol. 82, 3 (1983), pp. 94–102. Also published as "Amerikanische Städte im Wandel: Die neue Stadtgeographie der achtziger Jahre," *Geographische Rundschau*, vol. 35, 4 (1983), pp. 142–150. English version reprinted in Raymond A. Mohl, ed., *The Making of Urban America* (Wilmington, Del.: Scholarly Resources, 1988), pp. 277–289.　　**4631**

Lewis, Peirce F., "The Galactic Metropolis," in Rutherford H. Platt and George Macinko, eds., *Beyond the Urban Fringe: Land-Use Issues of Nonmetropolitan America* (Minneapolis: University of Minnesota Press, 1983), pp. 23–49.　　**4632**

Expansion of the system of cities

Nelson, Howard J., "Town Founding and the American Frontier," *Yearbook of the Association of Pacific Coast Geographers*, vol. 36 (1974), pp. 7–24.　　**4633**

Meyer, David R., "A Dynamic Model of the Integration of Frontier Urban Places into the United States System of Cities," *Economic Geography*, vol. 56, 2 (1980), pp. 120–140.　　**4634**

Integration of the system of cities

Pred, Allan R., "Large-City Interdependence and the Preelectronic Diffusion of Innovations in the U.S.," *Geographical Analysis*, vol. 3, 2 (1971), pp. 165–181.　　**4635**

Pred, Allan R., *Urban Growth and the Circulation of Information: The United States System of*

Cities, 1790–1840 (Cambridge: Harvard University Press, 1973), 348 pp.   **4636**

Pred, Allan R., *Urban Growth and City Systems in the United States: 1840–1860* (Cambridge: Harvard University Press, 1980), 282 pp.   **4637**

Differentiation within the system of cities

Semple, R. Keith, and Alan G. Phipps, "The Spatial Evolution of Corporate Headquarters within an Urban System," *Urban Geography*, vol. 3, 3 (1982), pp. 258–279. [Focus on 1957–1979]   **4638**

Faloon, Terrence P., "Changes in the Functional Specialization of American Cities, 1950–1980," Master's thesis, University of South Carolina, 1984.   **4639**

Persky, Joseph, and Ronald Moses, "Specialized Industrial Cities in the United States, 1860–1930," *Journal of Historical Geography*, vol. 10, 1 (1984), pp. 37–51.   **4640**

Bessler, Paul P., "Shifts in Corporate Headquarters, 1957–1983," Master's thesis, University of Arizona, 1987.   **4641**

Thielke, Paul D., "Changing Pattern of U.S. Corporate Headquarters, 1957–1986," Master's thesis, California State University–Northridge, 1988.
                                                            4642

Special-function towns

Hubbard, George D., "The Precious Metals as a Geographic Factor in the Settlement and Development of Towns in the United States," *Scottish Geographical Magazine*, vol. 26, 9 (1910), pp. 449–466.   **4643**

Mahnke, Hans-Peter, *Die Haupstädte und die führenden Städte der U.S.A.* (Stuttgart: Stuttgarter Geographische Studien, no. 78, 1970), 167 pp.   **4644**

Mahnke, Hans-Peter, "Hauptstadtverlegungen in den USA," *Geographische Rundschau*, vol. 24, 9 (1972), pp. 366–371.   **4645**

Warren, William, "The Railroad Town: A Study of Urban Response to Changes in Technology, Operating Procedures, and Demand for Railroad Service in the Post World War II Period," Ph.D. diss., University of North Carolina, 1972.
                                                            4646

Francaviglia, Richard V., "County Seat Centrality as a Regional Trait," *Geographical Survey*, vol. 2, 2 (1973), pp. 1–21.   **4647**

Alanen, Arnold R., "The Classification of Company Communities in a Resource Region of the United States: An Historical Assessment," *Proceedings of Historical Geography: Twenty-fourth International Geographical Congress, Section 9*

(Tokyo: International Geographical Union, 1981), pp. 252–256.   **4648**

TOWN GROWTH

General

Dunkle, John R., *Historical Cities* (Garden City, N.Y.: Nelson Doubleday, 1959), 64 pp.   **4649**

Wissink, Gerardus A., *America's Cities in Perspective: With Special Reference to the Development of Their Fringe Areas* (Assen: Van Gorcum, 1962), 320 pp.   **4650**

Suburban expansion

Muller, Peter O., "The Evolution of American Suburbs: A Geographical Interpretation," *Urbanism: Past and Present*, no. 4 (1977), pp. 1–10. **4651**

Jackson, Kenneth T., "Federal Subsidy and the Suburban Dream: The First Quarter-Century of Government Intervention in the Housing Market," *Records of the Columbia Historical Society of Washington, D.C.*, vol. 50 (1980), pp. 345–358.
                                                            4652

Muller, Peter O., "The Historical Evolution of American Suburbs," in his *Contemporary Suburban America* (Englewood Cliffs, N.J.: Prentice-Hall, 1981), pp. 19–60.   **4653**

Erickson, Rodney A., "The Evolution of the Suburban Space Economy," *Urban Geography*, vol. 4, 2 (1983), pp. 95–121. [Focus on 1920s–1980s] **4654**

Muller, Peter O., "Turning the American City Inside Out," *Journal of Urban History*, vol. 13, 2 (1987), pp. 348–353.   **4655**

Harris, Richard S., "American Suburbs: A Sketch of a New Interpretation," *Journal of Urban History*, vol. 15, 1 (1988), pp. 98–103.   **4656**

URBAN ECONOMIC STRUCTURE

General

Meyer, David R., "The Rise of the Industrial Metropolis: The Myth and the Reality," *Social Forces*, vol. 68, 3 (1990), pp. 731–752.   **4657**

Commercial patterns

Vance, James E., Jr., "Emerging Patterns of Commercial Structure in American Cities," *Lund Studies in Geography*, ser. B, no. 24 (1962), pp. 485–518.   **4658**

Perry, James A., "A Quantitative Analysis and Comparison of Some Aspects of Commercial Land Use Change in New Brunswick, New Jersey, and Lansing, Michigan, 1900–1960," Master's thesis, Rutgers University, 1964.   **4659**

Central business district

Ford, Larry R., "Individual Decisions in the Creation of the American Downtown," *Geography*, vol. 58, 4 (1973), pp. 324–327.   **4660**

Sauder, Robert A., "Geographic Change on the Downtown Waterfronts of Boston, New Orleans, and San Francisco," Ph.D. diss., University of Oregon, 1973.   **4661**

Bowden, Martyn J., "Growth of the Central Districts of Large Cities," in Leo F. Schnore, ed., *The New Urban History: Quantitative Explorations by American Historians* (Princeton: Princeton University Press, 1975), pp. 63–88.   **4662**

Sauder, Robert A., "Waterfront Subregions in Late Nineteenth Century Boston, New Orleans, and San Francisco," *Ecumene*, vol. 13 (1981), pp. 18–27.   **4663**

Robertson, Kent A., "The Downtown Hotel: Evolution and Recent Trends in the Large American City," in C. S. Yadav, ed., *Morphology of Towns* (New Delhi: Concept Publishing Co., 1987), pp. 115–134.   **4664**

Retail

Pyle, Jane, "Farmers' Markets in the United States: Functional Anachronisms," *Geographical Review*, vol. 61, 2 (1971), pp. 167–197.   **4665**

Cohen, Yehoshua S., *Diffusion of an Innovation in an Urban System: The Spread of Planned Regional Shopping Centers in the United States, 1949–1968* (Chicago: University of Chicago Department of Geography, Research Paper no. 140, 1972), 136 pp.   **4666**

Robertson, Kent A., "Downtown Retail Activity in Large American Cities, 1954–1977," *Geographical Review*, vol. 73, 3 (1983), pp. 314–323.   **4667**

Buckwalter, Donald W., "Geographical Changes in the Retail Structure of Medium-Sized Metropolitan Areas, 1958–1982," Ph.D. diss., University of Tennessee, 1988.   **4668**

Manufacturing

Pred, Allan R., "Manufacturing in the American Mercantile City: 1800–1840," *Annals of the Association of American Geographers*, vol. 56, 2 (1966), pp. 307–338.   **4669**

Transportation

Muller, Peter O., "Transportation and Urban Growth: The Shaping of the American Metropolis," *Focus*, vol. 36, 2 (1986), pp. 8–17.   **4670**

Vance, James E., Jr., "Human Mobility and the Shaping of Our Cities," in John Fraser Hart, ed.,

Our Changing Cities (Baltimore: Johns Hopkins University Press, 1991), pp. 67–85.   **4671**

Open space

Londa, Kathleen, "Urban Parks: Their Historical Development and Geographic Distribution in American Cities," Master's thesis, Syracuse University, 1979.   **4672**

URBAN SOCIAL STRUCTURE

General

Weiss, Edwin T., "The City and Its Cultural Role: Spatial and Conceptual Implications," Master's thesis, Clark University, 1971.   **4673**

Lampard, Eric E., "Some Aspects of Urban Social Structure and Morphology in the Historical Development of Cities in the United States," *Cahiers bruxellois: Revue d'histoire urbaine*, vol. 22 (1977), pp. 73–115.   **4674**

Muller, Edward K., "Sharpening the Focus on Mid-Nineteenth Century Urban Life: A Review Essay," *Historical Geography*, vol. 8, 2 (1978), pp. 1–16.   **4675**

Ley, David F., "Liberal Ideology and the Post-Industrial City," *Annals of the Association of American Geographers*, vol. 70, 2 (1980), pp. 238–258.   **4676**

Lloyd, William J., "Understanding Late Nineteenth-Century American Cities," *Geographical Review*, vol. 71, 4 (1981), pp. 460–471.   **4677**

Radford, John P., "The Social Geography of the Nineteenth Century U.S. City," in David T. Herbert and Ronald J. Johnston, eds., *Geography and the Urban Environment: Progress in Research and Applications, vol. 4* (N.Y.: John Wiley & Sons, 1981), pp. 257–293.   **4678**

Ward, David, "Social Structure and Social Geography in Large Cities of the U.S. Urban-Industrial Heartland," in David Ward and John Radford, *North American Cities in the Victorian Age* (Norwich, England: Geo Books, Historical Geography Research Series, no. 12, 1983), pp. 1–31.   **4679**

Harvey, David W., "Flexible Accumulation through Urbanization: Reflections on 'Post-Modernism' in the American City," *Antipode*, vol. 19, 3 (1987), pp. 260–286.   **4680**

Ward, David, *Poverty, Ethnicity, and the American City, 1840–1925: Changing Conceptions of the Slum and Ghetto* (New York: Cambridge University Press, 1989), 288 pp.   **4681**

Ward, David, "Social Reform, Social Surveys, and the Discovery of the Modern City," *Annals of the Association of American Geographers*, vol. 80, 4 (1990), pp. 491–503.   **4682**

Occupational structure

Ward, David, "Some Locational Implications of the Ethnic Division of Labor in Mid-Nineteenth Century American Cities," in Ralph E. Ehrenberg, ed., *Pattern and Process: Research in Historical Geography* (Washington, D.C.: Howard University Press, 1975), pp. 258–270.   **4683**

Ward, David, "Ethnic Pluralism and the Division of Labor in U.S. Cities, 1870–1880," Discussion Paper, Seminar on the Cultural Division of Labor, University of Washington, Seattle (1976), 30 pp.   **4684**

Ward, David, "Ethnicity Redefined: The Impact of the Division of Labor on Urban Migrants," *Proceedings of the New England–St. Lawrence Valley Division, Association of American Geographers*, vol. 4 (1976), pp. 3–7.   **4685**

Saueressig-Schreuder, Yda, "Labor Segmentation, Ethnic Division of Labor and Residential Segregation in American Cities in the Early Twentieth Century," *Professional Geographer*, vol. 41, 2 (1989), pp. 131–142.   **4686**

Residential segregation

Zunz, Olivier, "Residential Segregation in the American Metropolis: Concentration, Dispersion, and Dominance," *Urban History Yearbook 1980* (1980), pp. 23–33.   **4687**

Immigrant neighborhoods

Ward, David, "The Emergence of Central Immigrant Ghettos in American Cities: 1840–1920," *Annals of the Association of American Geographers*, vol. 58, 2 (1968), pp. 343–359.   **4688**

Ward, David, "The Internal Spatial Differentiation of Immigrant Residential Districts," *Northwestern University Department of Geography Special Publications*, no. 3 (1970), pp. 24–42. Reprinted, with omissions, in David Ward, ed., *Geographic Perspectives on America's Past: Readings on the Historical Geography of the United States* (New York: Oxford University Press, 1979), pp. 335–343.   **4689**

Femminella, Francis X., "The Immigrant and the Urban Melting Pot," in Melvin I. Urofsky, ed., *Perspectives on Urban America* (Garden City, N.Y.: Anchor Books, 1973), pp. 43–65. Reprinted, with omissions, in David Ward, ed., *Geographic Perspectives on America's Past: Readings on the Historical Geography of the United States* (New York: Oxford University Press, 1979), pp. 61–69.   **4690**

Ward, David, "The Ethnic Ghetto in the United States: Past and Present," *Transactions of the Institute of British Geographers*, n.s. vol. 7, 3 (1982), pp. 257–275.   **4691**

African American neighborhoods

Rose, Harold M., "The All-Negro Town: Its Evolution and Function," *Geographical Review*, vol. 55, 3 (1965), pp. 362–381.   **4692**

Rose, Harold M., "The Origins and Patterns of Development of Urban Black Social Areas," *Journal of Geography*, vol. 68, 6 (1969), pp. 326–332.   **4693**

Deskins, Donald R., "The Black Sub-Community: A Microcosm," in Joe T. Darden, ed., *The Ghetto: Readings with Interpretations* (Port Washington, N.Y.: Kennikat Press, 1981), pp. 32–56.   **4694**

Housing

Clark, William A. V., "The Dynamics of Rental Housing Areas in U.S. Cities, 1940–1960," Ph.D. diss., University of Illinois, 1964.   **4695**

Groth, Paul E., "Forbidden Housing: The Evolution and Exclusion of Hotels, Boarding Houses, and Rooming Houses in America's Urban Residential Culture, 1880–1930," Ph.D. diss., University of California–Berkeley, 1983.   **4696**

Daly, G., "Housing Politics and Pressure Groups: The Impacts of Central–Local Government Relations and Reformers on American Public Housing Policy, 1933–1953," Ph.D. diss., University of Cambridge, 1985.   **4697**

Ford, Larry R., "Housing and Inner City Population Change in Columbus and San Diego," *Yearbook of the Association of Pacific Coast Geographers*, vol. 50 (1988), pp. 105–115. [Focus on 1960–1980]   **4698**

Seager, Jonquil K., "'Father's Chair': Domestic Reform and Housing Change in the Progressive Era," Ph.D. diss., Clark University, 1988.   **4699**

Harris, Richard S., "Working-Class Home Ownership in the American Metropolis," *Journal of Urban History*, vol. 17, 1 (1990), pp. 46–69.   **4700**

Social life

Pred, Allan R., "The Impact of Technological and Institutional Innovations on Life Content: Some Time-Geographic Observations," *Geographical Analysis*, vol. 10, 4 (1978), pp. 345–372.   **4701**

Pred, Allan R., "Production, Family, and 'Free-time Projects': A Time-Geographic Perspective on the Individual and Societal Change in Nineteenth-Century U.S. Cities," *Journal of Historical Geography*, vol. 7, 1 (1981), pp. 3–36. Reprinted in revised form in Allan R. Pred, *Mak-*

ing Histories and Constructing Human Geographies: The Local Transformation of Practice, Power Relations, and Consciousness (Boulder: Westview Press, 1990), pp. 76–125.   4702

Marston, Sallie A., "Adapted Citizens: Discourse and the Production of Meaning among Nineteenth Century American Urban Immigrants," Transactions of the Institute of British Geographers, n.s. vol. 14, 4 (1989), pp. 435–445.   4703

Labor activity

Homenuck, P. Henry M., "Institutional Spatial Organization: Case Study of the United Steelworkers of America, 1936–1966," Ph.D. diss., University of Cincinnati, 1969.   4704

Bennett, Sari J., and Carville V. Earle, "The Geography of Strikes in the United States, 1881–1894," Journal of Interdisciplinary History, vol. 13, 1 (1982–1983), pp. 63–84.   4705

Social amenities

Bassett, Thomas J., "Vacant Lot Cultivation: Community Gardening in America, 1893–1978," Master's thesis, University of Califronia–Berkeley, 1979.   4706

Bassett, Thomas J., "Reaping on the Margins: A Century of Community Gardening in America," Landscape, vol. 25, 2 (1981), pp. 1–8.   4707

Suburban impulse

Walker, Richard A., "The Suburban Solution: Urban Geography and Urban Reform in the Capitalist Development of the United States," Ph.D. diss., Johns Hopkins University, 1977.   4708

Walker, Richard A., "The Transformation of Urban Structure in the Nineteenth Century, and the Beginning of Suburbanization," in Kevin R. Cox, ed., Urbanization and Conflict in Market Societies (Chicago: Maaroufa Press, 1978), pp. 165–211.   4709

Winsberg, Morton D., "The Suburbanization of the Irish in Boston, Chicago, and New York," Éire-Ireland, vol. 21, 3 (1986), pp. 90–104. [Focus on 1950–1980]   4710

TOWNSCAPE

General

McDermott, George L., "The Morphology and Evolution of the Company Town," Proceedings of the New York–New Jersey Division, Association of American Geographers, vol. 4 (1971), pp. 90–98.   4711

Conzen, Michael P., "Analytical Approaches to the Urban Landscape," in Karl W. Butzer, ed., Di-

mensions of Human Geography: Essays on Some Familiar and Neglected Themes (Chicago: University of Chicago Department of Geography, Research Paper no. 186, 1978), 128–165. [Focus on United States]   4712

Rubin, Barbara, "Aesthetic Ideology and Urban Design," Annals of the Association of American Geographers, vol. 69, 3 (1979), pp. 339–361. Reprinted in Dell Upton and John Michael Vlach, eds., Common Places: Readings in American Vernacular Architecture (Athens: University of Georgia Press, 1986), pp. 482–508. [Focus from the late nineteenth century to the 1970s]   4713

Conzen, Michael P., "The Morphology of Nineteenth Century Cities in the United States," in Woodrow Borah, Jorge Hardoy, and Gilbert A. Stelter, eds., Urbanization in the Americas: The Background in Comparative Perspective (Ottawa: National Museum of Man, 1980), pp. 119–141; volume also issued as a special number of the Urban History Review, 1980.   4714

Muller, Edward K., "Distinctive Downtown," Geographical Magazine, vol. 53, 11 (1980), pp. 747–755.   4715

Bowden, Martyn J., "Geographical Change in Cities Following Disaster," in Alan R. H. Baker and Mark Billinge, eds., Period and Place: Research Methods in Historical Geography (Cambridge: Cambridge University Press, 1982), pp. 114–126 and 331–332.   4716

Muller, Edward K., "The Americanization of the City," in Michael P. Conzen, ed., The Making of the American Landscape (Boston: Unwin Hyman, 1990), pp. 269–292.   4717

Ground plan

Stanislawski, Dan, "Early Spanish Town Planning in the New World," Geographical Review, vol. 37, 1 (1947), pp. 96–105.   4718

Schretter, Howard A., "Circular Corporate Limits in the United States: Their Origin, Distribution and Implications," Master's thesis, University of Georgia, 1959.   4719

Nelson, Howard J., "Walled Cities of the United States," Annals of the Association of American Geographers, vol. 51, 1 (1961), pp. 1–22.   4720

Reps, John W., The Making of Urban America: A History of City Planning in the United States (Princeton: Princeton University Press, 1965), 574 pp.   4721

Price, Edward T., "The Central Courthouse Square in the American County Seat," Geographical Review, vol. 58, 1 (1968), pp. 29–60. Reprinted in Dell Upton and John Michael Vlach, eds., Common Places: Readings in American Vernacular

Architecture (Athens: University of Georgia Press, 1986), pp. 124–145.   **4722**

Groth, Paul E., "Streetgrids as Frameworks for Urban Variety," *Harvard Architectural Review*, vol. 2 (1981), pp. 68–75.   **4723**

Conzen, Michael P., "Town-Plan Analysis in an American Setting: Cadastral Processes in Boston and Omaha, 1630–1930," in Terry R. Slater, ed., *The Built Form of Western Cities: Essays for M. R. G. Conzen on the Occasion of His Eightieth Birthday* (Leicester: Leicester University Press, 1990), pp. 142–170.   **4724**

Groth, Paul E., "Lot, Yard, and Garden: American Distinctions," *Landscape*, vol. 30, 3 (1990), pp. 29–35.   **4725**

Groth, Paul E., "Parking Gardens/Parking Lots," in Mark Francis and Randolph T. Hester, eds., *Meanings of the Garden: Idea, Place, and Action* (Cambridge: MIT Press, 1990), pp. 130–137.   **4726**

Building types

Gerling, Walter, *Das Amerikanische Hochhaus: Seine Entwicklung und Bedeutung* (Würzburg: Triltsch, 1949), 58 pp.   **4727**

Ford, Larry R., "The Diffusion of the Skyscraper as an Urban Symbol," *Yearbook of the Association of Pacific Coast Geographers*, vol. 35 (1973), pp. 49–60.   **4728**

Ford, Larry R., "The Urban Housetype as an Illustration of the Concentric Zone Model: Comments on the Perception of Architectural Continuity," *Journal of Geography*, vol. 73, 2 (1974), pp. 29–39.   **4729**

Ford, Larry R., "The Urban Skyline as a City Classification System," *Journal of Geography*, vol. 75, 3 (1976), pp. 154–164.   **4730**

Jakle, John A., "The American Gasoline Station: 1920 to 1970," *Journal of American Culture*, vol. 1, 3 (1978), pp. 520–542.   **4731**

Bastian, Robert W., "The Prairie Style House: Spatial Diffusion of a Minor Design," *Journal of Cultural Geography*, vol. 1, 1 (1980), pp. 50–65.   **4732**

Bastian, Robert W., "Urban House Types as a Research Focus in Historical Geography," *Environmental Review*, vol. 4, 2 (1980), pp. 27–34.   **4733**

Ford, Larry R., and Richard D. Fusch, "Architecture and the Geography of the American City," *Geographical Review*, vol. 73, 5 (1983), pp. 324–340.   **4734**

Ford, Larry R., "Architecture and Geography: Toward a Mutual Concern for Space and Place,"

Yearbook of the Association of Pacific Coast Geographers, vol. 46 (1984), pp. 7–33.   **4735**

Ford, Larry R., "Multiunit Housing in the American City," *Geographical Review*, vol. 76, 4 (1986), pp. 390–407.   **4736**

Groth, Paul E., "'Marketplace' Vernacular Design: The Case of Downtown Rooming Houses," in Camille Wells, ed., *Perspectives in Vernacular Architecture*, vol. 2 (Columbia: University of Missouri Press, 1986), pp. 179–191.   **4737**

Raitz, Karl B., and John Paul Jones III, "The City Hotel as Landscape Artifact and Community Symbol," *Journal of Cultural Geography*, vol. 9, 1 (1988), pp. 17–36.   **4738**

Land-use morphology

MacDonald, Kent, "The Commercial Strip from Main Street to Television Road," *Landscape*, vol. 28, 2 (1985), pp. 12–19.   **4739**

Wood, Joseph S., "Suburbanization of Center City," *Geographical Review*, vol. 78, 3 (1988), pp. 325–330.   **4740**

Other themes

Zube, Ervin H., "The Natural History of Urban Trees," *Natural History* (Nov. 1973), pp. 48–51.   **4741**

Alanen, Arnold R., "Landscape Architects, Model Industrial Villages, and Welfare Capitalism in Early Twentieth-Century America," in Margaret McAvin, ed., *Landscape and Architecture: Sharing Common Ground, Defining Turf, Charting New Paths*, Proceedings of the Annual Conference, Council of Educators in Landscape Architecture, 1987 (Washington, D.C.: Council of Educators in Landscape Architecture, 1988), pp. 186–190.   **4742**

RECREATION & TOURISM

Movies

Gomery, Douglas, "Movie Audiences, Urban Geography, and the History of the American Film," *Velvet Light Trap*, vol. 19 (1982), pp. 23–29.   **4743**

Organized sports

McDevitt, Thomas E., "A Geographic Analysis of Professional Baseball within the United States, 1930–1955," Master's thesis, Southern Illinois University, 1959.   **4744**

Miller, Mark M., "A Spatial Analysis of Golf Facility Development in the United States, 1931–1970," Master's thesis, Oklahoma State University, 1972.   **4745**

Goudge, Theodore L., "A Geographical Analysis of Major College Football Programs: The Parameters of Success, 1952–1983," Ed.D. diss., Oklahoma State University, 1984.   4746

Adams, Robert L. A., and John F. Rooney, Jr., "Evolution of American Golf Facilities," *Geographical Review*, vol. 75, 4 (1985), pp. 419–438.   4747

Touring

McKenzie, Roderick C., "The Development of Automobile Road Guides in the United States," Master's thesis, University of California–Los Angeles, 1963.   4748

Frederic, Paul B., "Geography and Living Historical Farm Sites," *Agricultural History*, vol. 48, 1 (1974), pp. 5–10.   4749

Hugill, Peter J., "The Rediscovery of America: Elite Automobiles Touring Early This Century," *Annals of Tourism Research*, vol. 12, 3 (1985), pp. 435–447.   4750

Resorts

Stansfield, Charles A., "The Development of Modern Seaside Resorts," *Parks and Recreation*, vol. 5, 10 (1972), pp. 43–46.   4751

Demars, Stanford E., "British Contributions to American Seaside Resorts," *Annals of Tourism Research*, vol. 6, 3 (1979), pp. 285–293.   4752

Demars, Stanford E., "Worship-by-the-Sea: Camp Meetings and Seaside Resorts in Nineteenth Century America," *Focus*, American Geographical Society, vol. 38, 4 (1988), pp. 15–20.   4753

Cultivation of wilderness

Schoenichen, Walther, "Aus der Entstehungsgeschichte der Nationalparke," *Petermanns Geographische Mitteilungen*, vol. 83, 4 (1949), pp. 175–177.   4754

Holz, Robert K., "Geographic Implication in the Historical Development of National Forests of the United States," *Journal of Geography*, vol. 64, 6 (1965), pp. 254–266.   4755

Thompson, Kenneth, "Wilderness and Health in the Nineteenth Century," *Journal of Historical Geography*, vol. 2, 2 (1976), pp. 145–162.   4756

PLANNING

General

Zube, Ervin H., "Landscape Aesthetics: Policy and Planning in the U.S.," in Jay Appleton, ed., *The Aesthetics of Landscape* (Oxford, England: Rural Planning Services, 1980), pp. 68–79.   4757

Steiner, F., G. Young, and Ervin H. Zube, "Ecological Planning: Retrospect and Prospect," *Landscape Journal*, vol. 7, 1 (1988), pp. 31–39.   4758

Planned communities

Alanen, Arnold R., "The Development of Planned Communities in the United States, 1900–1967," Master's thesis, University of Minnesota, 1968.   4759

Alanen, Arnold R., "New Towns and Planned Communities," in William H. Tishler, ed., *American Landscape Architecture: Designers and Places* (Washington, D.C.: Preservation Press, 1989), pp. 176–179.   4760

Historic preservation

Ford, Larry R., "Historic Preservation and the Sense of Place," *Growth and Change*, vol. 5, 2 (1974), pp. 33–37.   4761

Ford, Larry R., "Historic Preservation and the Stream of Time: The Role of the Geographer," *Historical Geography*, vol. 5, 1 (1975), pp. 1–15.   4762

Lewis, Peirce F., "The Future of the Past: Our Clouded Vision of Historic Preservation," *Pioneer America*, vol. 7, 2 (1975), pp. 1–20.   4763

Hofmeister, Burkhard, "Die Erhaltung historisch wertvoller Bausubstanz in den Städten der USA," *Erde*, vol. 108 (1977), pp. 129–150.   4764

Ford, Larry R., "Urban Preservation and the Geography of the City in the United States," *Progress in Human Geography*, vol. 3, 3 (1979), pp. 211–238.   4765

Carlson, Alvar W., "An Analysis of Historic Preservation in the U.S. as Reflected by the National Register of Historical Places," *Journal of American Culture*, vol. 3, 2 (1980), pp. 245–267.   4766

Ford, Larry R., "Historic Districts and Urban Design," *Environmental Review*, vol. 4, 2 (1980), pp. 20–26.   4767

Datel, Robin E., "Historic Districts in Three American and Two Western European Cities: A Geographical Study," Ph.D. diss., University of Minnesota, 1983.   4768

Lamme, Ary J., III, *America's Historic Landscapes: Community Power and the Preservation of Four National Historic Sites* (Knoxville: University of Tennessee Press, 1989), 213 pp.   4769

Lamme, Ary J., III, "Preserving Special Places," *Geographical Review*, vol. 79, 2 (1989), pp. 195–209.   4770

Wood, Joseph S., "Providing Substance: Historic Preservation as Cultural Environmentalism,"

North American Culture, vol. 4, 2 (1989), pp. 81–87.
4771

PLACE NAMES

General

Kohl, Johann Georg, "Historical Notes on the Ancient and Modern Names with Which the Regions, Countries, Territories, and States along the Coasts of the North American Union Have Been Designated," *National Intelligencer,* vol. 57, 8410 (Nov. 6, 1856), p. 4; 8411 (Nov. 8, 1856), p. 4; and 8412 (Nov. 11, 1856), p. 4.
4772

Staples, Hamilton B., "Origin of the Names of the States of the Union," *Proceedings of the American Antiquarian Society,* n.s. vol. 1 (1882), pp. 366–383.
4773

Field, David D., "On the Nomenclature of Cities and Towns in the United States," *Journal of the American Geographical Society,* vol. 17 (1885), pp. 1–16.
4774

Coxe, A. Cleveland, "American Geographical Names," *Forum* (New York), vol. 4 (1887), pp. 67–77.
4775

Gannett, Henry, *The Origin of Certain Place Names in the United States* (Washington, D.C.: United States Geological Survey Bulletin no. 197, ser. F, Geography no. 32, 1902), 280 pp. Revised as Bulletin no. 258, ser. F, Geography no. 45, 1905, 334 pp. Reprinted Baltimore: Genealogical Publishing Co., 1970.
4776

Whitbeck, Ray H., "Geographic Names in the United States and the Stories They Tell," *National Geographic Magazine,* vol. 16, 3 (1905), pp. 100–104.
4777

Bell, Laura, "Some Geographical Names and Their Significance," *Bulletin of the Geographical Society of Philadelphia,* vol. 18 (1920), pp. 31–34.
4778

Lawrence, Frederick W., "The Origins of American State Names," *National Geographic Magazine,* vol. 38, 2 (1920), pp. 105–143.
4779

Holt, Alfred H., *American Place Names* (New York: Thomas Y. Crowell Co., 1938), 222 pp.
4780

Stewart, George R., *Names on the Land: A Historical Account of Place-Naming in the United States* (New York: Random House, 1945), 418 pp.
4781

Quimby, Myron, *Scratch Ankle, U.S.A.: American Place Names and Their Derivation* (South Brunswick, N.J.: A. S. Barnes, 1969), 390 pp.
4782

Taft, William Howard, *County Names: An Historical Perspective; An Essay* (n.p.: National Association of Counties, 1982), 66 pp.
4783

Names of Indian provenance

Boyd, Stephen G., *Indian Local Names, with Their Interpretation* (York, Pa.: The author, 1885), 70 pp.
4784

Lawson, James (Chief Night Sun), *Handbook of Indian Place Names in America* (Wisconsin Dells: n.p., 1970), 32 pp.
4785

European ethnic provenance

Shelburne, Mause E., "Some French Place-Names in the United States," Master's thesis, University of Chicago, 1929.
4786

Lyra, Elzbieta, and Francis Zik Lyra, "Polish Place-Names in the U.S.A.," *Geographica Polonica,* vol. 11 (1967), pp. 29–39.
4787

Coulet du Gard, René, *Dictionary of French Place Names in the USA* (Newark, Del.: Éditions des deux mondes et Slavuta, 1986), 431 pp.
4788

Schmocker, Erdmann, and Kim-Chan Nguyen, "Swiss Related Place Names in the USA," *Swiss-American Historical Society Newsletter,* vol. 22, 1 (1986), pp. 10–47.
4789

Stump, Roger W., "Pluralism in the American Place-Name Cover: Ethnic Variations in Catholic Church Names," *North American Culture,* vol. 2, 2 (1986), pp. 126–140.
4790

Geographical distribution and regional variations

Whitbeck, Ray H., "Regional Peculiarities in Place Names," *Bulletin of the American Geographical Society,* vol. 43, 4 (1911), pp. 273–281.
4791

Zelinsky, Wilbur, "Classical Town Names in the United States: The Historical Geography of an American Idea," *Geographical Review,* vol. 57, 4 (1967), pp. 463–495.
4792

Leighly, John B., "Town Names of Colonial New England in the West," *Annals of the Association of American Geographers,* vol. 68, 2 (1978), pp. 233–248.
4793

Zelinsky, Wilbur, "Nationalism in the American Place-Name Cover," *Names,* vol. 31, 1 (1983), pp. 1–28.
4794

Vogel, Virgil J., "Indian Trails and Place Names," *Names,* vol. 33, 1–2 (1985), pp. 39–50.
4795

Selected themes

Martin, Lawrence, "The Dates of Naming Places and Things for George Washington," in U.S. George Washington Bicentennial Commission, *History of the George Washington Bicentennial Celebration,* Literature Series, vol. 3 (Washington, D.C., 1932), pp. 308–312.
4796

Alexander, Gerard L., *Nicknames of American Cities, Towns, and Villages, Past and Present* (New York: Special Libraries Association, 1951), 74 pp. **4797**

Burrill, Meredith F., "Toponymic Generics," *Names*, vol. 4 (1956), pp. 129–137, 226–240. **4798**

McMullen, Edwin W., "The Term Prairie in the United States," *Names*, vol. 5, 1 (1957), pp. 27–46. **4799**

Burrill, Meredith F., "Generic Terms in United States Watercourse Names," *Sixth International Congress of Onomastic Sciences, Munich, 1958*, vol. 2 (1961), pp. 175–180. **4800**

Price, Edward T., "A Geography of Color," *Geographical Review*, vol. 54, 4 (1964), pp. 590–592. [Chromotoponyms] **4801**

Kane, Joseph N., and Gerard L. Alexander, *Nicknames and Sobriquets of U.S. Cities and States* (Metuchen, N.J.: Scarecrow Press, 1965), 341 pp. Revised 1970, 456 pp. **4802**

Brunn, Stanley D., and James O. Wheeler, "Notes on the Geography of Religious Town Names in the U.S.," *Names*, vol. 14, 4 (1966), pp. 197–202. **4803**

McDavid, Raven I., Jr., and Virginia McDavid, "Cracker and Hoosier," *Names*, vol. 21, 3 (1973), pp. 161–167. **4804**

Leighly, John B., "Biblical Place Names in the United States," *Names*, vol. 27, 1 (1979), pp. 46–59. **4805**

Zelinsky, Wilbur, "By Their Names You Shall Know Them: A Toponymic Approach to the American Land and Ethos," *New York Folklore*, vol. 8, 1 & 2 (1982), pp. 85–96. **4806**

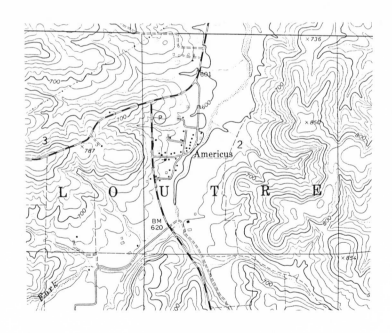

THE EAST

(INCLUDING THE ATLANTIC SEABOARD AND THE
NORTHEAST QUADRANT OF THE UNITED STATES)

GENERAL

See also 1149, 1151

Kulikoff, Allan, *Tobacco and Slaves: The Development of Southern Cultures in the Chesapeake, 1680–1800* (Chapel Hill: University of North Carolina Press, for the Institute of Early American History and Culture, 1986), 449 pp.   **4807**

ENVIRONMENTAL CHANGE

Brown, Ralph Hall, "The Seaboard Climate in the View of 1800," *Annals of the Association of American Geographers*, vol. 41, 3 (1951), pp. 217–232.   **4808**

Wahl, Eberhard W., "A Comparison of the Climate of the Eastern United States during the 1830s with the Current Normals," *Monthly Weather Review*, vol. 96 (1968), pp. 73–82.   **4809**

Meade, R. H., and Stanley W. Trimble, "Changes in Sediment Loads in Rivers of the Atlantic Drainage of the United States since 1900," in *Effects of Man on the Interface of the Hydrological Cycle with the Physical Environment*, International Association of Scientific Hydrology, Publication no. 113 (1974), pp. 99–104.   **4810**

Vines, R. G., "Rainfall Patterns in the Eastern United States," *Climatic Change*, vol. 6, 1 (1984), pp. 79–98. [1880–1960]   **4811**

NATIVE PEOPLES & WHITE RELATIONS

Janke, Robert A., "Prehistoric Origins of the Chippewa Indians," *Geographical Bulletin*, vol. 19 (1980), pp. 37–43.   **4812**

EXPLORATION & MAPPING

See also 1275–1284

Brown, Ralph Hall, "The De Brahm Charts of the Atlantic Ocean, 1772–1776," *Geographical Review*, vol. 28, 1 (1938), pp. 124–132.   **4813**

POPULAR IMAGES & EVALUATION

Brown, Ralph Hall, "Materials Bearing upon the Geography of the Atlantic Seaboard, 1790 to 1810," *Annals of the Association of American Geographers*, vol. 28, 3 (1938), pp. 201–231.   **4814**

Peters, Bernard C., "Changing Ideas about the Use of Vegetation as an Indicator of Soil Quality: Example of New York and Michigan," *Journal of Geography*, vol. 72, 2 (1973), pp. 18–30.   **4815**

REGIONAL SETTLEMENT

Sauer, Carl O., "The Settlement of the Humid East," in *Climate and Man: Yearbook of Agriculture 1941* (Washington, D.C.: Government Printing Office, 1942), pp. 157–166. Reprinted in Carl O. Sauer, *Selected Essays, 1963–1975*, ed. Bob Callahan (Berkeley, Calif.: Turtle Island Foundation, for the Netzahaulcoyotl Historical Society, 1981), pp. 3–15.   **4816**

Isaac, Erich, "Jamestown and the Mid-Atlantic Coast: A Geographic Reconsideration," *Journal of Geography*, vol. 57, 1 (1958), pp. 17–28.   **4817**

Merrens, H. Roy, "Settlement of the Colonial Atlantic Seaboard," in Ralph E. Ehrenberg, ed., *Pattern and Process: Research in Historical Geography* (Washington, D.C.: Howard University Press, 1975), pp. 235–243.   **4818**

POPULATION

Hauk, Sister Mary Ursula, "Changing Patterns of Catholic Population in the Eastern United States (1790–1950)," Ph.D. diss., Clark University, 1958.   **4819**

Hudson, John C., "Migration to an American Frontier," *Annals of the Association of American Geographers*, vol. 66, 2 (1976), pp. 242–265. Reprinted, with omissions, in David Ward, ed., *Geographic Perspectives on America's Past: Readings on the Historical Geography of the United States* (New York: Oxford University Press, 1979), pp. 94–113.   **4820**

RURAL & REGIONAL SOCIAL GEOGRAPHY

Price, Edward T., "Mixed Blood Racial Islands of the Eastern United States as to Origin, Localization, and Persistence," Ph.D. diss., University of California–Berkeley, 1950.   **4821**

Price, Edward T., "A Geographic Analysis of White-Negro-Indian Racial Mixtures in the Eastern United States," *Annals of the Associa-*

tion of American Geographers, vol. 43, 2 (1953), pp. 138–155.   4822

Tweedie, Stephen W., "The Geography of Religious Groups in New York, Pennsylvania, and Ohio: Persistence and Change, 1890–1965," Ph.D. diss., Syracuse University, 1969.   4823

Tweedie, Stephen W., "The Geography of Religious Groups in New York, Pennsylvania, and Ohio: Persistence and Change, 1890–1965," *Proceedings of the New York–New Jersey Division, Association of American Geographers*, vol. 2 (1969), pp. 121–132.   4824

Meyer, Douglas K., and Judith W. Meyer, "American Cultural Themes: Midwest and New England Culture Regions," *Bulletin of the Illinois Geographical Society*, vol. 21, 2 (1979), pp. 28–36.
4825

Rudnicki, Ryan, "Peopling Industrial America: Formation of Italian and Polish Settlements in the Manufacturing Heartland of the United States," Ph.D. diss., Pennsylvania State University, 1979.   4826

Tank, Heide, *Die Entwicklung der Wirtschaftsstruktur einer traditionellen Sozialgruppe: Das Beispiel der Old Order Amish in Ohio, Indiana, und Pennsylvania, USA* (Berlin: Freie Universität Berlin, Geographisches Institut, Abhandlungen no. 27, 1979), 155 pp.   4827

POLITICAL & ADMINISTRATIVE GEOGRAPHY

See also 1387–1388, 3953

Mitchell, Robert D., "American Origins and Regional Institutions: Seventeenth-Century Chesapeake," *Annals of the Association of American Geographers*, vol. 73, 3 (1983), pp. 404–420.   4828

ECONOMIC DEVELOPMENT

Skaggs, David C., "John Semple and the Development of the Potomac Valley, 1750–1773," *Virginia Magazine of History and Biography*, vol. 92, 3 (1984), pp. 282–308.   4829

LAND & LAND USE

Hart, John Fraser, "Loss and Abandonment of Cleared Farm Land in the Eastern United States," *Annals of the Association of American Geographers*, vol. 58, 3 (1968), pp. 417–440. [Focus on 1910–1959]   4830

Trimble, Stanley W., "Perspectives on the History of Soil Erosion Control in the Eastern United States," *Agricultural History*, vol. 59 (1985), pp. 162–180.   4831

EXTRACTIVE ACTIVITY

See also 1410

Gabriel, Ralph H., "Geographic Influences in the Development of the Menhaden Fishery of the Eastern Coast of the United States," *Geographical Review*, vol. 10, 2 (1920), pp. 91–100.   4832

Deasy, George F., and Phyllis R. Griess, "Local and Regional Differences in Long Term Bituminous Coal Production Prospects in the Eastern United States," *Annals of the Association of American Geographers*, vol. 57, 3 (1967), pp. 519–533. [Focus on 1898–1963]   4833

AGRICULTURE

Baker, Oliver E., "Agricultural Regions of North America: Part V—The Hay and Dairying Region," *Economic Geography*, vol. 4, 1 (1928), pp. 44–73.   4834

Baker, Oliver E., "Agricultural Regions of North America: Part VII—The Middle Atlantic Trucking Region," *Economic Geography*, vol. 5, 1 (1929), pp. 36–69.   4835

Monmonier, Mark S., and George A. Schnell, "Dairying, Urbanization, and Recent Agricultural Change in the Northeast," *Proceedings of the Middle States Division of the Association of American Geographers*, vol. 15 (1981), pp. 28–31.
4836

Rumney, Thomas A., "Regional Agricultural Change in Virginia, Maryland, and Delaware," *Virginia Geographer*, vol. 22, 2 (1990), pp. 44–52. [Focus on 1964–1987]   4837

LANDSCAPE

Zelinsky, Wilbur, "Where the South Begins: The Northern Limit of the Cis-Appalachian South in Terms of Settlement Landscape," *Social Forces*, vol. 30, 2 (1951), pp. 172–178.   4838

Kniffen, Fred B., and Henry H. Glassie, "Building in Wood in the Eastern United States: A Time-Place Perspective," *Geographical Review*, vol. 56, 1 (1966), pp. 40–66. Reprinted, with omissions, in Thomas J. Schlereth, ed., *Material Culture Studies in America* (Nashville: American Association for State and Local History, 1982), pp. 174–182; and in Dell Upton and John Michael Vlach, eds., *Common Places: Readings in American Vernacular Architecture* (Athens: University of Georgia Press, 1986), pp. 159–181.   4839

Meigs, Peveril, III, "Historical Geography of Tide Mills on the Atlantic Coast," *American Philosophical Society Yearbook 1970* (Philadelphia: American Philosophical Society, 1971), pp. 462–464.   4840

Ainsley, W. Frank, Jr., "Folk Architecture in the Eastern United States," *Independent Republic Quarterly*, vol. 14, 1 (1980), pp. 4–6.　　**4841**

Noble, Allan G., and Brian Coffey, "The Use of Cobblestones as a Folk Building Material," *Pioneer America Society Transactions*, vol. 9 (1986), pp. 45–51.　　**4842**

Mattson, Richard L., "The Gable Front and Upright and Wing: An Historical Geography of Two Common American House Types," Ph.D. diss., University of Illinois, 1988. [New York, Michigan, Minnesota]　　**4843**

COMMUNICATIONS

See 1429, 1431

TOWNSCAPE

Reps, John W., *Tidewater Towns: City Planning in Colonial Virginia and Maryland* (Charlottesville: Colonial Williamsburg Foundation and the University Press of Virginia, 1972), 345 pp.　　**4844**

Ohman, Marian M., "Diffusion of Foursquare Courthouses to the Midwest, 1785–1885," *Geographical Review*, vol. 72, 2 (1982), pp. 171–189.　　**4845**

Jakle, John A., Robert W. Bastian and Douglas K. Meyer, *Common Houses in America's Small Towns: The Atlantic Seaboard to the Mississippi Valley* (Athens: University of Georgia Press, 1989), 238 pp.　　**4846**

THE NORTHEAST

ENVIRONMENTAL CHANGE

Nelson, J. Gordon, "Man and Geomorphic Process in the Chemung River Valley, New York and Pennsylvania," *Annals of the Association of American Geographers*, vol. 56, 1 (1966), pp. 24–32. **4847**

NATIVE PEOPLES & WHITE RELATIONS

Day, Gordon M., "The Indian as an Ecological Factor in the Northeastern Forest," *Ecology*, vol. 34, 2 (1953), pp. 329–346. **4848**

Hoffman, Bernard G., "Ancient Tribes Revisited: A Summary of Indian Distribution and Movement in the Northeastern United States from 1534 to 1779, Parts I–III," *Ethnohistory*, vol. 14, 1 & 2 (1967), pp. 1–46. **4849**

Aquila, Richard, "The Iroquois as Geographic Middlemen: A Research Note," *Indiana Magazine of History*, vol. 80, 1 (1984), pp. 51–60. **4850**

EXPLORATION & MAPPING

See also **3954**

Brown, Ralph Hall, "Early Maps of the United States: The Ebeling-Sotzmann Maps of the Northern Seaboard States," *Geographical Review*, vol. 30, 3 (1940), pp. 471–479. **4851**

Trindell, Roger T., "Pehr Lindeström, Geographer on the Delaware," *Bulletin of the Special Libraries Association, Geography and Map Division*, no. 68 (1967), pp. 6–9. **4852**

Monmonier, Mark S., "Street Maps and Private-Sector Map Making: A Case Study of Two Firms," *Cartographica*, vol. 18, 3 (1981), pp. 34–52. **4853**

Wainright, Nicholas B., "Mason and Dixon's Map," *Princeton University Library Chronicle*, vol. 45, 1 (1983), pp. 28–32. **4854**

POPULAR IMAGES & EVALUATION

LeBlanc, Robert G., "The Differential Perception of Salt Marshes by the Folk and Elite in the Nineteenth Century," *Proceedings of the Association of American Geographers*, vol. 5 (1973), pp. 138–143. [Northeastern states] **4855**

Bodle, Wayne, "The Myth of the Middle Colonies Reconsidered: The Process of Regionalization in Early America," *Pennsylvania Magazine of History and Biography*, vol. 113, 4 (1989), pp. 527–548. **4856**

REGIONAL SETTLEMENT

Odhner, Clas T., "Om den svenske Koloni Nya Sverige," *Geografisk tijdskrift* (Denmark), vol. 3 (1879), pp. 49–54. [Focus on the Swedish colony of New Sweden] **4857**

LeConte, René, "La Nouvelle Belgique: 1—Les origines de la colonisation hollandaise (1609–1618)"; "2—La fondation de Nieuw Amsterdam par Peter Minnewyt (1623–1632)," *Bulletin de la Société royale belge de géographie*, vol. 50 (1926), pp. 134–144; "La Nouvelle Belgique: 3—La companie des Indes Occidentales et sa politique coloniale"; "4—Les successeurs de Minnewyt (1632–1655)"; "5—Histoire de la Nouvelle-Suède (1624–1671)"; 6—Fin de la domination Hollandaise (1655–1674)," vol. 51 (1927), pp. 18–27, 69–85. **4858**

Kury, Theodore W., "Iron and Settlement: The New York–New Jersey Highlands in the Eighteenth Century," in H. Jesse Walker and William G. Haage, eds., *Man and Cultural Heritage: Papers in Honor of Fred B. Kniffen* (Baton Rouge: Louisiana State University, Geoscience & Man, vol. 5, 1974), pp. 7–24. **4859**

Lord, Philip, *War over Walloomscoick: Land Use and Settlement Pattern on the Bennington Battlefield, 1777* (Albany: New York State Museum, Bulletin no. 473, 1989), 190 pp. [Focus on the Walloomac River Valley, Vermont and New York] **4860**

POPULATION

Lobeck, Armin K., "The Physiographic Influence upon the Distribution of Population in Maryland and Pennsylvania," *Geographical Review*, vol. 16, 2 (1926), pp. 94–101. [Considers 1900–1920] **4861**

Lamb, Richard F., "Patterns of Population Redistribution in Non-Metropolitan New York and New England, 1950–1975," *Proceedings of the Middle States Division, Association of American Geographers*, vol. 11 (1977), pp. 54–59. **4862**

Monmonier, Mark S., and George A. Schnell, "The Increasing Importance of Mortality in Population Trends: The North-Eastern U.S., 1940–1974," *Proceedings of the Middle States Division, Association of American Geographers*, vol. 11 (1977), pp. 49–53. **4863**

Condran, Gretchen, and Eileen Crimmins, "Mortality Differentials between Rural and Urban Areas of States in the Northeastern United States, 1890–1900," *Journal of Historical Geography*, vol. 6, 2 (1980), pp. 179–202. **4864**

Schnell, George A., and Mark S. Monmonier, "Population Turnaround in the Northeast: A Cartographic Analysis," *Proceedings of the Middle States Division, Association of American Geographers*, vol. 15 (1981), pp. 80–85. **4865**

RURAL & REGIONAL SOCIAL GEOGRAPHY

Nelson, Helge M. O., "Delawares Svenskarna och deras attlingors amerikanisering," in *Fran skilda tider: Studies tillagnade Hjalmar F. Holmquist* (Stockholm: Diakonistyrelsos Bokforlag, 1938), 654 pp. **4866**

Zelinsky, Wilbur, "Cultural Variation in Personal Name Patterns in the Eastern United States," *Annals of the Association of American Geographers*, vol. 60, 1 (1970), pp. 743–769. [Focus on 1790–1968] **4867**

Christiansen, Jane K., "Founding of Roman Catholic Parishes in Central New York and Adjacent Pennsylvania, 1654–1970," Master's thesis, Syracuse University, 1973. **4868**

Earle, Carville V., and Sari J. Bennett, "Labor Power and Locality in the Gilded Age: The Northeastern United States, 1881–1894," *Social History/Histoire sociale*, vol. 25, 30 (1982), pp. 383–405. **4869**

POLITICAL & ADMINISTRATIVE GEOGRAPHY

Mayo, Lawrence S., "The Forty-Fifth Parallel: A Detail of the Unguarded Boundary," *Geographical Review*, vol. 13 (1923), pp. 255–265. [New York and Vermont] **4870**

McManis, Douglas R., "Regional Reaction to National Law: The Embargo and Northern New York and New England," *Professional Geographer*, vol. 17, 4 (1965), pp. 6–8. [Focus on the American trade embargo against Britain and France, 1807–1809] **4871**

Hilliard, Sam B., "A Robust New Nation, 1783–1820," in Robert D. Mitchell and Paul A. Groves, eds., *North America: The Historical Geography of a Changing Continent* (Totowa, N.J.: Rowman & Littlefield, 1987), pp. 149–171. **4872**

ECONOMIC DEVELOPMENT

Mulligan, William, et al., "Mapping the Economic System of the Mid-Atlantic: A Preliminary Re-

port," *Historical Methods*, vol. 12, 3 (1979), pp. 127–128. **4873**

Groves, Paul A., "The Northeast and Regional Integration, 1800–1860," in Robert D. Mitchell and Paul A. Groves, eds., *North America: The Historical Geography of a Changing Continent* (Totowa, N.J.: Rowman & Littlefield, 1987), pp. 198–219. **4874**

RESOURCE MANAGEMENT

Macinko, George, "Resource Management and Conservation: The Approach of the Brandywine Valley Association," *Land Economics*, vol. 40, 3 (1964), pp. 318–324. **4875**

Quinn, Mary Louise, "Water Management and Use in the Upper Delaware River Basin, 1890–1970," Ph.D. diss., University of California–Berkeley, 1976. [Pennsylvania and New York] **4876**

AGRICULTURE

Monmonier, Mark S., and George S. Schnell, "Spatial-Temporal Trends in Farm Mechanization: The Tractor in New York and Pennsylvania, 1930–1964," *Proceedings of the New England–St. Lawrence Valley Division, Association of American Geographers*, vol. 1 (1971), pp. 2–9. **4877**

Monmonier, Mark S., and George S. Schnell, "The Tractor in New York and Pennsylvania, 1930–1969: A Study of Geographic Trends in Agricultural Mechanization," *Proceedings of the Association of American Geographers*, vol. 4 (1972), pp. 70–75. **4878**

Schnell, George A., and Mark S. Monmonier, "Agricultural Change in the Northeast, 1954–1974," *Proceedings of the Middle States Division, Association of American Geographers*, vol. 12 (1978), pp. 85–89. **4879**

LANDSCAPE

Griswold, Erwin N., "Hunting Boundaries with Car and Camera in the Northeastern United States," *Geographical Review*, vol. 29, 3 (1939), pp. 353–382. [Boundary markers] **4880**

Pillsbury, Richard R., *Field Guide to Folk Architecture of the Northern United States* (Hanover: Dartmouth College Publications in Geography, no. 8, 1970), 99 pp. **4881**

Glassie, Henry H., "Eighteenth-Century Cultural Process in Delaware Valley Folk Building," *Winterthur Portfolio*, vol. 7 (1972), pp. 29–57. Reprinted in Dell Upton and John Michael Vlach, eds., *Common Places: Readings in Amer-*

ican Vernacular Architecture (Athens: University of Georgia Press, 1986), pp. 395–425.　**4882**

Noble, Allen G., "A Tentative Classification of Dutch Colonial Rural Houses in New York and New Jersey," Ohio Geographers: Recent Research Themes, vol. 7 (1979), pp. 31–40.　**4883**

Noble, Allen G., "Variance in Floor Plans of Dutch Houses of the Colonial Period," Pioneer America Society Transactions, vol. 3 (1980), pp. 46–56.　**4884**

O'Brien, Raymond J., American Sublime: Landscape and Scenery of the Lower Hudson Valley (New York: Columbia University Press, 1981), 353 pp.　**4885**

Matchak, Stephen, "Folk Housing in the Northeast," Ph.D. diss., University of North Carolina, 1982.　**4886**

Noble, Allen G., and Gayle Seymour, "Distribution of Barn Types in the Northeastern United States," Geographical Review, vol. 72, 2 (1982), pp. 155–170.　**4887**

Lewis, Peirce F., "The Northeast and the Making of American Geographical Habits," in Michael P. Conzen, ed., The Making of the American Landscape (Boston: Unwin Hyman, 1990), pp. 80–103.　**4888**

COMMUNICATIONS & TRADE

Brigham, Albert Perry, "The Eastern Gateway of the United States," Geographical Journal, vol. 13, 5 (1899), pp. 513–524. Reprinted in Journal of School Geography, vol. 4, 4 (1900), pp. 127–137.　**4889**

Brigham, Albert Perry, "The Great Roads across the Appalachians," Bulletin of the American Geographical Society, vol. 37, 6 (1905), pp. 321–339.　**4890**

Brigham, Albert Perry, From Trail to Railway through the Appalachians (Boston: Ginn & Co., 1907), 188 pp.　**4891**

Raup, Hallock F., "The Susquehanna Corridor: A Neglected Trans-Appalachian Route," Geographical Review, vol. 30, 3 (1940), pp. 439–450.　**4892**

Monmonier, Mark S., "Railroad Abandonment in Delmarva: The Effect of Orientation on the Probability of Link Severance in a Transport Network," Proceedings of the Pennsylvania Academy of Science, vol. 44 (1970), pp. 27–31. [Focus on 1869–1969]　**4893**

Monmonier, Mark S., "Maps in the New York Times, 1860–1980: A Study in the History of Journalistic Cartography," Proceedings of the Penn-

sylvania Academy of Science, vol. 58 (1984), pp. 79–83.　**4894**

Monmonier, Mark S., "The Geography of Change in the Newspaper Industry of the Northeast United States, 1940–1980," Proceedings of the Pennsylvania Academy of Science, vol. 60 (1986), pp. 55–59.　**4895**

Monmonier, Mark S., "The Geography of Group Ownership of Daily Newspapers in the Northeast United States, 1940–1985," Proceedings of the Pennsylvania Academy of Science, vol. 61 (1987), pp. 73–77.　**4896**

MANUFACTURING & INDUSTRIALIZATION

Kury, Theodore W., "Historical Geography of the Iron Industry in the New York–New Jersey Highlands: 1700–1900," Ph.D. diss., Louisiana State University, 1968.　**4897**

Cochran, Thomas D., "Early Industrialization in the Delaware and Susquehanna River Areas: A Regional Analysis," Social Science History, vol. 1, 3 (1977), pp. 283–306.　**4898**

URBAN NETWORKS & URBANIZATION

Browning, Clyde E., Population and Urbanized Area Growth in Megalopolis, 1950–1970 (Chapel Hill: University of North Carolina Department of Geography, Studies in Geography, no. 7, 1974), 97 pp.　**4899**

Frantz, Klaus, Die Großstadt Angloamerikas im 18. und 19. Jahrhundert: Strukturwandlungen und sozialräumliche Entwicklungsprozesse anhand ausgewählter Beispiele der Nordostküste (Stuttgart: Franz Steiner Verlag, 1987, Erdkundliches Wissen, vol. 77), 200 pp.　**4900**

URBAN ECONOMIC STRUCTURE

Meyer, Judith W., and Lawrence A. Brown, "Diffusion Agency Establishment: The Case of Friendly Ice Cream and Public Sector Diffusion Processes," Socio-Economic Planning Sciences, vol. 13, 5 (1979), pp. 241–249. [Focus on the northeastern United States, 1936–1974]　**4901**

Domosh, Mona, "Shaping the Commercial City: Retail Districts in Nineteenth-Century New York and Boston," Annals of the Association of American Geographers, vol. 80, 2 (1990), pp. 268–284.　**4902**

URBAN SOCIAL STRUCTURE

Frantz, Klaus, "Sozio-ökonomische Strukturen der angloamerikanischen Großstadt im Wandel des 19. Jahrhunderts: Dargestellt an Beispielen der Nordostküste," in Hans-Wilhelm Windhorst and William H. Berentsen, eds., *Beiträge zur räumlichen Prozeßforschung in den USA* (Vechta: Vechta Druckerei und Verlag, Zentralverband der Deutschen Geographen, Arbeitskreis USA, Vechtaer Arbeiten zur Geographie und Regionalwissenschaft, vol. 2, 1986), pp. 57–68.   **4903**

RECREATION & TOURISM

O'Brien, Raymond J., "The Role of Highland Aesthetics in the Creation of an Interstate Park: Geographic Conception in the Lower Hudson (1783–1909) and the Evolution of a Regional Recreation Landscape," Ph.D. diss., Rutgers University, 1975.   **4904**

PLANNING

Lipman, Jacob G., "Social and Economic Factors in Land-Use Planning in the Northeastern States," *Economic Geography*, vol. 11, 3 (1935), pp. 217–226.   **4905**

PLACE NAMES

Zelinsky, Wilbur, "Some Problems in the Distribution of Generic Terms in the Place-Names of the Northeastern United States," *Annals of the Association of American Geographers*, vol. 45, 4 (1955), pp. 319–349. Reprinted in Philip L. Wagner and Marvin W. Mikesell, eds., *Readings in Cultural Geography* (Chicago: University of Chicago Press, 1962), pp. 129–156.   **4906**

NEW ENGLAND

GENERAL

See also 1353

Alden, Edmund K., "Influence of Physical Features on New England's Development," *New England Magazine*, n.s. vol. 8 (1893), pp. 653–656.   **4907**

Shaler, Nathaniel Southgate, "Environment and Man in New England," *North American Review*, vol. 62, 475 (1896), pp. 727–739.   **4908**

Adams, James T., "The Historical Background," in John K. Wright, ed., *New England's Prospect: 1933* (New York: American Geographical Society, Special Publication no. 16, 1933), pp. 1–13.   **4909**

Wright, John K., "The Changing Geography of New England," in John K. Wright, ed., *New England's Prospect: 1933* (New York: American Geographical Society, Special Publication no. 16, 1933), pp. 459–475.   **4910**

Dodge, Stanley D., "The Frontier of New England in the Seventeenth and Eighteenth Centuries and Its Significance in American History," *Papers of the Michigan Academy of Science, Arts, and Letters*, vol. 28 (1942), pp. 435–440.   **4911**

Higbee, Edward C., "The Three Earths of New England," *Geographical Review*, vol. 42, 3 (1952), pp. 425–438. [Indian, colonial, modern]   **4912**

Boesch, Hans, "New England," *Geographica Helvetica*, vol. 11, 1 (1956), pp. 68–74.   **4913**

McManis, Douglas R., *Colonial New England: A Historical Geography* (New York: Oxford University Press, 1975), 159 pp.   **4914**

ENVIRONMENTAL CHANGE

Dieffenbach, Ferdinand, "Die vulkanischen Erscheinungen in Neu-England von 1638–1870," *Das Ausland*, vol. 47, 11 (1874), pp. 219–220. **4915**

Baron, William, "Eighteenth-Century New England Climate Variation and Its Suggested Impact on Society," *Maine Historical Society Quarterly*, vol. 21, 4 (1982), pp. 201–218.   **4916**

Smith, David C., et al., "Climate Fluctuations and Agricultural Change in Southern and Central New England, 1765–1880," *Maine Historical Society Quarterly*, vol. 21, 4 (1982), pp. 179–200. **4917**

NATIVE PEOPLES & WHITE RELATIONS

Withington, Ann F., "New England: Indians and Europeans, 1524–1675," Master's thesis, University of California–Berkeley, 1972.   **4918**

Doran, Michael F., and Berndt H. Künnecke, "The Stone Enigmas of New England," *Anthropological Journal of Canada*, vol. 15, 1 (1977), pp. 2–19.   **4919**

Cronon, William J., *Changes in the Land: Indians, Colonists, and the Ecology of New England* (New York: Hill & Wang, 1983), 241 pp.   **4920**

EXPLORATION & MAPPING

Boesch, Hans, "Eine alte Karte von Neuengland," *Geographica Helvetica*, vol. 11, 3 (1956), pp. 215–217.   **4921**

DeVorsey, Louis, Jr., "William de Brahm's Continuation of the Atlantic Pilot: An Empirically Supported Eighteenth Century Model of North Atlantic Surface Circulation," in Mary Sears and Daniel Merriman, eds., *Oceanography: The Past* (New York: Springer-Verlag, 1980), pp. 718–733.   **4922**

Danforth, Susan, "The First Official Maps of Maine and Massachusetts," *Imago Mundi*, vol. 35 (1983), pp. 37–57.   **4923**

Monmonier, Mark S., "Federal-State Cost-Sharing and the Geography of Cartography in New Hampshire and Vermont," *Proceedings of the Pennsylvania Academy of Science*, vol. 57 (1983), pp. 93–98. [Focus on 1885–1950]   **4924**

POPULAR IMAGES & EVALUATION

McManis, Douglas R., *European Impressions of the New England Coast, 1497–1620* (Chicago: University of Chicago Department of Geography, Research Paper no. 139, 1972), 147 pp. **4925**

Conron, John, "Contemplative Landscape: New England, 1870–1960," *Proceedings of the New England–St. Lawrence Valley Division, Association of American Geographers*, vol. 7 (1977), pp. 3–15.   **4926**

REGIONAL SETTLEMENT

Marsh, George Perkins, *The Goths of New England* (Middlebury, Vt.: J. Cobb, 1843), 39 pp. **4927**

James, Preston E., "The Blackstone Valley: A Study in Chorography in Southern New England," *Annals of the Association of American Geographers*, vol. 19, 2 (1929), pp. 67–110. Reprinted in Donald W. Meinig, ed., *On Geography: Selected Writings of Preston E. James* (Syracuse: Syracuse University Press, 1971), pp. 132–180.
4928

Whittlesey, Derwent S., "Coast Land and Interior Mountain Valley: A Geographical Study of Two Typical Localities in Northern New England," in John K. Wright, ed., *New England's Prospect* (New York: American Geographical Society, 1933), pp. 446–458. [Lancaster, N.H., and Ellsworth, Me.]
4929

Scofield, Edna Lois, "The Origin of Settlement Patterns in Rural New England," *Geographical Review*, vol. 28, 4 (1938), pp. 652–663.
4930

Herbst, Joseph C., "Hill Town—Valley Town: A Study in Historical Geography in New England," Master's thesis, Syracuse University, 1950.
4931

Morris, Francis Grave, "Some Aspects of the Rural Settlement of New England in Colonial Times," in L. Dudley Stamp and S. W. Wooldridge, eds., *London Essays in Geography: Rodwell Jones Memorial Volume* (Cambridge, Mass.: Harvard University Press, 1951), pp. 219–227.
4932

Barton, Bonnie, "New England Settlement: An Inquiry into the Comparability of Geographical Methodologies," Ph.D. diss., University of Michigan, 1973.
4933

Barton, Bonnie, *The Comparability of Geographic Methodologies: A Study of New England Settlement* (Ann Arbor: University of Michigan Department of Geography Publications, no. 20, 1977), 161 pp. [Focus on 1650–1800]
4934

Barton, Bonnie, "The Creation of Centrality," *Annals of the Association of American Geographers*, vol. 68, 1 (1978), pp. 34–44. [Focus on 1650–1800]
4935

Wood, Joseph S., "The Origin of the New England Village," Ph.D. diss., Pennsylvania State University, 1978.
4936

Wood, Joseph S., "Village and Community in Early Colonial New England," *Journal of Historical Geography*, vol. 8, 4 (1982), pp. 333–346. Reprinted in Robert Blair St. George, ed., *Material Life in America, 1600–1860* (Boston: Northeastern University Press, 1988), pp. 159–169.
4937

Wood, Joseph S., "Elaboration of a Settlement System: The New England Village in the Federal Period," *Journal of Historical Geography*, vol. 10, 4 (1984), pp. 331–356.
4938

Bell, Michael M., "Did New England Go Downhill?" *Geographical Review*, vol. 79, 4 (1989), pp. 450–466.
4939

POPULATION

See also 4862

Dodge, Stanley D., "A Study of Population in Vermont and New Hampshire," *Papers of the Michigan Academy of Science, Arts, and Letters*, vol. 18 (1932), pp. 131–136.
4940

Wilson, Harold F., "Population Trends in Northwestern New England, 1790–1930" *Geographical Review*, vol. 24, 2 (1934), pp. 272–277.
4941

Dodge, Stanley D., "A Study of Population Regions in New England on a New Basis," *Annals of the Association of American Geographers*, vol. 25, 4 (1935), pp. 197–210.
4942

Whitney, Herbert A., "Estimating Pre-Census Populations: A Method Suggested and Applied to the Towns of Rhode Island and Plymouth Colonies in 1689," *Annals of the Association of American Geographers*, vol. 55, 1 (1965), pp. 179–189.
4943

Vicero, Ralph D., "Immigration of French Canadians to New England, 1840–1900: A Geographical Analysis," Ph.D. diss., University of Wisconsin–Madison, 1968.
4944

Florin, John W., *Death in New England: Regional Variations in Mortality* (Chapel Hill: University of North Carolina Department of Geography, Studies in Geography, no. 3, 1971), 172 pp.
4945

Lewis, George K., "Population Change in Northern New England," *Annals of the Association of American Geographers*, vol. 62, 2 (1972), pp. 307–322. Reissued in John Fraser Hart, ed., *Regions of the United States* (New York: Harper & Row, 1972), same pagination. [Emphasis on 1940–1970]
4946

O'Keefe, Doris N., "The Geographic Mobility of Marriage Partners in Colonial New England," Master's thesis, Syracuse University, 1976.
4947

O'Keefe, Doris N., "Marriage and Migration in Colonial New England: A Study in Historical Population Geography," Syracuse University Department of Geography Discussion Paper no. 16 (1976), 42 pp.
4948

O'Keefe, Doris N., "Patterns of Marriage Migration in Colonial New England," *Proceedings of the New England–St. Lawrence Valley Division, Association of American Geographers*, vol. 6 (1976), pp. 7–9.
4949

Miller, Roger P., and Arlene C. Rengert, "Farm to Factory: Female Industrial Migration in Early Nineteenth Century New England," in Arlene C. Rengert and Janice Monk, eds., *Women and Spatial Change* (Dubuque: Kendall/Hunt, 1982), pp. 29–31.
4950

Adams, John W., and Alice B. Kasakoff, "Migration and the Family in Colonial New England:

The View from Genealogies," *Journal of Family History*, vol. 9, 1 (1984), pp. 24–43. **4951**

Darlington, James W., "Down from the Hills and into the Nation: The Migratory Behavior of Early Nineteenth Century New England College Students," Ph.D. diss., University of Kentucky, 1990. **4952**

RURAL & REGIONAL SOCIAL GEOGRAPHY

Evans, E. Estyn, "Old Ireland and New England," *Ulster Journal of Archaeology*, 3d ser., vol. 12 (1949), pp. 104–112. **4953**

Vicero, Ralph D., "Sources statistiques pour l'étude de l'immigration et du peuplement Canadien-Français en Nouvelle-Angleterre au cours du XIXe siècle," *Recherches sociographiques*, vol. 12, 3 (1971), pp. 361–372. **4954**

Mooers, Richard E., "Positively and Negatively Permeable Political Barriers to the Expansion Diffusion of Unitarianism in Early New England," *Proceedings of the Middle States Division, Association of American Geographers*, vol. 9 (1975), pp. 21–25. **4955**

Koelsch, William A., "The New England Meteorological Society, 1884–96: A Study in Professionalism," in Brian W. Blouet, ed., *The Origins of Academic Geography in the United States* (Hamden, Conn.: Shoestring Press, 1981), pp. 89–106. **4956**

Sorrell, Richard S., "The Survivance of French Canadians in New England (1865–1930): History, Geography and Demography as Destiny," *Ethnic and Racial Studies*, vol. 4, 1 (1981), pp. 91–109. **4957**

POLITICAL & ADMINISTRATIVE GEOGRAPHY

See also **4871**

Cushing, Sumner W., "The Boundaries of the New England States," *Annals of the Association of American Geographers*, vol. 10, 1 (1920), pp. 17–40. **4958**

Grochol, Andrea, "Jerusalem without Walls: A Reconsideration of the Puritan Model for the New England Towns," Master's thesis, University of Wisconsin–Madison, 1974. **4959**

LeBlanc, Robert G., "Geopolitical Conceptions and Imperial Ambitions of French-Canadian Nationalists in the Nineteenth Century: The Francophone Conquest of New England," *American Review of Canadian Studies*, vol. 15, 3 (1985), pp. 280–311. **4960**

LAND

Logan, Richard F., "Abandonment of Agricultural Lands in the Uplands of Western New England," Ph.D. diss., Harvard University, 1948. **4961**

EXTRACTIVE ACTIVITY

Ramsdell, Louis G., "Forest and Forest Resources as Factors in the Economic Development of New England," Master's thesis, University of Chicago, 1925. **4962**

Dodge, Stanley D., "The Geography of the Codfishing Industry in Colonial New England," *Bulletin of the Philadelphia Geographical Society*, vol. 25, 1 (1927), pp. 43–50. **4963**

Ackerman, Edward A., "Depletion in New England Fisheries," *Economic Geography*, vol. 14, 3 (1938), pp. 233–238. **4964**

AGRICULTURE

Gardula, Robert J., "Trends in the Nature and Intensity of Agricultural Activity in New England for the Period 1930–1960," Master's thesis, Clark University, 1962. **4965**

Lewis, Thomas R., Jr., "Declining Cigar Tobacco Production in Southern New England," *Journal of Geography*, vol. 79, 3 (1980), pp. 108-111. Reprinted in *Near the Long Tidal River: Readings in the Historical Geography of Central Connecticut* (Washington, D.C.: University Press of America, 1981), pp. 119–128. [Focus on 1950–1979] **4966**

LANDSCAPE

New England town features

Brodeur, David D., "Geographic Consequences of the Location of Some New England Town Commons and Greens," Ph.D. diss., Clark University, 1963. **4967**

Brodeur, David D., "Evolution of the New England Town Common: 1630–1966," *Professional Geographer*, vol. 19, 6 (1967), pp. 313–318. Reprinted in Christopher L. Salter, ed., *The Cultural Landscape* (Belmont, Calif.: Duxbury Press, 1971), pp. 196–201. **4968**

Nostrand, Richard L., "The Colonial New England Town," *Journal of Geography*, vol. 72, 7 (1973), pp. 45–53. **4969**

Stilgoe, John R., "The Puritan Townscape: Ideal and Reality," *Landscape*, vol. 20, 3 (1976), pp. 3–7. **4970**

Domosh, Mona, and Martyn J. Bowden, "Meetinghouse and Townhouse in New England: Architect's Territory and the Diffusion Process,"

Proceedings of the New England–St. Lawrence Valley Division, Association of American Geographers, vol. 7 (1977), pp. 24–30. **4971**

Wood, Joseph S., "The New England Village as an American Vernacular Form," in Camille Wells, ed., Perspectives on Vernacular Architecture, II (Columbia: University of Missouri Press, 1986), pp. 54–63. **4972**

Wood, Joseph S., "The Three Faces of the New England Village," North American Culture, vol. 3, 1 (1987), pp. 3–14. **4973**

Other themes

Zelinsky, Wilbur, "The New England Connecting Barn," Geographical Review, vol. 48, 4 (1958), pp. 540–553. **4974**

Stilgoe, John R., "Jack-o-Lanterns to Surveyors: The Secularization of Landscape Boundaries," Environmental Review, vol. 1, 1 (1976), pp. 14–31. **4975**

Stilgoe, John R., "The Wildering of Rural New England, 1850–1950," Proceedings of the New England–St. Lawrence Valley Division, Association of American Geographers, vol. 10 (1980), pp. 1–6. **4976**

Stilgoe, John R., "A New England Coastal Wilderness," Geographical Review, vol. 71, 1 (1981), pp. 33–50. **4977**

Krim, Arthur J., "Diffusion of Garden Cemeteries in New England," Proceedings of the New England–St. Lawrence Valley Division, Association of American Geographers, vol. 13 (1983), pp. 38–44. **4978**

COMMUNICATIONS & TRADE

Lalor, Pierce C., "The Effect of Physiography upon the Railroad Pattern of New England," Master's thesis, Clark University, 1950. **4979**

MANUFACTURING & INDUSTRIALIZATION

Keir, R. Malcolm, "Some Influences of the Sea upon the Industries of New England," Geographical Review, vol. 5, 5 (1918), pp. 399–404. **4980**

Cammett, Stuart H., "Geographic Factors Determining the Trend of Manufacturing in the Blackstone Valley," Master's thesis, Clark University, 1924. **4981**

Botts, Adelbert K., "New England Water Power: Facts and Traditions," Journal of Geography, vol. 34, 7 (1935), pp. 278–285. **4982**

Fairchild, Wilma B., "Changes in Industry in the Upper Housatonic Valley," Master's thesis, Clark University, 1937. **4983**

Kelly, Lenore H., "The Industrial Decline of New England," Master's thesis, Clark University, 1950. **4984**

Wallace, William H., "Merrimack Valley Manufacturing: Past and Present," Economic Geography, vol. 37, 4 (1961), pp. 283–308. **4985**

Frederic, Paul B., "Historical Geography of the Northern New England Sweet Corn Canning Industry," Master's thesis, Southern Illinois University, 1968. **4986**

LeBlanc, Robert G., "The Location of Manufacturing in New England in the Nineteenth Century," Ph.D. diss., University of Minnesota, 1968. **4987**

LeBlanc, Robert G., Location of Manufacturing in New England in the Nineteenth Century (Hanover: Dartmouth University Geographical Publications, no. 7, 1969), 173 pp. **4988**

URBAN NETWORKS & INDUSTRIALIZATION

McDonaugh, John P., "Differential Growth in New England Cotton Textile Cities," Proceedings of the New England–St. Lawrence Valley Division, Association of American Geographers, vol. 6 (1976), pp. 35–38. **4989**

URBAN SOCIAL STRUCTURE

Warren, Stacey, "Housing and Ideology: The Menace of the Three-Decker," Master's thesis, Clark University, 1988. **4990**

TOWNSCAPE

Krim, Arthur J., "The Three Decker as Urban Architecture in New England," Monadnock, vol. 44 (1970), pp. 45–55. **4991**

RECREATION & TOURISM

Demars, Stanford E., "Nineteenth Century Shore Resorts on Narragansett Bay," Proceedings of the New England–St. Lawrence Valley Division, Association of American Geographers, vol. 5 (1975), pp. 51–55. **4992**

Demars, Stanford E., "Changing Housing Patterns in New England Shore Resorts," Proceedings of the New England–St. Lawrence Valley Division, Association of American Geographers, vol. 6 (1976), pp. 31–34. [Nineteenth to mid-twentieth centuries] **4993**

Demars, Stanford E., "The Seaside Resort in New England: Evolution of a Settlement Form," *Proceedings of the New England–St. Lawrence Valley Division, Association of American Geographers*, vol. 10 (1980), pp. 28–31.   **4994**

Koelsch, William A., "Antebellum Harvard Students and the Recreational Exploration of the New England Landscape," *Journal of Historical Geography*, vol. 8, 4 (1982), pp. 362–372.   **4995**

PLACE NAMES

Trumbull, James S., "The Composition of Indian Geographical Names, Illustrated from the Algonkin Languages," *Connecticut Historical Society Collections*, vol. 2 (1870), pp. 1–50.   **4996**

Douglas-Lithgow, Robert A., *Dictionary of American-Indian Place and Proper Names in New England* (Salem, Mass.: Salem Press Co., 1909), 400 pp.   **4997**

Huden, John C., *Indian Place Names of New England* (New York: Museum of the American Indian, 1962), 408 pp.   **4998**

Leighly, John B., "New England Town Names Derived from Personal Names," *Names*, vol. 18, 3 (1970), pp. 155–174.   **4999**

Cerney, James W., "The Pattern of Indian-Derived Town Names in New England," *Proceedings of the New England–St. Lawrence Valley Division, Association of American Geographers*, vol. 3–4 (1975), pp. 21–26.   **5000**

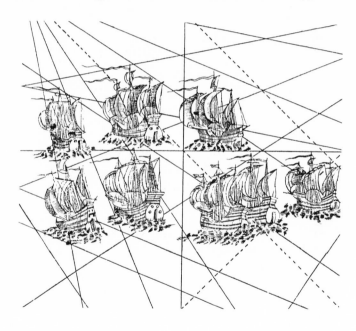

MAINE

GENERAL

Culbert, James J., "Geographic Influences in the History of Kittery, Maine," Master's thesis, Clark University, 1938.   5001

Culbert, James J., "The Coastal Features of Southwestern Maine and Their Influence upon Human Occupancy," Ph.D. diss., Clark University, 1939.   5002

Dalrymple, Paul, "An Historical Geography of Monhegan Island, Maine," Master's thesis, Syracuse University, 1952.   5003

Tobey, Ray W., "A Geographic Study of Fairfield, Maine," Master's thesis, Clark University, 1953.   5004

ENVIRONMENTAL CHANGE

Fobes, Charles B., "Historic Forest Fires in Maine," *Economic Geography*, vol. 24, 4 (1948), pp. 269–273. [Focus on 1762–1903]   5005

Smith, David C., et al., "Climatic Stress and Maine Agriculture, 1785–1885," in T. M. L. Wigley, M. J. Ingram, and G. Farmer, eds., *Climate and History: Studies in Past Climates and Their Impact on Man* (Cambridge: Cambridge University Press, 1981), pp. 450–464.   5006

EXPLORATION & MAPPING

See also 4923

Kohl, Johann Georg, *A History of the Discovery of Maine: A History of the Discovery of the East Coast of North America, Particularly the Coast of Maine, from the Northmen of 900 to the Charter of Gilbert in 1578* (Portland: Collections of the Maine Historical Society, 2d ser., 1869), 535 pp.   5007

Wise, Donald, "Surveying and Mapping the International Border in Northeast Maine, 1817–18," *Surveying and Mapping*, vol. 40, 4 (1980), pp. 419–427.   5008

REGIONAL SETTLEMENT

Konrad, Victor A., "From French Canadian to Franco-American: Late Nineteenth Century Settlement Change in the Upper St. John Valley, Maine," *Proceedings of the New England–St. Lawrence Valley Division, Association of American Geographers*, vol. 10 (1980), pp. 15–22.   5009

POPULATION

Kohn, Clyde F., "Katahdin Iron Works, Maine: A Study in Population Distribution," *Papers of the Michigan Academy of Science, Arts, and Letters*, vol. 25 (1939), pp. 397–406.   5010

Fobes, Charles B., "Path of the Settlement and Distribution of Population of Maine," *Economic Geography*, vol. 20, 1 (1944), pp. 65–69.   5011

Allen, James P., "Migration Fields of French Canadian Immigrants to Southern Maine," *Geographical Review*, vol. 62, 3 (1972), pp. 366–383.   5012

Allen, James P., "Franco-Americans in Maine: A Geographical Perspective," *Acadiensis*, vol. 4, 1 (1974), pp. 32–66.   5013

Frederic, Paul B., "Post Civil War Intra-Town Population Movements in Central Maine," *Proceedings of the New England–St. Lawrence Valley Division, Association of American Geographers*, vol. 9 (1979), pp. 34–43.   5014

RURAL & REGIONAL SOCIAL GEOGRAPHY

Allen, James P., "Variations in Catholic-Protestant Proportions among Maine Towns," *Proceedings of the Association of American Geographers*, vol. 3 (1971), pp. 15–18.   5015

Vicero, Ralph D., "Le recensement d'Odule LaPlante," *Recherches sociographiques*, vol. 12, 3 (1971), pp. 373–377. [French Canadians in Maine in 1908]   5016

POLITICAL & ADMINISTRATIVE GEOGRAPHY

See also 1391

McIntosh, Terry L., "The Electoral Geography of Maine, 1940–1960," Master's thesis, University of Chicago, 1967.   5017

LAND

Candee, Richard M., "Land Surveys of William and John Godsoe of Kittery, Maine: 1689–1769," in Peter Benes, ed., *New England Prospect: Maps, Place Names, and the Historical Landscape* (Boston: Boston University and the Dublin Seminar for New England Folklife, 1982), pp. 9–46.   5018

EXTRACTIVE ACTIVITY

Finch, Grant E., and George F. Howe, "The Lime Industry at Rockland, Maine," *Economic Geography*, vol. 6, 4 (1930), pp. 389–397. [Focus on 1729–1930]   **5019**

AGRICULTURE

Wilson, Ella M., "The Aroostook Valley: A Study in Potatoes," *Geographical Review*, vol. 16, 2 (1926), pp. 196–205.   **5020**

Wallach, Bret, "The Potato Landscape: Aroostook County, Maine," *Landscape*, vol. 23, 1 (1979), pp. 15–22.   **5021**

Smith, David C., and Anne Bridges, "Salt Marsh Dykes as a Factor in Eastern Maine Agriculture," *Maine Historical Society Quarterly*, vol. 21, 4 (1982), pp. 219–226.   **5022**

LANDSCAPE

Philbrick, Allen K., "Some Geographical Aspects of House Architectural Styles in Maine," Master's thesis, University of Chicago, 1941.   **5023**

Hubka, Thomas, "The Connected Farm Buildings in Southwestern Maine," *Pioneer America*, vol. 9, 2 (1977), pp. 143–178.   **5024**

Konrad, Victor A., "Against the Tide: French Canadian Barn Building Tradition in the St. John Valley of Maine," *American Review of Canadian Studies*, vol. 12, 2 (1982), pp. 22–36.   **5025**

COMMUNICATIONS & TRADE

Janelle, Donald G., "Temporal and Spatial Coordination of Stage Coach Service in Maine: 1826–1829," *International Geography '76*, sec. 9, *Historical Section* (Moscow: Twenty-third International Geographical Union, 1976), pp. 56–59. **5026**

Janelle, Donald G., "Stagecoach Operations in Maine, 1826–1829," *Proceedings of the Association of American Geographers*, vol. 6 (1977), pp. 15–18.   **5027**

Anderson, Hayden, "Penobscot Waterways: Canals and Waterway Improvement on the Penobscot River, 1816–1921," *Maine Historical Society Quarterly*, vol. 19, 1 (1979), pp. 21–46.   **5028**

TOWN GROWTH

Halkyard, Neil W., "Bath and the Lower Kennebec," Master's thesis, Clark University, 1951.   **5029**

Marentette, David B., "An Historical Geography of Bath, Maine: 1600 to 1920," Ph.D. diss., University of Oregon, 1983.   **5030**

URBAN ECONOMIC STRUCTURE

Small, Comstock, "Changing Functions of Boothbay Harbor: Major Aspects of the Historico-Economic Geography of an Area on the Ria Coast of Maine," Master's thesis, Syracuse University, 1951.   **5031**

URBAN SOCIAL STRUCTURE

Sobel, Joel, "Occupational and Nativity Group Residence in Nineteenth Century Portland, Maine," *Iowa Geographic*, vol. 29 (1972), pp. 15–19.   **5032**

RECREATION & TOURISM

Judd, Richard W., "Reshaping Maine's Landscape: Rural Culture, Tourism, and Conservation, 1890–1929," *Journal of Forest History*, vol. 32, 4 (1988), pp. 180–190.   **5033**

PLACE NAMES

Chadbourne, Ava H., *Maine Place Names and the Peopling of Its Towns* (Portland: B. Wheelwright Co., 1955), 530 pp. Revised 1970.   **5034**

Churchill, Edwin, "Evolution of Maine Place Names," *Maine Historical Society Quarterly*, vol. 29, 2 (1989), pp. 66–91.   **5035**

NEW HAMPSHIRE

GENERAL

Perry, Robert F., "A Study in Historical Geography of Old Number Four: Charlestown, New Hampshire," Master's thesis, Syracuse University, 1950.   5036

Wallace, William H., "A Hard Land for a Tough People: A Historical Geography of New Hampshire," *New Hampshire Profiles*, vol. 24, 4 (1975), pp. 21–32.   5037

EXPLORATION & MAPPING

See 4924

REGIONAL SETTLEMENT

Goldthwait, James W., "A Town That Has Gone Down Hill," *Geographical Review*, vol. 17, 4 (1927), pp. 527–552. [Lyme, 1790–1925]   5038

Wallace, William H., "Some Aspects of Colonial Settlement in New Hampshire," *Proceedings of the New England–St. Lawrence Valley Division, Association of American Geographers*, vol. 7 (1977), pp. 16–24.   5039

POPULATION

See 4940

LAND & LAND USE

Torbert, Edward N., "The Evolution of Land Utilization in Lebanon, New Hampshire," Ph.D. diss., University of Chicago, 1931.   5040

Torbert, Edward N., "The Evolution of Land Utilization in Lebanon, New Hampshire," *Geographical Review*, vol. 25, 2 (1935), pp. 209–230.   5041

LANDSCAPE

Willits, Ruth C., "The Old Hayes Farm: Abandoned," *Bulletin of the Philadephia Geographical Society*, vol. 19, 1 (1921), pp. 9–13. [Located in the White Mountains]   5042

Wallace, William H., *Commons and Meeting Houses in New Hampshire* (Durham: University of New Hampshire Department of Geography, for the Eastern Historical Geography Association Annual Meeting, September 1991), 25 pp. and 24 leaves of illustrations.   5043

Wallace, William H., *Commons and Meeting Houses in New Hampshire: Field Excursion* (Durham: University of New Hampshire Department of Geography, for the Eastern Historical Geography Association Annual Meeting, September 1991), 46 pp. [Focus on southern New Hampshire]   5044

PLACE NAMES

Hunt, Elmer M., *New Hampshire Town Names and Whence They Came* (Peterborough: Noone House, 1971), 282 pp.   5045

VERMONT

GENERAL

See also 1144

The state

Lamson, Genevieve, "Geographic Influences in the Early History of Vermont," Master's thesis, University of Chicago, 1922.				**5046**

Local areas

Dodge, Stanley D., "The Vermont Valley: A Chorographical Study," *Papers of the Michigan Academy of Science, Arts, and Letters*, vol. 16 (1931), pp. 241–274.				**5047**

ENVIRONMENTAL CHANGE

Siccama, Thomas, "Presettlement and Present Forest Vegetation in Northern Vermont with Special Reference to Chittenden County," *American Midland Naturalist*, vol. 85, 1 (1971), pp. 153–172.				**5048**

NATIVE PEOPLES & WHITE RELATIONS

Calloway, Colin G., "Green Mountain Diaspora: Indian Population Movements in Vermont, ca.1600–1800," *Vermont History*, vol. 54, 4 (1986), pp. 197–228.				**5049**

EXPLORATION & MAPPING

See also 4924

Cobb, David A., "Vermont Maps Prior to 1900: An Annotated Cartobibliography," Master's thesis, University of Vermont, 1970.				**5050**

Shea, Philip, "A New and Accurate Map of Philip's Grant," *Vermont History*, vol. 53, 1 (1985), pp. 36–42.				**5051**

POPULAR IMAGES & EVALUATION

Gade, Daniel W., "L'image du Vermont: Mythologie américaine et réalité géographique," *Cahiers de géographie du Québec*, vol. 21, nos. 53–54 (1977), pp. 221–242.				**5052**

REGIONAL SETTLEMENT

See also 4860

Andrews, M. L., "The Evolution of Settlement in Orange County, Vermont, 1760–1960," Master's thesis, McGill University, 1964.				**5053**

POPULATION

See also 4940

Stillwell, Lewis D., "Migration from Vermont, 1776–1860," *Proceedings of the Vermont Historical Society*, vol. 5, 2 (1937), pp. 63–245.				**5054**

Meeks, Harold A., "An Isochronic Map of Vermont Settlement," *Vermont History*, vol. 38, 2 (1970), pp. 95–102.				**5055**

Bassett, T. D. Seymour, "Migration to Vermont, 1761–1836," *Vermont Geographer*, vol. 2 (1975), pp. 7–20.				**5056**

RURAL & REGIONAL SOCIAL GEOGRAPHY

Vicero, Ralph D., "French-Canadian Settlement in Vermont Prior to the Civil War," *Professional Geographer*, vol. 23, 4 (1971), pp. 290–294.				**5057**

Meyer, Douglas K., "Union Colony, 1836–1870: Pattern and Process in Growth," *Vermont History*, vol. 41, 3 (1973), pp. 147–157.				**5058**

POLITICAL & ADMINISTRATIVE GEOGRAPHY

Bigelow, Bruce L., "Abolition and Prohibition Themes for an Historical Geography of Vermont, 1841–1850," Master's thesis, Pennsylvania State University, 1970.				**5059**

Laks, Richard, and Harold A. Meeks, "The Line Which Separates Vermonters from Canadians: A Short History of Vermont's Northern Border with Quebec," *Vermont History*, vol. 44, 2 (1976), pp. 71–77.				**5060**

ECONOMIC DEVELOPMENT

See also 1404

Tucker, Robert G., "Hydroelectric Power and the Development of the Utility Industry in Vermont: A Study in Historical Geography," Master's thesis, 1986.				**5061**

RESOURCE MANAGEMENT

May, Julie A., and Robert R. Churchill, "The Spatial and Temporal Structure of Solid-Waste

Disposal Facilities in Vermont: 1900–1980," *Proceedings of the New England–St. Lawrence Valley Division, Association of American Geographers*, vol. 14 (1984), pp. 108–116.   5062

LAND & LAND USE

Meeks, Harold A., "A Land Use History," in his *Time and Change in Vermont: A Human Geography* (Chester, Conn.: Globe Pequot Press, 1986), pp. 5–200.   5063

Meeks, Harold A., *Vermont's Land and Resources* (Shelburne, Vt.: New England Press, 1986), 332 pp.   5064

AGRICULTURE

Illick, J. Rowland, "Agricultural Trends in the Southern Champlain Valley of Vermont, 1940–1980," *Proceedings of the New England–St. Lawrence Valley Division, Association of American Geographers*, vol. 13 (1983), pp. 12–21.   5065

Rumney, Thomas A., "The Hops Boom in Nineteenth Century Vermont," *Vermont History*, vol. 56, 1 (1988), pp. 36–41.   5066

LANDSCAPE

Meyer, John, "The Village Green Ensemble in Northern Vermont," *Vermont Geographer*, vol. 2 (1975), pp. 21–42.   5067

McHenry, Stewart G., "Vermont Barns: A Cultural Landscape Analysis," *Proceedings of the New England–St. Lawrence Valley Division, Association of American Geographers*, vol. 6 (1976), pp. 19–21.   5068

McHenry, Stewart G., "The Colonial Dutch Landscape Legacy in Vermont," *Proceedings of the New England–St. Lawrence Valley Division, Association of American Geographers*, vol. 7 (1977), pp. 37–44.   5069

McHenry, Stewart G., "Eighteenth Century Field Patterns as Vernacular Art," *Old-Time New England*, vol. 69, 1–2 (Summer-Fall 1978), pp. 1–21. Reprinted in Dell Upton and John Michael Vlach, eds., *Common Places: Readings in American Vernacular Architecture* (Athens: University of Georgia Press, 1986), pp. 107–123.   5070

McHenry, Stewart G., "Vermont Barns: A Cultural Landscape Analysis," *Vermont History*, vol. 46, 3 (1978), pp. 151–156.   5071

Dorney, Jane E., "The Stone Wall Landscape of the Green Mountains," Master's thesis, University of Vermont, 1988.   5072

COMMUNICATIONS & TRADE

Wilson, Harold F., "The Roads of Windsor," *Geographical Review*, vol. 21, 3 (1931), pp. 379–397. [Focus on 1763–1930]   5073

Wood, Joseph S., "Road Network and Regional Interaction in Vermont: 1796–1824," Master's thesis, University of Vermont, 1973.   5074

Wood, Joseph S., "The Road Network and Interaction in Vermont: 1796–1824," *Vermont Geographer*, vol. 2 (1975), pp. 53–64.   5075

MANUFACTURING & INDUSTRIALIZATION

Steponaitis, Louis W., Jr., "The Textile Industry in Vermont, 1790–1973: Its Development, Diffusion, and Decline," Master's thesis, University of Vermont, 1975.   5076

Tear, Jacqueline D., "Spatial and Structural Changes in Vermont Manufacturing since World War II," Master's thesis, University of Vermont, 1981.   5077

URBAN NETWORKS & URBANIZATION

LaRose, Bruce L., "The Emergence of the Vermont Settlement Pattern, 1609–1830," Master's thesis, Clark University, 1967.   5078

Bowden, Martyn J., Bruce L. LaRose, and Brian Mishara, "The Development of Competition between Central Places on the Frontier: Vermont, 1790–1830," *Proceedings of the Association of American Geographers*, vol. 3 (1971), pp. 32–38.   5079

TOWN GROWTH

Orr, David W., "The Port of Burlington, Vermont: Site and Situation; A Study in Historical Geography," Master's thesis, University of Vermont, 1972.   5080

Orr, David W., "Historical Geography of the Lakeport of Burlington, Vermont," *Vermont Geographer*, vol. 2 (1975), pp. 43–52.   5081

URBAN ECONOMIC STRUCTURE

Baker, Susan R., "The Changing Retail Structure of Burlington, Vermont, 1885–1969," *Proceedings of the New England–St. Lawrence Valley Division, Association of American Geographers*, vol. 14 (1984), pp. 78–90.   5082

Baker, Susan R., "The Evolving Retail Structure of Burlington, Vermont, 1885 to 1969," Master's thesis, University of Vermont, 1985.　　5083

RECREATION & TOURISM

Meeks, Harold A., "Stagnant, Smelly, and Successful: Vermont's Mineral Springs," *Vermont History*, vol. 47, 1 (1979), pp. 5–20.　　5084

PLACE NAMES

Leighly, John B., "Gallic Place-Names for Vermont, 1785," *Names*, vol. 21 (1973), pp. 65–74. Reprinted, with emendations, in *Vermont History*, vol. 42, 1 (1974), pp. 12–21.　　5085

Swift, Esther M., *Vermont Place-Names: Footprints of History* (Brattleboro: S. Greene Press, 1977), 701 pp.　　5086

Seymour-Bassett, Thomas D., "Why the Vermont Mountains Were Called Green," *Vermont Geographer*, vol. 3 (1984), pp. 1–6.　　5087

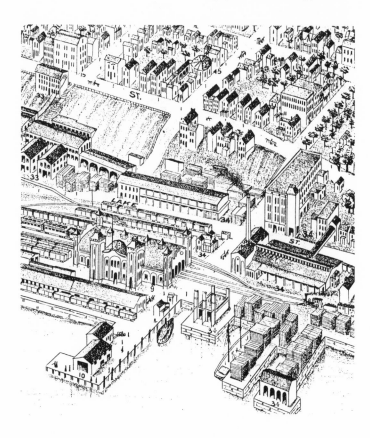

MASSACHUSETTS

GENERAL

See also 1324

The state

Keir, R. Malcolm, "Some Influences of Environment in Massachusetts," Ph.D. diss., University of Pennsylvania, 1917.   5088

Keir, R. Malcolm, "Some Responses to Environment in Massachusetts," *Bulletin of the Philadelphia Geographical Society*, vol. 15, 4 (1917), pp. 167–185.   5089

Smaller areas

Orr, William, Jr., "The Geographic Features of the Connecticut Valley in Western Massachusetts," *Journal of Geography*, vol. 1, 3 (1897), pp. 72–78.
                                                                      5090

Brigham, Albert Perry, "Cape Cod and the Old Colony," *Geographical Review*, vol. 10, 1 (1920), pp. 1–22.   5091

Brigham, Albert Perry, *Cape Cod and the Old Colony* (New York: G. P. Putnam's Sons, 1920), 284 pp.   5092

Clune, Mary C., "The Geographic Factors in the Development of the Massachusetts Towns of the Connecticut Valley," Ph.D. diss., Clark University, 1922.   5093

Saunders, Richard M., "Historical Geography of Cape Ann," Master's thesis, Clark University, 1925.   5094

Madigan, Thomas E., "Change and Growth in a New England Upland Town: A Geographic Study of Ware, Massachusetts," Master's thesis, Ohio State University, 1954.   5095

Spector, Anthony J., "An East Coast Contrast: Franklin County, Massachusetts in the Early Nineteenth Century," in Michael P. Conzen and Linda S. Lim, eds., *Illinois Canal Country: The Early Years in Comparative Perspective* (Chicago: University of Chicago Committee on Geographical Studies, Studies on the Illinois & Michigan Canal Corridor, no. 5, 1991), pp. 117-136.   5096

ENVIRONMENTAL CHANGE

Hubbard, Edwin L., "The Effects of Numerous Old Mill Dams on Lower Basin Stream Development: 250 Years of Industrial Use of the French River and its Tributaries, Southern Worcester

County, Massachusetts," Ph.D. diss., Clark University, 1979.   5097

NATIVE PEOPLES & WHITE RELATIONS

Hearn, Lea T., "Life of the Aborigines along the Taunton River Basin," Master's thesis, Clark University, 1948.   5098

EXPLORATION & MAPPING

See also 4923

Reps, John W., "Boston by Bostonians: The Printed Plans and Views of the Colonial City by Its Artists, Cartographers, Engravers, and Publishers," in Walter Muir Whitehill and Sinclair H. Hitchings, eds., *Boston Prints and Printmakers, 1670–1775* (Boston: Colonial Society of Massachusetts, Publications, vol. 46, 1973), pp. 3–56.
                                                                      5099

Meigs, Peveril, III, "John G. Hales, Boston Geographer and Surveyor, 1785–1832," *New England Historical and Genealogical Register*, vol. 129, 1 (1975), pp. 23–29.   5100

Cumming, William P., "Colonial Charting of the Massachusetts Coast," in P. C. F. Smith, ed., *Seafaring in Colonial Massachusetts* (Boston: Colonial Society of Massachusetts, 1980), pp. 67–118.
                                                                      5101

POPULAR IMAGES & EVALUATION

Hoyt, Joseph B., "The Historical Geography of Berkshire County, Massachusetts: A Study of Man's Changing Evaluation of a Physical Setting," Ph.D. diss., Clark University, 1954.   5102

Lloyd, William J., "A Social-Literary Geography of Late Nineteenth-Century Boston," in Douglas C. D. Pocock, ed., *Humanistic Geography and Literature: Essays on the Experience of Place* (Totowa, N.J.: Barnes & Noble, 1981), pp. 173–189.   5103

REGIONAL SETTLEMENT

Klimm, Lester E., "The Relation between Certain Population Changes and the Physical Environment in Hampden, Hampshire, and Franklin Counties, Massachusetts, 1790–1925," Ph.D. diss., University of Pennsylvania, 1930.   5104

Botts, Adelbert K., "Northbridge, Massachusetts: A Town That Moved Downhill," *Journal of Geography*, vol. 33, 7 (1934), pp. 249–260. Reprinted

in George J. Miller, ed., *Human Geography Studies: The United States* (Bloomington, Ill.: McKnight & McKnight, Geographic Education Series, 1935), pp. 28–39. [Focus on c.1800–1930]
5105

Al-Khashab, Wafiq H., "Population and Settlement of Holden, Massachusetts," Master's thesis, Clark University, 1955.
5106

Vaughn, Thomas, "A Test of the Dispersion Hypothesis on the Settlement Patterns of Colonial New England," Master's thesis, Boston University, 1972. [Focus on Andover, 1650-1693, and Brockton, 1710-1750]
5107

Swedlund, Alan C., "Population Growth and Settlement Pattern in Franklin and Hampshire Counties, Massachusetts, 1650–1850," *American Antiquity*, vol. 40, 2 (1975), pp. 22–33.
5108

POPULATION

See also **1344, 4943**

Rimbert, Sylvie, "L'immigration franco-canadienne au Massachusetts," *Revue canadienne de géographie*, vol. 8, 3–4 (1954), pp. 75–85.
5109

Laing, Jean, "The Pattern of Population Trends in Massachusetts," *Economic Geography*, vol. 31, 3 (1955), pp. 265–271. [Focus on 1870–1950]
5110

Seig, Louis, "Population Change in the Springfield-Chicopee-Holyoke Commuter Region," *Rocky Mountain Social Science Journal*, vol. 7, 1 (1970), pp. 77–88. [Focus on 1790–1970]
5111

Kelly, Cathy, "Marriage Migration in Massachusetts, 1765–1790," Syracuse University Department of Geography Discussion Paper no. 30 (1977), 51 pp.
5112

Kelly, Cathy, "Migration of Marriage Partners: Massachusetts, 1765–1790," Master's thesis, Syracuse University, 1977.
5113

RURAL & REGIONAL SOCIAL GEOGRAPHY

Van Cleef, Eugene, "The Finns of Cape Cod," *New England Quarterly*, vol. 6, 3 (1933), pp. 597–601.
5114

Brodeur, David D., "The Decline of Private Estates in Eastern Essex County, Massachusetts," Master's thesis, Clark University, 1960.
5115

Fletcher, R. Louise, "Shakerland: A Topographic History," *Landscape*, vol. 21, 3 (1977), pp. 36–44. [Focus on the eighteenth and nineteenth centuries]
5116

Hunter, John M., and Gary W. Shannon, "Exercises on Distance Decay Using Mental Health

Historical Data," *Journal of Geography*, vol. 83, 6 (1984), pp. 277–285.
5117

Hunter, John M., "Need and Demand for Mental Health Care: Massachusetts, 1854," *Geographical Review*, vol. 77, 2 (1987), pp. 139–156.
5118

POLITICAL & ADMINISTRATIVE GEOGRAPHY

Kasperson, Roger E., "The Know-Nothing Movement in Massachusetts, 1853–1857: A Study in Historical-Political Geography," Master's thesis, University of Chicago, 1961.
5119

McCutcheon, Henry R., "Town Formation in Eastern Massachusetts, 1630–1802: A Case Study in Political Area Organization," Ph.D. diss., Clark University, 1970.
5120

ECONOMIC DEVELOPMENT

Meigs, Peveril, III, "Energy in Early Boston," *New England Historical and Genealogical Register*, vol. 128, 2 (1974), pp. 83–90. [Focus on tide mills]
5121

Peters, Kim M., "Economic Development in the Boston Subregion, 1760–1850," Master's thesis, University of Wisconsin–Madison, 1983.
5122

RESOURCE MANAGEMENT

Boucher, Phyllis R., "Plymouth: A Study of Historical Landmarks as a Factor in Land Use," Master's thesis, Clark University, 1955.
5123

LAND & LAND USE

Land tenure

Farnsworth, Albert H., "Geographic Factors Influencing the Evolution of Land Tenure at Wellfleet, Massachusetts," Master's thesis, Clark University, 1940.
5124

Lowenthal, David, "The Common and Undivided Lands of Nantucket," *Geographical Review*, vol. 46, 3 (1956), pp. 399–403.
5125

Greven, Philip, Jr., "Old Patterns in the New World: The Distribution of Land in Seventeenth-Century Andover," *Essex Institute Historical Collections*, vol. 101 (1965), pp. 133–48. Reprinted, with omissions, in David Ward, ed., *Geographic Perspectives on America's Past: Readings on the Historical Geography of the United States* (New York: Oxford University Press, 1979), pp. 121–128.
5126

Hall, John, "The Three Rank System of Land Distribution in Colonial Swansea, Massachusetts,"

Rhode Island History, vol. 43, 1 (1984), pp. 3–17.
5127

Land use

Roper, Mary A., "Land Utilization of the Town of Princeton, Massachusetts," Master's thesis, Clark University, 1944. **5128**

Ma Thin Kyi, "Changes in Agricultural Land Utilization in Hampshire County, Massachusetts," Ph.D. diss., Clark University, 1952. **5129**

Al-Mayah, Ali M., "Agricultural Land Use, Town of Holden, Worcester County, Massachusetts," Master's thesis, Clark University, 1956. **5130**

Vincent, David E., "Lake Quinsigamond: An Assessment of Past and Present Land Use," Master's thesis, Clark University, 1963. **5131**

Saurino, Mary A., "Land Use Change in Three Connecticut River Valley Towns, 1940–1980," *Proceedings of the New England–St. Lawrence Valley Division, Association of American Geographers*, vol. 12 (1982), pp. 1–18. [Amherst, Hadley, and South Hadley] **5132**

Kelly, Cathy, "A Case Study of Changing Land Use: Nineteenth Century Berkshire County, Massachusetts," *Proceedings of the New England–St. Lawrence Valley Division, Association of American Geographers*, vol. 15 (1985), pp. 49–56. **5133**

AGRICULTURE

Hickey, Kevin L., "Von Thünen on the Boston Fringe, 1860–1880; With Emphasis on Farmer Persistence as a Factor in Agricultural Change," Master's thesis, Boston University, 1972. **5134**

LANDSCAPE

Whitehill, Walter M., "The Topography of Essex County in 1859," *Essex Institute Historical Collections*, vol. 95, 2 (1959), pp. 69–81. **5135**

Raup, Hugh M., "The View from John Sanderson's Farm: A Perspective for the Use of Land," *Journal of Forest History*, vol. 10, 1 (1966), pp. 2–11. [Petersham, Mass.] **5136**

St. Pierre, Susan M., "Cultural Landscape Change at Salem, Massachusetts, from 1626 to 1660," Master's thesis, Western Illinois University, 1979. **5137**

Zimmerman, Sarah, et al., *Historical and Archeological Resources of the Connecticut Valley* (Boston: Massachusetts Historical Commission, 1984), 321 pp. **5138**

Steinitz, Michael P., "Landmark and Shelter: Domestic Architecture in the Cultural Landscape of the Central Uplands of Massachusetts in the Eighteenth Century," Ph.D. diss., Clark University, 1988. **5139**

Steinitz, Michael P., "Rethinking Geographical Approaches to the Common House: The Evidence from Eighteenth-Century Massachusetts," in Thomas Carter and Bernard L. Herman, eds., *Perspectives in Vernacular Architecture, III* (Columbia: University of Missouri Press, for the Vernacular Architecture Forum, 1989), pp. 16–26. **5140**

Garrison, J. Ritchie, *Landscape and Material Life in Franklin County, Massachusetts, 1770–1860* (Knoxville: University of Tennessee Press, 1991), 320 pp. **5141**

COMMUNICATIONS & TRADE

Transport

Babson, Thomas, "Evolution of Cape Ann Roads and Transportation, 1623–1955," *Essex Institute Historical Collections*, vol. 91, 4 (1955), pp. 302–328. **5142**

Fayne, Francis A., "Onshore Aids to Navigation along Outer Cape Cod; A Human Response to Its Shipwrecks: A Study in Historical Geography," Master's thesis, University of Vermont, 1980. **5143**

Berman, Mildred, "Salem's Maritime Activities: A Bentley-Eye View," *Essex Institute Historical Collections*, vol. 119, 1 (1983), pp. 18–27. **5144**

Newspapers

Lotstein, Enid L., "An Analysis of Newspaper Information on the Blizzard of 1888: A Modification of Needham's Cosmopolite-Localite Model," *Proceedings of the New England–St. Lawrence Valley Division, Association of American Geographers*, vol. 15 (1985), pp. 66–75. **5145**

Trade

Blodgett, Michael L., "Greenfield, Massachusetts: Its Merchants and Functions, 1790–1836," *Proceedings of the New England–St. Lawrence Valley Division, Association of American Geographers*, vol. 6 (1976), pp. 28–31. **5146**

Rose, Gregory S., "Reconstructing a Retail Trade Area: Tucker's General Store, 1850–1860," *Professional Geographer*, vol. 39, 1 (1987), pp. 33–40. [Dartmouth, Bristol Co.] **5147**

MANUFACTURING & INDUSTRIALIZATION

Spence, Vina E., "The Manufacturing Industries of the City of Chicopee, Massachusetts," Master's thesis, Clark University, 1930. **5148**

Botts, Adelbert K., "Industrial Geography of Northbridge, Massachusetts," Master's thesis, Clark University, 1931. **5149**

Gronvold, Eunice, "The Industrial Development of the Upper French River Valley," Master's thesis, Clark University, 1931. [Environs of Worcester] **5150**

Cash, Myrtle, "Industrial Geography of Clinton, Massachusetts," Master's thesis, Clark University, 1932. **5151**

Waites, Sara F., "The Industrial Geography of Millbury, Massachusetts," Master's thesis, Clark University, 1933. **5152**

Myers, Merle W., "The Industrial Geography of the Town of Grafton," Master's thesis, Clark University, 1937. **5153**

Huffington, Paul, and J. Nelson Clifford, "Evolution of Shipbuilding in Southeastern Massachusetts," *Economic Geography*, vol. 15, 4 (1939), pp. 362–378. **5154**

Potter, Elaine I., "Industrial Development of Dalton, Massachusetts," Master's thesis, Clark University, 1958. **5155**

Erickson, Marcia D., "The Changing Significance of Manufacturing in the Millers River Valley, Massachusetts," Master's thesis, Clark University, 1959. **5156**

Gardula, Robert J., "Intraurban Spatial Patterns of Industrial Structural Expenditures, Worcester, Massachusetts, 1944–1972," Ph.D. diss., Clark University, 1975. **5157**

Bathelt, Harald, "Industrieller Wandel in der Region Boston: Ein Beitrag zum Standortsverhalten von Schlüsseltechnologie-Industrien," *Geographische Zeitschrift*, vol. 78 (1990), pp. 150–175. **5158**

TOWN GROWTH

Boston and environs

Gulliver, Frederic P., "The Geographical Development of Boston," *Journal of Geography*, vol. 2, 6 (1903), pp. 323–329. **5159**

Ackerman, Edward A., "Sequent Occupance of a Boston Suburban Community," *Economic Geography*, vol. 17, 1 (1941), pp. 61–74. [Concord] **5160**

Vance, James E., Jr., "The Growth of Suburbanization West of Boston: A Geographic Study of Transportation-Settlement Relationships," Ph.D. diss., Clark University, 1952. **5161**

Conzen, Michael P., "Town into Suburb: Boston's Expanding Fringe," in Clyde E. Browning, ed., *Population and Urbanized Area Growth in Megalopolis, 1950–1970* (Chapel Hill: University of North Carolina, Studies in Geography, no. 7 (1974), pp. 37–49. **5162**

Conzen, Michael P., "Time and Place," in Michael P. Conzen and George K. Lewis, *Boston: A Geographical Portrait* (Cambridge, Mass.: Ballinger Publishing Co., 1976), pp. 3–17. **5163**

Other centers

Waterman, Nancy M., "Evolution and Delimitation of Quinsigamond Village," Master's thesis, Clark University, 1952. **5164**

Kent, Lillian W., "Fitchburg and Leominster, Massachusetts: A Comparative Study of Two Small New England Cities," Master's thesis, Clark University, 1964. **5165**

Seig, Louis, "Concepts of Change and the Historical Method in Geography: The Case of Springfield, Massachusetts," Ph.D. diss., University of Minnesota, 1968. **5166**

URBAN ECONOMIC STRUCTURE

See also 1447, 1466, 4661, 4663, 4902

Boston

Shurtleff, Arthur A., "The Boston Park System," *Journal of Geography*, vol. 2, 6 (1903), pp. 302–314. **5167**

Lanier, Mary Jean, "The Earlier Development of Boston as a Commercial Center," Ph.D. diss., University of Chicago, 1924. **5168**

Vance, James E., Jr., "Labor-Shed, Employment Field, and Dynamic Analysis in Urban Geography," *Economic Geography*, vol. 36, 3 (1960), pp. 189–200. [Focus on Natick, 1880s–1950] **5169**

Ward, David, "The Industrial Revolution and the Emergence of Boston's Central Business District," *Economic Geography*, vol. 42, 2 (1966), pp. 152–171. **5170**

Hoffman, Stephen, "The Locational Behavior of Machinery Firms in Boston, 1850–1880," Master's thesis, Boston University, 1976. **5171**

Worcester

Chin, Eugene S. T., "Distribution and Movement of Drug Stores in Worcester, Massachusetts, 1900–1950," Master's Thesis, Clark University, 1956. **5172**

Tucker, Grady O., "Development of the Central Business Area of Worcester, Massachusetts," Ph.D. diss., Clark University, 1958. **5173**

Other centers

Means, George R., "The Industrial Development of Webster, Massachusetts," Master's thesis, Clark University, 1932. 5174

Clifford, J. Nelson, "The Evolution of Industry at Quincy, Massachusetts," Master's thesis, Clark University, 1938. 5175

Clifford, J. Nelson, "The Granite Industry of Quincy, Massachusetts," *Economic Geography*, vol. 15, 2 (1939), pp. 146–152. [Focus on 1837–1936] 5176

Withington, William A., "The Impact of Residential Growth on Land Use in a Suburb, 1930–1953: Winchester, Massachusetts," Ph.D. diss., Northwestern University, 1955. 5177

Peddle, James A., "The Development and Growth of Functional Areas in Everett, Massachusetts from 1880 to 1960," Master's thesis, Miami University of Ohio, 1965. 5178

Vance, James E., Jr., "Housing the Worker: The Employment Linkage as a Force in Urban Structure," *Economic Geography*, vol. 42, 4 (1966), pp. 294–325. [Focus in part on Lowell and Holyoke, 1820s–1850s] 5179

Parker, Margaret T., "Lowell: A Study in Industrial Development, " Ph.D. diss., University of Chicago, 1939. Published under the same title in a University of Chicago Libraries Private Edition, 1940, 238 pp.; republished New York: Kennikat Press, 1970. 5180

Donnell, Robert P., "Locational Response to Catastrophe: The Dynamics of Locational Change in the Shoe and Leather Industry of Salem, Massachusetts, after the Conflagration of June 25, 1914," Master's thesis, Clark University, 1971. 5181

Donnell, Robert P., "Locational Response to Catastrophe: The Shoe and Leather Industry of Salem, Massachusetts, after the Conflagration of June 25, 1914," Syracuse University Department of Geography Discussion Paper, no. 20 (1976), 17 pp. Revised under the title "Locational Response to Catastrophe: The Shoe and Leather Industry of Salem after the Conflagration of June 25, 1914," *Essex Institute Historical Collections*, vol. 113, 2 (1977), pp. 105–116. 5182

URBAN SOCIAL STRUCTURE

See also 4710

Boston

Murphey, Rhoads, "Boston's Chinatown," *Economic Geography*, vol. 28, 3 (1952), pp. 244–255. [Focus on 1835–1950] 5183

Ward, David, "Nineteenth Century Boston: A Study in the Role of Antecedent and Adjacent Conditions in the Spatial Aspects of Urban Growth," Ph.D. diss., University of Wisconsin–Madison, 1963. 5184

Ward, David, "Antecedence and Adjacence: Locational Attributes of Central Residential Districts in Nineteenth Century Boston," *Proceedings of the Twenty-fourth International Geographical Union* (London) (1964), pp. 277–278. 5185

Radford, John P., "Black in Boston," *Journal of Interdisciplinary History*, vol. 12, 4 (1982), pp. 677–684. 5186

Pred, Allan R., "Structuration, Biography Formation, and Knowledge: Observations on Port Growth during the Late Mercantile Period," *Environment and Planning D: Society and Space*, vol. 2 (1984), pp. 251–275. Revised as "Biography Formation, Knowledge Acquisition, and the Growth and Transformation of Cities during the Late Mercantile Period: The Case of Boston, 1783–1812," in Allan R. Pred, *Making Histories and Constructing Human Geographies: The Local Transformation of Practice, Power Relations, and Consciousness* (Boulder: Westview Press, 1990), pp. 41–75. 5187

Worcester

Zeller, Rose, "Changes in the Ethnic Composition and Character of Worcester's Population," Ph.D. diss., Clark University, 1940. 5188

Thompson, Bryan, "Cultural Ties as Determinants of Immigrant Settlement in Urban Areas: A Case Study of the Growth of an Italian Immigrant Neighborhood in Worcester, Massachusetts, 1875–1922," Ph.D. diss., Clark University, 1971. 5189

Weiss, Edwin T., "Patterns and Processes of High Value Residential Districts: The Case of Worcester, 1713–1970," Ph.D. diss., Clark University, 1973. 5190

Solomon, Leslie D., "The Structure of the Spatial Delivery of Medical Services: The Case of Maternity Services in Worcester, Massachusetts, between 1940 and 1970," Ph.D. diss., Clark University, 1974. 5191

Meyer, William B., and Michael Brown, "Locational Conflict in a Nineteenth Century City," *Political Geography Quarterly*, vol. 8, 2 (1989), pp. 107–122. [Worcester, 1871–1875] 5192

Other centers

Fonseca, James W., "The Portuguese Community in New Bedford, Massachusetts," *Proceedings of the New England–St. Lawrence Valley Divi-*

sion, *Association of American Geographers*, vol. 6 (1976), pp. 21–24.   **5193**

Berman, Mildred, "The Shape of Dr. Bentley's Salem, 1774–1819," *Proceedings of the New England–St. Lawrence Valley Division, Association of American Geographers*, vol. 7 (1977), pp. 31–36.   **5194**

Geib, Susan, "Landscape and Faction: Spatial Transformation in William Bentley's Salem," *Essex Institute Historical Collections,* vol. 113, 3 (1977), pp. 163–180.   **5195**

Marston, Sallie A., "Adopted Citizens: Community and the Development of Political Consciousness among the Irish of Lowell, Massachusetts, 1839–1885," Ph.D. diss., University of Colorado, 1986.   **5196**

Marston, Sallie A., "Neighborhood and Politics: Irish Ethnicity in Nineteenth Century Lowell, Massachusetts," *Annals of the Association of American Geographers*, vol. 78, 3 (1988), pp. 414–432.   **5197**

Marston, Sallie A., and Andrew Kirby, "Urbanization, Industrialization, and the Social Creation of a Space Economy: A Reconstruction of the Historical Development of Lowell and Lawrence, Massachusetts," *Urban Geography*, vol. 9, 4 (1988), pp. 358–375.   **5198**

Marston, Sallie A., "Public Rituals and Community Power: St. Patrick's Day Parades in Lowell, Massachusetts, 1841–1874," *Political Geography Quarterly*, vol. 8, 3 (1989), pp. 255–270.   **5199**

TOWNSCAPE

See also 4724

Metropolitan Boston

Warner, Sam B., *Streetcar Suburbs: The Process of Growth in Boston, 1870–1900* (Cambridge: Harvard University Press, 1962), 236 pp.   **5200**

Whitehill, Walter Muir, *Boston: A Topographical History* (Cambridge: Belknap Press, 1968), 299 pp.   **5201**

Hobart, Stephen P., "The Role of Inertia and Shape as Modifiers of Zonal Land Use: The Case of the Abandoned North Shore Railroad," Master's thesis, Clark University, 1971.   **5202**

Krim, Arthur J., *Survey of Architectural History in Cambridge: Report Five, Northwest Cambridge* (Cambridge: MIT Press and Cambridge Historical Commission, 1977), 206 pp.   **5203**

Krim, Arthur J., *The Three-Deckers of Dorchester* (Boston: Boston Landmarks Commission and

Boston Redevelopment Authority, 1977), 77 pp.   **5204**

Krim, Arthur J., *Roadside Architecture of Memorial Drive* (Boston: Boston University American Vernacular Institute, Commercial Archeology, 1979), 7 pp. [Pamphlet]   **5205**

Gable, Frank J., "Landfill Projects in the Port of Boston: The South Boston Flats, 1863–1920," Master's thesis, Louisiana State University, 1980.   **5206**

Sauder, Robert A., "The Use of Sanborn Maps in Reconstructing 'Geographies of the Past': Boston's Waterfront from 1867 to 1972," *Journal of Geography*, vol. 79, 6 (1980), pp. 204–213.   **5207**

Krim, Arthur J., *Cambridge Street: Highway in the City* (Boston: Society for Commercial Archeology, 1981), 4 pp. [Pamphlet]   **5208**

Bradley, James W., Arthur J. Krim, Peter Stott, and Sarah Zimmerman, *The Historical and Archeological Resources of the Boston Area* (Boston: Massachusetts Historical Commission, 1982), 264 pp.   **5209**

Worcester

Balk, Helen H., "The Expansion of Worcester and Its Effect on the Surrounding Towns," Ph.D. diss., Clark University, 1944.   **5210**

Balk, Helen H., "Rurbanization of Worcester's Environs," *Economic Geography*, vol. 21, 2 (1945), pp. 104–116. [Focus on 1765–1940]   **5211**

Roberge, Roger A., "The Three-Decker: Structural Correlate of Worcester's Industrial Revolution," Master's thesis, Clark University, 1965.   **5212**

RECREATION & TOURISM

Alexander, Lewis M., "The Impact of Tourism on the Economy of Cape Cod, Massachusetts," *Economic Geography*, vol. 29, 4 (1953), pp. 320–326.   **5213**

PLANNING

Natoli, Salvatore J., "Effects of Zoning upon the Development of Urban Land Use Patterns: A Case Study of Worcester, Massachusetts," Ph.D. diss., Clark University, 1967.   **5214**

Natoli, Salvatore J., "Zoning and the Development of Urban Land Use Patterns," *Economic Geography*, vol. 47, 2 (1971), pp. 171–184. [Focus on 1925–1963]   **5215**

PLACE NAMES

Writers' Program, *The Origin of Massachusetts Place Names of the State, Counties, Cities, and*

Towns (New York: Harlan Publications, for the Works Project Administration, 1941), 55 pp.

5216

Meigs, Peveril, III, "The Cove Names of Walden," *Thoreau Society Bulletin*, vol. 104 (Summer 1968), pp. 5–7.

5217

Green, Eugene, and Rosemary M. Green, "Place Names and Dialects in Massachusetts: Some Complementary Patterns," *Names*, vol. 19, 4 (1971), pp. 240–251.

5218

Stilgoe, John R., "Place Names in the Wilderness: Scituate, Massachusetts," *Places: A Literary Journal of Geography and Travel*, vol. 2 (1975), pp. 20–22.

5219

Krim, Arthur J., "Acculturation of the New England Landscape: Native and English Toponymy of Eastern Massachusetts," in Peter Benes, ed., *New England Prospect: Maps, Places, Names, and Its Historical Landscape* (Boston: Boston University and the Dublin Seminar for New England Folklife, 1982), pp. 69–88.

5220

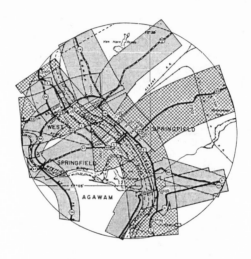

RHODE ISLAND

GENERAL

Sibley, Edward A., "Aquidneck, the Island of
Rhode Island: A Study in Historical Geography,"
Master's thesis, Clark University, 1950. **5221**

REGIONAL SETTLEMENT

Jensen, J. Granville, "Settlement Pattern of the
Providence Region as an Adjustment to Its Geography," Ph.D. diss., Clark University, 1946.
5222

POPULATION

See also **4943**

Whitney, Herbert A., "The Narragansett Region:
Concentrations of Population, 1635–1885," Ph.D.
diss., University of Michigan, 1962. **5223**

POLITICAL & ADMINISTRATIVE GEOGRAPHY

Ullman, Edward L., "The Historical Geography of
the Eastern Boundary of Rhode Island," *Research Studies of the State College of Washington, Pullman*, vol. 4 (1936), pp. 67–87. **5224**

Ullman, Edward L., "The Eastern Rhode Island–
Massachusetts Boundary Zone," *Geographical
Review*, vol. 29, 2 (1939), pp. 291–302. **5225**

LAND & LAND USE

Jackson, Eric P., "The Trend of Land Utilization in
Rhode Island and the Increasing Importance of
Geographic Factors," Master's thesis, Clark
University, 1923. **5226**

Jackson, Eric P., "Early Uses of Land in Rhode Island," *Bulletin of the Geographical Society of
Philadelphia*, vol. 24 (1926), pp. 69–87. **5227**

LANDSCAPE

Nebiker, Irene, "The Imprint of European Man on
the Landscape of North Smithfield, Rhode Island, 1660–1720," Master's thesis, McGill University, 1974. **5228**

COMMUNICATIONS & TRADE

Whitney, Herbert A., "Shifts in Transportation
Routes: The Rhode Island Example," *Proceed-

ings of the Pennsylvania Academy of Science,
vol. 38, 2 (1965), pp. 188–193. **5229**

MANUFACTURING & INDUSTRIALIZATION

Black, Lloyd D., "Evolution of Industry in Burrill-
ville, Rhode Island," Master's thesis, Clark University, 1936. **5230**

Sullivan, Robert J., "The Historic and Continuing
Impact of Industrialization and Water Supply
within the Pawtucket River Basin," *Proceedings
of the New England–St. Lawrence Valley Division, Association of American Geographers*, vol.
12 (1982), pp. 27–38. **5231**

TOWN GROWTH

Higbee, Olive B., "Kingston: The Historical Geography of an Entrepreneurial Village," Master's
thesis, University of Rhode Island, 1977. **5232**

URBAN ECONOMIC STRUCTURE

Donovan, Dennis J., "The Relocation of Firms in
Selected Growth Industries in Rhode Island,
1947–1972: A Geographical Analysis," Ph.D.
diss., University of Rhode Island, 1973. **5233**

Cranston, Kenneth C., "The Costume Jewelry In-
dustry in the Providence Area: Its History and
Character," *Proceedings of the New England–
St. Lawrence Valley Division, Association of
American Geographers*, vol. 9 (1979), pp. 20–23.
5234

PLANNING

Krausse, Gerald H., "College Hill, Providence: An
Assessment of Inner-City Historic Preservation," *Proceedings of the New England–St.
Lawrence Valley Division, Association of American Geographers*, vol. 6 (1976), pp. 38–42. **5235**

PLACE NAMES

Kohl, Johann Georg, "How Rhode Island Was
Named," *Magazine of American History*, vol. 9
(1883), pp. 81–93. **5236**

CONNECTICUT

GENERAL

The state

Lewis, Thomas R., Jr., and John E. Harmon, "Population and Settlement before 1800," "Population and Settlement 1800 to 1982," and "Toward an Industrial Landscape," in their *Connecticut: A Geography* (Boulder: Westview Press, 1986), pp. 47–101.   **5237**

Smaller areas

Diettrich, Sigismond D., "Historical Geography of the Thames River Valley, Connecticut," Ph.D. diss., Clark University, 1931.   **5238**

Harwood, Ernest M., "A Study of the Geography of Litchfield, Connecticut," Master's thesis, Syracuse University, 1937.   **5239**

Silberfein, Marilyn, "The Evolution of the Modern Civilization Pattern in Central Connecticut," Master's thesis, Syracuse University, 1965.   **5240**

Boucher, Robert, "Historical Geography of Mill River," Master's thesis, Connecticut State College, 1966.   **5241**

Lewis, Thomas R., Jr., "From Suffield to Saybrook: An Historical Geography of the Connecticut River Valley in Connecticut before 1800," Ph.D. diss., Rutgers University, 1978. Portions published in his *Near the Long Tidal River: Readings in the Historical Geography of Central Connecticut* (Washington, D.C.: University Press of America, 1981), pp. 1–67.   **5242**

Lewis, Thomas R., Jr., ed., *Near the Long Tidal River: Readings in the Historical Geography of Central Connecticut* (Washington, D.C.: University Press of America, 1981), 147 pp.   **5243**

Lewis, Thomas R., Jr., *Mainstream and Ebb: Readings in the Geography of Connecticut* (Needham Heights, Mass.: Ginn Press, 1986), 137 pp.   **5244**

ENVIRONMENTAL CHANGE

Goldthwait, James W., "The Gathering of Floods in the Connecticut River System," *Geographical Review*, vol. 18, 3 (1928), pp. 428–445. [Emphasis on 1771–1927]   **5245**

Bowden, Martyn J., "Legacies of Man: Environmental Relationships in the Hartford Region," in Sondra A. Stave, ed., *Hartford: The City and the Region* (Hartford: University of Hartford, 1979), pp. 17–20.   **5246**

POPULAR IMAGES & EVALUATION

Lewis, Thomas R., Jr., "Changing Environmental Perception of the Connecticut River Valley, 1635–1835," *Proceedings of the New England–St. Lawrence Valley Division, Association of American Geographers*, vol. 14 (1984), pp. 37–45.   **5247**

REGIONAL SETTLEMENT

Huka, Elizabeth C., "The Changing Geography of an Old New England Town: East Hadden, Connecticut," Master's thesis, Clark University, 1959.   **5248**

POPULATION

Monroe, Charles B., et al., "A Preliminary Trend Surface Analysis of Settlement Dynamics in Colonial Connecticut," *Proceedings of the New England–St. Lawrence Valley Division, Association of American Geographers*, vol. 6 (1976), pp. 10–15.   **5249**

Sutherland, John F., "Cheney Brothers Was the World: Migration and Settlement in Manchester, Connecticut, at the Turn of the Century," *Proceedings of the New England–St. Lawrence Valley Division, Association of American Geographers*, vol. 10 (1980), pp. 10–14.   **5250**

Yacher, Leon I., "Population Change in Fairfield County, Connecticut, 1940–1980," *Proceedings of the New England–St. Lawrence Valley Division, Association of American Geographers*, vol. 17 (1987), pp. 84–92.   **5251**

RURAL & REGIONAL SOCIAL GEOGHRAPHY

Berg, Carl G., "The Swedish Settlement in Northeastern Connecticut," Master's thesis, Clark University, 1942.   **5252**

Moberg, Wensel W., "Swedish Elements in the Land Utilization of Northeastern Connecticut," Master's thesis, Clark University, 1942.   **5253**

POLITICAL & ADMINISTRATIVE GEOGRAPHY

Natunewicz, Henry, "Political Geography of the Colony and State of Connecticut," Ph.D. diss., Columbia Teachers College, 1954.   **5254**

ECONOMIC DEVELOPMENT

Butler, Ann, "A History of the Uses of the Quinnipiac River for Water Power," Master's thesis, Southern Connecticut State College, 1970. **5255**

LANDSCAPE

Lewis, Thomas R., Jr., "Pre–Nineteenth Century House Types in the Connecticut River Valley," *Proceedings of the New England–St. Lawrence Valley Division, Association of American Geographers*, vol. 5 (1975), pp. 68–72. Reprinted as "Overhang, 'I', and Gambrel: Comments on Pre–Nineteenth Century Connecticut Valley House Types," in his *Near the Long Tidal River: Readings in the Historical Geography of Central Connecticut* (Washington, D.C.: University Press of America, 1981), pp. 69–80. **5256**

Derby, Nancy, "Housetypes Prior to 1800 in Windsor, Connecticut," *Proceedings of the New England–St. Lawrence Valley Division, Association of American Geographers*, vol. 8 (1977), pp. 55–61. **5257**

Lewis, Thomas R., Jr., "To Planters of Moderate Means: The Cottage as a Dominant Folk House in Connecticut before 1900," *Proceedings of the New England–St. Lawrence Valley Division, Association of American Geographers*, vol. 10 (1980), pp. 23–27. **5258**

Lewis, Thomas R., Jr., "The Landscape and Environment of the Connecticut River Valley," in Gerald Ward and William Hosley, Jr., eds., *The Great River* (Wadsworth: Atheneum, 1985), pp. 3–15. **5259**

Wickstrand, Norman M., "Notes and Sketches of Connecticut Blast Furnaces," *Connecticut Historical Society Bulletin*, vol. 51, 3 (1986), pp. 135–192. **5260**

Lewis, Thomas R., Jr., "Connecticut Landscapes and American History," *Yankee Forum* (Connecticut Council for the Social Studies), vol. 8 (1987), pp. 29–33. **5261**

COMMUNICATIONS & TRADE

Lewis, Thomas R., Jr., "A Glimpse of Cheney's Goat," *Bulletin of the Connecticut League of Historical Societies*, vol. 23, 1 (1971), pp. 9–10. **5262**

Lewis, Thomas R., Jr., "Manchester's Iron Goat," *Bulletin of the Connecticut Historical Society*, vol. 41, 4 (1976), pp. 97–106. Reprinted in his *Near the Long Tidal River: Readings in the Historical Geography of Central Connecticut* (Washington, D.C.: University Press of America, 1981), pp. 93–105. **5263**

Lewis, Thomas R., Jr., *Silk along Steel: The Story of the South Manchester Railroad* (Chester, Conn.: Globe Pequot Press, for Manchester Community College Press, 1976), 64 pp. **5264**

MANUFACTURING & INDUSTRIALIZATION

Fairchild, Wilma Belden, "Changes in Industry in the Upper Housatonic Valley," Master's thesis, Clark University, 1937. **5265**

Meyer, David R., "Urban Industrial Growth of Coastal Connecticut in the Nineteenth Century," *Long Island Sound: The People and the Environment*, Proceedings of Public Policy Symposium, Oceanic Society (1978), pp. 139–148. **5266**

Meyer, David R., "Connecticut as a Regional Industrial Complex," *Proceedings of the New England–St. Lawrence Valley Division, Association of American Geographers*, vol. 10 (1980), pp. 7–9. **5267**

Goff, John V., "Traces of the Shipyard Workers: Shipbuilding in the Connecticut River Valley, 1800–1850," *Bulletin of the Connecticut Historical Society*, vol. 46, 1 (1981), pp. 1–32. **5268**

URBAN NETWORKS & URBANIZATION

Genthe, Martha Krug, "Valley Towns of Connecticut," *Bulletin of the American Geographical Society*, vol. 39, 9 (1907), pp. 513–544. **5269**

Currey, Florence, "The Urban System of Colonial Connecticut," Master's thesis, York University, 1978. **5270**

TOWN GROWTH

Lewis, Thomas R., Jr., "Looms, Life, and Landscape: A Glimpse of the Growth of a New England Industrial Village," *Proceedings of the New England–St. Lawrence Valley Division, Association of American Geographers*, vol. 3 (1973–1974), pp. 32–37. Reprinted in his *Near the Long Tidal River: Readings in the Historical Geography of Central Connecticut* (Washington, D.C.: University Press of America, 1981), pp. 81–92. [Manchester] **5271**

Meyer, David R., *From Farm to Factory to Urban Pastoralism: Urban Change in Central Connecticut* (Cambridge: Ballinger, 1976), 57 pp. **5272**

Meyer, David R., "Image and the Physical Environment," in Sondra A. Stave, ed., *Hartford, the City and Region: Past, Present, Future* (Hartford: University of Hartford, 1979), pp. 13–17. **5273**

URBAN ECONOMIC STRUCTURE

Lewis, Thomas R., Jr., "The Nineteenth Century Marine Propeller Industry in Manchester, Connecticut," *Bulletin of the Connecticut Historical Society*, vol. 45, 3 (1980), pp. 90–96. Reprinted in his *Near the Long Tidal River: Readings in the Historical Geography of Central Connecticut* (Washington, D.C.: University Press of America, 1981), pp. 107–117.   **5274**

URBAN SOCIAL STRUCTURE

Carley, K. W., Timothy J. Rickard, and S. P. Taboriso, "The Austrian-Burgenlander Neighborhood in New Britain, Connecticut, 1900–1920," *Proceedings of the New England–St. Lawrence Valley Division, Association of American Geographers*, vol. 6 (1976), pp. 24–28.   **5275**

TOWNSCAPE

Brickman, Barbara, "The Nine Squares of New Haven," Master's thesis, Southern Connecticut State College, 1968.   **5276**

PLACE NAMES

Dexter, Franklin B., "The History of Connecticut, as Illustrated by the Names of Her Towns," *Proceedings of the American Antiquarian Society*, n.s. vol. 3, 1885, pp. 421–448.   **5277**

NEW YORK

GENERAL

See also 1143, 1145

The State

Seymour, Horatio, "Topography and History of the State of New York," *Bulletin of the American Geographical and Statistical Society*, vol. 2 (1857), pp. 128–157. **5278**

Whitbeck, Ray H., "Geographical Influences in the Development of New York State," *Journal of Geography*, vol. 9, 5 (1911), pp. 119–124. **5279**

Meinig, Donald W., "The Colonial Period," "Geography of Expansion," and "Elaboration and Change," in John H. Thompson, ed., *Geography of New York State* (Syracuse: Syracuse University Press, 1966), pp. 121–199. Revised 1977. **5280**

Meinig, Donald W., "New York and Its Neighbors: Some Problems of Regional Interpretation," in Manfred Jonas and Robert Wells, eds., *New Opportunities in a New Nation: The Development of New York after the Revolution* (Schenectady: Union College Press, 1982), pp. 69–108. **5281**

Smaller areas

Von Engeln, Oscar D., "The Geography of the Ithaca, New York, Region," *Annals of the Association of American Geographers*, vol. 16, 3 (1926), pp. 124–150. **5282**

Bothwell, Lucy, "The Historical Geography of Manlius Township," Master's thesis, Syracuse University, 1935. **5283**

Roberts, Kenneth A., "The Historical Geography of the Mohawk Valley," Master's thesis, Syracuse University, 1935. **5284**

Fuchs, Roland J., "Clermont Township, New York: A Study in Historical Geography," Master's thesis, Clark University, 1957. **5285**

Shapiro, Missy E., "Time Past: People, Life, and Landscape in Northern Lysander, New York, during the Nineteenth Century," Master's thesis, Syracuse University, 1977. **5286**

ENVIRONMENTAL CHANGE

See also 4847

Rostlund, Erhard, "Henry Hudson's Comment on Salmon in the Hudson River, September 1609," *Copeia*, no. 3 (1953), pp. 192–193. **5287**

NATIVE PEOPLES & WHITE RELATIONS

See also 1193, 1198

Chi, Sech Choo, "Settlement Geography of the Iroquois in Central New York: 1600–1779," Master's thesis, Syracuse University, 1965. **5288**

Raybeck, Robert J., "The Indian," in John H. Thompson, ed., *Geography of New York State* (Syracuse: Syracuse University Press, 1966), pp. 113–120. Revised 1977. **5289**

EXPLORATION & MAPPING

Wieder, Frederik C., "Onderzoek naar de oudste kaarten van de omgeving van New York," *Tijdschrift van het Koninklijk Nederlandsch Aardrijkskundig Genootschap*, vol. 2 (1918), p. 235. **5290**

Ristow, Walter W., "Simon de Witt: Pioneer American Cartographer," *Canadian Cartographer*, vol. 5, 2 (1968), pp. 90–107. **5291**

Cumming, William P., "The Montresor-Ratzer-Sauthier Sequence of Maps of New York City, 1766–76," *Imago Mundi*, vol. 31 (1979), pp. 55–65. **5292**

Ristow, Walter W., "Otto Lindberg: Finno-American Road Map Publisher," in Kerkko Hakulin and Arvo Peltonen, eds., *Papers of the Nordenskiöld Seminar on the History of Cartography and the Maintenance of Cartographic Archives, Sept. 12–15, 1979* (Helsinki: Nordenskiöld-Samfundet, Finland, 1981), pp. 177–193. **5293**

Bourcier, Paul G., *History in the Mapping: Four Centuries of Adirondack Cartography* (Blue Mountain Lake, N.Y.: Adirondack Museum, 1986), 69 pp. **5294**

POPULAR IMAGES & EVALUATION

See also 1310–1314, 4815, 8169

Rural

Rood, Elliot S., "The Genesee Country, 1788–1811: Perceptual Framework of Residents and Non-

Residents," Master's thesis, Syracuse University, 1971.   **5295**

O'Brien, Raymond, "The Role of West Point in the Evolution of a Hudson Valley Aesthetic," *Proceedings of the Middle States Division, Association of American Geographers,* vol. 8 (1974), pp. 94–97.   **5296**

Urban

Stokes, Isaac N. P., *The Iconography of Manhattan Island, 1498–1909,* 6 vols. (New York: R. H. Dodd, 1915–1928).   **5297**

Krim, Arthur J., "Coney Island of the Mind and Related Urban Districts," *Monadnock,* vol. 43 (1969), pp. 8–24.   **5298**

Domosh, Mona, "Imagining New York's First Skyscrapers, 1875–1910," *Journal of Historical Geography,* vol. 13, 3 (1987), pp. 233–248.   **5299**

Domosh, Mona, "Those Sudden Peaks That Scrape the Sky: The Changing Imagery of New York's First Skyscrapers," in Leo Zonn, ed., *Place Images in Media: Portrayal, Experience and Meaning* (Totowa, N.J.: Rowman & Littlefield, 1990), pp. 9–30.   **5300**

REGIONAL SETTLEMENT

See also 1332, 4858–4860

Upstate

Hanlon, Eleanor E., "A Geography of the Sequent Occupance of the Southern Littoral of Oneida Lake," Master's thesis, Syracuse University, 1938.   **5301**

White, Russell A., "The Sequent Occupance of the Peekskill, New York, Area through 1900," Master's thesis, Columbia University, 1962.   **5302**

Hanner, John, "Cultural Change and the Early Settlement of New Netherland, 1624 to 1664," Master's thesis, University of Chicago, 1973. **5303**

Rumney, Thomas A., "Post-Frontier Adjustment in Regional Settlement Structure: A Case Study of Clinton County, New York, 1850–1880," Ph.D. diss., University of Maryland, 1980.   **5304**

Wyckoff, William K., "Joseph Ellicott and the Western New York Frontier: Environmental Assessment, Geographical Strategies, and Authored Landscapes, 1797–1811," Ph.D. diss., Syracuse University, 1982.   **5305**

Wyckoff, William K., "Land Promoters as Regional Planners: Development Theory on the Western New York Frontier, 1793–1800," Syracuse University Department of Geography Discussion Paper no. 77 (1982), 44 pp.   **5306**

Wyckoff, William K., *The Developer's Frontier: The Making of the Western New York Frontier* (New Haven: Yale University Press, 1988), 239 pp.   **5307**

Barnet, David G., "The New World Dutch in Albany, New York: A Geographical Model of Conquest and Culture Change, 1644–1754," Master's thesis, Syracuse University, 1989.   **5308**

Schein, Richard H., "A Historical Geography of Central New York: Patterns and Processes of Colonization on the New Military Tract, 1782–1820," Ph.D. diss., Syracuse University, 1989.
                                                       5309

Downstate

"Holländische Anklänge in der Geographie Amerikas," *Das Ausland,* vol. 45, 23 (1872), pp. 549–551. [Focus on New Amsterdam in the seventeenth century]   **5310**

Wauwermans, Henri E., "Une colonie néderlandaise: New York et la Nouvelle-Belgique," *Bulletin de la Société géographie d'Anvers,* vol. 4 (1879), pp. 175–200.   **5311**

Bergman, Edward F., and Thomas W. Pohl, *A Geography of the New York Metropolitan Region* (Dubuque: Kendall/Hunt, 1975), 205 pp.
                                                       5312

POPULATION

See also 1348, 4862

Brigham, Albert Perry, "The Population of New York State," *Geographical Review,* vol. 2, 2 (1916), pp. 208–217. [Covers 1790–1910]   **5313**

Straw, H. Thompson, "A Study of the Population Growth of New York State," *Papers of the Michigan Academy of Science, Arts, and Letters,* vol. 21 (1935), pp. 397–400. [Focus on 1790–1930] **5314**

Unterberg, Lester I., "An Analysis of Some Aspects of the Changing Population of Nassau and Suffolk Counties, Long Island, for the Period 1930–1957," Master's thesis, Clark University, 1961.   **5315**

Kortum, Gerhard, "Sozial-geographische Aspekte der Auswanderung von den Nordfriesischen Inseln in die USA unter besonderer Berücksichtigung des Zielraumes New York," *Nordfriesisches Jahrbuch,* n.s. vol. 13 (1977), pp. 9–48. **5316**

Yacher, Leon I., "Population Change in Oswego County, 1940–1970," *Proceedings of the Middle States Division, Association of American Geographers,* vol. 12 (1978), pp. 98–102.   **5317**

Davenport, David P., "Population Persistence and Migration in New York State: 1855–1860," Ph.D. diss., University of Illinois, 1983.   **5318**

Davenport, David P., "Tracing Rural New York's Out-Migrants, 1855–1860," *Historical Methods*, vol. 17, 2 (1984), pp. 59–67.   **5319**

Rumney, Thomas A., "Demographic Measures for the Identification of Post-Frontier Regions," *Pennsylvania Geographer*, vol. 22, 1 & 2 (1984), pp. 21–30.   **5320**

Davenport, David P., "Duration of Residence in the 1855 Census of New York State," *Historical Methods*, vol. 18, 1 (1985), pp. 5–12.   **5321**

Widdis, Randy, "We Breathe the Same Air: Eastern Ontario Migration to Watertown, New York," *New York History*, vol. 68, 3 (1987), pp. 261–280.   **5322**

Widdis, Randy, "With Scarcely a Ripple: English Canadians in Northern New York State at the Beginning of the Twentieth Century," *Journal of Historical Geography*, vol. 13, 2 (1987), pp. 169–192.   **5323**

Davenport, David P., "Migration to Albany, New York, 1850–1855," *Social Science History*, vol. 13, 2 (1989), pp. 159–185.   **5324**

RURAL & REGIONAL SOCIAL GEOGRAPHY

See also **4823, 4868**

General

Brownell, Joseph W., and William R. Stanley, "A Cartographic Analysis of Changing Student Hinterlands of the S.U.N.Y. Colleges of Arts and Sciences," *Proceedings of the Eighth Annual Meeting of the New York–New Jersey Division of the Association of American Geographers*, vol. 1 (1968), pp. 74–93. [Focus on 1923–1966] **5325**

Hoffmann, Phillip P., "School District Reorganization in Cortland County, New York, 1930–1970: A Geographic Analysis, " Master's thesis, Syracuse University, 1976.   **5326**

Hinshalwood, Sophia G., "The Dutch Culture Area of the Mid-Hudson Valley," Ph.D. diss., Rutgers University, 1981.   **5327**

Schlereth, Thomas J., "Chautauqua: A Middle Landscape of the Middle Class," *North American Culture*, vol. 3, 2 (1987), pp. 3–17.   **5328**

Nickerson, Michael G., "Sermons, Systems and Strategies: The Geographic Strategies of the Methodist Episcopal Church in Its Expansion into New York State, 1788–1810," Ph.D. diss., Syracuse University, 1988.   **5329**

Manhattan Island

Smith, Daniel R., "The Spatial Dynamics of the Black Communities of Manhattan Island, 1626–

1776," Master's thesis, Rutgers University, 1981.   **5330**

POLITICAL & ADMINISTRATIVE GEOGRAPHY

See also **4871**

Brigham, Albert Perry, "The Valleys of New York in the American Revolution," *Journal of Geography*, vol. 27, 1 (1928), pp. 15–23.   **5331**

Lipton, Selma, and G. D. Scharf, "Geographical Influences in the Saratoga Campaign," Master's thesis, Columbia University, 1934.   **5332**

Miles, Edward J., "Political Regionalism in New York State, 1860–1954," Ph.D. diss., Syracuse University, 1958.   **5333**

Pell, John H. G., "Fort Ticonderoga: Key to a Continent," *Geographical Magazine*, vol. 31, 3 (1958), pp. 124–133.   **5334**

Boorstein, Margaret F., "Responses of Public Money Flows to Population Shifts in the New York Metropolitan Region, 1956 to 1978," *Proceedings of the Middle States Division of the Association of American Geographers*, vol. 16 (1982), pp. 10–25.   **5335**

ECONOMIC DEVELOPMENT

See also **1401**

Perejda, Andrew D., "The Salt Industry Turnpike, Erie and Oswego Canals, and Their Relationships to the Growth of Syracuse in the Canal Period, 1825–1850," Master's thesis, Syracuse University, 1939.   **5336**

Wyckoff, William K., "Frontier Milling in Western New York," *Geographical Review*, vol. 76, 1 (1986), pp. 73–93.   **5337**

LAND & LAND USE

Land survey

Wyckoff, William K., "Assessing Land Quality in Western New York: The Township Survey of 1797–1799," *Surveying and Mapping*, vol. 41, 3 (1981), pp. 315–325.   **5338**

Wyckoff, William K., "Land Subdivision on the Holland Purchase in Western New York State, 1797–1820," *Journal of Historical Geography*, vol. 12, 2 (1986), pp. 142–161.   **5339**

Land use

Fountain, Lawrence F., "Evolution of Land Utilization in the Adirondack Massif," Ph.D. diss., Clark University, 1941.   **5340**

Silvernail, George R., "The Agricultural Land Use of the Western Finger Lakes Region of New York, 1600–1959," Ph.D. diss., University of North Carolina, 1960. **5341**

Hover, Roger G., "A Geographical Study of New York State Agricultural Land Use Changes, 1860–1960," Master's thesis, Indiana University of Pennsylvania, 1970. **5342**

Pompi, Louis W., "A Quantitative Analysis of Agricultural Land Use in Western New York State: 1850," Master's thesis, State University of New York–Buffalo, 1970. **5343**

EXTRACTIVE ACTIVITY

Dinsdale, Evelyn M., "The Lumber Industry of Northern New York: A Geographical Examination of Its History and Technology," Ph.D. diss., Syracuse University, 1963. **5344**

Dinsdale, Evelyn M., "Spatial Patterns of Technological Change: The Lumber Industry of Northern New York," *Economic Geography*, vol. 41, 3 (1965), pp. 252–274. [Focus on c.1800–1930] **5345**

AGRICULTURE

See also 4877–4878

Dahlberg, Richard E., "The Concord Grape Industry of the Chautauqua-Erie Area," *Economic Geography*, vol. 37, 2 (1961), pp. 150–169. [Focus on 1900–1960] **5346**

Bresson, Marcelle M., "L'évolution agricole de Dutchess County, New York," *Annales de géographie*, vol. 71, 387 (1962), pp. 500–511. [Focus on 1609–1960] **5347**

Durand, Loyal, Jr., "The Historical and Economic Geography of Dairying in the North Country of New York State," *Geographical Review*, vol. 57, 1 (1967), pp. 24–47. **5348**

Leamon, J. Harold, "The Growth of Agricultural Specialization in Western New York: 1840–1860," Master's thesis, State University of New York–Buffalo, 1970. **5349**

Leamon, J. Harold, and Edgar C. Conkling, "Transport Change and Agricultural Specialization," *Annals of the Association of American Geographers*, vol. 65, 3 (1975), pp. 425–432. [Western New York, 1840–1860] **5350**

Rumney, Thomas A., "Agricultural Production and Locational Stability: Hops in New York State during the Nineteenth Century," *Kansas Geographer*, vol. 18 (1983), pp. 5–16. **5351**

LANDSCAPE

See also 4883, 4885, 8092

McDonald, Sister Mary Aquin, "The Distribution of Early Houses in the Vicinity of the Town of Newburgh, New York," Master's thesis, Catholic University of New York, 1965. **5352**

Thompson, John H., "The Rural Landscape," in John H. Thompson, ed., *Geography of New York State* (Syracuse: Syracuse University Press, 1966), pp. 358–369. Revised 1977. **5353**

Glassie, Henry H., "The Variation of Concepts within Tradition: Barn Building in Otsego County, New York," in H. Jesse Walker and William G. Haag, eds., *Man and Cultural Heritage: Papers in Honor of Fred B. Kniffen* (Baton Rouge: Louisiana State University School of Geoscience, Geoscience & Man, vol. 5, 1974), pp. 177–235. **5354**

Hugill, Peter J., "Landscape as 'Gesture': The Management of Conduct by an Elite," *Proceedings of the Association of American Geographers*, vol. 8 (1976), pp. 99–102. [Focus on Cazenovia, N.Y.] **5355**

Hugill, Peter J., "A Small Town Landscape as Sustained Gesture on the Part of a Dominant Social Group: Cazenovia, New York, 1794–1976," Ph.D. diss., Syracuse University, 1977. **5356**

Hugill, Peter J., "Houses in Cazenovia: The Effects of Time and Class," *Landscape*, vol. 24, 2 (1980), pp. 10–15. **5357**

VanDuzer, Edward F., "The Cobblestone House," *Proceedings of the Middle States Division, Association of American Geographers*, vol. 15 (1981), pp. 92–97. **5358**

Darlington, James W., "Hops and Hop Houses in Upstate New York," *Material Culture*, vol. 16, 1 (1984), pp. 25–42. **5359**

Murray, Sharon L., "Farms, Fields, and Fences: The Changing Agricultural Landscape of Onondaga County, New York," Master's thesis, Syracuse University, 1986. **5360**

Coffey, Brian, and Allan G. Noble, "Residential Building Materials in New York State, 1855–1875," *Material Culture*, vol. 21, 1 (1989), pp. 3–21. **5361**

COMMUNICATIONS & TRADE

See also 1431, 1433

Hayes, Isaac I., "The Waterways of New York," *Journal of the American Geographical Society*, vol. 13 (1881), pp. 93–109. **5362**

Morgan, Richard P., *Decline of the Commerce of the Port of New York* (Urbana: University of Illinois, University Studies, vol. 1, 2, 1901), 17pp. **5363**

MacFarlane, Charles T., "The Erie Canal," *Journal of Geography*, vol. 10, 7 (1912), pp. 219–228. [Focus on 1784–1912] **5364**

Rich, John L., "An Instance of the Changing Value of Geographical Location," *Journal of Geography*, vol. 15, 6 (1917), pp. 185–189. [Hobart Quadrangle, Catskill Mountains, 1870–1917] **5365**

Miller, William J., "Significance of the Gorge at Little Falls, New York," *Journal of Geography*, vol. 18, 4 (1919), pp. 156–158. [Since Amerindian times] **5366**

Torbert, Edward N., "The Earlier Evolution of Highways and Transportation through the Ontario-Mohawk Funnel," Master's thesis, University of Chicago, 1927. **5367**

McCarthy, Albert J. P., "The Oswego River: A Study in Historical Geography," Ph.D. diss., St. Louis University, 1965. **5368**

Darlington, James W., "A Railroad Geography: The New York, Ontario, and Western Railway," Master's thesis, Syracuse University, 1974. **5369**

Darlington, James W., "Railroads and Their Location: An Example of Failure," *Proceedings of the Middle States Division, Association of American Geographers*, vol. 8 (1974), pp. 20–26. [Focus on the Oswego Midland Railroad, c. 1867–1875] **5370**

Ruelke, Stephen P., "Local Transport Development: An Exercise in Historical Geography," *Proceedings of the Middle States Division, Association of American Geographers*, vol. 8 (1974), pp. 103–107. [Focus on New Palz, 1790–1900] **5371**

Hugill, Peter J., "The Elite, the Automobile, and the Good Roads Movement in New York: The Development and Transformation of a Technological Complex, 1909–1913," Syracuse University Department of Geography Discussion Paper no. 70 (1981), 28 pp. **5372**

MANUFACTURING & INDUSTRIALIZATION

See also **4897**

Roorbach, George B., "Geographic Influences in the Development of the Manufacturing Industry of the Mohawk Valley," *Journal of Geography*, vol. 10, 3 (1911), pp. 80–86. **5373**

Brown, Olin T., "The Industrial Conquest of New York's Southern Tier," Ph.D. diss., Cornell University, 1930. **5374**

Moravek, John R., "The Iron Industry as a Geographic Force in the Adirondack-Champlain

Region of New York State, 1800–1971," Ph.D. diss., University of Tennessee, 1976. **5375**

URBAN NETWORKS & URBANIZATION

Tarr, Ralph S., "Location of the Towns and Cities of Central New York," *Bulletin of the American Geographical Society*, vol. 42, 10 (1910), pp. 738–764. **5376**

Htoo, Tin, "Changes in the Distribution and Functions of Nucleated Settlements in Lewis County, New York between 1900 and 1950," Ph.D. diss., Syracuse University, 1954. **5377**

Lundin, Herbert J., "Stages of Dynamics in the Growth of Lower Order Central Places: The St. Lawrence Region, New York," Ph.D. diss., Syracuse University, 1962. **5378**

Miller, Roberta Balstad, *City and Hinterland: A Case Study of Urban Growth and Regional Development* (Westport, Conn.: Greenwood Press, 1979), 179 pp. [Syracuse and its immediate hinterland, 1830–1860] **5379**

TOWN GROWTH

Buffalo

Piper, P. F., "The Development of Buffalo," *Journal of Geography*, vol. 10, 7 (1912), pp. 241–244. **5380**

Kemp, Harold S., "Queen City of the Lakes: A Geographic Pageant," *Journal of Geography*, vol. 30, 3 (1931), pp. 93–110. Reprinted in George J. Miller, ed., *Human Geography Studies: The United States* (Bloomington, Ill.: McKnight & McKnight, Geographic Education Series, 1935), pp. 1–18. [Buffalo, N.Y.] **5381**

Whittemore, Katheryne Thomas, "Buffalo," in John H. Thompson, ed., *Geography of New York State* (Syracuse: Syracuse University Press, 1966), pp. 407–422. Revised 1977. **5382**

New York City

Virlet d'Aoust, P.-T., "Fondation de la ville de New York, en 1623, par une colonie des Flamandes et Wallons," *Comptes-rendus de la Société de géographie de Paris*, vol. 10 (1891), pp. 311–316. **5383**

Emerson, Frederick V., "A Geographic Interpretation of New York City," Ph.D. diss., University of Chicago, 1907. **5384**

Emerson, Frederick V., "A Geographic Interpretation of New York City," *Bulletin of the American Geographical Society*, vol. 40, 9 (1908), pp. 587–612; vol. 40, 12 (1908); and vol. 41, 1 (1909), pp. 3–21. **5385**

Poole, Sidman P., "Geographic Interpretation of New Amsterdam," *Bulletin of the Philadelphia Geographical Society*, vol. 32, 1 (1934), pp. 42–64. **5386**

Fellner, Albert, "Die Entwicklung New Yorks zur größten Handelsstadt der Welt," *Geographische Rundschau*, vol. 10, 7 (1958), pp. 261–266. **5387**

McNee, Robert B., "New York," in John H. Thompson, ed., *Geography of New York State* (Syracuse: Syracuse University Press, 1966), pp. 423–457. Revised 1977. **5388**

Lampard, Eric E., "The New York Metropolis in Transformation: History and Prospect; A Study in Historical Particularity," in H.-J. Ewers, ed., *The Future of the Metropolis* (Berlin: Walter de Gruyter & Co., 1986), pp. 27–110. **5389**

Chase, Jeanne, "New York, du port à ville: La construction de l'espace urbain, 1750–1820," *Annales: Economies, sociétés, civilisations*, vol. 44, 4 (1989), pp. 793–822. **5390**

Syracuse

Faigle, Eric H., "Some Aspects of the Urban Geography of Syracuse," *Papers of the Michigan Academy of Science, Arts, and Letters*, vol. 23 (1937), pp. 349–359. **5391**

Poole, Sidman P., "Successive Settlement Patterns on the Site of Syracuse," *Journal of Geography*, vol. 37, 3 (1938), pp. 99–108. **5392**

DeLaubenfels, David J., "25 Jahre Wandlung in der Geographie der Stadt Syracuse, New York," *Raumforschung und Raumordnung*, vol. 21 (1963), pp. 225–228. **5393**

DeLaubenfels, David J., "Syracuse," in John H. Thompson, ed., *Geography of New York State* (Syracuse: Syracuse University Press, 1966), pp. 469–479. Revised 1977. **5394**

Other centers

Mueller, Wilma N., "The Historical Geography of Liverpool, New York," Master's thesis, Syracuse University, 1934. **5395**

Stone, Kirk H., "Cortland, New York: A Study of City Growth," *Papers of the Michigan Academy of Science, Arts, and Letters*, vol. 24, 3 (1938), pp. 61–70. **5396**

Johnson, Robert S., "Ogdensburg and the Ogdensburg Gateway: A Study in Geographic Situation," *Economic Geography*, vol. 30, 3 (1954), pp. 262–277. **5397**

Hall, Robert B., Jr., "Rochester," in John H. Thompson, ed., *Geography of New York State* (Syracuse: Syracuse University Press, 1966), pp. 458–468. Revised 1977. **5398**

McFarlane, Sidley K., "Utica," in John H. Thompson, ed., *Geography of New York State* (Syracuse: Syracuse University Press, 1966), pp. 480–488. Revised 1977. [Covers Utica-Rome metropolitan area] **5399**

Ebner, Kenneth R., "An Historical Geographic Study of a Mid-Hudson City: Newburgh, New York," *Proceedings of the Middle States Division, Association of American Geographers*, vol. 2 (1969), pp. 107–120. **5400**

Merwick, Donna, *Possessing Albany, 1630–1710: The Dutch and English Experiences* (Cambridge: Cambridge University Press, 1990), 312 pp. **5401**

URBAN ECONOMIC STRUCTURE

See also 4902

Buffalo

O'Day, Laura, "Buffalo as a Flour Milling Center," *Economic Geography*, vol. 8, 1 (1932), pp. 81–93. [Focus on 1898–1930] **5402**

Svec, M. Melvina, "The Port of Buffalo: Where the Water Routes and Trucking Routes of the Automobile Carriers Meet," *Journal of Geography*, vol. 37, 5 (1937), pp. 173–179. [Focus on the 1920s and 1930s] **5403**

Cowen, David J., "The Urban Land Use of a Section of Delaware Avenue, Buffalo, New York, 1900–1965," Master's thesis, State University of New York–Buffalo, 1968. **5404**

Langdale, John V., "Impact of the Telegraph on the Buffalo Agricultural Commodity Market, 1846–1848," *Professional Geographer*, vol. 31, 2 (1979), pp. 165–169. **5405**

Metropolitan New York

Frey, John W., "The Port of New York," *Journal of Geography*, vol. 21, 6 (1922), pp. 207–213. [Focus on 1621–1920] **5406**

Malon, Patricia E., "The Growth of Manufacturing in Manhattan, 1860–1900: An Analysis of Factoral Changes and Urban Structure," Ph.D. diss., Columbia University, 1981. **5407**

DeBarbieux, Bernard, "I.B.M. à la compagne: L'évolution du Dutchess County (État de New York), 1940–1984," *Annales de géographie*, vol. 94, 523 (1985), pp. 270–297. **5408**

Other centers

Carls, J. Norman, and Walter W. Ristow, "The Industrial Geography of Seneca Falls, New York," *Economic Geography*, vol. 12, 3 (1936), pp. 287–293. [Focus on 1790–1930] **5409**

Schneider, Noreen F., "An Industrial Study of Fulton, New York," Master's thesis, Clark University, 1942. **5410**

Dillman, Robert J., "Factors Involved in Spatial and Temporal Variations in Residential Land Use and Land Values in Smithtown Township, New York, 1930–1960," Master's thesis, Pennsylvania State University, 1970. **5411**

URBAN SOCIAL STRUCTURE

See also 4710

Albany

Merwick, Donna, "Dutch Townsmen and Land Use: A Spatial Perspective on Seventeenth-Century Albany, New York," *William and Mary Quarterly*, 3d ser., vol. 37, 1 (1980), pp. 53–78. **5412**

Buffalo

Long, Harriet R., "Changes in Character and Composition of Buffalo's Population," Master's thesis, Clark University, 1941. **5413**

Stein, Gregory P., "Ethnicity and the Growth of the Roman Catholic Church in the Buffalo, New York, Urbanized Area," *Proceedings of the Middle States Division, Association of American Geographers*, vol. 8 (1974), pp. 111–114. **5414**

Yox, Andrew, "Ethnic Loyalties of the Alsatians in Buffalo, 1829–1855," *Yearbook of German-American Studies*, vol. 20 (1985), pp. 105–123. **5415**

New York City

Gerling, Walter, "Über den Strukturwandel der Stadtbevölkerung von New York in der Zeit von 1750–1850," in Walter Gerling, *Kulturgeographische Untersuchungen* (Würzburg: Verlag der Stahel'schen Universitäts-Buchhandlung, 1963), pp. 7–32. **5416**

McMahon, Marie, "An Historical Geography of Greenwich Village from the Seventeenth to the Twentieth Century," Master's thesis, Columbia University, 1969. **5417**

Ward, David, "The Internal Spatial Structure of Immigrant Residential Districts in the Late Nineteenth Century," *Geographical Analysis*, vol. 1, 4 (1969), pp. 337–353. **5418**

Freedman, Margaret R., "The Effect of Geographic Barriers on the Population Distribution of Upper Manhattan, 1950–1970," *Proceedings of the Middle States Division, Association of American Geographers*, vol. 7 (1973), pp. 88–93. **5419**

Tom, Henry, "Colonia Incognita: The Formation of Chinatown, New York City, 1850–1890," Master's thesis, University of Maryland, 1975. **5420**

Bergman, Edward F., "Shifting Lower Manhattan Ghettoes," *Proceedings of the Middle States Division, Association of American Geographers*, vol. 11 (1977), pp. 71–73. [Focus from the 1840s to 1969] **5421**

Chase, Jeanne, "L'accumulation des fortunes dans la ville de New York de 1820 à 1850 et ses effets sur le développement urbain," *Espaces et sociétés*, nos. 28–29 (1979), pp. 9–34. **5422**

Frantz, Klaus, "Das Ausmaß der europäischen Immigration in die Großstädte der USA: Dargestellt am Beispiel von New York City zwischen 1855–1920," *Innsbrucker Geographische Studien*, vol. 5 (1979), pp. 199–213. **5423**

Boorstein, Margaret F., "Responses of Public Money Flows to Population Shifts in the New York Metropolitan Region: 1956–1978," *Proceedings of the Middle States Division, Association of American Geographers*, vol. 15 (1981), pp. 10–25. **5424**

Gabaccia, Donna, "Sicilians in Space: Environmental Change and Family Geography," *Journal of Social History*, vol. 16, 2 (1982), pp. 53–66. **5425**

Gilfoyle, Timothy, "The Urban Geography of Commercial Sex: Prostitution in New York City, 1790–1860," *Journal of Urban History*, vol. 13, 4 (1987), pp. 371–393. **5426**

Rothschild, Nan A., *New York City Neighborhoods: The Eighteenth Century* (San Diego: Academic Press, 1990), 264 pp. **5427**

Warf, Barney L., "The Reconstruction of Social Ecology and Neighborhood Change in Brooklyn," *Environment and Planning D: Society and Space*, vol. 8, 1 (1990), pp. 73–96. **5428**

Syracuse

Bigelow, Bruce L., "Changing Spatial Endogamy of Polish Americans: A Case Study in Syracuse, New York, 1940–1970," Syracuse University Department of Geography Discussion Paper no. 19 (1976), 24 pp. **5429**

Mesinger, Jonathan S., "The Jewish Community in Syracuse, 1850–1880: The Growth and Structure of an Urban Ethnic Region," Ph.D. diss., Syracuse University, 1977. **5430**

Mesinger, Jonathan S., "Peddlers and Merchants: The Geography of Work in a Nineteenth Century Jewish Community," Syracuse University Geography Department Discussion Paper no. 38 (1977), 74 pp. [Syracuse] **5431**

Bigelow, Bruce L., "Ethnic Stratification in a Pedestrian City: A Social Geography of Syracuse in 1860," Ph.D. diss., Syracuse University, 1978.
5432

Clarke, Keith C., "Population Density Dynamics in Syracuse, 1900–1970: A Trend Surface Approach," Master's thesis, University of Michigan, 1979.
5433

Bigelow, Bruce L., "Ethnic Separation in a Pedestrian City: A Social Geography of Syracuse, New York in 1860," Syracuse University Department of Geography Discussion Paper no. 93 (1989), 34 pp.
5434

TOWNSCAPE

New York City

Muir, John C., "Development of a Nineteenth-Century Rowhouse Suburb: The Park Slope Historic District of Brooklyn," *Proceedings of the Middle States Division, Association of American Geographers*, vol. 9 (1975), pp. 11–16. [Focus on 1868–1916]
5435

Domosh, Mona, "The Skyscrapers of New York, 1880–1910," *Proceedings of the New England–St. Lawrence Valley Division, Association of American Geographers*, vol. 13 (1983), pp. 22–28.
5436

Domosh, Mona, "Scrapers of the Sky: The Symbolic and Functional Structures of Lower Manhattan," Ph.D. diss., Clark University, 1985.
5437

Cardia, Clara, *Ils ont construit New York: histoire de la métropole au XIXe siècle* (Genève: Georg Éditeur, Collection Histoire/Urbanisme, 1987), 239 pp.
5438

Domosh, Mona, "The Symbolism of the Skyscraper: Case Studies of New York's First Tall Buildings," *Journal of Urban History*, vol. 14, 3 (1988), pp. 321–345.
5439

Domosh, Mona, "A Method for Interpreting Landscape: A Case Study of the New York World Building," *Area*, vol. 22, 4 (1989), pp. 347–355.
5440

Domosh, Mona, "New York's First Skyscrapers: Conflict in Design of the American Commercial Landscape," *Landscape*, vol. 30, 2 (1989), pp. 34–39.
5441

Other centers

Thomas, Katheryne C., "Geographic Influences in the Building of Buffalo Harbor," Ph.D. diss., Clark University, 1936.
5442

Mano, Jo Margaret, "Succession in Suburban Patterns: A Micro-Scale Approach," *Proceedings of the Middle States Division, Association of American Geographers*, vol. 14 (1980), pp. 48–52. [Focus on Rockland Co., 1955–1976]
5443

Johnson, Kenneth A., "The Changing Relationship between Residential Patterns and the Built Environment: A Case Study of Metropolitan Syracuse, 1950–1970," Ph.D. diss., Syracuse University, 1981.
5444

Stump, Roger W., "The Evolution of Albany's Religious Landscape," in Anne F. Roberts and Marcia W. Cockrell, eds., *Historic Albany: Its Churches and Synagogues* (Albany: Library Communications Services, 1986), pp. 2–19.
5445

RECREATION & TOURISM

See also **4904**

Heiman, Michael K., "Production Confronts Consumption: Landscape Perception and Social Conflict in the Hudson Valley," *Environment and Planning D: Society and Space*, vol. 7, 2 (1989), pp. 165–178.
5446

Johnson, Kenneth A., "Origins of Tourism in the Catskill Mountains," *Journal of Cultural Geography*, vol. 11, 1 (1990), pp. 5–16.
5447

PLANNING

Lindstrom, Eric A., "The Olmsted Legacy of Nineteenth-Century City Parks in Buffalo, New York," Master's thesis, State University of New York–Buffalo, 1983.
5448

Jacobson, Daniel, "The Pastoral in the City: Frederick Law Olmsted and the Development of Central Park," *East Lakes Geographer*, vol. 20 (1985), pp. 70–77.
5449

PLACE NAMES

See also **1477–1478**

Beauchamp, William M., *Aboriginal Place Names of New York* (Albany: New York State Education Department, New York State Museum Bulletin no. 108, 1907), 333 pp.
5450

Raymond, Lyle S., Jr., "Tug Hill: Survival of a Folk Names and Landform Terminology," *Proceedings of the Middle States Division, Association of American Geographers*, vol. 9 (1975), pp. 100–103.
5451

Gordon, Jeffrey J., "Onondaga Iroquois Place-Names: An Approach to Historical and Contemporary Indian Landscape Perception," *Names*, vol. 32, 3 (1984), pp. 218–233.
5452

Harder, Kelsie B., "French Colonial Names in New York," *Proceedings of the French Colonial Historical Society*, vol. 11, 1 (1985), pp. 19–24.
5453

NEW JERSEY

GENERAL

The state

Whitbeck, Ray H., "Geographical Influences in the Development of New Jersey," *Journal of Geography*, vol. 6, 6 (1908), pp. 177–182.   **5454**

Wacker, Peter O., "New Jersey's Cultural Landscape before 1800," *Proceedings of the Second Annual Symposium of the New Jersey Historical Commission* (Newark: New Jersey Historical Society, 1971), pp. 35–62.   **5455**

Wacker, Peter O., *The Cultural Geography of Eighteenth Century New Jersey* (Trenton: New Jersey Historical Commission, 1975), 24 pp. **5456**

Wacker, Peter O., *Land and People: A Cultural Geography of Preindustrial New Jersey: Origins and Settlement Patterns* (New Brunswick: Rutgers University Press, 1975), 499 pp.   **5457**

Kelland, Frank S., and Marylin C. Kelland, "The Early Influences (to 1783)," in their *New Jersey: Garden or Suburb?* (Dubuque: Kendall/Hunt, 1978), pp. 61–78.   **5458**

Stansfield, Charles A., "Early Settlement," "The Cultural Landscape," "Population Characteristics," "Transportation," "Agriculture," and "Industrial Development," in his *New Jersey: A Geography* (Boulder: Westview Press, 1983), pp. 11–24, 43–62, 69–90, 99–115, 121–127, and 139–149.   **5459**

Smaller areas

Muntz, Alfred P., "The Changing Geography of the New Jersey Woodlands, 1600–1900," Ph.D. diss., University of Wisconsin–Madison, 1959.   **5460**

Trindell, Roger T., "Historical Geography of Southern New Jersey as Related to Its Colonial Ports," Ph.D. diss., Louisiana State University, 1966.   **5461**

Wacker, Peter O. "Forest, Forge, and Farm: An Historical Geography of the Musconetcong Valley, New Jersey," Ph.D. diss., Louisiana State University, 1966.   **5462**

Wacker, Peter O., *The Musconetcong Valley of New Jersey: A Historical Geography* (New Brunswick: Rutgers University Press, 1968), 207 pp.   **5463**

ENVIRONMENTAL CHANGE

Jacobson, Daniel, "The Pollution Problem of the Passaic River," *Proceedings of the New Jersey Historical Society*, vol. 76, 3 (1958), pp. 186–198.   **5464**

EXPLORATION & MAPPING

Guthorn, Peter J., "Some Notable New Jersey Maps of the Dutch Colonial Period," *Proceedings of the New Jersey Historical Society*, vol. 80, 2 (1962), pp. 102–110.   **5465**

Rice, Howard C., ed., *New Jersey Road Maps of the Eighteenth Century* (Princeton: Princeton University Library, 1970), 48 pp.   **5466**

Snyder, John P., *The Mapping of New Jersey: The Men and the Art* (New Brunswick: Rutgers University Press, 1973), 234 pp.   **5467**

POPULAR IMAGES & EVALUATION

Vining, James W., "Early American Geographers and New Jersey Agriculture," *Directions* (Rider College, Lawrenceville), vol. 10, 1 (1981), pp. 10–20.   **5468**

REGIONAL SETTLEMENT

See also **4858–4859**

Brush, John E., "Some Aspects of the Growth and Morphology of Villages in Central New Jersey," *Proceedings of the New York–New Jersey Division, Association of American Geographers*, vol. 3 (1970), pp. 14–27.   **5469**

Kury, Theodore W., "Early Settlement in the Highlands: An Iron Maker–Farmer Sequence?" *Pioneer America*, vol. 2, 1 (1970), pp. 7–14.   **5470**

Kury, Theodore W., "Iron as a Factor in New Jersey Settlement," *Proceedings of the Second Annual Symposium of the New Jersey Historical Commission* (1970), pp. 63–79.   **5471**

Rutsch, Edward S., "The Colonial Plantation Settlement Pattern in New Jersey: Iron and Agricultural Examples," in William D. Wright, ed., *Economic and Social History of Colonial New Jersey* (Trenton: New Jersey Historical Commission, 1974), pp. 10–23.   **5472**

Wacker, Peter O., "Early Settlement Patterns in the Highlands," in Lorraine A. Caruso, ed., *Celebrate the Highlands* (Morristown: Association of New Jersey Environmental Commission, 1984), pp. 17–22.   **5473**

POPULATION

Wacker, Peter O., "The
the Black Population c
A Preliminary View," *Proceedings of the Association of American Geographers*, vol. 3 (1971), pp. 174–178.   **5474**

Wacker, Peter O., "Patterns and Problems in the Historical Geography of the Afro-American Population of New Jersey, 1726–1860," in Ralph E. Ehrenberg, ed., *Pattern and Process: Research in Historical Geography* (Washington, D.C.: Howard University Press, 1975), pp. 25–72. **5475**

RURAL & REGIONAL SOCIAL GEOGRAPHY

Martin, Theodora, "Quaker Settlement in New Jersey: Origins and Dispersals," Master's thesis, Rutgers University, 1969.   **5476**

Wacker, Peter O., "A Preliminary View of the Possible Association between Cultural Background and Agriculture in New Jersey during the Latter Part of the Eighteenth Century," *Proceedings of the New York–New Jersey Division, Association of American Geographers*, vol. 4 (1971), pp. 48–57.   **5477**

Wacker, Peter O., "The Dutch Culture Area in the Northeast, 1609–1800," *New Jersey History*, vol. 104, 1 (1986), pp. 1–21.   **5478**

ECONOMIC DEVELOPMENT

Kury, Theodore W., "Anthracite, Iron, and the Morris Canal," *Pioneer America*, vol. 3, 2 (1971), pp. 46–53.   **5479**

Levy, Robin, "Location of Research and Development Plants in New Jersey, 1950–1982," Master's thesis, Columbia University, 1984.   **5480**

Wacker, Peter O., "The New Jersey Taxable List of 1751," *New Jersey History*, vol. 107, 1 (1989), pp. 23–47.   **5481**

LAND & LAND USE

Sickler, Mary A., "Changes in Agricultural Land in Gloucester County, New Jersey," Master's thesis, Clark University, 1964.   **5482**

Wacker, Peter O., "Human Exploitation of the New Jersey Pine Barrens before 1900," in Richard T. T. Forman, ed., *Pine Barrens: Ecosystem and Landscape* (New York: Academic Press, 1979), pp. 3–23.   **5483**

Wacker, Peter O., "Land Use in Seventeenth and Eighteenth Century New Jersey," *New Jersey Folklore*, vol. 2 (1981), pp. 11–12.   **5484**

ˉIVE ACTIVITY

Highland Forests: Four
Centuries or Change," *Proceedings of the New York–New Jersey Division, Association of American Geographers*, vol. 3 (1970), pp. 28–37.   **5485**

Wacker, Peter O., "New Jersey's Forest," in Richard C. Davids, ed., *Encyclopedia of American Forest and Conservation History* (New York: Macmillan, 1983), pp. 485–487.   **5486**

LANDSCAPE

See also **4883–4885**

Wacker, Peter O., and Roger T. Trindell, "The Log House in New Jersey: Origins and Diffusion," *Keystone Folklore Quarterly*, vol. 13, 4 (1969), pp. 248–268.   **5487**

Wacker, Peter O., "Cultural and Commercial Regional Associations of Traditional Smokehouses in New Jersey," *Pioneer America*, vol. 3, 2 (1971), pp. 25–34.   **5488**

Wacker, Peter O., "Folk Architecture as an Indicator of Culture Area and Culture Diffusion: Dutch Barns and Barracks in New Jersey," *Pioneer America*, vol. 5, 2 (1973), pp. 37–47.   **5489**

Wacker, Peter O., "Traditional House and Barn Types in New Jersey: Keys to Acculturation, Past Culturogeographic Regions, and Settlement History," in H. Jesse Walker and William G. Haag, eds., *Man and Cultural Heritage: Papers in Honor of Fred B. Kniffen* (Baton Rouge: Louisiana State University School of Geoscience, Geoscience & Man, vol. 5, 1974), pp. 163–176.   **5490**

Wacker, Peter O., "Dutch Material Culture in New Jersey," *Journal of Popular Culture*, vol. 11, 4 (1978), pp. 948–958.   **5491**

Wacker, Peter O., "Relations between Cultural Origins, Relative Wealth, and the Size, Form, and Materials of Construction of Rural Dwellings in New Jersey during the Eighteenth Century," in C. Higounet, ed., *Géographie historique de village et de la maison rurale* (Paris: Centre de la recherche scientifique, 1979), pp. 201–231.   **5492**

COMMUNICATIONS & TRADE

Paglieri, Betty, "New Jersey Canals of the Nineteenth Century," Master's thesis, Indiana University, 1955.   **5493**

Veit, Richard F., *The Old Canals of New Jersey: A Historical Geography* (Little Falls: New Jersey Geographical Press, 1963), 106 pp.   **5494**

Trindell, Roger T., "Transportation Development and Hinterland Piracy: An Example from Colonial North America," *Journal of Transport History*, 2d ser., vol. 7, 4 (1966), pp. 205–217. [West New Jersey ports, especially Salem and Greenwich, and Philadelphia]   **5495**

MANUFACTURING & INDUSTRIALIZATION

See also **4897–4898**

DeVorsey, Louis, Jr., "Historical Geography of the Iron Industry of New Jersey (1780–1860)," Master's thesis, Indiana University, 1954.   **5496**

Muntz, Alfred P., "Forest and Iron: The Charcoal Iron Industry of the New Jersey Highlands," *Geografiska annaler*, vol. 42, 4 (1960), pp. 315–323.   **5497**

Kury, Theodore W., "Technology and Location in the Early American Iron Industry: An Example from Ringwood Manor, New Jersey," *Proceedings of the New York–New Jersey Division of the Association of American Geographers*, vol. 2 (1969), pp. 79–90.   **5498**

Kury, Theodore W., "The Long Pond Iron Works: A North Jersey Plantation," *Pioneer America*, vol. 2, 2 (1970), pp. 11–19.   **5499**

URBAN NETWORKS & URBANIZATION

Trindell, Roger T., "Historical Geography of Southern New Jersey as Related to Its Colonial Ports," Ph.D. diss., Louisiana State University, 1966.   **5500**

Trindell, Roger T., "The Ports of Salem and Greenwich in the Eighteenth Century," *New Jersey History*, vol. 86, 4 (1968), pp. 199–214.   **5501**

TOWN GROWTH

Moreland, Andrew S., "The Human Response to a Seaboard Situation: Atlantic City, New Jersey," Master's thesis, Clark University, 1951.   **5502**

Jacobson, Daniel, "Origins of the Town of Newark," *Proceedings of the New Jersey Historical Society*, vol. 75, 3 (1957), pp. 158–169.   **5503**

Turk, Jessie R., "Trenton, New Jersey, in the Nineteenth Century: The Significance of Location in the Historical Geography of a City," Ph.D. diss., Columbia University, 1964.   **5504**

Wacker, Peter O., "New Brunswick as an Eighteenth-Century Port," in Ruth M. Patt, ed., *The Tercentennial Lectures* (New Brunswick, N.J.: City of New Brunswick, 1982), pp. 2–8.   **5505**

URBAN ECONOMIC STRUCTURE

See **4659**

URBAN SOCIAL STRUCTURE

Smith, David B., "The Hungarians in New Brunswick, New Jersey, to 1920: A Social Geography," Master's thesis, Rutgers University, 1965.   **5506**

Clark, Thomas A., "Suburban Destinations of Black Migrants: Towards a Political Economy of Exclusion," *Proceedings of the Middle States Division, Association of American Geographers*, vol. 14 (1980), pp. 71–79. [Focus on 1930–1970]   **5507**

Bolen, William J. E., "The Changing Geography of Italian Immigrants in the United States: A Case Study of the Ironbound Colony, Newark, New Jersey," Ph.D. diss., Rutgers University, 1986.   **5508**

TOWNSCAPE

Wacker, Peter O., "Early Street Patterns in Pennsylvania and New Jersey: A Comparison," *Proceedings of the New York–New Jersey Division, Association of American Geographers*, vol. 3 (1970), pp. 1–13.   **5509**

RECREATION & TOURISM

See also **4904**

Stanfield, Charles A., "New Jersey's Evolving 'Leisureopolis'," in J. Matznetter, ed., *Studies in the Geography of Tourism* (Frankfurt: Selbstverlag des Seminars für Wirtschaftsgeographie der Johann Wolfgang Göthe-Universität, Frankfurter Wirtschafts- und Sozialgeographische Schriften, vol. 17, 1974), pp. 305–317.   **5510**

Stansfield, Charles A., "The Development of New Jersey Seashore Resorts," *Echoes of History (Pioneer America Society)*, vol. 5, 3 (1975), pp. 46–50.   **5511**

Stansfield, Charles A., "Pitman Grove: A Camp Meeting as Urban Nucleus," *Pioneer America*, vol. 7, 1 (1975), pp. 36–44. [Near Trenton and Philadelphia]   **5512**

Stansfield, Charles A., "Atlantic City and the Resort Cycle: Background to the Legalization of Gambling," *Annals of Tourism Research*, vol. 5, 2 (1978), pp. 238–251.   **5513**

Stansfield, Charles A., "Cape May: Selling History by the Sea," *Journal of Cultural Geography*, vol. 11, 1 (1990), pp. 25–38.   **5514**

PLACE NAMES

Writers' Program, *The Origin of New Jersey Place Names* (Trenton: New Jersey State Library Commission, for the Works Project Administration, 1939), 41 pp.   **5515**

Becker, Donald W., *Indian Place-Names in New Jersey* (Cedar Grove, N.J.: Phillips-Campbell Publishing Co., 1964), 111 pp.   **5516**

PENNSYLVANIA

GENERAL

The state

Kloss, Heinz, "Nationalität und Boden in Pennsylvania," *Petermanns Geographische Mitteilungen*, vol. 77, 1 (1931), pp. 20–21. **5517**

Smaller areas

James, Henry F., "The Kishacoquillas Valley: A Study in Human Geography," *Bulletin of the Philadelphia Geographical Society*, vol. 28, 4 (1930), pp. 223–239. **5518**

Rampon, William J., "The Historical Geography of Swissvale, Pennsylvania," Master's thesis, University of Oklahoma, 1959. **5519**

Schmieder, Allen A., "The Historical Geography of the Erie Triangle," Ph.D. diss., Ohio State University, 1963. **5520**

Lemon, James T., "A Rural Geography of Southeastern Pennsylvania in the Eighteenth Century: The Contributions of Cultural Inheritance, Social Structure, Economic Conditions, and Physical Resources," Ph.D. diss., University of Wisconsin–Madison, 1964. **5521**

Mitchell, Lawrence C., "A Historical Geography of Cambria County, Pennsylvania," Master's thesis, Michigan State University, 1965. **5522**

Lemon, James T., *The Best Poor Man's Country: A Geographical Study of Early Southeastern Pennsylvania* (Baltimore: Johns Hopkins University Press, 1972), 295 pp. Reprinted New York: W. W. Norton, 1976). **5523**

Pillsbury, Richard R., "The Pennsylvania Culture Area: A Reappraisal," *North American Culture*, vol. 3, 2 (1987), pp. 37–54. **5524**

ENVIRONMENTAL CHANGE

See **4847**

NATIVE PEOPLES & WHITE RELATIONS

Stephens, John D., "Comparison of the Upper Ohio Valley Monongahela Culture to One of Its Components—The Johnston Site," *Pennsylvania Geographer*, vol. 6, 1 (1968), pp. 20–25. **5525**

EXPLORATION & MAPPING

Garrison, Hazel S., "Cartography of Pennsylvania before 1800," *Pennsylvania Magazine of History and Biography*, vol. 59 (1935), pp. 255–283. **5526**

Stephenson, Richard W., "Charles Varlé: Nineteenth Century Cartographer," *Proceedings of the American Congress on Surveying and Mapping, Thirty-Second Annual Meeting, Washington, D.C., 1971* (Washington, D.C.: American Congress on Surveying and Mapping, 1972), pp. 189–198. **5527**

Lewis, Peirce F., "A Map for Revolutionaries," in Robert Secor, ed., *Pennsylvania, 1776* (University Park: Pennsylvania State University Press, 1975), pp. 80–89. **5528**

Monmonier, Mark S., "Private-Sector Mapping of Pennsylvania: A Selective Cartographic History from 1870 to 1974," *Proceedings of the Pennsylvania Academy of Science*, vol. 55 (1981), pp. 69–74. **5529**

Monmonier, Mark S., "Topographic Map Coverage of Pennsylvania: A Study in Cartographic Evolution," *Proceedings of the Pennsylvania Academy of Science*, vol. 56 (1982), pp. 61–66. **5530**

Lewis, Cindy, "A Study of Early Erie History through Its Cartography," *Journal of Erie Studies*, vol. 14, 1 (1985), pp. 31–64. **5531**

Daniels, Ted, "Advertisements for American Selves: Nineteenth-Century Pennsylvania County Atlases," *Landscape*, vol. 29, 3 (1987), pp. 17–23. **5532**

Muller, Edward K., "A County Revisited," Introduction to repr. ed. of *Atlas of the County of Allegany* (Philadelphia: G. M. Hopkins, 1876), reprinted in 1988 by the Historical Society of Western Pennsylvania. **5533**

POPULAR IMAGES & EVALUATION

Vining, James W., "Early Views of Pennsylvania's Agricultural Geography," *Pennsylvania Geographer*, vol. 21, 1 & 2 (1983), pp. 20–27. **5534**

Richards, Penny, "Perception and Cartographic Depiction in the Eighteenth Century: Pennsylvania's Northern Frontier, 1750–1782," Master's thesis, Pennsylvania State University, 1990. **5535**

REGIONAL SETTLEMENT

Raup, Hallock F., "The Pennsylvania-Dutch of Northampton County: Settlement Forms and Culture Pattern," *Bulletin of the Geographical Society of Philadelphia*, vol. 36, 1 (1938), pp. 1–15.   **5536**

Graff, John, "Settlement Patterns in West Deer Township, 1900–1957," Master's thesis, University of Pittsburgh, 1958.   **5537**

Mash, Donald, "A Sequent Occupance Study of Sewickley, Pennsylvania," Master's thesis, University of Pittsburgh, 1961.   **5538**

Lewis, Peirce F., "The Land of Penn's Woods," and "The Early Settlers," in Robert Secor, ed., *Pennsylvania, 1776* (University Park: Pennsylvania State University Press, 1975), pp. 17–31.   **5539**

Ham, Marilyn P., "An Analysis of Nineteenth Century Abandoned Settlement in Allegany County, Pennsylvania," Master's thesis, University of Pittsburgh, 1980.   **5540**

POPULATION

See also **4861**

Willard, Michael, "Geographic Analysis of Selected Aspects of Population Change in Fayette County, from 1900 to 1960," Master's thesis, Pennsylvania State University, 1963.   **5541**

Florin, John W., "The Advance of Frontier Settlement in Pennsylvania, 1638–1850," Master's thesis, Pennsylvania State University, 1966.   **5542**

Hornberger, Mark A., "The Spatial Distribution of Ethnic Groups in Selected Counties in Pennsylvania, 1800–1880: A Geographic Interpretation," Ph.D. diss., Pennsylvania State University, 1974.   **5543**

Hovinen, Elizabeth J., "Migration of Quakers from Pennsylvania to Upper Canada, 1800–1820," Master's thesis, York University, 1976.   **5544**

Florin, John W., *The Advance of Frontier Settlement in Pennsylvania, 1638–1850: A Geographical Interpretation* (University Park: Pennsylvania State University Department of Geography Paper no. 14, 1977), 108 pp.   **5545**

Schnell, George A., "Fertility and Levels of Development in Mid-Nineteenth Century Pennsylvania," *Proceedings of the Pennsylvania Academy of Science*, vol. 51 (1977), pp. 70–74.   **5546**

Hornberger, Mark A., "Germans in Pennsylvania, 1800, 1850, and 1880: A Spatial Perspective," *Yearbook of German-American Studies*, vol. 24 (1989), pp. 97–104.   **5547**

RURAL & REGIONAL SOCIAL GEOGRAPHY

See also **4823–4824, 4827, 4868**

Ethnic & community patterns

Lemon, James T., "The Agricultural Practices of National Groups in Eighteenth-Century Southeastern Pennsylvania," *Geographical Review*, vol. 56, 4 (1966), pp. 467–496. Reprinted, with omissions, in David Ward, ed., *Geographic Perspectives on America's Past: Readings on the Historical Geography of the United States* (New York: Oxford University Press, 1979), pp. 129–147.   **5548**

Lemon, James T., "Household Consumption in Eighteenth Century America and Its Relationship to Production and Trade: The Situation among Farmers in Southeastern Pennsylvania," *Agricultural History*, vol. 41, 1 (1967), pp. 59–70.   **5549**

Hannon, Thomas J., "The Process of Ethnic Assimilation in Selected Rural Christian Congregations, 1800–1976: A Western Pennsylvania Case Study," Ph.D. diss., University of Pittsburgh, 1977.   **5550**

Kolar, Walter, "The Role of Pennsylvania in the History of the Tambura in America," *Pennsylvania Geographer*, vol. 16, 3 (1978), pp. 7–16. [The tambura is a musical instrument indigenous to Croatia]   **5551**

Lemon, James T., "The Weakness of Place and Community in Early Pennsylvania," in James R. Gibson, ed., *European Settlement and Development in North America: Essays in Geographical Change in Honour and Memory of Andrew Hill Clark* (Toronto: University of Toronto Press, 1978), pp. 190–207.   **5552**

Marsh, Ben, "Continuity and Decline in the Anthracite Towns of Pennsylvania," *Annals of the Association of American Geographers*, vol. 77, 3 (1987), pp. 337–352. [Focus on the period since the 1920s]   **5553**

Purvis, Thomas L., "Patterns of Ethnic Settlement in Late Eighteenth-Century Pennsylvania," *Western Pennsylvania Historical Magazine*, vol. 70, 2 (1987), pp. 107–122.   **5554**

German (Pennsylvania Dutch) communities

Lohmann, Martin, *Die Bedeutung der deutschen Ansiedlungen in Pennsylvanien* (Stuttgart: Ausland und Heimat Verlags-Aktiengesellschaft, 1923), 153 pp.   **5555**

Meynen, Emil, "Die deutschen Pioniere Pennsylvaniens," *Die Westmark: Monatsschrift für deutsche Kultur*, vol. 3, 2 (1935), pp. 383–385.   **5556**

Raup, Hallock F., "Settlement and Settlement Forms of the Pennsylvania Dutch at the Forks of the Delaware, Northampton County, Pennsylvania," Ph.D. diss., University of California–Berkeley, 1935. **5557**

Meynen, Emil, "Das pennsylvaniendeutsche Bauernland," *Deutsches Archiv für Landes- und Volksforschung*, vol. 3 (1939), pp. 253–292. **5558**

Johnson, Hildegard Binder, "The Germantown Protest of 1688 against Negro Slavery," *Pennsylvania Magazine of History and Biography*, vol. 65, 2 (1941), pp. 144–156. **5559**

Hopple, Lee C., "Plain Dutch Settlements in Southeastern Pennsylvania," *Pennsylvania Geographer*, vol. 9, 3 (1971), pp. 1–5. **5560**

Hopple, Lee C., "Spatial Development and Internal Spatial Organization of the Southwestern Pennsylvania Plain Dutch Community," Ph.D. diss., Pennsylvania State University, 1971. **5561**

Hopple, Lee C., "Spatial History of the Schwenkfelders," *Pennsylvania Geographer*, vol. 13, 4 (1975), pp. 2–18. **5562**

Hopple, Lee C., "Spatial Organization of the Southern Pennsylvania Plain Dutch Group Culture Region to 1975," *Pennsylvania Folklife*, vol. 29, 1 (1979), pp. 13–26. **5563**

Vossen, Joachim, "Feldforschung; Einsichten und Erfahrungen beim Studium einer religiösen Minorität: Das Beispiel der Old Order Amish in SE–Pennsylvania," in Werner Kreisel, ed., *Geisteshaltung und Umwelt: Festschrift zum 65. Geburtstag von Manfred Büttner* (Aachen: Alano, Abhandlungen zur Geschichte der Geowissenschaften und Religion, Umwelt-Forschung, vol. 1, 1988), pp. 455–468. **5564**

Vossen, Joachim, "Eine religiöse Minderheit im Kräftefeld der amerikanischen Gesellschaft: Die Old Order Amish in Lancaster County, Pennsylvania," in Gisbert Rinschede and Kurt Rudolph, eds., *Beiträge zur Religion: Umwelt-Forschung II* (Berlin: Dietrich Reimer Verlag, Geographia Religionum, vol. 7, 1989), pp. 187–203. **5565**

POLITICAL & ADMINISTRATIVE GEOGRAPHY

Lefferts, Walter, "The Story of Pennsylvania's Southern Boundary," *Bulletin of the Philadelphia Geographical Society*, vol. 18, 3 (1920), pp. 94–99. **5566**

Miller, Vincent P., "Reflections on the Sequent Occupance of Local Government," *Pennsylvania Geographer*, vol. 17, 1 (1979), pp. 13–19. [Focus on the Pittsburgh region] **5567**

ECONOMIC DEVELOPMENT

Rolfe, D., "Geologic Influences in the Economic Development of the Pennsylvania Piedmont Plateau," *Bulletin of the Philadelphia Geographical Society*, vol. 13, 4 (1915), pp. 133–154. **5568**

Lemon, James T., and Gary Nash, "The Distribution of Wealth in Eighteenth Century America: A Century of Changes in Chester County, Pennsylvania, 1693–1802," *Journal of Social History*, vol. 2, 1 (1968), pp. 1–24. **5569**

Schnell, George A., "Geographic Associations between Urban-Industrial Development, the Mining Industry, and Fertility in Pennsylvania, 1880," *Proceedings of the Pennsylvania Academy of Science*, vol. 52 (1978), pp. 78–84. **5570**

Muller, Edward K., "Historical Aspects of Regional Structural Change in the Pittsburgh Region," in Joachim Hesse, ed., *Regional Structural Change and Industrial Policy in International Perspective: United States, Great Britain, France, and the Federal Republic of Germany* (Baden-Baden: Nomos-Verlag, 1988), pp. 17–48. **5571**

LAND & LAND USE

Mason, Carol Y., "Land Economy of Amberson Valley, Pennsylvania," *Economic Geography*, vol. 12, 3 (1936), pp. 265–272. [Focus on 1730s–1930s] **5572**

Darden, Joe T., "The Cemeteries of Pittsburgh: A Study in Historical Geography," Master's thesis, University of Pittsburgh, 1970. **5573**

EXTRACTIVE ACTIVITY

Oilfields

Miller, E. Willard, "The Economic Geography of the Bradford (Pennsylvania) Oil Region," Ph.D. diss., Ohio State University, 1942. **5574**

Miller, E. Willard, "Economic Geography of the Bradford Oil Region," *Economic Geography*, vol. 19, 2 (1943), pp. 177–186. [Focus on 1875–1940] **5575**

Coalfields

McCauley, Ray L., "The Natural and Cultural Factors That Have Affected Coal Production in Westmoreland County from 1860 to 1950," Master's thesis, University of Pittsburgh, 1950. **5576**

Miller, E. Willard, "The Southern Anthracite Region: A Problem Region," *Economic Geography*, vol. 31, 4 (1955), pp. 331–350. [Focus on 1850–1950] **5577**

Griess, Phyliss R., and George F. Deasy, "Past, Present, and Future Foci of Bituminous Coal Strip Mining in Pennsylvania," *Proceedings of the Pennsylvania Academy of Science*, vol. 32 (1958), pp. 108–114. **5578**

Miller, E. Willard, "Trends in the Coal Mining Industry of the Upper Susquehanna Basin (West Branch), 1925–1962," *Proceedings of the Pennsylvania Academy of Science*, vol. 38, 2 (1965), pp. 227–235. **5579**

Miller, E. Willard, "Employment Trends in Primary Activities of the Appalachian Coal Mining Region, 1940–1960," *Proceedings of the Pennsylvania Academy of Science*, vol. 41 (1967), pp. 119–122. **5580**

AGRICULTURE

See also **4877–4878**

James, Henry F., "The Agricultural Industry of Southeastern Pennsylvania: IV—Colonial Settlers"; "VI—Historical Introduction," *Bulletin of the Philadelphia Geographical Society*, vol. 26, 2 (1928), pp. 123–147; and 3 (1928), pp. 87–126. **5581**

Misra, R., "Agricultural Development in a Traditional Society: A Theoretical and Empirical Analysis of Processes of Agricultural Development and Change in Lancaster County, Pennsylvania," Ph.D. diss., University of Maryland, 1964. **5582**

Berry, David, "Idling of Farmland in the Philadelphia Region, 1930–1970," Regional Science Research Institute, Discussion Paper no. 88 (1976). **5583**

Good, David, "The Localization of Tobacco Production in Lancaster County," *Pennsylvania History*, vol. 49, 3 (1982), pp. 190–200. **5584**

LANDSCAPE

General

Lewis, Peirce F., and Ben Marsh, "Slices through Time: The Physical and Cultural Landscapes of Central and Eastern Pennsylvania," in Roman Cybriwsky, ed., *The Philadelphia Region: Selected Essays and Field Trip Itineraries* (Washington, D.C.: Association of American Geographers, 1979), pp. 1–50. **5585**

O'Brien, Raymond J., *Bucks County: A Journey through Paradise, from the Peaceable Kingdom to the Suburban Dream* (Dubuque: Kendall/Hunt, 1988), 178 pp. **5586**

Pennsylvania Dutch country

Wasielewski, Hans Th. v., "Das obere Conestogatal: Ein Stück deutschpennsylvanischer Kulturlandschaft," *Mitteilungen der Geographischen*

Gesellschaft in München, vol. 32 (1939), pp. 165–233. **5587**

Hovinen, Elizabeth J., and Gary R. Hovinen, *Pennsylvania Dutch Country: A Pictorial History* (Lancaster: Pennsylvania Publishers, 1986), 203 pp. **5588**

Housing

Pillsbury, Richard R., "The Construction Materials of the Rural Folk Housing of the Pennsylvania Culture Region," *Pioneer America*, vol. 8, 2 (1976), pp. 98–106. **5589**

Pillsbury, Richard R., "Patterns in the Folk and Vernacular House Forms of the Pennsylvania Culture Region," *Pioneer America*, vol. 9, 1 (1977), pp. 12–31. **5590**

Stetson, George, "The 1704 House of William Brinton, the Younger," *Pennsylvania Geographer*, vol. 17, 3 (1979), pp. 7–11. [Birmingham Twp., Chester Co.; rare American example of late medieval–style stone house with leaded glass casement windows] **5591**

Barns and other structures

Sloane, Eric P., "The First Covered Bridge in America," *Geographical Review*, vol. 49, 3 (1959), pp. 315–321. [Toll bridge over the Schuylkill River at Philadelphia] **5592**

Glass, Joseph W., "The Pennsylvania Culture Region: A Geographical Interpretation of Barns and Farmhouses," Ph.D. diss., Pennsylvania State University, 1971. **5593**

Noble, Allen G., and Brian Coffey, "Barn and Silo Types in Pennsylvania," *Pennsylvania Geographer*, vol. 12, 3 (1974), pp. 20–29. **5594**

Ensminger, Robert, "The Pennsylvania Barn: A Study in the Continuity of Form," *Pennsylvania Geographer*, vol. 21, 1–2 (1983), pp. 14–20. **5595**

Glass, Joseph W., *The Pennsylvania Culture Region: A View from the Barn* (Ann Arbor: University Microfilms International Research Press, 1986), 255 pp. **5596**

COMMUNICATIONS & TRADE

Trade

Schwartz, Mabel K., "Environmental Adjustment Reflected in the Character and Conduct of the Trade of Pittsburgh in the Pre-Railroad Days," Master's thesis, University of Chicago, 1924. **5597**

McTernan, Donald, "Andrew Depuy's Eighteenth Century Frontier Store," *Pioneer America*, vol. 4, 1 (1972), pp. 23–28. [Lower Smithfield] **5598**

Transport

Parkins, Almon E., "The Development of Transportation in Pennsylvania," *Bulletin of the Geographical Society of Philadelphia*, vol. 14, 3 (1916), pp. 92–114; 4 (1916), pp. 148–168; and vol. 15, 1 (1917), pp. 1–18.   **5599**

Myers, Richmond E., "Geography of Transportation in the Susquehanna River Corridor, Pennsylvania: 1700–1900," Ph.D. diss., Pennsylvania State University, 1951.   **5600**

Ruth, David H., "Development of Transportation in Blair County, Pennsylvania," Master's thesis, Indiana University of Pennsylvania, 1966.   **5601**

Filani, Michael O., "Highway Network Development and Urban Growth in Pennsylvania, 1920–1960," Master's thesis, Pennsylvania State University, 1970.   **5602**

Heatley, Richard T., "The Union Railroad Company of East Pittsburgh, Pennsylvania: An Historical Geography Analysis," Master's thesis, Indiana University of Pennsylvania, 1976.   **5603**

Pawling, Richard N., "The Geographic Influences upon the Development and Decline of the Union Canal," *Pennsylvania Geographer*, vol. 22, 1–2 (1984), pp. 14–21.   **5604**

Ballas, Donald J., "The Western Division of the Pennsylvania Canal: An Historical Geography," *Pennsylvania Geographer*, vol. 24, 1 & 2 (1986), pp. 27–34.   **5605**

MANUFACTURING & INDUSTRIALIZATION

See also **4898**

White, C. Langdon, "The Iron and Steel Industry of the Pittsburgh District," *Economic Geography*, vol. 4, 2 (1928), pp. 115–139. [Focus on 1860s–1925]   **5606**

Miller, E. Willard, "The Industrial Development of the Allegheny Valley of Western Pennsylvania," *Economic Geography*, vol. 19, 4 (1943), pp. 388–404. [Focus on 1870–1942]   **5607**

Miller, E. Willard, "The Industrial Structure of the Bradford Oil Region," *Western Pennsylvania Historical Magazine*, vol. 26 (1943), pp. 59–79.   **5608**

Miller, E. Willard, "Connellsville Beehive Coke Region: A Declining Mineral Economy," *Economic Geography*, vol. 29, 2 (1953), pp. 144–158.   **5609**

Meisel, Jay L., "The Iron and Steel Industry in Pennsylvania from 1716 to 1865," Master's thesis, Indiana University, 1960.   **5610**

Thompson, Andrew R., "The Geographical Influence upon the Rise and Decline of the Grist and Flour Milling Industry in Bucks County, Pennsylvania: A Historical Sequence," Master's thesis, West Chester State College, 1963.   **5611**

Davis, George S., "Factors of Location and Regionalization of the Pennsylvania Paper Industry, 1690–1961," Master's thesis, Pennsylvania State University, 1966.   **5612**

Slick, Max H., "Manufactural Diversification in the Allentown-Bethlehem-Easton Standard Metropolitan Statistical Area: The 1915–1960 Period," Ph.D. diss., Pennsylvania State University, 1967.   **5613**

Sabatos, J., "A Historical Geographic Analysis of Selected Manufacturing Industries of Indiana County, Pennsylvania, since 1800," Master's thesis, Indiana University of Pennsylvania, 1968.   **5614**

Slick, Max H., "An Analysis of the Changing Manufacturing Structure within the Four Major Nodes of the Allentown-Bethlehem-Easton SMSA," *Pennsylvania Geographer*, vol. 6, 4 (1968), pp. 6–13. [Focus on 1910–1960]   **5615**

Slick, Max H., "A Comparative Analysis of Methodology for Measuring Manufactural Diversification," *Proceedings of the Pennsylvania Academy of Science*, vol. 42 (1968), pp. 178–183. [Focus on the Lehigh Valley, 1915–1960]   **5616**

Thompson, Andrew R., "Changing Geography of Grist Milling in Bucks County, Pennsylvania," *Pennsylvania Geographer*, vol. 8, 4 (1970), pp. 1–12.   **5617**

Patton, Spiro G., "Comparative Advantage and Urban Industrialization: Reading, Allentown, and Lancaster in the Nineteenth Century," *Pennsylvania History*, vol. 50, 2 (1983), pp. 148–169.   **5618**

Warren, Kenneth, "The Business Career of Henry Clay Frick," *Pittsburgh History*, vol. 73, 1 (1990), pp. 3–15.   **5619**

URBAN NETWORKS & URBANIZATION

Cummings, Hubertis, "Pennsylvania: Network of Canal Ports," *Pennsylvania History*, vol. 21, 3 (1954), pp. 260–271.   **5620**

Geizer, Bernard P., "Central Places of Central Bucks County, Pennsylvania: Their Evolution and Classification," Master's thesis, Rutgers University, 1963.   **5621**

Lemon, James T., "Urbanization and the Development of Eighteenth-Century Southeastern Pennsylvania and Adjacent Delaware," *William* and Mary Quarterly, 3d ser., vol. 24, 4 (1967), pp. 501–542.   **5622**

Harper, R. Eugene, "Town Development in Early Western Pennsylvania," *Western Pennsylvania Historical Magazine*, vol. 71, 1 (1988), pp. 3–26.
                                                     5623

Muller, Edward K., "Metropolis and Region: A Framework for Enquiry into Western Pennsylvania," in Samuel P. Hays, ed., *City at the Point: Essays on the Social History of Pittsburgh* (Pittsburgh: University of Pittsburgh Press, 1989), pp. 181–211.   **5624**

TOWN GROWTH

Philadelphia

Keir, R. Malcolm, "The Causes for the Growth of Philadelphia as an Industrial Center," *Bulletin of the Philadelphia Geographical Society*, vol. 13, 3 (1915), pp. 91–109.   **5625**

Brown, Ralph Hall, "Philadelphia," *Journal of Geography*, vol. 21, 9 (1922), pp. 214–218.   **5626**

Williams, Frank E., "Historical Geography of the Philadelphia Region," Ph.D. diss., University of Wisconsin, 1927.   **5627**

Williams, Frank E., "Suburban Industrial Development of Philadelphia's Delaware County," *Bulletin of the Philadelphia Geographical Society*, vol. 25, 3 (1927), pp. 123–133. [Focus on the period after 1775]   **5628**

Alexandre, M., "Philadelphie: Le site et son utilisation," *Bulletin de l'Association de géographes français*, vol. 33, 56 (1932), pp. 75–80.   **5629**

Klimm, Lester E., "The Physical Site of Penn's 'Greene Towne'," *Bulletin of the Philadelphia Geographical Society*, vol. 33, 1 (1935), pp. 1–8.
                                                     5630

Starkey, Otis P., "The Situation and the Growth of Philadelphia," *Bulletin of the Philadelphia Geographical Society*, vol. 33, 1 (1935), pp. 9–15.   **5631**

Miller, Roger P., and Joseph Siry, "The Emerging Suburb: West Philadelphia, 1850–1880," *Pennsylvania History*, vol. 47, 2 (1980), pp. 99–145. **5632**

Hovinen, Gary R., "Suburbanization in Greater Philadelphia, 1880–1941," *Journal of Historical Geography*, vol. 11, 2 (1985), pp. 174–195.
                                                     5633

Pittsburgh

Miller, E. Willard, "Pittsburgh: Patterns of Evolution," *Pennsylvania Geographer*, vol. 19, 3 (1981), pp. 6–20.   **5634**

Shirey, Ruth I. "Pittsburgh: Renaissance, Redevelopment, and Revitalization, 1945–1981," *Penn-*

sylvania Geographer, vol. 19, 3 (1981), pp. 35–45.
                                                     5635

Other centers

Meynen, Emil, "Germantown," *Deutsche Arbeit*, vol. 24, 4 (1934), pp. 176–183.   **5636**

Meynen, Emil, "Germantown, Pennsylvanien, 1683–1933," *Heimat: Zeitschrift für niederrheinische Heimatpflege*, vol. 13 (1934), pp. 105–112.   **5637**

Wood, Donald S., "A Geographical Study of the Economic and Urban Evolution of McKeesport, Pennsylvania, from Frontier Settlement to Industrial City, 1758–1900," Master's thesis, University of Pittsburgh, 1950.   **5638**

Plankchorn, William F., "A Geographic Study of the Growth of Greater Williamsport, Pennsylvania," Ph.D. diss., Pennsylvania State University, 1957.   **5639**

Enman, John A., Jr., "The Shape, Structure, and Function of a Pennsylvania Company Town," *Proceedings of the Pennsylvania Academy of Science*, vol. 42 (1968), pp. 167–170. [Continental no. 2, Connellsville region, 1903–1968]   **5640**

Lewis, Peirce F., "Small Town in Pennsylvania," *Annals of the Association of American Geographers*, vol. 62, 2 (1972), pp. 323–351. Reissued in John Fraser Hart, ed., *Regions of the United States* (New York: Harper & Row, 1972), same pagination.   **5641**

Lord, Arthur, "Donegal Mills: A Case Study in Historical Geography," *Journal of the Lancaster County Historical Society*, vol. 81 (1977), pp. 117–137.   **5642**

Smith, Joe B., "The Growth and Development of York City from 1741 to 1890," *Pennsylvania Geographer*, vol. 25, 1 & 2 (1987), pp. 8–12.   **5643**

URBAN ECONOMIC STRUCTURE

Philadelphia

Talarcheck, Gary M., "Urban Parks and Land Use: An Historical Geography of Philadelphia's Public Squares," Master's thesis, Temple University, 1975.   **5644**

Jucha, Robert, "The Anatomy of a Streetcar Suburb: A Development History of Shadyside, 1852–1916," *West Pennsylvania Historical Magazine*, vol. 62, 4 (1979), pp. 301–320.   **5645**

Scranton, Philip, "Beyond Anecdotes and Aggregates: The Pattern of Industrial Decline in Philadelphia Textiles, 1916–1931," *Antipode*, vol. 18, 3 (1986), pp. 284–310.   **5646**

Other centers

Mattingly, Paul F., "Delimitation and Movement of CBD Boundaries through Time: The Harrisburg Example," *Professional Geographer*, vol. 16, 3 (1964), pp. 9–13.　　　　　**5647**

Obler, Kenneth E., "Inn, Hotel, and Motel Clusters in Somerset County, Pennsylvania: A Geographical Sequent Occupance Analysis," Master's thesis, University of Pennsylvania, 1971.　　**5648**

Kozakowski, Stephen F., "Work Force and Transportation: Case Study of Bridesburg, 1850–1930," Master's thesis, Temple University, 1976.　　**5649**

Tarr, Joel A., *Transportation Innovation and Changing Spatial Patterns in Pittsburgh, 1850–1934* (Chicago: Public Works Historical Society, Essays in Public Works History, no. 6, 1978), 64 pp.　　　　　**5650**

Mosher, Anne E., "Capital Transformation and the Restructuring of Place: The Creation of a Model Industrial Town," Ph.D. diss., Pennsylvania State University, 1989. [Vandergrift]　　**5651**

Wolfram-Seifert, Ursel, "Pittsburgh: Der wirtschaftliche und städtebauliche Wandel einer amerikanischen Industriestadt zur High Tech- und Dienstleistungsmetropole," in Frank N. Nagel, ed., *Der nordatlantische Raum: Festschrift für Gerhard Overbeck* (Hamburg: Mitteilungen der Geographische Gesellschaft in Hamburg, vol. 80, 1990), pp. 113–137.　　**5652**

URBAN SOCIAL STRUCTURE

Philadelphia

Johnson, Leon C., "Black Migration, Spatial Organization and Perception, and Philadelphia's Urban Environment, 1638–1930," Master's thesis, University of Washington, 1973.　　**5653**

Storbeck, James E., "Age Structure of Philadelphia, 1930–1970," Master's thesis, Temple University, 1975.　　　　　**5654**

Miller, Roger P., "A Time-Geographic Assessment of the Impact of Horsecar Transportation on Suburban Non-Heads-of-Household in Philadelphia, 1850–1860," Ph.D. diss., University of California–Berkeley, 1979.　　**5655**

Herschberg, Theodore, ed., *Philadelphia: Work Space, Family, and Group Experience in the Nineteenth Century* (New York: Oxford University Press, 1981), 525 pp.　　**5656**

Miller, Roger P., "Household Activity Patterns in Nineteenth-Century Suburbs: A Time-Geographic Exploration," *Annals of the Association of American Geographers*, vol. 72, 3 (1982), pp. 355–371.　　　　　**5657**

Miller, Roger P., "The Hoover in the Garden: Middle-Class Women and Suburbanization, 1850–1920," *Environment and Planning D: Society and Space*, vol. 1, 1 (1983), pp. 73–87.　　**5658**

Pack, Janet R., "Urban Spatial Transformation: Philadelphia, 1850–1880, Heterogeneity to Homogeneity?" *Social Science History*, vol. 8, 4 (1984), pp. 425–454.　　　　**5659**

Pittsburgh

Wolfe, Jacqueline, "The Changing Pattern of Residence of the Negro in Pittsburgh, with Emphasis on the Period 1930–1960," Master's thesis, University of Pittsburgh, 1964.　　**5660**

Fitzpatrick, Walter J., "Places of Worship in the City of Pittsburgh, Pennsylvania: A Study of Changes in Location and Distribution, 1910–1960," Master's thesis, University of Pittsburgh, 1967.　　　　　**5661**

Kuntz, Leonard I., "The Changing Pattern of Distribution of the Jewish Population of Pittsburgh from Earliest Settlement to 1963," Ph.D. diss., Louisiana State University, 1970.　　**5662**

Darden, Joe T., "Factors in the Location of Pittsburgh's Cemeteries," *Virginia Geographer*, vol. 7, 2 (1972), pp. 3–8. [Focus on 1850–1900]　　**5663**

Snyder, Frank S., "Spatial Distribution of Foreign-Born Whites in the City of Pittsburgh, Pennsylvania, 1910–1960," Ph.D. diss., University of Pittsburgh, 1973.　　　　　**5664**

Masson, Elizabeth J., "Episcopal Church Development and Church Neighborhood Change: Pittsburgh, Pennsylvania, 1870–1975," Master's thesis, University of Pittsburgh, 1976.　　**5665**

Kory, William B., "Spatial Distribution and Mobility of the Aged in Pittsburgh, Pennsylvania, 1940–1970," Ph.D. diss., University of Pittsburgh, 1977.　　　　　**5666**

Swauger, John, "Pittsburgh's Residential Pattern in 1815," *Annals of the Association of American Geographers*, vol. 68, 2 (1978), pp. 265–277.　　**5667**

Other centers

Costanzo, Anthony C., "A Geographic Study of the Italian Community in Washington, Pennsylvania: 1900–1970," Master's thesis, Pennsylvania State University, 1973.　　　　**5668**

TOWNSCAPE

See also **5509**

Regional

Pillsbury, Richard R., "The Market or Public Square in Pennsylvania, 1682–1815," *Proceed-*

ings of the Pennsylvania Academy of Sciences,
vol. 41 (1967), pp. 116–118.   **5669**

Pillsbury, Richard R., "The Urban Street Pattern of
Pennsylvania before 1815: A Study in Cultural
Geography," Ph.D. diss., Pennsylvania State
University, 1968.   **5670**

Pillsbury, Richard R., "The Urban Street Pattern as
a Culture Indicator: Pennsylvania, 1682–1815,"
Annals of the Association of American Geographers, vol. 60, 3 (1970), pp. 428–446.   **5671**

Pillsbury, Richard R., "Urban Street Patterns and
Topography: A Pennsylvania Case Study," *Professional Geographer*, vol. 22, 1 (1970), pp. 21–25.
                                           5672

Elbow, Gary S., "What Happens to the Company
Town When the Company Leaves? The
Changing Landscapes of Pittsburgh Area Company Towns," *Places*, vol. 3, 2 (1976), pp. 19–25.
                                           5673

Zelinsky, Wilbur, "The Pennsylvania Town: An
Overdue Geographical Account," *Geographical
Review*, vol. 67, 2 (1977), pp. 127–147.   **5674**

Demarest, David, and Eugene Levy, "A Relict Industrial Landscape: Pittsburgh's Coke Region,"
Landscape, vol. 29, 2 (1986), pp. 29–36. [Focus
from the 1870s to the 1910s]   **5675**

Mulrooney, Margaret M., "A Legacy of Coal: The
Coal Company Town of Southwestern Pennsylvania," in Thomas Carter and Bernard L. Herman, eds., *Perspectives in Vernacular Architecture, IV* (Columbia: University of Missouri Press,
for the Vernacular Architecture Forum, 1991),
pp. 130–137.   **5676**

Philadelphia

Reps, John W., "William Penn and the Planning
of Philadelphia," *Town Planning Review*, vol. 27,
1 (1956), pp. 27–39.   **5677**

Johnston, Norman J., "The Caste and Class of the
Urban Form of Historic Philadelphia," *Journal
of the American Institute of Planners*, vol. 32, 6
(1966), pp. 334–349.   **5678**

Beauregard, Robert A., "The Spatial Transformation of Postwar Philadelphia," in Robert A.
Beauregard, ed., *Atop the Urban Hierarchy*

(Totowa, N.J.: Rowman & Littlefield, 1989), pp.
195–238.   **5679**

Other centers

Crist, Anna, "The Influence of the Hershey Estates
on the Morphological Development of the Town
of Hershey, Pennsylvania," Master's thesis,
Syracuse University, 1948.   **5680**

Buvinger, Bruce J., "Street Patterns of Pittsburgh,"
Master's thesis, University of Pittsburgh, 1972.
                                           5681

RECREATION & TOURISM

Hovinen, Gary R., "Tourism Cycles in Lancaster
County, Pennsylvania," *Canadian Geographer*,
vol. 25, 3 (1981), pp. 283–286.   **5682**

Hovinen, Gary R., "Visitor Cycles: Outlook for
Tourism in Lancaster County," *Annals of Tourism Research*, vol. 9, 4 (1982), pp. 565–583. [Focus
on 1930s–1980]   **5683**

Leib, Jonathan I., "The Historical Geography of
Minor League Baseball in Pennsylvania: 1902–
1989," *Pennsylvania Geographer*, vol. 28, 1
(1990), pp. 3–14.   **5684**

Miller, E. Willard, "Golf in Pennsylvania," *Pennsylvania Geographer*, vol. 28, 1 (1990), pp. 42–49.
                                           5685

PLANNING

Shirey, George S., "The Historic Preservation of
Stone Iron Furnaces in Clarion County: Helen
Furnace, a Case Study," *Pennsylvania Geographer*, vol. 17, 3 (1979), pp. 19–24.   **5686**

PLACE NAMES

Espenshade, Abraham H., *Pennsylvania Place
Names* (State College: Pennsylvania State College Studies in History and Political Science, no.
1, 1925), 375 pp. Reprinted Baltimore: Genealogical Publishing Co., 1970.   **5687**

Pillsbury, Richard R., "The Street Name System of
Pennsylvania before 1820," *Names*, vol. 17, 3
(1969), pp. 214–222.   **5688**

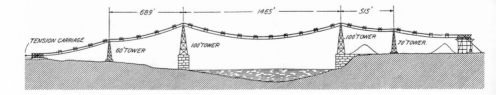

DELAWARE

ENVIRONMENTAL CHANGE

French, Gregory, "Historical Shoreline Changes in Response to Environmental Conditions in West Delaware Bay," Master's thesis, Mankato State University, 1990.   5689

NATIVE PEOPLES & WHITE RELATIONS

Porter, Frank W., Jr., "The Formation of the Nanticoke Indian Community at Indian River Inlet, Sussex County, Delaware," Ph.D. diss., University of Maryland, 1978.   5690

EXPLORATION & MAPPING

Jillson, Willard R., "Filson's Map of Wilmington, Delaware," *Filson Club Historical Quarterly*, vol. 7 (1933), pp. 209–213.   5691

Kohlin, Harald, "First Maps of Delaware: A Swedish Colony in North America," *Imago Mundi*, vol. 5 (1948), pp. 78–82.   5692

Munroe, John A., "Pierre Charles Varlé and His Map of Delaware," *Delaware History*, vol. 22, 1 (1986), pp. 22–38.   5693

REGIONAL SETTLEMENT

See 4858

AGRICULTURE

See 4837

LANDSCAPE

Quinn, Judith, "Traversing the Landscape in Federal Delaware," *Delaware History*, vol. 23, 1 (1988), pp. 39–61.   5694

MANUFACTURING & INDUSTRIALIZATION

Henderson, George L., "Continuity and Change in a Delaware Shipbuilding Town: Milton, Delaware, 1870–1910," Master's thesis, University of Delaware, 1987.   5695

URBAN NETWORKS & URBANIZATION

See 4659

TOWN GROWTH

Rodney, Richard S., "Historic Notes Relating to New Castle, Delaware," *Bulletin of the Philadelphia Geographical Society*, vol. 17, 4 (1919), pp. 138–142.   5696

URBAN SOCIAL STRUCTURE

Schreuder, Yda, "Immigrant Employment and Residential Patterns in Wilmington, Delaware, 1880–1910," *Proceedings of the Middle States Division, Association of American Geographers*, vol. 20 (1986), pp. 44–53.   5697

Schreuder, Yda, "Wilmington's Immigrant Settlement, 1880–1920," *Delaware History*, vol. 23, 2 (1988), pp. 140–166.   5698

Schreuder, Yda, "The Impact of Labor Segmentation on the Ethnic Division of Labor and the Immigrant Residential Community: Polish Leather Workers in Wilmington, Delaware, in the Early Twentieth Century," *Journal of Historical Geography*, vol. 16, 4 (1990), pp. 402–424.   5699

PLACE NAMES

Dunlap, Arthur R., *Dutch and Swedish Place-Names in Delaware* (Newark: University of Delaware Press, for the Institute of Delaware History and Culture, 1956), 66 pp.   5700

MARYLAND

GENERAL

The state

Mitchell, Robert D., and Edward K. Muller, "Interpreting Maryland's Past: Praxis and Desiderata," in Robert D. Mitchell and Edward K. Muller, eds., *Geographical Perspectives on Maryland's Past* (College Park: University of Maryland Department of Geography, Occasional Paper no. 4, 1979), pp. 1–50.   5701

Mitchell, Robert D., and Edward K. Muller, eds., *Geographical Perspectives on Maryland's Past* (College Park: University of Maryland Department of Geography, Occasional Paper no. 4, 1979), 187 pp.   5702

DiLisio, James E., "Maryland's Past in Today's Landscape," in his *Maryland: A Geography* (Boulder: Westview Press, 1983), pp. 141–152.   5703

Smaller areas

Raymond, John A., "An Historical Geography of the Eastern Shore of Maryland," Master's thesis, Syracuse University, 1968.   5704

ENVIRONMENTAL CHANGE

Gottschalk, L. C., "Effects of Soil Erosion on Navigation in Upper Chesapeake Bay," *Geographical Review*, vol. 35, 2 (1945), pp. 219–238. [Emphasis on 1846–1938]   5705

Costa, John E., "Effects of Agriculture on Erosion and Sedimentation in the Piedmont Province, Maryland," *Bulletin of the Geological Society of America*, vol. 86 (1975), pp. 1281–1286.   5706

NATIVE PEOPLES & WHITE RELATIONS

Porter, Frank W., Jr., "A Century of Accommodation: The Nanticoke Indians in Colonial Maryland," *Maryland Historical Magazine*, vol. 74, 2 (1979), pp. 175–192.   5707

Porter, Frank W., Jr., "Strategies for Survival: The Nanticoke Indians in a Hostile World," *Ethnohistory*, vol. 26, 4 (1979), pp. 325–346.   5708

Porter, Frank W., Jr., "Behind the Frontier: Indian Survivals in Maryland," *Maryland Historical Magazine*, vol. 75, 1 (1980), pp. 42–54.   5709

EXPLORATION & MAPPING

Cumming, William P., "Early Maps of the Chesapeake Bay Region: Their Relation to Settlement and Society," in David B. Quinn, ed., *Early Maryland in a Wider World* (Detroit: Wayne State University Press, 1982), pp. 267–310.   5710

Gibbons, Virginia S., "Lithography and the City Map: Baltimore, 1850–1900," Master's thesis, University of Maryland, 1983.   5711

REGIONAL SETTLEMENT

See also 5879

Warman, Henry J., "The Population and Land Utilization of the Manor Counties of Maryland," Ph.D. diss., Clark University, 1945. [Harford and Cecil Cos., 1660–1940]   5712

Isaac, Erich, "The First Century of Settlement of Kent Island," Ph.D. diss., Johns Hopkins University, 1957.   5713

Isaac, Erich, "Kent Island: Part I—The Period of Settlement; Part II—Settlements and Landholding under the Proprietary," *Maryland Historical Magazine*, vol. 52, 2 (1957), pp. 93–119; 3, 210–232. [In Chesapeake Bay, 1639–1919]   5714

Earle, Carville V., *The Evolution of a Tidewater Settlement System: All Hallow's Parish, Maryland, 1650–1783* (Chicago: University of Chicago Department of Geography, Research Paper no. 170, 1975), 239 pp.   5715

Porter, Frank W., Jr., "From Backcountry to County: The Delayed Settlement of Western Maryland," *Maryland Historical Magazine*, vol. 70, 4 (1975), pp. 329–349.   5716

Porter, Frank W., Jr., "The Maryland Frontier, 1722–1732: Prelude to Settlement in Western Maryland," in Robert D. Mitchell and Edward K. Muller, eds., *Geographical Perspectives on Maryland's Past* (College Park: University of Maryland Department of Geography, Occasional Paper no. 4, 1979), pp. 90–107.   5717

POPULATION

See also 4861

Warman, Henry J., "Population of the Manor Counties of Maryland," *Economic Geography*, vol. 25, 1 (1949), pp. 23–40.   5718

Buford, Carolyn B., "The Distribution of Negroes in Maryland, 1850–1950," Master's thesis, Catholic University of America, 1956.   **5719**

Kavula, Sister Mary Verne, "A Geographic Analysis of the Population of Maryland, 1930–1960," Catholic University of America, 1966.   **5720**

Marks, Bayly, "The Rage for Kentucky: Emigration from St. Mary's County, 1790–1810," in Robert D. Mitchell and Edward K. Muller, eds., *Geographical Perspectives on Maryland's Past* (College Park: University of Maryland Department of Geography, Occasional Paper no. 4, 1979), pp. 108–128.   **5721**

RURAL & REGIONAL SOCIAL GEOGRAPHY

Schwartzberg, Joseph E., "A Geographic Study of Old Order Amish and Stauffer Mennonite Communities in Southern Maryland," Master's thesis, University of Maryland, 1951.   **5722**

Jamieson, Andrew, "The Impact of Race on the Location of High Status Blacks in Prince George's County, 1960–1980," Master's thesis, University of Maryland, 1988.   **5723**

Pickett, James E., "Smith Island and Social Change in the Twentieth Century: A Cultural-Historical Geography," Master's thesis, Towson State University, 1990.   **5724**

LAND & LAND USE

Singleton, C. B., Jr., "An Evolution of Land Use in Kent County, Maryland," Master's thesis, University of Maryland, 1953.   **5725**

Edmonds, Anne C., "The Land Holdings of the Ridgelys of Hampton, 1726–1843," Master's thesis, Johns Hopkins University, 1957. [Baltimore Co.]   **5726**

Donnelly, Ralph, "The Colonial Land Patent System in Maryland," *Surveying and Mapping*, vol. 40, 1 (1980), pp. 51–68.   **5727**

EXTRACTIVE ACTIVITY

Fast, Nathan, "Oyster Production and Cultch Division in Nineteenth Century Maryland," Ph.D. diss., Johns Hopkins University, 1959.   **5728**

AGRICULTURE

See also **4837**

Love, Ann G., "A Century of Agricultural Progress in a Rural Community: Sandy Spring, Maryland, 1844–1949," Master's thesis, University of Maryland, 1950.   **5729**

Whisler, O. C., "Changes in Agriculture: Calvert County, Maryland, 1940–1960," Master's thesis, University of Maryland, 1965.   **5730**

Kolbo, Allan D., "Response of Commercial Agriculture to Urban Impact in the Rural-Urban Fringe of Baltimore City, 1930–1970," Ph.D. diss., University of Maryland, 1972.   **5731**

COMMUNICATIONS & TRADE

Brune, Basel H., "Early Tobacco Landings along Patuxent River, Maryland," Master's thesis, University of Maryland, 1972.   **5732**

Brune, Basel H., "The Changing Spatial Organization of Early Tobacco Marketing in the Patuxent River Basin," in Robert D. Mitchell and Edward K. Muller, eds., *Geographical Perspectives on Maryland's Past* (College Park: University of Maryland Department of Geography, Occasional Paper no. 4, 1979), pp. 78–89.   **5733**

Baughman, Charles A., "The Development of an Artificial Water Transportation Facility along the Potomac River: The Chesapeake and Ohio Canal," Master's thesis, University of Chicago, 1982.   **5734**

Hayden, Robert S., "Natural and Cultural Changes in Sequential Land Use on the Chesapeake and Ohio Canal, *Virginia Geographer*, vol. 16, 2 (1984), pp. 12–18.   **5735**

MANUFACTURING & INDUSTRIALIZATION

Hahn, Roland H., and Christine Wellems, "Hochtechnologie im Baltimore-Washington Korridor: Entwicklung, Standortsbedingungen, und räumliche Muster," in Hans-Wilhelm Windhorst, ed., *Arbeiten zur Kulturgeographie der USA* (Vechta: Vechta Druckerei und Verlag, Zentralverband der Deutschen Geographen, Arbeitskreis USA, Vechtaer Arbeiten zur Geographie und Regionalwissenschaft, vol. 10, 1990), pp. 85–98.   **5736**

URBAN NETWORKS & URBANIZATION

Marks, Bayly, "Rural Response to Urban Penetration: Baltimore and St. Mary's County, Maryland, 1790–1840," *Journal of Historical Geography*, vol. 8, 2 (1982), pp. 113–127.   **5737**

TOWN GROWTH

Baltimore

Blood, Pearle, "Factors in the Economic Development of Baltimore, Maryland," *Economic Geography*, vol. 13, 2 (1937), pp. 187–208.   **5738**

Olson, Sherry H., "Baltimore Imitates the Spider," *Annals of the Association of American Geographers*, vol. 69, 4 (1979), pp. 557–574. 5739

Olson, Sherry H., *Baltimore: The Building of an American City* (Baltimore: Johns Hopkins University Press, 1980), 432 pp. 5740

Other centers

Biddle, John F., "Historical Geography of Bladensburg, Maryland," Master's thesis, Catholic University of America, 1954. 5741

URBAN ECONOMIC STRUCTURE

Baltimore

Mowll, Jack O., "The Economic Development of Eighteenth Century Baltimore," Ph.D. diss., Johns Hopkins University, 1956. 5742

Enedy, Joseph D., "The Department Store in Metropolitan Baltimore, 1945 to the Present: A Geographical Analysis," Ph.D. diss., Kent State University, 1973. 5743

Faull, James, "The Structural Growth of the Port of Baltimore, 1729–1814," Master's thesis, University of Maryland, 1973. 5744

Headman, Joseph I., Jr., "The Location of Playgrounds and Parks in Baltimore, 1897–1910," Master's thesis, University of Maryland, 1976. 5745

Muller, Edward K., and Paul A. Groves, "The Changing Location of the Clothing Industry: A Link to the Social Geography of Baltimore in the Nineteenth Century," *Maryland Historical Magazine*, vol. 71, 4 (1976), pp. 403–420. 5746

Babinski, Gregory, "The Development of Transportation Facilities as a Stimulus to Growth in Baltimore, 1800–1853," Master's thesis, Wayne State University, 1977. 5747

Muller, Edward K., and Paul A. Groves, "The Emergence of Industrial Districts in Mid-Nineteenth Century Baltimore," *Geographical Review*, vol. 69, 2 (1979), pp. 159–178. 5748

Muller, Edward K., "Spatial Order before Industrialization: Baltimore's Central District, 1833–1860," *Working Papers*, Regional Economic History Research Center, Eleutherian Mills-Hagley Foundation, Wilmington, Delaware, vol. 4, 2 (1981), pp. 100–139. 5749

Erickson, Rodney A., and Marylynn Gentry, "Suburban Nucleations," *Geographical Review*, vol. 75, 1 (1985), pp. 19–31. [Focus on Baltimore, 1957–1980] 5750

Vill, Martha J., "Building Enterprise in Late Nineteenth-Century Baltimore," *Journal of Historical Geography*, vol. 12, 2 (1986), pp. 162–181. 5751

Gillies, Charles F., "The Motor Freight and Port of Baltimore, Maryland: Thirty Years of Spatial Change," Master's thesis, University of Maryland, 1989. 5752

URBAN SOCIAL STRUCTURE

Baltimore

Kendall, Mary, "Two Decades of Change in the Urban Lutheran Church of Baltimore City, 1950–1970," Master's thesis, Johns Hopkins University, 1970. 5753

Dyce, Cedric, "The Geographic History of the Negro Middle Class in West Baltimore, 1880–1970," Master's thesis, Syracuse University, 1973. 5754

Vill, Martha J., "Property Ownership in German Residential Areas in Baltimore, Maryland, in the Late Nineteenth Century," Ph.D. diss., University of Maryland, 1976. 5755

Beirne, D. Randall, "Residential Growth and Stability in the Baltimore Industrial Community of Canton during the Late Nineteenth Century," *Maryland Historical Magazine*, vol. 74, 1 (1979), pp. 39–51. 5756

Beirne, D. Randall, "Residential Stability among Urban Workers: Industrial Linkages in Hampden-Woodbury, Baltimore, 1880–1930," in Robert D. Mitchell and Edward K. Muller, eds., *Geographical Perspectives on Maryland's Past* (College Park: University of Maryland Department of Geography, Occasional Paper no. 4, 1979), pp. 168–187. 5757

Peebles, Lucy V., "Leisure Time and Indoor Recreational Activities of Blacks: Perceptions and References: Baltimore, 1940–1978," Master's thesis, University of Maryland, 1979. 5758

Vill, Martha J., "Immigrants and Ownership: Home Mortgage Financing in Baltimore, 1865–1914," in Robert D. Mitchell and Edward K. Muller, eds., *Geographical Perspectives on Maryland's Past* (College Park: University of Maryland Department of Geography, Occasional Paper no. 4, 1979), pp. 150–167. 5759

Beirne, D. Randall, "Late Nineteenth Century Industrial Communities in Baltimore," *Maryland Historian*, vol. 11, 1 (1980), pp. 38–49. 5760

Torrieri, Nancy K., "Cultural Change and Residential Dispersal: The Survival of Italian-American Culture in Baltimore," Ph.D. diss., University of Maryland, 1982. 5761

Steffens, Charles, "Who Owns the Waterfront: Property Relations in Fell's Point, Baltimore, 1783," *Urbanism: Past and Present*, no. 15 (1983), pp. 12–17. **5762**

Beirne, D. Randall, "The Impact of Black Labor on European Immigration into Baltimore's Oldtown, 1790–1910," *Maryland Historical Magazine*, vol. 83, 4 (1988), pp. 331–345. **5763**

Other centers

Ives, Sallie M., "The Formation of a Black Community in Annapolis, 1870–1885," in Robert D. Mitchell and Edward K. Muller, eds., *Geographical Perspectives on Maryland's Past* (College Park: University of Maryland Department of Geography, Occasional Paper no. 4, 1979), pp. 129–149. **5764**

Beirne, D. Randall, "Hampden-Woodbury: The Mill Village in an Urban Setting," *Maryland Historical Magazine*, vol. 77, 1 (1982), pp. 6–26. **5765**

Brennand, Mark, "Employment Stability and Community Institutions in a Company Town: Brunswick, Maryland, 1880–1920," Master's thesis, University of Maryland, 1983. **5766**

TOWNSCAPE

See also **4844**

Vill, Martha J., "Residential Development on a Landed Estate: The Case of Baltimore's 'Har- lem'," *Maryland Historical Magazine*, vol. 77, 3 (1982), pp. 266–278. **5767**

PLANNING

Cox, Richard J., "Trouble on the Chain Gang: City Surveying, Maps, and the Absence of Urban Planning in Baltimore, 1730–1823; With a Checklist of Maps of the Period," *Maryland Historical Magazine*, vol. 81, 1 (1986), pp. 8–49. **5768**

PLACE NAMES

Bigbee, Janet H., "Seventeenth Century Place Names: Culture and Process on the Eastern Shore," Master's thesis, University of Maryland, 1970. **5769**

Gritzner, Janet H., "Seventeenth Century Generic Place Names: Culture and Process on the Eastern Shore," *Names*, vol. 20, 4 (1972), pp. 231–239. **5770**

Gritzner, Janet H., "Perception of Landscape through the Medium of Language: Seventeenth-Century Toponymy of the Eastern Shore," in Robert D. Mitchell and Edward K. Muller, eds., *Geographical Perspectives on Maryland's Past* (College Park: University of Maryland Department of Geography, Occasional Paper no. 4, 1979), pp. 51–70. **5771**

Hamill, Kenny, *The Placenames of Maryland: Their Origin and Meaning* (Baltimore: Maryland Historical Society, 1984), 352 pp. **5772**

———— DISTRICT OF COLUMBIA ————

GENERAL

Baker, Marcus, "The Historical Development of the National Capital," *National Geographic Magazine*, vol. 9, 7 (1898), pp. 323–329.   5773

Moore, Charles, "The Transformation of Washington: A Glance at the History and along the Vista of the Future of the Nation's Capital," *National Geographic Magazine*, vol. 43, 6 (1923), pp. 569–595.   5774

Hay, Frances S., "Some Geographic Factors in the History of Washington, D.C.," *Journal of Geography*, vol. 27, 12 (1928), pp. 359–368.   5775

Ahnert, Frank, "Washington, D.C.: Entwicklung und Gegenwartsbild der amerikanischen Hauptstadt," *Erdkunde*, vol. 12, 1 (1958), pp. 1–26.   5776

Groves, Paul A., *Washington between the Wars* (Washington, D.C.: Intac, for the Associates for Renewal in Education,, 1980), 90 pp.   5777

Groves, Paul A., "The Federal Capital Comes of Age," in Keith Melder, ed., *City of Magnificent Intentions: A History of the District of Columbia* (Washington, D.C.: Intac, for the Associates for Renewal in Education, 1983), pp. 304–420.   5778

EXPLORATION & MAPPING

Ehrenberg, Ralph E., "Nicholas King: First Surveyor of the City of Washington, 1803–1812," *Columbia Historical Society Records*, vol. 69–70 (1969–1970), pp. 31–64.   5779

Ehrenberg, Ralph E., "Mapping the Nation's Capital: The Surveyor's Office, 1791–1818," *Quarterly Journal of the Library of Congress*, vol. 36, 3 (1979), pp. 279–319.   5780

POLITICAL & ADMINISTRATIVE GEOGRAPHY

Whitbeck, Ray H., "Geographical Considerations in Selecting the Site for the National Capital," *Journal of Geography*, vol. 13, 8 (1915), pp. 260–261.   5781

Merrens, H. Roy, "The Locating of the Federal Capital of the United States," Master's thesis, University of Maryland, 1957.   5782

Stephenson, Richard W., "America's First Federal Map Library," *Meridian: Journal of the Map &*

Geography Round Table of the American Library Association, vol. 1 (1989), pp. 3–15.   5783

URBAN ECONOMIC STRUCTURE

Hughes, Anthony, "The Delimitation of the Central Business District of Washington, D.C., over Time," Master's thesis, University of Maryland, 1966.   5784

URBAN SOCIAL STRUCTURE

Matthews, Diller G., "The Distribution of the Negro Population of the District of Columbia, 1800–1960," Master's thesis, Catholic University of America, 1967.   5785

Radford, John P., "Patterns of White–Non-White Residential Segregation in Washington, D.C., in the Late Nineteenth Century," Master's thesis, University of Maryland, 1967.   5786

Brown, Letitia W., "Residence Patterns of Negroes in the District of Columbia, 1800–1860," *Records of the Columbia Historical Society of Washington, D.C., 1969–1970*, vol. 69–70 (1971), pp. 66–79.   5787

Groves, Paul A., "Alley Population: An Element in the Social and Physical Structure of Late Nineteenth Century Washington," in W. P. Adams and F. M. Helleiner, eds., *International Geography 1972*, vol. 1, sec. 5, *Historical Geography* (Toronto: University of Toronto Press, for the International Geographical Union, 1972), pp. 422–423.   5788

Borchert, James, "The Rise and Fall of Washington's Inhabited Alleys, 1852–1972," *Records of the Columbia Historical Society of Washington, D.C., 1971–1972*, vol. 48 (1973), pp. 267–288.   5789

Groves, Paul A., "The 'Hidden' Population: Washington Alley Dwellers in the Late Nineteenth Century," *Professional Geographer*, vol. 26, 3 (1974), pp. 270–276.   5790

Dobson, Kenneth E., "Journey-to-Work Patterns of Black Federal Employees in Early Twentieth Century Washington, D.C.," Master's thesis, University of Maryland, 1975.   5791

Groves, Paul A., and Edward K. Muller, "The Evolution of Black Residential Areas in Late Nineteenth Century Cities," *Journal of Historical Geography*, vol. 1, 2 (1975), pp. 169–192.   5792

Groves, Paul A., "The Development of a Black Residential Community in Southwest Washington: 1860–1897," *Records of the Columbia Historical Society of Washington, D.C., 1973–1974,* vol. 49 (1976), pp. 260–275. **5793**

Borchert, James, *Alley Life in Washington: Family, Community, Religion, and Folklife in the City, 1850–1970* (Urbana: University of Illinois Press, 1980), 326 pp. **5794**

TOWNSCAPE

Byrnes, John J., "Pennsylvania Avenue in 1860: A Study in Historical Geography," Master's thesis, Catholic University of America, 1956. **5795**

Beaujeu-Garnier, Jacqueline, "Les leçons de Washington," *La vie urbaine,* n.s. (1968), pt. 1, pp. 1–31. **5796**

Borchert, James, "Alley Landscapes of Washington," *Landscape,* vol. 23, 3 (1979), pp. 3–10. Reprinted in Dell Upton and John Michael Vlach, eds., *Common Places: Readings in American Vernacular Architecture* (Athens: University of Georgia Press, 1986), pp. 281–291. [Focus on 1897–1970] **5797**

Stephenson, Richard W., "The Delineation of a Grand Plan," *Quarterly Journal of the Library of Congress,* vol. 36, 3 (1979), pp. 207–224. [L'Enfant plan of Washington, D.C.] **5798**

Borchert, James, "Builders and Owners of Alley Dwellings in Washington, D.C., 1877–1892," *Records of the Columbia Historical Society of Washington, D.C.,* vol. 50 (1980), pp. 345–358. **5799**

Levy, Anneli M., "Washington, D.C., and the Growth of Its Early Suburbs: 1860–1920," Master's thesis, University of Maryland, 1980. **5800**

PLANNING

Ehrenberg, Ralph E., and Herman R. Friis, "Nicholas King and His Wharfing Plans of the City of Washington, 1797," *Records of the Columbia Historical Society of Washington, D.C.,* vol. 66–67 (1966–1968), pp. 34–46. **5801**

Reps, John W., *Monumental Washington: The Planning and Development of the Capital Center* (Princeton, N.J.: Princeton University Press, 1967), 221 pp. **5802**

APPALACHIA

GENERAL

Semple, Ellen Churchill, "The Influence of the Appalachian Barrier upon Colonial History," *Journal of School Geography*, vol. 1, 1 (1897), pp. 33–41.　　　　5803

Rank, John L., "The Cumberland Narrows as a Factor in the Development of the United States," Master's thesis, Columbia University, 1922.　　　　5804

Mitchell, Robert D., "The View from the East," in Robert D. Mitchell and Milton B. Newton, *The Appalachian Frontier: Views from the East and the Southwest* (London: Institute of British Geographers, Historical Geography Research Group, Historical Geography Research Series, no. 21, 1988), pp. 3–42.　　　　5805

Mitchell, Robert D., and Milton B. Newton, Jr., *The Appalachian Frontier: Views from the East and the Southwest* (London: Institute of British Geographers, Historical Geography Research Group, Historical Geography Research Series, no. 21, 1988), 64 pp.　　　　5806

Newton, Milton B., Jr., "The View from the Southwest," in Robert D. Mitchell and Milton B. Newton, *The Appalachian Frontier: Views from the East and the Southwest* (London: Institute of British Geographers, Historical Geography Research Group, Historical Geography Research Series, no. 21, 1988), pp. 43–64.　　　　5807

Hsiung, David C., "How Isolated Was Appalachia?: Upper East Tennessee, 1780–1835," *Appalachian Journal*, vol. 16, 4 (1989), pp. 336–349.　　　　5808

Mitchell, Robert D., "Introduction: Revisionism and Regionalism," in Robert D. Mitchell, ed., *Appalachian Frontiers: Settlement, Society, and Development in the Pre-Industrial Era* (Lexington: University Press of Kentucky, 1991), pp. 1–22.　　　　5809

Mitchell, Robert D., ed., *Appalachian Frontiers: Settlement, Society, and Development in the Pre-Industrial Era* (Lexington: University Press of Kentucky, 1991), 350 pp.　　　　5810

NATIVE PEOPLES & WHITE RELATIONS

Robison, William C., "Cultural Plant Geography of the Middle Appalachians," Ph.D. diss., Boston University, 1960.　　　　5811

REGIONAL SETTLEMENT

Wilhelm, Eugene J., "Folk Settlements in the Blue Ridge Mountains," *Appalachian Journal*, vol. 5 (1978), pp. 204–245.　　　　5812

RURAL & REGIONAL SOCIAL GEOGRAPHY

Price, Edward T., "Root Digging in the Appalachians: The Geography of Botanical Drugs," *Geographical Review*, vol. 50, 1 (1960), pp. 1–20.　5813

Lewis, Helen Matthews, "Subcultures of the Southern Appalachians," *Virginia Geographer*, vol. 3, 1 (1968), pp. 2–8.　　　　5814

Wilhelm, Eugene J., "Folk Geography of the Blue Ridge Mountains," Ph.D. diss., Texas A & M University, 1971.　　　　5815

Brinkman, Leonard W., "Home Manufactures as an Indication of an Emerging Appalachian Subculture, 1840–1870," *West Georgia College Studies in the Social Sciences*, vol. 12 (1973), pp. 50–58.　　　　5816

Vogeler, Ingolf K., "The Peasant Culture of Appalachia and Its Survival," *Antipode*, vol. 5, 1 (1973), pp. 17–24.　　　　5817

Wilhelm, Eugene J., "Folk Culture History of the Blue Ridge Mountains," *Appalachian Journal*, vol. 2 (1975), pp. 192–222.　　　　5818

Pudup, Mary Beth, "The Boundaries of Class in Preindustrial Appalachia," *Journal of Historical Geography*, vol. 15, 2 (1989), pp. 139–162.　　5819

ECONOMIC DEVELOPMENT

Simon, Richard, "The Labour Process and Uneven Development: The Appalachian Coal Fields, 1880–1930," *International Journal of Urban and Regional Research*, vol. 4, 1 (1980), pp. 46–71.　　　　5820

Pudup, Mary Beth, "The Limits of Subsistence: Agriculture and Industrialization in Central Appalachia," *Agricultural History*, vol. 64, 1 (1990), pp. 61–89.　　　　5821

LAND & LAND USE

Hart, John Fraser, "Land Rotation in Appalachia," *Geographical Review*, vol. 67, 2 (1977), pp. 148–166. [Focus on 1928–1967]　　　　5822

EXTRACTIVE ACTIVITY

Miller, E. Willard, "Industrial Evolution of the Appalachian Coal Mining Region, 1940–1960," in José A. Sporck, ed., *Mélanges de géographie physique, humaine, économique, appliquée offerts à M. Omer Tulippe*, vol. 2 (Gembloux, Belgium: Éditions J. Duculot, 1967), pp. 63–73.

5823

Otto, John S., "The Decline of Forest Farming in Southern Appalachia," *Journal of Forest History*, vol. 27, 1 (1983), pp. 18–27.

5824

RECREATION & TOURISM

Foresta, Ronald A., "Transformation of the Appalachian Trail," *Geographical Review*, vol. 77, 1 (1987), pp. 76–85.

5825

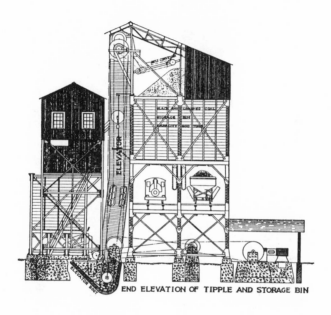

END ELEVATION OF TIPPLE AND STORAGE BIN

THE SOUTH

GENERAL

Campbell, Edna F., "Historical Geography of the Lower Mississippi Valley in the Pre-Steamboat Period," Master's thesis, University of Chicago, 1916. **5826**

Parkins, Almon E., "The Antebellum South: A Geographic Interpretation," *Annals of the Association of American Geographers*, vol. 21, 1 (1931), pp. 1–35. **5827**

Parkins, Almon E., *The South: Its Economic-Geographic Development* (New York: John Wiley & Sons, 1938), 528 pp. Revised 1949. Reprinted Westport, Conn.: Greenwood Press, 1970. **5828**

Morris, Francis Grave, "The Human Geography of the Cotton Belt," *Geography*, vol. 34, 3 (1939), pp. 146–150. [Focus on the eighteenth century to 1936] **5829**

Boesch, Hans, "Der Süden der Vereinigten Staaten," *Geographica Helvetica*, vol. 1, 1 (1946), pp. 30–45. **5830**

Pfeifer, Gottfried, "Historische Grundlagen der kulturgeographischen Individualität des Südostens der Vereinigten Staaten," *Petermanns Geographische Mitteilungen*, vol. 98, 4 (1954), pp. 301–312. Reprinted in Gerd Kohlhepp, ed., *Beiträge zur Kulturgeographie der Neuen Welt: Ausgewählte Arbeiten von Gottfried Pfeifer* (Berlin: Dietrich Reimer, 1981), pp. 136–166. **5831**

Pfeifer, Gottfried, "Die kulturgeographische Stellung des alten Südostens der Vereinigten Staaten," in Theodor Kraus and Ernst Weigt, eds., *Verhandlungen des Deutschen Geographentages, 1953*, vol. 29 (Wiesbaden: Franz Steiner, 1955), pp. 67–82. **5832**

Prunty, Merle C., Jr., "Two American Souths: The Past and the Future," *Southeastern Geographer*, vol. 17, 1 (1977), pp. 1–24. **5833**

Dunbar, Gary S., "Fall Line," in D. C. Roller and R. W. Twyman, eds., *Encyclopedia of Southern History* (Baton Rouge: Louisiana State University Press, 1979), pp. 419–420. **5834**

Colten, Craig, E., "Where the South Ends: A Critique of Regionalizing in Cultural Geography," Syracuse University Department of Geography, Discussion Paper no. 66 (1980), 32 pp. **5835**

Cruickshank, Alistair B., "Development of the Deep South: A Reappraisal," *Scottish Geo-*

graphical Magazine, vol. 96, 2 (1980), pp. 91–104. **5836**

Aiken, Charles S., "The Rural South as Seen by a Historical Geographer," *Proceedings of the National Rural Studies Committee*, vol. 2 (1989), pp. 11–21. **5837**

Otto, John S., *The Southern Frontiers, 1607–1860: The Agricultural Evolution of the Colonial and Antebellum South* (New York: Greenwood, 1989), 177 pp. **5838**

ENVIRONMENTAL CHANGE

General

Rostlund, Erhard, "The Geographic Range of the Historic Bison in the Southeast," *Annals of the Association of American Geographers*, vol. 50, 4 (1960), pp. 395–407. **5839**

Prunty, Merle C., Jr., "Some Geographic Views of the Role of Fire in Settlement Processes in the South," in *Proceedings of the Fourth Annual Tall Timbers Fire Ecology Conference* (Tallahassee: Tall Timbers Research Station, 1965), pp. 161–168. **5840**

Adkins, Howard G., "The Imported Fire Ant in the Southern United States," *Annals of the Association of American Geographers*, vol. 60, 3 (1970), pp. 578–592. [Focus on 1900–1968] **5841**

Strahler, Alan H., "Forests of the Fairfax Line," *Annals of the Association of American Geographers*, vol. 62, 4 (1972), pp. 664–684. [Virginia and West Virginia, 1746–1970] **5842**

Pine, W. M., "Atmospheric Determinants and the History of the Old South," *South Carolina Historical Magazine*, vol. 90, 4 (1989), pp. 313–321. [Effects of air mass changes on sailing ships, trade, and port prosperity in the colonial era] **5843**

Soil degradation & erosion

Morris, Francis Grave, "Soil Erosion in South-Eastern United States," *Geographical Journal*, vol. 90, 3 (1937), pp. 363–370. [Focus on 1848–1936] **5844**

Trimble, Stanley W., *Man-Induced Erosion on the Southern Piedmont, 1770–1970* (Ankeny, Iowa: Soil Conservation Service, 1971), 180 pp. **5845**

Trimble, Stanley W., "Man-Induced Soil Erosion on the Southern Piedmont of the USA: A Perspective," in W. P. Adams and F. M. Helleiner, eds., *International Geography, 1972*, vol. 1, sec. 5, *Historical Geography* (Toronto: University of Toronto Press, for the International Geographical Union, 1972), pp. 454–457. **5846**

Trimble, Stanley W., "A Geographic Analysis of Erosive Land Use on the Southern Piedmont, ca.1700 to the Present," Ph.D. diss., University of Georgia, 1973. **5847**

Trimble, Stanley W., "A Volumetric Estimate of Man-Induced Soil Erosion from the Southern Piedmont," in U.S. Department of Agriculture, *Present and Prospective Technology for Predicting Sediment Yields and Sources* (Houston: U.S. Department of Agriculture, Agricultural Research Service Publication S-40, 1975), pp. 142–154. **5848**

Earle, Carville V., "The Myth of the Southern Soil Miner: Macrohistory, Agricultural Innovation, and Environmental Change," in Donald Worster, ed., *The Ends of the Earth: Perspectives on Modern Environmental History* (Cambridge: Cambridge University Press, 1988), pp. 175–210. **5849**

NATIVE PEOPLES & WHITE RELATIONS

Wilms, Douglas C., "A Note on the District Boundaries of the Cherokee Nation, 1820," *Appalachian Journal*, vol. 2 (1975), pp. 284–285. **5850**

Goodwin, Gary C., *Cherokees in Transition: A Study of Changing Culture and Environment Prior to 1775* (Chicago: University of Chicago Department of Geography, Research Paper no. 181, 1977), 221 pp. **5851**

Wilms, Douglas C., "Agrarian Progress in the Cherokee Nation Prior to Removal," *West Georgia College Studies in the Social Sciences*, vol. 16 (1977), pp. 1–16. **5852**

Wilms, Douglas C., "Cherokee Acculturation and Changing Land Use Practices," *Chronicles of Oklahoma*, vol. 56, 3 (1978), pp. 331–343. **5853**

Jacobson, Daniel, "Estimating Populations of Native Americans through Time: The Alabama and Coushatta," *East Lakes Geographer*, vol. 21 (1986), pp. 84–92. **5854**

Jacobson, Daniel, "The Migrations and Changing Culture of the Alabama and Coushatta, 1760–1900," *Journal of Cultural Geography*, vol. 6, 2 (1986), pp. 51–66. **5855**

Neuman, Robert W., "Indians and the Landscape," in Charles R. Wilson and William Ferris, eds., *Encyclopedia of Southern Culture* (Chapel Hill: University of North Carolina Press, 1989), p. 547. **5856**

Pillsbury, Richard R., "Cherokee Settlement," in Charles R. Wilson and William Ferris, eds., *Encyclopedia of Southern Culture* (Chapel Hill: University of North Carolina Press, 1989), pp. 567–568. **5857**

EXPLORATION & MAPPING

Cumming, William P., "Geographical Misconceptions of the Southeast in the Cartography of the Seventeenth and Eighteenth Centuries," *Journal of Southern History*, vol. 4 (1938), pp. 476–492. **5858**

Corbitt, David L., *Explorations, Descriptions, and Attempted Settlements of Carolina, 1584–1590* (Raleigh: Department of Archives and History, 1953), 136 pp. **5859**

Stout, Wilbur W., "Lamhatty's Road Map," *Southern Quarterly*, vol. 2, 3 (1964), pp. 247–254. [Indian map, c. 1707, showing route from northwest Florida to Virginia] **5860**

Cumming, William P., "Mapping of the Southeast: The First Two Centuries," *Southeastern Geographer*, vol. 6 (1966), pp. 3–19. **5861**

DeVorsey, Louis, Jr. "The Colonial Southeast on 'An Accurate General Map,'" *Southeastern Geographer*, vol. 6 (1966), pp. 20–32. **5862**

Friis, Herman R., "Highlights of the Geographical and Cartographical Activities of the Federal Government in the Southeastern United States: 1776–1865," *Southeastern Geographer*, vol. 6 (1966), pp. 41–57. **5863**

Ristow, Walter W., "State Maps of the Southeast to 1833," *Southeastern Geographer*, vol. 6 (1966), pp. 33–40. **5864**

DeVorsey, Louis, Jr., "William Gerard de Brahm: Eccentric Genius of Southeastern Geography," *Southeastern Geographer*, vol. 10, 1 (1970), pp. 21–29. **5865**

DeVorsey, Louis, Jr., *De Brahm's Report of the General Survey in the Southern District of North America* (Columbus: University of South Carolina Press, 1971), 325 pp. **5866**

DeVorsey, Louis, Jr., "Early Maps as a Source in the Reconstruction of Southern Indian Landscapes," in C. M. Hudson, ed., *Red, White, and Black* (Athens: University of Georgia Press, 1971), pp. 12–30. **5867**

DeVorsey, Louis, Jr., "Dating the Emergence of a Savannah River Island: An Hypothesis in Forensic Historical Geography," *Environmental Review*, vol. 4, 2 (1980), pp. 6–19. **5868**

POPULAR IMAGES & EVALUATION

Aiken, Charles S., "Faulkner's Yoknapatawpha County: Geographical Fact into Fiction," *Geographical Review*, vol. 67, 1 (1977), pp. 1–21. **5869**

Aiken, Charles S., "Faulkner's Yoknapatawpha County: A Place in the American South," *Geographical Review*, vol. 69, 3 (1979), pp. 332–348. **5870**

Aiken, Charles S., "A Geographical Approach to William Faulkner's 'The Bear,'" *Geographical Review*, vol. 71, 4 (1981), pp. 446–459. **5871**

Aiken, Charles S., "The Image of the Plantation in Southern Fiction: The Case of William Faulkner," *Proceedings of the Tall Timbers Ecology and Management Conference* (Tallahassee: Tall Timbers Research Station, 1982), pp. 189–206. **5872**

Hall, John W., "Geographical Views of Red River Valley, 1873," *North Louisiana Historical Society Journal*, vol. 13, 4 (1982), pp. 107–117. **5873**

Ferris, William, "The Dogtrot: A Mythic Image in Southern Culture," *Southern Quarterly*, vol. 25, 1 (1986), pp. 72–85. **5874**

Walters, William D., "Unsurpassed Locations: Gulf Coast Townsite Advertisements, 1835–1837," *Pioneer America Society Transactions*, vol. 12 (1989), pp. 65–72. **5875**

REGIONAL SETTLEMENT

Scott, Elton M., "The Geography of Settlement in a Portion of the Texas-Louisiana Coastal Plain," Ph.D. diss., University of Wisconsin, 1941. **5876**

Sharma, Jitendra K., "Geographic Changes in Rural Settlement between 1939 and 1971 in a Sample Strip across Southeast Tennessee and Southwest North Carolina," Ph.D. diss., University of Georgia, 1973. **5877**

Wood, Perry S., "The Growth and Decline of Small Communities in the Southern Allegheny Mountains," Ph.D. diss., University of Nebraska, 1973. **5878**

Denecke, Dietrich, "Prozesse der Entstehung und Standortverschiebung zentraler Orte in Gebieten höher Instabilität des räumlichfunktionalen Gefüges: Virginia und Maryland vom Beginn der Kolonisation bis heute," in Carl Schott, ed., *Beiträge zur Geographie Nordamerikas* (Marburg: Marburger Geographischen Schriften, no. 66, 1976), pp. 175–200. [Focus from 1607 to the 1970s] **5879**

Ainsley, W. Frank, Jr., "Pulsating Patterns of Land Occupancy: The Impacts of Farm Colonization Experiments on the Rural South," *Pioneer America Society Transactions*, vol. 10 (1987), pp. 43–52. **5880**

POPULATION

See also 1360–1361

Bollinger, Clyde J., "A Synoptic Chart of Population Change in the Gulf Southwest," *Texas Geographic Magazine*, vol. 6, 1 (Spring 1942), pp. 9–12. [Focus on 1920–1940] **5881**

Owsley, Frank L., "The Pattern of Migration and Settlement on the Southern Frontier," *Journal of Southern History*, vol. 11, 2 (1945), pp. 147–176. **5882**

Mather, Eugene Cotton, and John Fraser Hart, "The People of the Deep South and the Border States," *Tijdschrift voor economische en sociale geografie*, vol. 45, 1 & 2 (1954), pp. 1–4. **5883**

Melvin, Ernest E., Kirk H. Stone, and Thomas F. Hardaway, *The South's Changing Population and the Georgia Example* (Athens: University of Georgia Institute of Community and Area Development and Department of Geography, 1978), 34 pp. [Focus on 1950–1970] **5884**

O'Sullivan, Patrick M., "Catholic Irish in the Deep South," *Ecumene*, vol. 13 (1981), pp. 42–49. **5885**

Shortridge, James R., and Roger W. Stump, "Westward Migration, 1750–1900," in Samuel S. Hill, ed., *The Encyclopedia of Religion in the South* (Macon, Ga.: Mercer University Press, 1984), pp. 473–477. **5886**

Boswell, Thomas D., "Cuban Settlement," in Charles R. Wilson and William Ferris, eds., *Encyclopedia of Southern Culture* (Chapel Hill: University of North Carolina Press, 1989), pp. 570–571. **5887**

Roseman, Curtis C., "Migration Patterns," in Charles R. Wilson and William Ferris, eds., *Encyclopedia of Southern Culture* (Chapel Hill: University of North Carolina Press, 1989), pp. 551–552. **5888**

RURAL & REGIONAL SOCIAL GEOGRAPHY

General

Newton, Milton B., Jr., "Cultural Preadaptation and the Upland South," in H. Jesse Walker and William G. Haag, eds., *Man and Cultural Heritage: Papers in Honor of Fred B. Kniffen* (Baton Rouge: Louisiana State University School of Geoscience, Geoscience & Man, vol. 5, 1974), pp. 143–154. **5889**

Otto, John S., and Nain Estelle Anderson, "The Diffusion of Upland South Folk Culture, 1790–1840," *Southeastern Geographer*, vol. 22, 2 (1982), pp. 89–98. **5890**

Stump, Roger W., and James R. Shortridge, "Geography of Southern Religion," in Samuel S. Hill, ed., *The Encyclopedia of Religion in the South* (Macon, Ga.: Mercer University Press, 1984), pp. 284–288. **5891**

Shortridge, James R., and Roger W. Stump, "Religious Regions," in Charles R. Wilson and William Ferris, eds., *The Encyclopedia of Southern Culture* (Chapel Hill: University of North Carolina Press, 1989), pp. 557–559. **5892**

Race & slavery

Price, Edward T., "The Melungeons: A Mixed Blood Strain of the Southern Appalachians," *Geographical Review*, vol. 41, 2 (1951), pp. 256–271. **5893**

Hazel, Joseph A., "The Geography of Negro Agricultural Slavery in Alabama, Florida, and Mississippi, circa 1860," Ph.D. diss., Columbia University, 1962. **5894**

Elgie, Robert A., "Racial Inequality within a Socio-Spatial System: The Southeastern United States, 1950–1970," Ph.D. diss., University of California–Berkeley, 1976. **5895**

Whelan, James P., Jr., "Plantation Slave Subsistence in the Old South and Louisiana," in Roland E. Chardon, ed., *Plantation Traits in the New World* (Baton Rouge: Louisiana State University Publications, Studies in Geography and Anthropology, vol. 23, 1983), pp. 113–126. **5896**

African American patterns

Phillips, Ulrich B., "The Origin and Growth of the Southern Black Belts," *American Historical Review*, vol. 11, 4 (1906), pp. 798–816. **5897**

Aiken, Charles S., "New Settlement Patterns of Rural Blacks in the American South," *Geographical Review*, vol. 75, 4 (1985), pp. 383–404. **5898**

Aiken, Charles S., "A New Type of Black Ghetto in the Plantation South," *Annals of the Association of American Geographers*, vol. 80, 2 (1990), pp. 223–246. **5899**

White ethnic patterns

Kollmorgen, Walter M., "A Reconnaissance of Some Cultural-Agricultural Islands in the South," *Economic Geography*, vol. 17, 4 (1941), pp. 409–430. **5900**

Kollmorgen, Walter M., "Agricultural-Cultural Islands in the South: Part II," *Economic Geography*, vol. 19, 3 (1943), pp. 109–117. **5901**

Kollmorgen, Walter M., "Immigrant Settlements in Southern Agriculture: A Commentary on the Significance of Cultural Islands in Agricultural History," *Agricultural History*, vol. 19, 2 (1945), pp. 69–78. **5902**

Otto, John S., "The Migration of the Southern Plain Folk: An Interdisciplinary Synthesis," *Journal of Southern History*, vol. 51, 2 (1985), pp. 183–200. **5903**

Curtis, James R., "Ethnic Geography," in Charles R. Wilson and William Ferris, eds., *Encyclopedia of Southern Culture* (Chapel Hill: University of North Carolina Press, 1989), pp. 541–542. **5904**

Consumption patterns

Hilliard, Sam B., "Hog Meat and Cornpone: Food Habits in the Antebellum South," *Proceedings of the American Philosophical Society*, vol. 113, 1 (1969), pp. 1–13. Reprinted, in expanded form, in Robert Blair St. George, ed., *Material Life in America, 1600–1860* (Boston: Northeastern University Press, 1988), pp. 311–332. **5905**

Carney, George O., "Country Music and the South: A Cultural Geography Perspective," *Journal of Cultural Geography*, vol. 1, 1 (1980), pp. 16–33. **5906**

POLITICAL & ADMINISTRATIVE GEOGRAPHY

General

Abernathy, Thomas P., "The Political Geography of Southern Jacksonianism," *East Tennessee Historical Society Publications*, vol. 3 (1931), pp. 35–41. **5907**

Towle, Jerry C., "The Areal Base of Southern Democratic Strength, 1920–1960," Master's thesis, Southern Illinois University, 1965. **5908**

Ingalls, Gerald L., "Spatial Change in Post War Southern Republican Voting Responses," Ph.D. diss., Michigan State University, 1973. **5909**

Geographical boundaries

Coulter, E. Merton, "The Georgia-Tennessee Boundary Line," *Georgia Historical Quarterly*, vol. 35, 4 (1951), pp. 269–306. **5910**

DeVorsey, Louis, Jr., "The Virginia-Cherokee Boundary of 1771: An Example of the Importance of Maps in the Interpretation of History," *East Tennessee Historical Society Publications*, vol. 33 (1961), pp. 2–16. **5911**

DeVorsey, Louis, Jr., "The Evolution of the Southern Indian Boundary Line in the British American Colonies, 1763–1775," Ph.D. diss., University
of London, 1965.   5912

DeVorsey, Louis, Jr., *The Indian Boundary in the
Southern Colonies, 1763–1775* (Chapel Hill: University of North Carolina Press, 1966), 267 pp.
                                                    5913

Wiggins, David H., "Running the North Carolina–
South Carolina Boundary: A Geographic Evalua-
tion," Master's thesis, University of North
Carolina–Chapel Hill, 1974.   5914

Winberry, John J., "Formation of the West
Virginia–Virginia Boundary," *Southeastern
Geographer*, vol. 17, 2 (1977), pp. 108–124.   5915

Vanderhill, Burke G., and Frank A. Unger, "The
Georgia-Florida Land Boundary: Product of
Controversy and Compromise," *West Georgia
College Studies in the Social Sciences*, vol. 18
(1979), pp. 59–74.   5916

DeVorsey, Louis, Jr., *The Georgia–South Carolina
Boundary: A Problem in Historical Geography*
(Athens: University of Georgia Press, 1982), 219
pp.   5917

Aiken, Charles S., "Race as a Factor in Municipal
Underbounding," *Annals of the Association of
American Geographers*, vol. 77, 4 (1987), pp. 564–
579.   5918

The Civil War

Emerson, Frederick V., "Physiographic Control of
the Chattanooga Campaign," *Journal of Geography*, vol. 4, 2 (1905), pp. 58–73.   5919

Emerson, Frederick V., "Geographic Influences on
the Atlanta Campaign," *Journal of Geography*,
vol. 4, 3 (1905), pp. 106–121.   5920

Matthews, William H., "Geography and Southern
Sectionalism in the Civil War," *Bulletin of the
Philadelphia Geographical Society*, vol. 26, 4
(1928), pp. 255–275.   5921

Hippen, James C., "The Influence of Geographical
Conditions upon Civil War Strategy in the Mississippi Delta," *Proceedings of the Oklahoma
Academy of Science for 1957*, vol. 38 (1958), pp.
128–131.   5922

Doyon, Roy, and Thomas W. Hodler, "Secession-
ist Sentiment and Slavery: A Geographic Analysis," *Georgia Historical Quarterly*, vol. 73, 2
(1989), pp. 323–348.   5923

ECONOMIC DEVELOPMENT

Gerhard, Hermann, *Die volkswirtschaftliche Entwicklung des Südens der Vereinigten Staaten
von Amerika von 1860 bis 1900* (Halle: Gebauer-
Schetschke Druckerei und Verlag, 1904), 99 pp.
                                                    5924

Polspoel, Lambert G., "Geo-economische
Structuurveranderingen in het Zuidoosten van
de Verenigde Staten," *Bulletin de la Société
belge d'études géographiques*, vol. 21, 1 (1952),
pp. 201–223. [Focus on 1909–1949]   5925

Earle, Carville V., and Ronald A. Hoffman, "Staple
Crops and Urban Development in the Eighteenth Century South," *Perspectives in American History*, vol. 10 (1976), pp. 7–78.   5926

Higgs, Robert W., "The Boll Weevil: The Cotton
Economy and Black Migration, 1910–1930,"
Agricultural History, vol. 50, 2 (1976), pp. 335–
350.   5927

Wheeler, James O., and Catherine L. Brown, "The
Metropolitan Corporate Hierarchy in the U.S.
South, 1960–1980," *Economic Geography*, vol. 61,
1 (1985), pp. 66–78.   5928

Aiken, Charles S., "Afro-American Slavery and the
Cotton Gin," in John D. Smith, ed., *Dictionary of
Afro-American Slavery* (Westport, Conn.:
Greenwood, 1988), pp. 151–152.   5929

Hugill, Peter J., "The Macro-Landscape of the
Wallerstein World Economy: King Cotton and
the American South," in Richard L. Nostrand
and Sam B. Hilliard, eds., *The American South*
(Baton Rouge: Louisiana State University School
of Geoscience, Geoscience & Man, vol. 25, 1988),
pp. 77–84.   5930

LAND & LAND USE

Land survey

Hilliard, Sam B., "An Introduction to Land Survey
Systems in the Southeast," *West Georgia College Studies in the Social Sciences*, vol. 12 (1973),
pp. 1–15.   5931

Price, Edward T., "Order Mid Chaos: Regularity in
Southern Colonial Land Surveys," *Technical
Papers of the American Congress on Surveying
and Mapping and the American Society For
Photogrammetry and Remote Sensing* (1985),
pp. 337–345.   5932

Land tenure

Wheeler, David L., and Clayton Loudon, "Land
Distribution in the Southern Colonies of America," *Bulletin of the Illinois Geographical Society*, vol. 11, 2 (1969), pp. 61–69.   5933

Fisher, James S., "Negro Farm Ownership in the
South," *Annals of the Association of American
Geographers*, vol. 63, 4 (1973), pp. 478–489.
[Focus on 1900–1969]   5934

Lockyer, C. Allan, "A Geographical Analysis of Black-Owned Farmland Loss in the Southeastern United States: 1910–1978," *Bulletin of the Association of North Dakota Geographers*, vol. 35 (1985), pp. 33–52.   5935

Holder, Gerald L., "Land Division," in Charles R. Wilson and William Ferris, eds., *Encyclopedia of Southern Culture* (Chapel Hill: University of North Carolina Press, 1989), pp. 547–548.   5936

Land use

Trimble, Stanley W., Frank H. Weirich, and Barbara L. Hoag, "Reforestation and the Reduction of Water Yields on the South Piedmont since c1940," *Water Resources Research*, vol. 23 (1987), pp. 425–437.   5937

Doughty, Robin W., "Land Use," in Charles R. Wilson and William Ferris, eds., *Encyclopedia of Southern Culture* (Chapel Hill: University of North Carolina Press, 1989), pp. 343–344.   5938

Land value

Murphy, Raymond E., "Land Values in the Blue Grass and Nashville Basins," *Economic Geography*, vol. 6, 2 (1930), pp. 191–203.   5939

EXTRACTIVE ACTIVITY

Oil

Bradley, Virginia, "The Petroleum Industry of the Gulf Coast Salt Dome Area," *Economic Geography*, vol. 15, 4 (1939), pp. 395–407.   5940

Lumbering

Könnecke, Michael, "Baumkulturen in den winterfeuchten Subtropen der Neuen Welt: Entwicklung im nördlichen Großen Längstal," *Die Erde*, vol. 118, 1 (1987), pp. 5–20. [Focus on 1945–1980]   5941

AGRICULTURE

General

Harper, Roland M., "Development of Agriculture in the Pine Barrens of the Southeastern United States," *Journal of Geography*, vol. 15, 2 (1916), pp. 42–48.   5942

Baker, Oliver E., "Agricultural Regions of North America: Part II—The South," *Economic Geography*, vol. 3, 1 (1927), pp. 50–86.   5943

Parkins, Almon E., "Southern Agriculture," in W. T. Couch, ed., *Culture in the South* (Chapel Hill: University of North Carolina Press, 1935), pp. 52–79.   5944

Hall, Arthur, "Terracing in the Southern Piedmont," *Agricultural History*, vol. 23, 2 (1949), pp. 96–109.   5945

Strack, Charles M., "Agricultural Changes in the TVA Area, 1930–1945," Ph.D. diss., Iowa University, 1950.   5946

Prunty, Merle C., Jr., "Some Quantitative Aspects of Farm Mechanization in the Southeastern Cotton Habitat, 1924–1949," *Memorandum Folio, Southeastern Division, Association of American Geographers*, vol. 5 (1953), pp. 53–59.   5947

Mather, Eugene Cotton, and John Fraser Hart, "Agriculture in the Deep South and the Border States," *Tijdschrift voor economische en sociale geografie*, vol. 45, 9 & 10 (1954), pp. 161–166. 5948

Lamb, Robert B., *The Mule in Southern Agriculture* (Berkeley: University of California Publications in Geography, vol. 15, 1963), 99 pp.   5949

Hilliard, Sam B., "Hog Meat and Hoecake: A Geographic View of Food Supply in the Heart of the Old South, 1840–1860," Ph.D. diss., University of Wisconsin–Madison, 1966.   5950

Hilliard, Sam B., *Hog Meat and Hoecake: Food Supply in the Old South, 1840–1860* (Carbondale: Southern Illinois University Press, 1972), 296 pp.   5951

Mitchell, Robert D., "Agricultural Regionalization: Origins and Diffusions in the Upper South before 1860," in W. P. Adams and F. M. Helleiner, eds., *International Geography 1972*, vol. 1, sec. 5, *Historical Geography* (Toronto: University of Toronto Press, for the International Geographical Union, 1972), pp. 740–742.   5952

Aiken, Charles S., "The Decline of Sharecropping in the Lower Mississippi Valley," in Sam B. Hilliard, ed., *Man and Environment in the Lower Mississippi Valley* (Baton Rouge: Louisiana State University School of Geoscience, Geoscience & Man, vol. 19, 1978), pp. 151–165.   5953

Hart, John Fraser, "Cropland Concentrations in the South," *Annals of the Association of American Geographers*, vol. 68, 4 (1978), pp. 505–517. [Focus on 1910–1974]   5954

Manlove, Robert A., "Spatial Changes in Cropland Harvested in Eight Southeastern States, 1939–1974," Master's thesis, University of Tennessee, 1978.   5955

Foust, J. Brady, and Ingolf K. Vogeler, "Prolegomenon to Future Research on Black Agriculture in the South," *West Georgia College Studies in the Social Sciences*, vol. 18 (1979), pp. 85–92. 5956

Phillips, Lynn R., "Agricultural Land Use Patterns in the Southern Piedmont, 1945–1982," Master's thesis, East Carolina University, 1985.   5957

Plantations

Prunty, Merle C., Jr., "The Renaissance of the Southern Plantation," *Geographical Review*, vol. 45, 4 (1955), pp. 459–491.　　　5958

Aiken, Charles S., "The Fragmented Neoplantation: A New Type of Farm Operation in the Southeast," *Southeastern Geographer*, vol. 11, 1 (1971), pp. 43–51. [Focus on 1944–1964]　　5959

Hart, John Fraser, "The Role of the Plantation in Southern Agriculture," *Proceedings of the Tall Timbers Ecology and Management Conference*, vol. 16 (Tallahassee, Fla.: Tall Timbers Research Station, 1979), pp. 1–19.　　　5960

Hilliard, Sam B., "The Plantation in Antebellum Southern Agriculture," *Proceedings of the Tall Timbers Ecology and Management Conference*, vol. 16 (Tallahassee, Fla.: Tall Timbers Research Station, 1979), pp. 127–139.　　　5961

Cotton

Erickson, Franklin C., "The Broken Cotton Belt," *Economic Geography*, vol. 24, 4 (1948), pp. 263–268. [Focus on 1865–1948]　　　5962

Prunty, Merle C., Jr., "Recent Quantitative Changes in the Cotton Regions of the Southeastern States," *Economic Geography*, vol. 27, 3 (1951), pp. 189–208. [Focus on 1924–1944]　　　　　　　　5963

Rothstein, Morton, "The Cotton Frontier of the Antebellum South: A Methodological Battleground," *Agricultural History*, vol. 44, 1 (1970), pp. 149–165. Reprinted, with omissions, in David Ward, ed., *Geographic Perspectives on America's Past: Readings on the Historical Geography of the United States* (New York: Oxford University Press, 1979), pp. 203–209.　　5964

Aiken, Charles S., "An Examination of the Role of the Eli Whitney Cotton Gin in the Origin of the United States Cotton Regions," *Proceedings of the Association of American Geographers*, vol. 3 (1971), pp. 5–9.　　　5965

Prunty, Merle C., Jr., and Charles S. Aiken, "The Demise of the Piedmont Cotton Region," *Annals of the Association of American Geographers*, vol. 62, 2 (1972), pp. 283–306. Reissued in John Fraser Hart, ed., *Regions of the United States* (New York: Harper & Row, 1972), same pagination. [Focus on the 1950s and 1960s]　5966

Aiken, Charles S., "The Evolution of Cotton Ginning in the Southeastern United States," *Geographical Review*, vol. 63, 2 (1973), pp. 196–224.　　　5967

Hart, John Fraser, "The Demise of King Cotton," *Annals of the Association of American Geogra-*

phers, vol. 67, 3 (1977), pp. 307–322. [Focus on 1880–1970]　　　5968

Aiken, Charles S., "Cotton Gins," in Charles R. Wilson and William Ferris, eds., *Encyclopedia of Southern Culture* (Chapel Hill: University of North Carolina Press, 1989), pp. 568–569.　5969

Tobacco

Ogilvie, Bruce C., "Development of the Tobacco Belt of Georgia and Florida: A Study in Economic Geography," Master's thesis, Clark University, 1949.　　　5970

Chestang, Ennis L., "Tobacco Industry," in Charles R. Wilson and William Ferris, eds., *Encyclopedia of Southern Culture* (Chapel Hill: University of North Carolina Press, 1989), pp. 753 754.　5971

Rice

Hilliard, Sam B., "The Tidewater Rice Plantation: An Ingenious Adaptation to Nature," in H. Jesse Walker, ed., *Coastal Resources* (Baton Rouge: Louisiana State University School of Geoscience, Geoscience & Man, vol. 12, 1975), pp. 57–66.　　　5972

Hilliard, Sam B., "Antebellum Tidewater Rice Culture in South Carolina and Georgia," in James R. Gibson, ed., *European Settlement and Development in North America: Essays in Geographical Change in Honour and Memory of Andrew Hill Clark* (Toronto: University of Toronto Press, 1978), pp. 98–115.　　　5973

Lee, Jeon, "The Historical Geography of Rice Culture in the American South," Ph.D. diss., Louisiana State University, 1988.　　　5974

Sugar

Rehder, John B., "Sugar Plantations," in Charles R. Wilson and William Ferris, eds., *Encyclopedia of Southern Culture* (Chapel Hill: University of North Carolina Press, 1989), pp. 576–577.　5975

Herding

Post, Lauren C., "Revolution in the Beef Cattle Industry in the South," *McNeese Review*, vol. 11 (1959), pp. 61–75.　　　5976

Hilliard, Sam B., "Pork in the Antebellum South: The Geography of Self-Sufficiency," *Annals of the Association of American Geographers*, vol. 59, 3 (1969), pp. 461–480.　　　5977

Jordan, Terry G., *Trails to Texas: Southern Roots of Western Cattle Ranching* (Lincoln: University of Nebraska Press, 1981), 220 pp.　　　5978

McWhiney, Grady, and Forrest McDonald, "Celtic Origins of Southern Herding Practices," *Jour-*

nal of Southern History, vol. 51, 2 (1985), pp. 165–182. **5979**

Poultry

Lord, J. Dennis, "Poultry," in Charles R. Wilson and William Ferris, eds., *Encyclopedia of Southern Culture* (Chapel Hill: University of North Carolina Press, 1989), pp. 28–29. **5980**

LANDSCAPE

General

Mather, Eugene Cotton, and John Fraser Hart, *Southeastern Guidebook* (Chicago: Rand McNally, for the International Geographical Union, 1952), 136 pp. **5981**

Hilliard, Sam B., "Plantations Created the South," *Geographical Magazine*, vol. 52, 6 (1980), pp. 409–416. **5982**

Pillsbury, Richard R., and Suzanne Andres, "The South as a Cultural Landscape," in Charles R. Wilson and William Ferris, eds., *Encyclopedia of Southern Culture* (Chapel Hill: University of North Carolina Press, 1989), pp. 533–541. **5983**

Rehder, John B., "Plantation Morphology," in Charles R. Wilson and William Ferris, eds., *Encyclopedia of Southern Culture* (Chapel Hill: University of North Carolina Press, 1989), pp. 554–555. **5984**

Hilliard, Sam B., "Plantations and the Moulding of the Southern Landscape," in Michael P. Conzen, ed., *The Making of the American Landscape* (Boston: Unwin Hyman, 1990), pp. 104–126. **5985**

Building types & materials

Wright, Martin, "The Log Cabin in the South," Master's thesis, Louisiana State University, 1950. **5986**

Anthony, Carl, "The Big House and the Slave Quarters: Part I—Prelude to New World Architecture"; "Part II—African Contributions to the New World," *Landscape*, vol. 20, 3 (1976), pp. 8–19; vol. 21, 1 (1976), pp. 9–15. **5987**

Vlach, John M., "The Shotgun House: An African Architectural Legacy: Part I"; and "Part II," *Pioneer America*, vol. 8, 1 (1976), pp. 47–56; and 2 (1976), pp. 57–70. Reprinted in Dell Upton and John Michael Vlach, eds., *Common Places: Readings in American Vernacular Architecture* (Athens: University of Georgia Press, 1986), pp. 58–78. **5988**

Bonner, James C., "House and Landscape Design in the Antebellum South," *Landscape*, vol. 21, 3 (1977), pp. 2–8. **5989**

Gritzner, Janet H., "Tabby in the Coastal Southeast: The Culture History of an American Building Material," Ph.D. diss., Louisiana State University, 1978. **5990**

Rehder, John B., and James R. O'Malley, "The Two-Story Log House in the Upland South," *Journal of Popular Culture*, vol. 11, 4 (1978), pp. 904–915. **5991**

Murray, M. Jeffrey, "The Diffusion of Georgian-Style Architecture from England to the West Indies and the Southern United States," in Roland E. Chardon, ed. *Studies in Historical Geography, I: Diffusion of Plantation Traits in the New World* (Baton Rouge: Louisiana State University Department of Geography and Anthropology, 1981), pp. 37–70. **5992**

Newton, Milton B., Jr., "Bungalow House," in Charles R. Wilson and William Ferris, eds., *Encyclopedia of Southern Culture* (Chapel Hill: University of North Carolina Press, 1989), pp. 496–497. **5993**

Newton, Milton B., Jr., "Dogtrot House," in Charles R. Wilson and William Ferris, eds., *Encyclopedia of Southern Culture* (Chapel Hill: University of North Carolina Press, 1989), pp. 498–499. **5994**

Newton, Milton B., Jr., "House Types," in Charles R. Wilson and William Ferris, eds., *Encyclopedia of Southern Culture* (Chapel Hill: University of North Carolina Press, 1989), pp. 481–482. **5995**

Newton, Milton B., Jr., "I–House," in Charles R. Wilson and William Ferris, eds., *Encyclopedia of Southern Culture* (Chapel Hill: University of North Carolina Press, 1989), p. 506. **5996**

Newton, Milton B., Jr., "Log Housing," in Charles R. Wilson and William Ferris, eds., *Enclyclopedia of Southern Culture* (Chapel Hill: University of North Carolina Press, 1989), pp. 550–551. **5997**

Newton, Milton B., Jr., "Shotgun House," in Charles R. Wilson and William Ferris, eds., *Encyclopedia of Southern Culture* (Chapel Hill: University of North Carolina Press, 1989), pp. 519–520. **5998**

Other features

Winberry, John J., and David Jones, "Rise and Decline of the 'Miracle Vine': Kudzu in the Southern Landscape," *Southeastern Geographer*, vol. 13, 2 (1973), pp. 61–70. **5999**

COMMUNICATIONS & TRADE

Trade

Lindstrom, Diane, "Southern Dependence upon Interregional Grain Supplies: A Review of the Trade Flows, 1840–1860," *Agricultural History*, vol. 44, 1 (1970), pp. 101–113. **6000**

Transport

Guardia, John E., "Successive Human Adjustments to Raft Conditions in the Lower Red River Valley," Master's thesis, University of Chicago, 1927.   6001

Browne, Walter A., "The Lower Mississippi as a Waterway," *Journal of Geography*, vol. 29, 4 (1930), pp. 155–163.   6002

Weaver, David C., "The Transport Expansion Sequence in Georgia and the Carolinas, 1670 to 1900: A Search for Spatial Regularities," Ph.D. diss., University of Florida, 1972.   6003

Weaver, David C., "Spatial Strategies in Railroad Planning in Georgia and the Carolinas, 1830–1860," *West Georgia College Studies in the Social Sciences*, vol. 18 (1979), pp. 9–24.   6004

MANUFACTURING & INDUSTRIALIZATION

General

Mather, Eugene Cotton, and John Fraser Hart, "Industry in the Deep South and the Border States," *Tijdschrift voor economische en sociale geografie*, vol. 45, 5 & 6 (1954), pp. 108–112.   6005

Bean, John L., "Structural and Spatial Changes in Manufacturing within the Western Gulf Coast Manufacturing District of the United States during the Twentieth Century," Ph.D. diss., University of Pittsburgh, 1967.   6006

Brand, Ulrich, *Die Entwicklung der Industrie in den Südstaaten der USA: Unter besonderer Berücksichtigung der petrochemischen Industrie* (Marburg: Marburger Geographischen Schriften, no. 36, 1968), 236 pp.   6007

Johnson, Merrill L., "Industrial Evolution in Selected Labor-Intensive Environments of the Southern Piedmont, 1947 to 1977," Ph.D. diss., University of Georgia, 1981.   6008

Individual industries

Lemert, Ben F., "Furniture Industry of the Southern Appalachian Piedmont," *Economic Geography*, vol. 10, 2 (1934), pp. 183–199.   6009

Lemert, Ben F., "The Knit-Goods Industry in the Southern States," *Economic Geography*, vol. 11, 4 (1935), pp. 368–388.   6010

Prunty, Merle C., Jr., and Carl F. Ojala, "The Rise of the Pine Plywood Industry in the South," *Southeastern Geographer*, vol. 8 (1968), pp. 11–22.   6011

Prunty, Merle C., Jr., "Pulp and Paper Industry," in D. C. Roller and R. W. Tugman, eds., *Encyclope-*

dia of Southern History (Baton Rouge: Louisiana State University Press, 1979), pp. 1013–1014. 6012

Smith, James L., "Historical Geography of the Southern Charcoal Iron Industry, 1800–1860," Ph.D. diss., University of Tennessee, 1982. 6013

Jumper, Sidney R., "Funiture Industry," in Charles R. Wilson and William Ferris, eds., *Encyclopedia of Southern Culture* (Chapel Hill: University of North Carolina Press, 1989), p. 742.   6014

Winberry, John J., "The Cultural Hearth of the Southern Pottery Tradition: The Historical Geographic Framework," in Catherine Wilson Horne, ed., *Crossroads of Clay: The Alkaline-Glazed Stoneware Tradition* (Columbia: McKissick Museum, 1989), pp. 5–15. [Some emphasis on western South Carolina]   6015

URBAN NETWORKS & URBANIZATION

See also 1446

Emory, Samuel T., Jr., "Topography and Towns of the Carolina Piedmont," *Economic Geography*, vol. 12, 1 (1936), pp. 91–97.   6016

Ernst, Joseph A., and H. Roy Merrens, "Camden's Turrets Pierce the Skies! The Urban Process in the Southern Colonies during the Eighteenth Century," *William and Mary Quarterly*, 3d ser., vol. 30 (1973), pp. 549–574. Reprinted, with omissions, in David Ward, ed., *Geographic Perspectives on America's Past: Readings on the Historical Geography of the United States* (New York: Oxford University Press, 1979), pp. 308–320. 6017

Earle, Carville V., and Ronald Hoffman, "The Urban South: The First Two Centuries," in Blaine A. Brownell and David R. Goldfield, eds., *The City in Southern History: The Development of Urban Civilization in the South* (Port Washington, N.Y.: Kennikat Press, 1977), pp. 23–51. 6018

Kovacik, Charles F., "The Declining Small Southern Town," *West Georgia College Studies in the Social Sciences*, vol. 16 (1977), pp. 35–44. 6019

Clark, Charles R., "Functional Change between 1950 and 1970: The South as a Regional Urban Complex," Master's thesis, University of Southern Mississippi, 1978.   6020

Kirby, Russell S., "Urban Growth and Economic Change in the Nineteenth Century South: The Hinterland of Memphis, Tennessee, 1830–1900," Ph.D. diss., University of Wisconsin–Madison, 1982.   6021

Meyer, David R., "The Industrial Retardation of Southern Cities, 1860–1880," *Explorations in Economic History*, vol. 25, 4 (1988), pp. 366–386. 6022

Meyer, David R., "Industry in Southern Cities in the Nineteenth Century," in Richard L. Nostrand and Sam B. Hilliard, eds., *The American South* (Baton Rouge: Louisiana State University School of Geoscience, Geoscience & Man, vol. 25, 1988), pp. 129–138. **6023**

Raitz, Karl B., "Towns and Villages," in Charles R. Wilson and William Ferris, eds., *Encyclopedia of Southern Culture* (Chapel Hill: University of North Carolina Press, 1989), pp. 565–567. **6024**

URBAN SOCIAL STRUCTURE

Kellogg, John, "Negro Urban Clusters in the Postbellum South," *Geographical Review*, vol. 67, 3 (1977), pp. 310–321. [Focus on Lexington, Atlanta, Richmond, and Durham, 1860–1970] **6025**

TOWNSCAPE

Winberry, John J., "Symbols in the Landscape: The Confederate Memorial," *Pioneer America Society Transactions*, vol. 5 (1982), pp. 9–15. **6026**

Winberry, John J., "'Lest We Forget': The Confederate Monument and the Southern Townscape," *Southeastern Geographer*, vol. 23, 2 (1983), pp. 107–121. **6027**

Bastian, Robert W., "Early Southern Skyscrapers: Symbols of Urban Growth in the Image of New York City?" in Richard L. Nostrand and Sam B. Hilliard, eds., *The American South* (Baton Rouge: Louisiana State University School of Geoscience, Geoscience & Man, vol. 25, 1988), pp. 151–158. **6028**

Pillsbury, Richard R., and Suzanne Andres, "Courthouse Square," in Charles R. Wilson and William Ferris, eds., *Encyclopedia of Southern Culture* (Chapel Hill: University of North Carolina Press, 1989), pp. 569–570. **6029**

RECREATION & TOURISM

Lawrence, Henry W., "Southern Spas: Sources of the American Resort Tradition," *Landscape*, vol. 27, 2 (1983), pp. 1–12. **6030**

Meyer-Arendt, Klaus, "Resort Evolution along the Gulf of Mexico Littoral: Historical, Morphologi-

cal, and Environmental Aspects," Ph.D. diss., Louisiana State University, 1987. **6031**

Meyer-Arendt, Klaus J., "Recreational Business Districts in Gulf of Mexico Seaside Resorts," *Journal of Cultural Geography*, vol. 11, 1 (1990), pp. 39–56. **6032**

PLANNING

General

Ripley, Wolfe M., "Changing the Face of Southern Appalachia: Urban Planning in Southwest Virginia and East Tennessee, 1890–1929," *Journal of the American Planning Association*, vol. 47, 3 (1981), pp. 252–265. **6033**

Tennessee Valley Authority

Roehrig, H. W., *Das Tennessee-Tal: Ein Beispiel amerikanischer Großraumplanung und Großraumordnung* (Bielefeld: F. Eiler, Arbeiten des Instituts für Raumforschung in Bonn, 1951), 247 pp. **6034**

Hessing, Franz J., "Drei Jahrzehnte Tennessee Valley Authority," *Raumforschung und Raumplanung*, vol. 24, 3 (1966), pp. 120–129. **6035**

Lenz, Karl, "50 Jahre Planungen im Tennessee-Tal," *Geographische Rundschau*, vol. 35, 4 (1983), pp. 56–64. **6036**

Bradshaw, Michael, "TVA at Fifty," *Geography*, vol. 69, 3 (1984), pp. 209–220. **6037**

PLACE NAMES

West, Robert C., "The Term 'Bayou' in the United States: A Study in the Geography of Place Names," *Annals of the Association of American Geographers*, vol. 44, 1 (1954), pp. 63–74. **6038**

Kolin, Philip C., "Jefferson Davis: From President to Place-Name," *Names*, vol. 25, 3 (1977), pp. 158–173. **6039**

Gulley, Harold E., "Southern Nationalism on the Landscape: County Names in Former Confederate States," *Names*, vol. 38, 3 (1990), pp. 231–242. **6040**

VIRGINIA

GENERAL

The state

Surface, George T., "Geographic Influence on the Economic History of Virginia," in his "Studies on the Geography of Virginia," Ph.D. diss., University of Pennsylvania, 1907, pp. 1–13. Published under the same title, Philadelphia, private edition.   6041

Gottmann, Jean, "Three and a Half Centuries of Change," chap. 2 in his *Virginia in Our Century*, 2d ed. (Charlottesville: University Press of Virginia, 1969), pp. 54–141.   6042

O'Mara, James, "The Riverine Myth in Interpretations of Eighteenth Century Virginia," *Southern Folklore Quarterly*, vol. 44 (1980), pp. 165–177.   6043

Ainsley, W. Frank, Jr., and P. Rouse, *Virginia History and Geography* (Morristown, N.J.: Silver, Burdett & Ginn, 1990), 448 pp.   6044

Smaller areas

Stone, Robert G., "An Historical-Geographic Interpretation of the Upper Big Sandy River Basin of Southwestern Virginia," Master's thesis, Ohio State University, 1931.   6045

Mitchell, Robert D., "The Upper Shenandoah Valley of Virginia during the Eighteenth Century: A Study in Historical Geography," Ph.D. diss., University of Wisconsin–Madison, 1969.   6046

Mitchell, Robert D., "The Shenandoah Valley Frontier," *Annals of the Association of American Geographers*, vol. 62, 3 (1972), pp. 461–486. Reprinted, with omissions, in David Ward, ed., *Geographic Perspectives on America's Past: Readings on the Historical Geography of the United States* (New York: Oxford University Press, 1979), pp. 148–166.   6047

Mitchell, Robert D., *Commercialism and Frontier: Perspectives on the Early Shenandoah Frontier* (Charlottesville: University Press of Virginia, 1977), 251 pp.   6048

Mitchell, Robert D., "The Shenandoah Valley," in D. C. Roller and R. W. Tugman, eds., *The Encyclopedia of Southern History* (Baton Rouge: Louisiana State University Press, 1979), p. 1099.   6049

Mitchell, Robert D., "The Pattern of Change in the Shenandoah Valley after the American Revolu-

tion," *Winchester-Frederick County Historical Society Journal*, vol. 2 (1987), pp. 33–42.   6050

ENVIRONMENTAL CHANGE

Wolfanger, Louis A., "Abandoned Land in a Region of Land Abandonment," *Economic Geography*, vol. 7, 2 (1931), pp. 166–176. [James River District, 1607-1930]   6051

Dunbar, Gary S., "Some Notes on Bison in Early Virginia," *Quarterly Bulletin of the Virginia Archeological Society*, vol. 18, 4 (1964), pp. 75–78.   6052

McDonald, Jerry N., and S. O. Bird, eds., *The Quaternary of Virginia: Symposium Volume* (Charlottesville: Virginia Division of Mineral Resources Publication no. 75, 1986), 137 pp.   6053

EXPLORATION & MAPPING

See also 5860

Ford, Worthington C., "Captain John Smith's Map of Virginia, 1612," *Geographical Review*, vol. 14, 3 (1924), pp. 433–443.   6054

Martin, Lawrence, "Warner's Map of the Rappahannock and Potomac Rivers," *William and Mary Quarterly Magazine*, 2d ser., vol. 19, 1 (1939), pp. 82–83.   6055

Roberts, Joseph K., "History of Geologic and Topographic Mapping in Virginia," *Bulletin of the Geological Society of America*, vol. 50, 3 (1939), p. 1931.   6056

Verner, Coolie, "The First Maps of Virginia, 1590–1673," *Virginia Magazine of History and Biography*, vol. 58, 1 (1950), pp. 3–15.   6057

Verner, Coolie, "Maps of Virginia in Mercator's Lesser Atlases," *Imago Mundi*, vol. 17 (1963), pp. 45–61.   6058

Burton, Arthur G., and Richard W. Stephenson, "John Ballendine's Eighteenth-Century Map of Virginia," *Quarterly Journal of the Library of Congress*, vol. 21, 3 (1964), pp. 174–178.   6059

Sanchez-Saaveda, E. M., *A Description of the Country: Virginia's Cartographers and Their Maps, 1607–1881* (Richmond: Virginia State Library, 1975), 130 pp. [9 maps and commentary]   6060

Harley, J. Brian, "George Washington, Map-Maker," *Geographical Magazine*, vol. 48, 10 (1976), pp. 588–594.   6061

Hanna, Jan L., "The Development of Virginia Road Maps," *Virginia Geographer*, vol. 15 (1983), pp. 25–44.   6062

Simpson, Alan, *The Mysteries of the 'Frenchman's Map' of Williamsburg, Virginia* (Williamsburg: Colonial Williamsburg Foundation, 1984), 42 pp.   6063

Herndon, G. Melvin, "William Tatham: Early Virginia Surveyor, Geographer, and Cartographer," *Virginia Geographer*, vol. 17, 2 (1985), pp. 27–41.   6064

Friis, Herman R., "Highlights of Matthew Fontaine Maury's Life as a Virginia Geographer in the Service of His Country and His State," *Virginia Geographer*, vol. 20, 2 (1988), pp. 27–32. [1806–1873]   6065

POPULAR IMAGES & EVALUATION

Greely, Adolphus Washington, "Jefferson as a Geographer," *National Geographic Magazine*, vol. 7, 6 (1896), pp. 269–271.   6066

Brown, Ralph Hall, "St. George Tucker *versus* Jedidiah Morse on the Subject of Williamsburg," *William & Mary Quarterly*, 2d ser., vol. 20, 4 (1940), pp. 487–491.   6067

Brown, Ralph Hall, "Jefferson's Notes on Virginia," *Geographical Review*, vol. 35, 3 (1945), pp. 467–473.   6068

Dunbar, Gary S., "Assessment of Virginia's Natural Qualities by Explorers and Early Settlers," in R. C. Simonini, ed., *Virginia in History and Tradition* (Farmville, Va.: Longwood College, 1958), pp. 65–84.   6069

Dunbar, Gary S., "Some Curious Analogies in Explorers' Preconceptions of Virginia," *Virginia Journal of Science*, vol. 9, 3 (1958), pp. 323–326. Reprinted in Christopher L. Salter, ed., *The Cultural Landscape* (Belmont, Calif.: Duxbury Press, 1971), pp. 18–20.   6070

Dunbar, Gary S., "The Popular Regions of Virginia," *University of Virginia Newsletter*, vol. 38, 3 (1961), pp. 9–12.   6071

Skelton, Raleigh A., "Ralegh [*sic*] as a Geographer," *Virginia Magazine of History and Biography*, vol. 71, 2 (1963), pp. 131–149.   6072

Vining, James W., "Virginia Landscape Curiosities: Views from the Early Geographies," *Virginia Geographer*, vol. 14, 1 (1982), pp. 39–47.   6073

Hawthorne, Marijean H., "Mining the Archives II: Changing Perceptions of Beach Lands in Virginia," *Virginia Geographer*, vol. 15 (1983), pp. 45–53.   6074

REGIONAL SETTLEMENT

See also 5879

Miller, LeRoy C., *The Shenandoah Valley in Virginia—An Economic-Geographic Interpretation* (Nashville: George Peabody College for Teachers, Abstract of Contribution to Education no. 236, 1939), 8 pp.   6075

Daniell, David S., "The Lost Colony," *Geographical Magazine*, vol. 13, 5 (1941), pp. 288–294. [Roanoke]   6076

Finkl, Charles W., "Sequent Occupance in Fauquier County, Virginia," Master's thesis, Oregon State University, 1966.   6077

Finkl, Charles W., "The Character of Settlement in Northern Fauquier County," *Virginia Geographer*, vol. 3, 2 (1968), pp. 2–7.   6078

Grim, Ronald E., "The Absence of Towns in Seventeenth-Century Virginia: The Emergence of Service Centers in York County," Ph.D. diss., University of Maryland, 1977.   6079

Wilhelm, Eugene J., "Shenandoah Resettlement," *Pioneer America*, vol. 14, 1 (1982), pp. 15–40.   6080

Cocks, Edmond D., "The Appomattox," *Virginia Geographer*, vol. 16, 1 (1984), pp. 57–67. [Focus on the Appomattox Basin]   6081

POPULATION

Surface, George T., "Racial and Regional Study of the Virginia Population," *Bulletin of the American Geographical Society*, vol. 39, 5 (1907), pp. 285–291.   6082

Vance, Rupert B., "The Changing Density of Virginia's Population: Urbanization and Migration," in Roscoe D. Hughes and Henry Leidheiser, Jr., eds., *Exploring Virginia's Human Resources* (Charlottesville: University Press of Virginia, 1965), pp. 35–53. Reprinted in John S. Reed and Daniel J. Singal, eds., *Regionalism and the South: Selected Papers of Rupert Vance* (Chapel Hill: University of North Carolina Press, 1982), pp. 233–249. [Focus on 1940–1960]   6083

Hardin, David S., "From Tidewater to Blue Ridge: The Expansion of Population in Eastern Virginia during the Early Eighteenth Century," Master's thesis, University of Tennessee, 1985.   6084

RURAL & REGIONAL SOCIAL GEOGRAPHY

Main, Jackson Turner, "The Distribution of Property in Post-Revolutionary Virginia," *Mississippi Valley Historical Review*, vol. 41, 2 (1954), pp. 241–258.   6085

Main, Jackson Turner, "The One Hundred," *William & Mary Quarterly*, 3d ser., vol. 11, 3 (1954), pp. 354–384. [The hundred wealthiest planters in Virginia in the 1780s] **6086**

Landing, James E., "Exploring Mennonite Settlements in Virginia," *Virginia Geographer*, vol. 4, 1 (1969), pp. 6–12. **6087**

Mitchell, Robert D., "Content and Context: Tidewater Characteristics in the Early Shenandoah Valley," *Maryland Historian*, vol. 5, 2 (1974), pp. 79–92. **6088**

Earle, Carville V., "Environment, Disease, and Mortality in Early Virginia," *Journal of Historical Geography*, vol. 5, 4 (1979), pp. 365–390. **6089**

Smith, James L., "Pocahontas: A Secluded Island Community," *Virginia Geographer*, vol. 14, 1 (1982), pp. 13–23. **6090**

POLITICAL & ADMINISTRATIVE GEOGRAPHY

See **5911, 5915**

General

Main, Jackson Turner, "Sections and Politics in Virginia, 1781–1787," *William & Mary Quarterly*, 3d ser., vol. 12, 1 (1955), pp. 96–112. **6091**

Doran, Michael F., "A Political Definition of Virginia's Nuclear Core," *Political Geography Quarterly*, vol. 6, 4 (1987), pp. 301–311. **6092**

Military

Emerson, Frederick V., "The Shenandoah Valley in the Civil War," *Journal of School Geography*, vol. 5, 6 (1901), pp. 208–214. **6093**

Carrington, George Baker, "Topography, Strategy, and Jackson: A Geographical Analysis of the Shenandoah Valley Campaign of 1862, and an Evaluation of the Strategic Potentialities of the Valley Today," Master's thesis, University of Virginia, 1949. **6094**

Shelton, Samuel W., "The Peninsula Campaign: A Study in Military Geography," Master's thesis, University of Virginia, 1956. **6095**

Calkins, Chris M., "A Geographic Description of the Petersburg Battlefields: June 1864–April 1865," *Virginia Geographer*, vol. 16, 1 (1984), pp. 43–56. **6096**

Dunbar, Gary S., "Resources of the Southern Fields and Forests: Local Remedies and Provisionment in the Confederate States of America," *Virginia Geographer*, vol. 17, 2 (1985), pp. 52–58. **6097**

Ansley, Mary, and Sandra Freed Pritchard, "Winter Weather at Valley Forge, 1777–1778: A Lesson in Climatic Reconstruction," *Journal of Geography*, vol. 86, 3 (1987), pp. 120–126. **6098**

ECONOMIC DEVELOPMENT

Hawthorne, Marijean, "Mining the Archives: Mills and Fish-ways in Virginia," *Virginia Geographer*, vol. 14 (1981), pp. 48–51. **6099**

Richetto, Jeffrey P., and Henry Moon, "Railroad Development in Central Virginia and Its Effect on the Redistribution of Tobacco Farming, 1840–1880," *Virginia Geographer*, vol. 17, 1 (1985), pp. 1–23. **6100**

RESOURCE MANAGEMENT

Hardin, David S., "Laws of Nature: Environmental Legislation in Colonial Virginia, 1619–1776," *Virginia Geographer*, vol. 22, 2 (1990), pp. 53–67. **6101**

LAND & LAND USE

Roberts, Lisa S., "Historical Land Use in Burke's Garden, Tazewell County, Virginia, 1880–1981," Master's thesis, Louisiana State University, 1981. **6102**

AGRICULTURE

See also **4837**

Mitchell, Robert D., "The Commercial Nature of Frontier Settlement in the Shenandoah Valley of Virginia," *Proceedings of the Association of American Geographers*, vol. 1 (1969), pp. 109–113. **6103**

Mitchell, Robert D., "Agricultural Change and the American Revolution: A Virginia Case Study," *Agricultural History*, vol. 47, 2 (1973), pp. 119–132. **6104**

Gouger, James B., III, "Agricultural Change in the Northern Neck of Virginia in the Eighteenth Century, 1700–1860: An Historical Geography," Ph.D. diss., University of Florida, 1976. **6105**

Gouger, James B., III, "The Northern Neck of Virginia: A Tidewater Grain-Farming Region in the Antebellum South," *West Georgia College Studies in Social Science*, vol. 16 (1977), pp. 73–90. **6106**

LANDSCAPE

See also **4844**

Gordon, Michael H., "The Upland Southern–Lowland Southern Culture Areas: A Field Study of Building Characteristics in Southern Virginia," Master's thesis, Rutgers University, 1968. **6107**

Glassie, Henry H., *Folk Housing in Middle Virginia* (Knoxville: University of Tennessee Press, 1975), 231 pp. **6108**

Grim, Ronald E., "George Washington's Potomac: Mount Vernon to Great Falls," in *Field Trip Guide, 1984 Annual Meetings of the Association of American Geographers* (Washington, D.C.: Association of American Geographers, 1984), pp. 75–83. **6109**

Upton, Dell, "White and Black Landscapes in Eighteenth-Century Virginia," *Places*, vol. 2 (1985), pp. 59–72. Reprinted in Robert Blair St. George, ed., *Material Life in America, 1600–1860* (Boston: Northeastern University Press, 1988), pp. 357–369. **6110**

Wells, Camille, "The Eighteenth-Century Landscape of Virginia's Northern Neck," *Northern Neck of Virginia Historical Magazine*," vol. 37, 1 (1987), pp. 4217–4255. **6111**

Upton, Dell, "New Views of the Virginia Landscape," *Virginia Magazine of History and Biography*, vol. 96, 4 (1988), pp. 403–470. **6112**

COMMUNICATIONS & TRADE

Wilhelm, Eugene J., "Pioneer Boats and Transportation on the Upper James River," *Pioneer America*, vol. 3, 1 (1971), pp. 39–47. **6113**

Farmer, Charles J., "Country Stores and Frontier Exchange Systems in Southside Virginia during the Eighteenth Century," Ph.D. diss., University of Maryland, 1984. **6114**

Farmer, Charles J., "Country Store Trading Patterns in Backcountry Southern Virginia during the Eighteenth Century," in Richard L. Nostrand and Sam B. Hilliard, eds., *The American South* (Baton Rouge: Louisiana State University School of Geoscience, Geoscience & Man, vol. 25, 1988), pp. 57–66. **6115**

Farmer, Charles J., "Persistence of Country Trade: The Failure of Towns to Develop in Southside Virginia during the Eighteenth Century," *Journal of Historical Geography*, vol. 14, 4 (1988), pp. 331–341. **6116**

URBAN NETWORKS & URBANIZATION

Grim, Ronald E., "The Origins and Early Development of the Virginia Fall-Line Towns," Master's thesis, University of Maryland, 1971. **6117**

O'Mara, James J., "Urbanization in Tidewater Virginia during the Eighteenth Century: A Study in Historical Geography," Ph.D. diss., York University, 1979. **6118**

O'Mara, James J., *An Historical Geography of Urban System Development: Tidewater Virginia in the Eighteenth Century* (Downsview: York University Department of Geography, 1983), 320 pp. **6119**

TOWN GROWTH

Fredericksburg

Armstrong, Thomas, "Antebellum Urban Promotion in Fredericksburg, Virginia," *Southeastern Geographer*, vol. 20, 1 (1980), pp. 58–74. Reprinted in *Virginia Geographer*, vol. 14 (1982), pp. 22–38. **6120**

London, Bruce, and Richard P. Palmieri, "Fredericksburg: The Ecological Foundations of Urban History," *Pioneer America Society Transactions*, vol. 3 (1980), pp. 122–139. **6121**

Lynchburg

DeBusk, Clinton E., "An Historical Geography of Lynchburg, Virginia," Master's thesis, University of Virginia, 1953. **6122**

Armstrong, Thomas, "Tobacco Growth and Urban Strategy: Antebellum Lynchburg, Virginia," *Virginia Geographer*, vol. 14, 1 (1982), pp. 1–12. **6123**

Scottsville

Goldstone, Robert L., "Historical Geography of Scottsville, Virginia: The Relation of Changing Transportation Patterns to a Riverine-Piedmont Community," Master's thesis, University of Virginia, 1953. **6124**

Landreth, Pamela Sue, "Scottsville: Early Transshipment Center for Piedmont Virginia," *Virginia Geographer*, vol. 7, 1 (1972), pp. 3–6. **6125**

Other centers

Riley, Edward M., "Suburban Development of Yorktown, Virginia, during the Colonial Period," *Virginia Magazine of History and Biography*, vol. 60, 4 (1952), pp. 522–536. **6126**

Price, Carolyn D., "Geographic Factors in the Evolution of Gordonsville," Master's thesis, University of Virginia, 1970. **6127**

Armstrong, Thomas, "In Pursuit of People: The Ante-Bellum Town Promotion of Staunton, Virginia," *Virginia Geographer*, vol. 12, 1 (1977), pp. 15–21. **6128**

Hanna, Jon, and Linda Slagle, "Matildaville, Virginia: An Extinct Town on the Potomac," *Virginia Geographer*, vol. 14, 1 (1982), pp. 24–38. [Focus on 1716–1839] **6129**

O'Mara, James J., "Town Founding in Seventeenth Century North America: Jamestown in Virginia," *Journal of Historical Geography*, vol. 8, 1 (1982), pp. 1–11. **6130**

URBAN ECONOMIC STRUCTURE

Ainsley, W. Frank, Jr., "Changing Land Use in Downtown Norfolk, Virginia: 1680–1930," Ph.D. diss., University of North Carolina–Chapel Hill, 1977. **6131**

Henderson, William D., "The Evolution of Petersburg's Economy, 1860–1900," *Virginia Geographer*, vol. 16, 1 (1984), pp. 23–42. **6132**

URBAN SOCIAL STRUCTURE

Fredericksburg

London, Bruce, and Richard P. Palmieri, "Fredericksburg's Urban History: A Reconstructed Residential Ecology," *Virginia Geographer*, vol. 14 (1982), pp. 1–4. **6133**

Bragdon, Jane V. V., Willam S. Chilton, Nancy Freeman, Doris L. Green, and Katherine Shiflett, "Fredericksburg in 1888: A Spatial Ecology," *Virginia Geographer*, vol. 14 (1982), pp. 5–7. **6134**

Warker, Kim, and Mickie Miller, "Residential Segregation in Fredericksburg, Virginia, 1880 and 1910," *Virginia Geographer*, vol. 14 (1982), pp. 8–13. **6135**

Myers, Mary Anne P., and Bruce London, "Fredericksburg in 1976: A Spatial Ecology," *Virginia Geographer*, vol. 14 (1982), pp. 14–21. **6136**

Petersburg

Edwards, Lucius, Jr., "Petersburg and Free Black Immigrants: 1748–1860," *Virginia Geographer*, vol. 16, 1 (1984), pp. 1–14. **6137**

Smith, James W., "The Role of Blacks in Petersburg's Carrying Trade and Service-Oriented Industry, 1800–1865," *Virginia Geographer*, vol. 16, 1 (1984), pp. 15–22. **6138**

Other centers

Glenn, Garrard, "The University of Virginia," *Geographical Magazine*, vol. 4, 1 (1936), pp. 58–72. [Charlottesville] **6139**

Organ, David J., "Truxton, Virginia, 1918–1921: The All-Black Town Phenomenon Revisited at a Critical Juncture in Evolution and Reconstruction of African-American Urban Historical Geography," Master's thesis, University of California–Berkeley, 1989. **6140**

TOWNSCAPE

Reps, John W., "Thomas Jefferson's Checkerboard Towns," *Journal of the Society of Architectural Historians*, vol. 20, 3 (1961), pp. 108–114. **6141**

Crotty, Anne R., "House Types in Old Alexandria," Master's thesis, Catholic University of America, 1971. **6142**

PLANNING

See **6033**

PLACE NAMES

Long, Charles M., *Virginia County Names: Two Hundred and Seventy Years of Virginia History* (New York: Neale Publishing Co., 1908), 207 pp. **6143**

Burrill, Meredith F., "Terminology of Virginia's Geographic Features," *Bulletin of the Virginia Geographical Society*, vol. 9 (1957), pp. 12–20. **6144**

Miller, Mary R., "Place-Names of the Northern Neck of Virginia: A Proposal for a Theory of Place-Naming," *Names*, vol. 24, 1 (1976), pp. 9–23. **6145**

Friberg, Justin C., and Donald J. Zeigler, "Tidewater: A Metropolitan Toponym for Southeast Virginia?" *Names*, vol. 36, 1 (1988), pp. 5–20. Reprinted in *Virginia Geographer*, vol., 22, 2 (1990), pp. 9–19. **6146**

WEST VIRGINIA

EXPLORATION & MAPPING

Norona, Delf, "Cartography of West Virginia," *West Virginia History*, vol. 9 (Jan. and Apr. 1948), pp. 99–127 and 187–223. **6147**

REGIONAL SETTLEMENT

Gillenwater, Mack H., "A Cultural and Historical Geography of Mining Settlements in the Poca-hontas Coalfield of Southern West Virginia, 1880–1930," Ph.D. diss., University of Tennesee, 1972. **6148**

Gillenwater, Mack H., "Mining Settlements of Southern West Virginia," in Howard G. Adkins, S. Ewing, and Chester E. Zimolzak, eds., *West Virginia and Appalachia: Selected Readings* (Dubuque: Kendall/Hunt, 1977), pp. 132–158. **6149**

RURAL & REGIONAL SOCIAL GEOGRAPHY

Pudup, Mary Beth, "Women's Work in the West Virginia Economy," *West Virginia History*, vol. 49 (1990), pp. 7–20. [Focus on 1870s–1980s] **6150**

POLITICAL & ADMINISTRATIVE GEOGRAPHY

See also **5915**

Russell, George H., "A Geographic Analysis of the Battle of Antietam," Master's thesis, Bowling Green State University, 1974. **6151**

EXTRACTIVE ACTIVITY

Wion, Diana, "A Time Series Analysis of Coal Production in West Virginia, 1900–1982," Master's thesis, West Virginia University, 1985. **6152**

URBAN ECONOMIC STRUCTURE

Downs, Margaret B., "Industrial Structure and Pattern of the Wheeling District: Its Evolution and Development, 1840–1950," Ph.D. diss., University of Maryland, 1957. **6153**

PLACE NAMES

Kenny, Hamill, *West Virginia Place Names: Their Origin and Meaning, Including the Nomenclature of the Streams and Mountains* (Piedmont, W.Va.: Place Name Press, 1945), 768 pp. **6154**

Gillenwater, Mack H., "Place Names as Cultural Indicators: The Case of the New River (West Virginia) Basin," *Virginia Geographer*, vol. 14 (1982), pp. 39–50. **6155**

Jansson, Quinith, and William Fernbach, *West Virginia Place Names* (Shepherdstown: J & F Enterprises, 1984), 87 pp. **6156**

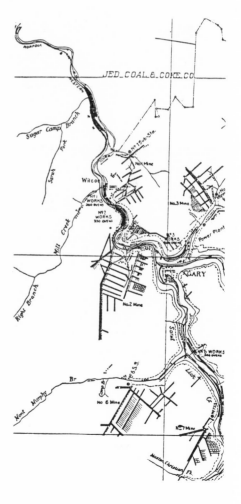

NORTH CAROLINA

GENERAL

The state

Merrens, H. Roy, "The Changing Geography of the Colony of North Carolina during the Eighteenth Century," Ph.D. diss., University of Wisconsin–Madison, 1962.   **6157**

Merrens, H. Roy, *Colonial North Carolina in the Eighteenth Century: A Study in Historical Geography* (Chapel Hill: University of North Carolina Press, 1964), 293 pp.   **6158**

Wilms, Douglas C., "The Geography of Early North Carolina," in Vernon M. Smith, Donald Steila, and Richard A. Stephenson, eds., *North Carolina: A Reader* (Geneva, Ill.: Paladin Press, 1975), pp. 3–9.   **6159**

Ainsley, W. Frank, Jr., and John W. Florin, *North Carolina: The Land and Its People* (Morristown, N.J.: Silver, Burdett & Ginn, 1988), 392 pp.   **6160**

Smaller areas

Norburn, Martha, "The Influence of the Physiographic Features of Western North Carolina on the Settlement and Development of the Region," Ph.D. diss., University of North Carolina, 1932.   **6161**

Dunbar, Gary S., "Cultural Geography of the North Carolina Outer Banks," Ph.D. diss., Louisiana State University, 1956.   **6162**

Dunbar, Gary S., *Historical Geography of the North Carolina Outer Banks* (Baton Rouge: Louisiana State University Coastal Studies, no. 3, 1958), 234 pp.   **6163**

Smith, Mary R., "A Study of the Historical Geography of Ocracoke Island and Ocracoke Inlet, North Carolina," *Virginia Geographer*, vol. 6, 1 (1971), pp. 15–18.   **6164**

ENVIRONMENTAL CHANGE

Dunbar, Gary S., "Thermal Belts in North Carolina," *Geographical Review*, vol. 56, 4 (1964), pp. 516–526.   **6165**

Dolan, Robert, and Kenton Bosserman, "Shoreline Erosion and the Lost Colony," *Annals of the Association of American Geographers*, vol. 62, 3 (1972), pp. 424–426. [North Carolina and Raleigh's 1585 settlement]   **6166**

Dolan, Robert, and Robert Glassen, "Oregon Inlet, North Carolina: A History of Coastal Change," *Southeastern Geographer*, vol. 13, 1 (1973), pp. 41–53.   **6167**

NATIVE PEOPLES & WHITE RELATIONS

Dunbar, Gary S., "The Hatteras Indians of North Carolina," *Ethnohistory*, vol. 7, 4 (1960), pp. 410–418.   **6168**

EXPLORATION & MAPPING

Ford, Worthington C., "Early Maps of Carolina," *Geographical Review*, vol. 16, 2 (1926), pp. 264–273.   **6169**

Cumming, William P., "The Earliest Permanent Settlement in Carolina: Nathaniel Batts and the Comberford Map," *American Historical Review*, vol. 45, 1 (1939), pp. 82–89.   **6170**

Dunbar, Gary S., "Silas McDowell and the Early Botanical Exploration of Western North Carolina," *North Carolina Historical Review*, vol. 41, 4 (1964), pp. 425–435.   **6171**

Cumming, William P., "Wimble's Maps and the Colonial Cartography of the North Carolina Coast," *North Carolina Historical Review*, vol. 46, 2 (1969), pp. 157–170.   **6172**

Merrens, H. Roy, and Herbert Paschal, "A Map-Maker's View of Anson County in 1769," *North Carolina Historical Review*, vol. 59, 3 (1982), pp. 271–278.   **6173**

Cumming, William P., *Mapping the North Carolina Coast: Sixteenth-Century Cartography and the Roanoke Voyages* (Raleigh: North Carolina Department of Cultural Resources, Division of Archives and History, 1988), 143 pp.   **6174**

REGIONAL SETTLEMENT

See **5877**

POPULATION

Rice, Gwenda Hedd, "Changing Mortality Patterns in North Carolina, 1920–1970,"Ph.D. diss., University of North Carolina, 1981.   **6175**

Cromartie, John, "Population Change in North Carolina's Coastal Plains, 1960–1980," Master's thesis, University of North Carolina, 1984.   **6176**

Gilmartin, Robin Mary, "North Carolina's Rural Nonfarm Population, 1950–1980," Master's thesis, University of North Carolina, 1984. **6177**

RURAL & REGIONAL SOCIAL GEOGRAPHY

See also **7372**

Morris, Francis Grave, and Phyllis Mary Morris, "Economic Conditions in North Carolina about 1780: Part I—Landholdings; Part II—Ownership of Town Lots, Slaves, and Cattle," *North Carolina Historical Review*, vol. 16, 2 (1939), pp. 107–133; 3, 296–327. **6178**

Ainsley, W. Frank, Jr., "The North Carolina Piedmont: An Island of Religious Diversity," Master's thesis, University of North Carolina, 1972. **6179**

Ainsley, W. Frank, Jr., and John W. Florin, "The North Carolina Piedmont: An Island of Religious Diversity," *West Georgia College Studies in the Social Sciences*, vol. 12 (1973), pp. 30–34. **6180**

Ainsley, W. Frank, Jr., "Own a Home in North Carolina: Image and Reality in Ethnic European Colonies," *Journal of Cultural Geography*, vol. 5, 2 (1985), pp. 61–70. **6181**

Efrid, Cathy M., "A Geography of Lay Midwifery in Appalachia, North Carolina, 1925–1950," Ph.D. diss., University of North Carolina, 1985. **6182**

POLITICAL & ADMINISTRATIVE GEOGRAPHY

See also **5914**

Goff, Chris, "The Geographic Origins of North Carolina Enlistments in the War between the States," Master's thesis, University of North Carolina, 1987. **6183**

LAND & LAND USE

Stafford, Dorothy A., "Contemporary Land Occupance Traits at St. Helena, North Carolina: Their Derivation and Evolution," Master's thesis, University of Georgia, 1967. **6184**

EXTRACTIVE ACTIVITY

Glass, Brent D., "'Poor Men with Rude Machinery': The Formative Years of the Gold Hill Mining District, 1842–1853," *North Carolina Historical Review*, vol. 61, 1 (1984), pp. 1–35. **6185**

AGRICULTURE

Landon, Charles E., "The Tobacco Growing Industry of North Carolina," *Economic Geography*, vol. 10, 3 (1934), pp. 239–253. [Focus on 1880–1930] **6186**

Holder, Gerald L., "The Tobacco Farm Complex in Lee County, North Carolina, 1938–1965," Master's thesis, University of Georgia, 1966. **6187**

Hart, John Fraser, and Ennis L. Chestang, "Rural Revolution in East Carolina," *Geographical Review*, vol. 68, 4 (1978), pp. 435–458. [Focus on 1928–1977] **6188**

LANDSCAPE

Dunbar, Gary S., "Colonial Carolina Cowpens," *Agricultural History*, vol. 35, 3 (1961), pp. 125–130. **6189**

Ainsley, W. Frank, Jr., "Vernacular Houses in Brunswick County, North Carolina," *Pioneer America Society Transactions*, vol. 4 (1981), pp. 26–41. **6190**

COMMUNICATIONS & TRADE

See also **6003–6004**

Kithcart, Phillip E., "An Historical Analysis of the Highway Network, North Carolina, 1770–1970," Master's thesis, University of Cincinnati, 1970. **6191**

MANUFACTURING & INDUSTRIALIZATION

Bynum, Jefferson, "Piedmont North Carolina and Textile Production," *Economic Geography*, vol. 4, 2 (1928), pp. 232–240. **6192**

Whitehurst, Jonathan H., "The Early Menhaden Industry of North Carolina: A Brief Study in Historical Geography," *Virginia Geographer*, vol. 5, 2 (1970), pp. 6–8. **6193**

Tuttle, Marcia L., "The Location of North Carolina's Nineteenth Century Cotton Products Industry," Master's thesis, University of North Carolina–Chapel Hill, 1974. **6194**

URBAN NETWORKS & URBANIZATION

See also **6017**

Logan, Byron E., "An Historical Geography of North Carolina Ports," Ph.D. diss., University of North Carolina, 1956. **6195**

TOWN GROWTH

Ebert, Charles C. V., "High Point's Evolution as a Furniture Town," Master's thesis, University of North Carolina, 1954. **6196**

Pattrick, C., "Growth Patterns of Raleigh, North Carolina," Ph.D. diss., University of North Carolina, 1964.   6197

Randall, Duncan P., "Geographic Factors in the Growth and Economy of Wilmington, North Carolina," Ph.D. diss., University of North Carolina, 1965.   6198

Randall, Duncan P., "Wilmington, North Carolina: The Historical Development of a Port City," *Annals of the Association of American Geographers*, vol. 58, 3 (1968), pp. 441–451.   6199

TOWNSCAPE

Ainsley, W. Frank, Jr., *The Historical Architecture of Warsaw, North Carolina* (Warsaw, N.C.: Warsaw Garden Club, 1983), 71 pp.   6200

Larson, Albert J., "The Courthouse of Northeastern North Carolina," *Pioneer America Society Transactions*, vol. 9 (1986), pp. 79–87.   6201

RECREATION & TOURISM

Colten, Craig E., "The Historical Geography of Seasonal Settlement in Henderson County, North Carolina: 1827–1977," Master's thesis, Louisiana State University, 1978.   6202

PLACE NAMES

Writers' Program, *How They Began: The Story of North Carolina County, Town, and Other Place Names* (Raleigh: North Carolina Department of Conservation and Development, and New York: Harlan Publications, 1941), 73 pp.   6203

290 CHARLOTTE, COLUMBIA AND AUGUSTA RAILWAY.

W. Johnston, President,
Charlotte, N. C.
Caleb Bouknight,
Superintendent.

C. H. Manson, Sec. and Treas.
E. R. Dorsey,
Gen. Freight and Ticket Ag't,
Columbia, S. C.

Trains Leave.				April, 1870.	Trains Arrive.			
Acc.	Acc.	Pas	Mls	STATIONS.	Frs.	Pas	Acc.	Acc.
	A. M.	A. M.				P. M.		P. M.
	10 30	10 15	0	...**Charlotte**[1]....		4 10		5 10
	11 15	10 55	11	.... Morrow's		3 40		4 30
	11 55	11 19	18	......Fort Mills.....		3 15		3 55
	12 50	11 49	26	..... Rock Hill......		2 44		3 10
	1 40	12 20	35	.......Smith's.......		2 12		2 15
	2 00	12 31	38	.......Lewis.......		2 02		1 55
	3 00	1 15	45	......**Chester**[2].....		1 35		12 55
	3 45	1 40	53	.... Cornwall's.....		12 48		11 30
	4 15	1 52	57	.... Black Stock ...		12 33		11 05
	4 40	2 05	60	....Yonguesville...		12 19		10 35
	5 00	2 18	64	.....White Oak		12 06		10 10
	5 15	2 28	67	...... Adger's.....		11 56		9 55
	6 05	2 46	72	.....Winnsboro.....		11 39		9 30
	6 35	3 08	78	......Simpson's		11 14		8 35
	7 15	3 32	84	.....Ridgeway.....		10 54		8 00
	7 55	3 56	91	.......Doko......		10 29		7 10
P. M.	8 25	4 15	97	.....Killian's.....		10 05	A. M.	6 30
10 00	P. M.	4 50	107	.....**Columbia**[3]....		9 40	4 20	5 40
11 20		5 40	124	......Lexington.....		8 35	2 55	A. M.
12 10		6 11	134	...Gilbert Hollow...		8 02	1 50	
12 50		6 33	141	.... Leesville......		7 38	12 55	
1 15		6 41	143	.... Batesville.....		7 31	12 30	
2 10		7 15	153	.....Ridge Spring ...		6 56	11 00	
3 10		7 43	162	......Johnston.....		6 26	9 35	
4 20		8 25	173	.....Mile's Mill.....		5 47	7 10	
5 20		8 56	183	.... Graniteville....		5 17	6 05	
6 30		9 40	195	.....**Augusta**[4]....		4 30	4 15	
A. M.		P. M.		[ARRIVE] [LEAVE]		A. M.	P. M.	

Standard of Time.—Clock in Supt.'s office at Columbia.

CONNECTIONS.

[1] At Charlotte, with North Carolina, and Wilmington, Charlotte and Rutherford Railways.
[2] At Chester, with King's Mountain Railway.
[2] At Chester, with Stages for Unionville, Glen Springs, Spartanburg, &c., on Mondays, Wednesdays and Fridays.
[3] At Columbia, with Greenville and Columbia Railway, and Columbia Branch of South Carolina Railway.
[4] At Augusta with Georgia and Augusta and Savannah Railways.

—————— SOUTH CAROLINA ——————

GENERAL

The state

Kovacik, Charles F., and John J. Winberry, "The Historical Setting," in their *South Carolina: A Geography* (Boulder: Westview Press, 1987), pp. 51–132.   **6204**

Smaller areas

Ristow, Walter W., "Geographic Studies in Orangeburg County, South Carolina," Ph.D. diss., Clark University, 1937.   **6205**

ENVIRONMENTAL CHANGE

Winberry, John J., "Changing Attitudes and Land Use Patterns in South Carolina's Freshwater Wetlands," in J. Tibbets and V. Beach, eds., *Wealth or Wastelands: South Carolina's Freshwater Wetlands* (Charleston: South Carolina Sea Grant Consortium, 1988), pp. 33–38.   **6206**

EXPLORATION & MAPPING

Cumming, William P., *Cartography of Colonial Carolina*, Inaugural Address, Kendall Collection, South Carolina Library, University of South Carolina (Columbia: University of South Carolina, 1961), 15 pp.   **6207**

POPULAR IMAGES & EVALUATION

Brown, Ralph Hall, "Governor Drayton's Contribution to Geography," *South Carolina Historical and Genealogical Magazine*, vol. 39, 2 (1938), pp. 68–72. [His book published in 1802]   **6208**

Merrens, H. Roy, "The Physical Environment of Early America: Images and Image-Makers in Colonial South Carolina," *Geographical Review*, vol. 59, 4 (1969), pp. 530–556.   **6209**

Merrens, H. Roy, "A View of Coastal Carolina in 1778: The Journal of Ebenezer Hazard," *South Carolina Historical Magazine*, vol. 73, 4 (1972), pp. 177–193.   **6210**

Kovacik, Charles F., and Lawrence Rowland, "Images of Colonial Port Royal, South Carolina," *Annals of the Association of American Geographers*, vol. 63, 3 (1973), pp. 331–340.   **6211**

Merrens, H. Roy, ed., *The Colonial South Carolina Scene: Comtemporary Views, 1697–1774* (Columbia: University of South Carolina Press, 1977), 295 pp.   **6212**

Winberry, John J., "The Reputation of Carolina Indigo," *South Carolina Historical Magazine*, vol. 80, 3 (1979), pp. 242–250.   **6213**

REGIONAL SETTLEMENT

Picklesmier, Parnell W., "Agglomerated Settlements in the New Bright Tobacco Belt," *Economic Geography*, vol. 22, 1 (1946), pp. 38–45. [Focus on 1900–1940]   **6214**

Morrison, Bruce, "The Influence of the Railroad upon the Rural Settlement Landscape of Sumter County, South Carolina: 1848–1978," Master's thesis, University of South Carolina, 1980.   **6215**

POPULATION

See also **5914, 5917**

Petty, Julian J., "The Growth and Distribution of Population in South Carolina," Ph.D. diss., Ohio State University, 1943.   **6216**

Higgins, W. Robert, "The Geographical Origins of Negro Slaves in Colonial South Carolina," *South Atlantic Quarterly*, vol. 70, 1 (1971), pp. 34–47.   **6217**

RURAL & REGIONAL SOCIAL GEOGRAPHY

Merrens, H. Roy, and George Terry, "Dying in Paradise: Malaria, Mortality, and the Perceptual Environment in Colonial South Carolina," *Journal of Southern History*, vol. 50, 4 (1984), pp. 533–550.   **6218**

ECONOMIC DEVELOPMENT

Ernst, Joseph A., and H. Roy Merrens, "The South Carolina Economy of the Middle Eighteenth Century: A View from Philadelphia," *West Georgia College Studies in the Social Sciences*, vol. 12 (1973), pp. 16–29.   **6219**

Carlton, David L., "The Piedmont and Waccamow Regions: An Economic Comparison," *South Carolina Historical Magazine*, vol. 88, 2 (1987), pp. 83–100.   **6220**

RESOURCE MANAGEMENT

Dunbar, Gary S., "Deer-Keeping in Early South Carolina," *Agricultural History*, vol. 36, 2 (1962), pp. 108–109.   **6221**

LAND & LAND USE

Land survey

Pett-Conklin, Linda Marie, "Cadastral Surveying in Colonial South Carolina: A Historical Geography," Ph.D. diss., Louisiana State University, 1986.   **6222**

Land use

Carpenter, James G., "The Rice Plantation Lands of Georgetown County, South Carolina: A Historical Geographic Study," Master's thesis, University of South Carolina, 1973.   **6223**

Kovacik, Charles F., "Land Use Change on the South Carolina Rice Plantation Lands," *International Geography '76*, sec. 9, *Historical Section* (Moscow: Twenty-third International Geographical Union, 1976), pp. 64–67.   **6224**

EXTRACTIVE ACTIVITY

Salter, Paul S., "A Historical Geography of the South Carolina Phosphate Industry," *Virginia Geographer*, vol. 4, 2 (1969), pp. 16–24.   **6225**

AGRICULTURE

See also **5973**

Ristow, Walter W., "The Rise and Decline of the Indigo Industry of South Carolina," *Yearbook of the Association of Pacific Coast Geographers*, vol. 2 (1936), p. 32.   **6226**

Mason, Robert E., "A Historical Geography of South Carolina's Sea Island Cotton Industry," Master's thesis, University of South Carolina, 1976.   **6227**

Brasington, Dalton K., "A Historical Geography of South Carolina's Inner Coastal Plain Cotton Region," Master's thesis, University of South Carolina, 1977.   **6228**

Winberry, John J., "Indigo in South Carolina: A Historical Geography," *Southeastern Geographer*, vol. 19, 2 (1979), pp. 91–102.   **6229**

Kovacik, Charles F., and Robert E. Mason, "Changes in the South Carolina Sea Island Cotton Industry," *Southeastern Geographer*, vol. 25, 2 (1985), pp. 77–104. [Focus on 1790s–1910s] **6230**

Otto, John S., "The Origins of Cattle-Ranching in Colonial South Carolina, 1670–1715," *South Carolina Historical Magazine*, vol. 87, 2 (1986), pp. 117–124.   **6231**

LANDSCAPE

Kovacik, Charles F., "South Carolina Rice Coast Landscape Changes," *Proceedings of the Tall Timbers Ecology and Management Conference*,

vol. 16 (Tallahassee, Fla.: Tall Timbers Research Station, 1979), pp. 47–65.   **6232**

COMMUNICATIONS & TRADE

See also **6003–6004**

Ford, Ralph W., "The Changing Geographic Pattern of South Carolina's Railroad System, 1860–1902," Master's thesis, University of South Carolina, 1986.   **6233**

MANUFACTURING & INDUSTRIALIZATION

See **6015**

URBAN NETWORKS & URBANIZATION

See also **6017**

Schulz, Judith H., "The Hinterland of Revolutionary Camden, South Carolina," *Southeastern Geographer*, vol. 16, 2 (1976), pp. 91–97.   **6234**

Collins, Frederick B., "Charleston and the Railroads: A Geographic Study of a South Atlantic Port and Its Strategies for Developing a Railroad System, 1820–1860," Master's thesis, University of South Carolina, 1977.   **6235**

Kovacik, Charles F., "Health Conditions and Town Growth in Colonial and Antebellum South Carolina," *Social Science and Medicine: Series D*, vol. 12, 2 (1978), pp. 131–136.   **6236**

Calhoun, Jeanne A., Martha A. Zierden, and Elizabeth A. Paysinger, "The Geographic Spread of Charleston's Mercantile Community, 1732–1767," *South Carolina Historical Magazine*, vol. 86, 3 (1985), pp. 182–220.   **6237**

TOWN GROWTH

Schulz, Judith H., "The Rise and Decline of Camden as South Carolina's Major Inland Trading Center, 1751–1829: A Historical Geographical Study," Master's thesis, University of South Carolina, 1972.   **6238**

Radford, John P., "Culture, Economy, and Urban Structure in Charleston, South Carolina, 1860–1880," Ph.D. diss., Clark University, 1974.   **6239**

Radford, John P., "Testing the Model of the Preindustrial City: The Case of Antebellum Charleston, South Carolina," *Transactions of the Institute of British Geographers*, n.s. vol. 4, 3 (1979), pp. 392–410.   **6240**

URBAN ECONOMIC STRUCTURE

McQuillan, David C., "The Street Railway and the Growth of Columbia, South Carolina, 1882–

1936," Master's thesis, University of South Carolina, 1975. **6241**

URBAN SOCIAL STRUCTURE

Radford, John P., "The Charlestown Planter in 1860," *South Carolina Historical Magazine*, vol. 75, 4 (1976), pp. 227–235. **6242**

Radford, John P., "Race, Residence, and Ideology: Charleston, South Carolina, in the Mid-Nineteenth Century," *Journal of Historical Geography*, vol. 2, 4 (1976), pp. 329–346. Reprinted, with omissions, in David Ward, ed., *Geographic Perspectives on America's Past: Readings on the Historical Geography of the United States* (New York: Oxford University Press, 1979), pp. 344–355. **6243**

Radford, John P., "Delicate Space: Race and Residence in Charleston, South Carolina, 1860–1880," *West Georgia College Studies in the Social Sciences*, vol. 16 (1977), pp. 17–38. **6244**

Seman, Paul F., "Structure and Spatial Distribution of Black-Owned Businesses in Columbia, South Carolina: 1900–1976," Master's thesis, University of South Carolina, 1977. **6245**

Radford, John P., "Social Structure and Urban Form: Charleston, 1860–1880," in Walter J.

Fraser and Winfred B. Moore, eds., *From the Old South to the New: Essays on the Transitional South* (Westport, Conn.: Greenwood Press, 1981), pp. 81–91. **6246**

Kovacik, Charles F., "Eating Out in South Carolina's Cities: The Last Fifty Years," *North American Culture*, vol. 4, 1 (1988), pp. 53–64. **6247**

PLANNING

Datel, Robin E., "Southern Regionalism and Historic Preservation in Charleston, South Carolina, 1920–1940," *Journal of Historical Geography*, vol. 16, 2 (1990), pp. 197–215. **6248**

PLACE NAMES

Writers' Program, *Palmetto Place Names* (Columbia, S.C.: Sloane Printing Co., 1941), 158 pp. **6249**

Dunbar, Gary S., "A Southern Geographical Word List," *American Speech*, vol. 36 (1961), pp. 293–296. [Focus on South Carolina] **6250**

DeVorsey, Louis, Jr., "Names Associated with the Pre-Revolutionary South Carolina–Cherokee Boundary Line," *Names in South Carolina*, vol. 18 (1971), pp. 13–15. **6251**

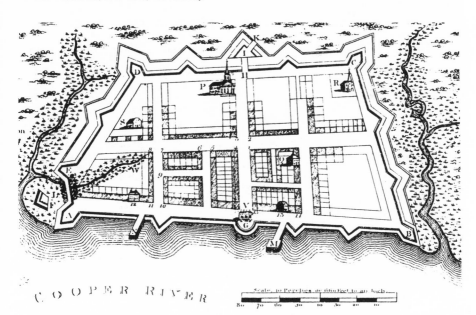

COOPER RIVER

GEORGIA

GENERAL

The state

DeVorsey, Louis, Jr., "On the Trail to Georgia's Past," in William G. Haynes, ed., *Man in the Landscape* (Darien: Darien MacIntosh County Bicentennial Committee, 1977), pp. 5–10. **6252**

DeVorsey, Louis, Jr., "A Land in Time," in Bill Weems, ed., *Georgia: The Home Place* (n.p.: Rapoport Printing Corporation, 1979), pp. 20–35. **6253**

Smaller areas

Elliot, Daniel, and Roy Doyon, *Archeology and Historical Geography of the Savannah River Floodplain near Augusta, Georgia* (Athens: University of Georgia Laboratory of Archeology Series, no. 22, 1981), 194 pp. **6254**

ENVIRONMENTAL CHANGE

Trimble, Stanley W., "The Alcovy River Swamps: The Result of Culturally Accelerated Sedimentation," *Bulletin of the Georgia Academy of Science*, vol. 28 (1970), pp. 131–141. **6255**

Trimble, Stanley W., *Culturally Accelerated Sedimentation on the Middle Georgia Piedmont* (Ft. Worth, Tex.: U.S. Department of Agriculture, Soil Conservation Service, 1971), 110 pp. **6256**

Trimble, Stanley W., "The Origin of the Alcovy River Swamps: A Discussion," *Southeastern Geology*, vol. 18 (1978), pp. 191–194. **6257**

Brook, George A., and Edward R. Luft, "Channel Pattern Changes along the Lower Oconee River, Georgia, 1805/7 to 1949," *Physical Geography*, vol. 8, 3 (1987), pp. 191–209. **6258**

NATIVE PEOPLES & WHITE RELATIONS

Gude, Mary B., "Georgia and the Cherokees," Master's thesis, University of Chicago, 1910. **6259**

Wilms, Douglas C., "Cherokee Indian Land Use in Georgia, 1800–1838," Ph.D. diss., University of Georgia, 1974. **6260**

Wilms, Douglas C., "Cherokee Settlement Patterns in Nineteenth Century Georgia," *Southeastern Geographer*, vol. 14, 1 (1974), pp. 46–53. **6261**

Pillsbury, Richard R., "The Europeanization of the Cherokee Settlement Landscape Prior to Removal: A Georgia Case Study," in Robert W.

Neuman, ed., *Historical Archaeology of the Eastern United States: Papers from the R. J. Russell Symposium* (Baton Rouge: Louisiana State University School of Geoscience, Geoscience & Man, vol. 23 (1983), pp. 59–69. **6262**

DeVorsey, Louis, Jr., "The Colonial Georgia Backcountry," in Edward Cashin, ed., *Colonial Augusta: Key of the Indian Country* (Macon: Mercer University Press, 1986), pp. 1–28. **6263**

EXPLORATION & MAPPING

DeVorsey, Louis, Jr., "William Gerard de Brahm: Surveyor-General and Man of Science in Royal Georgia," *Bulletin of the Georgia Academy of Science*, vol. 34 (1976), pp. 204–209. **6264**

DeVorsey, Louis, Jr., "Maps in Colonial Promotion: James Edward Oglethorpe's Use of Maps in 'Selling' the Georgia Scheme," *Imago Mundi*, vol. 38 (1986), pp. 35–45. **6265**

DeVorsey, Louis, Jr., "Oglethorpe and the Earliest Maps of Georgia," in Phinizy Spalding and Harvey Jackson, eds., *Oglethorpe in Perspective* (Tuscaloosa: University of Alabama Press, 1989), pp. 22–43. **6266**

Baine, Rodney M., and Louis DeVorsey, Jr., "The Provenance and Historical Accuracy of *A View of Savannah* as It Stood the 29th of March, 1734," *Georgia Historical Quarterly*, vol. 73, 4 (1989), pp. 784–813. **6267**

POPULAR IMAGES & EVALUATION

Johnson, Hildegard Binder, "Die Haltung der Salzburger in Georgia zur Sklaverei, 1734–1750," *Mitteilungen der Gesellschaft für Salzburger Landeskunde*, vol. 76 (1936), pp. 183–196. **6268**

Miller, Cynthia A., "Tybee Island, Georgia: Changing Images and Land Use, 1733–1895," Master's thesis, University of Georgia, 1986. **6269**

REGIONAL SETTLEMENT

Zelinsky, Wilbur, "Settlement Patterns of Georgia," Ph.D. diss., University of California–Berkeley, 1953. **6270**

Christensen, David F., *Rural Occupance in Transition: Sumter and Lee Counties, Georgia* (Chicago: University of Chicago Department of Geography, Research Paper no. 43, 1956), 160 pp. **6271**

Noble, William A., "Sequent Occupance of Hopeton-Altama, 1816–1956," Master's thesis, University of Georgia, 1957. **6272**

Cooper, Sherwin H., "The Rural Settlement of the Lower Savannah River Basin in Georgia," Ph.D. diss., University of Michigan, 1960. **6273**

Cooper, Sherwin H., "The Rural Settlement of the Savannah Country," *Papers of the Michigan Academy of Science, Arts, and Letters*, vol. 47 (1962), pp. 413–427. **6274**

Mitchell, Ruthanne L., "Settlement Geography of the Richmond Hill Plantation, Bryan County, Georgia," Master's thesis, Georgia State University, 1984. **6275**

Douglas, Robert W., "Antebellum Paired Plantations along Coastal Georgia," in Richard L. Nostrand and Sam B. Hilliard, eds., *The American South* (Baton Rouge: Louisiana State University School of Geoscience, Geoscience & Man, vol. 25, 1988), pp. 67–76. **6276**

POPULATION

Zelinsky, Wilbur, "An Isochronic Map of Georgia Settlement, 1750–1850," *Georgia Historical Quarterly*, vol. 35, 3 (1951), pp. 191–195. **6277**

Hart, John Fraser, "Migration to the Blacktop: Population Redistribution in the South," *Landscape*, vol. 25, 3 (1981), pp. 15–19. [Carroll Co., 1921–1973] **6278**

Brown, Catherine L., "A Geographical Analysis of the Chinese in Georgia, 1865–1980," Master's thesis, University of Georgia, 1982. **6279**

RURAL & REGIONAL SOCIAL GEOGRAPHY

Scott, Ralph C., Jr., "The Quaker Settlement of Wrightsborough, Georgia," *Georgia Historical Quarterly*, vol. 56, 2 (1972), pp. 210–223. **6280**

POLITICAL & ADMINISTRATIVE GEOGRAPHY

See also **5910, 5916–5917**

Politics

Phillips, Ulrich B., "Georgia and States Rights: A Study of the Political History of Georgia from the Revolution to the Civil War, with Particular Regard to Federal Regulations," *Annual Report of the American Historical Association for the Year 1901*, vol. 2 (Washington, D.C.: Government Printing Office, 1902), pp. 3–224. **6281**

Johnson, Zachary T., "Geographic Factors in Georgia Politics in 1850," *Georgia Historical Quarterly*, vol. 17, 1 (1933), pp. 26–36. **6282**

Hunt, Roger A., "Vox pinuum: A Geographical Analysis of Voter Turnout in Georgia's Presidential Elections, 1940–1972," Master's thesis, University of Georgia, 1980. **6283**

Offord, John, "State Welfare Expenditures and the Geography of Social Well-Being in Georgia, 1950–1970," Master's thesis, University of Georgia, 1981. **6284**

Boundaries

DeVorsey, Louis, Jr., "Indian Boundaries in Colonial Georgia," *Georgia Historical Quarterly*, vol. 54, 1 (1970), pp. 63–78. **6285**

Vanderhill, Burke G., and Frank A. Unger, "Georgia's Crenelated County Boundaries," *West Georgia College Studies in the Social Sciences*, vol. 16 (1977), pp. 59–73. **6286**

ECONOMIC DEVELOPMENT

Clout, Hugh D., "L'héritage de la production colonnière en Géorgia, USA," *Norois*, vol. 21, 84 (1974), pp. 585–605. **6287**

Jeanne, Donald G., "The Culture History of Grist Milling in Northwest Georgia," Ph.D. diss., Louisiana State University, 1974. **6288**

DeVorsey, Louis, Jr., "Early Water-Powered Industries in Athens and Clarke County," *Papers of the Athens Historical Society*, vol. 2 (1979), pp. 39–57. **6289**

Crawford, George B., "Cotton, Land, and Sustenance: Toward the Limits of Abundance in Late Antebellum Georgia," *Georgia Historical Quarterly*, vol. 72, 2 (1988), pp. 215–247. **6290**

LAND & LAND USE

Land survey

Hilliard, Sam B., "Headright Grants and Surveying in Northeastern Georgia," *Geographical Review*, vol. 72, 4 (1982), pp. 416–429. **6291**

Hilliard, Sam B., "Land Grants and Surveying," in *History of Franklin County, Georgia* (Roswell, Ga.: WH Wolfe Associates, for the Franklin County Historical Society, 1986), pp. 74–87. **6292**

Land tenure

Wilms, Douglas C., "Georgia's Land Lottery of 1832," *Chronicles of Oklahoma*, vol. 52, 1 (1974), pp. 52–60. **6293**

Engerrand, Steven, "The Evolution of Landholding Patterns on the Georgia Piedmont, 1805–1830," *Southeastern Geographer*, vol. 15, 2 (1975), pp. 73–80.   **6294**

Holder, Gerald L., "Georgia Land Lottery," in Charles R. Wilson and William Ferris, eds., *Encyclopedia of Southern Culture* (Chapel Hill: University of North Carolina Press, 1989), pp. 572.   **6295**

Land use

Hart, John Fraser, "Land Use Change in a Piedmont County," *Annals of the Association of American Geographers*, vol. 70, 4 (1980), pp. 492–527. [Carroll Co., 1930–1974]   **6296**

AGRICULTURE

See also **5970**

Black, Blanton E., "The Rise and Decline of Plantation Agriculture in Coastal Georgia," Master's thesis, University of Chicago, 1937.   **6297**

Prunty, Merle C., Jr., "Land Management at Antebellum Hopeton Plantation in the Light of the Soil Exhaustion Thesis," *Memorandum Folio, Southeastern Division, Association of American Geographers*, vol. 11 (1959), pp. 97–101.   **6298**

Hilliard, Sam B., "Birdsong: Sequent Occupance on a Southwestern Georgia Plantation," Master's thesis, University of Georgia, 1961.   **6299**

Farr, James T., "Shifts in the Spatial Distribution of Soybean Production in Georgia, 1929–1967," Master's thesis, University of Georgia, 1969. **6300**

Wilms, Douglas C., "The Development of Rice Culture in Eighteenth Century Georgia," *Southeastern Geographer*, vol. 12, 1 (1972), pp. 45–57.
6301

Pfeifer, Gottfried, "Die Wirtschaftsformation des Baumwollgürtels in Georgia und deren Entwicklung in Raum und Zeit," in *Der Wirtschaftsraum: Beiträge zu Methoden und Anwendung eines geographischen Forschungsansatzes* (Festschrift für Erik Otremba) (Wiesbaden: Franz Steiner Verlag, Erdkundliches Wissen, Beihefte zur Geographischen Zeitschrift, vol. 41, 1975), pp. 150–169. Reprinted in Gerd Kohlhepp, ed., *Beiträge zur Kulturgeographie der Neuen Welt: Ausgewählte Arbeiten von Gottfried Pfeifer* (Berlin: Dietrich Reimer, 1981), pp. 167–188.   **6302**

LANDSCAPE

Zelinsky, Wilbur, "The Log House in Georgia," *Geographical Review*, vol. 43, 2 (1953), pp. 173–193. Reprinted in abbreviated form in Robert S.

Platt, ed., *Field Study in American Geography* (Chicago: University of Chicago Department of Geography, Research Paper no. 61, 1959), pp. 367–377.   **6303**

Zelinsky, Wilbur, "The Greek Revival House in Georgia," *Journal of the Society of Architectural Historians*, vol. 13, 1 (1954), pp. 9–12.   **6304**

DeLaubenfels, David J., "Where Sherman Passed By," *Geographical Review*, vol. 47, 3 (1957), pp. 381–395. Reprinted in Fred E. Dohrs and Lawrence M. Sommers, eds., *Cultural Geography: Selected Readings* (New York: Thomas Y. Crowell Co., 1967), pp. 42–54. [Land use and landscape change in central Georgia, 1865–1950]
6305

Holder, Gerald L., "The Eighteenth Century Landscape in Northeast Georgia," *Pioneer America*, vol. 13, 1 (1981), pp. 39–48.   **6306**

Pillsbury, Richard R., "Farrar Lumber Company, Farrar-Made Houses: A Georgia Product," *Pioneer America*, vol. 13, 1 (1981), pp. 49–61. [Focus on the company's 1918 catalog]   **6307**

Stone, Kirk H., "The Geographical Inheritance of Current Rural House Densities in Eastern Georgia," *Georgia Historical Quarterly*, vol. 66, 2 (1982), pp. 196–216.   **6308**

COMMUNICATIONS & TRADE

See also **4522, 6003–6004**

Liesendahl, James A., "Expansion of the Paved Road in the State Highway System of Georgia," Master's thesis, University of Georgia, 1964. **6309**

Mealor, W. Theodore, "Functional and Spatial Patterns of Georgia Shortline Railroads, 1915–1978," *West Georgia College Studies in the Social Sciences*, vol. 18 (1979), pp. 25–42.   **6310**

MANUFACTURING & INDUSTRIALIZATION

Dobson, Jeffrey, and Roy Doyon, "Expansion of the Pine Oleoresin Industry in Georgia: 1842 to ca.1900," *West Georgia Studies in the Social Sciences*, vol. 18 (1979), pp. 43–58.   **6311**

Park, Sam Ock, and James O. Wheeler, "The Filtering Down Process in Georgia: The Third Stage in the Product Life Cycle," *Professional Geographer*, vol. 35, 1 (1983), pp. 18–31.   **6312**

URBAN NETWORKS & URBANIZATION

Holder, Gerald L., "The Fall Zone Towns of Georgia: An Historical Geography," Ph.D. diss., University of Georgia, 1973.   **6313**

Holder, Gerald L., "State Planned Trading Centers in Pioneer Georgia," *Pioneer America*, vol. 14, 3 (1982), pp. 115–124. **6314**

Allen, Daniel S., "Georgia Urban Industrial Growth and Structure, 1860–1880," Master's thesis, University of Georgia, 1990. **6315**

TOWN GROWTH

Watkins, Edgar, "Geography, Railroads, and Men Made Atlanta," *Atlanta Historical Bulletin*, vol. 8 (1948), pp. 71–81. **6316**

Roddy, William A., "Urban Fringe Expansion in Clarke County, Georgia, 1938–1979," Master's thesis, University of Georgia, 1981. **6317**

DeVine, Jerry, "Town Development in Winegrass, Georgia, 1870–1900," *Journal of Southwestern Georgia History*, vol. 1 (1983), pp. 1–22. **6318**

URBAN ECONOMIC STRUCTURE

Fehrenback, Joseph, "The Reconstruction of Past Urban Land Use in Athens, Georgia, Utilizing Sanborn Fire Insurance Maps," Master's thesis, University of Georgia, 1977. **6319**

Wheeler, James O., and Sam Ock Park, "Intrametropolitan Location Change in Manufacturing: Atlanta, 1958 to 1976," *Southeastern Geographer*, vol. 21, 1 (1981), pp. 10–25. **6320**

Porter, Layne K., "From Bedroom Community to Suburban Business Center: A Geographical Analysis of the Buckhead Community in Atlanta, Georgia, 1920–1988," Master's thesis, Georgia State University, 1989. **6321**

URBAN SOCIAL STRUCTURE

O'Connor, Michael J., "The Measurement and Significance of Racial Residential Barriers in Atlanta, 1890–1970," Ph.D. diss., University of Georgia, 1977. **6322**

TOWNSCAPE

Regional

Reps, John W., "Town Planning in Georgia," *Town Planning Review*, vol. 30, 4 (1960), pp. 273–285. **6323**

Sears, Joan Niles, "Town Planning in White and Habersham Counties, Georgia," *Georgia Historical Quarterly* vol. 54, 1 (1970), pp. 20–40. **6324**

Pillsbury, Richard R., "The Morphology of the Piedmont Georgia County Seat before 1860," *Southeastern Geographer*, vol. 18, 2 (1978), pp. 115–124. **6325**

Sears, Joan Niles, *The First Hundred Years of Town Planning in Georgia* (Atlanta: Cherokee Publishing Co., 1979), 220 pp. **6326**

Larson, Albert J., "Influences on the Architectural Style of Georgia County Courthouses," in Richard L. Nostrand and Sam B. Hilliard, eds., *The American South* (Baton Rouge: Louisiana State University School of Geoscience, Geoscience & Man, vol. 25, 1988), pp. 119–128. **6327**

Atlanta

Dillon, Patrick M., "The Morphogenesis of Atlanta's Northwest Industrial Rail Corridor," Master's thesis, University of Georgia, 1979. **6328**

Laws, Kevin, "The Origin of the Street Grid in Atlanta's Urban Core," *Southeastern Geographer*, vol. 19, 2 (1979), pp. 69–79. **6329**

PLACE NAMES

Goff, John H., *Placenames of Georgia: Essays of John H. Goff* (Athens: University of Georgia Press, 1975), 495 pp. **6330**

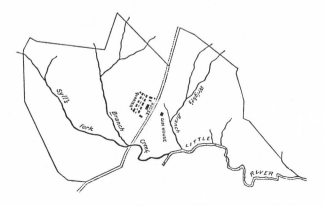

FLORIDA

GENERAL

The state

DeVorsey, Louis, Jr., "British East Florida on the Eve of Revolution," in Samuel Proctor, ed., *Eighteenth Century Florida and Its Borderlands* (Gainesville: University of Florida Press, 1974), pp. 78–101.   **6331**

Marcus, Robert, and Edward A. Fernald, "Florida's Historical Background," in their *Florida: A Geographical Approach* (Dubuque: Kendall/Hunt, 1975), pp. 13–22.   **6332**

Smaller areas

Bingham, Millicent Todd, "La Floride du sud-est et la ville de Miami," in *Mélanges géographiques offerts par ses élèves à Raoul Blanchard à l'occasion du vingt-cinquième anniversaire de l'Institut de géographie alpine de Grenoble* (Grenoble: l'Institute, 1932), pp. 89–133.   **6333**

Gricouroff, Nadine, "Historical Geography of the Lower St. John's Valley," Master's thesis, University of Florida, 1951.   **6334**

Upchurch, John C., "Middle Florida: An Historical Geography of the Area between the Apalachicola and Suwanee Rivers," Ph.D. diss., University of Tennessee, 1971.   **6335**

Schaleman, Harry J., Jr., "Cedar Key, Florida: A Study of Time and Place, Boom and Bust," *Florida Geographer*, vol. 19 (1985), pp. 6–10.   **6336**

ENVIRONMENTAL CHANGE

Segretto, Peter S., "The Relationship between Urbanization and Stream Flow in the Hillsborough River Basin, Florida, from 1940 to 1970," Ph.D. diss., University of Florida, 1977.   **6337**

NATIVE PEOPLES & WHITE RELATIONS

Craig, Alan K., and Christopher Peeples, "Ethno-Ecologic Change among the Seminoles, 1740–1840," in H. Jesse Walker and William G. Haag, eds., *Man and Cultural Heritage: Papers in Honor of Fred B. Kniffen* (Baton Rouge: Louisiana State University School of Geoscience, Geoscience & Man, vol. 5, 1974), pp. 83–96.   **6338**

Richards, Storm, "Geographic Techniques for Differentiating Archeological Sites in North-Central Florida," *Florida Geographer*, vol. 14, 1 (1980), pp. 14–19.   **6339**

EXPLORATION & MAPPING

See also **5860**

Scisco, L. D., "The Track of Ponce de Leon in 1513," *Bulletin of the American Geographical Society*, vol. 45, 10 (1913), pp. 721–735.   **6340**

Reuter, Otto S., "Ist das nordmännische Weinland in Florida zu suchen?" *Petermanns Geographische Mitteilungen*, vol. 89, 1 (1943), pp. 34–38.   **6341**

True, David O., "Some Early Maps Relating to Florida," *Imago Mundi*, vol. 11 (1954), pp. 73–84.   **6342**

Cumming, William P., "The Parreus Map (1562) of French Florida," *Imago Mundi*, vol. 17 (1963), pp. 27–40.   **6343**

DeVorsey, Louis, Jr., "La Florida Revealed: The De Brahm Surveys of British East Florida," in W. P. Adams and F. M. Helleiner, eds., *International Geography, 1972*, vol. 1, sec. 5, *Historical Geography* (Toronto: University of Toronto Press, for the International Geographical Union, 1972), pp. 411–412.   **6344**

DeVorsey, Louis, Jr., "A Colorful Resident of British St. Augustine: William Gerard de Brahm," *Escribano*, vol. 12 (1975), pp. 1–24.   **6345**

DeVorsey, Louis, Jr., "La Florida Revealed: The De Brahm Survey of British East Florida, 1765–1771," in Ralph E. Ehrenberg, ed., *Pattern and Process: Research in Historical Geography* (Washington, D.C.: Howard University Press, 1975), pp. 87–102.   **6346**

Herbert, John R., "Vicente Sebastian Pintado, Surveyor General of Spanish West Florida, 1805–17: The Man and His Maps," *Imago Mundi*, vol. 39 (1987), pp. 50–72.   **6347**

POPULAR IMAGES & EVALUATION

Kixmiller, Patricia Elaine, "Anastasia Island, Florida: A Case Study in Historical Perception of Resources and Resistances," Master's thesis, Florida Atlantic University, 1973.   **6348**

Lamme, Ary J., III, "Literary Resources for Historical Geography: A Florida Example," *Florida Geographer*, vol. 12 (1978), pp. 11–16.   **6349**

Lamme, Ary J., III, "The Image of Florida," in Ronald Foreman, ed., *First Citizens and Other Florida Folk: Essays on Florida Folklife* (Tallahassee: Florida Division of Archives, 1984), pp. 17–22.   **6350**

REGIONAL SETTLEMENT

Upchurch, John C., "Some Aspects of Early Exploration, Settlement, and Economic Development within the Forbes Purchase," Master's thesis, Florida State University, 1965.　　　　　6351

Unger, Frank, "Some Aspects of Land Acquisition and Settlement in Territorial Florida: The St. Joseph Community," Master's thesis, Florida State University, 1974.　　　　　6352

POPULATION

Harper, Roland M., "The Population of Florida: Regional Composition and Growth as Influenced by Soil, Climate, and Mineral Discoveries," *Geographical Review*, vol. 2, 5 (1916), pp. 361–367. [Focus on 1830–1915]　　　6353

Winsberg, Morton D., "The Non-Hispanic White Elderly in Southern Florida, 1950–1980," *Geographical Review*, vol. 73, 4 (1983), pp. 447–449.　　　　　6354

Winsberg, Morton D., "Relative Growth and Distribution of Florida's European Born," *Florida Geographer*, vol. 18, 1 (1984), pp. 16–21.　　6355

RURAL & REGIONAL SOCIAL GEOGRAPHY

See 5894

POLITICAL & ADMINISTRATIVE GEOGRAPHY

See also 5916

DeVorsey, Louis, Jr., "Florida's Seaward Boundary: A Problem in Applied Historical Geography," *Professional Geographer*, vol. 25, 3 (1973), pp. 214–220.　　　　　6356

Miller, Craig, "Extension of the National Land Survey System to Colonial West Florida: The Evolution and Influence of Colonial Land Policy," Master's thesis, Florida State University, 1979.　　　　　6357

ECONOMIC DEVELOPMENT

Varney, Charles B., "Economic and Historical Geography of the Gulf Coast of Florida: Cedar Keys to St. Marks," Ph.D. diss., Clark University, 1963.　　　　　6358

Amelung, Evasusanne, "History of Economic Development of the Sanford, Florida, Area," Master's thesis, University of Florida, 1971.　　6359

RESOURCE MANAGEMENT

Brueckheimer, William R., "The Quail Plantations of the Thomasville-Tallahassee-Albany Regions," *Proceedings of the Tall Timbers Ecology and Management Conference*, vol. 16 (Tallahassee: Tall Timbers Research Station, 1979), pp. 141–165.　　　　　6360

LAND & LAND USE

Dicken, Samuel N., "Central Florida Farm Landscape," *Economic Geography*, vol. 11, 2 (1935), pp. 173–182. [Focus on 1893–1932]　　6361

Okerson, Barbara B., "A Historical Geography of Land Use Changes: Santa Rosa Island, Florida, from Prehistoric Times to Present," Master's thesis, Memphis State University, 1988.　　6362

AGRICULTURE

See also 5970

Hicks, W. T., "The Development of the Tung Oil Industry in Florida," *Journal of Geography*, vol. 31, 1 (1932), pp. 27–35. [Focus on 1905–1930] 6363

Mealor, W. Theodore, "Open-Range Ranching and Its Contemporary Successors in South Florida," Ph.D. diss., University of Georgia, 1972.　　　　　6364

Harris, James W., "The Florida Cattle Industry: A Transition Economy, 1840–1890," Master's thesis, University of Chicago, 1974.　　6365

Mealor, W. Theodore, and Merle C. Prunty, Jr., "Open-Range Ranching in Southern Florida," *Annals of the Association of American Geographers*, vol. 66, 3 (1976), pp. 360–376.　　6366

Anderson, James R., "Plantation Agriculture in the Middle Suwanee Basin of Florida, 1825–50," *Proceedings of the Tall Timbers Ecology and Management Conference*, vol. 16 (Tallahassee: Tall Timbers Research Station, 1979), pp. 21–45　　　　　6367

Sheldon, Samuel R., "Spatial and Temporal Perspectives on Florida's Sugarcane Industry," *Florida Geographer*, vol. 15 (1981), pp. 1–6.　6368

Otto, John S., "Florida's Cattle-Ranching Frontier: Hillsborough County," *Florida Historical Quarterly*, vol. 63, 1 (1984), pp. 71–83.　　6369

Otto, John S., "Traditional Cattle-Herding Practices in Southern Florida," *Journal of American Folklore*, vol. 97, 385 (1984), pp. 291–309.　6370

Otto, John S., "Florida's Cattle-Ranching Frontier: Manatee and Brevard Counties (1860)," *Florida Historical Quarterly*, vol. 64, 1 (1985), pp. 48–61.　　　　　6371

Sheldon, Samuel R., "Sugarcane Cultivation in East Florida: Perceptions and Realities," *Florida Geographer*, vol. 19 (1985), pp. 28–35.　6372

Otto, John S., "Open-Range Cattle Herding in Antebellum South Florida 1842–1860," *Southeastern Geographer*, vol. 26, 1 (1986), pp. 55–67.　**6373**

Otto, John S., "Open-Range Cattle Herding in Southern Florida," *Florida Historical Quarterly*, vol. 65, 3 (1987), pp. 317–337.　**6374**

LANDSCAPE

Boniface, Brian, "A Landscape Reconstruction of Spanish Florida, c.1700," Master's thesis, University of Georgia, 1971.　**6375**

Miller, Craig, and Patrick O'Sullivan, "The Obliteration of Colonial West Florida," *Florida Geographer*, vol. 14, 2 (1980), pp. 1–9.　**6376**

COMMUNICATIONS & TRADE

Stanaback, Richard, "Postal Operations in Territorial Florida, 1821–1845," *Florida Historical Quarterly*, vol. 52, 2 (1973), pp. 157–174.　**6377**

Vanderhill, Burke G., "The Alachua Trail: A Reconstruction," *Florida Historical Quarterly*, vol. 55, 4 (1977), pp. 423–438.　**6378**

Richards, Storm, and Jeanne Fillman-Richards, "Steamboats and Regional Development: The Ocklawaha and St. Johns Rivers in the Nineteenth Century," *Florida Geographer*, vol. 16, 1 (1982), pp. 33–39.　**6379**

Vanderhill, Burke G., "The Alachua–St. Mary's Road," *Florida Historical Quarterly*, vol. 66, 1 (1987), pp. 50–67.　**6380**

URBAN NETWORKS & URBANIZATION

Vanderhill, Burke G., "The Ports of the St. Marks River, Florida," *Southeastern Geographer*, vol. 5 (1965), pp. 15–23.　**6381**

Clark, Terry, "An Assessment of the Influence of Tallahassee's Retail Sector on Its Surrounding Smaller Communities between 1953 and 1977," Master's thesis, Florida State University, 1980.　**6382**

TOWN GROWTH

Dunkle, John R., "St. Augustine, Florida: A Study in Historical Geography," Ph.D. diss., Clark University, 1955.　**6383**

Selber, Truman D., "Historical and Economic Geography of Masarytown, Florida," Master's thesis, University of Florida, 1957.　**6384**

Dunkle, John R., "Population Change as an Element in the Historical Geography of St. Augustine," *Florida Historical Quarterly*, vol. 37, 1 (1958), pp. 3–32. [Focus on 1595–1950]　**6385**

Young, Eric M., "An Historical Geographic Study of Miami, Florida, 1896–1920," Master's thesis, Miami University, 1990.　**6386**

URBAN ECONOMIC STRUCTURE

Hurst, Robert, "Mapping Old St. Joseph, Its Railroads, and Environs," *Florida Historical Quarterly*, vol. 39, 4 (1961), pp. 354–365.　**6387**

Ollry, Jan, "Changes in the Geographic Distribution of Selected Retail and Service Establishments in the Tallahassee Urban Area, 1949–1969," Master's thesis, Florida State University, 1970.　**6388**

URBAN SOCIAL STRUCTURE

Rosenthal, Lisa J., "The Revitalization of South Miami Beach, Florida," Master's thesis, University of Chicago, 1985.　**6389**

TOWNSCAPE

Lloyd, Robert B., "Development of the Plan of Pensacola during the Colonial Era, 1559–1821," *Florida Historical Quarterly*, vol. 64, 3 (1986), pp. 253–272.　**6390**

Lamme, Ary J., III, "Power to Preserve Landscapes: The St. Augustine Experience," *North American Culture*, vol. 4, 2 (1988), pp. 38–49.　**6391**

Larson, Albert J., "The County Courthouses of Florida's Panhandle," *Pioneer America Society Transactions*, vol. 12 (1989), pp. 55–63.　**6392**

RECREATION & TOURISM

Vanderhill, Burke G., "The Historic Spas of Florida," *West Georgia College Studies in the Social Sciences*, vol. 12 (1973), pp. 59–77.　**6393**

PLACE NAMES

Read, William A., *Florida Place-Names of Indian Origin and Seminole Personal Names* (Baton Rouge: Louisiana State University Press, Louisiana State University Studies, no. 11, 1934), 83 pp.　**6394**

McMullen, Edwin W., *English Topographical Terms in Florida, 1563–1874* (Gainesville: University of Florida Press, 1953), 227 pp.　**6395**

Chardon, Roland E., "Notes on South Florida Place Names: Norris Cut," *Tequesta*, vol. 37 (1977), pp. 57–67.　**6396**

Bloodworth, Bertha E., and Alton C. Morris, *Places in the Sun: The History and Romance of Florida Place-Names* (Gainesville: University Presses of Florida, 1978), 209 pp.　**6397**

ALABAMA

GENERAL

The state

Tower, J. Allen, "The Shaping of Alabama," *Alabama Review*, vol. 12, 2 (1959), pp. 132–139.   **6398**

Smaller areas

Gibson, J. Sullivan, "Alabama Black Belt: Its Geographic Status," *Economic Geography*, vol. 17, 1 (1941), pp. 1–23.   **6399**

EXPLORATION & MAPPING

Holmes, Jack D. L., "Charting Mobile Bay and River," *Alabama Historical Quarterly*, vol. 44, 3 & 4 (1982), pp. 143–170.   **6400**

POPULAR IMAGES & EVALUATION

Rostlund, Erhard, "The Myth of a Natural Prairie Belt in Alabama: An Interpretation of Historical Records," *Annals of the Association of American Geographers*, vol. 47, 4 (1957), pp. 392–411.   **6401**

REGIONAL SETTLEMENT

Allman, John M., "Yeoman Regions in the Antebellum Deep South: Settlement and Economy in Northern Alabama, 1815–1860," Ph.D. diss., University of Maryland, 1979.   **6402**

Oszuscik, Phillippe, "Eighteenth Century British on the Eastern Shore of Mobile Bay," *Pioneer America Society Transactions*, vol. 12 (1989), pp. 73–81.   **6403**

POPULATION

Woodruff, James F., "Some Characteristics of the Alabama Slave Population in 1850," *Geographical Review*, vol. 52, 4 (1962), pp. 379–388.   **6404**

Hazel, Joseph A., "Semi-Micro Studies of Counties from the Manuscripts of the Census of 1860," *Professional Geographer*, vol. 17, 4 (1965), pp. 15–19.   **6405**

Hackett, Berkeley, "Walker County, Alabama, 1850–1950: A Migration Study," Master's thesis, University of Alabama, 1974.   **6406**

RURAL & REGIONAL SOCIAL GEOGRAPHY

See also **5894**

Kollmorgen, Walter M., *The German Settlement in Cullman County, Alabama: An Agricultural*

Island in the Cotton Belt (Washington, D.C.: Department of Agriculture, Bureau of Agricultural Economics, 1941), 66 pp.   **6407**

Tower, J. Allen, and Walter Wolf, "Ethnic Groups in Cullman County, Alabama," *Geographical Review*, vol. 33, 2 (1943), pp. 276–285.   **6408**

Cobbs, Hamner, "Geography of the Vine and Olive Colony," *Alabama Review*, vol. 14, 1 (1961), pp. 83–97. [Focus on Demopolis, Greene, and Marengo counties., 1817–1830]   **6409**

Pearson, Christopher P., "The Ku Klux Klan in Alabama, 1867–1972: Spatial Variation in the Intensity of Racial Violence," Master's thesis, University of Chicago, 1983.   **6410**

Oszuscik, Phillippe, "The Carolina Heritage in Mobile and Southwest Alabama," *Pioneer American Society Transactions*, vol. 9 (1986), pp. 63–70.   **6411**

LAND & LAND USE

Smith, Warren I., "Land Patterns in Ante-Bellum Montgomery County, Alabama," *Alabama Review*, vol. 8 (1955), pp. 196–208.   **6412**

Doster, James F., "Land Titles and Public Land Sales in Early Alabama," *Alabama Review*, vol. 16, 2 (1963), pp. 108–124.   **6413**

Rumney, Thomas A., "The Vine and Olive Land Grants of Alabama: Geographical Ideal Versus Reality," *Southeastern Geographer*, vol. 20, 2 (1980), pp. 120–133.   **6414**

AGRICULTURE

Tower, J. Allen, "Alabama's Shifting Cotton Belt," *Alabama Review*, vol. 1 (1948), pp. 27–38. [Focus on 1808–1944]   **6415**

Tower, J. Allen, "Cotton Change in Alabama, 1879–1946," *Economic Geography*, vol. 26, 1 (1950), pp. 6–28.   **6416**

Stickney, Hazel L., "The Conversion from Cotton to Cattle Economy in Alabama Black Belt, 1930–1960," Ph.D. diss., Clark University, 1961.   **6417**

Perry, John L., "Crop Combination Regions in Alabama, 1934–1964," Master's thesis, University of Alabama, 1968.   **6418**

LANDSCAPE

Wilson, Eugene M., "Folk Houses of Northern Alabama," Ph.D. diss., Louisiana State University, 1935.   **6419**

TOWNSCAPE

Nelson, Marshall T., "Morphological Evolution of a Depressed Commercial Retail Core: A Case Study of the CBD of Mobile, Alabama," Master's thesis, University of Alabama, 1974. **6420**

PLACE NAMES

Patterson, Lucy A. H., "A Study of Some Place Names of Southeastern Lee County, Alabama," Master's thesis, Auburn University, 1963. **6421**

Read, William A., *Indian Place Names in Alabama* (Baton Rouge: Louisiana State University Press, Louisiana State University Studies, no. 29, 1937), 84 pp. Revised 1984, 107 pp. **6422**

Foscue, Virginia O., *Place Names in Alabama* (Tuscaloosa: University of Alabama Press, 1989), 175 pp. **6423**

MISSISSIPPI

GENERAL

The state

Loewen, James, "Cultural Geography and the Study of Mississippi History and Social Structure," *Mississippi Geographer*, vol. 2, 1 (1974), pp. 27–32. **6424**

Smaller areas

Kelley, Arthell, and Robert C. Spillman, "Sequent Occupancy of the Piney Woods in Southeastern Mississippi, 1805 to 1976," *Mississippi Geographer*, vol. 4 (1976), pp. 25–42. **6425**

Kelley, Arthell, "Sequent Occupancy of the Yazoo Basin, Mississippi, 1830 to 1976," *Mississippi Geographer*, vol. 6 (1978), pp. 3–18. **6426**

Cobb, James C., "Delta," in Charles R. Wilson and William Ferris, eds., *Encyclopedia of Southern Culture* (Chapel Hill: University of North Carolina Press, 1989), p. 571. **6427**

ENVIRONMENTAL CHANGE

Yodis, Elaine, "Historic Changes in Channel Morphology of Mississippi River Tributaries: Southwestern Mississippi," Ph.D. diss., Louisiana State University, 1990. **6428**

NATIVE PEOPLES & WHITE RELATIONS

McKee, Jesse O., "The Choctaw Indians: A Geographical Study in Cultural Change," *Southern Quarterly*, vol. 9, 2 (1971), pp. 107–141. **6429**

Greenwell, Dale, "Pre-historic Cultural Diffusion and Migration in Southeast Mississippi," *Mississippi Geographer*, vol. 2 (1974), pp. 19–26. **6430**

McKee, Jesse O., and Jon A. Schlenker, *The Choctaws: Cultural Evolution of a Native American Tribe* (Jackson: University Press of Mississippi, 1980), 223 pp. **6431**

McKee, Jesse O., and Steve Murray, "Economic Progress and Development of the Choctaw since 1945," in Samuel J. Wells and Roseanna Tubby, eds., *After Removal: The Choctaw in Mississippi* (Jackson: University Press of Mississippi, 1986), pp. 122–136. **6432**

McKee, Jesse O., "The Choctaw: Self Determination and Socioeconomic Development," in Thomas E. Ross and Tyrel G. Moore, eds., *A Cultural Geography of North American Indians* (Boulder: Westview Press, 1987), pp. 173–190. **6433**

McKee, Jesse O., *The Choctaw* (New York: Chelsea House, 1989), 103 pp. **6434**

POPULAR IMAGES & EVALUATION

McKee, Jesse O., and Penny Prenshaw, eds., *Sense of Place: Mississippi* (Jackson: University Press of Mississippi, 1979), 229 pp. **6435**

Mealor, W. Theodore, Jr., "Myths of Mississippi's Rural Landscape: Change and Challenge," *Southern Quarterly*, vol. 17, 3 & 4 (1979), pp. 189–215. [Focus on 1939–1974] **6436**

Vining, James W., "Mississippi Agriculture in the Early American Geographies," *Mississippi Geographer*, vol. 10 (1982), pp. 18–23. **6437**

REGIONAL SETTLEMENT

Brewer, Olen B., "The Peopling of Mississippi," Master's thesis, George Peabody College for Teachers, 1933. **6438**

Halsell, Willie D., "Migration into, and Settlement of, LeFlore County, 1833–1876," *Journal of Mississippi History*, vol. 9, 4 (1947), pp. 219–237. **6439**

Halsell, Willie D., "Migration into, and Settlement of, LeFlore County in the Later Periods, 1876–1920," *Journal of Mississippi History*, vol. 10, 3 (1948), pp. 240–260. **6440**

Kelley, Arthell, "Levee Building and the Settlement of the Yazoo Basin," *Southern Quarterly*, vol. 1, 4 (1962), pp. 285–308. [Focus on 1816–1930] **6441**

POPULATION

Lowry, Mark, II, "Population and Race in Mississippi, 1948–1960," *Annals of the Association of American Geographers*, vol. 61, 3 (1971), pp. 576–588. **6442**

Lang, Marvel L., "Population Trends in Jasper County, Mississippi, 1833–1970: A Historical Geographical Perspective," *Journal of Mississippi History*, vol. 43, 4 (1981), pp. 294–308. **6443**

RURAL & REGIONAL SOCIAL GEOGRAPHY

See also **5894**

Kelley, Arthell, "Sullivan-Kilrain Fight, Richburg, Mississippi, July 8, 1889," *Southern Quarterly*, vol. 8, 2 (1970), pp. 135–144. [Last ever bare-knuckle world championship prize fight, and why it took place in Richburg] **6444**

Lowry, Mark, II, "Schools in Transition," *Annals of the Association of American Geographers,* vol. 63, 2 (1973), pp. 167–180. [Focus on 1939–1968]
6445

Lang, Marvel L., "Historic Settlement and Residential Segregation in Local Neighborhoods of Jasper County, Mississippi, 1900–1977," Ph.D. diss., Michigan State University, 1979.   **6446**

AGRICULTURE

Aiken, Charles S., "Transitional Plantation Occupance in Tate County, Mississippi," Master's thesis, University of Georgia, 1962.   **6447**

Gilbert, Dennis W., "Agricultural Land Use Changes in DeSoto County, Mississippi, 1949–1969," Master's thesis, Memphis State University, 1970.   **6448**

Israel, Kenneth D., "The Cattle Industry of Mississippi: Its Origin and Its Changes through Time up to 1850," Master's thesis, University of Southern Mississippi, 1970.   **6449**

LANDSCAPE

Hudson, John C., "The Yazoo Delta as Plantation Country," *Proceedings of the Tall Timbers and Ecology and Management Conference,* vol. 16 (Tallahassee: Tall Timbers Research Station, 1979), pp. 34–52.   **6450**

Newton, Milton B., Jr., "Water-Powered Sawmills and Related Structures in the Piney Woods," in Noel Polk, ed., *Mississippi's Piney Woods: A Human Perspective* (Jackson: University Press of Mississippi, 1986), pp. 155–172.   **6451**

COMMUNICATIONS & TRADE

Odom, M., "The Introduction and Expansion of Railroad Lines in Mississippi, 1830–1973," *Mississippi Geographer,* vol. 2 (1974), pp. 51–60.   **6452**

MANUFACTURING & INDUSTRIALIZATION

McKee, Jesse O., "A Historical Geography of the Areal Shifts in the Mean Point Location of Manufacturing Employment in Mississippi for 1940–1950–1960," *Journal of Mississippi History,* vol. 31, 4 (1969), pp. 302–320.   **6453**

URBAN NETWORKS & URBANIZATION

Adkins, Howard G., "The Historical Geography of Extinct Towns in Mississippi," Ph.D. diss., University of Tennessee, 1972.   **6454**

Adkins, Howard G., "The Geographic Base of Urban Retardation in Mississippi, 1800–1840," *West Georgia College Studies in the Social Sciences,* vol. 12 (1973), pp. 35–49.   **6455**

Adkins, Howard G., "The Historical Geography of Extinct Towns in Mississippi," *Southern Quarterly,* vol. 17, 3–4 (1979), pp. 123–152. [Focus on 1770–1970]   **6456**

Lang, Marvel L., "The Development of Small Towns as a Settlement Process in Mississippi: A Case Study," *Mississippi Geographer,* vol. 9 (1981), pp. 5–14. [Focus on Jasper Co., 1833–1923]   **6457**

TOWN GROWTH

James, Preston E., "Vicksburg: A Study in Urban Geography," *Geographical Review,* vol. 21, 2 (1931), pp. 234–243.   **6458**

Schaeper, Herbert R., "The Historical Geography of Ocean Springs, Mississippi," Master's thesis, University of Southern Mississippi, 1965.   **6459**

Neff, Guy C., "The Historical Geography of Hattiesburg, Mississippi," Master's thesis, University of Southern Mississippi, 1968.   **6460**

URBAN ECONOMIC STRUCTURE

Mitlin, Lucille L., "Historical Development of Land Use in Starkville, Mississippi: A Small University City," Master's thesis, Mississippi State University, 1975.   **6461**

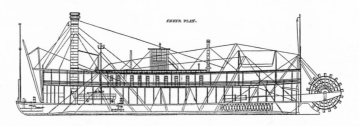

TENNESSEE

GENERAL

The state

Frank, Sadie A., "The Founding of Tennessee," *Journal of Geography*, vol. 7, 2 (1908), pp. 34–36. **6462**

Smaller areas

Hardiman, Charles E., "Historical Geography of Ruskin Cave, Tennessee," Master's thesis, University of Tennessee, 1964. **6463**

Wallach, Bret, "The Slighted Mountains of Upper East Tennessee," *Annals of the Association of American Geographers*, vol. 71, 3 (1981), pp. 359–373. **6464**

ENVIRONMENTAL CHANGE

Foehner, Nora L., "The Historical Geography of Environmental Change in the Copper Basin," Master's thesis, University of Tennessee, 1980. **6465**

Barnhardt, Michael L., "Historical Sedimentation in West Tennessee Gullies," *Southeastern Geographer*, vol. 28, 1 (1988), pp. 1–18. **6466**

EXPLORATION & MAPPING

Heppart, E. D., "Tennessee Valley Surveying, 1745 to 1783," *Surveying and Mapping*, vol. 35 (1975), pp. 347–354. **6467**

Wells, Ann H., "Early Maps of Tennessee, 1794–1799," *Tennessee Historical Quarterly*, vol. 35, 2 (1976), pp. 123–143. **6468**

POPULAR IMAGES & EVALUATION

Aiken, Charles S., "The Transformation of James Agee's Knoxville," *Geographical Review*, vol. 73, 2 (1983), pp. 150–165. **6469**

REGIONAL SETTLEMENT

See also **5877**

Van Benthuysen, R. N., "Sequent Occupance of Tellico Plains, Tennessee," Master's thesis, University of Tennessee, 1951. **6470**

Prunty, Merle C., Jr., "Initial Settlement Pattern in the Obion–Forked Deer Confluence Area, Tennessee," *Memorandum Folio, Southeastern*

Division, Association of American Geographers, vol. 10 (1958), pp. 60–64. **6471**

Icenogle, David W., "Rural Nonfarm Population and Settlement in Upper East Tennessee," Ph.D. diss., Louisiana State University, 1970. **6472**

POPULATION

Straw, H. Thompson, "The Population Distribution and Change in the Eastern Highland Rim Plateau of Tennessee," *Proceedings of the Eighth American Scientific Congress*, vol. 9 (Washington, D.C.: Department of State, 1943), pp. 145-155. **6473**

RURAL & REGIONAL SOCIAL GEOGRAPHY

Kollmorgen, Walter M., *The German-Swiss in Franklin County, Tennessee: A Study of the Significance of Cultural Considerations in Farming Enterprises* (Washington, D.C.: Department of Agriculture, Bureau of Agricultural Economics, 1940), 113 pp. **6474**

Kollmorgen, Walter M., "Observations on Cultural Islands in Terms of Tennessee Agriculture," *East Tennessee Historical Society Publications*, vol. 16 (1944), pp. 65–78. **6475**

POLITICAL & ADMINISTRATIVE GEOGRAPHY

See also **5910**

Chambers, William T., "Attempts at Political Adjustment to Pioneer Environment in Tennessee," Master's thesis, University of Chicago, 1924. **6476**

ECONOMIC DEVELOPMENT

Dobson, Jerome E., "The Changing Control of Economic Activity in the Gatlinburg, Tennessee, Area, 1930–1973," Ph.D. diss., University of Tennessee, 1975. **6477**

Moore, Tyrel G., "Role of Ferryboat Landings in East Tennessee's Economic Development, 1790–1870," *West Georgia College Studies in the Social Sciences*, vol. 18 (1979), pp. 1–18. **6478**

Buckwalter, Donald W., "Effects of Early Nineteenth Century Transportation Disadvantage on the Agriculture of Eastern Tennessee," *South-*

eastern Geographer, vol. 27, 1 (1987), pp. 18–37.
6479

EXTRACTIVE ACTIVITY

Schulman, Steven, "The Lumber Industry of the Upper Cumberland River Valley," *Tennessee Historical Quarterly*, vol. 32, 3 (1973), pp. 255–264.
6480

Schulman, Steven, "Rafting Logs on the Upper Cumberland River," *Pioneer America*, vol. 6, 1 (1974), pp. 14–24.
6481

AGRICULTURE

Plümacher, D., "Zur Geschichte des Weinbaues in Tennessee," *Das Ausland*, vol. 59, 12 (1886), pp. 226–227. [Focus on the Swiss colony in Grundy Co.]
6482

Glendinning, Robert M., and Edward N. Torbert, "Agricultural Problems in Grainger County, Tennessee," *Economic Geography*, vol. 14, 2 (1938), pp. 159–166.
6483

Prunty, Merle C., Jr., "Evolution of the Agricultural Geography of Dyer County, Tennessee," Ph.D. diss., Clark University, 1944.
6484

Prunty, Merle C., Jr., "Physical Bases of Agriculture in Dyer County, Tennessee," *Journal of the Tennessee Academy of Science*, vol. 23 (1948), pp. 215–235.
6485

LANDSCAPE

Scofield, Edna Lois, "The Evolution and Development of Tennessee Houses," *Journal of the Tennessee Academy of Science*, vol. 11, 4 (1936), pp. 229–240.
6486

Hulon, Richard, "Middle Tennessee and the Dog-Trot House," *Pioneer America*, vol. 7, 2 (1975), pp. 37–46.
6487

Rehder, John B., John T. Morgan, and Joy L. Medford, "The Decline of Smokehouses in Grainger County, Tennessee," *West Georgia College Studies in the Social Sciences*, vol. 18 (1979), pp. 75–83.
6488

Morgan, John T., "The Decline of Log House Construction in Blount County, Tennessee," Ph.D. diss., University of Tennessee, 1986.
6489

Trimble, Stanley W., "Ante-Bellum Domestic Architecture in Middle Tennessee," in Richard L. Nostrand and Sam B. Hilliard, eds., *The American South* (Baton Rouge: Louisiana State University School of Geoscience, Geoscience & Man, vol. 25, 1988), pp. 97–118.
6490

Morgan, John T., *The Log House in East Tennessee* (Knoxville: University of Tennessee Press, 1990), 177 pp.
6491

Morgan, John T., "Log House Construction in Blount County, Tennessee," in Robert D. Mitchell, ed., *Appalachian Frontiers: Settlement, Society, and Development in the Pre-Industrial Era* (Lexington: University Press of Kentucky, 1991), pp. 201–221.
6492

COMMUNICATIONS & TRADE

Martin, G. C., "The Effect of Physiography on the Trade Routes of Eastern Tennessee," Master's thesis, University of Tennessee, 1932.
6493

Moore, Tyrel G., "The Role of Ferry Crossings in the Development of the Transportation Network in East Tennessee, 1790–1974," Master's thesis, University of Tennessee, 1975.
6494

URBAN NETWORKS & URBANIZATION

See also **6021**

Hodgson, Julia, *A Comparison of Three Tennessee Urban Centers: Goodlettsville, Franklin, and Clarksville* (Nashville: George Peabody College for Teachers, Abstract of Contribution to Education no. 240, 1939), 15 pp.
6495

TOWN GROWTH

Wright, Caroline M., "Nashville: Its History, Growth, and Prosperity," *Journal of School Geography*, vol. 5, 6 (1901), pp. 201–207.
6496

Johnson, R. W., "Geographic Influences in the Location and Growth of the City of Memphis," *Journal of Geography*, vol. 27, 3 (1928), pp. 85–97.
6497

Foscue, Edwin J., "Gatlinburg: A Mountain Community," *Economic Geography*, vol. 21, 3 (1945), pp. 192–205.
6498

Bacon, H. Phillip, "The Historical Geography of Antebellum Nashville," Ph.D. diss., George Peabody College for Teachers, 1955.
6499

Bacon, H. Phillip, "Some Problems of Adjustment to Nashville's Site and Situation, 1780–1860," *Tennessee Historical Quarterly*, vol. 15, 4 (1956), pp. 322–329.
6500

Kane, Kevin D., "Oakwood: Knoxville's Industrial Suburb of the Labor Aristocracy, 1902–1917," Master's thesis, University of Tennessee, 1984.
6501

Kane, Kevin D., and Thomas L. Bell, "Suburbs for a Labor Elite," *Geographical Review*, vol. 75, 3 (1985), pp. 319–334. [Oakwood, Knoxville] **6502**

URBAN ECONOMIC GROWTH

Bacon, H. Phillip, "Nashville's Trade at the Beginning of the Nineteenth Century," *Tennessee Historical Quarterly*, vol. 15, 1 (1956), pp. 30–36.
6503

Thornton, Charles A., "The Role of Transportation, 1790–1962: Implications in the Decentralization and Centralization of Selected Cities in East Tennessee," Ph.D. diss., University of Tennessee, 1970.
6504

Doering, Thomas R., "Historical Geography of Chemical Manufacturing in Metropolitan Memphis, Tennessee, 1939–1968," Master's thesis, Memphis State University, 1971.
6505

Honea, Robert B., "The Evolution of Industrial Land Use within the Knoxville Metropolitan Region: An Analysis Using Aerial Photography and Historical Data for the Purpose of Land Use Modeling," Ph.D. diss., University of Florida, 1975.
6506

PLANNING

See 6033

TOWNSCAPE

Bacon, H. Phillip, "The Townscape of Nashville, Tennessee, on the Eve of the Civil War," *Journal of Geography*, vol. 56, 8 (1957), pp. 353–363. 6507

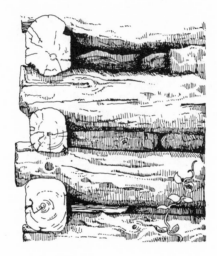

KENTUCKY

GENERAL

The state

Shaler, Nathaniel Southgate, *Kentucky: A Pioneer Commonwealth* (Boston: Houghton Mifflin Co., 1884), 433 pp.   **6508**

Smaller areas

Schockel, Bernard H., "Changing Conditions in the Kentucky Mountains," *Proceedings of the Indiana Academy of Science for 1914* (1915), pp. 109–131.   **6509**

Davis, Darrell H., "The Geography of the Jackson Purchase of Kentucky," Ph.D. diss., University of Michigan, 1923.   **6510**

Davis, Darrell H.,*The Geography of the Jackson Purchase of Kentucky* (Frankfort: Kentucky Geological Survey, Geological Reports, ser. 6, no. 9, 1923), 181 pp.   **6511**

Davis, Darrell H., *The Geography of the Mountains of Eastern Kentucky* (Frankfort: Kentucky Geological Survey, Geological Reports, ser. 6, no. 18, 1924), 180 pp.   **6512**

Davis, Darrell H., "The Changing Role of the Kentucky Mountains and the Passing of the Kentucky Mountaineer," *Journal of Geography*, vol. 24, 2 (1925), pp. 41–52. [Focus from colonial times to the 1920s]   **6513**

Burroughs, Wilbur G., *The Geography of the Kentucky Knobs* (Frankfort: Kentucky Geological Survey, Geological Reports, ser. 6, no. 19, 1926), 284 pp.   **6514**

Davis, Darrell H., *The Geography of the Blue Grass Region of Kentucky* (Frankfort: Kentucky Geological Survey, Geological Reports, ser. 6, no. 23, 1927), 215 pp.   **6515**

Sauer, Carl O., *The Geography of the Pennyroyal* (Frankfort: Kentucky State Geological Survey, Geological Reports, ser. 6, no. 25, 1927), 303 pp.   **6516**

EXPLORATION & MAPPING

Jillson, Willard R., "Early Kentucky Maps," *Register of the Kentucky Historical Society*, vol. 47 (1949), pp. 265–293; vol. 48 (1950), pp. 32–52.   **6517**

POPULAR IMAGES & EVALUATION

Dunbar, Gary S., "Henry Clay on Kentucky Bluegrass, 1838," *Agricultural History*, vol. 51, 3 (1977), pp. 520–523.   **6518**

REGIONAL SETTLEMENT

See also **7049**

Boertman, Charles S., "The Sequence of the Human Occupance in Wayne County, Kentucky: An Historical Study," Ph.D. diss., University of Michigan, 1934.   **6519**

Davis, Darrell H., "A Study of the Succession of Human Activities in the Kentucky Mountains: A Dissected Highland Area," *Journal of Geography*, vol. 29, 3 (1930), pp. 85–100. Reprinted in George J. Miller, ed., *Human Geography Studies: The United States* (Bloomington, Ill.: McKnight & McKnight, Geographic Education Series, 1935), pp. 71–86.   **6520**

Dicken, Samuel N., "The Kentucky Barrens," *Bulletin of the Philadelphia Geographical Society*, vol. 33, 2 (1935), pp. 42–51.   **6521**

Wilson, Leonard S., "Settlement Forms in the Northwest Cumberland Plateau of Kentucky," *Proceedings of the Minnesota Academy of Science*, vol. 6 (1938), pp. 5–12.   **6522**

Raitz, Karl B., and Peter C. Smith, "Negro Hamlets and Agricultural Estates in Kentucky's Inner Bluegrass," *Geographical Review*, vol. 64, 2 (1974), pp. 217–234.   **6523**

POPULATION

See also **5721**

Barnhart, John D., "The Migration of Kentuckians across the Ohio River," *Filson Club Historical Quarterly*, vol. 25 (1951), pp. 24–32.   **6524**

Lawson, Hughie G., "Geographical Origins of White Migrants to Trigg and Calloway Counties in the Antebellum Period," *Filson Club Historical Quarterly*, vol. 57, 3 (1983), pp. 286–304.   **6525**

RURAL & REGIONAL SOCIAL GEOGRAPHY

Semple, Ellen Churchill, "The Anglo-Saxons of the Kentucky Mountains: A Study in Anthropogeography," *Geographical Journal*, vol. 17, 6 (1901), pp. 588–623. Reprinted in *Bulletin of the American Geographical Society*, vol. 42, 8 (1910), pp. 561–594; and in abbreviated form in Robert S. Platt, ed., *Field Study in American Geography* (Chicago: University of Chicago Department of Geography, Research Paper no. 61, 1959), pp. 60–77.   **6526**

Adams, Neilam D., "A Historical Description of the Areal Distribution of the Churches of Warren County, Kentucky," Master's thesis, Western Kentucky University, 1971. **6527**

Shannon, Gary W., "County Population/Physician Ratios in Kentucky, 1847–1976," *Southeastern Geographer*, vol. 22, 1 (1982), pp. 68–86. **6528**

Pudup, Mary Beth, "Land before Coal: Class and Regional Development in Southeast Kentucky," Ph.D. diss., University of California–Berkeley, 1987. **6529**

Pudup, Mary Beth, "Social Class and Economic Development in Southeastern Kentucky, 1820–1880," in Robert D. Mitchell, ed., *Appalachian Frontiers: Settlement, Society, and Development in the Pre-Industrial Era* (Lexington: University Press of Kentucky, 1991), pp. 235–260. **6530**

POLITICAL & ADMINISTRATIVE GEOGRAPHY

Singlas, Sudesh K., "Geographical Analysis of the State-Administered Roads in Kentucky, 1920 to 1970," Master's thesis, Western Kentucky University, 1972. **6531**

ECONOMIC DEVELOPMENT

Moore, Tyrel G., "An Historical Geography of Economic Development in Appalachian Kentucky, 1800–1930," Ph.D. diss., University of Tennessee, 1984. **6532**

Moore, Tyrel G., "Development and Change in Appalachian Kentucky's Economy: 1870–1890," *Southeastern Geographer*, vol. 30, 2 (1990), pp. 121–139. **6533**

Moore, Tyrel G., "Economic Development in Appalachian Kentucky, 1820–1880," in Robert D. Mitchell, ed., *Appalachian Frontiers: Settlement, Society, and Development in the Pre-Industrial Era* (Lexington: University Press of Kentucky, 1991), pp. 222–234. **6534**

LAND & LAND USE

Hart, John Fraser, "Abandonment of Farmland in Kentucky," *Southeastern Geographer*, vol. 4 (1964), pp. 1–10. [Focus on 1890–1960] **6535**

Hart, John Fraser, "Abandonment of Farm Land on the Appalachian Fringe of Kentucky," in L. Dethier, ed., *Mélanges de géographie, physique, humaine, économique, appliquée, offerts à M. Omer Tulippe* (Gembloux, Belgium: J. Duculat, 1968), pp. 352–360. **6536**

AGRICULTURE

Whitaker, J. Russell, "The Development of the Tobacco Industry in Kentucky: A Geographical

Interpretation," *Bulletin of the Philadelphia Geographical Society*, vol. 27, 1 (1929), pp. 15–42. **6537**

Raitz, Karl B., and Nancy O'Malley, "An Index of Soil Production Potential as Applied to Historic Agricultural Adaptation: A Kentucky Example," *Historical Methods*, vol. 18, 4 (1985), pp. 137–146. **6538**

Moore, Tyrel G., "Home Manufactures in Appalachian Kentucky's Agricultural Economy, 1840–1870," *Proceedings of the Third Conference on Appalachian Geography* (March 1986), pp. 107–115. **6539**

LANDSCAPE

Williamson, Duane, "A Study of the Stone Fence as a Landscape Feature of Fayette County, Kentucky," Master's thesis, University of Kentucky, 1967. **6540**

Worboys, Paul S., "The Historical and Cultural Implications of Cemeteries, Calloway County, Kentucky, 1820–1965," Master's thesis, Murray State University, 1973. **6541**

Raitz, Karl B., "The Barns of Barren County," *Landscape*, vol. 22, 2 (1978), pp. 19–26. **6542**

Murray-Wooley, Carolyn, and Karl B. Raitz, *Rock Fences of the Bluegrass* (Lexington: University Press of Kentucky, 1992), 220 pp. **6543**

MANUFACTURING & INDUSTRIALIZATION

Zimmer, Dietrich M., *Die Industrialisierung der Bluegrass Region von Kentucky* (Heidelberg: Heidelberger Geographische Arbeiten, no. 31, 1970), 196 pp. [Focus on 1815–1940] **6544**

TOWN GROWTH

Semple, Ellen Churchill, "Louisville: A Study in Economic Geography," *Journal of School Geography*, vol. 4, 9 (1900), pp. 361–370. **6545**

Holt, Etelka, "The Settlement at the Falls of the Ohio, 1819–1824: A Geographical Interpretation," Master's thesis, University of Chicago, 1930. **6546**

Thornthwaite, Charles Warren, "Louisville, Kentucky: A Study in Urban Geography," Ph.D. diss., University of California–Berkeley, 1930. **6547**

Boertman, C. Stewart, and Henry M. Kendell, "The Somerset-Ferguson Urban Area in Southeastern Kentucky," *Papers of the Michigan Academy of Science, Arts, and Letters*, vol. 21 (1935), pp. 293–302. **6548**

Jacobson, Daniel, "The Historical Geography of Ashland," *Kentucky Engineer*, vol. 18 (May 1956), pp. 25–27, 50–52.   **6549**

URBAN ECONOMIC STRUCTURE

Dakan, A. William, "Evolution of a Trade Area: Predicting New Sites with a Space-Time Perspective," *Papers & Proceedings of Applied Geography Conferences*, vol. 11 (1988), pp. 1–9. [Louisville, 1950–1988]   **6550**

URBAN SOCIAL STRUCTURE

Kellogg, John, "The Formation of Black Residential Areas in Lexington, Kentucky, 1865–1887,"

Journal of Southern History, vol. 48, 1 (1982), pp. 21–52.   **6551**

PLACE NAMES

Rennick, Robert M., *Kentucky Place Names* (Lexington: University Press of Kentucky, 1984), 375 pp.   **6552**

Leighly, John B., *German Family Names in Kentucky Place Names* (New York: American Name Society, Monograph 2, 1987), 84 pp.   **6553**

MISSOURI

GENERAL

The state

Emerson, Frederick V., "A Geographical Interpretation of Missouri," *Geographical Journal*, vol. 41, 1 (1913), pp. 39–48; and 2 (1913), pp. 130–145.
6554

Ellis, James F., "The Influence of Environment on the Settlement of Missouri," Ph.D. diss., St. Louis University, 1929.
6555

Ellis, James F., *The Influence of Environment on the Settlement of Missouri* (St. Louis: Webster Publishing Co., 1929), 180 pp.
6556

Knox, Ray, "Exploring Virgin Missouri," *Missouri Geographer*, vol. 20, 2 (Spring 1974), p. 9.
6557

Rafferty, Milton D., "Boundaries and Land Surveys," and "Settlement," in his *Missouri: A Geography* (Boulder: Westview Press, 1983), pp. 39–47 and 49–64.
6558

Smaller areas

Sauer, Carl O., "The Geography of the Ozark Highland of Missouri," Ph.D. diss., University of Chicago, 1915.
6559

Sauer, Carl O., *The Geography of the Ozark Highland of Missouri* (Chicago: Geographical Society of Chicago, Bulletin no. 7, 1920), 245 pp. Reprinted Greenwood Press, 1960.
6560

Kersten, Earl W., "Changing Economy and Landscape in a Missouri Ozarks Area," *Annals of the Association of American Geographers*, vol. 48, 4 (1958), pp. 398–418.
6561

Conoyer, Johyn W., *The St. Louis Gateway: A Geographic Interpretation of the St. Louis 1:250,000 Topographic Map* (Normal, Ill.: National Council for Geographic Education, "Geography through Maps" series, Special Publication no. 14, 1967), 38 pp.
6562

Schroeder, Walter A., *The Eastern Ozarks: A Geographic Interpretation of the Rolla 1:250,000 Topographic Map* (Normal, Ill.: National Council for Geographic Education, "Geography through Maps" series, Special Publication no. 13, 1967), 40 pp.
6563

Walke, Bruno, "Historical Geography of St. Genevieve County, Missouri," Master's thesis, Southern Illinois University, 1969.
6564

Rafferty, Milton D., "The Ozarks: Geographical Change in an American Backwoods Region," *Proceedings of Historical Geography: Twenty-fourth International Geographical Congress, Section 9* (Tokyo: International Geographical Union, 1981), pp. 189–195.
6565

Rafferty, Milton D., "A Changing Ozarks," in Charles R. Wilson and William Ferris, eds., *Encyclopedia of Southern Culture* (Chapel Hill: University of North Carolina Press, 1989), pp. 552–554.
6566

ENVIRONMENTAL CHANGE

Schroeder, Walter A., *Presettlement Prairie of Missouri* (Jefferson City: Missouri Department of Conservation, Natural History Series, no. 2, 1981), 37 pp.
6567

Driever, Steven, and Danny M. Vaughan, "Flood Hazard in Kansas City since 1880," *Geographical Review*, vol. 78, 1 (1988), pp. 1–19.
6568

EXPLORATION & MAPPING

Wood, W. Raymond, "William Clark's Mapping in Missouri, 1803–1804," *Missouri Historical Review*, vol. 76, 3 (1982), pp. 241–252.
6569

Reps, John W., *Saint Louis Illustrated: Nineteenth-Century Engravings and Lithographs of a Mississippi River Metropolis* (Columbia: University of Missouri Press, 1989), 189 pp.
6570

POPULAR IMAGES & EVALUATION

Trexler, Harrison A., "Missouri in the Old Geographies," *Missouri Historical Review*, vol. 32, 2 (1937), pp. 148–155.
6571

Griffin, Rodney D., "A Garden and a Desert: Early Environmental Perceptions of Missouri," *Missouri Geographer*, vol. 21, 1 (Fall 1974), pp. 10-18.
6572

REGIONAL SETTLEMENT

Bratton, Sam T., and W. O. Smith, "Historical Geography of Salt River Community, Audrain County, Missouri," *Missouri Historical Review*, vol. 23 (1928), pp. 91–98.
6573

Bratton, Sam T., and Martha Langenderfer, "The Herman, Missouri, Region," *Bulletin of the Philadelphia Geographical Society*, vol. 29, 2 (1931), pp. 115–129.
6574

Johnson, Hugh N., "Sequent Occupance of the St. Francis Mining Region," Ph.D. diss., St. Louis University, 1950.
6575

Schroeder, Walter A., "Spread of Settlement in Howard County, Missouri, 1810–1859," *Missouri Historical Review*, vol. 63, 1 (1968), pp. 1–37. **6576**

Collins, Charles D., "Settlement Geography of Stone County, Missouri, 1800–1860," Master's thesis, University of Arkansas, 1971. **6577**

Clendenen, Harbert L., "Settlement Morphology of the Southern Courtois Hills, Missouri, 1820–1860," Ph.D. diss., Louisiana State University, 1973. **6578**

Rafferty, Milton D., "Population and Settlement Changes in Two Ozark Localities," *Rural Sociology*, vol. 38, 1 (1973), pp. 46–56. [Buck Prairie Twp., Lawrence Co.; and Linn Twp., Christian Co., 1879–1968] **6579**

Rafferty, Milton D., and Dennis J. Hrebec, "Logan Creek: A Missouri Ozark Valley Revisited," *Journal of Geography*, vol. 72, 7 (1973), pp. 7–17. **6580**

Shortridge, James R., "The Expansion of the Settlement Frontier in Missouri," *Missouri Historical Review*, vol. 75, 1 (1980), pp. 64–90. **6581**

O'Brien, Michael J., ed., *Grassland, Forest, and Historical Settlement: An Analysis of Dynamics in Northeast Missouri* (Lincoln: University of Nebraska Press, 1984), 345 pp. **6582**

POPULATION

Mattingly, Paul F., "Population Trends of Missouri," *Journal of Geography*, vol. 55, 2 (1956), pp. 80–84. [Focus on 1810–1950] **6583**

Bench, Cecil C., "Population Distribution in Early Missouri," Master's thesis, Clark University, 1971. **6584**

Gerlach, Russel L., "Population Origins in Rural Missouri," *Missouri Historical Review*, vol. 71, 1 (1976), pp. 1–21. **6585**

Gerlach, Russel L., "Origins of Early Ozark Settlers," *Bittersweet (Lebanon High School, Mo.)*, vol. 4 (1977), pp. 12–18. **6586**

Gerlach, Russel L., *Settlement Patterns in Missouri: A Study of Population Origins* (Columbia: University of Missouri Press, 1986), 88 pp. **6587**

Schroeder, Walter A., "Missouri: Center of Population of the United States," *Missouri Historical Review*, vol. 81, 3 (1987), pp. 328–334. **6588**

Amonker, Ravindra G., and Diane L. Balduzy, "Migration Patterns of Southwest Missouri's Older Population," *Missouri Geographer*, vol. 34, (1990). **6589**

RURAL & REGIONAL SOCIAL GEOGRAPHY

Emerson, Frederick V., "Life along a Graded River," *Bulletin of the American Geographical Society*, vol. 44, 9 (1912), pp. 674–681; and 10 (1912), pp. 761–768. [Focus from the 1820s to 1912 along the Glasgow-Booneville section of the Missouri River] **6590**

Gerlach, Russel L., "German Settlements in the Ozarks," *Rundschau (National Carl Schurz Association)*, vol. 3 (1973), pp. 5–7. **6591**

Gerlach, Russel L., "Rural Ethnic and Religious Groups as Cultural Islands in the Ozarks of Missouri: Their Emergence and Persistence," Ph.D. diss., University of Nebraska–Lincoln, 1974. **6592**

Gerlach, Russel L., *Immigrants in the Ozarks: A Study in Ethnic Geography* (Columbia: University of Missouri Press, 1976), 206 pp. **6593**

Gold, Gerald L., "Lead Mining and the Survival and Demise of French in Rural Missouri (Les gens qui ont pioché le tuf)," *Cahiers de géographie du Québec*, vol. 23, 59 (1979), pp. 331–342. **6594**

Price, Cynthia, and James Price, "Investigation of Settlement and Subsistence Systems in the Ozark Border Region of Southeast Missouri during the First Half of the Nineteenth Century: The Widow Harris Cabin Project," *Ethnohistory*, vol. 27, 3 (1981), pp. 237–258. **6595**

Gerlach, Russel L., "The Ozark Scotch-Irish: The Subconscious Persistence of an Ethnic Culture," *Pioneer America Society Transactions*, vol. 7 (1984), pp. 47–57. **6596**

DeBres, Karen J., "From Germans to Americans: The Creation and Destruction of Three Ethnic Communities," Ph.D. diss., Columbia University, 1986. [Hermann] **6597**

Anderson, Timothy G., "Westphalia, Missouri: The Historical Geography of a German Community," Master's thesis, University of Oklahoma, 1990. **6598**

POLITICAL & ADMINISTRATIVE GEOGRAPHY

Crisler, Robert M., "Republican Areas in Missouri," *Missouri Historical Review*, vol. 42, 4 (1948), pp. 299–309. **6599**

ECONOMIC DEVELOPMENT

Powers, Robert Wayne, "Property Value and Paved Roads in Northern Boone County," *Missouri Geographer*, vol. 20, 2 (Spring 1974), pp. 25–32. **6600**

Ohman, Marian M., "Missouri County Organization, 1812–1876," *Missouri Historical Review*, vol. 76, 3 (1982), pp. 253–281. **6601**

LAND & LAND USE

Cozzens, Arthur B., "Conservation in German Settlements of the Missouri Ozarks," *Geographical Review*, vol. 33, 2 (1943), pp. 286–298. [Focus on the transition from folk to modern practices]
6602

Schroeder, Walter A., "The Changing Size of Rural Property in Missouri," *Missouri Geographer*, vol. 22, 1 (Fall 1975), pp. 50-54.
6603

Coble, Dale, "Changing Land Use in the Past Twenty Years in Douglas County, Missouri," *Missouri Geographer*, vol. 24, 2 (Fall 1977), p. 28.
6604

Schroeder, Walter A., "Order in the Orientation of Pre-American Land Grants in the Ste. Genevieve District, Missouri," in Michael O. Roark, ed., *French and Germans in the Mississippi Valley: Landscape and Culture Tradition* (Cape Girardeau: Southeast Missouri State University, Center for Regional History and Culture Heritage, 1988), pp. 125–136.
6605

EXTRACTIVE ACTIVITY

Bratton, Sam T., "Coal in Missouri," *Missouri Historical Review*, vol. 22 (1928), pp. 150–156.
6606

Roark, Michael O., "Early American Lead Mining in Southeastern Missouri," *Pioneer America Society Transactions*, vol. 5 (1982), pp. 55–62.
6607

Roark, Michael O., "The Effect of Lead and Iron Mining on the Cultural Development of Eastern Missouri, 1860–1880," *Pioneer America Society Transactions*, vol. 11 (1988), pp. 9–17.
6608

AGRICULTURE

Hudson, Charles E., "A Geographic Study Examining the Major Elements Involved in the Rise of Cotton Production in Southeast Missouri, 1922–1925," Master's thesis, Western Michigan University, 1967.
6609

Rafferty, Milton D., "Missouri's Black Walnut Kernel Industry," *Missouri Historical Review*, vol. 63, 2 (1969), pp. 214–226.
6610

Rafferty, Milton D., "The Black Walnut Kernel Industry: The Modernization of a Pioneer Custom," *Pioneer America*, vol. 5, 1 (1973), pp. 23–32.
6611

Rafferty, Milton D., "Agricultural Change in the Western Ozarks," *Missouri Historical Review*, vol. 69, 3 (1975), pp. 299–322. [Focus on 1850–1967]
6612

LANDSCAPE

See also **8587–8589**

Miller, E. Joan Wilson, "Folk Materials as Documentation in the Historical Geography of the Ozarks," Ph.D. diss., University of North Carolina, 1965.
6613

Miller, E. Joan Wilson, "The Ozark Culture Region as Revealed by Traditional Materials," *Annals of the Association of American Geographers*, vol. 58, 1 (1968), pp. 51–77.
6614

Rafferty, Milton D., "Ozark House Types," *Missouri Geographer*, vol. 19, 2 (Spring 1973), pp. 6–37.
6615

Johnson, C., "Missouri-French Houses: Some Relict Features of Early Settlement," *Pioneer America*, vol. 6, 2 (1974), pp. 1–11.
6616

DeBres, Karen, "Cycles of Construction: Creating and Recreating Landscapes in Rural Missouri," *Proceedings of the Middle States Division, Association of American Geographers*, vol. 14 (1980), pp. 53–56. [Focus on Washington, Mo.]
6617

Roark, Michael O., "Imprint of the French in North America: Long-Lots in the Mid-Missouri Valley," in Michael O. Roark, ed., *French and German in the Mississippi Valley: Landscape and Cultural Traditions* (Cape Girardeau: Southeast Missouri State University, Center for Regional History and Cultural Heritage, 1988), pp. 111–124.
6618

Denny, James M., "The Georgian Cottage in Missouri: An Obscure but Persistent Alternative to the I-House in the Upper South," *Pioneer America Society Transactions*, vol. 13 (1990), pp. 63–70.
6619

COMMUNICATIONS & TRADE

Bratton, Sam T., "Inefficiency of Water Transportation in Missouri: A Geographical Factor in the Development of Railroads," *Missouri Historical Review*, vol. 14 (1919), pp. 82–88.
6620

Bellovich, Steven J., "The Establishment and Development of the Main Colonial-Territorial Routes of Lead Movement in Eastern Missouri, 1700–1965," Master's thesis, Southern Illinois University, 1970.
6621

MANUFACTURING & INDUSTRIALIZATION

Cozzens, Arthur B., "Chronology of Ironmaking," *Missouri Historical Review*, vol. 36, 2 (1941), pp. 214–220.
6622

Cozzens, Arthur B., "The Iron Industry of Missouri," *Missouri Historical Review*, vol. 35, 4 (1941), pp. 509–538; vol. 36, 1 (1941), pp. 48–60. **6623**

Prante, Mary C., "Maramec Ironworks: An Example in Migration of the Iron Industry before Carnegie," *Bulletin of the Illinois Geographical Society*, vol. 29, 1 (1987), pp. 25–35. **6624**

URBAN NETWORKS & URBANIZATION

See also 8442

Thomas, Lewis F., "Decline of St. Louis as Midwest Metropolis," *Economic Geography*, vol. 25, 2 (1949), pp. 118–127. **6625**

Smith, Russell E., "The Towns of the Missouri Valley: An Element of the Historical Geography of Missouri," Master's thesis, University of Missouri, 1957. **6626**

Morrow, Lynn, "New Madrid and Its Hinterland, 1783–1826," *Bulletin of the Missouri Historical Society*, vol. 36, 4 (1980), pp. 241–250. **6627**

Rafferty, Milton D., "Population Trends of Missouri Towns," in Michael O. Roark, ed., *Cultural Geography of Missouri* (Cape Girardeau: Southeast Missouri State University, Center for Regional History and Cultural Heritage, 1983), pp. 59–76. **6628**

TOWN GROWTH

Semple, Ellen Churchill, "Geographic Influences in the Development of St. Louis," *Journal of Geography*, vol. 3, 6 (1904), pp. 290–300. **6629**

Brannon, Fred K., "Geographic Influences in the Development of St. Louis, Missouri," Master's thesis, University of Chicago, 1916. **6630**

Johnson, Elmer H., "St. Louis," *Journal of Geography*, vol. 21, 9 (1922), pp. 233–236. **6631**

Franklin, Lillie, "Rocheport, Missouri: An Illustration of Economic Adjustment to Environment," *Missouri Historical Review*, vol. 19, 1 (1924), pp. 3–11. **6632**

Johnson, Alan H., "Rocheport, Missouri: A Study in Historical Economic Geography," Master's thesis, University of Missouri, 1962. **6633**

Fuller, Michael J., and Doris W. Ewing, "Community History of the Old Town District of Lebanon, Missouri," *Missouri Geographer*, vol. 22, 2 (Spring 1976), pp. 36–43. **6634**

URBAN ECONOMIC STRUCTURE

Thomas, Lewis F., "The Sequence of Areal Occupancy in a Section of St. Louis, Missouri," *An-*

nals of the Association of American Geographers, vol. 21, 1 (1931), pp. 75–90. **6635**

Kearns, Kevin C., "The Acquisition of St. Louis' Forest Park," *Missouri Historical Review*, vol. 62, 2 (1968), pp. 95–106. **6636**

URBAN SOCIAL STRUCTURE

Howe, Gary C., "The Negro Ghetto: The Dynamics of Its Spatial Distribution in St. Louis, 1940, 1950, 1960," Master's thesis, Southern Illinois University, 1968. **6637**

TOWNSCAPE

Larimore, Ann E., "The Cultural Geography of St. Charles, Missouri: House Types," Master's thesis, University of Chicago, 1955. **6638**

Reps, John W., "New Madrid on the Mississippi: American Eighteenth Century Planning on the Spanish Frontier," *Journal of the Society of Architectural Historians*, vol. 18, 1 (1959), pp. 21–26. **6639**

Smith, Stuart A., "The Changing 'Urban' Landscape in the Rural Missouri Ozarks: The Example of Houston," Master's thesis, University of Missouri–Columbia, 1990. **6640**

RECREATION & TOURISM

Rafferty, Milton D., "The Historical Geography of the Ozark Tourism-Recreation Industry," *Frankfurter Wirtschafts- und Sozialgeographische Schriften*, vol. 41 (1982), pp. 89–107. **6641**

PLACE NAMES

Sauer, Carl O., "Origin of the Name 'Ozark'," *Missouri Historical Review*, vol. 22, 4 (1928), p. 550. **6642**

Ramsey, Robert L., et al., *Introduction to a Survey of Missouri Place Names* (Columbia: University of Missouri Studies, vol. 9, 1, 1934), 124 pp. **6643**

Doiron, Claude J., Jr., "Some Missouri Places and Place Names, *Missouri Geographer*, vol. 22, 1 (Fall 1975), pp. 11-20. **6644**

Schroeder, Walter A., "The Missouri Place Name Survey," *Missouri Geographer*, vol. 22, 1 (Fall 1975), pp. 38-40. **6645**

Schroeder, Walter A., "Panther Hallow and Dead Elm Street: Plant and Animal Place Names in Missouri," *Missouri Historical Review*, vol. 73, 3 (1979), pp. 321–347. **6646**

ARKANSAS

GENERAL

Harrison, Robert W., and Walter M. Kollmorgen, "Socio-Economic History of Cypress Creek Drainage District and Related Districts of Southeast Arkansas," *Arkansas Historical Quarterly*, vol. 7, 1 (1948), pp. 20–52.   **6647**

Holder, Virgil H., "Historical Geography of the Lower White River Valley," Master's thesis, University of Arkansas, 1965.   **6648**

McConnell, John G., "The Fort Smith Area, 1780–1961: A Historical Geography," Master's thesis, University of Toronto, 1965.   **6649**

Holder, Virgil H., "Historical Geography of the Lower White River," *Arkansas Historical Quarterly*, vol. 27, 2 (1968), pp. 132–145.   **6650**

Harnish, Harry E., "Historical Geography of the Upper White River Valley," Master's thesis, University of Arkansas, 1978.   **6651**

ENVIRONMENTAL CHANGE

Reid, James W., *The Problem of Droughts in Arkansas Agriculture* (Nashville: George Peabody College for Teachers, Abstract of Contribution to Education no. 229, 1939), 9 pp. [Focus on 1897–1939]   **6652**

Phillips, Charles A., "Drought Periodicity in Arkansas as Inferred from Tree-Ring Indices: 1530–1980," Master's thesis, University of Arkansas, 1986.   **6653**

EXPLORATION & MAPPING

Loberg, David L., "The Mapping of Arkansas, 1541–1900," Master's thesis, University of Arkansas, 1976.   **6654**

REGIONAL SETTLEMENT

McClelland, Audrey M., "Washington County, Arkansas: A Study in Sequent Occupance," Master's thesis, University of Arkansas, 1974.   **6655**

Pilcher, Bruce F., "The Settlement Geography of Prairie Township, Washington County, Arkansas," Master's thesis, University of Arkansas, 1974.   **6656**

Hudson, James F., "Settlement Geography of Madison County, Arkansas, 1836–1860," Master's thesis, University of Arkansas, 1976.   **6657**

POPULATION

Walz, Robert B., "Migration into Arkansas, 1820–1880: Incentives and Means of Travel," *Arkansas Historical Quarterly*, vol. 17, 4 (1958), pp. 309–324.   **6658**

Schiefer, Carl L., "Washington County, Arkansas: A Geography of Population Change, 1840–1970," Master's thesis, 1975.   **6659**

Gray, Lissa C., "Population Growth, Pope County, Arkansas, with Emphasis on Migration, 1920–1976," Master's thesis, University of Arkansas, 1977.   **6660**

Silva, Michael F., "Black Arkansas Population Change, 1900–1970," Master's thesis, University of Arkansas, 1981.   **6661**

POLITICAL & ADMINISTRATIVE GEOGRAPHY

Dorr, Guy E., "Issei, Nissei, and Arkansas: A Geographic Study of the Wartime Relocation of Japanese-Americans in Southeast Arkansas, 1942–1945," Master's thesis, University of Arkansas, 1977.   **6662**

LAND & LAND USE

Harrison, Robert W., and Walter M. Kollmorgen, "Land Reclamation in Arkansas under the Swamp Land Grant of 1850," *Arkansas Historical Quarterly*, vol. 6, 4 (1947), pp. 369–418.   **6663**

AGRICULTURE

Hewes, Leslie, "Tontitown: Ozark Vineyard Center," *Economic Geography*, vol. 29, 2 (1953), pp. 125–143.   **6664**

Green, D. Brooks, "Irrigation Experiment in Arkansas: A Preliminary Investigation," *Arkansas Historical Quarterly*, vol. 45, 3 (1986), pp. 261–268.   **6665**

LANDSCAPE

Tebbetts, Diane, "Traditional Houses of Independence County, Arkansas," *Pioneer America*, vol. 10, 1 (1978), pp. 36–55.   **6666**

COMMUNICATIONS & TRADE

Green, D. Brooks, and David Dempsey, "The Butterfield Overland Mail Route through Faulkner

County," *Faulkner Facts and Fiddlings,* vol. 24
(1982), pp. 10–22.   **6667**

URBAN NETWORKS & URBANIZATION

Buell, Michaele A., "A Historical Geography of
Selected Small Towns in Benton County, Arkansas," Master's thesis, University of Arkansas,
1990.   **6668**

TOWN GROWTH

Minton, Hubert L., "The Evolution of Conway,
Arkansas," Ph.D. diss., University of Chicago,
1937. Published under the same title, as a University of Chicago Libraries Private Edition,
1937), 68 pp.   **6669**

TOWNSCAPE

Green, D. Brooks, "Architectural Change in Conway from 1880 to 1950," *Faulkner Facts and Fiddlings,* vol. 27 (1985), pp. 1–10.   **6670**

PLACE NAMES

Miller, E. Joan Wilson, "The Naming of the Land
in the Arkansas Ozarks: A Study in Cultural Process," *Annals of the Association of American
Geographers,* vol. 59, 2 (1969), pp. 240–251.   **6671**

Dickinson, Samuel D., "Colonial Arkansas Place
Names," *Arkansas Historical Quarterly,* vol. 48,
2 (1989), pp. 137–168.   **6672**

LOUISIANA

GENERAL

The state

Serruys, Edmond, "La Louisiane sous la domination espagnole," *Bulletin de la Société royale belge de géographie*, vol. 17 (1893), pp. 164–177.
6673

Kniffen, Fred B., *Louisiana: Its Land and People* (Baton Rouge: Louisiana State University Press, 1968), pp. 100–182.
6674

Smaller areas

Post, Lauren C., "Cultural Geography of the Prairies of Southwest Louisiana," Ph.D. diss., University of California–Berkeley, 1937.
6675

Post, Lauren C., "The Rice Country of Southwestern Louisiana," *Geographical Review*, vol. 30, 4 (1940), pp. 574–590. [Focus on 1890–1940]
6676

Blume, Helmut, *Die Entwicklung der Kulturlandschaft des Mississippideltas in kolonialer Zeit unter besonderer Berücksichtigung der deutschen Siedlung* (Kiel: Schriften des Geographischen Instituts der Universität Kiel, vol. 16, 3 (1956), 123 pp. Translated and published as *The German Coast during the Colonial Era, 1722–1803* (Destrehan, La.: German-American Coast Historical and Genealogical Society, 1990), 165 pp.
6677

Reilly, Timothy F., "An Historical Geography of the Morgan City Area, 1700–1950," in *Outer Continental Shelf Impacts, Morgan City, Louisiana* (Washington, D.C.: United States Department of Commerce, SPO-76–12, 1976–1977).
6678

Comeaux, Malcolm L., "Atchafalaya Basin Swamp," in Charles R. Wilson and William Ferris, eds., *Encyclopedia of Southern Culture* (Chapel Hill: University of North Carolina Press, 1989), pp. 375–376.
6679

ENVIRONMENTAL CHANGE

Post, Lauren C., "The Domestic Animals and Plants of French Louisiana as Mentioned in the Literature with Reference to Sources, Varieties, and Uses," *Louisiana Historical Quarterly*, vol. 16, 4 (1933), pp. 554–586.
6680

Russell, Richard J., "Larto Lake: An Old Mississippi Channel," *Louisiana Conservation Review*, vol. 3 (1933), pp. 18–21; 46. Reprinted in H. Jesse

Walker and Milton B. Newton, Jr., eds., *Environment and Culture* (Baton Rouge: Louisiana State University, Department of Geography and Anthropology, 1978), pp. 65–68.
6681

Sternberg, Hilgard O., "The Point Coupée Cut-Off in Historical Writings," *Louisiana Historical Quarterly*, vol. 28, 1 (1945), pp. 69–84.
6682

Harrison, Robert W., and Walter M. Kollmorgen, "Past and Present Drainage Reclamation in the Coastal Marshlands of the Mississippi River Delta," *Journal of Land and Public Utility Economics*, vol. 23, 3 (1947), pp. 297–320.
6683

McIntire, William G., "Methods of Correlating Cultural Remains with States of Coastal Development," *Second Coastal Geography Conference* (Baton Rouge: Louisiana State University, Coastal Studies Institute, 1959), pp. 341–359. Reprinted in H. Jesse Walker and Milton B. Newton, Jr., eds., *Environment and Culture* (Baton Rouge: Louisiana State University, Department of Geography and Anthropology, 1978), pp. 117–125.
6684

Comeaux, Malcolm L., "Les Acadiens Louisianais: L'impact de l'environnement," *Revue de Louisiane/Louisiana Review*, vol. 6, 2 (1977), pp. 163–178.
6685

Detro, Randall A., "New Orleans Drainage and Reclamation: A 200-Year Problem," *Zeitschrift für Geomorphologie*. vol. 34, suppl. (1980), pp. 87–96.
6686

Faust, Marie N., "Changes in Cross-Sectional Elements of the Mississippi River Channel, 1880–1975," Master's thesis, Lousiana State University, 1983.
6687

NATIVE PEOPLES & WHITE RELATIONS

Kniffen, Fred B., "The Historic Indian Tribes of Louisiana," *Louisiana Conservation Review*, vol. 55, 3 (1935), pp. 5–12.
6688

Kniffen, Fred B., "The Indian Mounds of Iberville Parish, Louisiana," *Louisiana Department of Conservation Geological Bulletin*, 13 (1938), pp. 189–206. Reprinted in H. Jesse Walker and Milton B. Newton, Jr., eds., *Environment and Culture* (Baton Rouge: Louisiana State University, Department of Geography and Anthropology, 1978), pp. 135–142.
6689

Kniffen, Fred B., "A Spanish (?) Spinner in Louisiana," *Southern Folklore Quarterly*, vol. 13

(1949), pp. 192–199. Reprinted in H. Jesse Walker and Milton B. Newton, Jr., eds., *Environment and Culture* (Baton Rouge: Louisiana State University, Department of Geography and Anthropology, 1978), pp. 169–173. 6690

Jacobson, Daniel, "Koasati Culture Changes," Ph.D. diss., Louisiana State University, 1954. 6691

McIntire, William G., "Prehistoric Settlements of Coastal Louisiana," Ph.D. diss., Louisiana State University, 1954. 6692

McIntire, William G., *Prehistoric Indian Settlements of the Changing Mississippi River Delta* (Baton Rouge: Louisiana State University Press, 1958), 128 pp. 6693

Post, Lauren C., "Some Notes on the Attakapas Indians of Southwest Louisiana," *Louisiana History*, vol. 3, 3 (1962), pp. 221–242. 6694

Jacobson, Daniel, Howard N. Martin, and Ralph H. Marsh, *Alabama-Coushatta (Creek) Indians: Ethnological Report and Statement of Testimony, Documents on the Alabama and Coushatta Tribes of Texas, History of Polk County, Texas* (New York: Garland Publishing Co., American Indian Ethnohistory Series: Southern and Southeast Indians, 1974), 361 pp. 6695

Curry-Roper, Janel M., "Cultural Change and the Houma Indians: A Historical and Ecological Examination," in Thomas E. Ross and Tyrel G. Moore, eds., *A Cultural Geography of North American Indians* (Boulder: Westview Press, 1987), pp. 227–242. 6696

Jacobson, Daniel, "Alabama and Coushatta Settlements in Louisiana," *Southern Studies*, vol. 26, 2 (1987), pp. 137–153. 6697

Jacobson, Daniel, "The Coushatta of Bayou Blue, 1884–1986," *East Lakes Geographer*, vol. 22 (1987), pp. 33–43. 6698

Kniffen, Fred B., et al., *The Historic Indian Tribes of Louisiana: From 1542 to the Present* (Baton Rouge: Louisiana State University Press, 1987), 324 pp. 6699

POPULAR IMAGES & EVALUATION

Comeaux, Malcolm L., "An Early View of the Atchafalaya: The Lt. Enoch Humphrey Expedition of 1805," *Attakapas Gazette*, vol. 11 (1976), pp. 152–163. 6700

Dunbar, Gary S., "Élisée Réclus in Louisiana," *Louisiana History*, vol. 23, 4 (1983), pp. 341–352. 6701

Estaville, Lawrence E., "Civil War Images of a Cajun Landscape: Bayous Lafourche and Terre-

bonne," *Attakapas Gazette*, vol. 21 (1986), pp. 64–68. 6702

REGIONAL SETTLEMENT

See also 1331, 5876

Phillips, Yvonne, "Settlement Succession in the Tensas Basin, Louisiana," Ph.D. diss., Louisiana State University, 1953. 6703

Blume, Helmut, "Deutsche Kolonisten im Mississippidelta," *Jahrbuch für Amerikastudien*, vol. 1 (1956), pp. 177–183. 6704

Knipmeyer, William B., "Cultural Succession in the Settlement of Southeastern Louisiana," Ph.D. diss., Louisiana State University, 1956. 6705

Taylor, James W., "The Agricultural Settlement Succession in the Prairies of Southwest Louisiana," Ph.D. diss., Louisiana State University, 1956. 6706

Wright, Martin, "Settlement Succession in Hill, Louisiana," Ph.D. diss., Louisiana State University, 1956. 6707

Gagliano, Sherwood M., "Occupance Sequence at Avery Island," Ph.D. diss., Louisiana State University, 1967. 6708

Newton, Milton B., Jr., "The Peasant Farm of St. Helena Parish, Louisiana: A Cultural Geography," Ph.D. diss., Louisiana State University, 1967. 6709

Lewis, John C., "The Settlement Succession of the Boeuf River Basin, Louisiana," Ph.D. diss., Louisiana State University, 1973. 6710

L'Herisson, Lawrence E., "The Evolution of the Texas Road and the Sequential Settlement Occupancy of Northwestern Louisiana, 1528–1819," Master's thesis, Louisiana State University, 1981. 6711

McCloskey, Kathleen G., "Early Acadian Settlement in St. James Parish, Louisiana," Master's thesis, Louisiana State University, 1981. 6712

Rawson, Paul, "Early French Settlers along Bayou Bartholomew," *Pioneer America Society Transactions*, vol. 8 (1985), pp. 91–97. 6713

Mires, Peter B., "Predicting the Past: The Geography of Settlement in Louisiana, 1690–1890, and Its Application to Historic Preservation," Ph.D. diss., Louisiana State University, 1988. 6714

POPULATION

Kyster, John S., "The Evolution of Louisiana Parishes in Relation to Population Growth and

Movements," Ph.D. diss., Louisiana State University, 1938. 6715

Oukada, Larbi, "The Territory and Population of French-Speaking Louisiana," *Revue de Louisiane/Louisiana Review*, vol. 7, 1 (1978), pp. 5–34. [Emphasis on the twentieth century] 6716

Lawrence, William F., "European Immigration Trends of Northeast Louisiana, 1880–1900," *Louisiana History*, vol. 26, 1 (1985), pp. 41–52. 6717

RURAL & REGIONAL SOCIAL GEOGRAPHY

See also 5896

French Louisiana and the Acadians

Kelley, Minnie, "Acadian South Lousiana," *Journal of Geography*, vol. 33, 3 (1934), pp. 81–90. Reprinted in George J. Miller, ed., *Human Geography Studies: The United States* (Bloomington, Ill.: McKnight & McKnight, Geographic Education Series, 1935), pp. 142–151. 6718

Kollmorgen, Walter M., and Robert W. Harrison, "French-Speaking Farmers of Southern Louisiana," *Economic Geography*, vol. 22, 3 (1946), pp. 153–160. 6719

Post, Lauren C., *Cajun Sketches from the Prairies of Southwest Louisiana* (Baton Rouge: Louisiana State University Press, 1962), 215 pp. Reprinted 1974. 6720

Comeaux, Malcolm L., *Atchafalaya Swamp Life: Settlement and Folk Occupations* (Baton Rouge: Louisiana State University School of Geoscience, Geoscience & Man, vol. 2, 1972), 111 pp. 6721

Comeaux, Malcolm L., "The Cajun Accordion," *Revue de Louisiane/Louisiana Review*, vol. 7, 2 (1978), pp. 117–128. 6722

Estaville, Lawrence E., "The Louisiana French Culture Region: Geographic Morphologies in the Nineteenth Century," Ph.D. diss., University of Oklahoma, 1984. 6723

Estaville, Lawrence E., "Mapping the Cajuns," *Southern Studies*, vol. 25, 2 (1986), pp. 163–171. 6724

Estaville, Lawrence E., "Mapping the Louisiana French," *Southeastern Geographer*, vol. 26, 2 (1986), pp. 90–113. 6725

Estaville, Lawrence E., "Changeless Cajuns: Nineteenth-Century Reality or Myth?" *Louisiana History*, vol. 28, 2 (1987), pp. 117–140. 6726

Estaville, Lawrence E., "The Louisiana French in 1900," *Journal of Historical Geography*, vol. 14, 4 (1988), pp. 342–360. 6727

Estaville, Lawrence E., "Were the Nineteenth-Century Cajuns Geographically Isolated?" in Richard L. Nostrand and Sam B. Hilliard, eds., *The American South* (Baton Rouge: Louisiana State University School of Geoscience, Geoscience & Man, vol. 25, 1988), pp. 85–96. 6728

Trepanier, Cecyle, "French Louisiana at the Threshold of the Twenty-First Century," Ph.D. diss., Pennsylvania State University, 1989. 6729

Estaville, Lawrence E., "The Louisiana French Language in the Nineteenth Century," *Southeastern Geographer*, vol. 30, 2 (1990), pp. 107–120. 6730

Estaville, Lawrence E., "The Louisiana French Region: National-Scale Boundaries," *Southern Studies*, n.s. vol. 1, 1 (1990), pp. 61–64. 6731

Other ethnic groups

LeConte, René, "Les Allemands à la Louisiane au XVIIIe siècle," *Bulletin de la Société de géographie de Québec*, vol. 18, 5 (1924), pp. 257–273. 6732

Jacobson, Daniel, "The Origin of the Koasati Community of Louisiana," *Ethnohistory*, vol. 7, 2 (1960), pp. 97–120. 6733

Johnson, Hildegard Binder, *French Louisiana and the Development of the German Triangle* (Minneapolis: University of Minnesota, Associates of the James Ford Bell Library, German-American Tricentennial Publication, 1983), 4 pp. and 2 plates. 6734

Din, Gilbert C., "The Canary Islander Settlements of Spanish Louisiana: An Overview," *Louisiana History*, vol. 27, 4 (1986), pp. 353–373. 6735

Folkways

Curry-Roper, Janel M., "Houma Blowguns and Baskets in the Mississippi River Delta," *Journal of Cultural Geography*, vol. 2, 2 (1982), pp. 13–22. 6736

Whelan, James P., Jr., "From Forest, Stream, and Sea: Aspects of Self-Sufficiency in the Nineteenth Century Louisiana Diet," Ph.D. diss., Louisiana State University, 1989. 6737

Sexton, Rocky, "Passing a Good Time in Southwest Louisiana: An Ethnohistoric and Humanistic Approach to the Study of Cajun Bars/Clubs as Place," Master's thesis, Louisiana State University, 1990. 6738

Labor relations

Penn, James R., "The Geographical Variation of Unionism in Louisiana: A Study of the Southern Claims Data," *Louisiana History*, vol. 30, 4

(1989), pp. 399–418. [Focus on Civil War claims] 6739

POLITICAL & ADMINISTRATIVE GEOGRAPHY

Musset, René, "Les vicissitudes de la Louisiane et les survivances du droit français en Louisiane," *Cahiers d'outre mer*, vol. 7, 4 (1954), pp. 406–408. 6740

ECONOMIC DEVELOPMENT

Bertrand, John, "Oil and Population in Southern Louisiana, 1901–1935," Master's thesis, Louisiana State University, 1952. 6741

Blume, Helmut, "Landwirtschaft und Wirtschaft in Louisiana unter französischer Kolonialverwaltung," *Erdkunde*, vol. 10, 3 (1956), pp. 177–185. 6742

LAND & LAND USE

Harrison, Robert W., and Walter M. Kollmorgen, "Drainage Reclamation in the Coastal Marshlands of the Mississippi River Delta," *Louisiana Historical Quarterly*, vol. 30, 2 (1947), pp. 654–709. 6743

Hall, John W., "Louisiana Survey Systems: Their Antecedents, Distributions, and Characteristics," Ph.D. diss., Louisiana State University, 1970. 6744

French, Carolyn, "Land Survey and Land Acquisition in the Florida Parishes of Louisiana," in Sam B. Hilliard, ed., *Man and Environment in the Lower Mississippi Valley* (Baton Rouge: Louisiana State University School of Geoscience, Geoscience & Man, vol. 19, 1978), pp. 107–122. 6745

Kruger, Darrell, "Disposal of the Public Domain in the Hill Country of Louisiana: Union Parish, 1826–1936," Master's thesis, Louisiana State University, 1990. 6746

EXTRACTIVE ACTIVITY

McCarter, John, and Fred B. Kniffen, "Louisiana Iron Rock," *Economic Geography*, vol. 29, 3 (1953), pp. 299–306. [Focus on 1820–1950] 6747

Stokes, George A., "Lumbering in Southwest Louisiana: A Study of the Industry as a Cultural-Geographic Factor," Ph.D. diss., Louisiana State University, 1954. 6748

Stokes, George A., "Lumbering and Western Louisiana Cultural Landscapes," *Annals of the Association of American Geographers*, vol. 47, 3 (1957), pp. 250–266. 6749

Gregory, Hiram F., Jr., "The Black River Commercial Fisheries: A Study in Cultural Geography," *Louisiana Studies*, vol. 5, 1 (1966), pp. 3–36. 6750

Mancil, Ervin, "An Historical Geography of Industrial Cypress Lumbering in Louisiana," Ph.D. diss., Louisiana State University, 1972. 6751

Wicker, Karen, "The Development of the Louisiana Oyster Industry in the Nineteenth Century," Ph.D. diss., Louisiana State University, 1979. 6752

AGRICULTURE

Sugar

Foscue, Edwin J., and Elizabeth Troth, "Sugar Plantations of the Irish Bend District, Louisiana," *Economic Geography*, vol. 12, 4 (1936), pp. 373–381. [Focus on 1751–1935] 6753

Blume, Helmut, *Zuckerrohranbau am unteren Mississippi (Louisiana's Sugar Bowl)* (Regensburg: M. L. Kallmünz, Münchner Geographische Hefte, no. 5, 1954), 69 pp. 6754

Rehder, John B., "Sugar Plantation Settlements of Southern Louisiana: A Cultural Geography," Ph.D. diss., Louisiana State University, 1971. 6755

Rehder, John B., "Sugar Plantations in Louisiana: Origin, Dispersal, and Responsible Location Factors," *West Georgia College Studies in the Social Sciences*, vol. 12 (1973), pp. 78–93. 6756

Shea, Philip, "The Louisiana Sugar Cane Industry, 1751–1970: A Study in Geographical Relationships," Ph.D. diss., Michigan State University, 1974. 6757

Schmitz, Mark, "Farm Interdependence in the Antebellum Sugar Sector," *Agricultural History*, vol. 52, 1 (1978), pp. 93–103. 6758

Hilliard, Sam B., "Site Characteristics and Spatial Stability of the Louisiana Sugarcane Industry," *Agricultural History*, vol. 53, 1 (1979), pp. 254–269. 6759

Rehder, John B., "Sugar Plantations in Louisiana," *Proceedings of the Tall Timbers Ecology and Management Conference*, vol. 16 (Tallahassee: Tall Timbers Research Station, 1979), pp. 111–123. 6760

Gaiennie, Betty, "Sugarcane Retreats South," *Louisiana History*, vol. 25, 1 (1984), pp. 76–78. 6761

Rice

Lee, Chan, "The Culture History of Rice, with Special Reference to Louisiana," Ph.D. diss., Louisiana State University, 1960. 6762

Mitcham, Samuel W., Jr., "The Origin and Evolution of the Southwestern Louisiana Rice Region, 1880–1920," Ph.D. diss., University of Tennessee, 1986. **6763**

Other crops

Chatterton, Harry J., "The Development of the Pepper Industry of Louisiana," *Journal of Geography*, vol. 38, 9 (1939), pp. 364–369. **6764**

Aldrich, Courtney C., W. W. DeBlieus, and Fred B. Kniffen, "The Spanish Moss Industry of Louisiana," *Economic Geography*, vol. 19, 4 (1943), pp. 347–357. **6765**

Kniffen, Fred B., and Malcolm L. Comeaux, *The Spanish Moss Folk Industry of Louisiana* (Baton Rouge: Louisiana State University, Museum of Geoscience, Mélanges, no. 12, 1979), 19 pp. **6766**

Cattle

Post, Lauren C., "The Old Cattle Industry in Southwest Louisiana," *McNeese Review*, vol. 9 (1957), pp. 43–55. **6767**

Post, Lauren C., "Cattle Branding in Southwest Louisiana," *McNeese Review*, vol. 10 (1958), pp. 101–117. **6768**

LANDSCAPE

Kniffen, Fred B., "Louisiana House Types," *Annals of the Association of American Geographers*, vol. 26, 4 (1936), pp. 179–193. Reprinted in Philip L. Wagner and Marvin W. Mikesell, eds., *Readings in Cultural Geography* (Chicago: University of Chicago Press, 1962), pp. 157–169. **6769**

Kniffen, Fred B., "The Outdoor Oven in Louisiana," *Louisiana History*, vol. 1, 1 (1960), pp. 25–35. **6770**

Kniffen, Fred B., "The Physiognomy of Rural Louisiana," *Louisiana History*, vol. 4, 4 (1963), pp. 291–300. Reprinted in H. Jesse Walker and Milton B. Newton, Jr., eds., *Environment and Culture* (Baton Rouge: Louisiana State University, Department of Geography and Anthropology, 1978), pp. 199–204. **6771**

Newton, Milton B., Jr., *Louisiana House Types: A Field Guide* (Baton Rouge: Louisiana State University Museum of Geoscience, Mélanges, no. 2, 1971), 18 pp. **6772**

Newton, Milton B., Jr., and C. N. Raphael, "Relic Roads of East Feliciana Parish, Louisiana," *Geographical Review*, vol. 61, 2 (1971), pp. 250–264. **6773**

Pulliam, Linda, and Milton B. Newton, Jr., *Country and Small Town Stores of Louisiana: Legacy of the Greek Revival and the Frontier* (Baton Rouge: Louisiana State University Museum of Geoscience, Mélanges, no. 7, 1973), 11 pp. **6774**

Allen, Danny, "A Study of Landscape Changes in Ouachita Parish, Louisiana to 1832," Ed.D. diss., Oklahoma State University, 1974. **6775**

Rehder, John B., "Diagnostic Landscape Traits of Sugar Plantations in Southern Louisiana," in Sam B. Hilliard, ed., *Man and Environment in the Lower Mississippi Valley* (Baton Rouge: Louisiana State University School of Geoscience, Geoscience & Man, vol. 19, 1978), pp. 135–150. **6776**

Reilly, Timothy F., "Historical Architectural Survey of East St. Mary Parish," in Robert Gramling and E. F. Stallings, eds., *East St. Mary Parish: Economic Growth and Stabilization Strategies* (Baton Rouge: Louisiana Department of Natural Resources, Coastal Resources Section, 1980). **6777**

Fricker, Jonathan, "The Origins of the Creole Raised Plantation House," *Louisiana History*, vol. 25, 2 (1984), pp. 137–153. **6778**

Sechrist, Gail S., "Church Buildings Enter the Urban Age: A Louisiana Example of the Church in Settlement Geography," Ph.D. diss., Louisiana State University, 1986. **6779**

Edwards, Jay D., "The Origins of the Louisiana Creole Cottage," in Michael O. Roark, ed., *French and Germans in the Mississippi Valley: Landscape and Cultural Traditions* (Cape Girardeau: Southeast Missouri State University, Center for Regional History and Cultural Heritage, 1988), pp. 9–60. **6780**

Oszuscik, Phillippe, "The French Creole Cottage and Its Caribbean Connection," in Michael O. Roark, ed., *French and Germans in the Mississippi Valley: Landscape and Cultural Traditions* (Cape Girardeau: Southeast Missouri State University, Center for Regional History and Cultural Heritage, 1988), pp. 61–78. **6781**

Wegner, Mark, "French and Spanish Influence on the Architecture of American Settlers in Louisiana," in Michael O. Roark, ed., *French and Germans in the Mississippi Valley: Landscape and Cultural Traditions* (Cape Girardeau: Southeast Missouri State University, Century for Regional History and Cultural Heritage, 1988), pp. 79–97. **6782**

Comeaux, Malcolm L., "The Cajun Barn," *Geographical Review*, vol. 79, 1 (1989), pp. 47–62. **6783**

COMMUNICATIONS & TRADE

Roads and water transport

Keller, Josephine, "Early Roads in the Parishes of East and West Feliciana and East Baton

Rouge," Master's thesis, Louisiana State University, 1936.   6784

Gritzner, Charles F., "Louisiana Waterway Crossings," *Louisiana Studies*, vol. 2, 4 (1963), pp. 213–232.   6785

Comeaux, Malcolm L., "The Atchafalaya River Raft," *Louisiana Studies*, vol. 9 (1970), pp. 217–227.   6786

Newton, Milton B., Jr., "Route Geography and the Routes of St. Helena Parish, Louisiana," *Annals of the Association of American Geographers*, vol. 60, 1 (1970), pp. 134–152.   6787

Casey, Powell, "Military Roads in the Florida Parishes of Louisiana," *Louisiana History*, vol. 15, 3 (1974), pp. 229–242.   6788

Comeaux, Malcolm L., "Folk Boats of Louisiana," in Nicholas Spitzer, ed., *Louisiana Folklife: A Guide to the State* (Baton Rouge: Louisiana Folklife Program, Division of the Arts, 1985), pp. 160–178.   6789

Jeter, Katherine, "Norris Ferry Road," *North Louisiana Historical Society Quarterly*, vol. 18, 1 (1987), pp. 11–29.   6790

Railroads

Estaville, Lawrence E., "A Strategic Railroad: The New Orleans, Jackson, & Great Northern in the Civil War," *Louisiana History*, vol. 14, 2 (1973), pp. 117–136.   6791

Estaville, Lawrence E., "A Small Contribution: Louisiana's Short Rural Railroads in the Civil War," *Louisiana History*, vol. 18, 1 (1977), pp. 87–103.   6792

Estaville, Lawrence E., "North Louisiana's Strategic Railroad: The Vicksburg, Shreveport, & Texas in the Civil War," *North Louisiana Historical Association Journal*, vol. 9, 4 (1978), pp. 177–192.   6793

Estaville, Lawrence E., *Confederate Neckties: Louisiana Railroads in the Civil War* (Ruston: McGinty Publications, Louisiana Tech University, 1989), 123 pp.   6794

Telephone

Paskoff, Paul F., "The Areal Spread of a Systematic Innovation: The Case of the Telephone in Louisiana, 1898–1913," in Sam B. Hilliard, ed., *Man and Environment in the Lower Mississippi Valley* (Baton Rouge: Louisiana State University School of Geoscience, Geoscience & Man, vol. 19, 1978), pp. 101–109.   6795

TOWN GROWTH

Campbell, Edna F., "New Orleans in Early Days," *Geographical Review*, vol. 10, 1 (1920), pp. 31–36.   6796

Campbell, Edna F., "New Orleans at the Time of the Louisiana Purchase," *Geographical Review*, vol. 11, 3 (1921), pp. 414–425.   6797

Guardia, John E., "Historic Natchitoches, Louisiana: Its Two-Century Raison d'être," *Journal of Geography*, vol. 33, 1 (1934), pp. 1–9. Reprinted in George J. Miller, ed., *Human Geography Studies: The United States* (Bloomington, Ill.: McKnight & McKnight, Geographic Education Series, 1935), pp. 133–141.   6798

Brown, Harry B., Jr., "Port Hudson: A Study in Historical Geography," Master's thesis, Louisiana State University, 1936.   6799

Brill, Dieter, *Baton Rouge, Louisiana: Aufstieg, Funktionen und Gestalt einer jungen Großstadt des neuen Industriegebiets im unteren Mississippi* (Kiel: Schriften des Geographischen Instituts der Universität Kiel, vol. 21, 2, 1963), 287 pp.   6800

URBAN ECONOMIC STRUCTURE

See also 4661, 4663

Baker, Everett, "Changes in Sales and Service Foci in Natchitoches, Louisiana, between 1890 and 1920," Master's thesis, Northeastern State University of Louisiana, 1973.   6801

Sauder, Robert A., "Municipal Markets in New Orleans," *Journal of Cultural Geography*, vol. 2, 1 (1981), pp. 82–95.   6802

Sauder, Robert A., "The Origin and Spread of the Public Market System in New Orleans," *Louisiana History*, vol. 22, 3 (1981), pp. 281–297.   6803

URBAN SOCIAL STRUCTURE

Thouez, Jean-Pierre, "Historique du développement sociale et économique du 'Vieux Carré'," *Revue de Louisiane/Louisiana Review*, vol. 1, 2 (1972), pp. 78–95.   6804

Sechrist, Gail S., "Changes in the Location and Role of Louisiana's Urban Churches, 1865–1940," in Richard L. Nostrand and Sam B. Hilliard, eds., *The American South* (Baton Rouge: Louisiana State University School of Geoscience, Geoscience & Man, vol. 25, 1988), pp. 139–150.   6805

TOWNSCAPE

See also 1461

Lewis, Peirce F., *New Orleans: The Making of an Urban Landscape* (Cambridge, Mass.: Ballinger, 1976), 115 pp.   6806

Sauder, Robert A., "Architecture and Urban Growth in Nineteenth Century New Orleans,"

Southeastern Geographer, vol. 17, 2 (1977), pp. 93–107.   **6807**

Sauder, Robert A., "New Orleans' Nineteenth Century Townscape," in Richard H. Kesel and Robert A. Sauder, eds., *A Field Guidebook for Louisiana* (Washington, D.C.: Association of American Geographers, 1978), pp. 117–120. **6808**

RECREATION & TOURISM

Meyer-Arendt, Klaus J., "The Grand Isle, Louisiana, Resort Cycle," *Annals of Tourism Research*, vol. 12, 3 (1985), pp. 449–465. [Focus on 1811–1984]   **6809**

PLANNING

Sauder, Robert A., and Teresa A. Wilkinson, "Preservation Planning and Geographical Change in New Orleans' Vieux Carré," *Urban Geography*, vol. 10, 1 (1989), pp. 41–61.   **6810**

PLACE NAMES

Read, William A., *Louisiana Place-Names of Indian Origin* (Baton Rouge: Louisiana State University Bulletin, n.s. vol. 19, 2, 1927), 72 pp.   **6811**

Sternberg, Hilgard O., "The Names 'False River' and 'Pointe Loupee': An Inquiry in Historical Geography," *Louisiana Historical Quarterly*, vol. 31, 3 (1948), pp. 598–605.   **6812**

Parkerson, Codman, *Those Strange Louisiana Names* (Baton Rouge: Claitors Publishing Division, 1969), 22 pp.   **6813**

Detro, Randall A., "Generic Terms in Louisiana Place Names: An Index to the Cultural Landscape," Ph.D. diss., Louisiana State University, 1970.   **6814**

Detro, Randall A., "Louisiana Toponymic Generics Delimit Culture Areas," *Names*, vol. 32, 4 (1984), pp. 367–391.   **6815**

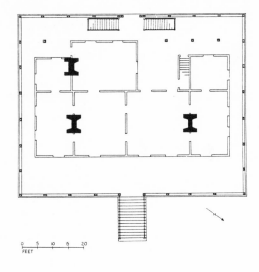

TEXAS

GENERAL

The state

Simonds, Frederic W., "Geographic Influences in the Development of Texas," *Journal of Geography*, vol. 10, 9 (1912), pp. 277–284.   6816

Shuler, Ellis N., "The Influence of the Shoreline, Rivers, and Springs on the Settlements and Early Development of Texas," *Texas Geographic Magazine*, vol. 4, 1 (Autumn 1940), pp. 26–31.   6817

Davenport, Harbert, "Geographic Notes on Spanish Texas: El Orcoquisac and Los Horconsitos," *Southwest Historical Quarterly*, vol. 50, 4 (1947), pp. 489–492.   6818

Meinig, Donald W., *Imperial Texas: An Interpretive Essay in Cultural Geography* (Austin: University of Texas Press, 1969), 145 pp.   6819

Smaller areas

Chambers, William T., "Lower Rio Grande Valley of Texas," *Economic Geography*, vol. 6, 4 (1930), pp. 364–373.   6820

Foscue, Edwin J., "Historical Geography of the Lower Rio Grande Valley of Texas," *Texas Geographic Magazine*, vol. 3, 1 (Spring 1939), pp. 1–15.   6821

Chambers, William T., "The Redlands of Central Eastern Texas," *Texas Geographic Magazine*, vol. 5, 2 (1941), pp. 1–15.   6822

White, Wayne R., "The Historical Geography of Marion County, Texas, 1830–1890: An Example from the Era of Steamboat Navigation on Inland Waters," Master's thesis, University of Texas, 1964.   6823

ENVIRONMENTAL CHANGE

Collier, Gerald L., "The Evolving East Texas Woodland," Ph.D. diss., University of Nebraska–Lincoln, 1964.   6824

Bryant, Vaughn M., and Robert K. Holz, "The Role of Pollen in the Reconstruction of Past Environments," *Pennsylvania Geographer*, vol. 6, 1 (1968), pp. 11–19. [Focus on southwest Texas]   6825

Schmid, James A., Jr., "The Wild Landscape of the Edwards Plateau of South Central Texas: A Study in Developing Livelihood Patterns and Ecological Change," Master's thesis, University of Chicago, 1969.   6826

Doughty, Robin W., *Wildlife and Man in Texas: Environmental Change and Conservation* (College Station: Texas A & M University Press, 1983), 246 pp.   6827

Cotter, John V., "Mosquitoes and Disease in the Lower Rio Grande Valley, 1846–1946," Ph.D. diss., University of Texas–Austin, 1986.   6828

Doughty, Robin W., "Settlement and Environmental Change in Texas, 1820–1900," *Southwestern Historical Quarterly*, vol. 89, 4 (1986), pp. 423–442.   6829

Frederick, Charles D., "An Investigation into the Paleoenvironmental History of the Austin Mastodon Site," Master's thesis, University of Texas–Austin, 1987.   6830

NATIVE PEOPLES & WHITE RELATIONS

Bryan, Kirk, "Stone Cultures near Cerro Pedernal and Their Geological Antiquity," *Texas Archaeological and Palinological Society Bulletin*, vol. 11 (1939), pp. 9–42.   6831

Ricklis, Robert A., "Historical Cultural Ecology of the Karankawan Indians of the Central Texas Coast: A Case Study of the Roots of Adaptive Change," Ph.D. diss., University of Texas–Austin, 1990.   6832

EXPLORATION & MAPPING

See also 8916

Ledbetter, Nan Thompson, "Three Generations of Texas Topographers," *Southwest Historical Quarterly*, vol. 64, 3 (Jan. 1961), pp. 384–387.   6833

Martin, Robert S., "Maps of an *Empresario*: Austin's Contribution to the Cartography of Texas," *Southwestern Historical Quarterly*, vol. 85, 4 (1982), pp. 371–400.   6834

Jackson, Jack, Robert S. Weddle, and Winston DeVille, *Mapping Texas and the Gulf Coast: The Contributions of Saint-Denis, Oliván, and LeMaire* (College Station: Texas A & M University Press, 1990), 92 pp.   6835

POPULAR IMAGES & EVALUATION

Krug, Vincenz F., "Early Contemporary Description and Concepts of the Geography of Texas," Master's thesis, University of Kansas, 1966.   6836

Jordan, Terry G., "Pioneer Evaluation of Vegetation in Frontier Texas," *Southwestern Historical Quarterly*, vol. 76, 3 (1973), pp. 233–254.   6837

Jordan, Terry G., "Vegetational Perception and Choice of Settlement Site in Frontier Texas," in Ralph E. Ehrenberg, ed., *Pattern and Process: Research in Historical Geography* (Washington, D.C.: Howard University Press, 1975), pp. 244–257. **6838**

Doughty, Robin W., *At Home in Texas: Early Views of the Land* (College Station: Texas A & M University Press, 1987), 164 pp. **6839**

REGIONAL SETTLEMENT

See also **5876**

Smith, Harriet, "Geographic Influences in the History of the Settlement of Black Prairie in Texas," *Journal of Geography*, vol. 19, 8 (1920), pp. 287–294. **6840**

Castañeda, Carlos E., "First European Settlement on the Rio Grande," *Texas Geographic Magazine*, vol. 9, 2 (1945), pp. 28–31. **6841**

Mitchell, Charles H., "The Role of Water in the Settlement of the Llano Estacado," Master's thesis, University of Texas, 1960. **6842**

Harris, Robert L., "The Panhandle Plains of Texas: A Study in Sequent Occupance," Master's thesis, University of Arkansas, 1962. **6843**

Jordan, Terry G., "Between the Forest and the Prairie," *Agricultural History*, vol. 38, 4 (1964), pp. 205–216. Reprinted, with omissions, in David Ward, ed., *Geographic Perspectives on America's Past: Readings on the Historical Geography of the United States* (New York: Oxford University Press, 1979), pp. 50–60. **6844**

Jordan, Terry G., "The Imprint of the Upper and Lower South on Mid-Nineteenth Century Texas," *Annals of the Association of American Geographers*, vol. 57, 4 (1967), pp. 667–690. Reprinted, with omissions, in David Ward, ed., *Geographic Perspectives on America's Past: Readings on the Historical Geography of the United States* (New York: Oxford University Press, 1979), pp. 210–226. **6845**

Jordan, Terry G., "The German Settlement of Texas after 1865," *Southwestern Historical Quarterly*, vol. 73, 2 (1969), pp. 193–212. **6846**

Hannaford, Jean T., "The Cultural Impact of European Settlement in Central Texas," Master's thesis, University of Texas, 1970. **6847**

Green, D. Brooks, "Agricultural Settlement: The Drylands," *Association of American Geographers Field Trip Guide, San Antonio, Texas* (1983), pp. 34–39. **6848**

POPULATION

Lathrop, Barnes F., *Migration into East Texas, 1835–1860: A Study from the United States Census* (Austin: Texas State Historical Association, 1949), 114 pp. **6849**

Grimes, Jeanne J., "One Hundred Years of Population Expansion in Texas: 1850–1950," Master's thesis, Southern Methodist University, 1953. **6850**

Gallaway, B. P., "Population Trends in the Western Cross Timbers of Texas, 1890–1960: Growth and Distribution," *Southwestern Historical Quarterly*, vol. 65, 3 (1962), pp. 333–347. **6851**

Jordan, Terry G., "The Pattern of Origins of the Adelsverein German Colonists," *Texana*, vol. 6 (1968), pp. 245–257. **6852**

Jordan, Terry G., "Population Origins in Texas, 1850," *Geographical Review*, vol. 59, 1 (1969), pp. 83–103. **6853**

Jordan, Terry G., "The German Element in Texas: An Overview," *Rice University Studies*, vol. 63 (1977), pp. 1–11. **6854**

Spillman, Robert C., "A Historical Geography of Mexican American Population Patterns in the South Texas Hispanic Borderland: 1850–1970," Master's thesis, University of Southern Mississippi, 1977. **6855**

Davidson, Claud M., "Population and Urban Growth on the Texas South Plains," *Ecumene*, vol. 11 (1979), pp. 12–27. **6856**

Spillman, Robert C., "Hispanic Population Patterns in Southern Texas, 1850–1970," Syracuse University Department of Geography Discussion Paper no. 57 (1979), 34 pp. **6857**

Jordan, Terry G., *Immigration to Texas* (Boston: American Press, 1980), 39 pp. Reprinted in Cary D. Wintz, ed., *Readings in Texas History* (Boston: American Press, 1983), pp. 93–130. **6858**

Jordan, Terry G., "The 1887 Census of Texas' Hispanic Population," *Aztlan*, vol. 12, 2 (1981), pp. 271–278. **6859**

Jordan, Terry G., "The Forgotten Texas State Census of 1887," *Southwestern Historical Quarterly*, vol. 85, 4 (1982), pp. 401–408. **6860**

Marner, Magnus, "Swedish Migrants to Texas," *Swedish-American Historical Quarterly*, vol. 38, 2 (1987), pp. 49–74. **6861**

RURAL & REGIONAL SOCIAL GEOGRAPHY

General

Jordan, Terry G., "Forest Folk, Prairie Folk: Rural Religious Cultures in North Texas," *Southwestern Historical Quarterly*, vol. 80, 2 (1976), pp. 135–162. **6862**

Jordan, Terry G., John Bean, and William Holmes, "Confluence of Cultures," in their *Texas: A Ge-*

ography (Boulder: Westview Press, 1984), pp.
69–94.   **6863**

Jordan, Terry G., "A Century and a Half of Ethnic
Change in Texas, 1836–1986," *Southwestern His-
torical Quarterly*, vol. 89, 4 (1986), pp. 385–417.
Reprinted in Ralph Wooster and Robert
Calvert, eds., *Texas Vistas* (Austin: Texas State
Historical Association, 1987), pp. 319–352.   **6864**

Jordan, Terry G., "Germans and Blacks in Texas,"
in Randall M. Miller, ed., *States of Progress:
Germans and Blacks in America over Three
HundredYears: Lectures from the Tricentennial
of the Germantown Protest against Slavery*
(Philadelphia: German Society of Pennsylvania,
1989), pp. 89–97.   **6865**

Germans

Jordan, Terry G., "The German Element of Gillespie County, Texas," Master's thesis, University
of Texas, 1961.   **6866**

Jordan, Terry G., "A Geographical Appraisal of
the Significance of German Settlement in
Nineteenth-Century Texas Agriculture," Ph.D.
diss., University of Wisconsin–Madison, 1965.
                                                        6867

Jordan, Terry G., *German Seed in Texas Soil: Immigrant Farmers in Nineteenth Century Texas*
(Austin: University of Texas Press, 1966), 237 pp.
                                                        6868

Wilhelm, Hubert G. H., "Organized German Settlement and Its Effects on the Frontier of South-
Central Texas," Ph.D. diss., Louisiana State University, 1968.   **6869**

Jordan, Terry G., "The Old World Antecedents of
the Fredericksburg Easter Fires," in Frances E.
Abernathy, ed., *The Folklore of Texan Cultures*
(Austin: Encino Press, 1974), pp. 151–154.   **6870**

Jordan, Terry G., "A Religious Geography of the
Hill Country Germans of Texas," in Frederick C.
Luebke, ed., *Ethnicity on the Great Plains*
(Lincoln: University of Nebraska Press, 1980),
pp. 109–128.   **6871**

Wilhelm, Hubert G. H., *Organized German Settlement and Its Effects on the Frontier of South-
Central Texas* (New York: Arno Press, 1980), 237
pp.   **6872**

Other groups

Nelson, Helge M. O., "Svenskar och svenskbygder; Texas," *Svensk geografisk årsbok*, vol. 15
(1939), pp. 67–99.   **6873**

Starczewska, Maria, "The Historical Geography of
the Oldest Polish Settlement in the United
States," *Polish Review*, vol. 12 (1967), pp. 11–40.
[Panna Maria, Karnes Co.]   **6874**

POLITICAL & ADMINISTRATIVE
GEOGRAPHY

Dillman, C. Daniel, "The Relationship of Early
Settlement on the Gulf Coastal Plain to the Use
of Rivers as County Boundaries in Texas," *Papers of the Michigan Academy of Science, Arts,
and Letters*, vol. 47 (1962), pp. 429–436.   **6875**

McKee, Jesse O., "The Rio Grande: The Political
Geography of a River Boundary," *Southern
Quarterly*, vol. 4, 1 (1965), pp. 29–40.   **6876**

Stephenson, Richard W., "The Mapping of the
Northwest Boundary of Texas, 1859–1860," *Terrae Incognitae*, vol. 6 (1974), pp. 39–50.   **6877**

ECONOMIC DEVELOPMENT

Jordan, Terry G., "The Texan Appalachia," *Annals
of the Association of American Geographers*,
vol. 60, 3 (1970), pp. 409–427.   **6878**

RESOURCE MANAGEMENT

Templer, Otis W., "Texas Surface Water Law: The
Legacy of the Past and Its Impact on Water Resource Management," *Historical Geography*,
vol. 8, 1 (1978), pp. 11–20.   **6879**

Doughty, Robin W., "Wildlife Conservation in
Late Nineteenth Century Texas: The Carp Experiment," *Southwestern Historical Quarterly*,
vol. 84, 2 (1980), pp. 169–196.   **6880**

Doughty, Robin W., and Larry L. Smith, "The
Nine-Banded Armadillo in Texas and the
South," *Journal of Cultural Geography*, vol. 2, 1
(1981), pp. 120–130.   **6881**

LAND & LAND USE

Land survey

Jordan, Terry G., "Antecedents of the Long-Lot in
Texas," *Annals of the Association of American
Geographers*, vol. 64, 1 (1974), pp. 70–86. **6882**

Jordan, Terry G., "Land Survey Patterns in Texas,"
in R. C. Eidt, Kashi N. Singh, and Rana P. B.
Singh, eds., *Man, Culture, and Settlement:
Festschrift to Professor R. L. Singh* (New Delhi:
Kalyani Publishers, 1977), pp. 141–146.   **6883**

Land use

Foscue, Edwin J., "Land Utilization in the Lower
Rio Grande Valley of Texas," *Economic Geography*, vol. 8, 1 (1932), pp. 1–11.   **6884**

Strong, Helen M., "A Land Use Record in the
Blackland Prairies of Texas," *Annals of the Association of American Geographers*, vol. 28, 2
(1938), pp. 128–136.   **6885**

Barnett, Sarah C., "Land Utilization and Sequent Occupance Description of Mesquite, Texas," Master's thesis, Southern Methodist University, 1967. **6886**

EXTRACTIVE ACTIVITY

Doughty, Robin W., "Sea Turtles in Texas: A Forgotten Commerce," *Southwestern Historical Quarterly*, vol. 88, 1 (1984), pp. 43–70. **6887**

AGRICULTURE

See also **5978**

Cultivation

Foscue, Edwin J., "Agricultural Geography of the Lower Rio Grande Valley of Texas," Ph.D. diss., Clark University, 1931. **6888**

Foscue, Edwin J., "Agricultural History of the Lower Rio Grande Valley Region," *Agricultural History*, vol. 8, 3 (1934), pp. 124–137. **6889**

Glick, Thomas F., *The Old World Background of the Irrigation System of San Antonio, Texas* (El Paso: Texas Western Press, 1972), 67 pp. **6890**

Holmes, William M., "An Historical Geography of Dry Farming on the Northern High Plains of Texas," Ph.D. diss., University of Texas–Austin, 1975. **6891**

Ranching

Jordan, Terry G., "The Origin of Anglo-American Cattle Ranching in Texas: A Documentation of Diffusion from the Lower South," *Economic Geography*, vol. 45, 1 (1969), pp. 63–87. **6892**

Jordan, Terry G., "Texas Influence in Nineteenth-Century Arizona Cattle Ranching," *Journal of the West*, vol. 14, 3 (1975), pp. 15–18. **6893**

Jordan, Terry G., "Early Northeast Texas and the Evolution of Western Ranching," *Annals of the Association of American Geographers*, vol. 67, 1 (1977), pp. 66–87. **6894**

LANDSCAPE

General

Schroeder, Klaus, "Spanische Einflüsse in der formalen Struktur der Kulturlandschaft des südlichsten Texas," in Julius Büdel and Horst Mensching, eds., *Verhandlungen des Deutschen Geographentages, Würzburg, 1957* (Wiesbaden: Franz Steiner, 1958), pp. 441–447. **6895**

Newton, Ada, "The Anglo-Irish House of the Rio Grande," *Pioneer America*, vol. 5, 1 (1973), pp. 33–38. **6896**

Jackson, John Brinckerhoff, *The Southern Landscape Tradition in Texas* (Forth Worth: Amon Carter Museum, 1980), 44 pp. **6897**

Hugill, Peter J., et al., "The Texas Golden Triangle," *Field Trip Guide, Association of American Geographers, Annual Meeting at San Antonio* (Washington, D.C.: Association of American Geographers, 1982), pp. 26–41. **6898**

Log buildings

Jordan, Terry G., "Log Construction in the East Cross Timbers of Texas," *Proceedings of the Pioneer America Society*, vol. 2 (1973), pp. 107–124. **6899**

Jordan, Terry G., "Log Corner-Timbering in Texas," *Pioneer America*, vol. 8, 1 (1976), pp. 8–18. **6900**

Jordan, Terry G., *Texas Log Buildings: A Folk Architecture* (Austin: University of Texas Press, 1978), 230 pp. **6901**

Jordan, Terry G., "Log Corner Notching in Texas," in Francis E. Abernathy, ed., *Built in Texas* (Waco: E-Heart Press and Texas Folklore Society, 1979), pp. 78–83. **6902**

Jordan, Terry G., et al., *Log Cabin Village: A History and Guide* (Austin: Texas State Historical Association, 1980), 146 pp. **6903**

Jordan, Terry G., "The Texas Log House and Barn," *Proceedings, Texana 1: The Frontier* (Austin: Texas Historical Commission, 1983), pp. 37–39. **6904**

German houses

Jordan, Terry G., "German Houses in Texas," *Landscape*, vol. 14 (1964), pp. 24–26. [Emphasis on the 1850s] **6905**

Wilhelm, Hubert G. H., "German Settlement and Folk Building Practices in the Hill Country of Texas," *Pioneer America*, vol. 3, 2 (1971), pp. 15–24. **6906**

Jordan, Terry G., "A Russian-German Folk House in North Texas," in Francis E. Abernathy, ed., *Built in Texas* (Waco: E-Heart Press Texas Folklore Society, 1979), pp. 136–138. **6907**

Jordan, Terry G., "German Folk Houses in the Texas Hill Country," in G. Lick and D. B. Reeves, eds., *German Culture in Texas: A Free Earth: Essays from the 1978 Southwest Symposium* (Boston: Twayne, 1980), pp. 103–120. **6908**

Jordan, Terry G., "The Hill Country Germans of Texas," *Association of American Geographers Field Trip Guide* (Washington, D.C.: Association of American Geographers, 1982), pp. 94–115. **6909**

Other features

Jordan, Terry G., "Windmills in Texas," *Agricultural History*, vol. 37, 2 (1963), pp. 80–85. 6910

Jordan, Terry G., "The Traditional Southern Rural Chapel in Texas," *Ecumene*, vol. 8 (1976), pp. 6–17. 6911

Jordan, Terry G., "'The Roses So Red and the Lillies So Fair': Southern Folk Cemeteries in Texas," *Southwestern Historical Quarterly*, vol. 83, 3 (1980), pp. 227–258. 6912

Jordan, Terry G., "A Forebay Bank Barn in Texas," *Pennsylvania Folklife*, vol. 30, 2 (1980–1981), pp. 72–77. 6913

Jordan, Terry G., *Texas Graveyards: A Cultural Legacy* (Austin: University of Texas Press, 1982), 147 pp. 6914

Jordan, Terry G., "A Gabled Folk House of the Mexico-Texas Borderland," *Yearbook of the Conference of Latin Americanist Geographers*, vol. 14 (1988), pp. 2–6. 6915

COMMUNICATIONS & TRADE

See also 4522, 8435

Richardson, Thomas C., "Cattle Trade of Texas," *Texas Geographic Magazine*, vol. 1, 2 (1937), pp. 16–29. 6916

Brown, Ralph Hall, "Texas Cattle Trails," *Texas Geographic Magazine*, vol. 10, 1 (1946), pp. 1–6. 6917

Williams, J. W., "The Butterfield Overland Mail Road across Texas," *Southwestern Historical Quarterly*, vol. 61, 1 (1957), pp. 1–19. 6918

Doran, Edwin B., Jr.,, "Shell Roads in Texas," *Geographical Review*, vol. 55, 2 (1965), pp. 23–240. [Emphasis on 1912–1963] 6919

Glasmeier, Amy, "The Role of Merchant Wholesalers in Industrial Agglomeration Formation," *Annals of the Association of American Geographers*, vol. 80, 3 (1990), pp. 394–417. [Focus on Austin, 1950–1988] 6920

MANUFACTURING & INDUSTRIALIZATION

Doerr, Arthur H., "The Origin and Development of the Lone Star Iron and Steel Works," *Proceedings of the Oklahoma Academy of Science for 1953*, vol. 34 (1955), pp. 238–239. 6921

Gierloff-Emden, Hans G., "Die Industrialisierung im Bereich der Golfküste von Texas," in Herbert Wilhelmy and Karl H. Schröder, eds., *Verhandlungen des Deutscher Geographentages Hamburg 1955* (Wiesbaden: Franz Steiner, 1957), pp. 423–431. [Focus on 1900–1950] 6922

Davidson, Claud M., "The Pattern and Evolution of the Wood-Pulp Industry in Texas," Master's thesis, University of Texas, 1966. 6923

URBAN NETWORKS & URBANIZATION

Hannemann, Max, *Die Seehäfen von Texas: Ihre geographischen Grundlagen, ihre Entwicklung und Bedeutung* (Frankfurt: Frankfurter Geographische Hefte, vol. 2, 1, 1928), 270 pp. [Emphasis on 1900–1925] 6924

Geiser, Samuel W., "Ghost-Towns and Lost Towns of Texas, 1840–1880," *Texas Geographic Magazine*, vol. 8, 1 (1944), pp. 9–20. 6925

TOWN GROWTH

Chambers, William T., "Kilgore, Texas: An Oil Boom Town," *Economic Geography*, vol. 9, 1 (1933), pp. 72–84. 6926

Foscue, Edwin J., "The Growth of Dallas, 1850–1930," *Field & Laboratory*, vol. 4 (1935), pp. 16–18. 6927

Grime, Sarah L., "El Paso: The Gateway," *Journal of Geography*, vol. 34, 9 (1935), pp. 364–369. 6928

Floyd, Willie M., "Thurber, Texas: An Abandoned Coal Field Town," *Texas Geographic Magazine*, vol. 3, 2 (1939), pp. 1–21. 6929

Chambers, William T., "San Antonio, Texas," *Economic Geography*, vol. 16, 3 (1940), pp. 291–298. 6930

Dillman, C. Daniel, "Occupance Phases of the Lower Rio Grande of Texas and Tamaulipas," *California Geographer*, vol. 12 (1971), pp. 30–37. [Focus on the twin cities of Brownsville-Matamoros] 6931

McMillan, Frank, "Calvert: An Historical Geography," Master's thesis, Texas A & M University, 1984. 6932

URBAN SOCIAL STRUCTURE

Manaster, Jane, "The Ethnic Geography of Austin, Texas, 1875–1910," Master's thesis, University of Texas–Austin, 1986. 6933

Arreola, Daniel D., "The Mexican American Cultural Capital," *Geographical Review*, vol. 77, 1 (1987), pp. 17–34. [San Antonio] 6934

McDonald, Darrel L., "The Historical Cultural Plant Geography of Urbanized Galveston: Implications of Gardening on a Subtropical Barrier Island," Ph.D. diss., Texas A & M University, 1989. 6935

TOWNSCAPE

Shannon, Susan K., "A Residential Age Structure Model Based on U.S. Building Cycles: 1890–

1969: An Examination and Test of the Adams Model in Dallas, Texas," Master's thesis, Indiana University, 1977.   6936

Hugill, Peter J., and Daryl L. Engel, "Historical San Antonio," *Field Trip Guide, Association of American Geographers, Annual Meeting at San Antonio* (Washington, D.C.: Association of American Geographers, 1982), pp. 83–93.   6937

Foote, Kenneth E., "Velocities of Change of a Built Environment, 1880–1980," *Urban Geography*, vol. 6, 3 (1985), pp. 220–245. [Austin]   6938

RECREATION & TOURISM

Valenza, Janet, "'Taking the Waters' at Texas Spas," *Journal of Cultural Geography*, vol. 11, 1 (1990), pp. 57–70.   6939

PLANNING

Williams, Cecil A., "A Geographic Analysis of the New Deal Rural Resettlement Communities of

Texas," Ph.D. diss., University of Oklahoma, 1973.   6940

PLACE NAMES

Fulmore, Zachary T., *The History and Geography of Texas as Told in County Names* (Austin: E. L. Steck, 1915), 312 pp.   6941

Jordan, Terry G., "The Origin of 'Motte' and 'Island' in Texan Vegetational Terminology," *Southern Folklore Quarterly*, vol. 36, 2 (1972), pp. 121–135.   6942

Jordan, Terry G., "The Origin of 'Motte' in Anglo-Texas Vegetational Terminology," in J. L. Dillard, ed., *Perspectives on American English* (The Hague: Mouton, 1980), pp. 163–173.   6943

Diem, John, "The Place-Names of Brazos County, Texas: 1821–1880," Master's thesis, Texas A & M University, 1981.   6944

THE EASTERN INTERIOR

(INCLUDING THE OHIO VALLEY)

EXPLORATION & MAPPING

Brown, Lloyd A., "Early Map Makers of the Ohio Valley," *Western Pennsylvania Historical Magazine*, vol. 43, 3 (1960), pp. 239–250.   6945

POPULAR IMAGES & EVALUATION

Jakle, John A., *Images of the Ohio Valley: A Historical Geography of Travel, 1740 to 1860* (New York: Oxford University Press, 1977), 217 pp. 6946

Jakle, John A., "Social Stereotypes and Place Images: People on the Transappalachian Frontier as Viewed by Travelers," in Leo Zonn, ed., *Place Images in the Media: Portrayal, Experience, and Meaning* (Totowa, N.J.: Rowman & Littlefield, 1990), pp. 83–104.   6947

REGIONAL SETTLEMENT

See also 1321

Wunderlich, Erich, "Die geographischen Grundlagen der Innerkolonisation in den Vereinigten Staaten," *Memorial Volume of the Transcontinental Excursion of 1912 of the American Geographical Society of New York* (New York: American Geographical Society, 1915), pp. 115–124.   6948

Jakle, John A., "Salt and the Initial Settlement of the Ohio Valley," Ph.D. diss., Indiana University, 1967.   6949

Jakle, John A., "Salt on the Ohio Valley Frontier, 1770–1820," *Annals of the Association of American Geographers*, vol. 59, 4 (1969), pp. 687–709.   6950

RURAL & REGIONAL SOCIAL GEOGRAPHY

Price, Edward T., "The Mixed-Blood Racial Strain of Carmel, Ohio, and Magoffin County, Kentucky," *Ohio Journal of Science*, vol. 50 (1951), pp. 281–290.   6951

Evans, E. Estyn, "The Scotch-Irish: Their Cultural Adaptation and Heritage in the American Old West," in E. R. R. Green, ed., *Essays in Scotch-Irish History* (London: Routledge & Kegan Paul, 1969), pp. 69–86.   6952

Welch, Richard W., "The Assimilation of an Ethnic Group in the German-Jewish Peddlers of the Upper Ohio Valley, 1790–1840: A Study in Historical Geography," Master's thesis, Michigan State University, 1972.   6953

ECONOMIC DEVELOPMENT

Hiatt, Frederick W., "The Ohio River as a Factor in the Early Development of the Eastern Interior," Master's thesis, University of Chicago, 1915.   6954

Earle, Carville V., "Regional Economic Development West of the Appalachians, 1815–1860," in Robert D. Mitchell and Paul A. Groves, eds., *North America: The Historical Geography of a Changing Continent* (Totowa, N.J.: Rowman & Littlefield, 1987), pp. 172–197.   6955

RESOURCE MANAGEMENT

Jakle, John A., "The American Bison and the Human Occupance of the Ohio Valley," *Proceedings of the American Philosophical Society*, vol. 112 (1968), pp. 299–305.   6956

EXTRACTIVE ACTIVITY

Roepke, Howard G., "Changing Pattern of Coal Production in the Eastern Interior Field," *Economic Geography*, vol. 31, 3 (1955), pp. 234–247. [Focus on 1885–1952]   6957

AGRICULTURE

Baker, Oliver E., "Agricultural Regions of North America: Part III—The Middle Country, Where South Meets North," *Economic Geography*, vol. 3, 3 (1927), pp. 309–339.   6958

Henlein, Paul C., "Shifting Range-Feeder Patterns in the Ohio Valley before 1860," *Agricultural History*, vol. 31 (1957), pp. 1–12.   6959

COMMUNICATIONS & TRADE

Turrentine, Haywood, "An Historical Examination of an Evolving Road Network: A Case Study of the Ohio Valley, 1750–1815," Master's thesis, University of Cincinnati, 1974.   6960

MANUFACTURING & INDUSTRIALIZATION

Harrison, Lucia, "The Salt Industry as a Factor in the History of the Interior to 1865," Master's thesis, University of Chicago, 1919.   6961

Gillenwater, Mack H., "The History of the Hanging Rock and Eastern Kentucky Ironmaking

Industry," Master's thesis, Marshall University, 1958.   **6962**

PLACE NAMES

Finnie, W. Bruce, "Ohio Valley Localisms: Topographical Terms, 1750–1800," *American Speech*, vol. 38, 3 (1963), pp. 178–187.   **6963**

Jakle, John A., "Salt-Derived Place Names in the Ohio Valley," *Names*, vol. 16 (1968), pp. 1–5. **6964**

Finnie, W. Bruce, *Topographic Terms in the Ohio Valley, 1748–1800* (University: University of Alabama Press, Publications of the American Dialect Society, no. 53, 1970), 119 pp.   **6965**

THE MISSISSIPPI VALLEY

GENERAL

Emerson, Frederick V., "Geographic Influences in the Mississippi Valley," *Proceedings of the Mississippi Valley Historical Association for the Year 1914–1915*, vol. 8 (1915), pp. 289–296. **6966**

Lukermann, Fred E., "The Meeting Ground of Three Cultures," in special issue on "The River: Images of the Mississippi," *Design Quarterly*, vols. 101, 102 (1976), pp. 18–19. [Covers 1810–1880] **6967**

Hudson, John C., "The Midland Prairies: Natural Resources and Urban Settlement," in P. Larson, ed., *The Spirit of H. H. Richardson on the Midland Prairies* (Ames: Iowa State University Press, 1988), pp. 122–137. **6968**

ENVIRONMENTAL CHANGE

Deckert, Emil, "Veränderungen des Mississippilaufes und des Mississippideltas," *Geographische Zeitschrift*, vol. 2, 10 (1896), pp. 587–588. [Focus on 1765–1887] **6969**

Stevens, M. A., Daryl B. Simons, and Stanley A. Schumm, "Man-Induced Changes of the Middle Mississippi River," *Proceedings of the American Society of Civil Engineers, Journal of Waterways Division*, vol. 101, WW2 (1975), pp. 119–133. **6970**

NATIVE PEOPLES & WHITE RELATIONS

See also **1199**

Robertson, D. A., "The Prehistoric Inhabitants of the Mississippi Valley, Part 1: The Mound Builders," *Journal of the American Geographical Society*, vol. 5 (1874), pp. 256–272. **6971**

Carter, George F., "The Distribution of Races of Maize among the Indians of the Mississippi Valley," *Transactions of the New York Academy of Sciences*, 2d ser., vol. 9 (1947), pp. 268–269. **6972**

EXPLORATION & MAPPING

Reed, Susan M., "British Cartography of the Mississippi Valley in the Eighteenth Century," *Mississippi Valley Historical Review*, vol. 2, 2 (1915), pp. 213–224. **6973**

Delanglez, Jean, "The Jolliet Lost Map of the Mississippi," *Middle America*, vol. 28 (1946), pp. 130–139. **6974**

Delanglez, Jean, "The Cartography of the Mississippi: Part I—The Maps of Coronelli"; "Part II—LaSalle and the Mississippi," *Mid-America*, vol. 30, 2 (1948), pp. 257–284; and vol. 31, 1 (1949), pp. 29–52. **6975**

DeVorsey, Louis, Jr., "The Impact of the La Salle Expedition of 1682 on European Cartography," in Patricia Galloway, ed., *La Salle and His Legacy: Frenchmen and Indians in the Lower Mississippi* (Jackson: University Press of Mississippi, 1982), pp. 60–76. **6976**

Wood, W. Raymond, "Nicholas de Finiels: Mapping the Mississippi and Missouri Rivers, 1797–1798," *Missouri Historical Review*, vol. 81, 4 (1987), pp. 387–402. **6977**

DeVorsey, Louis, Jr., "La Salle's Cartography of the Lower Mississippi River," in Richard L. Nostrand and Sam B. Hilliard, eds., *The American South* (Baton Rouge: Louisiana State University School of Geoscience, Geoscience & Man, vol. 25, 1988), pp. 5–24. **6978**

REGIONAL SETTLEMENT

Thoman, Richard S., *The Changing Occupance Pattern of the Tri-State Area, Missouri, Kansas, and Oklahoma* (Chicago: University of Chicago Department of Geography, Research Paper no. 31, 1953), 139 pp. **6979**

Birch, Brian P., "Farmstead Settlement in the North American Corn Belt," *Southampton Research Series in Geography*, vol. 3 (1966), pp. 25–57. **6980**

Kniffen, Fred B., "The Lower Mississippi Valley: European Settlement, Utilization, and Modification," in H. Jesse Walker and Randall A. Detro, eds., *Cultural Diffusion and Landscapes: Selections by Fred B. Kniffen* (Baton Rouge: Louisiana State University Geoscience Publications, Geoscience & Man, vol. 27, 1990), pp. 3–34. **6981**

POPULATION

Thompson, Ian B., "The Genesis of the Population Structure of the Corn Belt," *Tijdschrift voor economische en sociale geografie*, vol. 54, 5 (1963), pp. 106–110. **6982**

Hart, John Fraser, "The Spread of the Frontier and the Growth of Population," in H. Jesse Walker and William G. Haag, eds., *Man and Cultural Heritage: Papers in Honor of Fred B. Kniffen*

(Baton Rouge: Louisiana State University School of Geoscience, Geoscience & Man, vol. 5, 1974), pp. 73–82.   **6983**

RURAL & REGIONAL SOCIAL GEOGRAPHY

Sauer, Carl O., "Homestead and Community on the Middle Border," edited version published in *Landscape*, vol. 12, 1 (1962), pp. 3–7; reprinted in John Leighly, ed., *Land and Life: A Selection from the Writings of Carl Ortwin Sauer* (Berkeley: University of California Press, 1963), pp. 32–41. Full version published in Howard W. Ottoson, ed., *Land Use Policy in the United States* (Lincoln: University of Nebraska Press, 1963), pp. 65-85; reprinted in Paul W. English and Robert C. Mayfield, eds., *Man, Space, and Environment: Concepts in Contemporary Human Geography* (New York: Oxford University Press, 1972), pp. 15–28; and in Carl O. Sauer, *Selected Essays, 1963–1975*, ed. Bob Callahan (Berkeley, Calif.: Turtle Island Foundation, for the Netzahaulcoyotl Historical Society, 1981), pp. 57–77.   **6984**

POLITICAL & ADMINISTRATIVE GEOGRAPHY

Bowman, Isaiah, "An American Boundary Dispute: Decision of the Supreme Court of the United States with Respect to the Texas-Oklahoma Boundary," *Geographical Review*, vol. 13, 2 (1923), pp. 161–189.   **6985**

ECONOMIC DEVELOPMENT

Adams, Russell B., "A Changing Economy," in special issue on "The River: Images of the Mississippi," *Design Quarterly*, vols. 101, 102 (1976), pp. 22–23. [Focus on the twentieth century]   **6986**

Knotwell, James O., "An Analysis of Change in Farmland Values from 1959–1982 in Missouri, Iowa, and Illinois," Master's thesis, Western Illinois University, 1989.   **6987**

EXTRACTIVE ACTIVITY

Comeaux, Malcolm L., "Hook-and-Line Fishing in the Mississippi River System," *Material Culture*, vol. 21, 1 (1989), pp. 23–45.   **6988**

Comeaux, Malcolm L., "Use of Hoop Nets in the Mississippi River Basin," *Journal of Cultural Geography*, vol. 10, 2 (1989), pp. 75–87.   **6989**

AGRICULTURE

Baker, Oliver E., "Agricultural Regions of North America: Part IV—The Corn Belt," *Economic Geography*, vol. 3, 4 (1927), pp. 447–465.   **6990**

Hart, John Fraser, "Change in the Corn Belt," *Geographical Review*, vol. 76, 1 (1986), pp. 51–72. [Emphasis on 1949–1982]   **6991**

LANDSCAPE

Roark, Michael O., ed., *French and Germans in the Mississippi Valley: Landscape and Cultural Traditions* (Cape Girardeau: Southeast Missouri State University, Center for Regional History and Cultural Heritage, 1988), 228 pp.   **6992**

Hudson, John C., "Settlement of the American Grassland," in Michael P. Conzen, ed., *The Making of the American Landscape* (Boston: Unwin Hyman, 1990), pp. 169–185.   **6993**

COMMUNICATIONS & TRADE

Appleton, John B., "The Declining Significance of the Mississippi as a Commercial Highway in the Middle of the Nineteenth Century," *Bulletin of the Philadelphia Geographical Society*, vol. 28, 4 (1930), pp. 267–284.   **6994**

Johnson, John A., "Pre-Steamboat Navigation on the Lower Mississippi River," Ph.D. diss., Louisiana State University, 1963.   **6995**

Hilliard, Sam B., "Antebellum Interregional Trade: The Mississippi River as an Example," in Ralph E. Ehrenberg, ed., *Pattern and Process: Research in Historical Geography* (Washington, D.C.: Howard University Press, 1975), pp. 202–214.   **6996**

Borchert, John R., "The Climax of the River Boat Era," in special issue on "The River: Images of the Mississippi," *Design Quarterly*, vols. 101, 102 (1976), pp. 20–21. [Focus on the year 1868] **6997**

Comeaux, Malcolm L., "Origin and Evolution of Mississippi River Fishing Craft," *Pioneer America*, vol. 10, 1 (1978), pp. 72–97.   **6998**

URBAN NETWORKS & URBANIZATION

Burghardt, Andrew F., "The Location of River Towns in the Central Lowland of the United States," *Annals of the Association of American Geographers*, vol. 49, 3 (1959), pp. 305–323.   **6999**

Jakle, John A., "Transportation and the Evolution of River Settlement along the Middle Mississippi River," Master's thesis, Southern Illinois University, 1963.   **7000**

TOWN GROWTH

Pierce, Bessie Louise, "Changing Urban Patterns in the Mississippi Valley," *Journal of Illinois State Historical Society*, vol. 43, 1 (1950), pp. 46–57.   **7001**

URBAN ECONOMIC STRUCTURE

Luman, Donald E., "One-Half Century of Change along the Middle Mississippi," *Journal of Geography*, vol. 80, 1 (1981), pp. 27–30. [St. Louis–East St. Louis]   7002

TOWNSCAPE

Larson, Albert J., "Influences on County Courthouse Styles in the Central Mississippi Valley," *Pioneer America Society Transactions*, vol. 8 (1985), pp. 55–67.   7003

Larson, Albert J., "Vernacular to High Style: Four County Courthouses of Mid-America," *Pioneer*

America Society Transactions, vol. 13 (1990), pp. 71–79.   7004

PLACE NAMES

Crissler, Robert M., "The Regional Status of Little Dixie in Missouri and Little Egypt in Illinois," *Journal of Geography*, vol. 49, 8 (1950), pp. 337–343.   7005

McDermott, John F., "The French Impress on Place Names in the Mississippi Valley," *Journal of the Illinois State Historical Society*, vol. 72, 3 (1979), pp. 225–234.   7006

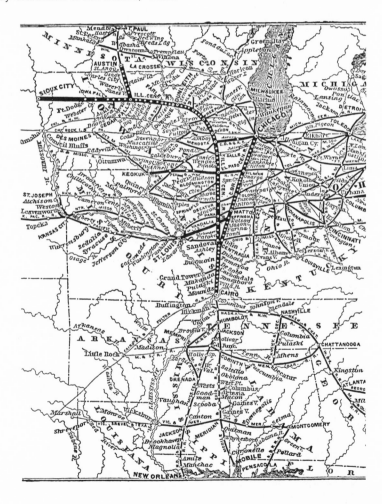

THE MIDDLE WEST

GENERAL

The region

Hart, John Fraser, "The Middle West," *Annals of the Association of American Geographers*, vol. 62, 2 (1972), pp. 258–282. Also in John Fraser Hart, ed., *Regions of the United States* (New York: Harper & Row, 1972), same pagination.
7007

Hudson, John C., "The Middle West as a Cultural Hybrid," *Pioneer America Society Transactions*, vol. 7 (1984), pp. 35–45.
7008

Shortridge, James R., "The Emergence of the Middle West as an American Regional Label," *Annals of the Association of American Geographers*, vol. 74, 2 (1984), pp. 209–220. [Focus on the period since 1880]
7009

Borchert, John R., "Persistent Places and Paths on the Midwestern Plain," *Journal of Geography*, vol. 87, 5 (1986), pp. 218–223.
7010

Borchert, John R., *America's Northern Heartland: An Economic and Historical Geography of the Upper Midwest* (Minneapolis: University of Minnesota Press, 1987), 250 pp.
7011

Shortridge, James R., *The Middle West: Its Meaning in American Culture* (Lawrence: University Press of Kansas, 1989), 201 pp.
7012

Smaller cross-state areas

Borchers, Irma T., "The Geography of the Lead and Zinc Region of the Upper Mississippi Valley," Master's thesis, University of Wisconsin–Madison, 1929.
7013

Swain, Harry and Eugene Cotton Mather, *St. Croix Border Country* (Prescott, Wis.: Trimbelle Press, 1968), 91 pp.
7014

Flader, Susan L., "An Ecosystem Perspective on Environment and Social Changes in the Great Lakes Forest," *Journal of Forest History*, vol. 27, 1 (1983), pp. 34–41.
7015

Hudson, John C., "Cultural Geography and the Upper Great Lakes Region," *Journal of Cultural Geography*, vol. 5, 1 (1984), pp. 19–32.
7016

ENVIRONMENTAL CHANGE

Vegetation

Gleason, Henry A., "The Vegetational History of the Middle West," *Annals of the Association of American Geographers*, vol. 12, 2 (1922), pp. 39–85.
7017

Meyer, Alfred H., "Fundament Vegetation of the Calumet Region of Northwest Indiana and Northeast Illinois," *Papers of the Michigan Academy of Science, Arts, and Letters*, vol. 36 (1952), pp. 177–182.
7018

Rivers and flooding

Alexander, Charles S., and Nelson R. Nunnally, "Channel Stability on the Lower Ohio River," *Annals of the Association of American Geographers*, vol. 62, 3 (1972), pp. 411–417. [1809–1965]
7019

Hirschboeck, Katherine K., "The Response of Flooding in the Upper Mississippi Valley to Twentieth Century Climatic Fluctuations, 1925–1969," Master's thesis, University of Wisconsin–Madison, 1975.
7020

Knox, James C., et al., *The Response of Floods and Sediment Yield to Climatic Variation and Land Use in the Upper Mississippi Valley* (Madison: University of Wisconsin, Institute for Environmental Studies, Report no. 52, 1975), 75 pp.
7021

Johnson, William C., "Historical Trends in Sediment Movement within Stream Systems of the Midwestern United States," *Papers & Proceedings of Applied Geography Conferences*, vol. 2 (1979), pp. 225–236. [Focus on 1850–1979]
7022

Magilligan, Francis J., IV, "Historical Floodplain Sedimentation in the Galena River Basin: Southwest Wisconsin, Northwest Illinois," Master's thesis, University of Wisconsin–Madison, 1983.
7023

Knox, James C., "Historical Valley Floor Sedimentation in the Upper Mississippi Valley," *Annals of the Association of American Geographers*, vol. 77, 2 (1987), pp. 224–244.
7024

Buckler, William R., "General Land Office Resurveys: A Methodology for Determining Long-Term Shoreland Recession Rates," *Papers & Proceedings of Applied Geography Conferences*, vol. 11 (1988), pp. 17–26. [Lake Michigan, 1827–1986]
7025

Knox, James C., "Climatic Influence on Upper Mississippi Valley Floods," in V. R. Baker, R. C. Kochel, and P. C. Patton, eds., *Flood Geomorphology* (New York: John Wiley and Sons, 1988), pp. 279–300.
7026

Knox, James C., "Long- and Short-Term Episodic Storage and Removal of Sediment in Watersheds of Southwestern Wisconsin and Northwestern Illinois," in R. F. Hadley and E. D. Ongley, eds., *Sediment and the Environment* (International Association of Scientific Hydrology, Publication no. 184, 1989), pp. 117–130. **7027**

Knox, James C., *Hydrologic and Geomorphic Implications of Climatic Change* (Fort Belvoir, Va.: U.S. Army Corps of Engineers, Institute for Water Resources, Report no. DACW 72-88-M-0754, 1990), 230 pp. **7028**

NATIVE PEOPLES & WHITE RELATIONS

Parkins, Almon E., "The Indians of the Great Lakes Region and Their Environment," *Geographical Review*, vol. 6, 6 (1916), pp. 504–512. **7029**

Fitting, James, and Charles Cleland, "Late Prehistoric Settlement Patterns in the Upper Great Lakes," *Ethnohistory*, vol. 16, 4 (1969), pp. 289–302. **7030**

Janke, Robert A., "Chippewa Land Losses," *Journal of Cultural Geography*, vol. 2, 2 (1982), pp. 84–100. **7031**

Van Voorhis, Eugene P., "The Hydrographic Factor in Ottawa Indian Culture and History, 1615–1836," Master's thesis, Bowling Green State University, 1983. **7032**

Pierce, Roxann, "An Historical Geography of Ojibway Land Cessions," Master's thesis, University of Minnesota, 1990. **7033**

EXPLORATION & MAPPING

Brown, Ralph Hall, "With Cass in the Northwest in 1820: The Journal of Charles C. Trowbridge, May 24 to September 13, 1820," *Minnesota History*, vol. 23 (1942). **7034**

Rogers, Richard R., "Historical Cartography of the Great Lakes (1569–1746)," *Papers of the Michigan Academy of Science, Arts, and Letters*, vol. 34 (1948), pp. 175–184. **7035**

Johnson, Deborah, "U.S. Lake Survey Nautical Charts: A Cartographic and Historical Analysis," Master's thesis, Michigan State University, 1982. **7036**

Conzen, Michael P., "Maps for the Masses: Alfred T. Andreas and the Midwestern County Atlas Trade," *Chicago Mapmakers: Essays on the Rise of the City's Map Trade* (Chicago: Chicago Historical Society, for the Chicago Map Society, 1984), pp. 46–63. Copublished in *Chicago History*, vol. 13, 1 (1984), pp. 46–63. **7037**

Bosse, David, "Dartmouth on the Mississippi: Speculators and Surveyors in British North

America," *Imago Mundi*, vol. 41 (1989), pp. 9–18. **7038**

Baruth, Christopher M., "The United States Lake Survey: Pattern and Process, 1841–1856," Ph.D. diss., University of Wisconsin–Milwaukee, 1990. **7039**

Harley, J. Brian, and Howard A. Deller, "The World by Lake Michigan," *Map Collector*, vol. 50 (1990), pp. 2–9. **7040**

POPULAR IMAGES & EVALUATION

See also **1315**

Johnson, Hildegard Binder, "Perceptions and Illustrations of the American Landscape in the Ohio Valley and the Midwest," in *This Land of Ours: The Acquisition and Disposition of the Public Domain* (Indianapolis: Indiana Historical Society, 1978), pp. 1–38. **7041**

Mahaffey, Charles G., "Changing Images of the Cutover: An Historical Geography of Resource Utilization in the Lake Superior Region, 1840–1930," Ph.D. diss., University of Wisconsin–Madison, 1978. **7042**

Mahaffey, Charles G., and Felice R. Bassuk, *Images of the Cutover: A Historical Geography of Resource Utilization in the Lake Superior Region, 1845–1930* (Madison: University of Wisconsin, Institute for Environmental Studies, Center for Geographic Analysis, Lake Superior Project, RF Monograph-76-15, IES Report 98, 1978), 38 pp. **7043**

Peters, Bernard C., "Revolt from the Wilderness: Romantic Travelers on Lake Superior," *Michigan Academician*, vol. 13 (1981), pp. 491–501. **7044**

Jakle, John A., "Images of Place: Symbolism and the Middle Western Metropolis," in Carl Patton and Barry Checkoway, eds., *The Metropolitan Midwest* (Urbana: University of Illinois Press, 1985), pp. 74–103. **7045**

Jakle, John A., "Childhood on the Middle Border: Remembered Small Town America," *Journal of Geography*, vol. 85, 4 (1986), pp. 159–163. **7046**

Mather, Eugene Cotton, "The Midwest: Images and Reality," *Journal of Geography*, vol. 85, 5 (1986), pp. 190–194. **7047**

Alanen, Arnold R., "Wilderness and Landscape: Finnish Immigrant Expressions in the American Midwest," *Terra*, vol. 101, 1 (1989), pp. 31–33. **7048**

REGIONAL SETTLEMENT

Peattie, Roderick, "The Human Significance of Maturity of a Plains Region," *Journal of Geography*, vol. 25, 5 (1926), pp. 176–183. [Ohio, Kentucky, Iowa] **7049**

Meyer, Alfred H., "The Kankakee Marsh of Northern Indiana and Illinois," Ph.D. diss., University of Michigan, 1934. 7050

Meyer, Alfred H., "The Kankakee 'Marsh' of Northern Indiana and Illinois," *Papers of the Michigan Academy of Science, Arts, and Letters*, vol. 21 (1935), pp. 359–396. Reprinted in abbreviated form in Robert S. Platt, ed., *Field Study in American Geography* (Chicago: University of Chicago Department of Geography, Research Paper no. 61, 1959), pp. 200–216. 7051

Hewes, Leslie, "The Northern Wet Prairie of the United States: Nature, Sources of Information, and Extent," *Annals of the Association of American Geographers*, vol. 41, 4 (1951), pp. 307–323. 7052

Meyer, Alfred H., "Circulation and Settlement Patterns of the Calumet–South Chicago Region of Northwest Indiana and Northeast Illinois," *Proceedings of the Eighth General Assembly— Seventeenth Congress of the International Geographical Union* (Washington, D.C.: International Geographical Union, 1952), pp. 538–544. 7053

Hewes, Leslie, "Die Entwässerung der Nördlichen naßen Prärien der Vereinigten Staaten: Eine Einführung," *Die Erde*, vol. 2 (1953), pp. 95–108. 7054

Meyer, Alfred H., "Circulation and Settlement Patterns of the Calumet Region of Northwest Indiana and Northeast Illinois (The Second Stage of Occupancy: Pioneer Settlement and Subsistance Economy, 1830–1850)," *Annals of the Association of American Geographers*, vol. 46, 3 (1956), pp. 312–356. 7055

Gentilcore, R. Louis, "Vincennes and French Settlement in the Old Northwest," *Annals of the Association of American Geographers*, vol. 47, 3 (1957), pp. 285–297. 7056

Kaups, Matti E., "Finnish Rural Settlement in the Lake Superior Area," Ph.D. diss., University of Minnesota, 1965. 7057

Birch, Brian P., "Characteristics of Rural Settlement in the Corn Belt of the North American Mid-West," Ph.D. diss., University of Durham, 1967. 7058

Kaups, Matti E., "Speculations and Geographic Myths: Patterns of Finnish Settlement in the Lake Superior Region," *Michigan Academician*, vol. 3, 3 (1971), pp. 77–91. 7059

Johnson, Hildegard Binder, "A Historical Perspective on Form and Function in Upper Midwest Rural Settlement," *Agricultural History*, vol. 48, 1 (1974), pp. 11–25. 7060

Ostergren, Robert C., "Geographic Perspectives on the History of Settlement in the Upper Midwest," *Upper Midwest History*, vol. 1 (1981), pp. 27–39. 7061

Lanegran, David A., and Anne Mosher-Sheridan, "The European Settlement of the Upper Mississippi River Valley: Cairo, Illinois, to Lake Itasca, Minnesota, 1540 to 1860," in John S. Wozniak, ed., *Historic Lifestyles in the Upper Mississippi River Valley* (Washington, D.C.: American University Press, 1983), pp. 3–57. 7062

Rohe, Randall E., "Settlement Pattern of Logging Camps in the Great Lakes Region," *Journal of Cultural Geography*, vol. 6, 1 (1985), pp. 79–107. 7063

Swierenga, Robert P., "The Settlement of the Old Northwest: Pluralism in a Featureless Plain," *Journal of the Early Republic*, vol. 9, 1 (1989), pp. 73–106. 7064

POPULATION

General

Sjaastad, Larry A., *Migrations and Population Growth in the Upper Midwest, 1930–1960* (Minneapolis: Upper Midwest Research and Development Council, Upper Midwest Economic Study, Paper no. 4, 1962), 40 pp. 7065

McNeal, Ilene C., "The Use of County Sex Ratios as an Indicator of Frontier Movement in the Great Lakes States, 1850–1890," Master's thesis, Pennsylvania State University, 1973. 7066

Brooks, William D., "A Regional Profile of Population Distribution and Trends in West Central Indiana and East Central Illinois," *Proceedings of the Indiana Academy of the Social Sciences, 1973*, vol. 5 (1974), pp. 82–90. [Covers 1950–1970] 7067

Borchert, John R., "Geographical Shifts in Midwestern Population in the Twentieth Century," in Curtis C. Roseman, ed., *Population Redistribution in the Midwest* (Ames: Iowa State University, North Central Regional Center for Rural Development, 1981), pp. 25–48. 7068

Ethnic distributions

Johnson, Hildegard Binder, "The Location of German Immigrants in the Middle West," *Annals of the Association of American Geographers*, vol. 41, 1 (1951), pp. 1–41. 7069

Alanen, Arnold R., "The Norwegian Connection: The Background in Arctic Norway for Early Finnish Emigration to the American Midwest," *Finnish-America*, vol. 6, 1 (1983–1984), pp. 20–30. 7070

Alanen, Arnold R., "Finns and Other Immigrant Groups in Communities of the American Upper Midwest," in Michael G. Karni, O. Loivukangas, and E. W. Laine, eds., *Finns in North America* (Turku, Finland: Institute of Migration, 1988), pp. 58–83.   7071

American-born distributions

Malmstrom, Vincent H., "When Vermont Went West," *Vermont Geographer*, vol. 2 (1975), pp. 1–6.   7072

Hudson, John C., "Yankeeland in the Middle West," *Journal of Geography*, vol. 85, 5 (1986), pp. 195–200.   7073

Hudson, John C., "North American Origins of Middlewestern Frontier Populations," *Annals of the Association of American Geographers*, vol. 78, 3 (1988), pp. 395–413.   7074

Rose, Gregory S., "The Southern Midwest as Pennsylvania Extended," *East Lakes Geographer*, vol. 23 (1988), pp. 53–70.   7075

RURAL & REGIONAL SOCIAL GEOGRAPHY

See also **1383**

General

Davis, Alva, "Dialect Distribution and Settlement Patterns in the Great Lakes Region," *Ohio History*, vol. 60 (1951), pp. 48–56.   7076

Sauer, Carl O., "Status and Change in the Rural Midwest: A Retrospect," *Mitteilungen der Österreichischen Geographischen Gesellschaft*, vol. 105, 3 (1963), pp. 357–365. Reprinted in Carl O. Sauer, *Selected Essays, 1963–1975*, ed. Bob Callahan (Berkeley, Calif.: Turtle Island Foundation, for the Netzahaulcoyotl Historical Society, 1981), pp. 78–91; and in Wilford A. Bladen and Pradyumna P. Karan, eds., *The Evolution of Geographic Thought in America: A Kentucky Root* (Dubuque, Iowa: Kendall/Hunt Publishing Co., 1983), pp. 115–122.   7077

Parker, William N., "From Northwest to Midwest: Social Bases of a Regional History," in William N. Parker, ed., *Essays in Nineteenth Century Economic History: The Old Northwest* (Athens: Ohio University Press, 1975), pp. 3–34. Reprinted, with omissions, in David Ward, ed., *Geographic Perspectives on America's Past: Readings on the Historical Geography of the United States* (New York: Oxford University Press, 1979), pp. 167–179.   7078

Rose, Gregory S., "The National Road Border between the North and the South in the Midwest by 1870," in Richard L. Nostrand and Sam B. Hilliard, eds., *The American South* (Baton Rouge: Louisiana State University School of

Geoscience, Geoscience & Man, vol. 25, 1988), pp. 159–167.   7079

Ethnic communities

Lewthwaite, Gordon R., "Midwestern Swiss Migrants and Foreign Cheese," *Yearbook of the Association of Pacific Coast Geographers*, vol. 34 (1972), pp. 41–60.   7080

Raitz, Karl B., "Ethnicity and the Diffusion and Distribution of Cigar Tobacco Production in Wisconsin and Ohio," *Tijdschrift voor economische en sociale geografie*, vol. 64, 5 (1973), pp. 295–306.   7081

Alanen, Arnold R., "The Development and Distribution of Finnish Consumers' Cooperatives in Michigan, Minnesota, and Wisconsin, 1903–1973," in Michael G. Karni, Matti E. Kaups, and D. Ollila, eds., *The Finnish Experience in the Western Great Lakes Region: New Perspectives* (Turku: Institute for Migration, 1975), pp. 103–130.   7082

Karni, Michael, Matti E. Kaups, and Douglas Ollila, eds., *The Finnish Experience in the Western Great Lakes Region: New Perspectives* (Turku, Finland: Institute for Migration, 1975), 232 pp.   7083

McQuillan, D. Aidan, "The Creation and Survival of French-Canadian Communities in the American Upper Midwest during the Nineteenth Century," *Cahiers de géographie du Québec*, vol. 23, 58 (1979), pp. 53–72.   7084

Alanen, Arnold R., "Finns and the Corporate Environment of the Lake Superior Region," in Michael G. Karni, ed., *Finnish Diaspora II: United States* (Toronto: Multicultural Historical Society of Ontario, 1981), pp. 33–61.   7085

Ostergren, Robert C., "The Immigrant Church as a Symbol of Community and Place in the Upper Midwest," *Great Plains Quarterly*, vol. 1, 4 (1981), pp. 225–238.   7086

Alanen, Arnold R., "Kaivosmichista maanviljelijoihin: Suomaliset siirtolaiset pohjoisten Suurtenjarvien alueella Yhdysvalloissa," *Terra*, vol. 94, 3 (1982), pp. 189–206.   7087

McQuillan, D. Aidan, "Les communautés Canadiennes-français du Midwest americain au dix-neuvième siècle," in Dean R. Louder and Eric Waddell, eds., *Du continent perdu à l'archipel retrouvé: Le Québec et l'Amérique français* (Quebec: Presses de l'Université Laval, Travaux du Département de géographie de l'Université, no. 6, 1983), pp. 97–115.   7088

Ostergren, Robert C., "The Transplanted Swedish Rural Community in the Upper Middle West," in Harold Runblom and Dag Blanck, eds., *Scandinavia Overseas: Patterns of Cultural Transfor-

mation in North America and Australia (Uppsala: Center for Multiethnic Research, Uppsala Multiethnic Papers, no. 7, 1986), pp. 18–39. **7089**

Ostergren, Robert C., "Environment, Culture, and Community: Research Issues and Method in the Study of Scandinavian Settlement in the Middle West," in S. E. Jorgensen, L. Scheving, and N. P. Stillings, eds., *From Scandinavia to America* (Odense: Odense University Press, 1987), pp. 176–198. **7090**

POLITICAL & ADMINISTRATIVE GEOGRAPHY

Eirich, Constance G., "A Study in Historico-Geography: The Establishing of the Ohio-Michigan Boundary Line," *Journal of Geography*, vol. 12, 1 (1913), pp. 5–8. **7091**

Jacobson, Daniel, *The Northwest Ordinance of 1787* (East Lansing: Michigan State University Alumni Association, 1987), 36 pp. **7092**

Lass, William E., "Minnesota's Separation from Wisconsin: Boundary Making on the Upper Mississippi Frontier," *Minnesota History*, vol. 50, 8 (1987), pp. 309–320. **7093**

Shelley, Fred M., and J. Clark Archer, "Sectionalism and Presidential Politics: Voting Patterns in Illinois, Indiana, and Ohio," *Journal of Interdisciplinary History*, vol. 20, 2 (1989), pp. 227–256. **7094**

ECONOMIC DEVELOPMENT

Libby, Orin G., "An Economic and Social Study of the Lead Region in Iowa, Illinois, and Wisconsin," *Transactions of the Wisconsin Academy of Sciences, Arts, and Letters*, vol. 13, 1 (1901), pp. 188–281. **7095**

Gates, Richard, "Historical Geography of Salt in the Old Northwest," Master's thesis, University of Wisconsin–Madison, 1966. **7096**

Wilson, Homer, "Population Dynamics and the Diffusion of Growth Impulses through an Urban System: The Case of a Mid-Western Region, 1910–1970," Master's thesis, University of Toledo, 1976. **7097**

Penn, James R., "Land, Labor, and Class in the Old Northwest: A Geographic Perspective," Ph.D. diss., University of Wisconsin–Madison, 1983. **7098**

LAND & LAND USE

Hart, John Fraser, "Cleared Farm Land in Upper Great Lakes States, 1910–1964," *Journal of the Minnesota Academy of Science*, vol. 36, 1 (1969), pp. 29–31. **7099**

Johnson, Hildegard Binder, *Order upon the Land: The U.S. Rectangular Land Survey and the Upper Mississippi Valley* (New York: Oxford University Press, 1976), 268 pp. **7100**

EXTRACTIVE INDUSTRY

Fishing

Hessen, Willard C., "The Commercial Fishing Industry of Lake Superior," Master's thesis, Clark University, 1950. **7101**

Mining

Miller, George J., "Some Geographic Influences of the Lake Superior Iron Ores," *Bulletin of the American Geographical Society*, vol. 46, 12 (1914), pp. 881–916. [Focus from the 1820s to the 1910s] **7102**

Schockel, Bernard H., "Settlement and Development of the Lead and Zinc Mining Region, with Special Emphasis upon Jo Daviess County, Illinois," *Mississippi Valley Historical Society Review*, vol. 4, 2 (1917), pp. 169–192. **7103**

Bastian, Robert W., "Technological Evolution and Resource Revaluation: Lake Superior Iron Ores," in W. P. Adams and F. M. Helleiner, eds., *International Geography 1972*, vol. 1, sec. 5, *Historical Geography* (Toronto: University of Toronto Press, for the International Geographical Union, 1972), pp. 396–398. **7104**

Lumbering

Rohe, Randall E., "The Upper Great Lakes Lumber Era," *Inland Seas*, vol. 40, 1 (1984), pp. 16–29. **7105**

Rohe, Randall E., "Archeology: A Key to the Great Lakes Lumber Era," *Wisconsin Archeologist*, vol. 66, 4 (1985), pp. 359–384. **7106**

Rohe, Randall E., "The Evolution of the Great Lakes Logging Camp, 1830–1930," *Journal of Forest History*, vol. 30, 1 (1986), pp. 17–28. **7107**

Rohe, Randall E., "Tramways and Pole Railroads: An Episode in the Technological History of the Great Lakes Lumber Era," *Upper Midwest History*, vol. 5 (1986), pp. 19–44. **7108**

AGRICULTURE

Weaver, John C., "Crop-Combination Regions for 1919 and 1929 in the Middle West," *Geographical Review*, vol. 44, 4 (1954), pp. 560–572. **7109**

Lewthwaite, Gordon R., "The Formation of Mid-Western Cheese-Specialty Areas," *Proceedings of the Oklahoma Academy of Science*, vol. 34 (1955), pp. 212–214. **7110**

Wallace, Henry A., "Corn and the Midwestern Farmer," *Landscape*, vol. 6, 3 (1957), pp. 9–12. **7111**

Bogue, Allan G., *From Prairie to Cornbelt: Farming on the Illinois and Iowa Prairies in the Nineteenth Century* (Chicago: University of Chicago Press, 1963), 310 pp. **7112**

Lewthwaite, Gordon R., "Cows in the Corn: The Emergence of the Tri-State Butter Region," *Proceedings of the Association of American Geographers*, vol. 7 (1975), pp. 113–117. **7113**

Hartnett, Sean, "Harvesting the New Land: A Geographical Appraisal of the Wheat Frontier in the Upper Midwest, 1835–1885," Master's thesis, University of Wisconsin–Madison, 1981. **7114**

Bogue, Margaret B., "The Lake and the Fruit: The Making of Three Farm-Type Areas," *Agricultural History*, vol. 59, 4 (1985), pp. 493–522. [Michigan, Wisconsin] **7115**

LANDSCAPE

General

Jakle, John A., *The Testing of a House Typing System in Two Middle Western Counties: A Comparative Analysis of Rural Houses* (Urbana: University of Illinois, Department of Geography Occasional Paper no. 11, 1976), 36 pp. **7116**

Noble, Allen G., "The Silo in the Eastern Midwest: Patterns of Evolution and Distribution," *Ohio Geographers: Recent Research Themes*, vol. 4 (1976), pp. 9–22. **7117**

Walters, William D., "Nineteenth Century Midwestern Brick," *Pioneer America*, vol. 14, 3 (1982), pp. 125–136. **7118**

Schlereth, Thomas J., "The New England Presence in the Midwest Landscape," *Old Northwest*, vol. 9, 2 (1983), pp. 125–142. **7119**

Baker, Sharon F., "From Horse to Horsepower: Farm Tractorization and the Rural Landscape in Minnesota and Surrounding States," Master's thesis, South Dakota State University, 1983. **7120**

Ethnic imprint

Johnson, Hildegard Binder, "Immigrant Tradition and Rural Middle Western Architecture," *American-German Review*, vol. 9, 5 (1943), pp. 17–20. **7121**

Mather, Eugene Cotton, and Matti E. Kaups, "The Finnish Sauna: A Cultural Index to Settlement," *Annals of the Association of American Geographers*, vol. 53, 4 (1963), pp. 494–504. **7122**

Alanen, Arnold R., and William Tishler, "Finnish Farmstead Organization in Old and New World Settings," *Journal of Cultural Geography*, vol. 1, 1 (1980), pp. 68–81. **7123**

Kaups, Matti E., "Finnish Log Houses in the Upper Middle West: 1890–1920," *Journal of Cultural Geography*, vol. 3, 2 (1983), pp. 2–26. **7124**

Noble, Allen G., "The Finnish Landscape of the Upper Great Lakes," *East Lakes Geographer*, vol. 18 (1983), pp. 14–24. **7125**

Kaups, Matti E., "Finns," in Del Upton, ed., *America's Architectural Roots: Ethnic Groups That Built America* (Washington, D.C.: National Trust for Historic Preservation, Preservation Press, 1986), pp. 124–129. **7126**

Kaups, Matti E., "Finnish Meadow-Hay Barns in the Lake Superior Region," *Journal of Cultural Geography*, vol. 10, 1 (1989), pp. 1–18. **7127**

Barns and Fences

Beck, Robert L., and George W. Webb, "Barn Door Decorations in the Boundary Junction Area of Indiana, Michigan, and Ohio: The Case of the Painted Arch," *Indiana State University, Department of Geography, Professional Paper* no. 9 (1977), pp. 3–12. **7128**

Hewes, Leslie, "Early Fencing on the Western Margin of the Prairie," *Annals of the Association of American Geographers*, vol. 71, 4 (1981), pp. 499–526. Reprinted with minor changes in *Nebraska History*, vol. 69, 3 (1982), pp. 301–348. **7129**

Hewes, Leslie, and Christian L. Jung, "Early Fencing on the Middle Western Prairie," *Annals of the Association of American Geographers*, vol. 71, 2 (1981), pp. 177–201. **7130**

Baltensperger, Bradley H., "Hedgerow Distribution and Removal in the Non-Forested Area of the Midwest," *Journal of Soil and Water Conservation*, vol. 42, 1 (1987), pp. 60–64. [Covers 1940–1980] **7131**

COMMUNICATIONS & TRADE

See also 1432

Atwood, Jane K., "The Development of the Commerce of the Great Lakes," Master's thesis, University of Chicago, 1915. **7132**

Hartshorne, Richard, "The Significance of Lake Transportation to the Grain Traffic of Chicago," *Economic Geography*, vol. 2, 2 (1926), pp. 274–291. **7133**

Morrison, Paul C., "Michigan Limestone in the Great Lakes Stone Trade," *Economic Geography*, vol. 18, 4 (1942), pp. 413–427. **7134**

Kistler, John M., "Variables Affecting the Design of Ohio River Boats, 1800 to 1965," Master's thesis, Miami University of Ohio, 1968. **7135**

Munski, Douglas C., "Modeling the Historical Geography of the Chicago and Eastern Illinois Railroad, 1849–1969," Ph.D. diss., University of Illinois, 1978. **7136**

Quastler, Imre E., "A Descriptive Model of Railroad Network Growth in the American Midwest, 1865–1910," *Journal of Geography*, vol. 77, 3 (1978), pp. 87–93. **7137**

Quastler, Imre E., *Pioneer of the Third Level: A History of Air Midwest* (San Diego: Commuter Airlines Press, 1980), 174 pp. **7138**

Zareczny, Frank, "The Evolution of Upper Great Lakes Passenger Travel: Historical Geography," Master's thesis, University of Wisconsin–Milwaukee, 1984. **7139**

Quastler, Imre E., *Air Midwest: The First Twenty Years* (San Diego: Airline Press of California, 1985), 298 pp. **7140**

Mayer, Harold M., "Trans-Atlantic Passenger Liners in the Great Lakes," *Soundings (Wisconsin Marine Historical Society)*, vol. 28, 4 (1988), pp. 1–4, 9–10. **7141**

MANUFACTURING & INDUSTRIALIZATION

Cutshall, Alden D., "Industrial Geography of the Lower Wabash Valley," *Economic Geography*, vol. 17 (1941), pp. 297–307. **7142**

Cutshall, Alden D., "The Manufacture of Clay Products in the Lower Wabash Valley," *Transactions of the Illinois State Academy of Science*, vol. 35 (1942), pp. 118–120. **7143**

Cutshall, Alden D., "The Manufacture of Food and Kindred Products in the Lower Wabash Valley," *Agricultural History*, vol. 18, 1 (1944), pp. 16–22. **7144**

Lukermann, Fred E., "The Changing Pattern of Flour Mill Location," *Northwestern Miller*, vol. 261, nos. 3, 4, 6, 8, 12, 13, 17 (1959), 21 maps. **7145**

Walsh, Margaret, "The Spatial Evolution of the Midwestern Pork Industry, 1835–75," *Journal of Historical Geography*, vol. 4, 1 (1978), pp. 1–22. **7146**

Hart, John Fraser, "Small Towns and Manufacturing," *Geographical Review*, vol. 78, 3 (1988), pp. 272–287. [Focus on the Middle West, 1950–1980] **7147**

Meyer, David R., "Midwestern Industrialization and the American Manufacturing Belt in the Nineteenth Century," *Journal of Economic History*, vol. 49, 4 (1989), pp. 921–937. **7148**

Casey, William, "Distribution of Upper Midwest Manufacturing Sites: Changes from 1960 to

1989," Master's thesis, University of Minnesota, 1990. **7149**

URBAN NETWORKS & URBANIZATION

Borchert, John R., *The Urbanization of the Upper Midwest, 1930–1960* (Minneapolis: Upper Midwest Research and Development Council, Upper Midwest Economic Study, Urban Report no. 2, 1963), 56 pp. **7150**

Conzen, Michael P., "Metropolitan Dominance in the American Midwest during the Later Nineteenth Century," Ph.D. diss., University of Wisconsin–Madison, 1972. [Chicago, Indianapolis, Milwaukee, and Des Moines] **7151**

Muller, Edward K., "The Development of Urban Settlement in a Newly Settled Region: The Middle Ohio Valley, 1800–1860," Ph.D. diss., University of Wisconsin–Madison, 1972. [Southwest Ohio and southeast Indiana] **7152**

Conzen, Michael P., "A Transport Interpretation of the Growth of Urban Regions: An American Example," *Journal of Historical Geography*, vol. 1, 4 (1975), pp. 361–382. **7153**

Muller, Edward K., "Selective Urban Growth in the Middle Ohio Valley, 1800–1860," *Geographical Review*, vol. 66, 2 (1976), pp. 178–199. Reprinted, with omissions, in David Ward, ed., *Geographic Perspectives on America's Past: Readings on the Historical Geography of the United States* (New York: Oxford University Press, 1979), pp. 291–307. **7154**

Baerwald, Thomas J., "County Seats in the Middle Western Urban System," *Geographical Bulletin*, vol. 14 (1977), pp. 6–15. **7155**

Sheridan, Anne Mosher, "The Development of Nucleated Settlement Systems: The Case of the Upper Mississippi Valley, 1800–1860," Master's thesis, Pennsylvania State University, 1984. **7156**

Mahoney, Timothy R., "Urban History in a Regional Context: River Towns on the Upper Mississippi, 1840–1860," *Journal of American History*, vol. 72, 2 (1985), pp. 318–339. **7157**

Mahoney, Timothy R., *River Towns in the Great West: The Structure of Provincial Urbanization in the American Midwest, 1820–1870* (New York: Cambridge University Press, 1989), 288 pp. **7158**

TOWN GROWTH

Espenshade, Edward B., "Urban Developments at the Upper Rapids of the Mississippi," Ph.D. diss., University of Chicago, 1943. Published under the same title, as a University of Chicago Department of Geography Private Edition, 1944, 185 pp. **7159**

URBAN SOCIAL STRUCTURE

McBride, Mary J., "Explorations of Urban Density in the Midwest, 1910–1960," Master's thesis, Indiana University, 1965.   **7160**

Adams, John S., "Residential Structure of Midwestern Cities," *Annals of the Association of American Geographers*, vol. 60, 1 (1970), pp. 37–62. [Focus on 1890–1960]   **7161**

Alanen, Arnold R., "Immigrant Gardens on a Mining Frontier," in Mark Francis and Randolph T. Hester, eds., *The Meaning of Gardens: Idea, Place, and Action* (Cambridge: MIT Press, 1990), pp. 160–166.   **7162**

TOWNSCAPE

Bastian, Robert W., "Storefront Remodeling in Small Midwestern Cities, 1890–1940," *Pioneer America Society Transactions*, vol. 1 (1978), pp. 1–14.   **7163**

PLANNING

Alanen, Arnold R., "The Planning of Company Communities in the Lake Superior Mining Region," *Journal of the American Planning Association*, vol. 45, 3 (1979), pp. 256–278.   **7164**

Alanen, Arnold R., "Physical Planning and Social Order on the Lake Superior Mining Frontier," in P. A. Miller and L. Diamond, eds., *The Frontier Landscape: Selected Proceedings of the Inter-national Federation of Landscape Architects Congress 1981* (Vancouver: University of British Columbia, 1982), pp. 120–127.   **7165**

PLACE NAMES

Meyer, Alfred H., "Toponymy in Sequent Occupance Geography: Calumet Region, Indiana-Illinois," *Proceedings of the Indiana Academy of Science*, vol. 54 (1945), pp. 142–159.   **7166**

Bastian, Robert W., "Generic Place-Names and the Northern-Midland Dialect Boundary in the Midwest," *Names*, vol. 25, 4 (1977), pp. 228–236.   **7167**

Kaups, Matti E., "Finnish Place Names as a Form of Ethnic Expression in the Middle West, 1880–1977," *Finnish America*, vol. 1 (1978), pp. 51–70.   **7168**

Hartley, Alan, "The Expansion of Ojibway and French Place Names into the Lake Superior Region in the Seventeenth Century," *Names*, vol. 28, 1 (1980), pp. 43–68.   **7169**

Rohe, Randall E., "Place-Names: Relics of the Great Lakes Lumber Era," *Journal of Forest History*, vol. 28, 3 (1984), pp. 126–135.   **7170**

Peters, Bernard C., "Moon Names of the Chippewa," *Names*, vol. 36, 1 & 2 (1988), pp. 51–60.   **7171**

Peters, Bernard C., "Wa-bish-kee-pe-nas and the Chippewa Reverence for Copper," *Michigan Historical Review*, vol. 15, 2 (1989), pp. 47–60.   **7172**

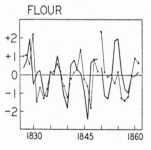

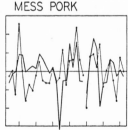

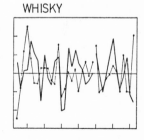

OHIO

GENERAL

The state

Carney, Frank, "Geographic Influences in the Development of Ohio," *Popular Science Monthly*, vol. 75 (1909), pp. 479–489. **7173**

Carney, Frank, "Geographic Influences in the Development of Ohio," *Journal of Geography*, vol. 9, 7 (1911), pp. 169–174. [A quite different treatment from that in the previous entry] **7174**

Hoke, George N., "The Ohio Valley in Relation to Early Ohio History," *Journal of Geography*, vol. 9, 7 (1911), pp. 180–182. **7175**

Peattie, Roderick, *Geography of Ohio* (Columbus: Geological Survey of Ohio, 4th ser., Bulletin no. 27, 1923), 137 pp. **7176**

Buchanan, Jim, "A Geography of the Ohio Lands of Virginia," *Virginia Geographer*, vol. 9, 2 (1974), pp. 3–6. [Focus on the 1780s] **7177**

Noble, Allen G., and Albert J. Korsok, eds., *Ohio: An American Heartland* (Columbus: State of Ohio Department of Natural Resources, Division of Geological Survey, 1975), 230 pp. **7178**

Earle, Carville V., "Ohio," *World Book Encyclopedia*, vol. 14 (1988), pp. 686–710. **7179**

Smaller areas

Bobula, Walter, "The Historical Geography of the Michigan Survey Region of Ohio," Master's thesis, Ohio State University, 1940. **7180**

Beck, James R., "The Dover–New Philadelphia, Ohio, Area," Ph.D. diss., University of Chicago, 1941. **7181**

Garland, John H., "The Western Reserve of Connecticut: Geography of a Political Relic," *Economic Geography*, vol. 19, 3 (1943), pp. 301–319. **7182**

EXPLORATION & MAPPING

Anderson, Russell H., "The Pease Map of the Connecticut Western Reserve," *Ohio History*, vol. 63, 3 (1954), pp. 270–278. **7183**

Ristow, Walter W., "Nineteenth Century Cadastral Maps in Ohio," *Papers of the Bibliographical Society of America*, vol. 59, 3 (1965), pp. 306–315. **7184**

Wittmann, John H., "Cartographic Development of Modern Road Maps, as Exemplified by Ohio Road Maps," Master's thesis, Ohio State University, 1965. **7185**

Sanders, James M., "Map Use in Ohio's Regional Newspapers, 1930–1985: Frequency, Thematic Content, and Geographic Focus," Master's thesis, University of Akron, 1990. **7186**

POPULAR IMAGES & EVALUATION

Ford, Larry R., and Richard D. Fusch, "Historic Preservation and the Inner City: The Perception of German Village by Those Just Beyond," *Proceedings of the Association of American Geographers*, vol. 8 (1976), pp. 110–114. **7187**

Ford, Larry R., and Richard D. Fusch, "Neighbors View: German Village," *Historic Preservation*, vol. 30, 3 (1978), pp. 37–41. **7188**

Jakle, John A., "Cincinnati in the 1830s: A Cognitive Map of Travellers," *Environmental Review*, vol. 3, 3 (1979), pp. 2–10. **7189**

Colten, Craig E., "The Steeple in the Grid: Landscape Awareness in Nineteenth Century Ohio," Ph.D. diss., Syracuse University, 1984. **7190**

Smith, Dennis A., "Pioneer Assessment and Utilization of Ohio's Tallgrass Prairies before 1850," Master's thesis, Miami University of Ohio, 1984. **7191**

REGIONAL SETTLEMENT

See also **7049**

Runkle, Evelyn, "Geographic Factors in the First Permanent Settlement in the Marietta Region, Ohio," Master's thesis, Ohio State University, 1938. **7192**

Richards, Wilfred G., The Settlement of the Miami Valley of Southwestern Ohio," Ph.D. diss., University of Chicago, 1948. Published under the same title, as a University of Chicago Department of Geography Private Edition, 1948, 146 pp. **7193**

Matthews, James S., *Expressions of Urbanism in the Sequent Occupance of Northeastern Ohio* (Chicago: University of Chicago Department of Geography, Research Paper no. 5, 1949), 179 pp. **7194**

George, Milton C., "The Settlement of the Connecticut Western Reserve of Ohio," Ph.D. diss., University of Michigan, 1950. **7195**

Reynolds, Esther C., "Settlement of Licking County to 1840," Master's thesis, Ohio State University, 1951. **7196**

Kaatz, Martin R., "The Settlement of the Black Swamp of Northwestern Ohio, since ca.1890," Ph.D. diss., University of Michigan, 1952. **7197**

Kaatz, Martin R., "The Settlement of the Black Swamp of Northwestern Ohio," *Historical Society of Northwestern Ohio Quarterly*, vol. 25, 1 (1952), pp. 22–36; 3 (1953), pp. 134–150; and 4 (1953), pp. 201–217. **7198**

Kaatz, Martin R., "The Black Swamp: A Study in Historical Geography," *Annals of the Association of American Geographers*, vol. 45, 1 (1955), pp. 1–35. **7199**

Rutherford, Larry L., "A Cartographic and Statistical Analysis of the Distribution of Houses as a Measure of Settlement Changes in Noble County, Ohio, 1875–1960," Master's thesis, University of Georgia, 1966. **7200**

Wilhelm, Hubert G. H., "Southeastern Ohio as a Settlement Region: An Historical-Geographical Interpretation," *Proceedings of the Pioneer America Society*, vol. 1 (1973), pp. 96–123. **7201**

Wilhelm, Hubert G. H., "Settlement Convergence and Residential Cultural Effects in South Central Ohio," *Ohio Geographers: Recent Research Themes*, vol. 3 (1975), pp. 62–72. **7202**

Barr, Ann, "New England Settlement Effects in Southeast Ohio," Master's thesis, Ohio University, 1980. **7203**

Bobersky, Alexander T., and David T. Stephens, "Cultural Faultline: An Examination of Early Settlement Patterns along the Boundary of the Western Reserve," *Pioneer America Society Transactions*, vol. 11 (1988), pp. 87–95. **7204**

Fabe, Joan H., "The Trial and Error Period of Euro-American Settlement in Hamilton County, Ohio, 1773–1795," Ph.D. diss., University of Cincinnati, 1988. **7205**

Boller, Robert, "Settlement Patterns and Building Types as a Result of Initial Occupance in South Central Ohio," Master's thesis, Ohio University, 1990. **7206**

POPULATION

Smith, Guy-Harold, "A Population Map of Ohio for 1920," *Geographical Review*, vol. 18, 3 (1928), pp. 422–427. **7207**

Smith, Guy-Harold, "Population Redistribution in Ohio, 1880–1930," in J. H. Sitterly, R. H. Baker, and J. I. Falconer, eds., *Major Land-Use Problem Areas and Land Utilization in Ohio, 1935*

(Columbus: Ohio Agricultural Experiment Stations, Bulletin no. 79, 1935), pp. 287–294. **7208**

Van Cleef, Eugene, "Finnish Population Movement in Ohio," *Baltic and Scandinavian Countries*, vol. 3 (1937), pp. 253–255. **7209**

Handel, Hazel G., "Geographic Factors in the Evolution of the Present Population Pattern of Ohio," Master's thesis, Clark University, 1941. **7210**

Colbourne, Fred W., "The Population Geography of Ohio: 1860–1920," Master's thesis, Miami University of Ohio, 1963. **7211**

Wolf, Laurence G., "Population Redistribution in Ohio: 1900–2000," Ph.D. diss., Syracuse University, 1966. **7212**

Heath, Marilyn S., "A Study of the Threshold Negro Population of Ohio, 1950–1970," Master's thesis, Bowling Green State University, 1973. **7213**

Brown, E. Leonard, "Quaker Migration to 'Miami Country,' 1798–1861," Ph.D. diss., Michigan State University, 1974. **7214**

Rose, Gregory S., "The County Origins of Migrants to Southeastern Ohio before 1850," *Ohio Geographers: Recent Research Themes*, vol. 16 (1988), pp. 24–41. **7215**

RURAL & REGIONAL SOCIAL GEOGRAPHY

See also **4823–4824, 4827, 7081**

General cultural patterns

Wilhelm, Hubert G. H., *The Origin and Distribution of Settlement Groups: Ohio, 1850* (Athens, Ohio: Cutler Hall, 1982), 262 pp. **7216**

Noble, Allen G., "Identifying Ethnic Regions in Ohio," *Ohio Geographers: Recent Research Themes*, vol. 12 (1984), pp. 18–29. **7217**

American regional traits

Spiro, James A., "New England in Ohio: Cultural Transplantation and Preservation in the Western Reserve and Hudson Township," Master's thesis, Michigan State University, 1974. **7218**

Wilhelm, Hubert G. H., "New England in Southeastern Ohio," *Pioneer America Society Transactions*, vol. 2 (1979), pp. 13–30. **7219**

European ethnic communities

Van Cleef, Eugene, "The Finns of Ohio," *Ohio Archeological and Historical Quarterly*, vol. 43, 4 (1934), pp. 452–460. **7220**

McManis, Douglas R., "Schoenbrunn: Ohio's Abortive Cultural Hearth," Master's thesis, Kent State University, 1955. **7221**

Wilhelm, Hubert G. H., "A Lower Saxon Settlement Region in Western Ohio," *Pioneer America Society Transactions*, vol. 4 (1981), pp. 1–10. **7222**

Wilhelm, Hubert G. H., "German Settlers in Ohio: The Initial Immigration Phase," *Ohio Geographers: Recent Research Themes*, vol. 11 (1983), pp. 21–31. **7223**

Gibb, Andrew, "Our Most Sanguine Expectations: The Rise and Fall of a Scottish Town in the Ohio Valley, 1800–1840," *Ohio Geographers: Recent Research Themes*, vol. 12 (1984), pp. 9–17. **7224**

Wilhelm, Hubert G. H., "The Route West: German Immigration in Ohio before 1850, with Emphasis on the Riverine Area," in Michael O. Roark, ed., *French and Germans in the Mississippi Valley: Landscape and Cultural Traditions* (Cape Girardeau: Southeast Missouri State University, Center for Regional History and Cultural Heritage, 1988), pp. 209–228. **7225**

Struble, Michael T., "Ty Chapels and the Residual Patterns of Welsh Settlement upon the Landscape of Southeastern Ohio," *Pioneer America Society Transactions*, vol. 12 (1989), pp. 21–28. **7226**

POLITICAL & ADMINISTRATIVE GEOGRAPHY

See also **7091, 7094**

Military

Smith, Guy-Harold, "George Washington at the Great Bend of the Ohio River," *Ohio Archeological and Historical Quarterly*, vol. 41, 4 (1932), pp. 655–667. **7227**

Smith, Guy-Harold, "Washington's Camp Sites on the Ohio River," *Ohio Archeological and Historical Quarterly*, vol. 41, 1 (1932), pp. 1–19. **7228**

Political

French, Richard, "The Virginia Military District as a Distinct Political Entity within Ohio, as Measured by Presidential Elections, 1804–1976," Master's thesis, Bowling Green State University, 1979. **7229**

Jonas, Andrew E., "Local Interests and State Territorial Structures: Integration and Fragmentation in Metropolitan Columbus, Ohio, in the Postwar Period," Ph.D. diss., Ohio State University, 1989. **7230**

ECONOMIC DEVELOPMENT

Morrison, Paul C., "Kelleys Island, Ohio: An Economy in Transition," *Economic Geography*, vol. 26, 2 (1950), pp. 105–124. [Focus on 1921–1947] **7231**

Denniston, Robert, "The Rise and Decline of Grist Milling: An Element of the Early Economy of Lake and Geauga Counties, Ohio," Master's thesis, Kent State University, 1967. **7232**

LAND & LAND USE

Land survey

Thrower, Norman J. W., "Contrasting Cadastral Survey Systems in Ohio and Their Effects on Rural Settlement," Ph.D. diss., University of Wisconsin–Madison, 1958. **7233**

Pattison, William D., "The Survey of the Seven Ranges," *Ohio Historical Quarterly*, vol. 68, 2 (1959), pp. 115–140. **7234**

Thrower, Norman J. W., *Original Survey and Land Subdivision: A Comparative Study of the Form and Effect of Contrasting Cadastral Surveys* (Chicago: Rand McNally & Co., for the Association of American Geographers, Monograph no. 4, 1966), 160 pp. **7235**

Cooper, Sherwin H., "The Survey Grid as a Control of Settlement and Circulation," in S. P. Chatterjee and S. P. DasGupta, eds., *Selected Papers of the International Geographical Congress*, vol. 3, *Population and Settlement Geography, Political and Historical Geography* (Calcutta: National Committee for Geography, 1971), pp. 71–78. **7236**

Land tenure

Hardenberg, Mark J., "Land Parcel Fragmentation as a Measure of Land Use Change in Appalachian Ohio, 1930–1976," Master's thesis, Ohio University, 1980. **7237**

Stephens, David T., and Alexander T. Bobersky, "Analysis of Land Sales, Steubenville Land Office, 1800–1820," *Pioneer American Society Transactions*, vol. 13 (1990), pp. 1–10. **7238**

Land use

Hudgins, Bert, "The South Bass Island Community (Put-in-Bay)," *Economic Geography*, vol. 19, 1 (1943), pp. 16–36. [Focus on 1850s–1940] **7239**

Reith, David J., "The Impact of Urbanization on Rural Land in Butler County, Ohio, 1940–1965," Master's thesis, Miami University of Ohio, 1966. **7240**

EXTRACTIVE ACTIVITY

Carmin, Robert L., "The Coal Mining Industry of Guernsey County, Ohio," *Economic Geography*, vol. 19, 3 (1943), pp. 292–300. [Focus on 1890–1940]   **7241**

Lewis, Donald W., "The Decline of the Lake Erie Commercial Fishing Industry in Ohio," Ph.D. diss., Ohio State University, 1966.   **7242**

AGRICULTURE

White, C. Langdon, and Clyde E. Cooper, "The Sheep Industry of Southeastern Ohio," *Economic Geography*, vol. 7, 3 (1931), pp. 263–272. [Focus on 1840–1930]   **7243**

Morrison, Paul C., "Viticulture in Ohio," *Economic Geography*, vol. 12, 1 (1936), pp. 71–85. [Focus on 1822–1934]   **7244**

Stover, Stephen L., "The Changing Regionalization of Sheep Husbandry in Ohio," Ph.D. diss., University of Wisconsin–Madison, 1960.   **7245**

Stover, Stephen L., "Early Sheep Husbandry in Ohio," *Agricultural History*, vol. 36, 2 (1962), pp. 101–107.   **7246**

Stover, Stephen L., "Ohio's Sheep Year: 1868," *Agricultural History*, vol. 38, 2 (1964), pp. 102–107.   **7247**

Beach, J. Richard, "The Sheep Industry in the Upper Ohio Area, 1770–1973: A Geographic Analysis," Ph.D. diss., University of Pittsburgh, 1975.   **7248**

Beach, J. Richard, *Two Hundred Years of Sheep Raising in the Upper Ohio Valley* (Monongahela: Bicentennial Commission of Washington County, Pennsylvania, 1976), 104 pp.   **7249**

LANDSCAPE

See also 7128

General

Raup, Hallock F., "Western Reserve Landscapes," in Will R. Folger, Mary H. Folger, and Harry F. Lupold, eds., *The Western Reserve Story* (Garrettsville, Ohio: Western Reserve Magazine, 1981), pp. 9–14.   **7250**

Noble, Allen G., "Landscape of Piety/Landscape of Profit: The Amish-Mennonite and Derived Landscapes of Northeastern Ohio," *East Lakes Geographer*, vol. 21 (1986), pp. 34–48.   **7251**

Noble, Allen G., and Debrah King, "Here Today, Gone Tomorrow: Determining the Disappearance Rate of Agricultural Structures in Pike County, Ohio," in Robert E. Walls, ed., *The Old Traditional Way of Life: Essays in Honor of Warren E. Roberts* (Bloomington: Trickster Press, Indiana University Folklore Institute, 1989), pp. 272–282.   **7252**

Houses

Noble, Allen G., "The Evolution and Classification of Nineteenth Century Housing in Ohio," *Journal of Geography*, vol. 74, 5 (1973), pp. 285–302.   **7253**

Gillespie, M. Gail, "Pre- and Post-Industrial Saltbox Houses as Features of Local Evolution in Athens County, Ohio," Master's thesis, Ohio University, 1985.   **7254**

Barns & other outbuildings

Noble, Allen G., "Barns and Square Silos in Northeast Ohio," *Pioneer America*, vol. 6, 2 (1974), pp. 12–21.   **7255**

Wilhelm, Hubert G. H., "The Pennsylvania-Dutch Barn in Southeastern Ohio," in H. Jesse Walker and William G. Haag, eds., *Man and Cultural Heritage: Papers in Honor of Fred B. Kniffen* (Baton Rouge: Louisiana State University School of Geoscience, Geoscience & Man, vol. 5, 1974), pp. 155–162.   **7256**

Coffey, Brian, "Nineteenth Century Barn Types in Geauga County, Ohio: A Study of the Cultural Landscape," Master's thesis, University of Akron, 1976.   **7257**

Noble, Allen G., "Barns as Elements of the Settlement Landscape of Rural Ohio," *Pioneer America*, vol. 9, 1 (1977), pp. 62–79.   **7258**

Noble, Allen G., and Albert J. Korsok, "Barn Variations in Columbiana County, Ohio," *East Lakes Geographer*, vol. 12 (1977), pp. 98–111.   **7259**

Carlson, Alvar W., "Designing Historic Rural Areas: A Survey of Northwestern Ohio Barns," *Landscape*, vol. 22, 3 (1978), pp. 29–33.   **7260**

Coffey, Brian, "Nineteenth-Century Barns of Geauga County, Ohio," *Pioneer America*, vol. 10, 2 (1978), pp. 53–63.   **7261**

Noble, Allen G., "Crib Death: The Demise of Elevated Corn Cribs in Pike County, Ohio," *East Lakes Geographer*, vol. 23 (1988), pp. 27–36. **7262**

Wilhelm, Hubert G. H., "Double Overhang Barns in Southeastern Ohio," *Pioneer America Society Transactions*, vol. 12 (1989), pp. 29–37.   **7263**

COMMUNICATIONS & TRADE

See also 4522

Chapman, Charles K., "Ohio Canals," *Journal of Geography*, vol. 17, 4 (1918), pp. 152–159.   **7264**

Ketcham, Hazel M., "The Evolution of the Transportation Routes between Presque Isle Bay and the Ohio River," Master's thesis, University of Chicago, 1932.　　　　　　　　　7265

Ray, John B., "Zane's Trace, 1796–1812: A Study in Historical Geography," Ph.D. diss., Indiana University, 1968.　　　　　　　　　7266

Brown, Lawrence A., et al., "The Diffusion of Cable Television in Ohio: A Case Study of Diffusion Agency Location Patterns and Processes of the Polynuclear Type," Economic Geography, vol. 50, 4 (1974), pp. 285–299. [Focus on 1950–1970]　　　　　　　　　7267

Ray, John B., "Trade Patterns along Zane's Trace, 1797–1812," Professional Geographer, vol. 22, 3 (1976), pp. 142–146.　　　　　　　　　7268

Kimmerly, David, "The Creation of a Canal Landscape: The Impact of the Hocking Canal on the Settlement of the Hocking River Valley, 1840–1870," Master's thesis, Ohio University, 1983.　　　　　　　　　7269

Ryan, Joseph A., II, "Development of Transportation Networks in the Cuyahoga Valley, 1820–1880," Master's thesis, Kent State University, 1989.　　　　　　　　　7270

MANUFACTURING & INDUSTRIALIZATION

General

Wright, Alfred J., "The Industrial Geography of the Middle Miami Valley, Ohio," Papers of the Michigan Academy of Science, Arts, and Letters, vol. 28 (1936), pp. 401–427.　　　7271

Tanger, Marjorie D., "Ohio's Eastern Lake Plains: The Industrial Evolution of a Commercial Shore," Master's thesis, Ohio State University, 1954.　　　　　　　　　7272

Price, Robert D., Jr., "The Analysis of the Inter-Urban Migration of Manufacturing Establishments in Hamilton County, 1949–1967," Master's thesis, University of Cincinnati, 1968.　　7273

Iron and Steel Industry

Stout, Wilber E., "The Charcoal Iron Industry of the Hanging Rock Iron District: Its Influence on the Early Development of the Ohio Valley," Ohio Archeological and Historical Quarterly, vol. 42, 1 (1933), pp. 72–104.　　　7274

Drobnock, George, "The Early Iron Industry of Vinton County, Ohio, and Its Effects on Land Tenure and Land Use," Master's thesis, Ohio University, 1979.　　　　　　　7275

Kotch, Joseph A., Jr., "The Mahoning Iron and Steel Industry," Proceedings of the Middle States Division, Association of American Geographers, vol. 15 (1981), pp. 43–47. [Focus on 1804–1977]　　　　　　　　　7276

Other industries

Lezius, Walter G., "Geography of Glass Manufacture at Toledo, Ohio," Economic Geography, vol. 13, 4 (1937), pp. 402–412. [Focus on 1888–1933]　　　　　　　　　7277

Rosell, Ruth F., "The Development of Paper Manufacture in the Miami Valley," Master's thesis, Miami University of Ohio, 1941.　　　7278

Frank, Ralph W., "The Rubber Industry of the Akron-Barberton Area: A Study of the Factors Related to Its Development, Distribution, and Localization," Ph.D. diss., Northwestern University, 1952.　　　　　　　　　7279

Willis, Patricia A., "Transformation of a Landscape: A Study of the Clay Industry in Tuscarawas County, Ohio, 1870–1940," Master's thesis, Kent State University, 1979.　　　7280

URBAN NETWORKS & URBANIZATION

See also 7152

Hessler, Sherry O., "Patterns of Transport and Urban Growth in the Miami Valley, Ohio, 1820–1880," Master's thesis, Johns Hopkins University, 1961.　　　　　　　　　7281

McElhoe, Forrest L., Jr., "A Comparative Study of the Geographic Factors in the Rise of Cities in the Hocking Valley, Ohio, with Special Reference to Their Locations and Sites," Ph.D. diss., Ohio State University, 1965.　　　7282

Salling, Mark, "Town Size and Growth in a Spatial System of Towns: Two Hypotheses and an Empirical Study in Southeastern Ohio, 1870 to 1900," Master's thesis, University of Cincinnati, 1973.　　　　　　　　　7283

TOWN GROWTH

Cincinnati

Fenneman, Nevin M., "Geographic Influences Affecting Early Cincinnati," Journal of Geography, vol. 9, 7 (1911), p. 192.　　　7284

Garbutt, Irving R., "The Development of Cincinnati," Journal of Geography, vol. 9, 7 (1911), pp. 182–183.　　　　　　　　　7285

Whitaker, J. Russell, "Cincinnati," Journal of Geography, vol. 21, 6 (1922), pp. 222–227.　　7286

Cleveland

Strong, Helen M., "The Geography of Cleveland," Ph.D. diss., University of Chicago, 1921. **7287**

Wood, George E., "Cleveland," *Journal of Geography*, vol. 21, 6 (1922), pp. 218–221. **7288**

Dureau, Agnès, "Cleveland–Ohio," *La vie urbaine*, vol. 16, 28 (1926), pp. 786–800. **7289**

Wilson, Lois D., "The Cleveland Area: A Geographic Study, 1796–1900," Master's thesis, Ohio State University, 1946. **7290**

Denton, William E., "The Growth and Development of Suburbia; An Explanation of the Growth Ring Concept: The Cleveland Metropolitan Area, 1950–1970," Master's thesis, Kent State University, 1976. **7291**

Goetz, Andrew R., "The Effect of Rail Transit on the Spatial Distribution of Population and Land Values in Cleveland, Ohio: 1900–1980," Master's thesis, Kent State University, 1984. **7292**

Other centers

Hoyt, Edith E., "Geographic Factors in the Origin and Development of Marietta, Ohio," Ph.D. diss., Clark University, 1928. **7293**

Curless, Irene, "The Evolution of Marion, Ohio," Master's thesis, Ohio State University, 1942. **7294**

Davey, Thomas E., "The Historical Geography of Marietta, Ohio," Master's thesis, Kent State University, 1949. **7295**

Appleby, Joseph, "A Historical Geography of Cambridge, Ohio," Master's thesis, Kent State University, 1950. **7296**

Hendrickson, George R., "Bowling Green, Ohio: Evolution and Function," Master's thesis, University of California–Los Angeles, 1950. **7297**

Summers, Leerie R., "Canal Fulton, Ohio: A Study of the Development of a Community," Master's thesis, Kent State University, 1953. **7298**

Andrick, David, "Historical-Geographical Study of Cuyahoga Falls, Ohio," Master's thesis, Kent State University, 1961. **7299**

Mould, David H., "The Company Town That Outlived the Company: Haydenville, Ohio," *Journal of Cultural Geography*, vol. 5, 2 (1985), pp. 71–86. **7300**

URBAN ECONOMIC STRUCTURE

Cincinnati

Homenuck, P. Henry M., "Historical Geography of the Cincinnati Pork Industry, 1810–1893," Master's thesis, University of Cincinnati, 1965. **7301**

Tunstall, Richard J., The Changing Composition of Retailing in Downtown Cincinnati, 1945–1977," Master's thesis, University of Cincinnati, 1979. **7302**

Miller, Glenn R., "Transportation and Urban Growth in Cincinnati, Ohio, 1788–1980," Ph.D. diss., University of Cincinnati, 1983. **7303**

Columbus

Hunker, Henry L., "Columbus, Ohio: The Industrial Evolution of a Commercial Center, Ph.D. diss., Ohio State University, 1953. **7304**

Hunker, Henry L., *Industrial Evolution of Columbus, Ohio* (Columbus: Ohio State University, College of Commerce, Bureau of Business Research and Administration, 1958), 260 pp. **7305**

Mair, Andrew, "Private Plans for Economic Development: Local Business Coalitions in Columbus, Ohio, 1870–1986," Ph.D. diss., Ohio State University, 1988. **7306**

Other centers

Heitz, Catherine L., "The Evolution of the Lima, Ohio, Oil Industry," Master's thesis, Miami University of Ohio, 1958. **7307**

Rowe, Elijah, "The Impact of the Railroad on the Pattern of Land Use and Development of Kent, Ohio," Ph.D. diss., Kent State University, 1972. **7308**

Grandfield, Irish, "Trends in Changing Floodplain Land Use in Athens, Ohio, 1939–1986," Master's thesis, Ohio University, 1987. **7309**

Miller, Harvey J., "An Anatomy of Commercial Decline: Structural Changes in the Youngstown Central Business District, 1960–1985," Master's thesis, Kent State University, 1987. **7310**

URBAN SOCIAL STRUCTURE

See also 4698

General

Colten, Craig E., "Shaping Sacred Space in Urban Ohio: 1788–1860," *Ohio Geographers: Recent Research Themes*, vol. 13 (1985), pp. 70–83. **7311**

Akron

Fuller, Ross N., "The Effect of Negro Migration on the Electoral Geography of Akron, Ohio, 1934–1964: An Application of the Lewis Method of Cartographic Analysis," Master's thesis, Kent State University, 1968. **7312**

Woolford, Warren L., "A Geographical Appraisal of Major Distributional Changes in the Akron,

Ohio, Black Population, 1930–1970," Master's thesis, University of Akron, 1974. **7313**

Cincinnati

Litzelman, David J., "The Location of High Status Residential Areas in Cincinnati, Ohio, 1892–1910," Master's thesis, University of Cincinnati, 1970. **7314**

Taylor, Henry, "Spatial Organization and the Residential Experience: Black Cincinnati in 1850," *Social Science History*, vol. 10, 1 (1988), pp. 45–70. **7315**

Cleveland

Sanders, Ralph A., "Spatial Trends in Age Structure Changes within the Cleveland Ghetto, 1940–1965," Master's thesis, Pennsylvania State University, 1968. **7316**

Sanders, Ralph A., and John S. Adams, "Age Structure in Expanding Ghetto-Space: Cleveland, Ohio, 1940–1965," *Southeastern Geographer*, vol. 11, 2 (1971), pp. 121–132. **7317**

Ekechuku, Godwin, "The Pattern of the Elderly in the City of Cleveland, Ohio," Master's thesis, University of Akron, 1980. **7318**

Skinner, James L., "The Background Characteristics of Doctors as a Contributing Factor to Their Changing Distribution in Western Cleveland, Ohio, SMSA, 1912–1969," Ph.D. diss., University of Florida, 1980. **7319**

Columbus

Null, Howard A., "The Evolution of the Market-Mohawk Blighted Area in Columbus, Ohio," Master's thesis, Ohio State University, 1956. **7320**

Sutcliffe, Michael O., "Neighborhood Activism in Sociohistorical Perspective: Columbus, Ohio, 1900–1980," Ph.D. diss., Ohio State University, 1984. **7321**

Bowman, Stuart, "Urban Progressive Reform in Columbus: The Restructuring of Municipal Government, 1912–1916," Master's thesis, Ohio State University, 1988. **7322**

Sutcliffe, Felicity Kitchin, "The Changing Spatial Structure of the Twentieth-Century Family: Columbus, Ohio," Ph.D. diss., Ohio State University, 1988. **7323**

Other centers

Ellis, Lewis S., "Social Areas and Spatial Changes in Toledo, Ohio: 1950–1970," Master's thesis, University of Toledo, 1973. **7324**

King, Thomas, "Mid Nineteenth Century Black Settlement in Xenia, Ohio: An Historical Geog-

raphy," Master's thesis, University of Colorado, 1983. **7325**

TOWNSCAPE

Morrison, Paul C., "A Morphological Study of Worthington, Ohio," *Ohio Journal of Science*, vol. 34 (1934), pp. 31–45. **7326**

Wright, Alfred J., "Ohio Town Patterns," *Geographical Review*, vol. 27, 4 (1937), pp. 615–624. **7327**

Reps, John W., "Urban Development in the Nineteenth Century: The Squaring of Circleville," *Journal of the Society of Architectural Historians*, vol. 14, 1 (1955), pp. 23–26. **7328**

Francaviglia, Richard V., "Some Notes on Open Space in the Nineteenth Century Ohio Town," *Ohio Woodlands*, vol. 11, 4 (1973), pp. 14–15. **7329**

Francaviglia, Richard V., "Main Street: The Origins," *Timeline* (Ohio Historical Society), vol. 5, 6 (1988–1989), pp. 28–39. **7330**

Francaviglia, Richard V., "Main Street: The Twentieth Century," *Timeline* (Ohio Historical Society), vol. 6, 1 (1989), pp. 28–43. **7331**

Noble, Allen G., and Jill Schuler, "Landscape of the Future: The Art Deco and Streamlined Styles in Akron, Ohio, 1920–1940," *East Lakes Geographer*, vol. 24 (1989), pp. 13–33. **7332**

Francaviglia, Richard V., "Mining Town Commercial Vernacular Architecture: The 'Overhang Porches' of Ohio's Hocking Mining District," *Pioneer America Society Transactions*, vol. 13 (1990), pp. 45–52. **7333**

PLANNING

Philley, Shirley H., "Change over Time in the Planned Community of Greenhills, Ohio," Master's thesis, University of Cincinnati, 1989. **7334**

PLACE NAMES

Martin, Maria Ewing, "Origins of Ohio Place Names," *Ohio Archaeological and Historical Quarterly*, vol. 14, 3 (1905), pp. 272–290. **7335**

Raup, Hallock F., "Names of Ohio's Streams," *Names*, vol. 5, 3 (1957), pp. 162–168. **7336**

Raup, Hallock F., "The Standardization of Spelling on Ohio Settlement and Stream Names of Indian Origin," *Names*, vol. 15, 1 (1967), pp. 8–11. **7337**

Raup, Hallock F., "An Overview of Ohio Place-Names," *Names*, vol. 30, 1 (1982), pp. 49–54. **7338**

INDIANA

GENERAL

The state

Dryer, Charles R., "Geographic Influences in the Development of Indiana," *Journal of Geography*, vol. 9, 1 (1910), pp. 17–22.   7339

Switzer, Jesse E., "Some Observations Concerning the Historical Geography of Indiana," *Proceedings of the Indiana Academy of Science*, vol. 51 (1942), pp. 207–214.   7340

Smaller areas

Visher, Stephen S., "Geography and Local History: A Case Study," *Indiana Historical Bulletin*, vol. 32 (1955), pp. 39–41. [Geographical influences in the development of Bloomington]   7341

Kiefer, Wayne E., "Historical Development of Northwest Indiana," in M. Reshkin and L. Strawhen, eds., *Environmental Perspectives: Northwest Indiana 1973* (Highland: Northwest Indiana Comprehensive Health Planning, 1973), 208 pp.   7342

ENVIRONMENTAL CHANGE

See also 7018

Butler, Amos W., "Indiana: A Century of Changes in the Aspects of Nature," in Charles R. Dryer, ed., *Studies in Indiana Geography* (Terre Haute: Inland Publishing Co., 1897), pp. 72–81.   7343

NATIVE PEOPLES & WHITE RELATIONS

Buls, Erwin J., "The Grand Portage Fur Traders' Route and Indian Reservation," *Proceedings of the Indiana Academy of Science*, vol. 59 (1960), pp. 225–229.   7344

EXPLORATION & MAPPING

Kingsbury, Robert C., "The County Atlas in Indiana," *Proceedings of the Indiana Academy of the Social Sciences, 1976*, vol. 11 (1977), pp. 81–90.   7345

Kingsbury, Robert C., "Sanborn Maps of Indiana, 1883–1950," *Proceedings of the Indiana Academy of the Social Sciences, 1977*, vol. 12 (1978), pp. 67–77.   7346

POPULAR IMAGES

Good, James K., "The Delimitation of Southern Indiana as an Historic, Contemporary, and Per-

ceptual Region," Ph.D. diss., Indiana State University, 1974.   7347

Rose, Gregory S., "Frontier Perception and Settlement in Northeastern Indiana, 1820–1850," Master's thesis, Michigan State University, 1977.   7348

Bigelow, Bruce L., "Nineteenth Century Indiana as Depicted by Edward Eggleston: Themes for Historical Geography," *Proceedings of the Indiana Academy of Social Sciences*, vol. 23 (1988), pp. 33–41.   7349

REGIONAL SETTLEMENT

See also 7050–7051, 7053, 7055–7056

Bergen, John V., "Some Aspects of Settlement Patterns: A Case Study in South-Central Indiana," *Proceedings of the Indiana Academy of Science*, vol. 68 (1958), pp. 285–288. [Rural dwellings in 1946–1947 in portions of Johnson, Shelby, Brown, and Bartholomew counties]   7350

Guernsey, Lee, "Settlement Changes Caused by Strip Coal Mining in Indiana," *Proceedings of the Indiana Academy of Science*, vol. 70 (1961), pp. 158–164. [Focus on 1920s–1960, with emphasis on the 1950s]   7351

Kiefer, Wayne E., "The Rural Settlement Geography of Rush County, Indiana," Ph.D. diss., Indiana University, 1967.   7352

Kiefer, Wayne E., *Rush County, Indiana: A Study in Rural Settlement Geography* (Bloomington: Indiana University Geography Department Monographs, vol. 2, 1969), 144 pp.   7353

Barton, Thomas F., "Population and Settlement Decline in Southwestern Indiana," *Proceedings of the Indiana Academy of Science*, vol. 79 (1970), pp. 318–324. [Focus on 1930–1960]   7354

POPULATION

See also 7067

Visher, Stephen S., "Distribution of the Birthplaces of Indianians of 1870," *Indiana Magazine of History*, vol. 26, 2 (1930), pp. 126–142.   7355

Visher, Stephen S., "Indiana's Population, 1850–1940: Sources and Dispersal," *Indiana Magazine of History*, vol. 38, 1 (1942), pp. 51–59.   7356

Visher, Stephen S., "Population Changes in Indiana, 1840–1940," *Proceedings of the Indiana*

Academy of Science, vol. 51 (1942), pp. 179–193.
7357

Visher, Stephen S., "Indiana County Contrasts in Population Changes," *Proceedings of the Indiana Academy of Science*, vol. 53 (1944), pp. 139–143. [Focus on 1870–1940] **7358**

Gentilcore, R. Louis, "Curves of Population Change in Indiana, 1850–1950," *Procceedings of the Indiana Academy of Science*, vol. 62 (1953), pp. 272–276. **7359**

Lal, Amrit, "Population Trends in Indiana's Villages of 1000–2500 in 1950," *Proceedings of the Indiana Academy of Science*, vol. 66 (1957), pp. 204–208. [Focus on 1900–1950] **7360**

Rose, Gregory S., "The Southern-ness of Hoosierdom: The Nativity of Settlement Groups in Indiana by 1850," Ph.D. diss., Michigan State University, 1981. **7361**

Rose, Gregory S., "Major Sources of Indiana's Settlers in 1850," *Pioneer America Society Transactions*, vol. 6 (1983), pp. 67–76. **7362**

Rose, Gregory S., "Hoosier Origins: The Nativity of Indiana's United States–Born Population in 1850," *Indiana Magazine of History*, vol. 81, 3 (1985), pp. 201–232. **7363**

Rose, Gregory S., "Upland Southerners: The County Origins of Southern Migrants to Indiana by 1850," *Indiana Magazine of History*, vol. 82, 3 (1986), pp. 242–263. **7364**

RURAL & REGIONAL SOCIAL GEOGRAPHY

See also **4827**

General

Visher, Stephen S., "Scientific Contributions Made by Indiana's Colleges and Universities, 1870–1950," *Proceedings of the Indiana Academy of Science*, vol. 62 (1953), pp. 277–278. **7365**

Visher, Stephen S., "Indiana's Yield of Eminent People Compared with That of Nearby States," *Proceedings of the Indiana Academy of Science*, vol. 72 (1963), pp. 240–242. **7366**

Wolins, Jason K., "Folk Culture as a Reflection of Early Migration to Parke County, Indiana," Master's thesis, Indiana State University, 1974. **7367**

Bergquist, James M., "Tracing the Origins of a Midwestern Culture: The Case of Central Indiana," *Indiana Magazine of History*, vol. 77, 1 (1981), pp. 1–32. **7368**

Wintsch, Susan, "A Meander around New Harmony," *Geographical Magazine*, vol. 56, 6 (1984), pp. 317–320. **7369**

Bigelow, Bruce L., and Gregory S. Rose, "The Geography of New School Presbyterians in Indiana in 1850: A Puzzling Map," *Proceedings of the Indiana Academy of Social Sciences*, vol. 20 (1985), pp. 85–90. **7370**

Bigelow, Bruce L., "The Disciples of Christ in Antebellum Indiana: Geographical Indicator of the Border South," *Journal of Cultural Geography*, vol. 7, 1 (1986), pp. 49–58. [Focus on 1845–1860] **7371**

Rose, Gregory S., "Quakers, North Carolinians, and Blacks in Indiana's Settlement Pattern," *Journal of Cultural Geography*, vol. 7, 1 (1986), pp. 35–48. [Focus on 1850] **7372**

Amish and Mennonite communities

Landing, James E., "Organization of an Old Order Amish-Beachey Amish Settlement: Nappanee, Indiana," Ph.D. diss., Pennsylvania State University, 1967. **7373**

Landing, James E., "The Old Order Amish Settlement at Nappanee, Indiana: Oldest in Indiana," *Mennonite Historical Bulletin*, vol. 30, 4 (1969), p. 5. **7374**

Landing, James E., "A Morphology of Cultural Disintegration among German-American Minorities in Elkhart County, Indiana," *Brethren Life and Thought*, vol. 18, 1 (1973), pp. 13–24. **7375**

Harper, Glen A., and Leslie H. Smith, "They Chose Wisely: Settlement Patterns and Land Use among Mennonite Settlers in Southern Adams County, Indiana," *Pioneer America Society Transactions*, vol. 11 (1988), pp. 73–81. **7376**

POLITICAL & ADMINISTRATIVE GEOGRAPHY

See also **7094**

Visher, Stephen S., "Geography of Indiana Governors," *Indiana Magazine of History*, vol. 35, 1 (1939), pp. 58–65. **7377**

Badertscher, John W., "An Analysis of the Geographic Factors Involved in William Henry Harrison's Military Campaign in Indiana from Fort Knox to Prophet's Town," Master's thesis, Indiana State University, 1969. **7378**

LAND & LAND USE

Guernsey, Lee, "Land Use Changes Caused by a Quarter Century of Strip Coal Mining in Indiana," *Proceedings of the Indiana Academy of Science*, vol. 69 (1960), pp. 200–209. [Focus on 1934–1959] **7379**

Schneider, Allan F., "Non-Congressional Land-Survey Divisions in Indiana," *Proceedings of the*

Indiana Academy of Science, vol. 74 (1965), pp. 248–254.   **7380**

Kiefer, Wayne E., "Land Use and Historical Geography of the Indiana Dunes National Lakeshore," in M. Reshkin, H. Feldman, W. Kiefer, and C. Krekeler, eds., *Basic Ecosystems Studies of the Indiana Dunes National Lakeshore* (Gary: Indiana University-Northwest, School of Public and Environmental Affairs, 1975), chap. 2, 60 pp.   **7381**

EXTRACTIVE ACTIVITY

Loring, Robert D., "The Growth of Strip Coal-Mining in Indiana," *Proceedings of the Indiana Academy of Science*, vol. 61 (1952), pp. 184–186. [Focus on 1914–1949]   **7382**

AGRICULTURE

Rose, John K., "Climate and Corn Yield in Indiana, 1887–1930," *Proceedings of the Indiana Academy of Science*, vol. 41 (1932), pp. 317–321.   **7383**

Bracken, Lawson E., "Some Geographical Factors in a Quarter Century of Indiana Harvests, 1926–50," *Proceedings of the Indiana Academy of Science*, vol. 62 (1953), pp. 256–265.   **7384**

Landing, James E., "Analysis of the Decline of the Commercial Mint Industry of Indiana since World War II," Master's thesis, Pennsylvania State University, 1963.   **7385**

LANDSCAPE

See also **7128**

Kriebel, Ralph M., "Indiana's Changing Landscape," *Proceedings of the Indiana Academy of Science*, vol. 56 (1947), pp. 95–105.   **7386**

Bastian, Robert W., "Indiana Folk Architecture: A Lower Midwestern Index," *Pioneer America*, vol. 9, 2 (1977), pp. 113–136.   **7387**

Noble, Allen G., and Victoria Hosler, "A Method for Estimating Distribution of Barn Styles: Indiana as a Case Study," *Geographical Survey*, vol. 6, 3 (1977), pp. 14–31.   **7388**

Richason, Benjamin F., Jr., "The Greenville Treaty Boundary Line and the Cultural Landscape of East Central and Southeastern Indiana," Ph.D. diss., Michigan State University, 1978.   **7389**

COMMUNICATIONS & TRADE

Dryer, Charles R., "The Maumee-Wabash Waterway," *Annals of the Association of American Geographers*, vol. 9 (1919), pp. 41–51.   **7390**

Hurlburt, Floyd, "Our Highways: An Indian Heritage," *Proceedings of the Indiana Academy of Science*, vol. 62 (1953), pp. 266–271.   **7391**

Lamme, Ary J., III, "Crossing the Wabash: The Role of Ferries since the Early Nineteenth Century," *Professional Geographer*, vol. 21, 6 (1969), pp. 401–405.   **7392**

MANUFACTURING & INDUSTRIALIZATION

Austin, George S., and John B. Patton, "History of Brick Manufacture in Indiana," *Proceedings of the Indiana Academy of Science*, vol. 81 (1972), pp. 229–237.   **7393**

McGregor, John R., "A Survey of Historical Industrial Sites in Western Indiana," *Proceedings of the Symposium on Ohio Valley Urban and Historic Archeology*, vol. 4 (1986), pp. 96–102.   **7394**

URBAN NETWORKS & URBANIZATION

See also **7151–7152**

Visher, Stephen S., "The Location of Indiana Towns and Cities," *Indiana Magazine of History*, vol. 51, 4 (1953), pp. 341–346.   **7395**

Weingartner, Ronald O., "Population Change of Indiana Incorporated Places, 1860–1960," Master's thesis, Indiana University, 1966.   **7396**

Chang, Kang-tsung, "A Probabilistic Approach to Spatial Theory: The Distribution of Places in Indiana, 1860–1960," Ph.D. diss., Clark University, 1971.   **7397**

Pal, Dilip K., "The Changing Pattern of Urban Diffusion in Indiana, 1940 to 1970: Causes and Implications," *Proceedings of the Indiana Academy of the Social Sciences, 1970*, vol. 5 (1971), pp. 67–83.   **7398**

TOWN GROWTH

Strain, Warren, "Some Geographical Influences in the Growth of Fort Wayne," *Journal of Geography*, vol. 28, 5 (1929), pp. 211–216.   **7399**

Cheadle, Queen V., "Gary: A Planned City," Master's thesis, University of Chicago, 1938.   **7400**

Cutshall, Alden D., "Vincennes: Historic City on the Wabash," *Scientific Monthly*, vol. 57 (1943), pp. 413–424.   **7401**

Arlen, Mary L., "Greencastle, Indiana: The Geography of Its Development," Master's thesis, Indiana University, 1949.   **7402**

Moulton, Benjamin, "Indianapolis: Its Evolving Functions and Functional Areas," Ph.D. diss., Indiana University, 1950.   **7403**

Barton, Thomas F., "Relative Location and the Growth of Terre Haute," *Proceedings of the Indiana Academy of Science*, vol. 60 (1951), pp. 236–238.   7404

Visher, Stephen S., "Changing Significance of Environmental Factors at Bloomington, Indiana," *Annals of the Association of American Geographers*, vol. 46, 4 (1956), pp. 411–416.   7405

Visher, Stephen S., "Geographic Influences, Changes in Bloomington, Indiana," *Proceedings of the Indiana Academy of Science*, vol. 71 (1962), pp. 265–270.   7406

Borders, Carl, "An Analysis of the Geographic Factors Involved in the Development of Vincennes, Indiana," Master's thesis, Indiana State University, 1969.   7407

URBAN ECONOMIC STRUCTURE

Miller, Harold V., "Industrial Development of New Albany, Indiana," Master's thesis, University of Chicago, 1934.   7408

Miller, Harold V., "Industrial Development of New Albany, Indiana," *Economic Geography*, vol. 14, 1 (1938), pp. 47–54.   7409

Cutshall, Alden D., "Terre Haute Iron and Steel: A Declining Industry," *Indiana Magazine of History*, vol. 37, 3 (1941), pp. 237–244.   7410

Schockel, Bernard H., "Manufactural Evansville, 1820–1933," Ph.D. diss., University of Chicago, 1947. Published under the same title, as a University of Chicago Department of Geography Private Edition, 1947), 263 pp.   7411

Harvey, Robert O., *Land Uses in Bloomington, Indiana, 1818–1950* (Bloomington: Indiana University School of Business, Bureau of Business Research, Indiana Business Studies, no. 33, 1951), 84 pp.   7412

Schockel, Bernard H., "Manufacturing Level of Manufactural Evansville," *Proceedings of the Indiana Academy of Science*, vol. 60 (1951), pp. 256–259. [Focus on 1860–1940]   7413

Dinkel, E. Michael, and Adelord J. Cantin, "The Changing Location Patterns of the Neighborhood Grocers in Terre Haute, Indiana: A Geographic Analysis," *Proceedings of the Indiana Academy of Science*, vol. 79 (1970), pp. 309–317. [Focus on 1900–1967]   7414

Dunn, Richard L., "The Distribution of Mobile Home Park Development in Vigo County, Indiana," *Proceedings of the Indiana Academy of Science*, vol. 80 (1971), pp. 362–364. [Focus on 1940–1970]   7415

McGregor, John R., "Evansville, Indiana, Historic Industrial Sites," *Proceedings of the Symposium*

on Ohio Valley Urban and Historic Archeology, vol. 5 (1987), pp. 105–111.   7416

URBAN SOCIAL STRUCTURE

Riley, Bernard W., "The Residence Pattern of the Instructional Staff at Indiana University during the Twentieth Century: In the City of Bloomington, Indiana," *Proceedings of the Indiana Academy of Science*, vol. 73 (1964), pp. 188–195.   7417

Brooks, William D., "The Polarization of Political and Educational Functions and Their Effect on Community Growth: The Courthouse, the University, and Bloomington, Indiana," *Proceedings of the Indiana Academy of the Social Sciences*, 1970, vol. 5 (1971), pp. 96–108.   7418

Landing, James E., "The Pioneer Urbanist: A Micro-Study in Entrepreneurial Historical Geography," in W. P. Adams and F. M. Helleiner, eds., *International Geography, 1972*, vol. 1, sec. 5, *Historical Geography* (Toronto: University of Toronto Press, for the International Geographical Union, 1972), p. 438. [Michigan City, 1828–1830s]   7419

Nordsieck, Evelyn M., "The Residential Location and Mobility of Blacks in Indianapolis, 1850–1880," Master's thesis, University of Maryland, 1975.   7420

Barrows, Robert, "Hurryin' Hoosiers and the American Pattern: Geographic Mobility in Indianapolis and Urban North America," *Social Science History*, vol. 5, 2 (1981), pp. 197–222.   7421

TOWNSCAPE

Landing, James E., "The Geometrical Geography of Michigan City, Indiana," *Indiana History Bulletin*, vol. 49, 2 (1972), pp. 15–21.   7422

Landing, James E., "A Micro-Historical Case Study of Urban Development, Morphology, and Entrepreneurial Activity: Michigan City, Indiana," *Bulletin of the Illinois Geographical Society*, vol. 14, 1 (1972), pp. 14–21.   7423

Bastian, Robert W., "Architecture and Class Structure in Late Nineteenth-Century Terre Haute, Indiana," *Geographical Review*, vol. 65, 2 (1975), pp. 166–179.   7424

Martinson, Tom L., and Susan L. Nelson, "The Scarcity of Sylvan Space in Machine-Age Muncie," *Places*, vol. 3, 2 (1976), pp. 43–46. [Focus on 1941–1969]   7425

RECREATION & TOURISM

Thornbury, William D., "The Mineral Waters and Health Resorts of Indiana: A Study in Historical

Geography," *Proceedings of the Indiana Academy of Science*, vol. 50 (1941), pp. 154–164. **7426**

Jenkinson, Roger, "Historical Geography of Indiana High School and Collegiate Basketball," Ed.D. diss., Oklahoma State University, 1974.
  7427

PLANNING

Jakle, John A., and Robert L. Janiskee, "Why Covered Bridges? Toward the Management of Historic Landscapes: The Case of Parke County,

Indiana," in Ralph E. Ehrenberg, ed., *Pattern and Process: Research in Historical Geography* (Washington, D.C.: Howard University Press, 1975), pp. 193–201. **7428**

PLACE NAMES

See also **7166**

Baker, Ronald L., and Marvin Carmony, *Indiana Place Names* (Bloomington: Indiana University Press, 1975), 196 pp. **7429**

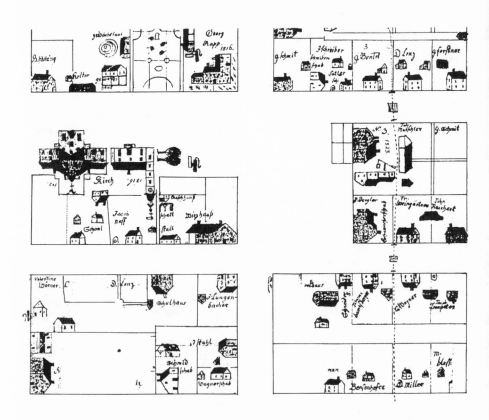

ILLINOIS

GENERAL

The state

Collins, Helen M., "Geographic Influence in the History of Illinois," Master's thesis, University of Chicago, 1908. **7430**

Ridgley, Douglas C., "Geographic Influences in the Development of Illinois," *Journal of Geography*, vol. 9, 8 (1911), pp. 209–214. **7431**

Clendening, R.onald J., "Historical Geography of the Illinois Country, 1673–1763," Master's thesis, Illinois State University, 1965. **7432**

Wheeler, David L., "The Illinois Country, 1673–1696," *Bulletin of the Illinois Geographical Society*, vol. 7, 1 (1965), pp. 42–47. **7433**

Cutshall, Alden D., "Milestones in the Development of Illinois," *Bulletin of the Illinois Geographical Society*, vol. 17, 2 (1975), pp. 3–7. **7434**

Cutshall, Alden D., "Historical Geography," in Ronald E. Nelson, ed., *Illinois: Land and Life in the Prairie State* (Dubuque: Kendall/Hunt, 1978), pp. 109–136. **7435**

Harris, Neil, and Michael P. Conzen, Introduction to *The WPA Guide to Illinois: The Federal Writers' Guide to 1930s Illinois* (New York: Pantheon Books, 1983), pp. xvii–xl. **7436**

Hornsley, A. Doyne, "Historical Portrait," in his *Illinois: A Geography* (Boulder: Westview Press, 1986), pp. 29–40. **7437**

Buisseret, David, *Historic Illinois from the Air* (Chicago: University of Chicago Press, 1990), 232 pp. **7438**

Smaller areas

Barrows, Harlan H., *Geography of the Middle Illinois Valley* (Urbana: Illinois State Geological Survey, Bulletin no. 15, 1910), 128 pp. **7439**

Hatch, Laura, "A Geographic Study of Du Page County, Illinois," Master's thesis, University of Chicago, 1911. **7440**

Sauer, Carl O., *Geography of the Upper Illinois Valley and History of Development* (Urbana: Illinois Geological Survey, Bulletin no. 27, 1916), 208 pp. Pp. 153-163 reprinted under the title "Conditions of Pioneer Life in the Upper Illinois Valley," in John Leighly, ed., *Land and Life: A Selection from the Writings of Carl Ortwin Sauer* (Berkeley: University of California Press, 1963), pp. 11-22. **7441**

Cloyer, Frank H., "Geographic Influences in the Settlement and Development of the Southern Counties of Illinois," Master's thesis, University of Chicago, 1920. **7442**

Smith, Marjorie C., "Historical Geography of Champaign County, Illinois," Ph.D. diss., University of Illinois, 1957. **7443**

Christensen, David E., and Robert M. Harper, eds., *The Mississippi–Ohio Confluence Area: A Geographic Interpretation of the Paducah 1:250,000 Topographic Map* (Normal, Ill.: National Council for Geographic Education, "Geography Through Maps" series, Special Publication no. 12, 1967), 49 pp. **7444**

Kircher, Harry B., *The Southern Illinois Prairies: A Geographic Interpretation of the Belleville 1:250,000 Topographic Map* (Normal, Ill.: National Council for Geographic Education, "Geography Through Maps" series, Special Publication no. 11, 1967), 39 pp. **7445**

Oakley, Dorothy, "The Historical Geography of McHenry County," Master's thesis, Northern Illinois University, 1972. **7446**

Conzen, Michael P., "The Historical and Geographical Development of the Illinois & Michigan Canal National Heritage Corridor," in Michael P. Conzen and Kay J. Carr, eds., *The Illinois & Michigan Canal National Heritage Corridor: A Guide to Its History and Sources* (Dekalb: Northern Illinois University Press, 1988), pp. 3–25. **7447**

Morris, Jo Ann, "Exploring the Historical Geography of Livingston County, Illinois," *Bulletin of the Illinois Geographical Society*, vol. 31, 2 (1989), pp. 3–13. **7448**

Conzen, Michael P., and Linda S. Lim, eds., *Illinois Canal Country: The Early Years in Comparative Perspective* (Chicago: University of Chicago Committee on Geographical Studies, Studies on the Illinois & Michigan Canal, no. 5, 1991), 155 pp. **7449**

ENVIRONMENTAL CHANGE

See also **7018, 7023, 7027**

General

Salisbury, Rollin D., and Harlan H. Barrows, *The Environment of Camp Grant* (Urbana: Illinois

Geological Survey, Bulletin no. 39, 1918), 75 pp. **7450**

Butzer, Karl W., "Geomorphology of the Lower Illinois Valley as a Spatial-Temporal Context for the Koster Archaic Site," *Illinois State Museum Reports of Investigations*, vol. 34 (1977), pp. 1–60. **7451**

Colten, Craig E., "Environmental Development in the East St. Louis Region, 1890–1930," *Environmental History Review*, vol. 14 , 1 & 2 (1990), pp. 93–114. **7452**

Climatic and hydrological change

Changnon, Stanley A., Jr., "Trends in Floods and Related Climatic Conditions in Illinois," *Climatic Change*, vol. 5, 4 (1983), pp. 341–364. **7453**

Changnon, Stanley A., Jr., "Climatic Fluctuations and Impacts: The Illinois Case," *American Meteorological Bulletin*, vol. 66, 2 (1985), pp. 142–151. **7454**

Hawkins-Coniglio, Maura, "The Impact of Urban and Suburban Land Use Change on Stream Discharge: The West Branch of the DuPage River, 1962–1983," Master's thesis, Western Illinois University, 1985. **7455**

Environmental pollution

Colten, Craig E., *Industrial Wastes in the Calumet Area: An Historical Geography, 1869–1970* (Illinois Hazardous Waste Research and Information Center, Research Report no. 1, 1985), 124 pp. **7456**

Colten, Craig E., "Documenting Historical Hazardous Wastes: Problems and Prospects in Illinois," *Papers & Proceedings of the Applied Geography Conference*, vol. 9 (1986), pp. 104–113. **7457**

Colten, Craig E., "Industrial Wastes in Southeast Chicago: Production and Disposal, 1870–1970," *Environmental Review*, vol. 10, 2 (1986), pp. 93–106. **7458**

Colten, Craig E., "Prehistoric Hazardous Waste in the Calumet Area: 1880–1970," *Bulletin of the Illinois Geographical Society*, vol. 28, 2 (1986), pp. 3–16. **7459**

Colten, Craig E., and Gerard B. Breen, *Historical Industrial Waste Disposal Practices in Winnebago County, Illinois, 1870–1980* (Illinois Hazardous Waste Research and Information Center, Research Report no. 11, 1986), 125 pp. **7460**

Colten, Craig E., "Industrial Middens in Illinois: The Search for Historical Hazardous Wastes, 1870–1980," *IA: The Journal for Industrial Archeology*, vol. 14 (1988), pp. 51–61. **7461**

Colten, Craig E., "Historical Geographic Identification of Hazardous Waste Disposal Sites: Illinois Examples," *Environmental Professional*, vol. 10 (1988), pp. 54–61. **7462**

Colten, Craig E., and Ted B. Samsel, *Historical Assessment of Hazardous Waste Management in Madison and St. Clair Counties, Illinois, 1890–1980* (Illinois Hazardous Waste Research and Information Center, Research Report no. 30, 1988), 81 pp. **7463**

NATIVE PEOPLES & WHITE RELATIONS

English, Thomas H., "The Cahokia Indian Mounds: A Plea for Their Preservation," *Geographical Review*, vol. 11, 2 (1921), pp. 207–211. **7464**

Woods, William I., "Prehistoric Settlement and Subsistence in the Cahokia Creek Drainage," Ph.D. diss., University of Wisconsin–Milwaukee, 1986. **7465**

EXPLORATION & MAPPING

Trewartha, Glenn T., "The Earliest Map of Galena, Illinois," *Wisconsin Magazine of History*, vol. 23, 1 (1939), pp. 40–43. **7466**

Fitchet, Duncan M., "100 Years and Rand McNally," *Surveying and Mapping*, vol. 16, 2 (1956), pp. 126–132. **7467**

Conzen, Michael P., ed., *Chicago Mapmakers: Essays on the Rise of the City's Map Trade* (Chicago: Chicago Historical Society, for the Chicago Map Society, 1984), 76 pp. **7468**

Conzen, Michael P., "Evolution of the Chicago Map Trade: An Introduction," *Chicago Mapmakers: Essays on the Rise of the City's Map Trade* (Chicago: Chicago Historical Society, for the Chicago Map Society, 1984), pp. 4–11. Co-published in *Chicago History*, vol. 13, 1 (1984), pp. 4–11. **7469**

Danzer, Gerald A., "Chicago's First Maps," in Michael P. Conzen, ed., *Chicago Mapmakers: Essays on the Rise of the City's Map Trade* (Chicago: Chicago Historical Society, for the Chicago Map Society, 1984), pp. 12–22. Copublished in *Chicago History*, vol. 13, 1 (1984), pp. 12–22. **7470**

Selmer, Marsha L., "Rufus Blanchard: Early Chicago Map Publisher," in Michael P. Conzen, ed., *Chicago Mapmakers: Essays on the Rise of the City's Map Trade* (Chicago: Chicago Historical Society, for the Chicago Map Society, 1984), pp. 23–31. Copublished in *Chicago History*, vol. 13, 1 (1984), pp. 23–31. **7471**

Danzer, Gerald A., "George F. Cram and the American Perception of Space," in Michael P. Conzen, ed., *Chicago Mapmakers: Essays on the Rise of the City's Map Trade* (Chicago: Chicago Historical Society, for the Chicago Map Society, 1984), pp. 32–45. Copublished in *Chicago History*, vol. 13, 1 (1984), pp. 32–45. **7472**

Peters, Cynthia H., "Rand, McNally and Company in the Nineteenth Century: Reaching for a National Market," in Michael P. Conzen, ed., *Chicago Mapmakers: Essays on the Rise of the City's Map Trade* (Chicago: Chicago Historical Society, for the Chicago Map Society, 1984), pp. 64–72. Copublished in *Chicago History*, vol. 13, 1 (1984), pp. 64–72. **7473**

Bergen, John V., "Maps and Their Makers in Early Illinois: The Burr Map and the Peck-Messinger Map," *Western Illinois Regional Studies*, vol. 10, 1 (1987), pp. 5–31. **7474**

POPULAR IMAGES & EVALUATION

McManis, Douglas R., *The Initial Evaluation and Utilization of the Illinois Prairies, 1815–1840* (Chicago: University of Chicago Department of Geography, Research Paper no. 94, 1964), 104 pp. **7475**

Birch, Brian P., "Initial Perception of Prairie: An English Settlement in Illinois," in Robert G. Ironside et al., eds., *Frontier Settlement* (Edmonton: University of Alberta, Department of Geography, 1974), pp. 178–194. **7476**

Vining, James W., "Illinois in the Early Geographies," *Bulletin of the Illinois Geographical Society*, vol. 21, 2 (1979), pp. 3–14. **7477**

Walters, William D., "Early Western Illinois Town Advertisements: A Geographical Inquiry," *Western Illinois Regional Studies*, vol. 8, 1 (1985), pp. 5–15. **7478**

Cohen, Shaul E., "Perceptions of Ottawa: A Sense of Place," in Michael P. Conzen, ed., *Focus on Ottawa: A Historical and Geographical Survey of Ottawa, Illinois, in the Twentieth Century* (Chicago: University of Chicago Committee on Geographical Studies, Studies on the Illinois & Michigan Canal Corridor, no. 1, 1987), pp. 67–70. **7479**

Winsor, Roger A., "Environmental Imagery of the Wet Prairie of East Central Illinois, 1820–1870," *Journal of Historical Geography*, vol. 13, 4 (1987), pp. 375–397. **7480**

Walters, William D., "A Contemporary View of the Changing Material Culture of Northern Illinois," *Material Culture*, vol. 20, 3 (1988), pp. 9–17. **7481**

Nelson, Caroline P. M., "Shake Lockport Out of the Box: Lockport and Dorothy Dow Fitzgerald," in Michael P. Conzen and Adam R. Daniel, eds., *Lockport Legacy: Themes in the Historical Geography of an Illinois Canal Town* (Chicago: University of Chicago Committee on Geographical Studies, Studies on the Illinois & Michigan Canal Corridor, no. 4, 1990), pp. 121–137. [The poet's image of her birthplace. Appendix presents world premier publication of two poems: a portion of Dow's autobiographical poem "The Flowers of Time, and Edgar Lee Masters' "The Illinois and Michigan Canal"] **7482**

REGIONAL SETTLEMENT

See also **7050–7051, 7053, 7055, 7062**

The state

Meyer, Douglas K., "Development of Settlement Patterns in Illinois, 1800–1850," *Illinois History*, vol. 27 (1973), pp. 27–29. **7483**

Meyer, Douglas K., "Development of Settlement Patterns on the Illinois Frontier," *Proceedings of the Association of American Geographers*, vol. 8 (1976), pp. 41–44. **7484**

French period

Henderson, John R., "The Cultural Landscape of French Settlement in the American Bottom," Master's thesis, Illinois State University, 1966. **7485**

Delehanty, James M., "Livelihood in the Region of Fort de Chartres under French Rule, 1720–1736," Master's thesis, University of Chicago, 1979. **7486**

Smaller areas

Emerson, Frederick V., "The Geographic Story of Kaskaskia," *Journal of Geography*, vol. 8, 9 (1910), pp. 193–201. **7487**

Schockel, Bernard H., "Settlement and Development of Jo Daviess County," Master's thesis, University of Chicago, 1913. **7488**

Schockel, Bernard H., "The Settlement and Development of Jo Daviess County, Illinois," in Arthur C. Trowbridge and Eugene W. Shaw, eds., *The Geology and Geography of the Galena and Elizabeth Quadrangle* (Urbana: Illinois Geological Survey, 1916), pp. 173–228. **7489**

Dodge, Stanley D., "Sequent Occupance of an Illinois Prairie," *Bulletin of the Geographic Society of Philadelphia*, vol. 29, 3 (1931), pp. 205–209. [Bureau Prairie, Bureau Co.] **7490**

Poggi, Edith M., "The Prairie Province of Illinois: A Study of Human Adjustment to the Natural Environment," Ph.D. diss., University of Illinois, 1931.   7491

Poggi, Edith M., "Settlement and Development of the Prairie Province of Illinois," *Transactions of the Illinois State Academy of Science*, vol. 24 (1932), pp. 401–409.   7492

Poggi, Edith M., *The Prairie Province of Illinois: A Study in Human Adjustment to the Natural Environment* (Urbana: University of Illinois, Bulletin vol. 31, 42, 1934), 124 pp.   7493

Hicken, Victor, "Geographic Factors in the Settlement of Western Illinois," *Bulletin of the Illinois Geographical Society*, vol. 2, 1 (1960), pp. 16–22.   7494

Gaither, Jack, "The Development of a Four County Area in Central Illinois, 1840–1880," Master's thesis, Illinois State University, 1964.   7495

Preno, Judith, "Settlement of Livingston County, Illinois, 1830–1880," Master's thesis, Illinois State University, 1965.   7496

Knepler, Jane, "Early Settlement and Development of Lexington Township, McLean County, Illinois," *Bulletin of the Illinois Geographical Society*, vol. 8, 2 (1966), pp. 8–14.   7497

Lutgens, F. K., "A Geographical Appraisal of the Morphology of the English Prairie Settlement," Master's thesis, Illinois State University, 1970.   7498

Birch, Brian P., "The Environment and Settlement of the Prairie-Woodland Transition Belt: A Case Study of Edwards County, Illinois," *Southampton Research Series in Geography*, vol. 6 (1971), pp. 3–31.   7499

Wheeler, David L., and Daniel Hager, "The Influence of Railroads on Prairie Settlement in Central Illinois," *Bulletin of the Illinois Geographical Society*, vol. 13, 2 (1971), pp. 30–35.   7500

Anderson, Gary I., "Sequent Occupance Reviewed: The Case of Clinton County, Illinois, 1840–1860," Master's thesis, Southern Illinois University at Edwardsville, 1973.   7501

Puckett, William, "Settlement History Development of the Cahokia Canal Drainage Area," *Bulletin of the Illinois Geographical Society*, vol. 21, 2 (1974), pp. 15–27.   7502

Park, Siyoung, "Perception of Land Quality and Settlement of Northern Pike County, 1821–1836," *Western Illinois Regional Studies*, vol. 3, 1 (1980), pp. 5–21.   7503

Conzen, Michael P., and Melissa J. Morales, eds., *Settling the Upper Illinois Valley: Patterns of Change in the I & M Canal Corridor, 1830–1900*

(Chicago: University of Chicago Committee on Geographical Studies, Studies on the Illinois & Michigan Canal Corridor, no. 3, 1989), 171 pp.   7504

POPULATION

See also 7067

Schwartz, Carroll, "Distribution of the Foreign-Born Population of Illinois, 1870–1950," Master's thesis, Southern Illinois University, 1959.   7505

Mattingly, Paul F., "Population Trends in the Hamlets and Villages of Illinois, 1940–1960," *Professional Geographer*, vol. 15, 6 (1963), pp. 17–21.   7506

Larson, Albert J., and Siim Sööt, "Centers of Population and the Historical Geography of Illinois," *Bulletin of the Illinois Geographical Society*, vol. 15, 2 (1973), pp. 34–52.   7507

Meyer, Douglas K., "Southern Illinois Migration Fields: The Shawnee Hills in 1850," *Professional Geographer*, vol. 28, 2 (1976), pp. 151–160.   7508

Larson, Albert J., and Siim Sööt, "Population and Social Geography: Historical Development of Social and Population Patterns," in Robert E. Nelson, ed., *Illinois: Land and Life in the Prairie State* (Dubuque: Kendall/Hunt, 1978), pp. 140–152.   7509

Strauss, Lee J., Jr., "Migration to LaSalle County, Illinois, 1820–1877: A Quantitative Study in Collective Biography," Master's thesis, University of Chicago, 1978.   7510

Meyer, Douglas K., "Immigrant Clusters in the Illinois Military Tract," *Pioneer America*, vol. 12, 2 (1980), pp. 97–112.   7511

Marcioni, Steven, "Net Migration in Non-Metropolitan Illinois, 1950–1976," Master's thesis, Western Illinois University, 1982.   7512

Meyer, Douglas K., "Persistence and Change in Migrant Patterns in a Transitional Culture Region of the Prairie State," *Bulletin of the Illinois Geographical Society*, vol. 26, 1 (1984), pp. 13–28. [Coles Co., 1850–1870]   7513

Gambone, Michael D., "The Immigrant Presence in Grundy County, 1850–1860," in Michael P. Conzen and Melissa J. Morales, eds., *Settling the Upper Illinois Valley: Patterns of Change in the I & M Canal Corridor, 1830–1900* (Chicago: University of Chicago Committee on Geographical Studies, Studies on the Illinois & Michigan Canal Corridor, no. 3, 1989), pp. 61–76.   7514

Nannini, Michael D., "The Ethnic and Regional Composition of LaSalle County, 1850–1860," in Michael P. Conzen and Melissa J. Morales, eds., *Settling the Upper Illinois Valley: Pattern of*

Change in the I & M Canal Corridor, 1830–1900 (Chicago: University of Chicago Committee on Geographical Studies, Studies on the Illinois & Michigan Canal Corridor, no. 3, 1989), pp. 77–90. **7515**

Meyer, Douglas K., "Illinois and the Great Migration," *Illinois History*, vol. 43 (1990), pp. 141–145. **7516**

RURAL & REGIONAL SOCIAL GEOGRAPHY

Culture regions

Tudor, William J., "Southern Illinois: A Cultural Area," *Transactions of the Illinois State Academy of Science*, vol. 42 (1949), pp. 140–144. **7517**

Larson, Albert J., "Northern Illinois as New England Extended: A Preliminary Report," *Pioneer America*, vol. 7, 1 (1975), pp. 45–51. **7518**

Meyer, Douglas K., "Illinois Culture Regions at Mid-Nineteenth Century," *Bulletin of the Illinois Geographical Society*, vol. 18, 2 (1976), pp. 3–13. **7519**

Ethnic communities

Nelson, Helge M. O., "Svensk bosättning: Chicago och norra Illinois," *Svensk geografisk årsbok*, vol. 16 (1940), pp. 108–151. **7520**

Nelson, Ronald E., "The Bishop Hill Colony and Its Pioneer Economy," *Swedish Pioneer Historical Quarterly*, vol. 18, 1 (1967), pp. 32–48. **7521**

Bettis, Norman C., "The Swiss Community of Highland, Illinois: A Study in Historical Geography," Master's thesis, Western Illinois University, 1968. **7522**

Bettis, Norman C., "The Swiss Community of Highland, Illinois: A Study in Historical Geography," *Bulletin of the Illinois Geographical Society*, vol. 12, 1 (1969), pp. 51–68. **7523**

Nelson, Ronald E., "The Role of Colonies in the Pioneer Settlement of Henry County, Illinois," Ph.D. diss., University of Nebraska, 1970. **7524**

Nelson, Ronald E., "Bishop Hill: Swedish Development of the Western Illinois Frontier," *Western Illinois Regional Studies*, vol. 1, 2 (1978), pp. 109–120. **7525**

Kantowicz, Edward, "A Fragment of French Canada on the Illinois Prairies," *Journal of the Illinois State Historical Society*, vol. 75, 4 (1982), pp. 263–276. [Kankakee Co.] **7526**

Nelson, Ronald E., "The Bishop Hill Colony: What They Found," *Western Illinois Regional Studies*, vol. 12, 2 (1989), pp. 36–45. **7527**

Nelson, Ronald E., "The Building of Bishop Hill," *Western Illinois Regional Studies*, vol. 12, 2 (1989), pp. 46–60. **7528**

Other features

Frazer, Timothy, "Language Variation in the Military Tract," *Western Illinois Regional Studies*, vol. 5, 1 (1982), pp. 54–64. **7529**

Jelks, Edward, "Route of the Zion's Camp March across Pike County, Illinois, June 1834," *Bulletin of the Illinois Geographical Society*, vol. 28, 2 (1986), pp. 17–40. **7530**

Langrock, David J., "The Progress of Public Education, 1836–1989," in Michael P. Conzen and Adam R. Daniel, eds., *Lockport Legacy: Themes in the Historical Geography of an Illinois Canal Town* (Chicago: University of Chicago Committee on Geographical Studies, Studies on the Illinois & Michigan Canal Corridor, no. 4, 1990), pp. 103–110. **7531**

POLITICAL & ADMINISTRATIVE GEOGRAPHY

See also **7094**

Political

Graetner, Norman A., "The Illinois Country and the Treaty of Paris of 1783," *Illinois Historical Journal*, vol. 78, 1 (1985), pp. 2–16. **7532**

Military

Piety, James, "The Development of Chicago's Camp Douglas Prisoner of War Camp: 1861–1865," *Bulletin of the Illinois Geographical Society*, vol. 21, 2 (1979), pp. 36–41. **7533**

Dunlop, Michael J., "The Effects of Two World Wars on the Community," in Michael P. Conzen, ed., *Focus on Ottawa: A Historical and Geographical Survey of Ottawa, Illinois, in the Twentieth Century* (Chicago: University of Chicago Committee on Geographical Studies, Studies on the Illinois & Michigan Canal Corridor, no. 1, 1987), pp. 64–66. **7534**

Kim, Ronald J., "The Corridor Goes to War: Patterns of Enlistment and Fatalities, with Special Reference to Grundy County," in Michael P. Conzen and Melissa J. Morales, ed., *Settling the Upper Illinois Valley: Patterns of Change in the I & M Canal Corridor, 1830–1900* (Chicago: University of Chicago Committee on Geographical Studies, Studies on the Illinois & Michigan Canal Corridor, no. 3, 1989), pp. 103–110. **7535**

Administrative

Sublett, Michael D., *Preserving the Territorial Integrity of Champaign County, Illinois: 1855–1867*

(Normal: Illinois State University Department of Geography, 1980), 16 pp.   **7536**

Sublett, Michael D., "Unorganized Illinois Counties," *Illinois Magazine*, vol. 21 (Mar.-Apr. 1982), pp. 33–38.   **7537**

Sublett, Michael D., "Marquette and Highland: Two of Illinois' Paper Counties," *Pioneer America Society Transactions*, vol. 8 (1985), pp. 77–84.
                                                                        7538

Sublett, Michael D., *Paper Counties: The Illinois Experience, 1825–1867* (New York: Peter Lang Publishers, American University Studies, ser. 25, Geography, vol. 4, 1990), 254 pp.   **7539**

ECONOMIC DEVELOPMENT

See also **7095**

Martens, Eva E., "The Influence of the Fox River of Illinois on the Settlement and Economy of Kane County," Master's thesis, Clark University, 1944.
                                                                        7540

Chaplin, Ronald L., "Spatial Changes in Coal Employment within Southern Illinois, 1900–1959," Master's thesis, Southern Illinois University, 1961.   **7541**

Fischer, Robert J., "The Relationship of Coal Mines and Rail Lines in Illinois to 1910," Master's thesis, Western Illinois University, 1975.
                                                                        7542

Walters, William D., and Floyd Mansberger, "Early Mill Locations in Northern Illinois," *Bulletin of the Illinois Geographical Society*, vol. 25, 2 (1983), pp. 3–12.   **7543**

RESOURCE MANAGEMENT

Braun, Elizabeth T., "Resource in the Land: From Upper Illinois Valley to National Heritage Corridor," in Michael P. Conzen and Linda S. Lim, eds., *Illinois Canal Country: The Early Years in Comparative Perspective* (Chicago: University of Chicago Committee on Geographical Studies, Studies on the Illinois & Michigan Canal Corridor, no. 5, 1991), pp. 139-148.   **7544**

LAND & LAND USE

Land tenure

Baker, William L., "Land Claims as Indicators of Settlement in Southwestern Illinois, circa 1809–13," *Bulletin of the Illinois Geographical Society*, vol. 16, 1 (1974), pp. 29–42.   **7545**

Rezab, Gordana, "Land Speculation in Fulton County, 1817–1832," *Western Illinois Regional Studies*, vol. 3, 1 (1980), pp. 22–35.   **7546**

Park, Siyoung, "Land Speculation in Western Illinois: Pike County, 1821–1835," *Journal of the Illinois Historical Society*, vol. 38, 2 (1984), pp. 115–128.   **7547**

Richardson, Katherine, "An Analysis of Land Parcel and Landscape Change in LaSalle County, 1859–1892," in Michael P. Conzen and Melissa J. Morales, eds., *Settling the Upper Illinois Valley: Patterns of Change in the I & M Canal Corridor, 1830–1900* (Chicago: University of Chicago Committee on Geographical Studies, Studies on the Illinois & Michigan Canal Corridor, no. 3, 1989), pp. 111–124.   **7548**

Hazen, Scott D., "Federal and State Land Sales in the Illinois River Valley: Patterns of Original Purchases in the Starved Rock–Utica Area," in Michael P. Conzen and Linda S. Lim, eds., *Illinois Canal Country: The Early Years in Comparative Perspective* (Chicago: University of Chicago Committee on Geographical Studies, Studies on the Illinois & Michigan Canal, no. 5, 1991), pp. 16-29.   **7549**

Kapper, Peter G., "Patterns of Original Land Purchase in the Vicinity of Peru–LaSalle" in Michael P. Conzen and Linda S. Lim, eds., *Illinois Canal Country: The Early Years in Comparative Perspective* (Chicago: University of Chicago Committee on Geographical Studies, Studies on the Illinois & Michigan Canal, no. 5, 1991), pp. 1-15.   **7550**

Land use

Bogue, Margaret B., "The Swamp Land Act and Wet Land Utilization in Illinois, 1850–1890," *Agricultural History*, vol. 25, 4 (1951), pp. 169–180.   **7551**

Knepler, Jane, "Stark County Historical Geography and Land Use Study," Master's thesis, Illinois State University, 1964.   **7552**

EXTRACTIVE ACTIVITY

See also **7103**

Sibley, David, "The Bituminous Coal Industry of Southern Illinois, 1880–1940: A Case Study in Industrial Organization," Master's thesis, Illinois State University, 1965.   **7553**

Colten, Craig E., "Harvesting the River: Geographic Themes in a Museum Exhibit," *Bulletin of the Illinois Geographical Society*, vol. 30, 2 (1988), pp. 3–10.   **7554**

Pote, Linda T., "The Celebrated Joliet Marble Fields: An Historical Geography of the Lower Des Plaines Valley Limestone Industry," in Michael P. Conzen, ed., *Time and Place in Joliet: Essays on the Geographical Evolution of the City*

(Chicago: University of Chicago Committee on Geographical Studies, Studies on the Illinois & Michigan Canal Corridor, no. 2, 1988), pp. 15–28. **7555**

Seymour, Whitney A., "In a Mine's Eye: An Historical Geography of Coal Mining in the Upper Illinois Valley," in Michael P. Conzen and Melissa J. Morales, eds., *Settling the Upper Illinois Valley: Patterns of Change in the I & M Canal Corridor, 1830–1900* (Chicago: University of Chicago Committee on Geographical Studies, Studies on the Illinois & Michigan Canal Corridor, no. 3, 1989), pp. 47–60. **7556**

Kelly, John H., "The Material Service Corporation Reshapes the Des Plaines Valley," in Michael P. Conzen and Adam R. Daniel, eds., *Lockport Legacy: Themes in the Historical Geography of an Illinois Canal Town* (Chicago: University of Chicago Committe on Geographical Studies, Studies on the Illinois & Michigan Canal Corridor, no. 4, 1990), pp. 93–102. **7557**

AGRICULTURE

See also 7112

The state

Nakagawa, August T., "Statistical Mapping of Illinois Agriculture, 1925–45," Master's thesis, University of Chicago, 1952. **7558**

Grotewold, Andreas, "Changing Patterns of Corn Yields per Acre: The Position of Illinois in the United States," *Transactions of the Illinois Academy of Science*, vol. 48 (1956), pp. 157–165. [Focus largely national, 1900–1952] **7559**

Roepke, Howard G., "Patterns of Agricultural Change in Illinois," *Transactions of the Illinois State Academy of Science*, vol. 49 (1956), pp. 98–103. [Focus on 1930–1954] **7560**

Powell, Lanny C., "An Examination of Factors Influencing the Temporal-Spatial Diffusion of Soybean Production in Illinois, 1930–1968," Ph.D. diss., University of Illinois, 1971. **7561**

Meyer, Douglas K., "Types of Farming on the Illinois Frontier," *Bulletin of the Illinois Geographical Society*, vol. 21, 1 (1979), pp. 9–17. **7562**

Mattingly, Paul F., "Disadoption of Milk Cows by Farmers in Illinois: 1930–1978," *Professional Geographer*, vol. 36, 1 (1984), pp. 40–50. **7563**

Mattingly, Paul F., and George Aspbury, "Some Devolution Similarities to Diffusion," *Geografiska annaler*, vol. 67B, 1 (1985), pp. 1–6. [Focus on the decline of dairy cows in Illinois, 1940–1978] **7564**

Mattingly, Paul F., "Patterns of Horse Devolution and Tractor Diffusion in Illinois, 1920–1982,"

Professional Geographer, vol. 39, 3 (1987), pp. 298–308. **7565**

Smaller areas

Hatch, Laura, "Geographical Factors in the Agriculture of DuPage County, Illinois," *Journal of Geography*, vol. 13, 7 (1915), pp. 216–223. **7566**

Colyer, Frank H., "The Cotton Industry of Southern Illinois," *Transactions of the Illinois State Academy of Science*, vol. 17 (1924), pp. 226–232. [Focus on 1839–1924] **7567**

Robertson, Ina C., "The Ozark Orchard Center of Southern Illinois," *Economic Geography*, vol. 4, 2 (1928), pp. 253–266. **7568**

Durand, Loyal, Jr., "Cheese Region of Northwestern Illinois," *Economic Geography*, vol. 22, 1 (1946), pp. 24–37. [Focus on 1870s–1940s] **7569**

Price, Dalias A., "Factors in the Establishment of Commercial Orcharding in Southern Illinois," *Transactions of the Illinois State Academy of Science*, vol. 48 (1956), pp. 149–156. [Focus on 1820s–1950s] **7570**

Noonan, W. R., "The Role of Soybeans in the Farm Economy of McLean County [Illinois], 1925–64," Master's thesis, Illinois State University, 1965. **7571**

Alderman, Ralph H., "The Beef Cattle Industry of McLean County, Illinois, 1815–1860," Master's thesis, Illinois State University, 1966. **7572**

Kolzow, David, "The Development of Commercial Dairying in Kane County, Illinois, 1850–1920," *Bulletin of the Illinois Geographical Society*, vol. 15, 1 (1973), pp. 41–53. **7573**

Winsor, Roger A., "The Drainage of the Wet Prairies of East Central Illinois: 1830–1920," Ph.D. diss., University of Illinois, 1975. **7574**

Swenson, Barbara G., "Sheep Production in West Central Illinois, 1860 to 1985: A Geographical Analysis," Master's thesis, Western Illinios University, 1985. **7575**

Yoder, Franklin L., "Beyond the Towpath: Farming along the Illinois & Michigan Canal," in Michael P. Conzen and Melissa J. Morales, eds., *Settling the Upper Illinois Valley: Patterns of Change in the I & M Canal Corridor, 1830–1900* (Chicago: University of Chicago Committee on Geographical Studies, Studies on the Illinois & Michigan Canal Corridor, no. 3, 1989), pp. 33–46. **7576**

Knox, Douglas W., "Farms Undermined: Agricultural Changes in Utica and Deer Park, 1860-1870," in Michael P. Conzen and Linda S. Lim, eds., *Illinois Canal Country: The Early Years in Comparative Perspective* (Chicago: University of Chicago Committee on Geographical Studies,

Studies on the Illinois & Michigan Canal, no. 5, 1991), pp. 33-45.   7577

Stock, Meegan E., "Farming in Ottawa Township in 1860," in Michael P. Conzen and Linda S. Lim, eds., *Illinois Canal Country: The Early Years in Comparative Perspective* (Chicago: University of Chicago Committee on Geographical Studies, Studies on the Illinois & Michigan Canal, no. 5, 1991), pp. 46-52.   7578

Krueger, Joseph D., "Farming in Rutland and Fall River Townships, LaSalle County, 1860," in Michael P. Conzen and Linda S. Lim, eds., *Illinois Canal Country: The Early Years in Comparative Perspective* (Chicago: University of Chicago Committee on Geographical Studies, Studies on the Illinois & Michigan Canal, no. 5, 1991), pp. 53-63.   7579

LANDSCAPE

General

Jakle, John A., "How to Read the Illinois Landscape," in Lachlan F. Blair and John A. Quinn, eds., *Historic Preservation: Setting, Legislation, and Techniques* (Urbana: University of Illinois, Bureau of Urban and Regional Planning Research, 1977), pp. 49-57.   7580

Jakle, John A., "The Illinois Landscape," in Ruth E. Knack, ed., *Preservation Illinois: A Guide to State & Local Resources* (Springfield: Illinois Department of Conservation, Division of Historic Sites, 1977), pp. 3-9.   7581

Conzen, Michael P., and David B. Hanson, "The Des Plaines Valley: Historical Landscapes of Business," *Bulletin of the Illinois Geographical Society*, vol. 23, 2 (1981), pp. 3-17.   7582

Cope, Lisa A., "The Changing Landscape of Central Western Will County, 1870-1910," in Michael P. Conzen and Melissa J. Morales, eds., *Settling the Upper Illinois Valley: Patterns of Change in the I & M Canal Corridor, 1830-1900* (Chicago: University of Chicago Committee on Geographical Studies, Studies on the Illinois & Michigan Canal Corridor, no. 3, 1989), pp. 133-140.   7583

Medzihradsky, Sofia M., "Landscape Change in the Lockport District, 1870-1910," in Michael P. Conzen and Melissa J. Morales, eds., *Settling the Upper Illinois Valley: Patterns of Change in the I & M Canal Corridor, 1830-1900* (Chicago: University of Chicago Committee on Geographical Studies, Studies on the Illinois & Michigan Canal Corridor, no. 3, 1989), pp. 125-132.   7584

Land patterns

Walters, William D., and Floyd Mansberger, "Initial Field Location in Illinois," *Agricultural History*, vol. 57, 3 (1983), pp. 289-296.   7585

Buildings & structures

Meyer, Douglas K., "Diffusion of Upland South Folk Housing in the Shawnee Hills of Southern Illinois," *Pioneer America*, vol. 7, 2 (1975), pp. 56-66.   7586

Meyer, Douglas K., "Folk Housing on the Illinois Frontier," *Pioneer American Society Transactions*, vol. 1 (1978), pp. 30-42.   7587

Schimmer, James R., and Allen G. Noble, "The Evolution of the Corn Crib, with Special Reference to Putnam County, Illinois," *Pioneer America Society Transactions*, vol. 7 (1984), pp. 21-33.   7588

Swenson, Russell G., "Wind Engines in Western Illinois," *Western Illinois Regional Studies*, vol. 7, 1 (1984), pp. 61-79.   7589

Meyer, Douglas K., "German Cottage Structure-Types in Southwest Illinois," in Michael O. Roark, ed., *French and Germans in the Mississippi Valley: Landscape and Cultural Traditions* (Cape Girardeau: Southwest Missouri State University, Center for Regional History and Cultural Heritage, 1988), pp. 191-208.   7590

Vining, James W., "An Architectural Classification of Third Generation Country Schools in Brown County," *Western Illinois Regional Studies*, vol. 12, 1 (1989), pp. 56-72.   7591

Vining, James W., "Country Schoolhouse Architecture: Testing a Classification," *Pioneer America Society Transactions*, vol. 12 (1989), pp. 11-20.   7592

Mansberger, Floyd, and Carol J. Dyson, "Archeology and the Built Environment: Documenting the Modernization of Illinois' Early Domestic Architecture," *Pioneer America Society Transactions*, vol. 13 (1990), pp. 81-88.   7593

Scully, Keith A., "Lessons from the Landscape: The Stone Arch Bridges of Monroe County, Illinois," *Illinois Historical Journal*, vol. 83, 2 (1990), pp. 112-126.   7594

COMMUNICATIONS & TRADE

See also 7133

General

Shaw, Fayette B., "Transportation in the Development of Joliet and Will County," *Journal of the Illinois Historical Society*, vol. 30, 1 (1937), pp. 85-134.   7595

Sanders, Eileen M., "Farm to Market in LaSalle County, Illinois," in Michael P. Conzen and Linda S. Lim, eds., *Illinois Canal Country: The Early Years in Comparative Perspective* (Chicago: University of Chicago Committee on Geographical Studies, Studies on the Illinois & Michigan Canal, no. 5, 1991), pp. 67-73. [Focus on 1850–1870]   7596

Waterways

Ashton, Bessie L., "The Geonomic Aspects of the Illinois Waterway," Master's thesis, University of Wisconsin–Madison, 1927.   7597

Piety, James, "Utilization of the Chicago Portage by Two Cultures: A Study in Historical Geography," *Bulletin of the Illinois Geographical Society*, vol. 15, 2 (1973), pp. 23–33.   7598

King, Charles, "Ferry Locations Enacted by the State of Illinois, 1819–1855," *Bulletin of the Illinois Geographical Society*, vol. 24, 2 (1982), pp. 32–41.   7599

Newton, Gerald A., John A. McFarland, and Donald W. Griffin, "The Hennepin Canal: New Life for an Old Waterway," *Western Illinois Regional Studies*, vol. 7, 2 (1984), pp. 34–46.   7600

Kamish, Allysa P., "The Chicago Sanitary and Ship Canal: Its Construction and Effects," in Michael P. Conzen and Adam R. Daniel, eds., *Lockport Legacy: Themes in the Historical Geography of an Illinois Canal Town* (Chicago: University of Chicago Committee on Geographical Studies, Studies on the Illinois & Michigan Canal Corridor, no. 4, 1990), pp. 76–86.   7601

Railroads

Gutgesell, William H., "Changing Pattern of Railroad Passenger Service in Southern Illinois, 1929–1959," Master's thesis, Southern Illinois University, 1960.   7602

Clark, Stewart A., "Illinois Shortline Railroads, 1840–1962," Master's thesis, University of Chicago, 1962.   7603

McClure, Matthew K., "The Transformation of Metropolitan Chicago's Railway Pattern," Master's thesis, University of Chicago, 1986.   7604

Barrionuevo, Carlos J., "From Boat to Boxcar: Railroads around the Illinois & Michigan Canal, 1850–1880," in Michael P. Conzen and Melissa J. Morales, eds., *Settling the Upper Illinois Valley: Patterns of Change in the I & M Canal Corridor, 1830–1900* (Chicago: University of Chicago Committee on Geographical Studies, Studies on the Illinois & Michigan Canal Corridor, no. 3, 1989), pp. 23–32.   7605

Air transport

Kirchherr, Eugene C., "Airport Land Use in the Chicago Metropolitan Area: A Study of the Historical Development, Characteristics, and Special Problems of a Land Use Type within a

Metropolitan Area," Ph.D. diss., Northwestern University, 1959.   7606

Kirchherr, Eugene C., "Variations in the Number and Distribution of Commercial Airports in the Chicago Area, 1951–1967," *Michigan Academician*, vol. 3, 1 (1970), pp. 83–93.   7607

Regional trade

Hausman, Sandra E., "Selling Products and Selling Place: Reflections of Commercial and Community Development in Joliet Newspapers," in Michael P. Conzen, ed., *Time and Place in Joliet: Essays on the Geographical Evolution of the City* (Chicago: University of Chicago Committee on Geographical Studies, Studies on the Illinois & Michigan Canal Corridor, no. 2, 1988), pp. 107–116.   7608

Walters, William D., "Advertisements and Artifacts: Some Thoughts on Nineteenth Century Wabash River Trade," in Charles Rohrbaugh and Thomas Emerson, eds., *Historical Archeology in Illinois* (Normal: Midwest Archeological Research Center, Report no. 5, Illinois Cultural Resources Study no. 6, 1988), pp. 11–18.   7609

Yuasa, Shigehiro, "The Commercial Pattern of the Illinois & Michigan Canal, 1848–1860," in Michael P. Conzen and Melissa J. Morales, eds., *Settling the Upper Illinois Valley: Patterns of Change in the I & M Canal Corridor, 1830–1900* (Chicago: University of Chicago Committee on Geographic Studies, Studies on the Illinois & Michigan Canal Corridor, 1989), pp. 9–22.   7610

Monckton, John T., "The Northern Illinois Grain Trade and the Nortons of Lockport: Entrepreneurs in a Regional Setting, 1840–1880," Master's thesis, University of Chicago, 1990.   7611

MANUFACTURING & INDUSTRIALIZATION

Bonnell, Clarence, "A Primitive Industry in Southeastern Illinois," *Transactions of the Illinois State Academy of Science*, vol. 21 (1928), pp. 337–339. [Focus on the salt industry]   7612

Lounsbury, John F., "The Pottery Industry in McDonough and Warren Counties, Illinois," *Transactions of the Illinois State Academy of Science*, vol. 40 (1947), pp. 100–106.   7613

Roepke, Howard G., "The Changing Distribution of Manufacturing in Illinois," *Transactions of the Illinois State Academy of Science*, vol. 48 (1956), pp. 134–143. [Focus on 1939–1951]   7614

Kunstmann, John W., "The Industrialization of Franklin Park, Illinois," Ph.D. diss., Northwestern University, 1964.   7615

Johnson, Richard D., "Changes in the Growth and Spatial Patterns of Manufacturing in Southern Illinois, 1939–1963," Master's thesis, Southern Illinois University, 1966. **7616**

McGregor, John R., *The Development and Present Structure of Kane County Manufacturing* (Geneva, Ill.: Kane County Planning Department, 1966), 34 pp. **7617**

Cutshall, Alden D., "Stages in the Industrial Development of Illinois," *Bulletin of the Illinois Geographical Society*, vol. 19, 1 (1977), pp. 74–76. **7618**

Walters, William D., "Abandoned Nineteenth Century Brick and Tile Works in Central Illinois: An Introduction from Local Sources," *Industrial Archeology Review*, vol. 4, 1 (1979–1980), pp. 70–80. **7619**

URBAN NETWORKS & URBANIZATION

See also **7151, 8104**

Urban networks

Branom, Mendel E., "A Geographic Interpretation of the Development of the Fox River Region," Master's thesis, University of Chicago, 1916. **7620**

Fellman, Jerome D., "The Urbanization of Illinois, 1870–1950," *Transactions of the Illinois Academy of Science*, vol. 49 (1956), pp. 92–97. **7621**

Harden, Jon M., "Population Trends and the Changing Functions of Small Western Illinois Central Places, 1890–1960," Master's thesis, Western Illinois University, 1969. **7622**

Walters, William D., "The Making of the Urban Pattern in Central Illinois: 1831–1895," *Bulletin of the Illinois Geographical Society*, vol. 19, 1 (1977), pp. 3–15. **7623**

Walters, William D., "The Fanciful Geography of 1836," *Old Northwest*, vol. 9, 4 (1983–1984), pp. 331–343. [Town platting in central Illinois, 1835–1837] **7624**

Bergen, John V., "College Towns and Campus Sites in Western Illinois," *Western Illinois Regional Studies*, vol. 13, 2 (1990), pp. 46–77. **7625**

City-hinterland relations

Comeaux, Malcolm L., "Impact of Transportation Activities upon the Historical Development of Cairo, Illinois," Master's thesis, Southern Illinois University, 1966. **7626**

Mayer, Harold M., "The Changing Role of Metropolitan Chicago in the Midwest and the Nation," *Bulletin of the Illinois Geographical Society*, vol. 17, 1 (1975), pp. 3–13. **7627**

Cronon, William J., "To Be the Central City: Chicago, 1848–1857," *Chicago History*, vol. 10, 3 (1981), pp. 130–140. **7628**

Cronon, William J., *Nature's Metropolis: Chicago and the Great West* (New York: W. W. Norton & Co., 1991), 530 pp. **7629**

TOWN GROWTH

Chicago

Kohl, Johann Georg, "Über die geographische Lage der Stadt Chicago," *Das Ausland*, vol. 44 (1871), pp. 745–750. **7630**

Sewell, Harriet, "Geographic Influences in the Development of Chicago," Master's thesis, University of Chicago, 1910. **7631**

Riley, Elmer A., "The Development of Chicago and Vicinity as a Manufacturing Center Prior to 1880," Ph.D. diss., University of Chicago, 1911. **7632**

Branom, Frederick K., "Some Geographic Factors in the Development of Chicago," *Journal of Geography*, vol. 20, 5 (1921), pp. 176–186. **7633**

Goode, J. Paul, *The Geographic Background of Chicago* (Chicago: University of Chicago Press, for the Chicago Real Estate Board, 1926), 70 pp. **7634**

Boesch, Hans H., "Chicago als Hafenstadt," *Geographica Helvetica*, vol. 11, 2 (1956), pp. 103–111. **7635**

Davis, James L., *The Elevated System and the Growth of Northern Chicago* (Chicago: Northwestern University Studies in Geography, no. 10, 1965), 180 pp. [Focus on 1895–1914] **7636**

Cutler, Irving, *Chicago: Metropolis of the Mid-Continent* Dubuque: Kendall/Hunt, 1973), 319 pp. **7637**

Cutler, Irving, "The Chicago Metropolitan Area: Historical Development," in Ronald E. Nelson, ed., *Illinois: Land and Life in the Prairie State* (Dubuque: Kendall/Hunt, 1978), pp. 277–289. **7638**

Mayer, Harold M., "The Launching of Chicago: The Situation and the Site," *Chicago History*, vol. 9, 2 (1980), pp. 68–79. **7639**

Conzen, Michael P., "The Changing Character of Metropolitan Chicago," *Journal of Geography*, vol. 85, 5 (1986), pp. 224–236. **7640**

Joliet

Conzen, Michael P., ed., *Time and Place in Joliet: Essays on the Geographical Evolution of the City* (Chicago: University of Chicago Committee on Geographical Studies, Studies on the Illinois &

Michigan Canal Corridor, no. 2, 1988), 151 pp.
7641

Hardick, Jane A., "Suburbanization and Annexation since 1930," in Michael P. Conzen, ed., *Time and Place in Joliet: Essays on the Geographical Evolution of the City* (Chicago: University of Chicago Committee on Geographical Studies, Studies on the Illinois & Michigan Canal Corridor, no. 2, 1988), pp. 99–106. **7642**

Lang, Peter M., "The Economy and Society of Joliet as an Early Commercial Center, 1834–1870," in Michael P. Conzen, ed., *Time and Place in Joliet: Essays on the Geographical Evolution of the City* (Chicago: University of Chicago Committee on Geographical Studies, Studies on the Illinois & Michigan Canal Corridor, no. 2, 1988), pp. 1–14. **7643**

Other centers

Dodge, Stanley D., "Bureau and the Princeton Community," Ph.D. diss., University of Chicago, 1926. **7644**

Dodge, Stanley D., "Bureau and the Princeton Community," *Annals of the Association of American Geographers*, vol. 22, 3 (1932), pp. 159–209. **7645**

Poggi, Edith M., "Decatur, Illinois: A Study in Urban Geography," *Bulletin of the Philadelphia Geographical Society*, vol. 32, 4 (1934), pp. 121–134. Reprinted in *Transactions of the Illinois State Academy of Science*, vol. 27 (1935), pp. 85–99. **7646**

Lathrope, Frances M., "An Urban Study of Danville, Illinois," Master's thesis, Clark University, 1940. **7647**

Cutshall, Alden D., "The Growth of Robinson, Illinois," *Transactions of the Illinois State Academy of Science*, vol. 34 (1941), pp. 145–146. **7648**

Kusch, Monica H., "Zion, Illinois: An Attempt at a Theocratic City," Ph.D. diss., University of California–Los Angeles, 1954. **7649**

Deizman, Thomas J., "Historical Geography of Forest Park, Illinois," Master's thesis, Northern Illinois University, 1962. **7650**

Robertson, Alfred C., "Historical Geography of Belleville, Illinois," Master's thesis, Illinois State University, 1962. **7651**

Hornberger, Mark A., "An Historical Geography of Carbondale, Illinois," Master's thesis, Southern Illinois University, 1966. **7652**

Carner, James, "Historical Geography of Cairo, Illinois, 1673–1900," Master's thesis, Illinois State University, 1968. **7653**

Krausse, Gerald H., "Galena, Illinois: Urban Land Use Change and Development of a Midwestern Mining Town, 1820–1970," Master's thesis, Northern Illinois University, 1970. **7654**

Itrick, Thomas J., "The Historical Geography of Bensenville, Illinois," Master's thesis, Northern Illinois University, 1971. **7655**

Krausse, Gerald H., "Historic Galena: A Study of Urban Change and Development in a Midwestern Mining Community," *Bulletin of the Illinois Geographical Society*, vol. 13, 2 (1971), pp. 3–19. **7656**

Monteith, Dean D., "The Changing Situation and Function of Colchester, Illinois, from the Nineteenth Century to the Present," Master's thesis, Western Illinois University, 1976. **7657**

Kirchherr, James, and Russell Foster, "Peru, Illinois: Its Developmental Geography," *Bulletin of the Illinois Geographical Society*, vol. 27, 2 (1985), pp. 3–17. **7658**

Conzen, Michael P., ed., *Focus on Ottawa: A Historical and Geographical Survey of Ottawa, Illinois, in the Twentieth Century* (Chicago: University of Chicago Committee on Geographical Studies, Studies on the Illinois & Michigan Canal Corridor, no. 1, 1987), 117 pp. **7659**

Germain, Mirah, "The Historical Growth and Spatial Evolution of Marseilles," in Michael P. Conzen and Melissa J. Morales, eds., *Settling the Upper Illinois Valley: Patterns of Change in the I & M Canal Corridor, 1830–1900* (Chicago: University of Chicago Committee on Geographical Studies, Studies on the Illinois & Michigan Canal Corridor, no. 3, 1989), pp. 141–164. **7660**

Conzen, Michael P., and Adam R. Daniel, eds., *Lockport Legacy: Themes in the Historical Geography of an Illinois Canal Town* (Chicago: University of Chicago Committee on Geographical Studies, Studies on the Illinois & Michigan Canal Corridor, no. 4, 1990), 163 pp. **7661**

URBAN ECONOMIC STRUCTURE

The state

Paquet, John F., "The Spatial Diffusion of McDonald's Restaurants in Illinois," Master's thesis, Illinois State University, 1981. **7662**

Comparative

Bohnert, John E., and Paul F. Mattingly, "Delimiting the CBD through Time," *Economic Geography*, vol. 40, 3 (1964), pp. 337–347. [Danville, Decatur, Galesburg, Champaign-Urbana, Bloomington-Normal, 1884–1962] **7663**

Walker, Juliet, "Occupational Distribution of Frontier Towns in Pike County: An 1850 Census Survey," *Western Illinois Regional Studies*, vol. 5, 2 (1982), pp. 146–171. **7664**

Chicago

Pattison, William D., "Land for the Dead of Chicago," Master's thesis, University of Chicago, 1952. **7665**

Pattison, William D., "The Cemeteries of Chicago: A Phase of Land Utilization," *Annals of the Association of American Geographers*, vol. 45, 3 (1955), pp. 245–257. **7666**

Yeates, Maurice H., "The Spatial Distribution of Chicago Land Values, 1910–1960," Ph.D. diss., Northwestern University, 1963. **7667**

Yeates, Maurice H., "Some Factors Affecting Spatial Distribution of Chicago Land Values, 1910–1960," *Economic Geography*, vol. 41, 1 (1965), pp. 57–70. **7668**

Schwartz, Bernard S., "An Historic and Descriptive Overview of the Electronics Industry in Chicago Prior to 1940," Master's thesis, Northeastern Illinois University, 1975. **7669**

Pudup, Mary Beth, "Packers and Reapers, Merchants and Manufacturers: Industrial Structuring and Location in an Era of Emergent Capitalism," Master's thesis, University of California–Berkeley, 1983. [Focus on Chicago] **7670**

Keating, Ann Durkin, "From City to Metropolis: Infrastructure and Residential Growth in Chicago," in Ann Durkin Keating, ed., *Infrastructure and Urban Growth in the Nineteenth Century* (Chicago: Public Works Historical Society, Essays in Public Works History, no. 14, 1985), pp. 3–27. **7671**

Joliet

Ellingson, James K., "The Spatial Evolution of the Central Business District," in Michael P. Conzen, ed., *Time and Place in Joliet: Essays on the Geographical Evolution of the City* (Chicago: University of Chicago Committee on Geographical Studies, Studies on the Illinois & Michigan Canal Corridor, no. 2, 1988), pp. 67–84. **7672**

Gossard, W. Bradley, "Etching the Corridors of 'Stone City': Waterways, Railroads, and Streets, 1839–1990," in Michael P. Conzen, ed., *Time and Place in Joliet: Essays on the Geographical Evolution of the City* (Chicago: University of Chicago Committee on Geographical Studies, Studies on the Illinois & Michigan Canal Corridor, no. 2, 1988), pp. 29–36. **7673**

Howicz, James J., "Forging the Public Sector: City Services and Their Buildings, 1854–1967," in

Michael P. Conzen, ed., *Time and Place in Joliet: Essays on the Geographical Evolution of the City* (Chicago: University of Chicago Committee on Geographical Studies, Studies on the Illinois & Michigan Canal Corridor, no. 2, 1988), pp. 45–58. **7674**

Kolodny, Mark A., "The Industrialization of Joliet: Steel and Its Dependencies, 1870–1920," in Michael P. Conzen, ed., *Time and Place in Joliet: Essays on the Geographical Evolution of the City* (Chicago: University of Chicago Committee on Geographical Studies, Studies on the Illinois & Michigan Canal Corridor, no. 2, 1988), pp. 37–44. **7675**

Lockport

Dodge, Mark A., "Four Canal Town Merchants: Gaylord, Martin, Lull, and Lynd," in Michael P. Conzen and Adam R. Daniel, eds., *Lockport Legacy: Themes in the Historical Geography of an Illinois Canal Town* (Chicago: University of Chicago Committee on Geographical Studies, Studies on the Illinois & Michigan Canal Corridor, no. 4, 1990), pp. 53–62. **7676**

Gómez, José A., "Texaco Comes to Lockport," in Michael P. Conzen and Adam R. Daniel, eds., *Lockport Legacy: Themes in the Historical Geography of an Illinois Canal Town* (Chicago: University of Chicago Committee on Geographical Studies, Studies on the Illinois & Michigan Canal Corridor, no. 4, 1990), pp. 87–92. **7677**

Hemachandra, Michelle K., "A New Shipment Just In: An Advertising Portrait of Early Retailing," in Michael P. Conzen and Adam R. Daniel, eds., *Lockport Legacy: Themes in the Historical Geography of an Illinois Canal Town* (Chicago: University of Chicago Committee on Geographical Studies, Studies on the Illinois & Michigan Canal Corridor, no. 4, 1990), pp. 63–69. **7678**

Monckton, John T., "Lockport's Captain of Industry: Hiram Norton and His Business Interests," in Michael P. Conzen and Adam R. Daniel, eds., *Lockport Legacy: Themes in the Historical Geography of an Illinois Canal Town* (Chicago: University of Chicago Committee on Geographical Studies, Studies on the Illinois & Michigan Canal Corridor, no. 4, 1990), pp. 36–52. **7679**

Ottawa

Dickerson, James E., "A City Equipped: Basic Services over Eighty-Five Years," in Michael P. Conzen, ed., *Focus on Ottawa: A Historical and Geographical Survey of Ottawa, Illinois, in the Twentieth Century* (Chicago: University of Chicago Committee on Geographical Studies, Studies on the Illinois & Michigan Canal Corridor, no. 1, 1987), pp. 49–57. **7680**

Forest, Benjamin, "Land Use and Residential Geography in 1900," in Michael P. Conzen, ed., *Focus on Ottawa: A Historical and Geographical Survey of Ottawa, Illinois, in the Twentieth Century* (Chicago: University of Chicago Committee on Geographical Studies, Studies on the Illinois & Michigan Canal Corridor, no. 1, 1987), pp. 30–35. **7681**

Walstra, Julie K., "The External World of Ottawa, 1900–1987," in Michael P. Conzen, ed., *Focus on Ottawa: A Historical and Geographical Survey of Ottawa, Illinois, in the Twentieth Century* (Chicago: University of Chicago Committee on Geographical Studies, Studies on the Illinois & Michigan Canal Corridor, no. 1, 1987), pp. 19–29. **7682**

Wolfe, Philip D., "Ottawa's Economy: Growth and Change in Commerce, Industry, and Government," in Michael P. Conzen, ed., *Focus on Ottawa: A Historical and Geographical Survey of Ottawa, Illinois, in the Twentieth Century* (Chicago: University of Chicago Committee on Geographical Studies, Studies on the Illinois & Michigan Canal Corridor, no. 1, 1987), pp. 11–18. **7683**

Other centers

Carlson, Carl F., "Aurora, Illinois: A Study in Sequent Land Use," Ph.D. diss., University of Chicago, 1940. Published under the same title, as a University of Chicago Libraries Private Edition, 1940), 121 pp. **7684**

Condit, Charles M., "The Evolution of Industries in Peoria, Illinois," Master's thesis, Miami University of Ohio, 1940. **7685**

Gleave, Geoffrey R., "The Central Business District of Springfield, Illinois, 1884–1959," Master's thesis, University of Illinois, 1959. **7686**

Simbo, Francis N. K., "Selected Aspects of Retail Trade in Bloomington-Normal, 1949–1974," Master's thesis, Illinois State University, 1975. **7687**

Mattson, Richard L., and John A. Jakle, "Good-bye to the Horse: The Transition from Horse-Related to Automobile-Related Businesses in an Urban Landscape," *Pioneer America Society Transactions*, vol. 2 (1979), pp. 31–51. [Champaign] **7688**

URBAN SOCIAL STRUCTURE

See also 4710

Chicago

Fujibayashi, Virginia I., "Occupational and Residential Changes of Chicago's Japanese-

American Evacuees," Master's thesis, University of Chicago, 1965. **7689**

Zentefis, Demetrios A., "Uptown Chicago: A Community in Transition, 1929–1970," Master's thesis, Western Illinois University, 1971. **7690**

Saurino, Mary A., "'The White City': Urban Space and Social Order at the Columbian Exposition," Master's thesis, University of Minnesota, 1985. **7691**

Jablonsky, Thomas J., "From *The Jungle* to the Council: A Historic Sense of Place," *Journal of Geography*, vol. 85, 5 (1986), pp. 237–244. **7692**

Grossman, James R., *Land of Hope: Chicago, Black Southerners, and the Great Migration* (Chicago: University of Chicago Press, 1989), 384 pp. **7693**

Jablonsky, Thomas J., "Making a Home in the Jungle: A Local Newspaper's Role in Using a Sense of Place to Foster Community," *Journal of Newspaper and Periodical History*, vol. 5, 3 (1989), pp. 17–28. **7694**

Meyerowitz, Joanne J., "Sexual Geography and Gender Economy: The Furnished Room Districts of Chicago, 1890–1920," *Gender and History*, vol. 2, 3 (1990), pp. 274–296. **7695**

Sklar, Kathryn Kish, "Hull-House Maps and Papers: Social Science as Women's Work in the 1890s," in Martin Bulmer, Kevin Bales, and Kathryn Kish Sklar, eds., *The Social Survey in Historical Perspective, 1880–1940* (Cambridge: Cambridge University Press, 1991), pp. 111–147. **7696**

Joliet

Goodwin, Tara L., "The Aging of the Built Environment: Residential Trends and Neighborhood Revitalization Efforts on Joliet's East Side," in Michael P. Conzen, ed., *Time and Place in Joliet: Essays on the Geographical Evolution of the City* (Chicago: University of Chicago Committee on Geographical Studies, Studies on the Illinois & Michigan Canal Corridor, no. 2, 1988), pp. 133–146. **7697**

Shibuya, Kumiko, "The Social Geography of Joliet and West Side Neighborhood Change," in Michael P. Conzen, ed., *Time and Place in Joliet: Essays on the Geographical Evolution of the City* (Chicago: University of Chicago Committee on Geographical Studies, Studies on the Illinois & Michigan Canal Corridor, no. 2, 1988), pp. 117–132. **7698**

Szydagis, Katarzyna C., "The Emerging Social Geography of Joliet before 1940," in Michael P. Conzen, ed., *Time and Place in Joliet: Essays on the Geographical Evolution of the City* (Chicago:

University of Chicago Committee on Geographical Studies, Studies on the Illinois & Michigan Canal Corridor, no. 2, 1988), pp. 59–66.　　**7699**

LaSalle–Peru

Guerin, Michael, "Community Development in the Corridor: LaSalle and Peru to 1860," in Michael P. Conzen and Melissa J. Morales, ed., *Settling the Upper Illinois Valley: Patterns of Change in the I & M Canal Corridor, 1830–1900* (Chicago: University of Chicago Committee on Geographical Studies, Studies on the Illinois & Michigan Canal Corridor, no. 3, 1989), pp. 91–102.　　**7700**

Morgan, John B., "The Development of LaSalle, 1850-1860: An Irish and Industrial Demeanor," in Michael P. Conzen and Linda S. Lim, eds., *Illinois Canal Country: The Early Years in Comparative Perspective* (Chicago: University of Chicago Committee on Geographical Studies, Studies on the Illinois & Michigan Canal Corridor, no. 5, 1991), pp. 91-104.　　**7701**

Lockport

Abramowitz, Max W., "Geographical and Occupational Mobility, 1850–1860," in Michael P. Conzen and Adam R. Daniel, eds., *Lockport Legacy: Themes in the Historical Geography of an Illinois Canal Town* (Chicago: University of Chicago Committee on Geographical Studies, Studies on the Illinois & Michigan Canal Corridor, no. 4, 1990), pp. 27–35.　　**7702**

Benedetti, Michael M., "Urban and Municipal Development, 1836–1900," in Michael P. Conzen and Adam R. Daniel, eds., *Lockport Legacy: Themes in the Historical Geography of an Illinois Canal Town* (Chicago: University of Chicago Committee on Geographical Studies, Studies on the Illinois & Michigan Canal Corridor, no. 4, 1990), pp. 6–13.　　**7703**

Carlson, Julie M., "Cultural Life of Lockport: Religious, Fraternal, and Social Organizations," in Michael P. Conzen and Adam R. Daniel, eds., *Lockport Legacy: Themes in the Historical Geography of an Illinois Canal Town* (Chicago: University of Chicago Committee on Geographical Studies, Studies on the Illinois & Michigan Canal Corridor, no. 4, 1990), pp. 111–120.　　**7704**

Rod, Adam S., "The First Generation: A Social History to 1860," in Michael P. Conzen and Adam R. Daniel, eds., *Lockport Legacy: Themes in the Historical Geography of an Illinois Canal Town* (Chicago: University of Chicago Committee on Geographical Studies, Studies on the Illinois & Michigan Canal Corridor, no. 4, 1990), pp. 21–26.　　**7705**

Schreier, Joshua S., "West Side Story: The Changing Composition of Those Who Lived on the Other Side of the Canal, 1880–1900," in Michael P. Conzen and Adam R. Daniel, eds., *Lockport Legacy: Themes in the Historical Geography of an Illinois Canal Town* (Chicago: University of Chicago Committee on Geographical Studies, Studies on the Illinois & Michigan Canal Corridor, no. 4, 1990), pp. 70–75.　　**7706**

Ottawa

Nootens, Natalie G., "Population and Employment Trends in Ottawa, 1900–1980," in Michael P. Conzen, ed., *Focus on Ottawa: A Historical and Geographical Survey of Ottawa, Illinois, in the Twentieth Century* (Chicago: University of Chicago Committee on Geographical Studies, Studies on the Illinois & Michigan Canal Corridor, no. 1, 1987), pp. 5–10.　　**7707**

Thale, Christopher P., "Social and Religious Geography, 1900–1985," in Michael P. Conzen, ed., *Focus on Ottawa: A Historical and Geographical Survey of Ottawa, Illinois, in the Twentieth Century* (Chicago: University of Chicago, Committee on Geographical Studies, Studies on the Illinois & Michigan Canal Corridor, no. 1, 1987), pp. 40–48.　　**7708**

Other centers

Moline, Norman T., *Mobility and the Small Town, 1900–1930* (Chicago: University of Chicago Department of Geography, Research Paper no. 132, 1971), 169 pp. [Oregon, Ill.]　　**7709**

Smith, Stephanie A., "Early Social Patterns in Marseilles," in Michael P. Conzen and Linda S. Lim, eds., *Illinois Canal Country: The Early Years in Comparative Perspective* (Chicago: University of Chicago Committee on Geographical Studies, Studies on the Illinois & Michigan Canal Corridor, no. 5, 1991), pp. 105-114.　　**7710**

TOWNSCAPE

General

Walters, William D., "Time and Town Squares," *Bulletin of the Illinois Geographical Society*, vol. 22, 2 (1980), pp. 19–23.　　**7711**

Larson, Albert J., "Prairie Temples of Justice: The County Courthouses of Illinois," *Bulletin of the Illinois Geographical Society*, vol. 29, 1 (1987), pp. 3–15.　　**7712**

Kaiser, Christopher P., "Town Platting in LaSalle County," in Michael P. Conzen and Linda S. Lim, eds., *Illinois Canal Country: The Early Years in Comparative Perspective* (Chicago: University of Chicago Committee on Geographical Studies, Studies on the Illinois & Michigan Canal, no. 5, 1991), pp. 77-81. **7713**

Schweiger, Richard A., "Grundy County Paper Towns," in Michael P. Conzen and Linda S. Lim, eds., *Illinois Canal Country: The Early Years in Comparative Perspective* (Chicago: University of Chicago Committee on Geographical Studies, Studies on the Illinois & Michigan Canal, no. 5, 1991), pp. 82-90. **7714**

Champaign-Urbana

Jakle, John A., "Gasoline Stations in the Champaign-Urbana Landscape: 1920 to 1970," *Bulletin of the Illinois Geographical Society*, vol. 20, 1 (1978), pp. 3–15. **7715**

Jakle, John A., and Richard L. Mattson, "The Evolution of a Commercial Strip," *Journal of Cultural Geography*, vol. 1, 2 (1981), pp. 12–25. [The strip connecting Champaign and Urbana, 1919–1979] **7716**

Jakle, John A., "Twentieth Century Revival Architecture: Housing the Gentry in a College Town," *Journal of Cultural Geography*, vol. 4, 1 (1983), pp. 28–43. [Urbana] **7717**

Chicago

Hoyt, Homer, *One Hundred Years of Land Values in Chicago: The Relationship of the Growth of Chicago to the Rise in Its Land Values, 1830–1933* (Chicago: University of Chicago Press, 1933), 519 pp. **7718**

Fellman, Jerome D., "Pre-Building Growth Patterns of Chicago," *Annals of the Association of American Geographers*, vol. 47, 1 (1957), pp. 59–82. **7719**

Mayer, Harold M., and Richard C. Wade, *Chicago: Growth of a Metropolis* (Chicago: University of Chicago Press, 1969), 510 pp. **7720**

Doherty, Prudence J., "Changing Land Use on Prairie Avenue: A Preliminary Study," Master's thesis, University of Chicago, 1979. **7721**

Petersen, Donald L., "Chicago's North Shore during the 1920s and 1950s: A Three Dimensional Approach to Urban Geography," Master's thesis, University of Chicago, 1990. **7722**

Lockport

Longmire, Stephen H., "The Pattern of Early Town Lot Sales, 1836–1850," in Michael P. Conzen and Adam R. Daniel, eds., *Lockport Legacy: Themes in the Historical Geography of an Illinois Canal Town* (Chicago: University of Chicago Committee on Geographical Studies, Studies on the Illinois & Michigan Canal Corridor, no. 4, 1990), pp. 14–20. **7723**

Petersen, Donald L., "Everything in Its Place: The Logic of Lockport's Evolved Spatial Structure," in Michael P. Conzen and Adam R. David, eds., *Lockport Legacy: Themes in the Historical Geography of an Illinois Canal Town* (Chicago: University of Chicago Committee on Geographical Studies, Studies on the Illinois & Michigan Canal Corridor, no. 4, 1990), pp. 138–157. **7724**

Other centers

Reps, John W., "Great Expectations and Hard Times: The Planning of Cairo, Illinois," *Journal of the Society of Architectural Historians*, vol. 16, 4 (1957), pp. 14–21. **7725**

Sarff, Jerry J., "The Morphology of Kewanee, Illinois, 1837–1969," Master's thesis, Western Illinois University, 1972. **7726**

Phillips, Webster P., "A Geographic Analysis of Fire as It Occurred in Peoria, Illinois, 1930 to 1974," Master's thesis, Western Illinois University, 1976. **7727**

Shick, Nancy Easter, and Douglas K. Meyer, *Pictorial Landscape History of Charleston, Illinois* (Charleston: Rardin Graphics for the Sesquicentennial Committee, 1985), 243 pp. **7728**

Walters, William D., "Change and Continuity in the Materials of Downtown Building: 1842–1910," *Pioneer America Society Transactions*, vol. 8 (1985), pp. 37–44. [Bloomington] **7729**

Fendrick, Peter S., "A Straining Coherency: Landscapes and Morphological Change in Ottawa," in Michael P. Conzen, ed., *Focus on Ottawa: A Historical and Geographical Survey of Ottawa, Illinois, in the Twentieth Century* (Chicago: University of Chicago Committee on Geographical Studies, Studies on the Illinois & Michigan Canal Corridor, no. 1, 1987), pp. 71–111. **7730**

RECREATION & TOURISM

Vining, James W., "The Search for Sulphur Springs," *Newsletter of the Schuyler-Brown Counties, Illinois Historical Society*, vol. 15, 2 (1981), pp. 3–5. **7731**

Vining, James W., "The Corporate Development of Ripley Mineral Springs," *Newsletter of the Schuyler-Brown Counties, Illinois Historical Society*, vol. 16, 1 (1982), pp. 12–14. **7732**

Vining, James W., "Siloam Springs: A Once Noted Health Resort," *Illinois*, vol. 21, 1 (1982), pp. 13–18. **7733**

Vining, James W., "Slater Burgesser and His Famous Spring," *Western Illinois Regional Studies*, vol. 5, 2 (1982), pp. 184–194. **7734**

Vining, James W., "Versailles Mineral Springs: An Historical Geography," *Pioneer America Society Transactions*, vol. 5 (1982), pp. 37–43.   **7735**

Kolodny, Mark A., "Changing Recreational Patterns, 1900–1987," in Michael P. Conzen, ed., *Focus on Ottawa: A Historical and Geographical Survey of Ottawa, Illinois, in the Twentieth Century* (Chicago: University of Chicago Committee on Geographical Studies, Studies on the Illinois & Michigan Canal Corridor, no. 1, 1987), pp. 58–62.   **7736**

PLANNING

Nowicki, Henry, "Influences of Zoning in the Recent Historical Geography of Glenview, Illinois," Master's thesis, University of Illinois, 1951.   **7737**

Kirchherr, Eugene C., "Nineteenth Century Technology and Design Applied to City Planning: The Development of Riverside and Pullman," in Edward J. Miller and Robert P. Wolensky, eds., *Proceedings of the 1984 Conference on the Small City and Regional Community*, vol. 6 (Stevens Point, Wisconsin: University of Wisconsin–Stevens Point Foundation Press, 1984), pp. 133–143.   **7738**

Daines, Sara A., "Historic Preservation and Chicago's Sheffield Neighborhood: A Brief Discussion of the Evolution of the American Preservation Movement and Its Impact upon the Landscape," Master's thesis, University of Chicago, 1987.   **7739**

Werner, Ralph, "Daniel Burnham und der Plan für Chicago," *Berichte zur Raumforschung und Raumplanung*, vol. 31, 1–2 (1987), pp. 44–48. **7740**

Arthur, Curtis L., "No Little Plans for Joliet, 1921 and 1959: Promise and Outcome," in Michael P. Conzen, ed., *Time and Place in Joliet: Essays on the Geographical Evolution of the City* (Chicago: University of Chicago Committee on Geographical Studies, Studies on the Illinois & Michigan Canal Corridor, no. 2, 1988), pp. 85–98.   **7741**

Mayer, Harold M., "Geography and City Planning Policy: A Chicago Case Study, 1939–1959," *Papers & Proceedings of Applied Geography Conferences*, vol. 12 (1989), pp. 61–66.   **7742**

PLACE NAMES

See also 7166

Ackerman, William K., *The Origin of Names of Stations on the Line of the Illinois-Central Railroad Company* (Chicago: Fergus Printing Co., 1884), 67 pp.   **7743**

Cutshall, Alden D., "Origin of Our State and County Names," *Illinois Bulletin of History*, vol. 6, 3 (1944), pp. 6–11.   **7744**

Vogel, Virgil J., *Indian Place Names in Illinois* (Springfield: Illinois State Historical Society, Pamphlet Series, no. 4, 1963), 176 pp.   **7745**

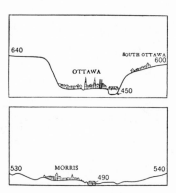

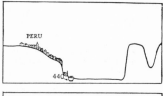

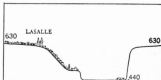

MICHIGAN

GENERAL

See also 1150

The state

Jefferson, Mark S., "Note on the Expansion of Michigan," *Report of the Michigan Academy of Science*, vol. 4 (1902), pp. 88–91. **7746**

Miller, George J., "Geographic Influences in the History of Michigan," Master's thesis, University of Chicago, 1909. **7747**

Smaller areas

Davis, Charles M., "The High Plains of Michigan," *Papers of the Michigan Academy of Science, Arts, and Letters*, vol. 21 (1935), pp. 303–342. **7748**

Cooper, Dennis G., "Geographic Influences on the History and Development of Isle Royale, Michigan," *Papers of the Michigan Academy of Science, Arts, and Letters*, vol. 24, 3 (1938), pp. 1–8. **7749**

Russell, Joseph A., "A Geographical Study of Delta County, Michigan," *Papers of the Michigan Academy of Science, Arts, and Letters*, vol. 24, 3 (1938), pp. 29–54. **7750**

Odenkirk, Thomas R., "A Historical Geography of Grand Ledge, Michigan," Master's thesis, Michigan State University, 1959. **7751**

Malik, Jahan A., "A Historical Geography of Ingham County, Michigan," Ph.D. diss., Michigan State University, 1961. **7752**

Ott, Michael, "A Historical Geography of Olivet, Michigan (From Early Nineteenth Century to 1873)," Master's thesis, Western Michigan University, 1972. **7753**

ENVIRONMENTAL CHANGE

Kenoyer, Leslie Alva, "Forest Distribution in South-Western Michigan as Interpreted from the Original Land Survey, 1826–32," *Papers of the Michigan Academy of Science, Arts, and Letters*, vol. 19 (1933), pp. 107–111. **7754**

Dick, W. Bruce, "A Study of the Original Vegetation of Wayne County, Michigan," *Papers of the Michigan Academy of Science, Arts, and Letters*, vol. 22 (1936), pp. 329–334. **7755**

Hudgins, Bert, "Old Detroit: Drainage and Land Forms," *Michigan History*, vol. 30, 2 (1946), pp. 348–368. **7756**

Davis, M. B., "Erosion Rates and Land Use History in Southern Michigan," *Environmental Conservation*, vol. 3 (1976), pp. 139–148. **7757**

Buckler, William R., "High Water Levels and Bluff Recession: Lake Michigan's Southeast Shore," *East Lakes Geographer*, vol. 22 (1987), pp. 157–177. **7758**

Stolle, Hans J., "Michigan Tornadoes, 1930–1969 and 1970–1980," *East Lakes Geographer*, vol. 22 (1987), pp. 88–102. **7759**

NATIVE PEOPLES & WHITE RELATIONS

Williams, David R., "A Late Pleistocene Geography of Southwestern Michigan: A Cultural and Historical Study," Master's thesis, Western Michigan University, 1969 **7760**

Peters, Bernard C., "Comments on the Distribution of Garden Beds in Kalamazoo County," *Ecumene*, vol. 12 (1980), pp. 31–37. [Prehistoric ridged fields] **7761**

Gribb, William J., "The Grand Traverse Band's Land Base: A Cultural-Historical Study of Land Transfer in Michigan," Ph.D. diss., Michigan State University, 1982. **7762**

EXPLORATION & MAPPING

Jenks, William L., "A Michigan Family of Mapmakers," *Michigan History Magazine*, vol. 11, 2 (1927), pp. 242–250. **7763**

Karpinski, Louis C., "Michigan and the Great Lakes upon the Map, 1636–1802," *Michigan History*, vol. 29, 3 (1945), pp. 291–312. **7764**

Barnett, LeRoy, "Milestones in Michigan Mapping," *Michigan History*, vol. 63, 5 (1979), pp. 29–38. **7765**

Sambrook, Richard, "Historical Lineaments in the Straits of Mackinac: An Investigation in Cultural Cartography," Master's thesis, Michigan State University, 1980. **7766**

Peters, Bernard C., *Lake Superior Journal: Bela Hubbard's Account of the 1840 Houghton Expedition* (Marquette: Northern Michigan University Press, 1983), 113 pp. **7767**

POPULAR IMAGES & EVALUATION

See also 4815

Peters, Bernard C., "Early American Impressions and Evaluations of the Landscape of Inner

Michigan, with Emphasis on Kalamazoo County," Ph.D. diss., Michigan State University, 1969. **7768**

Peters, Bernard C., "Folk Poetry as a Source for the Settlement Geographer: Example of Kalamazoo County, Michigan," *Professional Geographer*, vol. 22, 4 (1970), pp. 204–205. **7769**

Peters, Bernard C., "No Trees on the Prairie: Persistence of Error in Landscape Terminology," *Michigan History*, vol. 54, 1 (1970), pp. 19–28. **7770**

Peters, Bernard C., "Pioneer Evaluation of the Kalamazoo County Landscape," *Michigan Academician*, vol. 3 (1970), pp. 15–25. **7771**

Peters, Bernard C., "Early Perception of a High Plain in Michigan," *Annals of the Association of American Geographers*, vol. 62, 1 (1972), pp. 57–60. **7772**

Peters, Bernard C., "Oak Openings or Barrens: Landscape Evaluation on the Michigan Frontier," *Proceedings of the Association of American Geographers*, vol. 4 (1972), pp. 84–86. **7773**

Peters, Bernard C., "Settler Attitude toward the Land as Revealed in the Pioneer Poetry of Kalamazoo County," *Michigan Academician*, vol. 6 (1973), 209–216. **7774**

Peters, Bernard C., "The Remaking of an Image: The Propaganda Campaign to Attract Settlers to Michigan, 1815–1840," *Geographical Survey*, vol. 3, 1 (1974), pp. 25–52. **7775**

Peters, Bernard C., "Michigan's Oak Openings: Pioneer Perceptions of a Vegetative Landscape," *Journal of Forest History*, vol. 22 (1978), pp. 18–23. **7776**

REGIONAL SETTLEMENT

Miller, George J., "Some Geographic Influences in the Settlement of Michigan and in the Distribution of Its Population," *Bulletin of the American Geographical Society*, vol. 45 (1913), pp. 321–348. **7777**

Whittlesey, Derwent S., "A Locality on a Stubborn Frontier at the Close of a Cycle of Settlement," *Geografiska annaler*, vol. 12 (1930), pp. 175–192. [Republic, Mich.] **7778**

Rasche, Herbert H., "Sequent Occupance at the Straits of Mackinac," Master's thesis, University of Wisconsin–Madison, 1934. **7779**

McGaugh, Maurice E., *The Settlement of the Saginaw Basin* (Chicago: University of Chicago Department of Geography, Research Paper no. 16, 1950), 407 pp. **7780**

Stilgenbauer, Floyd A., and Stephen Scherer, "Northville: An Example of a Changing Settlement Pattern," *Michigan History*, vol. 34, 3 (1950), pp. 203–212. **7781**

Hart, John Fraser, "A Rural Retreat for Northern Negroes," *Geographical Review*, vol. 50, 2 (1960), pp. 147–168. [Lake Co., 1920–1957] **7782**

McCauley, David C., "The River Raisin Settlement, 1796–1812: A French Cultural Area," Master's thesis, Eastern Michigan University, 1968. **7783**

Berg, Richard C., "The Origin of Stoney Creek, Michigan," Master's thesis, Eastern Michigan University, 1973. **7784**

Dooley, Mary T., "The Andrews Bailiwick: A Geographic Study of Migration to and Settlement of Northern Macomb County, Michigan, 1810–1850, as Perceived by Selected Participants," Ph.D. diss., Michigan State University, 1975. **7785**

POPULATION

Freeman, Otis W., "A Geographic Study of the Growth and Distribution of Population in Michigan," *Report of the Michigan Academy of Science*, vol. 15 (1913), pp. 39–53. [Focus on 1820–1910] **7786**

Maybee, Rolland, "Population Growth and Distribution in Lower Michigan," *Papers of the Michigan Academy of Sciences, Arts, and Letters*, vol. 31 (1945), pp. 253–268. **7787**

Perejda, Andrew, "Sources and Dispersal of Michigan's Population," *Michigan History*, vol. 32, 4 (1948), pp. 355–366. **7788**

Enedy, Joseph D., "Population Growth and Decline in Washtenaw County, 1830–1840 and 1870–1880," Master's thesis, Michigan State University, 1967. **7789**

Wheeler, James O., and Stanley D. Brunn, "Negro Migration into Rural Southwestern Michigan," *Geographical Review*, vol. 58, 2 (1968), pp. 214–230. [Focus on c. 1900–1960] **7790**

Knuth, Clarence P., "Early Immigration and Current Residential Patterns of Negroes in Southwestern Michigan," Ph.D. diss., University of Michigan, 1969. **7791**

Wheeler, James O., and Stanley D. Brunn, "An Agricultural Ghetto: Negroes in Cass County, Michigan, 1845–1968," *Geographical Review*, vol. 59, 3 (1969), pp. 317–329. **7792**

Kovacik, Charles F., "A Historical Geography of the Foreign-Born in the Thumb of Michigan, with Particular Reference to Canadians, 1850–

1880," Ph.D. diss., Michigan State University, 1970.   7793

Johnson, Paula Ann, "Declining Fertility in Michigan, 1884 to 1970: A Test of the Diffusion and Adjustment Hypotheses," Master's thesis, Pennsylvania State University, 1973.   7794

Rose, Gregory S., "South Central Michigan Yankees," *Michigan History*, vol. 70, 2 (1986), pp. 32–39.   7795

Dickason, David G., "Downsizing Motown, 1960–1985: Population Trends in Michigan," *East Lakes Geographer*, vol. 22 (1987), pp. 203–215.   7796

Quandt, Elder, John T. Houdek, and Laurence Rosen, "Immigrant Settlers in Southwestern Michigan, 1850–1880," *East Lakes Geographer*, vol. 22 (1987), pp. 178–189.   7797

Rose, Gregory S., "The County Origins of Southern Michigan's Settlers, 1800–1850," *East Lakes Geographer*, vol. 22 (1987), pp. 74–87.   7798

Rose, Gregory S., "The Origins of Canadian Settlers in Southern Michigan, 1820–1850," *Ontario History*, vol. 79, 1 (1987), pp. 31–52.   7799

RURAL & REGIONAL SOCIAL GEOGRAPHY

See also 7082

Wilson, Leonard S., "Eben: A Finnish Community in the Upper Peninsula of Michigan," *Papers of the Michigan Academy of Science, Arts, and Letters*, vol. 19 (1933), pp. 367–375.   7800

Bjorklund, Elaine M., "Ideology and Culture Exemplified in Southwestern Michigan," *Annals of the Association of American Geographers*, vol. 54, 2 (1964), pp. 227–241. Reprinted in Fred E. Dohrs and Lawrence M. Sommers, eds., *Cultural Geography: Selected Readings* (New York: Thomas Y. Crowell Co., 1967), pp. 251–272.   7801

Mackun, Stanley, "The Changing Patterns of Polish Settlements in the Greater Detroit Area: Geographic Study of the Assimilation of an Ethnic Group," Ph.D. diss., University of Michigan, 1964.   7802

Moline, Norman T., "Finnish Settlement in Upper Michigan," Master's thesis, University of Chicago, 1966.   7803

Kaups, Matti E., and Eugene Cotton Mather, "Eben: Thirty Years Later in a Finnish Community in the Upper Peninsula of Michigan," *Economic Geography*, vol. 44, 1 (1968), pp. 57–70.   7804

DeForth, Peter, "The Spatial Evolution of the German-American Culture Region in Clinton

and Ionia Counties, Michigan," Master's thesis, Michigan State University, 1970.   7805

Yli-Jokkpii, Pentti, "The Cultural Geography of Kaleva, a Finnish Immigrant Community in Michigan," *Acta geographica* (Helsinki), vol. 22 (1971), pp. 1–24.   7806

Evans, Sydney K., "The Reorganization of Michigan Rural Schools: Educational Central Place Increase," Master's thesis, Eastern Michigan University, 1972. [Focus on 1912–1970]   7807

Johnson, Howard G., "A Historical Geography of the Franconian Colonies of the Saginaw Valley, Michigan," Ph.D. diss., Michigan State University, 1972.   7808

Penzkofer, Mary Elizabeth, "The Evolution of the Gull Lake Community, 1900–1975," Master's thesis, Western Michigan University, 1975. 7809

Bossa, Wayne E., "Dutch Immigration and Migration: The Establishment of Dutch Communities in Southwestern Michigan," *Proceedings of the New England–St. Lawrence Valley Division, Association of American Geographers*, vol. 6 (1976), pp. 46–48.   7810

Houdek, John T., and Charles F. Heller, "Searching for Nineteenth-Century Farm Tenants: An Evaluation of Methods," *Historical Methods*, vol. 19, 2 (1986), pp. 55–61. [Prairie Ronde and Wakshma Townships, southwestern Michigan]   7811

Nutter, David C., "Malaria in Michigan," Master's thesis, Michigan State University, 1988.   7812

Dandekar, Hemalata C., and Mary Bockstahler, "The Changing Farmscape: A Case Study of German Farmers in Southeast Michigan," *Michigan History*, vol. 74, 1 (1990), pp. 42–47. [Focus on the Raab farmstead, Bridgewater Twp., Washtenaw Co., 1848–1990]   7813

POLITICAL & ADMINISTRATIVE GEOGRAPHY

See also 7091

Miller, George J., "The Establishment of Michigan's Boundaries: A Study in Historical Geography," *Bulletin of the American Geographical Society*, vol. 43, 5 (1911), pp. 339–350.   7814

Shepherd, Glenn J., "An Electoral Geography of Wayne County, Michigan, 1932–1972," Master's thesis, Eastern Michigan University, 1975. 7815

ECONOMIC DEVELOPMENT

Whitaker, J. Russell, "The Relation of Agriculture to Mining in the Upper Peninsula of Michigan,"

Journal of Geography, vol. 25, 1 (1926), pp. 21–30. [Focus on 1880s–1920s]   **7816**

Daoust, Charles F., "Transition in Central Michigan: Agriculture to Industry," Master's thesis, University of Chicago, 1954.   **7817**

Kubicki, Dale L., "An Early Intracounty Railroad Network and the Development of Fruit Culture: Van Buren County, Michigan," Master's thesis, Western Michigan University, 1969.   **7818**

Kendall, Joan M., "Nonemployment Income as a Factor in the Economic Base of Michigan Counties, 1959–1986," Master's thesis, Michigan State University, 1989.   **7819**

LAND & LAND USE

Land Survey

Jacobson, Daniel, "Michigan Meridian and Base Line: A Study in Historical Geography," *East Lakes Geographer*, vol. 22 (1987), pp. 37–52.   **7820**

Land Tenure

McMurray, Kenneth C., and Mary Greenshields, "Some Geographic Relationships of Tax Delinquency in Michigan," *Papers of the Michigan Academy of Science, Arts, and Letters*, vol. 14 (1930), pp. 377–387. [Focus on 1880–1920]   **7821**

McIntire, George S., "A History of Tax-Delinquent Land in Township 24 North, Range 1 East, Ogeman County, Michigan," *Papers of the Michigan Academy of Science, Arts, and Letters*, vol. 25 (1939), pp. 417–436.   **7822**

Heller, Charles F., and F. S. Moore, "Continuity in Rural Land Ownership: Western Kalamazoo County, Michigan, 1830–1861," *Michigan History*, vol. 56, 3 (1972), pp. 230–246.   **7823**

Peters, Bernard C., "Early Town-Site Speculation in Kalamazoo County," *Michigan History*, vol. 56, 3 (1972), pp. 201–215.   **7824**

Peters, Bernard C., "The Fever Period of Land Speculation in Kalamazoo County: 1835–37," *Michigan Academician*, vol. 8, 3 (1976), pp. 287–301.   **7825**

Land Use

Dick, W. Bruce, "A Study of Settlement and Land Use in Livingston County, Michigan," *Papers of the Michigan Academy of Science, Arts and Letters*, vol. 26 (1940), pp. 345–400.   **7826**

Vanderhill, Burke G., "A Survey of Land Use and Land Ownership on Bois Blanc Island," *Papers of the Michigan Academy of Science, Arts, and Letters*, vol. 35 (1949), pp. 235–249.   **7827**

Lemerand, Martin, "Land Utilization in the Allegan State Forest: A Historical Geography," Master's thesis, Western Michigan University, 1965.   **7828**

Wuersching, Karl, "Internal and External Factors Determining Past and Future Land Use and Settlement Patterns of Washtenaw County, Michigan," Ph.D. diss., University of Michigan, 1967.   **7829**

EXTRACTIVE ACTIVITY

Mining

Hinsdale, Elizur B., "Native Copper of Michigan," *Journal of the American Geographical Society*, vol. 23 (1891), pp. 324–338.   **7830**

Goodman, Robert J., "The Discovery and Early Exploitation of Iron Ore on the Marquette Range, Marquette County, Michigan," *Papers of the Michigan Academy of Science, Arts, and Letters*, vol. 37 (1951), pp. 161–165.   **7831**

Lumbering

Cook, Charles W., "The Influence of the Lumber Industry upon the Salt Industry of Michigan," *Journal of Geography*, vol. 15, 4 (1916), pp. 117–125.   **7832**

Maybee, Rolland, "Michigan's White Pine Era, 1840–1900," *Michigan History*, vol. 43 (1959), pp. 385–432.   **7833**

Kromm, David E., "Sequences of Forest Utilization in Northern Michigan," *Canadian Geographer*, vol. 12, 3 (1968), pp. 144–157.   **7834**

Neithercut, Mark, "The White Pine Industry and the Transformation of Nineteenth-Century Michigan," Ph.D. diss., University of British Columbia, 1983.   **7835**

Krog, Carl, "The Development of Lumbering in the Nicolet National Forest," *Wisconsin Geographer*, vol. 1 (1985), pp. 56–71.   **7836**

Quarrying

Morrison, Paul C., "Michigan Limestone Industry," *Economic Geography*, vol. 18, 3 (1942), pp. 259–274. [Focus on 1900–1937]   **7837**

AGRICULTURE

See also **1421**, **7115**

Stilgenbauer, Floyd A., "The Michigan Sugar Beet Industry," *Economic Geography*, vol. 3, 4 (1927), pp. 486–506. [Focus on 1900–1924]   **7838**

Hudgins, Bert, "Bean Production in Michigan," *Economic Geography*, vol. 9, 3 (1933), pp. 265–272. [Focus on 1850–1930]   **7839**

Deasy, George F., "Agriculture in Luce County, Michigan, 1880 to 1930: A Study of Agricultural

Development in the Upper Great Lakes Region," *Agricultural History*, vol. 34, 1 (1950), pp. 29–41. **7840**

Olmstead, Clarence W., "The Pattern of Orchards in Michigan: An Historical-Geographic Study of the Development of a Pattern of Land Use," Ph.D. diss., University of Michigan, 1951. **7841**

Heimonen, Henry S., "Agricultural Trends in the Upper Peninsula," *Michigan History*, vol. 41, 1 (1957), pp. 45–52. **7842**

Ball, John M., "Changes in Sugar Beet Production in Michigan, 1899–1958," *Papers of the Michigan Academy of Science, Arts, and Letters*, vol. 45 (1960), pp. 137–144. **7843**

Senninger, Earl J., "The Chicory Industry of Michigan," *Papers of the Michigan Academy of Science, Arts, and Letters*, vol. 45 (1960), pp. 145–153. [Focus on 1890s–1950s] **7844**

Landing, James E., "The Decline of the Commercial Mint Industry in Michigan," *Professional Geographer*, vol. 15, 4 (1963), pp. 21–25. **7845**

Wiseman, Robert F., "The Evolution and Character of the Bedding Plants Industry in Kalamazoo County, Michigan," Master's thesis, Western Michigan University, 1969. **7846**

Henley, Ronald L., and Carl F. Ojala, "The Beet Sugar Industry of Michigan: A Geographical Analysis," *Michigan Academician*, vol. 6, 3 (1974), pp. 321–332. [Focus on 1899–1970] **7847**

Heller, Charles F., and John T. Houdek, "When Wheat Was King: An Analysis of Michigan's Wheat Belt in 1885," *East Lakes Geographer*, vol. 24 (1989), pp. 34–47. **7848**

LANDSCAPE

See also **7128, 8083**

Decker, Keith M., "Early Pioneer Homesteads in Central Michigan," *Papers of the Michigan Academy of Science, Arts, and Letters*, vol. 44 (1959), pp. 315–321. **7849**

Kyser, Dewayne, "Relict Forms in the Central Michigan Rural Landscape," *Michigan Academician*, vol. 2, 2 (1969), pp. 57–65. **7850**

McLennan, Marshall S., "Vernacular Architecture: Common House Types in Southern Michigan," in C. Kurt Dewhurst and Yvonne Lockwood, eds., *Michigan Folklife Reader* (East Lansing: Michigan State University Press, 1987), pp. 15–46. **7851**

COMMUNICATIONS & TRADE

See also **7134**

Field, Arthur, "Road Patterns of the Southern Peninsula of Michigan," *Papers of the Michigan Academy of Science, Arts, and Letters*, vol. 14 (1930), pp. 305–328. **7852**

Sheldon, Samuel R., "The Michigan Central Railroad and Washtenaw County's Changing Economic Geography from 1820 to 1850," Master's thesis, Eastern Michigan University, 1967. **7853**

Smith, H. Roger, "Diminishing Time-Space and Functional Change in the Haslett–Lake Lansing, Michigan, Area," *Papers of the Michigan Academy of Science, Arts, and Letters*, vol. 52 (1967), pp. 297–311. [Focus on 1840–1960] **7854**

Leatherberry, Earl C., "Freeway Development in Detroit Metropolitan Area, 1940–1970: Impact on the Central City," Master's thesis, University of Michigan, 1973. **7855**

MANUFACTURING & INDUSTRIALIZATION

Morrison, Paul C., "Cement Plant Migration in Michigan," *Economic Geography*, vol. 21, 1 (1945), pp. 1–16. [Focus on 1872–1940] **7856**

Boas, Charles W., "Locational Patterns of the Michigan Passenger Automobile Industry, 1900–1957," *Papers of the Michigan Academy of Science, Arts, and Letters*, vol. 44 (1959), pp. 303–314. **7857**

Seaton, Lynn E., "The Industrial Evolution of Washtenaw County, Michigan," Master's thesis, Eastern Michigan University, 1964. **7858**

Wigglesworth, Eugene J., "The Geographical Factors Influencing the Location and Growth of the Dow Chemical Company in Midland, Michigan," Master's thesis, Eastern Michigan University, 1966. **7859**

Wheeler, James O., "Spatial Changes in Manufacturing: The Michigan Example, 1840–1963," *Land Economics*, vol. 47 (1971), pp. 193–198. **7860**

Kurzhals, Richard D., "The Furniture Industry of Grand Rapids: An Historical Geography," Ph.D. diss., Michigan State University, 1977. **7861**

Bloomfield, Gerald T., "Shaping the Character of a City: The Automobile Industry and Detroit, 1900–1920," *Michigan Quarterly Review*, vol. 25, 2 (1986), pp. 167–181. **7862**

Thompson, John, "The Bay City Land Dredge and Dredge Works: Perspectives on the Machines of Land Drainage," *Michigan Historical Review*, vol. 12, 2 (1986), pp. 21–43. **7863**

URBAN NETWORKS & URBANIZATION

Davis, Charles M., "The Cities and Towns of the High Plains of Michigan," *Geographical Review*, vol. 28, 4 (1938), pp. 664–673. [Focus on 1900–1935]   **7864**

Reynolds, Robert B., "Central Places of the Flint Metropolitan Community: Their Classification and Areas of Dominance in 1900 and 1960," Ph.D. diss., University of Michigan, 1963.   **7865**

Mastran, Shelley S., "Changes in Accessibility and Relative Growth: The Centers of Southern Michigan, 1840–1900," Master's thesis, George Washington University, 1974.   **7866**

TOWN GROWTH

Detroit

Parkins, Almon E., "The Historical Geography of Detroit," Ph.D. diss., University of Chicago, 1914. Published under the same title, as a University of Chicago Libraries Private Edition, 1914.   **7867**

Parkins, Almon E., *The Historical Geography of Detroit* (Lansing: Michigan Historical Commission, University Series no. 3, 1918), 356 pp. Reprinted Port Washington, N.Y.: Kennikat Press, 1970).   **7868**

Hudgins, Bert, "Evolution of Metropolitan Detroit," *Economic Geography*, vol. 21, 3 (1945), pp. 206–220.   **7869**

Maday, Robert C., "An Historical Geography of Hamtramck Township," Master's thesis, University of Michigan, 1977.   **7870**

Grand Rapids

Ellis, Grace F., "Why is Grand Rapids?" *Journal of Geography*, vol. 11, 2 (1912), pp. 45–48.   **7871**

Bailey, Perry L., "The Role of the Economic Geographic Factors in the Origin and Growth of Grand Rapids, Michigan," Ph.D. diss., Ohio State University, 1955.   **7872**

Other centers

Whitaker, J. Russell, "Negaunee, Michigan: An Urban Center Dominated by Iron Mining," *Bulletin of the Philadelphia Geographical Society*, vol. 29, 2 (1931), pp. 137–174.   **7873**

Cooper, Dennis G., and Floyd A. Stilgenbauer, "The Urban Geography of Saginaw, Michigan," *Papers of the Michigan Academy of Science, Arts, and Letters*, vol. 20 (1934), pp. 297–312.   **7874**

Straw, H. Thompson, "Hillsdale: An Urban Study of a Small Mid-Western Town," *Journal of Geography*, vol. 34, 8 (1935), pp. 324–334. [Focus on 1850–1935]   **7875**

Straw, H. Thompson, "Battle Creek: A Study in Urban Geography, Part 2: Origin and Development, and Functional Interpretation," *Papers of*

the *Michigan Academy of Science, Arts, and Letters*, vol. 24, 3 (1938), pp. 71–92.   **7876**

Glasgow, James A., "Muskegon, Michigan: The Evolution of a Lake Port," Ph.D. diss., University of Chicago, 1939. Published under the same title, as a University of Chicago Libraries Private Edition, 1939, 102 pp.   **7877**

Ballert, Albert G., "The Geographic Foundations and Developments of Monroe, Michigan," Master's thesis, Syracuse University, 1940.   **7878**

Santer, Richard A., "A Historical Geography of Jackson, Michigan: A Study on the Changing Character of an American City, 1829–1969," Ph.D. diss., Michigan State University, 1970.   **7879**

Sinclair, Robert, Robert Shipton, and Helen Willis, "A Case Study of Urban Expansion in Southwestern Macomb County," *Michigan Academician*, vol. 4, 2 (1971), pp. 161–182. [On the northern margin of the City of Detroit, 1948–1968]   **7880**

URBAN ECONOMIC STRUCTURE

See also **4659**

Detroit

Hudgins, Bert, "A Geographic Study of the Water Supply Problem of Detroit, Michigan," Ph.D. diss., Clark University, 1930.   **7881**

Hudgins, Bert, "Historical Geography of the Detroit Water Supply," *Michigan History Magazine*, vol. 20, 4 (1936), pp. 351–381.   **7882**

Wilson, Leonard S., "Functional Areas of Detroit, 1890–1933," *Papers of the Michigan Academy of Science, Arts, and Letters*, vol. 22 (1936), pp. 397–409.   **7883**

Kocher, Eric, "Growth and Shifting of the Business Area of Detroit," *Michigan History Magazine*, vol. 21, 1 (1937), pp. 103–109. [Focus on 1810–1890]   **7884**

Dain, Floyd R., "An Economic Study of Detroit, 1815–1825," Master's thesis, Wayne State University, 1943.   **7885**

Wenglowski, David, "Factors Influencing the Spatial Extent of the Urban Cemetery: An Historical Analysis of Burial Ground Development in the Detroit Metropolitan Area, 1871–1970," Master's thesis, Wayne State University, 1972.   **7886**

Herron, Janet, "Decision Making and the Geography of Parks: Detroit, 1806–1975," Master's thesis, Wayne State University, 1976.   **7887**

Bloomfield, Gerald T., "The Business Side of Henry Ford," *Herald (Greenfield Village and Henry Ford Museum)*, vol. 8, 2 (1979), pp. 6–13.   **7888**

Rii, Hae Un, "Genesis, Early Growth, and Impact of the Transportation System on Detroit, 1805–1900," Ph.D. diss., Michigan State University, 1982.   7889

Other centers

Rolfe, Eldred, "Analysis of the Spatial Distribution of Neighborhood Parks in Lansing, 1920–1960," *Papers of the Michigan Academy of Science, Arts, and Letters*, vol. 50 (1965), pp. 479–491. 7890

URBAN SOCIAL STRUCTURE

Ann Arbor

Deskins, Donald R., "Negro Settlement in Ann Arbor [1850–1960]," Master's thesis, University of Michigan, 1962.   7891

Jones, Michael J., "The Pattern and Process of Residential Growth in Ann Arbor, 1920–1970," Master's thesis, Wayne State University, 1975.   7892

Battle Creek

Gaston, Juanita, "The Changing Residential Pattern of Blacks in Battle Creek, Michigan: A Study in Historical Geography," Ph.D. diss., Michigan State University, 1977.   7893

Gaston, Juanita, and Walter C. Farrell, "Residential Patterns of Blacks in Battle Creek, Michigan, 1850–1930," *Proceedings of the Pennsylvania Academy of Science*, vol. 51 (1977), pp. 79–84.   7894

Detroit

Humphrey, N. D., "The Migration and Settlement of Detroit Mexicans," *Economic Geography*, vol. 19, 4 (1943), pp. 358–361. [Focus on 1910–1935]   7895

Deskins, Donald R., "Race, Residence, and Workplace in Detroit, 1880 to 1965," *Economic Geography*, vol. 48, 1 (1972), pp. 79–94.   7896

Deskins, Donald R., *Residential Mobility of Negroes in Detroit, 1837–1965* (Ann Arbor: University of Michigan, Department of Geography, Michigan Geographical Publications, no. 5, 1972), 297 pp.   7897

Ham, Robert C., "Area-Specific Crime Rates for the Detroit Metropolitan Region, 1930–1970," Ph.D. diss., University of Michigan, 1976.   7898

Sinclair, Robert, "Ghetto Expansion and the Urban Landscape in Detroit," in Erhart Winkler and Herwig Lechleitner, eds., *Beiträge zur Wirtschaftsgeographie* (Vienna: Ferdinand Hirt, Wiener Geographische Schriften, nos. 46–48, 1976), pp. 191–202. [Focus on 1940–1970]   7899

Deskins, Donald R., "An Index of City Structure Based on Empirical Observations," in Gyorgy

Enyedi, ed., *Urban Development in the U.S.A. and Hungary* (Budapest: Akademiai Kiado, 1978), pp. 155–168. [Occupational centroids for Detroit, 1850–1970]   7900

Schneider, John C., *Detroit and the Problem of Order, 1830–1880: A Geography of Crime, Riots, and Policing* (Lincoln: University of Nebraska Press, 1980), 171 pp.   7901

Zunz, Olivier, *The Changing Face of Inequality: Urbanization, Industrial Development, and Immigrants in Detroit, 1880–1920* (Chicago: University of Chicago Press, 1982), 481 pp.   7902

Zunz, Olivier, "Croissance urbaine et mutations sociale dans l'amérique industrielle: Detroit de 1880 à 1920," *Bulletin d'information de la Société de Demographie Historique*, vol. 36 (1982), pp. 23–28.   7903

Darden, Joe T., et al., *Detroit: Race and Uneven Development* (Philadelphia: Temple University Press, 1987), 317 pp. [Focus on 1915 to the 1980s, with emphasis on the post–World War II phase]   7904

Nathalang, Matrini, "Where Did the Doctors Go? Primary Physician Relocation, Detroit, 1950–1980," Ph.D. diss., University of Kentucky, 1988.   7905

Kalamazoo

Jakle, John A., and James O. Wheeler, "The Changing Residential Structure of the Dutch Population in Kalamazoo," *Annals of the Association of American Geographers*, vol. 59, 3 (1969), pp. 441–460. [Focus on 1873–1965]   7906

Jakle, John A., and James O. Wheeler, "The Dutch in Kalamazoo, Michigan: A Study of Spatial Barriers to Acculturation," *Tijdschrift voor economische en sociale geografie*, vol. 60, 4 (1969), pp. 249–254. [Focus on 1870–1965]   7907

Lansing

Meyer, Douglas K., "The Changing Negro Residential Patterns in Lansing, Michigan, 1850–1969," Ph.D. diss., Michigan State University, 1970.   7908

Meyer, Douglas K., "Evolution of a Permanent Negro Community in Lansing," *Michigan History*, vol. 55, 2 (1971), pp. 141–154.   7909

Meyer, Douglas K., "Changing Negro Residential Patterns in Michigan's Capital, 1915–1970," *Michigan History*, vol. 56, 2 (1972), pp. 151–167.   7910

Other centers

Lewis, Peirce F., "Impact of Negro Migration on the Electoral Geography of Flint, Michigan, 1932–1962: A Cartographic Analysis," *Annals of the Association of American Geographers*, vol. 55, 1 (1965), pp. 1–25.   **7911**

Veness-Randall, April René, "The Socio-Spatial Lifecycle of a Company Town: Calumet, Michigan," Master's thesis, Michigan State University, 1979. [Focus on 1880–1930]   **7912**

TOWNSCAPE

Reps, John W., "Town Planning in the Wilderness: Detroit, 1805–1830," *Town Planning Review*, vol. 25, 4 (1955), pp. 240–250.   **7913**

Lambert, Gordon A., "157 Years of Real Estate Subdividing and Urban Expansion in Oakland County, Michigan, 1819–1976," Master's thesis, Wayne State University, 1979.   **7914**

Deskins, Donald R., "Morphogenesis of a Black Ghetto," *Urban Geography*, vol. 2, 2 (1981), pp. 95–114.   **7915**

RECREATION & TOURISM

Coulson, Lois E., "Evolution of the Recreational Occupance of Berrien County, Michigan, with Emphasis on the Present Recreational Landscape," Ph.D. diss., University of Illinois, 1959.   **7916**

PLACE NAMES

Leestma, Roger, "Origin of Dutch Place Names in Allegan and Ottawa Counties, Michigan," *Papers of the Michigan Academy of Science, Arts, and Letters*, vol. 34 (1948), pp. 147–151.   **7917**

Kaups, Matti E., "Finnish Place Names in Michigan," *Michigan History*, vol. 51, 4 (1967), pp. 335–347.   **7918**

Peters, Bernard C., "Relic Names on the Landscape: The Prairies of Kalamazoo County," *Names*, vol. 20, 1 (1972), pp. 60–61.   **7919**

Peters, Bernard C., "The Origin and Meaning of the Term 'Marais' as Used on the Lake Superior

Shoreline of Marquette," *Michigan Academician*, vol. 13, 1 (1980), pp. 7–16.   **7920**

Peters, Bernard C., "Voyageur Place Names in the Great Lakes with Emphasis on Michigan's Lake Superior Shoreline," *Papers of the North Central Names Institute*, vol. 1 (1980), pp. 64–76.   **7921**

Peters, Bernard C., "The Origin and Meaning of Place Names along the Pictured Rocks National Shoreline," *Michigan Academician*, vol. 14 (1981), pp. 41–55.   **7922**

Peters, Bernard C., "The Origin of Some Stream Names along Michigan's Lake Superior Shoreline," *Inland Seas*, vol. 37, 1 (1981), pp. 6–12. **7923**

Peters, Bernard C., "Michigan Place Names from the American Rectangular Survey System," *Papers of the North Central Name Institute*, vol. 3 (1982), pp. 30–43.   **7924**

Peters, Bernard C., "The Origin and Meaning of Chippewa Place Names along the Lake Superior Shore Line between Grand Island and Pointe Abbaye," *Names*, vol. 32, 3 (1984), pp. 234–251.   **7925**

Peters, Bernard C., "The Origin and Meaning of Chippewa and French Place Names along the Shoreline of the Keweenaw Peninsula," *Michigan Academician*, vol. 17, 2 (1985), pp. 195–211.   **7926**

Peters, Bernard C., "The Origin and Meaning of Place Names along the Lake Superior Shoreline between Keweenaw Portage and Montreal River," *Michigan Academician*, vol. 18, 2 (1986), pp. 411–429.   **7927**

Romig, Walter, *Michigan Place Names: The History of the Founding and the Naming of More than Five Thousand Past and Present Michigan Communities* (Grosse Point, Mich.: Wayne State University Press, 1986), 673 pp.   **7928**

Peters, Bernard C., "The Origin and Meaning of the Name 'Sault Sainte Marie'," *Michigan Academician*, vol. 19, 2 (1987), pp. 253–257.   **7929**

WISCONSIN

GENERAL

The state

Dopp, Mary, "Geographic Influences in the Development of Wisconsin," Master's thesis, University of Chicago, 1910.　　　　　　　**7930**

Dopp, Mary, "Geographical Influences in the Development of Wisconsin," *Bulletin of the American Geographical Society*, vol. 45, 6 (1913), pp. 401–412; 7, pp. 490–499; 8, pp. 585–609; 9, pp. 653–663; 10, pp. 736–749; 11, pp. 831–846; and 12, pp. 902–920.　　　　　　　**7931**

Stickle, B. A., "The Influence of the Mississippi River in the Development of Wisconsin," *Journal of Geography*, vol. 12, 8 (1914), pp. 274–279.　　　　　　　**7932**

Uber, Harvey A., "Environmental Factors in the Development of Wisconsin," Ph.D. diss., Marquette University, 1937.　　　　　　　**7933**

Uber, Harvey A., *Environmental Factors in the Development of Wisconsin* (Milwaukee: Marquette University Press, 1937), 265 pp.　　　**7934**

Hofmeister, Burkhard, "Wisconsin: Eine kulturgeographische Skizze," *Jahrbuch für Amerikastudien*, vol. 4 (1959), pp. 249–283.　　**7935**

Vogeler, Ingolf K., "Historical Landscapes," "The Northwoods Region," and "The Southern Agricultural Region," in his *Wisconsin: A Geography* (Boulder: Westview Press, 1987), pp. 51–83, 84–114, and 124–131.　　　　　　　**7936**

Smaller areas

McConnell, Wallace R., "Geography of the Winnebago and Lower Fox River Valley," *Journal of Geography*, vol. 12, 8 (1914), pp. 262–267.　　**7937**

Whitbeck, Ray H., *The Geography of the Fox-Winnebago Valley* (Madison: Wisconsin Geological and Natural History Survey, Bulletin no. 42, Education Series no. 5, 1915), 115 pp.　　**7938**

Blanchard, William O., "A Geographic Interpretation of the Cuesta of Southwestern Wisconsin," Ph.D. diss., University of Wisconsin–Madison, 1921.　　　　　　　**7939**

Whitbeck, Ray H., *The Geography and Economic Development of Southeastern Wisconsin* (Madison: Wisconsin Geological and Natural History Survey, Bulletin no. 58, 1921), 243 pp.　　　　　　　**7940**

Blanchard, William O., "Man and Topography in Southwestern Wisconsin," *Transactions of the Illinois State Academy of Science*, vol. 15 (1922), pp. 393–395.　　　　　　　**7941**

Blanchard, William O., *The Geography of Southwestern Wisconsin* (Madison: Wisconsin Geological and Natural History Survey, Bulletin no. 65, 1924), 117 pp.　　　　　　　**7942**

Schafer, Joseph, *Wisconsin Domesday Book Town Studies*, vol. 1 (Madison: State Historical Society of Wisconsin, 1924), 168 pp.　　**7943**

Schafer, Joseph, *Four Wisconsin Counties: Prairie and Forest* (Madison: State Historical Society of Wisconsin, Wisconsin Domesday Book, General Studies, vol. 2, 1927), 429 pp.　　**7944**

Schafer, Joseph, *The Wisconsin Lead Mining Region* (Madison: State Historical Society of Wisconsin, Wisconsin Domesday Book, General Studies, vol. 3, 1932), 341 pp.　　**7945**

Mather, Eugene Cotton, John Fraser Hart, and Hildegard Binder Johnson, *Upper Coulee Country* (Prescott, Wis.: Pierce County Geographical Society, 1975), 101 pp.　　**7946**

ENVIRONMENTAL CHANGE

See also **7023, 7027**

General

LeMaire, Minnie E., "History of the Natural Setting of LaCrosse, Wisconsin," *LaCrosse County Historical Society Sketches*, ser. 6 (1942), pp. 73–75.　　　　　　　**7947**

Mather, Eugene Cotton, "Coulees and the Coulee Country of Wisconsin," *Wisconsin Academy Review*, vol. 22 (1976), pp. 22–25.　　**7948**

Climate

Villmow, Jack R., "Wisconsin's Greatest Heat Wave," *Transactions of the Wisconsin Academy of Sciences, Arts, and Letters*, vol. 70 (1982), pp. 167–171.　　　　　　　**7949**

Moran, Joseph M., and E. Lee Somerville, "Nineteenth-Century Temperature Record at Fort Howard, Green Bay, Wisconsin," *Transactions of the Wisconsin Academy of Sciences, Arts, and Letters*, vol. 75 (1987), pp. 79–89.　　**7950**

Villmow, Jack R., "Wisconsin's Coldest Five Weeks," *Transactions of the Wisconsin Acad-*

emy of Sciences, Arts, and Letters, vol. 70 (1982), pp. 172–176.   **7951**

Vegetation

Trewartha, Glenn T., "The Vegetal Cover of the Driftless Cuestaform Hill Land: Pre-settlement Record and Post-Glacial Evolution," *Transactions of the Wisconsin Academy of Sciences, Arts, and Letters*, vol. 32 (1940), pp. 361–382. **7952**

Icke, Paul W., "Original Forest Vegetation in a Glaciated Area," *Transactions of the Illinois State Academy of Science*, vol. 34 (1941), pp. 147–148. [Vilas and Oneida counties]   **7953**

Stearns, Forest W., "Ninety Years Change in a Northern Hardwood Forest in Wisconsin," *Ecology*, vol. 30, 3 (1949), pp. 350–358.   **7954**

Finley, Robert W., "The Original Forest Cover of Wisconsin," Ph.D. diss., University of Wisconsin–Madison, 1951.   **7955**

Puhala, Robert, "Conceptual Geography in an Historical Perspective: A Sequent Occupance Case Study of Horicon Marsh," Master's thesis, University of Illinois–Chicago, 1979.   **7956**

Puhala, Robert, "Conceptual Geography in an Historical Perspective: A Sequent Occupance Case Study of Horicon Marsh," *Bulletin of the Illinois Geographical Society*, vol. 22, 1 (1980), pp. 26–42.   **7957**

Hanron, Kevin F., "A Reconstruction of the Black Woods of Wisconsin, 1847–1849," Master's thesis, University of Minnesota, 1981.   **7958**

Kasbarian, John A., "Forest History at Flambeau River, Sawyer County, Wisconsin," Master's thesis, University of Wisconsin–Madison, 1987.   **7959**

Liegel, Konrad, "Land Use and Vegetational Change on the Aldo Leopold Memorial Reserve," *Transactions of the Wisconsin Academy of Sciences, Arts, and Letters*, vol. 76 (1988), pp. 47–68.   **7960**

Erosion & sedimentation

Happ, Stafford C., "Effects of Sedimentation on Floods in the Kickapoo Valley, Wisconsin," *Journal of Geology*, vol. 52, 1 (1944), pp. 53–68.   **7961**

Knox, James C., "Valley Alluviation in Southwestern Wisconsin," *Annals of the Association of American Geographers*, vol. 62, 3 (1972), pp. 401–410.   **7962**

Kay, Paul A., "Hydrological and Morphological Changes during the Historical Period in Ellis Branch, Southwest Wisconsin," Master's thesis, University of Wisconsin–Madison, 1973.   **7963**

Trimble, Stanley W., "Response of Coon Creek, Wisconsin, to Soil Conservation Measures," in Barbara Borowiecki, ed., *Landscapes of Wisconsin: Field Trip Guide for the 71st Annual Association of American Geographers Convention* (Washington, D.C.: Association of American Geographers, 1975), pp. 24–29.   **7964**

Johnson, William C., "The Impact of Environmental Change on Fluvial Systems: Kickapoo River, Wisconsin," Ph.D. diss., University of Wisconsin–Madison, 1976.   **7965**

Trimble, Stanley W., "Modern Stream and Valley Sedimentation in the Driftless Area, Wisconsin, USA," *Proceedings of the Twenty-Third International Geographical Congress*, vol. 1, *Geomorphology and Paleogeography* (Moscow: International Geographical Union, 1976), pp. 228–231.
7966

Trimble, Stanley W., "Sedimentation in Coon Creek Valley, Wisconsin," *Proceedings of the Third Federal Interagency Sedimentation Conference, Colorado* (Washington, D.C.: Water Resources Council, 1976), pp. 100–112.   **7967**

Knox, James C., "Human Impacts on Wisconsin Stream Channels," *Annals of the Association of American Geographers*, vol. 67, 3 (1977), pp. 323–342.   **7968**

Knox, James, S. J. Cary, and Francis J. Magilligan IV, *Climatic Variation and the Mobility and Storage of Sediment in Watersheds* (Madison: University of Wisconsin Water Resources Center, Technical Report 81–03, 1981), 56 pp.   **7969**

Trimble, Stanley W., "Changes in Sediment Storage in the Coon Creek Basin, Driftless Area, Wisconsin, 1853 to 1975," *Science*, vol. 214, 4517 (1981), pp. 181–183.   **7970**

Trimble, Stanley W., and Steven W. Lund, *Soil Conservation and the Reduction of Erosion and Sedimentation in the Coon Creek Basin, Wisconsin* (Washington, D.C.: U.S. Geological Survey, Professional Paper no. 1234, 1982), 35 pp.
7971

Trimble, Stanley W., and Steven W. Lund, "Soil Conservation in the Coon Creek Basin, Wisconsin," *Journal of Soil and Water Conservation*, vol. 37, 6 (1982), pp. 355–356.   **7972**

Trimble, Stanley W., "A Sediment Budget for Coon Creek Basin in the Driftless Area, Wisconsin, 1853–1977," *American Journal of Science*, vol. 283, 5 (1983), pp. 454–474.   **7973**

Wolbert, George B., "Geomorphology of Alluvial Fans in Arrow Branch Basin, Southwest Wisconsin," Master's thesis, University of Wisconsin–Madison, 1986.   **7974**

Fauna

Kay, Jeanne C., "The Land of La Baye: The Ecological Impact of the Green Bay Fur Trade, 1634–1836," Ph.D. diss., University of Wisconsin–Madison, 1977.   **7975**

NATIVE PEOPLES & WHITE RELATIONS

See also **3965**

Kay, Jeanne C., "Indian Responses to a Mining Frontier," in W. W. Savage and S. I. Thompson, eds., *The Frontier: Comparative Studies*, vol. 2 (Norman: University of Oklahoma Press, 1979), pp. 193–203.   **7976**

Kay, Jeanne C., "Wisconsin Indian Hunting Patterns, 1634–1836," *Annals of the Association of American Geographers*, vol. 69, 3 (1979), pp. 402–418.   **7977**

Deller, Howard A., "Indian Peoples of the Upper Door Peninsula and the Landscape They Created," *Bulletin of the Wisconsin Council for Geographic Education, 1979* (1980), pp. 63–78.   **7978**

Kay, Jeanne C., "John Lawe, Green Bay Trader," *Wisconsin Magazine of History*, vol. 64, 1 (1980), pp. 3–27.   **7979**

Dorney, John R., "The Impact of Native Americans on Presettlement Vegetation in Southeastern Wisconsin," *Transactions of the Wisconsin Academy of Sciences, Arts, and Letters*, vol. 69 (1981), pp. 26–36.   **7980**

Kay, Jeanne C., "The Ecological Basis of Menominee Ethnobotany," *Journal of Cultural Geography*, vol. 2, 2 (1982), pp. 1–12.   **7981**

EXPLORATION & MAPPING

Smith, Alice E., "Two Wisconsin Map Makers," *Wisconsin Magazine of History*, vol. 29, 4 (1946), pp. 402–406.   **7982**

Friis, Herman R., "The David Dale Owen Map of Southwestern Wisconsin," *Prologue: The Journal of the National Archives*, vol. 1, 1 (1969), pp. 9–28.   **7983**

Marini, Michael F., "The History and Development of the Official State of Wisconsin Highway Map," Master's thesis, University of Wisconsin–Madison, 1974.   **7984**

Beckman, Thomas, *Milwaukee Illustrated: Panoramic and Bird's Eye Views of a Midwestern Metropolis, 1844–1908* (Milwaukee: Milwaukee Art Center, 1978), 68 pp.   **7985**

Baruth, Christopher M., "Mapping of Wisconsin since 1832," Master's thesis, University of Wisconsin–Milwaukee, 1980.   **7986**

Dorney, John R., "Increase A. Lapham's Pioneer Observations and Maps of Land Forms and Natural Disturbances," *Transactions of the Wisconsin Academy of Sciences, Arts, and Letters*, vol. 71, 2 (1983), pp. 25–30.   **7987**

Edmonds, Michael, "Increase A. Lapham and the Mapping of Wisconsin," *Wisconsin Magazine of History*, vol. 68, 3 (1985), pp. 163–187.   **7988**

Durbin, Richard, "Mapping the Wisconsin River," *Wisconsin Magazine of History*, vol. 70, 4 (1987), pp. 243–269.   **7989**

Prell, Renae, "History and Survey of Historical Vegetation Mapping in Wisconsin," *Wisconsin Geographer*, vol. 5 (1989), pp. 60–68.   **7990**

Rosen, Carol, "Mapping Wisconsin's Bedrock: 1839–1983," *Wisconsin Geographer*, vol. 5 (1989), pp. 16–28.   **7991**

POPULAR IMAGES & EVALUATION

Calkins, Charles F., "Perception of the Prairie in a Letter from Prairieville," *Transactions of the Wisconsin Academy of Sciences, Arts, and Letters*, vol. 67 (1979), pp. 63–68.   **7992**

Deller, Howard A., "Wisconsin as Portrayed in the Disturnell Guidebooks, 1857–1874," *Bulletin of the Wisconsin Council for Geographic Education, 1984* (1984), pp. 25–34.   **7993**

Tuan, Yi-Fu, "A Sense of Place," in Gretchen Holstein Schoff and Yi-Fu Tuan, *Two Essays on a Sense of Place* (Madison: Wisconsin Humanities Committee, 1989), pp. 1–13.   **7994**

Brinkman, Robert, and Howard A. Deller, "Alfred Ward's Wisconsin: Images of the Gilded Age," *Wisconsin Academy Review*, vol. 36, 3 (1990), pp. 3–7.   **7995**

Rosen, Carol, "Images of Wisconsin's Settlement Frontier," Ph.D. diss., University of Wisconsin–Milwaukee, 1990.   **7996**

REGIONAL SETTLEMENT

Trewartha, Glenn T., "French Settlement in the Driftless Hill Land," *Annals of the Association of American Geographers*, vol. 28, 3 (1938), pp. 179–200.   **7997**

Trewartha, Glenn T., "A Second Epoch of Destructive Occupance in the Driftless Hill Land (1760–1832): Period of British, Spanish, and Early American Control," *Annals of the Association of American Geographers*, vol. 30, 2 (1940), pp. 109–142.   **7998**

Bertrand, Kenneth J., "Rural Agglomerated Settlements in the Eastern Lake Shore Red Clay Dairy

Region of Wisconsin," *Transactions of the Wisconsin Academy of Sciences, Arts, and Letters*, vol. 34 (1942), pp. 47–62. **7999**

Trewartha, Glenn T., "Population and Settlements in the Upper Mississippi Hill Land during the Period of Destructive Exploitation (1670–1832)," *Proceedings of the Eighth American Scientific Congress* (1942), pp. 183–196. **8000**

Burns, Bert E., "Early and Contemporary Rural Occupance of Kenosha County, Wisconsin," Master's thesis, University of Nebraska, 1949. **8001**

Helgeson, Arlan C., "Nineteenth Century Land Colonization in Northern Wisconsin," *Wisconsin Magazine of History*, vol. 36, 2 (1953), pp. 115–121. **8002**

Every, Donovan R., "Changes in the Geography of Hamlets in South-Western Wisconsin: 1937–1964," Master's thesis, University of Wisconsin–Madison, 1973. **8003**

Hart, John Fraser, "People and Farms," in E. Cotton Mather, John Fraser Hart, and Hildegard Binder Johnson, *Upper Coulee Country* (Prescott, Wis.: Trimbelle Press, 1975), pp. 47–79. **8004**

Johnson, Hildegard Binder, "Settlement," in Eugene Cotton Mather, John Fraser Hart, and Hildegard Binder Johnson, *Upper Coulee Country* (Prescott, Wis.: Trimbelle Press, 1975), pp. 81–101. **8005**

Alanen, Arnold R., "Communities and Settlements on Wisconsin's Gogebic Iron Range Frontier, 1884–1894," *Wisconsin Academy Review*, vol. 30, 1 (1984), pp. 70–72. **8006**

Saueressig-Schreuder, Yda, "Immigration and Frontier Development: Dutch Catholic Settlement in the Fox River Valley of Wisconsin in the Mid-Nineteenth Century," *Upper Midwest History*, vol. 5 (1986), pp. 45–59. **8007**

Osterman, Jeffrey, "Historic Settlement Patterns of German Catholics and Lutherans in Eastern Wisconsin," *Wisconsin Geographer*, vol. 3 (1987), pp. 13–23. **8008**

Schreuder, Yda, *Dutch Catholic Immigrant Settlement in Wisconsin, 1850–1905* (New York: Garland, 1989), 195 pp. **8009**

POPULATION

Levi, Kate Everest, "Geographical Origin of German Immigration to Wisconsin," *Collections of the State Historical Society of Wisconsin*, vol. 14 (1898), pp. 341–493. **8010**

Smith, Guy-Harold, "The Settlement and Distribution of Population in Wisconsin: A Geographical Interpretation," Ph.D. diss., University of Wisconsin, 1927. **8011**

Smith, Guy-Harold, "The Populating of Wisconsin," *Geographical Review*, vol. 18, 3 (1928), pp. 402–421. Published in an expanded version as "The Settlement and the Distribution of the Population in Wisconsin," *Transactions of the Wisconsin Academy of Sciences, Arts, and Letters*, vol. 24 (1929), pp. 53–107. **8012**

Smith, Guy-Harold, "Notes on the Distribution of the German-Born in Wisconsin in 1905," *Wisconsin Magazine of History*, vol. 13, 2 (1929), pp. 107–120. **8013**

Smith, Guy-Harold, "Notes on the Distribution of the Foreign-Born Scandinavian in Wisconsin in 1905," *Wisconsin Magazine of History*, vol. 14, 4 (1930–1931), pp. 419–436. **8014**

Read, Mary Jo, "A Population Study of the Driftless Hill Land during the Pioneer Period, 1832–1860," Ph.D. diss., University of Wisconsin, 1941. **8015**

Polk, Robert R., "A Geographical Analysis of Population Change in the Hill Land of Western Wisconsin, 1870–1950," Ph.D. diss., University of Wisconsin, 1964. **8016**

Hess, Elmer B., "Historical Background: Wisconsin Population Distribution," *Proceedings of the Indiana Academy of Science*, vol. 74 (1965), pp. 278–282. **8017**

RURAL & REGIONAL SOCIAL GEOGRAPHY

See also 7081–7082

Town & country relations

Galpin, Charles J., *The Social Anatomy of an Agricultural Community* (Madison: University of Wisconsin Agricultural Experiment Station Research Bulletin no. 34, 1915), 34 pp. [Focus on Walworth Co.] **8018**

Kolb, John H., *Rural Primary Groups: A Study of Agricultural Neighborhoods* (Madison: University of Wisconsin Agricultural Experiment Station Research Bulletin no. 51, 1921), 81 pp. [Focus on Dane Co., c. 1840–1920] **8019**

Kolb, John H., and C. J. Bornman, *Rural Religious Organization: A Study of the Origin and Development of Religious Groups* (Madison: University of Wisconsin Agricultural Experiment Station Research Bulletin no. 60, 1924), 63 pp. [Focus on Dane Co., 1850–1924] **8020**

Kolb, John H., and R. A. Polson, *Trends in Town-Country Relations* (Madison: University of Wisconsin Agricultural Experiment Station Research Bulletin no. 117, 1933), 37 pp. [Focus on Walworth Co., 1913–1929] **8021**

Kolb, John H., *Trends of Country Neighborhoods: A Restudy of Rural Primary Groups, 1921–1931* (Madison: University of Wisconsin Agricultural Experiment Station Research Bulletin no. 120, 1933), 56 pp. [Focus on Dane Co.] **8022**

Kolb, John H., and Douglas G. Marshall, *Neighborhood-Community Relationships in Rural Society* (Madison: University of Wisconsin Agricultural Experiment Station Research Bulletin no. 154, 1944), 55 pp. [Focus on Dane Co., 1921–1941] **8023**

Kolb, John H., and LeRoy J. Day, *Interdependence in Town and Country Relations in Rural Society: A Study of Trends in Walworth County, Wisconsin, 1911–13 to 1947–48* (Madison: University of Wisconsin Agricultural Research Station Bulletin no. 172, 1950), 52 pp. **8024**

Kolb, John H., *Neighborhood-Family Relations in Rural Society: A Review of Trends in Dane County, Wisconsin over a Thirty-Five Year Period* (Madison: University of Wisconsin Agricultural Experiment Station Research Bulletin no. 201, 1957), 24 pp. **8025**

Ethnic communities

Boesch, Hans H., "New Glarus (Green County, Wisconsin): Eine schweizer Siedlung in den Vereinigten Staaten," in Ernst Winkler, ed., *Das schweizer Dorf: Beiträge zur Erkenntnis seines Wesens* (Zurich: Atlantis Verlag, 1941), pp. 286–299. **8026**

Nelson, Helge M. O., "Gustaf Unonius, Pine Lake–kolonien och Wisconsins svenska befolkning: till hundraårsminnet av den svenska emigrationen till Nordamerika," *Svensk geografisk årsbok*, vol. 17 (1941), pp. 125–141. **8027**

Brunnschweiler, Dieter, *New Glarus (Wisconsin), Gründung, Entwicklung und heutiger Zustand einer Schweizerkolonie im amerikanischen Mittelwesten* (Zurich: Buchdruckerei Fluntern; also Geographisches Institut der Universität Zürich, Arbeiten, ser. A, no. 71, 1954), 106 pp. **8028**

Vogeler, Ingolf K., "A Study of the Influence of Ethnicity and Religion on Farm Land Transfers in Western Wisconsin," Master's thesis, University of Minnesota, 1970. **8029**

Raitz, Karl B., and Eugene Cotton Mather, "Norwegians and Tobacco in Western Wisconsin," *Annals of the Association of American Geographers*, vol. 61, 4 (1971), pp. 684–696. **8030**

Perret, Maurice E., "Cultural Diversity in Central Wisconsin," *Transactions of the Wisconsin Academy of Sciences, Arts, and Letters*, vol. 61

(1973), pp. 45–58. [Focus on Portage Co., 1876–1972] **8031**

Alanen, Arnold R., "Back to the Land: Rural Finnish Settlement in Wisconsin," *Transactions of the Wisconsin Academy of Sciences, Arts, and Letters*, vol. 65 (1977), pp. 180–203. **8032**

Legreid, Anne, "Ethnicity, Religious Affiliations, and Rural Settlement Formation, 1880–1905: Six Wisconsin Townships," Master's thesis, University of Wisconsin–Madison, 1979. **8033**

Legreid, Anne, and David Ward, "Religious Schism and the Development of Rural Immigrant Communities: Norwegian Lutherans in Western Wisconsin, 1880–1905," *Upper Midwest History*, vol. 2 (1982), pp. 13–29. **8034**

Saueressig, Yda, "Emigration, Settlement, and Assimilation of Dutch Catholic Immigrants in Wisconsin, 1850–1905," Ph.D. diss., University of Wisconsin–Madison, 1982. **8035**

Gallusser, Werner A., "Die Buffalo County: Ein Siedlungsgebiet für schweizer Auswanderer im westlichen Wisconsin," in Klaus Aerni et al., eds., *Der Mensch in der Landschaft: Festschrift für Georges Grosjean* (Bern: Jahrbuch der Geographischen Gesellschaft von Bern, no. 55, 1983–1985), pp. 287–300. **8036**

Legreid, Anne, "Ethnicity, Religious Affiliation, and the Development of Rural Immigrant Communities: An Analysis of Religious Schism amongst Norwegian Lutherans in Western Wisconsin, the Late Nineteenth Century," Ph.D. diss., University of Wisconsin–Madison, 1985. **8037**

Saueressig-Schreuder, Yda, "Dutch Catholic Settlement in Wisconsin," in Robert P. Swierenga, ed., *The Dutch in America: Immigration, Settlement, and Cultural Change* (New Brunswick: Rutgers University Press, 1985), pp. 105–124. **8038**

Knowles, Anne K., "Welsh Settlement in Waukesha County, Wisconsin, 1840–1873," Master's thesis, University of Wisconsin–Madison, 1989. **8039**

POLITICAL & ADMINISTRATIVE GEOGRAPHY

See also **7093**

Martin, Lawrence, "The Michigan-Wisconsin Boundary Case in the Supreme Court of the United States, 1923–26," *Annals of the Association of American Geographers*, vol. 20, 3 (1930), pp. 105–163. **8040**

Gallusser, Werner A., "Der Wiederaufbau der nordamerikanischen Zivilisationslandschaft durch staatliche Maßnahmen, am Beispiel von Wisconsin," *Erdkunde*, vol. 32, 2 (1978), pp. 142–157. [Focus on soil conservation history since the 1930s]   8041

ECONOMIC DEVELOPMENT

See also 7095

RESOURCE MANAGEMENT

Baker, John P., "An Analysis of the Surface Hydrology in the Galena Watershed, 1940–1987," Master's thesis, University of Wisconsin–Madison, 1990. [Influence on soil conservation practices]   8042

LAND & LAND USE

Herrmann, Reuben M., "Changing Land Use Patterns in Genessee Township, Wisconsin, 1914–1967," Master's thesis, Arizona State University, 1969.   8043

Penn, James R., "The Initial Evolution and Utilization of Land on the Prairie Border: A Study of Walworth County, Wisconsin," Master's thesis, University of Wisconsin–Madison, 1977.   8044

Hartnett, Sean, "Land Ownership Change on the Wisconsin Frontier: A Historical Geography of Landownership in Turtle and LaPrairie Townships, 1839–1890," Ph.D. diss., University of Wisconsin–Madison, 1989. [Rock Co.]   8045

EXTRACTIVE ACTIVITY

Fur trade

Branom, Mendel E., "Trade and Travel in the Fox River Region during the Fur Trading Period," Master's thesis, University of Chicago, 1916.   8046

Kay, Jeanne C., "The American Fur Company and the Decline of the Green Bay Trade," in Thomas C. Buckley, ed., *Rendezvous: Selected Papers of the Fourth North American Fur Trade Conference* (St. Paul: The Conference, 1981), pp. 73–82.   8047

Mining

Sanford, C. M., "The Wisconsin Lead and Zinc District," *Journal of Geography*, vol. 9, 3 (1910), pp. 74–76.   8048

Schubring, Selma L., "A Statistical Study of Lead and Zinc Mining in Wisconsin," Ph.D. diss., University of Wisconsin, 1920.   8049

Schubring, Selma L., "A Statistical Study of Lead and Zinc Mining in Wisconsin," *Transactions of*

the *Wisconsin Academy of Sciences, Arts, and Letters*, vol. 22 (1926), pp. 9–98.   8050

Watson, Charles F., "The Evolution of the Lead and Zinc Mining Industry of Southwestern Wisconsin," Master's thesis, University of Chicago, 1928.   8051

Fatzinger, Dale R., "Historical Geography of Lead and Zinc Mining in Southwest Wisconsin, 1820–1920: A Century of Change," Ph.D. diss., Michigan State University, 1971.   8052

Alanen, Arnold R., "Northern Mining, 1880s–1960s," in Ingolf Vogeler, ed., *Wisconsin: A Geography* (Boulder: Westview Press, 1986), pp. 97–103.   8053

Lumbering

Hofmeister, Burkhard, "Forst- und Holzwirtschaft im Staate Wisconsin," *Die Erde*, vol. 91, 4 (1960), pp. 258–276.   8054

Rohe, Randall E., "Lumbering's Impact on the Landscape of the Wolf River Area of Northeastern Wisconsin," Master's thesis, University of Colorado, 1971.   8055

Rohe, Randall E., "The Landscape and the Era of Lumbering in Northeastern Wisconsin," *Geographical Bulletin*, vol. 4 (1972), pp. 1–27.   8056

Rohe, Randall E., "The Myth of the Wild Wolf: Logging and River Improvement on a Wisconsin River," *Great Lakes Review*, vol. 10, 2 (1984), pp. 24–35.   8057

Hartwig, Laura, "Historic Logging Site Detection in the Chequamegon National Forest with Air Photo Reading," Master's thesis, University of Wisconsin–Madison, 1986.   8058

Rohe, Randall E., "Man and Nature: Lumbering and Half Moon Lake," *Wisconsin Geographer*, vol. 3 (1987), pp. 49–65.   8059

Rohe, Randall E., "White Lake: Lumber Center on the Soo, Part 1," *Soo*, vol. 10 (Jan. 1988), pp. 30–49; "Part 2" (Apr. 1988), pp. 26–51.   8060

AGRICULTURE

See also 1420, 7115

General

Durand, Loyal, Jr., "The Retreat of Agriculture in Milwaukee County, Wisconsin," *Transactions of the Wisconsin Academy of Sciences, Arts, and Letters*, vol. 51 (1962), pp. 197–218. [Focus on 1925–1961]   8061

Durand, Loyal, Jr., "The Landscapes of Retreat in Milwaukee County," *Transactions of the Wisconsin Academy of Sciences, Arts, and Letters*,

vol. 52A (1963), pp. 79–87. [Focus on 1875–1960]
8062

Stover, Stephen L., "Changing Regionalization of Sheep Husbandry in Wisconsin," *Transactions of the Wisconsin Academy of Sciences, Arts, and Letters*, vol. 52 (1963), pp. 111–132. [Focus on 1850–1962]
8063

Johansen, Harley E., "Spatial Diffusion of Contour Strip Cropping in Wisconsin," Master's thesis, University of Wisconsin–Madison, 1969.
8064

Conzen, Michael P., "Urban Influence upon Frontier and Commercial Agriculture: Blooming Grove, Wisconsin, in the Later Nineteenth Century," Master's thesis, University of Wisconsin–Madison, 1970.
8065

Conzen, Michael P., *Frontier Farming in an Urban Shadow: The Influence of Madison's Proximity on the Agricultural Development of Blooming Grove, Wisconsin* (Madison: State Historical Society of Wisconsin, 1971), 235 pp.
8066

Johansen, Harley E., "Diffusion of Strip Cropping in Southwestern Wisconsin," *Annals of the Association of American Geographers*, vol. 61, 4 (1971), pp. 671–683.
8067

Fonstad, Todd A. "The Central Wisconsin Farms Project," *Bulletin of the Wisconsin Council for Geographic Education, 1984* (1984), pp. 44–49.
8068

Bogue, Margaret B., "The Lure of the Cherry: The Making of a Farm Type Area," in Thomas R. McKay and Deborah E. Kmetz, eds., *Agricultural Diversity in Wisconsin* (Madison: State Historical Society of Wisconsin, 1987), pp. 62–71.
8069

Found, R. F., "Strawberry Fortunes and Misfortunes in Jackson County, Wisconsin, 1930–1986," *Wisconsin Geographer*, vol. 3 (1987), pp. 1–12.
8070

McKay, Thomas R., and Deborah E. Kmetz, eds., *Agricultural Diversity in Wisconsin* (Madison: State Historical Society of Wisconsin, 1987), 93 pp.
8071

Rohe, Randall E., "Lumber Company Farms and the Development of Agriculture in Wisconsin," *Wisconsin and Its Region: Proceedings of the Annual Institute of Wisconsin Studies Conference* (1989), pp. 144–166.
8072

Dairy Farming

Trewartha, Glenn T., "The Dairy Industry of Wisconsin as a Geographic Adjustment," Ph.D. diss., University of Wisconsin–Madison, 1924.
8073

Trewartha, Glenn T., "The Dairy Industry of Wisconsin as a Geographic Adjustment," *Bulletin of*

the *Philadelphia Geographical Society*, vol. 23, 4 (1925), pp. 93–119.
8074

Trewartha, Glenn T., "The Green County, Wisconsin, Foreign Cheese Industry," *Economic Geography*, vol. 2, 2 (1926), pp. 292–308. [Focus on 1845–1923]
8075

Durand, Loyal, Jr., "The Cheese Manufacturing Regions of Wisconsin, 1850–1950," *Transactions of the Wisconsin Academy of Sciences, Arts, and Letters*, vol. 42 (1953), pp. 109–130.
8076

Lewthwaite, Gordon R., "The Localization of Butter and Cheese Production in Wisconsin," *Proceedings of the First (New Zealand) Geography Conference* (1955), pp. 57–60.
8077

Lewthwaite, Gordon R., "Wisconsin Cheese and Farm Type: A Locational Hypothesis," *Economic Geography*, vol. 40, 2 (1964), pp. 95–112. [Focus on 1895–1950]
8078

Cross, John A., "Wisconsin's Changing Dairy Industry and the Dairy Termination Program," *Transactions of the Wisconsin Academy of Sciences, Arts, and Letters*, vol. 77 (1989), pp. 11–26. [Focus on 1930–1985]
8079

LANDSCAPE

Fish, Norman S., "The History of the Silo in Wisconsin," *Wisconsin Magazine of History*, vol. 8, 2 (1924), pp. 160–170.
8080

Durand, Loyal, Jr., "Dairy Barns of Southeastern Wisconsin," *Economic Geography*, vol. 19, 1 (1943), pp. 37–44.
8081

Collins, Charles N., "The Influence of Drumlin Topography on Field Patterns in Dodge County, Wisconsin," *Transactions of the Wisconsin Academy of Sciences, Arts, and Letters*, vol. 69 (1971), pp. 55–66.
8082

Kaups, Matti E., "From Savusaunas to Contemporary Saunas: A Century of Sauna Traditions in Minnesota, Michigan, and Wisconsin," in Harold Teir, Yrjo Collan, and Pirkko Voltakari, eds., *Sauna Studies: Papers Read at the Sixth International Sauna Congress in Helsinki* (Helsinki: Sauna Seura, 1974), pp. 34–56.
8083

Perret, Maurice E., "Cemeteries: A Source of Geographic Information," *Transactions of the Wisconsin Academy of Sciences, Arts, and Letters*, vol. 63 (1975), pp. 139–161.
8084

Raitz, Karl B., "The Wisconsin Tobacco Shed: A Key to Ethnic Settlement and Diffusion," *Landscape*, vol. 20, 1 (1975), pp. 32–37.
8085

Calkins, Charles F., and William G. Laatsch, "The Hop Houses of Waukesha County, Wisconsin," *Pioneer America*, vol. 9, 2 (1977), pp. 180–192.
8086

Martin, George G., "The Evolving Spatial Distribution of Cemeteries in Waukesha County in Wisconsin, 1835–1976," Master's thesis, Michigan State University, 1978. **8087**

Calkins, Charles F., and William G. Laatsch, "The Belgian Outdoors Ovens of Northeastern Wisconsin," *Pioneer America Society Transactions*, vol. 2 (1979), pp. 1–12. **8088**

Hart, John Fraser, "Features of the Door County Landscape," *Pioneer America Society Transactions*, vol. 4 (1981), pp. 20–25. **8089**

Johnson, Paul R., "Communal Imprints on the Wisconsin Landscape: St. Nazianz, 1854–1873," *Bulletin of the Wisconsin Council for Geographic Education, 1984* (1984), pp. 34–43. **8090**

Johnson, Paul R., "St. Nazianz, Wisconsin: Landscape Persistence in a German Communal Settlement, 1854–1983," Ph.D. diss., University of Oklahoma, 1984. **8091**

Perkins, Martin, "Cobblestone Architecture: A Southeastern Wisconsin Extension of Western New York's Masonry Building Tradition," *Pioneer American Society Transactions*, vol. 10 (1987), pp. 1–8. **8092**

Eiseley, Jane, and William Tishler, "The Honey Creek Swiss Settlement in Sauk County: An Expression of Cultural Norms in Rural Wisconsin," *Wisconsin Magazine of History*, vol. 73, 1 (1989), pp. 3–20. **8093**

COMMUNICATIONS & TRADE

Perret, Maurice E., "Développement et déclin des chemins de fer dans le Wisconsin," *Geographica helvetica*, vol. 23, 3 (1968), pp. 13–117. **8094**

Krog, Carl, "The Development of a Railroad System North of Green Bay," *Geographical Perspectives*, vol. 39 (1977), pp. 27–34. **8095**

Rohe, Randall E., "The Geographical Impact of Log Transportation: The River Driving Era in Wisconsin," *Wisconsin Academy Review*, vol. 27, 4 (1981), pp. 17–24. **8096**

Rohe, Randall E., "Wisconsin's First Logging Railroad: An Addendum," *Chips and Sawdust*, vol. 11 (1988), pp. 2–7. **8097**

MANUFACTURING & INDUSTRIALIZATION

Whitbeck, Ray H., "Industries of Wisconsin and Their Geographic Basis," *Annals of the Association of American Geographers*, vol. 2 (1912), pp. 55–64. **8098**

Watson, Charles F., "The Lumbering and Wood-Working Industries (of Wisconsin)," *Journal of Geography*, vol. 12, 8 (1914), pp. 235–241. **8099**

Exworthy, Kenneth, "The Evolution of Manufactural Adjustments at the Mouth of the Menominee River," Master's thesis, University of Chicago, 1936. **8100**

Ihde, Aaron J., and James W. Conners, "Chemical Industry in Early Wisconsin," *Transactions of the Wisconsin Academy of Sciences, Arts, and Letters*, vol. 44 (1955), pp. 5–20. **8101**

Baldwin, William O., "Historical Geography of the Brewing Industry: Focus on Wisconsin," Ph.D. diss., University of Illinois, 1966. **8102**

Walsh, Margaret, *The Manufacturing Frontier: Pioneer Industry in Antebellum Wisconsin, 1830–1860* (Madison: State Historical Society of Wisconsin, 1972), 263 pp. **8103**

URBAN NETWORKS & URBANIZATION

See also **7151**

Cutler, Irving, "The Chicago-Milwaukee Corridor: A Geographic Study of Intermetropolitan Coalescence," Ph.D. diss., Northwestern University, 1964. **8104**

Conzen, Michael P., "Capital Flows and the Developing Urban Hierarchy: State Bank Capital in Wisconsin, 1854–1895," *Economic Geography*, vol. 51, 4 (1975), pp. 321–338. **8105**

Kirby, Russell S., "Variable Urban Growth in Southeastern Wisconsin: 1850–1880," Master's thesis, University of Wisconsin–Madison, 1977. **8106**

Detwyler, Thomas, "Corporate Colonization of Small Cities," in Robert P. Wolensky and Edward J. Miller, eds., *Proceedings of the 1982 Conference on the Small City and Regional Community*, vol. 5 (Stevens Point: University of Wisconsin–Stevens Point Foundation Press, 1982), pp. 143–156. **8107**

Rohe, Randall E., "Lumber Company Towns in Wisconsin," *Old Northwest*, vol. 10, 4 (1984–1985), pp. 409–437. **8108**

TOWN GROWTH

Gould, Lucius T., "The Making of Milwaukee," *Journal of Geography*, vol. 12, 8 (1914), pp. 279–288. **8109**

Trewartha, Glenn T., "The Prairie du Chien Terrace: Geography of a Confluence Site," *Annals of the Association of American Geographers*, vol. 22, 2 (1932), pp. 119–158. **8110**

Shaw, Reginald M., "The Historical Geography of Superior, Wisconsin," Ph.D. diss., University of Wisconsin, 1938. **8111**

Fass, Eleanor L., "Geographic Elements in the Areal Expansion of Milwaukee," Master's thesis, Clark University, 1944. **8112**

Rohe, Randall E., "Heineman: The Life and Death of a Lumber Town," *Proceedings of the Tenth Annual Meeting of the Forest History Association of Wisconsin* (1985), pp. 18–25. **8113**

Zeidler, Frank P., "Milwaukee's South Side: A Historical Look," *Milwaukee History*, vol. 8, 2 & 3 (1985), pp. 56–84. **8114**

Rohe, Randall E., "Oshkosh: The Rise and Decline of a Lumber Center," *Proceedings of the Thirteenth Annual Meeting of the Forest History Association of Wisconsin* (1988), pp. 31–41. **8115**

Rohe, Randall E., "The Boom and Bust of Peshtigo Harbor," *Proceedings of the Fourteenth Annual Meeting of the Forest History Association of Wisconsin* (1989), pp. 15–31. **8116**

URBAN ECONOMIC STRUCTURE

Conzen, Michael P., and Kathleen Neils Conzen, "Geographical Structure in Nineteenth-Century Urban Retailing: Milwaukee, 1836–90," *Journal of Historical Geography*, vol. 5, 1 (1979), pp. 45–66. **8117**

Stetzer, Donald F., "Employment in Professional Services in Wisconsin Cities, 1950–1980," in Edward J. Miller and Robert P. Wolensky, eds., *Proceedings of the Sixth Conference on the Small City and Regional Community*, vol. 6 (Stevens Point: University of Wisconsin–Stevens Point Foundation Press, 1985), pp. 127–132. **8118**

Stetzer, Donald F., "Manufacturing in Small Wisconsin Cities," in Robert P. Wolensky and Edward J. Miller, eds., *Proceedings of the Conference on the Small City and Regional Community*, vol. 7 (Stevens Point: University of Wisconsin–Stevens Point Foundation Press, 1987), pp. 222–225. [1954–1982] **8119**

URBAN SOCIAL STRUCTURE

Schultz, Gwen, "Evolution of the Areal Patterns of German and Polish Settlement in Milwaukee," *Erdkunde*, vol. 10, 2 (1956), pp. 136–141. **8120**

Rauch, Sister Dolores, "Impact of Population Changes in the Central Area of Milwaukee upon Catholic Parochial Schools, 1940–1970," Master's thesis, University of Wisconsin–Milwaukee, 1968. **8121**

Hansell, Charles R., and William A. V. Clark, "The Expansion of the Negro Ghetto in Milwaukee," *Tijdschrift voor economische en sociale geografie*, vol. 61, 5 (1970), pp. 267–277. **8122**

Sebanc, James, "Immigration and the Emergence of Yugoslav Social Communities in Wisconsin, 1900–1971," Master's thesis, University of Wisconsin–Milwaukee, 1972. **8123**

Todd, William J., "A Factor Analysis of Black-White Polarization in Milwaukee, 1950–1970," *Bulletin of the Illinois Geographical Society*, vol. 14, 2 (1972), pp. 17–29. **8124**

Todd, William J., "Factor-Analytic Black-White Polarization in Milwaukee, 1950 to 1970," Master's thesis, Indiana State University, 1972. **8125**

Conzen, Kathleen Neils, "Mapping Manuscript Census Data for Nineteenth Century Cities," *Historical Geography*, vol. 4, 1 (1974), pp. 1–7. [Milwaukee] **8126**

Conzen, Kathleen Neils, "Patterns of Residence in Early Milwaukee," in Leo F. Schnore, ed., *The New Urban History: Quantitative Explorations by American Historians* (Princeton: Princeton University Press, 1975), pp. 145–183. **8127**

Conzen, Kathleen Neils, *Immigrant Milwaukee, 1836–1860: Accommodation and Community in a Frontier City* (Cambridge: Harvard University Press, 1976), 300 pp. **8128**

Mayer, Jonathan D., "The Journey-to-Work, Ethnicity, and Occupation in Milwaukee, 1860–1900," Ph.D. diss., University of Michigan, 1977. **8129**

Gurda, John, "Change at the River Mouth: Ethnic Succession on Milwaukee's Jones Island, 1700 to 1922," Master's thesis, University of Wisconsin–Milwaukee, 1978. **8130**

Botts, Howard A., "Commercial Structure and Ethnic Residential Patterns in the Shaping of Milwaukee, 1880–1900," Ph.D. diss., University of Wisconsin–Madison, 1985. **8131**

Mahon, Richard, "Class and Context in Nineteenth-Century Urban Out-Migration: Madison, Wisconsin, 1860–1870," Master's thesis, University of Wisconsin–Madison, 1985. **8132**

Cooper, Fiona M. B., "Ethnic and Sexual Divisions of Labor: Milwaukee, 1880–1905," Master's thesis, University of Wisconsin–Madison, 1986. **8133**

Rohe, Randall E., "Myths and Realities: Life in Wisconsin's Boom and Bust Lumber Towns," *Wisconsin and Its Region: Proceedings of the Annual Institute of Wisconsin Studies Conference* (1988), pp. 285–318. **8134**

TOWNSCAPE

Conzen, Michael P., "The Spatial Effects of Antecedent Conditions upon Urban Growth," Master's thesis, University of Wisconsin–Madison, 1968. [Focus on Madison, Wis., 1836–1920] **8135**

Reisser, Craig T., "Immigrants and House Form in Northeast Milwaukee, 1885–1916," Master's thesis, University of Wisconsin–Milwaukee, 1977. **8136**

DeJulio, Mary A., "Prairie du Chien and the Rediscovery of Its French Log Houses," in Michael O. Roark, ed., *French and Germans in the Mississippi Valley: Landscape and Cultural Traditions* (Cape Girardeau: Southeast Missouri State University, Center for Regional History and Cultural Heritage, 1988), pp. 98–110. **8137**

Zellie, Carole Smith, "Nineteenth-Century Townsite Plans in Southern Wisconsin: A Typology and Analysis," Master's thesis, University of Wisconsin–Madison, 1989. **8138**

Vogeler, Ingolf K., "The Character of Place: Building Materials and Architectural Characteristics in Eau Claire, Wisconsin," *Material Culture*, vol. 22, 1 (1990), pp. 1–22. **8139**

RECREATION & TOURISM

Alanen, Arnold R., and Paul Skidmore, "The Development of Urban Pathways in Madison and Dane County, Wisconsin, 1893–1987," in *Parkways: Past, Present, Future: Proceedings of the Second Biennial Linear Park Conference, 1987* (Boone, N.C.: Appalachian Consortium Press, 1988), pp. 137–146. **8140**

PLANNING

Carner, Bettyann, "Rural Land Zoning in Vilas County, Wisconsin, 1933–54: A Case History,"

Master's thesis, University of Chicago, 1955. **8141**

Alanen, Arnold R., and Thomas Reltin, "Kohler, Wisconsin: Planning and Paternalism in a Model Industrial Village," *Journal of the American Institute of Planners*, vol. 44, 2 (1978), pp. 145–159. **8142**

Eden, Joseph A., and Arnold R. Alanen, "Looking Backward at a New Deal Town: Greendale, Wisconsin, 1935–1980," *Journal of the American Planning Association*, vol. 49, 1 (1983), pp. 40–58. **8143**

Alanen, Arnold R., and Joseph A. Eden, *Main Street Ready-Made: The New Deal Community of Greendale, Wisconsin* (Madison: State Historical Society of Wisconsin, 1987), 156 pp. **8144**

PLACE NAMES

Taube, Edward, "The Name Wisconsin," *Names*, vol. 15, 3 (1967), pp. 173–181. **8145**

Gard, Robert E., and Leland G. Sorden, *The Romance of Wisconsin Place Names* (New York: October House, 1968), 144 pp. Reprinted Minoqua, Wis.: Northword, 1988. **8146**

Hoefer, J., "The Generic Use of the Term Coulee in Western Wisconsin," *Wisconsin Geographer*, vol. 1 (1985), pp. 35–40. **8147**

Rohe, Randall E., "Names on the Land: A Legacy of the Wisconsin Lumber Era," *Voyageur: Historical Review of Brown County and Northeastern Wisconsin*, vol. 2 (1985), pp. 17–24. **8148**

Rohe, Randall E., "Toponymy and the U.S. Land Survey in Wisconsin," *Names*, vol. 36, 1 & 2 (1988), pp. 43–50. **8149**

MINNESOTA

GENERAL

The state

Posey, Chessley J., "The Influence of Geographic Factors in the Development of Minnesota," *Minnesota History Bulletin*, vol. 2 (1918), pp. 443–453. **8150**

Borchert, John R., *Minnesota's Changing Geography* (Minneapolis: University of Minnesota Press, 1959), 191 pp. **8151**

Clark, Clifford E., ed., *Minnesota in a Century of Change* (St. Paul: Minnesota Historical Society Press, 1989), 607 pp. **8152**

Smaller areas

Colby, Charles C., "Geography of Southeastern Minnesota," Ph.D. diss., University of Chicago, 1917. **8153**

ENVIRONMENTAL CHANGE

Davis, Darrell H., "Return of the Forest in Northeastern Minnesota," *Economic Geography*, vol. 16, 2 (1940), pp. 171–187. [Focus on 1918–1938] **8154**

Moline, Robert T., "The Modification of the Wet Prairie in Southern Minnesota," Master's thesis, University of Minnesota, 1969. **8155**

Waddington, Jean C. B., "Vegetational Changes Associated with Settlement and Land Clearance in Minnesota over the Last 125 Years: A Comparison of Historical and Sedimentary Records," Ph.D. diss., University of Minnesota, 1978. **8156**

Baker, Donald G., Bruce F. Watson, and Richard H. Skaggs, "The Minnesota Long-Term Temperature Record," *Climatic Change*, vol. 7, 2 (1985), pp. 225–236. **8157**

Skaggs, Richard H., and Donald G. Baker, "Fluctuations in the Length of the Growing Season in Minnesota," *Climatic Change*, vol. 7, 4 (1988), pp. 403–414. [Focus on 1899–1982] **8158**

NATIVE PEOPLES & WHITE RELATIONS

Brower, Jacob V., "Prehistoric Man at the Headwaters of the Mississippi River," *Journal of the Manchester Geographical Society*, vol. 11, 1 (1895), pp. 3–80. **8159**

Brown, Ralph Hall, "Some Aspects of Minnesota Prehistory," *Minnesota History*, vol. 15, 2 (1934), pp. 148–156. **8160**

Korgen, Mali, "Adjustment to Environment by Prehistoric Indians in Minnesota," Master's thesis, Clark University, 1947. **8161**

Sherman, Merle, "A Geographic Study of the Red Lake Chippewa Indian Band of Minnesota," *Proceedings of the Minnesota Academy of Science*, vol. 30, 1 (1962), pp. 60–66. **8162**

Kaups, Matti E., "Ojibwa Fisheries on St. Louis River, Minnesota: 1800–1835," *Journal of Cultural Geography*, vol. 5, 1 (1984), pp. 61–84. **8163**

Youngbear-Tibbets, Holly, "Every Place Has Its Story . . . Every Place Has Its Struggle: An Experimental Historical Geography of the Anishinabeg of the White Earth, Minnesota, Indian Reservation, 1580–1920," Master's thesis, University of Wisconsin–Madison, 1988. **8164**

EXPLORATION & MAPPING

Treude, Mai, Introduction to *Windows to the Past: A Bibliography of Minnesota County Atlases* (Minneapolis: Center for Urban and Regional Affairs, University of Minnesota, 1980), pp. 1–40. **8165**

POPULAR IMAGES & EVALUATION

See also **1306**

Brown, Ralph Hall, "Fact and Fancy in Early Accounts of Minnesota's Climate," *Minnesota History*, vol. 17, 3 (1936), pp. 243–261. **8166**

Stein, Gregory P., "Lake Minnetonka: Historical Perceptions of an Urban Lake," Ph.D. diss., University of Minnesota, 1971. **8167**

Pyle, Jane, "Perception and Change in a Minnesota Landscape," *Geographical Survey*, vol. 2, 1 (1973), pp. 27–40. **8168**

Stein, Gregory P., "Two New York Images of Frontier Minnesota, 1852," *Proceedings of the Middle States Division, Association of American Geographers*, vol. 6 (1973), pp. 70–74. **8169**

Richter, Bonnie, ed., *Saint Paul Omnibus: Images of the Changing City* (St. Paul: Old Town Restorations, Inc., 1979), 144 pp. **8170**

REGIONAL SETTLEMENT

See also **7062**

Posey, Chessley J., "Geographic Influences in the Exploration and Early Development of Minnesota," *Journal of Geography*, vol. 14, 6 (1916), pp. 214–217.   8171

Laine, Oliver H., "Geographic Characteristics of Finnish Settlement and Land Use in St. Louis County, Minnesota," Master's thesis, Clark University, 1949.   8172

Meeks, Harold A., "Railroad Expansion and Agricultural Settlement in Minnesota, 1860–1910," *Proceedings of the Minnesota Academy of Science*, vol. 27 (1959), pp. 22–37.   8173

Borchert, John R., *A Quarter-Century of Change in the Finland Community of Northeastern Minnesota* (Duluth: Social Sciences Research Trust Fund at the University of Minnesota–Duluth, 1960), unpaged.   8174

Stein, Gregory P., "Historical Settlement Patterns on Lake Minnetonka, Minnesota," *Proceedings of the Middle States Division, Association of American Geographers*, vol. 7 (1973), pp. 59–62.   8175

Rozycki, Anthony T., "The Evolution of the Hamlets of Stearns County, Minnesota," Master's thesis, University of Minnesota, 1977.   8176

POPULATION

General

Wilson, Leonard S., "Some Notes on the Growth of Population in Minnesota," *Geographical Review*, vol. 30, 4 (1940), pp. 660–664. [Focus on 1850–1930]   8177

Rikkinen, Kalevi, "Population Changes in the Incorporated Hamlets of Minnesota, 1930–1960," *Acta geographica* (Helsinki), vol. 19, 4 (1968), pp. 1–31.   8178

Rikkinen, Kalevi, and Arnold R. Alanen, "Changing Age Structures in a Rural-Urban Continuum," *Geografiska annaler*, vol. 51B, 2 (1969), pp. 57–71. [Minnesota, 1930–1960]   8179

Bastian, Robert W., "Mesabi Mine Locations: An Example of Population Reconstructions," *Proceedings of the Association of American Geographers*, vol. 5 (1973), pp. 10–13. [Focus on 1910–1955]   8180

Hickey, John J., and Frederic R. Steinhauser, "The Demographic Characteristics of 1860 New Ulm, Minnesota, Germans," *Journal of the Minnesota Academy of Science*, vol. 46, 2 (1980), pp. 12–15.   8181

Ethnic distributions

Johnson, Hildegard Binder, "The Distribution of the German Pioneer Population in Minnesota," *Rural Sociology*, vol. 6, 1 (1941), pp. 16–34. [Focus on 1850–1860]   8182

Johnson, Hildegard Binder, "Factors Influencing the Distribution of the German Pioneer Population in Minnesota," *Agricultural History*, vol. 19, 1 (1945), pp. 39–57.   8183

Albert, Michael D., "The Japanese," in June D. Holmquist, ed., *They Chose Minnesota: A Survey of the State's Ethnic Groups* (St. Paul: Minnesota Historical Society Press, 1981), pp. 558–571.   8184

Thornquist, Lisa M., "Ethnic Settlement of Western Wright County, 1860–1905," Master's thesis, University of Minnesota, 1983.   8185

Migration

Johnson, Hildegard Binder, "Eduard Pelz and German Emigration," *Minnesota History*, vol. 31, 4 (1950), pp. 222–230.   8186

Ostergren, Robert C., "Kinship Networks and Migration: A Nineteenth-Century Swedish Example," *Social Science History*, vol. 6, 3 (1982), pp. 292–320. [Isanti Co.]   8187

RURAL & REGIONAL SOCIAL GEOGRAPHY

See also 1381, 7082

Culture regions

Vogeler, Ingolf K., "The Roman Catholic Culture Region of Central Minnesota," *Pioneer America*, vol. 8, 2 (1976), pp. 71–83.   8188

Ethnic communities

Davis, Darrell H., "The Finland Community, Minnesota," *Geographical Review*, vol. 25, 3 (1935), pp. 382–394. [Lake Co., 1895–1935]   8189

Nelson, Helge M. O., "Minnesotas bebyggarde. Med sorskild hansyn till svenskars, norrmans och tyskars andel i densamma," *Svensk geografisk årsbok*, vol. 13 (1937), pp. 164–190. [English summary]   8190

Johnson, Hildegard Binder, "The Carver County German Reading Society," *Minnesota History*, vol. 24, 3 (1943), pp. 214–225.   8191

Johnson, Hildegard Binder, "Intermarriages between German Pioneers and Other Nationalities in Minnesota in 1860 and 1870," *American Journal of Sociology*, vol. 51, 4 (1946), pp. 299–304.   8192

Mead, William R., "A Finnish Settlement in Central Minnesota," *Acta geographica* (Helsinki), vol. 13, 3 (1954), pp. 1–16. [In Meeker and Wright counties, 1855–1920]   8193

Brown, Robert H., "The Upsala, Minnesota, Community: A Case Study in Rural Dynamics,"

Annals of the Association of American Geographers, vol. 57, 2 (1967), pp. 267–300.　　**8194**

Ostergren, Robert C., "Cultural Homogeneity and Population Stability among Swedish Immigrants in Chisago County," *Minnesota History*, vol. 43, 7 (1973), pp. 255–269.　　**8195**

Rice, John G., *Patterns of Ethnicity in a Minnesota County, 1880–1905* (Umeå, Sweden: University of Umeå Geographical Report no. 4, 1973), 98 pp.
　　8196

Ostergren, Robert C., "Rattvik to Isanti: A Community Transplanted," Ph.D. diss., University of Minnesota, 1976.　　**8197**

Rice, John G., "The Role of Culture and Community in Frontier Prairie Farming," *Journal of Historical Geography*, vol. 3, 2 (1977), pp. 155–176. Reprinted, with omissions, in David Ward, ed., *Geographic Perspectives on America's Past: Readings on the Historical Geography of the United States* (New York: Oxford University Press, 1979), pp. 188–202.　　**8198**

Rice, John G., "Marriage Behavior and the Persistence of Swedish Communities in Minnesota," in Nils Hasselmo, ed., *Perspectives on Swedish Immigration: Proceedings of the International Conference on the Swedish Heritage in the Upper Midwest* (Chicago: Swedish Pioneer Historical Society, 1978), pp. 136–150.　　**8199**

Gjerde, Jon, "The Effect of Community on Migration: Three Minnesota Townships, 1885–1905," *Journal of Historical Geography*, vol. 5, 4 (1979), pp. 403–422.　　**8200**

Ostergren, Robert C., "A Community Transplanted: The Formative Experience of a Swedish Immigrant Community in the Upper Middle West," *Journal of Historical Geography*, vol. 5, 2 (1979), pp. 189–212. [Isanti Co.]　　**8201**

Johnson, Hildegard Binder, "The Germans," in June Drenning Holmquist, ed., *They Chose Minnesota: A Survey of the State's Ethnic Groups* (St. Paul: Minnesota Historical Society, 1981), pp. 153–184.　　**8202**

Ostergren, Robert C., "Land and Family in Rural Immigrant Communities," *Annals of the Association of American Geographers*, vol. 71, 3 (1981), pp. 400–411. [Isanti Co., 1881–1915]　　**8203**

Rice, John G., "The Old-Stock Americans," in June Drenning Holmquist, ed., *They Chose Minnesota: A Survey of the State's Ethnic Groups* (St. Paul: Minnesota Historical Society, 1981), pp. 55–72.　　**8204**

Ostergren, Robert C., *A Community Transplanted: The Trans-Atlantic Experience of a Swedish Immigrant Settlement in the Upper Middle West, 1835–1915* (Madison: University of Wis-

consin Press, 1988), 400 pp.; also published at Uppsala, Sweden: Acta Universitatis Upsaliensis, Studia Multiethnica, no. 4, 1988.　　**8205**

McFarlane, Larry A., "The Fairmount Colony in Martin County, Minnesota, in the 1870s," *Kansas History*, vol. 12, 3 (1989), pp. 166–174.　　**8206**

POLITICAL & ADMINISTRATIVE GEOGRAPHY

See also **7093**

Hill, Alfred J., "Historico-Geographical Memorandum Concerning the Creation of New Counties in Northern Minnesota," *Journal of the Manchester Geographical Society* [England], vol. 5 (1889), pp. 214–216.　　**8207**

Johnson, Hildegard Binder, "The Election of 1860 and the Germans in Minnesota," *Minnesota History*, vol. 28, 1 (1947), pp. 20–36. Reprinted in Frederick C. Luebke, ed., *Ethnic Voters and the Election of Lincoln* (Lincoln: University of Nebraska Press, 1971), pp. 92–109.　　**8208**

ECONOMIC DEVELOPMENT

Baerwald, Thomas J., "Forces at Work on the Landscape," in Clifford E. Clark, ed., *Minnesota in a Century of Change: The State and Its People since 1900* (St. Paul: Minnesota Historical Society Press, 1989), pp. 19–54.　　**8209**

RESOURCE MANAGEMENT

Carroll, Jane L., "Dams and Damages: The Ojibway, the United States, and the Mississippi Headwaters Reservoirs," *Minnesota History*, vol. 52, 1 (1990), pp. 3–15.　　**8210**

LAND & LAND USE

Land survey

Johnson, Hildegard Binder, "Rational and Ecological Aspects of the Quarter Section: An Example from Minnesota," *Geographical Review*, vol. 47, 3 (1957), pp. 330–348.　　**8211**

Land tenure

Dingman, Charles, "Land Alienation in Houston County, Minnesota: Preferences in Land Selection," *Geographical Bulletin*, vol. 4 (1972), pp. 45–49.　　**8212**

Rice, John G., "The Effect of Land Alienation on Settlement," *Annals of the Association of American Geographers*, vol. 68, 1 (1978), pp. 61–72.
　　8213

Jacobi, Judith M., "Historic Aspects of Land Alienation in Southern Minnesota," Master's thesis, University of Minnesota, 1983.   **8214**

Curry-Roper, Janel M., "A Historical Geography of Land Ownership in Minnesota: The Influence of the Timber and Stone Act," Ph.D. diss., University of Minnesota, 1985.   **8215**

Curry-Roper, Janel M., "The Impact of the Timber and Stone Act on Public Ownership in Northern Minnesota," *Journal of Forest History*, vol. 33, 2 (1989), pp. 70–80.   **8216**

EXTRACTIVE INDUSTRIES

Mining

Landis, Paul H., "Cultural Adjustments to the Mesabi Resources," *Economic Geography*, vol. 11, 2 (1935), pp. 167–172. [Focus on 1855–1935]
                                                              8217

Szczepaniak, Regina, "Historical Background and Present Trends in Iron Ore Mining in Minnesota," Master's thesis, Northeastern Illinois University, 1971.   **8218**

Lumbering

Cheyney, Edward G., "The Development of the Lumber Industry in Minnesota," *Journal of Geography*, vol. 14, 6 (1916), pp. 189–195.   **8219**

Belthius, Lyda, "Some Interpretations of a Map on Minnesota Sawmilling," *Journal of the Minnesota Academy of Science*, vol. 32, 2 (1965), pp. 106–108.   **8220**

Krenz, Duane A., "An Historical Geographic Study of the Virginia and Rainy Lake Company: The Last Major White Pine Operation in the Great Lakes Region," Master's thesis, Mankato State University, 1969.   **8221**

Fisheries

Kaups, Matti E., "Norwegian Immigrants and the Development of Commercial Fisheries along the North Shore of Lake Superior, 1870–1895," in Harald Naess, ed., *Norwegian Influence on the Upper Midwest* (Duluth: University of Minnesota–Duluth, 1976), pp. 21–34.   **8222**

Kaups, Matti E., "North Shore Commercial Fishing, 1849–1870," *Minnesota History*, vol. 46, 2 (1978), pp. 43–58.   **8223**

AGRICULTURE

See also **7120**

Washburn, R. M., "Dairying in Minnesota," *Journal of Geography*, vol. 14, 6 (1916), pp. 206–211. [Focus on 1850–1910]   **8224**

Colby, Charles C., "Agricultural Adjustments to the Natural Environment in Southeastern Minnesota during the Period of Bonanza Wheat Farming," *Transactions of the Illinois State Academy of Science*, vol. 17 (1924), pp. 213–225.
                                                              8225

Fause, Asbjorn, and George S. Corfield, "The Potato Industry in Minnesota," *Economic Geography*, vol. 13, 4 (1937), pp. 393–401. [Focus on 1860–1933]   **8226**

Johnson, Hildegard Binder, "King Wheat in Southeastern Minnesota: A Case Study of Pioneer Agriculture," *Annals of the Association of American Geographers*, vol. 47, 4 (1957), pp. 350–362.   **8227**

Tideman, Philip L., "An Example of Crop Dynamics in Minnesota: The Soybean," *Proceedings of the Minnesota Academy of Science*, vol. 31, 2 (1964), pp. 147–152. [Focus on 1934–1959]   **8228**

Rikkinen, Kalevi, "Kalevala, Minnesota: Agricultural Geography in Transition," *Acta geographica* (Helsinki), vol. 19, 5 (1969), pp. 1–55. [1930–1960]   **8229**

LANDSCAPE

See also **8083**

Kaups, Matti E., "A Finnish Riihi in Minnesota," *Journal of the Minnesota Academy of Science*, vol. 38, 2 & 3 (1972), pp. 66–71.   **8230**

Kaups, Matti E., "A Finnish Savusauna in Minnesota," *Minnesota History*, vol. 45, 1 (1976), pp. 11–20.   **8231**

Vogeler, Ingolf K., and Thomas P. Dockendorff, "Central Minnesota: Relic Tobacco Shed Region," *Pioneer America*, vol. 10, 2 (1978), pp. 76–83.   **8232**

Dockendorff, Thomas P., "Upper Mississippi Valley Landscape: A Legacy of German Catholic Settlement in Central Minnesota," *Pioneer America Society Transactions*, vol. 8 (1985), pp. 85–90.   **8233**

Dockendorff, Thomas P., "Century Farms: A Central Minnesota Experience," *Pioneer American Society Transactions*, vol. 11 (1988), pp. 82–86.
                                                              8234

Martens, Steve C., "Material Procurement and Farmstead Development: Effect of Indigenous Material on the Appearance of German Brick Farmhouses in Carver County, Minnesota," *Pioneer America Society Transactions*, vol. 13 (1990), pp. 11–22.   **8235**

COMMUNICATIONS & TRADE

Primmer, George H., "Pioneer Roads Centering at Duluth," *Minnesota History*, vol. 16, 3 (1935), pp. 282–299. [Focus on 1850–1934]   **8236**

Primmer, George H., "Railways at the Head of Lake Superior," *Economic Geography*, vol. 13, 3 (1937), pp. 269–280. **8237**

Kaups, Matti E., and Kalevi Rikkinen, "Decline of Railroad Passenger Services in Minnesota," *Journal of the Minnesota Academy of Science*, vol. 35, 1 (1968), pp. 42–46. [Focus on 1934–1966] **8238**

Rikkinen, Kalevi, "Decline of Railroad Passenger Traffic in Minnesota," *Acta geographica* (Helsinki), vol. 19, 3 (1968), pp. 1–52. [Focus on 1934–1956] **8239**

Francaviglia, Richard V., "Some Comments on the Historic and Geographic Importance of Railroads in Minnesota," *Minnesota History*, vol. 43, 2 (1972), pp. 58–62. **8240**

MANUFACTURING & INDUSTRIALIZATION

Hagen, Dennis J., "Historical Geographic Study of the Clay Related Industries of the Mankato Region," Master's thesis, Mankato State University, 1975. **8241**

Dick, Charles F., "A Geographical Analysis of the Development of the Brewing Industry of Minnesota," Ph.D. diss., University of Minnesota, 1981. **8242**

URBAN NETWORKS & URBANIZATION

Zimmerman, Carl C., *Farm Trade Centers in Minnesota, 1905–1929* (Minneapolis: University of Minnesota Agricultural Experiment Station, Bulletin no. 269, 1930), 69 pp. **8243**

Lively, Charles E., *Growth and Decline of Farm Trade Centers in Minnesota, 1905–1930* (Minneapolis: University of Minnesota Agricultural Experiment Station, Bulletin no. 287, 1932), pp. 1–48. **8244**

Weis, Billy D., "A Historical Geography of Rail and Highway Transportation at Bemidji, Minnesota," Master's thesis, University of North Dakota, 1967. **8245**

Deul, Scott W., "The Development of Small Urban Centers in a Western Region: The Minnesota and St. Croix River Valley, 1850–1905," Master's thesis, University of Wisconsin–Madison, 1978. **8246**

Alanen, Arnold R., "The 'Locations': Company Communities on Minnesota's Iron Ranges," *Minnesota History*, vol. 48, 3 (1982), pp. 94–107. **8247**

Harvey, Thomas W., "The Making of Railroad Towns in Minnesota's Red River Valley, Master's thesis, Pennsylvania State University, 1982. **8248**

Borchert, John R., "The Network of Urban Centers," in Clifford E. Clark, ed., *Minnesota in a Century of Change: The State and Its People since 1900* (St. Paul: Minnesota Historical Society Press, 1989), pp. 55–98. **8249**

Harvey, Thomas W., "Small-Town Minnesota," in Clifford E. Clark, ed., *Minnesota in a Century of Change: The State and Its People since 1900* (St. Paul: Minnesota Historical Society Press, 1989), pp. 99–128. **8250**

TOWN GROWTH

Minneapolis and St. Paul

Brown, Earl D., "The Twin Cities: Minneapolis and St. Paul," *Journal of Geography*, vol. 21, 6 (1922), pp. 227–232. **8251**

Bergsmark, Daniel R., "Minneapolis: The Mill City," *Economic Geography*, vol. 3, 3 (1927), pp. 391–396. **8252**

Borchert, John R., "The Twin-Cities Urbanized Area: Past, Present, Future," *Geographical Review*, vol. 51, 1 (1961), pp. 47–70. [Focus on 1900–1960] **8253**

Johnson, Hildegard Binder, "Die Twin Cities am oberen Mississippi," *Geographische Zeitschrift*, vol. 54, 4 (1966), pp. 269–294. **8254**

Borchert, John R., David Gebhart, David A. Lanegran, and Judith A. Martin, *The Legacy of Minneapolis: Preservation amid Change* (Minneapolis: Voyager Press, 1983), 195 pp. **8255**

New Ulm

Johnson, Hildegard Binder, "The Founding of New Ulm, Minnesota," *American-German Review*, vol. 12, 5 (1946), pp. 8–12. **8256**

Schafer, Franz, and Ursula Mulla, "New Ulm in Minnesota: Stadtgründung württembergischer Emigranten in den USA," *Mitteilungen der Geographischen Gesellschaft in München*, vol. 71 (1986), pp. 167–186. **8257**

Other centers

Primmer, George H., "The Influence of Location on the Evolution of Duluth, Minnesota," Ph.D. diss., Clark University, 1933. **8258**

Wilson, Leonard S., "Faribault, Minnesota: The Sequent Occupance of a Representative Landscape Unit," *Proceedings of the Minnesota Academy of Science*, vol. 7 (1939), pp. 77–82. **8259**

Fletcher, Merna Irene, "Rochester: A Professional Town," *Economic Geography*, vol. 23, 2 (1947), pp. 143–151. **8260**

Brown, Robert H., "Some Aspects of the Dynamic Geography of St. Cloud, Minnesota," *Proceedings of the Minnesota Academy of Science*, vols. 25, 26 (1957–1958), pp. 389–391. [Focus on 1854–1945]   8261

Alanen, Arnold R., "The Rise and Demise of a Company Town," *Professional Geographer*, vol. 29, 1 (1977), pp. 32–39. [Morgan Park]   8262

URBAN ECONOMIC STRUCTURE

See also 1456–1457

Borchert, John R., *Belt Line Commercial-Industrial Development: A Case Study in the Minneapolis–St. Paul Metropolitan Area* (Minneapolis: University of Minnesota Highway Research Project, 1960), 87 pp.   8263

Prestwich, Roger, "The Manufacturing Industry of the Twin Cities: Changes in Locational Emphases, 1946–1967," Master's thesis, University of Minnesota, 1968.   8264

Prestwich, Roger, "Postwar Industrial Locations in the Minneapolis–St. Paul Area," *Journal of the Minnesota Academy of Science*, vol. 37, 1 (1970–1971), pp. 40–45.   8265

Wagner, Philip L., "Historical Geography of Apartment Housing in Minneapolis, Late Nineteenth–Early Twentieth Centuries," Ph.D. diss., University of Minnesota, 1990.   8266

URBAN SOCIAL STRUCTURE

See also 1456–1457

Duluth

Kaups, Matti E., "Europeans in Duluth, 1870," in Ryck Lydecker and Lawrence Sommers, eds., *Duluth Sketches of the Past: A Bicentennial Collection* (Duluth: American Revolution Bicentennial Commission, 1976), pp. 70–81.   8267

Kaups, Matti E., "Swedish Immigrants in Duluth," in Nils Hasseland, ed., *Perspectives on Swedish Immigration* (Chicago: Swedish Pioneer Historical Society, 1978), pp. 165–198.   8268

Minneapolis and St. Paul

Lanegran, David A., and Ernest Sandeen, *The Lake District of Minneapolis: A Neighborhood History* (Minneapolis: Living Historical Museum, 1979), 112 pp.   8269

Hathaway, James T., "The Evolution of Drinking Places in the Twin Cities: From the Advent of White Settlement to the Present," Ph.D. diss., University of Minnesota, 1982.   8270

Lanegran, David A., *St. Anthony Park: Portrait of a Community* (St. Paul: District 12 Community Council and the St. Anthony Park Association, 1987), 137 pp.   8271

Van Drasek, Barbara, "Social Structure and Residence in Minneapolis, 1860–1940," Master's thesis, University of Minnesota, 1990.   8272

Other centers

Schloff, Linda M., "Overcoming Geography: Jewish Religious Life in Four Market Towns," *Minnesota History*, vol. 51, 1 (1988), pp. 3–14. [Mankato, Faribault, Austin, Albert Lea, 1880s-1950s]   8273

Alanen, Arnold R., "Years of Change on the Iron Range," in Clifford E. Clark, ed., *Minnesota in a Century of Change: The State and Its People since 1900* (St. Paul: Minnesota Historical Society, 1989), pp. 155–194.   8274

TOWNSCAPE

Harvey, Thomas W., "Railroad Towns: Urban Form on the Prairie," *Landscape*, vol. 27, 3 (1983), pp. 26–34. [Focus on the 1880s]   8275

RECREATION & TOURISM

Kaups, Matti E., "Evolution of Smelt-O-Mania on Lake Superior's North Shore," *Journal of Popular Culture*, vol. 11, 4 (1978), pp. 959–976.   8276

PLANNING

Alanen, Arnold R., "Sixty Years of Transition in a Planned Company Town," in Ryck Lydecker and Lawrence Sommers, eds., *Duluth Sketches of the Past: A Bicentennial Collection* (Duluth: American Revolution Bicentennial Commission, 1976), pp. 185–192.   8277

Martin, Judith A., and Anthony Goddard, *Past Choices, Present Landscapes: The Impact of Urban Renewal on the Twin Cities* (Minneapolis: University of Minnesota Center for Urban and Regional Affairs, 1989), 211 pp.   8278

PLACE NAMES

Upham, Warren, *Minnesota Geographic Names: Their Origin and Historic Significance* (St. Paul: Minnesota Historical Society, 1920), 735 pp. Revised 1969, 788 pp.   8279

Kaups, Matti E., "Finnish Place Names in Minnesota: A Study in Cultural Transfer," *Geographical Review*, vol. 56, 3 (1966), pp. 377–397.   8280

Rippley, LaVern, and Rainer Schmeissner, *German Place Names in Minnesota* (Northfield: St. Olaf's College Department of German, 1989), 106 pp.   8281

IOWA

GENERAL

Aitchinson, Alison E., "Geographic Influences in the Settlement and Development of Dubuque County," Master's thesis, University of Chicago, 1914. **8282**

ENVIRONMENTAL CHANGE

Bettis, E. Arthur, III, "Pedogenesis in Late Prehistoric Indian Mounds, Upper Mississippi Valley," *Physical Geography*, vol. 9, 3 (1988), pp. 263–279. [Focus on northeastern Iowa] **8283**

REGIONAL SETTLEMENT

See also 7049

Hewes, Leslie, "Some Features of Early Woodland and Prairie Settlement in a Central Iowa County," *Annals of the Association of American Geographers*, vol. 40, 1 (1950), pp. 40–57. **8284**

Hewes, Leslie, and Phillip E. Frandson, "Occupying the Wet Prairie: The Role of Artificial Drainage in Story County, Iowa," *Annals of the Association of American Geographers*, vol. 42, 1 (1952), pp. 24–50. **8285**

Hudson, John C., "A Location Theory for Rural Settlement," *Annals of the Association of American Geographers*, vol. 59, 2 (1969), pp. 365–381. [Six sample counties in eastern Iowa, 1870–1960] **8286**

Gamble, Janice, "The Iowa Wet Prairie and the Problem of Early Settlement," *Geographical Perspectives*, vol. 30 (1972), pp. 51–55. **8287**

POPULATION

See also 8542

Heusinkveld, Harriet M., "The Historical Geography of Population in Marion, Mahaska, and Monroe Counties in Iowa," Ph.D. diss., University of Iowa, 1958. **8288**

RURAL & REGIONAL SOCIAL GEOGRAPHY

Davis, Darrell H., "Amana: A Study in Occupance," *Economic Geography*, vol. 12, 3 (1936), pp. 217–230. **8289**

Lowenberg, Carla, "The Historical Analysis of the Mennonite Cultural Landscape of Franklin Township, Lee County, Iowa," Master's thesis, University of Nebraska, 1971. **8290**

Clark, Robert E., "A Cultural and Historical Geography of the Amana Colony, Iowa," Ph.D. diss., University of Nebraska–Lincoln, 1974. **8291**

Reed, James P., "The Role of One English Family in the Settlement and Development of Northwestern Iowa," Master's thesis, University of Nebraska–Omaha, 1974. **8292**

ECONOMIC DEVELOPMENT

See also 7095

EXTRACTIVE ACTIVITY

Clutter, Allen, III, "The Impact of Coal Mining on Mahaska and Keokuk Counties, Iowa, 1875–1900," Master's thesis, Eastern Michigan University, 1973. **8293**

AGRICULTURE

See also 7112

LANDSCAPE

Fox, Rodney, "A Landscape in Transition," *Landscape*, vol. 8, 3 (1959), pp. 1–5. [The loss of farmsteads, schools, and churches in Iowa, with emphasis on 1930–1950] **8294**

Jung, Christian L., "The Historical Geography of Iowa Fences: Pioneer Enclosures to 1895," Master's thesis, University of Nebraska–Lincoln, 1967. **8295**

Rueber, Bruce E., "Factors Influencing Barn Styles in Fayette County, Iowa," Master's thesis, San Diego State University, 1974. **8296**

COMMUNICATIONS & TRADE

Cooper, Clare C., "The Role of Railroads in the Settlement of Iowa: A Study in Historical Geography," Master's thesis, University of Nebraska–Lincoln, 1958. **8297**

MANUFACTURING & INDUSTRIALIZATION

Page, Brian K., "Cornbelt Industrialization and Urban Growth: An Historical Geography of Wapello County, Iowa," Master's thesis, University of California–Berkeley, 1988. **8298**

URBAN NETWORKS & URBANIZATION

See also 7151

Laska, John A., "The Development of the Pattern of Retail Trade Centers in a Selected Area of Southwestern Iowa," Master's thesis, University of Chicago, 1958.   8299

Blome, Donald A., "An Analysis of the Changing Spatial Relationships of Iowa Towns, 1900–1960," Ph.D. diss., University of Iowa, 1963.   8300

Salisbury, Neil E., and Gerard Rushton, *Growth and Decline of Iowa Villages: A Pilot Study* (Iowa City: State University of Iowa, Department of Geography, Publication no. 4, 1963). [Focus on two sample areas in east central and southwestern Iowa, 1870–1960]   8301

Weiskind, Stewart, "Settlement Changes and Spatial Behavior in Iowa, 1930–1960," Master's thesis, Ohio State University, 1969.   8302

Webber, M. J., "Population Growth and Town Location in an Agricultural Community: Iowa, 1840–1960," *Geographical Analysis*, vol. 4, 2 (1972), pp. 134–155.   8303

Conzen, Michael P., "Local Migration Systems in Nineteenth Century Iowa," *Geographical Review*, vol. 64, 3 (1974), pp. 339–361.   8304

Hellyer, David L., "Geographic Aspects of Farm Service Centers in Clinton County, Iowa, 1941–

1973," Master's thesis, Western Illinois University, 1976.   8305

URBAN ECONOMIC STRUCTURE

Nelson, Howard J., "The Economic Development of Des Moines," *Iowa Journal of History*, vol. 48, 3 (1950), pp. 193–220.   8306

URBAN SOCIAL STRUCTURE

Johnson, Hildegard Binder, "The Claus Groth Guild of Davenport, Iowa," *American-German Review*, vol. 11, 2 (1944), pp. 26–29. [German-American sick-relief society]   8307

Johnson, Hildegard Binder, "German Forty-Eighters in Davenport," *Iowa Journal of History*, vol. 44, 1 (1946), pp. 3–60.   8308

Hartshorn, Truman A., "Urban Blight: The Structure and Change of Substandard Housing in Cedar Rapids, Iowa, 1940–1960," Ph.D. diss., University of Iowa, 1968.   8309

PLACE NAMES

Vogel, Virgil J., *Iowa Place Names of Indian Origin* (Iowa City: University of Iowa Press, 1983), 150 pp.   8310

THE WEST

GENERAL

The West as a whole

Ratzel, Friedrich, "Die Entwicklung des Westens der Vereinigten Staaten," *Globus*, vol. 36 (1879), pp. 237–238. **8311**

Brigham, Albert Perry, "The Geographic Importance of the Louisiana Purchase," *Journal of Geography*, vol. 3, 6 (1904), pp. 243–251. **8312**

Berkhofer, Robert F., Jr., "Space, Time, Culture, and the New Frontier," *Agricultural History*, vol. 38, 1 (1964), pp. 21–30. Reprinted, with omissions, in David Ward, ed., *Geographic Perspectives on America's Past: Readings on the Historical Geography of the United States* (New York: Oxford University Press, 1979), pp. 40–49. **8313**

Meinig, Donald W., "American Wests: Preface to a Geographical Introduction," *Annals of the Association of American Geographers*, vol. 62, 2 (1972), pp. 159–184. Reissued in John Fraser Hart, ed., *Regions of the United States* (New York: Harper & Row, 1972), same pagination. Reprinted, with omissions, in David Ward, ed., *Geographic Perspectives on America's Past: Readings on the Historical Geography of the United States* (New York: Oxford University Press, 1979), pp. 227–246. **8314**

Nash, Gerald D., "Where's the West?" *Historian*, vol. 49, 1 (1986), pp. 1–9. **8315**

Hornbeck, David, Jr., "The Far West, 1840–1920," in Robert D. Mitchell and Paul A. Groves, eds., *North America: The Historical Geography of a Changing Continent* (Totowa, N.J.: Rowman & Littlefield, 1987), pp. 279–298. **8316**

Southern borderlands

Nostrand, Richard L., "The Hispanic-American Borderland: A Regional Historical Geography," Ph.D. diss., University of California–Los Angeles, 1968. **8317**

Nostrand, Richard L., "The Hispanic-American Borderland: Delimitation of an American Culture Region," *Annals of the Association of American Geographers*, vol. 60, 4 (1970), pp. 638–661. **8318**

Nostrand, Richard L., "The Borderlands in Perspective," in Gary S. Elbow, ed., *International Aspects of Development in Latin America: Geographical Perspectives*, Proceedings of the Conference of Latin Americanist Geographers, vol. 6 (1977), pp. 9–28. **8319**

Nostrand, Richard L., "The Spanish Borderlands," in Robert D. Mitchell and Paul A. Groves, eds., *North America: The Historical Geography of a Changing Continent* (Totowa, N.J.: Rowman & Littlefield, 1987), pp. 48–64. **8320**

ENVIRONMENTAL CHANGE

McKnight, Tom L., "The Feral Horse in Anglo-America," *Geographical Review*, vol. 46, 1 (1956), pp. 506–525. [Emphasis on the western U.S.A., 1929–1950] **8321**

Rohe, Randall E., "Man as Geomorphic Agent: Hydraulic Mining in the American West," *Pacific Historian*, vol. 27, 1 (1983), pp. 5–16. **8322**

McGregor, Kent M., "Drought during the 1930s and 1950s in the Central United States," *Physical Geography*, vol. 6, 3 (1985), pp. 288–301. [Covers 1932–1957] **8323**

NATIVE PEOPLES & WHITE RELATIONS

Rostlund, Erhard, "Fishing among Primitive Peoples: A Theme in Cultural Geography," *Yearbook of the Association of Pacific Coast Geographers*, vol. 10 (1948), pp. 26–32. **8324**

Deutsch, Herman, "Indian and White in the Inland Empire: The Contest for the Land, 1880–1912," *Pacific Northwest Quarterly*, vol. 47, 1 (1956), pp. 44–51. **8325**

Hilliard, Sam B., "Indian Land Cessions West of the Mississippi," *Journal of the West*, vol. 10, 3 (1971), pp. 493–510. **8326**

Stafford, John W., "Crow Cultural Change: A Geographical Analysis," Ph.D. diss., Michigan State University, 1971. **8327**

Wills, Berndt L., "Native Americans and Early Explorers," *Bulletin of the Association of North Dakota Geographers*, vol. 27 (1977), pp. 1–12. **8328**

White, Richard, *The Roots of Dependency: Subsistence, Environment, and Social Change among the Choctaws, Pawnees, and Navajos* (Lincoln: University of Nebraska, 1983), 433 pp. **8329**

Dorn, Ronald I., and David Whitley, "Chronometric and Relative Age Determination of Petroglyphs in the Western United States," *Annals of the Association of American Geographers*, vol. 74, 2 (1984), pp. 308–322.   **8330**

EXPLORATION & MAPPING

Exploration

Howland, A. C., "Explorations within the Louisiana Purchase," *Journal of Geography*, vol. 3, 6 (1904), pp. 261–270.   **8331**

Gannett, Henry, "Early Western Explorers and the Railroads," *Bulletin of the American Geographical Society*, vol. 37, 12 (1905), pp. 716–718.   **8332**

Gilbert, Edmund W., "Geographical Influence on the Exploration of America West of the Mississippi, 1800–1850," B.Litt. thesis, University of Oxford, 1928.   **8333**

Gilbert, Edmund W., "Animal Life and the Exploration of Western America," *Scottish Geographical Magazine*, vol. 47, 1 (1931), pp. 19–28.   **8334**

Gilbert, Edmund W., *The Exploration of Western America, 1800–1850: An Historical Geography* (New York: Cooper Square Publications, 1933), 233 pp.   **8335**

Friis, Herman R., and Suzanna Pitzer, *Federal Exploration of the American West before 1880* (Washington, D.C.: National Archives, Publication no. 64–6, 1963), 31 pp.   **8336**

Goetzmann, William H., *Exploration and Empire: The Explorer and the Scientist in the Winning of the American West* (New York: Alfred A. Knopf, 1966), 656 pp.   **8337**

Friis, Herman R., "The Documents and Reports of the United States Congress: A Primary Source of Information on Travel in the West, 1783–1861," in John F. McDermott, ed., *Travelers on the Western Frontier* (Urbana: University of Illinois Press, 1970), pp. 112–167.   **8338**

Bruman, Henry J., *Alexander von Humboldt and the Exploration of the American West* (Los Angeles: University of California Library Private Edition, 1971), 10 pp.   **8339**

Allen, John L., "An Analysis of the Exploratory Process: The Lewis and Clark Expedition of 1804–1806," *Geographical Review*, vol. 62, 1 (1972), pp. 13–39.   **8340**

Zernal, John J., "The Path of a Pathfinder: Walker's Route to California in 1833," Master's thesis, Oregon State University, 1974.   **8341**

Allen, John L., *Passage through the Garden: Lewis and Clark and the Image of the Northwest* (Urbana: University of Illinois Press, 1975), 412 pp.   **8342**

Allen, John L., "The Summer of Decision, 1805," *We Proceeded On*, vol. 2, 3 (1976), pp. 8–11.   **8343**

Allen, John L., "The Illy-Smelling Sea: Indians, Information, and Early Search for the Northwest Passage," *Man in the Northwest*, vol. 33 (1987), pp. 127–135.   **8344**

Smith, Melvyn T., "Before Powell: Exploration of the Colorado River," *Utah Historical Quarterly*, vol. 55, 2 (1987), pp. 105–119.   **8345**

Allen, John L., *Jedediah Smith and the Mountain Men of the American West* (New York: Chelsea House, 1990), 112 pp.   **8346**

Mapping

Abel, Annie H., "A New Lewis and Clark Map," *Geographical Review*, vol. 1, 5 (1916), pp. 329–345.   **8347**

Friis, Herman R., "Cartographic and Geographic Activities of the Lewis and Clark Expedition," *Journal of the Washington Academy of Sciences*, vol. 44 (1954), pp. 338–351.   **8348**

Wheat, Carl S., *Mapping the American West, 1540–1857: A Preliminary Study* (Worcester: American Antiquarian Society, 1954), 194 pp.   **8349**

Friis, Herman R., "The United States (Stephen H. Long's) Exploring Expedition: 1819–1820: The Unpublished Manuscript Map of 1820–22," *California Geographer*, vol. 8 (1967), pp. 75–87.   **8350**

McDermott, Paul D., and Ronald E. Grim, "Maps of the Mullan Road," *Proceedings of the American Congress on Surveying and Mapping*, vol. 36 (1976), pp. 212–226. [Montana, Idaho, Washington]   **8351**

Garver, John B., Jr., "Isaac McCoy: Forgotten Mapper of the Trans-Missouri West," *Portolan*, no. 9 (1987), pp. 11–16.   **8352**

POPULAR IMAGES & EVALUATION

General

Smith, Henry Nash, *Virgin Land: The American West as Symbol and Myth* (Cambridge, Mass.: Harvard University Press, 1950), 305 pp. Reprinted 1970.   **8353**

Bowden, Martyn J., "The Perception of the Western Interior of the United States, 1800–1870: A Problem in Historical Geosophy," *Proceedings of the Association of American Geographers*, vol. 1 (1969), pp. 16–21.   **8354**

Allen, John L., "Geographical Knowledge and American Images of the Louisiana Territory,"

Western Historical Quarterly, vol. 2, 2 (1971), pp. 151–170. Reprinted, with omissions, in David Ward, ed., *Geographic Perspectives on America's Past: Readings on the Historical Geography of the United States* (New York: Oxford University Press, 1979), pp. 33–39. **8355**

Allen, John L., "Of This Enterprise: American Images of the Lewis and Clark Expeditions," in W. Willingham, ed., *Enlightenment Science in the American Northwest* (Portland, Oreg.: Lewis & Clark College, 1984), pp. 29–43. **8356**

Image-makers

Leighly, John B., "John Muir's Image of the West," *Annals of the American Association of Geographers*, vol. 48, 4 (1958), pp. 309–318. **8357**

Pattison, William D., "Westward by Rail with Professor Sedgwick: A Lantern Journey of 1873," *Historical Society of Southern California Quarterly*, vol. 42, 4 (1960), pp. 335–349. **8358**

Friis, Herman R., "The Image of the American West at Mid-Century (1840–60): A Product of Scientific Geographical Exploration by the United States Government," in John F. McDermott, ed., *The Frontier Re-Examined* (Urbana: University of Illinois, 1967), pp. 49–63. **8359**

Allen, John L., "Thomas Jefferson and the Passage to India: A Pre-Exploratory Image," in Ralph E. Ehrenberg, ed., *Pattern and Process: Research in Historical Geography* (Washington, D.C.: Howard University Press, 1975), pp. 103–113. **8360**

Birch, Brian P., "From Old England to Old Faithful: A Victorian Englishman's View of the West," *Annals of Wyoming*, vol. 54, 1 (1982), pp. 2–9. **8361**

Writers' imagery

Sellars, Richard W., "The Interrelationship of Literature, History, and Geography in Western Writing," *Western Historical Quarterly*, vol. 4, 2 (1973), pp. 171–185. **8362**

Cragg, Barbara, "Mary Hallock Foote's Images of the Old West," *Landscape*, vol. 24, 3 (1980), pp. 42–47. **8363**

Schmitt-von Mühlenfels, Astrid, "Geographie und Literatur: Der nachrevolutionäre Westen Nordamerikas bei Gilbert Imlay," in Hans-Wilhelm Windhorst and William H. Berentsen, eds., *Beiträge zur räumlichen Prozeßforschung in den USA* (Vechta: Vechta Druckerei und Verlag, Zentralverband der Deutschen Geographen, Arbeitskreis USA, Vechtaer Arbeiten zur Geographie und Regionalwissenschaft, vol. 2, 1986), pp. 121–138. **8364**

Artists' imagery

Logan, Linda D'A., "The Geographical Imagination of Frederic Remington: A Chapter in the Geosophy of the American West," Ph.D. diss., Clark University, 1987. **8365**

Mauduy, Jacques, and Gérard Henriet, *Géographies du western: Une nation en marche* (Paris: Éditions Nathan, 1989), 254 pp. **8366**

Krygier, John B., "The Landscape Images of Baron Frederick W. von Egloffstein, Topographic Artist, in the Transmississippi West, 1853–1859," Master's thesis, University of Wisconsin–Madison, 1990. **8367**

Irrigation movement

Rickard, Timothy J., "Perceptions and Results of the Irrigation Movement in the Western U.S., 1891–1914," Ph.D. diss., University of Kansas, 1974. **8368**

REGIONAL SETTLEMENT

General

Green, D. Brooks, "The Settlement of Teton Valley, Idaho-Wyoming," Master's thesis, Brigham Young University, 1974. **8369**

Freedom, Gary S., "Military Reservation and Settlement," *Periodical: Journal of the Council on America's Military Past*, vol. 12, 3 (1983), pp. 38–46. **8370**

Mormon settlement morphology

Nelson, Lowry, *The Mormon Village: A Pattern and Technique of Land Settlement* (Salt Lake City: University of Utah Press, 1952), 296 pp. **8371**

Rosenvall, Lynn A., "Mormon Settlement Patterns: 1830–1900," Ph.D. diss., University of California–Berkeley, 1972. **8372**

Jackson, Richard H., and Robert Layton, "The Mormon Village: Analysis of a Settlement Type," *Professional Geographer*, vol. 28, 2 (1976), pp. 136–141. **8373**

Rosenvall, Lynn A., "Defunct Mormon Settlements, 1830–1930," in Richard H. Jackson, ed., *The Mormon Role in the Settlement of the West* (Provo, Utah: Brigham Young University Press, Charles Redd Monographs in Western History, no. 9, 1978), pp. 51–74. **8374**

Jackson, Richard H., "The Mormon Village: Genesis and Antecedents of the City of Zion Plan," *Brigham Young University Studies*, vol. 17 (1977), pp. 223–240. **8375**

Bennion, Lowell C., "Mormon Country a Century Ago: A Geographer's View," in Thomas G. Alexander, ed., *The Mormon People* (Provo: Brig-

ham Young University Press, 1980), pp. 1–26.
8376

POPULATION

Packer, E. B., "Middle Class British Immigration to the Trans-Mississippi West, 1870–1900," Master's thesis, University of London, 1967.   8377

Bennion, Lowell C., and Dean R. Louder, "Mapping Mormons across the Modern West," in Richard H. Jackson, ed., *The Mormon Role in the Settlement of the West* (Provo: Brigham Young University Press, Charles Redd Monographs in Western History, no. 9, 1978), pp. 135–169.   8378

Hudson, John C., "The Study of Western Frontier Population," in Jerome O. Steffen, ed., *The American West: New Perspectives* (Norman: University of Oklahoma Press, 1978), pp. 35–66.
8379

Birch, Brian P., "An English Approach to the American Frontier," *Journal of Historical Geography*, vol. 7, 4 (1981), pp. 397–406.   8380

Rohe, Randall E., "Goldrush Migrations and Goldfield Populations in the American West, 1849–1880," *Geographical Bulletin*, vol. 28, 1 (1986), pp. 5–29.   8381

RURAL & REGIONAL SOCIAL GEOGRAPHY

General

Renner, George T., "Chinese Influence in the Development of the Western United States," *Annals of the American Academy of Political and Social Science*, vol. 152 (1930), pp. 356–369.   8382

Women in the West

Wilkinson, Nancy Lee, "Women on the Oregon Trail," *Landscape*, vol. 23, 1 (1979), pp. 42–47.
8383

Norwood, Vera, "Women's Place: Continuity and Change in Response to Western Landscapes," in Schlissel, Lillian, Vicki L. Ruiz, and Janice Monk, eds., *Western Women: Their Land, Their Lives* (Albuquerque: University of New Mexico, 1988), pp. 155–181.   8384

Schlissel, Lillian, Vicki L. Ruiz, and Janice Monk, eds., *Western Women: Their Land, Their Lives* (Albuquerque: University of New Mexico, 1988), 354 pp.   8385

Simmons, Alexy, *Red Light Ladies: Settlement Patterns and Material Culture on the Mining Frontier* (Corvallis: Oregon State University Department of Anthropology, Anthropology Northwest, vol. 4, 1989), 150 pp.   8386

Mormon genesis in the West

Petersen, B. L., "A Geographical Study of the Mormon Migration from Nauvoo, Illinois, to the Great Salt Lake Valley," Master's thesis, University of California–Los Angeles, 1941.   8387

Jackson, Richard H., "The Overland Journey," in Richard H. Jackson, ed., *The Mormon Role in the Settlement of the West* (Provo, Utah: Brigham Young University Press, Charles Redd Monographs in Western History, no. 9, 1978), pp. 1–27.   8388

Mormon culture region

Meinig, Donald W., "The Mormon Culture Region: Strategies and Patterns in the Geography of the American West, 1847–1967," *Annals of the Association of American Geographers*, vol. 55, 2 (1965), pp. 191–220. Reprinted in Fred E. Dohrs and Lawrence M. Sommers, eds., *Cultural Geography: Selected Readings* (New York: Thomas Y. Crowell Co., 1967), pp. 515–556.   8389

Johnson, Paul T., "An Analysis of the Spread of the Church of Jesus Christ of Latter-Day Saints from Salt Lake City, Utah, Utilizing a Diffusion Model," Ph.D. diss., University of Iowa, 1966.
8390

Jackson, Richard H., "Religion and Landscape in the Mormon Cultural Region," in Karl W. Butzer, ed., *Dimensions of Human Geography: Essays on Some Familiar and Neglected Themes* (Chicago: University of Chicago Department of Geography, Research Paper no. 186, 1978), pp. 100–127.   8391

Jackson, Richard H., ed., *The Mormon Role in the Settlement of the West* (Provo: Brigham Young University Press, Charles Redd Monographs in Western History, no. 9, 1978), 224 pp.   8392

Jackson, Richard H., "Religion and Settlement in the American West: The Mormon Example," in Manfred Büttner, K. Hoheisel, U. Kopf, Gisbert Rinschede, and A. Slevers, eds., *Religion und Siedlungsraum*, vol. 2 (Berlin: Dietrich Reimer Verlag, 1986), pp. 250–267.   8393

Mormon communities

Nelson, Lowry, "The Mormon Village: A Study in Social Origins," *Proceedings of the Utah Academy of Science*, vol. 7 (1930), pp. 11–37.   8394

Rathjen, M. Randall, "Evolution and Development of the Mormon Welfare Farms," Ph.D. diss., Michigan State University, 1969.   8395

POLITICAL & ADMINISTRATIVE GEOGRAPHY

See also 1390

Romanet du Caillaud, F., "Les limites au nord-ouest de la Lousiane cédée par la France aux États-Unis en 1803," *Report of the Eighth International Geographical Congress, Held in the United States, 1904* (Washington, D.C.: Government Printing Office, 1905), pp. 939–940. **8396**

Klotz, Otto, "The History of the Forty-Ninth Parallel Survey West of the Rocky Mountains," *Geographical Review*, vol. 3, 5 (1917), pp. 382–387. **8397**

Pfeifer, Gottfried, "Die politisch-geographische Entwicklung der Vereinigten Staaten westlich des Mississippi," *Geographische Zeitschrift*, vol. 41, 10 (1935), pp. 361–380. Reprinted in Gerd Kohlhepp, ed., *Beiträge zur Kulturgeographie der Neuen Welt: Ausgewählte Arbeiten von Gottfried Pfeifer* (Berlin: Dietrich Reimer, 1981), pp. 69–88. **8398**

Rosenvall, Lynn A., "The Creation and Evolution of Interstate Boundaries in the Western United States," *Proceedings of the Annual Conference of the Association of Canadian Map Libraries, June 25–30, 1973* (1974), pp. 31–43. **8399**

Handley, Lawrence R., "The Mormon State of Deseret: A Study in Political Geography," *Geographical Bulletin*, vol. 10 (1975), pp. 2–12. **8400**

LAND & LAND USE

Sutton, Imre, "Land Tenure in the West: Continuity and Change," *Journal of the West*, vol. 9, 1 (1970), pp. 1–23. **8401**

McIntosh, C. Barron, "Use and Abuse of the Timber Culture Act," *Annals of the Association of American Geographers*, vol. 65, 3 (1975), pp. 347–362. **8402**

Sauder, Robert A., and Rose M. Sauder, "Regional Variations in Land Alienation: The Agricultural College Act of 1862," *Journal of Historical Geography*, vol. 12, 4 (1986), pp. 365–380. **8403**

Sauder, Robert A., and Rose M. Sauder, "The Morrill Act's Influence on Public Land Dispersal after 1870," *Agricultural History*, vol. 61, 1 (1987), pp. 34–49. **8404**

EXTRACTIVE ACTIVITY

Fur trade

Wishart, David J., "The Fur Trade of the West, 1807–1840: A Geographical Synthesis," in David H. Miller and Jerome O. Steffen, eds., *The Frontier: Comparative Studies* (Norman: University of Oklahoma Press, 1977), pp. 161–200. **8405**

Wishart, David J., *The Fur Trade of the American West, 1807–1840: A Geographical Synthesis*

(Lincoln: University of Nebraska Press, 1979), 237 pp. **8406**

Mining

Rohe, Randall E., "The Geographical Impact of Placer Mining in the American West, 1848–1974," Ph.D. diss., University of Colorado, 1978. **8407**

Rohe, Randall E., "After the Gold Rush: Chinese Mining in the Far West, 1850–1890," *Montana*, vol. 32, 1 (1982), pp. 2–19. **8408**

Rohe, Randall E., "Gold Dredging in the American West: Origin and Diffusion," *Pacific Historian*, vol. 28, 1 (1984), pp. 5–17. **8409**

Rohe, Randall E., "Just Scratching the Surface: Geographers and the Mining West," *Geographical Bulletin*, vol. 26, 2 (1984), pp. 35–46. **8410**

Rohe, Randall E., "Hydraulicking in the American West: The Development and Diffusion of a Mining Technique," *Montana*, vol. 35, 1 (1985), pp. 18–35. **8411**

Rohe, Randall E., "Origins and Diffusion of Traditional Placer Mining in the West," *Material Culture*, vol. 18, 3 (1986), pp. 127–166. **8412**

AGRICULTURE

Baker, Oliver E., "Agricultural Regions of North America: Part X—The Grazing and Irrigated Crops Region," *Economic Geography*, vol. 7, 4 (1931), pp. 325–364; and vol. 8, 4 (1932), pp. 325–377. **8413**

Brayer, Herbert O., "British Cattle Ranches in America," *Geographical Magazine*, vol. 20, 4 (1947), pp. 125–131. [Focus on the western U.S.A., 1879–1900] **8414**

Kniffen, Fred B., "The Western Cattle Complex: Notes on Differentiation and Diffusion," *Western Folklore*, vol. 12, 3 (1953), pp. 179–185. Reprinted in H. Jesse Walker and Milton B. Newton, Jr., eds., *Environment and Culture* (Baton Rouge: Louisiana State University, Department of Geography and Anthropology, 1978), pp. 237–240. **8415**

Meinig, Donald W., "The Growth of Agricultural Regions in the Far West, 1850–1910," *Journal of Geography*, vol. 54, 5 (1955), pp. 211–232. **8416**

Gómez-Ibañez, Daniel A., "The Rise and Decline of Transhumance in the United States," Master's thesis, University of Wisconsin–Madison, 1967. . **8417**

Gregor, Howard F., "The Industrial Farm as a Western Institution," *Journal of the West*, vol. 9, 1 (1970), pp. 78–92. **8418**

Harper, Kelly C., "The Mormon Role in Irrigation Beginnings and Diffusions in the Western States: An Historical Geography," Master's thesis, Brigham Young University, 1974. **8419**

Jackson, Richard H., "Mormon Indian Farms," in Jerry N. McDonald and Tony Lazewski, eds., *Geographical Perspectives on Native Americans: Topics and Resources* (Washington, D.C.: Association of American Geographers, Associated Committee of Native Americans, no. 1, 1976), pp. 41–54. **8420**

Rinschede, Gisbert, "Formen der Wandervieh-wirtschaft in den westlichen USA," *Zeitschrift für Agrargeographie*, vol. 4 (1986), pp. 1–41. **8421**

Rinschede, Gisbert, "Wanderviehwirtschaft in den westlichen USA," in Hans-Wilhelm Windhorst and William H. Berentsen, eds., *Beiträge zur räumlichen Prozeßforschung in den USA* (Vechta: Vechta Druckerei und Verlag, Zentralverband der Deutschen Geographen, Arbeitskreis USA, Vechtaer Arbeiten zur Geographie und Regionalwissenschaft, vol. 2, 1986), pp. 121–138. **8422**

LANDSCAPE

General

Francaviglia, Richard V., "Western Barns: Architectural Form and Climatic Considerations," *Yearbook of the Association of Pacific Coast Geographers*, vol. 34 (1972), pp. 153–160. **8423**

Bowden, Martyn J., "Creating Cowboy Country," *Geographical Magazine*, vol. 52, 10 (1980), pp. 693–701. **8424**

Rohe, Randall E., "Man and the Land: Mining's Impact in the Far West," *Arizona and the West*, vol. 28, 4 (1986), pp. 299–338. **8425**

Arreola, Daniel D., "Mexican American House-scapes," *Geographical Review*, vol. 78, 3 (1988), pp. 299–315. **8426**

Parsons, James J., "Hillside Letters in the Western Landscape," *Landscape*, vol. 30, 1 (1988), pp. 15–23. [Focus on 1905–1988] **8427**

Hornbeck, David, Jr., "Spanish Legacy in the Borderlands," in Michael P. Conzen, ed., *The Making of the American Landscape* (Boston: Unwin Hyman, 1990), pp. 51–62. **8428**

Wescoat, James L., "Challenging the Desert," in Michael P. Conzen, ed., *The Making of the American Landscape* (Boston: Unwin Hyman, 1990), pp. 186–203. **8429**

Mormon landscapes

Francaviglia, Richard V., "The Mormon Landscape: Existence, Creation, and Perception of a Unique Image in the American West," Ph.D. diss., University of Oregon, 1970. **8430**

Francaviglia, Richard V., "Mormon Central-Hall Houses in the American West," *Annals of the Association of American Geographers*, vol. 61, 1 (1971), pp. 65–71. **8431**

Rosenvall, Lynn A., "Mormon Settlement Plats: Their Design and Origin," *Great Plains–Rocky Mountain Geographical Journal*, vol. 1 (1972), pp. 88–93. **8432**

Pitman, Leon S., "A Survey of Nineteenth-Century Folk Housing in the Mormon Culture Region," Ph.D. diss., Louisiana State University, 1973. **8433**

COMMUNICATIONS & TRADE

General

Vance, James E., Jr., "The Oregon Trail and Union Pacific Railroad: A Contrast in Purpose," *Annals of the Association of American Geographers*, vol. 51, 4 (1961), pp. 357–379. **8434**

Roads & trails

Castañeda, Carlos E., "Communications between Santa Fe and San Antonio in the Eighteenth Century," *Texas Geographic Magazine*, vol. 5, 1 (1941), pp. 17–38. **8435**

Stewart, George R., Introduction to T. H. Jefferson, *Map of the Emigrant Road from Independence, Mo., to San Francisco, California* (San Francisco: California Historical Society, 1945), pp. i-xi. **8436**

Raburn, Robert A., "Motor Freight and Urban Morphogenesis with Reference to California and the West," Ph.D. diss., University of California–Berkeley, 1988. **8437**

Railroads

Partsch, Joseph, "Die Nordpazifische Bahn: Die geographischen Bedingungen ihres Werdens und ihres Wirkens," *Memorial Volume of the Transcontinental Excursion of 1912 of the American Geographical Society of New York* (New York: American Geographical Society, 1915), pp. 201–221. **8438**

Pattison, William D., "The Pacific Railroad Rediscovered," *Geographical Review*, vol. 52, 1 (1962), pp. 25–36. **8439**

Airways

Elliott, Harold M., "The Historical Geography of Western Airlines," *Yearbook of the Association of Pacific Coast Geographers*, vol. 43 (1981), pp. 77–100. **8440**

URBAN NETWORKS & URBANIZATION

Nußbaum, Fritz, "Bemerkungen über Lage und Entwicklung einiger Städte in den westlichen Vereinigten Staaten," *Memorial Volume of the Transcontinental Excursion of 1912 of the American Geographical Society of New York* (New York: American Geographical Society, 1915), pp. 147–161. **8441**

Wells, Eugene T., "St. Louis and Cities West, 1820–1880: A Study in History and Geography," Ph.D. diss. (History), University of Kansas, 1950. **8442**

Chow, Willard T., "Urban Evolution in the Northern Sierra Foothills," Master's thesis, University of California–Berkeley, 1970. **8443**

Rohe, Randall E., "Feeding the Miners: The Development of Supply Centers for the Goldfields," *Annals of Wyoming*, vol. 57, 1 (1985), pp. 40–59. **8444**

TOWNSCAPE

Rosenvall, Lynn A., "Joseph Smith's Influence on Mormon City Planning," *Ensign of the Church of Jesus Christ of the Latter Day Saints*, vol. 4, 6 (1974), p. 26. **8445**

Reps, John W., "Bonanza Towns: Urban Planning on the Western Mining Frontier," in Ralph E. Ehrenberg, ed., *Pattern and Process: Research in Historical Geography* (Washington, D.C.:

Howard University Press, 1975), pp. 271–289. **8446**

Brownridge, Dennis R., "Secret Societies and Their Impact on the Architectural Landscape of the West," Ph.D. diss., University of Oregon, 1976. **8447**

Reps, John W., *Cities of the American West: A History of Frontier Urban Planning* (Princeton: Princeton University Press, 1979), 827 pp. **8448**

Rohe, Randall E., "The Geography and Material Culture of the Western Mining Town," *Material Culture*, vol. 16, 3 (1984), pp. 99–120. **8449**

RECREATION & TOURISM

Jakle, John A., "Touring by Automobile in 1932: The American West as Stereotype," *Annals of Tourism Research*, vol. 8, 4 (1981), pp. 534–549. [Focus on a trip from St. Paul, Minnesota, to San Francisco] **8450**

Fifer, J. Valerie, *American Progress: The Growth of the Transport, Tourist, and Information Industries in the Nineteenth Century West Seen through the Life and Times of George A. Crofutt, Pioneer Publicist of the Transcontinent Age* (Chester, Conn.: Globe Pequot Press, 1988), 472 pp. **8451**

Demars, Stanford E., *The Tourist in Yosemite, 1855–1985* (Salt Lake City: University of Utah Press, 1991), 168 pp. **8452**

———— THE GREAT PLAINS ————

GENERAL

Visher, Stephen S., "Notes on the Geography of the Red River Valley," *Journal of Geography*, vol. 14, 6 (1916), pp. 202–205.   **8453**

Webb, Walter Prescott, *The Great Plains* (Boston: Ginn & Co., 1931), 525 pp.   **8454**

Moehlman, Arthur H., "The Red River of the North," *Geographical Review*, vol. 25, 1 (1935), pp. 79–91.   **8455**

Thornthwaite, Charles Warren, "Climate and Settlement in the Great Plains," in *Climate and Man: 1941 Yearbook of Agriculture* (Washington, D.C.: Government Printing Office, 1941), pp. 177–187.   **8456**

Mather, Eugene Cotton, "The American Great Plains," *Annals of the Association of American Geographers*, vol. 62, 2 (1972), pp. 237–257. Reissued in John Fraser Hart, ed., *Regions of the United States* (New York: Harper & Row, 1972), same pagination.   **8457**

Hewes, Leslie, "The Great Plains One Hundred Years after Major John Wesley Powell," in Brian W. Blouet and Merlin P. Lawson, eds., *Images of the Plains: The Role of Human Nature in Settlement* (Lincoln: University of Nebraska Press, 1975), pp. 203–214.   **8458**

Hudson, John C., "Landscape Organization of the Great Plains: A Reexamination of the Humid Area Institutions Thesis," in Donald Deskins et al., eds., *Geographic Humanism, Analysis, and Social Action: A Half Century of Geography at Michigan* (Ann Arbor: University of Michigan Geography Publication no. 17, 1977), pp. 149–177.   **8459**

ENVIRONMENTAL CHANGE

See also 1157, 1166, 1169–1174

General

Riebsame, William E., "The United States Great Plains," in Billie Lee Turner II, ed., *The Earth as Transformed by Human Action: Global and Regional Changes in the Biosphere over the Past Three Hundred Years* (New York: Cambridge University Press, 1990), pp. 561–575.   **8460**

Climate

Smith, J. Warren, "Rainfall of the Great Plains in Relation to Cultivation," *Annals of the Associa-*

tion of American Geographers, vol. 10 (1920), pp. 69–74.   **8461**

Van Royen, William, "Prehistoric Droughts in the Central Great Plains," *Geographical Review*, vol. 27, 4 (1937), pp. 637–650.   **8462**

Trewartha, Glenn T., "Climate and Settlement of the Subhumid Lands," in *Climate and Man: 1941 Yearbook of Agriculture* (Washington, D.C.: Government Printing Office, 1941), pp. 167–176.   **8463**

Frisby, Emily M., "Weather-Crop Relationships: Forecasting Spring-Wheat Yield in the Northern Great Plains of the United States," *Transactions of the Institute of British Geographers*, vol. 17 (1951), pp. 79–96. [Focus on North and South Dakota and Montana, 1929–1946]   **8464**

Bryson, Reid A., D. A. Baerreis, and Wayne M. Wendland, "The Character of Late Glacial and Postglacial Climatic Changes," in W. Dort and J. K. Jones, eds., *Pleistocene and Recent Environments of the Central Great Plains* (Lawrence: University of Kansas Press, University of Kansas Department of Geology Special Publication no. 3, 1970), pp. 53–74.   **8465**

Kollmorgen, Walter M., and Johanna Kollmorgen, "Landscape Meteorology in the Plains Area," *Annals of the Association of American Geographers*, vol. 63, 4 (1973), pp. 424–441.   **8466**

Bowden, Martyn J., et al., "The Effect of Climate Fluctuations on Human Populations," in T. M. L. Wigley, M. J. Ingram, and G. Farmer, eds., *Climate and History: Studies in Past Climates and Their Impact on Man* (Cambridge: Cambridge University Press, 1981), pp. 479–513. [Focus on the Great Plains, 1890–1970]   **8467**

Bryson, Reid A., "Chinook Climates and Plains People," *Great Plains Quarterly*, vol. 1, 1 (1981), pp. 5–15.   **8468**

Warrick, Richard A., and Martyn J. Bowden, "The Changing Aspects of Droughts in the Great Plains," in Merlin P. Lawson and M. Baker, eds., *The Great Plains: Perspectives and Prospects* (Lincoln: University of Nebraska Press, 1981), pp. 111–137.   **8469**

Barry, Roger G., "Climatic Environments of the Great Plains, Past and Present," in *Transactions of the Nebraska Academy of Sciences*, vol. 11 (1983), pp. 45–55. [Volume title: *Man and the Changing Environments in the Great Plains*]   **8470**

Schafer, Thomas C., "Impact of Prolonged Drought upon Selected Great Plains Counties, 1890–1960," Master's thesis, University of Nebraska–Omaha, 1990.   **8471**

Fauna

Alford, John J., "The American Bison: An Ice Age Survivor," *Proceedings of the Association of American Geographers*, vol. 5 (1973), pp. 1–5.   **8472**

Alford, John J., "The Geography of Mastadon Extinction," *Professional Geographer*, vol. 26, 4 (1974), pp. 425–429.   **8473**

Landforms, flora, and fire

Duncanson, Henry B., "Observations on the Shifting of the Channel of the Missouri River since 1883," *Science*, vol. 29, 752 (1909), pp. 869–871.   **8474**

Malin, James C., "Soil, Animal, and Plant Relations of the Grassland, Historically Reconsidered," *Scientific Monthly*, vol. 76, 4 (1953), pp. 207–220.   **8475**

Phillips, Walter S., *Vegetational Changes in the Northern Great Plains: Photographic Documentation* (Tucson: University of Arizona, Agricultural Experiment Station, Report no. 214, 1963), 185 pp.   **8476**

Droze, W. H., "Changing the Plains Environment: The Afforestation of the Trans-Mississippi West," *Agricultural History*, vol. 51, 1 (1977), pp. 6–22.   **8477**

NATIVE PEOPLES & WHITE RELATIONS

Prehistoric occupance

Bell, Robert, "Precolumbian Prairie Settlements in the Great Plains," *Great Plains Journal*, vol. 2, 1 (1962), pp. 22–28.   **8478**

Reider, Richard G., "Some Geographic Themes in the Prehistory of the Great Plains," *Pennsylvania Geographer*, vol. 6, 1 (1968), pp. 6–10.   **8479**

Gillaspie, Emmet A., Jr., "Prehistoric Settlement Patterns in the Middle Missouri Regions of North and South Dakota, A.D. 700–1675," Master's thesis, University of Nebraska, 1972.   **8480**

Contact period

Markevich, Sandra C., "The Variable Effect of European Acculturation upon the Subsistence and Non-Subsistence Economies of the Northern Plains, 1591–1805," Master's thesis, University of Wisconsin–Madison, 1972.   **8481**

Ballas, Donald J., "Early Agriculture and Livestock Raising among the Teton Dakota Indians," *Bulletin of the Illinois Geographical Society*, vol. 15, 2 (1973), pp. 29–39.   **8482**

Moore, Conrad T., "Communication: A Major Reason for Indian Grass Fires in the American West, 1535–1890," *Proceedings of the Association of American Geographers*, vol. 5 (1973), pp. 181–185.   **8483**

Glassner, Martin I., "The Mandan Migrations: Pre-Conquest to 1876," *Journal of the West*, vol. 13, 1 (1974), pp. 25–46.   **8484**

Glassner, Martin I., "The New Mandan Migrations: From Hunting Expeditions to Relocation," *Journal of the West*, vol. 13, 2 (1974), pp. 59–74.   **8485**

Glassner, Martin I., "Population Figures for Mandan Indians," *Indian Historian*, vol. 7, 2 (1974), pp. 41–46. [Focus on 1738–1970]   **8486**

Wishart, David J., "Cultures in Co-operation and Conflict: Indians in the Fur Trade on the Northern Great Plains, 1807–1840," *Journal of Historical Geography*, vol. 2, 4 (1976), pp. 311–328.   **8487**

Barnett, LeRoy, "The Buffalo Bone Commerce of the Northern Great Plains," Ph.D. diss., Michigan State University, 1979.   **8488**

White, Richard, "The Cultural Landscape of the Pawnees," *Great Plains Quarterly*, vol. 2, 1 (1982), pp. 31–40.   **8489**

Ballas, Donald J., "Changing Ecology and Land-Use among the Teton Dakota Indians, 1680–1900," *Bulletin of the Illinois Geographical Society*, vol. 27, 2 (1985), pp. 35–47.   **8490**

Parks, Douglas R., and Waldo R. Wedel, "Pawnee Geography: Historical and Sacred," *Great Plains Quarterly*, vol. 5, 3 (1985), pp. 143–176.   **8491**

Dagel, Kenneth C., "Ethnogeography of Middle Missouri River Indians: 1738–1889," Master's thesis, University of North Dakota, 1988.   **8492**

Native dispossessions

Wishart, David J., "The Dispossession of the Pawnee," *Annals of the Association of American Geographers*, vol. 69, 3 (1979), pp. 382–401.   **8493**

Wishart, David J., "The Pawnee Claims Case, 1947–64," in Imre Sutton, ed., *Irredeemable America: The Indians' Estate and Land Claims* (Albuquerque: University of New Mexico Press, 1986), pp. 157–186.   **8494**

Wishart, David J., "Compensation for Dispossession: Payments to the Indians for Their Lands on the Central and Northern Great Plains in the

Nineteenth Century," *National Geographic Research*, vol. 6, 1 (1990), pp. 94–109.　　8495

EXPLORATION & MAPPING

Exploration

Lewis, G. Malcolm, "Early American Exploration and the Cis-Rocky Mountain Desert, 1803–1823," *Great Plains Journal*, vol. 5, 1 (1965), pp. 1–11.　　8496

Allen, John L., "Lewis and Clark on the Upper Missouri: Decision at the Marias," *Montana*, vol. 21, 3 (1971), pp. 2–17.　　8497

Allen, John L., "Exploration and the Creation of Geographical Images of the Great Plains: Comments on the Role of Subjectivity," in Brian W. Blouet and Merlin P. Lawson, eds., *Images of the Plains: The Role of Human Nature in Settlement* (Lincoln: University of Nebraska Press, 1975), pp. 3–12.　　8498

Mapping

Hamilton, Raphael N., "The Early Cartography of the Missouri Valley," *American Historical Review*, vol. 39, 4 (1934), pp. 645–662.　　8499

Diller, A., "A New Map of the Missouri River Drawn in 1795," *Imago Mundi*, vol. 12 (1955), pp. 175–180.　　8500

Friis, Herman R., "The Role of the United States Topographical Engineers in Compiling a Cartographic Image of the Plains Region," in Brian W. Blouet and Merlin P. Lawson, eds., *Images of the Plains: The Role of Human Nature in Settlement* (Lincoln: University of Nebraska Press, 1975), pp. 59–74.　　8501

Lewis, G. Malcolm, "Changing National Perspectives and the Mapping of the Great Plains between 1785 and 1795," *Cartographica*, vol. 17, 3 (1980), pp. 1–31.　　8502

Allen, John L., "Patterns of Promise: Mapping the Plains and Prairies, 1800–1860," *Great Plains Quarterly*, vol. 4, 1 (1984), pp. 5–28. Reprinted in Frederick C. Luebke, Frances Kaye, and Gary E. Moulton, eds., *Mapping the North American Plains: Essays in the History of Cartography* (Norman: University of Oklahoma Press, 1987), pp. 41–62.　　8503

Lewis, G. Malcolm, "Indian Maps: Their Place in the History of Plains Cartography," *Great Plains Quarterly*, vol. 4, 2 (1984), pp. 91–108. Reprinted in Frederick C. Luebke, Frances Kaye, and Gary E. Moulton, eds., *Mapping the North American Plains: Essays in the History of Cartography*

(Norman: University of Oklahoma Press, 1987), pp. 63–80.　　8504

Wood, W. Raymond, "Mapping the Missouri River through the Great Plains, 1673–1895," *Great Plains Quarterly*, vol. 4, 1 (1984), pp. 29–42. Reprinted in Frederick C. Luebke, Frances Kaye, and Gary E. Moulton, eds., *Mapping the North American Plains: Essays in the History of Cartography* (Norman: University of Oklahoma Press, 1987), pp. 27–40.　　8505

Grim, Ronald E., "Mapping Kansas and Nebraska: The Role of the General Land Office," *Great Plains Quarterly*, vol. 5, 3 (1985), pp. 177–197. Reprinted in Frederick C. Luebke, Frances Kaye, and Gary E. Moulton, eds., *Mapping the North American Plains: Essays in the History of Cartography* (Norman: University of Oklahoma Press, 1987), pp. 127–144.　　8506

Ehrenberg, Ralph E., "Exploratory Mapping of the Great Plains before 1800," in Frederick C. Luebke, Frances Kaye, and Gary E. Moulton, eds., *Mapping the North American Plains: Essays in the History of Cartography* (Norman: University of Oklahoma Press, 1987), pp. 3–26.　　8507

Garver, John B., Jr., "Practical Military Geographers and Mappers of the Trans-Missouri West, 1820–1860," in Frederick C. Luebke, Frances Kaye, and Gary E. Moulton, eds., *Mapping the North American Plains: Essays in the History of Cartography* (Norman: University of Oklahoma Press, 1987), pp. 111–126.　　8508

POPULAR IMAGES & EVALUATION

General

Kollmorgen, Walter M., "Some Geographic Misconceptions of the Climate of Nebraska and the Great Plains," Master's thesis, University of Nebraska, 1933.　　8509

Lewis, G. Malcolm, "Changing Emphases in the Description of the Natural Environment of the American Great Plains Area," *Transactions of the Institute of British Geographers*, vol. 30 (1962), pp. 75–90.　　8510

Lewis, G. Malcolm, "Regional Ideas and Reality in the Cis-Rocky Mountain West," *Transactions of the Institute of British Geographers*, vol. 38 (1966), pp. 135–150.　　8511

Lewis, G. Malcolm, "The Great Plains Region and Its Image of Flatness," *Journal of the West*, vol. 6, 1 (1967), pp. 11–26.　　8512

Bowden, Martyn J., "The Great American Desert and the American Frontier, 1800–1882: Popular Images of the Plains and Places in the Westward Movement," in Tamara K. Hareven, ed.,

Anonymous Americans: Explorations in Nineteenth Century Social History (Englewood Cliffs, N.J.: Prentice-Hall, 1971), pp. 48–79.　　8513

Lawson, Merlin P., "A Behavioralist Interpretation of Pike's Geographical Knowledge of the Interior of the Louisiana Purchase," *Great Plains–Rocky Mountain Geographical Journal*, vol. 1 (1972), pp. 58–64.　　8514

Blouet, Brian W., and Merlin P. Lawson, eds., *Images of the Plains: The Role of Human Nature in Settlement* (Lincoln: University of Nebraska Press, 1975), 214 pp.　　8515

Bowden, Martyn J., "Desert Wheat Belt, Plains Corn Belt: Environment Cognition and Behavior of Settlers in the Plains Margin, 1850–90," in Brian W. Blouet and Merlin P. Lawson, eds., *Images of the Plains: The Role of Human Nature in Settlement* (Lincoln: University of Nebraska Press, 1975), pp. 189–202.　　8516

Davis, John F., "Constructing the British View of the Great Plains," in Brian W. Blouet and Merlin P. Lawson, eds., *Images of the Plains: The Role of Human Nature in Settlement* (Lincoln: University of Nebraska Press, 1975), pp. 181–188.　　8517

Jackson, Richard H., "Mormon Perception and Settlement of the Great Plains," in Brian W. Blouet and Merlin P. Lawson, eds., *Images of the Plains: The Role of Human Nature in Settlement* (Lincoln: University of Nebraska Press, 1975), pp. 137–147.　　8518

Lawson, Merlin P., "Toward a Geosophic Climate of the Great American Desert: The Plains Climate of the Forty-Niners," in Brian W. Blouet and Merlin P. Lawson, eds., *Images of the Plains: The Role of Human Nature in Settlement* (Lincoln: University of Nebraska Press, 1975), pp. 101–114.　　8519

Lewis, G. Malcolm, "The Recognition and Delimitation of the Northern Interior Grasslands during the Eighteenth Century," in Brian W. Blouet and Merlin P. Lawson, eds., *Images of the Plains: The Role of Human Nature in Settlement* (Lincoln: University of Nebraska Press, 1975), pp. 23–44.　　8520

Wishart, David J., "Images of the Northern Great Plains from the Fur Trade, 1807–43," in Brian W. Blouet and Merlin P. Lawson, eds., *Images of the Plains: The Role of Human Nature in Settlement* (Lincoln: University of Nebraska Press, 1975), pp. 45–55.　　8521

Bowden, Martyn J., "The Great American Desert in the American Mind: The Historiography of a Geographical Notion," in David Lowenthal and Martyn J. Bowden, eds., *Geographies of the Mind: Essays in Historical Geosophy in Honor of John Kirtland Wright* (New York: Oxford University Press, 1976), pp. 119–148.　　8522

Lewis, G. Malcolm, "First Impressions of the Great Plains and Prairies," in J. Wreford Watson and Timothy O'Riordan, eds., *The American Environment: Perspectives and Policies* (New York: John Wiley & Sons, 1976), pp. 37–46.　　8523

Lawson, Merlin P., and Charles Stockton, "Desert Myth and Climatic Reality," *Annals of the Association of American Geographers*, vol. 71, 4 (1981), pp. 527–535.　　8524

Allen, John L., "The Garden-Desert Continuum: Competing Views of the Great Plains in the Nineteenth Century," *Great Plains Quarterly*, vol. 5, 4 (1985), pp. 207–220.　　8525

Image-makers

Lewis, G. Malcolm, "William Gilpin and the Concept of the Great Plains Region," *Annals of the Association of American Geographers*, vol. 56, 1 (1966), pp. 33–51.　　8526

Carlson, Alvar W., "Roosevelt and the Badlands: The Persistence of Error in Geographic Location," *Journal of the West*, vol. 9, 4 (1970), pp. 469–486. [Focus on North and South Dakota]　　8527

Baltensperger, Bradley H., "Plains Promoters and Plain Folk: Pre-Migration and Post-Settlement Images of the Central Great Plains," Ph.D. diss., Clark University, 1975.　　8528

Communicating imagery

Wyckoff, William K., "The Garden and the Desert in the Imaginative Literature of the Great Plains," *Proceedings of the Middle States Division, Association of American Geographers*, vol. 12 (1978), pp. 94–97.　　8529

Lewis, G. Malcolm, "The Cognition and Communication of Former Ideas about the Great Plains," in Brian W. Blouet and Frederick C. Luebke, eds., *The Great Plains: Environment and Culture* (Lincoln: University of Nebraska Press, 1979), pp. 27–42.　　8530

Baltensperger, Bradley H., "Newspaper Images of the Central Great Plains in the Late Nineteenth Century," *Journal of the West*, vol. 19, 2 (1980), pp. 64–70. Reprinted in William H. Lyon, ed., *Journalism in the West* (Manhattan, Kans.: Sunflower University Press, 1980), pp. 64–70.　　8531

Jeffrey, Julie Roy, "'There is Some Splendid Scenery': Women's Responses to the Great Plains Landscape," *Great Plains Quarterly*, vol. 8, 2 (1988), pp. 69–78.　　8532

Influence of imagery on settlement behavior

Dopson, Eileen H., "Nineteenth Century Images of the Northern Plains: Impacts on Settlement Patterns," Master's thesis, University of North Dakota, 1979. **8533**

REGIONAL SETTLEMENT

See also 1320, 1334

Wishart, David J., "The Changing Position and Nature of the Frontier of Settlement on the Eastern Margins of the Northern and Central Great Plains, 1854–1920," Master's thesis, University of Nebraska, 1968. **8534**

Wishart, David J., "The Changing Position of the Frontier of Settlement on the Eastern Margins of the Central and Northern Great Plains, 1840–1890," *Professional Geographer*, vol. 21, 3 (1969), pp. 153–157. **8535**

Hewes, Leslie, "Siedlung und Landnutzung in den Great Plains (USA)," *Geographische Rundschau*, vol. 23, 10 (1971), pp. 385–399. **8536**

Hudson, John C., "Two Dakota Homestead Frontiers," *Annals of the Association of American Geographers*, vol. 63, 4 (1973), pp. 442–462. [Bowman Co., North Dakota; and Sanborn Co., South Dakota] **8537**

Blouet, Brian W., and Frederick C. Luebke, eds., *The Great Plains: Environment and Culture* (Lincoln: University of Nebraska Press, 1979), 246 pp. **8538**

Roet, Jeffrey B., "Agricultural Settlement on the Dry Farming Frontier, 1900–1920," Ph.D. diss., Northwestern University, 1982. **8539**

Wishart, David J., "Settling the Great Plains, 1850–1930," in Robert D. Mitchell and Paul A. Groves, eds., *North America: The Historical Geography of a Changing Continent* (Totowa, N.J.: Rowman & Littlefield, 1987), pp. 255–278. **8540**

POPULATION

Wishart, David J., A. Warren, and Robert H. Stoddard, "An Attempted Definition of a Frontier Using a Wave Analogy," *Rocky Mountain Social Science Journal*, vol. 6 (1969), pp. 73–81. **8541**

Westfall, John E., "The Demographic Inflection: Iowa and Nebraska," *Proceedings of the Association of American Geographers*, vol. 2 (1970), pp. 149–152. **8542**

Joyes, Aldon W., "The Great Plains: Source Areas and Destinations of Interstate Migrants, 1940–1970," Master's thesis, Bowling Green State University, 1974. **8543**

Hudson, John C., "Who Was 'Forest-Man?' Sources of Migration to the Plains," *Great Plains Quarterly*, vol. 6, 2 (1986), pp. 69–83. **8544**

RURAL & REGIONAL SOCIAL GEOGRAPHY

See also 9138

Allen, Agnes M., "Domestic Economy of the Prairie Pioneers," Master's thesis, Clark University, 1934. **8545**

Nelson, Helge M. O., "Svensk nybyggesveksambet: Nebraska och Dakota-staterna," *Svensk geografisk årsbok*, vol. 14 (1938), pp. 174–191. **8546**

Luebke, Frederick C., ed., *Ethnicity on the Great Plains* (Lincoln: University of Nebraska Press, 1980), 237 pp. **8547**

Manzo, Joseph T., "Native Americans, Euro-Americans: Some Shared Attitudes towards Life in the Prairies," *American Studies*, vol. 23, 2 (1982), pp. 39–48. **8548**

Baltensperger, Bradley H., "Germans on the Great Plains: Environment and Acculturation," *Marburger Geographische Schriften*, vol. 96 (1985), pp. 220–232. **8549**

Shortridge, James R., "Cowboy, Yeoman, Pawn, and Hick: Myth and Contradictions in Great Plains Life," *Focus* (American Geographical Society), vol. 35, 4 (1985), pp. 22–27. **8550**

Riley, Glenda, *The Female Frontier: A Comparative View of Women on the Prairie and the Plains* (Lawrence: University Press of Kansas, 1988), 299 pp. **8551**

Shortridge, James R., "The Heart of the Prairie: Culture Areas in the Central and Northern Great Plains," *Great Plains Quarterly*, vol. 8, 4 (1988), pp. 206–221. **8552**

POLITICAL & ADMINISTRATIVE GEOGRAPHY

See also 1389

Freedom, Gary S., "U.S. Military Forts on the Northern Great Plains, 1866–1891: An Historical Geography," Ph.D. diss., University of Tennessee, 1976. **8553**

Wade, Arthur P., "The Military Command Structure: The Great Plains, 1853–1891," *Journal of the West*, vol. 15, 3 (1976), pp. 5–22. **8554**

Freedom, Gary S., "Military Forts and Logistical Self-Sufficiency on the Northern Great Plains, 1866–1891," *North Dakota History*, vol. 50, 2 (1983), pp. 4–11. **8555**

Freedom, Gary S., "Moving Men and Supplies: Military Transportation on the Northern Great Plains, 1866–1891," *South Dakota History*, vol. 14, 2 (1984), pp. 114–133. 8556

ECONOMIC DEVELOPMENT

See also 1400

Freedom, Gary S., "Economic Impact of Military Forts on the Northern Great Plains, 1866–91," *McNeese Review*, vol. 24 (1977–1978), pp. 40–49. 8557

Osborne, Brian S., "The Kansas-Colorado Power and Railroad Project: A Multi-Functional Plan for the Development of the Arkansas Valley," *Pioneer America*, vol. 6, 2 (1974), pp. 22–33. 8558

Windhorst, Hans-Wilhelm, "Wandlungen in der wirtschaftlichen Inwertsetzung der nordamerikanischen Prärien und Great Plains," *Zeitschrift für Wirtschaftsgeographie*, vol. 21, 1 (1977), pp. 4–15. 8559

RESOURCE MANAGEMENT

See also 1405

Hewes, Leslie, "The Conservation Reserve of the American Soil Bank as an Indicator of Regions of Maladjustment in Agriculture, with Particular Reference to the Great Plains," in Erhart Winkler and Herwig Lechleitner, eds., *Beiträge zur Wirtschaftsgeographie: Festschrift Leopold G. Scheidl zum 60. Geburtstag*, vol. 2 (Wien: Wiener Geographische Schriften, vols. 43–48, 1967), pp. 331–346. 8560

Lewis, Michael E., "The National Grasslands in the Old Dust Bowl: A Long Term Evaluation of Agricultural Adjustment through Landscape Change," Ph.D. diss., University of Oklahoma, 1988. 8561

Lewis, Michael E., "National Grasslands in the Dust Bowl," *Geographical Review*, vol. 79, 2 (1989), pp. 161–171. [Focus on the twentieth century] 8562

LAND & LAND USE

Roet, Jeffrey B., "Land Quality and Land Alienation on the Dry Farming Frontier," *Professional Geographer*, vol. 37, 2 (1985), pp. 173–182. 8563

Baltensperger, Bradley H., "Farm Consolidation in the Northern and Central States of the Great Plains," *Great Plains Quarterly*, vol. 7, 4 (1987), pp. 256–265. 8564

EXTRACTIVE ACTIVITY

Guthe, Otto E., "The Black Hills of South Dakota and Wyoming," *Papers of the Michigan Academy of Science, Arts, and Letters*, vol. 20 (1934), pp. 343–376. 8565

Wishart, David J., "An Historical Geography of the Fur Trade on the Upper Missouri, 1807–1843," Ph.D. diss., University of Nebraska, 1971. 8566

Chambers, Robert W., "The Changing Geography of the Fur Trade in the Upper Missouri Country before 1835," Master's thesis, University of British Columbia, 1980. 8567

AGRICULTURE

See also 1415

General

Baker, Oliver E., "Agricultural Regions of North America: Part VI—The Spring Wheat Region," *Economic Geography*, vol. 4, 4 (1928), pp. 399–433. 8568

Kollmorgen, Walter M., "The Woodsman's Assaults on the Domain of the Cattleman," *Annals of the Association of American Geographers*, vol. 59, 2 (1969), pp. 215–239. Reprinted in Barbara Gutmann Rosenkrantz and William A. Koelsch, eds., *American Habitat: A Historical Perspective* (New York: Free Press, 1973), pp. 187–217. 8569

Wishart, David J., "Agriculture at the Trading Posts on the Upper Missouri Prior to 1843," *Agricultural History*, vol. 47, 1 (1973), pp. 57–62. 8570

Baltensperger, Bradley H., "Agricultural Adjustments to Great Plains Drought, 1870–1990," in Brian W. Blouet and Frederick C. Luebke, eds., *The Great Plains: Environment and Culture* (Lincoln: University of Nebraska Press, 1979), pp. 43–60. 8571

Hewes, Leslie, "Agricultural Risk in the Great Plains," in Brian W. Blouet and Frederick C. Luebke, eds., *The Great Plains: Environment and Culture* (Lincoln: University of Nebraska Press, 1979), pp. 157–186. 8572

Rickard, Timothy J., "The Great Plains as Part of an Irrigated Western Empire," in Brian W. Blouet and Frederick C. Luebke, eds., *The Great Plains: Environment and Culture* (Lincoln: University of Nebraska Press, 1979), pp. 81–98. 8573

Baltensperger, Bradley H., "Agricultural Change among Great Plains Russian Germans," *Annals of the Association of American Geographers*, vol. 73, 1 (1983), pp. 75–88. 8574

Cattle

Prator, Moina M., "The Development of the Cattle Industry of the Great Plains," Master's thesis, University of Chicago, 1918. 8575

Post, Lauren C., "The Upgrading of Beef Cattle on the Great Plains," *California Geographer*, vol. 2, 1 (1961), pp. 1–8.   8576

Wheeler, David L., "The Origin and Development of the Cattle Feeding Industry in the Southern High Plains," *Panhandle-Plains Historical Review*, vol. 49 (1976), pp. 81–90.   8577

Cultivation

Baker, Oliver E., "The Agriculture of the Great Plains Region," *Annals of the Association of American Geographers*, vol. 13, 3 (1923), pp. 110–167.   8578

Tideman, Philip L., "Wheat on the Northern Agricultural Frontier, 1840–1920," Ph.D. diss., University of Nebraska, 1967.   8579

Roet, Jeffrey B, "Agriculture on the Dry Farming Frontier, 1900–1920," *Bulletin of the Association of North Dakota Geographers*, vol. 29 (1979), pp. 19–35.   8580

Sidewalk & suitcase farming

Kollmorgen, Walter M., and George F. Jenks, "Sidewalk Farming in Toole County, Montana, and Traill County, North Dakota," *Annals of the Association of American Geographers*, vol. 48, 3 (1958), pp. 209–231.   8581

Hewes, Leslie, *The Suitcase Farming Frontier: A Study in the Historical Geography of the Central Great Plains* (Lincoln: University of Nebraska Press, 1973), 281 pp.   8582

Hewes, Leslie, "Early Suitcase Farming in the Central Great Plains," *Agricultural History*, vol. 51, 1 (1977), pp. 23–37.   8583

LANDSCAPE

General

Hewes, Leslie, "Transformation of an Agrarian Landscape: The Suitcase-Farming Frontier of the Central Great Plains," in W. P. Adams and F. M. Helleiner, eds., *International Geography 1972*, vol. 1, sec. 5, *Historical Geography* (Toronto: University of Toronto Press, for the International Geographical Union, 1972), pp. 432–434.   8584

Housing

Mears, Louise Wilhelmina, "The Sod House as a Form of Shelter: Where? What? Why?" *Journal of Geography*, vol. 14, 10 (1916), pp. 385–389. 8585

Gates, Donald S., "The Sod House," *Journal of Geography*, vol. 32, 9 (1933), pp. 353–359. Reprinted in George J. Miller, ed., *Human Geography Studies: The United States* (Bloomington,

Ill.: McKnight & McKnight, Geographic Education Series, 1935), pp. 209–215.   8586

Shortridge, James R., "Traditional Rural Houses along the Missouri-Kansas Border," *Journal of Cultural Geography*, vol. 1, 1 (1980), pp. 105–137.   8587

Noble, Allen G., "Pioneer Settlement on the Plains: Sod Dugouts and Sod Houses," *Pioneer America Society Transactions*, vol. 4 (1981), pp. 11–19.   8588

Shortridge, James R., "Some Relationships Between External Housing Characteristics and House Types," *Pioneer America*, vol. 13, 2 (1981), pp. 1–28. [Kansas-Missouri border area]   8589

Trees and shelterbelts

Lang, James B., "The Shelterbelt Project in the Southern Great Plains, 1934–1970: A Geographic Appraisal," Master's thesis, University of Oklahoma, 1971.   8590

Ferrill, Martha Jean Williams, "The Myth of Tree Planting on the Great Plains," Ph.D. diss., University of Nebraska–Lincoln, 1988.   8591

COMMUNICATIONS & TRADE

See also 1432

Gard, Wayne, "Retracing the Chisholm Trail," *Southwestern Historical Quarterly*, vol. 60, 1 (1956), pp. 53–68.   8592

Thaller, Michael L., "Structure and Process in Railroad Network Development under Competition: The Case of the Granger Railroads," Ph.D. diss., University of Wisconsin–Milwaukee, 1973. 8593

Murphey, Frances A., "Steam Navigation and Trade Networks on the Upper Missouri River, 1819–1887: A Primary Factor in the Development of the Northern Plains," Master's thesis, San Francisco State University, 1982.   8594

Kirby, Russell S., "Nineteenth-Century Patterns of Railroad Development on the Great Plains," *Great Plains Quarterly*, vol. 3, 3 (1983), pp. 157–170.   8595

Baruth, Wilma F., "Straight as the Crow Flies: Historical Geography of the Kansas City Southern Railway Company," Master's thesis, Kansas State University, 1986.   8596

URBAN NETWORKS & URBANIZATION

Hudson, John C., "The Plains Country Town," in Brian W. Blouet and Frederick C. Luebke, eds., *The Great Plains: Environment and Culture* (Lincoln: University of Nebraska Press, 1979), pp. 99–118.   8597

Hudson, John C., "Towns of the Western Railroads," *Great Plains Quarterly*, vol. 2, 1 (1982), pp. 41–54.   **8598**

Larsen, Lawrence, and Roger Johnson, "Obstacles to Urbanization on the Northern Great Plains of the United States," *North Dakota History*, vol. 50, 3 (1983), pp. 14–22.   **8599**

Hudson, John C., *Plains Country Towns* (Minneapolis: University of Minnesota Press, 1985), 189 pp.   **8600**

Hudson, John C., "New Grain Networks in an Old Urban System," in John Fraser Hart, ed., *Our Changing Cities* (Baltimore: Johns Hopkins University Press, 1991), pp. 86–107.   **8601**

PLANNING

Quinn, M.-L., "Federal Drought Planning in the Great Plains: A First Look," *Climatic Change*, vol. 4, 3 (1982), pp. 273–296.   **8602**

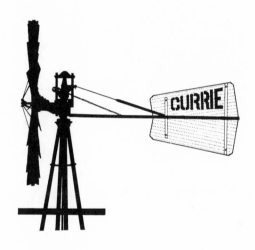

NORTH DAKOTA

GENERAL

Babcock, Harold E., "The Historical Geography of Devil's Lake, North Dakota," Master's thesis, University of Washington, 1952.   8603

NATIVE PEOPLES & WHITE RELATIONS

See 8527

POPULAR IMAGES & EVALUATION

See 1307, 8527

REGIONAL SETTLEMENT

See also 8537

Wangberg, Louis M., "The Historical Geography of Selected Farms in the Larimore, North Dakota, Area," Master's thesis, University of North Dakota, 1966.   8604

Johnson, Gary E., "Settlement of the Land," *Bulletin of the Association of North Dakota Geographers*, vol. 27 (1977), pp. 13–18.   8605

Vyzralek, Frank E., "The Use of Federal Census Data as an Aid to Determining Settlement Patterns in North Dakota, 1880–1920," *Bulletin of the Association of North Dakota Geographers*, vol. 28 (1978), pp. 68–72.   8606

POPULATION

Connor, T. Dwight, "The Population of North Dakota from 1890 to 1960: A Geographical Study," Master's thesis, University of North Dakota, 1963.   8607

Sherman, William C., "Ethnic Distribution in Western North Dakota," *North Dakota History*, vol. 46, 1 (1979), pp. 4–12.   8608

RURAL & REGIONAL SOCIAL GEOGRAPHY

See 8546

ECONOMIC DEVELOPMENT

Carlson, Alvar W., "Lignite Coal as an Enabling Factor in the Settlement of Western North Dakota," *Great Plains Journal*, vol. 11, 2 (1972), pp. 145–153.   8609

Hudson, John C., "North Dakota's Frontier Fuels," *Bulletin of the Association of North Dakota Geographers*, vol. 28 (1978), pp. 1–15.   8610

LAND & LAND USE

Schimmer, James R., "A Geography of Tree Claims in Grand Forks County, North Dakota," Master's thesis, University of North Dakota, 1989.   8611

AGRICULTURE

See also 8581

Johnson, Gary E., "The Bonanza Farms and Cattle Empires: Exploitation of North Dakota's Land Resource Base," *Bulletin of the Association of North Dakota Geographers*, vol. 27 (1977), pp. 19–26.   8612

LANDSCAPE

Hudson, John C., "Frontier Housing in North Dakota," *North Dakota History*, vol. 42, 1 (1975), pp. 4–15.   8613

Carlson, Alvar W., "German-Russian Houses in Western North Dakota," *Pioneer America*, vol. 13, 2 (1981), pp. 49–60.   8614

COMMUNICATIONS & TRADE

Hudson, John C., "North Dakota's Railway War of 1905," *North Dakota History*, vol. 48, 1 (1981), pp. 4–19.   8615

URBAN NETWORKS & URBANIZATION

Troseth, Christopher, "A Study of the Growth and Decline of North Dakota Towns, 1920–1970," Master's thesis, University of North Dakota, 1980.   8616

URBAN ECONOMIC STRUCTURE

Mower, Roland D., "North Dakota Central Places, 1870–1920: Land Use Changes and Expanding Opportunities," *Bulletin of the Association of North Dakota Geographers*, vol. 27 (1977), pp. 41–51.   8617

PLACE NAMES

Williams, Mary A., *Origins of North Dakota Place Names* (Washburn, N.Dak.: Bismark Tribune, 1966), 354 pp.   8618

Wick, Douglas A., *North Dakota Place Names* (Fargo: Prairie House, 1988), 239 pp.   8619

SOUTH DAKOTA

GENERAL

The state

Visher, Stephen S., "Historical Geography or the Evolution of Present Conditions," in his *The Geography of South Dakota* (Vermillion: University of South Dakota, South Dakota State Geological and Natural History Survey, Bulletin no. 8, 1918), pp. 129–162. **8620**

Smaller areas

Edwards, Mildred M. L., "The Historical Geography of the Black Hills," Master's thesis, University of Oklahoma, 1958. **8621**

Gritzner, Charles F., "Physical Geography," in *Brookings County History* (Freeman, S.Dak.: Pine Hill Press, 1989), pp. 1–6. **8622**

ENVIRONMENTAL CHANGE

Hillestad, Linda K., "The Changing Impact of Natural Disasters in Brookings County, South Dakota," Master's thesis, South Dakota State University, 1982. **8623**

Brown, Richard, "The Enduring Frontier: The Impact of Weather on South Dakota History and Literature," *South Dakota History*, vol. 15, 1 & 2 (1985), pp. 26–57. **8624**

Borkowski, Ralph, "The Original Survey Notes of Beadle County as a Geographical Reference," Master's thesis, South Dakota State University, 1987. **8625**

NATIVE PEOPLES & WHITE RELATIONS

See also **8480**

Coleman, John M., "The Missouri Valley of South Dakota: Its Human Geography at Euro-American Contact," Ph.D. diss., Indiana University, 1968. **8626**

Vogeler, Ingolf K., and Terry Simmons, "Settlement Morphology of South Dakota Indian Reservations," *Yearbook of the Association of Pacific Coast Geographers*, vol. 37 (1975), pp. 91–108. **8627**

Alex, Lynn Marie, "Prehistoric and Early Historic Farming and Settlement Patterns," *South Dakota History*, vol. 13, 1 & 2 (1983), pp. 4–21. **8628**

POPULAR IMAGES & EVALUATION

See also **8527**

Ward, Freeman, "South Dakota and Some Misapprehensions," *Geographical Review*, vol. 17, 2 (1927), pp. 236–250. **8629**

REGIONAL SETTLEMENT

See also **8537**

Hamburg, James F., "The Influence of Railroads upon the Processes and Patterns of Settlement in South Dakota," Ph.D. diss., University of North Carolina, 1968. **8630**

Ballas, Donald J., "A Cultural Geography of Todd County, South Dakota, and the Rosebud Sioux Indian Reservation," Ph.D. diss., University of Nebraska, 1970. **8631**

Hamburg, James F., "Railroads and the Settlement of South Dakota during the Great Dakota Boom, 1878–1887," *Great Plains–Rocky Mountain Geographical Journal*, vol. 1 (1972), pp. 40–45. Republished, with additions, in *South Dakota History*, vol. 5, 2 (1975), pp. 165–178. **8632**

Smith, James R., "Homesteading in South Dakota: The Andersons in Stanley County," *Bulletin of the Association of North Dakota Geographers*, vol. 28 (1978), pp. 27–54. **8633**

Hamburg, James F., *The Influence of Railroads upon the Processes and Patterns of Settlement in South Dakota* (New York: Arno Press, 1981), 487 pp. **8634**

Ostergren, Robert C., "Settlement and Ethnicity Patterns on the Agricultural Frontiers of South Dakota," *South Dakota History*, vol. 13, 1 & 2 (1983), pp. 49–82. **8635**

Anderson, Scott A., "South Dakota Hutterites: A Study in Diffusion and Settlement," Master's thesis, Brigham Young University, 1987. **8636**

Lockwood, Catherine M., "South Dakota's Evolving Settlement Landscape: Primary Factors of Site Selection," Master's thesis, South Dakota State University, 1989. **8637**

POPULATION

Rahim, Abdur, "Population Trends in South Dakota Counties, 1880–1890: A Geographical Analysis," Master's thesis, South Dakota State University, 1987. **8638**

RURAL & REGIONAL SOCIAL GEOGRAPHY

See also 1371, 8546

Landis, Paul H., *South Dakota Town-Country Relations, 1901–1931* (Brookings: South Dakota State College Agricultural Experiment Station, Bulletin no. 274, 1932), 47 pp.   8639

Cobb, Douglas S., "The Jamesville Bruderhof: A Hutterian Agricultural Colony," *Journal of the West*, vol. 9, 1 (1970), pp. 60–77.   8640

Ostergren, Robert C., "Prairie Bound: Migration Patterns to a Swedish Settlement on the Dakota Frontier," in Frederick C. Luebke, ed., *Ethnicity on the Great Plains* (Lincoln: University of Nebraska Press, 1980), pp. 73–91. [Dalesburg, Clay Co.]   8641

POLITICAL & ADMINISTRATIVE GEOGRAPHY

Visher, Stephen S., "Geographic Influence Affecting the Choice of South Dakota's Boundaries," *South Dakota Historical Collections*, vol. 9 (1918), pp. 380–385.   8642

LAND & LAND USE

Salonen, Debra, "Taking Hold: A Study of Land Acquisition, Land Ownership, and Community Development in Northeast Brookings County (1876–1916)," Master's thesis, South Dakota State University, 1977.   8643

EXTRACTIVE ACTIVITY

See also 8565

Guthe, Otto E., "Lead and Rapid City: A Study of Contrasting Settlements within the Black Hills Region," *Papers of the Michigan Academy of Science, Arts, and Letters*, vol. 18 (1932), pp. 143–155.   8644

Kovates, Julius A., "Black Hills Gold Mining, 1876–1935: Toward a Time-Space Model," Ph.D. diss., University of Oklahoma, 1978.   8645

AGRICULTURE

Lee, Chak Po, "Frontier Agriculture, 1880–1910: An Investigation of Human and Environmental Factors in the Process of Agricultural Evolution in Davison County, South Dakota," Master's thesis, South Dakota State University, 1986. 8646

URBAN NETWORKS & URBANIZATION

Ruth, Gerald D., "Market Hierarchies in South Dakota: A Study in History and Spatial Analyses," Ph.D. diss., Indiana University, 1972.   8647

Hamburg, James F., "Papertowns in South Dakota," *Journal of the West*, vol. 16, 1 (1977), pp. 40–42.   8648

Year, Peggy E., "Ghost Towns in South Dakota: A Geographic Perspective," Master's thesis, South Dakota State University, 1981.   8649

TOWN GROWTH

Wade, Louise C., "Small-Town Survival on the Great Plains: Miller, Dakota Territory, in the 1880s," *South Dakota History*, vol. 16, 4 (1986), pp. 317–350.   8650

Gao, Jianling, "The Development of the City of Volga, South Dakota," Master's thesis, University of South Dakota, 1990.   8651

PLACE NAMES

Writers' Program, *South Dakota Place-Names* (Vermillion: University of South Dakota, for the Works Project Administration, 1940), unpaged.   8652

Hamburg, James F., "Postmasters' Names and South Dakota Place-Names," *Names*, vol. 21, 1 (1973), pp. 59–64.   8653

NEBRASKA

GENERAL

The state

Condra, George E., "Geographic Influences in the Development of Nebraska," *Journal of Geography*, vol. 9, 4 (1910), pp. 85–92.   8654

Luebke, Frederick C., "Time, Place, and Culture in Nebraska History," *Nebraska History*, vol. 69, 4 (1988), pp. 150–168.   8655

Smaller areas

Mears, Louise Wilhelmina, "Some Geographical Influences in the Development of Southeastern Nebraska: Nemaha County in Particular," Master's thesis, University of Nebraska, 1912.   8656

Brand, Donald D., *The History of Scotts Bluff, Nebraska* (Berkeley: National Park Service, Field Division of Education, 1934), 83 pp.   8657

McKinley, John L., "The Influence of the Platte River upon the History of the Valley," Ph.D. diss., University of Nebraska, 1935.   8658

Heathcote, Ronald L., "The Historical Geography of Two Nebraska Counties," Master's thesis, University of Nebraska, 1959.   8659

ENVIRONMENTAL CHANGE

Schmieding, Arthur C., "Geographic Patterns of Failure of Wheat and Corn in Nebraska, 1931–1952," Master's thesis, University of Nebraska, 1954.   8660

Lawson, Merlin P., et al., *Nebraska Droughts: A Study of Their Past Chronological and Spatial Extent with Implications for the Future* (Lincoln: University of Nebraska Department of Geography Occasional Paper no. 1, 1977), 147 pp.   8661

NATIVE PEOPLES & WHITE RELATIONS

Gilmore, Melvin R., "A Glimpse at Nebraska Indian Geography," *Journal of Geography*, vol. 13, 6 (1915), pp. 179–185.   8662

EXPLORATION & MAPPING

See also 8506

McIntosh, C. Barron, "The Route of a Sand Hills Bone Hunt: The Yale College Expedition of 1870," *Nebraska History*, vol. 69, 2 (1988), pp. 84–94.   8663

POPULAR IMAGES & EVALUATION

See also 8509

Bowen, Marshall E., "Changes in Resource Evaluation as Keys to Selected Aspects of Geographic Change: The Case of Sheridan County, Nebraska, 1875–1925," Ph.D. diss., Boston University, 1970.   8664

Bowen, Marshall E., "Environmental Perception and Geographic Change in Southwest Sheridan County," *Nebraska History*, vol. 51, 3 (1970), pp. 319–338.   8665

Bowen, Marshall E., "Environment and Perception: Some Insights into Geographic Change in the Westernmost Nebraska Sandhills," *Pennsylvania Geographer*, vol. 9, 1 (1971), pp. 6–14.   8666

Bowen, Marshall E., "Cognitive Factors and Utilization of the Nebraska Potash Lakes," *Bulletin of the Illinois Geographical Society*, vol. 14, 1 (1972), pp. 3–13.   8667

Krone, Patricia L., "The Humanistic Perspective in Historical Geography: Willa Cather's Nebraska, 1880–1970," *Ohio Geographers: Recent Research Themes*, vol. 7 (1979), pp. 41–46.   8668

REGIONAL SETTLEMENT

McKim, V. Calvin, "The Geography of the Pine Ridge Country of Nebraska," Ph.D. diss., University of Nebraska–Lincoln, 1934.   8669

Jenkins, George R., "Settlement of the Nebraska Section of the Great Plains," Master's thesis, University of Wisconsin, 1938.   8670

Richardson, C. Howard, "The Nebraska Prairies: Dilemma to Early Territorial Farmers," *Nebraska History*, vol. 50, 4 (1969), pp. 359–372. 8671

Bellovich, Steven J., "A Geographic Appraisal of Settlement within the Union Pacific Land Grant in Eastern Nebraska, 1869–1890," Ph.D. diss., University of Nebraska–Lincoln, 1974.   8672

Davis, John F., "The Role of the Railroad in the Settling of Nebraska, 1860–1900," in Robert G. Ironside et al., eds., *Frontier Settlement* (Edmonton: University of Alberta Department of Geography, 1974), pp. 164–177.   8673

Piellusch, Frederick B., "The Great American Desert and Nebraska Settlement," *Proceedings of the Middle States Division, Association of*

American Geographers, vol. 11 (1977), pp. 10–15.
8674

Baltensperger, Bradley H., "Settlement: Occupance, Utilization, and Adaptation," in his *Nebraska: A Geography* (Boulder: Westview Press, 1984), pp. 37–68.
8675

Rumney, Thomas A., "Salt and Settlement in Nineteenth-Century Nebraska," *Material Culture*, vol. 16, 1 (1984), pp. 43–54.
8676

Clark, Robert D., "The Settlement of Blackwood Township, Hayes County, Nebraska, 1878–1907," *Nebraska History*, vol. 66, 1 (1985), pp. 74–110.
8677

POPULATION

See also 8542

Anderson, Esther S., "The Significance of Some Population Changes in Nebraska since 1880," *Journal of Geography*, vol. 21, 7 (1922), pp. 254–263.
8678

Hinkle, Edmund D., "Changing Pattern of Population Distribution in Nebraska, 1930–1960," Master's thesis, University of Nebraska, 1963.
8679

Larson, Albert J., and Siim Sööt, "The Use of Population Centers of Gravity in Historical Geographic Analysis: The Nebraska Case," *Geographical Perspectives*, vol. 32 (1973), pp. 23–34.
8680

Wishart, David J., "The Age and Sex Composition of the Population on the Nebraska Frontier, 1860–1880," *Nebraska History*, vol. 54, 1 (1973), pp. 107–119.
8681

Bremer, Richard G., "Patterns of Spatial Mobility: A Case Study of Nebraska Farmers, 1890–1970," *Agricultural History*, vol. 48, 4 (1974), pp. 529–542.
8682

Barndt, Paul E., "Some Characteristics of the Farm Population in Nebraska Territory, 1854–1860," Master's thesis, University of Nebraska–Omaha, 1977.
8683

Baltensperger, Bradley H., "Population: Sources, Characteristics, and Trends," in his *Nebraska: A Geography* (Boulder: Westview Press, 1984), pp. 69–78.
8684

RURAL & REGIONAL SOCIAL GEOGRAPHY

See also 8546

Stoddard, Robert H., "Changing Patterns of Some Rural Churches," *Rocky Mountain Social Science Journal*, vol. 7, 1 (1970), pp. 61–68. [Nemaha Co., 1850–1965]
8685

Gerlach, Jerry D., "The Changing Role of the Tavern in the Cultural Landscape of Rural Ne-

braska," Ph.D. diss., University of Oklahoma, 1974.
8686

Baltensperger, Bradley H., "Agricultural Change among Nebraska Immigrants, 1880–1900," in Frederick C. Luebke, ed., *Ethnicity on the Great Plains* (Lincoln: University of Nebraska Press, 1980), pp. 170–189. Reprinted in *Journal of the American Historical Society of Germans from Russia*, vol. 5, 4 (1982), pp. 40–48.
8687

Gerlach, Jerry D., "The Frontier Saloon: A Nebraska Study," *Ecumene*, vol. 13, 1 (1981), pp. 4–11.
8688

ECONOMIC DEVELOPMENT

Melvin, Earl E., "The Geographic Factors Operative in the Development of Hall County, Nebraska," Master's thesis, University of Nebraska, 1926.
8689

LAND & LAND USE

Land survey

Richardson, C. Howard, "Early Settlement of Eastern Nebraska Territory: A Geographical Study Based on the Original Land Survey," Ph.D. diss., University of Nebraska–Lincoln, 1968.
8690

Land tenure

Bowen, Marshall E., "The Kinkaid Act and the Southern Sheridan County Sandhills of Nebraska," *Rocky Mountain Social Science Journal*, vol. 9, 1 (1972), pp. 39–49.
8691

McIntosh, C. Barron, "Forest Lieu Selections in the Sand Hills of Nebraska," *Annals of the Association of American Geographers*, vol. 64, 1 (1974), pp. 87–99. [Focus on 1897–1905]
8692

McIntosh, C. Barron, "Patterns from Land Alienation Maps," *Annals of the Association of American Geographers*, vol. 66, 4 (1976), pp. 570–582. [Sandhills, 1879–1915]
8693

McIntosh, C. Barron, "One Man's Sequential Land Alienation on the Great Plains," *Geographical Review*, vol. 71, 4 (1981), pp. 427–445. [Sheridan Co., 1884–1907]
8694

Egbert, Stephen L., "The Resettlement of Nance County: Land Alienation Patterns, 1878–1913," Master's thesis, University of Nebraska, 1983.
8695

Brooks, Helen, "Land Alienation Patterns in the Nebraska Sand Hills South of the Platte: A Geographic Analysis of Public Land Disposal, 1870–1904," Master's thesis, University of Nebraska–Lincoln, 1986.
8696

Land use

Sherfey, Christine G., "The Evolution of Land Utilization in the Nebraska Panhandle," Master's thesis, University of Chicago, 1941. 8697

Bowden, Martyn J., "The Changes of Land Use of Jefferson County, Nebraska, 1857–1957," Master's thesis, University of Nebraska–Lincoln, 1959. 8698

Albrecht, Horst D., "Agricultural Land Use Change in Cass County, Nebraska, 1860–1970," Master's thesis, University of Nebraska–Omaha, 1972. 8699

Piellusch, Frederick B., "Frontier and Settled Land Use in Nebraska, 1880–1885," Ph.D. diss., University of Nebraska–Lincoln, 1974. 8700

AGRICULTURE

Hewes, Leslie, and Arthur C. Schmieding, "Risk in the Central Great Plains: Geographical Patterns of Wheat Failure in Nebraska, 1931–52," *Geographical Review*, vol. 46, 3 (1956), pp. 375–387. 8701

Hewes, Leslie, "Wheat Failure in Western Nebraska, 1931–54," *Annals of the Association of American Geographers*, vol. 48, 4 (1958), pp. 375–397. 8702

Brandhorst, L. Carl, "The North Platte Oasis: Notes on the Geography and History of an Irrigated District," *Agricultural History*, vol. 51, 1 (1977), pp. 166–172. 8703

LANDSCAPE

Riedesel, Gordon, "The Geography of Saunders County Rural Cemeteries from 1859," *Nebraska History*, vol. 61, 2 (1980), pp. 215–228. 8704

COMMUNICATIONS & TRADE

Pioneer trails

Krouch, Mildred, "The Geography of the Oregon Trail in Nebraska," Master's thesis, University of Nebraska, 1933. 8705

Steele, Olga, "The Geography of the Mormon Trail across Nebraska," Master's thesis, University of Nebraska, 1933. 8706

Railroads

Hanson, Raus M., "The Relationship of Geographic Factors to Railway Developments in Nebraska," Master's thesis, University of Nebraska, 1927. 8707

Newspapers

Duhaime, Paula J., "Making Nowhere Somewhere: Newspapers as Indicators of Settlement in Nineteenth-Century Nebraska," Ph.D. diss., Pennsylvania State University, 1986. 8708

URBAN NETWORKS & URBANIZATION

Larson, Albert J., "The Hamlets of Nebraska," Ph.D. diss., University of Nebraska–Lincoln, 1969. 8709

Ward, Denis M., "A Spatial Analysis of County Seat Location in Nebraska, 1854–1930," Ph.D. diss., University of Nebraska–Lincoln, 1973. 8710

TOWN GROWTH

Lincoln

McDill, Ruth, "A Geographic Interpretation of Some of the Factors Effective in the Location and Development of Lincoln, Nebraska," Master's thesis, University of Nebraska, 1925. 8711

Hewes, Leslie, "The Lincoln, Nebraska, Area," in *Transcontinental Excursion Guidebook* (International Geographical Congress, International Geographical Union, Publication no. 4, 1952), pp. 26–37. 8712

Strzygowski, Walter, "Lincoln, Nebraska: Die Entwicklung einer amerikanischen Stadt," *Mitteilungen der Österreichischen Geographischen Gesellschaft*, vol. 105 (1963), pp. 166–179. 8713

Omaha

Knight, Ella Bartlett, "Geographic Factors in the Location and Growth of Omaha," Ph.D. diss., Clark University, 1924. 8714

Clayburn, Ansel B., "Geographic Influences in the Development of Omaha, Nebraska," Master's thesis, University of Nebraska, 1928. 8715

Other centers

Burrill, Helen Adriance, "A Geographic Interpretation of the Location and Development of Fremont, Nebraska," Master's thesis, University of Nebraska, 1927. 8716

Bowen, Marshall E., "Sandhills Potash Town: The Rise and Fall of Antioch, Nebraska," *Kansas Geographer*, vol. 7 (1972), pp. 5–17. 8717

URBAN ECONOMIC STRUCTURE

Harding, George E., "A Geographic Interpretation of the Industrial Development of Lincoln, Nebraska," Master's thesis, University of Nebraska, 1926. 8718

Robertson, Catherine S., "The Development of a Commercial Landscape in Lincoln, Nebraska, 1880–1920," Master's thesis, University of Nebraska–Lincoln, 1983.　　　8719

Hawley, Rebecca Dawn, "Land Use Changes through Time: Mapping the Hard Core CBD of Omaha, Nebraska, 1940–1980," Master's thesis, University of Nebraska–Omaha, 1986.　　8720

URBAN SOCIAL STRUCTURE

Fimple, Kathleen L., "Midwestern Mosaic: A Study of the Homogeneity of Ethnic Populations in Omaha, Nebraska, 1880," Master's thesis, South Dakota State University, 1978.　　8721

Schneider, John C., "Skidrow as an Urban Neighborhood, 1880–1960," *Urbanism: Past and Present*, vol. 9, 1 (1984), pp. 10–20. [Focus on Omaha]　　8722

Fimple, Kathleen L., "An Analysis of the Changing Spatial Dimensions of Ethnic Neighborhoods in Omaha, Nebraska, 1880–1990," Ph.D. diss., University of Nebraska–Lincoln, 1989.　　8723

TOWNSCAPE

See also 4724

Barton, Thomas F., "The Sequential Landscapes and Land Utilization of Hastings, Nebraska: An Urban Center Dominated by a Great Plains Environment," Ph.D. diss., University of Nebraska–Lincoln, 1935.　　8724

Baker, William B., "The Areal Growth of Omaha, Nebraska, with Emphasis on the Westside Area, Ph.D. diss., University of Nebraska, 1958.　　8725

Nollen, Keith, "Changing Land Use Patterns of Northwest Omaha, 1950–1970," Master's thesis, University of Nebraska–Omaha, 1972.　　8726

PLACE NAMES

Gilmore, Melvin R., "The Aboriginal Geography of the Nebraska Country," *Proceedings of the Mississippi Valley Historical Association*, vol. 6 (1912–1913), pp. 317–331.　　8727

Gilmore, Melvin R., "Some Indian Place Names in Nebraska," *Publications of the Nebraska State Historical Society*, vol. 19 (1919), pp. 130–139.　　8728

Fitzpatrick, Lilian Linder, *Nebraska Place-Names* (Lincoln: University of Nebraska Studies in Language, Literature, and Criticism, no. 6, 1925), 166 pp. Reprinted 1960.　　8729

Link, John T., "The Toponymy of Nebraska," Ph.D. diss., University of Nebraska, 1932.　　8730

Link, John T., *The Origin of the Place Names of Nebraska* (Lincoln: Nebraska Geological Survey, Bulletin no. 7, 2d ser., 1933), 186 pp.　　8731

Writers' Program, *Origin of Nebraska Place Names* (Lincoln: Nebraska State Historical Society, 1938), 28 pp.　　8732

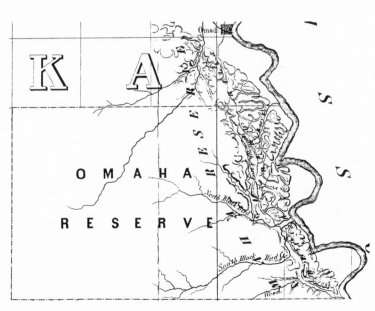

KANSAS

GENERAL

The state

Self, Huber, "The Geographical and Historical Background," in his *Environment and Man in Kansas: A Geographical Analysis* (Lawrence: Regents Press of Kansas, 1978), pp. 4–33. **8733**

Shortridge, James R., "Vernacular Regions in Kansas," *American Studies*, vol. 21, 1 (1980), pp. 73–94. **8734**

Shortridge, James R., Introduction to *The WPA Guide to Kansas: The Federal Writers' Project Guide to 1930s Kansas* (Lawrence: University Press of Kansas, 1984), 12 pp. **8735**

Smaller areas

Hudgins, Bert, "The Geography of LaBelle County, Kansas," Master's thesis, University of Chicago, 1921. **8736**

Malin, James C., "An Introduction to the History of the Bluestem-Pasture Region of Kansas: A Study in Adaptation to Geographical Environment," *Kansas Historical Quarterly*, vol. 11, 1 (1942), pp. 3–28. **8737**

Wood, Perry S., "Historical Geography of Pottawatomie County, Kansas," Master's thesis, Kansas State University, 1967. **8738**

ENVIRONMENTAL CHANGE

Malin, James C., "Dust Storms: Part One, 1850–1860"; "Part Two, 1861–1880"; "Part Three, 1881–1900," *Kansas Historical Quarterly*, vol. 14, 2 (1946), pp. 129–144; 3, pp. 265–296; 4, pp. 391–413. **8739**

Kirk, Henry C., "The Dust Bowl Years: A Study of Their Effects on Scott County, Kansas," *Kansas Geographer*, vol. 15 (1980), pp. 5–15. **8740**

Martin, Charles W., "Historic Channel Change in the Medicine Lodge River Basin, Kansas, 1871–1983," Master's thesis, University of Kansas, 1985. **8741**

McGregor, Kent M., "The Effect of Climatic Change on Cropping Structure of Shawnee County, Kansas: A Bayseian Model," *Agricultural History*, vol. 63, 2 (1989), pp. 202–216. **8742**

NATIVE PEOPLES & WHITE RELATIONS

Smith, Robert, "The Migration of the Wyandot Indians," *Kansas Geographer*, vol. 8 (1973), pp. 19–31. **8743**

Manzo, Joseph T., "Emigrant Indian Objections to Kansas Residence," *Kansas History*, vol. 4, 4 (1981), pp. 246–254. **8744**

EXPLORATION & MAPPING

See also **8506**

Fruehauf, Erich, "Early Surveys in Kansas," *Kansas History*, vol. 5, 2 (1982), pp. 121–138. **8745**

McCleary, George F., Jr., "Pursuing the Cheyenne: Mapping Tribes, Trails, the 1857 Expedition, and the Battle of Solomon's Fork," *Meridian*, vol. 4 (1990), pp. 3–28. **8746**

POPULAR IMAGES & EVALUATION

Schmidt, Nicholas J., Jr., "Evolving Geographic Concepts of the Kansas Area, with Emphasis on the Land Literature of the Santa Fe Railroad," Master's thesis, University of Kansas, 1949. **8747**

Coulson, Michael R. C., "Geographic Concepts of Kansas Prior to 1803," Master's thesis, University of Kansas, 1962. **8748**

Lambert, Patricia, "Ho for Kansas! The Origins and Spread of 'Kansas Fever,' 1870–1880," Syracuse University Department of Geography Discussion Paper no. 44 (1978), 39 pp. **8749**

McQuillan, D. Aidan, "The Interface of Physical and Historical Geography: The Analysis of Farming Decisions in Response to Drought Hazards on the Margins of the Great Plains," in Alan R. H. Baker and Mark Billinge, eds., *Period and Process: Research Methods in Historical Geography* (London: Cambridge University Press, 1982), pp. 136–144. **8750**

Wherry, Peg, "At Home on the Range: Reactions of Pioneer Women to the Kansas Plains Landscape," *Kansas Quarterly*, vol. 18, 3 (1986), pp. 71–79. **8751**

Birch, Brian P., "Popularizing the Plains: News of Kansas in England," *Kansas History*, vol. 10, 4 (1987–1988), pp. 262–274. **8752**

REGIONAL SETTLEMENT

Kollmorgen, Walter M., and George F. Jenks, "A Geographic Study of Population and Settlement Changes in Sherman County, Kansas," *Transactions of the Kansas Academy of Sciences*, vol. 54 (1951), pp. 449–494; 55 (1952), pp. 1–37. **8753**

Gregory, Katheryn A., "Population, Settlement, and Movement in the Great Plains Area of Kansas from 1870–1900," Master's thesis, Pennsylvania State University, 1966.   8754

Garver, John B., Jr., "The Role of the U.S. Army in the Colonization of the Trans-Mississippi West: Kansas, 1823–1861," *Proceedings of the Eighth Annual Meeting of the New York–New Jersey Division of the Association of American Geographers,* vol. 1 (1968), pp. 30–53.   8755

Petersen, Albert J., Jr., "The German-Russian Settlement Pattern in Ellis County, Kansas," *Rocky Mountain Social Science Journal,* vol. 5, 1 (1968), pp. 52–62.   8756

Petersen, Albert J., Jr., "German-Russian Catholic Colonization in Western Kansas: A Settlement Geography," Ph.D. diss., Louisiana State University, 1970.   8757

Brandhorst, L. Carl, "Settlement and Landscape Change on a Sub-Humid Grassland: Lincoln County, Kansas," Ph.D. diss., University of Nebraska–Lincoln, 1974.   8758

Powell, William E., "European Settlement in the Cherokee-Crawford Coal Field of Southeastern Kansas," *Kansas Historical Quarterly,* vol. 41, 2 (1975), pp. 150–165.   8759

Garver, John B., Jr., "The Role of the United States Army in the Colonization of the Trans-Missouri West: Kansas, 1804–1861," Ph.D. diss., Syracuse University, 1981.   8760

POPULATION

McQuillan, D. Aidan, "The Mobility of Immigrants and Americans: A Comparison of Farmers on the Kansas Frontier," *Agricultural History,* vol. 53, 3 (1979), pp. 576–596.   8761

Swann, Patricia Lambert, "Place and Population Mixing in Post Frontier Societies: Kansas, 1870–1900," Ph.D. diss., Syracuse University, 1989.
                                                    8762

Harrier, Donald R., "An Analysis of Spatial Distribution of Rural Farm Population in Decatur County, Kansas: 1900–1988," Master's thesis, Kansas State University, 1990.   8763

RURAL & REGIONAL SOCIAL GEOGRAPHY

Malin, James C., "The Adaptation of the Agricultural System to Sub-humid Environment: Illustrated by the Activities of the Wayne Township Farmers' Club of Edwards County, Kansas, 1886–1893," *Agricultural History,* vol. 10, 3 (1936), pp. 118–141.   8764

Shortridge, James R., "The Post Office Frontier in Kansas," *Journal of the West,* vol. 13, 3 (1974), pp. 83–97.   8765

McQuillan, D. Aidan, "Adaptation of Three Immigrant Groups to Farming in Central Kansas, 1875–1925," Ph.D. diss., University of Wisconsin–Madison, 1975.   8766

McQuillan, D. Aidan, "Farm Size and Work Ethic: Measuring the Success of Immigrant Farmers on the American Grasslands, 1875–1925," *Journal of Historical Geography,* vol. 4, 1 (1978), pp. 57–76.   8767

McQuillan, D. Aidan, "Territory and Ethnic Identity: Some New Measures of an Old Theme in the Cultural Geography of the United States," in James R. Gibson, ed., *European Settlement and Development in North America: Essays in Honour and Memory of Andrew Hill Clark* (Toronto: University of Toronto Press, 1978), pp. 136–169.
                                                    8768

Phillips, Paul, "Relationship of Environmental Factors to Healthfulness: Kansas, 1850–1900," *Kansas Geographer,* vol. 13 (1978), pp. 5–16.   8769

McQuillan, D. Aidan, *Prevailing over Time: Ethnic Adjustments on the Kansas Prairies, 1875–1925* (Lincoln: University of Nebraska Press, 1990), 292 pp.   8770

POLITICAL & ADMINISTRATIVE GEOGRAPHY

Schoewe, Walter H., "The Geography of Kansas, Part 1: Political Geography," *Transactions of the Kansas Academy of Science,* vol. 51, 3 (1948), pp. 253–288.   8771

ECONOMIC DEVELOPMENT

See also 8558

RESOURCE MANAGEMENT

Sorenson, Curtis J., and Glen A. Marotz, "Changes in Shelterbelt Mileage Statistics over Four Decades in Kansas," *Journal of Soil and Water Conservation,* vol. 32 (1977), pp. 276–281. [Focus on 1935–1974]   8772

LAND & LAND USE

Swenson, Russell G., "Land Ownership among Ethnic Groups in Cloud County, Kansas, 1885–1975," *Kansas Geographer,* vol. 16 (1981), pp. 45–55.   8773

EXTRACTIVE ACTIVITY

Stanley, William R., "The Historical and Economic Geography of the Salt Industry in Kansas," Master's thesis, University of Nebraska–Lincoln, 1962. 8774

Powell, William E., "The Historical Geography of the Impact of Coal Mining upon the Cherokee-Crawford Coal Field of Southeast Kansas," Ph.D. diss., University of Nebraska, 1970. 8775

Powell, William E., "Coal and Pioneer Settlement in Southeasternmost Kansas," *Ecumene*, vol. 9 (1977), pp. 6–16. 8776

AGRICULTURE

Malin, James C., "Beginnings of Winter Wheat Production in the Upper Kansas and Lower Smoky Hill River Valleys: A Study in Adaptation to Geographical Environment," *Kansas Historical Quarterly*, vol. 10, 3 (1941), pp. 227–259. 8777

Malin, James C., *Winter Wheat in the Golden Belt of Kansas: A Study in Adaptation to Subhumid Geographical Environment* (Lawrence: University of Kansas Press, 1944), 290 pp. 8778

Hodgkins, Jordan A., "Geographic-Historic Study of Farm Unit Size in Kanwaka Township, Douglas County, Kansas," Master's thesis, University of Kansas, 1949. 8779

Marple, Robert, "The Corn-Wheat Ratio in Kansas, 1879 and 1959: A Study in Historical Geography," *Great Plains Journal*, vol. 8, 2 (1969), pp. 79–86. 8780

Rubright, Lynnell, "Development of Farming Systems in Western Kansas, 1885–1915," Ph.D. diss., University of Wisconsin–Madison, 1977. 8781

Hines, M. Elizabeth, "Farming and Ranching in Morton County through 1915: The Historical Geography of a High Plains Frontier," Master's thesis, University of Kansas, 1985. 8782

Hickey, Joseph V., and Charles E. Webb, "The Transition from Farming to Ranching in the Kansas Flint Hills: Two Case Studies," *Great Plains Quarterly*, vol. 7, 4 (1987), pp. 244–255. 8783

LANDSCAPE

See also 8587, 8589

Webb, Robert M., "Deep Dry Wells on the High Plains of Kansas," *Landscape*, vol. 18, 2 (1969), pp. 27–28. [Focus on the 1880s] 8784

Rafferty, Milton D., "Limestone Fenceposts of the Smoky Hill Region of Kansas," *Pioneer America*, vol. 6, 1 (1974), pp. 40–45. 8785

Petersen, Albert J., Jr., "The German-Russian House in Kansas: A Study in Persistence of Form," *Pioneer America*, vol. 8, 1 (1976), pp. 19–27. 8786

Cyr, John R., "Historic Landscapes of Cloud County, Kansas," Master's thesis, Kansas State University, 1981. 8787

Martin, Brenda Stevens, "The Impact of Mennonite Settlement on the Cultural Landscape of Kansas," Master's thesis, Kansas State University, 1988. 8788

Shortridge, James R., *Kaw Valley Landscapes: A Traveler's Guide to Northeastern Kansas* (Lawrence: University Press of Kansas, 1988), 240 pp. 8789

COMMUNICATIONS & TRADE

Illgner, Rick, "Railroad Developments in Westmoreland, Kansas," *Kansas Geographer*, vol. 12 (1977), pp. 5–14. 8790

Quastler, Imre E., *The Railroads of Lawrence, Kansas, 1854–1900: A Case Study in the Causes and Consequences of an Unsuccessful American Urban Railroad Program* (Lawrence: Coronado Press, 1979), 424 pp. 8791

URBAN NETWORKS & URBANIZATION

Larson, Sara C., "The Lost Towns of Finney County," *Proceedings of the Kansas Academy of Science*, vol. 66, 3 (1963), pp. 409–416. 8792

Robinson, Correl, III, "Some Responses of the LaCrosse, Kansas, Business Community to the Historical Alterations of the Trade Territory Population," Master's thesis, University of Kansas, 1970. 8793

Groop, Richard E., "Small Town Population Change in Kansas, 1950–1970," Ph.D. diss., University of Kansas, 1976. 8794

Dotzauer, Peter J., "The Impact of Location Relative to Cities on Village Population Change in Kansas, 1950–1976," Master's thesis, Kansas State University, 1980. 8795

URBAN ECONOMIC STRUCTURE

Dashiell, Samuel C., "Urban and Industrial Geography of Leavenworth, Kansas," Master's thesis, Clark University, 1982. 8796

URBAN SOCIAL STRUCTURE

Manzo, Joseph T., "Sequent Occupance in Kansas City, Kansas: A Historical Geography of Strawberry Hill," *Kansas History*, vol. 4, 1 (1981), pp. 20–29. 8797

TOWNSCAPE

Parks, Sharon, "Morphology of a City Changing: Lawrence, Kansas," *Kansas Geographer*, vol. 14 (1979), pp. 29–35.   8798

Schmiedeler, Thomas L., "Origin and Evolution of Town Forms in North-Central Kansas, 1860–1900," Ph.D. diss., University of Kansas, 1990.   8799

PLACE NAMES

Rydjord, John, *Indian Place Names: Their Origin, Evolution, and Meanings, Collected in Kansas* from the Siouan, Algonquian, Shoshonean, Caddoan, Iroquoian, and Other Tongues (Norman: University of Oklahoma Press, 1968), 380 pp.   8800

Rydjord, John, *Kansas Place-Names* (Norman: University of Oklahoma Press, 1972), 613 pp.   8801

McCoy, Sandra Van Meter, and Jon Hults, *1001 Kansas Place Names* (Lawrence: University Press of Kansas , 1989), 223 pp.   8802

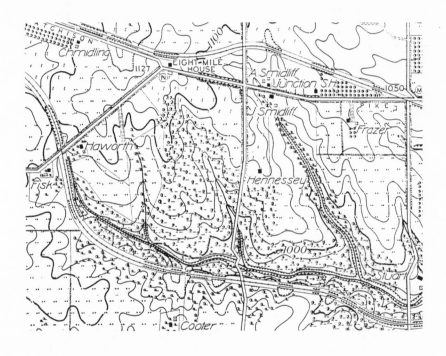

OKLAHOMA

GENERAL

The state

Rosenberg, H., "Oklahoma: Die Entwicklung vom Indianer-Reservat zur modernen Kulturlandschaft," in Dietrich Hafemann, H. Kastrup, and R. Klöpper, eds., *Festgabe zum 65. Geburtstag Professor Wolfgang Panzer* (Braunschweig: Georg Westermann Verlag, Mainzer Geographische Studien, 1961), pp. 26–45. [1828–1950]   8803

Doran, Michael F., "The Origins of Culture Areas in Oklahoma, 1830–1900," Ph.D. diss., University of Oregon, 1974.   8804

Stadler, Stephen J., "The Pulse of Oklahoma: Huntington's Theory in a Modern Setting," *Indiana State University Department of Geography Papers*, vol. 17 (1985), pp. 47–60.   8805

Zdordkowski, R. Todd, and George O. Carney, "This Land Is My Land: Oklahoma's Changing Vernacular Regions," *Journal of Cultural Geography*, vol. 5, 2 (1985), pp. 97–106.   8806

Smaller areas

Blair, Paul E., "Historical Geography of the Glenn Pool Area, Oklahoma," Master's thesis, University of Oklahoma, 1961.   8807

Carney, Champ C., "Historical Geography of the Chickasaw Lands of Oklahoma," Ph.D. diss., Indiana University, 1961.   8808

ENVIRONMENTAL CHANGE

Doerr, Arthur H., "Dry Conditions in Oklahoma in the 1930s and 1950s as Delimited by the Original Thornthwaite Climatic Classification," *Great Plains Journal*, vol. 2, 2 (1963), pp. 67–76.   8809

Brown, William R., Jr., "Natural History of the Canadian River," *Panhandle-Plains Historical Review*, vol. 61, 1 (1988), pp. 1–16.   8810

NATIVE PEOPLES & WHITE RELATIONS

Hewes, Leslie, "Geography of the Cherokee Country of Oklahoma," Ph.D. diss., University of California–Berkeley, 1940.   8811

Hewes, Leslie, "Indian Land in the Cherokee Country of Oklahoma," *Economic Geography*, vol. 18, 4 (1942), pp. 401–412. [Focus on 1903–1940]   8812

Hewes, Leslie, "The Oklahoma Ozarks as the Land of the Cherokees," *Geographical Review*, vol. 32, 3 (1942), pp. 269–281. [Focus on 1830–1936]   8813

Hewes, Leslie, "Cherokee Occupance in the Oklahoma Ozarks and Prairie Plains," *Chronicles of Oklahoma*, vol. 22, 3 (1944), pp. 324–337.   8814

Evans, Oren F., "Some Factors That Controlled the Location of the Villages of the Pre-Historic People of Central Oklahoma," *Proceedings of the Oklahoma Academy of Science for 1952*, vol. 33 (1954), pp. 320–322.   8815

Burrill, Robert M., "The Establishment of Ranching on the Osage Indian Reservation," *Geographical Review*, vol. 62, 4 (1972), pp. 524–543. [Focus on 1860s–1890s]   8816

Doran, Michael F., "Population Statistics of Nineteenth Century Indian Territory," *Chronicles of Oklahoma*, vol. 53, 4 (1975–1976), pp. 492–515.   8817

Doran, Michael F., "Antebellum Cattle Herding in the Indian Territory," *Geographical Review*, vol. 66, 1 (1976), pp. 48–58.   8818

Roark, Michael O., "Nineteenth Century Population Distributions of the Five Civilized Tribes in Indian Territory, Oklahoma," Syracuse University Department of Geography Discussion Paper no. 15 (1976), 23 pp.   8819

Doran, Michael F., "Negro Slaves of the Five Civilized Tribes," *Annals of the Association of American Geographers*, vol. 68, 3 (1978), pp. 335–350.   8820

Hewes, Leslie, *Occupying the Cherokee Country of Oklahoma* (Lincoln: University of Nebraska Studies, n.s. no. 57, 1978), 77 pp.   8821

Roark, Michael O., "Oklahoma Territory: Frontier Development, Migration, and Culture Areas," Ph.D. diss., Syracuse University, 1979.   8822

EXPLORATION & MAPPING

Burrill, Robert M., "The Osage Pasture Map," *Chronicles of Oklahoma*, vol. 53, 2 (1975), pp. 204–211.   8823

Wise, Donald, "Bird's Eye Views of Oklahoma Towns," *Chronicles of Oklahoma*, vol. 67, 3 (1989), pp. 228–247.   8824

REGIONAL SETTLEMENT

See also 8814, 8821–8822

Morris, John W., *The Agglomerated Settlements of the Greater Seminole Area* (Nashville: George Peabody College for Teachers, Abstract of Contribution to Education no. 301, 1941), 8 pp.
8825

Kott, Richard F., "The Sequent Occupance of Tinker Air Force Base: A Case Study," Master's thesis, University of Oklahoma, 1959. 8826

Coling, Jerome F., "Rural Settlement in the Vicinity of Coalgate, Oklahoma," *Proceedings of the Oklahoma Academy of Science for 1967*, vol. 48 (1969), pp. 165–169. [Focus on 1880–1920] 8827

POPULATION

See also 8817, 8819

Morris, John W., "Population Changes in the Greater Seminole Area, 1920 to 1940," *Proceedings of the Oklahoma Academy of Science for 1941*, vol. 22 (1942), pp. 185–188. 8828

Morris, John W., "Population Trends in the Washita Basin," *Proceedings of the Oklahoma Academy of Science for 1951*, vol. 32 (1952), pp. 136–138. [Focus on 1910–1975] 8829

Hale, Douglas, "European Immigrants in Oklahoma: A Survey," *Chronicles of Oklahoma*, vol. 53, 2 (1975), pp. 179–203. 8830

RURAL & REGIONAL SOCIAL GEOGRAPHY

See also 8820

Lynch, Russell W., "Czech Farmers in Oklahoma: A Comparative Study of the Stability of a Czech Farm Group in Lincoln County, Oklahoma, and the Factors Relating to Stability," Ph.D. diss., Columbia University, 1942. Published with same title in *Bulletin, Oklahoma A & M College*, vol. 39, 13 (1942), 119 pp. 8831

Hewes, Leslie, "A Cultural Fault Line in the Cherokee Country," *Economic Geography*, vol. 19, 2 (1943), pp. 136–142. 8832

Morris, John W., "Seminole Oil Field Camps," *Economic Geography*, vol. 19, 2 (1943), pp. 129–135. [In the greater Seminole area, 1920–1943] 8833

Branson, Vanda K., "The Amish of Thomas, Oklahoma: A Study in Cultural Geography," Master's thesis, University of Oklahoma, 1967. 8834

Carney, George O., "Crumb Bosses and Collar Peckers: Folklife of Old-Time Oil Field Pipelines," *North American Culture*, vol. 5, 1 (1989), pp. 31–50. 8835

POLITICAL & ADMINISTRATIVE GEOGRAPHY

Stephens, Elizabeth P., "The Historical Geography of the Boundaries of Oklahoma," Master's thesis, University of Oklahoma, 1964. 8836

ECONOMIC DEVELOPMENT

Gould, Charles N., "Oklahoma: An Example of Arrested Development," *Economic Geography*, vol. 2, 3 (1926), pp. 426–450. [Focus on 1850–1925] 8837

LAND & LAND USE

See also 8812–8813

Myles, Edward L., "Changing Land Use Patterns in Cleveland County, Oklahoma, 1937 vs. 1957," Master's thesis, University of Oklahoma, 1960. 8838

EXTRACTIVE ACTIVITY

Keso, Edward E., "The Old and the New Oil Field Community," *Journal of Geography*, vol. 38, 4 (1939), pp. 156–163. 8839

AGRICULTURE

See also 8816, 8818

General

Bieberdorf, G. A., "History of the Distribution of the Mexican Boll Weevil in Oklahoma," *Proceedings of the Oklahoma Academy of Science*, vol. 7 (1927), pp. 29–34. 8840

Williams, Cecil A., "The Production and Distribution of Grain Sorghums in Oklahoma, 1907–1965," Master's thesis, University of Oklahoma, 1966. 8841

Cotton

Britton, Robert L., "Regional Changes in Cotton Acreage in Oklahoma between 1910 and 1920," *Proceedings of the Oklahoma Academy of Science*, vol. 9 (1929), pp. 104–105. 8842

Webb, Charles E., "Distribution of Cotton Production in Oklahoma, 1907–1962," Master's thesis, University of Oklahoma, 1963. 8843

Garner, Robert V., "The Changing Cotton Belt of Southeast Oklahoma," *Proceedings of the Oklahoma Academy of Science for 1965*, vol. 46 (1966), pp. 191–193. 8844

Ranching

Burrill, Robert M., "Grassland Empires: The Geography of Ranching in Osage County, Oklahoma,

1872–1965," Ph.D. diss., University of Kansas,
1970.   8845

LANDSCAPE

Carney, George O., *Cushing Oil Field: A Historic Preservation Survey* (Stillwater: Panic Press, 1981), 115 pp.   8846

Carney, George O., "Shotgun Houses in Payne County," *Payne County, Oklahoma, Historical Review*, vol. 2 (1981), pp. 30–38.   8847

Carney, George O., "Historic Properties of the Cushing Oil Field," *Payne County, Oklahoma, Historical Review*, vol. 4 (1983), pp. 20–25.   8848

Carney, George O., "The Shotgun House in Oklahoma," *Journal of Cultural Geography*, vol. 4, 1 (1983), pp. 57–71.   8849

Crumby, Peggy D., "The I–House in Oklahoma: A Geographic Study in Folk House Typology," Master's thesis, Oklahoma State University, 1987.   8850

COMMUNICATIONS & TRADE

Tennant, H. S., "History of the Chisholm Trail," *Chronicles of Oklahoma*, vol. 14, 1 (1936), pp. 108–122. [Oklahoma portion]   8851

Gardner, Charles, "Railroad Abandonment in Oklahoma," Master's thesis, University of Oklahoma, 1958.   8852

Thompson, Gary L., "The Chisholm Trail in Geographical Perspective," *Proceedings of the Oklahoma Academy of Science for 1961*, vol. 42 (1962), pp. 253–259. [Oklahoma portion]   8853

MANUFACTURING & INDUSTRIALIZATION

Creveling, Harold F., "Centers of Industrial Growth in Oklahoma, 1919 to 1939," *Proceedings of the Oklahoma Academy of Science for 1946*, vol. 27 (1947), pp. 84–86.   8854

URBAN NETWORKS & URBANIZATION

Olson, Ralph E., "The Functional Decline of Oklahoma Villages: A Case Study," *Proceedings of the Oklahoma Academy of Science for 1951*, vol. 32 (1952), pp. 132–136. [Focus on 1930–1950]   8855

Brandt, Donald P., "Population Trends of Incorporated Agglomerations (1,000–2,500) of Oklahoma, 1920–1960," Master's thesis, University of Oklahoma, 1964.   8856

TOWN GROWTH

Coling, Jerome F., "A Historical Geography of Coalgate, Oklahoma," Master's thesis, University of Oklahoma, 1966.   8857

Coling, Jerome F., "Coalgate, Oklahoma: Some Aspects of Its Historical Geography," *Proceedings of the Oklahoma Academy of Science for 1966*, vol. 47 (1968), pp. 368–370.   8858

Nardone, Kathryn, "Tulsa, Oklahoma: Some Aspects of Its Urban Settlement," *Proceedings of the Oklahoma Academy of Science for 1966*, vol. 47 (1968), pp. 378–381.   8859

Meuter, Ralph F., "The Functional Evolution of Seminole, Oklahoma," *Proceedings of the Oklahoma Academy of Science for 1967*, vol. 48 (1969), pp. 184–187. [Focus on 1910–1960]   8860

Clark, Blue, "Buffalo: A 'Place' Designated County Seat by the Constitution of Oklahoma," *Chronicles of Oklahoma*, vol. 51, 1 (1973), pp. 2–20. 8861

Morris, John W., ed., *Cities of Oklahoma* (Oklahoma City: Oklahoma Historical Society. 1979), 170 pp.   8862

TOWNSCAPE

DiLisio, James E., and Estele Wall, "The Origin of Street Patterns in Norman, Oklahoma," *Places*, vol. 3, 2 (1976), pp. 37–42.   8863

PLACE NAMES

Wright, Muriel H., "Some Geographic Names of French Origin in Oklahoma," *Chronicles of Oklahoma*, vol. 7, 2 (1929), pp. 188–193.   8864

Shirk, George H., *Oklahoma Place Names* (Norman: University of Oklahoma Press, 1965), 233 pp.   8865

Carney, George O., "From Slapout to Bug Tussle: Place Names on the Oklahoma Landscape," *Places*, vol. 3, 2 (1976), pp. 30–37.   8866

THE SOUTHWEST

GENERAL

Sauer, Carl O., "The Relation of Man to Nature in the Southwest: A Conference," *Huntington Library Quarterly*, vol. 8, 2 (1945), pp. 116–149. **8867**

Carter, George F., "Man, Time, and Change in the Far Southwest," *Annals of the Association of American Geographers*, vol. 49, 3, pt. 2 (1959), pp. 8–30. **8868**

Sauer, Carl O., "Comments on Paul Kirschoff's Gatherers and Farmers in the Greater Southwest," *American Anthropologist*, vol. 56 (1964), pp. 553–556. Reprinted in Carl O. Sauer, *Selected Essays, 1963–1975*, ed. Bob Callahan (Berkeley, Calif.: Turtle Island Foundation, for the Netzahaulcoyotl Historical Society, 1981), pp. 159–163. **8869**

White, Russell A., "El Paso del Norte: The Geography of a Pass and Border Area through 1906," Ph.D. diss., Columbia University, 1968. **8870**

Meinig, Donald W., *Southwest: Three Peoples in Geographical Change, 1600–1970* (New York: Oxford University Press, 1971), 151 pp. **8871**

Nostrand, Richard L., "A Changing Culture Region," in Ellwyn R. Stoddard, Richard L. Nostrand, and Jonathan P. West, *Borderlands Sourcebook: A Guide to the Literature on Northern Mexico and the American Southwest* (Norman: University of Oklahoma Press, 1983), pp. 6–15. **8872**

Lewis, Michael E., and Craig L. Torbenson, "Cultural Antecedents of J. W. Powell's Arid Lands Report," *Journal of Geography*, vol. 89, 2 (1990), pp. 74–80. **8873**

ENVIRONMENTAL CHANGE

Huntington, Ellsworth, "The Fluctuating Climate of North America: Part I—The Ruins of the Hohokam"; "Part II—The Succession of Civilization"; "Part III—The Evidence of the Trees," *Geographical Journal*, vol. 40, 3 (1912), pp. 264–280; 4, pp. 392–401 and 401–411. **8874**

Huntington, Ellsworth, "The Physical Environment of the Southwest in Pre-Columbian Days," *Records of the Past*, vol. 11, 3 (May-June 1912), pp. 128–141. **8875**

Bryan, Kirk, "Date of Channel Trenching (Arroyo Cutting) in the Arid Southwest," *Science*, n. s. vol. 57 (1925), pp. 339–344. **8876**

Shreve, Forrest, and Arthur L. Hinckley, "Thirty Years of Change in Desert Vegetation," *Ecology*, vol. 18 (1937), pp. 463–478. **8877**

Leopold, Luna, "Vegetation of Southwestern Watersheds in the Nineteenth Century," *Geographical Review*, vol. 41, 2 (1951), pp. 295–316. **8878**

Cooper, Charles F., "Changes in Vegetation, Structure, and Growth of Southwestern Pine Forests since White Settlement," *Ecological Monographs*, vol. 30 (1960), pp. 129–164. **8879**

Smiley, T. L., "Evidences of Climatic Fluctuations in Southwestern Prehistory," *Annals of the New York Academy of Sciences*, vol. 95, 1 (1961), pp. 697–704. **8880**

Woodbury, R. B., "Climatic Changes and Prehistoric Agriculture in the Southwestern United States," *Annals of the New York Academy of Sciences*, vol. 95, 1 (1961), pp. 705–709. **8881**

Harris, David R., "Recent Invasions in the Arid and Semi-Arid Southwest of the United States," *Annals of the Association of American Geographers*, vol. 56, 3 (1966), pp. 408–422. Reprinted in Thomas R. Detwyler, ed., *Man's Impact on Environment* (New York: McGraw-Hill Book Co., 1971), pp. 459–475. [1860–1960] **8882**

Bull, William B., and K. M. Scott, "Impact of Mining Gravel from Urban Stream Beds in the Southwestern United States," *Geology*, vol. 2, 4 (1974), pp. 171–174. **8883**

Cooke, Ronald U., and Richard W. Reeves, *Arroyos and Environmental Change in the American South-West* (Oxford: Oxford University Press, 1976), 213 pp. **8884**

NATIVE PEOPLES & WHITE RELATIONS

Prehistoric settlement

Stevenson, James, "Ancient Inhabitants of the Southwest," *Journal of the American Geographical Society*, vol. 18 (1886), pp. 329–342. **8885**

Ober, Frederick A., "Ancient Cities of America," *Journal of the American Geographical Society*, vol. 20 (1888), pp. 39–74. **8886**

Mindeleff, Cosmos, "Origin of the Cliff Dwellings," *Journal of the American Geographical Society*, vol. 30 (1890), pp. 111–126. **8887**

Haas, William H., "The Cliff-Dweller and His Habitat," *Annals of the Association of American Geographers*, vol. 16, 4 (1926), pp. 167–215. 8888

Brand, Donald D., "Prehistoric Trade in the Southwest," *New Mexico Business Review*, vol. 4 (1935), pp. 202–209. 8889

Brand, Donald D., "Aboriginal Trade Routes for Sea Shells in the Southwest," *Yearbook of the Association of Pacific Coast Geographers*, vol. 4 (1938), pp. 3–10. 8890

Bryan, Kirk, "Pre-Columbian Agriculture in the Southwest, as Conditioned by Periods of Alluviation," *Annals of the Association of American Geographers*, vol. 31, 4 (1941), pp. 219–242. Also published in *Proceedings of the Eighth American Scientific Congress, 1940*, vol. 2 (Washington, D.C.: Department of State, 1942), pp. 57–74. 8891

Carter, George F., "Plant Geography and Culture History in the American Southwest," Ph.D. diss., University of California–Berkeley, 1942. 8892

Carter, George F., and Edgar Anderson, "A Preliminary Survey of Maize in the Southwestern United States," *Annals of the Missouri Botanical Garden*, no. 32 (1945), pp. 297–322. 8893

Carter, George F., *Plant Geography and Culture History in the American Southwest* (New York: Viking Fund Publications, Publications in Anthropology no. 5, 1945), 140 pp. Reprinted by Johnson Reprint Co., 1964. 8894

Jett, Stephen C., "Pueblo Indian Migrations: An Evaluation of the Possible Physical and Cultural Determinants," *American Antiquity*, vol. 29, 3 (1964), pp. 281–300. 8895

Ross, Stanley H., "Prehistoric Trade Routes between Mesoamerica and the American Southwest: A Tentative Assessment," *California Geographer*, vol. 8, 1 (1967), pp. 9–19. 8896

Ross, Stanley H., "Metallurgical Beginnings: The Case of Copper in the Prehistoric American Southwest," *Annals of the Association of American Geographers*, vol. 58, 2 (1968), pp. 360–370. 8897

Aschmann, Homer, "Athapaskan Expansion in the Southwest," *Yearbook of the Association of Pacific Coast Geographers*, vol. 32 (1970), pp. 79–98. 8898

Historic period

Spencer, Virginia Evelyn, "The Geography of Navajo Dwelling Types, with Special Reference to Black Creek Valley, Arizona-New Mexico," Master's thesis, University of California–Davis, 1969. 8899

Spencer, Virginia Evelyn, and Stephen C. Jett, "Navajo Dwellings of Rural Black Creek Valley, Arizona–New Mexico," *Plateau*, vol. 43, 4 (1971), pp. 159–175. 8900

Jett, Stephen C., "The Destruction of Navajo Orchards in 1869," *Arizona and the West*, vol. 16, 4 (1974), pp. 365–378. 8901

Jett, Stephen C., *Interwoven Heritage: A Bicentennial Exhibition of Southwestern Indian Basketry and Textile Arts* (Davis: University of California–Davis Memorial Art Gallery, 1976), 44 pp. 8902

Jett, Stephen C., "History of Fruit Tree Raising among the Navajo," *Agricultural History*, vol. 51, 4 (1977), pp. 681–701. 8903

Jett, Stephen C., "Navajo Seasonal Migration Patterns," *Kiva*, vol. 44, 1 (1978), pp. 65–75. 8904

Jett, Stephen C., "The Origins of Navajo Settlement Patterns," *Annals of the Association of American Geographers*, vol. 68, 3 (1978), pp. 351–362. 8905

Jett, Stephen C., "The Navajo Homestead: Situation and Site," *Yearbook of the Association of Pacific Coast Geographers*, vol. 42 (1980), pp. 101–118. 8906

Jett, Stephen C., and Virginia Evelyn Spencer, *Navajo Architecture: Forms, History, Distributions* (Tucson: University of Arizona Press, 1981), 289 pp. 8907

Jett, Stephen C., "Making the 'Stars' of Navajo Planetaria," *Kiva*, vol. 50, 1 (1984), pp. 25–40. 8908

Graf, William L., "Fluvial Erosion and Federal Public Policy in the Navajo Nation," *Physical Geography*, vol. 7, 2 (1986), pp. 97–115. 8909

Nablan, G. P., "Papago Indian Desert Agriculture and Water Control in the Sonoran Desert, 1697–1934," *Applied Geography*, vol. 6, 1 (1986), pp. 43–60. 8910

Jett, Stephen C., "Cultural Fusion in Native American Folk Architecture: The Navajo Hogan," in Thomas G. Ross and Tyrel G. Moore, eds., *A Cultural Geography of North American Indians* (Boulder: Westview Press, 1987), pp. 243–256. 8911

Seig, Louis, "Spatial Manifestation of Cultural Differences: The Navajo-Hopi Land Dispute," *North American Culture*, vol. 3, 1 (1987), pp. 15–28. 8912

EXPLORATION & MAPPING

Dellenbaugh, Frederick S., "The True Route of Coronado's March," *Journal of the American Geographical Society*, vol. 29 (1897), pp. 399–431. 8913

Brand, Donald D., "Contemporaries of Coronado and his Entrada," *New Mexico Anthropologist*, vol. 3, 1 (1939), pp. 72–80. 8914

Strout, Clevy L., "The Coronado Expedition: Following the Geography Described in the Spanish Journals," *Great Plains Journal*, vol. 14, 1 (1974), pp. 2–31. 8915

Martin, James C., and Robert S. Martin, *Maps of Texas and the Southwest, 1513–1900* (Albuquerque: University of New Mexico Press, for Amon Carter Museum, 1984), 173 pp. 8916

Garver, John B., Jr., "Mapping the Southwest: A Twentieth Century Historical Geographic Perspective," in Donna P. Koepp, ed., *Exploration and Mapping of the American West: Selected Essays* (Chicago: Speculum Orbis Press, Occasional Paper no. 1, 1986), pp. 170–182. 8917

POPULAR IMAGES & EVALUATION

Zube, Ervin H., "An Explanation of Southwestern Landscape Images," *Landscape Journal*, vol. 1, 1 (1982), pp. 31–40. 8918

Norwood, Vera, and Janice Monk, eds., *The Desert Is No Lady: Southwestern Landscapes in Women's Writing and Art* (New Haven: Yale University Press, 1987), 281 pp. 8919

REGIONAL SETTLEMENT

Jones, L. Rodwell, "Notes on the Geographical Factors Which Controlled the Spanish Advance into Northern Mexico and Southern California," *Scottish Geographical Magazine*, vol. 39, 3 (1923), pp. 159–172. 8920

West, Robert C., "A Geographical Analysis of the Western Interior Path of Spanish Northward Expansion in New Spain," Master's thesis, University of California–Los Angeles, 1938. 8921

Shrode, Ida May, "Early Settlement of California and the Southwest," in Clifford M. Zierer, ed., *California and the Southwest* (New York: John Wiley & Sons, 1956), pp. 101–121. 8922

McGee, Ralph C., "Colonial Organization and Regional Development: Factors in the Historical Geography of the American Southwest," Master's thesis, University of California–Berkeley, 1979. 8923

Carlson, Alvar W., "Rural Settlements and Land Use," in Ellwyn R. Stoddard, Richard L. Nostrand, and Jonathan P. West, *Borderlands Sourcebook: A Guide to the Literature on Northern Mexico and the American Southwest* (Norman: University of Oklahoma Press, 1983), pp. 105–110. 8924

Nostrand, Richard L., "The Century of Hispano Expansion," *New Mexico Historical Review*, vol. 62, 4 (1987), pp. 361–386. 8925

POPULATION

Broadbent, Elizabeth, "Mexican Population in the Southwestern United States," *Texas Geographic Magazine*, vol. 5, 2 (1941), pp. 16–24. [Focus on 1910–1930] 8926

Nostrand, Richard L., "Mexican Americans circa 1850," *Annals of the Association of American Geographers*, vol. 65, 3 (1975), pp. 378–390. 8927

Nostrand, Richard L., "The Hispano Homeland in 1900," *Annals of the Association of American Geographers*, vol. 70, 3 (1980), pp. 382–396. 8928

RURAL & REGIONAL SOCIAL GEOGRAPHY

Nostrand, Richard L., *Los Chicanos: Geografía Histórica Regional*, Sep./Sentintas, 306 (Mexico, D.F.: Edimex, S.A., 1976), 178 pp. 8929

Carney, George O., "The Southwest in American Country Music: Regional Innovators and Stylistic Contributions," in *Southwest Cultural Heritage Festival: Selected Faculty Papers* (Stillwater: Oklahoma State University Press, 1982), pp. 813–838. 8930

POLITICAL & ADMINISTRATIVE GEOGRAPHY

Boundaries

Thomas, Benjamin E., "The California-Nevada Boundary," *Annals of the Association of American Geographers*, vol. 42, 1 (1952), pp. 51–68. 8931

Comeaux, Malcolm L., "Attempts to Establish and Change a Western Boundary," *Annals of the Association of American Geographers*, vol. 72, 2 (1982), pp. 254–271. [The Arizona-Utah-Nevada line, 37°N latitude] 8932

Comeaux, Malcolm L., "Selection of the Arizona-Utah Boundary," *Journal of Arizona History*, vol. 24, 3 (1983), pp. 237–254. 8933

Gadsden Purchase

Hazard, Joseph T., "Historical Geography of the Gadsden Purchase," *Yearbook of the Association of Pacific Coast Geographers*, vol. 2 (1936), p. 24. 8934

Taylor, James W., "Geographic Bases of the Gadsden Purchase," *Journal of Geography*, vol. 57, 8 (1958), pp. 402–410. 8935

Hannon, Ralph L., "The Gadsden Purchase 1854–1884: A Historical Geographic Justification,"

Master's thesis, Arizona State University, 1966.
8936

RESOURCE MANAGEMENT

Pisani, D. J., "Irrigation, Water Rights, and the Betrayal of Indian Allotment," *Environmental Review*, vol. 10, 3 (1986), pp. 157–176. **8937**

LAND & LAND USE

Burns, Elizabeth K., and Rebecca Dawn Hawley, "Population Density and Land Consumption Trends in the Metropolitan Southwest," *Computers, Environment and Urban Systems*, vol. 13, 4 (1989), pp. 231–242. [Covers 1950–1980] **8938**

AGRICULTURE

Hansen, Brooks K., "A Geographical Analysis of the Emergence and Subsequent Disappearance of the Cotton Industry in the Virgin River Basin, 1856–1901," Master's thesis, Brigham Young University, 1967. **8939**

LANDSCAPE

Hoover, J. Wenger, "House and Village Types of the Southwest as Conditioned by Aridity," *Scientific Monthly*, vol. 40 (1935), pp. 237–249. **8940**

Conway, A. W., "Southwestern Colonial Farms," *Landscape*, vol. 1, 1 (1951), pp. 6–9. **8941**

Gritzner, Charles F., "Cultural Landscapes," in Ellwyn R. Stoddard, Richard L. Nostrand, and Jonathan P. West, *Borderlands Sourcebook: A Guide to the Literature on Northern Mexico and the American Southwest* (Norman: University of Oklahoma Press, 1983), pp. 116–120. **8942**

COMMUNICATIONS & TRADE

Best, Thomas D., "The Role of the Atchison, Topeka, and Santa Fe Railway System in the Economic Development of the Southwestern United States: 1859–1954," Ph.D. diss., Northwestern University, 1959. **8943**

Quastler, Imre E., "The Geography of Rail Passenger Services in California and Nevada, 1900–1970," *California Geographer*, vol. 18 (1978), pp. 55–83. **8944**

MANUFACTURING & INDUSTRIALIZATION

Creveling, Harold F., "Pattern of Industrial Development in the Southwest, 1919–1939," Master's thesis, University of Oklahoma, 1947. **8945**

URBAN NETWORKS & URBANIZATION

Cruz, Gilbert R., *Let There Be Towns: Spanish Municipal Origins in the American Southwest, 1610–1810* (College Station: Texas A & M University Press, 1989), 236 pp. **8946**

TOWNSCAPE

Lambert, Marjorie F., "Cities before Columbus: Prehistoric Town Planning in the Puebloan Southwest," *Landscape*, vol. 3, 2 (1953–1954), pp. 12–15. **8947**

RECREATION & TOURISM

Jett, Stephen C., "Culture and Tourism in the Navajo Country," *Journal of Cultural Geography*, vol. 11, 1 (1990), pp. 85–108. **8948**

PLACE NAMES

Hill, Robert T., "Descriptive Topographic Terms of Spanish America," *National Geographic Magazine*, vol. 7, 9 (1896), pp. 291–302. [Focus on Texas and New Mexico] **8949**

Pearce, Thomas M., "Spanish Place Name Patterns in the Southwest," *Names*, vol. 3, 4 (1955), pp. 201–209. **8950**

Jett, Stephen C., "An Analysis of Navajo Place-Names," *Names*, vol. 18, 3 (1970), pp. 175–184. **8951**

———— THE MOUNTAIN WEST ————

GENERAL

Bogardus, James F., "The Great Basin," *Economic Geography*, vol. 6, 4 (1930), pp. 321–337.   8952

Ives, Ronald L., "Geography and History in the Arid West," *American West*, vol. 1, 2 (1964), pp. 54–63.   8953

Durrenberger, Robert, "The Colorado Plateau," *Annals of the Association of American Geographers*, vol. 62, 2 (1972), pp. 211–236. Reissued in John Fraser Hart, ed., *Regions of the United States* (New York: Harper & Row, 1972), same pagination.   8954

ENVIRONMENTAL CHANGE

Aschmann, Homer, "Great Basin Climates in Relation to Human Occupance," *Reports of the University of California Archeological Survey*, no. 42 (1958), pp. 23–40.   8955

Lawson, Merlin P., "A Dendroclimatological Interpretation of the Great American Desert," *Proceedings of the Association of American Geographers*, vol. 3 (1971), pp. 109–114.   8956

Lawson, Merlin P., "The Climate of the Great American Desert," Ph.D. diss., Clark University, 1973.   8957

Lawson, Merlin P., *The Climate of the Great American Desert: Reconstruction of the Climate of Western Interior United States, 1800–1850* (Lincoln: University of Nebraska Studies, n.s. no. 46, 1974), 134 pp.   8958

POPULAR IMAGES & EVALUATION

Lang, Anna, "William Blake's Desert of the Colorado River," *California Geographer*, vol. 21 (1981), pp. 81–94.   8959

Sauder, Robert A., "Sod Land Versus Sagebrush: Early Land Appraisal and Pioneer Settlement in an Arid Intermontaine Frontier," *Journal of Historical Geography*, vol. 15, 4 (1989), pp. 402–419.   8960

REGIONAL SETTLEMENT

Aschmann, Homer, "The Head of the Colorado Delta," in S. Robert Eyre and Glanville R. J. Jones, eds., *Geography as Human Ecology* (New York: St. Martin's Press, 1966), pp. 231–263.   8961

POPULATION

Winsberg, Morton D., "European Immigration to the Mountain States, 1850–1980—Changing Patterns," *Journal of the West*, vol. 25, 1 (1986), pp. 103–106.   8962

POLITICAL & ADMINISTRATIVE GEOGRAPHY

Green, D. Brooks, "The Idaho-Wyoming Boundary: A Problem in Location," *Idaho Yesteryears*, vol. 23 (1979), pp. 10–14.   8963

ECONOMIC DEVELOPMENT

Rinschede, Gisbert, "Die saisonale Nutzung des Hochgebirgsraum der USA durch Viehwirtschaft und Tourismus," *Frankfurter Wirtschafts- und Sozialgeographische Schriften*, vol. 36 (1981), pp. 173–212.   8964

Rinschede, Gisbert, *Die Wanderviehwirtschaft im gebirgigen Westen der USA und ihre Auswirkungen im Naturraum* (Regensburg: F. Pustet, Eichstätter Beiträge, Abteilung Geographie, vol. 10, 1984).   8965

AGRICULTURE

Rinschede, Gisbert, "The Migratory Livestock Industry in the Mountain West of the United States," *Mitteilungsblatt des Arbeitskreises USA im Zentralverband der Deutschen Geographen*, vol. 6 (1987), pp. 9–41.   8966

LANDSCAPE

Kilpinen, Jon T., "Material Folk Culture in the Adaptive Strategy of the Rocky Mountain Valley Ranching Frontier," Master's thesis, University of Texas–Austin, 1990. [Focus on the built landscape 1880–1920]   8967

COMMUNICATIONS & TRADE

Douglas, James, "Historical and Geographical Features of the Rocky Mountain Railroads," *Journal of the American Geographical Society*, vol. 17 (1885), pp. 299–342.   8968

Grey, Alan H., "A Railroad across the Mountains: Choosing the Route of the Union Pacific over the Eastern Rockies," Ph.D. diss., University of Wisconsin–Madison, 1963.   8969

Corkran, Robert S., "Rail Route Selection in the Northern Rocky Mountains, 1853–1890," Master's thesis, University of Chicago, 1968.　**8970**

McCaw, David H., "Air Passenger Flows in the Mountain West, 1962–1982," Master's thesis, University of Georgia, 1984.　**8971**

URBAN NETWORKS & URBANIZATION

Elliott, Harold M., "Changing Spatial Structure in the Rocky Mountain Regional System," Year-book of the Association of Pacific Coast Geographers, vol. 48 (1986), pp. 149–167. [Focus on 1940–1980]　**8972**

PLACE NAMES

Koch, Elers, "Geographic Names of Western Montana and Northern Idaho," Oregon Historical Quarterly, vol. 49, 1 (1948), pp. 50–62.　**8973**

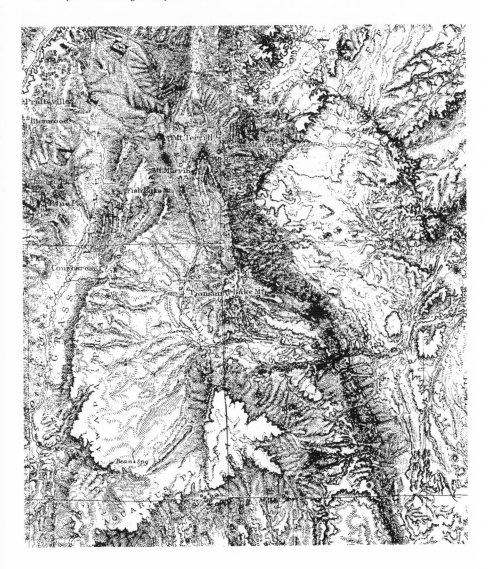

NEW MEXICO

GENERAL

Brown, Ralph Hall, "A Southwestern Oasis: The Roswell Region, New Mexico," *Geographical Review*, vol. 26, 4 (1936), pp. 610–619. [Focus from 1905 to the 1930s]   8974

Jackson, John Brinckerhoff, "High Plains Country: A Sketch of the Geography, Physical and Human, of Union County, New Mexico," *Landscape*, vol. 3, 3 (1954), pp. 11–22.   8975

Widdison, Jerold G., "Historical Geography of the Middle Rio Puerco Valley, New Mexico," Master's thesis, University of Colorado, 1958.   8976

Widdison, Jerold G., "Historical Geography of the Middle Rio Puerco Valley, New Mexico," *New Mexico Historical Review*, vol. 34, 4 (1959), pp. 248–284.   8977

Carlson, Alvar W., "The Rio Arriba: A Geographic Appraisal of the Spanish-American Homeland (Upper Rio Grande Valley, New Mexico)," Ph.D. diss., University of Minnesota, 1971.   8978

Carlson, Alvar W., *The Spanish-American Homeland: Four Centuries in New Mexico's Rio Arriba* (Baltimore: Johns Hopkins University Press, 1990), 294 pp.   8979

ENVIRONMENTAL CHANGE

Bryan, Kirk, "Historical Evidence of Changes in the Channel of Rio Puerco, A Tributary of the Rio Grande in New Mexico," *Journal of Geology*, vol. 36 (1928), pp. 265–282.   8980

Tuan, Yi-Fu, "New Mexican Gullies: A Critical Review and Some Recent Observations," *Annals of the Association of American Geographers*, vol. 56, 4 (1966), pp. 573–597.   8981

Denevan, William M., "Livestock Numbers in Nineteenth Century New Mexico and the Problem of Gullying in the Southwest," *Annals of the Association of American Geographers*, vol. 57, 4 (1967), pp. 691–703.   8982

York, John C., and William A. Dick-Pedie, "Vegetation Changes in Southern New Mexico during the Past Hundred Years," in W. G. McGinnies and B. J. Goldman, eds., *Arid Lands in Perspective* (Tucson: University of Arizona Press, 1969), pp. 157–166.   8983

McCraw, David J., "A Phytogeography History of Larrea in Southwestern New Mexico, Illustrating the Historical Expansion of the Chihuahuan

Desert," Master's thesis, University of New Mexico, 1985.   8984

NATIVE PEOPLES & WHITE RELATIONS

Pre-Spanish settlements

Duff, U. Francis, "The Prehistoric Ruins of the Rio Tularosa," *Journal of the American Geographical Society*, vol. 29 (1897), pp. 261–270.   8985

Fewkes, J. Walter, "The Ruined Pueblo in New Mexico Discovered by Vargas in 1692," *Bulletin of the American Geographical Society*, vol. 34, 2 (1902), pp. 217–222.   8986

Fliedner, Dietrich, "Über die Entstehung der Siedlungsformen und Siedlungsräume im Bereich der Pueblo-Indianer New Mexicos (USA)," *Göttinger Geographische Abhandlungen*, vol. 60 (1972), pp. 467–481.   8987

Fliedner, Dietrich, *Der Aufbau der vorspanischen Siedlungs- und Wirtschaftslandschaft im Kulturraum der Pueblo-Indianer: Eine historisch-geographische Interpretation wüstgefallener Ortsstellen und Feldflächen im Jemez-Gebiet, New Mexico* (Saarbrücken: Arbeiten aus dem Geographischen Institut der Universität des Saarlandes, vol. 19, 1974), 63 pp.   8988

Fliedner, Dietrich, "Pre-Spanish Pueblos in New Mexico," *Annals of the Association of American Geographers*, vol. 65, 3 (1975), pp. 363–377.   8989

Jett, Stephen C., *House of Three Turkeys: Anasazi Redoubt* (Santa Barbara, Cal.: Capra Press, 1977), 63 pp.   8990

Nelson, Bonnie K., "A Spatial Analysis of the Classic Mimbres Sites along the Rio Mimbres of Southwestern New Mexico," Master's thesis, Florida State University, 1977.   8991

Fliedner, Dietrich, "Geosystemforschung und menschliches Verhalten," *Geographische Zeitschrift*, vol. 67, 1 (1979), pp. 29–42. [Focus on Pueblo Pecos, 1250–1838]   8992

Jett, Stephen C., and Peter Mogle, "The Exotic Origins of Fishes Depicted on Prehistoric Mimbres Pottery from New Mexico," *American Antiquity*, vol. 51, 4 (1986), pp. 688–720.   8993

Modern settlements

Ingersoll, Ernest, "The Village Indians of New Mexico," *Journal of the American Geographical Society*, vol. 7 (1875), pp. 114–126.   8994

Henderson, Martha L., "Landscape Changes in the Mescalero Apache Reservation: Eastern Apache Adaptation to Federal Indian Policy," Ph.D. diss., Louisiana State University, 1988.
8995

Henderson, Martha L., "Settlement Patterns on the Mescalero Apache Reservation since 1883," *Geographical Review*, vol. 80, 3 (1990), pp. 226–238.
8996

Magnaghi, Russell M., "Plains Indians in New Mexico: The Genizaro Experience," *Great Plains Quarterly*, vol. 10, 2 (1990), pp. 86–95.
8997

EXPLORATION & MAPPING

Simpson, James H., "The Ruins to Be Found in New Mexico and the Explorations of Francisco Vasquez de Coronado in Search of the Seven Cities of Cibola," *Journal of the American Geographical Society*, vol. 5 (1874), pp. 194–216.
8998

Sauer, Carl O., "The Discovery of New Mexico Reconsidered," *New Mexico Historical Review*, vol. 12, 3 (1937), pp. 270–287.
8999

Sauer, Carl O., "The Credibility of the Fray Marcos Account," *New Mexico Historical Review*, vol. 16, 2 (1941), pp. 233–243.
9000

POPULAR IMAGES & EVALUATION

Tuan, Yi-Fu, and Cyril E. Everard, "New Mexico's Climate: The Appreciation of a Resource," *Natural Resources Journal*, vol. 4, 3 (1964), pp. 268–308.
9001

REGIONAL SETTLEMENT

Rubright, Lynnell, "A Sequent Occupance of the Espanola Valley, New Mexico," Master's thesis, University of Colorado, 1967.
9002

Simmons, Marc, "Settlement Patterns and Village Plans in Colonial New Mexico," *Journal of the West*, vol. 8, 1 (1969), pp. 7–21.
9003

McDonald, Jerry N., "Sequential Land Use of the Philmont Scout Ranch Region, Northeastern New Mexico," Master's thesis, University of Texas–Austin, 1972.
9004

Fliedner, Dietrich, *Die Kolonisierung New Mexicos durch die Spanier: Ein Beitrag zum Problem der Entstehung von antropogenen Räumen* (Saarbrücken: Arbeiten aus dem Geographischen Institut der Universität des Saarlandes, vol. 21, 1975), 98 pp.
9005

Carlson, Alvar W., "Spanish Colonization and the Abiquiu Grant, New Mexico, 1754–1970," *Philippine Geographical Journal*, vol. 20, 2 (1976), pp. 61–68.
9006

Carlson, Alvar W., "El Rancho and Vadito: Spanish Settlements on Indian Land Grants," *El Palacio*, vol. 85, 1 (1979), pp. 28–39.
9007

McDonald, Jerry N., "La Jicarilla," *Journal of Cultural Geography*, vol. 2, 2 (1982), pp. 40–57.
9008

POPULATION

Culbert, James J., "Distribution of Spanish-American Population in New Mexico," *Economic Geography*, vol. 19, 2 (1943), pp. 171–176. [Focus on 1744–1940]
9009

RURAL & REGIONAL SOCIAL GEOGRAPHY

Hornbeck, David, Jr., "Spatial Manifestation of Acculturative Processes in the Upper Pecos Valley, New Mexico, 1840–1880," Ph.D. diss., University of Nebraska–Lincoln, 1974.
9010

Carlson, Alvar W., "Corrales, New Mexico: Transition in a Spanish-American Community," *Red River Valley Historical Review*, vol. 4 (1979), pp. 88–99.
9011

Nostrand, Richard L., "El Cerrito Revisited," *New Mexico Historical Review*, vol. 57, 2 (1982), pp. 109–122.
9012

Anderson, H. Allen, "The Encomienda in New Mexico, 1598–1680," *New Mexico Historical Review*, vol. 60, 4 (1985), pp. 353–377.
9013

POLITICAL & ADMINISTRATIVE GEOGRAPHY

McPherson, Robert, "Boundaries, Bonanzas, and Bickering: Consolidation of the Northern Navajo Frontier, 1870–1905," *New Mexico Historical Review*, vol. 62, 2 (1987), pp. 169–190.
9014

RESOURCE MANAGEMENT

Sauri-Pujol, David, "From Majordomos to State Engineers: Historical Change in New Mexico Water Rights," Master's thesis, Clark University, 1990.
9015

LAND & LAND USE

Land survey

McKim, V. Calvin, "Geographic Background of Spanish Grants, Taos County, New Mexico," *Bulletin of the Geological Society of America*, vol. 69, 2 (1958), pp. 1765–1766.
9016

Carlson, Alvar W., "Long-Lots in the Rio Arriba," *Annals of the Association of American Geographers*, vol. 65, 1 (1975), pp. 48–57.
9017

Land tenure

Carlson, Alvar W., "Spanish-American Acquisition of Cropland within the Northern Pueblo Indian Grants, New Mexico," *Ethnohistory*, vol. 22, 2 (1975), pp. 95–110.　　　　9018

Land use

Dunham, Harold H., *A Historical Study of Land Use Eastward of the Taos Indians' Pueblo Land Grant Prior to 1848* (New York: Garland, 1974), 29 pp.　　　　9019

Meszaros, Laura, "Vegetation and Land Use History of the Upper Pecos Area, New Mexico," Master's thesis, University of New Mexico, 1989.　　　　9020

EXTRACTIVE ACTIVITY

Milbauer, John A., "The Historical Geography of the Silver City Mining Region of New Mexico," Ph.D. diss., University of California–Riverside, 1983.　　　　9021

AGRICULTURE

Foscue, Edwin J., "The Mesilla Valley of New Mexico: A Study in Aridity and Irrigation," *Economic Geography*, vol. 7, 1 (1931), pp. 1–27.　　　　9022

Culbert, James J., "Pinto Beans in the Estancia Valley of New Mexico," *Economic Geography*, vol. 17, 1 (1941), pp. 50–60.　　　　9023

Carlson, Alvar W., "New Mexico's Sheep Industry 1850–1900: Its Role in the History of the Territory," *New Mexico Historical Review*, vol. 44, 1 (1969), pp. 25–49.　　　　9024

LANDSCAPE

Conway, A. W., "A Northern New Mexico House Type," *Landscape*, vol. 1, 2 (1951), pp. 20–21.　　　　9025

Jackson, John Brinckerhoff, "Pueblo Architecture and Our Own," *Landscape*, vol. 3, 2 (1953–1954), pp. 20–25.　　　　9026

DeBorhegyi, Stephen, "The Evolution of a Landscape," *Landscape*, vol. 4, 1 (1954), pp. 24–30. [Near Chimayo in Santa Fe Co.]　　　　9027

Gritzner, Charles F., "Spanish Log Housing in New Mexico," Ph.D. diss., Louisiana State University, 1969.　　　　9028

Gritzner, Charles F., "Log Housing in New Mexico," *Pioneer America*, vol. 3, 2 (1971), pp. 54–62.　　　　9029

Gritzner, Charles F., "Construction Materials in a Folk Housing Tradition: Considerations Governing Their Selection in New Mexico," *Pioneer America*, vol. 6, 1 (1974), pp. 25–39.　　　　9030

Gritzner, Charles F., "Hispano Gristmills in New Mexico," *Annals of the Association of American Geographers*, vol. 64, 4 (1974), pp. 514–524.　　　9031

Gritzner, Charles F., "Hispanic Log Construction of New Mexico," *El Palacio*, vol. 85, 4 (1979–1980), pp. 20–29.　　　　9032

Wilson, Chris, and David Kammer, *Community and Continuity: The History, Architecture, and Cultural Landscape of La Terra Amarilla* (Santa Fe: New Mexico Historic Preservation Division, 1989), 122 pp.　　　　9033

COMMUNICATIONS & TRADE

See also 8435

Scott, Wayne, "Case-History of a Superhighway," *Landscape*, vol. 6, 2 (1956–1957), pp. 5–7.　　　9034

URBAN NETWORKS & URBANIZATION

Coburn, Frances M., "The Influence of Transportation on the Historical Geography of Las Vegas, New Mexico," Master's thesis, University of Colorado, 1977.　　　　9035

TOWN GROWTH

Rex, Heather, "Albuquerque, New Mexico: From Respiratory Haven to Respiratory Challenge," Master's thesis, University of New Mexico, 1988.　　　　9036

URBAN ECONOMIC STRUCTURE

Hughes, James C., "Three Stages of Land Use in Santa Fe, New Mexico, 1610–1967," Master's thesis, University of Kansas, 1968.　　　　9037

PLACE NAMES

Chávez, Fray Angélico, "Saints' Names in New Mexico Geography," *El Palacio*, vol. 56, 11 (1949), pp. 323–335.　　　　9038

Chávez, Fray Angélico, "New Mexico Place-Names from Spanish Proper Names," *El Palacio*, vol. 56, 12 (1949), pp. 367–382.　　　　9039

Chávez, Fray Angélico, "New Mexico Religious Place-Names Other Than Those of Saints," *El Palacio*, vol. 57, 1 (1950), pp. 24–26.　　　　9040

Chávez, Fray Angélico, "Neo-Mexicanism in New Mexico Place Names," *El Palacio*, vol. 57, 3 (1950), pp. 67–79.　　　　9041

Chávez, Fray Angélico, "Aztec or Nahuatl Words in New Mexico Place Names," *El Palacio*, vol. 57, 4 (1950), pp. 109–112. **9042**

Pearce, Thomas M., *New Mexico Place Names: A Geographical Dictionary* (Albuquerque: University of New Mexico Press, 1965), 187 pp. **9043**

Herrick, Robert L., "Cultural Aspects of Place Names: New Mexico," *Names*, vol. 31, 4 (1983), pp. 271–278. **9044**

Steele, Thomas J., "Naming of Places in Spanish New Mexico," in Marta Weigle, ed., *Hispanic Arts and Ethnohistory in the Southwest* (Santa Fe: Ancient City Press, 1983), pp. 293–302. **9045**

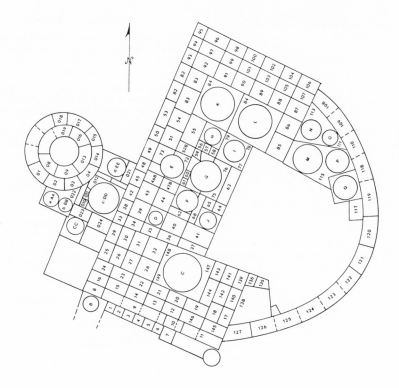

ARIZONA

GENERAL

The state

Wyllys, Rufus K., "The Historical Geography of Arizona," *Pacific Historical Review*, vol. 21, 2 (1952), pp. 121–127.   **9046**

Smaller areas

Bufkin, Donald H., "Geographic Change at Yuma Crossing, 1849–1966," *Arizona and the West*, vol. 28, 2 (1986), pp. 155–160.   **9047**

ENVIRONMENTAL CHANGE

Colton, Harold S., "Sunset Crater: The Effect of a Volcanic Eruption on an Ancient Pueblo People," *Geographical Review*, vol. 22, 4 (1932), pp. 582–590. [Focus on 700–875 A.D.]   **9048**

Schroeder, Albert H., "Man and Environment in the Verde Valley," *Landscape*, vol. 3, 2 (1953–1954), pp. 16–19.   **9049**

Campbell, Ian A., "Climate and Overgrazing on the Shonto Plateau, Arizona," *Professional Geographer*, vol. 22, 3 (1970), pp. 132–141. [Focus on 1500–1960]   **9050**

Burkham, D. E., *Channel Changes of the Gila River in Safford Valley, Arizona, 1846–1970* (Washington, D.C.: U.S. Geological Survey, Professional Paper no. 655–G, 1972).   **9051**

Bahre, Conrad J., and David E. Bradbury, "Vegetation Change along the Arizona-Sonora Boundary," *Annals of the Association of American Geographers*, vol. 68, 2 (1978), pp. 145–165. [Focus on 1892–1976]   **9052**

Hsui, Sheng-I, "Urbanization and Its Effects on the Climate of Phoenix," Ph.D. diss., Arizona State University, 1979.   **9053**

Francaviglia, Richard V., "The Upper San Pedro River Valley: A Century of Environmental Change in Cochise County, Arizona," *Cochise County Historical and Archeological Society Quarterly*, vol. 14, 2 (1984), pp. 8–26.   **9054**

Bahre, Conrad J., *A Legacy of Change: Historic Human Impact on Vegetation of the Arizona Borderlands.* (Tucson: University of Arizona Press, 1991), 231 pp.   **9055**

NATIVE PEOPLES & WHITE RELATIONS

See also 3965, 9047

Prehistoric settlements

Colton, Harold S., "The Geography of Certain Ruins near the San Francisco Mountains, Arizona," *Bulletin of the Philadelphia Geographical Society*, vol. 16, 2 (1918), pp. 37–60.   **9056**

Sauer, Carl O., and Donald D. Brand, "Pueblo Sites in Southeastern Arizona," *California Publications in Geography*, vol. 3, 7 (1930), pp. 415–459. Reprinted in abbreviated form in Robert S. Platt, ed., *Field Study in American Geography* (Chicago: University of Chicago Department of Geography, Research Paper no. 61, 1959), pp. 140–160.   **9057**

Munson, Esther M., "Aboriginal Economic Geography of the Hopi," Master's thesis, University of California–Berkeley, 1933.   **9058**

Hoover, J. Wenger, "Cerros de Trincheras of the Arizona Pagueria," *Geographical Review*, vol. 31, 2 (1941), pp. 228–239. [Prehistory to 1884]   **9059**

Reeve, Frank D., "Early Navaho Geography," *New Mexico Historical Review*, vol. 31, 4 (1956), pp. 290–309.   **9060**

Ross, Stanley H., "The Prehistoric Use of Copper in Arizona," Ph.D. diss., University of California–Los Angeles, 1963.   **9061**

Historic era

McIntire, Elliot G., "Changes in an American Peasant Society: The Hopi Farmer," *Oregon Geographer*, vol. 1, 2 (1967), pp. 9–13.   **9062**

Hasse, Michel L., "Raiders to Ranchers: The Historical Geography of the Arizona Apache Adoption of Cattle," Master's thesis, Arizona State University, 1968.   **9063**

McIntire, Elliot G., "The Impact of Cultural Change on the Land Use Patterns of the Hopi Indians," Ph.D. diss., University of Oregon, 1968.   **9064**

McIntire, Elliot G., and Sandra Gordan, "The Hopi Snake Dance: 1883," *Plateau*, vol. 41, 1 (1968), pp. 27–33.   **9065**

McIntire, Elliot G., "Hopi Colonization on the Colorado River," *California Geographer*, vol. 10, 1 (1969), pp. 7–14. [Covers 1945–1965]   **9066**

McIntire, Elliot G., "The Hopi Villages of Arizona: A Study in Changing Patterns," *Proceedings of the Association of American Geographers*, vol. 1 (1969), pp. 95–99.   9067

Willey, Elizabeth Scowcroft, "The Lands and History of the Hopi Indians," Master's thesis, University of Utah, 1969.   9068

Ressler, John Q., "Moenkopi: Sequent Occupance, Landscape Change, and the View of the Environment in an Oasis on the Western Navajo Reservation, Arizona," Master's thesis, University of Oregon, 1970.   9069

McIntire, Elliot G., "Changing Patterns of Hopi Indian Settlement," *Annals of the Association of American Geographers*, vol. 61, 3 (1971), pp. 510–521. [Focus on 1870–1970]   9070

Aschmann, Homer, "Terrain and Ecological Conditions in the Western Apache Range," *Apache Indians V* (New York: Garland, American Indian Ethnohistory Series, 1974), pp. 233–260.   9071

Aschmann, Homer, "Environment and Ecology in the Northern Tonto Claim Area," *Apache Indians V* (New York: Garland, American Indian Ethnohistory Series, 1974), pp. 167–232. [Verde Valley]   9072

Jett, Stephen C., "War Dogs in the Spanish Expedition Mural, Canyon del Muerto, Arizona?" *Kiva*, vol. 46, 4 (1981), pp. 273–280.   9073

Noble, Allen G., "Navajo Housing: Example of Environmental Adjustments," *Ohio Geographers: Recent Research Themes*, vol. 9 (1981), pp. 17–26.   9074

McIntire, Elliot G., "First Mesa Hopis in 1900: A Demographic Reconstruction," *Journal of Cultural Geography*, vol. 2, 2 (1982), pp. 58–71.   9075

Bahre, Conrad J., "Wild Hay Harvesting in Southern Arizona: A Casualty of the March of Progress," *Journal of Arizona History*, vol. 29, 1 (1987), pp. 69–78.   9076

McIntire, Elliot G., "Early Twentieth Century Hopi Population," in Thomas E. Ross and Tyrel G. Moore, eds., *A Cultural Geography of Native Americans* (Boulder: Westview Press, 1987), pp. 275–295.   9077

EXPLORATION & MAPPING

Sauer, Carl O., "Spanish Expeditions into the Arizona Apacheria," *Arizona Historical Review*, vol. 6, 1 (1935), pp. 3–13.   9078

Bufkin, Donald H., "Phoenix and the Salt River Valley: A Cartographer's View," *Journal of Arizona History*, vol. 18, 3 (1977), pp. 295–298.   9079

POPULAR IMAGES & EVALUATION

Zube, Ervin H., and Christina B. Kennedy, "Changing Images of the Arizona Landscape," in Leo Zonn, ed., *Place Images in the Media: Portrayal, Experience, and Meaning* (Totowa, N.J.: Rowman & Littlefield, 1990), pp. 183–206.   9080

REGIONAL SETTLEMENT

Allen, Agnes M., "The Sequence of Human Occupancy in the Middle Rio Verde Valley, Arizona," Ph.D. diss., Clark University, 1937.   9081

Rogers, William M., "Historical Land Occupance of the Upper San Pedro River Valley since 1870," Master's thesis, University of Arizona, 1965.   9082

Ormrod, Richard K., "The Nineteenth-Century Arizona Mining Frontier: A Study in Settlement Geography," Master's thesis, Arizona State University, 1966.   9083

Harris, Jonathan L., "The Persistence of Mining Settlements in the Arizona Landscape," Master's thesis, University of Arizona, 1971.   9084

Morris, Matthew O., "Mormon Exploration and Settlement in the Little Colorado Basin of Arizona," Master's thesis, Arizona State University, 1972.   9085

Comeaux, Malcolm L., "Early Settlement of the Land," in his *Arizona: A Geography* (Boulder: Westview Press, 1981), pp. 59–126.   9086

Hoy, Bill, "Sonoyta and Santo Domingo: A Story of Two Sonoran Towns and the River That Ran By," *Journal of Arizona History*, vol. 31, 2 (1990), pp. 117–140.   9087

RURAL & REGIONAL SOCIAL GEOGRAPHY

Noden, Richard B., "The Kansas Settlement, Cochise County, Arizona: A Study in Historical Geography," Master's thesis, California State University–Fresno, 1971.   9088

POLITICAL & ADMINISTRATIVE GEOGRAPHY

See also 8932–8933

RESOURCE MANAGEMENT

Wehmeier, Eckhard, "Die Region Phoenix: Entwicklung und Strukturwandel unter dem Aspekt der Wasserversorgung," *Geographische Rundschau*, vol, 39, 7–8 (1987), pp. 435–442.   9089

LAND & LAND USE

Famisa, Zacchaeus S., "The Conversion of Agricultural Land to Non-Agricultural Uses in the Phoenix-Tucson Corridor, 1940–1975," Ph.D. diss., Arizona State University, 1976.　9090

Bahre, Conrad J., "Land Use History of the Research Ranch, Elgine, Arizona," *Journal of the Arizona Academy of Science*, vol. 12, suppl. 2 (1977), pp. 1–32.　9091

Raynak, Thomas, "The Impact of Urbanization on Agricultural Land Use, Chandler, Arizona, 1954–1984," Master's thesis, Arizona State University, 1985.　9092

EXTRACTIVE ACTIVITY

Francaviglia, Richard V., "Copper Mining and Landscape Evolution: A Century of Change in the Warren Mining District, Arizona," *Journal of Arizona History*, vol. 23, 3 (1982), pp. 267–298.　9093

Francaviglia, Richard V., "Time Exposures: The Evolving Landscape of an Arizona Copper Mining District," in Harley E. Johansen, Olen P. Matthews, and Gundars Rudzitis, eds., *Mineral Resource Development: Geopolitics, Economics, and Policy* (Boulder: Westview Press: 1987), pp. 258–268. [Warren Mining District, Bisbee area]　9094

AGRICULTURE

Shapiro, Erik-Anders, "Cotton in Arizona: A Historical Geography," Master's thesis, University of Arizona, 1989.　9095

LANDSCAPE

Gelpke, Richard B., "The Mormon Impact on the Arizona Landscape," Master's thesis, University of Arizona, 1973.　9096

Hirt, Paul, "The Transformation of a Landscape: Culture and Ecology in Southeast Arizona," *Environmental Review*, vol. 13, 3 & 4 (1989), pp. 167–189.　9097

COMMUNICATIONS & TRADE

Wahmann, Russell, "Railroading in the Verde Valley, 1894–1951," *Journal of Arizona History*, vol. 12, 3 (1971), pp. 153–166.　9098

URBAN NETWORKS & URBANIZATION

Sargent, Charles S., Jr., "Towns of the Salt River Valley, 1870–1930," *Historical Geography Newsletter*, vol. 5, 2 (1975), pp. 1–9.　9099

TOWN GROWTH

Parker, Margaret T., "Tucson: City of Sunshine," *Economic Geography*, vol. 24, 2 (1948), pp. 79–113.　9100

Newkirk, William, "Historical Geography of Bisbee, Arizona," Master's thesis, University of Arizona, 1966.　9101

URBAN ECONOMIC STRUCTURE

Gibson, Lay James, "Tucson's Evolving Commercial Base, 1883–1914: A Map Analysis," *Historical Geography Newsletter*, vol. 5, 2 (1975), pp. 10–17.　9102

Volckmann, Steven R., "Historical Development of the Land Uses within the Commercial 'Strip' of Speedway Boulevard, Tucson, Arizona," Master's thesis, University of Arizona, 1977.　9103

Ehrlich, Jonathan D., "Changing Form and Function in the Central Business District of Tempe, Arizona, 1940–1980," Master's thesis, University of Vermont, 1980.　9104

Russell, Peter L., "Downtown's Downtown: A Historical Geography of the Phoenix, Arizona, Central Business District, 1890–1986," Master's thesis, Arizona State University, 1986.　9105

URBAN SOCIAL STRUCTURE

Morehouse, Barbara J., "Landscape as Text: A Sociogeographic Study of the Santa Cruz River within the Vicinity of Tucson, Arizona," Master's thesis, University of Arizona, 1990.　9106

TOWNSCAPE

Deitch, Lewis, "Evolution of House Types in Tucson, Arizona," Master's thesis, University of Arizona, 1966.　9107

Hecht, Melvin F., "The Decline of the Grass Lawn Tradition in Tucson," *Landscape*, vol. 19, 3 (1975), pp. 3–10. [Focus on the twentieth century]　9108

McPherson, E. Gregory, and Renée A. Haip, "Emerging Desert Landscape in Tucson," *Geographical Review*, vol. 79, 4 (1989), pp. 435–449. [Focus on 1870s–1980s]　9109

PLACE NAMES

Barnes, Will C., *Arizona Place Names* (Tucson: University of Arizona, 1935), 503 pp. Reprinted by the University of Arizona Press, 1988.　9110

COLORADO

GENERAL

The state

Griffiths, Mel, and Lynnell Rubright, "Settlement History," in their *Colorado: A Geography* (Boulder: Westview Press, 1983), pp. 169–188. **9111**

ENVIRONMENTAL CHANGE

Mernitz, Scott, "The Impact of Coal Mining on Marshall, Colorado, and Vicinity: An Historical Geography of Environmental Change," Master's thesis, University of Colorado, 1971. **9112**

Smith, Charles R., "Effects of Man on the Geomorphology of the Rampart Range, Colorado," Ph.D. diss., University of Georgia, 1977. **9113**

Graf, William L., "Mining and Channel Response," *Annals of the Association of American Geographers*, vol. 69, 2 (1979), pp. 262–275. [Focus on Central City, 1859–1974] **9114**

Nadler, C. T., and Stanley A. Schumm, "Metamorphosis of South Platte and Arkansas Rivers, Eastern Colorado," *Physical Geography*, vol. 2, 2 (1981), pp. 95–115. [Evidence from 1823–1980] **9115**

Veblen, Thomas T., and Diane C. Lorenz, "Anthropogenic Disturbance and Recovery Patterns in Montane Forests, Colorado Front Range," *Physical Geography*, vol. 7, 1 (1986), pp. 1–24. [Boulder, mid-nineteenth century to 1985] **9116**

Goldblum, David, "Fire History of a Ponderosa Pine/Douglas-Fir Forest in the Colorado Front Range," Master's thesis, University of Colorado, 1990. **9117**

Veblen, Thomas T., and Diane C. Lorenz, *The Colorado Front Range: A Century of Ecological Change* (Salt Lake City: University of Utah Press, 1990), 210 pp. **9118**

NATIVE PEOPLES & WHITE RELATIONS

Birdsall, Williams R., "The Cliff Dwellers of the Canyons of the Mesa Verde," *Journal of the American Geographical Society*, vol. 23 (1891), pp. 584–620. **9119**

Atwood, Wallace W., "A Geographic Study of the Mesa Verde," *Annals of the Association of American Geographers*, vol. 1 (1911), pp. 95–100. [Historical study of the cliff dwellers in the area of present-day Mesa Verde National Park] **9120**

EXPLORATION & MAPPING

Davidson, Levette J., "Colorado Cartography," *Colorado Magazine*, vol. 32 (1955), pp. 178–190 and 256–265. **9121**

Wyckoff, William K., "Mapping the 'New' El Dorado: Pikes Peak Promotional Cartography, 1859–1861," *Imago Mundi*, vol. 40 (1988), pp. 32–45. **9122**

REGIONAL SETTLEMENT

Lantis, David W., "The San Luis Valley, Colorado: Sequent Occupance in an Intermontaine Basin," Ph.D. diss., Ohio State University, 1950. **9123**

Boucher, Bertrand P., "The Sequent Occupance of Baca County, Colorado," Master's thesis, University of Colorado, 1951. **9124**

DePuy, LoAnn, "The Sequent Occupance of the Lower Cache La Poudre Valley, Colorado," Master's thesis, University of Denver, 1957. **9125**

Cadle, James K., "Sequent Occupance of the Idaho Springs Area in Central Colorado," Master's thesis, University of Colorado, 1961. **9126**

Farquhar, Peter, "The Sequent Occupance of Browns Park," Master's thesis, University of Colorado, 1962. **9127**

Taylor, Robert G., "Sequent Occupance of the Cripple Creek Gold Mining District, Colorado," Ph.D. diss., Indiana University, 1962. **9128**

Carlson, Alvar W., "Rural Settlement Patterns in the San Luis Valley: A Comparative Study," *Colorado Magazine*, vol. 44, 3 (1967), 111–128. **9129**

Andrews, John P., "History of Spanish Settlement and Land Use in the Upper Culebra Basin of the San Luis Valley, Costilla County, Colorado," Master's thesis, University of Colorado, 1972. **9130**

POPULATION

Ives, Ronald L., "Population Changes in a Mountain County," *Economic Geography*, vol. 18, 3 (1942), pp. 298–306. [Grand Co., 1860–1940] **9131**

Werden, Dorothie M., "Cartographic Interpretation of the Population Distribution Patterns of the State of Colorado, 1860–1950," Master's thesis, University of Colorado, 1953. **9132**

Loeffler, M. John, "The Population Syndromes on the Colorado Piedmont," *Annals of the Association of American Geographers*, vol. 55, 1 (1965), pp. 26–66. [Focus on 1870–1960] 9133

Matsuda, Shigeharu T., "Japanese Settlement in the Colorado Piedmont Area," Master's thesis, Syracuse University, 1967. 9134

Wayne, George, "Negro Migration and Colonization in Colorado, 1870–1930," *Journal of the West*, vol. 15, 1 (1976), pp. 102–120. 9135

DeLuca, John, "Colorado's Population Changes since Statehood," *Missouri Geographer*, vol. 34 (1990). 9136

RURAL & REGIONAL SOCIAL GEOGRAPHY

Carlson, Alvar W., "Seasonal Farm Labor in the San Luis Valley," *Annals of the Association of American Geographers*, vol. 63, 1 (1973), pp. 97–108. 9137

Norris, Melvin E., "Dearfield, Colorado: The Evolution of a Rural Black Settlement: An Historical Geography of Black Colonization on the Great Plains," Ph.D. diss., University of Colorado, 1980. 9138

ECONOMIC DEVELOPMENT

See also 8558

Osborne, Brian S., "Frying Pan–Arkansas Project: The Twentieth Century Frontier of Colorado," *Wessex Geographer*, vol. 6 (1965), pp. 58–65. 9139

Saa, Oscar R., "Bijou Creek Area, Colorado: The Evolution of an Irrigated Landscape," Master's thesis, University of Colorado, 1969. 9140

RESOURCE MANAGEMENT

Poulton, Curt A., "A Historical Geographic Approach to the Study of the Institutionalization of the Doctrine of Prior Appropriation: The Emergence of Appropriative Water Rights in Colorado Springs, Colorado," Ph.D. diss., University of Minnesota, 1990. 9141

LAND & LAND USE

Davis, Charles M., "Land Utilization in North Park, Colorado," *Economic Geography*, vol. 13, 4 (1937), pp. 379–384. [Focus on 1918–1933] 9142

Davis, Charles M., "Land Ownership in Middle Park, Colorado," *Economic Geography*, vol. 17, 2 (1941), pp. 169–179. [Focus on 1860–1935] 9143

Davis, Charles M., "Changes in Land Utilization on the Plateau of Northwestern Colorado," *Economic Geography*, vol. 18, 4 (1942), pp. 379–388. [Focus on 1870–1931] 9144

Hewes, Leslie, "A Traverse across Kit Carson County, Colorado, with Notes on Land Use on the Margin of the Old Dust Bowl, 1939–1940 and 1962," *Economic Geography*, vol. 39, 4 (1963), pp. 332–340. 9145

EXTRACTIVE ACTIVITY

Christians, William F., "A Geographic Interpretation of the Cripple Creek District," Master's thesis, University of Chicago, 1932. 9146

Gunnell, E. Mitchell, "Ecological and Historical Aspects of Leadville, Colorado, as Typifying the Pure Saxicultural Adjustment," *Transactions of the Illinois State Academy of Science*, vol. 32 (1939), pp. 139–140. 9147

Hoffmeister, Harold A., "Central City Mining Area," *Economic Geography*, vol. 16, 1 (1940), pp. 96–104. [Focus on 1859–1935] 9148

Ashbaugh, James G., "The Historical Geography of the Cripple Creek Mining Area," Master's thesis, University of Colorado, 1953. 9149

Biggins, James, "Historical Geography of the Georgetown, Colorado, Silver Mining Area," Ph.D. diss., University of Colorado, 1972. 9150

AGRICULTURE

Davis, Charles M., "Dry-land Wheat in Northwestern Colorado," *Papers of the Michigan Academy of Science, Arts, and Letters*, vol. 27 (1941), pp. 345–350. [Focus on 1910–1935] 9151

LANDSCAPE

Pritchard, Sandra Freed, "Landscape Changes in Summit County, Colorado, 1859 to the Present: A Historical Geography," Ph.D. diss., University of Oregon, 1982. 9152

COMMUNICATIONS & TRADE

Brown, Ralph Hall, "Colorado Mountain Passes," *Colorado Magazine*, vol. 6 (1929), pp. 227–237. 9153

Brown, Ralph Hall, "Trans-Montane Routes of Colorado," *Economic Geography*, vol. 7, 4 (1931), pp. 412–424. [Focus on 1806–1927] 9154

Due, John F., "The Carson and Colorado Railroad," *Economic Geography*, vol. 27, 3 (1951), pp. 251–267. [Focus on 1880–1950] 9155

Grey, Alan H., "Denver and the Locating of the Union Pacific Railroad, 1862–1866," *Rocky Mountain Social Science Journal*, vol. 6, 2 (1969), pp. 51–59. **9156**

Kindquist, Cathy E., "The Stony Pass Route: An Historical Geography, 1860–1985," Master's thesis, University of Colorado, 1986. **9157**

Kindquist, Cathy E., *Stoney Pass* (Silverton, Colorado: San Juan County Book Co., 1987), 134 pp. **9158**

MANUFACTURING & INDUSTRIALIZATION

Cook, Stephen R., "The Historical and Economic Geography of the Brewing Industry in the Denver Region, 1859–1987," Master's thesis, University of Colorado, 1987. **9159**

URBAN NETWORKS & URBANIZATION

Wyckoff, William K., "Incorporation as a Factor in Formation of an Urban System," *Geographical Review*, vol. 77, 3 (1987), pp. 279–292. [Business incorporations in Colorado, 1859–1879] **9160**

Wyckoff, William K., "Revising the Meyer Model: Denver and the National Urban System, 1859–1879," *Urban Geography*, vol. 9, 1 (1988), pp. 1–18. **9161**

Wyckoff, William K., "Central Place Theory and the Location of Services in Colorado in 1899," *Social Science Journal*, vol. 26, 4 (1989), pp. 383–398. **9162**

TOWN GROWTH

Brown, Ralph Hall, "Monte Vista: Sixty Years of a Colorado Community," *Geographical Review*, vol. 18, 4 (1928), pp. 567–568. **9163**

Stoeckly, Erika, "Boulder: A Study in Historical Geography," Master's thesis, University of Colorado, 1938. **9164**

Brion, Irene J., "The Historical Geography of Leadville, Colorado," Master's thesis, University of Colorado, 1953. **9165**

Trindell, Roger T., "Sequent Occupance of Pueblo, Colorado," Master's thesis, University of Colorado, 1960. **9166**

McBroom, Emmertt G., "A Geographic Perspective of Nederland, a Colorado Mountain Town, 1870–1968," Master's thesis, University of Nebraska, 1969. **9167**

URBAN ECONOMIC STRUCTURE

McCracken, Michael W., "Chain Growth and Competitive Strategy: Metropolitan Denver Supermarket Chains, 1950–1980," Master's thesis, University of Colorado, 1982. **9168**

URBAN SOCIAL STRUCTURE

Lyles, Lionel D., "An Historical Urban Geographical Analysis of Black Neighborhood Development in Denver, 1860–1970," Ph.D. diss., University of Colorado, 1977. **9169**

Gruntfest, Eve C., "Changes in Flood Plain Land Use and Flood Hazard Adjustment in Denver and Boulder, Colorado, 1958–1979," Ph.D. diss., University of Colorado, 1982. **9170**

RECREATION & TOURISM

Leu, Del Q., "A Full Land for a Rich Society: The Evolution of the Bureau of Land Management's Recreation Program in Southwestern Colorado," Master's thesis, University of Wisconsin–Madison, 1986. **9171**

Hartmann, Rudi, "Vom Bergbauort zur Fremdenverkehrsgemeinde: Goldgräber- und Westernstädte als Ausgangspunkt touristischer Entwicklungen in den Colorado Rocky Mountains," in Rudi Hartmann, ed., *Forschungsperspektiven der nordamerikanischen Fremdenverkehrsgeographie* (Trier: Geographische Gesellschaft Trier, Materialien zur Fremdenverkehrsgeographie, vol. 20, 1989), pp. 125–153. **9172**

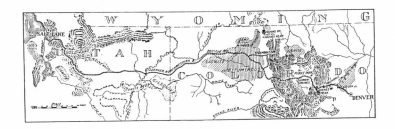

UTAH

Hodson, Dean R., "The Origin of Non-Mormon Settlement in Utah: 1847–1896," Ph.D. diss., Michigan State University, 1971. **9195**

Rosenvall, Lynn A., "Interstate Boundaries and Settlement Patterns: The Example of Utah," in Roger Leigh, ed., *Malaspina Papers: Studies in Human and Physical Geography* (Vancouver: Tantalus Research, B.C. Geographical Series, no. 17, 1973), pp. 35–50. [Focus from 1847 to the 1870s] **9196**

Blake, John T., "A Geographic Sketch of Early Utah Settlement," Master's thesis, Brigham Young University, 1974. **9197**

Wahlquist, Wayne L., "Settlement Processes in the Mormon Core Area, 1847–1890," Ph.D. diss., University of Nebraska–Lincoln, 1974. **9198**

Shelley, Wayne R., "The Development and Failure of Historic Agricultural Communities of Utah: A Case Study of Johns Valley, Utah," Master's thesis, Brigham Young University, 1989. **9199**

POPULATION

White, C. Langdon, "The Distribution of Population in the Salt Lake Oasis," *Journal of Geography*, vol. 27, 1 (1928), pp. 1–14. [Focus on 1847–1928] **9200**

Gregory, Herbert E., "Population of Southern Utah," *Economic Geography*, vol. 21, 1 (1945), pp. 29–57. [Focus on 1851–1940] **9201**

Peterson, Wayne L., "Population Growth in the Mormon Core Area, 1847–1890," in Richard H. Jackson, ed., *The Mormon Role in the Settlement of the West* (Provo: Brigham Young University Press, Charles Redd Monographs in Western History, no. 9, 1978), pp. 107–134. **9202**

Maxfield, Brent W., "Population Movement and Growth in Utah County, Utah, 1940–1980," Master's thesis, Brigham Young University, 1981. **9203**

RURAL & REGIONAL SOCIAL GEOGRAPHY

Seeman, Albert L., "Communities in the Salt Lake Basin," *Economic Geography*, vol. 14, 3 (1938), pp. 300–308. [Focus on 1847–1937] **9204**

Rogers, Peter, "Danish Settlement in Northern Utah," Master's thesis, University of California–Berkeley, 1970. **9205**

Rice, Cindy, "A Geographic Appraisal of the Acculturation Process of Scandinavians in the Sanpete Valley, Utah, 1850–1900," Master's thesis, University of Utah, 1973. **9206**

Jackson, Richard H., "Utah's Harshlands, Hearth of Greatness," *Utah Historical Quarterly*, vol. 49, 1 (1981), pp. 4–25. **9207**

Bennion, Lowell C., "The Incidence of Mormon Polygamy in 1880: Dixie Versus Davis Stake," *Journal of Mormon History*, vol. 11, 1 (1984), pp. 27–32. **9208**

POLITICAL & ADMINISTRATIVE GEOGRAPHY

See also **8932–8933**

Hanson, George H., "The Geographic Factor and Its Influence on Utah Administrative Units," *Yearbook of the Association of Pacific Coast Geographers*, vol. 3 (1937), pp. 3–8. **9209**

Brightman, George F., "The Boundaries of Utah," *Economic Geography*, vol. 17, 1 (1940), pp. 87–95. **9210**

Allen, James B., "The Evolution of County Boundaries in Utah," *Utah Historical Quarterly*, vol. 23, 3 (1955), pp. 261–278. **9211**

Greer, Deon C., "The Political Geography of the Relicted Lands of the Great Salt Lake," *Journal of Geography*, vol. 71, 3 (1972), pp. 161–166. Reprinted, with minor omissions, in *California Geographer*, vol. 14 (1973), pp. 81–91. [Focus on 1865–1973] **9212**

Fisher, Albert L., Boundaries and Utah: Sense or Nonsense?" *Encyclia* (Utah Academy of Sciences, Arts, and Letters), vol. 56 (1979), pp. 127–133. [Focus on 1850–1979] **9213**

RESOURCE MANAGEMENT

Speth, William W., "Environment, Culture, and the Mormon in Early Utah: A Study in Cultural Adaptation," *Yearbook of the Association of Pacific Coast Geographers*, vol. 29 (1967), pp. 53–67. **9214**

Williams, Clinton K., "Distribution and Water Use of the Spanish Fork River, Utah, 1900–1968," Master's thesis, Brigham Young University, 1972. **9215**

LAND & LAND USE

Skousen, Ervin M., "Trend Surface Analysis of Residential Subdivision in the Salt Lake Valley: 1887 to 1972," Master's thesis, University of Utah, 1974. **9216**

Buchanan, Robert M., "Agricultural Land Conversion in the Salt Lake Valley: Policies and Practices, 1950–1980," Master's thesis, University of Utah, 1982. **9217**

AGRICULTURE

See also 9299

White, C. Langdon, "The Agricultural Geography of the Salt Lake Oasis," *Journal of the Scientific Laboratories of Denison University*, vol. 24, art. 4 (1925), pp. 117–283. **9218**

White, C. Langdon, "Transhumance in the Sheep Industry of the Salt Lake Region," *Economic Geography*, vol. 2, 3 (1926), pp. 414–425. [Focus on 1848–1925] **9219**

Wride, Charles H., "The Agricultural Geography of Utah County, 1849–1960," Master's thesis, Brigham Young University, 1961. **9220**

Reed, Carl W., "Geography of Turkey Raising in the Sanpete Valley: A Study in Time and Space," Master's thesis, Brigham Young University, 1971. **9221**

Strässer, Manfred, *Die Bewässerungslandschaft der Wasatch Oase in Utah* (Freiburg i. Br.: Hans Ferdinand Schulz Verlag, Freiburger Geographische Arbeiten, vol. 4, 1972), 246 pp. [Focus on 1847–1970] **9222**

Strässer, Manfred, "Die Feldbewässerung des Mormonenlandes: Utah in Wandel der Zeit," *Zeitschrift für Wirtschaftegeographie*, vol. 19, 3 (1975), pp. 87–90. [Focus on 1847–1970] **9223**

Strässer, Manfred, "Die Bewässerungswirtschaft der Mormonen," *Geographie im Unterricht*, vol. 1, 7 (1976), pp. 181–191. **9224**

LANDSCAPE

Geddes, Joseph A., "Modifications of the Early Utah Farm Village," *Yearbook of the Association of Pacific Coast Geographers*, vol. 8 (1942), pp. 15–22. **9225**

Spencer, Joseph E., "House Types of Southern Utah," *Geographical Review*, vol. 35, 3 (1945), pp. 444–457. **9226**

Rice, Cindy, "Spring City: A Look at a Nineteenth-Century Mormon Village," *Utah Historical Quarterly*, vol. 43, 3 (1975), pp. 260–277. **9227**

MANUFACTURING & INDUSTRIALIZATION

White, C. Langdon, "The Insular Integrity of Industry in the Salt Lake Oasis," *Economic Geography*, vol. 1, 2 (1925), pp. 206–235. [Focus on 1848–1925] **9228**

URBAN NETWORKS & URBANIZATION

Harris, Chauncy D., "Location of Salt Lake City," *Economic Geography*, vol. 17, 2 (1941), pp. 204–212. **9229**

Layton, Robert, "The Historical Geography of the Salt Lake Milkshed," *Yearbook of the Association of Pacific Coast Geographers*, vol. 14 (1952), pp. 34–39. **9230**

Bennion, Lowell C., and Merrill K. Ridd, "Utah's Dynamic Dixie: Satellite of Salt Lake, Las Vegas, or Los Angeles?" *Utah Historical Quarterly*, vol. 47, 3 (1979), pp. 310–327. **9231**

TOWN GROWTH

Chesnutwood, Charles M., "A Historical Approach to the Urban Geography of Brigham City, Utah," Master's thesis, University of Utah, 1950. **9232**

Boyce, Ronald R., "An Historical Geography of Greater Salt Lake City," Master's thesis, University of Utah, 1957. **9233**

URBAN SOCIAL STRUCTURE

Wright, Paul A., "The Growth and Distribution of the Mormon and Non-Mormon Population in Salt Lake City," Master's thesis, University of Chicago, 1970. **9234**

Kuhn, Robert J., "The Location of Multifamily Housing in the Salt Lake Valley, 1900–1975," Master's thesis, University of Utah, 1976. **9235**

Burns, Elizabeth K., and Jeanne C. Kay, "Land Ownership Trends in Salt Lake City's Changing Central Business District," *Yearbook of the Association of Pacific Coast Geographers*, vol. 43 (1981), pp. 23–35. **9236**

TOWNSCAPE

Schuster, Stephen, "The Evolution of Mormon City Planning and Salt Lake City, Utah, 1833–1877," Master's thesis, University of Utah, 1967. **9237**

RECREATION & TOURISM

Jackson, Richard H., "Great Salt Lake and Great Salt Lake City: American Curiosities," *Utah Historical Quarterly*, vol. 56, 2 (1988), pp. 128–147. **9238**

PLACE NAMES

Palmer, William R., "Indian Names in Utah Geography," *Utah Historical Quarterly*, vol. 1, 1 (1928), pp. 5–26. **9239**

Writers' Program, *Origins of Utah Place Names*, 3d ed. (Salt Lake City: Utah State Department of Public Instruction, 1940), 47 pp. **9240**

Buss, Walter R., "The Fascination of Utah Place Names," *Encyclia* (Utah Academy of Sciences, Arts, and Letters), vol. 63 (1986), pp. 194–199. **9241**

NEVADA

GENERAL

Bowen, Marshall E., "The Heritage of an Empty Land: Independence Valley, Nevada," *Journal of Cultural Geography*, vol. 6, 2 (1986), pp. 67–79.
9242

ENVIRONMENTAL CHANGE

Bowen, Marshall E., "Jackrabbit Invasion of a Nevada Agricultural Community," *Ecumene*, vol. 12 (1980), pp. 6–16.
9243

NATIVE PEOPLES & WHITE RELATIONS

Carter, George F., "Archaeology in the Reno Area in Relation to the Age of Man in America and the Culture Sequence in America," *Proceedings of the American Philosophical Society*, vol. 102 (1958), pp. 174–192.
9244

REGIONAL SETTLEMENT

Weaver, John C., "Silver Peak and Blair: Desert Mining Communities," *Economic Geography*, vol. 15, 1 (1939), pp. 80–84. [Focus on 1863–1939]
9245

Peters, Lillian L., "Settlement Patterns in Nevada," Master's thesis, University of Chicago, 1947.
9246

Kersten, Earl W., "The Early Settlement of Aurora, Nevada, and Nearby Mining Camps," *Annals of the Association of American Geographers*, vol. 54, 4 (1964), pp. 490–507.
9247

Bowen, Marshall E., "Turnover of Pioneers and Property in a Marginal Nevada Farming Community," *Yearbook of the Association of Pacific Coast Geographers*, vol. 42 (1980), pp. 45–58. **9248**

Bowen, Marshall E., "Dryland Homesteading on Tobar Flat," *Northeastern Nevada Historical Society Quarterly 1981*, no. 4 (1981), pp. 118–140.
9249

Bowen, Marshall E., "Pioneer Success and Failure in a Northeastern Nevada Valley," *Pioneer America Society Transactions*, vol. 9 (1986), pp. 23–29.
9250

Bowen, Marshall E., "The Desert Homestead as a Non-Farm Residence," *Nevada Historical Society Quarterly*, vol. 31, 3 (1988), pp. 198–211. **9251**

POLITICAL & ADMINISTRATIVE GEOGRAPHY

See also **8931–8932**

Hill, James E., "Nevada South of 37 Degrees North: An Unprecedented Political Blunder," *Yearbook of the Association of Pacific Coast Geographers*, vol. 35 (1973), pp. 61–74.
9252

Mottaz, Stan, "County Evolution in Nevada," *Nevada Historical Society Quarterly*, vol. 21, 1 (1978), pp. 25–50.
9253

ECONOMIC DEVELOPMENT

Kersten, Earl W., "Nevada Then and Now: Forging an Economy," *Yearbook of the Association of Pacific Coast Geographers*, vol. 47 (1985), pp. 7–26. [Focus on 1860–1983]
9254

LAND & LAND USE

Thomas, David, "Historic and Prehistoric Land-Use Patterns in the Reese River Valley," *Nevada Historical Society Quarterly*, vol. 30, 2 (1987), pp. 111–117.
9255

AGRICULTURE

Bowen, Marshall E., "Elko County's Dry Farming Experimental Station," *Northeastern Nevada Historical Society Quarterly*, vol. 2, 1 (1979), pp. 35–51.
9256

Rowley, William D., "Opposition to Arid Land Irrigation in Nevada, 1890–1900," *Yearbook of the Association of Pacific Coast Geographers*, vol. 43 (1981), pp. 113–123.
9257

Bowen, Marshall E., "A Backward Step: From Irrigation to Dry Farming in the Nevada Desert," *Agricultural History*, vol. 63, 2 (1989), pp. 231–242.
9258

COMMUNICATIONS & TRADE

See also **8944**

Eigenheer, Richard A., "Eastward the Frontier: Historic Nevada Post Office Locations, 1860–1910," *Nevada Historical Society Quarterly*, vol. 25, 4 (1982), pp. 315–326.
9259

TOWN GROWTH

Moehring, Eugene P., "Suburban Resorts and the Triumph of Las Vegas," *Halcyon*, vol. 10 (1988), pp. 201–214. [Focus on 1920–1960]   **9260**

PLACE NAMES

Carlson, Helen S., *Nevada Place Names: A Geographical Dictionary* (Reno: University of Nevada Press, 1974), 282 pp. Revised 1985.   **9261**

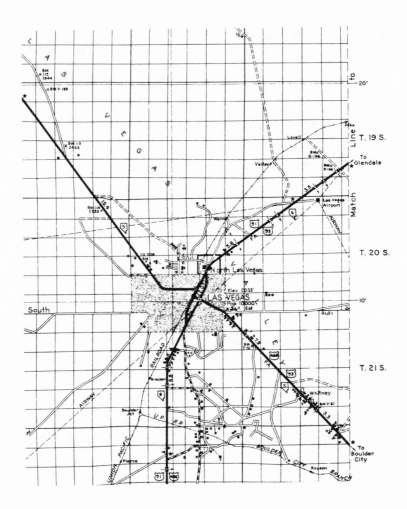

WYOMING

GENERAL

Barry, J. Nielson, "Wyoming: The Completed Puzzle," *Bulletin of the Philadelphia Geographical Society*, vol. 30, 3 (1932), pp. 153–156. [Focus on territorial evolution] **9262**

POPULAR IMAGES & EVALUATION

Bowen, Marshall E., "Perception and Mormon Pioneering in the Big Horn Basin: Cowley Flat, Wyoming," *Great Plains–Rocky Mountain Geographical Journal*, vol. 1 (1972), pp. 14–18. **9263**

Birch, Brian P., "Crossing Wyoming with the Forty-Niners: Cornish Impressions of the Trek West," *Annals of Wyoming*, vol. 59, 2 (1987), pp. 8–15. **9264**

REGIONAL SETTLEMENT

See also **8369**

Bowen, Marshall E., "On the Outer Rim of Zion: Mormon Occupance of Burlington Flat, Wyoming," *Philippine Geographical Journal*, vol. 16, 2 (1972), pp. 55–66. **9265**

Brown, Robert H., "Population Dynamics," and "Sequential Occupance," in his *Wyoming: A Geography* (Boulder: Westview Press, 1980), pp. 53–74 and 37–45. **9266**

POPULATION

Bowen, Marshall E., "Migration to and from a Northern Wyoming Mormon Community, 1900–1925," *Pioneer America*, vol. 9, 2 (1977), pp. 208–227. **9267**

POPULATION & ADMINISTRATIVE GEOGRAPHY

See **8963**

RESOURCE MANAGEMENT

Greenquist, Connie Marie, "The American Pronghorn Antelope in Wyoming: A History of Human Influences and Management," Ph.D. diss., University of Oregon, 1983. **9268**

EXTRACTIVE ACTIVITY

See **8565**

COMMUNICATIONS & TRADE

Gilbert, Edmund W., "South Pass: A Study in the Historical Geography of the United States," *Scottish Geographical Magazine*, vol. 45, 3 (1929), pp. 144–154. **9269**

Grey, Alan H., "The Union Pacific Railroad and South Pass," *Kansas Quarterly*, vol. 2, 3 (1970), pp. 46–57. **9270**

Braatz, Ned E., "Historical Geography of Transportation in the Laramie Basin," Master's thesis, University of Wyoming, 1972. **9271**

TOWN GROWTH

Logan, Byron E., "Cheyenne, Wyoming: A Study in Historical and Urban Geography," Master's thesis, University of Colorado, 1952. **9272**

TOWNSCAPE

Bowen, Marshall E., "Trees for a Desert Town," *Virginia Geographer*, vol. 9, 1 (1974), pp. 3–7. [Cowley, 1900–1915] **9273**

PLACE NAMES

Urbanek, Mae Bobb, *Wyoming Place Names* (Missoula: Mountain Press Publishing Co., 1988), 233 pp. **9274**

MONTANA

GENERAL

The state

Freeman, Otis W., "Montana: A Study of the Geographic Factors Influencing the State," *Bulletin of the Philadelphia Geographical Society*, vol. 12, 4 (1914), pp. 129–165.   **9275**

Smaller areas

Bowman, Isaiah, "Jordan Country," *Geographical Review*, vol. 21, 1 (1931), pp. 22–55.   **9276**

Alwin, John A., "Jordan Country: A Golden Anniversary Look," *Annals of the Association of American Geographers*, vol. 71, 4 (1981), pp. 479–498.   **9277**

ENVIRONMENTAL CHANGE

Knapp, Paul A., "Natural Recovery of Compacted Soils in Semiarid Montana," *Physical Geography*, vol. 10, 2 (1989), pp. 165–175. [Evidence from five southwest Montana ghost towns—Aldridge, Castle, Revenue Flats, Rochester, and Storrs—all abandoned between 1910 and 1941]   **9278**

NATIVE PEOPLES & WHITE RELATIONS

See also **3965**

Lang, William L., "Where Did the Nez Perces go in Yellowstone in 1877?" *Montana*, vol. 40, 1 (1990), pp. 14–21.   **9279**

EXPLORATION & MAPPING

See also **8351**

POPULAR IMAGES & EVALUATION

Cragg, Barbara, "Richard Hugo's 'Triggering Towns': A Poet's Landscape of Montana," *Yearbook of the Association of Pacific Coast Geographers*, vol. 46 (1984), pp. 51–61.   **9280**

Cragg, Barbara, "Sacred Place, Virgin Land, and Triggering Towns: The Literature of Montana as Geographic Text," Ph.D. diss., University of Oregon, 1986.   **9281**

POLITICAL & ADMINISTRATIVE GEOGRAPHY

Bren, Glen D., "The Battle of the Little Big Horn: A Retrospect (Historical Geography)," Master's thesis, South Dakota State University, 1970. **9282**

LAND & LAND USE

Oliver, A. Russell, "Land Utilization in Judith Basin, Montana," *Yearbook of the Association of Pacific Coast Geographers*, vol. 3 (1937), pp. 16–18. [Focus on 1880–1935]   **9283**

EXTRACTIVE ACTIVITY

Alwin, John A., "Pelts, Provisions, and Perceptions: The Hudson's Bay Company Mandan Indian Trade, 1795–1812," *Montana*, vol. 29, 3 (1979), pp. 16–27.   **9284**

Wyckoff, William K., and D. R. Lageson, "Retrograde Mineral Exploration and Settlement of Western and Central Montana during the Late Nineteenth Century," *Centennial Field Conference Guidebook* (Montana Geological Society, 1989), pp. 5–18.   **9285**

AGRICULTURE

See **8581**

LANDSCAPE

Knudson, Harold S., "Barns as an Index to Ethnic Origins in Western Montana," Master's thesis, University of Montana, 1969.   **9286**

Alwin, John A., "Montana's Beaverslide Hay Stacker," *Journal of Cultural Geography*, vol. 3, 1 (1982), pp. 42–50.   **9287**

COMMUNICATIONS & TRADE

Alwin, John A., "Post Office Locations and the Historical Geographer: A Montana Example," *Professional Geographer*, vol. 26, 2 (1974), pp. 183–186.   **9288**

URBAN NETWORKS & URBANIZATION

See also **9231**

Alwin, John A., "Pattern of Montana's Towns, 1860 to 1920," Master's thesis, University of Montana, 1972.   **9289**

TOWN GROWTH

Winchell, Alexander N., "Why is Butte?" *Journal of Geography*, vol. 10, 3 (1911), pp. 86–88.   **9290**

TOWNSCAPE

Leeper, Joseph S., "The Changing Urban Land-scape of Butte, Montana," Ph.D. diss., University of Oregon, 1974.   9291

Hudson, John C., "Main Streets of the Yellowstone Valley," *Montana,* vol. 35, 4 (1985), pp. 56–67.
                    9292

PLACE NAMES

See also **8973**

Cheney, Roberta Carkeek, *Names on the Face of Montana: The Story of Montana's Place Names* (Missoula: University of Montana Publications in History, 1971), 275 pp.   9293

Cheney, Roberta Carkeek, "A Century of Montana History in Her Placenames," *Names,* vol. 37, 2 (1989), pp. 155–164.   9294

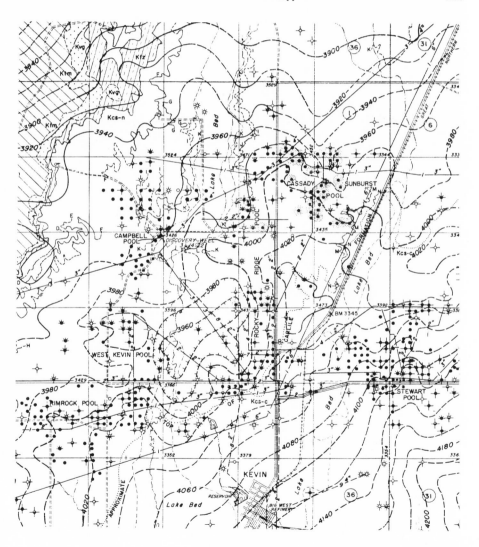

—————————— IDAHO ——————————

GENERAL

Mansfield, George R., "Geography of Southeastern Idaho," *Annals of the Association of American Geographers*, vol. 15, 2 (1925), pp. 51–64. **9295**

EXPLORATION & MAPPING

See **8351**

REGIONAL SETTLEMENT

See **8369**

RURAL & REGIONAL SOCIAL GEOGRAPHY

McFeeley, Sarah A., "The Spatial Distribution of Churches in Rural Latah County, Idaho, 1870–1980," Master's thesis, University of Idaho, 1980. **9296**

POLITICAL & ADMINISTRATIVE GEOGRAPHY

See also **8963**

Thomas, Benjamin E., "Boundaries and Internal Problems of Idaho," *Geographical Review*, vol. 39, 1 (1949), pp. 99–109. **9297**

LAND & LAND USE

West, Keith D., "Land Alienation and Fractionated Heirship in Nez Perce Country: A Study of Resource Control," Master's thesis, University of Idaho, 1982. **9298**

AGRICULTURE

Valora, Peter J., "A Historical Geography of Agriculture in the Upper Snake River Valley, Idaho, Including a Comparison with Cache Valley, Utah/Idaho," Ph.D. diss., University of Colorado, 1986. **9299**

LANDSCAPE

Attebury, Jennifer, "Log Construction in the Sawtooth Valley of Idaho," *Pioneer America*, vol. 8, 1 (1976), pp. 36–46. **9300**

URBAN NETWORKS & URBANIZATION

Wrigley, Robert, Jr., "Pocatello, Idaho, as a Railroad Center," *Economic Geography*, vol. 19, 4 (1943), pp. 325–336. [Focus on 1872–1940] **9301**

PLACE NAMES

See also **8973**

Kramer, Fritz L., *Idaho Town Names* (Boise: Idaho State Historical Department, Twenty-Third Biennial Report, 1953), pp. 14–114. **9302**

Boone, Lalia, *Idaho Place Names: A Geographical Dictionary* (Moscow: University of Idaho Press, 1988), 413 pp. **9303**

—— THE PACIFIC NORTHWEST ——

(& PACIFIC COAST, PACIFIC BASIN)

GENERAL

See also 1148

Duboc, Jessie L., "Geographic Background of History in the Pacific Northwest," *Journal of Geography*, vol. 46, 9 (1947), pp. 338–347. **9304**

Gastil, Raymond D., "The Pacific Northwest as a Cultural Region," *Pacific Northwest Quarterly*, vol. 64, 4 (1973), pp. 147–156. **9305**

Jordan, H. Glenn, "Geographic Setting for the Pacific Basin Frontier," *Journal of the West*, vol. 15, 3 (1976), pp. 5–14. **9306**

ENVIRONMENTAL CHANGE

See also 1160

Jillson, Willard R., "The Volcanic Activity of Mount St. Helens and Mount Hood in Historic Times," *Geographical Review*, vol. 3, 4 (1917), pp. 481–485. **9307**

Schulman, Edmund, "Runoff Histories in Tree Rings of the Pacific Slope," *Geographical Review*, vol. 35, 1 (1945), pp. 59–73. **9308**

Bennett, Charles F., "Some Post-1850 Human Influences on Pacific Coast Zoogeography," *Yearbook of the Association of Pacific Coast Geographers*, vol. 25 (1963), pp. 31–36. **9309**

Graumlich, Lisa J., "Precipitation Variation in the Pacific Northwest (1675–1975) as Reconstructed from Tree Rings," *Annals of the Association of American Geographers*, vol. 77, 1 (1987), pp. 19–29. **9310**

NATIVE PEOPLES & WHITE RELATIONS

Waterman, Thomas T., "The Geographical Names Used by the Indians of the Pacific Coast," *Geographical Review*, vol. 12, 2 (1922), pp. 175–194. **9311**

Merriam, Willis B., "Some Environmental Influences in the Cultural Development of the Haida," *Yearbook of the Association of Pacific Coast Geographers*, vol. 8 (1942), pp. 23–26. **9312**

Gibson, James R., "European Dependence upon American Natives: The Case of Russian America," *Ethnohistory*, vol. 25, 4 (1978), pp. 359–386. **9313**

Gibson, James R., *Russian Dependence upon the Natives of Russian America* (Washington, D.C.: Kennan Institute for Advanced Russian Studies, Occasional Paper no. 70, 1979), 37 pp. **9314**

EXPLORATION & MAPPING

See also 1285–1288

Kingston, C. S., "Explorations, Political Adjustments, and Settlement," in Otis W. Freeman and Howard H. Martin, eds., *The Pacific Northwest: A Regional, Human, and Economic Survey of Resources and Development* (New York: John Wiley & Sons, 1942), pp. 14–37. **9315**

Wagner, Henry R., "George Davidson, Geographer of the Northwest Coast of America," *California Historical Society Quarterly*, vol. 11, 4 (1932), pp. 299–320. **9316**

Freeman, Otis W., "Maps and Their Use in Pacific Northwest History," *Pacific Northwest Quarterly*, vol. 42, 3 (1951), pp. 242–246. **9317**

Ehrenberg, Ralph E., "Our Heritage in Maps: Sketch of Part of the Missouri and Yellowstone Rivers with a Description of the Country," *Prologue: The Journal of the National Archives*, vol. 3, 2 (1971), pp. 73–79. **9318**

Holmes, Kenneth L., "Francis Drake's Course in the North Pacific, 1579," *Geographical Bulletin*, vol. 17 (1979), pp. 5–41. **9319**

Ronda, James, "A Chart in His Way: Indian Cartography and the Lewis and Clark Expedition," *Great Plains Quarterly*, vol. 4, 1 (1984), pp. 43–53. Reprinted in Frederick C. Luebke, Frances Kaye, and Gary E. Moulton, eds., *Mapping the North American Plains: Essays in the History of Cartography* (Norman: University of Oklahoma Press, 1987), pp. 81–91. **9320**

Ehrenberg, Ralph E., "Surveying and Charting the Pacific Basin," in Herman J. Viola and Carolyn Margolis, eds., *Magnificent Voyagers: The U.S. Exploring Expedition, 1838–1842* (Washington, D.C.: Smithsonian Institute Press, 1985), pp. 164–187. **9321**

Matthewson, Sandra, "From Myth to Reality: Mapping the Northwest, 1790–1850," Master's thesis, Oregon State University, 1990. **9322**

POPULAR IMAGES & EVALUATION

Allen, John L., "The Geographical Images of the American Northwest, 1673 to 1806: An Historical Geography," Ph.D. diss., Clark University, 1969.
9323

Dunbar, Gary S., "Isotherms and Politics: Perception of the Northwest in the 1850s," in A. W. Rasporich and H. C. Klassen, eds., *Prairie Perspectives: Selected Papers of the Western Canadian Studies Conferences, 1970–71* (Toronto: Holt, Rinehart, and Winston, 1973), pp. 80–101.
9324

REGIONAL SETTLEMENT

See also 1324, 1338–1339

Colonization

Merriam, Willis B., "Historical Geography of Russian America," *Yearbook of the Association of Pacific Coast Geographers*, vol. 3 (1937), pp. 18–23.
9325

Settlement morphology

Erickson, Kenneth A., "Morphology of Lumber Settlement in Western Oregon and Washington," Ph.D. diss., University of California–Berkeley, 1965.
9326

Prasanna, Subbarayan, "Morphologies of the Settlement Landscape in the Columbia Basin Project Area," Ph.D. diss., University of Washington, 1976.
9327

RURAL & REGIONAL SOCIAL GEOGRAPHY

See also 1377–1378

Stratton, David, "Hells Canyon: The Missing Link in Pacific Northwest Regionalism," *Idaho Yesteryears*, vol. 28, 3 (1984), pp. 2–9.
9328

POLITICAL & ADMINISTRATIVE GEOGRAPHY

See also 1395

Deutsch, Herman, "The Evolution of Territorial and State Boundaries in the Inland Empire of the Pacific Northwest," *Pacific Northwest Quarterly*, vol. 51, 3 (1960), pp. 115–131.
9329

Freeman, William H., "An Analysis of Military Land Use Policy and Practice in the Pacific Northwest, 1849–1940," Ph.D. diss., University of Washington, 1974.
9330

Updegraff, Nancy A., "The Evolution between 1935 and 1965 of Federal Legislation to Control Water Pollution and Its Relationship to Water Quality Regulation in the Lower Columbia River," Ph.D. diss., Oregon State University, 1976.
9331

Freeman, William H., "Accessibility and Transportation: An Analysis of Military Land Use Policy and Practice in the Pacific Northwest, 1849–1970," in James W. Scott, ed., *Transportation in the Puget Sound Region: Past, Present, and Future* (Bellingham: Western Washington State University Center for Pacific Northwest Studies, 1977), pp. 38–61.
9332

Freeman, William H., "Army Air Power in the Pacific Northwest, 1920–1940: A Practical Example of the Development of the Site Selection Rationale for Regional Military Airdromes in the United States: 1920–1940," *Aerospace Historian*, vol. 25, 3 (Sept. 1978), pp. 167–175.
9333

ECONOMIC DEVELOPMENT

Bridges, John L., "Regional Development and Socioeconomic Well-Being in the Pacific Northwest, 1950–1980," Master's thesis, University of Georgia, 1986.
9334

Warf, Barney L., "Regional Transformation, Everyday Life, and Pacific Northwest Lumber Production," *Annals of the Association of American Geographers*, vol. 78, 2 (1988), pp. 326–346. [Focus on 1870–1984]
9335

RESOURCE MANAGEMENT

Macinko, George, "The Columbia Basin Project: Expectations, Realizations, Implications," *Geographical Review*, vol. 53, 2 (1963), pp. 185–199.
9336

Macinko, George, "The Columbia Basin Project Reappraised," in *United Nations Interregional Seminar on River Basin and Interbasin Development: Policies and Planning* (Budapest: United Nations, 1976), pp. 211–216.
9337

EXTRACTIVE ACTIVITY

See also 1408, 1411, 1413

Freeman, Otis W., "Salmon Industry of the Pacific Coast," *Economic Geography*, vol. 11, 2 (1935), pp. 109–129.
9338

Damron, John E., "The Emergence of Salmon Trolling on the American Northwest Coast: A Maritime Historical Geography," Ph.D. diss., University of Oregon, 1975.
9339

AGRICULTURE

See also 1417–1418, 1422

Baker, Oliver E., "Agricultural Regions of North America: Part IX—The North Pacific Hay and Pasture Region," *Economic Geography*, vol. 7, 2 (1931), pp. 109–153.   9340

Baker, Oliver E., "Agricultural Regions of North America: Part XI—The Columbia Plateau Wheat Region," *Economic Geography*, vol. 9, 2 (1933), pp. 167–197.   9341

LANDSCAPE

Rostlund, Erhard, "The Changing Forest Landscape," *Landscape*, vol. 4, 2 (1954–1955), pp. 30–35.   9342

COMMUNICATIONS

See 1434, 1436

MANUFACTURING & INDUSTRIALIZATION

Freeman, Otis W., "The Pacific Northwest Pea Industry," *Economic Geography*, vol. 19, 2 (1943), pp. 118–128.   9343

Monahan, Robert L., "Locational Changes in the Forest Products Industries of the Pacific Northwest," *Yearbook of the Association of Pacific Coast Geographers*, vol. 28 (1966), pp. 29–40. [Focus on 1925–1965]   9344

TOWNSCAPE

Turbeville, Daniel E., III, "Cities of Kindling: Geographical Implications of the Urban Fire Hazard on the Pacific Northwest Coast Frontier, 1851–1920," Ph.D. diss., Simon Fraser University, 1986.   9345

PLACE NAMES

Writers' Program, *Geographical Names in the Coastal Areas of California, Oregon, and Washington* (Washington, D.C.: U.S. Department of Commerce, 1940), 94 pp.   9346

——— WASHINGTON ———

GENERAL

See also 1147

Rockie, William A., "Man's Effect on the Palouse," *Geographical Review*, vol. 29, 1 (1939), pp. 34–45. 9347

Atkinson, Burton W., "The Historical Geography of the Snohomish River Valley," Master's thesis, University of Washington, 1940. 9348

Meinig, Donald W., "The Walla Walla Country: 1805–1900: A Century of Man and the Land," Ph.D. diss., University of Washington, 1954. 9349

Hazeltine, Jean, "The Historical and Regional Geography of the Willapa Bay Area," Ph.D. diss., Ohio State University, 1956. 9350

Meinig, Donald W., *The Great Columbia Plain: A Historical Geography, 1805–1910* (Seattle: University of Washington Press, 1968), 576 pp. 9351

ENVIRONMENTAL CHANGE

Dart, John O., "The Changing Hydrologic Pattern of the Renton-Sumner Lowland, Washington," *Yearbook of the Association of Pacific Coast Geographers*, vol. 14 (1952), pp. 19–23. [Focus on 1906–1950] 9352

Smelser, Curtis R., "Sequent Occupance of the Nooksack River Valley and the Influence of Man on the Rate of Sediment Delivery to Bellingham Bay," Master's thesis, Western Washington College, 1970. 9353

DiDominico, Anthony T., "Vegetation Patterns at the Time of American Settlement in the Nooksack Lowland, Wheaton County, Washington," Master's thesis, University of Washington, 1982. 9354

Burg, Mary Ellen, "Habitat Change in the Nisqually River Delta and Estuary since the Mid-1800s," Master's thesis, University of Washington, 1984. 9355

NATIVE PEOPLES & WHITE RELATIONS

See 9361

EXPLORATION & MAPPING

See 1289, 8351

POPULAR IMAGES & EVALUATION

Meinig, Donald W., "The Evolution of Understanding an Environment: Climates and Wheat Culture in the Columbia Plateau," *Yearbook of the Association of Pacific Coast Geographers*, vol. 16 (1954), pp. 25–34. 9356

Meinig, Donald W., "Isaac J. Stevens, Practical Geographer of the Early Northwest," *Geographical Review*, vol. 45, 4 (1955), pp. 542–558. 9357

REGIONAL SETTLEMENT

See also 9326

Seeman, Albert L., and Harold E. Tennant, "Changing Frontier in the Columbia Basin," *Economic Geography*, vol. 14, 4 (1938), pp. 419–427. 9358

Meinig, Donald W., "Environment and Settlement in the Palouse, 1868–1910," Master's thesis, University of Washington, 1950. 9359

Hartwich, Gordon, "Early Settlement in the Puyallup Valley," Master's thesis, University of Washington, 1972. 9360

Tremaine, David G., "Indian and Pioneer Settlement of the Nooksack Lowland, Washington, to 1890," Master's thesis, Western Washington State College, 1974. 9361

POPULATION

Mapes, Carl H., "Population Growth in the Puget Sound Region," *Yearbook of the Association of Pacific Coast Geographers*, vol. 2 (1936), pp. 15–18. [Focus on 1850–1930] 9362

Mapes, Carl H., "A Map Interpretation of Population Growth and Distribution in the Puget Sound Region," Ph.D. diss., University of Washington, 1943. 9363

Duffy, Sister Ellen J., "An Isochronic Map of Settlement in Washington State," Master's thesis, Catholic University of America, 1964. 9364

Bryant, Nathaniel H., "Black Migration and the Settlement of the Puget Sound Country," Master's thesis, University of Washington, 1972. 9365

RURAL & REGIONAL SOCIAL GEOGRAPHY

Anderson, Burton L., "The Scandinavian and Dutch Rural Settlements in the Stillaguamish and Nooksack Valleys of Western Washington," Ph.D. diss., University of Washington, 1957. 9366

White, Richard, *Land Use, Environment, and Social Change: The Shaping of Island County, Washington* (Seattle: University of Washington, 1980), 234 pp. 9367

POLITICAL & ADMINISTRATIVE GEOGRAPHY

Bauer, Carl J., "Labor without Brains: Water Development, Law, and Policy in Washington State, 1890–1935," Master's thesis, University of Wisconsin–Madison, 1988. 9368

ECONOMIC DEVELOPMENT

Ekman, Leonard C., "Migratory Work Waves in the Skykomish Valley," *Yearbook of the Association of Pacific Coast Geographers*, vol. 2 (1936), pp. 5–10. [Focus on 1860–1936] 9369

EXTRACTIVE ACTIVITY

Corson, Donald L., "The Western Washington Coal Industry, 1875–1935: A Study of an Ephemeral Industry," Master's thesis, California State University–Los Angeles, 1974. 9370

Pridgeon, Rodney, "The Coal Mining Industry in Washington: A Study in Historical and Economic Geography," Master's thesis, Western Washington University, 1978. 9371

AGRICULTURE

Lechner, H. J., "Some Geographic Influences of Eastern Washington in Relation to Agriculture," *Journal of Geography*, vol. 14, 9 (1916), pp. 362–364. 9372

Whitley, Edward C., "Agricultural Geography of the Kittitas Valley, Washington," *Pacific Northwest Quarterly*, vol. 41, 1 (1950), pp. 3–18. 9373

Brandt, Theodore R., "Components of Change in the Agriculture of the Puget Sound Region, Washington, 1945–1980," in Nigel M. Waters, ed., *Aspects of Human Geography: The Kelowna Papers, 1981* (Vancouver: Tantalus Research, B.C. Geographical Series, no. 34, 1982), pp. 27–42. 9374

Macinko, George, "The Ebb and Flow of Wheat Farming in the Big Bend, Washington," *Agricultural History*, vol. 59, 2 (1985), pp. 215–228. 9375

COMMUNICATIONS & TRADE

Meinig, Donald W., "Wheat Sacks Out to Sea: The Early Export Trade from the Walla Walla Country," *Pacific Northwest Quarterly*, vol. 45, 1 (1954), pp. 13–18. 9376

Turbeville, Daniel E., III, "The Electric Railway Era in Northwest Washington, 1890–1930," Master's thesis, Western Washington State College, 1976. 9377

Heiges, Harvey E., "The Railroad to Monte Christo," in James W. Scott, ed., *Transportation in the Puget Sound Region: Past, Present, and Future* (Bellingham: Western Washington State University Center for Pacific Northwest Studies, 1977), pp. 102–109. 9378

Turbeville, Daniel E., III, "The Rise and Decline of Electric Railways in Northeastern Washington, 1890–1938," in James W. Scott, ed., *Transportation in the Puget Sound Region: Past, Present, and Future* (Bellingham: Western Washington University, Center for Pacific Northwest Studies, 1977), pp. 84–101. 9379

Turbeville, Daniel E., III, *The Electric Railway Era in Northwest Washington, 1890–1930* (Bellingham: Western Washington University, Center for Pacific Northwest Studies, 1979), 199 pp. 9380

Grant, Patrick S., "The Evolution of Ferry Service in the San Juan Islands, Washington: A Study in Historical Geography," Master's thesis, Western Washington University, 1981. 9381

MANUFACTURING & INDUSTRIALIZATION

Scott, James W., and Daniel E. Turbeville III, *Early Industries of Bellingham Bay and Whatcom County: A Photographic Essay* (Bellingham: Fourth Corner Registry, 1980), 167 pp. 9382

URBAN NETWORKS & URBANIZATION

Gregory, William M., "The Growth of the Cities of Washington," *Journal of Geography*, vol. 14, 9 (1916), pp. 348–353. 9383

Renner, George T., "Cities of the Puget Basin," *Economic Geography*, vol. 11, 3 (1935), pp. 280–283. 9384

Landis, Paul H., *Washington Farm Trade Centers, 1900–1935* (Pullman: Washington Agricultural Experimentation Station, Bulletin no. 360, 1938), 40 pp. 9385

TOWN GROWTH

Smith, Guy-Harold, "Seattle," *Journal of Geography*, vol. 21, 6 (1922), pp. 237–241. 9386

Dickson, Belle L., "The 'Why' of Spokane," *Journal of Geography*, vol. 30, 4 (1931), pp. 151–160. 9387

Buckley, Wallace T., "The Historical Geography of Spokane, an Inland Metropolis," *Bulletin of the Geographical Society of Philadelphia*, vol. 30, 2 (1932), pp. 59–69.   **9388**

Ekman, Leonard C., "The Occupance and Abandonment of Tye: A Cascade Mountain Community," *Yearbook of the Association of Pacific Coast Geographers*, vol. 3 (1937), pp. 28–29. [Focus on 1893–1925]   **9389**

Combs, Herbert L., Jr., "The Historical Geography of Port Townsend, Washington," Master's thesis, University of Washington, 1951.   **9390**

Pohl, Thomas W., "Seattle, 1851–1861: A Frontier Community," Ph.D. diss., University of Washington, 1970.   **9391**

Pederson, Eldor O., "Terminus: Transportation and the Growth of Tacoma," in James W. Scott, ed., *Transportation in the Puget Sound Region: Past, Present, and Future* (Bellingham: Western Washington State University Center for Pacific Northwest Studies, 1977), pp. 62–83.   **9392**

Fullerton, Janet Elda, "Transit and Settlement in Seattle, 1871–1941," Master's thesis, University of Washington, 1982.   **9393**

Newman, John, "Port Townsend, Washington: A Humanistic Interpretation of Its Historical Geography from the Mid-Nineteenth Century to the Present," Master's thesis, Western Washington University, 1990.   **9394**

URBAN ECONOMIC STRUCTURE

Miletich, Fred P., "The Historical and Economic Geography of Port Angeles, Washington," Master's thesis, University of Washington, 1954. **9395**

Merriam, Willis B., "Urban-Use Evolution of the Union Bay Lowlands, Seattle," in Julian V. Minghi, ed., *The Geographer and the Public Environment* (Vancouver: Tantalus Research, B.C. Geographical Series, no. 7, 1966), pp. 51–54.   **9396**

Goss, Lawrence E., Jr., "The Rise and Fall of Downtown Tacoma: Its Causes and Consequences,"

Master's thesis, University of Washington, 1969.   **9397**

Fansler, David A., "Downtown Retailing: A Quarter Century of Decline (Seattle)," Master's thesis, University of Washington, 1976.   **9398**

URBAN SOCIAL STRUCTURE

Schultz, Ronald R., "The Locational Behavior of Physician Establishments: An Analysis of Growth and Change in Physician Supply in the Seattle Metropolitan Area, 1950–1970," Ph.D. diss., University of Washington, 1971.   **9399**

Cohn, Lori Etta, "Residential Patterns of the Jewish Community of the Seattle Area, 1910–1980," Master's thesis, University of Washington, 1982.   **9400**

TOWNSCAPE

McElhoe, Forrest L., Jr., "Physical Modifications of Site Necessitated by the Urban Growth of Seattle," Master's thesis, University of Washington, 1950.   **9401**

PLACE NAMES

Meany, Edmond S., *Origin of Washington Geographic Names* (Seattle: University of Washington Press, 1923), 357 pp.   **9402**

Oliphant, J. Orin, "Notes on Early Settlements and on Geographic Names of Eastern Washington," *Pacific Northwest Quarterly*, vol. 22, 3 (1931), pp. 172–202.   **9403**

Phillips, James W., *Washington State Place Names* (Seattle: University of Washington Press, 1971), 167 pp.   **9404**

Hitchman, Robert, *Place Names of Washington* (Tacoma: Washington State Historical Society, 1985), 340 pp.   **9405**

Smith, Grant, "Density Variations of Indian Placenames: Spokane County and the State of Washington," *Names*, vol. 37, 2 (1989), pp. 139–154.   **9406**

OREGON

GENERAL

The state

Mitchell, John H. (Senator), "Oregon: Its History, Geography, and Resources," *National Geographic Magazine*, vol. 6 (Apr. 1895), pp. 239–284.   **9407**

Dicken, Samuel N., and Emily Dicken, *The Making of Oregon: A Study in Historical Geography* (Portland: Oregon Historical Society, 1979), 208 pp.   **9408**

Smaller areas

Merriam, Willis B., "Notes on the Historical Geography of Rogue River Valley," *Oregon Historical Quarterly*, vol. 52, 4 (1941), pp. 317–322.   **9409**

Buckles, James S., "Historical Geography of the Fort Rock Valley, 1900–1941," Master's thesis, University of Oregon, 1959.   **9410**

Dicken, Samuel N., and Emily F. Dicken, *The Legacy of Ancient Lake Modoc: An Historical Geography of the Klamath Lakes Basin* (Eugene: University of Oregon Bookstore; and Klamath Falls, Oreg.: Shaw Stationery Co., 1985), 161 pp.   **9411**

ENVIRONMENTAL CHANGE

Johannessen, Carl L., William Davenport, Artimus Millet, and Steven McWilliams, "The Vegetation of the Willamette Valley," *Annals of the Association of American Geographers*, vol. 61, 2 (1971), pp. 286–302.   **9412**

Terich, Thomas A., "Bayocean Spit, Tillamook, Oregon: Early Economic Development and Erosion History," Master's thesis, Oregon State University, 1973.   **9413**

Towle, Jerry C., "Woodland in the Willamette Valley: An Historical Geography," Ph.D. diss., University of Oregon, 1974.   **9414**

Cole, David N., "Man's Impact on Wilderness Vegetation: An Example from Eagle Cap Wilderness, Northwestern Oregon," Ph.D. diss., University of Oregon, 1976.   **9415**

Burke, Constance J., "Historic Fires in the Central Western Cascades, Oregon," Master's thesis, Oregon State University, 1979.   **9416**

Towle, Jerry C., "Changing Geography of Willamette Valley Woodlands," *Oregon Historical Quarterly*, vol. 83, 1 (1982), pp. 67–87.   **9417**

Butler, Sally A., "A Cultural History of the American Urban Forest Using Eugene, Oregon, as a Case Study," Master's thesis, University of Oregon, 1987.   **9418**

Towle, Jerry C., "The Great Failure: Nineteenth Century Dispersals of the Pacific Salmon," *California Geographer*, vol. 27 (1987), pp. 75–96. **9419**

NATIVE PEOPLES & WHITE RELATIONS

Sutherland, John, "Umatilla Agricultural Landscapes, 1700–1973: An Historical Geography of a Region of the Oregon Country," Master's thesis, University of Oregon, 1973.   **9420**

Dicken, Samuel N., "Oregon Geography before White Settlement, 1770–1840," in Thomas Vaughn, ed., *The Western Shore: Oregon Country Essays Honoring the American Revolution* (Portland: Oregon Historical Society and American Revolution Bicentennial Commission of Oregon, 1975), pp. 1–17.   **9421**

Kenney, James B., "The Umatilla Indian Reservation, 1855–1976: Factors Contributing to a Diminished Land Resource Base," Ph.D. diss., Oregon State University, 1977.   **9422**

EXPLORATION & MAPPING

Hazeltine, Jean, "The Discovery and Cartographical Recognition of Shoalwater Bay," *Oregon Historical Quarterly*, vol. 58, 3 (1957), pp. 251–263.   **9423**

Ward, Robert, "Drake and the Oregon Coast," *Geographical Magazine*, vol. 53, 10 (1981), pp. 645–650.   **9424**

POPULAR IMAGES & EVALUATION

Carr, Keith, "Changing Environmental Perceptions, Attitudes, and Values in Oregon's Willamette Valley: 1800–1978," Master's thesis, University of Oregon, 1977.   **9425**

REGIONAL SETTLEMENT

See also 9326

Black, Lloyd D., "The Peopling of the Middle Willamette Valley, Oregon," Ph.D. diss., University of Michigan, 1940.   **9426**

Gierhart, John W., "Sequent Occupance with Special Reference to the Problems of Land Use in

the Lower Siuslaw Valley, Oregon," Master's
thesis, Syracuse University, 1949.   9427

Eggleston, Dale C., "Harney County, Oregon:
Some Aspects of Sequent Occupancy and Land
Use," Master's thesis, University of Oregon,
1970.   9428

Bowen, William A., "Migration and Settlement on
a Far Western Frontier: Oregon to 1890," Ph.D.
diss., University of California–Berkeley, 1972.
                                             9429

Tetzlaff, Thomas, "Settlement and Landscape
Transitions: The Coquille Valley, Oregon," Master's thesis, University of Oregon, 1973.   9430

Price, Donald C., "Development of Settlement in
Curry County, Oregon," Master's thesis, University of Oregon, 1977.   9431

Bowen, William A., *The Willamette Valley: Migration and Settlement on the Oregon Frontier*
(Seattle: University of Washington Press, 1978),
120 pp.   9432

Scott, James W., "The Missionary as Pioneer: An
Assessment of the Achievement and Impact of
the Protestant Missions in the Settlement of the
Oregon Country East of the Cascades," in James
W. Scott, ed., *Pacific Northwest Themes: Historical Essays in Honor of Keith A. Murray* (Bellingham: Western Washington University Center
for Pacific Northwest Studies, 1978), pp. 71–82.
                                             9433

Towle, Jerry C., "Settlement and Subsistence in the
Willamette Valley," *Northwest Anthropological
Research Notes*, vol. 19 (1979), pp. 12–21. 9434

Hatton, Raymond R., "Climatic Variations and Agricultural Settlement in Southeastern Oregon,"
Ph.D. diss., University of Oregon, 1989.   9435

POPULATION

Black, Lloyd D., "Middle Willamette Valley Population Growth," *Oregon Historical Quarterly*,
vol. 43, 1 (1942), pp. 40–55.   9436

Adams, Georgia E., "Two Isochronic Maps of Settlement in Oregon," *Yearbook of the Association of Pacific Coast Geographers*, vol. 18 (1956),
pp. 36–41.   9437

Bowen, William A., "The Oregon Frontiersman: A
Demographic View," in Thomas Vaughn, ed.,
*The Western Shore: Oregon Country Essays
Honoring the American Revolution* (Portland:
Oregon Historical Society and American Revo-
lution Bicentennial Commission of Oregon,
1975), pp. 181–197.   9438

RURAL & REGIONAL SOCIAL GEOGRAPHY

Olson, John A., "The Danish Settlement in Junction City, Oregon," Master's thesis, University of
Oregon, 1968.   9439

Brown, Pia Tollo, "Art Festivals and Land Use in
Oregon," *Yearbook of the Association of Pacific
Coast Geographers*, vol. 41 (1979), pp. 49–64.
[Focus on 1950–1976]   9440

McConnell, Gregory, "An Historical Geography of
the Chinese in Oregon," Master's thesis, University of Oregon, 1979.   9441

POLITICAL & ADMINISTRATIVE
GEOGRAPHY

Abbott, David R., "Political Regionalism in Lane
County, Oregon, 1932–1960," Master's thesis,
University of Oregon, 1963.   9442

Sorenson, Charles, "Oregon Partisan Electoral
Geography, 1946–1978," Master's thesis, University of Oregon, 1979.   9443

Bourke, Paul F., and Donald A. DeBats, "The
Structures of Political Involvement in the Nineteenth Century: A Frontier Case," *Perspectives
in American History*, n.s. vol. 3 (1987), pp. 207–
238. [Focus on Washington Co., 1855–1859]   9444

ECONOMIC DEVELOPMENT

Roberson, James J., "Historical Geography of
Banking in Oregon," Master's thesis, University
of Oregon, 1971.   9445

RESOURCE MANAGEMENT

Blok, Jack H., "The Evolution of Agricultural Resource Use Strategies in the Willamette Valley,"
Ph.D. diss., Oregon State University, 1973. 9446

LAND & LAND USE

Head, Harlow Z., "The Oregon Donation Acts:
Background, Development, and Application,"
Master's thesis, University of Oregon, 1969. 9447

EXTRACTIVE ACTIVITY

Clevinger, Woodrow R., "Locational Change in the
Douglas Fir Lumber Industry," *Yearbook of the
Association of Pacific Coast Geographers*, vol. 15
(1953), pp. 23–31. [Focus on 1924–1947]   9448

Erikson, Kenneth A., "Isochrones of Logging on
the Pacific Slope of Oregon, 1890–1940," *Yearbook of the Association of Pacific Coast Geographers*, vol. 19 (1957), pp. 19–24.   9449

AGRICULTURE

Highsmith, Richard M., Jr., "Irrigation in the Willamette Valley," *Geographical Review*, vol. 46, 1 (1956), pp. 98–110. [Emphasis on 1929–1950] **9450**

Renwick, William R., II, "Changes in Deschutes County Irrigation Agriculture since 1950," Master's thesis, Oregon State University, 1975. **9451**

Reynolds, Wes L., "Evolution of the Grass Seed Landscape: A Historical Geography of Agriculture in the Southern Willamette Valley," Master's thesis, University of Oregon, 1977. **9452**

LANDSCAPE

White, Wayne R., "Gardens in the Valley: A Study of Some Folk Landscapes in the Willamette Valley of Oregon," Ph.D. diss., University of Oregon, 1977. **9453**

COMMUNICATIONS & TRADE

Throckmorton, Harold L., "The Interurbans of Portland, Oregon: A Historical Geography," Master's thesis, University of Oregon, 1962. **9454**

Due, John F., "The City of Prineville Railway and the Economic Development of Crook County," *Economic Geography*, vol. 43, 2 (1967), pp. 170–181. [Focus on 1911–1960] **9455**

Dicken, Samuel N., *Pioneer Trails of the Oregon Coast* (Portland: Oregon Historical Society, 1971), 77 pp. **9456**

MANUFACTURING & INDUSTRIALIZATION

Mbogho, Archie, "Sawmilling in Lane County, Oregon: A Geographical Examination of Its Development," Master's thesis, University of Oregon, 1965. **9457**

URBAN NETWORKS & URBANIZATION

Smith, Everett G., Jr., "An Urban Interpretation of Oregon Settlement," *Yearbook of the Association of Pacific Coast Geographers*, vol. 29 (1967), pp. 43–52. **9458**

Helbock, Richard W., "The Evolution of Nodal Settlement Distribution in the Willamette Valley of Oregon, 1850–1900," Ph.D. diss., University of Pittsburgh, 1973. **9459**

Holtgrieve, Donald G., "The Effects of the Railroads on Small Town Population Changes: Linn County, Oregon," *Yearbook of the Association of Pacific Coast Geographers*, vol. 35 (1973), pp. 87–102. **9460**

Holtgrieve, Donald G., "Historical Geography of Transportation Routes and Town Populations in

Oregon's Willamette Valley," Ph.D. diss., University of Oregon, 1973. **9461**

Keeler, Elizabeth L., "Willamette Valley River Towns and Steamboats," Master's thesis, University of Oregon, 1985. **9462**

TOWN GROWTH

Kapuscinski, Pearl B., "A Method for Analyzing Changes in the Urban Fringe: Albany, Oregon, 1936–1975," Master's thesis, Oregon State University, 1978. **9463**

Dicken, Samuel N., "Klamath Falls and Altamont, Oregon," *Yearbook of the Association of Pacific Coast Geographers*, vol. 47 (1985), pp. 27–38. **9464**

TOWNSCAPE

Bailey, Barbara R., "The Evolution of Small Town Main Streets," Ph.D. diss., University of Oregon, 1977. **9465**

Urquhart, Alvin W., "Stripping the Urban Landscape," *Yearbook of the Association of Pacific Coast Geographers*, vol. 43 (1981), pp. 7–22. [Eugene, 1910–1978] **9466**

Sharrard, Sally, "Of City Greens and Time: The Form and Function of City Parks of Western Oregon," Master's thesis, University of Oregon, 1979. **9467**

Hilden, Clark G., "An Historical Geography of Small Town Main Streets in the Willamette Valley, Oregon," Ph.D. diss., University of Oregon, 1980. **9468**

Bailey, Barbara R., *Main Street Northeastern Oregon: The Founding and Development of Small Towns* (Portland: Oregon Historical Society, 1982), 219 pp. **9469**

McEarchern, Philip D., "Silverton: The Morphology of an Oregon Town," Master's thesis, University of Oregon, 1990. **9470**

PLACE NAMES

McArthur, Lewis A., "Oregon Geographic Names," *Oregon Historical Quarterly*, vol. 26 (1925), pp. 309–423; vol. 27 (1926), ; vol. 28 (1927). **9471**

McArthur, Lewis A., *Oregon Geographic Names*, (Portland, 1928), 450 pp. Fourth edition, Oregon Historical Society, 1974, 835 pp. **9472**

Martinson, Tom L., "Wendling, Oregon: Ephemeral Place but Persistent Name," *Places*, vol. 2 (1975), pp. 23–25. **9473**

Oakes, Dennis J., "Site Abandonment: Placename Evidence in Oregon," Master's thesis, University of Oregon, 1988. **9474**

CALIFORNIA

GENERAL

The state

Ratzel, Friedrich, "Über Kalifornien," *Jahresbericht der Geographischen Gesellschaft in München*, vol. 6–7 (1877), pp. 124–148. Reprinted in Hans Helmolt, ed., *Kleine Schriften von Friedrich Ratzel* (Munich: R. Oldenbourg, 1906), pp. 1–18. 9475

Chamberlain, James F., "Geographic Influences in the Development of California," *Journal of Geography*, vol. 9, 10 (1911), pp. 253–261. 9476

Whitmoyer, Clinton B., "The Influence of Geographical Conditions upon the History of California," Master's thesis, University of California–Berkeley, 1912. 9477

Huntington, Ellsworth, "Gold, Distance, and Climate as Social Influences in California," in Jerome Davis and Harry E. Barnes, eds., *Readings in Sociology* (Boston: D. C. Heath & Co., 1927), pp. 310–312. Reprinted from Ellsworth Huntington, *The Character of Races* (New York: Charles Scribner's Sons, 1924), pp. 327–330. 9478

Bates, Lana, "The Historical Geography of California, 1513–1835," Master's thesis, University of California–Berkeley, 1931. 9479

Baugh, Ruth E., "Geographic Factors in the Evolution of California," *Journal of Geography*, vol. 54, 3 (1955), pp. 133–140. 9480

Parsons, James J., "The Uniqueness of California," *American Quarterly*, vol. 7, 1 (1955), pp. 45–55. 9481

Hornbeck, David, Jr., and Julia Costello, "Alta California: An Overview," in David H. Thomas, ed., *Columbian Consequences: Archeological and Historical Perspectives on the Spanish Southwest*, vol. 1 (Washington, D.C.: Smithsonian Institution, 1989), pp. 423–433. 9482

Smaller areas

Broek, Jan O. M., *The Santa Clara Valley, California: A Study in Landscape Change* (Utrecht: A. Oosthek's Uitgevers-Mij., 1932), 184 pp. 9483

Nida, Richard H., "The Escondido–San Pasqual–San Bernardo Area: A Study in Historical Geography of San Diego County, California," Master's thesis, University of California–Berkeley, 1935. 9484

Glendinning, Robert M., "The Role of Death Valley," *Economic Geography*, vol. 16, 3 (1940), pp. 299–311. [Focus on 1849–1939] 9485

Karinen, Arthur E., "The Historical Geography of the Mendocino Coast," Master's thesis, University of California–Berkeley, 1948. 9486

Roy, Jean-Marie, "La grande vallée de Californie," *Canadian Geographer*, vol. 4 (1954), pp. 63–76. 9487

Price, Edward T., "The Future of California's Southland," *Annals of the Association of American Geographers*, vol. 49, 3 (1959), pt. 2, pp. 101–116. [Focus on 1850–1950] 9488

MacGraw, Frank M., "The Santa Clara Valley: An Historical and Geographical Appraisal," Master's thesis, Stanford University, 1961. 9489

Guzman, Louis E., "San Fernando Valley: Two Hundred Years in Transition," *California Geographer*, vol. 3 (1962), pp. 55–58. 9490

Dillane, Allan P., "A Historical Geography of the El Cajon Valley, San Diego County, California," Master's thesis, San Diego State College, 1964. 9491

Pease, Robert W., *Modoc Country: A Geographic Time Continuum on the California Volcanic Tableland* (Berkeley: University of California Publications in Geography, no. 17, 1965), 304 pp. 9492

Nathan, Elroy, "A Historical Geography of Cohasset Ridge," Master's thesis, California State University–Chico, 1966. 9493

Howatt, Elizabeth A., "A Historical Geography of Alpine County, California, and the 'Alpine-Nevada Alliance'," Master's thesis, University of California–Berkeley, 1968. 9494

Rustvold, Marjorie M., "San Pasqual Valley: Rancheria to Greenbelt," Master's thesis, California State University–San Diego, 1968. 9495

Hedgecock, David G., "The Fresno Plain, 1868–1885: A Cultural-Geographic Interpretation," Master's thesis, California State University–Fresno, 1972. 9496

Parsons, James J., "The California Gold Country," *Geographical Review*, vol. 62, 2 (1972), pp. 269–271. 9497

Preston, William L., *Vanishing Landscape: Land and Life in the Tulare Lake Basin* (Berkeley: University of California Press, 1981), 278 pp. 9498

Dilsaver, Lary M., "After the Gold Rush," *Geographical Review*, vol. 75, 1 (1985), pp. 1–18. 9499

Parsons, James J., "A Geographer Looks at the San Joaquin Valley," *Geographical Review*, vol. 76, 4 (1986), pp. 371–389. **9500**

ENVIRONMENTAL CHANGE

General

Aschmann, Homer, "The Evolution of a Wild Landscape, and Its Persistence, in Southern California," *Annals of the Association of American Geographers*, vol. 49, 3, pt. 2 (1959), pp. 34–56. **9501**

Sanders, Norman, "Port Hueneme, California: A Study in Coastal Anthropogeomorphology," *Yearbook of the Association of Pacific Coast Geographers*, vol. 28 (1966), pp. 119–134. [Focus on 1938–1964] **9502**

Aschmann, Homer, "Purpose of Southern California Landscape," *Journal of Geography*, vol. 66, 6 (1967), pp. 311–317. **9503**

Place, John L., "Man's Role in Geomorphic Change on the Shoreline of Los Angeles County, California," Ph.D. diss., University of California–Los Angeles, 1970. **9504**

Gordon, Burton L., *Monterey Bay Area: Natural History and Cultural Imprints* (Pacific Grove, Calif.: Boxwood Press, 1975), 321 pp. Revised 1979. **9505**

Stine, Scott W., "The Past 4000 Years at Mono Lake," Ph.D. diss., University of California–Berkeley, 1987. **9506**

Climate, drought, and fire

Grainger, Orman E., "Climatic Variation in California: Looking Ahead to 2000 AD," *Physical Geography*, vol. 2, 1 (1981), pp. 47–61. **9507**

Shelton, M. L., "Hydroclimatic Analysis of Severe Drought in the Sacramento River Basin, California," *Physical Geography*, vol. 5, 3 (1984), pp. 262–286. [Focus on the droughts of 1924 and 1977] **9508**

Rowntree, Lester B., "A Crop-Based Rainfall Chronology for Pre–Instrumental Record Southern California," *Climatic Change*, vol. 7, 3 (1985), pp. 327–342. **9509**

Rowntree, Lester B., "Drought during California's Mission Period, 1769–1834," *Journal of California and Great Basin Anthropology*, vol. 7, 1 (1985), pp. 7–20. **9510**

Minnich, Richard A., "Fire Behavior in Southern California: Chaparral before Fire Control; The Mount Wilson Burns at the Turn of the Century," *Annals of the Association of American Geographers*, vol. 77, 4 (1987), pp. 599–618. **9511**

Minnich, Richard A., *The Biogeography of Fire in the San Bernardino Mountains of California* (Berkeley: University of California Publications in Geography, no. 28, 1988), 120 pp. **9512**

Vegetation

Sempler, Heinrich, "Die Veränderungen welche der Mensch in der Flora Kaliforniens bewirkt hat," *Petermanns Geographische Mitteilungen*, vol. 34, 8 (1888), pp. 239–243; 9, pp. 276–283; and 10, pp. 302–312. **9513**

Robison, William C., "Historical Geography of the Redwood Forest of the Santa Cruz Mountains," Master's thesis, University of California–Berkeley, 1949. **9514**

Thompson, Kenneth, "Riparian Forest of the Sacramento Valley, California," *Annals of the Association of American Geographers*, vol. 51, 3 (1961), pp. 294–315. **9515**

McIntire, Elliot G., "The Rise and Fall of the California Eucalypt," *Proceedings of the Association of American Geographers*, vol. 5 (1973), pp. 155–159. **9516**

Dodge, John M., "Vegetational Changes Associated with Land Use and Fire History in San Diego County," Ph.D. diss., University of California–Riverside, 1975. **9517**

Wester, Lyndon L., "Changing Vegetation Patterns on the West Side and South End of the San Joaquin Valley in Historic Times," Ph.D. diss., University of California–Los Angeles, 1975. **9518**

Aschmann, Homer, "Man's Impact on the Southern California Flora," in June Latting, ed., *Plant Communities in Southern California* (Berkeley: California Native Plant Society, Special Publication no. 2, 1976), pp. 40–48. **9519**

Vale, Thomas R., "Forest Changes in the Warner Mountains, California," *Annals of the Association of American Geographers*, vol. 67, 1 (1977), pp. 28–45. [Focus on 1870–1970] **9520**

Bradbury, David E., "The Evolution and Persistence of a Local Sage/Chamise Community Pattern in Southern California," *Yearbook of the Association of Pacific Coast Geographers*, vol. 40 (1978), pp. 39–56. [Focus on 1931–1972] **9521**

Rossi, Randall S., "Land Use and Vegetation Change in the Oak Woodland–Savanna of Northern San Luis Obispo County, California (1774–1978)," Ph.D. diss., University of California–Berkeley, 1979. **9522**

Rossi, Randall S., "History of Cultural Influences on the Distribution and Reproduction of Oaks in California," *Proceedings of the Symposium*

on the Management, Utilization, and Ecology of
California Oaks, Claremont, California, June 15,
1979 (Berkeley: U.S. Forest Service, Pacific
Southwest Forest and Range Experiment Station, 1980), pp. 7–18.   9523

Brothers, Timothy S., "Historical Change in the
Owens River Riparian Woodland," Master's
thesis, University of California–Los Angeles,
1981.   9524

Nedeff, Nicole E., "The Historical Extent of Riparian Forest Vegetation along the Lower Stanislaus River, California," Master's thesis, University of California–Berkeley, 1984.   9525

Burns, Charmion B., "A History of Exotic Conifer
Plantations in the San Gabriel Mountains of
California," Master's thesis, University of
California–Los Angeles, 1987.   9526

Drainage, sedimentation, & flooding

Gilbert, Grove K., Hydraulic Mining Débris in the
Sierra Nevada (Washington, D.C.: U.S. Geological Survey, Professional Paper no. 105, 1917), 154
pp.   9527

Thompson, Kenneth, "Historic Flooding in the
Sacramento Valley," Pacific Historical Review,
vol. 29, 4 (1960), pp. 349–360.   9528

Bull, William B., "History and Causes of Channel
Trenching in Western Fresno County, California," American Journal of Science, vol. 262, 2
(1964), pp. 249–258.   9529

James, L. Allan, "Historical Transport and Storage
of Hydraulic Mining Sediment in the Bear
River, California," Ph.D. diss., University of
Wisconsin–Madison, 1988.   9530

Fauna

Emory, Jerry, "The California Condor: A History of
Decline," California Geographer, vol. 28 (1988),
pp. 43–68.   9531

Earthquakes

Chamberlain, James F., "California Earthquakes,"
Journal of School Geography, vol. 4, 2 (1900), pp.
58–63.   9532

NATIVE PEOPLES & WHITE RELATIONS

Prehistoric settlements

Carter, George F., "Evidence for Pleistocene Man
in Southern California," Geographical Review,
vol. 40, 1 (1950), pp. 84–102.   9533

Carter, George F., Pleistocene Man at San Diego,
California (Baltimore: Johns Hopkins University
Press, 1957), 400 pp.   9534

Hoover, Robert, "Prehistoric Land Use Patterns in
the Morro Bay Watershed, San Luis Obispo
County, California," California Geographer, vol.
17 (1977), pp. 83–96.   9535

Hornbeck, David, Jr., "The California Indian before European Contact," Journal of Cultural Geography, vol. 2, 2 (1982), pp. 23–39.   9536

Preston, William L., "Infinidad de Gentiles: Aboriginal Population in the Tulare Basin," Yearbook of the Association of Pacific Coast Geographers, vol. 51 (1989), pp. 79–100.   9537

Modern period

Jones, Stanley J., "Some Regional Aspects of Native California," Scottish Geographical Magazine, vol. 67, 1 (1951), pp. 19–30.   9538

Reith, Gertrude L., "The Ventura Chumash: An
Example of Geographic Adaptation," California
Geographer, vol. 5 (1964), pp. 53–56.   9539

Sutton, Imre, "Land Tenure and Changing Occupance on Indian Reservations in Southern California," Ph.D. diss., University of California–Los
Angeles, 1965.   9540

Edwards, Clinton R., "Early European Contacts
with the Indians of the Bodega-Tomales Region,
California," Indian Historian, vol. 2, 1 (1969), pp.
12–16.   9541

Sutton, Imre, "The Cartographic Factor in Indian
Land Tenure: Some Examples from Southern
California," American Indian Culture and Re-
search Journal, vol. 12, 2 (1988), pp. 53–80.   9542

Preston, William L., "The Tulare Lake Basin: An
Aboriginal Cornucopia," California Geographer,
vol. 30 (1990), pp. 1–24. [Focus on the late eighteenth century]   9543

Trafzer, Clifford E., and Richard L. Carrico, "American Indians: The County's First Residents," in
Philip R. Pryde, ed., San Diego: An Introduction
to the Region, 3d ed. (Dubuque: Kendall-Hunt
Publishing Co., 1992), pp. 51–67.   9544

EXPLORATION & MAPPING

Exploration

Davidson, George, The Discovery of Humboldt
Bay, California (San Francisco: Publications of
the Geographical Society of the Pacific, 1891), 16
pp.   9545

Raup, Hallock F., "The Delayed Discovery of San
Francisco Bay," California Historical Society
Quarterly, vol. 27, 4 (1948), pp. 289–296.   9546

Thrower, Norman J. W., "Sir Francis Drake in California and England," California Geographer,
vol. 20 (1980), pp. 81–87.   9547

Block, Robert H., "The Whitney Survey: A Geographical Exploration of California, 1860–74," *History of Geography Newsletter*, vol. 1 (1981), pp. 29–37. **9548**

Davies, Arthur, "The Golden Hind and the Tello on the Coasts of California," *Geographical Journal*, vol. 148, 2 (1981), pp. 219–224. **9549**

Block, Robert H., "The Whitney Survey of California, 1860–74: A Study of Environmental Science and Exploration," Ph.D. diss., University of California–Los Angeles, 1982. **9550**

Kelsey, Harry, "Mapping the California Coast: The Voyages of Discovery, 1533–1543," *Arizona and the West*, vol. 26, 4 (1984), pp. 307–324. **9551**

Mapping

Heizer, Robert F., "Alexander S. Taylor's Map of California Indian Tribes, 1864," *California Historical Society Quarterly*, vol. 20, 2 (1941), pp. 171–180. **9552**

Harlow, Neal, "The Maps of San Francisco Bay and the Town of Yerba Buena to One Hundred Years Ago," *Pacific Historical Review*, vol. 16, 4 (1947), pp. 365–378. **9553**

Donkin, Robin A., "The Diseño: A Source for the Geography of California, 1830–46," *Mid-America*, vol. 40, 2 (1958), pp. 92–105. **9554**

Carter, George F., "California as an Island," *Masterkey for Indian Lore and History*, vol. 38 (1964), pp. 74–78. **9555**

Leighly, John B., *California as an Island* (San Francisco: Book Club of California, 1972), 154 pp. **9556**

Lockmann, Ronald F., "Some Eighteenth Century Maps of Pacific North America: The La Perouse Expedition in California," *Historical Geography*, vol. 5, 1 (1975), pp. 16–24. **9557**

Padick, Clement, "Vertical Aerial Imagery of the Los Angeles Area: A Historical Perspective," *California Geographer*, vol. 21 (1981), pp. 30–46. **9558**

Harlow, Neal, *Maps of the Pueblo Lands of San Diego, 1602–1874* (Los Angeles: Dawson's Book Shop, 1987), 244 pp. **9559**

POPULAR IMAGES & EVALUATION

General

Vance, James E., Jr., "California and the Search for the Ideal," *Annals of the Association of American Geographers*, vol. 62, 2 (1972), pp. 185–210. Reissued in John Fraser Hart, ed., *Regions of the United States* (New York: Harper & Row, 1972), same pagination. **9560**

Thompson, Kenneth, "Negative Perceptions of Early California," *California Geographer*, vol. 18 (1978), pp. 1–15. **9561**

Ford, Larry R., and Ernst C. Griffin, "The Ghettoization of Paradise," *Geographical Review*, vol. 69, 2 (1979), pp. 140–158. [Focus on 1950–1975] **9562**

Oliver, Virginia, "Literary Landscapes of Hispanic California," *California Geographer*, vol. 20 (1980), pp. 53–61. [Focus on 1820s–1840s] **9563**

Edwards, Benjamin G., "The Great Wrong Place: Images of Southern California in the 1930s," Master's thesis, University of California–Los Angeles, 1981. **9564**

Cross-cultural perceptions

Oliver, Virginia, "Foreigners' Images of Hispanic California, 1800–1846," Master's thesis, California State University–Northridge, 1978. **9565**

Little, William T., "Spain's Fantastic Vision and the Mythic Creation of California," *California Geographer*, vol. 27 (1987), pp. 1–38. **9566**

Climate and health

Thompson, Kenneth, "Insalubrious California: Perception and Reality," *Annals of the Association of American Geographers*, vol. 59, 1 (1969), pp. 50–64. [Focus on the nineteenth century] **9567**

Thompson, Kenneth, "Irrigation as a Menace to Health in California: A Nineteenth Century View," *Geographical Review*, vol. 59, 2 (1969), pp. 195–214. **9568**

Blackburn, David, "The History of the Perception of Comfort and the Climate of California," Master's thesis, California State University–Northridge, 1979. **9569**

Sauder, Robert A., "Powell's Vision of Arid Land Settlement Reexamined: Owens' Valley, California," *Yearbook of the Association of Pacific Coast Geographers*, vol. 52 (1990), pp. 65–90. **9570**

Agriculture

Quastler, Imre E., "American Images of California Agriculture, 1800–1890," Ph.D. diss., University of Kansas, 1970. **9571**

Quastler, Imre E., "The Core Area of Images Concept and American Perceptions of California Agriculture, 1800–1890," *Proceedings of the Association of American Geographers*, vol. 4 (1972), pp. 91–95. **9572**

Thompson, Kenneth, "The Perception of the Agricultural Environment," *Agricultural History*, vol. 49, 1 (1975), pp. 230–237. **9573**

Eigenheer, Richard A., "Early Perceptions of Agricultural Resources in the Central Valley of California," Ph.D. diss., University of California–Davis, 1976.   9574

Thompson, Kenneth, and Richard A. Eigenheer, "The Agricultural Promise of the Sacramento Valley: Some Early Views," *Journal of the West*, vol. 18, 4 (1979), pp. 33–41.   9575

Starrs, Paul F., "The Navel of California and Other Oranges: Images of California and the Orange Crate," *California Geographer*, vol. 28 (1988), pp. 1–41.   9576

Transport

Carpenter, Nevin S., "Images of the Spatial Impact of the Railroad: San Diego, 1851–1873," Master's thesis, San Diego State University, 1975.   9577

Floyd, Donald R., "A Surge of Hope: Public Reaction to Arguments for Construction of Narrow-Gauged Railroads in California, 1870–1873," *California Geographer*, vol. 25 (1985), pp. 65–84. 9578

Urban imagery

Krim, Arthur J., "Imagery in Search of a City: The Geography of Los Angeles, 1921–1971," Ph.D. diss., Clark University, 1980.   9579

Russell, Peter L., "From Mean Streets to Freeways: Los Angeles in American Detective Fiction," *California Geographer*, vol. 30 (1990), pp. 73–92. [Focus on 1920s–1990]   9580

REGIONAL SETTLEMENT

See also 8920, 8922

General

Shrode, Ida May, "The Sequent Occupance of the Rancho Azusa Duarte: A Segment of the Upper San Gabriel Valley of California," Ph.D. diss., University of Chicago, 1948. Published under the same title, as a University of Chicago Department of Geography Private Edition, 1948, 164 pp.   9581

LeResche, J. H., "The Lower Ventura River Valley, California: A Study in Changing Occupance," Master's thesis, University of California–Los Angeles, 1951.   9582

Thompson, John, "The Settlement Geography of San Gorgonio Pass, Southern California," Master's thesis, University of California–Berkeley, 1951.   9583

Simoons, Frederick J., "The Settlement of the Clear Lake Upland of California," Master's thesis, University of California–Berkeley, 1952. 9584

Mikesell, Marvin W., "The Santa Barbara Area, California: A Study of Changing Culture Patterns to 1865," Master's thesis, University of California–Los Angeles, 1953.   9585

Thompson, John, "The Settlement Geography of the Sacramento–San Joaquin Delta," *Bulletin of the California Council of Geography Teachers*, vol. 4 (1956), pp. 3–7.   9586

Graham, C. John, "The Settlement of Merced County, California," Master's thesis, University of California–Los Angeles, 1957.   9587

Thompson, John, "The Settlement Geography of the Sacramento–San Joaquin Delta," Ph.D. diss., Stanford University, 1958.   9588

Trussell, Margaret E., "The Settlement of the Bodega Bay Region," Master's thesis, University of California–Berkeley, 1960.   9589

Ketteringham, William J., "The Settlement Geography of the Napa Valley," Master's thesis, Stanford University, 1961.   9590

Nostrand, Richard L., "A Settlement Geography of the Santa Ynez Valley, California," Master's thesis, University of California–Los Angeles, 1964.   9591

White, C. Langdon, "Sequent Occupance in the Santa Clara Valley, California," *Journal of the Graduate Research Center, Southern Methodist University*, vol. 34 (1965), pp. 277–299.   9592

Nostrand, Richard L., "The Santa Ynez Valley: Hinterland of Coastal California," *Southern California Quarterly*, vol. 48, 1 (1966), pp. 37–56.   9593

Holland, John, "Sequent Occupance of Big Meadows, Plumas County, California," Master's thesis, California State University–Chico, 1967. 9594

McKinnon, Richard M., "The Historical Geography of Settlement in the Foothills of Tuolomne County, California," Master's thesis, University of California–Berkeley, 1967.   9595

Wallick, Phillip K., "The Sequent Occupance of Salinas Valley," Master's thesis, California State University–San Francisco, 1968.   9596

Pfeifer, Gottfried, "Frontera del Norte Kaliforniens, 1800–1846: Russen, Spanier und Angelsachsen," in *Beiträge zur Geographie der Tropen und Subtropen: Festschrift für Herbert Wilhelmy* (Tübingen: Tübinger Geographische Studien, vol. 34, 1970), pp. 255–278. Reprinted in Gerd Kohlhepp, ed., *Beiträge zur Kulturgeographie der Neuen Welt: Ausgewählte Arbeiten von Gottfried Pfeifer* (Berlin: Dietrich Reimer, 1981), pp. 89–114.   9597

Seivertson, Bruce, "Pajaro Valley, California: The Sequent Occupance of a Coastal Agricultural

Basin," Master's thesis, California State University–Chico, 1970. **9598**

McKenzie, Roderick C., "The San Pasqual Grant: The Sequent Occupance of a Portion of the Mission San Gabriel Archangel Lands through Two Centuries," Ph.D. diss., University of California–Los Angeles, 1972. **9599**

Russell, John H., "A Sequent Occupance Study of Stanislaus County, California," Master's thesis, California State University–Fullerton, 1977. **9600**

Fletcher, Thomas C., "The Mono Basin in the Nineteenth Century: Discovery, Settlement, Land Use," Master's thesis, University of California–Berkeley, 1982. **9601**

Gruber, Gerald R., "Kolonisation und Bewässerung im San Joaquin Valley, Kalifornien," *Frankfurter Wirtschafts- und Sozialgeographische Schriften*, vol. 42 (1982), pp. 149–191. **9602**

Boam, Kay, "A Sequent Occupance of the Clear Lake Basin," Master's thesis, California State University–Chico, 1989. **9603**

McMonagle, Richard, "Historical Geography of Bucks Lake Wilderness Area," Master's thesis, California State University–Chico, 1989. **9604**

Weakley, Scott A., "Lompoc, California: A Study of Landscape Change Using Cross-Sections through Time," Master's thesis, Brigham Young University, 1990. **9605**

Spanish and Mexican period

Davidson, George, *The Discovery of San Francisco Bay, the Rediscovery of the Port of Monterey, the Establishment of the Presidio, and the Founding of the Mission of San Francisco* (San Francisco: Geographical Society of the Pacific, Transactions & Proceedings, 2d ser., vol. 4, May 1907), 154 pp. **9606**

Raup, Hallock F., "Rancho Los Palos Verdes," *Historical Society of Southern California Quarterly*, vol. 19, 1 (1937), pp. 7–21. **9607**

Carpenter, Bruce R., "Rancho Encino: Its Historical Geography," Master's thesis, University of California–Los Angeles, 1948. **9608**

Mikesell, Marvin W., "Franciscan Colonization at Santa Barbara," *Historical Society of Southern California Quarterly*, vol. 37, 3 (1955), pp. 211–222. **9609**

Walder, Margaret F., "The Historical Geography of Mission San Juan Capistrano, California," Master's thesis, University of California–Los Angeles, 1958. **9610**

Donkin, Robin A., "The Contribution of the Franciscan Missions to the Settlement of Alta California Colonization (1769–1823)," *Revista de Historia de America*, vol. 52 (1961), pp. 373–393. **9611**

Gentilcore, R. Louis, "Missions and Mission Lands of Alta California," *Annals of the Association of American Geographers*, vol. 51, 1 (1961), pp. 46–72. **9612**

Stokle, Gerald, "Mission San Jose and the Livermore Valley, 1798–1842: Demography and Ecology of a Mission Hinterland," Master's thesis, University of California–Berkeley, 1968. **9613**

Hornbeck, David, Jr., "Mission Population of Alta California, 1810–1830," *Historical Geography*, vol. 8, 1 (suppl.) (1978), 1 map. **9614**

Taugher, Michael F., "The Settlement Frontier of Hispanic California to 1890," Master's thesis, California State University–Northridge, 1979. **9615**

Aiken, S. Robert, "The Spanish Missions of Alta California: Rise, Fall, and Restoration," *Pioneer America*, vol. 15, 1 (1983), pp. 3–19. **9616**

Hornbeck, David, Jr., "Early Mission Settlement," in Francis Weber, ed., *Some Reminiscences about Fray Junipero Serra* (Santa Barbara: Kimberly Press and California Catholic Conference, 1985), pp. 55–66. **9617**

Hornbeck, David, Jr., "Economic Growth and Change at the Missions of Alta California, 1769–1846," in David H. Thomas, ed., *Columbian Consequences: Archeological and Historical Perspectives on the Spanish Borderlands West*, vol. 1 (Washington, D.C.: Smithsonian Institution, 1989), pp. 303–331. **9618**

Other ethnic colonization

Schofer, Allen A., "Finnish Settlement in Northern California," Master's thesis, University of California–Berkeley, 1966. **9619**

Anglo period

Walker, Gerald E., "Rural Settlement in the Far West, 1850–1880: Sonoma County," Ph.D. diss., University of California–Berkeley, 1970. **9620**

Birch, Brian P., "From Frontier to Arcadia: The Settling of the Backcountry of San Diego, California (1850–1930)," in Robert C. Eidt, Kashi N. Singh, and Rana P. B. Singh, eds., *Man, Culture, and Settlement: Festschrift to Professor R. L. Singh* (New Delhi: Kalyani Publishers, 1977), pp. 97–117. **9621**

POPULATION

See also 1354

Branchi, Camillo, "Gli Italiani nella storia della California," *Universo*, vol. 36, 6 (1956), pp. 421–432. **9622**

Lewthwaite, Gordon R., Christiane Mainzer and Patrick Holland, "From Polynesia to California: Samoan Migration and Its Sequel," *Journal of Pacific History*, vol. 8 (1973), pp. 133–157.　9623

Smith, Paul A., "Negro Settlement in Los Angeles, California, 1890 to 1930," Master's thesis, California State University–Northridge, 1973.　9624

Westfall, John E., "Historical Population Estimation Using Electoral Data," *Proceedings of the Association of American Geographers*, vol. 5 (1973), pp. 291–295. [San Francisco and Sierra Co.]　9625

Hornbeck, David, Jr., "A Population Map of California, 1798," *California Geographer*, vol. 14 (1973–1974), pp. 52–53.　9626

Book, Susan, "The Chinese in Butte County, 1869–1920," Master's thesis, California State University–Chico, 1974.　9627

Walker, Gerald E., "Migrants and Places of Birth: A Methodological Note," *Professional Geographer*, vol. 27, 1 (1975), pp. 58–64. [Focus on Sonoma Co., 1860–1880]　9628

Hornbeck, David, Jr., and Mary L. Tucey, "The Submergence of a People: Migration and Occupational Structure in California, 1850," *Pacific Historical Review*, vol. 46, 3 (1977), pp. 471–484.　9629

McGovern, Carolyn, "Comparing Population Pyramids: Two Techniques and a Test on Alta, California, Data from 1790 and the 1830s," Syracuse University Department of Geography Discussion Paper no. 53 (1978), 28 pp.　9630

McGovern, Carolyn, "Hispanic Population at Alta, California, 1790–1830," Master's thesis, California State University–Northridge, 1978.　9631

Dilsaver, Lary M., "Post–Gold Rush Population Changes in a Sierra Nevada Mining Region," *Yearbook of the Association of Pacific Coast Geographers*, vol. 45 (1983), pp. 101–116.　9632

Warf, Barney L., "Restructuring and the Nonmetropolitan Turnaround: The California Evidence," *Yearbook of the Association of Pacific Coast Geographers*, vol. 48 (1986), pp. 125–147. [Focus on 1910–1977]　9633

Griffin, Ernst C., "Peopling the Region: San Diego's Population Patterns," in Philip R. Pryde, ed., *San Diego: An Introduction to the Region*, 3d ed. (Dubuque: Kendall-Hunt Publishing Co., 1992), pp. 69–83.　9634

RURAL & REGIONAL SOCIAL GEOGRAPHY

Physical and mental health

Thompson, Kenneth, "The Australian Fever Tree in California: Eucalypts and Malaria Prophylaxis," *Annals of the Association of American Geographers*, vol. 60, 2 (1970), pp. 230–244. [Focus on the 1870s and 1880s]　9635

Thompson, Kenneth, "Climatotherapy in California," *California Historical Quarterly*, vol. 50, 2 (1971), pp. 111–130.　9636

Thompson, Kenneth, "Early California and the Causes of Insanity," *Southern California Quarterly*, vol. 58, 1 (1976), pp. 45–62.　9637

Religious activity

Heising, Heldemar, *Missionierung und Diözesanbildung in Kalifornien* (Münster: Westfälische Geographische Studien, vol. 14, 1958), 116 pp.　9638

Smith, George, Jr., "The Journey to Worship: An Historical-Geographical Study of the Effects of Transportation Patterns and Modes upon Selected Churches in Santa Clara County, California," Master's thesis, San Jose State University, 1984.　9639

Ethnic communities

Monaco, James, "The Changing Ethnic Character of Butte County's Gold Mining Community, 1848–1880," Master's thesis, California State University–Chico, 1986.　9640

German communities

Raup, Hallock F., "The German Colonization of Anaheim, California," *University of California Publications in Geography*, vol. 6, 3 (1932), pp. 123–146.　9641

Raup, Hallock F., "Anaheim: A German Community of Frontier California, " *American-German Review*, vol. 12, 2 (1945), pp. 7–11.　9642

Italian & Italian Swiss communities

Perret, Maurice E., "The Italian Swiss Colonies in California," Master's thesis, University of California–Berkeley, 1942.　9643

Perret, Maurice E., *Les colonies tessinoises en Californie* (Lausanne: F. Rouge et Cie, 1950), 304 pp.　9644

Raup, Hallock F., "The Italian-Swiss in California," *California Historical Society Quarterly*, vol. 30, 4 (1951), pp. 305–314.　9645

Barlow, Robert S., "Historical and Regional Analysis of the Italian Role in California Viticulture and Ecology," Master's thesis, University of California–Berkeley, 1964.　9646

Cornish & Welsh communities

Harries, Norman H., "Cornish and Welsh Mining Settlements in California," Master's thesis, University of California–Berkeley, 1956.　9647

Japanese communities

Nishi, Midori, "Japanese Settlement in the Los Angeles Area," *Yearbook of the Association of Pacific Coast Geographers*, vol. 20 (1958), pp. 35–48. [Focus on 1890–1950]   9648

Itamura, Sadao, "The Settlement Pattern of the Japanese in the Yuba-Sutter Area of California," Master's thesis, California State University–Chico, 1971.   9649

Hachimura, Keiko, "Japanese Farming in Fresno County, California: Prewar and Postwar Patterns," Master's thesis, California State University–Fresno, 1981.   9650

Yagasaki, Noritaka, "Japanese Truck Farmers and Ethnic Cooperativism in Southern California," *Chigaku Zasshi* (Journal of Geography, Tokyo), vol. 92, 2 (1983), pp. 73–90.   9651

Mennonite communities

Nachtigall, Gary B., "Mennonite Migration and Settlements of California," Master's thesis, California State University–Fresno, 1972.   9652

Chinese communities

Hardwick, Susan Wiley, *Chinese Settlement in Butte County, California: 1860–1920* (San Francisco: R & E Research Associates, 1976), 141 pp.   9653

Portuguese communities

Graves, Alvin, "Immigrants in Agriculture: The Portuguese Californians, 1850–1970s," Ph.D. diss., University of California–Los Angeles, 1977.   9654

Socialist communities

Kaizer, William, "The Kaweak Cooperative Colony: A Geographical Appraisal of Nineteenth Century Socialism in the Mountains," *California Geographer*, vol. 17 (1977), pp. 63–72.   9655

POLITICAL & ADMINISTRATIVE GEOGRAPHY

See also 8931

Dana, Mary A., "California Boundaries, Past and Present: Their Relation to Geographic Conditions," Master's thesis, University of California–Berkeley, 1919.   9656

Westfall, John E., "Estimating Minor Civil Divisions Boundaries through the Manuscript Censuses Schedules: A Methodological Note," *Historical Geography*, vol. 3, 1 (1973), pp. 3–6. [Sierra Co., 1870]   9657

Bruman, Henry J., "Sovereign California: The State's Most Plausible Alternative Scenario," in Henry J. Bruman and Clement W. Meighan,

Early California: Perception and Reality; Papers Read at a Clark Library Seminar 12 May 1979 (Los Angeles: University of California–Los Angeles, William Andrews Clark Memorial Library, 1981), pp. 1–41. Reprinted in *California Geographer*, vol. 26 (1986), pp. 1–43.   9658

Wolfe, Deborah, "A Locational Analysis of Foreign Government Representatives in the San Francisco Bay Area, 1925–1985," Master's thesis, San Francisco State University, 1988.   9659

ECONOMIC DEVELOPMENT

See also 1403

Brandt, Gladys, "The San Fernando Valley: A Study in Changing Adjustment between Its Economic Life and Its Natural Environment," Master's thesis, University of Chicago, 1928.   9660

Calef, Wesley, "The Salines of Southeastern California," *Economic Geography*, vol. 27, 1 (1951), pp. 43–64.   9661

Gentilcore, R. Louis, "Ontario, California, and the Agricultural Boom of the 1880s," *Agricultural History*, vol. 34, 2 (1960), pp. 77–87.   9662

Harrow, David R., "Shasta County, California: An Economic Geography of the Formative Years, 1850–1900," Master's thesis, Chico State College, 1968.   9663

Steger, Paul R., "A Historical Geography of the Bank of America's Branch Bank System, 1904–1970," Master's thesis, Oklahoma State University, 1977.   9664

Dilsaver, Lary M., "From Boom to Bust: Post Gold Rush Patterns of Adjustment in a California Mining Region," Ph.D. diss., Louisiana State University, 1982.   9665

RESOURCE MANAGEMENT

Water

Gregor, Howard F., "The Southern California Water Problem in the Oxnard Area," *Geographical Review*, 42, 1 (1952), pp. 16–32.   9666

Thomas, William L., Jr., "Competition for a Desert Lake: The Salton Sea, California," *California Geographer*, vol. 2 (1961), pp. 31–39. [Focus on 1907–1956]   9667

Gregor, Howard F., "Water and the California Paradox," in Cary McWilliams, ed., *The California Revolution* (New York: Grossman Publishers, 1968), pp. 159–171.   9668

Pagenhart, Thomas, "Historical Geography of Water Use in the Yuba River Basin, California," Ph.D. diss., University of California–Berkeley, 1969.   9669

Reclamation

Thompson, John, "Reclamation Sequence in the Sacramento–San Joaquin Delta," *California Geographer*, vol. 6 (1965), pp. 29–35.　　　9670

Forest conservation

Shafer, Elsa H., "The Civilian Conservation Corps in the Angeles National Forest," Master's thesis, California State University–Los Angeles, 1966.
　　　9671

Lockmann, Ronald F., "Changing Evaluations of Resources and the Establishment of National Forests in California's Transverse Ranges, 1875 to 1911," Ph.D. diss., University of California–Los Angeles, 1972.　　　9672

Lockmann, Ronald F., "Improving Nature in Southern California: Early Attempts to Ameliorate the Forest Resource in the Transverse Ranges," *Southern California Quarterly*, vol. 58, 4 (1976), pp. 485–498.　　　9673

Johnson, Sharon G., "The Land Use History of the Northern California Coast Range Preserve, Mendocino County, California," Master's thesis, San Francisco State University, 1979.　　　9674

Energy

Guinness, P., "The Changing Location of Power Plants in California," *Geography*, vol. 65, 3 (1980), pp. 217–220. [Focus on 1950–1980]　　　9675

Groenendaal, Gayle G., "California's First Fuel Crisis and Eucalyptus Plantings," Master's thesis, California State University–Northridge, 1985.　　　9676

National parks

Vankat, John L., "Fire and Man in Sequoia National Park," *Annals of the Association of American Geographers*, vol. 67, 1 (1977), pp. 17–27. [Focus from the 1860s to the 1960s]　　　9677

Dilsaver, Lary M., "Land-Use Conflict in the Kings River Canyon," *California Geographer*, vol. 26 (1986), pp. 59–80.　　　9678

Dilsaver, Lary M., "The Evolution of Land Use in Giant Forest, Sequoia National Park," *Yearbook of the Association of Pacific Coast Geographers*, vol. 49 (1987), pp. 35–50.　　　9679

Vale, Thomas R., "Vegetation Change and Park Purposes in the High Elevations of Yosemite National Park," *Annals of the Association of American Geographers*, vol. 77, 1 (1987), pp. 1–18. [Focus from 1903 to the 1980s]　　　9680

Dilsaver, Lary M., "Conservation Conflict and the Founding of Kings Canyon National Park," *California History*, vol. 69, 2 (1990), pp. 196–205.　9681

Dilsaver, Lary M., "Development and Ecology in a Mountain National Park," *Proceedings of the International Geographical Union Subcommission on Highland and High Latitude Zones*, vol. 1 (1990), pp. 35–50.　　　9682

Dilsaver, Lary M., and Douglas Strong, "Sequoia and Kings Canyon National Parks: 100 Years of Preservation and Resource Management," *California History*, vol. 69, 2 (1990), pp. 98–117.　9683

Dilsaver, Lary M., and William Tweed, *Challenge of the Big Trees: A Resource History of Sequoia and Kings Canyon National Parks* (Three Rivers, Calif.: Sequoia Natural History Association, 1990), 379 pp.　　　9684

LAND & LAND USE

Land survey

Lightfoot, James E., "Survey and Subdivision in Southern California: The San Gabriel Valley as an Example, 1848–1880," Ph.D. diss., University of California–Los Angeles, 1985.　　　9685

Land tenure

Wallach, Bret, "The Central Pacific Land Grant in Placer County, California," Master's thesis, University of California–Berkeley, 1966.　　　9686

Hornbeck, David, Jr., "Mexican-American Land Tenure Conflict in California," *Journal of Geography*, vol. 75, 4 (1976), pp. 209–221.　　　9687

Hornbeck, David, Jr., "Land Tenure and Rancho Expansion in Alta California, 1784–1846," *Journal of Historical Geography*, vol. 4, 4 (1978), pp. 371–390.　　　9688

Hornbeck, David, Jr., "The Patenting of California's Private Land Claims, 1851–1885," *Geographical Review*, vol. 69, 4 (1979), pp. 434–448.
　　　9689

Liebman, Ellen, "The Evolution of Large Agricultural Holdings in California," Ph.D. diss., University of California–Berkeley, 1981.　　　9690

Liebman, Ellen, *California Farmland: A History of Large Agricultural Landholdings* (Totowa, N.J.: Roman and Allenheld, 1983), 224 pp.　　　9691

Sauder, Robert A., "The Impact of the Agricultural College Act on Land Alienation in California," *Professional Geographer*, vol. 36, 1 (1984), pp. 28–39.　　　9692

Hornbeck, David, Jr., "California Rancheros and the Unlanded: Who Lived in Arcadia?" in *Early California Reflections* (San Juan Capistrano: Orange County Regional Library, 1988), pp. 23–36.　　　9693

Sauder, Robert A., "Patenting an Arid Frontier: Use and Abuse of the Public Land Laws in Owens Valley, California," *Annals of the Association of American Geographers*, vol. 79, 4 (1989), pp. 544–569.   **9694**

Wischemann, Trudy, "The Role of Land Tenure in Regional Development: Arvin and Dinuba Revisited," *California Geographer*, vol. 30 (1990), pp. 25–52. [Focus on 1860–1900]   **9695**

Land use

Baugh, Ruth E., "Land Use Changes in the Bishop Area of Owens Valley, California," *Economic Geography*, vol. 13, 1 (1937), pp. 17–34. [Focus on 1860s–1933]   **9696**

Goodan, Douglas, and Theodore C. Shatto, "Changing Land Use in Ygnacio Valley, California," *Economic Geography*, vol. 24, 2 (1948), pp. 135–148.   **9697**

Burcham, Levi T., "Historical Backgrounds of Range Land Use in California," *Journal of Range Management*, vol. 9, 2 (1956), pp. 81–86.   **9698**

Burcham, Levi T., *California Range Land: An Historico-Ecological Study of the Range Resource of California* (Sacramento: California Division of Forestry, 1957), 261 pp.   **9699**

Gregor, Howard F., "Push to the Desert," *Science*, vol. 129 (1959), pp. 1329–1339. [Land-use expansion]   **9700**

Henson, Raymond V., "Mission Valley, San Diego County, California: A Study in Its Changing Land-Use from 1769 to 1960," Master's thesis, University of California–Los Angeles, 1960.   **9701**

Moulton, Lawrence E., "The Vina District, Tehama County, California: Evolution of Land Use on a Small Segment of the Middle Sacramento Valley," Master's thesis, California State University–Chico, 1969.   **9702**

Scott, Frank L., "Visible Relics of Past Land Use in the Mother Lode Area, California," Ph.D. diss., University of California–Los Angeles, 1970.   **9703**

Burns, Carl S., "Historical Land Use Modifications in the Amadar Valley, California," Master's thesis, California State University–Hayward, 1975.   **9704**

Van Kampen, Carol, "From Dairy Valley to Chino: An Example of Urbanization in Southern California's Dairy Land," *California Geographer*, vol. 17 (1977), pp. 39–48. [Focus on 1920s–1977]   **9705**

Exline, Christopher H., "Sinclair's 'Von Thunen and Urban Sprawl': The Conversion of Agricultural Land to Suburban Uses in Sonoma County, California, 1950–1970," *California Geographer*, vol. 23 (1983), pp. 14–35.   **9706**

EXTRACTIVE ACTIVITY

Mining

Jones, Stanley J., "The Gold Country of the Sierra Nevada in California," *Transactions of the Institute of British Geographers*, vol. 15 (1949), pp. 115–139.   **9707**

MacKinnon, Richard M., "The Sonoran Miners: A Case of Historical Accident in the California Gold Rush," *California Geographer*, vol. 11 (1970), pp. 21–28.   **9708**

May, Philip, "California Gold: The Evolution of the Placer Mining Industry," *Proceedings of the Royal Geographical Society of Australasia, South Australia Branch*, vol. 71 (1970), pp. 27–42.   **9709**

Kristofors, Kris V., "The Copper Mining Era in Shasta County, California, 1896–1919: An Environmental Impact Study," Master's thesis, California State University–Chico, 1973.   **9710**

Lumbering

Warren, Judith L., "An Historical Geography of the Lumber Industry of the Plumas-Lassen Region," Master's thesis, University of California–Berkeley, 1971.   **9711**

Fisheries & Whaling

Nash, Robert A., "The Chinese Shrimp Fishery in California," Ph.D. diss., University of California–Los Angeles, 1973.   **9712**

Nichols, Thomas L., "California Shore Whaling, 1854 to 1900," Master's thesis, California State University–Northridge, 1982.   **9713**

Hunting

Stine, Scott W., "Hunting and the Faunal Landscape: Subsistence and Commercial Venery in Early California," Master's thesis, University of California–Berkeley, 1979.   **9714**

Oilfields

Wallach, Bret, "The West Side Oil Fields of California," *Geographical Review*, vol. 70, 1 (1980), pp. 50–59. [Focus on c. 1900–1980]   **9715**

AGRICULTURE

General

Baker, Oliver E., "Agricultural Regions of North America: Part VIII—The Pacific Subtropical

Crops Region," *Economic Geography*, vol. 6, 1 (1930), pp. 166–190; 3 (1930), pp. 278–308. **9716**

Pfeifer, Gottfried, *Räumliche Gliederung der Landwirtschaft im nördlichen Kalifornien* (Leipzig: Wissenschaftliche Veröffentlichungen der Gesellschaft für Erdkunde zu Leipzig, vol. 10, 1936), 309 pp. **9717**

Gregor, Howard F., "Agricultural Shifts in the Ventura Lowland of California," *Economic Geography*, vol. 29, 4 (1953), pp. 340–361. [Focus on 1850–1950] **9718**

Willis, Harry W., "Evolution of Corporate Agriculture in the San Joaquin Valley, California," Master's thesis, University of California–Los Angeles, 1953. **9719**

Gregor, Howard F., "The Local-Supply Agriculture of California," *Annals of the Association of American Geographers*, 47, 3 (1957), pp. 267–276. **9720**

Blossom, Herbert H., "The Agricultural Development of the Coachella Valley, California," Master's thesis, University of California–Berkeley, 1959. **9721**

Eder, Herbert M., "Some Aspects of the Persistence of Agriculture in the San Fernando Valley," Master's thesis, University of California–Los Angeles, 1960. **9722**

Gregor, Howard F., "Urbanization of Southern California Agriculture," *Tijdschrift voor economische en sociale geografie*, 54, 12 (1963), pp. 273–278. **9723**

Aldabbagh, Abdul W., "The Development of Agriculture in the Coachella Valley, California, Before and After the Importation of the Colorado River Water," Master's thesis, Clark University, 1967. **9724**

Fitzsimmons, Margaret L., "Agriculture in the Pueblo of Los Angeles, 1781–1847," Master's thesis, California State University–Northridge, 1975. **9725**

Hornbeck, David, Jr., and Mary L. Tucey, "Agriculture in Hispanic California, 1850," *California Geographer*, vol. 15 (1975), pp. 52–59. **9726**

Rowntree, Lester B., and Robert A. Raburn, "Rainfall Variability and California Mission Agriculture: An Analysis from Harvest and Tree Ring Data," *Yearbook of the Association of Pacific Coast Geographers*, vol. 42 (1980), pp. 31–44. [Focus on 1780–1910] **9727**

Dilsaver, Lary M., "Food Supply Regions for the California Gold Rush," *California Geographer*, vol. 23 (1983), pp. 36–50. **9728**

Thompson, John, and Edward A. Dutra, *The Tule Breakers: The Story of the California Dredge* (Stockton, Calif.: University of the Pacific, for the Stockton Corral of Westerners, 1983), 368 pp. **9729**

Thompson, John, "Introducing the 'Tule Breakers' of California," *Pioneer America Society Transactions*, vol. 7 (1984), pp. 13–20. **9730**

Quesada, William G., "The Agricultural Lands and Farming Practices of Mission San Jose, 1820–1830," Master's thesis, University of California–Berkeley, 1985. **9731**

Dilsaver, Lary M., "The Development of Agriculture in a Gold Rush Region," *Yearbook of the Association of Pacific Coast Geographers*, vol. 48 (1986), pp. 67–88. **9732**

Könnecke, Michael, "Phasen landwirtschaftlicher Inwertsetzung des Sacramentotals," *Zeitschrift für Wirtschaftsgeographie*, vol. 30, 2 (1986), pp. 35–48. **9733**

Sauder, Robert A., "The Agricultural Colonization of a Great Basin Frontier: Economic Organization and Environmental Alteration in Owens Valley, California, 1860–1925," *Agricultural History*, vol. 64, 1 (1990), pp. 78–101. **9734**

Windhorst, Hans-Wilhelm, "Die Ausbreitung des mechanischen Vollernters fur Industrietomaten in Kalifornien: Eine agrartechnologische Innovation und ihe Wirkungen," *Erdkunde*, vol. 44, 1 (1990), pp. 23–37. [Focus on 1950–1987] **9735**

Grains

Saunders, Margery H., "California Wheat, 1867–1910: Influence of Transportation on the Export Trade and the Location of Producing Areas," Master's thesis, University of California–Berkeley, 1960. **9736**

Dairying

Raup, Hallock F., "The Italian-Swiss Dairymen of San Luis Obispo County, California," *Yearbook of the Association of Pacific Coast Geographers*, vol. 1 (1935), pp. 3–8. **9737**

Copley, Richard, "An Historical Geography of the Dairy Industry of Stanislaus County, California," Master's thesis, University of California–Berkeley, 1961. **9738**

Livestock

Menzel, Marion Lee Jones, "The Historical Geography of the Sheep Industry in California in the Nineteenth Century," Master's thesis, University of California–Berkeley, 1944. **9739**

Burcham, Levi T., *Range Livestock Population of California, 1850–1950* (Sacramento: California Division of Forestry, 1955), 18 pp. **9740**

Burcham, Levi T., "Historical Geography of the Range Livestock Industry of California," Ph.D.

diss., University of California–Berkeley, 1956. **9741**

Burcham, Levi T., "The Advent of Sheep in California," *California Livestock News*, vol. 33, 24 (1957), sec. 2, pp. 13, 15. **9742**

Burcham, Levi T., "Cattle and Range Forage in California, 1770–1880," *Agricultural History*, 35, 3 (1961), pp. 140–149. **9743**

Burcham, Levi T., "Cattle Ranching in the Early Days of California," *American Hereford Journal*, vol. 55, 5 (1964), pp. 440–462. **9744**

Orchards

El-Gammal, Farouk M., "Changes in the Distributional Patterns of Fruit Agriculture in California, 1939–59," Master's thesis, Clark University, 1963. **9745**

Meleen, Nathan H., "The Changing Geography of the California Prune Industry," Master's thesis, Clark University, 1964. **9746**

Bowen, William A., "The Evolution of a Cultural Landscape: The Valley Fruit District of Solano County, California," Master's thesis, University of California–Berkeley, 1966. **9747**

Vineyards

Gibson, David J., "The Development of the Livermore Valley Wine District," Master's thesis, University of California–Davis, 1969. **9748**

Dorel, Gérard, "Le vignoble Californien," *Cahiers d'outre mer*, vol. 30, 1 (1977), pp. 5–30. [Focus on 1950–1973] **9749**

Eysberg, Cees D., *The California Wine Economy: Natural Opportunities and Socio-Cultural Constraints—A Regional Geographic Analysis of Its Origins and Perspectives* (Amsterdam: Koninklijk Nederlands Aardrijkskundig Genootschap and Geografisch Instituut Rijksuniversiteit Utrecht, 1990), 267 pp. **9750**

Specialty crops

Parsons, James J., "The California Hop Industry: Its Eighty Years of Development and Expansion," Master's thesis, University of California–Berkeley, 1939. **9751**

Parsons, James J., "Hops in Early California Agriculture," *Agricultural History*, vol. 14, 3 (1940), pp. 110–116. **9752**

Tyner, Gerald E., "The Historical Development of California's Herb Industry," *California Geographer*, vol. 16 (1976), pp. 43–51. **9753**

Yagasaki, Noritaka, "Evolution of Japanese Floriculture in Northern California," Master's thesis, University of California–Berkeley, 1978. **9754**

Yagasaki, Noritaka, "Formation of the Japanese Floriculture in Northern California: Role of the Ethnic Organization in Immigrant Agriculture," *Chigaku Zasshi* (Journal of Geography, Tokyo), vol. 89, 3 (1980), pp. 149–166. **9755**

Yagasaki, Noritaka, "Evolution of Japanese Floriculture in Southern California," *Jimbun Chiri* (Human Geography, Kyoto), vol. 35, 1 (1983), pp. 1–22. **9756**

Aron, Robert H., "The Changing Location of California Almond Production," *California Geographer*, vol. 28 (1988), pp. 69–94. [Focus on 1890–1987] **9757**

Eggs

Doughty, Robin W., "San Francisco's Nineteenth-Century Egg Basket: The Farallons," *Geographical Review*, vol. 61, 4 (1971), pp. 554–572. **9758**

Doughty, Robin W., "The Farallons and the Boston Men," *California Historical Review*, vol. 53, 4 (1974), pp. 306–316. **9759**

LANDSCAPE

General

Nelson, Howard J., "The Spread of an Artificial Landscape over Southern California," *Annals of the Association of American Geographers*, vol. 49, 1 (1959), pp. 80–99. **9760**

Raup, Hallock F., "The Transformation of Southern California to a Cultivated Land," *Annals of the Association of American Geographers*, vol. 49, 3 (1959), pt. 2, pp. 58–79. **9761**

Preston, Richard E., "The Changing Landscape of the San Fernando Valley between 1930 and 1964," *California Geographer*, vol. 6 (1965), pp. 59–72. **9762**

Miller, Crane S., "The Changing Landscape of the Simi Valley, California, from 1795 to 1968," Master's thesis, University of California–Los Angeles, 1968. **9763**

Hornbeck, David, Jr., "Landscape Changes in the Pajaro Valley, 1840–1880: A Study in Change Processes," Master's thesis, California State University–Fresno, 1969. **9764**

Scott, Frank L., "California Gold Mining Landscapes," *California Geographer*, vol. 12 (1971), pp. 38–44. **9765**

Johnson, Donald L., "Landscape Evolution on San Miguel Island, California," Ph.D. diss., University of Kansas, 1972. **9766**

Hornbeck, David, Jr., "California's Landscape Heritage," *Places*, vol. 3, 2 (1976), pp. 26–29. **9767**

Hornbeck, David, Jr., and Phillip Kane, *Missions, Mountains, and Monterrey: A Guide to Coastal California's Changing Landscapes* (Prepared for the National Council for Geographic Education, 1976), 41 pp.   9768

Hornbeck, David, Jr., Howard Botts, Martin Kenzer, and Virginia Oliver, *Cultural Landscapes of the Santa Barbara Coast, 1760–1890* (Northridge, Calif.: Field Guide for CUKANZUS '79, An International Conference for Historical Geography, 1979), 49 pp.   9769

Hornbeck, David, Jr., "The Ordinary Landscape of Hispanic California," in Nicholas Magalousis, ed., *Early California Reflections: A Series of Lectures Held at the San Juan Capistrano Branch of the Orange County Public Library* (San Juan Capistrano: Orange County Public Library, 1987), pp. 1–13.   9770

Nelson, Patricia W., "Relics in the Southern California Landscape," Master's thesis, California State University–Fullerton, 1987.   9771

Land draining

Bartz, Fritz, "Die Polderlandschaft des Deltas des Sacramento–San Joaquin: Das Holland Kalifornien," *Erdkunde*, vol. 6, 4 (1952), pp. 247–260.   9772

Buildings & building materials

Passarello, John, "Adaptation of House Type to Changing Function: A Sequence of Chicken House Styles in Petaluma," *California Geographer*, vol. 5 (1964), pp. 69–74.   9773

Fredericks, Robert, "Nineteenth-Century Stonework in California's Napa Valley," *California Geographer*, vol. 10 (1969), pp. 39–48.   9774

Pitman, Leon S., "Domestic Tankhouses of Rural California," *Pioneer America*, vol. 8, 2 (1976), pp. 84–97.   9775

Hornbeck, David, Jr., Michael Taugher, and Howard Botts, "Missions of the Santa Barbara Coast," *Field Guide for the Association of American Geographers Meetings, Los Angeles* (Washington, D.C.: Association of American Geographers, 1981), pp. 61–66.   9776

Ethnic signatures

Arreola, Daniel D., "The Chinese Role in Creating the Early Cultural Landscape of the Sacramento–San Joaquin Delta," *California Geographer*, vol. 15 (1975), pp. 1–15.   9777

COMMUNICATIONS & TRADE

See also **8437, 8944**

General

Garrison, Jeanne, "Barstow, California: A Transportation Focus in a Desert Environment," *Economic Geography*, vol. 29, 2 (1953), pp. 159–167. [Focus on 1775–1950]   9778

Simoons, Frederick J., "Development of Transportation Routes in the Clear Lake Area," *California Historical Society Quarterly*, vol. 32, 4 (1953), pp. 363–371.   9779

Búnkse, Edmund V., "Humboldt Bay Region: A Study of Pioneer Transportation," Master's thesis, University of California–Berkeley, 1966.   9780

Gilman, Harold F., "Origins and Persistence of a Transit Region: Eastern Mojave Desert of California," Ph.D. diss., University of California–Riverside, 1977.   9781

Quastler, Imre E., "San Diegans on the Move: Transportation in the County," in Philip R. Pryde, ed., *San Diego: An Introduction to the Region*, 3d ed. (Dubuque: Kendall-Hunt Publishing Co., 1992), pp. 165–184.   9782

Railroads

Smith, Howard G., "The Role of Interurban Railways in the Los Angeles Area," Master's thesis, California State University–Northridge, 1965.   9783

Floyd, Donald R., *California Narrow-Gauge: The Historic Role of Narrow-Gauge Railroads in California's Transportation Network* (Mountain View, Calif.: Gibson Press, 1970), 118 pp.   9784

Quastler, Imre E., "The Areal Distribution of Railroad Abandonments in California since 1920," *California Geographer*, vol. 11 (1970), pp. 35–42.   9785

Floyd, Donald R., "A Surge of Hope: Public Reaction to Arguments for Construction of Narrow-Gauge Railroads in California, 1870–1873," *California Geographer*, vol. 25 (1985), pp. 65–84. 9786

Road transport

Fitzsimmons, Allan K., "The Automobile and the Roads of Yosemite Valley," *California Geographer*, vol. 11 (1970), pp. 43–50. [Focus on 1913–1966]   9787

Water transport

Sargent, Charles S., Jr., "The Evolution of Water Transportation and Ports in the San Francisco

Bay Area, California, 1848–1880," Master's thesis, University of California–Berkeley, 1966. **9788**

Potter, Daniel, "Steam Navigation on the Lower San Joaquin River circa 1846 to 1900," Master's thesis, California State University–Hayward, 1989. **9789**

MANUFACTURING & INDUSTRIALIZATION

McQueeny, Theresa F., "The Industrial Development of the Mill River Valley," Master's thesis, Clark University, 1930. **9790**

Ketron, Robert G., "Locational and Historical Aspects of the Quick Frozen Vegetable Processing Industry of California," Master's thesis, University of Arizona, 1968. **9791**

Beaton, Joseph P., "Why the Movies Chose Hollywood," *Journal of Cultural Geography*, vol. 4, 1 (1983), pp. 99–109. **9792**

Cardellino, Joan E., "Industrial Location: A Case Study of the California Fruit and Vegetable Canning Industry, 1860–1984," Master's thesis, University of California–Berkeley, 1984. **9793**

Christopherson, Susan, and Michael Storper, "The City as Studio, the World as Back Lot: The Impact of Vertical Disintegration on the Location of the Motion Picture Industry," *Environment and Planning D: Society and Space*, vol. 4, 3 (1986), pp. 305–320. [Focus on c. 1900–1984] **9794**

Morales, R., "The Los Angeles Automobile Industry in Historical Perspective," *Environment and Planning D: Society and Space*, vol. 4, 3 (1986), pp. 289–303. **9795**

URBAN NETWORKS & URBANIZATION

See also **9231**

Smith, James, "Some Geographic Influences in the Location and Development of Certain Towns and Cities of California," Master's thesis, University of California–Berkeley, 1911. **9796**

Wilhelmy, Herbert, "Die Goldrauschstädte der 'Mother Lode' in Kalifornien," in Wilhelm Lauer, ed., *Beiträge zur Geographie der Neuen Welt: Oskar Schmieder zum 70. Geburtstag* (Kiel: Schriften des Geographischen Instituts der Universität Kiel, vol. 20, 1961), pp. 55–71. **9797**

Mason, Peter F., "Urban Development in the Central Valley, 1950–1972: Toward the Completion of the California Ecumenopolis," *Great Plains–Rocky Mountain Geographical Journal*, vol. 2 (1973), pp. 71–79. **9798**

Smith, Richard H., "Towns along the Tracks: Railroad Strategy and Town Promotion in the San Joaquin Valley, California," Ph.D. diss., University of California–Los Angeles, 1976. **9799**

TOWN GROWTH

Los Angeles

Snyder, William H., "The Geographical Determinants of Los Angeles," *Journal of Geography*, vol. 9, 10 (1911), pp. 275–277. **9800**

Miller, Willis H., "The Pattern of Metropolitan Los Angeles," *Bulletin of the Philadelphia Geographical Society*, vol. 31, 1 (1933), pp. 27–31. **9801**

Wagner, Anton, *Los Angeles: Werden, Leben und Gestalt der Zweimillionenstadt in Südkalifornien* (Kiel: Schriften des Geographischen Instituts der Universität Kiel, no. 3, 1935), 295 pp. **9802**

Preston, Richard E., "The Changing Form and Structure of the Southern California Metropolis," *California Geographer*, vol. 12 (1971), pp. 5–20; 13 (1972), pp. 32–47. [Focus on 1940–1970] **9803**

Nelson, Howard J., "The Two Pueblos of Los Angeles: Agricultural Village and Embryo Town," *Southern California Quarterly*, vol. 59, 1 (1977), pp. 1–11. **9804**

Marchand, Bernard, "L'émergence de Los Angeles (1940–1970): Croissance spatiale, rente foncière, et ségrégation sociale," *Annales de géographie*, vol. 96, 538 (1987), pp. 711–724. **9805**

Sacramento

Kabitzsch, Gesine, "Old Sacramento: Genese des ältesten Teils von Kaliforniens Hauptstadt Sacramento," in Christoph Jentsch, ed., *Beiträge zur Geographischen Methode und Landeskunde: Festgabe für Gudrun Höhl* (Mannheim: Geographisches Institut der Universität Mannheim, Mannheimer Geographische Arbeiten, vol. 1, 1977), pp. 465–473. **9806**

San Diego

Suhl, Alvena M., "Historical Geography of San Diego," Master's thesis, University of California–Berkeley, 1928. **9807**

Mirkowich, Nicholas, "Urban Growth in the San Diego Region," *Economic Geography*, vol. 18, 3 (1941), pp. 308–310. **9808**

Winterhouse, John, "The Historical Geography of San Diego: Some Aspects of Landscape Change Prior to 1850," Master's thesis, California State University–San Diego, 1972. **9809**

San Francisco

Ruhl, Alfred, "San Francisco," *Memorial Volume of the Transcontinental Excursion of 1912 of the American Geographical Society of New York* (New York: American Geographical Society, 1915), pp. 287–311.   9810

Jackson, Eric P., "The Early Historical Geography of San Francisco," *Journal of Geography*, vol. 26, 1 (1927), pp. 12–22.   9811

Vance, James E., Jr., *Geography and Urban Evolution in the San Francisco Bay Area* (Berkeley: University of California, Institute of Governmental Studies, 1964), 89 pp.   9812

Burns, Elizabeth K., "The Process of Suburban Residential Development: The San Francisco Peninsula," *Great Plains–Rocky Mountain Geographical Journal*, vol. 3 (1974), pp. 10–17.   9813

Burns, Elizabeth K., "The Process of Suburban Residential Development: The San Francisco Peninsula, 1860–1970," Ph.D. diss., University of California–Berkeley, 1974.   9814

Burns, Elizabeth K., "Subdivision Activity on the San Francisco Peninsula, 1860–1970," *Yearbook of the Association of Pacific Coast Geographers*, vol. 39 (1977), pp. 17–32.   9815

Ventura

Reith, Gertrude L., "Evolution of a California City: Ventura," *Yearbook of the Association of Pacific Coast Geographers*, vol. 24 (1962), pp. 15–20. 9816

Reith, Gertrude L., "Geographic Factors in the Historical Development of Ventura, California," Ph.D. diss., Clark University, 1963.   9817

Other centers

Gerlach, Arch C., "Growth of El Segundo, California," *Economic Geography*, vol. 16, 2 (1940), pp. 225–230.   9818

Raup, Hallock F., "San Bernardino, California: Settlement and Growth of a Pass-Site City," *University of California Publications in Geography*, vol. 8 (1940), pp. 1–64.   9819

Day, Dorothy M., "Azuza: The Ranch That Became a City," Master's thesis, Clark University, 1953.   9820

Jensen, Thomas A., "Palm Springs, California: Its Evolution and Function," Master's thesis, University of California–Los Angeles, 1954.   9821

Mikesell, Marvin W., "The Changing Role of the Port of Santa Barbara," *Historical Society of Southern California Quarterly*, vol. 36, 3 (1954), pp. 238–244.   9822

Gentilcore, R. Louis, "Ontario, California, and the Agricultural Boom of the 1880s," *Agricultural History*, vol. 34, 2 (1960), pp. 77–87.   9823

Hellmann, Margery Saunders, "Port Costa: California's Wheat Center," *California Geographer*, vol. 4 (1963), pp. 63–65.   9824

Merlin, Imelda B., "Alameda: Historical Geography of a California City," Master's thesis, University of California–Berkeley, 1964.   9825

Loeser, Cornelius J., "The Historical Geography of Newport Beach, California," Ph.D. diss., University of California–Los Angeles, 1965.   9826

Lockmann, Ronald F., "Burbank, California: An Historical Geography," Master's thesis, University of California–Los Angeles, 1967.   9827

Vieira, Richard, "Gridley, California: Evolution of a Mid-Sacramento Valley Farm Town," Master's thesis, California State University–Chico, 1968.   9828

Hancock, Raymond J., "Orland, California: An Historical Geography," Master's thesis, California State University–Chico, 1970.   9829

Weed, Abner, "Weed: The Evolution of a Company Town," Master's thesis, California State University–Chico, 1974.   9830

Young, Jann Ellen, "An Historical Geography of Fullerton, California, Through Incorporation in 1904," Master's thesis, California State University–Fullerton, 1976.   9831

Goss, Roger A. E., "The Impact of Technological Change on a Desert Town: The Growth and Decline of Amboy, California," Master's thesis, University of California–Los Angeles, 1977. 9832

Hainline, Ingrid, "Claremont the Beautiful," Master's thesis, California State University–Fullerton, 1977. [Focus on 1887–1977]   9833

Curtis, James R., "Alviso, California: A Study in Cultural-Historical Geography," Ph.D. diss., University of California–Los Angeles, 1978. 9834

Curtis, James R., "Whatever Happened to Port San Jose?" *California Geographer*, vol. 18 (1978), pp. 35–42.   9835

Glass, Stephen, "Soda Springs: Sequential Land Use," *California Geographer*, vol. 20 (1980), pp. 10–27.   9836

Aiken, S. Robert, "Bodie: From Bonanza to Ghost Town," *Focus* (American Geographical Society), vol. 35, 3 (1985), pp. 20–27.   9837

URBAN ECONOMIC STRUCTURE

See also 4661, 4663

Los Angeles

Zierer, Clifford H., "The Los Angeles Harbor Fishing Center," *Economic Geography*, vol. 10, 4 (1934), pp. 402–418. [Focus on 1893–1932]   9838

Miller, Willis H., "Competition for the Ocean Trade of Los Angeles," *Economic Geography*, vol. 13, 4 (1937), pp. 325–333. [Focus on 1781–1911] 9839

McDannold, Thomas A., "Development of the Los Angeles Chinatown: 1850–1970," Master's thesis, California State University–Northridge, 1973. 9840

Parker, Carl, III. "The Spatial Structure of Housing: Los Angeles, 1931–1970," Ph.D. diss., University of California–Los Angeles, 1975. 9841

Miller, Willis H., "The Port of Los Angeles–Long Beach in 1929 and 1979: A Comparative Study," *Southern California Quarterly*, vol. 65, 4 (1983), pp. 341–478. 9842

Sacramento

Hardwick, Susan Wiley, "Suburban Commercial Development in the Shadow of Downtown Sacramento," *Yearbook of the Association of Pacific Coast Geographers*, vol. 49 (1987), pp. 51–63. [Focus on 1930–1985] 9843

San Francisco

Elgie, Robert A., "The Development of Manufacturing in San Francisco, 1848–1880: Locational Factors and Urban Spatial Structure," Master's thesis, University of California–Berkeley, 1966. 9844

Bowden, Martyn J., "The Dynamics of City Growth: An Historical Geography of the San Francisco Central District, 1850–1931," Ph.D. diss., University of California–Berkeley, 1967. 9845

Bowden, Martyn J., "Downtown through Time: Delimitation, Expansion, and Internal Growth," *Economic Geography*, vol. 47, 2 (1971), pp. 121–135. 9846

Bowden, Martyn J., "Persistence, Failure, and Mobility in the Inner City: Preliminary Notes," in Ralph E. Ehrenberg, ed., *Pattern and Process: Research in Historical Geography* (Washington, D.C.: Howard University Press, 1975), pp. 169–192. Reprinted, with omissions, in David Ward, ed., *Geographic Perspectives on America's Past: Readings on the Historical Geography of the United States* (New York: Oxford University Press, 1979), pp. 321–334. 9847

Bloom, Khaled, "Market-Oriented Agriculture in Nineteenth Century San Francisco," *Yearbook of the Association of Pacific Coast Geographers*, vol. 44 (1982), pp. 75–92. 9848

Other centers

Henderson, Arvin C., Jr., "Evolution of Commercial Nucleation in San Jose, California," Master's thesis, California State University–San Jose, 1970. 9849

Kennedy, John H., "Historical Development of the Pacific Palisades Commercial Core Area," Master's thesis, University of California–Los Angeles, 1973. 9850

Botts, Howard A., "Monterey's Evolving Commercial Structure, 1885–1926," Master's thesis, California State University–Northridge, 1977. 9851

Ward, David A., "An Analysis of the South Pasadena Central Business District from 1895 to the Present Time," Master's thesis, University of California–Los Angeles, 1978. 9852

Fearing, Wendy, "Industrialization and Daily Bread: Bakeries and Household Provisioning in Oakland, 1880–1930," Master's thesis, University of California–Berkeley, 1986. 9853

Boboricken, Sherry A., "A Comparative Analysis of the Central Business Districts of Hollister, Watsonville, Santa Cruz, and Los Gatos, 1960 and 1988," Master's thesis, San Jose State University, 1989. 9854

URBAN SOCIAL STRUCTURE

See also 4698

Los Angeles

Dakan, A. William, "Electoral and Population Geography of South–Central Los Angeles," *Yearbook of the Association of Pacific Coast Geographers*, vol. 31 (1969), pp. 135–143. [Focus on 1932–1966] 9855

Dakan, A. William , "Electoral and Population Geography of South-Central Los Angeles, 1932–1966," Master's thesis, University of California–Los Angeles, 1970. 9856

Gordon, Roni E., "Residential Mobility in Los Angeles: 1920–1930," Master's thesis, University of California–Los Angeles, 1976. 9857

Konovnitzian, Peter, "The Russian Orthodox Community in Los Angeles, 1922–1985," Master's thesis, California State University–Los Angeles, 1988. 9858

San Francisco

Dunbar, Gary S., "The Rival Geographical Societies of Fin-de-Siècle San Francisco," *Yearbook of the Association of Pacific Coast Geographers*, vol. 40 (1978), pp. 57–64. 9859

Burns, Elizabeth K., "The Enduring Affluent Suburb," *Landscape*, vol. 24, 1 (1980), pp. 33–41. [Focus on 1900–1980] 9860

Leyland, Robert C., "Puerto Ricans in the San Francisco Bay Area, California: An Historical and Cultural Geography," Master's thesis, California State University–Hayward, 1980.　　9861

Shumsky, Neil L., and Larry M. Springer, "San Francisco's Zone of Prostitution, 1880–1934," *Journal of Historical Geography*, vol. 7, 1 (1981), pp. 71–89.　　9862

Godfrey, Brian J., "Inner-City Neighborhoods in Transition: The Morphogenesis of San Francisco's Ethnic and Nonconformist Communities," Ph.D. diss., University of California–Berkeley, 1984.　　9863

Godfrey, Brian J., "Inner-City Revitalization and Cultural Succession: The Evolution of San Francisco's Haight-Ashbury District," *Yearbook of the Association of Pacific Coast Geographers*, vol. 46 (1984), pp. 79–91.　　9864

Godfrey, Brian J., "Ethnic Identities and Ethnic Enclaves: The Morphogenesis of San Francisco's Hispanic Barrio," *Yearbook of the Association of Latin Americanist Geographers*, vol. 11 (1985), pp. 45–53.　　9865

Dobkin, Marjorie, "Biography Formation and Daily Life in a Frontier City: The Joint Constitution of Society and Subjects in San Francisco, 1848–1858," Ph.D. diss., University of California–Berkeley, 1988.　　9866

Godfrey, Brian J., *Neighborhoods in Transition: The Making of San Francisco's Ethnic and Non-Conformist Communities* (Berkeley: University of California Publications in Geography, no. 27, 1988), 233 pp.　　9867

Other centers

Halme, Kalervo R., "Environmental Hazards and Urban Development: A Historical, Spatial, and Systems View of the City of Long Beach," Master's thesis, California State University–Long Beach, 1974.　　9868

Tucey, Mary L., and David Hornbeck, Jr., "Anglo Immigration and the Hispanic Town: A Study of Urban Change in Monterey, California, 1835–1850," *Social Science Journal*, vol. 13, 2 (1976), pp. 1–8.　　9869

Hardwick, Susan Wiley, "A Geographical Interpretation of Ethnic Settlement in an Urban Landscape: Russians in Sacramento," *California Geographer*, vol. 19 (1979), pp. 87–104. [Focus on 1950–1970]　　9870

LaClaire, Charles K., "Stages of Neighborhood Development: The 'Westside' of the City of Bernardino," Master's thesis, California State University, 1985. [Focus on the period since 1950]　　9871

Gaubatz, Piper R., "The Geography of Neighborhood Change: Idora Park in the Twentieth Century," Master's thesis, University of California–Berkeley, 1986.　　9872

TOWNSCAPE

General

Foster, Richard H., Jr., "The Persistence of Mexican Land Grant Boundaries in the Present Day Landscape," Master's thesis, California State University–San Francisco, 1968.　　9873

Barnett, Roger T., "The Libertarian Suburb: Deliberate Disorder," *Landscape*, vol. 22, 3 (1978), pp. 44–48. [Focus from the 1910s to the 1970s]　　9874

Whitehead, Richard S., "Alta California's Four Fortresses," *Southern California Quarterly*, vol. 65, 1 (1983), pp. 67–94.　　9875

Los Angeles

Baugh, Ruth E., "Site of Early Los Angeles," *Economic Geography*, vol. 18, 1 (1942), pp. 87–96.　　9876

Brown, Robert G., "The California Bungalow in Los Angeles: A Study in Origins and Classification," Master's thesis, University of California–Los Angeles, 1964.　　9877

Nelson, Howard J., et al., "Remnants of the Ranchos in the Urban Pattern of the Los Angeles Area," *California Geographer*, vol. 5 (1964), pp. 1–9.　　9878

Rutledge, William H., "Morphology during the Growth of the Los Angeles Conurbation, 1900–1970, with Single-Family Houses Viewed as Composing City Form," Ph.D. diss., University of California–Berkeley, 1975.　　9879

Rubin, Barbara, "A Chronology of Architecture in Los Angeles," *Annals of the Association of American Geographers*, vol. 67, 4 (1977), pp. 521–537.　　9880

Padick, Clement, "Vertical Aerial Photography of the Los Angeles Area: A Historical Perspective," *California Geographer*, vol. 21 (1981), pp. 30–46. [Focus on 1938–1976]　　9881

Young, Terrence G., "Constructing an Urban Forest: A Cultural Biogeography in Middle-Class Los Angeles, 1930–1980," Master's thesis, University of California–Los Angeles, 1987.　　9882

San Diego

Ford, Larry R., and James R. Curtis, "Bungalow Courts in San Diego: Monitoring a Sense of

Place," *Journal of San Diego History*, vol. 34, 2 (1988), pp. 78–92.   **9883**

Ford, Larry R., "The Visions of the Builders: The Historical Evolution of the San Diego Cityscape," in Philip R. Pryde, ed., *San Diego: An Introduction to the Region*, 3d ed. (Dubuque: Kendall-Hunt Publishing Co., 1992), pp. 185–203.   **9884**

San Francisco

Bowden, Martyn J., "Reconstruction Following Catastrophe: The Laissez-Faire Rebuilding of Downtown San Francisco after the Earthquake and Fire of 1906," *Proceedings of the Association of American Geographers*, vol. 2 (1970), pp. 22–26.   **9885**

Foster, Richard H., Jr., "Wartime Trailer Housing in the San Francisco Bay Area," *Geographical Review*, vol. 70, 3 (1980), pp. 276–290.   **9886**

Baker, Simon, "San Francisco in Ruins: The 1906 Aerial Photographs of Sherrill Harbison," *Landscape*, vol. 30, 2 (1989), pp. 9–14.   **9887**

Other centers

Rutledge, William H., "The Role of House Types in the Formation of Residential Areas in Oakland," Master's thesis, University of California–Berkeley, 1964.   **9888**

Barnett, Roger T., "Suburban Subdivision: The Morphogenesis of Housing in Stockton, 1850–1950," Ph.D. diss., University of California–Berkeley, 1973.   **9889**

RECREATION & TOURISM

Anderson, Roy W., "The Historical Geography of the California Spas: Fountains of Health in the Central Coast Ranges," Master's thesis, University of California–Berkeley, 1965.   **9890**

Charnofsky, Kim, "California Mineral and Hot Springs: Historical and Geographical Considerations in Their Perception, Location, and Development," Master's thesis, University of California–Berkeley, 1989.   **9891**

Wyckoff, William K., "Summer Home Settings as Cultural Landscape: Southern California in the 1930s," *California Geographer*, vol. 29 (1989), pp. 1–19.   **9892**

PLACE NAMES

Sanchez, Nellie van de Grift, *Spanish and Indian Place Names of California: Their Meaning and Their Romance* (San Francisco: A. M. Robertson, 1914), 445 pp. Reprinted Salem, New Hampshire: Ayer Co. Publishers, 1976.   **9893**

Kroeber, Alfred L., "California Place Names of Indian Origin," *University of California Publications in American Archeology and Ethnology*, vol. 12, 2 (1916), 69 pp.   **9894**

Putnam, Ruth, "California: The Name," *University of California Publications in History*, vol. 4, 4 (1917), pp. 293–365.   **9895**

Waterman, Thomas T., "Yurok Geography," *University of California Publications in American Archeology and Ethnology*, vol. 16, 5 (1920), pp. 177–314.   **9896**

Kniffen, Fred B., "Achomawi Geography," *University of California Publications in American Archaeology and Ethnology*, vol. 23, 5 (1928), pp. 297–322.   **9897**

Wells, Harry Laurenz, *California Names: Over Two Thousand Five Hundred Place Names . . . in the Golden State* (Los Angeles: Kellaway-Ide-Jones Co., 1934), 94 pp.   **9898**

Raup, Hallock F., "Place Names of the California Gold Rush," *Geographical Review*, vol. 35, 4 (1945), pp. 653–658.   **9899**

Raup, Hallock F., and William B. Pounds, "The Northernmost Spanish Frontier in California: As Shown by the Distribution of Geographic Names," *California Historical Society Quarterly*, vol. 32, 1 (1953), pp. 43–48.   **9900**

Gudde, Erwin G., *California Place Names: The Origin and Etymology of Current Geographical Names* (Berkeley: University of California Press, 1960), 383 pp. Reprinted 1969.   **9901**

Edwards, Clinton R., "Wandering Toponyms: El Puerto de la Bodega and Bodega Bay," *Pacific Historical Review*, vol. 33, 3 (1964), pp. 253–272; vol. 35, 3 (1966), p. 345.   **9902**

Smith, Everett G., Jr., "Street Names in California," *Yearbook of the Association of Pacific Coast Geographers*, vol. 37 (1975), pp. 77–90.   **9903**

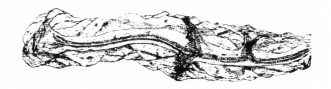

ALASKA

GENERAL

See also 1148, 3897

The state

Martin, Lawrence, "Geographic Influences in Alaska," *Journal of Geography*, vol. 9, 3 (1910), pp. 65–70.   9904

Lynch, Donald F., "The Historical Geography of New Russia: 1780–1837," Ph.D. diss., Yale University, 1964.   9905

Smaller areas

Critchfield, Howard J., "Seward Peninsula: Threshold of the Hemisphere," *Economic Geography*, vol. 25, 4 (1949), pp. 275–284. [Focus on 1899–1949]   9906

Lenz, Mary, "The Kuskokwim [River]," *Alaska Geographic*, vol. 15, 4 (1988), pp. 6–73.   9907

Simpson, Sherry, "From Bonanza until the Lights Go Out," *Alaska Geographic*, vol. 17, 2 (1990), pp. 16–45. [Focus from the 1880s to the 1940s] 9908

ENVIRONMENTAL CHANGE

See also 1160

Smith, Philip S., "Settlements and Climate of the Seward Peninsula, Alaska," *Bulletin of the Philadelphia Geographical Society*, vol. 5, 2 (1907), pp. 10–20.   9909

Schenck, Adolph, "Der Ausbruch des Vulkans Katmai in Alaska in Jahre 1912 und das Tal der Zehntausend Dämpfe," *Geographische Zeitschrift*, vol. 34, 10 (1928), pp. 613–616.   9910

Haag, William G., "The Bering Strait Land Bridge," *Scientific American*, vol. 206, 1 (1962), pp. 112–123. Reprinted in H. Jesse Walker and Milton B. Newton, Jr., eds., *Environment and Culture* (Baton Rouge: Louisiana State University, Department of Geography and Anthropology, 1978), pp. 227–232.   9911

Nelson, Fritz, and Sam I. Outcalt, "Anthropogenic Geomorphology in Northern Alaska," *Physical Geography*, vol. 3, 1 (1982), pp. 17–48.   9912

NATIVE PEOPLES & WHITE RELATIONS

Jenness, Diamond, "The Eskimos of Northern Alaska: A Study in the Effect of Civilization,"

Geographical Review, vol. 5, 2 (1918), pp. 89–101. [Focus on 1883–1918]   9913

Coppock, Henry A., "Interactions between Russians and Native Americans in Alaska, 1741–1840," Ph.D. diss., Michigan State University, 1970.   9914

EXPLORATION & MAPPING

See also 1285–1289

Brooks, Alfred H., "The Influence of Geography on the Exploration and Settlement of Alaska," *Bulletin of the American Geographical Society*, vol. 38, 2 (1906), pp. 102–105.   9915

Foote, Don C., "Exploration and Resource Utilization in Northwestern Arctic Alaska before 1855," Ph.D. diss., McGill University, 1965.   9916

Fedorova, Svetlana G., "Geographic Exploration," in *The Russian Population in Alaska and California: Late Eighteenth Century–1867*, Trans. Richard A. Pierce and A. S. Dennelly (Kingston, Ont.: Limestone Press, 1973), pp. 249–261.   9917

Gibson, James R., "Vitus Bering (1681–1741)," *Arctic*, vol. 35, 3 (1982), pp. 438–439.   9918

Pool, Rollo, "Earliest Inhabitants, First Explorers," *Alaska Geographic*, vol. 15, 1 (1988), pp. 58–69.   9919

POPULAR IMAGES & EVALUATION

Shortridge, James R., "American Perceptions of the Agricultural Potential of Alaska, 1867–1958," Ph.D. diss., University of Kansas, 1972.   9920

Shortridge, James R., "The Evaluation of the Agricultural Potential of Alaska, 1867–1897," *Pacific Northwest Quarterly*, vol. 68, 2 (1977), pp. 88–98.   9921

Shortridge, James R., "The Alaskan Agricultural Empire: An American Agrarian Vision, 1898–1929," *Pacific Northwest Quarterly*, vol. 69, 4 (1978), pp. 145–158.   9922

REGIONAL SETTLEMENT

See also 1324, 1338–1339

Lantis, David W., "Settlement of Alaska: Past, Present, Future," Master's thesis, University of Cincinnati, 1948.   9923

Stone, Kirk H., "Populating Alaska: The United States Phase," *Geographical Review*, vol. 42, 3 (1952), pp. 384–404.   9924

Monahan, Robert L., "The Development of Settlement in the Fairbanks Area, Alaska: A Study of Permanence," Ph.D. diss., McGill University, 1959.   9925

Gibson, James R., "Diversification on the Frontier: Russian America in the Middle of the Nineteenth Century," in James H. Bater and R. A. French, eds., *Studies in Russian Historical Geography*, vol. 1 (New York: Academic Press, 1983), pp. 197–238.   9926

Gibson, James R., "Colonial Russian America," in Mary C. Mangusson and Stephen W. Haycox, eds., *Interpreting Alaska's History: An Anthology* (Anchorage: Alaska Pacific University Press, 1989), pp. 110–121.   9927

Gibson, James R., "Tsarist Russia in Colonial America: Critical Constraints," in Alan Wood, ed., *The History of Siberia: Colonization, Settlement and Society* (London: Croom Helm, 1990), pp. 92–116.   9928

King, Robert, "Westerners Arrive," *Alaska Geographic*, vol. 17, 1 (1990), pp. 32–37. [Focus on the period after 1818]   9929

POPULATION

Barbeau, Marius, "The Aleutian Route of Migration into America," *Geographical Review*, vol. 35, 3 (1945), pp. 424–443.   9930

Bruyere, Donald E., "The Trend of Population in Southeastern Alaska," Ph.D. diss., University of Michigan, 1958. [Focus on the period from the eighteenth century to the 1950s]   9931

RURAL & REGIONAL SOCIAL GEOGRAPHY

See also 1377–1378

Stone, Kirk H., "Alaskan Group Settlement: The Matanuska Valley Colony," Ph.D. diss., University of Michigan, 1949.   9932

Gibson, James R., "Russian Dependence upon the Natives of Alaska," in S. Frederick Starr, ed., *Russia's American Colony* (Durham: Duke University Press, 1987), pp. 77–104.   9933

POLITICAL & ADMINISTRATIVE GEOGRAPHY

See also 1395

Begg, Alexander, "Review of the Alaska Boundary Question," *Scottish Geographical Magazine*, vol. 17, 2 (1901), pp. 86–96.   9934

Tompkins, Stuart R., "Drawing the Alaskan Boundary," *Canadian Historical Review*, vol. 26, 1 (1945), pp. 1–24.   9935

Gibson, James R., "Why the Russians Sold Alaska," *Wilson Quarterly*, vol. 3, 3 (1979), pp. 179–188.   9936

Gibson, James R., "The Sale of Russian America to the United States," *Acta slavica japonica*, vol. 1 (1983), pp. 15–37. Reprinted in S. Frederick Starr, ed., *Russia's American Colony* (Durham: Duke University Press, 1987), pp. 271–294.   9937

Bolkhovitinov, Nikolay N., "The Crimean War and the Emergence of Proposals for the Sale of Russian America, 1853–1861," *Pacific Historical Review*, vol. 59, 1 (1990), pp. 15–49.   9938

ECONOMIC DEVELOPMENT

See also 1402

Wolfanger, Louis A., "Economic Regions of Alaska," *Economic Geography*, vol. 2, 4 (1926), pp. 508–536.   9939

Bruyere, Donald E., "The Influence of Economic Change on the Population of Southern Alaska," *California Geographer*, vol. 3 (1962), pp. 33–39.   9940

Francis, Karl E., "Geographic Factors as Retardants to the Development of Alaska's Mineral Industries," Master's thesis, Oregon State University, 1964.   9941

Danver, Susan C., "The Historical Geography of Misty Fiords National Monument and Wilderness and Its Relationship to the Economy of Ketchikan, Alaska," Master's thesis, University of Washington, 1986.   9942

Lewis, Carol E., and Roger W. Pearson, "Three Development Models for Alaska's Agriculture Industry," *Yearbook of the Association of Pacific Coast Geographers*, vol. 52 (1990), pp. 109–124. [Focus on 1960–1988]   9943

RESOURCE MANAGEMENT

See 9916

LAND & LAND USE

Haynes, James B., "The Alaska Native Claims Settlement Act and Changing Patterns of Land Ownership in Alaska," *Professional Geographer*, vol. 28, 1 (1976), pp. 66–71.   9944

EXTRACTIVE ACTIVITY

See also 1408, 1411, 1413

Hadley, Jack, "Whaling off the Alaska Coast,"
Bulletin of the American Geographical Society,
vol. 47, 12 (1915), pp. 905–921. [Focus on 1848–
1915]   **9945**

Hawn, Barbara, "Historical Geography of Tin Mining, Seward Peninsula, Alaska," Master's thesis,
Oregon State University, 1956.   **9946**

Utermohle, George, Jr., "The Establishment of
Central Places in the Seward Peninsula and the
Interior of Alaska as a Result of the Placer Gold
Development in These Regions," Master's the-
sis, Arizona State University, 1967.   **9947**

Gibson, James R., "Sables to Sea Otters: Russia
Enters the Pacific," *Alaska Review,* vol. 3, 2
(1968–1969), pp. 203–217.   **9948**

Bundtzen, Thomas K., "A History of Mining in the
Kantishan Hills," *Alaska Geographic,* vol. 15, 3
(1988), pp. 51–61.   **9949**

AGRICULTURE

See also 1422

Seeman, Albert L., "Development of Reindeer Activities in Alaska," *Economic Geography,* vol. 9, 3
(1933), pp. 292–302. [Focus on 1883–1918]   **9950**

Francis, Karl E., "Outpost Agriculture: The Case of
Alaska," *Geographical Review,* vol. 57, 4 (1967),
pp. 496–505.   **9951**

Ehlers, Eckart, "Agrarkolonisation und Agrarlandschaft in Alaska: Probleme und Entwicklungstendenzen der Landwirtschaft in hohen
Breiten," *Geographische Zeitschrift,* vol. 61
(1973), pp. 195–219.   **9952**

Shortridge, James R., "The Collapse of Frontier
Agriculture in Alaska," *Annals of the Association of American Geographers,* vol. 66, 4 (1976),
pp. 583–604.   **9953**

COMMUNICATIONS & TRADE

See also 1436

Merriam, Willis B., "Some Recent Trends in Alaskan Commerce," *Economic Geography,* vol. 14,
4 (1938), pp. 413–418. [Focus on 1916–1938]   **9954**

Monahan, Robert L., "The Role of Transportation
in the Fairbanks Area," *Yearbook of the Association of Pacific Coast Geographers,* vol. 21
(1959), pp. 7–21. [Focus on 1885–1958]   **9955**

URBAN NETWORKS & URBANIZATION

Becker, Hans, "Kollektive Gründungen von
Goldgräber-Städten um die Wende zum 20.
Jahrhundert in Alaska," *Alte Stadt,* vol. 8 (1981),
pp. 1–12.   **9956**

Pearson, Roger W., "Distance and Dissent: Alaska's Capital Move," *Yearbook of the Association
of Pacific Coast Geographers,* vol. 48 (1986), pp.
89–105.   **9957**

TOWN GROWTH

Foscue, Edwin J., "The Development and Decline
of Skagway, Alaska," *Economic Geography,* vol.
10, 4 (1934), pp. 419–428. [Focus on 1896–1934]
                                                 9958

Bruyere, Donald E., "The Sequent Occupance of
Skagway, Alaska," *Papers of the Michigan Academy of Science, Arts, and Letters,* vol. 45 (1960),
pp. 155–168.   **9959**

Simpson, Sherry, "Juneau Matures," *Alaska Geographic,* vol. 17, 2 (1990), pp. 46–55. [Focus from
the 1940s to the 1980s]   **9960**

PLACE NAMES

See also 1473

Baker, Marcus, *Alaska Geographical Names*
(Washington, D.C.: Government Printing Office,
Twenty-First Annual Report of the United States
Geological Survey, 1899–1900), 509 pp.   **9961**

Writers' Program, *Geographical Names in the
Coastal Areas of Alaska* (Washington, D.C.:
Works Project Administration, 1943), 133 pp. **9962**

Schorr, Alan, *Alaska Place Names* (College: University of Alaska, Elmer E. Rasmuson Library,
Occasional Papers, no. 2, 1974), 32 pp.   **9963**

HAWAII

GENERAL

The state

Coan, Titus M., "The Hawaiian Islands: Their Geography, Their Volcanoes, and Their People," *Bulletin of the American Geographical Society*, vol. 21, 2 (1889), pp. 149–166. **9964**

Baldwin, Charles W., *Geography of the Hawaiian Islands* (New York: American Book Co., 1908), 128 pp. **9965**

[Note: The best modern interpretation of Hawaii's historical geography is that offered in the first four chapters of W. Kreisel, 1984 (in German); see below under "Rural & Regional Social Geography"]

Smaller areas

Holland, Jerald, "Land and Livelihood: The Kona Coast about 1825," Master's thesis, University of Hawaii, 1971. **9966**

ENVIRONMENTAL CHANGE

Coulter, John Wesley, "The Eruption of Kilauea, December 23, 1931," *Bulletin of the Geographical Society of Philadelphia*, vol. 30 (1932), pp. 195–199. **9967**

Kreisel, Werner, "Cultivated Plants as Indicators in the Reconstruction of the Progression of Settlement in Oceania: The Example of the Sweet Potato (*ipomoea batatas*)," *Tijdschrift voor economische en sociale geografie*, vol. 72, 5 (1981), pp. 266–278. **9968**

Giambelluca, Thomas W., "Water Balance of the Pearl Harbor–Honolulu Basin, 1946–1975," Ph.D. diss., University of Hawaii, 1983. **9969**

Nagata, Kenneth M., "Early Plant Introductions in Hawai'i," *Hawaiian Journal of History*, vol. 19 (1985), pp. 35–61. **9970**

Mueller-Dombois, D., "Waldsterben auf Hawaii," *Geographische Rundschau*, vol. 39, 1 (1987), pp. 39–43. [Focus on 1965–1985] **9971**

Terry, Ronald N., "The Legacy of the Hawaiian Cultivator in Windward Valleys of Hawaii," Ph.D. diss., Louisiana State University, 1988. [Focus on Kohala] **9972**

NATIVE PEOPLES & WHITE RELATIONS

Coan, Titus M., "Hawaiian Ethnography," *Bulletin of the American Geographical Society*, vol. 31, 1 (1899), pp. 24–30. **9973**

Lind, Karin, "First Hawaiians Could Have Migrated from B.C.," *Canadian Geographic*, vol. 98, 1 (1979), pp. 8–17. **9974**

EXPLORATION & MAPPING

Best, Elsdon, "Polynesian Navigators: Their Exploration and Settlement of the Pacific," *Geographical Review*, vol. 5, 3 (1918), pp. 169–182. **9975**

Taylor, Albert P., ed., *The Hawaiian Islands* (Honolulu: Captain Cook Sesquicentennial Commission and Archives of Hawaii Commission, 1930), 93 pp. **9976**

Buck, Peter H., "Cook's Discovery of the Hawaiian Islands," *Bulletin of the Bernice P. Bishop Museum* (Honolulu), no. 186 (1945), pp. 26–44. **9977**

Healy, Jack R., "The Mapping of the Hawaiian Islands from 1778 to 1848," Master's thesis, University of Hawaii, 1959. **9978**

Lewis, David, "Polynesian Navigational Methods," *Journal of the Polynesian Society*, vol. 73, 4 (1964), pp. 364–373. **9979**

Fitzpatrick, Gary L., *The Early Mapping of Hawai'i*, with contributions by Riley Moffat (Honolulu: Editions Limited, Palapala'aina, vol. 1, 1986), 160 pp. Reissued New York: Kegan Paul International, 1987. **9980**

POPULAR IMAGES & EVALUATION

Shin, Myongsup, "Hawaii: A Study of Images and Anti-Images, With a Special Focus on Its Dry Lands," Ph.D. diss., University of Minnesota, 1979. **9981**

Pi'iana'ia, I. Abraham, "Place in Hawaiian Folk Songs," *Mana: A South Pacific Journal of Language and Literature*, vol. 5, 2 (1980), pp. 43–52. **9982**

Cox, Helen Amelia, "Western Conceptual Geographies of the Hawaiian Islands, 1778–1874," Ph.D. diss., University of Utah, 1987. **9983**

REGIONAL SETTLEMENT

Chun, Paul Ming Pok, "Sequent Occupance in Waihee Valley, Oahu," Master's thesis, University of Hawaii, 1954. **9984**

Emery, Byron E., "Intensification of Settlement and Land Utilization since 1930 in Manoa Valley, Honolulu," Master's thesis, University of Hawaii, 1956. **9985**

Morgan, Joseph R., "Sequent Occupance: Two Centuries of Dualism," in his *Hawaii: A Geography* (Boulder, Colo.: Westview Press, 1983), pp. 187–195.   9986

POPULATION

See also 1354, 1357

General

Freeman, Otis W., "The Peopling of Hawaii," *Journal of Geography*, vol. 27, 4 (1928), pp. 125–141.   9987

Kolb, Albert, "Die farbige Bevölkerung der hawaiischen Inseln," *Weltwirtschaftliches Archiv: Zeitschrift des Instituts für Weltwirtschaft*, vol. 55, 1 (1942), pp. 178–214.   9988

Myerson, Jack, "Depopulation among the Native Hawaiians," Master's thesis, University of California–Los Angeles, 1953.   9989

Nordyke, Eleanor C., *The Peopling of Hawai'i* (Honolulu: University Press of Hawaii for the East-West Center, 1977), 221 pp. Revised 1989, 329 pp.   9990

Modern migrations

Kreisel, Werner, "Die Samoanische Einwanderung nach Hawaii: Ursachen und Probleme," in Rudolph Grulich et al., eds., *Volksgruppen und Minderheiten: Theodor Veiter zum 70. Geburtstag* (Kiel: LiteraturSpiegel no. 20, 1977), pp. 124–147.   9991

Wright, Paul A., "Residents Leave Paradise: A Study of Outmigration from Hawaii to the Mainland," Ph.D. diss., University of Hawaii, 1979. [Focus on 1940s–1979]   9992

RURAL & REGIONAL SOCIAL GEOGRAPHY

General

Lind, Andrew W., *An Island Community: Ecological Succession in Hawaii* (Chicago: University of Chicago Press, 1938), 337 pp. [Focus on 1850–1930]   9993

Myerson, Jack, and Joseph E. Spencer, "The Impact of Disease upon the Hawaiian Islanders: A Study in Medical Geography," *Yearbook of the Association of Pacific Coast Geographers*, vol. 13 (1951), p. 44.   9994

Ethnic groups & assimilation

Coulter, John Wesley, and B. B. M. Kim, "The Koreans in Hawaii," *Proceedings of the Hawaiian Academy of Science*, Bishop Museum Special Publication no. 21 (1933), pp. 9–10.   9995

Coulter, John Wesley, and Chee Kwon Chun, *Chinese Rice Farmers in Hawaii* (Honolulu:

University of Hawaii, Research Publication no. 16, 1937), 70 pp. [Focus on 1858–1935]   9996

Kolb, Albert, "Die germanische Bevölkerung der hawaiischen Inseln mit besonderer Berücksichtigung des Deutschtums," *Deutsches Archiv für Landes- und Volksforschung*, vol. 5 (1941), pp. 72–79.   9997

Huetz de Lemps, Christian, "Les Chinois aux Hawaii," in *Études de géographie tropicale offerts à Pierre Gourou* (Paris: Moutons, 1972), pp. 183–208. [Focus on 1853–1967]   9998

Kreisel, Werner, "Assimilation in Hawaii am Beispiel des Vordringens der englischen Sprache," *Sociologus*, n.s., vol. 30, 1 (1980), pp. 29–52. [Focus on 1846–1976]   9999

Kreisel, Werner, "Eine Minderheit auf der Suche nach ihrer Identität: Die Hawaiianer," in Frank Ahnert and Reinhart Zschocke, eds., *Festschrift für Felix Mohnheim zum 65. Geburtstag* (Aachen: Geographisches Institut der Rheinland–Westfalen Technische Hochschule Aachen, Aachener Geographische Arbeiten no. 14, pt. 2, 1981), pp. 639–661.   10000

Kreisel, Werner, *Die Ethnischen Gruppen der Hawaii-Inseln: Ihre Entwicklung und Bedeutung für Wirtschaftsstruktur und Kulturlandschaft* (Wiesbaden: Franz Steiner Verlag, Erdkundliches Wissen no. 68, 1984), 462 pp. [Focus on 1778–1980]   10001

Other themes

Kahn, Daniel, "Steel Guitar Development," *Ha'-ilono Mele* (March 1976), pp. 6–7; (April 1976), pp. 4–6; and (May 1976), pp. 1–4. [Historical and geographical development of this instrument, which had its origin in Hawaii]   10002

Heatwole, Charles A., "In Pele'realm: Reflections on Traditional Hawaiian Religion," *Focus (American Geographical Society)*, vol. 38, 3 (1988), pp. 6–11.   10003

POLITICAL & ADMINISTRATIVE GEOGRAPHY

Jones, Stephen B., "Geography and Politics in the Hawaiian Islands," *Geographical Review*, vol. 28, 2 (1938), pp. 193–213.   10004

Jones, Stephen B., and Klaus Mehnert, "Hawaii and the Pacific: A Survey of Political Geography," *Geographical Review*, vol. 30, 3 (1940), pp. 358–375.   10005

ECONOMIC DEVELOPMENT

Freeman, Otis W., *The Economic Geography of Hawaii* (Honolulu: University of Hawaii, Research Publication no. 2, 1927), 87 pp. [Focus on 1899–1919]   10006

Coulter, John Wesley, *Population and Utilization of Land and Sea in Hawaii, 1853* (Honolulu: Bernice P. Bishop Museum, Bulletin no. 88, 1931), 33 pp.   10007

LAND & LAND USE

Coulter, John Wesley, *Land Utilization in the Hawaiian Islands* (Honolulu: University of Hawaii, Research Publication no. 8, 1933), 140 pp. [Focus on 1906–1933]   10008

Bottenfield, Vernon C., "Changing Patterns of Land Utilization on Molokai," Master's thesis, University of Hawaii, 1958.   10009

Devaney, Dennis M., et al., *Kane'ohe: A History of Change, 1778–1950* (Honolulu: Bishop Museum Department of Anthropology, 1976), 271 pp. Revised: Bess Press, 1982. [Land and water use in Kaneohe Bay to 1950]   10010

Rigler, Malia A., "Land Tenure and Land Use in the Ahupua'a of Moanalua, O'ahu, during the Great Mahele, 1848–1855," Master's thesis, University of Hawaii, 1990.   10011

AGRICULTURE

Coulter, John Wesley, "Pineapple Industry in Hawaii," *Economic Geography*, vol. 10, 3 (1934), pp. 288–296. [Focus on 1883–1934]   10012

Wilson, James N., "Pineapple Industry of Hawaii," *Economic Geography*, vol. 24, 4 (1948), pp. 251–262. [Focus on 1900–1948]   10013

Newman, Thomas Stell, *Hawaiian Fishing and Farming on the Island of Hawaii in AD 1778* (Honolulu: Hawaii Division of Parks, 1970), 305 pp.   10014

Newman, Thomas Stell, "Hawaii Island Agricultural Zones in AD 1823: An Ethnohistorical Study," *Ethnohistory*, vol. 18, 4 (1971), pp. 335–351.   10015

Blume, Helmut, "Die Zuckerwirtschaft von Fiji und Hawaii: Konvergenzen und Divergenzen zweier tropischer pazifischen Inselräume," *Geographische Zeitschrift*, vol. 68, 4 (1980), pp. 284–304. [Focus on 1950–1978]   10016

Huetz de Lemps, Christian, "De la primauté des plantations à l'économie de services: L'exemple du Hawaii," in "Groupe de recherche sur la 'Viabilité des pays insulaires'," *Iles tropicales: Insularité, insularisme; Colloque* (Bordeaux-Talence: Université Bordeaux III, Centre de recherche des espaces tropicaux, iles et archipels, no. 8, 1987), pp. 361–398. [Focus on 1946–1986]   10017

LANDSCAPE

Kolb, Albert, "Bild und Werden der Wirtschaftslandschaft auf den Hawaiischen Inseln," *Wissenschaftliche Veröffentlichen des Deutsches Museums für Länderkunde*, n.s., vol. 5 (1938), pp. 141–160. [Focus on 1778–1936]   10018

Newman, Thomas Sell, "Two Early Hawaiian Field Systems on Hawaii Island," *Journal of the Polynesian Society*, vol. 81 (1972), pp. 87–89.   10019

COMMUNICATIONS & TRADE

Uttley, Marguerite Elizabeth, "The Geographic Basis of Hawaiian Commerce," Master's thesis, University of Chicago, 1921. [Focus on 1778–1920]   10020

Sturgell, Charles W., "The Geographic Development of the Port of Honolulu," Master's thesis, University of Hawaii, 1983.   10021

URBAN NETWORKS & URBANIZATION

Chow, Willard T., "Urbanization: Six Propositions," in Joseph R. Morgan, ed. *Hawaii: A Geography* (Boulder, Colo.: Westview Press, 1983), pp. 167–185.   10022

TOWN GROWTH

General

Kornhauser, David H., "Urban Problems of the Pacific Basin: Some Examples from Hawaii," *Science Reports of Tohoku University*, 7th ser. (Geography), vol. 22 (1972), pp. 231–249. [Focus on 1920–1970]   10023

Honolulu

Kreisel, Werner, "Stadtentwicklung in Hawaii am Beispiel Honolulus," in Werner Kreisel, W. D. Sick, and J. Stadelbauer, eds., *Siedlungsgeographische Studien: Festschrift für Gabrielle Schwartz* (Berlin: Walter de Gruyter, 1979), pp. 309–340.   10024

Kim, K. E., and K. Lowry, "Honolulu," *Cities*, vol. 7, 4 (1990), pp. 274–282.   10025

Beechert, Edward D., *Honolulu: Crossroads of the Pacific* (Columbia: University of South Carolina Press, 1991), 210 pp. [Includes many maps and landscape photographs]   10026

URBAN ECONOMIC STRUCTURE

Greer, Richard A., *Downtown Profile: Honolulu, A Century Ago* (Honolulu: Kamehameha Schools Press, 1966), 67 pp.   10027

URBAN SOCIAL STRUCTURE

Kreisel, Werner, "Honolulus Chinatown: Ein Stadtteil im Wandel," *Erdkunde*, vol. 31, 2 (1977), pp. 102–120. [Focus on 1810–1970]   **10028**

TOWNSCAPE

Peterson, Charles E., "Pioneer Prefabs in Honolulu," *Hawaiian Journal of History*, vol. 5 (1971), pp. 24–38.   **10029**

Wilcox, Gaylord, "Business and Buildings: Downtown Honolulu's Old Fashioned Block," *Hawaiian Journal of History*, vol. 6 (1972), pp. 3–27.
10030

RECREATION & TOURISM

Coller, Richard W., "Waikiki: A Study of Invasion and Succession as Applied to a Tourist Area," Master's thesis, University of Hawaii, 1952. **10031**

Huetz de Lemps, Christian, "Le tourisme dans l'Archipel des Hawaii," *Cahiers d'outre-mer*, vol. 17, 1 (1964), pp. 9–57. [Focus on 1929–1962] **10032**

Farrell, Bryan H., "The Tourist Ghettos of Hawaii," in M. C. R. Edgell and B. H. Farrell, eds., *Themes on Pacific Islands* (Victoria: University of Victoria Department of Geography, Western Geographical Series, vol. 10, 1974), pp. 181–221. [Focus on 1950s–1975]   **10033**

Chow, Willard T., "Tourism and Regional Planning: The Legend of Hawaii," *Proceedings of the Fifth Pacific Regional Science Conference, Vancouver 1977* (Bellingham: Western Washington University, 1978), pp. 349–368.   **10034**

Kreisel, Werner, "Fremdenverkehr in Hawaii: Entwicklung und Perspektiven," *Erdkunde*, vol.

34, 4 (1980), pp. 299–309. [Focus on 1940–1978]
10035

PLANNING

See also **10034**

Inagaki, John Y., "Economic Planning and Development in Hawaii, 1937–1957," Master's thesis, University of Hawaii, 1957.   **10036**

Mauk, John C., "Hawaii's State Land Use Regulations and Urban Development Patterns of Oahu," Master's thesis, California State University–Long Beach, 1979.   **10037**

PLACE NAMES

Coulter, John Wesley, "Hawaiian Toponymy," in his *Gazetteer of the Territory of Hawaii* (Honolulu: University of Hawaii, 1935), pp. 231–237.
10038

Pukui, Mary Kawena, and Samuel H. Elbert, *Place Names of Hawai'i* (Honolulu: University Press of Hawaii, 1966), 53 pp. Revised 1974, 289 pp.
10039

Elbert, Samuel, "Hawaii Place Names," *Working Papers in Linguistics*, vol. 3 (1971), pp. 1–87.
10040

Elbert, Samuel, "Connotative Values of Hawaiian Place Names," in *Directions in Pacific Traditional Literature: Essays in Honor of Katherine Luomala* (Honolulu: Bishop Museum, Special Publication no. 62, 1976), pp. 117–133.   **10041**

Comer, Wayne, "Wai'anea Town Origins," *Imua*, vol. 2, 1 (1980), pp. 34–37.   **10042**

Budnick, Rich., comp., *Hawaiian Street Names* (Honolulu: Aloha Publishing, 1989), 170 pp. **10043**

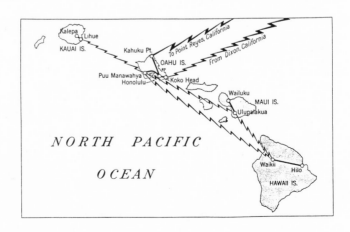

Alepa · Lihue · KAUAI IS. · Kahuku Pt. · To Point Reyes, California · From Dixon, California · OAHU IS. · Puu Manawahya · Honolulu · Koko Head · Wailuku · MAUI IS. · Ulupalakua

NORTH PACIFIC

OCEAN

Waikii · Hilo · HAWAII IS.

PART VI

INDEXES

Author Index

Numbers refer to individual citation entries in the Bibliography.

Author as subject

Author Index

Subject Index

Amerindians. *See* Indians
Amish: agriculture, 5582; Beachey Amish, 7373; landscapes, 4456, 7251; and Mennonites, 4194–4202, 7251; quilts, 4202; role of migration, 4199; settlements, 1322, 8834; viability, 4198. *See also* Amish, Old Order
Amish, Old Order: communities, 4194, 5564–5565, 5722, 7374; distribution, 4200; economic patterns, 4827; population, 4197; settlement organization, 7373
Anaheim, Calif., 9641–9642
Anasazi redoubts, 8990
Anastasia Island, Fla., 6348
Ancient cities, 8886
Ancient inhabitants, 8885
Anderson family, homesteaders, 8633
Andover, Mass., 5107; 5126
Andreas, Alfred T., atlas maker, 7037
Andrews Bailiwick, Mich., 7785
Angeles National Forest, Calif., 9671
Anglo migration, to Hispanic towns, 9869
Anglo-America, colonial origins of, 1138. *See also* North America
Anglo-Irish houses, 6896
Anglo-Saxons, 6526
Animal drives, 4412
Animals: domesticated, 3929; domestication, 3780; and exploration, 8334; French era, 6680; themes in American history, 3906
Anishinabeg Indians, 8164
Ann Arbor, Mich., 7891–7892
Annapolis Valley, N.S., 2017
Annapolis, Md., 5764
Annexation, and suburbanization, 3440, 3444, 7642
Anson Co., N.C., 6173
Antelope, human influence on, 9268
Anthracite coal: and iron and canals, 5479; region, 5577; towns, 5553
Anthropogenic disturbances, of forests, 9116
Anthropogeography, 133, 140, 445, 455, 629, 6526
Anthropogeomorphology, coastal, 9502, 9504, 9912
Anticosti, Quebec, 2442
Antietam, battle of, 6151
Antioch, Nebr., 8717
Antislavery protest (1688), 5559
Apache Indians: adoption of cattle, 9063; environment and ecology, 9071–9072; Mescalero Apache Reservation, N.Mex., 8995–8996; settlements, 8995–8996

Apalachicola River, Fla., 6335
Apartment districts, 3445
Apartment housing, 8266
APPALACHIA, 5803–5825, 6182, 6532–6534, 6536, 6539, 7238; routes through, 4890–4892; Southern, 6033; Texan, 6878
Appalachian barrier, influence on colonial history, 5803
Appalachian coal-mining region, employment trends, 5580
Appalachian frontiers, 5805–5807, 5809–5810
Appalachian Piedmont, 6009
Appalachian Trail, 5825
Applied historical geography, 45, 6356; forensic studies, 5868
Appomattox Basin, Va., 6081
Aquidneck, R.I., 5221
Arch, painted (barn decoration), 7128
Archeological sites, 6339
Archeology, 2219, 2487–2488, 2761, 3029; of early domestic architecture, 7593; resources, 5138
Archipelago, metaphor of Canada as, 1509
Architectural styles: Art Deco, 7332; Georgian, 5992, 6619; high style, 3652; Greek revival, 6304; ornamentation, 2602, 3189, 7128; Streamlined, 7332. *See also* House types
Architecture: antebellum domestic, 6490; bluenose, 2030; change in small towns, 6670; and the city, 4734–4735; courthouses, 6327; eighteenth-century domestic, 5139; and ideology, 2185; industrial, 1725; late medieval, 5591; mail-order, 4473; pre-1800, 5257; preservation, 1451, 1729, 3655; regional, 2088, 4886, 6108; regionalism in, 4465; role of secret societies in, 8447; surveys, 6777
Architecture, ethnic, 3187; Anglo-Irish, 6896; Chinese, 3668; Creole, 6780–6781; Doukhobor, 3590; Finnish, 7124; French, 6616, 6782; German, 7590; German-Russian, 8614, 8786; Hispanic, 9032; immigrant influence, 7121; Métis, 3185; Mexican American, 8426; Mennonite, 3274; Mormon, 8431, 8433; Navajo, 8899–8900, 8907, 8911; Pueblo, 9026; Spanish, 6782, 9028; Ukrainian, 3186, 3188–3190, 3274, 3415–3416
Architecture, folk. *See* Architecture, ethnic; Architecture, vernacular; Barns; Folk housing; House types
Architecture, rural. *See* Architecture, ethnic;

Architecture, vernacular; Barns; House types
Architecture, urban, 2039, 3013, 4734–4735, 5203, 6200, 7724, 8139. *See also* Building types; House types
Architecture, vernacular, 64, 225, 1424, 1426–1427, 1666, 1883–1885, 1959–1961, 2030, 2171, 2602, 2604, 2607, 3185–3190, 3274, 3415–3418, 3590, 3593–3595, 3654, 3659–3660, 4468–4469, 4471–4472, 4475, 4479, 5139–5140, 5589–5590, 5994, 5996, 6190, 6303, 6419, 6487, 6490, 6615, 6666, 7126, 7586–7587, 7851, 8433, 8585–8588, 8613, 8847, 8849–8850, 9029–9030. *See also* Architecture, ethnic; Barns; Folk housing; House types
Archives, railroad, 4528–4529
Arctic explorers: general, 3734, 3739; Sir John E. Franklin, 3732; German, 3742; maps of, 3740, 3743–3744; Sir William E. Parry, 3728; Émile Petiotot, 3741; Sir James Clark Ross, 3727
Areal growth, urban, 8725
Areal political structure, 5120; influence on urban patterns, 4284
Arid lands: bibliography, 8767; opposition to irrigation in, 9257; patenting patterns in frontier, 9694; Powell's view of settlement of, 9570; scientific studies, 8873
Aridity, regional, 8809
Aristocracy, labor, 6501 6502
ARIZONA, 9045–9110
ARKANSAS, 6647–6672
Arkansas River, Colo., 9115
Arkansas Valley, 8558
Armadillo, 6881
Army: air power, 9333; cantonments, 4294; posts and American culture, 4295; role in Western imagery, 8755
Aroostook Co., Maine, 5020
Arrested development. *See* Retardation
Arroyos: cutting, 8876; and environmental change, 8884
Art: festivals, 9440; and identity, 1562–1563, 3111, 3114, 3116; painting, 2105; and settlement, 3232; women's, 8919
Artificial landscapes, spread, 9760
Artisan unions, 1453
Artists, 5099; Baron Frederick von Egloffstein, 8367; Frederic Remington, 8365
Arvin, Calif., 9695
Asbestos industry, 2303, 2405
Ashland, Ky., 6549
Asian migration, 1597
Assessment rolls, as sources for

Number ranges indicate: Canada, 1479–3860

church, 4230, 4233
Christian Science: distribution, 4231; origin and spread, 4228,
Christmas observance, 4242
Chromotoponyms, 4801
Chumash Indians, 9539
Church of England, land policy, 3570
Church of Jesus Christ of Latter-Day Saints. *See* Mormon church
Churches: architecture, 4460; buildings, 6779; church colleges, 4251; and cultural geography, 2736; distribution of rural, 9296; evolving patterns, 5661; and journey to worship, 9639; local distribution, 6527; reuse of rural, 1381; urban, 6805; loss of, 8294
Churchill, Man., 3286, 3767
Cigar tobacco production, 7081: decline in, 4966
Cincinnati, Ohio, 7189, 7284–7286, 7301–7303, 7314–7315
Cinema audiences, 4743
Cinq-Mars, Marc Antoine Sicre de, maps by, 1909
Circleville, Ohio, 7328
Circuit riders, 2911
Circulation, regional, 7053, 7055
Cities. *See* entries under **Town Growth; Townscape; Urban Economic Structure; Urban Social Structure; Urban Networks and Urbanization** and entries under individual cities in regional, provincial, and state sections of the bibliography. Special aspects: American, 4650; Americanization, 4717; ancient, 8886; capital, 4644–4645; commercial structure, 4658; comparative study of small, 5165; and culture areas, 1442; as cultural centers, 4673; development as commercial centers, 5168; differential growth of cotton textile, 4989; and disasters, 4716; as economic control points, 4627; economic development, 5738; ethnic composition, 5188; external relations, 4618; functional specialization, 4639; gateway, 4617; general growth, 4597–4599, 4601, 4607; general perspectives, 4677; growth of functional areas, 5178; growth through industrialization, 4563; historical, 4649; historical perspectives, 4602; imagery, 8170; industrial retardation, 6022; industrialization, 4618–4620, 5180; industry in, 6023; locational conflict, 5192; manufacturing in small, 8119; modernity of Victorian, 1449; panoramic maps,

1291, 1293; pre-Columbian, 8947; public sector, 7674, 7680; regional location, 7395, 7397; social geography, 4678–4679; and social reform, 4682; social structure and morphology, 4674, 4679; and social surveys, 4682; spatial transformation, 5679; special function, 4643–4648; specialized industrial, 4640; walled, 4720
Citizenship: and gender in nation building, 4287; and immigrants, 4703
City-building process, 2398, 5741; and the cityscape, 9884
City form, reflected in single-family houses, 9879
City-hinterland relations, 5379, 5624, 7626–7629
City planning: colonial, 4844; history, 4721; Mormon, 8445, 9237; policy, 7742. *See also* Town planning
City plans, 7741
City services, 7680
City surveying, 5768, 5780
Cityscapes. *See* Urban morphology; *also* entries under **Townscape** in regional, provincial, and state sections of the bibliography
Civil War: battle of Antietam, 6151; battlefields, 6096, 6151; compensation claims, 6739; economic impact, 4329; enlistments, 6183; historical atlases of, 949–955; map use, 4296–4297; maps and mapping, 4016–4019, 4045, 5919–5923; military strategy, 6094–6096; military supply, 6097; Shenandoah Valley, 6093–6094; strategic railroads, 6791–6794; strategy, 5922
Civilian Conservation Corps, 9671
Claremont, Calif., 9833
Clarion Co., Pa., 5686
Clark, George Rogers, atlas of campaign, 1029
Clark, William, mapping, 6569
Clarke Co., Ga., 6289, 6317
Clarksville, Tenn., 6495
Class relations: boundaries in preindustrial regions, 5819; in the countryside, 2007, 2026, 4238; and ethnicity, 3290, 3296–3297; and ethnicity and property, 2372; and homeownership, 1511, 2368–2369, 2371, 2373, 4239; and housing, 2370, 2737, 2819, 3006, 3012, 3637, 3650, 3661, 3665; Jewish ethnicity and, 2836; in mining towns, 1781; and occupation and residence, 2375, 2384; and regional development, 6529–6530; relation to land and

labor, 7098; and residence, 1715, 2037, 2076, 2387, 2392, 2394; and residential mobility, 2383; urban spatial segregation, 2739; and urban architecture, 7424; and urban development, 3003, 3637; middle-class women, 5658. *See also* Elites; Middle class; Working class
Classical place names, 4792
Claus Groth Guild, 8307
Clay industry, 7280, 8241; manufacture, 7143
Clay, Henry, and regional description, 6518
Clear Lake Basin, Calif., 9584, 9603, 9779
Cleared farmland, 7099
Clemens, Samuel, writer, 4092
Clergy, 2127, 2131
Clermont Township, N.Y., 5285
Cleveland, Ohio, 7287–7292, 7316–7319
Cleveland Co., Okla., 8838
Cliff dwellers, 8887–8888, 9119–9120
Clifford Sifton, role in immigration, 1633
Climate: and agricultural settlement, 9435; in the colonial period, 3925; and corn yields, 7383; and floods, 7026, 7453; freezing and breakup, 3080, 3782, 3786–3787; and human comfort, 9569; and human occupance, 8955; impact of urbanization on urban, 9053; and Indians, 2103; influence in American history, 3915–3917; influence on American settlement, 3917; misconceptions, 8509; and overgrazing, 9050; perceptions of, 8166, 8519, 9569; and politics, 3106–3107; reconstruction, 3219, 6098; as resource, 9001; seaboard, 4808–4809; and settlement, 1485, 1501, 2084, 2664, 3106–3107, 3110, 3124, 3313, 3456, 3463; settlement and dry summer, 4107; temperature records, 1744, 2101, 9182; and wheat culture, 9356
Climatic change, 1165, 1745, 3788, 3924, 8465; effect on cropping structure, 8742; hydrological and geomorphological implications, 7028; and precontact agriculture, 8881; twentieth-century, 1162; views on forests and, 3922. *See also* Climatic variations
Climatic comparisons, 4809
Climatic environments, 8470
Climatic stress, and agriculture, 5006
Climatic variations, 3917, 3919, 3923, 8874; agricultural impact, 4917; and flooding, 7020–7021; human impacts, 8467; precontact,

8880–8881; regional impacts, 7454; regional patterns, 9507; social impact, 4916
Climatotherapy, 9636
Clinton, Mass., 5151
Clinton Co., Iowa, 8305
Clinton Co., Ill., 7501
Clinton Co., Mich., 7805
Clinton Co., N.Y., 5304
Clipper ships, effect on American shipping, 4525
Clothing industry, 1820, 1825–1826, 2636, 2813, 2836, 5746
Cloud Co., Kans., 8773, 8787
Clubs: and bars, 6738; farmers', 8764
Coachella Valley, Calif., 9721, 9724
Coal: influence on manufacturing location, 2625; iron and canals and anthracite, 5479; transport of, 2621
Coal Branch, Alta., 3349
Coal industry: employment, 7541; production, 5576, 5579, 6152, 6957; long-term bituminous production, 4833
Coal mines, relation to rail lines, 7542
Coal mining, 2021–2023, 3341, 3349, 3407–3408, 3650, 7241, 8293, 8775–8776, 9370–9371; bituminous, 7553, 7556; as geomorphological agent, 3932; environmental impact, 9112; regions of, industrial evolution of, 5823; and pioneer settlement, 8776; growth of strip, 7382; regional resources, 6606; role in land-use and settlement changes, 7379, 7351
Coal towns, 5676
Coalfields, 5576–5580; Cherokee-Crawford, Kans., 8759, 8775; labor and development of, 5820; Pocahontas, W.Va., 6148
Coalgate, Okla., 8827, 8857–8858
Coalitions, business, 7306
Coast Ranges, Calif., 9890
Coastal change, 6167
Coastal charts, 5101, 6400; atlases of, 948
Coastal development, and cultural remains, 6684
Coastal features, influence on human occupance, 5002
Coastal mapping, 6174
Coastal marshlands, 6683, 6743
Coastal navigation, effect of soil erosion on, 5705
Coastal wilderness, 4977
Cobblestone architecture and buildings, 4841, 5358, 8092
Cobourg, Ont., 2722
Cochise Co., Ariz., 9054, 9088
Cod fishery, colonial, 4963
Cognition: and communication, 8530; factors, 8667. See also

Evaluations; Geosophy, historical; Images; Perceptions
Cohasset Ridge, Calif., 9493
Colchester, Ill., 7657
Cold summers, 3920
Cold waves, 7951
Coles Co., Ill., 7513
Collective biography, 7510
College towns, 7625
Colleges: African American, 4250; basketball, 7427; campus sites, 7625; Congregational, 4252; Presbyterian, 4252; residential patterns of faculties, 7417; scientific contributions, 7365; student migration, 4952
Colonial era (Can.), 1138; British policies, 2546, 2553; cities, 2350; construction trends, 2599, 2601; environmental attitudes, 1300; land appraisal, 2882, 3570; settlements, 1863, 2897; merchant communities, 1966; unrest, 2543; vegetation, 2877
Colonial era (U.S.): 1138, 3887–3888, 3890, 4914, 5280, 6158, 6376; agriculture, 5838, 6189, 6231, 8941; archeology, 53; archives, 194; atlases and maps, 927–929, 987, 1109, 5101, 5465, 5862, 6063, 6172, 6207, 6265; climate, 3925, 5843; demography, 4947–4949, 4951, 6218; farms, 8941; fishing, 4963; health, 6236; households, 4182; house types, 4474, 4883–4884; Indian boundaries, 6285; Indians, 5707; iron and agricultural plantation types, 5472; land and land surveys, 5727, 5932, 6222, 6357; mountain barriers, 5803; New Belgium, 4858; organization, 8923; perceptions, 6209, 6211–6212; place names, 4793, 5453, 6672; population, 4121, 6217; ports, 5461, 5495, 5500–5501, 5505; regional development, 4312, 8923; regional settlement, 4818, 5249, 6263, 6677; roads, 6621; rural settlement, 4115, 4932, 4937, 4969, 5039, 5069, 5107, 5127, 9003; Russian America, 9927–9928; towns, 4613, 4844, 5099, 5270, 6126, 6390
Colonial revival architecture, 4474
Colonies: ethnic, 6181; Franconian, 7808
Colonists, Indians and ecology, 4920
Colonization, 5309: agents, 1346; farm experiments, 5880; German ethnic, 9641–9642; German-Russian ethnic, 8757; mental images in, 1299; regional land, 8002; roads, 2326, 2515; Spanish, 9005–9006; and vegetation

changes, 8156; of wheatlands, 1336
Color in place names, 4801
COLORADO, 9111–9172
Colorado Basin, 9085
Colorado Delta, 8961
Colorado Piedmont, 9133–9134
Colorado Plateau, 8954
Colorado River water, exportation, 9724
Colorado River, 8345, 9066
Colorado Springs, Colo., 9141
Columbia, S.C., 6241, 6245
Columbia Basin, 1434, 9358
Columbia Basin Project, 9327, 9336–9337
Columbia Plain, 9341, 9351, 9356
Columbia River, Oreg.-Wash., 9331
Columbian encounter, and maps, 1247
Columbian Exposition (1893), World's, 7691
Columbiana Co., Ohio, 7259
Columbus, Christopher, 1214, 1228, 1243, 1246; geographical conceptions, 1222; landfall in New World, 1223; voyages, 1235, 1246
Columbus, Ohio, 4698, 7230, 7304–7306, 7320–7323
Comberford map, 6170
Comer, George, 3724; diary of, 3763
Comfort, climate and human, 9569
Command structure, regional military, 8554
Commerce. See entries under Communications and trade in regional, provincial, and state sections of the bibliography. Special aspects: buffalo bone, 8488; decline in riverine, 6994; development of lake, 7132; geographic influences in early American, 4554; history of American, 4555
Commercial agriculture, response to urban fringe expansion, 5731
Commercial buildings, 10030
Commercial cities: development, 4615; industrial evolution, 7304–7305
Commercial cores, urban. See Central business districts
Commercial development: suburban-style near suburban downtowns, 9843; urban, 8719
Commercial fisheries, 6750, 7101, 7242, 8222–8223
Commercial mapmaking, 4020–4032
Commercial sector, African American-owned, 6245
Commercial sex, 5426
Commercial strips, 7716, 9103, 9466; history, 4739
Commercial structure: and ethnic residential patterns, 8131; urban,

Number ranges indicate: Canada, 1479–3860

5622, 5742, 5858, 5926, 6017, 6043, 6046, 6059, 6084, 6105, 6110–6111, 6114–6116, 6118–6119, 6157–6158, 6219, 6301, 6306, 6331, 6403, 6639, 6973, 8435, 8520, 9543, 9557
Eiricksson, Leifr, explorer, 1238
El Cajon Valley, Calif., 9491
El Cerrito, N.Mex., 9012
El Paso, Tex., 6928
El Paso del Norte, N.Mex.-Tex., 8870
El Puerto de la Bodega, Calif., 9902
El Rancho, N.Mex., 9007
El Segundo, Calif., 9818
Elderly, 1608, 1711, 2122, 3625; migration patterns, 6589; regional patterns, 4175, 6352; spatial patterns of urban, 7318; urban pattern and mobility, 5666
Elections: atlas of, 1065; bias, 2552; and voting, 4291–4293
Electoral data, use in population estimates, 9625
Electoral geography, 5017; effect of African American migration on, 7312, 7911; local level, 7815; state level, 9443; urban, 9855–9856
Electric interurban railways, 9454; era, 9377, 9379–9380; local patterns, 9783; systems, 4530
Electric power industry, 3423, 3559, 3562; dammed lakes as sources, 4341; evolution of capacity 1640; hydroelectric, 5061; power plants, siting, 4345, 9675; power projects, 8558; urban, 2404
Electronics industry, 7669
Elevated railroads, and urban development, 7636
Elevators, grain, 3184, 3278–3279
Elgine, Ariz., 9091
Elites: and early automobile, 5372; automobile touring, 4750; in college towns, 7717; eminent people, regional yields, 7366; landed gentry, 4239; landscapes shaped by, 4458, 4461, 5355–5357; neighborhoods, 3635, 3666; rancheros, 9693; wealthy planters, 6086
Elizabethtown Township, Ont., 2701
Elkhart Co., Ind., 7375
Elko Co., Nev., 9256
Ellicott, Joseph, land developer, 5305
Ellis Co., Kans., 8756
Emancipation, 4186. See also Underground railroad
Embargoes, trade, 4871
Emigrant road, 8436
Emigrants: British, 4139; Indians, objections to residence in Kansas, 8744
Emigration: Dutch, 4147; German to

the U.S., 4130, 4132; Scots and assisted, 2517; Welsh, 4140
Employment fields, 5169
Employment: in coal industry, 7541; immigrant patterns, 5697, 5699; and migration, 5179, 5250; in regional manufacturing, 6453; regional trends in primary activities, 5580; stability in company towns, 5766; urban service, 8118
Encomienda, 9013
Endogamy, Polish Americans, 5429
Energy: early development, 5121; and industrial location, 2628, 2631; production, 9675–9676; sources, 4341–4345; dammed lakes as sources, 4341
Engineered tomatoes, diffusion of, 9735
English: distribution, 2533; family role in settlement, 8292; frontier settlers, 9597; imprint on American landscapes, 4452, 4454; migration, 1925–1926, 1928–1929, 1934, 1943, 1980; migration from Canada to U.S., 4144; perceptions of the West, 8361; prairie settlement patterns, 7498; propinquity of settlement, 2532; settlement, 3551; urban settlement, 5401
Engravers, 5099
Engravings, of cities, 6570
Enlistments, geography of military, 6183
Entertainment industry. See Motion picture industry
Entrepreneurship, and urban growth, 2801, 7419, 7423
Environment: adjustment to, 8737, 8770; attitudes toward, 1301–1302, 9425; and culture, 8538; and disease, 6089; and ecology, 9072; and health, 4098, 8769; images of early physical, 6208; and humans, 4907, 9049; and land use, 3400, 9367; population changes and physical 5104; pre-Columbian physical, 8875; and regional settlement, 9359; responses to, 5089; and settlement, 3237, 6829; and social change, 9367; and society, 2515
Environmental amenities, in nonmetropolitan development, 4319
Environmental change. See entries under this title in regional, provincial, and state sections of the bibliography
Environmental determinism, 220, 536–538, 1132. See also Geographic influences

Environmental hazards: natural disasters, 8623; earthquakes, 9532, 9885, 9887; fire, 3082, 5181, 5840, 7727, 9117, 9345, 9416, 9511–9512, 9517, 9677, 9885, 9887; floods, 5245, 6568, 7020–7021, 7453, 7961, 9528; hazardous wastes, 7457, 7461–7462; industrial waste, 3935; precontact hazardous waste, 7459; urban, 4716, 9868, 9885; volcanoes, 1163, 4915, 9048, 9307, 9910, 9964
Environmental influences: concept of, 496, 506, 518, 629, 662; studies of, 1483–1485, 1500, 1685, 1742, 1748, 1839, 2109, 2197, 2240, 2321–2322, 2749, 2808, 3213, 3468, 3479, 5088–5089. See also Geographic influences
Environmental legislation, colonial, 6101
Environmental perceptions, 1301–1302, 5247, 8665–8666, 9425; methodology, 507; of Mormon pioneers, 9188–9189; regional, 6572; wet prairies, 7480
Environmental science, and exploration, 9550
Environmental understanding, evolution of, 9356
Environmentalism. See Environmental influences; Geographic influences; see also under **Resource Management**, in regional, provincial, and state sections of the bibliography
Environments, built. See Urban morphology
Ephemeral industry, 9370
Episcopal church, and neighborhood change, 5665
Erie, Pa., 5531
Erie Canal, 5336, 5364; capacity and use, 1431; compared with Welland Canal, 1433
Erie Triangle, Pa., 2869, 5520
Erosion. See Soil erosion
Escondido, Calif., 9484
Eskimos. See Inuit
Espanola Valley, N.Mex., 9002
Essex Co., Ont., 2874, 2877, 2913, 2928–2932, 2934, 2941–2942
Essex Co., Mass., 5115, 5135
Estancia Valley, N.Mex., 9023
Estates, agricultural, 652; private, 5115
Estevan, Sask., 3341
Ethnic and racial minorities, bibliography, 19
Ethnic assimilation, 7802; 8035; rural Christian congregations, 5550; among German-Jewish peddlers, 6953
Ethnic communities: agricultural

photographer, 9887
Harbors: building of, 5442; changing functions, 5031
Harney Co., Oreg., 9427
Harrisburg, Pa., 5647
Harrison, William Henry, military campaign, 7378
Harrisse, Henry, cartographer, 4030
Hartford, Conn., 5273
Hartford, Conn., region, 5246
Harvard students, and landscape recreation, 4995
Harvests, time series, 7384, 9727
Hastings, Nebr., 8724
Hastings Co., Ont., 2694
Hatteras Indians, 6168
Hattiesburg, Miss., 6460
HAWAII, 9964–10043
Hawaii (Island), Hawaii, 10014–10015
Hawaiians: migrations, 1357, 3540; minority identity of, 10000; origins in British Columbia, 9974; traditional religion, 10003
Hawkesbury Townships, East & West, Ont., 2675
Hay and dairying region, 4834
Hay and pasture regions, 9340
Hay River, N.W.T., 3848, 3854, 3858
Hay stackers, beaverslide, 9287
Haydenville, Ohio, 7300
Hayes Co., Nebr., 8677
Hayes Farm, Old, N.H., 5042
Hazard, Ebenezer, author, 6210
Hazardous wastes, 7457, 7461; disposal sites, 7462; management of, 3933, 7463; precontact, 7459
Hazards. See Environmental hazards
Headright grants, 6291
Health: and environment, 8769; migration, 4153; resorts, 7426, 7731–7735, 9890; threat from irrigation, 9568; and urban growth, 6236
Heartland, 7011; immigrants in manufacturing, 4826; urban-industrial, cities in, 4679
Heartland-hinterland concept. See Core-Periphery concept
Heat waves, 7949
Hedgerows
Hedges, 67, 7131; Osage orange, 4499
Heineman, Wis., 8113
Helen Furnace, Pa., 5686
Hell's Canyon, Idaho-Oreg., 9328
Henderson Co., N.C., 6202
Hennepin, Louis, explorer, 3973
Hennepin Canal, Ill., 7600
Henry Co., Ill., 7524
Herb growing, 9753
Herding, Celtic origins of Southern, 5979

Herman, Mo., 6574, 6597
Hershey Estates, influence on urban morphology, 5680
Hershey, Pa., 5680
Hicks, 8550
Hierarchies, corporate and urban, 4327
High Plains (Mich.), 7748, 7864; perceptions, 7772
High Point, N.C., 6196
High-status urban residential areas, 7314
High-technology industry, 5158; regions of, 5736; urban, 5652
Highland aesthetics, lower Hudson Valley, 4904
Highland, Ill., 7522–7523
Highway maps, 4046–4048, 7984
Highway networks, 6191; development and urban growth, 5602; evolution, 5367; paved roads in, 6309
Highways: and automobiles, 4500–4508; expenditures on, 2008; Indian antecedents, 7391
Hiking trails, 5825
Hill towns, 4931, 4939, 5095
Hill, La., 6707
Hillsborough River Basin, Fla., 6337
Hillsdale, Mich., 7875
Hillside letters, 8427
Hind, Henry Youle, 3099
Hinterland piracy, effect of port competition on, 5495
Hinterlands, urban, 5379, 6021, 6234, 6627, 7153
Hispanic areas, foreigners' impressions, 9656
Hispanic barrios, 9865
Hispanic landscapes, 9770
Hispanic settlement frontier, 9615
Hispanic towns, Anglo migration to, 9869
Hispanics: 8317–8318; distribution, 4172, 6857, 6859; literary landscape images, 9563; population, 9631
Hispano gristmills, 9031
Hispano homeland, 8928; expansion of, 8925
Historic districts, and urban design, 4767
Historic landscapes, 4427–4438, 4769; management of, 7428
Historic places, perception of, 4095
Historic preservation, 48; as cultural environmentalism, 4771; iron furnaces, 5686; in North American cities, 1451; settlement history in, 6714; and Southern regionalism, 6248; and the Supreme Court, 4306; urban, 5235
Historic preservation: inner city,

7187; urban neighborhoods, 7739, 8255
Historic urban cores, 9806
Historical archeology, bibliography, 53
Historical atlases. See Atlases
Historical geography: applied, 212, 219, 233, 236, 1729, 1889, 1891, 2393, 2649, 2656, 2743, 2766–2767, 2792, 2854–2855, 2962, 3212, 3454, 3526, 3655; archival work in, 210; and early American history, 181, 194; in Canada, 76–79, 82; ethics in, 233; field research, 159, 656, 663, 699; forensic, 5868; history of, 73, 76, 117, 196, 235; map use in, 86, 92, 114; methodology, 68, 72, 74, 83–85, 88–90, 95–101, 103–104, 106–107, 109–110, 115–116, 155, 158, 161–163, 169, 171, 179–180, 182–183, 185, 189–191, 196–198, 200, 204, 206, 209, 213, 215–216, 221, 230, 232, 234, 238, 241–243, 245, 546, 740; in North America, 68–71, 73, 117; organizations for, 224; perception in, 91; relation to social studies, 167, 1850; of the United States, 195, 3877, 3879, 3881, 3884, 3886; atlas, 3876; urban past, 92–93
Historical geosophy. See Geosophy, historical; also Cognition; Evaluations; Images; Perceptions
Historical landmarks, role in land use, 5123
Historical resources, regional, 5209
Historical villages, 1891
History: geographic factors in, 136; marketing of, 5514
Hocking Canal, Ohio, 7269
Hocking mining district, Ohio, 7333
Hocking Valley, Ohio, 7269, 7282, 7333
Hoecake, 5950–5951
Hog meat, 5905, 5950–5951
Hogan, Navajo, 8911
Hohokam people, 3937; settlements, 8874
Holden, Mass., 5106, 5130
Holland Purchase, N.Y., 5307, 5339
Hollister, Calif., 9854
Hollow Landing, Ont., 2800
Hollywood, Calif., 9792
Holyoke, Mass., 5111, 5179
Home manufactures, 5816, 6539
Home mortgage financing, immigrant, 5759
Homelands, Hispano, 8928; Spanish American, 8978–8979
Homeownership, 2819–2821; boom in, 2818; in cities, 1716; and class, 1511, 2368, –2369, 2371, 2373; diffusion, 1459; ethnic, 6181; working class, 1717, 4700

Number ranges indicate: Canada, 1479–3860

Number ranges indicate: Canada, 1479–3860

Military surveys, British North America, 1260
Military tracts (land compensation for veterans): New York, 5309; Illinois, 7511, 7529; Virginia (in Ohio), 7229
Milk cows, disadoption, 7563–7564
Milksheds, urban, 9230
Mill dams, effect on lower basin stream development, 5097
Mill locations, 7543
Mill River, Conn., 5241
Mill River Valley, Calif., 9790
Mill villages, urban, 5765
Millbury, Mass., 5152
Miller, Dakota Territory, 8650
Millers River Valley, Mass., 5156
Milling, frontier, 5337
Mills, changing patterns of flour, 7145
Mills, early, 6099
Milton, Del., 5695
Milwaukee, Wis., 7151, 7985, 8109, 8112, 8114, 8117, 8120, 8122, 8124–8131, 8133–8134
Milwaukee Co., Wis., 8061–8062
Mimbres culture, 8991, 8993; pottery, 8993
Mine locations, 8180
Mineral and hot springs, 9891
Mineral economy, local, 5609
Mineral exploitation, retarded, 9941
Mineral exploration, 9285
Mineral springs, 5084, 7426, 7731–7735. See also Spas
Mining districts, 6575, 8053, 9148; company communities, 8247; company towns in, 7164; population changes, 9632; post–gold rush adjustments, 9665
Mining frontiers, 9083; Indian responses to, 7976; prostitutes on, 8386
Mining industry, coal, 7241
Mining landscapes, 4449
Mining regions: coal, 5577, 5580, 5823, 8293, 8759, 8775; copper, 9093–9094; gold, 6185, 9128; iron, 8180, 8217; lead, 6594, 7103, 7945; silver, 1950, 9021; tin, 9946
Mining settlements, 9083–9084; coalfield, 6148–6149; Cornish and Welsh, 9647; desert, 9245
Mining towns, 1827, 2471, 3521, 3584, 3685, 3687, 3769; commercial architecture, 7333, community development, 3060; company, 7164; material culture, 8449, mine encroachment on, 2405; tourism, 9172
Mining: camps, 9247; and channel response, 9114; Chinese, 6408; debris, hydraulic, 9530; early

American lead, 6607; geographical approaches, 8410; gold, 8645; and human fertility, 5570; hydraulic, 8322, 8411; impact on land, 8425; spatial patterns of, 3583; iron ore, 8217–8218; landscapes and copper, 9093–9094; local history, 9949; machines and equipment, 2637; regional growth of strip coal, 7382; regional impact of placer, 8407–8412; regional relation to agriculture, 7816; strip coal, role in land-use changes, 7379
Minneapolis, Minn., 8251–8255, 8263–8266, 8269–8270, 8272
MINNESOTA, 8150–8281
Minnewyt, Peter, 4858
Minor league baseball, 5684
Minorities. See individual ethnic groups
Mint growing, 7385, 7845
Miramichi, N.B., 2051; origin of name, 2079
Misconceptions: cartographic, 5858; climatic, 8509; regional, 8629. See also Myths
Mission period, drought patterns, 9510
Mission San Gabriel Archangel, Calif., 9599
Mission San Jose, Calif., 9613, 9731
Mission San Juan Capistrano, Calif., 9610
Mission Valley, Calif., 9701
Missionaries, as pioneers, 9433
Missionizing, and diocese-building, 9638
Missions: agriculture, 9731; agriculture and climatic variability, 9727; Church of England, 3794; and economic growth, 9618; founding, 9606; landscapes, 9768, 9776; maps of Spanish, 1099; and mission lands, 9612; populations, 9614; settlement, 9617; settlement role of Franciscan, 9609, 9611–9612; Spanish, 9616
Missiquoi Co., Quebec, 2248
Mississauga, Ont., 2855
Mississauga Indians, 2666
MISSISSIPPI, 6424–6461
Mississippi Basin, empires in, 1132
Mississippi Delta, 6677, 6683, 6693, 6704, 6736, 6969; Civil War strategy, 5923
Mississippi-Ohio river confluence area, 7444
Mississippi River, 6002, 6969–6970, 6994–7000, 7002, 8159; changing channels of tributaries, 6428; channels and cutoffs, 6681–6682,

6687; discovery of by Hennepin, 3973; upper rapids, 7159
MISSISSIPPI VALLEY, 5826, 5953, 6966–7006; Upper, 7020–7021, 7024, 7026, 7062, 7095, 7100, 7156–7157, 7467
MISSOURI, 6554–6646
Missouri River, 6590, 8474, 8492, 8497, 8500, 8505, 8566–8567, 8570, 8594
Missouri Valley, 8480, 8499, 8626
Misty Fjords National Monument and Wilderness, Alaska, 9942
Mixed-blood populations, 4821–4822, 5893, 6951
Mobile, Ala., 6411, 6420
Mobile Bay, Ala., 6400, 6403
Mobile home industry, 4594
Mobile home parks, 7415
Mobility, general spatial, 4518; of marriage partners, 4947; and urban form, 4671
Mobility, geographical, 1581, 1584, 1598, 1775–1776, 1779, 1869–1871, 1873, 1879, 1927, 1936, 2002, 2074, 2090, 2092, 2114, 2118, 2142, 2263–2264, 2383, 2443, 2447–2450, 2484, 2535, 2569, 2679–2680, 2682–2684, 2688, 2733 2770, 2902, 2906, 3224, 3256–3257, 3327, 3329, 3385–3387, 3840
Mobility, residential, 2826–2838, 3000, 3442–3443, 3448; of urban African Americans, 7420
Mobility, social, 1936, 2036, 2070, 2136, 2684, 2688, 2770
Model industrial towns, 5651
Model industrial villages, 4742
Modernization, 1896; role of public policy in, 4300
Modoc, Calif., region, 9492
Moenkopi, Ariz., 9069
Mohawk Valley, N.Y., 5284, 5373
Mojave Desert, Calif., 9781
Molokai, Hawaii, 10009
Money flows, role of population shifts in changing public, 5335
Monhegan Island, Maine, 5003
Mono Basin, Calif., 9601
Mono Lake, Calif., 9506
Mono Township, Ont., 2773
Monongahela Culture, 5525
Monopoly capitalism, decline, 4568
Monroe, Mich., 7878
Monroe Co., Iowa, 8288
Monroe Co., Ill., 7594
Montague Township, Ont., 2677
MONTANA, 9275–9294
Monte Christo, Wash., 9378
Monte Vista, Colo., 1963
Monterey, Calif., 9768, 9851, 9869
Monterey Bay, Calif., 9505
Montgomery, L. M., writer, 1979

Number ranges indicate: Canada, 1479–3860

Number ranges indicate: Canada, 1479–3860

Sawmills, waterpowered, 2428, 6451
Sawtooth Valley, Idaho, 9300
Sawyer Co., Wis., 7959
Saxicultural adjustments, 9147
Say, Hugh. *See* Day, John
Scandinavians: acculturation, 9206;
    immigrant distribution, 8014;
    migration, 3136; rural settlements,
    9366; settlement, 3382, 7090;
    settlers, 1605, 3273, 3389
Scenery: lower Hudson Valley, 4885;
    and women, 8532
Schoenbrunn, Ohio, 7221
Scholarly cartography, 4049–4051
School geographies, 2236–2237
Schools: architecture of country,
    7591–7592; Catholic parochial,
    8121; loss of, 8294; and settlement,
    3155; in transition, 6445;
    reorganization of rural, 5326, 7807;
    and urban residential
    development, 3632
Schuylkill River, Pa., 5592
Schwenkfelder family, spatial
    history, 5562
Scientists, and exploration, 8337
Scituate, Mass., 5219
Scotch-Irish: cultural adaptation in
    Old West, 6952; cultural
    persistence, 6596; in the New
    World, 1372. *See also* Ulster-Scots
Scots: migration, 1587–1588, 1864,
    1868, 1874, 1982, 1999, 2001, 2003,
    2280, 2517–2518, 2521, 2531, 3134,
    3327; place names of, 2658;
    propinquity of settlement, 2531;
    response to Credit Union
    Movement, 2005; settlement, 2530,
    2536, 7224
Scott Co., Kans., 8740
Scotts Bluff, Nebr., 8657
Scottsville, Va., 6124–6125
Scurvy, 3826
Sea: influence on industry, 4980; and
    land, 3900; resources, 10007
Sea ice, 3789–3790
Sea-island cotton, 6227–6230
Sea shells, trade in, 8890
Sea turtles, commerce in, 6887
Seaboard climate, 4808–4809
Seaboard environment, perception,
    4077
Seal fishery, Newfoundland, 1941,
    1947, 1950, 1963
Seale, R. W., map of North America,
    3799
Seaports, 6924
Seaside resorts, 4992, 5511, 6032;
    British connection, 1468; and camp
    meetings, 4753; development,
    4751–4753; morphology of North
    America, 1468
Seasonal activity, of farmers, 2591

Seasonal land use, ranching and
    tourism, 8964
Seasonal migration. *See*
    Transhumance
Seasonal settlements, 6202
Seattle, Wash., 9386, 9391, 9393,
    9396, 9398–9401
Seaward boundaries, 6356
Secessionism, and slavery, 5923
Secret societies: role in architecture,
    8447; urban, 7704
Sectarian ideology, and church
    architecture, 4460
Section: and party in presidential
    elections, 4292; significance in
    American history, 3868–3869. *See
    also* Regions
Sectional thesis, 164, 491
Sectionalism: in American history,
    3866, 3868–3869, 4276–4277; effect
    on presidential elections, 4280;
    and presidential politics, 7094;
    Southern, 5912; U.S. Congress,
    4279. *See also* Regionalism
Sections and politics, 6091
Sedgwick, Professor, traveler, 8358
Sediment changes, Eastern fluvial,
    4810
Sediment movement, riverine, 7022
Sediment yield, and climatic
    fluctuation, 7021
Sedimentation: culturally
    accelerated, 6255–6256; effect of
    agriculture, 5706; floodplain, 7023;
    historical gully, 6466; history,
    7961, 7966–7974
Segregation: rural residential racial,
    6446; urban racial residential,
    5786; urban social, 9805
Seigneurial system, 2166, 2193, 2269,
    2279, 2289, 2292–2293, 2299–2301
Selective growth of towns in North
    America, 1443
Self-built urban homes, 2821
Self-determination, Choctaw
    Indians, 6433
Self-sufficiency: food, 6737;
    geography of, 5977; military forts
    and logistical, 8555
Seminole, Okla., 8825, 8828, 8860
Seminole area, Okla., 8833
Seminole Indians: ethnoecological
    change, 6338; place names, 6394
Semple, Ellen Churchill,
    geographer, 3875
Semple, John, promoter, 4829
Seneca Falls, N.Y., 5409
Sense of place, 2501, 6435, 7479, 7649,
    7692, 7694, 7994, 9883
Sequent occupance approach: concept
    of, 145, 151, 698, 2038, 2418; studies
    in, 2896, 2957, 2972, 3522, 5160,
    5301–5302, 5538, 5567, 5648, 6077,

6272, 6299, 6425–6426, 6470, 6519,
6575, 6635, 6655, 6708, 6711, 6843,
6886, 6931, 6979, 7053, 7055, 7166,
7194, 7206, 7490, 7501, 7684, 7779,
7956–7957, 7998, 8259, 8724, 8797,
8826, 9002, 9004, 9069, 9081–9082,
9123–9128, 9166, 9191, 9266, 9353,
9427–9428, 9483, 9581–9582, 9592,
9594, 9596, 9598–9600, 9603, 9959,
9984, 9986
Sequoia National Park, 9677, 9679,
    9683–9684
Serra, Father Junipero, 3974
Service centers, emergence of
    seventeenth century, 6079
Services: economy, 4328; regional,
    9162; and residential patterns,
    2828, 2861; urban, 5652, 7680; urban
    employment in, 8118
Settlement. *See* entries under
    Regional Settlement in regional,
    provincial, and state sections of
    the bibliography. Special aspects:
    Acadian (La.), 6712;
    agglomerated, 6214; and altitude,
    1317; atlas of, 1055; and climate,
    4107, 8456, 8463; and economy,
    6402; French Canadian, 5057;
    beginnings of American, 4101; coal
    and pioneer, 8776; colonies, 7524;
    commercial nature of frontier,
    6103; convergence, 7201; decline,
    7354; delayed, 5716; dispersion
    hypothesis, 5107; Dutch Catholic,
    8007, 8009; dynamics, 6582; effect
    of physiography, 6161; effects,
    regional images, 8533; English
    family role in, 8292; and
    environment, 6829; environment
    and regional, 9359; environmental
    influence on regional, 6555–6556;
    and ethnicity, 8635; evolution,
    5053; expansion, 5096, 6581;
    Finnish, 8172, 8193, 9619; French,
    7056, 7997; frontier, 5542, 5545,
    8534–8535; frontier, Hispanic,
    9615; German, 8233; of the
    grasslands, 6993; Hutterite, 8636;
    impact of canals on regional, 7269;
    and landscape change, 8758; and
    levee building, 6441; local, 7785,
    8827; methodology, 111, 184, 187–
    188, 205, 226; Mennonite, 8788; and
    military reservations, 8370;
    Mormon role in, 8392–8393;
    pioneer, 7055; plantations, 6275;
    and population, 5106; precontact,
    7465; promotion, regional, 7775; in
    provincial context, 3518; Pueblo
    Indians, 8987–8988; Quaker, 5476;
    redistribution, 5105, 5038;
    regional, 5470, 6472; retarded,
    5716; role of human nature, 8515;

Number ranges indicate: Canada, 1479–3860

Spanish moss industry, 6765–6766
Spanish municipal origins, 8946
Spanish place names, 9045, 9893, 9900
Spanish proper names: atlas of, 1040; as place names, 9039
Spanish settlement patterns, local, 9130
Spanish spinners, 6690
Spanish town planning, 4718, 6639
Sparrows, 3931; conservation of the English, 4339
Spas, 6939; historic, 6393; perceptions of, 9891; regional patterns, 9890; source of resort tradition, 6030. See also Mineral springs
Spatial systems in American history, 3902, 3907
Specialty farming, 4414–4421
Speculation: in land, 2570, 2572, 2927, 2929, 2931–2932, 2934, 2942, 3009; town-site, 7824
Speculators: appraisals of land, 2669; land, 7038
Spinners, Spanish, 6690
Spokane, Wash., 9387–9388
Spokane Co., Wash., 9406
Sports, high school and collegiate basketball, 7427
Spring City, Utah, 9227
Spring wheat region, 1415
Springfield, Ill., 7686
Springfield, Mass., 5111, 5166
Squatter settlement, 3318, 3321
Stagecoach service, 5026–5027
Stanislaus Co., Calif., 9600
Stanislaus River, Calif., 9525
Stanley Co., S.Dak., 8633
Stansburg expedition, 9187
Stanstead Township, Quebec, 2243
Staples: and national development, 2153, 4323; production and subsistence, 2013; and regional development, 2558; and urban development, 2035, 4324, 5926. See also individual natural resources
Stark Co., Ill., 7552
Starkville, Miss., 6461
Starved Rock, Ill., 7549
State-building, 4281–4287; Mormon concepts of, 8400; western in Revolutionary era, 4282
States: administration of roads, 6531; boundaries, 4274, 5224–5225, 5566, 5914–5917, 7093, 7814, 8399, 8642, 8836, 8931–8933, 9934–9935; capital relocation, 9957; censuses, 6859–6860; evolution, 4872; maps of, 5864; official maps of, 4923; origins of names, 4773, 4779; rankings of, 4097; sovereignty, 9658; state corporations and

regional development, 2458; states' rights, 6281
Statistical cartography, 3998; atlas (1870), 3996
Stauffer Mennonite communities, 5722
Staunton, Va., 6128
Steamboats: and regional development, 6379, 9789; and river towns, 9462; and trade networks, 8594
Stearns Co., Minn., 8176
Steel guitar development, 10002
Steel industry, 4583–4584, 7675
Steeples, church, 7190
Steinbeck, John, novelist, 4088
Stereotypes, regional, 8450
Steubenville, Ohio, 7238
Stevens, Isaac J., early geographer, 9357
Stillaguamish Valley, Wash., 9366
Stockton, Calif., 9889
Stone: bridges, 7594; cultures, ancient, 6831; fences and walls, 6540, 6543, 8785, 5072; grave markers, 2031; houses, 4842, 5358, 5591, 7590, 8092, 9774; iron furnaces, 5686; iron rock, 6747; legislation, 8215–8216; relics, 4919; trade, 7134, 7555, 7837
Stone Co., Mo., 6577
Stoney Creek, Mich., 7784
Stoney Pass route, Colo., 9157–9158
Storefront remodeling, 7163
Stores, metropolitan pattern of department, 5743
Storms, dust, 8739
Storrs, Mont., 9278
Story Co., Iowa, 8285
Strait of Belle Isle, 1953
Straits of Mackinac, 7766, 7779
Strathcona, Alta., 3363, 3440
Strawberry growing, 8070
Stream channels, human impacts on, 7968
Stream discharge, impact of urban development, 7455
Stream flow and urbanization, 6337
Stream sedimentation rates, 3919
Street grids, 4723, 7190, 7422; origins, 6329
Street lighting, 1456–1457
Street maps, 4853
Street names, 5688, 9903, 10043
Street patterns, 1463, 5670–5672, 5681; early, 5509; origins, 8863
Street railways, 6241; diffusion in North America, 1441; and urban development, 2843
Streetcar suburbs, 1466, 5200, 5645
Streetcars, 2958, 2991; and urban development, 2808–2809, 3300
Strikes, geography of, 4705

Strip-cropping, contour, 8064, 8067
Strip-mining, coal, 7351; bituminous, 5578; regional growth, 7382; role in land-use changes, 7379
Structural analysis: of agriculture, 1664; of cities, 1709
Structural change, in manufacturing, 1819, 2627, 2989; mining machinery and equipment, 2637
Structuration, in urban setting, 5187
Student catchment areas, 5325
Subcultures, regional, 5814, 5816
Subdivision: urban land, 2841, 3301, 3458, 3460, premature, 3301, suburban, 9815
Subhumid environment: agricultural adjustment to, 8764, 8777–8778; climate and settlement, 8462
Subsistence: agriculture, 5821; community, 6595; economies, 5821, 7055, 8481; and industrialization, 5821; precontact, 7465; and settlement, 9434; slave, 5896
Subtropical crop region, 9716
Suburban destinations, African American, 5507
Suburban dream, 5586; federal subsidy, 4652
Suburban home ownership, 2820
Suburban life, 3010
Suburban subdivisions, role in urban morphogenesis, 9815, 9889
Suburban-style commercial redevelopment, near downtowns, 9843
Suburbanization, 1465, 5161, 5633, 9813–9814; African American, 5507; and annexation, 3440, 3444, 7642; beginnings, 4709; Canadian, 1718; of center city, 4740, 9843; effect on political party base 4307; growth of, 5161–5162; Irish, 4710; metropolitan, 5633; and middle-class women, 5658; morphology of, 3014; role of federal government in, 4652; role of transport in, 5161; solution for urban problems, 4708; of towns, 5162; and urban reform, 4708
Suburbia, creation of, 2851
Suburbs. See entries under Town Growth in regional, provincial, and state sections of the bibliography. Special aspects: affluent, 9860; American, 5160–5162, 5177, 5200, 5632, 5800, 6126, 6321, 6501–6502; blue-collar, 3661, 3665; business nucleations, 5750, 6321; Canadian, 2392, 2394, 2791, 2837, 2840, 2842, 2844, 3629, 3661, 3665; colonial era, 6126; corporate, 2840; early, 2394, 5800; emergent, 5632–5633; evolution, 4651, 4653–

Number ranges indicate: Canada, 1479–3860

Number ranges indicate: Canada, 1479–3860

THE UNIVERSITY OF CHICAGO

GEOGRAPHY RESEARCH PAPERS

(Lithographed, 6 x 9 inches)

Titles in Print

166. BEDNARZ, ROBERT S. *The Effect of Air Pollution on Property Value in Chicago.* 1975. viii + 111 p.

167. HANNEMANN, MANFRED. *The Diffusion of the Reformation in Southwestern Germany, 1518-1534.* 1975. ix + 235 p.

168. SUBLETT, MICHAEL D. *Farmers on the Road: Interfarm Migration and the Farming of Noncontiguous Lands in Three Midwestern Townships. 1939-1969.* 1975. xiii + 214 p.

169. STETZER, DONALD FOSTER. *Special Districts in Cook County: Toward a Geography of Local Government.* 1975. xi + 177 p.

172. COHEN, YEHOSHUA S., and BRIAN J. L. BERRY. *Spatial Components of Manufacturing Change.* 1975. vi + 262 p.

173. HAYES, CHARLES R. *The Dispersed City: The Case of Piedmont, North Carolina.* 1976. ix + 157 p.

174. CARGO, DOUGLAS B. *Solid Wastes: Factors Influencing Generation Rates.* 1977. 100 p.

176. MORGAN, DAVID J. *Patterns of Population Distribution: A Residential Preference Model and Its Dynamic.* 1978. xiii + 200 p.

177. STOKES, HOUSTON H.; DONALD W. JONES; and HUGH M. NEUBURGER. *Unemployment and Adjustment in the Labor Market: A Comparison between the Regional and National Responses.* 1975. ix + 125 p.

181. GOODWIN, GARY C. *Cherokees in Transition: A Study of Changing Culture and Environment Prior to 1775.* 1977. ix + 207 p.

183. HAIGH, MARTIN J. *The Evolution of Slopes on Artificial Landforms, Blaenavon, U.K.* 1978. xiv + 293 p.

184. FINK, L. DEE. *Listening to the Learner: An Exploratory Study of Personal Meaning in College Geography Courses.* 1977. ix + 186 p.

185. HELGREN, DAVID M. *Rivers of Diamonds: An Alluvial History of the Lower Vaal Basin, South Africa.* 1979. xix + 389 p.

186. BUTZER, KARL W., ed. *Dimensions of Human Geography: Essays on Some Familiar and Neglected Themes.* 1978. vii + 190 p.

187. MITSUHASHI, SETSUKO. *Japanese Commodity Flows.* 1978. x + 172 p.

188. CARIS, SUSAN L. *Community Attitudes toward Pollution.* 1978. xii + 211 p.

189. REES, PHILIP M. *Residential Patterns in American Cities: 1960.* 1979. xvi + 405 p.

190. KANNE, EDWARD A. *Fresh Food for Nicosia.* 1979. x + 106 p.

192. KIRCHNER, JOHN A. *Sugar and Seasonal Labor Migration: The Case of Tucumán, Argentina.* 1980. xii + 174 p.

194. HARRIS, CHAUNCY D. *Annotated World List of Selected Current Geographical Serials, Fourth Edition. 1980.* 1980. iv + 165 p.

196. LEUNG, CHI-KEUNG, and NORTON S. GINSBURG, eds. *China: Urbanizations and National Development.* 1980. ix + 283 p.

197. DAICHES, SOL. *People in Distress: A Geographical Perspective on Psychological Well-being.* 1981. xiv + 199 p.

198. JOHNSON, JOSEPH T. *Location and Trade Theory: Industrial Location, Comparative Advantage, and the Geographic Pattern of Production in the United States.* 1981. xi + 107 p.

199-200. STEVENSON, ARTHUR J. *The New York–Newark Air Freight System.* 1982. xvi + 440 p.

201. LICATE, JACK A. *Creation of a Mexican Landscape: Territorial Organization and Settlement in the Eastern Puebla Basin, 1520-1605.* 1981. x + 143 p.

202. RUDZITIS, GUNDARS. *Residential Location Determinants of the Older Population.* 1982. x + 117 p.

204. DAHMANN, DONALD C. *Locals and Cosmopolitans: Patterns of Spatial Mobility during the Transition from Youth to Early Adulthood.* 1982. xiii + 146 p.

206. HARRIS, CHAUNCY D. *Bibliography of Geography. Part II: Regional. Volume 1. The United States of America.* 1984. viii + 178 p.

207-208. WHEATLEY, PAUL. *Nagara and Commandery: Origins of the Southeast Asian Urban Traditions.* 1983. xv + 472 p.

209. SAARINEN, THOMAS F.; DAVID SEAMON; and JAMES L. SELL, eds. *Environmental Perception and Behavior: An Inventory and Prospect.* 1984. x + 263 p.

210. WESCOAT, JAMES L., JR. *Integrated Water Development: Water Use and Conservation Practice in Western Colorado.* 1984. xi + 239 p.

211. DEMKO, GEORGE J., and ROLAND J. FUCHS, eds. *Geographical Studies on the Soviet Union: Essays in Honor of Chauncy D. Harris.* 1984. vii + 294 p.

212. HOLMES, ROLAND C. *Irrigation in Southern Peru: The Chili Basin.* 1986. ix + 199 p.

213. EDMONDS, RICHARD LOUIS. *Northern Frontiers of Qing China and Tokugawa Japan: A Comparative Study of Frontier Policy.* 1985. xi + 209 p.

214. FREEMAN, DONALD B., and GLEN B. NORCLIFFE. *Rural Enterprise in Kenya: Development and Spatial Organization of the Nonfarm Sector.* 1985. xiv + 180 p.

215. COHEN, YEHOSHUA S., and AMNON SHINAR. *Neighborhoods and Friendship Networks: A Study of Three Residential Neighborhoods in Jerusalem.* 1985. ix + 137 p.

216. OBERMEYER, NANCY J. *Bureaucrats, Clients, and Geography: The Bailly Nuclear Power Plant Battle in Northern Indiana.* 1989. x + 135 p.

217-218. CONZEN, MICHAEL P., ed. *World Patterns of Modern Urban Change: Essays in Honor of Chauncy D. Harris.* 1986. x + 479 p.

219. KOMOGUCHI, YOSHIMI. *Agricultural Systems in the Tamil Nadu: A Case Study of Peruvalanallur Village.* 1986. xvi + 175 p.

220. GINSBURG, NORTON; JAMES OSBORN; and GRANT BLANK. *Geographic Perspectives on the Wealth of Nations.* 1986. ix + 133 p.

221. BAYLSON, JOSHUA C. *Territorial Allocation by Imperial Rivalry: The Human Legacy in the Near East.* 1987. xi + 138 p.

222. DORN, MARILYN APRIL. *The Administrative Partitioning of Costa Rica: Politics and Planners in the 1970s.* 1989. xi + 126 p.

223. ASTROTH, JOSEPH H., JR. *Understanding Peasant Agriculture: An Integrated Land-Use Model for the Punjab.* 1990. xiii + 173 p.

224. PLATT, RUTHERFORD H.; SHEILA G. PELCZARSKI; and BARBARA K. BURBANK, eds. *Cities on the Beach: Management Issues of Developed Coastal Barriers.* 1987. vii + 324 p.

225. LATZ, GIL. *Agricultural Development in Japan: The Land Improvement District in Concept and Practice.* 1989. viii + 135 p.

226. GRITZNER, JEFFREY A. *The West African Sahel: Human Agency and Environmental Change.* 1988. xii + 170 p.

227. MURPHY, ALEXANDER B. *The Regional Dynamics of Language Differentiation in Belgium: A Study in Cultural-Political Geography.* 1988. xiii + 249 p.

228-229. BISHOP, BARRY C. *Karnali under Stress: Livelihood Strategies and Seasonal Rhythms in a Changing Nepal Himalaya.* 1990. xviii + 460 p.

230. MUELLER-WILLE, CHRISTOPHER. *Natural Landscape Amenities and Suburban Growth: Metropolitan Chicago, 1970-1980.* 1990. xi + 153 p.

231. WILKINSON, M. JUSTIN. *Paleoenvironments in the Namib Desert: The Lower Tumas Basin in the Late Cenozoic.* 1990. xv + 196 p.

232. DUBOIS, RANDOM. *Soil Erosion in a Coastal River Basin: A Case Study from the Philippines.* 1990. xii + 138 p.

233. PALM, RISA, AND MICHAEL E. HODGSON. *After a California Earthquake: Attitude and Behavior Change.* 1992. xii + 130 p.

234. KUMMER, DAVID M. *Deforestation in the Postwar Philippines.* 1992. xviii + 179 p.

235. CONZEN, MICHAEL P., THOMAS A. RUMNEY, AND GRAEME WYNN. *A Scholar's Guide to Geographical Writing on the American and Canadian Past.* 1993. xiii + 751 p.